T0312191

MATHEMATICAL METHODS AND MODELS FOR ECONOMISTS

This book is intended as a textbook for a first-year Ph.D. course in mathematics for economists and as a reference for graduate students in economics. It provides a self-contained, rigorous treatment of most of the concepts and techniques required to follow the standard first-year theory sequence in microeconomics and macroeconomics. The topics covered include an introduction to analysis in metric spaces, differential calculus, comparative statics, convexity, static optimization, dynamical systems, and dynamic optimization. The book includes a large number of applications to standard economic models and more than two hundred problems that are fully worked out.

Angel de la Fuente is Assistant Professor of Economics at the Instituto de Análisis Económica (CSIC), Adjunct Professor at the Department of Economics of the Universidad Autónoma de Barcelona, and Research Affiliate at the Centre for Economic Policy Research (CEPR), London. Besides his interest in mathematical economics, he specializes in growth and regional economics. Professor de la Fuente has published in the *Journal of Monetary Economics*, the *Journal of Economic Dynamics and Control*, *Economic Policy*, *Revista Española de Economía*, and *Investigaciones Económicas*, among other journals.

A mis padres

MATHEMATICAL METHODS AND MODELS FOR ECONOMISTS

ANGEL DE LA FUENTE

Instituto de Análisis Económica (CSIC), Barcelona

CAMBRIDGE
UNIVERSITY PRESS

CAMBRIDGE
UNIVERSITY PRESS

University Printing House, Cambridge CB2 8BS, United Kingdom

One Liberty Plaza, 20th Floor, New York, NY 10006, USA

477 Williamstown Road, Port Melbourne, VIC 3207, Australia

314-321, 3rd Floor, Plot 3, Splendor Forum, Jasola District Centre, New Delhi - 110025, India

79 Anson Road, #06-04/06, Singapore 079906

Cambridge University Press is part of the University of Cambridge.

It furthers the University's mission by disseminating knowledge in the pursuit of education, learning and research at the highest international levels of excellence.

www.cambridge.org
Information on this title: www.cambridge.org/9780521585293

© Angel de la Fuente 2000

First published 2000
14th printing 2018

A catalogue record for this publication is available from the British Library

Library of Congress Cataloging in Publication data
Fuente, Angel de la. Mathematical methods and
models for economists / Angel de la Fuente.
p.   cm.
Includes index.
ISBN 0-521-58512-0 (hb.) – ISBN 0-521-58529-5 (pb.)
1. Economics – Statistical methods.
2. Mathematical models.
I. Title.
HB137.F83   1999
330´.01´51 – dc21   98-52086
CIP

ISBN 978-0-521-58529-3 Paperback

Contents

Preface and Acknowledgments

Much of the time of the average graduate student in economics is spent learning a new language, that of mathematics. Although the investment does eventually pay off in many ways, the learning process can be quite painful. I know because I have been there. I remember the long nights spent puzzling over the mysteries of the Hamiltonian, the frustration of not understanding a single one of the papers in my second macroeconomics reading list, the culture shock that came with the transition from the undergraduate textbooks, with their familiar diagrams and intuitive explanations, into Debreu's *Theory of Value*, and my despair before the terse and incredibly dry prose of the mathematics texts where I sought enlightenment about the arcane properties of contractions.

This book is an attempt to make the transition into graduate economics somewhat less painful. Although some of my readers may never believe me, I have tried to do a number of things that should make their lives a bit easier. The first has been to collect in one place, with a homogeneous notation, most of the mathematical concepts, results, and techniques that are required to follow the standard first- and second-year theory courses. I have also tried to organize this material into a logical sequence and have illustrated its applications to some of the standard models. And last but not least, I have attempted to provide rigorous proofs for most of the results as a way to get the reader used to formal reasoning. Although a lot of effort has gone into making the text as clear as possible, the result is still far from entertaining. Most students without a good undergraduate background in mathematics are likely to find the going a bit rough at times. They have all my sympathy and the assurance that it does build character.

This book has been long in the making. It started out as a set of notes that I wrote for myself during my first year at Penn. Those notes were then refined for the benefit of my younger classmates when I became a teaching assistant, and they finally grew into lecture notes when I had the misfortune to graduate and was forced onto the other side of the lectern. Along the way,

I have had a lot of help. Much of the core material can be traced back to class lectures by Richard Kihlstrom, George Mailath, Beth Allen, David Cass, Maurice Obstfeld, Allan Drazen, Costas Azariadis, and Randy Wright. The first typed version of these notes was compiled jointly with Francis Bloch over a long and sticky Philadelphia summer as a reference for an introductory summer course for incoming students. Francis had the good sense to jump ship right after that, but some of his material is still here in one form or another. Several colleagues and friends have had the patience to read through various portions of the manuscript and have made many useful comments and suggestions. Among these, I would especially like to thank David Pérez and Maite Naranjo, who has also contributed a couple of the more difficult proofs. Thanks are also due to several generations of students at the Universidad Autónoma de Barcelona and various other places, who, while sweating through successive versions of this manuscript, have helped me to improve it in various ways and have detected a fair number of errors, as well as the usual typos. Finally, I would like to thank Conchi Rodriguez, Tere Lorenz, and the rest of the staff at the Instituto de Análisis Económica for their secretarial support and for their heroic behavior at the Xerox machine.

Part I

Preliminaries

1

Review of Basic Concepts

This chapter reviews some basic concepts that will be used throughout the text. One of its central themes is that relations and functions can be used to introduce different types of "structures" in sets. Thus relations of a certain type can be used to order sets according to criteria like precedence, size, or goodness; algebraic operations are defined using functions, and a function that formalizes the notion of distance between two elements of a set can be used to define topological concepts like convergence and continuity. In addition, we also introduce some simple notions of logic and discuss several methods of proof that will be used extensively later on.

1. Sets

A *set* is a collection of objects we call elements. We will denote sets by capital letters, and elements by lowercase letters. If x is an element of a set X, we write $x \in X$, and $x \notin X$ otherwise. A set A is a *subset* of X if all elements of A belong to X. This is written $A \subseteq X$ (A is contained in X). Formally, we can write

$$A \subseteq X \Leftrightarrow (x \in A \Rightarrow x \in X)$$

where the one-way arrow ($\Rightarrow$) denotes implication, and the two-way arrow ($\Leftrightarrow$) indicates equivalence. Two sets, A and B, are equal if they have the same elements, that is, $A = B$ if and only if $A \subseteq B$ and $B \subseteq A$. The symbol $\varnothing$ denotes the *empty set*, a set with no elements. By convention, $\varnothing$ is a subset of any set X.

Given a set X, the *power set* of X, written $P(X)$ or 2^X, is the set consisting of all the subsets A of X. A class or *family of sets* in X is a subset of $P(X)$, that is, a set whose elements are subsets of X. We will use "hollow" capital letters to denote families of sets. For example,

$$\mathbb{A} = \{A_i; A_i \subseteq X, i \in I\}$$

3

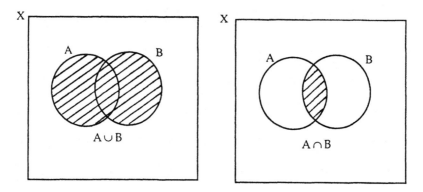

Figure 1.1. Union and intersection of two sets.

where I is some index set, such as the set of all natural numbers smaller than some given number n.

In what follows we will take as given some set X (the universal set), and assuming that "there is nothing" outside X, we will work with its subsets. Given two subsets of X, A and B, we define their *union*, $A \cup B$, as the set

$$A \cup B = \{x \in X;\ x \in A \text{ or } x \in B\}$$

That is, $A \cup B$ is the set of elements of X that belong to A or to B or to both. Similarly, the *intersection* of A and B, denoted by $A \cap B$, is the set whose elements belong to both sets at the same time:

$$A \cap B = \{x \in X;\ x \in A \text{ and } x \in B\}$$

These concepts can be extended in a natural way to classes of more than two sets. Given a family of subsets of X, $\mathbb{A} = \{A_i;\ i \in I\}$, its union and intersection are given respectively by

$$\cup \mathbb{A} = \cup_{i \in I} A_i = \{x \in X;\ \exists i \in I \text{ s.th. } x \in A_i\} \quad \text{and}$$
$$\cap \mathbb{A} = \cap_{i \in I} A_i = \{x \in X;\ x \in A_i \ \forall i \in I\}$$

where the *existential quantifier* "$\exists$" means "there exists some," the *universal quantifier* "$\forall$" means "for all," and "s.th." means "such that." That is, x is an element of the union $\cup \mathbb{A}$ if it belongs to at least one of the sets in the family $\mathbb{A}$, and it is an element of the intersection if it belongs to all sets in the class.

The following theorem summarizes the basic properties of unions and intersections of sets.

Theorem 1.1. Properties of unions and intersections of sets. Let $\mathbb{A}$, $\mathbb{B}$, *and* $\mathbb{C}$ *be three subsets of* X. *Then the following properties hold:*

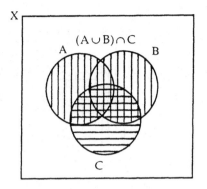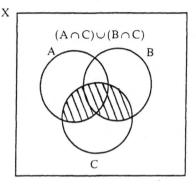

Figure 1.2. Distributive law.

(i) Commutative law: $A \cup B = B \cup A$ *and* $A \cap B = B \cap A$.

(ii) Associative law: $(A \cup B) \cup C = A \cup (B \cup C) = A \cup B \cup C$ *and* $(A \cap B) \cap C = A \cap (B \cap C) = A \cap B \cap C$.

(iii) Distributive law: $(A \cup B) \cap C = (A \cap C) \cup (B \cap C)$ *and* $(A \cap B) \cup C = (A \cup C) \cap (B \cup C)$.

Two sets A and B are *disjoint* if they have no elements in common, that is, if $A \cap B = \varnothing$. More generally, given a family of sets, $\mathbb{A} = \{A_i; i \in I\}$ in X, we say that the elements of $\mathbb{A}$ are *pairwise disjoint* if

$$A_i \cap A_j = \varnothing \ \forall \, i \neq j$$

We will sometimes use the notation $A \cup\!\!\!\cup B$ to indicate the union of disjoint sets. The expression $\cup\!\!\!\cup_{i \in I} A_i$ will denote the union of a family of pairwise-disjoint sets.

A *partition* of X is a class of pairwise-disjoint sets in X whose union is X itself; that is, $\mathbb{A} = \{A_i; i \in I\}$ is a partition of X if

$$\forall \, i \neq j, A_i \cap A_j = \varnothing \quad \text{and} \quad \cup\!\!\!\cup_i A_i = X$$

Given two sets A and B in X, their *difference* $A \sim B$ (or $A - B$ or $A \backslash B$) is the set of elements of A that do not belong to B:

$$A \sim B = \{x \in X; \ x \in A \text{ and } x \notin B\}$$

The *complement* of A (relative to X) is the set A^c or $\sim A$ of elements of X that do not belong to A:

$$\sim A = A^c = \{x \in X; \ x \notin A\}$$

Hence we have

$$A \sim B = A \cap (\sim B) \quad \text{and} \quad \sim A = X \sim A$$

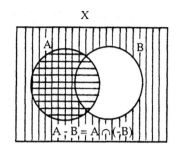

Figure 1.3. $A \sim B = A \cap (\sim B)$.

Let $\mathbb{A} = \{A_i;\ i = 1, 2, \ldots\}$ be a class of sets in X, and let $\mathbb{C} = \{A_i^c;\ i = 1, 2, \ldots\}$ be the family formed by the complements of the elements of $\mathbb{A}$. The following result says that the complement of the union of $\mathbb{A}$ is equal to the intersection of $\mathbb{C}$, and the complement of the intersection of $\mathbb{A}$ is the union of $\mathbb{C}$.

Theorem 1.2. Duality principle or De Morgan's laws. Let $\mathbb{A} = \{A_i;\ i \in I\}$ be a family of sets in X; then

(i) $\sim(\cup_{i \in I} A_i) = \cap_{i \in I}(\sim A_i)$, and
(ii) $\sim(\cap_{i \in I} A_i) = \cup_{i \in I}(\sim A_i)$.

This result also holds when we consider complements relative to some set that is not the universal set. Hence, if $\mathbb{A} = \{A_i;\ i \in I\}$ is a family of subsets of some set Y, then

(i) $Y \sim (\cup_{i \in I} A_i) = \cap_{i \in I}(Y \sim A_i)$, and
(ii) $Y \sim (\cap_{i \in I} A_i) = \cup_{i \in I}(Y \sim A_i)$.

2. A Bit of Logic

In this section we introduce some basic notions of logic that are often used in proofs.

(a) *Properties and Quantifiers*

Fix a set X, and let P be a *property* such that for each element x of X, the statement "x has property P" is either true or false (but not both at once, and not neither). If property P holds for x, we say that $P(x)$ is true and write $P(x)$. With each such property P we can associate the set P_T of elements of X for which $P(x)$ is true:

$$P_T = \{x \in X;\ P(x)\}$$

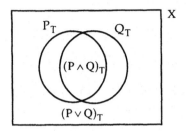

Figure 1.4. Sets associated with composite properties.

Similarly, with every subset A of X we can associate the property "being an element of A." In this manner we can establish a correspondence between sets and properties that will allow us to identify logical operations with set operations.

Given a property P, its *negation* $\neg P$ ("not P") is another property such that $\neg P(x)$ is true if and only if $P(x)$ is false. Because for any x in X precisely one of the two properties P and $\neg P$ will hold, the set associated with $\neg P$ is the complement of P_T:

$$(\neg P)_T = \{x \in X;\ \neg P(x) \text{ is true}\} = \{x \in X;\ P(x) \text{ is false}\} = {\sim}P_T$$

Therefore, P_T and $(\neg P)_T$ form a partition of X. That is, for any property P,

$$(\neg P)_T \cap P_T = \varnothing \quad \text{and} \quad (\neg P)_T \cup P_T = X$$

The *logical connectives* "and" ($\wedge$) and "or" ($\vee$) can be used to construct composite properties. Given two properties P and Q, their *conjunction* $P \wedge Q$ ("P and Q") is the property that holds if and only if both P and Q hold at the same time. Hence, the set associated with $P \wedge Q$ is the intersection of the sets associated with the two original properties. That is,

$$\begin{aligned} (P \wedge Q)_T &= \{x \in X;\ P(x) \text{ and } Q(x)\} = \{x \in X;\ P(x)\} \cap \{x \in X;\ Q(x)\} \\ &= P_T \cap Q_T \end{aligned}$$

In a similar way, we define the (nonexclusive) *disjunction* of P and Q, $P \vee Q$ ("P or Q"), as the property such that $(P \vee Q)(x)$ is true whenever $P(x)$ or $Q(x)$ or both hold. Hence, the set associated with the disjunction of P and Q is the union of P_T and Q_T:

$$\begin{aligned} (P \vee Q)_T &= \{x \in X;\ P(x) \text{ or } Q(x)\} = \{x \in X;\ P(x)\} \cup \{x \in X;\ Q(x)\} \\ &= P_T \cup Q_T \end{aligned}$$

To construct the negation of a composite property, we can make use of De Morgan's laws. From Theorem 1.2 we have

$${\sim}(P_T \cup Q_T) = ({\sim}P_T) \cap ({\sim}Q_T) \quad \text{and} \quad {\sim}(P_T \cap Q_T) = ({\sim}P_T) \cup ({\sim}Q_T)$$

from where

$$\neg(P \vee Q) = (\neg P) \wedge (\neg Q) \quad \text{and} \quad \neg(P \wedge Q) = (\neg P) \vee (\neg Q)$$

That is, not having the property "*P* or *Q*" is equivalent to not having either one, and not having the property "*P* and *Q*" is the same as lacking at least one of them.

Quantifiers are often used to indicate that all or some of the elements of a given set have a certain property. To say that all the elements of set *A* have property *P*, we use the universal quantifier ($\forall$) and write

$$\forall\, x \in A, \; P(x) \qquad \text{(i.e., for all } x \text{ in } A, \; P(x) \text{ is true)} \tag{1}$$

To say that some elements of *A* have a given property, we use the existential quantifier ($\exists$):[1]

$$\exists\, x \in A, \text{ s.th. } P(x) \qquad \text{(i.e., there is at least one element } x \text{ of } A \\ \text{such that } P(x) \text{ is true)} \tag{2}$$

Quantifiers can be seen as generalizations of logical connectives. Hence, if *A* is a finite set of the form $\{x_1, x_2, \ldots, x_n\}$, the statements (1) and (2) are equivalent to

$$P(x_1) \wedge P(x_2) \wedge \ldots \wedge P(x_n) \quad \text{and} \quad P(x_1) \vee P(x_2) \vee \ldots \vee P(x_n)$$

respectively. The earlier notation, however, has the advantage of being more compact and can also be used for infinite sets.

Expressions involving several quantifiers are commonly encountered. For example, the statement

$$\forall\, x \in A, \; \exists\, y \in B \text{ s.th. } P(x, y) \tag{3}$$

means that "for all *x* in *A*, there exists an element *y* in *B* such that the pair (x, y) has property *P*." In these cases, it is important to keep in mind that the order in which quantifiers appear matters. Thus the statement

$$\exists\, y \in B \text{ s.th. } \forall\, x \in A, \; P(x, y) \tag{4}$$

("there exists an element *y* in *B* such that for each *x* in *A*, the pair (x, y) has property *P*") is different from (3): In the first case, the choice of *y* may depend on the given value of *x*, whereas in (4) we are asserting the existence of at least one *y* that will work for all possible values of *x*. If we let *A* and *B* be the set of real numbers, and *P* the property that $x + y = 0$, for example, statement (3) is true (with $y = -x$), but (4) is false.

We often want to negate statements involving quantifiers. If it is not true that all the elements of a set *A* have property *P*, then clearly it must be the case that some elements of *A* have property $\neg P$. Hence

$$\neg[\forall\, x \in A, \; P(x)] \Leftrightarrow \exists\, x \in A \text{ s.th. } \neg P(x)$$

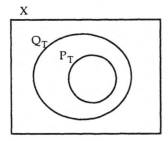

Figure 1.5. Implication as set inclusion.

Similarly, if there exist no elements of A with property P, all elements of the set must satisfy $\neg P$. That is,

$$\neg[\exists x \in A, \text{ s.th. } P(x)] \Leftrightarrow \forall x \in A, \neg P(x)$$

Hence, to negate a statement that makes use of quantifiers, we replace the $\forall$'s with $\exists$'s, and vice versa, and negate the properties. The same principle applies to statements involving several quantifiers. For example,

$$\neg(\forall x \in A, \exists y \in B, \text{ s.th. } P(x, y)) \Leftrightarrow \exists x \in A \text{ s.th. } \neg(\exists y \in B \text{ s.th. } P(x, y))$$
$$\Leftrightarrow \exists x \in A \text{ s.th. } \forall y \in B, \neg P(x, y)$$

That is, we begin with the statement "for all x in A, there exists an element y in B such that the pair (x, y) has property P." If that is not true, then there must exist some x in A such that for all y in B the pair (x, y) does not have property P.

(b) Implication

We often make statements of the type "property P implies property Q" – meaning that all elements that have property P also satisfy Q. This statement can be written "$P \Rightarrow Q$" – an expression that can also be read as

"if P then Q,"
"P is a sufficient condition for Q," or
"Q is a necessary condition for P."

In terms of the associated sets, "$P \Rightarrow Q$" means that

$$P_T \subseteq Q_T$$

Using quantifiers, the statement $P \Rightarrow Q$ can also be written

$$\forall x \in P_T, Q(x)$$

That is, if all elements x with property P also satisfy Q, then P_T must be contained in the set Q_T, and vice versa.

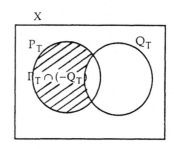

Figure 1.6.

To express "$P \Rightarrow Q$" in terms of an equivalent property that will be useful later, observe that

$$P_T \subseteq Q_T \quad \text{if and only if } (\sim P_T) \cup Q_T = X$$

where X is the universal set. The proof of this equivalence is left as an exercise, but the result should be intuitively clear, for if Q_T contains P_T, all points that lie outside Q_T will necessarily be outside P_T. Hence the statement $P \Rightarrow Q$ is true if and only if

$$x \in (\sim P_T) \cup Q_T \; \forall \, x \in X$$

or, equivalently, the property $(\neg P) \vee Q$ always holds. Figure 1.6 tries to clarify this result.

The *negation* of $P \Rightarrow Q$, written $P \nRightarrow Q$ or $\neg(P \Rightarrow Q)$, is true whenever there exists at least one x that satisfies P but not Q (that is, when $\exists \, x \in P_T$ s.th. $\neg Q(x)$). Drawing on our previous discussion, this is equivalent to saying that $P \nRightarrow Q$ is true when the negation of $(\neg P) \vee Q$ is true for some x in X. Applying De Morgan's laws,

$$\neg((\neg P) \vee Q) = P \wedge (\neg Q)$$

which implies that $P \nRightarrow Q$ is equivalent to

$$P_T \cap (\sim Q_T) \neq \varnothing$$

This result is readily apparent using a Venn diagram: As illustrated in Figure 1.6, if P_T is not a subset of Q_T, then there must be elements of P_T outside Q_T; hence the intersection of P_T and $\sim Q_T$ cannot be empty, and vice versa.

In addition to its negation, there are other statements related to the implication $P \Rightarrow Q$. They are

(i) its *converse*: $Q \Rightarrow P$,
(ii) its *inverse*: $\neg P \Rightarrow \neg Q$, and
(iii) its *contrapositive* statement: $\neg Q \Rightarrow \neg P$.

If both the implication $P \Rightarrow Q$ and its converse $Q \Rightarrow P$ are true, we say that P and Q are *equivalent* and write $P \Leftrightarrow Q$.

A statement and its contrapositive are equivalent, as is easily seen by applying the equivalence

$$A \subseteq B \Leftrightarrow (\sim B) \subseteq (\sim A)$$

to the sets associated with the two properties. This observation is useful because sometimes it is easier to prove the contrapositive than the original statement.

(c) Methods of Proof

There are several methods that are often used to prove that a statement of the form $P \Rightarrow Q$ or $P \Leftrightarrow Q$ is true. One of the most common is the *deductive method*, in which we start by assuming that P holds and use this information to verify that Q is also true. Because it is difficult to be much more specific at this level of generality, we shall consider a simple example. There will be many others later.

Example 2.1. Proof of De Morgan's first law. Let $\mathbb{A} = \{A_i; i \in I\}$ be a family of sets in X. We want to prove that

$$\sim(\cup_i A_i) = \cap_i(\sim A_i)$$

That is, we want to show that any element of $\sim(\cup_i A_i)$ also belongs to $\cap_i(\sim A_i)$, and vice versa. For this, it suffices to verify that the definitions of the two sets are equivalent:

$$x \in \sim(\cup_i A_i) \Leftrightarrow x \notin \cup_i A_i \Leftrightarrow \neg(\exists i \in I \text{ s.th. } x \in A_i)$$
$$\Leftrightarrow \forall i \in I, \, x \notin A_i \Leftrightarrow \forall i \in I, \, x \in \sim A_i$$
$$\Leftrightarrow x \in \cap_i(\sim A_i)$$

which is what we wanted to show. In words:

  (i) Take an arbitrary x in the complement of $\cup_i A_i$. By definition, x is not an element of $\cup_i A_i$. Negating the definition of the union of a family of sets (x belongs to $\cup_i A_i$ if it is an element of any of the A_i's), we obtain that
 (ii) x does not belong to any of the A_i's; this is the same as saying that for each i, x belongs to the complement of A_i, which in turn is equivalent to the statement that
(iii) x is an element of the intersection of the complements of the A_i's, $\cap_i(\sim A_i)$.
 (iv) Finally, because this is true for any x in $\cup_i A_i$, the set of all such x's (i.e., $\cup_i A_i$) must be contained in $\cap_i(\sim A_i)$.

Notice that the reasoning is also valid in the opposite direction. Hence we have proved that

$$x \in \sim(\cup_i A_i) \Rightarrow x \in \cap_i(\sim A_i); \quad \text{that is,} \quad \sim(\cup_i A_i) \subseteq \cap_i(\sim A_i)$$

and

$$x \in \cap_i(\sim A_i) \Rightarrow x \in \sim(\cup_i A_i); \quad \text{that is,} \quad \cap_i(\sim A_i) \subseteq \sim(\cup_i A_i)$$

and we can conclude that the two sets are equal.   □

Problem 2.2. Prove the following equivalence (X is the universal set):

$$P \subseteq Q \Leftrightarrow (\sim P) \cup Q = X$$

Problem 2.3. Prove the second of De Morgan's laws: Let $\mathbb{A} = \{A_i; i \in I\}$ be a family of sets in X. Then $\sim(\cap_i A_i) = \cup_i(\sim A_i)$.

The following example shows the usefulness of the equivalence between an implication and its *contrapositive*.

Theorem 2.4. Given two arbitrary real numbers a *and* b, *we have*

$$\forall \varepsilon > 0, \ a \leq b + \varepsilon \Rightarrow a \leq b \quad (P \Rightarrow Q)$$

Proof. The contrapositive of this statement ($\neg Q \Rightarrow \neg P$) can be written

$$a > b \Rightarrow \exists \varepsilon > 0, \ a > b + \varepsilon$$

This is very easy to prove. Because $a > b$, $a - b > 0$, and there exist real numbers ε such that $0 < \varepsilon < a - b$ (e.g., $(a - b)/2$). For any such number we have

$$b + \varepsilon < b + (a - b) = a \qquad \qquad □$$

Another method that is often useful for establishing properties associated with the set of natural numbers is based on the following axiom.

Axiom 2.5. The principle of induction. Let P *be a property that natural numbers (or positive integers) may or may not have. If*

(i) there exists some natural number n_0 *such that* P(n_0) *holds, and*
(ii) for any natural number, P(n) $\Rightarrow$ P(n + 1),

then P *holds for all natural numbers larger than or equal to* n_0.

That is, to prove statements of the form "all natural numbers larger than or equal to n_0 have property P," it is enough to establish that the property holds for n_0 and that if it holds for n it will also do so for $n + 1$. Notice that this is really a statement about the structure of the set of natural numbers. It tells us that the set of natural numbers larger than or equal to n_0 is the set $\{n_0, n_0 + 1, (n_0 + 1) + 1, \ldots\}$ (i.e., that this set can be constructed recursively by adding 1 to the previous element, starting from n_0). If we start from zero, this property can be taken as a definition of the set $\mathbb{N}$ of natural numbers and can therefore be seen as an axiom or basic assumption. It does, however, provide a simple way to establish many useful results, as illustrated by the following example.

Example 2.6. A proof by induction. We shall show that for any positive integer k,

$$\sum_{n=1}^{k} n = \frac{k(k+1)}{2} \tag{1}$$

(where n takes on all integer values from 1 to k). The formula clearly holds for 1, because then it simply says that

$$1 = \frac{1(1+1)}{2}$$

Next we will assume that (1) holds for an arbitrary k and show that this implies that it also holds for $k + 1$. For this, we add $(k + 1)$ to both sides of (1) and rearrange terms to get

$$\left(\sum_{n=1}^{k} n\right) + (k+1) = \frac{k(k+1)}{2} + (k+1) \Rightarrow \sum_{n=1}^{k+1} n = (k+1)\left(1 + \frac{k}{2}\right) = \frac{(k+1)(k+2)}{2}$$

which completes the proof. $\square$

An indirect strategy that is often useful is the *proof by contradiction*. To show that $P \Rightarrow Q$, it is sufficient to show that its negation, $P \nRightarrow Q$, yields a contradiction, that is, a statement of the form $R \wedge (\neg R)$, which can never be true. Intuitively, the idea is that if a given premise leads to a contradiction, then it cannot possibly be correct. Formally, if we can show that $P \nRightarrow Q$ leads to a contradiction, we will have shown that

$$P \wedge (\neg Q) \Rightarrow R \wedge (\neg R)$$

(where we are making use of an equivalence derived earlier). But then the contrapositive statement

$$(\neg R) \vee R \Rightarrow Q \vee (\neg P)$$

will also be true. And because the first property is always true (for any x and R, either R or $\neg R$ will be true), the second (which, as we have seen, is equivalent to $P \Rightarrow Q$) will always hold. As an example, we will prove the following result.

Theorem 2.7. The well-ordering principle. Every nonempty set of positive integers contains a least element.

Proof. Let P be a nonempty set of positive integers, and define S as the set of all positive integers that are strictly smaller than all elements of P. That is,

$$S = \{n \in \mathbb{Z}_+; \; n < p \; \forall \; p \in P\}$$

To prove the theorem, we first assume that P does not have a smallest element and attempt to show that this implies that S is the entire set of positive integers. But that would be a contradiction, for then S would contain the set P (which is nonempty by assumption), implying that for any number p in P we would have $p < p$, which clearly is impossible.

Assuming that P has no smallest element, we will proceed by induction:

(i) We observe that 1, which is the smallest positive integer, must belong to S.

(ii) Next, let k be an arbitrary positive integer. We will show that if k belongs to S, then so does $k + 1$. We proceed by contradiction: Suppose k is strictly smaller than any element of P, but $k + 1$ is not (i.e., $k \in S$, but $k + 1 \notin S$).

Then ($k + 1 \notin S$ implies that) there exists a number $p_1 \in P$ such that $k + 1 \geq p_1$. Moreover, because P has no least element, there exists some other number $p_2 \in P$ such that $p_2 < p_1$. Combining these two inequalities,

$$p_2 < p_1 \leq k + 1$$
$$\Rightarrow p_2 < k + 1 \tag{1}$$

Now, because both p_2 and k are integers, (1) implies

$$p_2 \leq k$$

and we conclude that k is not strictly smaller than every element of P. Hence, we have reached a contradiction, and we conclude that $k \in S$ implies $k + 1 \in S$.

Given (i) and (ii), it follows by induction that S is the whole of $\mathbb{Z}_+$. Because this leads to a contradiction, we conclude that P must have a least element.   □

Problem 2.8. The following modification of the induction principle is sometimes useful: Let P be a property that natural numbers (or positive integers) may or may not have. If

(i) $P(0)$ holds and

(ii) if P holds for all integers $k = 0, 1, \ldots, n - 1$, then it also holds for n.

Then P holds for all natural numbers.

Complete the following proof of this result: Let S be the set of nonnegative integers for which $P(n)$ is false. We want to show that S is the empty set. Suppose that S is not empty, and use the well-ordering principle and assumptions (i) and (ii) to reach a contradiction.

Problem 2.9. Use the modified induction principle to prove that any integer larger than 1 is either a prime number (it has no integer divisors other than 1) or the product of prime numbers.

3. Relations

Given two sets X and Y, their *Cartesian product* $X \times Y$ is the set of all ordered pairs formed by an element of X followed by one of Y. That is,

$$X \times Y = \{(x, y); \ x \in X \text{ and } y \in Y\}$$

A (binary) *relation* from X to Y is a subset R of $X \times Y$. In many cases we work with relations defined on $X \times X$. In this case, we speak of a relation defined on X.

If $(x, y) \in R$, we often write xRy or $y \in R(x)$ and say that y is an *image* of x. The image set of x is given by

$$R(x) = \{y \in Y; \ (x, y) \in R\}$$

If R is a relation from X to Y, its inverse relation, R^{-1}, is a relation from Y to X defined by

$$R^{-1} = \{(y, x); \ (x, y) \in R\}$$

Let R be a relation from X to Y. If A is a subset of X, the image of A under R is the subset of Y given by

$$R(A) = \{y \in Y; \ \exists x \in A \text{ s.th. } (x, y) \in R\} = \cup_{x \in A} R(x)$$

If B is a subset of Y, the inverse image of B under R is its image set under R^{-1}:

$$R^{-1}(B) = \{x \in X; \ \exists y \in B \text{ s.th. } (x, y) \in R\} = \cup_{y \in B} R^{-1}(y)$$

The inverse image of Y (i.e., the set of points of X that each has at least one image in Y) is the *domain* of the relation:

$$D_R = R^{-1}(Y) = \{x \in X;\ R(x) \neq \varnothing\}$$

And the *image* of X under R is the range of R:

$$R_R = R(X) = \{y \in Y;\ R^{-1}(y) \neq \varnothing\}$$

Given two relations R and S defined on the product set $X \times Y$, we say that S is a *subrelation* of R if $S \subseteq R$ or, equivalently, if $xSy \Rightarrow xRy$. We can also say that S is a restriction of R, or that R is an extension of S. For example, weak vector dominance ($\geq$), defined by

$$x \geq y \Leftrightarrow x_i \geq y_i\ \forall i = 1, \ldots, n$$

is a binary relation defined on $\mathbb{R}^n \times \mathbb{R}^n$. Strict vector dominance ($>$), defined in a similar way, but with strict inequalities, is a subrelation of weak vector dominance ($\geq$), because $x > y$ implies $x \geq y$.

Let R be a relation from X to Y, and S a relation from Y to Z. Their *composition*, $R \circ S$ is the relation from X to Z given by

$$R \circ S = \{(x, z);\ \exists\, y \in Y\ \text{s.th. } (x, y) \in R \text{ and } (y, z) \in S\}$$

Intuitively, the concept of "relation" provides a way to formalize the idea that two objects (typically two elements of the same set) stand in a certain relationship to each other. For example, if x and y are real numbers, one may be larger than the other. If x and y denote consumption bundles, a given consumer may prefer one to the other. The notation xRy, interpreted as "x stands in a certain relation to y," is therefore more suggestive than the notation $(x, y) \in R$, although they are equivalent. However, the formal definition of "relation as a set" is convenient from a mathematical point of view. It allows us, for example, to think in terms of subsets of R, or to decompose R in smaller "factors."

As we will see, the notion of relation is a basic instrument that can be used to define different types of structures on a set. In Section 4 we will introduce the concept of "function" as a special type of relation. That, in turn, will allow us to introduce an algebraic or topological structure in a set by defining functions with convenient properties that we will call "operations" or "metrics." Before getting into these subjects, the discussion in the rest of this section will focus on two types of relations that can be used to impose a certain "order" in a given set. An *equivalence relation* allows us to partition a set into a collection of subsets of "equivalent" elements, and an *order relation* allows us to classify the elements of a set according to criteria of preference and goodness or precedence and size. Because such relations are defined in terms of certain properties that relations may have, we begin by introducing these properties.

Definition 3.1. Let R be a binary relation defined on X. We say that R is

reflexive if $\forall\, x \in X, xRx$,
symmetric if $\forall\, x, y \in X, xRy \Leftrightarrow yRx$,
antisymmetric if $\forall\, x, y \in X, (xRy$ and $yRx) \Rightarrow x = y$, and
transitive if $\forall\, x, y, z \in X, (xRy$ and $yRz) \Rightarrow xRz$.

(a) Equivalence Relations and Decomposition of a Set into Classes

Definition 3.2. Equivalence relation. A binary relation R defined on a set X is an equivalence relation if it is reflexive, symmetric, and transitive.

Sometimes we are interested in decomposing a given set into a collection of pairwise-disjoint sets whose union is equal to the original set (i.e., into a *partition*). Such a partition of a set is called a decomposition of the set into (equivalence) classes. A natural way to achieve such a partition is to specify an equivalence relation R on X and then assign to each class all those elements that are related to each other under R.

Theorem 3.3. Partition of a set into classes. A set X *can be partitioned into classes by using an equivalence relation* R *as a criterion for assigning two elements to the same class. Conversely, every partition of a set defines an equivalence relation on it.*

Proof. Let R be an equivalence relation on X. For each a in X, define the set

$$C_a = \{x \in X;\ xRa\}$$

It is obvious that each element of X belongs to at least one such set, and also that some of these sets may be equal. To prove that the relation defines a partition, we must show that any two such sets, C_a and C_b, are either disjoint or identical (if aRb).

Suppose C_a and C_b have a common element, say c. By assumption, cRa and cRb. By symmetry, aRc, and by transitivity,

$$(aRc \text{ and } cRb) \Rightarrow aRb$$

Hence a and b are in the same class of elements, and we conclude that if C_a and C_b have any common elements, they are the same set. That is, the pairwise-disjoint sets of this type form a partition of X into equivalence classes.

We observe that every partition of X into pairwise-disjoint classes determines a binary relation on X, where xRy means that x and y belong to the same class. It is clear that this relation is reflexive, symmetric, and transitive (i.e., is an equivalence relation).   □

Definition 3.4. Quotient set. Let X be a set, and R an equivalence relation on X that determines a partition of X into classes. The set of equivalence classes under R is called the quotient set of X with respect to R.

(b) Order Relations and Ordered Sets

A class of binary relations of particular interest is the one that allows us to formalize the idea that some elements of a set dominate (or are "larger than") others. Such a relation is called an "order relation," and a set in which an order relation has been defined is called an ordered set.

Let "≥" be a binary relation on the set X. We interpret the expression $x \geq y$ as saying that, in some relevant way, x dominates y, is larger than y, or comes after it. Equivalently, we can work with the inverse relation "≤," where $x \leq y$ is equivalent to $y \geq x$ and indicates that x is "smaller" than y or precedes it. We now define two common types of order relations.

Definition 3.5. Preordering. A binary relation "≥" defined on a set X is a partial preordering or quasiordering if it is reflexive and transitive, that is, if

$$\forall\, x, y, z \in X, \; x \geq x \text{ and } [(x \geq y \text{ and } y \geq z) \Rightarrow x \geq z]$$

We say that X is partially preordered by "≥." If, in addition, any pair of elements x and y of X are comparable under the relation, that is, if

$$\forall\, x, y, \in X, \; x \geq y \text{ or } y \geq x \text{ or both}$$

then "≥" is a complete or total preordering, and we say that X is totally preordered by "≥."

Definition 3.6. Ordering. A binary relation "≥" defined on a set X is a partial ordering if it is reflexive, transitive, and antisymmetric, that is, if it is a partial preordering and, moreover,

$$\forall\, x, y \in X, (x \geq y \text{ and } y \geq x) \Rightarrow x = y$$

We then say that X is partially ordered by "≥." If, in addition, any pair of elements of X are comparable under the relation, "≥" is a complete or total ordering, and we say that X is totally ordered by it.[2]

The standard order relation defined on the set of real numbers is a complete ordering. This relation is antisymmetric, for given any two real numbers α and β, $\alpha \geq \beta$ and $\beta \geq \alpha$ imply $\alpha = \beta$.

Notice that the only difference between a preordering and an ordering is that the preordering need not be antisymmetric; that is, it is possible to have $x \geq y$, $y \geq x$, and $x \neq y$. In this case, we write $x \sim y$ and say that x and y are *equivalent*.

A preordering can be decomposed into its symmetric and asymmetric components by defining the following two subrelations:

$$x > y \text{ if and only if } x \geq y \text{ and } y \not\geq x$$

$$x \sim y \text{ if and only if } x \geq y \text{ and } y \geq x$$

(where $y \not\geq x$ means "not $y \geq x$"). In the context of the theory of preferences, these relations would be called the strict preference and indifference relations.

In an ordered set, the concept of the "best" or "largest" element makes sense. Hence, we can talk of maximization with respect to an order relation. We must be a bit careful, however, for if the order relation is not complete, some elements of the set may not be comparable. In this case, we cannot speak of a "maximum," but we can still define some closely related concepts.

Definition 3.7. Maximal and minimal elements. Let X be a set partially preordered by a relation "$\geq$." An element $\bar{x}$ of X is maximal (with respect to "$\geq$") if no other element of X dominates it strictly, that is, if

$$x \geq \bar{x} \Rightarrow x \sim \bar{x} \qquad (\text{or } x = \bar{x} \text{ for an ordering})$$

Similarly, an element $\underline{x}$ of X is minimal if no other element strictly precedes it, that is, if

$$x \leq \underline{x} \Rightarrow x \sim \underline{x} \qquad (\text{or } x = \underline{x} \text{ for an ordering})$$

where "$\leq$" is the inverse relation of "$\geq$."

Definition 3.8. Largest and smallest elements. Let X be a set partially preordered by "$\geq$." An element $\bar{z}$ of X is a largest or last element of X if it dominates every element of X (i.e., if $\forall x \in X, \bar{z} \geq x$). An element $\underline{z}$ of X is a least or first element of X if it precedes every element of X (i.e., if $\forall x \in X$, $\underline{z} \leq x$).

Notice that a largest element must be maximal, but a maximal element may not be largest if the preordering is partial, for some elements of X may not be comparable with it. If the preordering is complete, however, maximal elements will also be largest. If the relation "$\geq$" is an ordering, the largest element, when it exists, is unique and is called the maximum. This need not be the case with a preordering, where we may find several largest elements that are equivalent but are different from each other. With the appropriate changes, all this is also true for minimal and smallest elements.

4. Functions

Among the most important types of relations are those we call functions. Intuitively, a function from a set X to a set Y is a rule that assigns to each element of X a unique element of Y. We say that y is the image of x under f, and write $y = f(x)$. Conversely, x is an element of the preimage or inverse image of y, written $x \in f^{-1}(y)$.

Definition 4.1. Function. Let X and Y be two sets. A function f from X to Y, written $f : X \longrightarrow Y$, is a relation from X to Y with the property that for each $x \in X$ there exists a unique element $y \in Y$ such that $(x, y) \in f$.

The image and preimage of a set under a given function, and the function's domain and range, are defined as for any relation. If f is a function from X to Y, its domain is X, and its range is the set $f(X)$. If A is a subset of X, its image set is the subset of Y formed by the images of its elements:

$$f(A) = \{y \in Y; \ \exists x \in A \text{ s.th. } y = f(x)\} = \cup_{x \in A} f(x)$$

Given a subset B of Y, its inverse image is the set $f^{-1}(B)$ formed by those elements of X with images in B:

$$f^{-1}(B) = \{x \in X; \ f(x) \in B\}$$

If x is an element of X, and R is a relation, the image of x, $R(x)$, may be any subset of Y, including the empty set. If R is a function, however, $R(x)$ contains exactly one point of Y. Hence, a relation R is a function if and only if its domain is the whole set X and, moreover,

$$(x, y_1) \in R \text{ and } (x, y_2) \in R \Rightarrow y_1 = y_2$$

or, equivalently,

$$\forall x \in X, \ \exists! \ y \in Y \text{ s.th. } y = f(x)$$

where "$\exists!$" means "there exists exactly one element."

Two functions f and g are equal if they are identical as sets, that is, if $f \subseteq g$ and $g \subseteq f$. This is the same as saying that f and g have the same domain and range and, moreover, for every x in $D_f = D_g$, we have $f(x) = g(x)$.

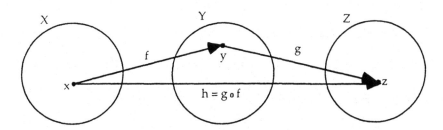

Figure 1.7. Composition of two functions.

If f is a function and, in addition, its range is the whole set Y, that is, if $f(X) = Y$, or

$$\forall\, y \in Y,\ \exists\, x \in X \text{ s.th. } y = f(x)$$

then we say that f is *surjective* or *onto* Y. We also say that f is *injective* or *one-to-one* if it always assigns different images to different elements of X, that is, if

$$\forall\, x_1, x_2 \in X,\ f(x_1) = f(x_2) \Rightarrow x_1 = x_2$$

or, equivalently, if $x_1 \neq x_2$ implies $f(x_1) \neq f(x_2)$. Finally, the function f is *bijective* if it is both "one-to-one" and "onto," that is, if each element of Y has an inverse image and that inverse image is unique.

Given a function f, its inverse relation $f^{-1} : y \longrightarrow x \in f^{-1}(y)$ may or may not be a function. If it is a function, f^{-1} is said to be the inverse function of f. If f is one-to-one, each y in $f(X)$ will have a unique inverse image in X, and therefore f^{-1} will be a function of $f(X)$ into X. If f is also "onto," f^{-1} will be a function from Y to X.

If f is a function of X into Y, and g is a function of Y into Z, their *composition*, $g \circ f$ is the function of X into Z defined by $(g \circ f)(x) = g[f(x)]$. The composition of two functions obeys the associative law, that is,

$$(h \circ g) \circ f = h \circ (g \circ f) = h \circ g \circ f$$

but it is generally not commutative.

We will now review some elementary results concerning the properties of the image sets and inverse-image sets under a function and introduce some concepts that are defined in terms of functions.

Theorem 4.2. Let $f : X \longrightarrow Y$ *be a function, and* $\mathbb{B} = \{B_i;\, i \in I\}$ *a family of subsets of* Y. *Then*

(i) $f^{-1}(\cup_{i \in I} B_i) = \cup_{i \in I} f^{-1}(B_i)$, *and*
(ii) $f^{-1}(\cap_{i \in I} B_i) = \cap_{i \in I} f^{-1}(B_i)$.

Proof

(i) $x \in f^{-1}(\cup_{i \in I} B_i) \Leftrightarrow f(x) \in \cup_{i \in I} B_i$
$\Leftrightarrow \exists_i \in I \text{ s.th. } f(x) \in B_i$
$\Leftrightarrow \exists_i \in I \text{ s.th. } x \in f^{-1}(B_i)$
$\Leftrightarrow x \in \cup_{i \in I} f^{-1}(B_i).$

(ii) $x \in f^{-1}(\cap_{i \in I} B_i) \Leftrightarrow f(x) \in \cap_{i \in I} B_i$
$\Leftrightarrow \forall i \in I, f(x) \in B_i$
$\Leftrightarrow \forall i \in I, x \in f^{-1}(B_i)$
$\Leftrightarrow x \in \cap_{i \in I} f^{-1}(B_i).$ □

Theorem 4.3. *Let* f $: X \longrightarrow Y$ *be a function, and* $\mathbb{A} = \{A_i; i \in I\}$ *a family of subsets of* X. *Then*

(i) $f(\cup_{i \in I} A_i) = \cup_{i \in I} f(A_i)$, *and*
(ii) $f(\cap_{i \in I} A_i) \subseteq \cap_{i \in I} f(A_i).$

Proof

(i) $y \in f(\cup_{i \in I} A_i) \Leftrightarrow \exists x \in \cup_{i \in I} A_i \text{ s.th. } f(x) = y$
$\Leftrightarrow \exists i \in I \text{ s.th. } f(x) = y \in f(A_i)$
$\Leftrightarrow y \in \cup_{i \in I} f(A_i).$

(ii) $y \in f(\cap_{i \in I} A_i) \Leftrightarrow \exists x \in \cap_{i \in I} A_i \text{ s.th. } f(x) = y$
$\Rightarrow \forall i \in I, \exists x_i \in A_i \text{ s.th. } f(x_i) = y$ (e.g., $x_i = x \; \forall_i$)
$\Leftrightarrow \forall i \in I, y \in f(A_i)$
$\Leftrightarrow y \in \cap_{i \in I} f(A_i).$ □

Problem 4.4. Explain why inclusion works only in one direction in the second part of Theorem 4.3, but in both directions in the first part.

(i) Give an example in which $\cap_{i \in I} f(A_i)$ is strictly larger than $f(\cap_{i \in I} A_i)$.
(ii) Prove that if f is one-to-one, then $\cap_{i \in I} f(A_i) = f(\cap_{i \in I} A_i)$.

Problem 4.5. Given a function $f : X \longrightarrow Y$, two subsets of X, A_1 and A_2, and two subsets of Y, B_1 and B_2, show that

(i) $f^{-1}(\sim B_1) = \sim f^{-1}(B_1)$,
(ii) $f^{-1}(B_1 \sim B_2) = f^{-1}(B_1) \sim f^{-1}(B_2)$, and
(iii) if f is bijective, then

$$f(\sim A_1) = \sim f(A_1) \quad \text{and} \quad f(A_1 \sim A_2) = f(A_1) \sim f(A_2)$$

What can we say if f is not bijective?

Problem 4.6. Let f be a function from X to Y, with A a subset of X, and B a subset of Y. Then

$$f[f^{-1}(B)] \subseteq B \quad \text{and} \quad A \subseteq f^{-1}[f(A)]$$

When are the two sets not equal to each other?

Sequences

A particularly useful family of functions is that formed by functions whose domain is the set of the natural numbers. Let X be an arbitrary set, and $\mathbb{N}$ the set of natural numbers. A function $s:\mathbb{N} \longrightarrow X$ is said to be a *sequence* in X. Intuitively, we can think of a sequence, or rather of its range, as an ordered set of elements of X. In the usual notation, x_i denotes the value of the sequence at i, that is, $s(i) = x_i$, and $\{x_n\}$ is used to indicate that we are talking about the sequence "as a whole."

It is sometimes useful to define a sequence recursively. That is, given a function f of X into itself, and an element a of X, there exists a unique sequence $\{x_n\}$ in X such that $x_0 = a$ and $x_{n+1} = f(x_n)$ for $n = 1, 2, \ldots$.

Occasionally we may want to work with a "subset" of a given sequence (i.e., with a subsequence). Formally, let $s:\mathbb{N} \longrightarrow X$ be a sequence, and consider a strictly increasing function $g:\mathbb{N} \longrightarrow \mathbb{N}$. The composite function given by $h(k) = s[g(k)]$ for any positive integer k is a *subsequence* of s. The usual notation for a subsequence of $\{x_n\}$ is $\{x_{n_k}\}$, with two subindices. Intuitively, a subsequence is a sequence formed by deleting some terms from the original one. For any $k = 1, 2, \ldots$, the increasing function $g(\ )$ selects some positive integer $n_k > n_{k-1}$, and we take the corresponding term of the original sequence to form $\{x_{n_k}\}$. For example, the even-numbered terms of a sequence form a subsequence.

Correspondences

A *correspondence* from X to Y is a function that to each element x of the set X assigns a subset of the set Y. Hence, a correspondence Ψ of X to Y, denoted by $\Psi:X \longrightarrow\!\!\!\!\!\rightarrow Y$, is a function $X \longrightarrow P(Y)$.

Alternatively, a relation Ψ of X to Y is a correspondence of X to Y if its domain is X, that is, if for all x in X we have $\Psi(x) \neq \varnothing$. Hence, every relation from X to Y is a correspondence defined on its domain D_R. We can also say that a function is a special case of correspondence in which the image set of each element of X is a singleton (i.e., a set formed by a single element).

Axiom of Choice

One of the basic assumptions of set theory is the so-called axiom of choice. It says that given an arbitrary collection $\mathbb{A}$ of nonempty sets in X, there is always a function f from $P(X)$ to X itself such that $f(A_i) \in A_i$ for each A_i in $\mathbb{A}$. That is, we assume the existence of a "selection function" f that chooses an element from each of the sets in $\mathbb{A}$. It seems reasonable to assume that this is always possible, but when we cannot give a specific selection criterion, we have to resort to the axiom of choice. This assumption is often used (in many cases implicitly) in proofs in which at some point we make a statement of the form "we take an element x_i from each of the sets A_i in a given class $\mathbb{A}$."

Finite, Infinite, and Countable Sets

When we count the number of elements of a set X, we associate with each element a natural number. In other words, counting the elements of a set X amounts to constructing a function from X to the set $\mathbb{N}$ of natural numbers. The generalization of this idea takes us to the concept of *cardinality* (or cardinal number) of a set.

We say that two sets A and B are *numerically equivalent* if there exists a bijective function of A onto B. If a set A is numerically equivalent to some subset of the set of positive integers, $\mathbb{Z}_+$, we say that A is a countable set. If this subset of $\mathbb{Z}_+$ is of the form $\{1, 2, \ldots, n\}$, the set is finite, and its cardinal number is simply the number of its elements. The empty set is considered finite, and its cardinal number is zero. If A is not numerically equivalent to $\{1, 2, \ldots, n\}$, we say that it is an infinite set.

Hence, a set A is *countable* if it is finite or if there exists a bijection from A to the entire set $\mathbb{Z}_+$ of the positive integers. In the second case, A is an infinite but countable set, and its cardinal number is called $\mathcal{N}_0$ ("aleph-zero"). There are also infinite sets that are not countable, such as the set $\mathbb{R}$ of real numbers.

Generalization of the Cartesian Product

We have defined the Cartesian product of two sets X and Y as the set of all ordered pairs of the form (x, y), where $x \in X$ and $y \in Y$. Suppose now that we are given a more general class of sets, $\mathbb{A} = \{A_i; A_i \subseteq X, i \in \mathrm{I}\}$. If the index set I is finite, say of the form $I = \{1, 2, \ldots, n\}$, the Cartesian product $A = \times_{i \in I} A_i$ is defined, as may be expected, as the set of all ordered n-tuples $x = (x_1, x_2, \ldots, x_n)$ such that $x_i \in A_i$ for each $i = 1, \ldots, n$. We say that x_i is the ith *coordinate* of x, and A_i the ith *component* of A. To generalize the concept to an arbitrary family of sets $\mathbb{A}$ (possibly infinite and not countable), we use the concept of function. Hence the Cartesian product $\times \mathbb{A}$ is defined as the set of all functions $f : I \longrightarrow \cup_{i \in I} A_i$ such that $f(i) \in A_i$ for each $i \in I$.

5. Algebraic Structures

In most applications, we work with numerical spaces, that is, sets whose elements are numbers, sequences of numbers, or numerical functions. It seems natural to impose an algebraic structure on such sets by defining operations.

In general terms, we can define an *algebraic structure* $A = \{(X_i), O\}$ as a collection formed by one or more sets X_i of (generally numeric) elements, together with a second set O of operations defined on the sets X_i. An *operation* is simply a function defined on the Cartesian product of two or more sets, and taking values in another set that may or may not be one of the preceding sets. Given a set X, an *n*-ary operation in X is a function $*: X^n \longrightarrow X$. For example, a binary operation in X is a function $*: X \times X \longrightarrow X$ that assigns to each pair of elements (x, y) of X a unique element z of X. We often write $z = x * y$. If "$*$" is a binary operation in X, we say that X is *closed* with respect to the operation "$*$," or that "$*$" is a law of internal composition.

We will now define some important algebraic structures. The different structures are characterized by different properties of the operations.

(a) Groups and Fields

Let X be a set, and "$*$" a binary operation defined on it. We say that "$*$" is an *associative* operation if

$$\forall x, y, z \in X, \ (x * y) * z = x * (y * z)$$

If this property holds, we can write expressions like $x * y * z$ without ambiguity. We say that "$*$" is *commutative* (or satisfies the commutative law) if the order of composition does not alter the result, that is, if

$$\forall x, y \in X, x * y = y * x$$

The operation "$*$" defined on X has an *identity element* if there exists an element e of X such that

$$\forall x \in X, x * e = x = e * x$$

Notice that the definition implies that the identity element, when it exists, is unique. To see this, assume that e and e' are both identity elements. Then, $e * e' = e'$ and $e * e' = e$, from where $e' = e * e' = e$.

An element x^s is the *symmetric* or *inverse element* of x with respect to "$*$" if the composition of the two is the identity element, that is, if

$$x * x^s = x^s * x = e$$

If the operation is associative, the inverse of x, when it exists, is unique, for if x^s and x^i are both inverses of x, we have

$$x^s = x^s * e = x^s * (x * x^i) = (x^s * x) * x^i = e * x^i = x^i$$

Let "$*$" and "$\oplus$" be two binary operations defined on a set X. We say that "$*$" is a *distributive law* with respect to "$\oplus$" if

$$\forall\, x, y, z \in X,\ x*(y \oplus z) = (x*y) \oplus (x*z) \text{ and } (y \oplus z)*x = (y*x) \oplus (z*x)$$

If "$*$" is commutative, these two properties (distributivity on the left and on the right) are equivalent.

Definition 5.1. Group and commutative group. Let G be a set, and "$*$" an operation defined on it. We say that $G = \{G, *\}$ is a group if G is closed under "$*$" and this operation is an associative law, endowed with an identity and with the property that every $x \in G$ has an inverse element with respect to "$*$." If, in addition, "$*$" is commutative, we say that $\{G, *\}$ is a commutative group.

Let $\{G, *\}$ be a group, and consider the restriction of "$*$" to some subset S of G. If S is closed with respect to "$*$" and $\{S, *\}$ satisfies the other conditions in the definition of group, we say that $\{S, *\}$ is a *subgroup* of $\{G, *\}$. Clearly, $\{S, *\}$ inherits the "manipulative" properties of $\{G, *\}$ (i.e., the associative and commutative laws); hence, in order to show that $\{S, *\}$ is a subgroup, it is sufficient to verify that S contains the identity e, and that for each x in S, its inverse is also in S.

Definition 5.2. Field. A field $F = \{F, +, \cdot\}$ is an algebraic structure formed by a set F together with two binary operations $(+, \cdot)$ defined on it, called addition and multiplication, respectively, which have the following properties:

I. The set F together with the operation of addition is a commutative group. The additive identity is called 0, and the symmetric element of each $\alpha \in F$ is denoted by $(-\alpha)$. That is, for every $\alpha, \beta, \gamma \in F$, the following properties hold:

   1. Associative property: $(\alpha + \beta) + \gamma = \alpha + (\beta + \gamma)$
   2. Commutative property: $\alpha + \beta = \beta + \alpha$
   3. Existence of the additive identity: $\exists!\ 0 \in F$ s.th. $\alpha + 0 = 0 + \alpha = \alpha\ \forall\ \alpha \in F$
   4. Existence of inverse elements: $\forall\ \alpha \in F, \exists!\ (-\alpha) \in F$ s.th. $\alpha + (-\alpha) = (-\alpha) + \alpha = 0$

II. Multiplication is an associative and commutative operation, endowed with an identity called 1 $(\neq 0)$, and every element α of F different from zero has a multiplicative inverse, written α^{-1} or $1/\alpha$. That is, $\forall\ \alpha, \beta, \gamma \in F$, we have the following:

   1. Associative property: $(\alpha \cdot \beta) \cdot \gamma = \alpha \cdot (\beta \cdot \gamma)$
   2. Commutative property: $\alpha \cdot \beta = \beta \cdot \alpha$
   3. Existence of a multiplicative identity: $\exists!\ 1 \in F$ s.th. $\alpha \cdot 1 = 1 \cdot \alpha = \alpha\ \forall\ \alpha \in F$

4. Existence of inverse elements: $\forall\, \alpha\, (\neq 0) \in F,\, \exists!\, \alpha^{-1} \in X$ s.th. $\alpha \cdot \alpha^{-1} = \alpha^{-1} \cdot \alpha = 1$

III. Multiplication is distributive with respect to addition:

$$\forall\, \alpha, \beta, \gamma \in F,\ \alpha \cdot (\beta + \gamma) = (\alpha \cdot \beta) + (\alpha \cdot \gamma) = \alpha \cdot \beta + \alpha \cdot \gamma$$

Let $F = \{F, +, \cdot\}$ be a field, and S a subset of F. We say that $\{S, +, \cdot\}$ is a *subfield* of F if $\{S, +, \cdot\}$ is a field on its own right, that is, if S is closed under both operations and the properties required in the definition hold. As before, if S is a subset of F, it will inherit the manipulative properties of F (i.e., the associative, commutative, and distributive properties will hold in S, because they hold in the whole F). To verify that a subset S of F gives rise to a subfield of F, therefore, it is sufficient to verify the existence of inverse and identity elements (with respect to addition and multiplication) and that S is closed under both operations.

The most common examples of fields are the real and complex numbers, with the standard definitions of addition and multiplication. In fact, the definition of "field" is based directly on the algebraic properties of the set of real numbers endowed with the standard operations.

All the basic properties of the operations of real numbers can be derived from the field axioms. For example:

(i) $\forall\, \alpha \in F, \alpha \cdot 0 = 0$: Let $\beta = \alpha \cdot 0$; by the distributive law, we have

$$\beta + \beta = \alpha \cdot 0 + \alpha \cdot 0 = \alpha \cdot (0 + 0) = \alpha \cdot 0 = \beta$$

Hence, $\beta + \beta = \beta$; adding the additive inverse of β to both sides of this expression, we have

$$-\beta + \beta = -\beta + \beta + \beta \Rightarrow 0 = 0 + \beta = \beta$$

(ii) $\forall\, \alpha \in F, (-1) \cdot \alpha = -\alpha$: Let $\gamma = (-1) \cdot \alpha$; then, using the existence of a zero element and the distributive law together with the previous result,

$$\alpha + \gamma = 1 \cdot \alpha + (-1) \cdot \alpha = \alpha \cdot (-1 + 1) = \alpha \cdot 0 = 0$$

from which we conclude that γ is the additive inverse of α.

Problem 5.3. Let "$*$" be a law of internal composition on X that satisfies the associative property and is endowed with an identity element. Prove that if x and y have symmetric elements x^s and y^s, then the symmetric element of $x * y$ is $y^s * x^s$.

Problem 5.4. Let X be an arbitrary set, and $\{G, *\}$ a group. Show that the set of functions of X into G, endowed with the operation defined by the composition of images, that is,

$$\forall\, x \in X,\ (f * g)(x) = f(x) * g(x)$$

is a group.

Problem 5.5. Show that the intersection of subgroups of G is a subgroup of G.

(b) Vector Spaces

Definition 5.6. Vector space. A vector or linear space V defined over a field F is a set V of elements called vectors, together with a binary operation $V \times V \longrightarrow V$ called vector addition, and an operation $F \times V \longrightarrow V$ called multiplication by a scalar (an element of the field F). These operations have the following properties:

I. Vector addition is a law of internal composition in V (i.e., V is closed under it), and $\{V, +\}$ is a commutative group, that is, for all $x, y, z \in V$, we have the following:

   1. Associative property: $x + (y + z) = (x + y) + z$
   2. Commutative property: $x + y = y + x$
   3. Existence of the additive identity: $\exists!\ \underline{0} \in V\!: x + \underline{0} = \underline{0} + x = x$
   4. Existence of inverse elements: $\forall\, x \in V, \exists!\ (-x)\!: x + (-x) = (-x) + x = \underline{0}$

II. For all $x, y \in V$ and for all $\alpha, \beta \in F$, we have the following:

   5. Double-distributive property:

   $$\alpha(x + y) = \alpha x + \alpha y \quad \text{and} \quad (\alpha + \beta)x = \alpha x + \beta x$$

   6. Associative law for scalars: $\alpha(\beta x) = (\alpha\beta)x$
   7. Neutrality of the scalar multiplicative identity, 1: $1x = x$

We will normally work with vector spaces defined over the field of real numbers. We will generally use Greek letters to denote scalars, and Latin letters to indicate vectors. Notice that we use the same symbol for vector addition and scalar addition; although they are different operations, this should not be a problem. Notice also that the dot ($\cdot$) is often omitted when multiplying a vector by a scalar.

Most vector spaces we will encounter in applications are special cases of the following space.

Theorem 5.7. Let X *be a nonempty set, and* F *a field. The set of all functions* $f : X \longrightarrow F$, *with addition and multiplication by a scalar defined by*

$$(f + g)(x) = f(x) + g(x) \quad \text{and} \quad (\alpha f)(x) = \alpha f(x)\ \forall\, x \in X$$

is a vector space over F.

It is obvious that most of the vector-space axioms hold given the properties of the field F. The zero element is the function z such that $z(x) = 0$ for every x in X; moreover, given an arbitrary function f, its additive inverse $(-f)$ is given by $(-f)(x) = -f(x)$.

If in Theorem 5.7 we take X to be the set of the first n positive integers and $F = \mathbb{R}$, we obtain the vector space $V_n(\mathbb{R})$, which is simply the set of vectors in $\mathbb{R}^n$ with vector addition and scalar multiplication defined component by component:

$$z = x + y \Leftrightarrow z^i = x^i + y^i \quad \text{and} \quad y = \alpha x \Leftrightarrow y^i = \alpha x^i \quad (\forall i = 1, \ldots, n)$$

If X is the set of natural numbers, and F is $\mathbb{R}$, we obtain the space of infinite real sequences, with vector addition and scalar multiplication defined term by term. With $X = \{(i, j); i = 1, \ldots, m, j = 1, \ldots, n\}$ we have the vector space of $m \times n$ matrices defined over a field F, with the usual definitions of matrix addition and multiplication by a scalar, and so forth.

In what follows, we will often suppress the distinction between the vector space V and the underlying set V (as we have already done in the case of fields). Let V be a vector space over a field F. If a subset S of V is a vector space under the same operations defined on V, we say that S is a *vector subspace* of V. Of course, S inherits the manipulative properties that hold on the whole of V; hence in order to establish that it is indeed a vector subspace, it is enough to verify that S is closed under addition and multiplication by a scalar, that the zero vector $\underline{0}$ is an element of S, and that for each x in S, $(-x)$ is also an element of X. In fact, it is even easier, as shown in the following result, whose proof is left as an exercise.

Theorem 5.8. Let V *be a vector space over a field* F, *and let* S *be a nonempty subset of* V. *Then* S *is a vector subspace of* V *if and only if*

$$\forall \alpha, \beta \in F \text{ and } \forall x, y \in S, \text{ we have } \alpha x + \beta y \in S.$$

Problem 5.9. Prove Theorem 5.8.

6. The Real Number System

Most of the spaces we will be working with are sets constructed in some way starting from the set $\mathbb{R}$ of real numbers. Hence, it is important to review the basic properties of this set. It is possible to construct $\mathbb{R}$ by starting with the natural numbers as undefined concepts, defining next the operations addition, multiplication, subtraction, and division, and introducing new numbers as it becomes necessary to ensure that these operations do not take us outside the set of "existing" numbers. In this manner we will arrive at the set $\mathbb{Q}$ of the rational numbers. It is then observed that even though each rational number can be represented as a point on a straight line, the converse statement is not true, suggesting that the set $\mathbb{Q}$ has, to put it informally, some holes in it. The problem also manifests itself through the impossibility of finding rational solutions to some simple equations (e.g., $x^2 = 2$). To "plug" these holes, we define the irrational numbers and then, finally, the set of real numbers as the union of the rational and irrational numbers.

It is also possible, although perhaps less instructive, to define $\mathbb{R}$ directly as a set that satisfies a number of properties or axioms. That is the path we will take here, because we will later make use of the properties of $\mathbb{R}$ rather than the method of its construction. The set $\mathbb{R}$ appears, then, as a set in which we have defined various structures: an algebraic structure that allows us to perform the usual operations of addition and multiplication, and an order structure, compatible with the cited operations, that permits us to say that some numbers are larger than others. These two sets of properties (which also hold for the rational numbers) are complemented by the so-called *axiom of completeness*, which completes the list of defining properties of $\mathbb{R}$. Intuitively, this third axiom is what allows us to establish the existence of a bijective function from $\mathbb{R}$ to the points of the line.

Problem 6.1. Show that there is no rational number $a = p/q$ (where p and q are integers with no common divisors) such that $a^2 = 2$. (By contradiction: Assume $p^2/q^2 = 2$, and show that this implies that both p and q are even, which contradicts our assumption. At some point, you will have to use the fact that the square of an odd integer is also odd. Prove it.)

(a) A Set of Axioms for the Real Number System

The set $\mathbb{R}$ can be defined as a complete ordered field, that is, a set that satisfies the three properties or axioms listed next. The existence of such a set can be established starting from the set of natural numbers, in several ways (e.g., Rudin, 1964, pp. 17ff.; Bartle, 1976, pp. 49–50).

Axiom 6.2. Field axioms. The set $\mathbb{R}$, endowed with the operations addition and multiplication, is a field. That is, both addition and multiplication are laws of internal composition (i.e., $\mathbb{R}$ is closed under these operations) that satisfy the associative and commutative properties and are endowed with identity and inverse elements (except for the zero element, the additive identity, which has no multiplicative inverse). Moreover, the following distributive property holds: For every α, β, $\gamma \in \mathbb{R}$, $(\alpha + \beta)\gamma = \alpha\gamma + \beta\gamma$.

Figure 1.8. The axiom of completeness.

Axiom 6.3. Order axioms. There exists a complete ordering[3] "≤" defined on $\mathbb{R}$ *that is compatible with addition and multiplication, in the following sense:*

$$\forall\, \alpha, \beta, \gamma \in \mathbb{R},\ \alpha \le \beta \Rightarrow \alpha + \gamma \le \beta + \gamma \quad and \quad (\alpha \le \beta \ and\ 0 \le \gamma) \Rightarrow \alpha\gamma \le \beta\gamma$$

That is, inequality between two numbers is preserved if (i) we add an arbitrary real number to both sides or (ii) we multiply both of them by a non-negative number. The zero element (0) is the additive identity.

Axiom 6.4. Axiom of completeness. Let L *and* H *be nonempty sets of real numbers, with the property that*

$$\forall\, l \in L\ and\ \forall\, h \in H,\ l \le h$$

Then there exists a real number α *such that*

$$\forall\, l \in L\ and\ \forall\, h \in H,\ l \le \alpha \le h$$

Problem 6.5. Let x, y, and z be arbitrary real numbers. Using the order axioms, show that the following statements are true:

(i) $(x \le y$ and $x' \le y') \Rightarrow x + x' \le y + y'$
(ii) $x \le y \Rightarrow -y \le -x$

(b) The Supremum Property

In this section we will explore some of the implications of the axiom of completeness. For this, we need to define some concepts that make use of the order axioms.

Definition 6.6. A bounded set and the bound of a set. Let X be a set of real numbers. If there exists a real number u (not necessarily in X) such that $x \le u$ for all x in X, we say that u is an upper bound of X and that the set X is bounded above. A lower bound l is defined in an analogous way, except that now we require that $x \ge l$ for all $x \in X$.

Observe that if u is an upper bound of a set X, then any number b larger than u is also an upper bound of X. Hence, if the set X is bounded above, it will have an infinite number of upper bounds. The smallest of all upper bounds of X is called the supremum (sup) of the set, written sup X.

Definition 6.7. Supremum and infimum. Let X be a set of real numbers that is bounded above. The number s is the supremum of X ($s = \sup X$) if it is its smallest upper bound, that is, if

(i) s is an upper bound for X: $\forall x \in X, x \leq s$, and
(ii) no number smaller than s is an upper bound of X:

$$\forall y < s, \exists x \in X \text{ s.th. } x > y$$

In the case of a set that is bounded below, the largest lower bound or infimum (inf) of the set is defined in an analogous manner.

Notice that if s is the supremum of X, then any number larger than s is not the least upper bound of X, and any number smaller than s is not an upper bound. Hence X must contain numbers that are arbitrarily close to s. It is also clear that if $A \subseteq B, A \neq \varnothing$, and B is bounded above, then A is also bounded above, and $\sup B \geq \sup A$.

The definitions of the upper bound and supremum of a set X do not require that these numbers belong to X. If X has a supremum s and s is an element of X, we call s the *maximum* of X and write $s = \max X$. For example, the interval $(0, 1]$ has a maximum equal to 1, whereas $(0, 1)$ has no maximum, although it does have a supremum (which is also 1).

We can now show that the axiom of completeness is equivalent to the statement that every nonempty set of real numbers that is bounded above has a supremum.

Theorem 6.8. The supremum property. Every nonempty set of real numbers that is bounded above has a supremum. This supremum is a real number.

Observing that $s = \sup X$ is equivalent to $-s = \inf(-X)$, where $-x \in -X$ if and only if $x \in X$, we see also that every nonempty set of real numbers that is bounded below has an infimum.

Proof. Let X be a nonempty set of real numbers with an upper bound, and define U as the set of upper bounds of X. By assumption, U is not empty, and by definition, $x \leq u$ for every $u \in U$ and every $x \in X$. By the axiom of completeness, there exists a real number α such that

$$x \leq \alpha \leq u \; \forall x \in X \text{ and } \forall u \in U$$

Because $x \leq \alpha$ for all x in X, α is an upper bound of X; moreover, because $\alpha \leq u$ for all u in the set U of upper bounds of X, α is the supremum of X. $\qquad \square$

Hence, the axiom of completeness guarantees the existence of a supremum for certain sets of real numbers. The following result shows that the supremum property implies the axiom of completeness, thus establishing the equivalence of the two properties.

Theorem 6.9. The supremum property implies the axiom of completeness.

Proof. Let L and H be nonempty sets of real numbers, with the property that $l \leq h$ for all l in L and all h in H. Then each h is an upper bound of L, and it follows that L has a supremum, with sup $L \leq h$ for all h in H. Next, because sup L is a lower bound of H, H has an infimum that cannot be smaller than sup L. Hence L has a supremum, H has an infimum, and

$$l \leq \sup L \leq \inf H \leq h \text{ for every } l \text{ in } L \text{ and every } h \text{ in } H$$

Putting $\alpha = \sup L$ or $\inf H$, or both when they coincide, we obtain the axiom of completeness. $\qquad\square$

The following results reveal two important implications of the axiom of completeness. Theorem 6.12, in particular, establishes the existence of real solutions to the equation $x^2 = 2$.

Theorem 6.10. The Archimedean property. The set $\mathbb{N}$ of the natural numbers is not bounded above (i.e., for any $x \in \mathbb{R}$, there exists a natural number n such that $n > x$).

Problem 6.11. Prove Theorem 6.10. Use the method of contradiction: If the result is false, then there exists a real number x that is an upper bound of $\mathbb{N}$. Use Theorem 6.9 and the definition of supremum to obtain a contradiction.

Theorem 6.12. Existence of $\sqrt{2}$. There exists a real number $x > 0$ such that $x^2 = 2$.

Proof. Let $Y = \{y \in \mathbb{R}; 0 \leq y^2 \leq 2\}$. The set Y is nonempty (because $0 \in Y$) and is bounded above (e.g., by 2, because $y > 2$ implies $y^2 > 2$). By the supremum property, Y has a supremum that we will call x. We will prove that $x^2 = 2$ by showing that we can exclude the other possibilities: If $x^2 < 2$, then we can find a number larger than x that lies in Y, and if $x^2 > 2$, we can find a positive number smaller than x that is an upper bound for Y. Because both of these statements contradict the fact that x is the least upper bound of Y, the result follows.

First, we will show that if $x^2 < 2$, then x cannot be the supremum of Y. Assume that $\sup Y = x$ and $x^2 < 2$. Then $2 - x^2 > 0$ and (by the Archimedean property) we can select a positive integer $n > 1$ such that

$$n > \frac{2x+1}{2-x^2} \iff \frac{2x+1}{n} < 2 - x^2 \tag{1}$$

Then, using (1), we have

$$\left(x + \frac{1}{n}\right)^2 = x^2 + \frac{2x}{n^2} + \frac{1}{n^2} \le x^2 + \frac{2x+1}{n} < x^2 + (2 - x^2) = 2$$

Hence, $0 < (x + (1/n))^2 < 2$, implying that $x + 1/n \in Y$. That is, we have found an element of Y larger than $x = \sup Y$, which is clearly impossible. Hence x^2 cannot be strictly smaller than 2.

Similarly, assume that $x^2 > 2$, and let m be a positive integer such that

$$m > \frac{1}{x} \quad \text{and} \quad m > \frac{2x}{x^2-2} \quad \left(\text{i.e., } x > \frac{1}{m} \text{ and } \frac{2x}{m} < x^2 - 2\right) \tag{2}$$

Then

$$\left(x - \frac{1}{m}\right)^2 = x^2 - \frac{2x}{m} + \frac{1}{m^2} > x^2 - \frac{2x}{m} > x^2 - (x^2 - 2) = 2$$

Hence $0 < x - (1/m)$, $(x - (1/m))^2 > 2$, and therefore $x - 1/m > y$ for all y in Y. We have found a positive number smaller than x that is an upper bound of Y. Because this contradicts the fact that x is the supremum of Y, it cannot be true that $x^2 > 2$. This leaves us with only the possibility that $x^2 = 2$. $\quad\square$

An extension of this argument can be used to establish the existence of nth roots of positive real numbers.

Problem 6.13. Let A and B be nonempty sets of real numbers, both of them bounded above, and let C be the set

$$C = \{c = a + b;\ a \in A,\ b \in B\}$$

Show that C has a supremum that is given by

$$\sup C = \sup A + \sup B$$

Problem 6.14. The semiopen interval $(a, b]$ is the set of real numbers x such that $a < x \le b$. Other intervals, such as (a, b) and $[a, b]$, are defined in an analogous manner. Show that a nonempty set S of real numbers is an interval if and only if whenever x and y are in S, any real number z such that $x < z < y$ lies also in S.

Hint: Let S be a set with the desired property, and define $a = \inf S$ (or $a = -\infty$ if S is not bounded below) and $b = \sup S$ (or $b = \infty$ if S is not bounded above). Using the definitions of supremum and infimum, show that $(a, b) \subseteq S \subseteq [a, b]$.

(c) Absolute Value

An important function defined on $\mathbb{R}$ is the one that assigns to each real number its absolute value. The function $|\cdot| : \mathbb{R} \longrightarrow \mathbb{R}$ is defined by $|x| = \max\{x, -x\}$ or

$$|x| = \begin{cases} x \text{ if } x \geq 0 \\ -x \text{ if } x < 0 \end{cases}$$

Among other things, the absolute-value function allows us to introduce the notion of distance between two numbers, because $|x - y|$ corresponds to the length of the real line segment that joins the points corresponding to x and y. As we will see in Chapter 2, once we have defined a measure of distance in a set, we can introduce a topological structure that will allow us to define concepts like continuity and convergence.

Problem 6.15. Show that if $a \geq 0$, then $|x| \leq a$ if and only if $-a \leq x \leq a$.

We will now establish a very important inequality.

Theorem 6.16. Triangle inequality for real numbers. Let x *and* y *be two real numbers; then*

$$|x + y| \leq |x| + |y|$$

Proof. By definition of absolute value, we have

$$-|x| \leq x \leq |x| \quad \text{and} \quad -|y| \leq y \leq |y|$$

Adding up these two inequalities, side by side,

$$-(|x| + |y|) \leq x + y \leq |x| + |y| \Rightarrow |x + y| \leq |x| + |y| \qquad \square$$

Problem 6.17. Given real numbers $x_i, i = 1, 2, \ldots, n$, show the following:

(i) $|\Sigma_{i=1}^{n} x_i| \leq \Sigma_{i=1}^{n} |x_i|$ (by induction using the triangle inequality),
(ii) $|a - c| \leq |a - b| + |b - c|$ (look for an adequate substitution in the triangle inequality).

7. Complex Numbers

We have seen that one of the reasons that motivate the construction of $\mathbb{R}$ is the desire for a number system in which the equation $x^2 = 2$ has a solution. A similar reason motivates the construction of the set of imaginary numbers. This set is a field that contains the square roots of negative numbers, including the solution to the equation $x^2 = -1$. In this section we will briefly discuss a "larger" number system, that of the complex numbers, which contains both the real numbers and the imaginary numbers. Because we will make rather limited use of complex numbers later in this book, we will simply introduce some basic notions, without proofs or much formal discussion.

A *complex number* is a number of the form

$$c = a + ib$$

where a and b are real numbers, and i is the imaginary unit, $i = \sqrt{-1}$. The number a is the *real part* of c (Re c), and b is its *imaginary part* (Im c). A complex vector $x = (c_1, \ldots, c_n)$ is simply a vector whose components are complex numbers.

The *conjugate* of a complex number $c = a + ib$ is the number $\bar{c} = a - ib$, with the sign of the imaginary part reversed. The conjugate of a complex vector $x = (c_1, \ldots, c_n)$ is $\bar{x} = (\bar{c}_1, \ldots, \bar{c}_n)$, the vector whose components are the complex conjugates of the components of the original vector.

The *modulus* of a complex number is the norm of the vector that represents it in the complex plane. That is,

$$|c| = r = \sqrt{a^2 + b^2}$$

Observe that a complex number and its conjugate have the same modulus and that the product of a complex number and its conjugate is the square of their common modulus:

$$(a + ib)(a - ib) = a^2 - b^2 i^2 = a^2 - b^2(-1) = a^2 + b^2 = r^2$$

It is often convenient to represent a complex number as a point with coordinates (a, b) in a plane (the *complex plane*) in which the vertical axis measures the imaginary component, and the horizontal axis the real component. Let θ be the angle formed by the vector representing a complex number c and the horizontal axis of the complex plane, as illustrated in Figure 1.9. We observe that

$$\cos \theta = a/r \Rightarrow a = r \cos \theta \quad \text{and} \quad \sin \theta = b/r \Rightarrow b = r \sin \theta$$

Hence we can write the number $c = a + ib$ in *trigonometric form*:

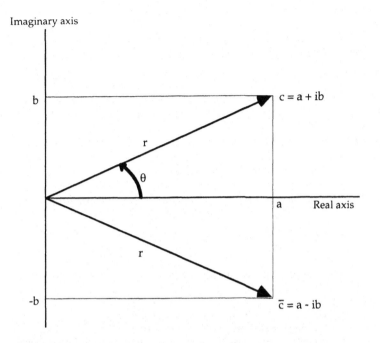

Figure 1.9. Graphical representation of a complex number.

$$c = a + ib = r\cos\theta + ir\sin\theta = r(\cos\theta + i\sin\theta)$$

Using the MacLaurin series representation of the sine, cosine, and exponential functions, we obtain *Euler's formula*:

$$e^{i\theta} = \cos\theta + i\sin\theta$$

which allows us to write the complex number c in yet another equivalent way:

$$c = a + ib = r(\cos\theta + i\sin\theta) = re^{i\theta}$$

Observe that the norm of $e^{i\theta}$ is $\sqrt{\cos^2\theta + \sin^2\theta} = 1$; thus $e^{i\theta}$ lies on the unit circumference in the complex plane. As the angle θ varies from 0 to 2π radians, the number $e^{i\theta}$ rotates around the origin at a constant distance equal to 1.

Bibliography

Apostol, T. 1974. *Mathematical Analysis*, 2nd ed. Reading, MA: Addison-Wesley.
Apostol, T. 1991. *Calculus*, vol. 1, 2nd ed. Barcelona: Ed. Reverté.
Bartle, R. 1976. *The Elements of Real Analysis*, 2nd ed. New York: Wiley.
Blackorby, C. 1989. "Orderings" and "Preorderings." In: J. Eatwell, M. Milgate, and

P. Newman (ed.), *The New Palgrave: Utility and Probability*. New York: Norton.

Bryant, V. 1990. *Yet Another Introduction to Analysis*. Cambridge University Press.

Clark, C. 1982. *Elementary Mathematical Analysis*, 2nd ed. Belmont, CA: Wadsworth.

Gemignani, M. 1972. *Elementary Topology*, 2nd ed. New York: Dover.

Haaser, N. B., and Sullivan, J. A. 1991. *Real Analysis*. New York: Dover.

Kolmogorov, A. N., and Fomin, S. V. 1970. *Introductory Real Analysis*. New York: Dover.

Lange, S. 1989. *Undergraduate Analysis*, 2nd ed. Berlin: Springer-Verlag.

Michel, P. 1984. *Cours de Mathématiques pour Economistes*. Paris: Economica.

Rudin, W. 1964. *Principles of Mathematical Analysis*, 2nd ed. New York: McGraw-Hill.

Yamane, T. 1977. *Matemáticas para economistas*, 2nd ed. Barcelona: Ariel.

Notes

1 The symbol "$\exists!$" is used to indicate that there is a unique element with a certain property. Thus, the expression $\exists! \, x \in A$ s.th. $P(x)$ means "there exists precisely one element of A that has property P.

2 Some authors use the term "ordering" to refer to what we call a "complete preordering." Then their "preordering" would mean "partial preordering" in our terminology. In applications to economic theory, usually there is no chance of confusion, because orderings (in our sense) are not used in the theory of consumer preferences.

3 A complete ordering on X is a reflexive, transitive, and antisymmetric binary relation with the property that any two elements of X are comparable under the relation. See Section 3(b).

2

Metric and Normed Spaces

The reader should be familiar with low-dimensional Euclidean spaces, particularly the real line and the Cartesian plane. Given two points, x and y, in one of these spaces, the distance between them, $d(x, y)$, is the length of the straight line segment that connects them. If x and y are real numbers, this corresponds to the absolute value of their difference, that is $d(x, y) = |x - y|$; if x and y are points in the plane with coordinates (x_1, x_2) and (y_1, y_2), respectively, the distance between them is given by the Euclidean norm of the difference vector:

$$d(x, y) = \|x - y\|_E = \sqrt{(x_1 - y_1)^2 + (x_2 - y_2)^2}$$

Equipped with a notion of distance, we can define two concepts of fundamental importance in mathematical analysis: continuity of a function, and limit of a sequence. Recall, for example, that a sequence $\{x_n\}$ of real numbers converges to a limit x if

$$\forall \varepsilon > 0, \ \exists N \text{ s.th. } n > N \Rightarrow |x_n - x| < \varepsilon$$

that is, if, given an arbitrarily small number $\varepsilon > 0$, there exists some positive integer N such that all terms in the sequence of order higher than N are contained within an open interval centered at x with radius ε. In a similar way, the definition of continuity also makes use of the concept of distance. We say that a function $f: \mathbb{R} \longrightarrow \mathbb{R}$ is continuous at a point x if

$$\forall \varepsilon > 0, \ \exists \delta > 0 \text{ s.th. } |y - x| < \delta \Rightarrow |f(y) - f(x)| < \varepsilon$$

Intuitively, a continuous function maps points that are close to each other into images that are also close by, and a sequence $\{x_n\}$ converges to x if by taking n large enough we can force x_n to be arbitrarily close to x. What is essential in both definitions is the notion of distance, rather than the specific formulas that define it. This observation suggests that if we can define an appropriate measure of distance, we can generalize con-

39

vergence, continuity, and other topological concepts to more complicated
sets without losing completely the geometric intuition we get from the study
of the plane. This takes us to the concept of metric space, which is simply a
set in which we have defined a useful notion of distance (i.e., one that preserves those properties of the familiar Euclidean distance we really need to
get useful results). Experience has shown that these basic properties are the
following:

   (i) The distance between two points is always nonnegative and is zero if and only
       if the two points are in fact the same.
  (ii) The distance from x to y is the same as the distance from y to x.
 (iii) The shortest route between two points is the straight line. One way to say this
       is as follows: Given any three points x, y, and z, it is always true that

$$d(x, z) \leq d(x, y) + d(y, z)$$

As we will see shortly, these three properties are sufficient to characterize a
distance function that will allow us to define all the important topological
concepts in a very general class of spaces.

1. Metric and Normed Spaces

Definition 1.1. Metric or distance function. A metric or distance function
defined on a set X is a real-valued, nonnegative function $d : X \times X \longrightarrow \mathbb{R}_+$
such that for every x, y, and z in X we have

  (i) $d(x, y) \geq 0$, with equality if and only if $x = y$,
 (ii) $d(x, y) = d(y, x)$,
(iii) $d(x, z) \leq d(x, y) + d(y, z)$ (triangle inequality).

Definition 1.2. Metric space. A metric space is a pair (X, d), where X is a
set, and d a metric defined on it.

Given a metric space (X, d) and a subset Y of X, it is clear that the restric-
tion of d to Y, denoted $d|_Y$, is a metric defined on Y. Hence the pair $(Y, d|_Y)$
is also a metric space, or a *metric subspace* of (X, d).

   We often work with sets endowed with both an algebraic structure
and a distance function. Such spaces are particularly useful because they
allow us to perform algebraic operations on their elements, in addition
to defining topological concepts like convergence or open sets. We now
introduce an important family of such sets, the so-called *normed vector
spaces*.

   We begin by defining a norm on the set of points X underlying a vector
space V. A norm is a function that assigns to each vector in X a nonnega-

tive real number that we interpret as its magnitude. It is therefore a generalization of the absolute value of a real number or the length of a vector in the plane.

Definition 1.3. Norm. Let V be a vector space, and X the underlying set of points. A real-valued function $\|\cdot\|: X \longrightarrow \mathbb{R}$ is called a norm if it satisfies the following properties for all x and y in X and any scalar α:

(i) nonnegativity: $\|x\| \geq 0$
(ii) only the zero vector has zero norm: $\|x\| = 0 \Leftrightarrow x = \underline{0}$
(iii) triangle inequality: $\|x + y\| \leq \|x\| + \|y\|$
(iv) $\|\alpha x\| = |\alpha| \|x\|$

Definition 1.4. Normed vector space. A normed vector space is a vector space V equipped with a norm.

A normed space naturally becomes a metric space if we define the distance between two vectors as the norm of their difference, that is,

$$d(x, y) = \|x - y\|$$

Observe that the function $d(\cdot, \cdot)$ automatically satisfies the definition of metric. We say that $d(\ )$ is the metric generated by the norm $\|\cdot\|$. When we speak of topological properties in a normed vector space, it will always be in terms of this metric.

The information that a certain set endowed with a distance function is a metric space can be very useful, because it allows us to use a lot of results that hold generally in metric spaces. Usually, verifying that such a pair is a metric space is fairly easy, except possibly for the triangle inequality. We will now consider some examples of useful metric spaces.

Example 1.5. n-dimensional Euclidean space. It is easy to go from the plane or three-dimensional space to a Euclidean space of arbitrary (but finite) dimension n. We shall denote this space by $E^n = (\mathbb{R}^n, d_E)$. That is, X is now the set of n-dimensional vectors

$$\mathbb{R}^n = \left\{ x = (x^1, x^2, \ldots, x^n); \; x^i \in \mathbb{R} \, \forall \, i = 1, \ldots, n \right\}$$

and the metric is the Euclidean distance between two vectors, defined as the Euclidean norm of their difference, $x - y = x + (-y)$:

$$d_E(x, y) = \|x - y\|_E = \sqrt{\sum_{i=1}^{n} (x^i - y^i)^2}$$

In order to show that $(\mathbb{R}^n, d_E)$ is indeed a metric space, it is sufficient to verify that $\|\cdot\|_E$ is a norm. It is obvious that $\|\cdot\|_E$ satifies the first two defining properties of a norm; verifying that the triangle inequality holds takes a bit more work. We begin by proving a related result.

Theorem 1.6. Cauchy-Schwarz inequality. Let α_i and β_i, $i = 1, \ldots, n$, be real numbers; then

$$\left(\sum_{i=1}^{n} \alpha_i \beta_i \right)^2 \leq \left(\sum_{i=1}^{n} \alpha_i^2 \right) \left(\sum_{i=1}^{n} \beta_i^2 \right)$$

Proof. For any real number λ, we have

$$0 \leq \sum_{i=1}^{n} (\alpha_i - \lambda \beta_i)^2 = \sum_{i=1}^{n} \alpha_i^2 - 2\lambda \sum_{i=1}^{n} \alpha_i \beta_i + \lambda^2 \sum_{i=1}^{n} \beta_i^2$$

Now, putting $\lambda = \sum_{i=1}^{n} \alpha_i \beta_i / \sum_{i=1}^{n} \beta_i^2$, we see that

$$\sum_{i=1}^{n} \alpha_i^2 - 2 \frac{\sum_{i=1}^{n} \alpha_i \beta_i}{\sum_{i=1}^{n} \beta_i^2} \sum_{i=1}^{n} \alpha_i \beta_i + \frac{\left(\sum_{i=1}^{n} \alpha_i \beta_i \right)^2}{\left(\sum_{i=1}^{n} \beta_i^2 \right)^2} \sum_{i=1}^{n} \beta_i^2 \geq 0 \quad \Leftrightarrow$$

$$\sum_{i=1}^{n} \alpha_i^2 - \frac{\left(\sum_{i=1}^{n} \alpha_i \beta_i \right)^2}{\sum_{i=1}^{n} \beta_i^2} \geq 0 \quad \Leftrightarrow \quad \left(\sum_{i=1}^{n} \alpha_i \beta_i \right)^2 \leq \left(\sum_{i=1}^{n} \alpha_i^2 \right) \left(\sum_{i=1}^{n} \beta_i^2 \right) \quad \square$$

Taking the square root on each side of the Cauchy-Schwarz inequality, we obtain

$$\sum_{i=1}^{n} \alpha_i \beta_i \leq \sqrt{\sum_{i=1}^{n} \alpha_i^2} \sqrt{\sum_{i=1}^{n} \beta_i^2}$$

Using this result, it is easy to verify that the triangle inequality holds in E^n. Given any three vectors $x, y, z \in \mathbb{R}^n$, we have

$$[d_E(x, z)]^2 = \sum_{i=1}^{n} (x^i - z^i)^2 = \sum_{i=1}^{n} [(x^i - y^i) + (y^i - z^i)]^2$$

$$= \sum_{i=1}^{n} (x^i - y^i)^2 + \sum_{i=1}^{n} (y^i - z^i)^2 + 2 \sum_{i=1}^{n} (x^i - y^i)(y^i - z^i)$$

$$\leq \sum_{i=1}^{n} (x^i - y^i)^2 + \sum_{i=1}^{n} (y^i - z^i)^2$$

$$+ 2 \sqrt{\sum_{i=1}^{n} (x^i - y^i)^2} \sqrt{\sum_{i=1}^{n} (y^i - z^i)^2}$$

$$= [d_E(x, y)]^2 + [d_E(y, z)]^2 + 2 d_E(x, y) d_E(y, z)$$

$$= [d_E(x, y) + d_E(y, z)]^2$$

which implies the desired result,

$$d_E(x, z) \leq d_E(x, y) + d_E(y, z) \qquad \square$$

Problem 1.7. The Cauchy-Schwarz-Bunyakovsky inequality. Let f and g be continuous functions $[a, b] \longrightarrow \mathbb{R}$. Adapt the preceding proof to establish the following analogue of Theorem 1.6 for integrals:

$$\left(\int_a^b f(x)g(x)\,dx\right)^2 \le \left(\int_a^b [f(x)]^2\,dx\right)\left(\int_a^b [g(x)]^2\,dx\right)$$

A given set (vector space) may have several different metrics (norms) defined on it. For example, an alternative to the Euclidean norm in $\mathbb{R}^n$ is the *sup norm*, defined for any $x \in \mathbb{R}^n$ as the absolute value of its largest component:

$$\|x\|_s = \max_i\{|x^i|;\ i = 1, 2, \ldots, n\}$$

Two norms $\|\cdot\|_1$ and $\|\cdot\|_2$ defined on the same vector space are said to be *Lipschitz-equivalent* if there exist positive real numbers m and M such that for any vector x, we have

$$m\|x\|_1 \le \|x\|_2 \le M\|x\|_1$$

Lipschitz-equivalent metrics are defined in an analogous manner. Intuitively, two metrics are Lipschitz-equivalent if they always agree on whether or not two given points are close to each other. As we will see later, this implies that equivalent metrics preserve such important properties as openness and convergence.

Problem 1.8. Show that the sup norm, $\|\cdot\|_s : \mathbb{R}^n \longrightarrow \mathbb{R}$, as defined earlier, is a norm.

Problem 1.9. Show that the sup norm $\|\cdot\|_s$ and the Euclidean norm $\|\cdot\|_E$ are Lipschitz-equivalent norms by proving that for any n-vector x, $\|x\|_s \le \|x\|_E \le \sqrt{n}\|x\|_s$.

Example 1.10. Product spaces. Let (X, d_1) and (Y, d_2) be metric spaces. We define the product space of these two spaces as the pair $(X \times Y, d_\pi)$ where the *product metric*, $d_\pi : X \times Y \longrightarrow \mathbb{R}_+$, is defined by

$$d_\pi[(x, y), (x', y')] = \sqrt{[d_1(x, x')]^2 + [d_2(y, y')]^2} \tag{1}$$

(or, alternatively, by $d_\pi = d_1 + d_2$ or $d_\pi = \max\{d_1, d_2\}$). This definition can be extended in the obvious way to the case of any finite number of metric spaces. The following problem asks the reader to verify that $(X \times Y, d_\pi)$ is itself a metric space.

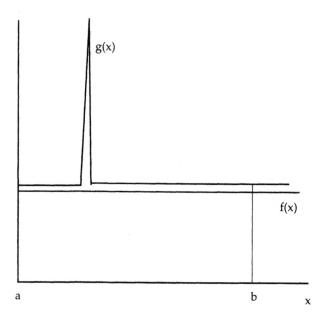

Figure 2.1.

Problem 1.11. Show that d_π is a metric.

Example 1.12. Some function spaces. It is often convenient to define a metric on a set of functions. For example, consider the set X of continuous functions $[a, b] \longrightarrow \mathbb{R}$. Two useful metrics on this set are the *sup metric*, defined for any f and g in X by

$$d_s(f, g) = \sup_{x \in [a,b]} |f(x) - g(x)|$$

and the L^2 *metric*, given by

$$d_2(f, g) = \left(\int_a^b [f(x) - g(x)]^2 \, dx \right)^{1/2}$$

Notice that these two metrics capture rather different ideas about what it means for two functions to be "close." According to the sup metric, $d_s(f, g)$ will be small only if f and g are close for all values of x, whereas in the L^2 metric it suffices that they be close on average over their domain. These two metrics are not equivalent, for functions that are arbitrarily close on average may be very far from each other over a small interval, as illustrated by Figure 2.1.

In some applications we are interested in how similar functions are in terms of both their values and their derivatives. If we let X be the set of functions $[a, b] \longrightarrow \mathbb{R}$ that are $r \geq 1$ times continuously differentiable (see Chapter 4), an appropriate metric can then be defined as follows. Given r, the C^i metric on X is defined, for $i \leq r$, by

$$d_i(f, g) = \sup_{x \in [a,b]} \{|f(x) - g(x)|, |f'(x) - g'(x)|, \ldots, |f^{(i)}(x) - g^{(i)}(x)|\}$$

where $f^{(i)}$ is the ith derivative of f. □

We conclude this section with some additional definitions. Given a metric space (X, d), the *open ball* with center at x and radius ε is the set

$$B_\varepsilon(x) = \{y \in X;\ d(x, y) < \varepsilon\}$$

The *closed ball* $B_\varepsilon[x]$ is defined in the same manner, but with a weak inequality. We will often write the ε-ball with center at x. Unless it is otherwise indicated, it will be understood that the ball is open.

A set S in a metric space is *bounded* if we can find a closed ball of finite radius that contains it. Formally, given a metric space (X, d), we say that a subset S of X is bounded if there exists some point x in X, and some real number B, such that $d(x, s) \leq B$ for all $s \in S$.[1] Equivalently, S is bounded if it has a finite diameter, where

$$\text{diam } S = \sup\{d(s, s');\ s, s' \in S\}$$

A function f from some set Z into (X, d) is bounded if $f(Z)$ is bounded.

Given a metric, we can define, in addition to the distance between two points, the *distance between a point and a set* or between two sets. Given a metric space (X, d), let A be a subset of X, and x some point in X. The distance from x to A is defined as

$$d(x, A) = \inf_{a \in A} d(x, a)$$

If A and B are two subsets of X, the distance between them is given by

$$d(A, B) = \inf_{a \in A} d(B, a) = \inf\{d(a, b);\ a \in A,\ b \in B\}$$

Problem 1.13. Prove that the union of any finite collection of bounded sets is bounded. (Prove it for two sets; the result then follows by induction. Draw a picture.)

Problem 1.14. Using the triangle inequality, show that for any x, y, and z in a normed vector space, the following are true:

(i) $\|x - y\| \geq \|x\| - \|y\|$ and (ii) $\|x - z\| \leq \|x - y\| + \|y - z\|$

Problem 1.15. Show that the set of bounded real sequences is a metric space, with the norm defined by $d(x, y) = \sup_n |x_n - y_n|$.

Problem 1.16. Let (X_2, d_2) be a metric space, X_1 a set, and $f : X_1 \longrightarrow X_2$ a one-to-one function. Define a function $d_1(\ )$ by

$$d_1(x, y) = d_2[f(x), f(y)] \, \forall \, x, y \in X_1$$

Show that (X_1, d_1) is a metric space.

Problem 1.17. Give an example of two sets A and B in a metric space such that $A \cap B = \varnothing$, but $d(A, B) = 0$.

Problem 1.18. Prove that the set $C[a, b]$ of continuous real functions defined on the interval $[a, b]$ is a metric space when the distance between two functions f and g is defined by

$$d(f, g) = \sup_{x \in [a,b]} |f(x) - g(x)|$$

Problem 1.19. Show that the following inequality holds for any $x \in \mathbb{R}^n$:

$$\|x\|_E \leq \sum_{i=1}^{n} |x_i|$$

Hint: Prove it directly for $n = 2$, and then proceed by induction.

2. Convergence of Sequences in Metric Spaces

We have seen that a sequence in X is a function $s : \mathbb{N} \longrightarrow X$ whose domain is the set of natural numbers and whose range is a subset of X. If (X, d) is a metric space, we can define convergence exactly as for sequences of real numbers.

Definition 2.1. Convergence in metric spaces. Let (X, d) be a metric space, and $\{x_n\}$ a sequence in X. We say that $\{x_n\}$ converges to $x \in X$, or that the sequence has limit x, if

$$\forall \, \varepsilon > 0, \, \exists \, N(\varepsilon) \text{ s.th. } n > N(\varepsilon) \Rightarrow d(x_n, x) < \varepsilon \qquad [\text{or}, x_n \in B_\varepsilon(x)]$$

If $\{x_n\}$ has limit x, we write $\{x_n\} \to x$ or $\lim_{n \to \infty} x_n = x$. A sequence that does not converge is said to diverge.

That is, a sequence is convergent if its terms get closer and closer to some point x, to the extent that, given an arbitrarily small number $\varepsilon > 0$, we can

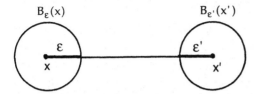

Figure 2.2.

always find some positive integer $N(\varepsilon)$ (which will in general depend on the chosen ε) such that all terms of the sequence of order higher than $N(\varepsilon)$ will lie within the ε-ball centered at x. Equivalently, the sequence $\{x_n\}$ of points of X has limit x if and only if the sequence of real numbers $\{d(x_n, x)\}$ converges to zero.

Problem 2.2. Using the formal definition of limit, show that

$$\text{(i)} \quad \lim_{n \to \infty} \frac{1}{n} = 0, \qquad \text{(ii)} \quad \lim_{n \to \infty} \frac{1}{\sqrt{n}} = 0, \qquad \text{(iii)} \quad \lim_{n \to \infty} \frac{n^2 + 2}{3n^2 + 4} = \frac{1}{3}$$

Imagine you are given some arbitrarily small ε. You must produce a positive integer N such that. . . .

Before we can speak of *the* limit of a sequence, we must show that it is uniquely defined. This is done in the following result, which shows that if a sequence has a limit, then it is unique.

Theorem 2.3. Uniqueness of the limit. A sequence $\{x_n\}$ in a metric space (X, d) has at most one limit.

Proof. We will prove the result by contradiction. Intuitively, $\{x_n\}$ cannot approach two different limits. If it did, we would be able to find terms of the sequence that would be, simultaneously, close to two "far-away" points.

Suppose $\{x_n\}$ had two different limits, x and x'. Then $d(x, x') > 0$, and we could construct two disjoint open balls, $B_\varepsilon(x)$ and $B_{\varepsilon'}(x')$, each centered at a different limit, as illustrated in Figure 2.2.[2] If both x and x' were limits of $\{x_n\}$, there would exist positive integers $N(\varepsilon)$ and $N(\varepsilon')$ such that $x_n \in B_\varepsilon(x)$ for all $n > N(\varepsilon)$ and $x_n \in B_{\varepsilon'}(x')$ for all $n > N(\varepsilon')$. It would follow that $x_n \in B_\varepsilon(x) \cap B_{\varepsilon'}(x') = \varnothing$ for all $n > \max\{N(\varepsilon), N(\varepsilon')\}$, but that would be impossible (we would have found an element of an empty set).

Problem 2.4. Let $\{x_n\}$ be a convergent sequence with limit x. Show that every subsequence of $\{x_n\}$ converges to x.

Theorem 2.5. Every convergent sequence in a metric space is bounded.

Proof. Assume $\{x_n\} \to x$. Then there exists some N such that $d(x_n, x) < 1$ for all $n > N$. Define

$$m = \max\{1, d(x_1, x), \ldots, d(x_N, x)\}$$

which is finite and well defined, because we are taking the maximum of a finite set of real numbers. By construction, $d(x_n, x) \leq m$ for all n; hence the bounded ball $B_m(x)$ contains the whole sequence, and the distance between any two terms of $\{x_n\}$ cannot exceed the ball's diameter; that is, for any x_i and x_k,

$$d(x_i, x_k) \leq d(x_i, x) + d(x, x_k) = 2m < \infty \qquad \qquad \square$$

We now introduce a concept closely related to that of limit. It is possible that a sequence may contain one or more convergent subsequences, even if it does not converge itself. We call the limits of such subsequences *cluster points* (of the original sequence).

Definition 2.6. Cluster point. Let $\{x_n\}$ be a sequence in a metric space (X, d), and c a point in X. We say that c is a cluster point of $\{x_n\}$ if any open ball with center at c contains infinitely many terms of the sequence. That is,

$$\forall \varepsilon > 0 \text{ and } \forall N, \ \exists n > N \text{ s.th. } x_n \in B_\varepsilon(c)$$

Note carefully the difference between the definitions of limit and cluster point: If x is the limit of $\{x_n\}$, any ε–ball around x will contain all terms of the sequence except for the first $N(\varepsilon)$. For a cluster point c, we require only that any ball around c contain an infinite number of points of the sequence. This is a weaker condition, for we may still have an infinite number of terms outside the ball. Hence, the limit of a sequence is a cluster point, but the converse statement need not be true. For example, the sequence defined by

$$x_n = 0 \text{ for } n \text{ even} \quad \text{and} \quad x_n = 1 \text{ for } n \text{ odd}$$

has two cluster points but does not converge.

Let y be the limit of some subsequence $\{x_{n_k}\}$ of $\{x_n\}$. Then y is a cluster point of $\{x_n\}$, because any $B_\varepsilon(y)$ will contain an infinite number of terms of $\{x_{n_k}\}$ and hence of $\{x_n\}$. In a metric space (but not necessarily in more general topological spaces), the converse statement is true.

Theorem 2.4. Let $\{x_n\}$ be a sequence in a metric space (X, d). If c is a cluster point of $\{x_n\}$, then there exists some subsequence $\{x_{n_k}\}$ of $\{x_n\}$ with limit c.

The proof of this result is an example of a *proof by construction*. To show that something exists, we show that we can construct it using the given assumptions.

Proof. If c is a cluster point of $\{x_n\}$, we have, by definition,

$$\forall\, \varepsilon > 0 \text{ and } \forall\, N,\ \exists\, n > N \text{ s.th. } x_n \in B_\varepsilon(c) \tag{1}$$

To construct a subsequence with limit c, consider a sequence of open balls with center at c and radius $1/k$, $\{B_{1/k}(c)\}$. It follows from (1) that for each k there exists some n_k such that $x_{n_k} \in B_{1/k}(c)$ and that, moreover, it is possible to choose $n_k > n_{k-1}$ for all k (so that $\{x_{n_k}\}$ is indeed a subsequence). As k increases without bound, the radius of the balls goes to zero, implying that $\{x_{n_k}\} \to c$. $\qquad\qquad\square$

3. Sequences in $\mathbb{R}$ and $\mathbb{R}^m$

Most spaces of interest in our applications are constructed starting from the real numbers. We shall therefore find it useful to establish some important properties of sequences in $\mathbb{R}$.

A sequence of real numbers $\{x_n\}$ is increasing if $x_{n+1} \geq x_n$ for all n, and decreasing if $x_{n+1} \leq x_n$. An increasing or decreasing sequence is said to be monotonic. The following result says that every increasing sequence of real numbers that is bounded above converges to its supremum. In the same way, it can be shown that every decreasing real sequence that is bounded below converges to its infimum. Hence, every monotonic bounded sequence of real numbers converges.

Theorem 3.1. Every increasing sequence of real numbers that is bounded above converges to its supremum.

If $\{x_n\}$ is increasing and has limit x, we often write $\{x_n\} \uparrow x$.

Proof. Let $\{x_n\}$ be an increasing real sequence, and assume that it is bounded above. By the supremum property,[3] $\{x_n\}$ has a supremum that we will call s. We want to show that s is the limit of the sequence, that is, that for any given $\varepsilon > 0$ we can find some positive integer N such that $x_n \in B_\varepsilon(s)$ for all $n \geq N$.

Fix some arbitrary $\varepsilon > 0$. By the definition of supremum, $x_n \leq s$ for all n; moreover, $s - \varepsilon$ is not an upper bound of $\{x_n\}$, so there exists some term x_N of the sequence such that $x_N > s - \varepsilon$. Finally, because $\{x_n\}$ is increasing, we have $x_n > s - \varepsilon$ for all $n \geq N$. We have shown that for the given ε, there exists some N such that

Figure 2.3.

$$n \geq N \Rightarrow s - \varepsilon < x_n \leq s < s + \varepsilon \Rightarrow |x - x_n| < \varepsilon$$

Finally, because ε is arbitrary, we conclude that $\{x_n\} \to s$.   □

A real sequence $\{x_n\}$ is bounded if it is bounded both above and below, that is, if there exist real numbers l and u such that

$$l \leq x_n \leq u \quad \text{for all } n \in \mathbb{N}$$

or, equivalently, if there exists some number B such that $|x_n| \leq B$ for all n. We have seen that every convergent sequence in a metric space is bounded. In general, the converse is not true: There exist bounded divergent sequences. However, for the case of $\mathbb{R}$, it can be shown that every bounded sequence contains at least one convergent subsequence. To prove this important result, we will need the following theorem:

Theorem 3.2. Every sequence of real numbers contains either an increasing subsequence or a decreasing subsequence, and possibly both.

Proof. Given an arbitrary sequence of real numbers $\{x_n\}$, define the set

$$S = \{s \in \mathbb{N}; \; x_s > x_n \, \forall \, n > s\}$$

To put an intuitive interpretation on S, imagine an infinite number of people seated in a very long line of seats in a movie theater, with the screen at the right "end" of the line, and interpret x_n as the height of the nth person in the line. Then S is the set of people who can see the movie (i.e., the subset of the audience consisting of individuals who are taller than all those in front of them). Notice that there are only two possibilities: Either an infinite number of people can see the movie, or only a finite number of them can. We will show that in the first case we can construct a decreasing subsequence of $\{x_n\}$, and in the second an increasing one.

Observe that the set $\{x_{n_k}; n_k \in S\}$, thought of as a (possibly finite) sequence, is always decreasing, by the definition of S, for if $n_k \in S$, we must have $x_{n_k} > x_{n_{k+1}}$. (Intuitively, the people who can see the screen must be arranged in order of decreasing height.) Hence, if S is unbounded (i.e., if we can always find another person farther down the line who can see the screen), we are done, for $\{x_{n_k}; n_k \in S\}$ is an (infinite) decreasing subsequence of $\{x_n\}$.

The other possibility is that S is finite (i.e., bounded above). By the supremum property, S then has a supremum that we call N (roughly, N is the last

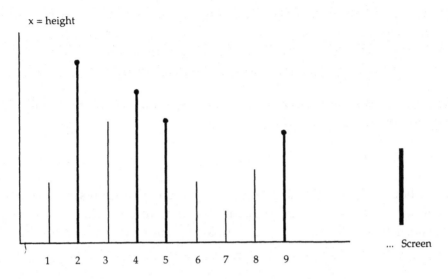

Figure 2.4. Construction of a decreasing subsequence.

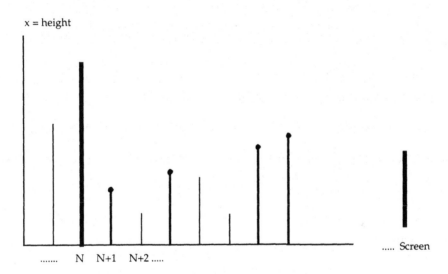

Figure 2.5. Construction of an increasing subsequence.

person who can see the screen). We will now construct an increasing sequence starting with the $(N+1)$th person. Put $k_1 = N+1$. Now, because person k_1 can't see ($k_1 \notin S$), there must exist a person farther down the line who is taller (i.e., $\exists\, n > k_1$ s.th. $x_n \geq x_{k_1}$). Call the first such person k_2. Now, $k_2 > N$ can't see either, so there must be an even taller person farther down, and so on. In this manner we can construct an increasing subsequence $\{x_{k_i}\}$, by starting with the first person who can't see and taking at each stage the individual who is blocking the view of the previous one.   □

Now, let $\{x_n\}$ be a bounded sequence of real numbers. The preceding theorem tells us that $\{x_n\}$ contains at least a monotonic subsequence. Clearly, this subsequence must be bounded, so we can apply Theorem 3.1 (or its analogue for decreasing sequences) to obtain the following result:

Theorem 3.3. Bolzano-Weierstrass. Every bounded real sequence contains at least one convergent subsequence.

Problem 3.4. We want to show that every real sequence $\{x_n\}$ contained in $[a, b]$ has a subsequence that converges to a point x in the interval. Because $\{x_n\}$ is bounded, the Bolzano-Weierstrass theorem ensures that it does indeed have a convergent subsequence. Assume that the limit of this subsequence lies outside $[a, b]$ (e.g., $x > b$). Show that this leads to a contradiction. (First, draw a picture.)

The following two results tell us that taking the limits of convergent sequences "preserves" weak inequalities and algebraic operations.

Theorem 3.5. Let $\{x_n\}$ and $\{y_n\}$ be convergent real sequences, with $\{x_n\} \to x$, and $\{y_n\} \to y$. If $x_n \le y_n$ for all n, then $x \le y$.

Proof. Fix some $\varepsilon > 0$. Because $\{x_n\} \to x$, and $\{y_n\} \to y$, there exist positive integers $N_x(\varepsilon/2)$ and $N_y(\varepsilon/2)$ such that

$$|x_n - x| < \varepsilon/2 \text{ for all } n > N_x(\varepsilon/2) \quad \text{and} \quad |y_n - y| < \varepsilon/2 \text{ for all } n > N_y(\varepsilon/2) \quad (1)$$

Putting $N = \max\{N_x(\varepsilon/2), N_y(\varepsilon/2)\}$, both inequalities in (1) hold simultaneously. Hence, for $n > N$, we have

$$x_n > x - \varepsilon/2 \quad \text{and} \quad y_n < y + \varepsilon/2 \qquad (2)$$

and we can write

$$x - y = (x - x_n) + (x_n - y_n) + (y_n - y) < \varepsilon \qquad (3)$$

because $x_n - y_n \le 0$ by assumption. Finally, because $x - y < \varepsilon$ for any positive ε, it must be true that $x - y \le 0$. $\qquad \square$

In fact, the assumptions of the theorem can be weakened: All we need is that there exist some N such that $x_n \le y_n$ for all $n > N$. Observe also that the theorem does not hold for strict inequalities. (Can you construct an example of two sequences that have the same limit even though $x_n < y_n$ for all n?)

Theorem 3.6. Let $\{x_n\}$ and $\{y_n\}$ be convergent real sequences, with $\{x_n\} \to x$ and $\{y_n\} \to y$. Then

(i) $\{x_n + y_n\} \to x + y$,

(ii) $\{x_n y_n\} \to xy$,

(iii) $\{x_n/y_n\} \to x/y$ *provided* $y \neq 0$ *and* $y_n \neq 0$ *for all* n.

Proof

(i) Using the triangle inequality, we can write

$$|(x_n + y_n) - (x + y)| = |(x_n - x) + (y_n - y)| \leq |x_n - x| + |y_n - y| \qquad (1)$$

Now, fix an arbitrary $\varepsilon > 0$. Because $\{x_n\} \to x$ and $\{y_n\} \to y$, there exist positive integers $N_x(\varepsilon/2)$ and $N_y(\varepsilon/2)$ such that

$$|x_n - x| < \varepsilon/2 \; \forall \, n > N_x(\varepsilon/2) \quad \text{and} \quad |y_n - y| < \varepsilon/2 \; \forall \, n > N_y(\varepsilon/2) \qquad (2)$$

Write $N = \max\{N_x(\varepsilon/2), N_y(\varepsilon/2)\}$. Then, for every $n > N$, both inequalities in (2) hold simultaneously, and we have, using (1):

$$|(x_n + y_n) - (x + y)| \leq |x_n - x| + |y_n - y| < \varepsilon/2 + \varepsilon/2 = \varepsilon$$

(ii) Proceeding in a similar fashion, we have

$$|x_n y_n - xy| = |x_n y_n - xy_n + xy_n - xy| = |(x_n - x)y_n + x(y_n - y)|$$
$$\leq |x_n - x||y_n| + |x||y_n - y| \qquad (3)$$

Fix some $\varepsilon > 0$. By assumption, $\{y_n\}$ is convergent and therefore bounded (Theorem 3.3); hence, there exists some positive number B such that

$$|y_n| \leq B \quad \text{for all } n \qquad (4)$$

Next, because both sequences converge, we can find an integer N_x such that

$$|x_n - x| < \frac{\varepsilon}{2B} \, \forall \, n > N_x \qquad (5)$$

and, provided $|x| \neq 0$, another N_y such that

$$|y_n - y| < \frac{\varepsilon}{2|x|} \, \forall \, n > N_y \qquad (6)$$

Put $N = \max\{N_x, N_y\}$ if $|x| \neq 0$, and $N = N_x$ otherwise. Going back to (3), we have, for any $n > N$:

$$|x_n y_n - xy| \leq |x_n - x||y_n| + |x||y_n - y| < \frac{\varepsilon}{2B} B + \frac{\varepsilon}{2|x|}|x| = \varepsilon$$

(if $|x| = 0$, the second term after the strict inequality is zero).

(iii) To establish the last part of the theorem, it is sufficient to show that $\{1/y_n\} \to 1/y$, provided $y \neq 0$ and no $y_n = 0$, and then use (ii). We now write

$$\left| \frac{1}{y_n} - \frac{1}{y} \right| = \left| \frac{y_n - y}{y_n y} \right| = \frac{|y_n - y|}{|y_n||y|} \qquad (7)$$

As before, we will now use the convergence of $\{y_n\}$ to put a bound on this expression. By definition of limit, we can find some N_1 such that

$$|y_n - y| < \frac{|y|}{2} \quad \text{for all } n > N_1 \tag{8}$$

Using the triangle inequality,

$$|y| = |(y - y_n) + y_n| \leq |y - y_n| + |y_n| \Rightarrow |y_n| \geq |y| - |y - y_n|$$

Using this expression and (8), we have that, for all $n > N_1$,

$$|y_n| \geq |y| - |y - y_n| > \frac{|y|}{2} \tag{9}$$

Next, fix some $\varepsilon > 0$. By the convergence of $\{y_n\}$, we can find some $N_2 > N_1$ such that for all $n > N_2$ we have

$$|y_n - y| < \frac{|y|^2 \varepsilon}{2} \tag{10}$$

Finally, substituting (9) and (10) into (7),

$$\left| \frac{1}{y_n} - \frac{1}{y} \right| = \frac{|y_n - y|}{|y_n||y|} < \frac{|y|^2 \varepsilon/2}{|y|^2/2} = \varepsilon \qquad \square$$

Clearly, if we replace one of the sequences by a constant, the proofs only become simpler. Hence, given any two real numbers α and β, we have

$$\{\alpha x_n\} \to \alpha x, \quad \{\alpha + x_n\} \to \alpha + x, \quad \text{and} \quad \{\alpha x_n + \beta y_n\} \to \alpha x + \beta y$$

Moreover,

$$\{x_n - y_n\} = \{x_n + (-1 y_n)\} \to x + (-y) = x - y$$

Notice also that the proofs make use of only some basic properties of the absolute value that are shared by any other norm. Hence, it is easy to adapt the foregoing arguments to show that the relevant parts of the last theorem hold for any normed vector space.

We have seen that convergent sequences are necessarily bounded. Hence, unbounded sequences do not have a limit in the proper sense, even if they "tend to infinity," a concept we now define precisely.

Definition 3.7. A sequence of real numbers $\{x_n\}$ tends to infinity, written $\{x_n\} \to \infty$, if for any number K there exists some integer $N(K)$ such that $x_n > K$ for all $n > N(K)$.

The following result is often helpful when we are trying to determine whether or not a given sequence tends to infinity. The proof is left as an exercise.

Theorem 3.8. Let $\{x_n\}$ be a sequence of positive real numbers. Then $\{x_n\} \to \infty$ if and only if $\{1/x_n\} \to 0$.

Problem 3.9. Prove Theorem 3.8.

In many applications we work with sequences in finite-dimensional Euclidean spaces. The following theorem says that in such spaces, a sequence of vectors converges if and only if each one of its coordinate sequences converges. By "coordinate sequences" we mean the real sequences whose terms are the components of each vector in the original sequence. This result can be extended to finite-dimensional normed vector spaces and to product spaces.

Theorem 3.10. A sequence $\{x_n\}$ in E^m converges to a vector $x = (x^1, x^2, \ldots, x^m)$ if and only if each coordinate sequence $\{x_n^i\}$ converges to x^i.

Proof. Note that $\{x_n\} \to x$ if and only if $\{x_n - x\} \to 0$. Hence, we can consider the case in which the limit x is the zero vector without any loss of generality.

- ($\rightarrow$) First, assume $\{x_n\} \to 0$, and fix some $\varepsilon > 0$. By the convergence of $\{x_n\}$ to 0, there exists some N such that $d_E(x_n, 0) < \varepsilon$ for all $n > N$, that is,

$$n > N \Rightarrow d_E(x_n, 0) = \sqrt{\sum\nolimits_{i=1}^{m} \left(x_n^i\right)^2} < \varepsilon$$

Now observe that for any $j = 1, \ldots, m$, we have $|x_n^j| = \sqrt{(x_n^j)^2} \leq \sqrt{\Sigma_{i=1}^m (x_n^i)^2}$. Hence it is also true that for $n > N$, we have $|x_n^j - 0| < \varepsilon$ for all $j = 1, \ldots, m$; that is, each of the coordinate sequences converges to the real number zero.

- ($\leftarrow$) Now assume that all the component sequences converge. Given some $\varepsilon > 0$, we can find positive integers N_i such that

$$\text{for each } i = 1, 2, \ldots, m, \ n > N_i \Rightarrow |x_n^i| < \varepsilon \ \sqrt{m} \tag{1}$$

If we now define $N = \max_i N_i$, (1) holds for all the component sequences, provided $n > N$. We have, then,

$$d_E(x_n, 0) = \sqrt{\sum\nolimits_{i=1}^{m} \left(x_n^i\right)^2} < \sqrt{m\varepsilon^2 \ m} = \varepsilon \quad \text{for all } n > N$$

Hence, $\{x_n^i\} \to 0$ for all i implies $\{x_n\} \to 0$. $\square$

Problem 3.11. Convergence in product spaces. Let (X, d_1) and (Y, d_2) be metric spaces, and consider the product space $(Z = X \times Y, d_\pi)$, with the *product metric* d_π defined by

$$d_\pi(z, z') = d_\pi[(x, y), (x', y')] = \sqrt{[d_1(x, x')]^2 + [d_2(y, y')]^2} \qquad (1)$$

Show that the sequence $\{z_n\} = \{(x_n, y_n)\}$ converges to $z = (x, y)$ in $(X \times Y, d_\pi)$ if and only if $\{x_n\}$ converges to x in (X, d) and $\{y_n\}$ converges to y in (Y, d).

Problem 3.12. Bolzano-Weierstrass in $\mathbb{E}^m$. Show that every bounded sequence in $\mathbb{E}^m$ contains at least one convergent subsequence.

To end this section, we consider the convergence properties of two commonly encountered families of real sequences.

Theorem 3.13. Let a *be a real number, and consider the sequence* $\{a^n\}$. *As* n $\to \infty$, *we have the following:*

(i) *If* $|a| < 1$, *then* $\{a^n\} \to 0$.
(ii) *If* a > 1, *then* $\{a^n\} \to \infty$.
(iii) *If* a ≤ -1, *then* $\{a^n\}$ *diverges.*

Problem 3.14. To prove this theorem, we need the following result, known as the *Bernoulli inequality*: For each positive integer n and any $x \ge -1$, $(1 + x)^n \ge 1 + nx$. Prove that this is true by induction. Where in the proof do you need the assumption that $x \ge -1$?

Problem 3.15. We can now prove Theorem 3.13. Hint: If $|a| < 1$ (and $a \ne 0$), we can write $|a| = 1/(1 + x)$ for some $x > 0$; if $a > 1$, then $a = 1 + x$ for some $x > 0$. Use the Bernoulli inequality.

Theorem 3.16. Let b *be a real number, and consider the sequence* $\{n^b\}$. *We then have the following:*

(i) *If* b < 0, *then* $\{n^b\} \to 0$.
(ii) *If* b > 0, *then* $\{n^b\} \to \infty$.

We will now show that when $b > 0$ and $a > 1$, the ratio a^n/n^b tends to infinity as $n \to \infty$; that is, the "exponential" function a^n grows faster than any power of n. First, however, we need the following result.

Theorem 3.17. Let $\{x_n\}$ *be a sequence of nonzero real numbers. If*

$$\lim_{n \to \infty} \left| \frac{x_{n+1}}{x_n} \right| = L < 1$$

then $\{x_n\} \to 0$.

Proof. Fix some $\varepsilon > 0$, and choose some $c \in (L, 1)$. Because $0 < |x_{n+1}/x_n| = |x_{n+1}|/|x_n| \to L < c$, there exists some N such that $|x_{n+1}| < c|x_n|$ for all $n > N$. By induction, we can write

$$|x_{N+k}| < c|x_{N+k-1}| < c^2|x_{N+k-2}| < \ldots < c^k|x_N| \tag{1}$$

for any $k > 0$. Now, because $c^k \to 0$ as $k \to \infty$, there exists some K such that $c^k < \varepsilon/|x_N|$ for all $k > K$. Thus, for $k > K$, we have

$$|x_{N+k}| < c^k|x_N| < \frac{\varepsilon}{|x_N|}|x_N| = \varepsilon$$

and $\{x_n\} \to 0$. $\square$

Theorem 3.18. Let $b > 0$ and $a > 1$; then $\{a^n/n^b\} \to \infty$.

Proof. Write $x_n = n^b/a^n$. We will show that $\{x_n\} \to 0$. By Theorem 3.8, this implies $\{1/x_n\} = \{a^n/n^b\} \to \infty$. Now,

$$\frac{x_{n+1}}{x_n} = \frac{(n+1)^b}{a^{n+1}}\frac{a^n}{n^b} = \frac{1}{a}\left(\frac{n+1}{n}\right)^b \quad \text{and therefore} \quad \lim_{n \to \infty}\frac{x_{n+1}}{x_n} = \frac{1}{a} < 1$$

By Theorem 3.17, we conclude that $\{x_n\} \to 0$. $\square$

Problem 3.19. Given a sequence of real numbers $\{x_n\}$, the sequence $\{S_N\}$, defined by $S_N = \Sigma_{n=0}^{N}x_n$, is called the sequence of partial sums of the infinite series $\Sigma_{n=0}^{\infty}x_n$. If $\{S_N\}$ converges to some (finite) limit S, then we write $\Sigma_{n=0}^{\infty}x_n = S$.

Consider the sequence $\{a^n; n = 0, 1, \ldots\}$, where $0 < a < 1$, and define S_N as before. Verify that $(1 - a)S_N = 1 - a^{N+1}$. Use this to show that $\Sigma_{n=0}^{\infty}a^n = 1/(1 - a)$.

Problem 3.20. Given the function

$$f(x) = \frac{x^2 + 2}{2x} \tag{1}$$

define a sequence $\{x_n\}$ of rational numbers by

$$x_1 = 1 \quad \text{and} \quad x_{n+1} = f(x_n) \quad \text{for all } n > 1 \tag{2}$$

We have, then,

$$x_2 = 1.5, \qquad x_3 = 1.417 \ldots \tag{3}$$

(i) Prove that if $\{x_n\}$ converges, then its limit is $x = \sqrt{2}$. (Complete the following expression: $x = \lim_{n \to \infty} x_{n+1} = \lim_{n \to \infty} f(x_n) = \ldots$.) We have seen in Chapter 1 (Problem 6.1) that $\sqrt{2}$ is not a rational number. Hence $\{x_n\}$ does not converge in $\mathbb{Q}$. We will show, however, that the given sequence has a real limit.

(ii) Prove that for $n \geq 2$ we have $x_n \geq \sqrt{2}$. (Show that $f(x) \geq \sqrt{2}$ using $a^2 + b^2 \geq 2ab$. Why?)

(iii) Calculate the value of $(x_{n+1} - x_n)$ as a function of x_n and x_{n-1}. Use the resulting expression to prove that for $n \geq 2$, $\{x_n\}$ is decreasing (by induction).

By the analogue of Theorem 3.1 for decreasing sequences bounded below, $\{x_n\}$ converges to a real number. Hence, there is a real number x such that $x^2 = 2$.

4. Open and Closed Sets

Definition 4.1. Open and closed sets. Let (X, d) be a metric space. A set A in X is open if for every $x \in A$ there exists an open ball centered at x that is contained in A, that is,

$$\forall x \in A, \ \exists \varepsilon > 0 \text{ s.th. } B_\varepsilon(x) \subseteq A$$

A set C in X is closed if its complement (C^c or $\sim C$) is open.

Intuitively, a set A is open if, starting from any point in it, any small movement still leaves us inside the set.[4] We will now establish some basic properties of open sets.

Theorem 4.2. Properties of open sets. Let (X, d) be a metric space. Then

  (i) $\emptyset$ and X are open in X,
  (ii) the union of an arbitrary (possibly infinite) family of open sets is open,
(iii) the intersection of a finite collection of open sets is open.

Proof

(i) This should be understood as a convention. X and $\emptyset$ are both open and closed in X.[5]

(ii) It is obvious: Let $\{A_i; A_i \subseteq X, i \in I\}$ be a family of open sets; then if $x \in \cup_i A_i$, x belongs to some particular A_i, and because A_i is open, there exists some $\varepsilon > 0$ such that $B_\varepsilon(x)$ is contained in A_i and therefore in $\cup_i A_i$.

(iii) Let $\{A_i; A_i \subseteq X, i = 1, \ldots, n\}$ be a finite family of open sets. We want to show that $A = \cap_{i=1}^n A_i$ is open. Take any point x in A; by definition, x belongs to each and all of the A_i's, and because these sets are all open, we can find open balls

$B_{\varepsilon i}(x)$ such that for each i, $B_{\varepsilon i}(x) \subseteq A_i$. Observe that the smallest such ball is contained in all the A_i's simultaneously, and hence in A. That is, if we put $\varepsilon = \min_i\{\varepsilon_i\}$, then

$$B_{\varepsilon}(x) \subseteq B_{\varepsilon i}(x) \subseteq A_i \ \forall \ i = 1, \ldots, n \Rightarrow B_{\varepsilon}(x) \subseteq \cap_{i=1}^{n} A_i = A$$

which shows that A is open.

The condition that the family of sets be finite is important. If we had an infinite number of sets, $\inf_i\{\varepsilon_i\}$ might be zero (note that the minimum might not exist). In that case, there might not be a ball small enough to do the job. For example, if we take the intersection of the infinite family of open intervals

$$\{(-1, 1), (-1/2, 1/2), \ldots, (-1/n, 1/n), \ldots\}$$

we end up with the set $\{0\}$, which is not open. $\qquad\qquad\square$

Using De Morgan's laws[6] and the previous result, it is easy to show that closed sets have the following properties:

Theorem 4.3. *Properties of closed sets.*

 (i) *$\varnothing$ and X are closed in X.*
 (ii) *The intersection of an arbitrary collection of closed sets is closed.*
 (iii) *The union of a finite family of closed sets is closed.*

Problem 4.4. Prove Theorem 4.3.

(a) Interior, Boundary, and Closure of a Set

Definition 4.5. Interior, exterior, boundary, and closure of a set. Let (X, d) be a metric space, and A a set in X. We say the following:

 (i) A point $x_i \in X$ is an *interior point* of A if there exists an open ball centered at x_i, $B_{\varepsilon}(x_i)$, that is contained in A. The set of all interior points of A is called the interior of A (int A).

$$x_i \in \text{int } A \Leftrightarrow \exists \varepsilon > 0 \text{ s.th. } B_{\varepsilon}(x_i) \subseteq A$$

 (ii) A point $x_e \in X$ is an *exterior point* of A if there exists some open ball around x_e that is contained in the complement of A ($\sim A$ or A^c). The set of all exterior points of A is called its exterior (ext A).

$$x_e \in \text{ext } A \Leftrightarrow \exists \varepsilon > 0 \text{ s.th. } B_{\varepsilon}(x_e) \subseteq (\sim A)$$

 (iii) A point $x_b \in X$ is a *boundary point* of A if any open ball around it intersects both A and its complement. The set of boundary points of A is called its boundary, written bdy A or ∂A.

$$x_b \in \partial A \Leftrightarrow \forall \varepsilon > 0, \ B_{\varepsilon}(x_b) \cap A \neq \varnothing \text{ and } B_{\varepsilon}(x_b) \cap (\sim A) \neq \varnothing$$

(iv) A point $x_c \in X$ is a *closure point* of A if any ε-ball around it contains at least one point in A. The set of closure points of a set is called its closure, written cl A or $\overline{A}$.

$$x_c \in \text{cl } A \Leftrightarrow \forall \varepsilon > 0, \ B_\varepsilon(x_c) \cap A \neq \varnothing$$

It is clear from the definition that int $A \subseteq A$: Because any interior point of A lies inside a ball contained in A, it must itself be in A; in the same manner, ext $A \subseteq (\sim A)$. Also, $A \subseteq$ cl A, for any open ball around a point $x \in A$ contains at least one element of A, namely x itself. Hence,

$$\text{int } A \subseteq A \subseteq \text{cl } A \tag{1}$$

On the other hand, a boundary point of A may belong either to A or to its complement, and the same is true of closure points.

It is also evident that the interior, exterior, and boundary of any set A in X constitute a partition of X; that is, they are disjoint sets, and

$$\text{int } A \cup \text{ext } A \cup \partial A = X \tag{2}$$

Finally, we have

$$\text{cl } A = \text{int } A \cup \partial A \tag{3}$$

and

$$\text{ext } A = \text{int}(\sim A) \tag{4}$$

Example 4.6. Let A be the closed ball $B_\varepsilon[x] = \{y \in X; d(x, y) \leq \varepsilon\}$. Then

$$\text{int } B_\varepsilon[x] = B_\varepsilon(x) = \{y \in X; d(x,y) < \varepsilon\}, \qquad \text{ext } B_\varepsilon(x) = \{y \in X; d(x,y) > \varepsilon\},$$
$$\text{bdy } B_\varepsilon[x] = \{y \in X; d(x, y) = \varepsilon\}, \qquad \text{cl } B_\varepsilon[x] = B_\varepsilon[x] \qquad \square$$

Problem 4.7. Prove that $\partial A = \text{cl } A \cap \text{cl}(\sim A)$.

Using the concepts of the interior and closure of a set, we obtain the following characterizations of open and closed sets:

Theorem 4.8

  (i) *int* A *is the largest open set contained in* A.
  (ii) A *is open if and only if* A = *int* A.
  (iii) *cl* A *is the smallest closed set that contains* A.
  (iv) A *is closed if and only if* A = *cl* A.

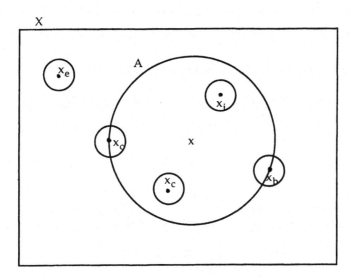

Figure 2.6. Interior, exterior, boundary, and closure points.

Proof

(i) First we show that int A is open. By definition of "interior," for each point $x_i \in$ int A there exists some open ball $B_\varepsilon(x_i)$ contained in A. To show that int A is open, we have to go one step further and verify that $B_\varepsilon(x_i)$ is contained in int A. Because an open ball is open set, around any point y in $B_\varepsilon(x_i)$ we can construct another open ball contained in $B_\varepsilon(x_i)$ and hence in A. It follows that any point $y \in B_\varepsilon(x_i)$ is an interior point and $B_\varepsilon(x_i)$ is indeed contained in A.

Next, we show that int A is the largest open subset of A. If B is any open subset of A, then all its points are by definition interior points of A. Hence, for any such set, $B \subseteq$ int A.

(ii) If $A =$ int A, then A is open, because int A is open. If A is open, then its largest open subset is A itself, and hence $A =$ int A. $\qquad\square$

Problem 4.9. Prove parts (iii) and (iv) of Theorem 4.8.

(b) Limit Points and Characterization of Closed Sets in Terms of Sequences

Definition 4.10. Limit points and derived set. Let (X, d) be a metric space, and A a set in X. A point x_L in X is said to be a limit (or cluster) point of A if every open ball around it contains at least one point of A distinct from x_L. The set of all limit points of A is called its derived set, denoted by $D(A)$:

$$x_L \in D(A) \Leftrightarrow \forall \varepsilon > 0, \; B_\varepsilon(x_L) \cap (A \setminus \{x_L\}) \neq \emptyset$$

Notice that this is more restrictive than the definition of closure point, because now the intersection of A and $B_\varepsilon(x_L)$ cannot be just the point x_L itself. Points for which this is the case are called *isolated points*. Hence, closure points are either limit points or isolated points.

Theorem 4.11. *Let (X, d) be a metric space, and A a set in X. A point $x_L \in X$ is a limit point of A if and only if there exists a sequence in $A\backslash\{x_L\}$ that converges to x_L.*

Proof

- $(\rightarrow)$ Assume that there exists a sequence $\{a_n\}$ in $A\backslash\{x_L\}$ (i.e., with $a_n \neq x_L$ for all n), with $\{a_n\} \rightarrow x_L$. Then for any given $\varepsilon > 0$ there exists some positive integer N_ε such that

$$d(a_n, x_L) < \varepsilon \quad \text{for all } n > N_\varepsilon$$

But then we have $B_\varepsilon(x_L) \cap (A\backslash\{x_L\}) \neq \emptyset$ for the given ε. Because this is true for any $\varepsilon > 0$, x_L is a limit point of A.

- $(\leftarrow)$ Assume that x_L is a limit point of A, that is,

$$\forall r > 0, \ B_r(x_L) \cap (A\backslash\{x_L\}) \neq \emptyset \tag{1}$$

We will show that we can construct a sequence with the desired properties. Put $r_1 = 1$; by (1), there exists some $a_1 \in B_{r_1}(x_L) \cap (A\backslash\{x_L\})$. Next, put

$$r_2 = \frac{d(a_1, x_L)}{2} \leq \frac{1}{2}$$

and, again by (1), there exists some $a_2 \in B_{r_2}(x_L) \cap (A\backslash\{x_L\})$. Continuing in this way, we can construct a sequence $\{a_n\}$ in $A\backslash\{x_L\}$ with the property that

$$0 < d(a_n, x_L) \leq \frac{1}{2^{n-1}}$$

Because $1/(2^{n-1}) \rightarrow 0$, so does $d(a_n, x_L)$, and therefore $\{a_n\} \rightarrow x_L$. $\qquad\square$

We will now obtain two useful, and closely related, characterizations of closed sets.

Theorem 4.12. *A set A in a metric space is closed if and only if it contains all its limit points.*

Proof

- $(\rightarrow)$ Assume that A is closed (i.e., its complement A^c is open). Then for any $x \in A^c$, there exists some $\varepsilon > 0$ such that

$$B_\varepsilon(x) \subseteq A^c \Leftrightarrow B_\varepsilon(x) \cap A = \emptyset$$

Hence, no point of A^c can be a limit point of A, and it follows that all such points must be contained in A.

- ($\leftarrow$) To show that if A contains all its limits points then A^c is open, we prove the contrapositive statement: If A^c is not open, then it contains some limit points of A.

  Suppose A^c is not open. Then, negating the definition of open set, there exist points in A^c with the property that no open ball around them lies entirely in A^c. Let x be one such point. For any $\varepsilon > 0$, the ball $B_\varepsilon(x)$ contains at least one point in A – necessarily different from x, because $x \in A^c$. Hence, x is a limit point of A lying in A^c. $\qquad\square$

Using Theorem 4.11, we can rephrase this last characterization of closedness in terms of sequences: A set A is closed if and only if every convergent sequence in A has its limit in A. This suggests a method that is sometimes convenient for showing that a given set A is closed: Consider an arbitrary convergent sequence contained in A, and use the set's properties to show that the limit is also contained in it.

Theorem 4.13. A set A in a metric space is closed if and only if every convergent sequence $\{x_n\}$ contained in A has its limit in A; that is, if $x_n \in A$ for all n and $\{x_n\} \to x$ imply that $x \in A$.

Proof. Assume that every convergent sequence $\{x_n\}$ contained in A has limit x in A. Then, in particular, this holds for all such sequences with the property that $x_n \neq x$ for all n. It follows that A contains all its limit points and is therefore closed.

Conversely, assume that A is closed, and let $\{x_n\}$ be a convergent sequence contained in A with limit x. If $x_n \neq x$ for all n, then x is a limit point of A and therefore belongs to A (because A is closed). Alternatively, $x = x_n$ for some n, and because $x_n \in A$, we have $x \in A$. $\qquad\square$

Problem 4.14. Show that in a metric space the closed ball $B_r[x]$ is a closed set. (Take a limit point a of $B_r[x]$ and consider an arbitrary sequence $\{x_n\}$ in $B_r[x]$ with limit a. Use the triangle inequality to show that a must be in $B_r[x]$.)

Problem 4.15. Let B be a nonempty set of real numbers bounded above. Let $s = \sup B$. Show that $s \in \overline{B}$. Notice that this implies that $s \in B$ if B is closed.

Problem 4.16. Let A be a set in a metric space (X, d). Show that if A is closed and $x \notin A$, then $d(x, A) > 0$.

Hint: Prove the contrapositive.

5. Limits of Functions

We shall now define the limit of a function between two metric spaces and show that it can be characterized in terms of the limits of sequences.

Definition 5.1. Limit of a function.[7] Let (X, d) and (Y, ρ) be two metric spaces, with A a set in X, f a function $A \longrightarrow Y$, and x^0 a (limit) point of A. We say that f has a limit y^0 as x approaches x^0 if

$$\forall \varepsilon > 0, \ \exists \delta_\varepsilon > 0 \text{ s.th. } 0 < d(x, x^0) < \delta_\varepsilon \Rightarrow \rho[f(x), y^0] < \varepsilon$$

We then write $f(x) \to y^0$ as $x \to x^0$, or $\lim_{x \to x^0} f(x) = y^0$.

Intuitively, $f(x)$ approaches y^0 as $x \to x^0$ if, by choosing x sufficiently close to x^0, we can bring $f(x)$ as close to y^0 as we want. Notice that nothing has been said in the definition about the value of f at x^0; in fact, x^0 may not even be in the domain of f. We require, however, that x^0 be a limit point of A so that we can always find points in the domain of f as close to x^0 as we want.

The following result shows that the limit of a function can be characterized in terms of the convergence of sequences.

Theorem 5.2. Let (X, d) and (Y, ρ) be two metric spaces, with f a function X $\longrightarrow$ Y, and x^0 a limit point of X. Then f has limit y^0 as x $\to x^0$ if and only if for every sequence $\{x_n\}$ that converges to x^0 in (X, d), with $x_n \neq x^0$, the sequence $\{f(x_n)\}$ converges to y^0 in (Y, ρ).

Proof

- $(\to)$ Assume that $\lim_{x \to x^0} f(x) = y^0$, and let $\{x_n\}$ be a sequence in X, with $x_n \neq x^0$ and $\{x_n\} \to x^0$. We want to show that $\{f(x_n)\} \to y^0$, that is, that

$$\forall \varepsilon > 0, \ \exists N(\varepsilon) \text{ s.th. } \rho[f(x_n), y^0] < \varepsilon \quad \text{for all } n > N(\varepsilon) \tag{1}$$

Fix some arbitrary $\varepsilon > 0$. By assumption, $f(x)$ has limit y^0 as $x \to x^0$, so we can bring $f(x)$ arbitrarily close to y^0 by choosing x sufficiently close to x^0; that is, for the given ε,

$$\exists \delta_\varepsilon > 0 \text{ s.th. } \rho[f(x), y^0] < \varepsilon \quad \text{for all } x \in B_{\delta_\varepsilon}(x^0) \backslash \{x^0\} \tag{2}$$

Finally, the fact that $\{x_n\} \to x^0$ guarantees that we can get x_n sufficiently close to x^0 by choosing n large enough. Formally, the convergence of $\{x_n\}$ implies that for the δ_ε in (2),

$$\exists N(\delta_\varepsilon) \text{ s.th. } x_n \in B_{\delta_\varepsilon}(x^0) \quad \text{for all } n > N(\delta_\varepsilon) \tag{3}$$

Now, (2) and (3) together imply (1) (with $N(\varepsilon) = N(\delta_\varepsilon)$), that is, $\{f(x_n)\} \to y^0$.

- $(\leftarrow)$ We now want to prove the following statement:

$[\forall \{x_n\}$ with $\{x_n\} \to x^0$ and $x_n \neq x^0$, we have $\{f(x_n)\} \to y^0] \Rightarrow \lim_{x \to x^0} f(x) = y^0$

It turns out to be easier to prove the contrapositive statement:

$$\lim_{x \to x^0} f(x) \neq y^0 \Rightarrow [\exists \{x_n\} \text{ with } x_n \neq x^0 \text{ and } \{x_n\} \to x^0, \text{ s.th. } \{f(x_n)\} \nrightarrow y^0]$$

That is, if y^0 is not the limit of f as $x \to x^0$, then there exist sequences with $\{x_n\} \to x^0$ and $x_n \neq x^0$ with the property that the image sequence $\{f(x_n)\}$ does not converge to y^0. Now, what does it mean to say that y^0 is not the limit of f as $x \to x^0$? Take the definition of limit,

$$\forall \varepsilon > 0, \ \exists \delta > 0 \text{ s.th. } \forall x \in B_\delta(x^0) \backslash \{x^0\} \text{ we have } \rho[f(x), y^0] < \varepsilon$$

and negate it, obtaining

$$\exists \varepsilon > 0 \text{ s.th. } \forall \delta > 0, \ \exists x \in B_\delta(x^0) \backslash \{x^0\} \text{ with } \rho[f(x), y^0] \geq \varepsilon \tag{4}$$

We will now show that if y^0 is not the limit of f as $x \to x^0$, then it is possible to find a sequence $\{x_n\}$ such that $\{x_n\} \to x^0$ and $x_n \neq x^0$, but $\{f(x_n)\} \nrightarrow y^0$. Choose some ε that works in (4), and consider a sequence of open balls centered at x^0 with radius $r_n = 1/n$. By (4), it is possible to pick for each n a point $x_n \in B_{1/n}(x^0)$ such that $\rho[f(x_n), y^0] \geq \varepsilon$. By construction, $\{x_n\} \to x^0$, but $\{f(x_n)\} \nrightarrow y^0$. $\square$

This result allows us to obtain some important properties of the limits of functions using earlier results about convergent sequences. We list some of these properties, leaving the proofs as exercises.

Theorem 5.3. Uniqueness of the limit. *Let* (X, d) *and* (Y, ρ) *be metric spaces, with* A *a set in* X, f *a function* A $\longrightarrow$ Y, *and* x^0 *a limit point of* A. *Then the limit of* f *as* x $\to$ x^0, *when it exists, is unique. That is, if* f(x) $\to$ y' *and* f(x) $\to$ y'' *as* x $\to$ x^0, *then* y' = y''.

Theorem 5.4. Algebra of limits. *Let* (X, d) *be a metric sapce, with* $(Y, \|\cdot\|)$ *a normed vector space,* f *and* g *functions* X $\longrightarrow$ Y, *and* x^0 *a limit point of* X. *Assume that* f(x) $\to$ a *and* g(x) $\to$ b *as* x $\to$ x^0. *Then*

(i) f(x) + g(x) $\to$ a + b *as* x $\to$ x^0, *and*
(ii) for any scalar λ, λf(x) $\to$ λa *as* x $\to$ x^0.

If $(Y, \|\cdot\|)$ *is* $\mathbb{R}$ *with the usual norm, then*

(iii) f(x)g(x) $\to$ ab *as* x $\to$ x^0, *and*
(iv) f(x)/g(x) $\to$ a/b *as* x $\to$ x^0, *provided* b $\neq$ 0.

Theorem 5.5. Preservation of equalities and inequalities. *Let* (X, d) *be a metric space, with* f *and* g *functions* X $\longrightarrow$ $\mathbb{R}$, *and* x^0 *a limit point of* X. *Then*

(i) *assume that there exists some $\varepsilon > 0$ such that* $f(x) = g(x)$ *for all* $x \in B_\varepsilon(x^0)\setminus\{x^0\}$
  and that $f(x) \to a$ *as* $x \to x^0$; *then* $g(x) \to a$ *as* $x \to x^0$, *and*
(ii) *assume that* $f(x) \to a$ *and* $g(x) \to b$ *as* $x \to x^0$. *If there exists some* $\varepsilon > 0$ *such that*
  $f(x) \le g(x)$ *for all* $x \in B_\varepsilon(x^0)\setminus\{x^0\}$, *then* $a \le b$.

Problem 5.6. Use the definition of the limit of a function to show that if

$$\lim_{x \to x^0} f(x) = a \quad \text{and} \quad \lim_{x \to x^0} g(x) = b$$

then $\lim_{x \to x^0}[f(x) + g(x)] = a + b$. Prove the same result using the analogous theorem for limits of sequences.

Limits at Infinity and Infinite Limits

Let f be a function $\mathbb{R} \longrightarrow \mathbb{R}$. We say that $f(x) \to y^0$ as $x \to \infty$ if for every $\varepsilon > 0$ there exists some $B > 0$ such that $|f(x) - y^0| < \varepsilon$ for all $x > B$. The limit of f as $x \to -\infty$ is defined in an analogous way.

The foregoing results concerning the preservation of inequalities and the algebra of limits have direct analogues for limits at infinity.

Next, let (X, d) be a metric space, with f a function $X \longrightarrow \mathbb{R}$, and x^0 a limit point of X. We say that $f(x) \to \infty$ as $x \to x^0$ if

$$\forall B > 0, \ \exists \delta > 0 \ \text{s.th.} \ f(x) > B \text{ for all } x \in B_\delta(x^0)\setminus\{x^0\}$$

In this case, we have to be more careful with the limits of sums, products, and quotients of functions. In particular, let f and g be functions $X \longrightarrow \mathbb{R}$, and x^0 a limit point of X. We have the following:

(i) If $\lim_{x \to x^0} f(x) = y^0$ and $\lim_{x \to x^0} g(x) = \infty$, then $\lim_{x \to x^0}[f(x) + g(x)] = \infty$, but if $\lim_{x \to x^0}$
   $f(x) = -\infty$, the limit of the sum may be anything.
(ii) If $\lim_{x \to x^0} f(x) = y^0 > 0$ and $\lim_{x \to x^0} g(x) = \infty$, then $\lim_{x \to x^0}[f(x)g(x)] = \infty$. However,
   if $\lim_{x \to x^0} f(x) = 0$, nothing can be said without studying f and g further.
(iii) If $\lim_{x \to x^0} f(x) = y^0 > 0$, $\lim_{x \to x^0} g(x) = 0$, and $g(x) \neq 0$ in some open ball around x^0,
   then $_{x \to x^0} f(x)/g(x) = \infty$.

6. Continuity in Metric Spaces

The familiar concept of continuity for a function from $\mathbb{R}$ to $\mathbb{R}$ can be extended in a natural way to functions mapping one metric space into another. In this section, we define continuity for functions between metric spaces, obtain some useful characterizations of continuous functions, and prove some important results concerning the properties of continuous real functions defined on an interval.

Definition 6.1. Continuous function. Let (X, d) and (Y, ρ) be metric spaces, and f a function $X \longrightarrow Y$. We say that f is continuous at a point $x^0 \in X$ if

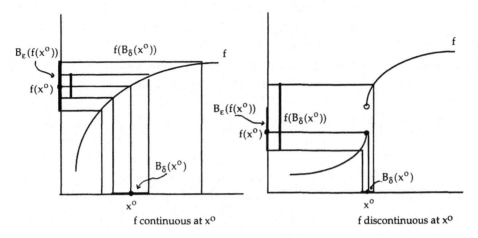

Figure 2.7.

$$\forall \varepsilon > 0, \ \exists \delta(x^0, \varepsilon) > 0 \text{ s.th. } d(x, x^0) < \delta(x^0, \varepsilon) \Rightarrow \rho[f(x), f(x^0)] < \varepsilon$$

The function f is continuous on a subset A of X if it is continuous at all points of A. If we speak simply of a continuous function, it is understood that the function is continuous at all points in its domain.[8]

Intuitively, a continuous function maps nearby points into images that are also close by. Hence, if f is continuous at x^0, a small change in x away from x^0 will not change the value of the function too much. The notation $\delta(x^0, \varepsilon)$ emphasizes that the value of δ that will work in each case will depend on the value of ε and on the point x^0.

The geometric intuition behind the definition is most easily captured by reformulating it in terms of open balls. Hence, a function f is continuous at x^0 if

$$\forall \varepsilon > 0, \ \exists \delta > 0 \text{ s.th. } x \in B_\delta(x^0) \Rightarrow f(x) \in B_\varepsilon(f(x^0))$$

or, equivalently, if

$$\forall \varepsilon > 0, \ \exists \delta > 0 \text{ s.th. } f(B_\delta(x^0)) \subseteq B_\varepsilon(f(x^0)) \tag{1}$$

That is, given an open ball around $f(x^0)$ with arbitrarily small radius ε, we can always find another ball with center at x^0 and radius δ whose image under f is contained in the first ball, $B_\varepsilon(f(x^0))$. The first panel of Figure 2.7 illustrates that this is always possible at a point of continuity. The second panel shows that if f is discontinuous at x^0, then it is impossible to find such a δ for any ε smaller than the jump in the function at x^0.

Problem 6.2. Preservation of sign. Let f be a continuous function from a metric space (X, d) to $\mathbb{R}$, with the usual metric. Prove (directly) that the set $\{x \in X; f(x) > 0\}$ is open. Intuitively, this result says that a continuous function that is strictly positive (or negative) at a point will maintain its sign within a sufficiently small ball around the original point.

Using the definition of the limit of a function and the characterization of limits of functions in terms of limits of sequences, we obtain immediately two useful characterizations of continuity. Loosely speaking, the first says that a function is continuous at a point if its value coincides with its limit, and the second says that a continuous function preserves convergence of sequences.

Theorem 6.3. Let (X, d) and (Y, ρ) be metric spaces, and f a function $X \longrightarrow Y$. Then f is continuous at a point x^0 in X if and only if either of the following (equivalent) statements is true:

(i) *$\mathrm{f}(x^0)$ is defined, and either x^0 is an isolated point or x^0 is a limit point of X and $\lim_{x \to x^0} \mathrm{f}(x) = \mathrm{f}(x^0)$.*
(ii) *For every sequence $\{x_n\}$ convergent to x^0 in (X, d), the sequence $\{\mathrm{f}(x_n)\}$ converges to $\mathrm{f}(x^0)$ in (Y, ρ).*

Hence, a function f is discontinuous at a limit point x^0 of X if the limit of f as $x \to x^0$ does not exist or if it exists but is not equal to the value of the function at x^0. For example, the function

$$f(x) = \frac{1}{x-1}$$

is discontinuous at $x = 1$ because it does not have a limit as $x \to 1$. The function defined by

$$g(x, y) = \frac{xy}{x^2 + y^2} \quad \text{for}(x, y) \neq (0, 0) \text{ and } f(0, 0) = 0$$

is discontinuous for the second reason. Notice that the sequence $\{(1/n, 1/n)\}$ converges to $(0, 0)$, but the image sequence $f(1/n, 1/n)$ does not approach 0.

Intuitively, a function is continuous except at points corresponding to "breaks" in its graph. Intuition, however, may occasionally need some help, as illustrated by the following example.

Example 6.4. Consider the function $f : \mathbb{R} \longrightarrow \mathbb{R}$, defined by $f(x) = 0$ if x is irrational, and by $f(x) = 1/q$ if x is the rational number p/q, where p and q are integers with no common factor and $q > 0$. We shall show that *f* is discontinuous at all rational numbers and continuous at all irrational ones.

What does it mean that a function is not continuous at a point x^0? Negating the definition of continuity, we obtain the following:

$$\exists \varepsilon > 0 \text{ s.th. } \forall \delta > 0, \; \exists x \in B_\delta(x^0) \text{ with the property that } \rho[f(x), f(x^0)] \geq \varepsilon$$

Hence, to establish discontinuity, we have to produce one such ε.

Now, Let $x^0 = p/q$ be a rational number, and choose $\varepsilon \leq 1/q$. Then, for any $\delta > 0$, the ball $B_\delta(x^0) = (x^0 - \delta, x^0 + \delta)$ contains at least an irrational number x^i. For this number, $|f(x^0) - f(x^i)| = 1/q \geq \varepsilon$.

Next, let x^0 be an irrational number, and fix some arbitrary $\varepsilon > 0$. The interval $B_\delta(x^0) = (x^0 - 1, x^0 + 1)$ contains finitely many rational numbers with denominator no greater than $1/\varepsilon$. Because x^0 is irrational and therefore cannot be any of these numbers, the distance between x^0 and the closest such number is a strictly positive number δ. Hence, any $x \in B_\delta(x^0)$ is either irrational or a rational number p/q with $q > 1/\varepsilon$. In the first case, $|f(x^0) - f(x)| = 0$, and in the second, $|f(x^0) - f(x)| = 1/q < \varepsilon$. $\qquad \square$

Problem 6.5. Let $f: \mathbb{R} \longrightarrow \mathbb{R}$ be the function defined by $f(x) = 1$ for x rational and by $f(x) = 0$ for x irrational. Show that f is discontinuous everywhere.

Hint: Recall that any interval in the real line contains both rational and irrational numbers.

Problem 6.6. Given a function $f: \mathbb{R} \longrightarrow \mathbb{R}$, define $g: \mathbb{R} \longrightarrow \mathbb{R}^2$ by $g(x) = (x, f(x))$. Use the sequential characterization of continuity to show that if f is continuous at some point x^0, then so is g.

Problem 6.7. Consider the finite-dimensional Euclidean space E^n. For any $k \in \{1, 2, \ldots, n\}$, the kth projection mapping, $p_k: \mathbb{R}^n \longrightarrow \mathbb{R}$, is defined for $x = (x_1, \ldots, x_n)$ by $p_k(x) = x_k$. Show that $p_k(\;)$ is a continuous function.

Problem 6.8. Show that in any normed vector space $(X, \|\cdot\|)$ the norm is a continuous function from X to $\mathbb{R}$.

Problem 6.9. Prove that if f is a continuous function, then for any set A, $f(\operatorname{cl} A) \subseteq \operatorname{cl}[f(A)]$.

Hint: Use the characterization of continuity in terms of inclusion relations among open balls given in expression (1) right after Definition 6.1.

Using the characterizations of continuity given in Theorem 6.3, it is very easy to prove some important results.

Theorem 6.10. Composite-function theorem. Let (X, d), (Y, d'), and (Z, d'') *be metric spaces. Given two functions* f : X $\longrightarrow$ Y *continuous at* $x^0 \in$ X *and* g : Y $\longrightarrow$ Z *continuous at* f(x^0) $\in$ Y, *the composite function* g $\circ$ f *is continuous at* x^0.

Proof. We will use the sequential characterization of continuity. Let $\{x_n\}$ be any sequence convergent to x^0 in (X, d). Because f is continuous at x^0, we have $\{f(x_n)\} \to f(x^0)$ for any such sequence. And because g is continuous at $f(x^0)$, $\{g[f(x_n)]\} \to g[f(x^0)]$ for any $\{x_n\}$ with $\{x_n\} \to x^0$. Hence, $g \circ f$ is continuous at x^0. $\qquad\qquad\qquad\qquad\qquad\qquad\qquad\qquad\qquad\qquad\quad$ $\square$

Problem 6.11. Let f and g be functions $\mathbb{R} \longrightarrow \mathbb{R}$, and assume that f is continuous at y^0 and that $g(x) \to y^0$ as $x \to \infty$. Show that $\lim_{x \to \infty} f[g(x)] = f(y^0)$.

Using the characterization of continuity in terms of limits and Theorem 5.4 on the algebra of limits, we obtain the following:

Theorem 6.12. Let (X, d) be a metric space, and (Y, $\|\cdot\|$) a normed vector *space. Given functions* f *and* g, X $\longrightarrow$ Y, *both continuous at* $x^0 \in$ X, *we have* *the following:*

(i) f + g *is continuous at* x^0, *and*
(ii) *for any scalar* λ, λf *is continuous at* x^0.

If (Y, $\|\cdot\|$) *is* $\mathbb{R}$ *with the usual norm, then*

(iii) f $\cdot$ g *is continuous at* x^0, *and*
(iv) f/g *is continuous at* x^0, *provided* g(x) $\neq 0$ *in some open ball around* x^0.

So far, we have been talking about continuity in local terms. That is, we defined the continuity of a function at a point and called the function continuous if it was continuous at all points in its domain. We shall now give a direct characterization of "global" continuity.

Theorem 6.13. Let (X, d) and (Y, ρ) be metric spaces, and f *a function* X $\longrightarrow$ Y. *Then* f *is continuous if and only if for every set* C *closed in* (Y, ρ) *the set* f^{-1}(C) *is closed in* (X, d).

That is, a function is continuous if and only if the inverse images of closed sets are closed. We emphasize that this is true only for inverse images. A

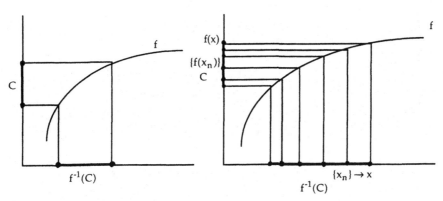

Figure 2.8.

continuous function does not necessarily map closed sets into closed sets, and a function that does map closed sets into closed sets is not necessarily continuous.

Proof

- $(\rightarrow)$ f continuous on $X \Rightarrow$ for any C closed in $Y, f^{-1}(C)$ is closed in X.

  Let C be an arbitrary closed set in (Y, ρ). We will show that $f^{-1}(C)$ is closed in (X, d) by verifying that it contains all its limit points. Let x be an arbitrary limit point of $f^{-1}(C)$; then (by Theorem 4.11) there exists a sequence $\{x_n\}$ in $f^{-1}(C)$ that converges to x. Because f is continuous, the sequence $\{f(x_n)\}$ converges to $f(x)$. By construction, $f(x_n) \in C$ for all n, and by assumption, C is closed. Hence, by Theorem 4.13, the limit $f(x)$ must lie in C. Now, $f(x) \in C \Leftrightarrow x \in f^{-1}(C)$, implying that $f^{-1}(C)$ contains all its limit points and is therefore closed.

- $(\leftarrow)$ For any C closed in $Y, f^{-1}(C)$ is closed in $X \Rightarrow f$ continuous on X.

  We will prove the contrapositive statement:

  > f discontinuous at some point x^0 in $X \Rightarrow \exists$ closed sets C in Y with $f^{-1}(C)$ not closed

Let f be discontinuous at some point x^0. Then (negating the characterization of continuity in terms of sequences) there exist sequences $\{x_n\} \to x^0$ in X with $\{f(x_n)\} \nrightarrow f(x^0)$. That is, there exists some $r > 0$ such that

$$\rho[f(x_n), f(x^0)] \geq r \quad \text{for all } n \tag{1}$$

(or at least for all n_k in some subsequence $\{x_{n_k}\}$ of $\{x_n\}$, in which case the argument goes through unchanged working with the subsequence).

We will use this fact to show that there exists a set with the desired properties. In particular, let C be the closure of the image sequence:

$$C = \text{cl}(\{f(x_n)\})$$

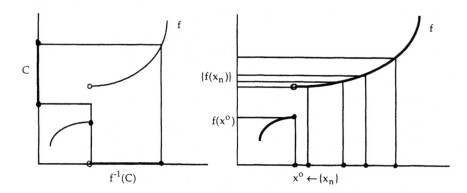

Figure 2.9.

Being the closure of a set, C is closed. We will prove that $f^{-1}(C)$ is not closed by showing that it does not contain all its limit points. In particular, we will show that x^0 is a limit point of $f^{-1}(C)$ but does not belong to this set. Note that because C contains $\{f(x_n)\}$, we have $x_n \in f^{-1}(C)$ for all n, and because $\{x_n\} \to x^0$, x^0 is a limit point of $f^{-1}(C)$. However, $f(x^0) \notin C$ (i.e., $f(x^0)$ is not a closure point of $\{f(x_n)\}$), for (1) implies $B_\varepsilon(f(x^0)) \cap \{f(x_n)\} = \varnothing$ for all $\varepsilon < r$. Hence, $x^0 \notin f^{-1}(C)$. $\square$

Taking complements of the appropriate sets, it is easy to obtain an equivalent characterization of continuity in terms of the inverse images of open sets.

Theorem 6.14. Let (X, d) and (Y, ρ) be metric spaces, and f a function $X \longrightarrow Y$. Then f is continuous if and only if for every set A open in (Y, ρ) the set $f^{-1}(A)$ is open in (X, d).

Problem 6.15. Using Theorem 6.13, prove Theorem 6.14.

Problem 6.16. Let (X, d) be a metric space, and $(Y, \|\cdot\|)$ a normed vector space with zero vector $\underline{0}$. Given a continuous function $f: X \longrightarrow Y$, adapt the proof of the characterization of continuity in terms of the inverse images of closed sets to show that the set $f^{-1}(\underline{0})$ is closed.

These last characterizations of continuity are of particular interest because they do not contain any explicit reference to a metric. In fact, when we work in general topological spaces (of which metric spaces are a subset), we begin with open (or closed) sets as a primitive concept and then define continuity in terms of their inverse images.

Uniform Continuity

A stronger concept of continuity that is sometimes useful is that of uniform continuity. We have seen that a function f between two metric spaces (X, d) and (Y, ρ) is continuous on a subset A of X if for all x and y in A we have

$$\forall \varepsilon > 0,\ \exists \delta(x, \varepsilon) > 0 \text{ s.th. } d(x, y) < \delta(x, \varepsilon) \Rightarrow \rho[f(x), f(y)] < \varepsilon \tag{1}$$

In general, the value of δ that satisfies (1) depends not only on the value chosen for ε, but also on the point x at which we are studying the function – hence the notation $\delta(x, \varepsilon)$. If it is possible to find some $\delta(\varepsilon)$ that for any given value of ε will work for any x in A, we say that the function is uniformly continuous on A. More formally, we have the following:

Definition 6.17. Uniformly continuous function. A function $f:(X, d) \longrightarrow (Y, \rho)$ is uniformly continuous on a subset A of X if for all $x, y \in A$ and for any $\varepsilon > 0$ there exists some number $\delta(\varepsilon) > 0$, independent of x, such that

$$d(x, y) < \delta(\varepsilon) \Rightarrow \rho[f(x), f(y)] < \varepsilon$$

It is clear that uniform continuity on a set implies continuity on the same set, but the converse statement is not true.

Lipschitz Functions

We now introduce a stronger notion of continuity that will be useful in Chapter 9.

Definition 6.18. Lipschitz and locally Lipschitz functions. Let X and Y be normed vector spaces, and E a subset of X. A function $f: X \longrightarrow Y$ is said to be Lipschitz on E if there exists a positive constant K such that for all x and y in E we have

$$\|f(x) - f(y)\| \leq K \|x - y\|$$

This condition is called a *Lipschitz condition*, and the constant K is a *Lipschitz constant* for f on E.

The function f is said to be locally Lipschitz on the set E if for each point x_0 in E there exists some $\varepsilon > 0$ and some $K_0 > 0$ such that $B_\varepsilon(x_0) \subseteq E$ and if for all x and y in $B_\varepsilon(x_0)$,

$$\|f(x) - f(y)\| \leq K_0 \|x - y\|$$

Problem 6.19. Show that a Lipschitz function is uniformly continuous (and therefore continuous).

Homeomorphisms

Definition 6.20. Homeomorphism. Let (X, d) and (Y, ρ) be metric spaces. A function $f : X \longrightarrow Y$ is called a homeomorphism if it is one-to-one and continuous and its inverse function is continuous on $f(X)$.

That is, a homeomorphism is a continuous function with a continuous inverse. The continuity of f implies that given two nearby points x' and x'' in X, their images $y' = f(x')$ and $y'' = f(x'')$ will also be close by. Given an arbitrary continuous function, however, it is possible that points that are far from each other will be mapped by the function into nearby points, or even into a single point. If f is a homeomorphism, that is impossible, for the inverse relation is also a continuous function. Hence, given two points in X, their images under a homeomorphism are close to each other if and only if the points themselves are not far away. Using the characterization of continuity in terms of sequences and inverse images of open sets, we obtain the following characterization of homeomorphism:

Theorem 6.21. A one-to-one function f : $(X, d) \longrightarrow (Y, \rho)$ *is a homeomorphism if and only if either of the following (equivalent) statements is true:*

(i) *For all* x $\in$ X, *the sequence* {x_n} *converges to* x *in* (X, d) *if and only if the image sequence* {f(x_n)} *converges to* f(x) *in* (Y, ρ).
(ii) *Given any open set* A_X *in* (X, d), *its image* f(A_X) *is open in* (Y, ρ), *and given any set* A_Y *open in* (Y, ρ), *its inverse image* $f^{-1}(A_Y)$ *is open in* (X, d).

Two metric spaces (X, d) and (Y, ρ) are homeomorphic if and only if there exists some homeomorphism h from X onto Y – that is, $Y = h(X)$ or h^{-1} must be defined on the whole set Y. The relation "being homeomorphic to" is an equivalence relation on the set of all metric spaces. Intuitively, two homeomorphic metric spaces are identical except for a continuous change of coordinates that preserves convergence and open sets. For many purposes, two homeomorphic metric (or topological) spaces are in fact equivalent. Properties of sets that are invariant under homeomorphisms are known as *topological properties.*

Some Properties of Continuous Real Functions

We will now establish some important properties of continuous real functions defined on an interval. In later sections we will see how they can be partially generalized to continuous functions defined on more general spaces.

In many applications, we are interested in finding the maximum (or minimum) of a real-valued function over some given set. In principle, however, a continuous function defined on an arbitrary set may not have a maximum. For the case of a continuous function from $\mathbb{R}$ to $\mathbb{R}$, we will show that a sufficient condition for the existence of a maximum over a set is that the set be a compact interval. We begin by showing that such a function must be bounded.

Theorem 6.22. Let $f: \mathbb{R} \longrightarrow \mathbb{R}$ *be defined and continuous on the closed and bounded interval [a, b]. Then* f *is bounded on [a, b]; that is, there exists some real number* M *such that* $|f(x)| \leq M$ *for all* x *in the interval.*

Proof. We will show that if f is both continuous and unbounded on the interval, we arrive at a contradiction. Suppose, for the sake of concreteness, that f is not bounded above on $[a, b]$. Then, for each positive integer n, there exists a point $x_n \in [a, b]$ such that $f(x_n) \geq n$. By the Bolzano-Weierstrass theorem, the bounded sequence $\{x_n\}$ has a convergent subsequence $\{x_{n_k}\}$ with limit x^0. Because $[a, b]$ is a closed set, moreover, we have $x^0 \in [a, b]$, by Theorem 4.13.

Now, by the continuity of f at x^0,

$$\lim_{k \to \infty} f(x_{n_k}) = f(x^0) \tag{1}$$

On the other hand, $\{x_{n_k}\}$ is a subsequence of $\{x_n\}$, and it must therefore be true that for each k, $f(x_{n_k}) \geq n_k > k$. Thus,

$$\lim_{k \to \infty} f(x_{n_k}) = \infty \tag{2}$$

and we have reached a contradiction. If f is continuous, it cannot be unbounded. $\square$

This result tells us that the set $\{f(x); x \in [a, b]\}$, being a nonempty and bounded set of real numbers, has a supremum (and an infimum). We will now show that the function also attains its supremum and infimum on the interval (i.e., it has both a maximum and a minimum on $[a, b]$).

Theorem 6.23. Extreme-value theorem. Let f *be a continuous real-valued function on the closed and bounded interval [a, b]. Then there exist points* x_M *and* x_m *in [a, b] such that for all* $x \in [a, b]$, $f(x_m) \leq f(x) \leq f(x_M)$.

Proof. We will prove the existence of a maximum. By Theorem 6.22 we know that $\mu = \sup_{x \in [a,b]} f(x)$ exists. We will now show that this value is achieved on the interval (i.e., $\exists \, x_M \in [a, b]$ such that $f(x_M) = \mu$).

Observe that no number smaller than μ is an upper bound of $\{f(x);$ $x \in [a, b]\}$. Hence, for each positive integer n, we can find some $x_n \in [a, b]$ such that

$$|f(x_n) - \mu| < 1/n \tag{1}$$

The sequence $\{x_n\} \subseteq [a, b]$ thus constructed is bounded and therefore has a convergent subsequence $\{x_{n_k}\}$ by the Bolzano-Weierstrass theorem. Call the limit of this subsequence x_M, and observe that because $[a, b]$ is closed, $x_M \in [a, b]$ (Theorem 4.13). It remains to show that $f(x_M) = \mu$.

Now, because $\{x_{n_k}\} \to x_M$ and f is continuous, we have $\{f(x_{n_k})\} \to f(x_M)$, that is,

$$\forall \varepsilon > 0, \ \exists N_\varepsilon \text{ s.th. } n_k > N_\varepsilon \Rightarrow |f(x_{n_k}) - f(x_M)| < \varepsilon \tag{2}$$

Next, by the triangle inequality, we can write

$$|f(x_M) - \mu| \le |f(x_M) - f(x_{n_k})| + |f(x_{n_k}) - \mu|$$

for any n_k. Now choose an arbitrary $\varepsilon > 0$. Using (1) and (2), we have that for all n_k greater than some N_ε,

$$0 \le |f(x_M) - \mu| \le |f(x_M) - f(x_{n_k})| + |f(x_{n_k}) - \mu| < \varepsilon + \frac{1}{n_k}$$

Because this inequality must hold for all $\varepsilon > 0$ and for arbitrarily large n_k, we conclude that $f(x_M) = \mu$. □

Theorem 6.24. Intermediate-value theorem. Let f *be a continuous real-valued function on the closed and bounded interval* [a, b]. *Then for each number* γ *(strictly) between* f(a) *and* f(b), *there exists a point* c $\in$ (a, b) *such that* f(c) = γ.

Proof. Assume, for concreteness, that $f(a) < \gamma < f(b)$, and let c be given by

$$c = \sup\{x \in [a, b]; f(x) \le \gamma\}$$

That is, c is roughly the largest number in the interval for which $f(x)$ is smaller than γ. Notice that the set $\{x \in [a, b]; f(x) \le \gamma\}$ is not empty, because it contains at least a, and it is bounded above by b. Hence, c is well defined by the supremum property. Notice also that, by construction, $f(x) > \gamma$ for all $x > c$.

To establish that $f(c) = \gamma$, we will use the sign-preservation property of continuous real-valued functions (Problem 6.2) to show that both $f(c) > \gamma$ and $f(c) < \gamma$ lead to a contradiction. In particular, if $f(c) < \gamma$, then c is not an

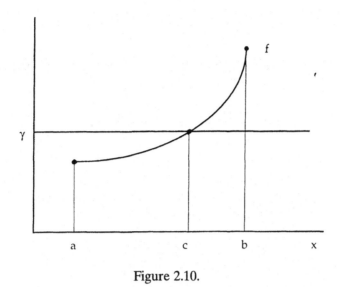

Figure 2.10.

upper bound of $\{x \in [a, b]; f(x) \le \gamma\}$, for there exists some $\delta > 0$ such that $f(c + \delta) < \gamma$ (Figure 2.10). Similarly, if $f(c) > \gamma$, then c cannot be the least upper bound of the given set, for then there exists some $\delta' > 0$ such that $f(x) > \gamma$ for all $x \in (c - \delta', c)$, and therefore $c - \delta'$ is a smaller upper bound for $\{x \in [a, b]; f(x) \le \gamma\}$ than c. Finally, because $f(a) < \gamma < f(b)$, c is neither of these points.

Problem 6.25. We will now give an alternative proof for the intermediate-value theorem. Let f be a real function of one variable defined and continuous on an interval $[a, b]$. Assume that $f(a) < 0 < f(b)$. To show that there exists some point c in (a, b) such that $f(c) = 0$, we construct two sequences $\{l_n\}$ and $\{u_n\}$ in the following way:

1. Put $l_1 = a$ and $u_1 = b$.
2. For each n, let $m_n = (l_n + u_n)/2$, and evaluate f at m_n. Then

    (a) if $f(m_n) > 0$, put $l_{n+1} = l_n$ and $u_{n+1} = m_n$,
    (b) if $f(m_n) < 0$, put $l_{n+1} = m_n$ and $u_{n+1} = u_n$, and
    (c) if $f(m_n) = 0$, stop.

(Draw a picture. What are we doing?) Using what we have learned about the limits of real sequences,

  (i) prove that $\{l_n\}$ and $\{u_n\}$ converge, and call their limits c' and c'';
  (ii) show that $c' = c''$ (i.e., both sequences converge to the same limit).

Hint: Show that $\{u_n - l_n\} \to 0$. Call the common limit of the two sequences c. We want to show that this is the point we want.

(iii) Use the continuity of f and the theorem on the preservation of inequalities to conclude that $f(c) = 0$.   □

Theorem 6.26. Let f be a continuous real function on the closed and bounded interval [a, b]. Then f([a, b]) is a closed interval.

Proof. By the extreme-value theorem, there exist points x_M and x_m in $[a, b]$ such that $f(x_M) \geq f(x)$ and $f(x_m) \leq f(x)$ for all $x \in [a, b]$. Put $M = f(x_M)$ and $m = f(x_m)$. Then both m and M belong to $f([a, b])$, and this set is contained in $[m, M]$. Let y be any point in $[m, M]$; by the intermediate-value theorem, there is some c_y in (a, b) such that $f(c_y) = y$. Hence, any such y is contained in $f([a, b])$, and the result follows.   □

Monotonic Functions

Let $f : \mathbb{R} \longrightarrow \mathbb{R}$ be defined on some interval $I = (a, b)$. We say that f is monotonically increasing if for any two points x and y in I, $x > y$ implies $f(x) \geq f(y)$, and monotonically decreasing if the second inequality is reversed. A function is *monotonic* in a given interval if it is either increasing or decreasing in it.

We will show that monotonic functions have one-sided limits at all points in the interior of their domain and are continuous almost everywhere.

Theorem 6.27. Let f be monotonically increasing on (a, b). Then the one-sided limits

$$f(x^+) = \lim_{y \to x^+} f(y) \quad and \quad f(x^-) = \lim_{y \to x^-} f(y)$$

exist at every point x of (a, b), and moreover,

$$sup\{f(s);\ a < s < x\} = f(x^-) \leq f(x) \leq f(x^+) = inf\{f(s);\ x < s < b\} \quad (1)$$

Furthermore, for any x and y in (a, b), with x < y, we have

$$f(x^+) \leq f(x^-) \quad (2)$$

Proof. Observe that the set $\{f(s);\ a < s < x\}$ is bounded above by $f(x)$ and therefore has a supremum that we will call μ. Clearly, $\mu \leq f(x)$. We want to show that μ is the limit of f as we approach x from the left, that is, that given any $\varepsilon > 0$, there exists some $\delta > 0$ such that

$$|f(y) - \mu| < \varepsilon \quad \text{for all } y \in (x - \delta, x)$$

For this, fix an arbitrary $\varepsilon > 0$. Because μ is the least upper bound of $\{f(s);\ a < s < x\}$, $\mu - \varepsilon$ is not an upper bound, and therefore there exists some $z \in (a, x)$ such that

$$\mu \geq f(z) > \mu - \varepsilon$$

Because f is increasing, moreover,

$$\mu - \varepsilon < f(z) \leq f(y) \leq \mu < \mu + \varepsilon \quad \text{for every } y \in (z, x)$$

and it follows that

$$|f(y) - \mu| < \varepsilon \quad \text{for all } y \in (z, x)$$

which is the first half of (1). The other half follows by the same reasoning.

Next, given two points x and y, with $x < y$, we have, by (1) and the monotonicity of the function, that

$$f(x^+) = \inf\{f(s); \ x < s < b\} = \inf\{f(s); \ x < s < y\}$$

and

$$f(y^-) = \sup\{f(s); \ a < s < y\} = \sup\{f(s); \ x < s < y\}$$

Comparing these expressions, we conclude that $f(x^+) \leq f(y^-)$. $\qquad\square$

Theorem 6.28. Let f *be monotonic on* (a, b). *Then the set of points of* (a, b) *at which* f *is discontinuous is at most countable.*

Proof. Suppose, for concreteness, that f is increasing, and let D be the set of points at which f is discontinuous. With each $x \in D$ we can associate a rational number $r(x)$ such that

$$f(x^-) < r(x) < f(x^+)$$

Because $x_1 < x_2$ implies $f(x_1^+) \leq f(x_2^-)$, we have that $r(x_1) \neq r(x_2)$ if $x_1 \neq x_2$. Hence, we have established a one-to-one correspondence between the set D and a subset of the rational numbers. Because the latter set is countable, so is D. $\qquad\square$

7. Complete Metric Spaces and the Contraction Mapping Theorem

Suppose we would like to know whether or not a given sequence $\{x_n\}$ in a metric space converges. If we proceed by applying the definition of convergence given in Section 2, we have to start by guessing what the limit of the sequence is. This is often difficult and frequently inconvenient, for we may want to *define* an object as the limit of a sequence, and we may be interested in its properties under conditions that are too general to allow a specific limit to be computed. Hence, it would be useful to develop convergence criteria that would not require us to guess the limit.

In this section we will show that in a certain class of spaces, known as complete spaces, convergence can be established by studying the behavior of the terms of a sequence, without specific reference to its limit. In these spaces, moreover, we have available an important fixed-point theorem (the contraction mapping theorem) that is useful in establishing the existence and uniqueness of solutions to certain types of equations that arise frequently in applications.

(a) Cauchy Sequences and Complete Metric Spaces

Definition 7.1. Cauchy convergence. A sequence $\{x_n\}$ in a metric space (X, d) is convergent in the sense of Cauchy (or is a Cauchy sequence, or, simply, "is Cauchy") if

$$\forall \varepsilon > 0, \ \exists N(\varepsilon) \text{ s.th. } \forall m, n > N(\varepsilon), \ d(x_m, x_n) < \varepsilon$$

That is, a sequence is Cauchy if its terms get closer and closer to each other. Intuitively, it is obvious that if the terms of a sequence are getting closer and closer to a limit, they will also be getting progressively closer to each other. At first sight, it would seem that this should also work the other way around, for if all the terms of a sequence beyond a certain order can be made to fit inside a ball of arbitrarily small radius, then the sequence must surely converge. However, the two concepts of convergence are not exactly equivalent. Given a metric space (X, d), it is true that every convergent sequence is Cauchy, but the converse statement is not true. Speaking loosely, the reason is that a Cauchy sequence may approach a limit "outside X" if this set has "holes" in it or does not contain its boundary. There is, however, an important class of metric spaces in which the two notions of convergence are equivalent. These are the so-called complete metric spaces. More formally, we have the following:

Theorem 7.2. Every convergent sequence in a metric space is Cauchy.

Proof. Let (X, d) be a metric space, and $\{x_n\}$ a convergent sequence in X with limit $x \in X$. Fix some arbitrary $\varepsilon > 0$; then, by the convergence of $\{x_n\}$, there exists some integer $N(\varepsilon/2)$ such that

$$\forall n > N(\varepsilon/2), \ d(x_n, x) < \varepsilon/2 \qquad (1)$$

Take any two terms of the sequence x_p, x_q with $p, q > N(\varepsilon/2)$; by the triangle inequality and (1), we have

$$d(x_p, x_q) \le d(x_p, x) + d(x, x_q) < \varepsilon$$

That is, given that $\{x_n\}$ converges to x, all terms of the sequence of a sufficiently high order will be close to the limit x, and therefore not far from each other. Hence the sequence is Cauchy.   □

In general, the converse statement is false in an arbitrary metric space. Spaces in which it does hold are said to be "complete."

Definition 7.3. Complete metric space and Banach space. A metric space (X, d) is complete if every Cauchy sequence contained in X converges to some point x in X.

A normed vector space that is complete (in its natural metric) is called a Banach space.

Example 7.4. A sequence of rational numbers may have an irrational limit. Hence, $\mathbb{Q}$ is not complete (see Problem 3.20).

Consider the metric space formed by $X = (0, 1]$ with the usual metric. The sequence $x_n = 1/n$ has limit 0, which is not in the interval. Hence, this space is not complete. If we add the point $\{0\}$ to obtain the closed interval $[0, 1]$, however, the resulting metric space is complete.   □

Theorem 7.5. *Every Cauchy sequence is bounded.*

Problem 7.6. Prove Theorem 7.5.

Problem 7.7. Prove that the sequence $\{x_n\}$ defined in Problem 3.20 is Cauchy. (Use the results from parts (ii) and (iii) of problem 3.20. An argument similar to the one used in the proof of the contraction mapping theorem in the next section will work.) Notice that the sequence $\{x_n\}$ converges in $\mathbb{R}$ (we know $\mathbb{R}$ is complete), but not in $\mathbb{Q}$ (which is not complete).

Theorem 7.8. *Let $\{x_n\}$ be a Cauchy sequence in a metric space. If $\{x_n\}$ has a convergent subsequence with limit x^0, then the sequence itself converges to x^0.*

Proof. Let $\{x_n\}$ be a Cauchy sequence in a metric space, and assume that $\{x_n\}$ has a convergent subsequence $\{x_{n_k}\}$ with limit x^0. We want to show that $\{x_n\} \to x^0$. The intuition is very simple: Because $\{x_{n_k}\} \to x^0$, all terms of the subsequence $\{x_{n_k}\}$ of sufficiently high order will be close to x^0; but because $\{x_n\}$ is Cauchy, all terms sufficiently far along in the sequence, even those not in $\{x_{n_k}\}$, cannot be very far from x^0.

Fix an arbitrary $\varepsilon > 0$; because $\{x_n\}$ is Cauchy, there is a positive integer $N_1(\varepsilon/2)$ such that

$$\forall m, n > N_1(\varepsilon/2), \; d(x_m, x_n) < \varepsilon/2 \tag{1}$$

and given that $\{x_{n_k}\} \to x^0$, for the same $\varepsilon/2$ there exists some $N_2(\varepsilon/2)$ such that

$$\forall n_k > N_2(\varepsilon/2), \; d(x_{n_k}, x^0) < \varepsilon/2 \tag{2}$$

Putting $N \equiv \max\{N_1, N_2\}$, (1) and (2) hold simultaneously for any $n > N$, and we have

$$\forall m, n_k > N, \; d(x_m, x_{n_k}) < \varepsilon/2 \text{ and } d(x_{n_k}, x^0) < \varepsilon/2 \tag{3}$$

Using (3) and the triangle inequality, we have, for the given ε and any $m > N$,

$$d(x_m, x^0) \leq d(x_m, x_{n_k}) + d(x_{n_k}, x^0) < \varepsilon$$

for any $n_k > N$. This proves the theorem: Notice that x_m is any term of sufficiently higher order in $\{x_n\}$ and need not be a term of the subsequence $\{x_{n_k}\}$ ☐

Example 7.4 suggests that there may be a connection between complete sets and closed sets. The following result establishes this connection.

Theorem 7.9. Let (X, d) *be a complete metric space, and* Y *a subset of* X. *Then* (Y, d) *is complete if and only if it is closed.*

Proof. Let $\{x_n\}$ be a Cauchy sequence in a closed subset Y of X. By the assumption that (X, d) is complete, $\{x_n\}$ converges to a point x in X. Because Y is closed and contains the sequence, it must also contain the limit (Theorem 4.13). Hence Y is complete.

If Y is complete, every Cauchy sequence contained in Y converges to a limit in Y. Being Cauchy (Theorem 7.2), every convergent sequence in Y has its limit in Y, which is therefore closed. ☐

We will now show that every finite-dimensional Euclidean space is complete. The first step – establishing the completeness of $\mathbb{R}$ with the usual metric – is immediate, given some previous results. The extension to E^m then follows easily by the equivalence between convergence in E^m and convergence of the coordinate sequences in $\mathbb{R}$.

Theorem 7.10. The set $\mathbb{R}$ *of the real numbers is complete with the usual metric.*

Proof. We want to show that every Cauchy sequence $\{x_n\}$ in $\mathbb{R}$ converges to a real limit. By Theorem 7.5, every such sequence is bounded. Hence, by the Bolzano-Weierstrass theorem, $\{x_n\}$ has a convergent subsequence $\{x_{n_k}\}$ with limit x in $\mathbb{R}$. By Theorem 7.8, "the whole sequence" converges to x, and the theorem follows. □

Theorem 7.11. *Any finite-dimensional Euclidean space* $E^m = (\mathbb{R}^m, d_E)$ *is complete.*

Proof. Let $\{x_k\}$, with $x_k = (x_k^1, x_k^2, \ldots, x_k^m) \in \mathbb{R}^m$, be a Cauchy sequence. For any $\varepsilon > 0$, there exists some positive integer $N(\varepsilon)$ such that

$$\forall\, p, q > N(\varepsilon),\ d_E(x_p, x_q) = \sqrt{\sum_{i=1}^{m}(x_p^i - x_q^i)^2} < \varepsilon$$

It follows that for any $j = 1, \ldots, m$,

$$\left|x_p^j - x_q^j\right| = \sqrt{\left(x_p^j - x_q^j\right)^2} \le \sqrt{\sum_{i=1}^{m}(x_p^i - x_q^i)^2} < \varepsilon$$

Hence, every component sequence $\{x_k^i\}$ is a Cauchy sequence in $\mathbb{R}$.

By the completeness of $\mathbb{R}$, each one of these sequences has a real limit, say $\{x_k^j\} \to x^j$. Define x as the vector whose components are the limits of these m real sequences, $x = (x^1, \ldots, x^m)$. We have seen (Theorem 3.10) that convergence in E^m is equivalent to convergence component by component; hence, $x \in \mathbb{R}^m$ is the limit of the vector sequence $\{x_k\}$. This shows that every Cauchy sequence in E^m converges to a point in $\mathbb{R}^m$. □

Let $C(X)$ be the space of bounded, continuous real-valued functions defined on a set X in $\mathbb{R}^n$. It is easy to show that this set, endowed with the *sup norm* defined by

$$\|f\|_s = \sup\{|f(x)|;\ x \in X\} \tag{1}$$

is a normed vector space. The following theorem shows that this normed space is complete. This result will be useful in Chapters 9 and 12.

Theorem 7.12. *Given a set* X *in* $\mathbb{R}^n$, *let* C(X) *be the set of bounded continuous functions* f: X $\longrightarrow$ R, *with the sup norm defined by (1). Then* [C(X), $\|\cdot\|_s$] *is a complete normed vector space.*

Proof. We know already that $[C(X), \|\cdot\|_s]$ is a normed vector space. To prove completeness, we need to show that every Cauchy sequence $\{f_n\}$ of bounded continuous functions converges in the sup norm. We will proceed in three steps: First, we construct a "candidate" function $f(\ )$ for the limit of the sequence; second, we verify that this function is bounded and continuous; third, we show that $\{f_n\} \to f$ in the sup norm.

- Given a Cauchy sequence of bounded continuous functions $\{f_n\}$, take some x in X and consider the sequence of real numbers $\{f_n(x)\}$. Note that given any positive integers m and n, we have

$$|f_m(x) - f_n(x)| \leq \sup\{|f_m(y) - f_n(y)|; \ y \in X\} \equiv \|f_m - f_n\|_s$$

Because $\{f_n\}$ is a Cauchy sequence, by choosing m and n high enough we can make $|f_m(x) - f_n(x)|$ arbitrarily small for any x. Hence, $\{f_n(x)\}$ is a Cauchy sequence of real numbers for any x, and because $\mathbb{R}$ is complete with the usual metric, $\{f_n(x)\}$ converges to some (finite) real limit, say $f(x)$.

We can therefore construct a function f that assigns to each x in X the limit $f(x)$ of the sequence of real numbers $\{f_n(x)\}$. This function, which is bounded by construction, will be our candidate for the limit of the sequence of functions $\{f_n\}$.

- To establish the continuity of f, fix an arbitrary point x in X and some $\varepsilon > 0$. Because $\{f_n\} \to f$ in the sup norm, there exists a positive integer N_1 such that $\|f - f_n\|_s < \varepsilon/3$ for all $n > N_1$. Hence,

$$|f_n(x) - f(x)| \leq \sup_y |f(y) - f_n(y)| \equiv \|f - f_n\|_s < \varepsilon/3 \tag{1}$$

for any x and all $n > N_1$. Moreover, because f_n is continuous, there is some $\delta_1 > 0$ such that for the given x,

$$|f_n(x) - f_n(y)| < \varepsilon/3 \quad \text{for all } y \text{ such that } \|x - y\|_E < \delta_1 \tag{2}$$

where $\|\cdot\|_E$ is the Euclidean norm in $\mathbb{R}^n$. Using (1), (2), and the triangle inequality, the continuity of f at x follows: For any $y \in B_{\delta_1}(x)$, and choosing $n > N_1$, we have

$$|f(x) - f(y)| \leq |f(x) - f_n(x)| + |f_n(x) - f_n(y)| + |f_n(y) - f(y)|$$
$$\leq \|f - f_n\|_s + |f_n(x) - f_n(y)| + \|f - f_n\|_s < \varepsilon$$

- Finally, we will show that $\|f - f_n\|_s \to 0$ as $n \to \infty$. Fix some $\varepsilon > 0$ and note that because $\{f_n\}$ is Cauchy, there is some N_2 such that

$$\|f_n - f_m\|_s < \varepsilon/2 \quad \text{for all } m, n > N_2 \tag{3}$$

By (3) and the triangle inequality, given any x in X, we have

$$|f_n(x) - f(x)| \leq |f_n(x) - f_m(x)| + |f_m(x) - f(x)| \leq \|f_n - f_m\| + |f_m(x) - f(x)|$$
$$< \varepsilon/2 + |f_m(x) - f(x)|$$

for all $m, n > N_2$. Moreover, because $\{f_m(x)\} \to f(x)$, we can choose m (separately for each x if need be) so that $|f_m(x) - f(x)| < \varepsilon/2$. Hence, N_2 is such that given any $n > N_2$,

$$|f_n(x) - f(x)| < \varepsilon \quad \text{for all } x \text{ in } X$$

Thus, for n sufficiently high, ε is an upper bound for $\{|f_n(x) - f(x)|; x \in X\}$, and because $\|f_n - f\|_s$ is the smallest such upper bound, we conclude that $\|f_n - f\|_s \leq \varepsilon$ for all $n > N_2$, that is, $\{f_n\} \to f$. $\qquad\square$

(b) Operators and the Contraction Mapping Theorem

A function $T : X \longrightarrow X$ from a metric space to itself is cometimes called an *operator*. We say that an operator is a contraction if its application to any two points of X brings them closer to each other. More formally, we have the following definition:

Definition 7.13. Contraction. Let (X, d) be a metric space, and $T : X \longrightarrow X$ an operator in it. We say that T is a contraction of modulus ß if for some ß $\in (0, 1)$ we have this: $\forall\, x, y \in X, d(Tx, Ty) \leq ßd(x, y)$. The notation Tx is sometimes used instead of $T(x)$.

Theorem 7.14. Every contraction is a continuous mapping.

Proof. Let T be a contraction on (X, d). We want to show that

$$\forall \varepsilon > 0, \ \exists \delta > 0 \text{ s.th. } d(x, y) < \delta \Rightarrow d(Tx, Ty) < \varepsilon$$

As T is a contraction, we have that for all $x, y \in X$ and some ß $\in (0, 1)$,

$$d(Tx, Ty) \leq ßd(x, y)$$

Given some ε, choose δ so that $\delta \leq \varepsilon/ß$; then the definition of continuity is satisfied, because

$$d(Tx, Ty) \leq ßd(x, y) < ß\delta \leq \varepsilon \qquad\square$$

Example 7.15. Let $f : [a, b] \longrightarrow [a, b]$ be a continuous function with positive slope always smaller than 1. Then f is a contraction, because $(f(y) - f(x))/(y - x) \leq ß < 1$. Figure 2.11 suggests that no matter how we draw it, f must cut the 45° line, that is, it must have at least one fixed point z such that $f(z) = z$.

Take any point x_0 in $[a, b]$ and define a sequence $\{x_n(x_0)\}$ recursively by

$$x_1 = f(x_0), x_2 = f(x_1), \ldots, x_{n+1} = f(x_n)$$

Graphically, the sequence is constructed as follows: Given the initial value x_0, we use the graph of the function to find the value of x_1; then we use the 45° line to project x_1 onto the horizontal axis, we go up again to

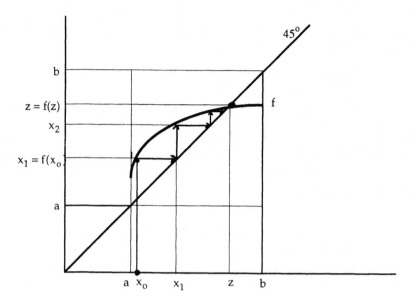

Figure 2.11. A contraction mapping.

the graph of f to find x_2, and so on. The figure suggests that no matter where we choose the initial point x_0 in $[a, b]$, the sequence converges to the fixed point z.   □

The following theorem says that this result can be generalized to any contraction defined on a complete metric space.

Theorem 7.16. Contraction mapping theorem. Let (X, d) be a complete metric space, and $T:X \longrightarrow X$ a contraction with modulus $\beta < 1$. Then

(i) T has precisely one fixed point x^* in X (i.e., $\exists! x^* \in X$ s.th. $Tx^* = x^*$), and
(ii) the sequence $\{x_n(x_0)\}$, defined by

$$x_1 = Tx_0, x_2 = Tx_1, \ldots, x_{n+1} = Tx_n$$

converges to x^* for any starting point x_0 in X.

Proof

• *Existence*: Take an arbitrary point x_0 in X and define the sequence $\{x_n(x_0)\}$ by

$$x_1 = Tx_0, x_2 = Tx_1, \ldots, x_{n+1} = Tx_n$$

We will first show that this sequence is Cauchy. Then, given that (X, d) is a complete metric space, the sequence converges to a point x^* in X. We will then show that x^* is a fixed point of T.

By using the definition of contraction repeatedly, we see that the distance between two successive terms of the sequence $\{x_n(x_0)\}$ is bounded and decreasing in n:

$$
\begin{aligned}
d(x_{n+1}, x_n) = d(Tx_n, Tx_{n-1}) &\le \text{ß}d(x_n, x_{n-1}) \\
= \text{ß}d(Tx_{n-1}, Tx_{n-2}) &\le \text{ß}^2 d(x_{n-1}, x_{n-2}) \\
&\le \ldots \le \text{ß}^n d(x_1, x_0)
\end{aligned}
\tag{1}
$$

Next, consider the distance between two arbitrary terms of the sequence, x_m and x_n, with $m < n$. Using the triangle inequality,

$$
\begin{aligned}
d(x_n, x_m) &\le \sum_{i=m}^{n-1} d(x_{i+1}, x_i) \quad \text{[by (1)]} \\
&\le \sum_{i=m}^{n-1} \text{ß}^i d(x_1, x_0) = \text{ß}^m d(x_1, x_0) \sum_{i=0}^{n-m-1} \text{ß}^i \\
&\le \text{ß}^m d(x_1, x_0) \sum_{i=0}^{\infty} \text{ß}^i = \frac{\text{ß}^m}{1 - \text{ß}} d(x_1, x_0)
\end{aligned}
\tag{2}
$$

Because $\text{ß} < 1$, $\text{ß}^m/(1 - \text{ß}) \to 0$ as $m \to \infty$. It follows that, given an arbitrary $\varepsilon > 0$, we can choose m and n sufficiently large that $d(x_m, x_n) < \varepsilon$; hence, $\{x_n(x_0)\}$ is Cauchy for any x_0, and given that (X, d) is complete by assumption, every such sequence will have a limit in X. Take one such point and call it x^*.

Next, we show that x^* is a fixed point of T. Being a contraction, T is continuous. Hence we can "take the limit out of the function" and write

$$
T(x^*) = T\left(\lim_{n \to \infty} x_n\right) = \lim_{n \to \infty} T(x_n) = \lim_{n \to \infty} x_{n+1} = x^*
$$

- *Uniqueness*: Nothing we have said so far implies uniqueness. It remains to show that x^* is independent of the choice of the initial point x_0 or, equivalently, that there is only one fixed point of T. We will prove that if T has two fixed points, they must be equal.

Assume that x' and x'' are both fixed points of T (i.e., $Tx' = x'$ and $Tx'' = x''$). Because T is a contraction, we have, for some $\text{ß} \in (0, 1)$,

$$
d(x', x'') = d(Tx', Tx'') \le \text{ß}d(x', x'')
$$

Because $\text{ß} < 1$, this can hold only if $d(x', x'') = 0$ (i.e., if $x' = x''$), for otherwise we would arrive at

$$
d(x', x'') < d(x', x'')
$$

a contradiction. $\qquad\qquad\square$

The following exercise generalizes this result. It is not necessary that T itself be a contraction; it is enough that its nth iteration (T^n) be a contraction for T to have precisely one fixed point. T^n is defined recursively by

$$
T^2 x = T(Tx), \, T^3 x = T[T(Tx)] = T(T^2 x), \ldots, T^{n+1} x = T(T^n x)
$$

Problem 7.17. Let (X, d) be a complete metric space, and $T: X \longrightarrow X$ a function whose nth iteration T^n is a contraction. Show that T has a unique fixed point.

The contraction mapping theorem is a very useful result. It can be used to prove the existence and uniqueness of solutions to several types of equations, including differential equations and some functional equations that arise in connection with dynamic-optimization problems. Moreover, the second part of the theorem suggests a method (the *method of successive approximations*) for calculating solutions to equations that can be written in the form $Tx = x$, where T is a contraction: Beginning with a convenient trial solution, we construct a sequence $\{x_n\}$ recursively with $x_{n+1} = Tx_n$. If we can find the limit of the sequence, we will also have found the solution to the equation. Otherwise, we can approximate the solution to any desired degree of accuracy by computing sufficiently many terms of the sequence.[9]

The following theorem says, loosely speaking, that if a continuity condition holds, we can do comparative statics with fixed points of contractions.

Theorem 7.18. Continuous dependence of the fixed point on parameters. Let (X, d) and (Ω, ρ) be two metric spaces, and $T(x, \alpha)$ a function $X \times \Omega \longrightarrow X$. If (X, d) is complete, if f is continuous in α, and if for each $\alpha \in \Omega$ the function T_α, defined by $T_\alpha(x) = T(x, \alpha)$ for each $x \in X$, is a contraction, then the solution function $z: \Omega \longrightarrow X$, with $x^* = z(\alpha)$, which gives the fixed point as a function of the parameters, is continuous.

Proof. Consider a convergent sequence of parameter values, $\{\alpha_n\} \to \alpha$. To establish the continuity of z, it is sufficient to show that

$$d[z(\alpha_n), z(\alpha)] \to 0 \quad \text{as } \{\alpha_n\} \to \alpha \tag{1}$$

By definition, the function z satisfies the identity $T_\alpha z(\alpha) \equiv z(\alpha)$ for any α. Using this expression in (1), we have

$$d[z(\alpha_n), z(\alpha)] = d[T_{\alpha_n} z(\alpha_n), T_\alpha z(\alpha)] \quad \text{(by the triangle inequality)}$$
$$\leq d[T_{\alpha_n} z(\alpha_n), T_{\alpha_n} z(\alpha)] + d[T_{\alpha_n} z(\alpha), T_\alpha z(\alpha)]$$
$$\leq ßd[z(\alpha_n), z(\alpha)] + d[T_{\alpha_n} z(\alpha), T_\alpha z(\alpha)]$$

where the second inequality uses the assumption that T_{α_n} is a contraction, with modulus $ß_n \leq ß \in (0, 1)$. Thus,

$$d[z(\alpha_n), z(\alpha)] \leq ßd[z(\alpha_n), z(\alpha)] + d[T_{\alpha_n} z(\alpha), T_\alpha z(\alpha)]$$

from where

$$d[z(\alpha_n), z(\alpha)] \le \frac{1}{1-\text{ß}} d[T_{\alpha_n} z(\alpha), T_\alpha z(\alpha)]$$

Now, T is continuous in α, so the right-hand side of this expression goes to zero as $\{\alpha_n\} \to \alpha$. Hence, (1) holds, and $z(\ )$ is continuous. □

Recall that given a complete metric space (X, d) and a closed subset C of X, (C, d) is also a complete metric space (Theorem 7.9). Now suppose that $T: X \longrightarrow X$ is a contraction and maps C into itself (i.e., if $x \in C$, then $Tx \in C$). In that case, T is a contraction on C, and the unique fixed point of T in X must lie in C. Sometimes this observation allows us to establish certain properties of a fixed point by applying the contraction mapping theorem twice – first in a "large" space X to establish existence, and then again in a closed subset of X in order to show that the fixed point has certain properties. For example, if (X, d) is the space of continuous real and bounded functions with the sup norm (see Section 1), then the subset of X formed by nondecreasing functions is closed. Hence, if a contraction T in (X, d) maps nondecreasing functions into nondecreasing functions, the fixed point of T will be a nondecreasing function.

It is not always easy to determine whether or not a given function is a contraction. The following theorem, due to Blackwell, gives sufficient conditions for an operator in a useful function space to be a contraction. The advantage of this result is that in some economic applications, Blackwell's conditions are very easy to verify.

Theorem 7.19. Blackwell's sufficient conditions for a contraction. Let B$(\mathbb{R}^n,$ $\mathbb{R})$ *be the set of bounded functions* f$:\mathbb{R}^n \longrightarrow \mathbb{R}$, *with the sup norm. If an operator* T$:$B$(\mathbb{R}^n, \mathbb{R}) \longrightarrow$ B$(\mathbb{R}^n, \mathbb{R})$ *satisfies the two conditions*

(i) monotonicity: $\forall$ f, g $\in$ B$(\mathbb{R}^n, \mathbb{R})$, f(x) $\le$ g(x) $\forall$ x $\Rightarrow$ Tf(x) $\le$ Tg(x) $\forall$x,
(ii) discounting: $\exists \beta \in (0, 1)$ *s.th.* $\forall$ f $\in$ B$(\mathbb{R}^n, \mathbb{R})$, x $\in \mathbb{R}^n$, *and* $\alpha \ge 0$, *we have*
$\quad$ T$[$f(x) $+ \alpha]$ $\le$ T$[$f(x)$]$ $+ \beta\alpha$

then T *is a contraction.*

Proof. For any $f, g \in B(\mathbb{R}^n, \mathbb{R})$, we have

$$f = g + (f - g) \le g + \|f - g\|$$

By assumptions (i) and (ii),

$$Tf \le T(g + \|f - g\|) \le Tg + \text{ß}\|f - g\| \Rightarrow Tf - Tg \le \text{ß}\|f - g\|$$

Interchanging the roles of f and g, we obtain, by the same logic,

$$Tg \leq T(f + \|g - f\|) \leq Tf + \beta\|g - f\| \Rightarrow Tf - Tg \geq -\beta\|f - g\|$$

Combining the two inequalities, we obtain the desired result:

$$\|Tf - Tg\| \leq \beta\|f - g\| \qquad\qquad \square$$

8. Compactness and the Extreme-Value Theorem

Let f be a real-valued function defined on some set in a metric space. A problem that frequently arises is that of finding the element of A that will maximize or minimize f. In order to guarantee that such a point exists, certain restrictions have to be placed on both the function and the set. For example, we have seen that if f is a function from a set of real numbers A to $\mathbb{R}$, a sufficient condition for the existence of a maximum is that f be continuous and A be a closed and bounded interval. One of the purposes of this section is to extend this result on continuous functions to more general sets. This brings us to the study of compactness.

(a) Compactness and Some Characterizations

To introduce the notion of compactness, we need some terminology.

Definition 8.1. Cover and open cover. A collection of sets $\mathbb{U} = \{U_i; i \in I\}$ in a metric space (X, d) is a cover of the set A if A is contained in its union, that is, if $A \subseteq \cup_{i \in I} U_i$. If all the sets U_i are open, the collection $\mathbb{U}$ is said to be an open cover of A.

Definition 8.2. Compact set. A set A in a metric space is compact if every open cover of A has a finite subcover. That is, A is compact if given *any* open cover $\mathbb{U} = \{U_i; i \in I\}$ of it, we can find a finite subset of $\mathbb{U}$, $\{U_1, \ldots, U_n\}$, that still covers A.

Notice that the definition does *not* say that a set is compact if it has a finite open cover. In fact, every set in a metric space (X, d) has a finite open cover, for the universal set X is open and covers any set in the space.

Example 8.3. $(0, 1)$ is not compact. The collection of open intervals $(1/n, 1)$ for $n \geq 2$ is an open cover of $(0, 1)$ because given any x in $(0, 1)$, there exists an integer n such that $n > 1/x$, and hence $x \in (1/n, 1)$. Thus, $(0, 1) = \cup_{n=2}^{\infty}(1/n, 1)$. However, no finite subcollection $\{(1/n_1, 1), \ldots, (1/n_k, 1)\}$ will suffice to cover $(0, 1)$, for the union of these sets is $(1/N, 1)$, where $N = \max_{1 \le i \le k} n_i$, and given any N there is some strictly positive real number x with $x < 1/N$. $\square$

A necessary prerequisite for the existence of a maximum of a function over a set is that the function be bounded on the set. To motivate the foregoing definition (i.e., to try to understand why sets with such strange properties may be useful), consider how we might go about extending the result given in Theorem 6.20 on the boundedness of a continuous function defined over an interval $[a, b]$ to a larger class of sets in an arbitrary metric space.

We begin by observing that a continuous function is locally bounded. Let $f: A \subseteq X \longrightarrow \mathbb{R}$ be continuous, and consider an arbitrary point a in A. Then, by the definition of continuity (with $\varepsilon = 1$), there exists a positive real number $\delta(a)$ (which depends both on the point chosen and on the particular function f we are working with) such that $|f(x) - f(a)| < 1$ for all $x \in B_{\delta(a)}(a)$. Hence, f is bounded in $B_{\delta(a)}(a)$ by $K_a = |f(a)| + 1$.

Now consider what happens when we try to extend this local boundedness property to the whole set A. The question is whether or not the continuity of f is sufficient to guarantee the existence of a bound K that will work for all x in A (for the given function). It is tempting to try to define K as the maximum of the K_a's over all points a in A, but that will not work in general, for there may be infinitely many such K_a's, and the set of such numbers may not have an upper bound. Notice, however, that the collection of open balls $\{B_{\delta(a)}(a)\}$ for all $a \in A$ is an open cover of A. If A is a compact set, there is a finite collection of such balls, $\{B_{\delta(a_1)}(a_1), \ldots, B_{\delta(a_n)}(a_n)\}$, that contains all points of A. In this case, the maximum of the (finite) set formed by the corresponding local bounds $\{K_{a_1}, \ldots, K_{a_n}\}$ is well defined and provides a global bound for the function on the set.

In conclusion, compactness allows us to replace an arbitrary open cover with a finite one. In some cases this is enough of a substitute for finiteness as to allow us to extend to infinite sets some properties that hold trivially in finite ones.

It is not always easy to work directly with the definition of compactness. In the remainder of this section we will develop some characterizations of compactness that frequently are more useful than our original definition. The first of these, known as sequential compactness, is valid in metric spaces, but not necessarily in more general topological spaces.

Definition 8.4. Sequential compactness. A set A in a metric space is sequentially compact if every sequence of elements of A has a convergent subsequence whose limit lies in A.

We will now show that compactness and sequential compactness (which is essentially the Bolzano-Weierstrass property) are equivalent in metric spaces. The first half of the equivalence is easily established.

Theorem 8.5. A compact set in a metric space is sequentially compact.

Proof. We will prove the contrapositive statement (a set A in a metric space that is not sequentially compact cannot be compact) by constructing an open cover of A with no finite subcover. If A is not sequentially compact, there is a sequence $\{x_n\}$ of points of A with the property that none of its subsequences converges to a point in A. Hence, no point of A is the limit of a subsequence of $\{x_n\}$, and it follows that for every x in A there exists an open ball $B_{\varepsilon(x)}(x)$ that contains only a finite number of elements of $\{x_n\}$. The family $\mathbb{B} = \{B_{\varepsilon(x)}(x); x \in A\}$ is an open cover of A. However, no finite subfamily of $\mathbb{B}$ can cover $\{x_n\}$ (and therefore A), for any such family will contain only a finite number of terms of $\{x_n\}$. Hence, A is not compact. $\qquad\square$

The converse result takes a bit more work. We begin with some definitions.

Definition 8.6. ε-net and totally bounded set. Given some $\varepsilon > 0$ and a set A in a metric space (X, d), an ε-net for A is a set of points E in X such that

$$A \subseteq \cup_{x \in E} B_\varepsilon(x)$$

A set A in (X, d) is totally bounded if it has a finite ε-net for any $\varepsilon > 0$.

That is, a set is totally bounded if it can be covered by a finite number of balls of arbitrarily small radius. Clearly, a totally bounded set is necessarily bounded, but the converse need not be true.

Definition 8.7. Lebesgue number for an open cover. Let A be a set in a metric space, and let $\mathbb{U}$ be an open cover of A. We say that a fixed real number $\varepsilon > 0$ is a Lebesgue number for $\mathbb{U}$ if for every x in A there exists a set $U(x)$ in $\mathbb{U}$ such that $B_\varepsilon(x) \subseteq U(x)$.

Hence, if $\mathbb{U}$ has a Lebesgue number, we can "replace" it with an open cover formed by balls of constant radius, which is often more convenient. Notice that if this "ball cover" has a finite subcover, so does the original one.

Example 8.8. Notice that an open cover may not have a Lebesgue number. As in the previous example, put $A = (0, 1)$ and consider the open cover

$\mathbb{U} = \{(1/n, 1); n \geq 2\}$. For any given $\varepsilon > 0$, choose $x < \varepsilon$; then $B_\varepsilon(x) = (0, x + \varepsilon)$ is not contained in $(1/n, 1)$ for any n.

Theorem 8.9. A sequentially compact set in a metric space is totally bounded.

Proof. We will show that if a set A is not totally bounded, then it cannot be sequentially compact – that is, if for some $\varepsilon > 0$ there is no finite ε-net for A, we can construct a sequence $\{x_n\}$ in A with no convergent subsequence.

Take any x_1 in A, and let $U_1 = B_\varepsilon(x_1)$. By assumption, B_1 does not cover A, so there is some $x_2 \in A$, with $x_2 \notin U_1$. Let $U_2 = B_\varepsilon(x_2)$; then $\{U_1, U_2\}$ is still not a cover of A, and therefore there is some $x_3 \in A$, with $x_3 \notin U_1 \cup U_2$. Put $U_3 = B_\varepsilon(x_3), \dots$, and so forth. By continuing in this fashion, we can construct a sequence $\{x_n\}$ with the property that $d(x_n, x_m) \geq \varepsilon$ for all n and m, as each new term of the sequence is chosen outside all the ε-balls centered at the previous terms. Clearly, this sequence has no Cauchy subsequences and therefore no convergent subsequences either. $\qquad\square$

Theorem 8.10. Any open cover of a sequentially compact set in a metric space has a Lebesgue number.

Proof. Let A be a set in a metric space (X, d) with an open cover $\mathbb{U}$. If $\mathbb{U}$ has no Lebesgue number, then for every $\varepsilon > 0$ there exists some point x in A such that no set U in $\mathbb{U}$ contains $B_\varepsilon(x)$. In particular, for each integer n, we can find some point x_n in A such that $B_{1/n}(x_n)$ is not contained in any $U \in \mathbb{U}$. We will show that if A is sequentially compact, no sequence in A can have this property. Hence, given sequential compactness of A, a Lebesgue number must exist for any open cover of it (or else we have a contradiction).

By the sequential compactness of A, any sequence $\{x_n\}$ of points in A contains a convergent subsequence $\{x_{n_k}\}$ with limit $x \in A$. Because $\mathbb{U}$ covers A, $x \in U_0$ for some $U_0 \in \mathbb{U}$, and because U_0 is open, there exists some integer m such that $B_{2/m}(x) \subseteq U_0$. We will show that $B_{1/n}(x_n) \subseteq U_0$ for some terms in the sequence by exploiting the fact that we can bring $\{x_{n_k}\}$ arbitrarily close to x and make $B_{1/n_k}(x_{n_k})$ arbitrarily small.

By the convergence of $\{x_{n_k}\}$ to x, there is some N such that

$$x_{n_k} \in B_{1/m}(x) \quad \text{for all } n_k > N$$

Choose $n_k > \max\{N, m\}$, and observe that for any point y in $B_{1/n_k}(x_{n_k})$ we have

$$d(y, x) \leq d(y, x_{n_k}) + d(x_{n_k}, x) < \frac{1}{n_k} + \frac{1}{m} < \frac{1}{m} + \frac{1}{m} = \frac{2}{m}$$

Hence, for n_k sufficiently high, we have $y \in B_{2/m}(x)$, but then

$$B_{1/n_k}(x_{n_k}) \subseteq B_{2/m}(x) \subseteq U_0$$

contradicting the nonexistence of a Lebesgue number.   □

We can now prove that sequential compactness implies compactness in a metric space.

Theorem 8.11. Any sequentially compact set in a metric space is compact.

Proof. Let $\mathbb{U}$ be an arbitrary open cover of a sequentially compact set A in a metric space. By Theorem 8.10, $\mathbb{U}$ has a Lebesgue number ε, and by Theorem 8.9 there exists a finite ε-net (for the same ε) $\{x_1, \ldots, x_n\}$ for A. For each $i = 1, \ldots, n$ there is some $U_i \in \mathbb{U}$ such that $B_\varepsilon(x_i) \subseteq U_i$, by the definition of Lebesgue number. Because $A \subseteq \cup_{i=1}^n B_\varepsilon(x_i) \subseteq \cup_{i=1}^n U_i$, $\mathbb{U}$ has a finite subcover $\{U_1, \ldots, U_n\}$.   □

We will now provide an alternative characterization of compactness in terms of a property of families of closed sets.

Definition 8.12. The finite-intersection property. A nonempty family of sets $\mathbb{A} = \{A_i; i \in I\}$ has the finite-intersection property if every (nonempty) finite subfamily of $\mathbb{A}$ has a nonempty intersection.

Theorem 8.13. A set C in a metric (or topological) space (X, d) *is compact if and only if every family of closed subsets of* X *that has the finite-intersection property has a nonempty intersection.*

Proof

- Suppose C is compact. To show that any family of closed subsets that has the finite-intersection property has a nonempty intersection, we will prove the following equivalent (contrapositive) statement: Let $\mathbb{A} = \{A_i; i \in I\}$ be a family of closed subsets of C with the property that $\cap \mathbb{A} = \cap_{i \in I} A_i = \varnothing$; then there exists *some* finite subfamily of $\mathbb{A}$ with an empty intersection – that is, there exists some finite set $J \subseteq I$ such that $\cap_{i \in J} A_i = \varnothing$.

  For each i, let $U_i = \sim A_i$ be the complement of the closed set A_i. Then each U_i is an open set, and we can write, using De Morgan's laws (Theorem 1.2 in Chapter 1),

$$C \subseteq X = \sim\varnothing = \sim(\cap_{i \in I} A_i) = \cup_{i \in I}(\sim A_i) = \cup_{i \in I} U_i$$

Hence, $\{U_i; i \in I\}$ is an open cover of C. Because C is compact, $\{U_i; i \in I\}$ contains a finite subcover of C. That is, there exists a finite set $J \subseteq I$ such that

$$C \subseteq \cup_{i \in J} U_i$$

which implies that

$$\cap_{i \in J} A_i = \sim(\cup_{i \in J} U_i) \subseteq \sim C \tag{1}$$

On the other hand, because each A_i is a subset of C, so is their intersection; hence, we have

$$\cap_{i \in J} A_i \subseteq C \tag{2}$$

Combining (1) and (2), we conclude that $\cap_{i \in J} A_i = \varnothing$, which establishes the desired result.

- For the converse, assume that C has the property that if the intersection of any family of closed subsets of C is empty, then the intersection of some finite subfamily of them is empty (we are using the contrapositive again). Let $\mathbb{U} = \{U_i; i \in I\}$ be an arbitrary open cover of C, so that

$$C \subseteq \cup_{i \in I} U_i$$

and observe that this implies that

$$\sim(\cup_{i \in I} U_i) \subseteq \sim C \tag{1}$$

Next, let

$$A_i = C \cap (\sim U_i)$$

for each i. Using (1) and De Morgan's laws, we have

$$\cap_{i \in I} A_i = \cap_{i \in I} (C \cap (\sim U_i)) = C \cap (\cap_{i \in I} (\sim U_i)) = C \cap (\sim(\cup_{i \in I} U_i)) \subseteq C \cap (\sim C) = \varnothing$$

Hence, $\mathbb{A} = \{A_i; i \in I\}$ is a family of closed subsets of C whose intersection is empty. By assumption, there exists some finite subfamily of $\mathbb{A}$ with an empty intersection; that is, there exists some finite set $J \subseteq I$ such that $\cap_{i \in J} A_i = \varnothing$, and it follows that

$$\cap_{i \in J} A_i = \cap_{i \in J} (C \cap (\sim U_i)) = C \cap (\cap_{i \in J} (\sim U_i)) = C \cap (\sim(\cup_{i \in J} U_i)) = \varnothing$$

This implies that C is contained in $\cup_{i \in J} U_i$. Hence, $\{U_i; i \in J\}$ is a finite subcover of $\{U_i; i \in I\}$, and we conclude that C is compact.

(b) Relationships with Other Topological Properties

In metric spaces, compactness is closely related to other topological properties, namely, closedness, completeness, and boundedness. In this section we spell out some of the interconnections among these properties.

Theorem 8.14. Any closed subset of a compact space is compact.

Proof. Given a metric space (X, d), let X be compact, and consider a closed subset C of X. Let $\mathbb{U} = \{U_i; i \in I\}$ be an arbitrary open cover of C. Because C

is closed, its complement C^c is open, and $\{U_i; i \in I\} \cup C^c$ is an open cover of X. As X is compact, this cover has a finite subcover $\{U_1, \ldots, U_n\} \cup C^c$. Then $\{U_1, \ldots, U_n\}$ is a finite subcover of C, which is therefore compact. $\qquad\square$

Theorem 8.15. A compact set in a metric space is closed.

(This result may not hold in more general topological spaces.)

Proof. Let A be a compact set in a metric space (X, d). We will prove that A is closed by showing that it contains all its limit points. Let x_L be an arbitrary limit point of A; by Theorem 4.11 there exists a sequence $\{x_n\}$ of points of A with limit x_L. By the (sequential) compactness of A, $\{x_n\}$ has a convergent subsequence with limit in A. By the uniqueness of the limit (see Problem 2.5), x_L is the limit of the subsequence and must therefore lie in A. $\qquad\square$

Theorem 8.16. A set in a metric space is compact if and only if it is complete and totally bounded.

Proof. We have already seen that a compact set is totally bounded. The proof that compactness implies completeness is left as an exercise. We now prove the converse implication (i.e., that a complete and totally bounded set in a metric space is compact).

Let C be complete and totally bounded. To establish (sequential) compactness, we need to show that any sequence $\{x_n\}$ in C has a subsequence converging to a point in C. And because we are assuming completeness, it is enough to show that given any sequence in C, we can produce a Cauchy subsequence, for completeness will then guarantee convergence.

Let $\{x_n\}$ be an arbitrary sequence in C. Because C is totally bounded, it can be covered by a finite number of balls of radius 1 (a 1-net). Among these balls, there must be one, say B_1, that contains infinitely many terms of the sequence. These infinitely many points of the original sequence form a new sequence that we call $\{x_n^1\}$. Next, we can cover B_1 with a finite number of balls of radius 1/2, and among these balls there must be one, say B_2, such that $B_1 \cap B_2$ contains an infinite number of points of $\{x_n^1\}$, forming a new sequence $\{x_n^2\}$. Continuing in this fashion, we obtain a sequence $\{B_i\}$ of balls with radius 1/i such that $B_1 \cap B_2 \cap \ldots \cap B_i$ contains infinitely many terms of the original sequence, yielding a new sequence $\{x_n^i\}$.

Consider now a "cross-sequence" $\{x_k^k\}$ formed by taking one element of each of these sequences (i.e., the kth term of $\{x_k^k\}$ is taken from $\{x_n^k\}$). We observe that, by construction,

$$x_k^k \in B_1 \cap B_2 \cap \ldots \cap B_k \quad \text{for each } k$$

Hence, given any positive integers p and q, with $p < q$, the terms x_p^p and x_q^q of $\{x_k^k\}$ are contained in the ball B_p (of radius $1/p$), and therefore

$$d(x_p^p, x_q^q) < 2/p$$

Hence, the subsequence $\{x_k^k\}$ is Cauchy: By taking p high enough, we can force all remaining terms of the sequence to fit inside a ball of arbitrarily small radius. By completeness, $\{x_k^k\}$ converges to a point in C. Hence, we have shown that an arbitrary sequence in C must contain a convergent subsequence with limit in C, thus establishing the sequential compactness of the set. $\qquad \square$

Problem 8.17. Show that a compact set in a metric space is complete.

Problem 8.18. Let A be a compact set, and let $\{A_n\}$ be a "decreasing sequence" of nonempty closed subsets of A such that $A_{n+1} \subseteq A_n$. Show that $\cup_{n=1}^{\infty} A_n$ is not empty.

From Theorems 8.9 and 8.15, we know that a compact set in a metric space is closed and bounded. The following result tells us that the converse is true for sets of real numbers, thereby establishing an important characterization of compact sets in $\mathbb{R}$ as those that are closed and bounded.

Theorem 8.19. Heine-Borel. Any closed and bounded set of real numbers is compact.

Proof. Note that any bounded set of real numbers must be contained in a closed interval $[a, b]$ with finite end points. Because we know that any closed subset of a compact set is compact, we need only show that $[a, b]$ is compact. By the Bolzano-Weierstrass theorem, any sequence contained in this (bounded) set contains a convergent subsequence, and because $[a, b]$ is closed, the subsequence converges to a point in the interval (Theorem 4.13), establishing sequential compactness (see Problem 3.4). $\qquad \square$

This result can be easily extended to any finite-dimensional Euclidean space.

Theorem 8.20. Any closed and bounded subset of $\mathbb{R}^m$ is compact.

Proof. Let A be a closed and bounded set in $\mathbb{R}^m$. Then there exists some number M such that $\|x\|_E \leq M$ for all x in A. Hence, A is contained in the cube of side M given by

$$C_m = I \times I \times \ldots \times I, \qquad \text{where } I = [-M, M]$$

As in the previous theorem, it is enough to show that C_m is compact, for the closedness of A then guarantees its compactness.

To simplify notation, let $m = 2$ (i.e., we will be working in the plane $\mathbb{R}^2$), and consider $C_2 = I \times I = [-M, M] \times [-M, M]$ and an arbitrary sequence $\{x_n\}$ in this set, with $x_n = (x_n^1, x_n^2)$. Observe that $\{x_n^1\}$ and $\{x_n^2\}$ are bounded sequences of real numbers contained in the compact set $I = [-M, M]$. By the Heine-Borel theorem, $\{x_n^1\}$ has a subsequence $\{x_{n_k}^1\}$ convergent to a limit x^1 in I, and the corresponding subsequence of $\{x_n^2\}$, $\{x_{n_k}^2\}$, has a convergent subsequence $\{x_{n_{k_j}}^2\}$ with limit x^2 in I. Putting $x_{n_{k_j}} = (x_{n_{k_j}}^1, x_{n_{k_j}}^2)$, it is clear that (by the equivalence between convergence in E^2 and coordinate-wise convergence in $\mathbb{R}$)

$$\{x_{n_{k_j}}\} \to (x^1, x^2) \in I \times I$$

that is, $\{x_n\}$ has a convergent subsequence with limit in C_2, which establishes the sequential compactness of C_2 and therefore of any closed and bounded set in the plane. The argument can be easily extended to any finite-dimensional Euclidean space. More generally, it can be shown that a finite product of compact sets is compact (in the sup metric).

(c) Continuous Functions on Compact Sets

Theorem 8.21. Let (X, d) and (Y, ρ) be metric spaces, and $f : X \longrightarrow Y$ a continuous function. If C is a compact set in (X, d), its image $f(C)$ is compact in (Y, ρ).

Proof. Let $\{y_n\}$ be an arbitrary sequence in $f(C)$, and consider a companion sequence formed by points x_n in C such that $f(x_n) = y_n$. By the sequential compactness of C, $\{x_n\}$ has a convergent subsequence, say $\{x_{n_k}\}$, with limit x in C. Then, by the continuity of f,

$$\lim_{k \to \infty} y_{n_k} = \lim_{k \to \infty} f(x_{n_k}) = f\left(\lim_{k \to \infty} x_{n_k}\right) = f(x) \in f(C)$$

Hence, $\{y_n\}$ has a subsequence $\{y_{n_k}\}$ that converges to a limit in $f(C)$. This establishes the sequential compactness of $f(C)$. $\square$

In the case of a real-valued function, the theorem says that the continuous image of a compact set is a compact interval or a collection of them. Because any such set of real numbers contains both its supremum and its infimum, we have the following important corollary:

Theorem 8.22. Extreme value (Weierstrass). Let C *be a compact set in a metric space, and* f: C $\longrightarrow$ $\mathbb{R}$ *a continuous function. Then* f *is bounded in* C *and attains both its maximum and its minimum in the set. That is, there exist points* x_M *and* x_m *in* C *such that*

$$f(x_M) = \sup f(C) \quad \text{and} \quad f(x_m) = \inf f(C)$$

Proof. We will prove the existence of a maximum. By the previous theorem, $f(C)$ is a compact set of real numbers and therefore is closed and bounded. Let β be its supremum. Then β is a limit point of $f(C)$. (Why? $\beta - 1/n$ is not an upper bound for $f(C)$). Because $f(C)$ is closed, it follows that β is contained in it, that is, there exists some point x_M in C such that $\beta = f(x_M)$. $\square$

Problem 8.23. Give an alternative proof for Theorem 8.21 using directly the definition of compactness. (Let $\{U_i; i \in I\}$ be an open cover of $f(C)$.)

Theorem 8.24. Let (X, d) *and* (Y, ρ) *be metric spaces, with* f: X $\longrightarrow$ Y *a continuous function, and* C *a compact set in* (X, d). *Then* f *is uniformly continuous on* C.

Proof. Let $\varepsilon > 0$ be given. Because f is continuous, for each point x in C we can find a positive number $\delta(x)$ such that

$$d(x, y) < \delta(x) \Rightarrow \rho[f(x), f(y)] < \varepsilon/2 \tag{1}$$

For each $x \in C$, let $B(x)$ be the set of all points y in C for which $d(x, y) < \delta(x)/2$. The collection of all such $B(x)$'s (one for each point in C) is an open cover of C, and because C is compact, there is a finite collection of points in C, say $\{x_1, \ldots, x_n\}$, such that

$$C \subseteq B(x_1) \cup \ldots \cup B(x_n) \tag{2}$$

Put

$$\delta = \frac{\min\{\delta(x_1), \ldots, \delta(x_n)\}}{2}$$

and observe that $\delta > 0$ because this is a finite collection of positive numbers (this is why we need compactness, it guarantees that we can find a finite subcover; note that the infimum of an infinite collection of positive numbers may be zero).

Let x and y be points in C such that $d(x, y) < \delta$. By (2), there is some point x_m such that $x \in B(x_m)$, and hence

$$d(x, x_m) < \frac{\delta(x_m)}{2} \tag{3}$$

Moreover,

$$d(y, x_m) \le d(y, x) + d(x, x_m) < \delta + \frac{\delta(x_m)}{2} \le \delta(x_m) \tag{4}$$

Hence, both x and y are sufficiently close to x_m that we can use (1) to conclude that

$$\rho[f(y), f(x)] \le \rho[f(y), f(x_m)] + \rho[f(x_m), f(x)] < \varepsilon \qquad \square$$

A similar argument will yield the following result.

Theorem 8.25. Show that if a function is locally Lipschitz on a compact set, then it is Lipschitz on the set (see Definition 6.18).

Problem 8.26. Compactness of the product space. Let (X, d_1) and (Y, d_2) be metric spaces, and consider the product space $(Z = X \times Y, d_\pi)$, with the *product metric d_π* defined by

$$d_\pi(z, z') = d_\pi[(x, y), (x', y')] = \sqrt{[d_1(x, x')]^2 + [d_2(y, y')]^2} \tag{1}$$

Show that the product space $(Z = X \times Y, d_\pi)$ is compact if and only if both (X, d_1) and (Y, d_2) are compact.

9. Connected Sets

A set is said to be connected if it consists of a single piece (i.e., if it is not made up of two or more "separate components"). The following definition makes this idea more precise.

Definition 9.1. Separated and connected sets. Two sets A and B in a metric space are said to be separated if both $A \cap \overline{B}$ and $\overline{A} \cap B$ are empty (i.e., if neither set has a point lying in the closure of the other). A set C in a metric space is said to be connected if it is not the union of two nonempty separated sets.

Notice that the condition for two sets to be separated is stronger than disjointedness but weaker than the requirement that the distance between them be strictly positive. Thus, the intervals $(-1, 0]$ and $(0, 1)$ are disjoint but not separated, because 0 lies in one interval and in the closure of the other.

The intervals $(-1, 0)$ and $(0, 1)$, however, are separated, but the distance between them is zero.

Connected sets on the real line have a particularly simple structure. As shown in our next result, the connected sets in $\mathbb{R}$ are precisely the intervals.

Theorem 9.2. A set S of real numbers is connected if and only if it is an interval.

Proof. Recall that a set I of real numbers is an interval if whenever x and y are in I, any real number z, with $x < z < y$, also lies in I (Problem 6.14 in Chapter 1).

- We first show that a set of real numbers that is not an interval is not connected. Let S be such a set. Then there exist real numbers x and y in S and $z \notin S$ such that $x < z < y$, and we can write S as the union of two components, as follows:

$$S = S_1 \cup S_2 \equiv [S \cap (-\infty, z)] \cup [S \cap (z, \infty)]$$

Notice that neither of these sets is empty, because S_1 contains at least x, and S_2 contains at least y. Moreover, S_1 and S_2 are separated, because $S_1 \subseteq (-\infty, z)$ and $S_2 \subseteq (z, \infty)$, and these intervals are separated (neither of them contains the only common boundary point, z). Hence S is not connected.

- To show that every interval is connected, we show that a nonconnected set cannot be an interval. Let E be a nonconnected set of real numbers. Then there exist nonempty separated sets A and B such that $A \cup B = E$. Pick $a \in A$ and $b \in B$, and assume (relabeling the sets if necessary) that $a < b$, as in Figure 2.12. To establish that E is not an interval, we will show that there is some real number $x \notin E$ with $a < x < b$.

We define

$$x = \sup\{A \cap [a, b]\}$$

Then (see Problem 4.15) we have $x \in \overline{A}$ and (because A and B are separated) $x \notin B$. Moreover, we have $a \leq x < b$. There are now two possibilities. If $x \notin A$, then we have found the desired number, for then $a < x < b$ and $x \notin E$. If $x \in A$, on the other hand, we have $x \notin \overline{B}$ (because A and B are separated), and it follows that x lies in the open set $\mathbb{R} \sim \overline{B}$. Hence, we can find some other point x' in this set (and therefore not in B) such that $a \leq x < x' < b$. This establishes the desired result.

Figure 2.12.

□

Our next result says that continuous functions preserve connectedness. Hence, one way to establish the connectedness of a set is by showing that it is the continuous image of another set that is known to be connected.

Theorem 9.3. *Let* $f:X \longrightarrow Y$ *be a continuous mapping between two metric spaces. If* C *is a connected subset of* X, *then* $f(C)$ *is connected.*

Proof. We will prove the contrapositive statement: If $f(C)$ is not connected, then neither is C. Suppose $f(C)$ is not connected. Then $f(C) = P \cup Q$, where P and Q are nonempty, separated subsets of Y, that is,

$$\overline{P} \cap Q = \varnothing \quad \text{and} \quad \overline{Q} \cap P = \varnothing$$

Let

$$A = C \cap f^{-1}(P) \quad \text{and} \quad B = C \cap f^{-1}(Q)$$

and notice that then

$$C = A \cup B$$

where neither A nor B is empty, and

$$f(A) = P \quad \text{and} \quad f(B) = Q$$

as illustrated in Figure 2.13.

Because $P \subseteq \overline{P}$ (where $\overline{P}$ is the closure of P), we have $A \subseteq f^{-1}[f(A)] = f^{-1}(P) \subseteq f^{-1}(\overline{P})$. Because f is continuous and $\overline{P}$ is closed, $f^{-1}(\overline{P})$ is closed, and it follows that $\overline{A} \subseteq f^{-1}(\overline{P})$. (Recall that the closure of A is the smallest closed set containing A.) Then we have $f(\overline{A}) \subseteq f[f^{-1}(\overline{P})] \subseteq \overline{P}$ (see Problem 4.6 in Chapter 1).

Collecting our results so far, we have

$$f(\overline{A}) \subseteq \overline{P}, f(B) = Q \quad \text{and} \quad \overline{P} \cap Q = \varnothing$$

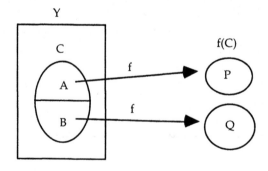

Figure 2.13.

We can therefore write

$$\varnothing = \overline{P} \cap Q = \overline{P} \cap f(B) \supseteq f(\overline{A}) \cap f(B)$$

Hence, $f(\overline{A}) \cap f(B) = \varnothing$, and this implies that $\overline{A} \cap B = \varnothing$, for if the latter set were not empty, any point z in $\overline{A} \cap B$ would have its image in $f(\overline{A}) \cap f(B)$, which could not therefore be empty.

A similar argument yields that $\overline{B} \cap A = \varnothing$. Hence $C = A \cup B$ is not connected, and the result follows. □

Let f be a continuous function from $\mathbb{R}$ to $\mathbb{R}$, and I an interval in the real line. By Theorem 9.3, $f(I)$ is also an interval and therefore contains all points lying between its end points. Thus the intermediate-value theorem (Theorem 6.22) is a special case of this result.

A concept closely related to connectedness, and often easier to check, is that of *arcwise connectedness*. A set C in a metric space is said to be arcwise-connected if any two points in it can be joined by a continuous curve lying entirely within the set. More formally, we have the following definition.

Definition 9.4. Arc and arcwise-connected set. A set A in a metric space is an arc if it is the image of a closed interval of the real line under a homeomorphism (a continuous function with a continuous inverse). A set B in a metric space is said to be arcwise-connected if given any two points x and y in B there is an arc containing x and y that is contained entirely in the set B.

Notice that an arc is connected, for it is the continous image of a connected set.

Our preceding result shows that every arcwise-connected set is connected. The converse statement, however, does not hold. As an example, consider the set $A \cup B$, where A is the graph of the function $y = \sin 1/x$ for $x > 0$, and B is the interval $(-1, 1)$ on the y axis of the Cartesian plane (Figure 2.14). As $x \to 0$, the amplitude of the sine waves decreases, and given any point b in B, we can find points in A arbitrarily close to b. Hence, $A \cup B$ is connected. It can be shown, however, that $A \cup B$ is not arcwise-connected (Sutherland, 1993, pp. 99–101).

Theorem 9.5. An arcwise-connected set in a metric space is connected.

Proof. We will prove the contrapositive statement that a nonconnected set in a metric space cannot be arcwise-connected.

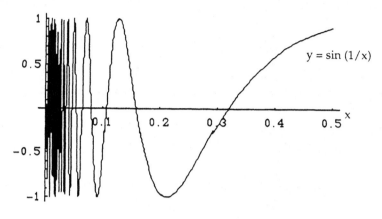

Figure 2.14.

Let D be a nonconnected set. Then there exist nonempty sets A and B such that $A \cup B = D$ and

$$\overline{A} \cap B = \varnothing = A \cap \overline{B} \tag{1}$$

Let a and b be arbitrary points of A and B, respectively, and let C be any subset of D that contains both a and b. We will show that D is not connected and cannot therefore be an arc.

Notice that $C \cap A$ and $C \cap B$ are nonempty sets (one contains at least a, and the other at least b), and

$$(C \cap A) \cup (C \cap B) = C \cap (A \cup B) = C \cap D = C$$

It remains to show that $C \cap A$ and $C \cap B$ are separated. For this, notice that any closure point of $C \cap A$ is a closure point of both C and A. Hence, $\mathrm{cl}(C \cap A) \subseteq \overline{C} \cap \overline{A}$. We can now write

$$\mathrm{cl}(C \cap A) \cap (C \cap B) \subseteq (\overline{C} \cap \overline{A}) \cap (\overline{C} \cap B) = \overline{C} \cap (\overline{A} \cap B) = \overline{C} \cap \varnothing = \varnothing$$

By the same argument, $(C \cap A) \cap \mathrm{cl}(C \cap B) = \varnothing$, and we conclude that C is not connected and cannot therefore be an arc. Hence, there is no arc containing a and b, and the set D is not arcwise-connected. $\qquad \square$

10. Equivalent Metrics and Norms

We have already noted that it is possible (and often convenient) to define several different metrics or norms in a given set. The question then arises as to when alternative metrics can be considered equivalent. In Section 1 we introduced the concept of Lipschitz equivalence for metrics and norms. We now introduce an alternative notion of equivalence (topological equivalence) and explore the relationship between these two concepts.

We will say that two metrics or norms are topologically equivalent if they preserve the basic topological properties of sets and functions. Formally, we will define topological equivalence in terms of the preservation of convergence and show that equivalent metrics also preserve continuity of functions and openness of sets.

Definition 10.1. Topologically equivalent metrics and norms. Let X be a nonempty set, and d_1 and d_2 two metrics defined on it. We will say that d_1 and d_2 are topologically equivalent if they preserve the convergence of sequences. That is, d_1 and d_2 are topologically equivalent if and only if the following condition holds: For any $x \in X$ and any sequence $\{x_n\}$ in X, $\{x_n\}$ converges to x in (X, d_1) if and only if it converges to x in (X, d_2).

Given a vector space X, two norms $\|\cdot\|_1$ and $\|\cdot\|_2$ defined on it are said to be topologically equivalent if the metrics they generate are topologically equivalent.

Theorem 10.2. Equivalent metrics preserve continuity. Let (Y, ρ) be a metric space, with X a nonempty set, and d_1 and d_2 two metrics defined on it. Then d_1 and d_2 are topologically equivalent if and only if given any two functions $f: X \longrightarrow Y$ and $g: Y \longrightarrow X$ we have that

(i) f is (d_1, ρ)-continuous if and only if it is (d_2, ρ)-continuous, and
(ii) g is (ρ, d_1)-continuous if and only if it is (ρ, d_2)-continuous.

Proof

- ($\rightarrow$) Assume that d_1 and d_2 are topologically equivalent metrics, and let $f: X \longrightarrow Y$ be a (d_1, ρ)-continuous function. We want to show that f is also (d_2, ρ)-continuous. By Theorem 6.3 (sequential characterization of continuity), the (d_1, ρ)-continuity of f implies that given any sequence $\{x_n\}$ convergent to x^0 in (X, d_1), the sequence $\{f(x_n)\}$ converges to $f(x^0)$ in (Y, ρ). By the equivalence of the metrics, any such sequence $\{x_n\}$ also converges to x^0 in (X, d_2), and because the image sequence $\{f(x_n)\}$ converges to $f(x^0)$ by assumption, the function f is continuous, again by Theorem 6.3. A similar argument can be made for functions $g: Y \longrightarrow X$.

- ($\leftarrow$) Assume that condition (i) holds, and consider a d_1-convergent sequence $\{x_n\}$ in X with limit x. We want to show that $\{x_n\}$ converges to x in (X, d_2). Let $I: X \longrightarrow X$, with $I(x) = x$, be the identity mapping in X. Because this function is clearly (d_1, d_1)-continuous, condition (i) implies that it is also (d_1, d_2)-continuous. Hence, by Theorem 6.3, the image sequence $\{I(x_n)\} = \{x_n\}$ converges to $I(x) = x$ in (X, d_2), which is the desired result. $\square$

Theorem 10.3. Equivalent metrics preserve open sets. Let X be a nonempty set, and d_1 and d_2 two metrics defined on it. Then a necessary and sufficient condition for d_1 and d_2 to be topologically equivalent is the following: A subset A of X is d_1-open if and only if it is d_2-open.

Problem 10.4. Prove Theorem 10.3. Hint: Use Theorem 10.2.

These results show that convergence and continuity do not really depend on the use of a specific metric per se, but rather on the topological equivalence class of metrics we are using or, equivalently, on the open-set structure of the space. As we have already noted, this property allows a more general treatment of many problems in a broad family of spaces (topological spaces) in which open sets are essentially the only primitive structures.

The next two results describe the relationship between topological equivalence and Lipschitz equivalence. The first theorem says that Lipschitz equivalence implies topological equivalence. The converse of this result does not hold in arbitrary metric spaces, but it does hold in normed vector spaces.

Theorem 10.5. Lipschitz equivalence implies topological equivalence. Let X be a nonempty set, and d_1 and d_2 two metrics defined on it. If d_1 and d_2 are Lipschitz-equivalent, that is, if there exist positive real numbers m and M such that

$$md_1(x, y) \leq d_2(x, y) \leq Md_1(x, y) \quad \text{for any } x, y \in X \tag{1}$$

then d_1 and d_2 are topologically equivalent.

Problem 10.6. Prove Theorem 10.5.

Theorem 10.7. Topological equivalence implies Lipschitz equivalence in vector spaces. Let X be a vector space, and $\|\cdot\|_1$ and $\|\cdot\|_2$ two norms defined on it. If $\|\cdot\|_1$ and $\|\cdot\|_2$ are topologically equivalent, then they are also Lipschitz-equivalent; that is, there exist positive constants m and M such that

$$m\|x\|_1 \leq \|x\|_2 \leq M\|x\|_1 \quad \text{for all } x \in X$$

Proof. We will prove the contrapositive statement: If $\|\cdot\|_1$ and $\|\cdot\|_2$ are not Lipschitz-equivalent, then they cannot be topologically equivalent – that is, we can then find a sequence $\{x_n\}$ that will converge to some limit x in the metric induced by $\|\cdot\|_1$ and will not converge to x in the metric induced by $\|\cdot\|_2$.

Suppose there is no constant M such that $\|x\|_2 \le M\|x\|_1$ for all x. Then for each positive integer n we can find some $x_n \in X$ with the property that

$$\|x_n\|_2 > n\|x_n\|_1 \tag{1}$$

Dividing both sides of (1) by $\|x_n\|_2$ and using the defining properties of the norm, we have

$$\left\|\frac{x_n}{\|x_n\|_2}\right\|_1 < \frac{1}{n} \quad \text{for all } n$$

which implies that the sequence $\{x_n/\|x_n\|_2\}$ converges to $\underline{0}$ in the metric induced by $\|\cdot\|_1$. On the other hand,

$$\left\|\frac{x_n}{\|x_n\|_2}\right\|_2 = \frac{\|x_n\|_2}{\|x_n\|_2} = 1 \quad \text{for all } n$$

So $\{x_n/\|x_n\|_2\}$ does not converge to $\underline{0}$ in the metric induced by $\|\cdot\|_2$. The same argument will work with the roles of $\|\cdot\|_1$ and $\|\cdot\|_2$ reversed. $\qquad\square$

Our next theorem says that all norms are equivalent in finite-dimensional vector spaces. This result is often useful because it allows us to choose whichever norm is more convenient for the problem at hand without having to worry about the validity of the results.

Theorem 10.8. Equivalence of all norms in $\mathbb{R}^n$. Let $\mathrm{N}:\mathbb{R}^n \to \mathbb{R}$ be any norm. Then there exist constants $m, M > 0$ such that

$$m\|x\|_E \le N(x) \le M\|x\|_E \quad \textit{for all } x \in \mathbb{R}^n \tag{1}$$

where $\|\cdot\|_E$ is the Euclidean norm in $\mathbb{R}^n$.

Proof. Recall from Problem 6.8 that a norm is a continuous function. By the extreme-value theorem (Theorem 8.24) it follows that $N(\ )$ achieves both a maximum M and a minimum m in the compact set

$$C = \left\{x \in \mathbb{R}^n;\ \|x\|_E \le 1\right\}$$

Now let x be an arbitrary vector in $\mathbb{R}^n$. If $x = \underline{0}$, then $N(\underline{0}) = \|\underline{0}\|_E = 0$, and (1) holds trivially. If $x \ne \underline{0}$, then $\|x\|_E = \alpha > 0$, and, using the defining properties of the norm, we can write

$$N(x) = N(\alpha\alpha^{-1}x) = \alpha N(\alpha^{-1}x)$$

Now, because $\|\alpha^{-1}x\|_E = \alpha^{-1}\|x\|_E = \|x\|_E/\|x\|_E = 1$, we have that $\alpha^{-1}x \in C$ and it follows that

$$m \le N(\alpha^{-1}x) \le M$$

from where

$$m \le \alpha^{-1} N(x) \le M$$

and, recalling that $\alpha = \|x\|_E$,

$$m\|x\|_E \le N(x) \le M\|x\|_E \qquad\qquad \square$$

11. Continuity of Correspondences in E^n

We saw in Chapter 1 that a correspondence $\Psi : X \to\to Y$ is a set-valued mapping, that is, a mapping that assigns to each point x in X a subset $\Psi(x)$ of Y. Suppose X and Y are metric spaces. Then a correspondence is said to be *closed-valued* (*compact-valued*) at a point x if the image set $\Psi(x)$ is closed (compact) in Y.

We would like to extend to the case of correspondences the standard notion of continuity for a single-valued mapping in a way that will preserve its intuitive interpretation. Hence, we would like to say that a correspondence Ψ is continuous if a small change in the argument x does not change the image set $\Psi(x)$ very much. To see how we can go about this, and to see the problems that arise, recall from Section 6 that a function is continuous if the inverse image of an open set is open. If we focus on a specific point in the domain of the function, this can be rephrased as follows: A function f is continuous at a point x if whenever x lies in the inverse image of an open set V, so does every point sufficiently close to it. If we try to apply this definition to correspondences, we immediately run into a difficulty: What is the inverse image of a set under a correspondence? Notice that there are two natural possibilities: We can define $\Psi^{-1}(V)$ as the set of all points x whose image set is totally contained in V, $\{x \in X; \Psi(x) \subseteq V\}$, or as the set of points whose image set is partially contained in V, $\{x \in X; \Psi(x) \cap V \ne \varnothing\}$. The first possibility is sometimes called the *upper* or *strong inverse* of V under Ψ, and the second is the *lower* or *weak inverse*. Each of these concepts of inverse gives rise to a different notion of (hemi-) continuity for correspondences, and we reserve the term "continuous" for a set-valued function that is hemicontinuous in both senses. Notice that both types of hemicontinuity reduce to the standard notion of continuity if Ψ is a single-valued mapping.

Definition 11.1. Continuity for correspondences.[10] Let X and Y be finite-dimensional Euclidean spaces, and let $\Psi : X \to\to Y$ be a correspondence. Then we say the following:

(i) Ψ is upper-hemicontinuous (uhc) at a point $x \in X$ if for every open set V containing $\Psi(x)$ there exists a neighborhood U of x such that $\Psi(x') \subseteq V$ for every $x' \in U$.

(ii) Ψ is lower-hemicontinuous (lhc) at a point $x \in X$ if for every open set V in Y with $\Psi(x) \cap V \neq \emptyset$ there exists a neighborhood U of x such that $\Psi(x') \cap V \neq \emptyset$ for every $x' \in U$.

(iii) Ψ is continuous at x if it is both uhc and lhc at this point.

A correspondence is continuous (uhc, lhc) if it is continuous (uhc, lhc) at each point in its domain.

Each type of hemicontinuity can be given a straightforward intuitive interpretation in terms of the restrictions placed on the "size" of the set $\Psi(x)$ as x changes. First, suppose that $\Psi()$ is uhc at some point x, and fix an appropriate open set V containing $\Psi(x)$. As we move from x to a nearby point x', the set V gives us an "upper bound" on the size of $\Psi(x')$, because we require that $\Psi(x')$ remain contained in V. Hence, upper hemicontinuity requires that the image set $\Psi(x)$ not "explode" (become suddenly much larger) with small changes in the argument, but allows this set to become suddenly much smaller. In the case of lower hemicontinuity, on the other hand, the set V acts as a "lower bound" on $\Psi(x')$, because the intersection of the image set with V cannot become empty. Hence, hemicontinuity rules out "implosions" of the image set (but not explosions).

Figure 2.15 may help clarify the meaning of these definitions. The correspondence Ψ is not uhc at x_1 (but it is lhc). To see this, fix an open set $V \supseteq \Psi(x_1)$ as in the figure, and notice that for any x_1' smaller than x_1 but arbitrarily close to it, the image set $\Psi(x_1')$ is not contained in V. Hence, $\Psi(x)$ "explodes" as we move away from x_1 to the left. On the other hand, φ is uhc at x_2 but not lhc, because as we move from this point to the left, the image set $\varphi(x)$ suddenly becomes much smaller.

We now develop some alternative characterizations of upper and lower

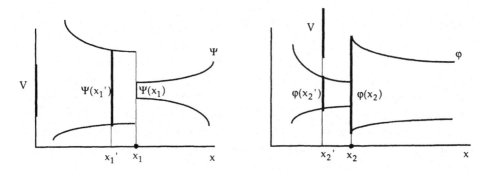

Figure 2.15. Failures of upper and lower hemicontinuity.

hemicontinuity that often are more convenient in applications than Definition 11.1. In all cases, the domain and range of the correspondence (the sets X and Y) are assumed to be finite-dimensional Euclidean spaces.

Theorem 11.2. A sequential characterization of upper hemicontinuity. A compact-valued correspondence $\Psi:X \rightarrow\rightarrow Y$ is uhc at x *if and only if for every sequence $\{x_n\}$ converging to* x, *every "companion sequence" $\{y_n\}$, with $y_n \in \Psi(x_n)$ for all* n, *has a convergent subsequence $\{y_{n_k}\}$ with limit in $\Psi(x)$.*

Proof

- Assume that Ψ is uhc at x, and let $\{x_n\}$ be a sequence converging to x, and $\{y_n\}$, with $y_n \in \Psi(x_n)$ for each n, an arbitrary companion sequence. We will first show that $\{y_n\}$ is bounded. By Theorems 3.3 and 3.10, this implies that $\{y_n\}$ has a convergent subsequence. We will then show that the limit of this subsequence lies in $\Psi(x)$.

  By assumption, $\Psi(x)$ is a compact and therefore bounded set. Hence there is a bounded and open set B that contains $\Psi(x)$. By the upper hemicontinuity of $\Psi(\ )$, there exists a neighborhood U of x such that $\Psi(z) \subseteq B$ for all $z \in U$. Now, because $\{x_n\} \to x$, there exists an integer N such that $x_n \in U$ for all $n > N$, and it follows that $\Psi(x_n) \subseteq B$ for $n > N$. Hence, any companion sequence $\{y_n; y_n \in \Psi(x_n)\}$ is bounded and therefore contains a convergent subsequence. Call this subsequence $\{y_{n_k}\}$, and let y be its limit.

  To show that $y \in \Psi(x)$, we will assume that such is not the case and obtain a contradiction. Suppose, then, that $y \notin \Psi(x)$. Because $\Psi(x)$ is (compact and therefore) closed, y cannot be a boundary point of $\Psi(x)$, and it follows that the distance between y and the set $\Psi(x)$ is strictly positive. Hence, we can construct a closed ε-ball around the set $\Psi(x)$.

  $$B_\varepsilon[\Psi(x)] = \bigcup_{a \in \Psi(x)} B_\varepsilon[a]$$

  that does not contain y by choosing ε such that

  $$0 < \varepsilon < \inf_{a \in \Psi(x)} d(a, y) = d(\Psi(x), y)$$

  Notice that the interior of $B_\varepsilon[\Psi(x)]$ is an open set that contains $\Psi(x)$.

  Now, because Ψ is uhc at x, and $\{x_n\} \to x$, $\Psi(x_n)$ will be contained in $B_\varepsilon[\Psi(x)]$ (actually, in its interior) for n sufficiently high. This, in turn, implies that the companion sequence $\{y_n; y_n \in \Psi(x_n)\}$ will be contained in $B_\varepsilon[\Psi(x)]$ for n high enough, and therefore so will the convergent subsequence $\{y_{n_k}\}$. Because $B_\varepsilon[\Psi(x)]$ is closed, it follows by Theorem 4.13 that y, which is the limit of $\{y_{n_k}\}$, will also belong to $B_\varepsilon[\Psi(x)]$. This contradicts the fact that $y \notin B_\varepsilon[\Psi(x)]$ by the construction of $B_\varepsilon[\Psi(x)]$.

- The second part of the theorem says that if a certain property concerning sequences holds, then the correspondence is uhc. It will be convenient to establish the equivalent (contrapositive) assertion that if Ψ is not uhc at x, then this property does not always hold.

For this, assume that Ψ is not uhc at x, that is, that there exists an open set V containing $\Psi(x)$ such that every neighborhood U of x contains a point z_u with $\Psi(z_u)$ not contained in V. Then we can choose a decreasing sequence of such neighborhoods $\{U_n\}$, with $U_{n+1} \subseteq U_n$ (say $U_n = B_{1/n}(x)$, an open ball with radius $1/n$ and center at x), and for each of them there is some point z_n with $\Psi(z_n)$ not contained in V. By construction, $\{z_n\} \rightarrow x$, but we can choose a companion sequence $\{y_n\}$, with $y_n \in \Psi(z_n)$, in such a way that $y_n \notin V$ (i.e., $y_n \in V^c$ for each n). Suppose now that $\{y_n\}$ has a convergent subsequence $\{y_{n_k}\}$, and call its limit y. Because $\{y_{n_k}\}$ is contained in the closed set V^c, its limit y must also lie on this set (by Theorem 4.13). Hence, $y \notin V$, and because V contains $\Psi(x)$, it follows that $y \notin \Psi(x)$. This establishes the desired result, for we have constructed a sequence $\{z_n\} \rightarrow x$ and a companion sequence $\{y_n \in \Psi(z_n)\}$ that can have no subsequence converging to a point in $\Psi(x)$. $\square$

Theorem 11.3. *A sequential characterization of lower hemicontinuity. A correspondence* $\Psi : X \rightarrow\!\!\!\rightarrow Y$ *is lhc at* x *if and only if for every sequence* $\{x_n\}$ *converging to* x *and every point* y $\in \Psi($x$)$ *there exists a companion sequence* $\{y_n\}$, *with* $y_n \in \Psi(x_n)$ *for all* n, *that converges to* y.

Proof

- Assume that Ψ is lhc at x; let $\{x_n\}$ be a sequence converging to x, and fix an arbitrary point in $\Psi(x)$, say y. For each integer k, let $B_{1/k}(y)$ be the open ball with radius $1/k$ and center at y. Clearly, $B_{1/k}(y) \cap \Psi(x)$ is nonempty, because it contains at least the point y. Because Ψ is lhc at x, for each k there exists a neighborhood U_k of x such that for each $z_k \in U_k$ we have $\Psi(z_k) \cap B_{1/k}(y) \neq \emptyset$. Because $\{x_n\} \rightarrow x$, we can find, for each given k, an integer n_k such that $x_n \in U_k$ for all $n \geq n_k$. These numbers, moreover, can be assigned so that $n_{k+1} > n_k$. Notice, moreover, that with $n \geq n_k$ we have $x_n \in U_k$, and this implies that $\Psi(x_n) \cap B_{1/k}(y)$ is nonempty. Hence, we can construct a companion sequence $\{y_n\}$, with y_n chosen from the set $\Psi(x_n) \cap B_{1/k}(y)$, for each n with $n_k < n_{k+1}$. As k, and hence n, increases, the radius of the balls $B_{1/k}(y)$ shrinks down to zero, which implies that $\{y_n\}$ converges to y.

- As in the preceding theorem, we prove the contrapositive of the desired result. Assume that Ψ is not lhc at x, that is, that there exists an open set V, with $\Psi(x) \cap V \neq \emptyset$, such that every neighborhood U of x contains a point z_u, with $\Psi(z_u) \cap V = \emptyset$. Taking a sequence of such neighborhoods, $U_n = B_{1/n}(x)$, and an appropriate point x_n in each of them, we obtain a sequence $\{x_n\}$ that converges to x by construction and has the property that $\Psi(x_n) \cap V = \emptyset$ for all n.

Hence, every companion sequence $\{y_n\}$, with $y_n \in \Psi(x_n)$, is contained in the complement of V, and if $\{y_n\}$ is convergent, the same must be true of its limit, because the complement of V is a closed set. It follows that no companion sequence of

$\{x_n\}$ can converge to a point in V. Hence, if we let y be a point in $\Psi(x) \cap V$, no convergent companion sequence can exist.   □

We now introduce another concept of continuity for correspondences, essentially by extending the sequential characterization of continuity for functions (the image of a sequence under the function converges to the image of the limit of the sequence). Before we state the definition, recall that the *graph* of the correspondence Ψ is the set

$$G_\Psi = \{(x, y) \in X \times Y; \ y \in \Psi(x)\}$$

Definition 11.4. A correspondence $\Psi : X \longrightarrow Y$ is said to be closed if its graph G_Ψ is closed in $X \times Y$; that Ψ is closed whenever

$$\left\langle \begin{array}{c} \{x_n\} \to x \\ y_n \in \Psi(x_n) \ \forall n \\ \{y_n\} \to y \end{array} \right\rangle \Rightarrow y \in \Psi(x)$$

Problem 11.5. Show that a closed correspondence is closed-valued.

Our next result shows that closedness is closely related to upper hemicontinuity. Because closedness is also fairly easy to check in many cases, a convenient way to show that a given correspondence is uhc is to establish its closedness and then apply Theorem 11.6.

Theorem 11.6. Relationship between closedness and upper hemicontinuity. Let $\Psi : X \longrightarrow Y$ be a nonempty valued and closed correspondence. If for any bounded set B in X the image set $\Psi(B)$ is bounded, then Ψ is uhc.

Notice that if the range Y of the correspondence is a compact space, the boundedness assumption is satisfied automatically.

Proof. Fix an arbitrary point x in X. Then $\Psi(x)$ is a closed set (by Problem 11.5) that is bounded (by assumption) and therefore compact. Hence, Ψ is compact-valued. Consider now a sequence $\{x_n\}$ converging to x and an arbitrary companion sequence $\{y_n\}$, with $y_n \in \Psi(x_n)$ for each n. To establish the desired result, we have to show that $\{y_n\}$ has a convergent subsequence with limit in $\Psi(x)$.

Because $\{x_n\} \to x$, there is a bounded set, say B, that contains both $\{x_n\}$ and x (Theorem 2.5). The image set $\Psi(B)$ contains the companion sequence and, by assumption, is bounded. Hence (by Theorems 3.3 and 3.10), $\{y_n\}$ has a convergent subsequence, say $\{y_{n_k}\}$, with limit y. Then $\{(x_{n_k}, y_{n_k})\}$ is a sequence in $G_\Psi \subseteq X \times Y$ converging to (x, y), and it follows from the closedness of the graph of Ψ that $(x, y) \in G_\Psi$ (i.e., that $y \in \Psi(x)$).   □

In the remainder of this section we list some useful properties of uhc correspondences.

Theorem 11.7. Let the correspondence $\Psi: X \twoheadrightarrow Y$ *be compact-valued and uhc, let* $\Gamma: X \twoheadrightarrow Y$ *be closed, and assume that* $\Psi(x) \cap \Gamma(x) \neq \emptyset$. *Then the intersection correspondence* $\Psi \cap \Gamma$, *defined by* $(\Psi \cap \Gamma)(x) = \Psi(x) \cap \Gamma(x)$, *is compact-valued and uhc.*

Problem 11.8. Prove Theorem 11.7. Notice that $\Psi(x) \cap \Gamma(x)$ is compact, by Theorem 8.12.

Theorem 11.9. Let the correspondence $\Psi: X \twoheadrightarrow Y$ *be compact-valued and uhc. Then the image under* Ψ *of a compact set* C,

$$\Psi(C) = \cup_{x \in C} \Psi(x)$$

is compact.

Problem 11.10. Prove Theorem 11.9. Hint: Use the sequential characterization of compactness and Theorem 11.2.

Theorem 11.11. Let the correspondences $\Psi_i: X \twoheadrightarrow Y$, *with* $i = 1, \ldots, n$, *be compact-valued and uhc at* x. *Then the sum correspondence* Ψ, *defined by* $\Psi(x) = \Sigma_{i=1}^n \Psi_i(x)$ *for each* x, *is compact-valued and uhc at* x.

Problem 11.12. Prove Theorem 11.11.
Let $\Psi: X \twoheadrightarrow Y$ and $\Gamma: Y \twoheadrightarrow Z$ be two correspondences. We define their *composition,* $\varphi = \Gamma \circ \Psi: X \twoheadrightarrow Z$ by

$$\varphi(x) = \Gamma \circ \Psi(x) = \Gamma[\Psi(x)] = \bigcup_{y \in \Psi(x)} \Gamma(y)$$

Theorem 11.13. Let $\Psi: X \twoheadrightarrow Y$ *and* $\Gamma: Y \twoheadrightarrow Z$ *be uhc at* x^0. *Then their composition* $\varphi = \Gamma \circ \Psi$ *is also uhc at* x^0.

Proof. Let W be an open set containing $\varphi(x^0)$, and let

$$U = \{x \in X;\ \varphi(x) \subseteq W\}$$

To establish the upper hemicontinuity of φ, we need to show that U is an open set. Let

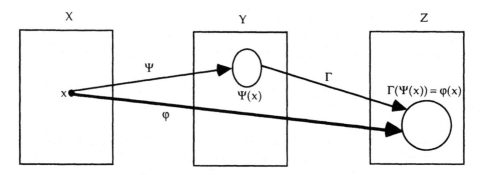

Figure 2.16. Composition of two correspondences.

$$V = \{y \in Y; \; \Gamma(y) \subseteq W\}$$

and observe that $\varphi(x) = \Gamma[\Psi(x)] \subseteq W$ if and only if $\Psi(x) \subseteq V$. Hence we have

$$U = \{x \in X; \; \Psi(x) \subseteq V\}$$

Now, because Γ is uhc, the openness of W implies the openness of V. Similarly, because V is open and Ψ is uhc, it follows that U is open, which establishes the desired result. □

Theorem 11.14. Let $\Gamma^i : X \to\to Y$, with $i = 1, \ldots, n$, be compact-valued and uhc correspondences. Then the product correspondence $\Gamma(\;)$, with $\Gamma(x) = \Gamma^1(x) \times \ldots \times \Gamma^n(x)$ for each x in X, is compact-valued and uhc.

Problem 11.15. Prove Theorem 11.14.

Bibliography

Apostol, T. 1974. *Mathematical Analysis*, 2nd ed. Reading, MA: Addison-Wesley.
Berge, C. 1966. *Espace Topologiques. Fonctions Multivoques*. Paris: Dunod.
Binmore, K. 1982. *Mathematical Analysis: A Straightforward Approach*, 2nd ed. Cambridge University Press.
Border, K. 1989. *Fixed Point Theorems with Applications to Economics and Game Theory*. Cambridge University Press.
Byrant, V. 1990. *Yet Another Introduction to Analysis*. Cambridge University. Press.
Clark, C. 1982. *Elementary Mathematical Analysis*, 2nd ed. Belmont, CA: Wadsworth.
Gemignani, M. 1972. *Elementary Topology*, 2nd ed. New York: Dover.
Giles, J. R. 1989. *Introduction to the Analysis of Metric Spaces*. Cambridge University Press.
Haaser, N., and Sullivan, J. 1991. *Real Analysis*. New York: Dover.

Hildenbrand, W. 1974. *Core and Equilibria of a Large Economy*. Princeton University Press.

Hildenbrand, W., and Kirman, A. 1976. *Introduction to Equilibrium Analysis. Variations on Themes by Edgeworth and Walras*. Amsterdam: North Holland.

Kolmogorov, A. N., and Fomin, S. V. 1970. *Introductory Real Analysis*. New York: Dover.

Lang, S. 1989. *Undergraduate Analysis*. Berlin: Springer-Verlag.

Michel, P. 1984. *Cours de Mathématiques pour Économistes*. Paris: Economica.

Nikaido, H. 1972. *Introduction to Sets and Mappings in Modern Economics*. Amsterdam: North Holland.

Protter, M., and Morrey, C. 1991. *A First Course in Real Analysis*, 2nd ed. Berlin: Springer-Verlag.

Royden, H. L. 1988. *Real Analysis*, 3rd ed. New York: Macmillan.

Rudin, W. 1964. *Principles of Mathematical Analysis*, 2nd ed. New York: McGraw-Hill.

Stirling, D. 1990. *Mathematical Analysis: A Fundamental and Straightforward Approach*. New York: Ellis Horwood.

Sutherland, W. 1993. *Introduction to Metric and Topological Spaces*. Oxford: Clarendon Press.

Notes

1 The choice of x is arbitrary: Notice that if S satisfies the definition of boundedness for some x, it will also satisfy it for any other point x' in X, with B replaced by $B + d(x, x')$, because $d(s, x') \leq d(s, x) + d(x, x')$. It should be noted that a given set may be bounded or unbounded depending on what metric we are using.

2 To guarantee that $B_\varepsilon(x) \cap B_{\varepsilon'}(x') = \varnothing$, it is enough to choose $\varepsilon, \varepsilon' < d(x, x')/2$.

3 Every nonempty set of real numbers that is bounded above has a least upper bound (see Chapter 1).

4 Note that openness is defined relative to a given metric space (X, d). It may be important to keep that in mind if X is itself embedded in a larger set. For example, let A be an "open circle" in a plane X, which is itself a subset of three-dimensional space Y. Then A is open in X, but not in Y, because any small movement in Y away from the X plane would take us out of A. However, any sufficiently small movement along the plane and away from a point in the circle will leave us inside A. If there is any possibility of ambiguity, we should say that a set A is open (or not) in X.

5 Note that in fact both X and $\varnothing$ satisfy the definition, but in a fairly strange way. It is true that around any point in $\varnothing$ we can construct an adequate open ball, or do anything we want, for that matter, because there is no such point. The same is true for X, for there is "nothing" outside it.

6 See Chapter 1.

7 Occasionally we may want to define the limit of f as x approaches x^0 through elements of a given set A. Right-handed and left-handed limits for functions in $\mathbb{R}$, for example, are defined in this way by requiring x to approach x^0 either from above or from below. More generally, we say that f tends to y^0 as x tends to x^0 for $x \in A$ if and only if x^0 is a limit point of A, and

$$\forall \varepsilon > 0, \ \exists \delta_\varepsilon > 0 \text{ s.th. } \rho[f(x), y^0] < \varepsilon \ \forall x \in A \text{ s.th. } d(x, x^0) < \delta_\varepsilon$$

8 As for limits, we may occasionally want to define continuity relative to a given set. We say that a function f is continuous *with respect to a set A* at a point x^0 if

$$\forall \varepsilon > 0, \ \exists \delta_\varepsilon > 0 \text{ s.th. } \rho[f(x), f(x^0)] < \varepsilon \ \forall x \in A \text{ s.th. } d(x, x^0) < \delta_\varepsilon$$

Right continuity and left continuity for real functions, for example, are defined in this way.

9 Given a contraction T with modulus β, let y be an arbitrary trial solution to the

equation $Tx = x$. If the true solution is x^*, it is easy to see by the argument used in the existence proof that

$$d(y, x^*) \le \frac{1}{1 - \beta} d(y, Ty)$$

10 The definition can be extended to the case of general metric spaces. Most of the results in this section continue to hold in this setting, but the proofs become more complicated. The interested reader is referred to Hildenbrand (1974) for a more general treatment.

3

Vector Spaces and Linear Transformations

The concept of a vector space was defined in Chapter 1. We begin this chapter with a brief review of the structure of vector spaces, focusing on the concept of basis. Then we turn to the study of linear functions.

1. Linear Independence and Bases

Let V be a vector space defined over the field F. A *family of vectors* in V, $\mathrm{x} = \{x_s \in V; s \in S\}$, is the range of a function f from an index set S to V such that $f(s) = x_s$. A *subfamily* of x is the range of the restriction of f to a subset S' of S. If S' is a finite set, we speak of a finite subfamily of x.

Let $\mathrm{x} = \{x_1, \ldots, x_n\}$ be a finite family of vectors in V. A *linear combination* of $x_1, \ldots, x_n$ is a vector of the form

$$y = \sum_{i=1}^{n} \alpha_i x_i$$

where $\alpha_1, \ldots, \alpha_n$ are scalars, and α_i is called the coefficient of the vector x_i.

We say that a finite family of vectors $\mathrm{x} = \{x_1, \ldots, x_n\}$ is *linearly dependent* if at least one of the vectors can be written as a linear combination of the rest. Equivalently, we say that $x_1, \ldots, x_n$ are linearly dependent if there exist scalars $\alpha_1, \ldots, \alpha_n$, not all zero, such that

$$\sum_{i=1}^{n} \alpha_i x_i = \underline{0}$$

For an infinite family $\mathrm{x} = \{x_s \in V; s \in S\}$, we say that x is linearly dependent if there exists at least one finite subfamily of x that is linearly dependent.

A family of vectors x in V is *linearly independent* if it is not linearly dependent; that is, if for every finite subfamily $\{x_s \in V; s \in S'\}$ of x we have that

$$\sum_{s \in S'} \alpha_s x_s = \underline{0} \implies \alpha_s = 0 \,\forall\, s \in S'$$

117

A subset W of V *spans* or *generates* V if every vector in V can be written as a linear combination of a finite number of elements of W, that is, if for every $x \in V$ there exist scalars $\alpha_1, \ldots, \alpha_n$ and vectors $w_1, \ldots, w_n$ in W such that

$$x = \sum_{i=1}^{n} \alpha_i w_i$$

We can now introduce a concept of "basis" that is valid for all vector spaces, even those of infinite dimension.

Definition 1.1. Hamel basis. A Hamel basis for a vector space V is a linearly independent family of vectors that spans V.

A Hamel basis is a useful concept because it allows us to write every element of V in a unique way as a linear combination of elements of the basis. Thus, once we have a basis, we "know" all the elements of V.

Theorem 1.2. Let $\mathbb{b} = \{v_s \in V; s \in S\}$ *be a Hamel basis for* V. *Then every nonzero vector* $x \in V$ *has a* unique *representation as a linear combination, with coefficients not all zero, of a finite number of vectors in* $\mathbb{b}$.

Proof. Let x be an arbitrary nonzero vector in V. Because (by definition of Hamel basis) $\mathbb{b}$ spans V, we know that x has at least one representation of the form

$$x = \sum_{s \in S_1} \alpha_s v_s$$

where S_1 is a finite subset of S, and $\alpha_s \neq 0$ for $s \in S_1$. Let us assume that there exists a second such representation

$$x = \sum_{s \in S_2} \beta_s v_s$$

where S_2 is another finite subset of S, and $\beta_s \neq 0$ for $s \in S_2$. We will show that these two representations must be equal.

Let $S_3 = S_1 \cup S_2$, and let $\alpha_s = 0$ for $s \in S_3 \sim S_1$ and $\beta_s = 0$ for $s \in S_3 \sim S_2$. We can then write both representations in terms of the same finite subfamily of $\mathbb{b}$:

$$x = \sum_{s \in S_3} \alpha_s v_s = \sum_{s \in S_3} \beta_s v_s$$

from which

$$\sum_{s \in S_3} (\alpha_s - \beta_s) v_s = \underline{0}$$

Because $\{v_s \in V; s \in S_3\}$ is a finite subfamily of a Hamel basis, it is linearly independent. Thus, the last expression implies that $\alpha_s - \beta_s = 0$ for all s. Hence, $\alpha_s = \beta_s$, and the representation is unique. $\square$

It can be shown that *every nontrivial vector space* $(V \neq \{\underline{0}\})$ *has a Hamel basis*, and that *all Hamel bases of V have the same cardinal number*. This cardinal number is therefore a property of the space V and is called its *dimension* (written dim V). A finite-dimensional Hamel basis (i.e., one that contains a finite number of vectors) is called a *basis*.

Although we will work mostly with finite-dimensional vector spaces, it is important to observe that certain vector spaces of interest are infinite-dimensional.

Example 1.3. Let F be a field, and consider the set

$$V_n(F) = \{v = (\alpha^1, \ldots, \alpha^n); \; \alpha^i \in F \; \forall \; i = 1, \ldots, n\}$$

Put

$$\delta_{ik} = 1 \text{ if } i = k \quad \text{and} \quad \delta_{ik} = 0 \text{ if } i \neq k$$

and define the vectors

$$e_p^n = (\delta_{1p}, \ldots, \delta_{pp}, \ldots, \delta_{np}) \quad \text{for } p \leq n$$

(i.e., the n-vector e_p^n has 1 as its pth component, and the others are zeros). If n is finite, it is easy to show that $V_n(F)$ is a vector space and the family $\{e_p^n; p = 1, \ldots, n\}$ is a basis (the *canonical basis*) for $V_n(F)$. If we go to the limit and put $n = \infty$, we obtain the infinite-dimensional vector space of the scalar sequences, $V_\infty(F)$. Observe that the infinite family $\{e_p^\infty; p = 1, \ldots, \infty\}$ of sequences with a single 1 and all the rest zeros is not a Hamel basis of $V_\infty(F)$, for it is impossible to write a sequence with an infinite number of terms different from zero as a linear combination of a finite number of sequences of the form e_p^∞. It is possible to show, however, that there is an extension of this family that is a Hamel basis for $V_\infty(F)$. $\square$

In the case of finite-dimensional vector spaces, bases have a very simple structure. In particular, we shall show that if V has dimension $n < \infty$, any collection of n linearly independent vectors in V is a basis for V.

Theorem 1.4. Let $v = \{v_1, \ldots, v_n\}$ *be a basis of* V; *then no set of more than* n *vectors in* V *is linearly independent.*

Proof. Let $x = \{x_1, \ldots, x_{n+1}\}$ be a collection of $n+1$ vectors in V. We can always find scalars $\beta_1, \ldots, \beta_{n+1}$ such that

$$\sum_{k=1}^{n+1} \beta_k x_k = \underline{0} \tag{1}$$

What we want to show is that there are β_k's that satisfy (1) and are not all zero.

Now, $\mathbb{v} = \{v_1, \ldots, v_n\}$ is a basis of V, and therefore each x_k has a unique representation as a linear combination of elements of $\mathbb{v}$. That is, there exist scalars α_{ik}, not all zero, such that for each $k = 1, \ldots, n+1$,

$$x_k = \sum_{i=1}^{n} \alpha_{ik} v_i \tag{2}$$

Substituting (2) into (1), we see that the β_k's must satisfy the following equality:

$$\underline{0} = \sum_{k=1}^{n+1} \beta_k \left(\sum_{i=1}^{n} \alpha_{ik} v_i \right) = \sum_{i=1}^{n} \left(\sum_{k=1}^{n+1} \beta_k \alpha_{ik} \right) v_i \tag{3}$$

Because $v_1, \ldots, v_n$ are linearly independent, (3) implies

$$\sum_{k=1}^{n+1} \beta_k \alpha_{ik} = 0 \ \forall \ i = 1, \ldots, n \tag{4}$$

Observe that (4) is a system of n equations in $n+1$ unknowns (the β_k's). As we will prove later (and the reader should already know), every such system has nontrivial solutions. Hence, it is possible to find β_k's not all zero that satisfy (1), and we conclude that $x_1, \ldots, x_{n+1}$ are linearly dependent.   □

This theorem implies that every basis for a finite-dimensional vector space has the same number of elements, for if this were not so, a basis with more elements than another one could not be a linearly independent family. Another almost immediate corollary of Theorem 1.4 is the following result:

Theorem 1.5. Let V *be a vector space of dimension* n. *Then any linearly independent family of* n *vectors in* V, $\mathbb{v} = \{v_1, \ldots, v_n\}$, *is a basis for* V.

Problem 1.6. Prove Theorem 1.5.

Example 1.7. Let F be a field. The set $F_{m \times n}$ of all matrices of dimension $m \times n$, $A = [a_{ik}]$ $(i = 1, \ldots, m; \ k = 1, \ldots, n)$, with matrix addition and multiplication by a scalar defined component by component, is a vector space. Moreover, the mn matrices E_{ik} with a 1 in the position ik and zeros in all other entries is a basis of $F_{m \times n}$ that therefore has dimension mn.

Problem 1.8. Prove the following result: Let X be a finite-dimensional normed linear space over the real field with basis $\{v_1, \ldots, v_m\}$. A sequence $\{x_n\}$, in X, with $x_n = \sum_{i=1}^m \alpha_i^n v_i$ (α_i^n *real*), converges to $x = \sum_{i=1}^m \alpha_i v_i$ if and only if each coordinate sequence $\{\alpha_i^n\}$ converges to α_i for each $i = 1, \ldots, m$. (It is sufficient to consider the case where $x = \underline{0}$.)

(i) Show that if $\{\alpha_i^n\} \to 0$ for all i, then $\{x_n\} \to \underline{0}$.

(ii) To prove the converse implication, suppose $\{x_n\} \to \underline{0}$, but for some k the coordinate sequence $\{\alpha_k^n\}$ does not converge to 0. Then there exists a subsequence of $\{x_n\}$ (for convenience of notation, still referred to as $\{x_n\}$ and some $r > 0$ such that $|\alpha_k^n| > r$ for all n. For each $n \in \mathbb{N}$, write

$$M_n = \max_i\{|\alpha_i^n|;\ 1 \le i \le m\}$$

and consider the sequence $\{y_n\}$, with $y_n = \dfrac{x_n}{M_n}$. Show that $\{y_n\} \to \underline{0}$.

(iii) Use the Bolzano-Weierstrass theorem to show that from $\{y_n\}$ we can choose a subsequence that converges coordinate-wise, but to a nonzero element. By the first part of the theorem, we have a contradiction.

Problem 1.9. Using the foregoing result and the completeness of $\mathbb{R}$, we will show that every finite-dimensional normed vector space over $\mathbb{R}$ is complete.

(i) First, show that if $\{x_n\}$ is Cauchy, then every coordinate sequence $\{\alpha_i^n\}$ is Cauchy. (Prove the contrapositive statement: If some coordinate sequence $\{\alpha_k^n\}$ is not Cauchy, then neither is $\{x_n\}$. Use the result in Problem 1.8.)

(ii) Using (i), Problem 1.8 again, and the completeness of $\mathbb{R}$, show that the desired result holds.

Affine Subspaces

Lex X be a vector space, and V a (vector) subspace of X. A set A of the form

$$A = x^0 + V = \left\{x \in X;\ x = x^0 + v,\ \text{where}\ x^0 \in X\ \text{and}\ v \in V\right\}$$

is an affine subspace of X "parallel" to V.

If $A = x^0 + V$ is an affine subspace of X, and $a_1, \ldots, a_n$ are vectors in A, then every linear combination of $a_1, \ldots, a_n$ is a vector of the form

$$x = \sum_{i=1}^n \alpha_i a_i = \sum_{i=1}^n \alpha_i(x^0 + v_i) = \left(\sum_{i=1}^n \alpha_i\right) x^0 + \sum_{i=1}^n \alpha_i v_i$$

where $v_i \in V$ for all i. As V is a vector space, we have $v = \sum_{i=1}^n \alpha_i v_i \in V$. If, in addition, we have $\sum_{i=1}^n \alpha_i = 1$, then $x = x^0 + v$, and therefore $x \in A$. That is, a linear combination $\sum_{i=1}^n \alpha_i a_i$ of vectors in an affine subspace of A belongs to A if and only if $\sum_{i=1}^n \alpha_i = 1$. A linear combination with this property is called an *affine combination*.

2. Linear Transformations

A function between two vector spaces is sometimes called a transformation. We now introduce an important class of transformations that, loosely speaking, preserve the algebraic structure of the set on which they are defined.

Definition 2.1. Linear transformation. Let X and Y be two vector spaces defined over the same field F. We say that a transformation $T: X \longrightarrow Y$ is linear if for all $x_1, x_2 \in X$ and any $\alpha, \beta \in F$, we have

$$T(\alpha x_1 + \beta x_2) = \alpha T(x_1) + \beta T(x_2)$$

This implies, of course, that

$$T(x_1 + x_2) = T(x_1) + T(x_2) \quad \text{and} \quad T(\alpha x_1) = \alpha T(x_1)$$

That is, given any two vectors, the image of their sum under a linear function is equal to the sum of their images, and the image of the product of a scalar and a vector is equal to the scalar times the image of the vector. It is in this sense that we can say that a linear function preserves the algebraic structure of the vector space on which it is defined.

Problem 2.2. Show that for any linear function T, we have $T(\underline{0}) = \underline{0}$.

We will denote by $L(X, Y)$ the set of all linear transformations from X to Y. This is a function space (i.e., a set whose elements are functions). However, we can still think of each linear function as a vector when we define addition and multiplication by a scalar in the usual way for functions.

Given two linear transformations $T_1, T_2 \in L(X, Y)$ and arbitrary scalars η and γ, the function $T = (\eta T_1 + \gamma T_2)$, defined by

$$T(x) = (\eta T_1 + \gamma T_2)(x) = \eta T_1(x) = \gamma T_2(x) \quad \text{for each } x \in X$$

maps X into Y. Moreover, $(\eta T_1 + \gamma T_2)$ is a linear transformation, for, given any two scalars α and β and vectors x_1 and x_2 in X, we have (using the linearity of T_1 and T_2)

$$
\begin{aligned}
T(\alpha x_1 + \beta x_2) &= (\eta T_1 + \gamma T_2)(\alpha x_1 + \beta x_2) = \eta T_1(\alpha x_1 + \beta x_2) + \gamma T_2(\alpha x_1 + \beta x_2) \\
&= \eta[\alpha T_1(x_1) + \beta T_1(x_2)] + \gamma[\alpha T_2(x_1) + \beta T_2(x_2)] \\
&= \alpha[\eta T_1(x_1) + \gamma T_2(x_1)] + \beta[\eta T_1(x_2) + \gamma T_2(x_2)] \\
&= \alpha(\eta T_1 + \gamma T_2)(x_1) + \beta(\eta T_1 + \gamma T_2)(x_2) = \alpha T(x_1) + \beta T(x_2)
\end{aligned}
$$

It follows that if $T_1, T_2 \in L(X, Y)$, then $\eta T_1 + \gamma T_2 \in L(X, Y)$. It is also obvious that the rest of the vector-space axioms are satisfied by $L(X, Y)$. For instance, the zero vector is the linear transformation that assigns to any x in X the zero vector in Y. We have, then, the following theorem.

Theorem 2.3. Lex X and Y be two vector spaces defined over the same field. The set $L(X, Y)$ of linear transformations from X to Y is a vector space.

Hence, every linear combination of linear functions is a linear function. It is also easy to see that the composition of linear functions is linear.

The *composition* of two linear functions is defined in the standard way. Let $R:X \longrightarrow Y$ and $S:Y \longrightarrow Z$ be two linear transformations. Then the composite mapping $S \circ R = T:X \longrightarrow Z$ is defined, as for any two functions, by $T(x) = S[R(x)]$.

Problem 2.4. Show that the composition of two linear functions is linear.

(a) Image and Kernel of a Linear Function

Definition 2.5. Given a linear function $T:X \longrightarrow Y$, its image (im) or range is the subset of Y given by

$$\text{im } T = T(X) = \{y \in Y;\ y = T(x) \text{ for some } x \in X\}$$

and its kernel or null space is the subset of X given by

$$\ker T = T^{-1}(\underline{0}) = \{x \in X;\ T(x) = \underline{0}\}$$

In other words, ker T is the set of solutions to the homogeneous linear system $T(x) = \underline{0}$, and im T is the set of vectors $y \in Y$ for which the system $T(x) = y$ has at least one solution. We will now show that both im T and ker T are vector spaces, and we will prove an important result that relates the dimension of these two spaces to that of the vector space X on which T is defined.

Theorem 2.6. Given a linear transformation $T:X \longrightarrow Y$, im T is a vector subspace of Y. If $X = \{x_1, \ldots, x_n\}$ is a basis for X, then $\{T(x_1), \ldots, T(x_n)\}$ spans im T.

Proof. Let y_1 and y_2 be vectors in $T(X)$. We want to show that $\alpha y_1 + \beta y_2 \in T(X)$ for any scalars α and β. Because $y_1, y_2 \in T(X)$, there exist $x_1, x_2 \in X$ such that $T(x_1) = y_1$ and $T(x_2) = y_2$. As X is a vector space, $\alpha x_1 + \beta x_2 \in X$, and by the linearity of T,

$$T(\alpha x_1 + \beta x_2) = \alpha T(x_1) + \beta T(x_2) = \alpha y_1 + \beta y_2$$

Hence, $\alpha y_1 + \beta x_2 \in T(X)$, and therefore $T(X)$ is a vector subspace of Y.

Consider an arbitrary vector $y = T(x)$ in $T(X)$, and let $\mathbf{x} = \{x_1, \ldots, x_n\}$ be a basis for X. Then $x \in X$ has a unique representation of the form $x = \sum_{i=1}^n \alpha_i x_i$. Using the linearity of T, we have

$$y = T(x) = T\left(\sum_{i=1}^n \alpha_i x_i\right) = \sum_{i=1}^n \alpha_i T(x_i)$$

Hence, any $T(x) \in \operatorname{im} T$ can be written as a linear combination of the images of the elements of a basis of X. $\qquad\square$

The *rank* of a family of vectors $\mathbf{v} = \{v_1, \ldots, v_n\}$ in a vector space V is the size of the largest independent family of vectors contained in $\mathbf{v}$. If there are r independent vectors in $\mathbf{v}$, they span a vector space of dimension r. Hence, the rank of $\{v_1, \ldots, v_n\}$ is also the dimension of the vector subspace formed by all the linear combinations of the vectors in $\mathbf{v}$.

Given a linear transformation $T: X \longrightarrow Y$ and a basis for X, $\{x_1, \ldots, x_n\}$, the rank of T is the dimension of its image space, $\operatorname{im} T$. By Theorem 2.6, the *rank* of T is equal to the number of linearly independent vectors in $\{T(x_1), \ldots, T(x_n)\}$.

Theorem 2.7. Given a linear transformation $T: X \longrightarrow Y$, *ker* T *is a vector subspace of* X.

Problem 2.8. Prove Theorem 2.7.

We conclude this section with a theorem which shows that there is a simple relationship among the dimensions of im T, ker T, and X (the space on which T is defined). In a later section we will consider the implications of this result for the dimension of the space of solutions to a system of linear equations.

Theorem 2.9. Let X *be a finite-dimensional vector space, and* $T: X \longrightarrow Y$ *a linear transformation. Then* $\dim X = \dim(\ker T) + \operatorname{rank} T$.

Proof. Put $\dim X = n$, $\dim(\ker T) = k$, and $\operatorname{rank} T = \dim(\operatorname{im} T) = r$. The theorem says, then, that $n = k + r$. Let $\{w_1, \ldots, w_r\}$ be a basis for im T, and $\{u_1, \ldots, u_k\}$ a basis for ker T (if the kernel is not equal to $\{\underline{0}\}$). Now, $w_i \in T(X)$, and therefore for each w_i there exists some $v_i \in X$ such that $T(v_i) = w_i$. We will show that

$$\mathbb{b} = \{v_1, \ldots, v_r;\ u_1, \ldots, u_k\}$$

is a basis for X, which establishes the theorem.

- First we show that $\mathbb{b}$ generates X. Let x be an arbitrary vector in X. Because $\{w_1, \ldots, w_r\}$ is a basis for $T(X)$, there exist unique scalars $\alpha_1, \ldots, \alpha_r$ such that

$$T(x) = \sum_{i=1}^{r} \alpha_i w_i = \sum_{i=1}^{r} \alpha_i T(v_i)$$

By the linearity of T,

$$T(x) = T\left(\sum_{i=1}^{r} \alpha_i v_i\right)$$

and, again by linearity, subtracting the right- from the left-hand side in the preceding expression,

$$T\left(x - \sum_{i=1}^{r} \alpha_i v_i\right) = \underline{0}$$

Thus, $x - \sum_{i=1}^{r} \alpha_i v_i \in \ker T$, and because $\{u_1, \ldots, u_k\}$ is a basis for $\ker T$, there exist scalars $\beta_1, \ldots, \beta_k$ such that

$$x - \sum_{i=1}^{r} \alpha_i v_i = \sum_{m=1}^{k} \beta_m u_m \Rightarrow x = \sum_{i=1}^{r} \alpha_i v_i + \sum_{m=1}^{k} \beta_m u_m$$

In conclusion, any x in X has a representation as a linear combination of elements of $\mathbb{b}$; hence $\mathbb{b}$ spans X.

- To prove that $\mathbb{b}$ is a basis for X, it remains to show that it is a linearly independent family. Whether or not that is the case, there exist scalars γ_i ($i = 1, \ldots, r$) and η_m ($m = 1, \ldots, k$) such that

$$\sum_{i=1}^{r} \gamma_i v_i + \sum_{m=1}^{k} \eta_m u_m = \underline{0} \tag{1}$$

What we want to show is that they must all be zero.

Applying T to both sides of (1), we have

$$T\left(\sum_{i=1}^{r} \gamma_i v_i + \sum_{m=1}^{k} \eta_m u_m\right) = \sum_{i=1}^{r} \gamma_i \, T(v_i) + \sum_{m=1}^{k} \eta_m \, T(u_m) = \underline{0} \tag{2}$$

Now, $u_m \in \ker T$, implying $T(u_m) = \underline{0}$ for all m, leaving us with

$$\sum_{i=1}^{r} \gamma_i \, T(v_i) = \sum_{i=1}^{r} \gamma_i \, w_i = \underline{0} \tag{3}$$

But the w_i's are linearly independent by assumption, so $\gamma_i = 0$ for all i, and (1) reduces to

$$\sum_{m=1}^{k} \eta_m u_m = \underline{0} \tag{4}$$

Finally, the u_m's are also linearly independent by assumption. Hence, $\eta_m = 0$ for all m, and we conclude that $\mathbb{b} = \{v_1, \ldots, v_r; u_1, \ldots, u_k\}$ is a linearly independent family. $\qquad\square$

(b) Inverse of a Linear Transformation

Definition 2.10. Inverse of a linear mapping. Let $T:X \longrightarrow Y$ be a linear mapping. We say that T is invertible if there exists a mapping S from Y to X such that

$$\forall x \in X,\ S[T(x)] = x \Leftrightarrow S \circ T = I_x \quad \text{and}$$
$$\forall y \in Y,\ T[S(y)] = y \Leftrightarrow T \circ S = I_y$$

where I_x and I_y are the identity mappings in X and Y, respectively (i.e., the functions that map each element in the corresponding space into itself).

The transformation S is called the inverse of T and is denoted T^{-1}. Clearly, if T^{-1} is the inverse of T, then T is the inverse of T^{-1}, and the relationships in the definition can be written

$$T^{-1}[T(x)] = x \quad \text{and} \quad T[T^{-1}(y)] = y$$

The following theorem shows that the inverse of a linear transformation is also a linear transformation.

Theorem 2.11. Let $T \in L(X, Y)$ *be an invertible linear function. Then the inverse map* $T^{-1}:Y \longrightarrow X$ *is linear; that is,* $T^{-1} \in L(Y, X)$.

Problem 2.12. Prove Theorem 2.11.

Recall that a transformation $T:X \longrightarrow Y$ is said to be injective or one-to-one if it does not map distinct elements of X into the same vector in Y, that is, T is one-to-one if

$$\forall x, x' \in X,\ x \neq x' \Rightarrow T(x) \neq T(x')$$

T is said to be surjective or "onto" if $T(X) = Y$ (i.e., if its range is the entire set Y).

Clearly, a linear transformation $T:X \longrightarrow Y$ is invertible if and only if it is both injective and surjective, for the inverse mapping is a well-defined function if and only if for each y in Y there exists a unique x in X such that $T(x) = y$.

We conclude with a useful necessary and sufficient condition for a linear mapping to be one-to-one.

Theorem 2.13. A linear transformation $T:X \longrightarrow Y$ *is one-to-one if and only if* $T(x) = \underline{0} \Rightarrow x = \underline{0}$, *that is, if ker* $T = \{\underline{0}\}$.

Problem 2.14. Prove Theorem 2.13. Hint: Recall that for any linear mapping T, we have $T(\underline{0}) = \underline{0}$.

3. Isomorphisms

We will now show that two vector spaces of the same dimension are "equivalent" from an algebraic point of view. Two particular cases of this result are of special interest in practice:

(i) Every vector space of finite dimension n defined over a field F, is equivalent to the space $V_n(F)$ defined in Example 1.3.
(ii) If X and Y are vector spaces defined over a field F, of finite dimensions n and m, respectively, the vector space of linear transformations from X to Y, $L(X, Y)$, is "equivalent" to the set of matrices of dimension $m \times n$ formed with elements of F.

Before getting into details, we need to make precise the notion of "equivalent" vector spaces.

Definition 3.1. Isomorphism and isomorphic vector spaces. Two vector spaces X and Y are isomorphic if there exists an invertible linear function (one-to-one and onto) from X to Y. A function with these properties is called an isomorphism.

Two isomorphic vector spaces are practically the same for algebraic purposes, for there exists an invertible function from X to Y that preserves algebraic operations in both directions. In particular, if T is an isomorphism from X onto Y, given any two vectors x_1 and x_2 in X, there exist unique vectors y_1 and y_2 in Y such that $y_1 = T(x_1)$ and $y_2 = T(x_2)$, and, vice versa, given any y_1, $y_2 \in Y$, there exist unique elements of X, x_1 and x_2, such that $x_1 = T^{-1}(y_1)$ and $x_2 = T^{-1}(y_2)$. Because both T and T^{-1} are linear functions, we have, moreover,

$$T(\alpha x_1 + \beta x_2) = \alpha T(x_1) + \beta T(x_2) = \alpha y_1 + \beta y_2$$
$$T^{-1}(\alpha y_1 + \beta y_2) = \alpha T^{-1}(y_1) + \beta T^{-1}(y_2) = \alpha x_1 + \beta x_2$$

and therefore $x = \alpha x_1 + \beta x_2$ if and only if $T(x) = y = \alpha y_1 + \beta y_2$.
We begin with a preliminary result.

Theorem 3.2. Let X *and* Y *be two vector spaces defined over the same field* F, *and let* x $= \{x_s \in$ X$; s \in$ S$\}$ *be a Hamel basis for* X. *Then a linear transformation* T$:$X $\longrightarrow$ Y *is completely defined by its value on* x, *that is:*

(i) *Given an arbitrary family* y $= \{y_s \in$ Y$; s \in$ S$\}$ *in* Y *with the same cardinal number as* x, *there exists a linear transformation* T $:$ X $\longrightarrow$ Y *such that* T$(x_s) = $ y_s *for each* s.

(ii) This transformation is unique. That is, if two linear transformations from X to Y, T and R, coincide in x (*i.e.,* $T(x_s) = R(x_s) \; \forall \; s \in S$), then they coincide for all $x \in X$.

Proof

- Let $x = \{x_s \in X; s \in S\}$ be a Hamel basis for X, and $y = \{y_s \in Y; s \in S\}$ a family of vectors in Y with the same cardinality as x. We define the function T from x onto y by

$$T(x_s) = y_s \; \forall \; s \in S$$

and extend it to the whole of X in the following way: Given an arbitrary $x \in X$ with representation

$$x = \sum_{s \in S'} \alpha_x x_s$$

(where the α_s's are scalars and S' is a finite subset of S), we define

$$T(x) = \sum_{s \in S'} \alpha_s T(x_s) = \sum_{s \in S'} \alpha_s y_s$$

The function $T : X \longrightarrow Y$ thus defined is linear. Given two vectors $x, y \in X$, with representations[1]

$$x = \sum_{s \in S'} \alpha_s x_s \quad \text{and} \quad y = \sum_{s \in S'} \beta_s x_s$$

and any two scalars δ and γ, we have

$$T(\gamma x + \delta y) = T\left(\gamma \sum_{s \in S'} \alpha_s x_s + \delta \sum_{s \in S'} \beta_s x_s\right) = T\left(\sum_{s \in S'} (\gamma \alpha_s + \delta \beta_s) x_s\right)$$
$$= \sum_{s \in S'} (\gamma \alpha_s + \delta \beta_s) T(x_s) = \gamma \sum_{s \in S'} \alpha_s T(x_s) + \delta \sum_{s \in S'} \beta_s T(x_s)$$
$$= \gamma T(x) + \delta T(y)$$

- Suppose R and T are two linear transformations such that

$$T(x_s) = R(x_s) \; \forall \; s \in S$$

Given an arbitrary $x \in X$, with representation $x = \Sigma_{s \in S'} \alpha_s x_s$, we have, using the linearity of T and S,

$$T(x) = \sum_{s \in S'} \alpha_s T(x_s) = \sum_{s \in S'} \alpha_s R(x_s) = R(x) \qquad \square$$

Theorem 3.3. *Two vector spaces* X *and* Y *defined over the same field are isomorphic if and only if they have the same dimension.*

Proof

- Assume T is an isomorphism from X onto Y, and let $x = \{x_s \in X; s \in S\}$ be a Hamel basis for X. We will prove that X and Y have the same dimension by showing that $T(x) = \{T(x_s) \in Y; x_s \in x\}$ is a Hamel basis for Y.

For any finite subset S' of S, we have

$$\sum_{s \in S'} \alpha_s T(x_s) = \underline{0} \Rightarrow T\left(\sum_{s \in S'} \alpha_s x_s\right) = \underline{0}$$

by the linearity of T, and given that T is invertible and therefore one-to-one and that $T(\underline{0}) = \underline{0}$, $T(x) = \underline{0}$ implies $x = \underline{0}$; hence $\sum_{s \in S'} \alpha_s x_s = \underline{0}$, and by the assumption that x is a linearly independent family,

$$\sum_{s \in S'} \alpha_s x_s = \underline{0} \Rightarrow \alpha_s = 0 \ \forall \ s \in S'$$

implying that $T(x) = \{T(x_s) \in Y; x_s \in x\}$ is a linearly independent family of vectors in Y.

Next, we show that $T(x)$ spans Y. Let y be an arbitrary vector in Y. Because T maps X onto Y, there exists some $x \in X$ such that $T(x) = y$. The vector x has a representation of the form

$$x = \sum_{s \in S'} \alpha_s x_s$$

where S' is a finite subset of S. By the linearity of T, we can write y as

$$y = T(x) = T\left(\sum_{s \in S'} \alpha_s x_s\right) = \sum_{s \in S'} \alpha_s T(x_s)$$

and it follows that every $y \in Y$ can be written as a linear combination of a finite number of elements of $T(x)$, which is therefore a Hamel basis for Y.

• Conversely, suppose that X and Y have the same dimension, and let $x = \{x_s \in X; s \in S\}$ and $y = \{y_s \in Y; s \in S\}$ be Hamel bases for the two spaces.[2] Define the function T from x onto y by $T(x_s) = y_s$ for each $x_s \in x$, and by $T(x) = \sum_{s \in S'} \alpha_s T(x_s)$ for an arbitrary $x = \sum_{s \in S'} \alpha_s x_s$ in X. By the preceding theorem, this function is linear, so we only have to establish its invertibility.

Suppose two vectors $x' = \sum_{s \in S'} \alpha_s x_s$ and $x'' = \sum_{s \in S'} \beta_s x_s$ have the same image under T. Then

$$T(x') = T(x') \Rightarrow \sum_{s \in S'} \alpha_s T(x_s) = \sum_{s \in S'} \beta_s T(x_s) \Rightarrow \sum_{s \in S'} (\alpha_s - \beta_s) y_s = \underline{0}$$

from which $\alpha_s - \beta_s = 0$ for all $s \in S'$, by the linear independence of the family y. Hence, $T(x') = T(x'')$ implies $x' = x''$, and T is one-to-one. Finally, we know that $T(X)$ is a vector subspace of Y spanned by $T(x)$ (Theorem 2.6). Because $T(x) = y$, which is a Hamel basis for Y, we have $T(X) = Y$, that is, T maps X onto Y. In conclusion, T is an isomorphism. $\square$

Let X be a vector space of finite dimension n defined over a field F. The simplest n-dimensional vector space defined over F is $V_n(F)$. The preceding result assures us that X and $V_n(F)$ are isomorphic. We will now verify directly that this is true. Along the way we will see what the isomorphism looks like and introduce the concept of coordinates.

If X is an n-dimensional vector space, then it has a basis formed by n vectors, $v = \{v_1, \ldots, v_n\}$, and every $x \in X$ has a unique representation as a linear combination of the elements of v; that is, there exist unique scalars $\alpha_1, \ldots, \alpha_n$ such that

$$x = \sum_{i=1}^{n} \alpha_i v_i$$

We say that α_i is the ith *coordinate* of x in basis v. We can now define a function, $\mathrm{crd}_v : X \to V_n(F)$, that assigns to each $x \in X$ its vector of coordinates in basis v:

$$\mathrm{crd}_v(x) = \underline{\alpha} = (\alpha_1, \ldots, \alpha_n)$$

The function crd_v is one-to-one because two vectors are equal if and only if they have the same coordinates, and it is onto because, given any $\underline{\alpha} = (\alpha_1, \ldots, \alpha_n)$ in $V_n(F)$, the linear combination $\sum_{i=1}^{n} \alpha_i v_i$ is a vector in X. Finally, crd_v is a linear function because, given arbitrary vectors $x, y \in X$, with coordinates $\underline{\alpha}$ and $\underline{\beta}$, respectively, and scalars γ and η, we have

$$\gamma x + \eta y = \gamma \left(\sum_{i=1}^{n} \alpha_i v_i \right) + \eta \left(\sum_{i=1}^{n} \beta_i v_i \right) = \sum_{i=1}^{n} (\gamma \alpha_i + \eta \beta_i) v_i$$

and therefore

$$\mathrm{crd}_v(\gamma x + \eta y) = \gamma \underline{\alpha} + \eta \underline{\beta} = \gamma \, \mathrm{crd}_v(x) + \eta \, \mathrm{cdr}_v(\dot{y})$$

We have proved the following theorem.

Theorem 3.4. *Every vector space of dimension* $n < \infty$ *defined over a field* F *is isomorphic to* $V_n(F)$.

Matrix Representation of a Linear Function

We have seen that the set $L(X, Y)$ of linear transformations between vector spaces is itself a vector space. We have also seen that the space $F_{m \times n}$ of $m \times n$ matrices defined over a field F is also a vector space. It is easy to show that if M is a matrix in $F_{m \times n}$, the function $L_M : V_n(F) \longrightarrow V_m(F)$, defined for all x in $V_n(F)$ by $L_M(x) = Mx$, is linear. We will now prove the converse result: With every linear transformation T between finite-dimensional vector spaces we can associate a matrix that, given bases for X and Y, represents T in a natural sense and is unique. We will also see that the function $Mtx_{w,v} : L(X, Y) \longrightarrow F_{m \times n}$ that assigns to a linear transformation in $L(X, Y)$ its matrix representation, given bases v and w for X and Y, respectively, is an isomorphism. This implies that, for many purposes, the theory of linear mappings between finite-dimensional spaces reduces to the study of matrices.

Let $T: X \longrightarrow Y$ be a linear transformation between finite-dimensional vector spaces (dim $X = n$, dim $Y = m$) defined over a field F. We fix bases $\mathbb{v} = \{v_1, \ldots, v_n\}$ for X and $\mathbb{w} = \{w_1, \ldots, w_m\}$ for Y and form the matrix M_T, with

$$\mathrm{col}_i(M_T) = \mathrm{crd}_\mathbb{w}(T(v_i))$$

Let x be a vector in X, with $\mathrm{crd}_\mathbb{v}(x) = \underline{\alpha}$. Using the linearity of $\mathrm{crd}(\ )$ and T, we have

$$M_T \mathrm{crd}_\mathbb{v}(x) = [\mathrm{crd}_\mathbb{w}(T(v_1)), \ldots, \mathrm{crd}_\mathbb{w}(T(v_n))]\begin{bmatrix} \alpha_1 \\ \cdots \\ \alpha_n \end{bmatrix} = \sum_{i=1}^n \alpha_i \mathrm{crd}_\mathbb{w}(T(v_i))$$

$$= \mathrm{crd}_\mathbb{w}\left(\sum_{i=1}^n \alpha_i T(v_i)\right) = \mathrm{crd}_\mathbb{w}\left(T\left(\sum_{i=1}^n \alpha_i v_i\right)\right) = \mathrm{crd}_\mathbb{w}(T(x))$$

Hence, the matrix M_T is such that for each x in X,

$$\mathrm{crd}_\mathbb{w}(T(x)) = M_T \mathrm{crd}_\mathbb{v}(x)$$

That is, given bases for X and Y, the (coordinate vector in basis $\mathbb{w}$ of the) image of x under T is simply the product of the matrix M_T and (the coordinate vector in basis $\mathbb{v}$ of) the vector x. Thus, we say that M_T is the matrix representation of T given bases $\mathbb{v}$ and $\mathbb{w}$ for X and Y, respectively.

We now define a function $Mtx_{\mathbb{w},\mathbb{v}} : L(X, Y) \longrightarrow F_{m \times n}$ by

$$Mtx_{\mathbb{w},\mathbb{v}}(T) = M_T \text{ s.th. } \mathrm{col}_i(M_T) = \mathrm{crd}_\mathbb{w}(T(v_i))$$

where v_i is the ith element of $\mathbb{v}$ (a basis for X).

It is easy to see that $Mtx_{\mathbb{w},\mathbb{v}}(T)$ is a linear function. Let S and T be two linear transformations, and M_T and M_S their matrix representations. For each $x \in X$ we have, then,

$$\mathrm{crd}_\mathbb{w}(T(x)) = M_T \mathrm{crd}_\mathbb{v}(x) \quad \text{and} \quad \mathrm{crd}_\mathbb{w}(S(x)) = M_S \mathrm{crd}_\mathbb{v}(x) \tag{1}$$

Using the linearity of $\mathrm{crd}(\ )$ and (1),

$$\mathrm{crd}_\mathbb{w}((\alpha T + \beta S)(x)) = \mathrm{crd}_\mathbb{w}(\alpha T(x) + \beta S(x)) = \alpha\, \mathrm{crd}_\mathbb{w}(T(x)) + \beta\, \mathrm{crd}_\mathbb{w}(S(x))$$
$$= \alpha M_T \mathrm{crd}_\mathbb{v}(x) + \beta M_S \mathrm{crd}_\mathbb{v}(x) = (\alpha M_T + \beta M_S)\mathrm{crd}_\mathbb{v}(x)$$

which shows that $\alpha M_T + \beta M_S$ is the matrix representation of $\alpha T + \beta S$ for the given bases; that is,

$$Mtx_{\mathbb{w},\mathbb{v}}(\alpha T + \beta S) = \alpha Mtx_{\mathbb{w},\mathbb{v}}(T) + \beta Mtx_{\mathbb{w},\mathbb{v}}(S)$$

Two linear transformations S and T have the same matrix representation if and only if they coincide in $\mathbb{v}$, that is, $S(v_i) = T(v_i)$ for all $v_i \in \mathbb{v}$. But then $S = T$ (Theorem 3.2), so $Mtx_{\mathbb{w},\mathbb{v}} T = Mtx_{\mathbb{w},\mathbb{v}} S$ implies $S = T$, and therefore Mtx is one-to-one. Finally, given an arbitrary matrix $M \in F_{m \times n}$ and bases $\mathbb{v} = \{v_1, \dots, v_n\}$ for X and $\mathbb{w} = \{w_1, \dots, w_m\}$ for Y, there exists a linear transformation L_M from X to Y such that $crd_{\mathbb{w}}(L_M(v_i)) = col_i(M)$ (Theorem 3.2). Hence, with each matrix in $F_{m \times n}$ we can associate a linear function from X to Y; that is, Mtx maps $F_{m \times n}$ onto $L(X, Y)$. In conclusion, we have the following theorem.

Theorem 3.5. Let X *and* Y *be vector spaces defined over the same field* F, *with dimensions* n *and* m, *respectively (both finite). Then* L(X, Y) *is isomorphic to* $F_{m \times n}$.

4. Linear Mappings between Normed Spaces

We now consider linear transformations between normed linear spaces. As may be expected, the algebraic properties of linear maps simplify the study of their continuity. Our first result says that a linear function is either always continuous or always discontinuous. Hence, to check its global continuity, it is sufficient to check local continuity at some convenient point, usually the zero vector. The reason for this is that given a linear transformation $T: X \longrightarrow Y$ and two points x and $y \in X$, linearity implies that $T(x) - T(y) = T(x - y)$. It follows that if X and Y are normed spaces, the distance between $T(x)$ and $T(y)$ depends only on the distance between x and y, not on the locations of these points.

Theorem 4.1. Let X *and* Y *be normed vector spaces, and* T *a linear mapping* X $\longrightarrow$ Y. *If* T *is continuous at some point* $x' \in$ X, *then it is (uniformly) continuous everywhere on* X.

Proof. Suppose T is continuous at some $x' \in X$, and fix some $\varepsilon > 0$. By continuity at x', there exists some $\delta > 0$ such that

$$\|T(y') - T(x')\| < \varepsilon \; \forall \; y' \in B_\delta(x')$$

Now consider some other point $x'' = x' + \Delta \in X$. Then $y'' = y' + \Delta \in B_\delta(x'')$ if and only if $y' \in B_\delta(x')$ and

$$T(y'') - T(x'') = T(y' + \Delta) - T(x' + \Delta) = T(y' - x') = T(y') - T(x')$$

Hence, for any $y'' \in B_\delta(x'')$ we have $\|T(y'') - T(x'')\| < \varepsilon$, and we conclude that T is continuous at x''.

Note that for give ε, the same δ will work everywhere. Hence, a continuous linear function is uniformly continuous.   □

We shall now establish a useful characterization of continuity for linear functions.

Definition 4.2. Bounded linear transformation. Let T be a linear transformation between two normed linear spaces, X and Y. We say that T is bounded if there exists some real number B such that

$$\forall x \in X, \|Tx\| \leq B\|x\|$$

that is, if T maps bounded sets in X into bounded sets in Y.

For linear functions, boundedness turns out to be equivalent to continuity.

Theorem 4.3. Let X and Y be normed vector spaces. A linear function $T : X \longrightarrow Y$ is continuous if and only if it is bounded.

Proof

- First, we show that a bounded mapping is continuous at $\underline{0}$ and therefore everywhere. If T is bounded, then there exists some $B > 0$ such that $\|Tx\| \leq B\|x\|$ for all $x \in X$. Fix an arbitrary $\varepsilon > 0$, and put $\delta = \varepsilon/B$ in the definition of continuity. Then, for any x with $\|x\| < \delta$, we have

$$\|Tx\| \leq B\|x\| < B\delta = \varepsilon$$

- To prove the second part of the theorem, we will show that if T is not bounded, then it cannot be continuous. If T is not bounded, then for each $n \in \mathbb{N}$ we can find some $x_n \in X$ such that

$$\|Tx_n\| > n\|x_n\|$$

By the linearity of T and the defining properties of the norm, this implies

$$\frac{1}{n\|x_n\|}\|T(x_n)\| = \left\|\frac{1}{n\|x_n\|}T(x_n)\right\| = \left\|T\left(\frac{x_n}{n\|x_n\|}\right)\right\| > 1$$

Now, the normalized vectors $x_n/\|x_n\|$ all have norm 1, implying that the sequence $\{x_n/(n\|x_n\|)\}$ converges to $\underline{0}$. By the preceding expression, however, the sequence $\{T(x_n/(n\|x_n\|))\}$ does not converge to $T(\underline{0}) = \underline{0}$, implying that T is not continuous. $\square$

The second part of the proof suggests a method for establishing that a given linear function T is discontinuous: We can try to find a sequence $\{x_n\}$ converging to $\underline{0}$, with $\{T(x_n)\} \nrightarrow \underline{0}$.

Problem 4.4. We will prove the following theorem: Given normed linear spaces X and Y and a linear function $T : X \longrightarrow Y$, the inverse function T^{-1}

exists and is a continuous linear mapping on $T(X)$ if and only if there exists some $m > 0$ such that $m\|x\| \leq \|Tx\|$.

(i) Using Theorem 2.13, show that if there exists some $m > 0$ such that $m\|x\| \leq \|Tx\|$, then T is one-to-one (and therefore invertible on $T(X)$).
(ii) Use Theorem 4.3 to show that T^{-1} is continuous on $T(X)$.
(iii) Using Theorem 4.3, show that if T^{-1} is continuous on $T(X)$, then there exists some $m > 0$ such that $m\|x\| \leq \|Tx\|$.

Theorem 4.5. A linear function from a finite-dimensional normed vector space into a normed vector space is continuous.

Proof. Let T be a linear function from a finite-dimensional normed vector space X, with basis $v = \{v_1, \ldots, v_m\}$, into a normed vector space Y. We will prove that T is continuous at $\underline{0}$ by showing that given any sequence $\{x_n\}$ of vectors in X with limit $\underline{0}$, the image sequence $\{Tx_n\}$ converges to $T(\underline{0}) = \underline{0}$ in Y. Each x_n has a representation of the form

$$x_n = \sum_{i=1}^{m} \alpha_i^n v_i$$

where α_i^n is a scalar. We know that in any finite-dimensional normed linear space, convergence is equivalent to coordinate-wise convergence, that is, $\{x_n\} \to \underline{0}$ if and only if $\{\alpha_i^n\} \to 0$ for all $i = 1, \ldots, m$ (see Problem 1.8). Now, for each n we have

$$0 \leq \|T(x_n)\| = \left\| T\left(\sum_{i=1}^{m} \alpha_i^n v_i \right) \right\| = \left\| \sum_{i=1}^{m} \alpha_i^n T(v_i) \right\| \leq \sum_{i=1}^{m} |\alpha_i^n| \|T(v_i)\|$$

And because $|\alpha_i^n| \to 0$ for all i, we have $\|T(x_n)\| \to 0$ or, equivalently, $\{Tx_n\} \to \underline{0}$. $\qquad\square$

(a) Linear Homeomorphisms

Given normed linear spaces X and Y, a linear mapping $T : X \longrightarrow Y$ is a topological isomorphism (or linear homeomorphism) if it is also a homeomorphism, that is, if it is continuous and invertible and has a continuous inverse. If there exists such a mapping between X and Y, we say that these two spaces are topologically isomorphic.

A linear homeomorphism is both a homeomorphism and an isomorphism. Hence, topologically isomorphic spaces are "equivalent" both in a topological sense and in an algebraic sense, because the mapping preserves closed and open sets and the convergence of sequences, as well as algebraic operations in both directions.

Given an m-dimensional normed linear space X defined over $\mathbb{R}$ with basis v, we have seen that the coordinate mapping $\mathrm{crd}_v : X \to \mathbb{R}^m$ that assigns to each $x \in X$ its vector of coordinates in basis v is an isomorphism (i.e., a linear and invertible function). Because X and $V_n(F)$ are finite-dimensional spaces, both the coordinate mapping and its inverse are continuous. It follows that crd_v is a linear homeomorphism, and we have the following theorem.

Theorem 4.6. All m-dimensional normed linear spaces over $\mathbb{R}$ are topologically isomorphic to $\mathrm{E}^m = (\mathbb{R}^m, \|\cdot\|_E)$.

Hence, for most purposes, the study of finite-dimensional vector spaces reduces to the study of $\mathbb{R}^m$.

(b) The Norm of a Linear Mapping

Let X and Y be two vector spaces. We have seen that the set $L(X, Y)$ of linear transformations from X to Y is a vector space. If X and Y are normed spaces, it seems natural to ask whether or not we can define a norm over $L(X, Y)$, that is, whether or not we can make $L(X, Y)$ into a normed space. While there is no "natural" way to define the "size" of a mapping, we can try defining the *norm* of a linear transformation T in terms of what it does to the norm of vectors. Thus, we write

$$\|T\| = \sup\left\{ \frac{\|T(x)\|}{\|x\|}; \ x \in X \text{ and } x \neq \underline{0} \right\} \tag{1}$$

Note that the symbol $\|\cdot\|$ has three different meanings in this expression: $\|x\|$ is the norm of a vector in X, $\|T(x)\|$ is the norm of a vector in Y, and $\|T\|$ is the "norm" (we still have to prove that it is really a norm) of a linear mapping. Intuitively, the ratio $\|T(x)\|/\|x\|$ tells us by how much the application of T to a vector x will increase or decrease its length, and we define the norm of T as the largest such ratio we can find.

To make sure that the supremum in (1) exists, we have to restrict $\|\cdot\|$ to a subset of $L(X, Y)$. Recall that a linear function T is bounded if there exists some $B > 0$ such that $\|Tx\| \leq B\|x\|$ for all x. If T is bounded, the smallest such B is its norm. Hence, we will define $\|\cdot\|$ on the set $B(X, Y)$ of bounded (i.e., continuous) linear functions from X to Y.

From the definition of $\|\cdot\|$, we see immediately that for any T in $B(X, Y)$ and any vector x in X, we have

$$\|T\| \geq \frac{\|Tx\|}{\|x\|} \Rightarrow \|Tx\| \leq \|T\|\|x\| \tag{2}$$

Theorem 4.7. Let $T: X \longrightarrow Y$ *be a bounded linear mapping, and* x *an arbitrary vector in* X. *Then* $\|T(x)\| \le \|T\| \, \|x\|$.

Using the defining properties of the norm (in Y) and the linearity of T, we see that

$$\frac{1}{\|x\|}\|T(x)\| = \left\|\frac{1}{\|x\|}T(x)\right\| = \left\|T\left(\frac{x}{\|x\|}\right)\right\|$$

Hence, we can write (note that $x/\|x\|$ has norm 1)

$$\|T\| = \sup\left\{\frac{\|Tx\|}{\|x\|}; \; x \in X, \; x \ne \underline{0}\right\} = \sup\{\|Tx\|; \; x \in X, \; \|x\| = 1\}$$
$$= {}^3\sup\{\|Tx\|; \; x \in X, \; \|x\| \le 1\}$$

We want to show that $(B(X, Y), \|\cdot\|)$ is a normed vector space. The first part of the proof is immediate: Because any linear combination of continuous linear functions is linear and continuous, $B(X, Y)$ is a vector subspace of $L(X, Y)$. It remains only to show that $\|\cdot\|$ is a norm in $B(X, Y)$. Clearly, $\|T\| \ge 0$ for any $T \in B(X, Y)$, because it is defined as the supremum of a set of nonnegative numbers. Moreover, for any scalar α,

$$\|\alpha T\| = \sup\{\|\alpha T(x)\|; \; \|x\| = 1\} = \sup\{|\alpha|\|T(x)\|; \; \|x\| = 1\}$$
$$= |\alpha|\sup\{\|T(x)\|; \; \|x\| = 1\} = |\alpha|\|T\|$$

Next, we check that the triangle inequality holds. For any T_1 and T_2 in $B(X, Y)$,

$$\|T_1 + T_2\| = \sup\{\|T_1(x) + T_2(x)\|; \; \|x\| = 1\} \le \sup\{\|T_1(x)\| + \|T_2(x)\|; \; \|x\| = 1\}$$
$$\le \sup\{\|T_1(x)\|; \; \|x\| = 1\} + \sup\{\|T_2(x)\|; \; \|x\| = 1\} = \|T_1\| + \|T_2\|$$

Finally, suppose $\|T\| = 0$; by (2), we have

$$\|T(x)\| \le \|T\| \, \|x\| = 0 \quad \text{for any } x$$

and so $T(x) = \underline{0}$ for all x. Thus $\|T\| = 0$ only for the function T_0 that maps every x in X into the zero element of Y – that is, for the zero vector in $L(X, Y)$. With this, we have verified that $\|\cdot\|$ satisfies all the defining properties of a norm, proving the following result:

Theorem 4.8. Let X *and* Y *be normed vector spaces. Then the set* B(X, Y) *of bounded linear mappings from* X *into* Y, *with the norm defined earlier, is a normed vector space.*

Given two finite-dimensional vector spaces X and Y over $\mathbb{R}$, with bases v and w, we have seen that $L(X, Y)$ and $B(X, Y)$ coincide and that the function $Mtx_{w,v} : L(X, Y) \longrightarrow \mathbb{R}_{m \times n}$ is an isomorphism. Next, we define a norm on $\mathbb{R}_{m \times n}$ by thinking of a matrix as an mn vector and using the Euclidean norm; that is, for $A = [a_{ik}]$ with $i = 1, \ldots, m$ and $k = 1, \ldots, n$, we write

$$\|A\| = \sqrt{\sum_{i=1}^{m} \sum_{k=1}^{n} \alpha_{ik}^2}$$

Then Theorem 4.5 implies that $Mtx(\ )$ is also a homeomorphism. Hence the theory of linear transformations between finite-dimensional vector spaces reduces, for most purposes, to the study of matrices.

(c) The Normed Vector Space $\mathbf{L}(R^m, R^m)$

Because $\mathbb{R}^n$ and $\mathbb{R}^m$ (equipped with the Euclidean norm) are finite-dimensional normed vector spaces, linear transformations in $L(\mathbb{R}^n, \mathbb{R}^m)$ are continuous (Theorem 4.5) and therefore bounded (Theorem 4.3). It follows that $L(\mathbb{R}^n, \mathbb{R}^m)$, equipped with the norm defined in the preceding section, is a normed vector space. In the remainder of this section we will study some properties of this space, concentrating on some results that will be needed in connection with the development of differential calculus in the next chapter.

In general, there is no practical way to compute the norm of a linear mapping. The following result, however, gives us some useful bounds for linear transformations in $L(\mathbb{R}^n, \mathbb{R}^m)$.

Theorem 4.9. Let $T \in L(R^n, R^m)$ *be a linear mapping, with standard matrix representation (i.e., relative to the canonical bases)* $A = [a_{ik}]$, *with* $i = 1, \ldots, m$ *and* $k = 1, \ldots, n$. *Let* μ *be the absolute value of the dominant element of* A,

$$\mu = max_{ik}\{|a_{ik}|; \ i = 1, \ldots m, \ k = 1, \ldots n\} \tag{1}$$

We have, then,

$$\mu \le \|T\| \le \mu\sqrt{mn}$$

Proof

- Given the standard bases in $\mathbb{R}^n$ and $\mathbb{R}^m$, T is represented by an $m \times n$ matrix, $A = [a_{ik}]$. The image of a vector x, $T(x) \in \mathbb{R}^m$, is the vector $y = Ax$ whose ith component is given by

$$y_i = \sum_{k=1}^{n} a_{ik} x_k$$

By the Cauchy-Schwarz inequality and the definition of μ in (1), we have

$$|y_i| = \left|\sum_{k=1}^n a_{ik}x_k\right| \le \sqrt{\sum_{k=1}^n a_{ik}^2}\sqrt{\sum_{k=1}^n x_k^2} = \sqrt{\sum_{k=1}^n a_{ik}^2}\,\|x\| \le \sqrt{n\mu^2}\,\|x\| = \mu\sqrt{n}\,\|x\| \quad (2)$$

for each i. Then

$$\|T(x)\| = \|y\| = \sqrt{\sum_{i=1}^m y_i^2} \le \sqrt{mn\mu^2\|x\|^2} = \mu\sqrt{mn}\,\|x\|$$

Finally, using the definition of the norm of a linear mapping, we observe that because $\mu\sqrt{mn}$ is an upper bound of $\|T(x)\|$ for any x with $\|x\| = 1$, we have

$$\|T\| = \sup\{\|T(x)\|;\ x \in \mathbb{R}^n,\ \|x\| = 1\} \le \mu\sqrt{mn}$$

- To get the lower bound on $\|T\|$, we consider what T does to the standard coordinate vectors in $\mathbb{R}^n$. Let $e^k = (0, 0, \ldots, 1, \ldots, 0)$ be the kth unit vector (with a single 1 in the kth component, and zeros elsewhere) and observe that (with A the standard representation of T) we have

$$\sigma_k = \|T(e^k)\| = \|Ae^k\| = \|(a_{1k}, \ldots, a_{mk})\| = \sqrt{\sum_{i=1}^m a_{ik}^2}$$

Hence σ_k is the norm of the vector corresponding to the kth column of A. Let

$$\sigma = \max_k \sigma_k$$

be the norm of the largest column vector of A. Because $\|T(x)\| = \sigma$ for some unit vector e^k (with norm 1), it follows that

$$\|T\| = \sup\{\|Tx\|;\ x \in \mathbb{R}^{n\cdot},\ \|x\| = 1\} \ge \sigma \quad (3)$$

Moreover,

$$\sigma_k = \sqrt{\sum_{i=1}^n a_{ik}^2} \ge \max_i |a_{ik}|$$

and therefore

$$\sigma = \max_k \sigma_k \ge \max_k[\max_i|a_{ik}|] = \mu$$

From this last inequality and (3), we obtain

$$\mu \le \sigma \le \|T\| \qquad \square$$

Given two functions $R \in L(\mathbb{R}^n, \mathbb{R}^m)$ and $S \in L(\mathbb{R}^m, \mathbb{R}^p)$, their composition $T = S \circ R$ is a linear function in $L(\mathbb{R}^n, \mathbb{R}^p)$, by Problem 2.4. In terms of their matrix representation, the composition of two linear mappings translates into a product. (In fact, the product of two matrices is defined so as to correspond to the composition of the corresponding linear operators.) Let $A_R, A_S,$ and A_T be the standard matrices associated with $R, S,$ and T; then

$$T(x) = S[R(x)] = A_S(A_R x) = (A_S A_R)x, \quad \text{so } A_T = A_S A_R$$

Using Theorem 4.7 we can get a bound on the norm of the composition of two linear mappings in terms of their respective norms. Observe that

$$\|T(x)\| = \|S(R(x))\| \le \|S\| \|R(x)\| \le \|S\| \|R\| \|x\|$$

for any x. Hence, $\|S\| \|R\|$ is an upper bound for $\|T(x)\|$ when $\|x\| = 1$, and it follows that

$$\|T\| = \|S \circ R\| \le \|S\| \|R\|$$

We have proved the following result:

Theorem 4.10. Let $R \in L(\mathbb{R}^n, \mathbb{R}^m)$ *and* $S \in L(\mathbb{R}^m, \mathbb{R}^p)$. *Then* $T = S \circ R \in L(\mathbb{R}^n, \mathbb{R}^p)$, *and* $\|T\| = \|S \circ R\| \le \|S\| \|R\|$.

Linear Operators in $\mathbb{R}^n$

A mapping from a space X into itself is often called an *operator*. In this section we will study some properties of linear operators in $\mathbb{R}^n$. The set of all such operators will be denoted by $L(\mathbb{R}^n)$. Because $L(\mathbb{R}^n)$ is just the vector space $L(\mathbb{R}^n, \mathbb{R}^n)$, earlier results apply. Certain additional properties follow from the fact that the domain and range spaces are the same.

If a linear operator $T \in L(\mathbb{R}^n)$ is invertible, then its inverse T^{-1} is also an element of $L(\mathbb{R}^n)$. Hence

$$T \circ T^{-1} = T^{-1} \circ T = I_n \tag{1}$$

that is, each invertible operator commutes with its inverse, and their composition is the identity operator in $\mathbb{R}^n$. Moreover, because $\|I_n\| = 1$, (1) yields (using Theorem 4.10)

$$\|I_n\| = 1 = \|T^{-1} \circ T\| \le \|T\| \|T^{-1}\| \Rightarrow \|T^{-1}\| \ge \frac{1}{\|T\|}$$

so the norm of the inverse of a linear operator is (weakly) larger than the inverse of the norm of the operator itself.

Each linear operator T in $\mathbb{R}^n$ is associated with a square n-matrix A. Hence the operator T is invertible if and only if the equation $y = Ax$ can be solved for a unique value of x for any given y. From elementary linear algebra we know that this is true if and only if the determinant $|A|$ does not vanish. In that case, the matrix A is nonsingular, and the solution of the system is given by $x = A^{-1}y$. Hence, invertible operators are those that are represented by invertible matrices.

If we let y be the zero vector in $\mathbb{R}^n$ ($\underline{0}_n$), the system $Ax = \underline{0}_n$ has always the trivial solution $x = \underline{0}_n$. If $|A| \neq 0$, then the trivial solution is unique, but if the determinant vanishes, then there are other solutions, and therefore T cannot be invertible, because it maps distinct vectors into zero. Recall also the relation

$$n = \dim \ker T + \operatorname{rank} T$$

If T is invertible, then rank $T = n$, and therefore dim ker T must be zero; that is, the kernel must be a subspace of dimension zero of $\mathbb{R}^n$, and hence ker $T = \{\underline{0}_n\}$. In conclusion, we have the following result:

Theorem 4.11. A necessary and sufficient condition for a linear operator $\mathrm{T}: R^n \longrightarrow R^n$ *to be invertible is that* T *map only the zero vector into the zero vector.*

If S and T are linear operators in $\mathbb{R}^n$, their composition $S \circ T$ is also a linear operator in $\mathbb{R}^n$, by Theorem 2.11. Moreover, the composition of two invertible operators is itself invertible. To show this is so, let T and S be invertible operators, and x any vector in $\mathbb{R}^n$ other than the zero vector $\underline{0}_n$. Because T is invertible and therefore one-to-one, $x \neq \underline{0}_n$ implies $T(x) \neq \underline{0}_n$, by Theorem 2.13; and because S is invertible, this implies in turn that $S(Tx) \neq \underline{0}_n$, and it follows that $S \circ T$ is invertible, by Theorem 4.11. Moreover,

$$(S \circ T) \circ (T^{-1} \circ S^{-1}) = S \circ (T \circ T^{-1}) \circ S^{-1} = S \circ I \circ S^{-1} = S \circ S^{-1} = I$$

so $(S \circ T)^{-1} = T^{-1} \circ S^{-1}$, that is, the inverse of the composition of two linear operators is the composition of their inverses in reverse order. We have, then, the following theorem.

Theorem 4.12. Let S *and* T *be invertible operators in* $\mathrm{L}(R^n)$. *Then the composition* $\mathrm{S} \circ \mathrm{T}$ *is also an invertible operator in* $\mathrm{L}(R^n)$, *and* $(\mathrm{S} \circ \mathrm{T})^{-1} = \mathrm{T}^{-1} \circ \mathrm{S}^{-1}$.

The set of all invertible operators in $L(\mathbb{R}^n)$ is denoted by $\Omega(\mathbb{R}^n)$. Because $L(\mathbb{R}^n)$ is a normed space, the concepts of open and closed sets are defined, as is the notion of continuity for functions mapping $L(\mathbb{R}^n)$ into itself. In the remainder of this section we will show that $\Omega(\mathbb{R}^n)$ is an open subset of $L(\mathbb{R}^n)$ and that the function that assigns its inverse to each invertible linear operator in $\mathbb{R}^n$ is continuous. These results will be needed in Chapter 4 in the proof of the inverse-function theorem. We begin with a preliminary result.

Lemma 4.13. Let T *be an operator in* $\mathrm{L}(R^n)$, *and* I *the identity mapping in* R^n.

(i) If $\|T\| < 1$, *then* $(I - T)$ *is invertible, and* $\|(I - T)^{-1}\| \le 1/(1 - \|T\|)$.

(ii) If $\|I - T\| < 1$, *then* T *is invertible.*

Proof

(i) Let $x \ne \underline{0}$ be an otherwise arbitrary vector in $\mathbb{R}^n$. We will show that if $\|T\| < 1$, then $(I - T)(x) \ne \underline{0}$. By Theorem 4.11, this implies that $(I - T)$ is invertible.

First, note that for arbitrary vectors x and y,

$$\|x\| - \|y\| = \|(x - y) + y\| - \|y\| \le \|x - y\| + \|y\| - \|y\| \Rightarrow \|x - y\| \ge \|x\| - \|y\|$$

Also, recall that

$$\|T(x)\| \le \|T\|\|x\|$$

Hence we have

$$\|(I - T)(x)\| = \|x - T(x)\| \ge \|x\| - \|T(x)\| \ge \|x\|(1 - \|T\|) > 0 \tag{1}$$

because $\|T\| < 1$ by assumption. Hence, $\|(I - T)(x)\| \ne 0$, and it follows that $(I - T)$ is invertible.

To get the bound on the norm of $(I - T)^{-1}$, replace x in (1) by $(I - T)^{-1}(y)$, where y is an arbitrary vector in $\mathbb{R}^n$. The left-hand side of this expression then becomes

$$\left\|(I - T) \circ (I - T)^{-1}(y)\right\| = \|I(y)\| = \|y\|$$

Hence, (1) yields

$$\|y\| \ge \left\|(I - T)^{-1}(y)\right\|(1 - \|T\|)$$

from which

$$\left\|(I - T)^{-1}(y)\right\| \le \frac{\|y\|}{1 - \|T\|}$$

Hence, $1/(1 - \|T\|)$ is an upper bound of $\|(I - T)^{-1}(y)\|$ for any y with $\|y\| = 1$, and it follows that

$$\left\|(I - T)^{-1}\right\| \le \frac{1}{1 - \|T\|}$$

as was to be shown.

(ii) Put $S = I - T$. Because $\|S\| = \|I - T\| < 1$, $(I - S)$ is invertible, by (i), but $I - S = I - (I - T) = T$. $\square$

Theorem 4.14. Let T *and* S *be linear operators in* $\mathbb{R}^n$. *If* T *is invertible and* S *satisfies*

$$\|T - S\| < 1/\|T^{-1}\|$$

then S *is also invertible. This implies that the set* $\Omega(\mathbb{R}^n)$ *is open in* $L(\mathbb{R}^n)$. *Moreover,*

$$\|S^{-1}\| \le \frac{\|T^{-1}\|}{1 - \|T^{-1} \circ (T - S)\|}$$

Notice that the theorem says that if T is invertible, then every operator S within an open ball with center at T and radius $1/\|T^{-1}\|$ is invertible. Hence the set of invertible operators is open. Although the reader may find it strange at first to think in these terms, the intuition should be clear. The openness of $\Omega(\mathbb{R}^n)$ means that if T is invertible, then any other linear operator S that is sufficiently close to T, in the sense that $\|S - T\|$ is "small," is also invertible. At this point, it may help to think in terms of the matrix representations of S and T: T is invertible if and only if $\det M_T \ne 0$; because the determinant is a continuous function of the entries of a matrix, any matrix M_S sufficiently similar to M_T has a nonzero determinant and is therefore invertible.

Proof. Because T is invertible, we can write

$$S = T - I \circ (T - S) = T \circ [I - T^{-1} \circ (T - S)] \tag{1}$$

By Theorem 4.10 and the assumptions of this theorem, we have

$$\|T^{-1} \circ (T - S)\| \le \|T^{-1}\| \|T - S\| < 1 \tag{2}$$

By Lemma 4.13, with $T^{-1} \circ (T - S)$ in place of T, this implies that $I - T^{-1} \circ (T - S)$ is invertible. But then (1) shows that S is the composition of two invertible operators and therefore is invertible itself, by Theorem 4.12.

Moreover, from (1) we have, by Theorem 4.12,

$$S^{-1} = [I - T^{-1} \circ (T - S)]^{-1} \circ T^{-1}$$

and hence

$$\|S^{-1}\| \le \left\| [I - T^{-1} \circ (T - S)]^{-1} \right\| \|T^{-1}\| \tag{3}$$

Using (2) and the inequality in part (i) of Lemma 4.13, with $T^{-1} \circ (T - S)$ in place of T, we have

$$\left\| [I - T^{-1} \circ (T - S)]^{-1} \right\| \le \frac{1}{1 - \|T^{-1} \circ (T - S)\|}$$

Substituting this expression into (3), we obtain the desired result:

$$\left\|S^{-1}\right\| \le \left\|\left[I - T^{-1}(T - S)\right]^{-1}\right\|\left\|T^{-1}\right\| \le \frac{\left\|T^{-1}\right\|}{1 - \left\|T^{-1} \circ (T - S)\right\|} \qquad \square$$

Thinking of an invertible operator as a point in the set $\Omega(\mathbb{R}^n)$, we can construct a function $(\ )^{-1} : \Omega(\mathbb{R}^n) \longrightarrow \Omega(\mathbb{R}^n)$ that assigns to each T in $\Omega(\mathbb{R}^n)$ its inverse T^{-1}. The next theorem tells us that this function is continuous; that is, for any $\varepsilon > 0$ we can find some $\delta > 0$ such that for S and T in $\Omega(\mathbb{R}^n)$,

$$\|S - T\| < \delta \Rightarrow \|S^{-1} - T^{-1}\| < \varepsilon$$

Intuitively, the continuity of the inversion mapping means that similar operators have similar inverses.

Theorem 4.15. The function $(\ )^{-1} : \Omega(\mathbb{R}^n) \longrightarrow \Omega(\mathbb{R}^n)$ that assigns to each invertible operator T its inverse T^{-1} is continuous.

Proof. Fix some T in $\Omega(\mathbb{R}^n)$, and observe that if we pick S so that

$$\|T - S\| < 1/\|T^{-1}\| \qquad (1)$$

then, by Theorem 4.14, S is invertible, and

$$\|S^{-1}\| \le \frac{\|T^{-1}\|}{1 - \|T^{-1} \circ (T - S)\|} \qquad (2)$$

If we strengthen (1) and require $\|T - S\| < 1/(2\|T^{-1}\|)$, then it can be seen from the proof of the preceding theorem that $\|T^{-1} \circ (T - S)\| < 1/2$, so (2), which still holds, becomes

$$\|S^{-1}\| \le \frac{\|T^{-1}\|}{1 - \|T^{-1} \circ (T - S)\|} \le 2\|T^{-1}\| \qquad (2')$$

Next, note that

$$T^{-1} \circ (T - S) \circ S^{-1} = (I - T^{-1} \circ S) \circ S^{-1} = S^{-1} - T^{-1}$$

and hence, by (2′),

$$\|S^{-1} - T^{-1}\| = \|T^{-1} \circ (T - S) \circ S^{-1}\| \le \|T^{-1}\|\|T - S\|\|S^{-1}\| < 2\|T^{-1}\|^2\|T - S\| \qquad (3)$$

Finally, fix some arbitrary $\varepsilon > 0$. If we choose

$$\delta = \frac{\varepsilon}{2\|T^{-1}\|^2}$$

then $\|S - T\| < \delta$ implies, using (3),

$$\|S^{-1} - T^{-1}\| < 2\|T^{-1}\|^2 \|T - S\| < \varepsilon$$

and we conclude that $(\ )^{-1}$ is continuous. $\qquad\qquad\qquad\qquad\qquad\qquad\quad\Box$

5. Change of Basis and Similarity

Let T be a linear mapping from a finite-dimensional vector space V into itself. We have seen that given a basis for V, the mapping T is represented by a square matrix. A change of basis, of course, yields a different matrix representation. In this section we investigate the relationships between different representations of a given linear mapping. This material will be useful in applications, as it is often convenient to change basis so as to obtain a simple representation of a given mapping.

We begin by exploring the effect of a change of basis on the coordinates of a vector. Let

$$\mathbb{a} = \{a_1, \dots, a_n\} \quad \text{and} \quad \mathbb{b} = \{b_1, \dots, b_n\}$$

be two bases for an n-dimensional vector space V. Because $\mathbb{a}$ is a basis, we can write each vector b_i of $\mathbb{b}$ as a linear combination of the elements of $\mathbb{a}$, that is, there exist scalars $q_{i1}, \dots, q_{in}$ such that

$$b_i = \sum_{k=1}^n q_{ik} a_k$$

Because this is true for each $i = 1, \dots, n$, there exists a matrix $Q = [q_{ik}]$ such that

$$\begin{bmatrix} b_i \\ \cdots \\ b_n \end{bmatrix} = \begin{bmatrix} q_{11} & \cdots & q_{1n} \\ \cdots & \cdots & \cdots \\ q_{n1} & \cdots & q_{nn} \end{bmatrix} \begin{bmatrix} a_1 \\ \cdots \\ a_n \end{bmatrix} = Q \begin{bmatrix} a_1 \\ \cdots \\ a_n \end{bmatrix} \qquad (1)$$

Next, let x be an arbitrary vector in V, with coordinate vector $\alpha = (\alpha_1, \dots, \alpha_n)^T$ in basis $\mathbb{a}$, and $\beta = (\beta_1, \dots, \beta_n)^T$ in basis $\mathbb{b}$. Then

$$x = \sum_{k=1}^n \alpha_k a_k = (\alpha_1, \dots, \alpha_n) \begin{bmatrix} a_1 \\ \cdots \\ a_n \end{bmatrix} = \alpha^T \begin{bmatrix} a_1 \\ \cdots \\ a_n \end{bmatrix}$$

Similarly, using (1),

$$x = \sum\nolimits_{k=1}^{n} \beta_k b_k = \beta^T \begin{bmatrix} b_1 \\ \cdots \\ b \end{bmatrix} = \beta^T Q \begin{bmatrix} a_1 \\ \cdots \\ a_n \end{bmatrix}$$

Because $A = [a_1, \ldots, a_n]^T$ is an invertible matrix by the linear independence of the elements of the basis, $\alpha^T A = \beta^T Q A$ implies $\alpha^T A A^{-1} = \beta^T Q A A^{-1}$, and therefore

$$\beta^T Q = \alpha^T$$

Taking transposes of both sides of this expression, and letting $Q^T = P$, we see that

$$\alpha = P\beta \tag{2}$$

Hence, the effect of a change of basis on the coordinates of a vector is to multiply the original coordinate vector by the transpose of the matrix Q that summarizes the relationship between the two bases. The following problem shows that the matrix P is invertible.

Problem 5.1. Show that the matrix P that represents a coordinate change is invertible. Hint: By the same argument we have used, there is a matrix Z such that $\beta = Z\alpha$.

Now, let $T: V \longrightarrow V$ be a linear mapping with matrix representation M_a in basis $\mathtt{a}$ and M_b in basis $\mathtt{b}$. Then, given an arbitrary vector x in V, its image $T(x)$ has coordinates $M_a \alpha$ in basis $\mathtt{a}$ and $M_b \beta$ in basis $\mathtt{b}$. By the previous discussion, these two coordinate vectors are related by

$$M_a \alpha = P M_b \beta$$

Substituting (2) in this expression,

$$M_a P \beta = P M_b \beta$$

and premultiplying both sides by P^{-1},

$$P^{-1} M_a P \beta = P^{-1} P M_b \beta = M_b \beta$$

Because this expression must hold for all vectors β, it follows that

$$P^{-1} M_a P = M_b \tag{3}$$

Hence, any two representations of the same linear mapping are related in a simple way: We can write one of them as the result of premultiplying and postmultiplying the other one by a matrix and its inverse.

Two matrices that satisfy relation (3) are said to be similar.

Definition 5.2. Two matrices A and B are said to be similar if there exists an invertible matrix P such that $P^{-1}AP = B$.

Hence, a change of basis alters the matrix representation of a linear mapping by a similarity transformation. In a later section we will see that it is often possible to find invertible matrices P that yield particularly convenient representations of a given linear mapping.

Problem 5.3. Show that similar matrices have the same determinant. (Recall that the determinant of the product of two matrices is the product of their determinants.)

6. Eigenvalues and Eigenvectors

Definition 6.1. Eigenvalues and eigenvectors. Let A be an $n \times n$ matrix, with e a nonzero n-vector, and λ a scalar (real or complex), such that

$$Ae = \lambda e \tag{1}$$

We then say that λ is an *eigenvalue* or *characteristic root* of A, and e an *eigenvector* or *characteristic vector* of A corresponding (or belonging) to the eigenvalue λ.

Rearranging (1), we see that the pair (λ, e) must satisfy the homogeneous system of equations

$$(A - \lambda I)e = \underline{0} \tag{2}$$

where I is the identity matrix. Notice that (2) is a homogeneous system of n equations in n unknowns (the components of e) and will therefore have nontrivial solutions only if λ is such that the coefficient matrix of the system is noninvertible, that is, if

$$|A - \lambda I| = 0 \tag{3}$$

for otherwise, $e = (A - \lambda I)^{-1}\underline{0} = \underline{0}$. Expanding the determinant $|A - \lambda I|$ in this expression, we obtain an nth-degree polynomial $p(\lambda)$, called the *characteristic polynomial* of A. Equation (3) (the *characteristic equation*) is therefore an nth-degree polynomial equation in λ, and, as such, it has n solutions, not necessarily all real or all distinct. Each of these solutions $(\lambda_i, i = 1, \ldots, n)$ is an eigenvalue of A. If an eigenvalue is repeated m times, we say that it has *multiplicity m*. The set of eigenvalues of A, $\{\lambda_i; i = 1, \ldots, n\}$, is sometimes called the *spectrum* of the matrix, denoted by $\sigma(A)$.

Having solved (3) for the eigenvalues of A, we can calculate the corresponding eigenvectors by solving the system

$$Ae_i = \lambda_i e_i \Leftrightarrow (A - \lambda_i I)e_i = \underline{0} \tag{4}$$

for each $i = 1, \ldots, n$. Observe that the characteristic vectors of a matrix are not uniquely defined. If e_i is an eigenvector of A associated with the eigenvalue λ_i, any vector of the form αe_i, where α is an arbitrary scalar, will also be a characteristic vector of A, for if we multiply A by αe_i, we obtain

$$A(\alpha e_i) = \alpha(Ae_i) = \alpha(\lambda_i e_i) = \lambda_i(\alpha e_i)$$

Hence, if e_i is an eigenvector of A, so is αe_i. The space of solutions of (4) corresponding to a given eigenvalue λ_i is called the *eigenspace* of A belonging to λ_i.

Problem 6.2. Show that the eigenspace of A corresponding to an eigenvalue λ is a vector space.

Problem 6.3. Show that if λ is an eigenvalue of A, then (i) λ^n is an eigenvalue of A^n, and (ii) λ^{-1} is an eigenvalue of A^{-1}.

The case of a 2×2 matrix is particularly simple and often useful in applications. Given the matrix

$$A = \begin{bmatrix} a_{11} & a_{12} \\ a_{21} & a_{22} \end{bmatrix}$$

its characteristic equation is

$$p(\lambda) = |A - \lambda I| = \begin{vmatrix} a_{11} - \lambda & a_{12} \\ a_{21} & a_{22} - \lambda \end{vmatrix} = (a_{11} - \lambda)(a_{22} - \lambda) - a_{12}a_{21}$$

$$= a_{11}a_{22} - \lambda a_{11} - \lambda a_{22} + \lambda^2 - a_{12}a_{21} - \lambda^2 - (a_{11} + a_{22})\lambda + (a_{11}a_{22} - a_{12}a_{21})$$

$$= \lambda^2 - (\text{tr } A)\lambda + \det A = 0$$

Using the quadratic formula, the eigenvalues of A are given by

$$\lambda_1, \lambda_2 = \frac{\text{tr} \pm \sqrt{(\text{tr})^2 - 4(\det)}}{2}$$

Given an eigenvalue λ_i, we now seek the corresponding eigenvectors e_i. To simplify things a bit, we can take advantage of the fact that eigenvectors are defined, at most, up to a multiplicative constant to normalize the second component of e_i to 1 ($e_{i2} = 1$). Hence, we want a vector $e_i = (e_{i1}, 1)$ such that $Ae_i = \lambda_i e_i$, that is, a solution of the system

$$\begin{bmatrix} a_{11} a_{12} \\ a_{21} a_{22} \end{bmatrix} \begin{bmatrix} e_{i1} \\ 1 \end{bmatrix} = \lambda_i \begin{bmatrix} e_{i1} \\ 1 \end{bmatrix}$$

or

$$a_{11} e_{i1} + a_{12} = \lambda_i e_{i1}$$
$$a_{21} e_{i1} + a_{22} = \lambda_i$$

Notice that there is only one unknown (e_{i1}). However, we know that the system must be consistent; hence, both equations have the same solutions, and we can solve whichever one is more convenient.

Problem 6.4. Find the eigenvalues and eigenvectors of the matrix

$$A = \begin{bmatrix} 3 & -2 & 0 \\ -2 & 3 & 0 \\ 0 & 0 & 5 \end{bmatrix}$$

The following theorems list some properties of eigenvalues and eigenvectors that will be useful in the study of linear dynamical systems.

Theorem 6.5. Let A *be a square matrix with real entries. Then, complex eigenvalues of* A, *if they exist, come in conjugate pairs. Moreover, the corresponding eigenvectors also come in conjugate pairs.*

Theorem 6.6. Let A = [a_{ij}] *be an* n × n *matrix. Then*

(i) *the product of the eigenvalues of* A *is equal to its determinant, that is,*

$$|A| = \Pi_{i=1}^{n} \lambda_i$$

(ii) *the sum of the eigenvalues of* A *is equal to its trace, that is,*

$$tr\, A \equiv \sum_{i=1}^{n} a_{ii} = \sum_{i=1}^{n} \lambda_i$$

(iii) *if* A *is a triangular matrix, then its eigenvalues are the coefficients in the principal diagonal of the matrix (i.e.,* $\lambda_i = a_{ii}$).

Proof. Let A be an $n \times n$ matrix. Then its characteristic polynomial is an nth-degree polynomial,

$$p(\lambda) = c_n \lambda^n + c_{n-1} \lambda^{n-1} + \ldots + c_1 \lambda + c_0$$

To prove (i) and (ii), we will write down two equivalent expressions for $p(\lambda)$ and compare their coefficients.

(i) First, let $\lambda_1, \ldots, \lambda_n$ be the eigenvalues of A. Because these numbers are, by definition, zeros of $p(\lambda)$, we can write

$$p(\lambda) = a(\lambda_1 - \lambda)(\lambda_2 - \lambda) \ldots (\lambda_n - \lambda) \tag{1}$$

for some number a. Using this expression, we see that

$$c_n = a(-1)^n \tag{2}$$
$$c_0 = p(0) = a\lambda_1\lambda_2 \ldots \lambda_n \tag{3}$$

Alternatively, we can also write

$$p(\lambda) = |A - \lambda I| = \begin{bmatrix} a_{11} - \lambda & a_{12} & \cdots & a_{1n} \\ a_{21} & a_{22} - \lambda & \cdots & a_{2n} \\ \cdots & \cdots & \cdots & \cdots \\ a_{n1} & a_{n2} & \cdots & a_{nn} - \lambda \end{bmatrix} \tag{4}$$

from which

$$c_0 = p(0) = \det A \tag{5}$$

Moreover, it can be shown by induction that this polynomial is of the form

$$p(\lambda) = (a_{11} - \lambda)(a_{22} - \lambda) \ldots (a_{nn} - \lambda) + \text{terms of order } n - 2 \text{ or lower in } \lambda \tag{6}$$

Inspection of this expression shows that

$$c_n = (-1)^n \tag{7}$$

Comparing (2) and (7), we see that

$$a = 1 \tag{8}$$

Equations (3) and (5) then imply, using (8), that

$$\lambda_1\lambda_2 \ldots \lambda_n = \det A \tag{9}$$

(ii) Next, consider the coefficient of λ^{n-1}, c_{n-1}. Comparing equations (1) and (6), we see that both expansions of the polynomial should yield similar expressions for c_{n-1}, with λ_i taking the role of a_{ii}. Using (1) with $a = 1$, we will show by induction that $c_{n-1} = (-1)^{n-1}(\Sigma_{i=1}^n \lambda_i)$. By the same argument, it can be shown that $c_{n-1} = (-1)^{n-1}(\Sigma_{i=1}^n a_{ii})$. Hence, it follows that $\operatorname{tr} A = \Sigma_{i=1}^n \lambda_i$, as was to be shown.

For each $k = 1, \ldots, n$, let

$$p_k(\lambda) = (\lambda_1 - \lambda)(\lambda_2 - \lambda) \ldots (\lambda_k - \lambda)$$

and observe that

$$p_{k+1}(\lambda) = p_k(\lambda)(\lambda_{k+1} - \lambda)$$

First, we verify that the desired result holds for $k = 2$. In this case, $p_k(\lambda)$ is of the form

$$p_2(\lambda) = (\lambda_1 - \lambda)(\lambda_2 - \lambda) = \lambda_1\lambda_2 - \lambda_1\lambda - \lambda\lambda_2 + \lambda^2 = \lambda^2 - (\lambda_1 + \lambda_2)\lambda + \lambda_1\lambda_2$$

and $c_{n-1} = c_1$ (the coefficient of λ) is indeed of the form

$$(-1)^{n-1}\left(\sum_{i=1}^{n}\lambda_i\right) = (-1)(\lambda_1 + \lambda_2)$$

Next we will assume that this result holds for k and show that this implies that it holds also for $k + 1$. Under our assumptions we have

$$p_k(\lambda) = (-1)^k\lambda^k + (-1)^{k-1}\left(\sum_{i=1}^{k}\lambda_i\right)\lambda^{k-1} + c_{k-2}\lambda^{k-2} + \ldots + c_1\lambda + c_0$$

Hence,

$$\begin{aligned}
p_{k+1}(\lambda) &= p_k(\lambda)(\lambda_{k+1} - \lambda) \\
&= \left[(-1)^k\lambda^k + (-1)^{k-1}\left(\sum_{i=1}^{k}\lambda_i\right)\lambda^{k-1} + c_{k-2}\lambda^{k-2} \ldots + c_1\lambda + c_0\right](\lambda_{k+1} - \lambda) \\
&= (-1)^{k+1}\lambda^{k+1} + \lambda_{k+1}(-1)^k\lambda^k + (-1)^k\left(\sum_{i=1}^{k}\lambda_i\right)\lambda^k + \ldots \\
&= (-1)^{k+1}\lambda^{k+1} + (-1)^k\left(\sum_{i=1}^{k}\lambda_i + \lambda_{k+1}\right)\lambda^k \ldots
\end{aligned}$$

which shows that the coefficient of λ^k is of the required form. This completes the proof.

(iii) Notice that in this case the characteristic equation reduces to $\Pi_{i=1}^{n}(a_{ii} - \lambda_i) = 0$. $\quad\square$

So far, we have talked about the eigenvalues and eigenvectors of a matrix, but in fact these concepts can be defined directly in terms of the underlying linear mapping. Let T be a linear function mapping an n-dimensional vector space V into itself. Given two bases of V, a and b, let M_a and M_b be the corresponding matrix representations of T. We have seen that M_a and M_b are similar matrices; that is, there exists an invertible matrix P (which is the transpose of the "change-of-basis" matrix) such that $M_b = P^{-1}M_aP$. Using this expression, it is easy to show that the two matrices have the same characteristic polynomial and therefore the same eigenvalues:

$$\begin{aligned}
|M_b - \lambda I| &= |P^{-1}M_aP - \lambda I| = |P^{-1}(M_a - \lambda I)P| = |P^{-1}||M_a - \lambda I||P| \\
&= |M_a - \lambda I||P^{-1}||P| = |M_a\lambda I|
\end{aligned}$$

Moreover, the eigenvectors of M_a and M_b represent the same element of V in the two bases we are considering. To see this, let x and y be eigenvectors of M_a and M_b belonging to the same eigenvalue, λ, that is, vectors such that

$$M_a x = \lambda x \quad \text{and} \quad M_b y = \lambda y$$

Then, because $M_b = P^{-1} M_a P$, we have

$$P^{-1} M_a P y = \lambda y \quad \text{and therefore} \quad M_a P y = \lambda P y$$

Hence, $x = Py$, and we conclude (see the previous section) that x and y represent the same vector under different bases.

Diagonalization of a Square Matrix

A matrix A is said to be diagonalizable if it is similar to a diagonal matrix, that is, if there exists an invertible matrix P such that $P^{-1}AP$ is diagonal.

Theorem 6.7. Let A *be an* $n \times n$ *matrix with* n *linearly independent eigenvectors. Then* A *is diagonalizable. Moreover, the diagonalizing matrix is the matrix* $E = [e_1, \ldots, e_n]$ *whose columns are the eigenvectors of* A, *and the resulting diagonal matrix is the matrix* $\Lambda = diag(\lambda_1, \ldots, \lambda_n)$, *with the eigenvalues of* A *in the principal diagonal, and zeros elsewhere. That is,* $E^{-1}AE = \Lambda$.

Proof. Because the eigenvectors of A are linearly independent by assumption, $E = [e_1, \ldots, e_n]$ is an invertible matrix, and therefore $E^{-1}AE = \Lambda$ is equivalent to $AE = E\Lambda$. We now verify that this expression holds. Using the definition of eigenvectors and eigenvalues,

$$AE = A[e_1, \ldots, e_n] = [Ae_1, \ldots, Ae_n] = [\lambda_1 e_1, \ldots, \lambda_n e_n]$$

$$= [e_1, \ldots, e_n] \begin{bmatrix} \lambda_1 & \cdots & 0 \\ \cdots & \cdots & \cdots \\ 0 & \cdots & \lambda_n \end{bmatrix} = E\Lambda \qquad \square$$

Theorem 6.8. Let A *be an* $n \times n$ *matrix. If the* n *eigenvalues of* A *are all distinct, then its eigenvectors* $e_1, \ldots, e_n$ *are linearly independent, and therefore* A *is diagonalizable.*

Proof. Recall that a set of vectors $e_1, \ldots, e_n$ is said to be linearly dependent if there exist scalars $\alpha_1, \ldots, \alpha_n$ not all zero, such that

$$\sum_{i=1}^{n} \alpha_i e_i = \underline{0}$$

and to be linearly independent if this expression holds only when all the scalars are zero.

For simplicity, let $n = 2$. There exist scalars α_1 and α_2 (possibly both zero) such that

$$\alpha_1 e_1 + \alpha_2 e_2 = \underline{0} \tag{1}$$

Multiplying both sides of (1) by A,

$$\alpha_1 A e_1 + \alpha_2 A e_2 = \underline{0} \Rightarrow \alpha_1 \lambda_1 e_1 + \alpha_2 \lambda_2 e_2 = \underline{0} \tag{2}$$

where λ_1 and λ_2 are the corresponding eigenvalues. Next, we multiply both sides of (1) by λ_2 and subtract the resulting equation from (2), obtaining

$$\alpha_1 \lambda_1 e_1 + \alpha_2 \lambda_2 e_2 - \alpha_1 \lambda_2 e_1 - \alpha_2 \lambda_2 e_2 = \alpha_1 (\lambda_1 - \lambda_2) e_1 = \underline{0}$$

Because $\lambda_1 \neq \lambda_2$ by assumption, and $e_1 \neq \underline{0}$, we must have $\alpha_1 = 0$. By the same argument, α_2 is also zero. Hence, the eigenvectors e_1 and e_2 belonging to different eigenvalues must be linearly independent.

A similar argument will work for any n: Assume that some linear combination of the n eigenvectors, $e_1, \ldots, e_n$, is equal to zero, multiply this combination by A, and subtract λ_n times the original linear combination from the resulting expression. This will leave a linear combination of $e_1, \ldots, e_{n-1}$ that is equal to zero. By repeating the process, we end up with the result that a multiple of e_1 is the zero vector, forcing $\alpha_1 = 0$ and, eventually, $\alpha_i = 0$ for all i. Hence, eigenvectors associated with distinct eigenvalues must be linearly independent. $\qquad\square$

Appendix: Polynomial Equations

A *polynomial* of degree n in x is a real or complex-valued function

$$p(x) = a_0 x^n + a_1 x^{n-1} + \ldots + a_{n-1} x + a_n \qquad \text{(with } a_0 \neq 0) \tag{1}$$

where the coefficients a_i are real or complex numbers. An equation of the form

$$p(x) = a_0 x^n + a_1 x^{n-1} + \ldots + a_{n-1} x + a_n = 0 \tag{2}$$

is called a *polynomial* or *algebraic equation*. The solutions or roots of the equation $p(x) = 0$ are the zeros of the polynomial $p(x)$.

Polynomial equations arise in the computation of the eigenvalues of a matrix and in other applications. A first question that arises in connection with such equations has to do with the existence of solutions to (2). It can be shown that a polynomial equation of degree n will always have n solutions, provided we allow for complex and repeated roots. In fact, complex numbers were "invented" to make sure that algebraic equations always have a solution. If the coefficients of $p(x)$ are real, moreover, any complex roots will come in conjugate pairs.

The solutions of the second-degree algebraic equation

$$ax^2 + bx + c = 0$$

can be obtained directly using the *quadratic formula*:

$$x_1, x_2 = \frac{-b \pm \sqrt{b^2 - 4ac}}{2a} \tag{3}$$

For the case of the third-degree equation,

$$z^3 + Az^2 + Bz + c = 0$$

there is a similar result. Observe first that by letting $z = x - (A/3)$, this equation can be written in the form

$$x^3 + ax + b = 0 \tag{4}$$

The roots of (4), then, must satisfy the *Cardano formula*:

$$x = \left(\frac{-b + \sqrt{\dfrac{4a^3 + 27b^2}{27}}}{2} \right)^{1/3} + \left(\frac{-b - \sqrt{\dfrac{4a^3 + 27b^2}{27}}}{2} \right)^{1/3} \tag{5}$$

Notice that there may be more than three numbers that satisfy this expression. Only three of them, however, will solve the original equation.

A more complicated formula exists for fourth-degree polynomial equations. For equations of a higher order, however, no explicit formulas are available.

Integer roots of a polynomial with integer coefficients are relatively easy to find. Observe that we can rewrite the equation

$$p(x) = a_0 x^n + a_1 x^{n-1} + \ldots + a_{n-1}x + a_n = 0 \tag{2}$$

in the form

$$x\left(a_0 x^{n-1} + a_1 x^{n-2} + \ldots + a_{n-1} \right) = -a_n$$

Assume that the coefficients of $p(x)$ are all integers and that x^* is an integer solution of (2). Then the expression inside the parentheses is an integer, and x^* must be a factor of the constant term a_n. It follows that in order to find the integer solutions of (2) (if they exist), it suffices to find all the integer factors of a_n. We can then insert each factor f_n in $p(x)$ to check whether or not it is indeed a zero of the polynomial. If it is, we can use this fact to simplify $p(x)$ by dividing it by $(x - f_n)$. In this manner, we can rewrite the original equation in the form

$$p(x) = q(x)(x - f_n)$$

where $q(x)$ is a polynomial of degree $n - 1$. If $p(x) = 0$ has enough integer roots, we may be able to write it as a product of a number of binomials of the form $(x - f_n)$ and a second- or third-degree polynomial $q(x)$. We can then use the quadratic formula or the Cardano formula to solve the equation $q(x) = 0$, thus finding the remaining solutions of the original equation.

We conclude this section with an algorithm that simplifies the task of dividing a polynomial $p(x)$ by a binomial of the form $(x - c)$. In general, the division of $p(x)$ by $(x - c)$ yields a quotient polynomial $q(x)$ of degree $n - 1$ and a constant remainder r, according to the formula

$$p(x) = q(x)(x - c) + r$$

Given $p(x)$ and c, we seek $q(x)$ and r. To illustrate the algorithm, let $p(x)$ be a third-degree polynomial. Then p and q are of the form

$$p(x) = a_0 x^3 + a_1 x^2 + a_2 x^2 + a_3 \quad \text{and} \quad q(x) = b_0 x^2 + b_1 x + b_2$$

To compute the values of r and the coefficients of $q(x)$, we construct the following table. The top row contains the coefficients of p. The first element of the third row is a_0. Then each element of the second row is obtained by multiplying the previous element of the third row by c. Each element of the third row is the sum of the corresponding elements of the first and second rows. The elements of the third row are the coefficients of $q(x)$, except for the last one, which is the remainder.

		a_1	a_2	a_3
c	a_0	ca_0	$ca_1 + c^2 a_0$	$ca_2 + c^2 a_1 + c^3 a_0$
	a_0	$a_1 + ca_0$	$a_2 + ca_1 + c^2 a_0$	$a_3 + ca_2 + c^2 a_1 + c^3 a_0$
	$(= b_0)$	$(= b_1)$	$(= b_2)$	$(= r)$

Bibliography

Anton, H. 1981. *Elementary Linear Algebra*, 3rd ed. New York: Wiley.
Apostol, T. 1984. *Calculus*, 2nd ed. Barcelona: Editorial Reverté.
Cullen, C. 1990. *Matrices and Linear Transformations*, 2nd ed. New York: Dover.
Giles, J. 1987. *Introduction to the Analysis of Metric Spaces*. Cambridge University Press.

Lang, S. 1986. *Introduction to Linear Algebra*, 2nd ed. Berlin: Springer-Verlag.

Maddox, I. 1988. *Elements of Functional Analysis*, 2nd ed. Cambridge University Press.

Michel, P. 1984. *Cours de Mathématiques pour Economistes*. Paris: Economica.

Schneider, H., and Barker, G. P. 1973. *Matrices and Linear Algebra*. New York: Dover.

Shilov, G. 1977. *Linear Algebra*. New York: Dover.

Sydsaeter, K. 1981. *Topics in Mathematical Analyis for Economists*. Orlando, FL: Academic Press.

Taylor, A., and Mann, R. *Advanced Calculus*. New York: Wiley.

Notes

1 We can assume, without loss of generality, that S' is the same set in both cases. If it were not so, we would have

$$x = \sum_{s \in S_1} \alpha_s x_s \quad \text{and} \quad y = \sum_{s \in S_2} \beta_s x_s$$

We could then define $S' = S_1 \cup S_2$ and put $\alpha_s = 0$ for $s \in S' \sim S_1$ and $\beta_s = 0$ for $s \in S' \sim S_2$.

2 Because X and Y have the same dimension, we can assume that the index set is the same for the Hamel bases of the two spaces.

3 Recall that for any scalar α, $\|\alpha x\| = |\alpha| \, \|x\|$; hence $\|T(\alpha x)\| = |\alpha| \, \|T(x)\|$. If $\|x\| \leq 1$, we can write $x = \alpha y$, where $|\alpha| \leq 1$ and $\|y\| = 1$ and therefore $\|T(x)\| \leq \|T(y)\|$. This is why we can replace the equality $\|x\| = 1$ by the inequality $\|x\| \leq 1$.

4

Differential Calculus

This chapter introduces the concept of differentiability and discusses some of its implications. After dealing briefly with the familiar case of univariate real functions, we extend the concept of differentiability to functions of $\mathbb{R}^n$ into $\mathbb{R}^m$. The key to the extension lies in the interpretation of differentiability in terms of the existence of a "good" linear approximation to a function at a point. We also show that important aspects of the local behavior of "sufficiently differentiable" functions are captured accurately by linear or quadratic approximations. This material has important applications to comparative statics and optimization.

1. Differentiable Univariate Real Functions

Let g be a univariate function, $g: \mathbb{R} \longrightarrow \mathbb{R}$. We want to make precise the notion of the slope of the function at a given point x. Given a second point y in the domain of g, the *difference quotient* $(g(y) - g(x))/(y - x)$ gives the slope of the secant to the function through the points $(x, g(x))$ and $(y, g(y))$. As we take points y closer and closer to x, the secant becomes a better approximation to the tangent to the graph of g at the point $(x, g(x))$, and in the limit the two coincide. Thus, we can define the derivative of g at x as the limit

$$g'(x) = \lim_{y \to x} \frac{g(y) - g(x)}{y - x} = \lim_{h \to 0} \frac{g(x + h) - g(x)}{h} \qquad (h \in \mathbb{R})$$

whenever it exists, and we can interpret it as the slope of the function at this point.

Definition 1.1. Derivative of a univariate function. Let $g: \mathbb{R} \longrightarrow \mathbb{R}$ be defined on an open interval I. We say that g is differentiable at a point x in I if the following limit exists:

156

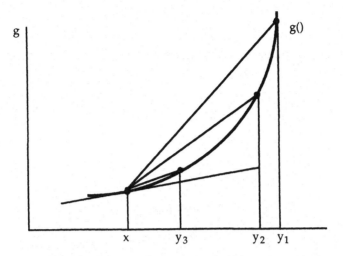

Figure 4.1. The derivative as the limit of the secant.

$$\lim_{h \to 0} \frac{g(x+h) - g(x)}{h} \qquad (h \in \mathbb{R})$$

When it does, we say that the value of the limit is the derivative of g at x, written $g'(x)$. If g is differentiable at each point in its domain, we say that the function is differentiable (on I).

Problem 1.2. Let f and g be functions $\mathbb{R} \longrightarrow \mathbb{R}$, and assume that they are both differentiable at some point x^0. Using the elementary properties of limits and the continuity of f and g at x, show that the product function p, defined by $p(x) = f(x)g(x)$, is differentiable at x^0 and that

$$p'(x^0) = f(x^0)g'(x^0) + f'(x^0)g(x^0)$$

Hint: $f(x)g(x) - f(x^0)g(x^0) = f(x)g(x) - f(x^0)g(x) + f(x^0)g(x) - f(x^0)g(x^0)$.

Problem 1.3. Let $f(x) = x^n$. Show by induction that $f'(x) = nx^{n-1}$. (First, prove it directly for $n = 2$.)

We will now establish some important properties of differentiable functions.

Theorem 1.4. Let f be a function $f : \mathbb{R} \supseteq I \longrightarrow \mathbb{R}$ *(I open). If f is differentiable at a point* $x \in I$, *then it is continuous at* x.

Proof. Given two points x and $x + h$ in I, we can write

$$f(x+h)-f(x)=\frac{f(x+h)-f(x)}{h}h$$

Taking limits as $h \to 0$, and applying earlier results on the algebra of limits, we have

$$\lim_{h\to 0} f(x+h)-f(x)=\left(\lim_{h\to 0}\frac{f(x+h)-f(x)}{h}\right)0 = f'(x)0 = 0$$

and therefore

$$\lim_{h\to 0} f(x+h)= f(x)$$

which establishes the continuity of f at x. $\square$

A point x^0 is a *local maximizer* of f if there exists some $\delta > 0$ such that $f(x^0) \geq f(x)$ for all $x \in B_\delta(x^0)$. The following result tells us that a zero derivative is a necessary condition for an interior maximum (minimum) of a differentiable function. (Notice that we exclude the end points of the interval, to avoid the possibility of corner maxima.)

Theorem 1.5. Necessary condition for an interior maximum. Let f *be a differentiable function* (a, b) $\longrightarrow$ $\mathbb{R}$, *and* x^0 *a local maximizer (minimizer) of* f. *Then* f$'$(x^0) = 0.

Proof. Suppose, for concreteness, that f has a local maximum at x^0. Then we have

$$f(x^0+h)-f(x^0)\leq 0 \;\forall\; h \text{ with } |h| < \delta$$

and therefore

$$\frac{f(x^0+h)-f(x^0)}{h}\leq 0 \quad \text{for } h \in (0,\ \delta)$$

$$\geq 0 \quad \text{for } h \in (-\delta,\ 0)$$

Taking limits as h approaches zero from above and from below, we have

$$\lim_{h\to 0^+}\frac{f(x^0+h)-f(x^0)}{h}\leq 0 \quad \text{and} \quad \lim_{h\to 0^-}\frac{f(x^0+h)-f(x^0)}{h}\geq 0$$

Now, because the function is differentiable, the limit of the difference quotient as $h \to 0$ exists and is given by the common value of the two one-sided limits. Hence,

$$0\leq f'(x^0)=\lim_{h\to 0}\frac{f(x^0+h)-f(x^0)}{h}\leq 0 \Rightarrow f'(x^0)=0 \qquad \square$$

Theorem 1.6. Rolle's theorem. Let f:[a, b] $\longrightarrow \mathbb{R}$ *be continuous and differentiable on* (a, b). *Assume* f(a) = f(b) = 0; *then there is some number* $\theta \in$ (a, b) *such that* f'(θ) = 0.

Proof. Because f is continuous on the compact set $I = [a, b]$, it attains both a maximum M and a minimum m on this interval. That is, there exist points x_m and x_M in $[a, b]$ with $f(x_m) = m$ and $f(x_M) = M$. If $f(x_m) = f(x_M) = 0$, then the function is constant on the interval, and $f'(x) = 0$ for all x in I. Otherwise, either $f(x_m) < 0$ for $x_m \in (a, b)$ and $f'(x_m) = 0$ (because x_m is a local minimizer) or $f(x_M) > 0$ for $x_M \in (a, b)$ and $f'(x_M) = 0$ (by Theorem 1.5), or both. $\qquad\square$

Using Rolle's theorem, it is easy to prove the following important result.

Theorem 1.7. Mean-value theorem. Let f:$\mathbb{R} \longrightarrow \mathbb{R}$ *be a differentiable function. If* a *and* b *are two points in* $\mathbb{R}$, *with* a < b, *then there is some number* $\theta \in$ (a, b) *such that* f'(θ) = (f(b) − f(a))/(b − a).

Proof. Define the function $\phi(\ )$ by

$$\phi(x) = f(x) - f(a) - \frac{f(b) - f(a)}{b - a}(x - a)$$

Because $\phi(\ )$ satisfies the assumptions of Rolle's theorem, there exists some point θ in (a, b) such that $\phi'(\theta) = 0$, that is,

$$\phi'(\theta) = f'(\theta) - \frac{f(b) - f(a)}{b - a} = 0 \Rightarrow f'(\theta) = \frac{f(b) - f(a)}{b - a} \qquad \square$$

The mean-value theorem gives us a way to relate the properties of a function to those of its derivative. The following problem provides an example of how this can be useful.

Problem 1.8. Let $f:\mathbb{R} \longrightarrow \mathbb{R}$ *be a differentiable function on an interval* I. Show that

(i) if $f'(x) = 0$ for each $x \in I$, then f is constant on the interval. Hint: Let x and y, with $x < y$, be two arbitrary points in I. Use the mean-value theorem to show that $f(x) = f(y)$,
(ii) if $f'(x) > 0$ on (a, b), then f is strictly increasing on (a, b).

Figure 4.2 gives a geometrical interpretation of the mean-value theorem. Putting $b = a + h$ in the formula given in the statement of the theorem, and rearranging terms, we have

$$f(b) = f(a) + f'(a + \lambda h)h$$

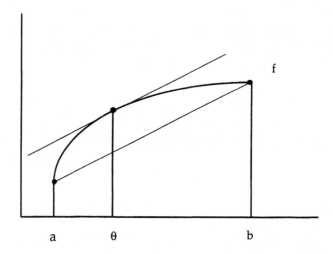

Figure 4.2. The mean-value theorem.

for some $\lambda \in (0, 1)$. The following theorem may be seen as an extension of this result.

Theorem 1.9. Taylor's formula for univariate functions. Let $f : \mathbb{R} \longrightarrow \mathbb{R}$ *be* n *times differentiable on an open interval* I. *For all* x *and* $x + h \in$ I *we have*

$$f(x+h) = f(x) + \sum_{k=1}^{n-1} \frac{f^{(k)}(x)}{k!} h^k + E_n \qquad (1)$$

where $f^{(k)}(x)$ *is the* kth *derivative of* f *evaluated at* x, *and the remainder or error term* E_n *is of the form*

$$E_n = \frac{f^{(n)}(x+\lambda h)}{n!} h^n$$

for some $\lambda \in (0, 1)$.

That is, the remainder has the same form as the other terms, except that the nth derivative is evaluated at some point between x and $x + h$.

Proof. Put $y = x + h$ and define the function $F(z)$ for z between x and y by

$$F(z) = f(y) - f(z) - \sum_{k=1}^{n-1} \frac{f^{(k)}(z)}{k!} (y-z)^k \qquad (2)$$

Then the theorem says that for some point $x + \lambda(y - x)$ between x and y,

$$F(x) = \frac{f^{(n)}(x+\lambda(y-x))}{n!} (y-x)^n \qquad (3)$$

First, observe that $F(y) = 0$ and that most terms in

$$F'(z) = -f'(z) - \sum_{k=1}^{n-1}\left(\frac{f^{(k)}(z)}{k!}k(y-z)^{k-1}(-1) + \frac{f^{(k+1)}(z)}{k!}(y-z)^k\right)$$

$$= -f'(z) + \sum_{k=1}^{n-1}\left(\frac{f^{(k)}(z)}{(k-1)!}(y-z)^{k-1} - \frac{f^{(k+1)}(z)}{k!}(y-z)^k\right)$$

$$= -f'(z) + \left(\frac{f'(z)}{1}1 - \frac{f''(z)}{1!}(y-z)\right) + \left(\frac{f''(z)}{1!}(y-z) - \frac{f^{(3)}(z)}{2!}(y-z)^2\right)$$

$$+ \left(\frac{f^{(3)}(z)}{2!}(y-z)^2 - \frac{f^{(4)}(z)}{3!}(y-z)^3\right) + \ldots + \left(\frac{f^{(n-2)}(z)}{(n-3)!}(y-z)^{n-3}\right)$$

$$- \frac{f^{(n-1)}(z)}{(n-2)!}(y-z)^{n-2}\right) + \left(\frac{f^{(n-1)}(z)}{(n-2)!}(y-z)^{n-2} - \frac{f^{(n)}(z)}{(n-1)!}(y-z)^{n-1}\right)$$

cancel, leaving us with:

$$F'(z) = -\frac{f^{(n)}(z)}{(n-1)!}(y-z)^{n-1} \tag{4}$$

Next, define the function

$$G(z) = F(z) - \left(\frac{y-z}{y-x}\right)^n F(x) \tag{5}$$

and observe that G is a continuous function on (x, y), with

$$G(y) = F(y) - 0 = 0 = F(x) - F(x) = G(x)$$

and

$$G'(z) = F'(z) - n\left(\frac{y-z}{y-x}\right)^{n-1}\frac{-1}{y-x}F(x) \tag{6}$$

By Rolle's theorem, there exists some $\lambda \in (0, 1)$ such that

$$G'(x + \lambda(y-x)) = 0$$

Expanding that expression using (4) and (6),

$$0 = G'(x+\lambda(y-x)) = F'(x+\lambda(y-x)) + n\left(\frac{y-x-\lambda(y-x)}{y-x}\right)^{n-1}\frac{1}{y-x}F(x)$$

$$\Rightarrow \frac{f^{(n)}(x+\lambda(y-x))}{(n-1)!}[y-x-\lambda(y-x)]^{n-1} = n\left(\frac{(1-\lambda)(y-x)}{y-x}\right)^{n-1}\frac{1}{y-x}F(x)$$

$$\Rightarrow \frac{f^{(n)}(x+\lambda(y-x))}{(n-1)!}[(1-\lambda)(y-x)]^{n-1} = n(1-\lambda)^{n-1}\frac{1}{y-x}F(x)$$

$$\Rightarrow \frac{f^{(n)}(x+\lambda(y-x))}{n!}(y-x)^n = F(x)$$

which is the desired result.   □

Taylor's theorem gives us a formula for constructing a polynomial approximation to a differentiable function. With $n = 2$, and omitting the remainder, we get

$$f(x+h) \cong f(x) + f'(x)h \tag{1}$$

The differentiability of f implies that the error term E_2 will be small. Hence the linear function in the right-hand side of (1) is guaranteed to be a decent approximation to $f(\ )$ near x. Higher-order approximations that use several derivatives will be even better.

Problem 1.10. A sufficient condition for a local maximum. Let $f: \mathbb{R} \longrightarrow \mathbb{R}$ be twice differentiable on some interval containing x^0. Assume, moreover, that $f'(x^0) = 0, f''(x^0) < 0$, and f'' is continuous at x^0. Use Problem 1.8 to show that x^0 is a local maximizer of f.

Problem 1.11. Let $f: \mathbb{R} \longrightarrow \mathbb{R}$ be $m+1$ times differentiable on an interval around the point x^0. Assume that for some $m > 1, f^{(m)}(x^0)$ is the first nonzero derivative of f at x^0, that is,

$$f'(x^0) = f''(x^0) = f^{(3)}(x^0) = \ldots = f^{(m-1)}(x^0) = 0 \quad \text{and} \quad f^{(m)}(x^0) \neq 0$$

Use Taylor's theorem to show that

(i) if m is even and $f^{(m)}(x^0) < 0$, then f has a local maximum at x^0,

(ii) if m is even and $f^{(m)}(x^0) > 0$, then f has a local minimum at x^0,

(iii) if m is odd, then f has neither a local maximum nor a local minimum at x^0.

Problem 1.12. Cauchy's mean-value theorem. Prove the following result: Let f and $g: [a, b] \to \mathbb{R}$ be differentiable on (a, b), and suppose that $g'(x) \neq 0$ for all x in (a, b). Then there is a point z in (a, b) such that

$$\frac{f(b) - f(a)}{g(b) - g(a)} = \frac{f'(z)}{g'(z)}$$

Hint: How do you have to modify the function $\phi(\ )$ in the proof of Theorem 1.7?

Problem 1.13. L'Hôpital's rule. Suppose f and g are continuous real-valued functions defined and differentiable on some open interval containing the point a and such that $f(a) = g(a) = 0$. Show that if $f'(x)/g'(x)$ tends to a limit as $x \to a$, so does $f(x)/g(x)$, and

$$\lim_{x \to a} \frac{f(x)}{g(x)} = \lim_{x \to a} \frac{f'(x)}{g'(x)}$$

Hint: Use Cauchy's mean-value theorem (Problem 1.12).

2. Partial and Directional Derivatives

We now want to extend the concept of differentiability at a point x from univariate functions to real-valued functions of n variables. One complication we immediately run into is that we now have to specify the direction along which we are approaching x. The problem does not arise in the real line because there we can approach x only from the left or from the right, and the derivative of the univariate function $g(\ )$ at x is defined as the common value of both one-sided limits whenever they coincide. In $\mathbb{R}^n$, however, we can approach a point from an infinite number of directions, and therefore we have to specify which one we are considering. This observation leads us to the concept of *directional derivative*, which we now define.

Let f be a function $\mathbb{R}^n \longrightarrow \mathbb{R}$, and fix two vectors x^0 and u in $\mathbb{R}^n$ with $\|u\| = 1$. We will interpret x^0 as a "point" in space, and u as a vector (an "arrow") describing a direction of movement in n-space, as illustrated in Figure 4.3. The set of points

$$L(x^0, u) = \{x(\alpha) \in \mathbb{R}^n; x(\alpha) = x^0 + \alpha u, \ \alpha \in \mathbb{R}\}$$

corresponds to the straight line through x^0 with direction u. Because u has norm 1, the parameter α measures the distance between a point $x(\alpha)$ in the line and x^0.

We will define the directional derivative of f at x^0 in the direction of u with the help of an auxiliary univariate function g whose derivative at zero gives us the slope of f as we move away from x^0 in the direction of u. We define $g : \mathbb{R} \longrightarrow \mathbb{R}$ by

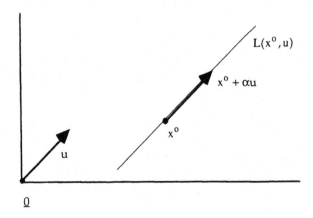

Figure 4.3.

$$g(\alpha) = f(x^0 + \alpha u)$$

When $n = 2$, the geometric interpretation is straightforward: The graph of f is a three-dimensional surface that we suppose to be oriented in such a way that the value of the function is measured vertically. The function g is the restriction of f to the line $L(x^0, u)$, and its graph is the curve obtained by cutting this surface with a vertical plane through x^0 and "parallel" to u. Then $g'(0)$ gives the slope of this curve at x^0 or, equivalently, the slope of the surface $\{(x_1, x_2, y); y = f(x_1, x_2)\}$ at the point $(x_1, x_2, f(x_1, x_2))$ when we move in the direction of u. We say that $g'(0)$ is the directional derivative of f at the point x^0 in the direction of u, and write $Df(x^0; u)$. More formally, we have the following:

Definition 2.1. Directional derivative. The directional derivative of $f \colon \mathbb{R}^n \longrightarrow \mathbb{R}$ in the direction of u at the point x^0 is defined by

$$Df(x^0; u) = \lim_{\alpha \to 0} \frac{f(x^0 + \alpha u) - f(x^0)}{\alpha}, \quad \text{where } \alpha \in \mathbb{R} \text{ and } \|u\| = 1$$

whenever this limit exists.

Because the only function of the vector u is that of indicating the direction of motion, we can assume that its norm is 1. This is not necessary for the definition per se, but it is a convenient way to normalize directional derivatives.

Problem 2.2. Let $f(x_1, x_2) = x_1 x_2$, $u = (3/5, 4/5)$, and $x^0 = (1, 2)$. Compute $Df(x^0; u)$ directly by taking the appropriate limits, and verify that the result is the same if you use the formula

$$Df(x^0; u) = \nabla f(x^0) u$$

(The definition of the gradient $\nabla f(x^0)$ follows after Problem 2.5.)

Directional derivatives in the direction of the coordinate axes are of special interest. The *partial derivative* of f with respect to its ith argument is defined as $Df(x; e^i)$, where e^i is a vector whose components are all zero except for the ith one, which is 1.

Definition 2.3. Partial derivative. Let f be a multivariate function $\mathbb{R}^n \longrightarrow \mathbb{R}$. The partial derivative of f with respect to its ith argument, x_i, at a point $x = (x_i, x_{-i})$, is the limit[1]

$$D_{x_i} f(x) = \lim_{\alpha \to 0} \frac{f(x_i + \alpha, x_{-i}) - f(x_i, x_{-i})}{\alpha}$$

whenever it exists.

There are several standard ways to write the partial derivative of f with respect to x_i. One of the most common notations uses subindices to indicate the variable with respect to which we are differentiating: $D_{x_i} f(x)$, $f_{x_i}(x)$, or $f_i(x)$. Another possibility is to write $\partial f(x) / \partial x_i$. In each case, we explicitly indicate the argument vector x to emphasize that the partial derivative is also a function of x. As it is not normally necessary to insist on this, the arguments are often omitted, and we write $D_{x_i} f$, f_{x_i}, or $\partial f / \partial x_i$.

Conceptually there is no difference between a partial derivative and the ordinary derivative of a univariate function. For given values of the other arguments x_{-i}, $f(x_i, x_{-i})$ is a function of a single variable, x_i. Fixing x_{-i} at a constant value $\bar{x}_{-i}$, and defining a new function g by $g(x_i) = f(x_i, \bar{x}_{-i})$, we have $g'(x_i) = f_i(x_i, \bar{x}_{-i})$. Hence the standard rules of differentiation for "normal" derivatives apply, without change, to partial derivatives, treating the other variables as constants. For example, if $f(x, y) = 3x^2 y + 4y^3$, then $f_x(x, y) = 6xy$, and $f_y(x, y) = 3x^2 + 12y^2$.

Problem 2.4. Given the functions

$$y = f(x_1, x_2) = \sin(x_1 x_2 + x_2^2), \qquad y = f(x_1, x_2) = x_1^2 x_2 + x_2^3 \ln x_1,$$
$$y = f(x_1, x_2) = \ln(x_2 + e^{x_1} x_2)$$

calculate, for each of them, the partial derivatives $\partial y / \partial x_1$ and $\partial y / \partial x_2$.

Problem 2.5. Find the points where all the partial derivatives of the function

$$f(x_1, x_2) = x_1^4 x_2 - x_1^2 x_2^3$$

are zero.

If all the partial derivatives of f exist and are continuous in some neighborhood of a point x^0, then the directional derivative at x^0 exists for all directions u and can be written as a linear combination of the partial derivatives. To see this, let

$$g(\alpha) = f(x^0 + \alpha u) = f(x_1^0 + \alpha u_1, \ldots, x_n^0 + \alpha u_n)$$

If the partial derivatives of f are continuous, then f is differentiable at x^0, and the chain rule yields

$$g'(\alpha) = f_1(x^0 + \alpha u) u_1 + \ldots + f_n(x^0 + \alpha u) u_n = \sum_{i=1}^{n} f_i(x^0 + \alpha u) u_i$$

(see Theorems 3.4 and 3.5 in Section 3). Hence,

$$Df(x^0; u) = g'(0) = \sum_{i=1}^{n} f_i(x^0) u_i \qquad (1)$$

If we define the *gradient vector* of f at x by

$$\nabla f(x) = (f_1(x), \ldots, f_n(x))$$

then (1) can be written as the scalar product of the gradient and the direction vector:

$$Df(x^0; u) = \nabla f(x)u \tag{2}$$

Using expression (2), we see that the gradient is the vector that points in the direction of steepest ascent or descent along the graph of the function. Given (2), the Cauchy-Schwarz inequality implies (using the convention that $\|u\| = 1$)

$$|Df(x; u)| = |\nabla f(x)u| \leq \|\nabla f(x)\| \, \|u\| = \|\nabla f(x)\| \tag{3}$$

Hence, the absolute value of the directional derivative cannot exceed the norm of the gradient. Moreover, if we consider the direction of the gradient, given by the normalized vector $g = \nabla f(x)/\|\nabla f(x)\|$, we have

$$|Df(x; g)| = |\nabla f(x)g| = \frac{\nabla f(x)\nabla f(x)}{\|\nabla f(x)\|} = \frac{\|\nabla f(x)\|^2}{\|\nabla f(x)\|} = \|\nabla f(x)\|$$

In this particular direction, therefore, the weak inequality in (3) holds as an equality. Thus, the gradient of f at x points in the direction in which the slope of f at x is largest in absolute value, and its norm is the absolute value of this slope.

Higher-Order Partials

Let f be a function $\mathbb{R}^n \longrightarrow \mathbb{R}$; then each one of its partial derivatives $f_i(x)$ is also a real-valued function of n variables, and the partials of $f_i(\ )$ can be defined exactly as for $f(\ )$. The partials of the $f_i(\ )$'s are the second partial derivatives of f, and we write $f_{ik}(x)$ or $\partial^2 f(x)/\partial x_i \partial x_k$ for $\partial f_i(x)/\partial x_k$.

In many cases of interest, symmetric cross-partials coincide, that is $f_{ik}(x) = f_{ki}(x)$, so the order of differentiation does not matter. The following result, a weak version of Schwarz's theorem, gives sufficient conditions for this property to hold.

Theorem 2.6. Let $f: \mathbb{R}^n \longrightarrow \mathbb{R}$ *be a function defined in an open neighborhood of a point* x^0. *Assume that the partial derivatives* $f_i(x)$, $f_k(x)$, $f_{ki}(x)$, *and* $f_{ik}(x)$ *are also defined in this neighborhood and that* $f_{ki}(x)$ *and* $f_{ik}(x)$ *are continuous at* x^0. *Then* $f_{ik}(x^0) = f_{ki}(x^0)$.

Proof. Because we will consider only two partials at a time, we can assume, with no loss of generality, that f is a function of two variables, say $f(x, y)$. We will work on a square of side h contained in the neighborhood of (x^0, y^0) mentioned in the statement of the theorem.

Consider the expression

$$D = f(x^0 + h, y^0 + h) - f(x^0 + h, y^0) - f(x^0, y^0 + h) + f(x^0, y^0)$$

To prove the theorem, we will use the mean-value theorem for univariate functions to derive two equivalent expressions for D in terms of symmetric cross-partials and conclude from their equality that $f_{xy}(x^0, y^0) = f_{yx}(x^0, y^0)$.

• If we define the function

$$\phi(x) = f(x, y^0 + h) - f(x, y^0)$$

we can write D in the form

$$D = \phi(x^0 + h) - \phi(x^0) \tag{1}$$

By assumption, ϕ is differentiable in the region in which we are working, with

$$\phi'(x) = f_x(x, y^0 + h) - f_x(x, y^0)$$

and applying the mean-value theorem for univariate functions, we have, for some $\lambda_1 \in (0, 1)$,

$$D = h\phi'(x^0 + \lambda_1 h) = h[f_x(x^0 + \lambda_1 h, y^0 + h) - f_x(x^0 + \lambda_1 h, y^0)] \tag{2}$$

Next, put

$$g(y) = f_x(x^0 + \lambda_1 h, y)$$

with derivative

$$g'(y) = f_{xy}(x^0 + \lambda_1 h, y)$$

and write (2) in the form

$$D = h[g(y^0 + h) - g(y^0)] \tag{3}$$

By the mean-value theorem, there is some $\lambda_2 \in (0, 1)$ for which we have

$$D = h^2 g'(y^0 + \lambda_2 h) = h^2 f_{xy}(x^0 + \lambda_1 h, y^0 + \lambda_2 h) \tag{4}$$

• In a similar manner, if we define $\gamma(\ )$ by

$$\gamma(y) = f(x^0 + h, y) - f(x^0, y)$$

we have $D = \gamma(y^0 + h) - \gamma(y^0)$, and by the same procedure used earlier we see that there exist $\lambda_3, \lambda_4 \in (0, 1)$ such that

$$D = h^2 f_{yx}(x^0 + \lambda_3 h, y^0 + \lambda_4 h) \tag{5}$$

Hence,

$$h^2 f_{xy}(x^0 + \lambda_1 h, y^0 + \lambda_2 h) = D = h^2 f_{yx}(x^0 + \lambda_3 h, y^0 + \lambda_4 h)$$

- Finally, we take limits for the preceding expression as $h \to 0$. Then the points at which we are evaluating the partials both approach (x^0, y^0), and because $f_{xy}(\ )$ and $f_{yx}(\ )$ are continuous by assumption, we have

$$f_{xy}(x^0, y^0) = \lim_{h \to 0} f_{xy}(x^0 + \lambda_1 h, y^0 + \lambda_2 h) = \lim_{h \to 0} f_{yx}(x^0 + \lambda_3 h, y^0 + \lambda_4 h) = f_{yx}(x^0, y^0)$$

Thus, symmetric cross-partials coincide at (x^0, y^0).   □

Directional Derivatives and Continuity

We began this section emphasizing the conceptual similarity between the directional derivatives of a multivariate function and the "normal" derivatives of univariate functions. The similarities end, however, when it comes to the connection between the existence of a derivative and continuity. We know that a function from $\mathbb{R}$ to $\mathbb{R}$ that is differentiable at a point x^0 is also continuous at x^0. For a function $\mathbb{R}^n \longrightarrow \mathbb{R}$, however, the existence of all partial derivatives, or even the existence of all directional derivatives at a point, is not sufficient to guarantee continuity, as shown by the following example.

Example 2.7. Consider the function

$$f(x,y) = \frac{xy^2}{x^2 + y^4} \quad \text{for } x \neq 0$$
$$= 0 \qquad \quad \text{for } x = 0$$

For any $u = (u_1, u_2)$ in R^2, the directional derivative of f at $(0, 0)$ is given by

$$\lim_{\alpha \to 0} \frac{f(\alpha u_1, \alpha u_2) - f(0, 0)}{\alpha} = \lim_{\alpha \to 0} \frac{(\alpha u_1)(\alpha u_2)^2}{\alpha[(\alpha u_1)^2 + (\alpha u_2)^4]}$$

$$= \lim_{\alpha \to 0} \frac{u_1 u_2^2}{u_1^2 + \alpha^2 u_2^4} = u_2^2/u_1 \quad \text{if } u_1 \neq 0$$

$$= 0 \qquad \qquad \qquad \text{if } u_1 = 0$$

Hence, $Df(0, 0; u)$ exists for all u. On the other hand, f has value $\frac{1}{2}$ at all points on the curve $x = y^2$ except at the origin, where it is zero. Hence, f is not continuous at $(0, 0)$.   □

It is possible to guarantee the continuity of f at a point by imposing additional conditions on the directional derivatives. For example, it can be shown, using an argument similar to that in the proof of Theorem 2.6, that a sufficient condition for the continuity of f at x^0 is that all its partial derivatives exist and be bounded on a neighborhood of x. It follows easily from this result that the continuity of the partial derivatives of f on some neighborhood of x^0 is sufficient for f to be continuous at x^0. Soon we will prove a stronger result.

The foregoing discussion suggests that it might be interesting to define a stronger concept of differentiability for multivariate functions. This will be done in the following section. For the moment, we observe that the existence of partial derivatives at a point x^0, or even of directional derivatives in all directions, is not sufficient for us to say that the function is *differentiable* at x^0.

3. Differentiability

We now turn to the general case where $f: \mathbb{R}^n \longrightarrow \mathbb{R}^m$ is a function of n variables whose value is an m-vector. We can think of the mapping f as a vector of component functions f^i, each of which is a real-valued function of n variables:

$$f = \left(f^1, \ldots, f^m \right)^T, \quad \text{where} \quad f^i: \mathbb{R}^n \longrightarrow \mathbb{R} \quad \text{for } i = 1, \ldots, m$$

We would like to define a concept of differentiability for functions $\mathbb{R}^n \longrightarrow \mathbb{R}^m$ that can be seen as a natural generalization of the derivative of a univariate function and that will preserve the implication of continuity without additional assumptions. As we will see, the key lies in defining differentiability in terms of the possibility of approximating the local behavior of f through a "linear"[2] function. We will then relate the resulting concept of derivative to the partial derivatives of the components of f.

Let us return for a moment to the definition of the derivative for a function $g: \mathbb{R} \longrightarrow \mathbb{R}$ and see if we can reinterpret it in a way that can be naturally extended to the multivariate case. A univariate real-valued function g is differentiable at a point x in its domain if the limit

$$\lim_{h \to 0} \frac{g(x+h) - g(x)}{h} \qquad (h \in \mathbb{R})$$

exists, that is, if it is equal to some real number a. This condition may be rephrased as follows: g is differentiable at x if there exists a real number a such that

$$\lim_{h \to 0} \frac{g(x+h) - [g(x) + ah]}{h} = 0 \tag{1}$$

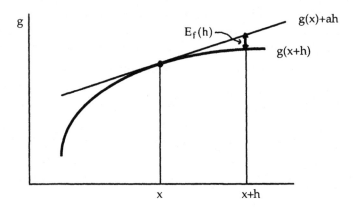

Figure 4.4. The derivative as a linear approximation.

To interpret this expression, fix some x, and suppose that we want to approximate the value of $g(x + h)$ by an affine function. One possibility is to use $g(x) + ah = g(x) + g'(x)h$ to approximate $g(x + h)$, as shown in Figure 4.4.

Expression (1) guarantees that the approximation will be good whenever h is small. If we denote the approximation error by

$$E_g(h) \equiv g(x + h) - [g(x) + ah]$$

then (1) can be written

$$\lim_{h \to 0} \frac{E_g(h)}{h} = 0 \tag{2}$$

which tells us that the approximation error goes to zero with h. Indeed, $E_g(h)$ goes to zero "faster" than h itself, a fact we sometimes indicate by writing $E_g(h) = o(h)$ (which reads "$E_g(h)$ is little-oh of h").

In summary, a function g is differentiable at x if for points close to x, $g(\ )$ admits a "good" approximation by an affine function or, equivalently, if the difference $g(x + h) - g(x)$ can be approximated by a linear function ah with an error that is of a smaller order of magnitude than h as $h \to 0$.

There is no difficulty in extending this notion of differentiability to mappings from $\mathbb{R}^n$ to $\mathbb{R}^m$. Before giving a formal definition, we want to emphasize the importance of the concept of differentiability for our purposes. Because differentiable functions admit good linear approximations, so do differentiable models. This gives us a tractable way to analyze them: When we use the calculus to study a nonlinear model, we are in fact constructing a linear approximation to it in some neighborhood of an equilibrium. The assumption that the behavioral functions in the model are differentiable means that the approximation error is small. The obvious limitation of the method is that it generally yields only local results, valid only in some small neighborhood of the initial solution.

Definition 3.1. Differentiability. A function $f: \mathbb{R}^n \supseteq X \longrightarrow \mathbb{R}^m$, where X is an open set, is differentiable at a point $x \in X$ if there exists a matrix A_x such that

$$\lim_{\|h\| \to 0} \frac{\|f(x+h) - f(x) - A_x h\|}{\|h\|} = 0 \tag{3}$$

where $h \in \mathbb{R}^n$ and $\|\cdot\|$ is the Euclidean norm of a vector, $\|x\| = \sqrt{\sum_{i=1}^n (x_i)^2}$. If f is differentiable at every point in its domain, we say that f is differentiable (on X).

There are two slightly different ways to think about the derivative of a mapping. Perhaps the most natural one is as a function whose value at each point is a matrix. If f is differentiable on X, we can define its derivative as the function

$$Df: \mathbb{R}^n \supseteq X \longrightarrow \mathbb{R}_{m \times n}$$

such that for each $x \in X$, $Df(x) = A_x$, where A_x is the matrix that satisfies (3) in Definition 3.1. In this interpretation, therefore, the derivative of a function at a point is a matrix, and Df is a function $X \longrightarrow \mathbb{R}_{mxn}$.

As we know, every matrix defines a linear transformation. We refer to the linear mapping defined by the derivative of f at x as the differential of f at x, written df_x. Hence, the differential of f at x is the function

$$df_x: \mathbb{R}^n \longrightarrow \mathbb{R}^m, \quad \text{with } df_x(h) = Df(x)h = A_x h$$

and its value at a point is a vector in $\mathbb{R}^m$. Thus, we can also think of the derivative as a mapping that to each x in X assigns the linear transformation df_x, represented by the matrix $Df(x)$. In this interpretation, the derivative Df is a mapping from X to the space $L(\mathbb{R}^n, \mathbb{R}^m)$ of linear functions from $\mathbb{R}^n$ into $\mathbb{R}^m$, with $x \longrightarrow df_x$.[3]

We can, as in the case of a univariate real function, interpret the differential as a linear approximation to the difference $f(x+h) - f(x)$. Expression (3) then guarantees that the approximation is good for "small" h. As before, if we denote the approximation error by

$$E_f(h) = f(x+h) - f(x) - df_x(h)$$

we can rewrite (3) in the form

$$\lim_{\|h\| \to 0} \frac{\|E_f(h)\|}{\|h\|} = 0 \tag{4}$$

That is, the (norm of the) error vector approaches zero faster than (the norm of) *h*.

It is now easy to check that differentiability implies continuity. We have

$$f(x+h) = f(x) + df_x(h) + E_f(h)$$

Taking the limit of this expression as $h \to \underline{0}$, we have that $E_f(h) \to \underline{0}$ by the differentiability of *f*, and $df_x(h) \to \underline{0}$ by the continuity of the linear mapping df_x and the fact that $df_x(\underline{0}) = \underline{0}$. Hence,

$$\lim_{h \to \underline{0}} f(x+h) = f(x)$$

and *f* is continuous at *x*. We have, then, the following theorem.

Theorem 3.2. Differentiability implies continuity. *Let* f : $\mathbb{R}^n \supseteq X \to \mathbb{R}^m$ (*X open*) *be differentiable at a point* x $\in$ X. *Then* f *is continuous at* x.

The following theorem relates the derivative of the mapping *f* to the partial derivatives of its component functions $f^1, \ldots, f^m$. An immediate implication of the theorem is that the matrix A_x that appears in the definition of differentiability is unique, and therefore the functions *Df* and df_x are well defined.

Theorem 3.3. *Let* f : $\mathbb{R}^n \supseteq X \longrightarrow \mathbb{R}^m$, (*X open*) *be a mapping, with component functions* $f^1, \ldots, f^m$. *Then* f *is differentiable at a point* x $\in$ X *if and only if each of these component functions is differentiable at* x. *Moreover, if* f *is differentiable at* x, *then the partial derivatives of the component functions exist at* x, *and the derivative of* f *at* x *is the matrix of first partial derivatives of the component functions evaluated at* x, *that is,*

$$Df(x) = \begin{bmatrix} Df^1(x) \\ \ldots \\ Df^m(x) \end{bmatrix} = \begin{bmatrix} \nabla f^1(x) \\ \ldots \\ \nabla f^m(x) \end{bmatrix} \equiv \begin{bmatrix} f^1_{x_1}(x) \ldots\ldots f^1_{x_n}(x) \\ \ldots\ldots \ldots\ldots \ldots\ldots \\ f^m_{x_1}(x) \ldots\ldots f^m_{x_n}(x) \end{bmatrix}$$

Note carefully what this expression says. Each row of the matrix $Df(x)$ is the vector $Df^j(x)$. This vector, thought of as a $1 \times n$ matrix, is the derivative of the function $f^j : \mathbb{R}^n \longrightarrow \mathbb{R}$. Moreover, the components of this vector are the partial derivatives of f^j.

The matrix of first partial derivatives of the component functions of *f* is known as the *Jacobian* of *f*.[4] The following symbols are sometimes used to refer to this matrix:

$$Df(x) = J^f(x) = \left[\frac{\partial(f^1, \ldots, f^m)}{\partial(x_1, \ldots, x_n)} \right]$$

When we are interested in a submatrix of $Df(x)$, we will use subindices to indicate the variables with respect to which we are differentiating. For example, if we partition $x = (y, z)$, the matrix of partial derivatives of $f^1, \ldots,$ f^m with respect to the components of z will be written $D_z^f(y, z)$ or $J_z^f(y, z)$.

Proof. Assume that f is differentiable at x. Then there exists a matrix $Df(x)$ such that

$$\lim_{\|h\| \to 0} \frac{\|f(x+h) - f(x) - Df(x)h\|}{\|h\|} = 0 \tag{1}$$

Denote the entries of $Df(x)$ by a_{ik} ($i = 1, \ldots, m$; $k = 1, \ldots, n$), and let $h = (h_1, \ldots, h_n)$. Then we have

$$Df(x)h = \left(\sum_{k=1}^{n} a_{1k} h_k, \ldots, \sum_{k=1}^{n} a_{mk} h_k \right)^T$$

and the ith component of the vector $f(x + h) - f(x) - Df(x)h$ is given by

$$f^i(x+h) - f^i(x) - \sum_{k=1}^{n} a_{ik} h_k$$

Observe that the absolute value of a component of a vector cannot exceed the Euclidean norm of the vector. Hence, (1) implies

$$\lim_{\|h\| \to 0} \frac{\left| f^i(x+h) - f^i(x) - \sum_{k=1}^{n} a_{ik} h_k \right|}{\|h\|} = 0 \tag{2}$$

which is precisely the definition of differentiability for the function f^i: $\mathbb{R}^n \longrightarrow \mathbb{R}$. Therefore, the component functions of f are differentiable.

To show that the coefficients a_{ik} of the matrix $Df(x)$ are the corresponding partial derivatives, we let h approach $\underline{0}$ along the sth coordinate axis (i.e., put $h_k = 0$ for all $k \neq s$). Then (2) implies

$$a_{is} = \lim_{h_s \to 0} \frac{f^i(x_s + h_s, x_{-s}) - f^i(x_s, x_{-s})}{h_s} \equiv f^i_{x_s}(x) \tag{3}$$

To establish sufficiency, note that the same logic will work in reverse. If all the component functions are differentiable, (2) holds, with $a_{is} = f^i_{x_s}(x)$; then (1) follows from (2) and from the observation that the Euclidean norm of a vector cannot be larger than the sum of the absolute values of its components.[5] $\square$

By Theorem 3.3, differentiability at a point implies the existence of all partial derivatives at that point. As we have seen, the converse statement is not true. However, the continuity of the partial derivatives is sufficient to guarantee differentiability, as shown in the following theorem.

Theorem 3.4. Let $f: \mathbb{R}^n \supseteq X \longrightarrow \mathbb{R}^m$, *(X open) be a mapping with component functions* $f^1, \ldots, f^m$. *If the partial derivatives of the component functions exist and are continuous on X, then* f *is differentiable on X.*

Proof. By the preceding theorem, a vector-valued function is differentiable at a point x^0 if and only if all its component functions are differentiable at x^0. Hence, it is sufficient to prove the theorem for the case of a real-valued function of n variables, $f: \mathbb{R}^n \supseteq X \longrightarrow \mathbb{R}$.

Fix some arbitrary x in X and some $\varepsilon > 0$. Because X is open and the partials of f are continuous, we can find some r such that the open ball $B_r(x)$ is contained in X and

$$|f_i(x+h) - f_i(x)| < \frac{\varepsilon}{n} \quad \text{for } i = 1, \ldots, n \tag{1}$$

for all $x + h \in B_r(x)$ (or, equivalently, for all h such that $\|h\| < r$).

Now, if f is differentiable, its derivative at x will be the gradient vector

$$\nabla f(x) = (f_1(x), \ldots, f_n(x))$$

Hence, what we want to prove is that

$$\lim_{\|h\| \to 0} \frac{|f(x+h) - f(x) - \nabla f(x)h|}{\|h\|} = 0 \tag{2}$$

We will work with the expression in the numerator. Let $h = (\alpha_1, \ldots, \alpha_n) = \sum_{i=1}^n \alpha_i e^i$, where e^i is the ith-unit coordinate vector in $\mathbb{R}^n$ (a vector with all zeros except for a 1 in the ith coordinate), and assume $\|h\| < r$. Next, define the n-vectors $v_0, \ldots, v_n$ by

$$v_0 = \underline{0} \quad \text{and} \quad v_k = (\alpha_1, \ldots, \alpha_k, 0, \ldots, 0) = \sum_{i=1}^k \alpha_i e^i \quad \text{for } k = 1, \ldots, n$$

Then, we can write[6]

$$f(x+h) - f(x) = \sum_{i=1}^n [f(x+v_i) - f(x+v_{i-1})] \tag{3}$$

Because $\|v_k\| \le \|h\| < r$ for all r and $B_r(x)$ is a convex set, the segments with end points $x + v_k$ all lie in $B_r(x)$, and therefore each partial $f_i(\ )$ of f exists and is continuous on the line segment connecting $x + v_i$ and $x + v_{i-1}$. Moreover, because along this segment of length α_i only the ith argument of f changes, we can use the one-dimensional mean-value theorem to conclude that for each $i = 1, \ldots, n$, there exists some $\theta_i \in (0, 1)$ such that

$$f(x+v_i) - f(x+v_{i-1}) = \alpha_i f_i(x + v_{i-1} + \theta_i \alpha_i v_i) \tag{4}$$

Using (3), (4), and (1) in the numerator of (2), we have, for $\|h\| < r$,

$$\left| f(x+h) - f(x) - \nabla f(x)h \right| = \left| \sum_{i=1}^{n} [f(x+v_i) - f(x+v_{i-1})] - \sum_{i=1}^{n} \alpha_i f_i(x) \right|$$

$$= \left| \sum_{i=1}^{n} \alpha_i [f_i(x+v_{i-1} + \theta_i \alpha_i v_i) - f_i(x)] \right|$$

$$\le \sum_{i=1}^{n} |\alpha_i| \| f_i(x+v_{i-1} + \theta_i \alpha_i v_i) - f_i(x) \| < \sum_{i=1}^{n} |\alpha_i| \frac{\varepsilon}{n} \le \varepsilon \|h\|$$

Hence,

$$\frac{|f(x+h) - f(x) - \nabla f(x)h|}{\|h\|} < \varepsilon \quad \text{for} \quad \|h\| < r$$

which is what we wanted to show. ☐

We conclude this section with some terminology and a few results for differentiable functions.

Critical and Regular Points and Values of a Function

As we will see later, some important results require assumptions concerning the rank of the Jacobian of a function, or, equivalently, that of its differential. In particular, it can be shown that if a function $f: \mathbb{R}^n \longrightarrow \mathbb{R}^m$ is differentiable at a point x and has a derivative matrix $Df(x)$ of rank m, then its local behavior is (loosely speaking) fully determined by that of its differential.

We now introduce some terms that will be useful later. Let $f: \mathbb{R}^n \supseteq X \longrightarrow \mathbb{R}^m$ (X open) be a differentiable function. A vector $x \in X$ is a *regular point* of f if the differential of f at x (i.e., the linear mapping $df_x \in L(\mathbb{R}^n, \mathbb{R}^m)$), is surjective (onto). If x is not a regular point of f (i.e., if df_x is not onto), then x is a *critical point* of f. A point $y \in \mathbb{R}^m$ is a *critical value* of f if it is the image of a critical point, and a *regular value* otherwise.

Recall that df_x is surjective (and therefore x is a regular point of f) if and only if the derivative $Df(x)$ has rank m. Hence the set of critical points of $f: \mathbb{R}^n \supseteq X \longrightarrow \mathbb{R}^m$ is given by

$$C_f = \{x \in X; \text{ rank } Df(x) < m\}$$

The set of critical values of f is $f(C_f)$, and the set of regular values is its complement, $\mathbb{R}^m \sim f(C_f)$. Note that if y is not the image of any point in X, then y is by definition a regular value of f, because a regular value is any point that is not a critical value, and y is a critical value of f if and only if $f^{-1}(y)$ contains at least one critical point, which is impossible if $f^{-1}(y)$ is the empty set.

This definition generalizes the standard concept of critical point used in the elementary calculus. If f is a multivariate real-valued function, the definition we have just given is equivalent to the condition that the gradient $\nabla f(x)$ be the zero vector, because this is the only case in which the components of $\nabla f(x)$ do not generate $\mathbb{R}$; if f is a univariate function, the condition reduces to $f'(x) = 0$. Note also that if f is a function from $\mathbb{R}^n$ into itself, then $Df(x)$ is a square matrix, and x is a critical point if $|Df(x)| = 0$.

The Chain Rule

In many cases we are interested in the derivatives of composite functions. The following result says that the composition of differentiable functions is differentiable, and its derivative is the product of the derivatives of the original functions.

Theorem 3.5. Let f *and* g *be two functions, with*

$$\text{f}: \mathbb{R}^n \supseteq \text{X} \longrightarrow \mathbb{R}^m \quad \text{and} \quad \text{g}: \mathbb{R}^m \supseteq \text{Y} \longrightarrow \mathbb{R}^p$$

where X *and* Y *are open sets, and* $\text{Y} \supseteq \text{f(X)}$. *Let* x^0 *be a point in* X, *put* $\text{y}^0 = \text{f}(\text{x}^0)$, *and define the composite function*

$$\text{F} = \text{g} \circ \text{f} \quad by \quad \text{F(x)} = \text{g}[\text{f(x)}] \quad \text{for each } \text{x} \in \text{X}$$

If f *is differentiable at* x^0, *and* g *at* y^0, *then* $\text{F} = \text{g} \circ \text{f}$ *is differentiable at* x^0, *and its derivative is given by*

$$\text{DF}(\text{x}^0) = \text{Dg}(\text{y}^0)\text{Df}(\text{x}^0)$$

Proof. We want to show that

$$\lim_{\|h\| \to 0} \frac{\|E_F(h)\|}{\|h\|} = \lim_{\|h\| \to 0} \frac{\|F(x^0 + h) - F(x^0) - Dg(y^0)Df(x^0)h\|}{\|h\|} = 0 \qquad (0)$$

for if this expression holds, F is differentiable at x^0, and its derivative is $Dg(y^0)Df(x^0)$. The basic idea is to show that the error $E_F(h)$ is "small" by relating it to the analogous terms for f and g, which are small by assumption.

For arbitrary $h \in \mathbb{R}^n$ and $k \in \mathbb{R}^m$, define

$$E_f(h) = f(x^0 + h) - f(x^0) - Df(x^0)h \qquad (1)$$

$$E_g(k) = g(y^0 + k) - g(y^0) - Dg(y^0)k \qquad (2)$$

The vectors $E_f(h)$ and $E_g(h)$ are the errors committed when we approximate f and g by their respective differentials. Because f and g are by assumption differentiable at x^0 and y^0, respectively, we know that these terms are small for h and k close to zero; in particular,

$$\varepsilon(h) = \frac{\|E_f(h)\|}{\|h\|} \to 0 \quad \text{as} \quad \|h\| \to 0 \qquad (3)$$

$$\eta(k) = \frac{\|E_g(k)\|}{\|k\|} \to 0 \quad \text{as } \|k\| \to 0 \tag{4}$$

Fix h and let

$$k = f(x^0 + h) - f(x^0) = f(x^0 + h) - y^0 \tag{5}$$

Then

$$
\begin{aligned}
\|k\| &= \|f(x^0 + h) - f(x^0)\| && \text{(by (1))} \\
&= \|E_f(h) + Df(x^0)h\| && \text{(by the triangle inequality)} \\
&\leq \|E_f(h)\| + \|Df(x^0)h\| && \text{(by (3))}^7 \\
&\leq \varepsilon(h)\|h\| + \|Df(x^0)\|\|h\| \\
&= \|h\|(\varepsilon(h) + \|Df(x^0)\|) \tag{6}
\end{aligned}
$$

Consider now the expression in the numerator of (0). We can write

$$
\begin{aligned}
E_F(h) &= F(x^0 + h) - F(x^0) - Dg(y^0)Df(x^0)h \\
&= g[f(x^0 + h)] - g[f(x^0)] - Dg(y^0)Df(x^0)h && \text{(by (5))} \\
&= g(y^0 + k) - g(y^0) - Dg(y^0)Df(x^0)h && \text{(by (2))} \\
&= E_g(k) + Dg(y^0)k - Dg(y^0)Df(x^0)h \\
&= E_g(k) + Dg(y^0)[f(x^0 + h) - f(x^0) - Df(x^0)h] && \text{(by (5))}
\end{aligned}
$$

from which

$$E_F(h) = E_g(k) + Dg(y^0)E_f(h) \tag{7}$$

This expression relates the approximation error for F to the analogous terms for f and g. Because each of the latter is small, so will be $E_F(h)$, which establishes the desired result. More formally, returning to (0) and using (7), we have

$$
\begin{aligned}
\frac{\|E_f(h)\|}{\|h\|} &= \frac{\|E_g(k) + Dg(y^0)E_f(h)\|}{\|h\|} && \text{(by (7))} \\
&\leq \frac{\|E_g(k)\| + \|Dg(y^0)\|\,\|E_f(h)\|}{\|h\|} && \text{(by (3) and (4))} \\
&= \frac{\eta(k)\|k\|}{\|h\|} + \varepsilon(h)\|D_g(y^0)\| && \text{(by (6))} \\
&= \eta(k)\{\varepsilon(h) + \|Df(x^0)\|\} + \varepsilon(h)\|Dg(y^0)\|
\end{aligned}
$$

Finally, suppose $\|h\| \to 0$. Then $\varepsilon(h) \to 0$, and, by (6), so does $\|k\|$, implying $\eta(k) \to 0$. Hence,

$$\lim_{\|h\| \to 0} \frac{\|E_F(h)\|}{\|h\|} = 0$$

which is what we wanted to show.   □

Problem 3.6. Let $w = f(x, y, z) = xy^2z$, with

$$x = r + 2s + t, \qquad y = 2r + 3s + t, \qquad z = 3r + s + t$$

Use the chain rule to calculate $\partial w/\partial r$, $\partial w/\partial s$, and $\partial w/\partial t$.

The Mean-Value Theorem

Given a function $g: \mathbb{R} \longrightarrow \mathbb{R}$ differentiable on an open interval I, the mean-value theorem says that for any x and y in I there exists some number z between x and y such that

$$f(y) - f(x) = f'(z)(y - x) \tag{1}$$

This formula continues to be valid for real functions of several variables, but it may not hold for mappings from $\mathbb{R}^n$ into $\mathbb{R}^m$. The following result tells us how (1) has to be modified in this case.

We will use the notation $L(x, y)$ to refer to the straight *line segment* that joins points x and y. That is, if $x, y \in \mathbb{R}^n$, then

$$L(x, y) = \{z \in \mathbb{R}^n;\ z = \lambda x + (1 - \lambda)y,\ \lambda \in [0,1]\}$$

Theorem 3.7. Mean-value theorem. Let $f: \mathbb{R}^n \longrightarrow \mathbb{R}^m$ *be differentiable on an open subset* X *of* $\mathbb{R}^n$, *and let* x *and* y *be two points in* X *such that* L(x, y) *is contained in* X. *Then for each vector* a *in* $\mathbb{R}^m$ *there exists a vector* z *in* L(x, y) *such that*

$$a[f(y) - f(x)] = a[Df(z)(y - x)] \tag{2}$$

Of course, if X *is a convex set, then* $X \supseteq L(x, y)$ *for all* x, y *in* X.

Problem 3.8. Complete the following proof of Theorem 3.7. Put $h = y - x$. As X is open and contains $L(x, y)$, there exists some $\delta > 0$ such that $x + \lambda h \in X$ for $\lambda \in (-\delta, 1 + \delta)$. Fix an arbitrary vector $a \in \mathbb{R}^m$, and define a real-valued function ϕ_a on the interval $(-\delta, 1 + \delta)$ by

$$\phi_a(\lambda) = af(x + \lambda h) = \sum_{i=1}^{m} a_i f^i(x + \lambda h)$$

By construction, $\phi_a(\ )$ is differentiable on $(-\delta, 1 + \delta)$. Compute its derivative, and apply the mean-value theorem for univariate functions to conclude that there exists some vector $z = x + \theta h$ for which (2) holds.   □

Theorem 3.9. Let $f: \mathbb{R}^n \longrightarrow \mathbb{R}^m$ *be a differentiable function on an open subset* X *of* $\mathbb{R}^n$, *and let* x *and* y *be two points in* X *such that* L(x, y) *is contained in* X. *Then there exists a vector* z *in* L(x, y) *such that*

$$\|f(y) - f(x)\| \le \|Df(z)(y - x)\| \le \|Df(z)\| \|y - x\| \tag{3}$$

Proof. If $f(x) = f(y)$, the result holds trivially. Otherwise, the mean-value theorem guarantees that for each vector $a \in \mathbb{R}^m$ there exists some vector $z \in L(x, y)$ such that

$$a[f(y) - f(x)] = a[Df(z)(y - x)]$$

Taking the absolute value of each side of this expression and using the Cauchy-Schwarz inequality, we have

$$|a(f(y) - f(x))| = |a(Df(z)(y - x))| \le \|a\| \|Df(z)(y - x)\| \tag{4}$$

Now, let a be the unit vector

$$a = \frac{(f(y) - f(x))^T}{\|f(y) - f(x)\|}$$

and observe that in this case

$$\begin{aligned} |a(f(y) - f(x))| &= \frac{1}{\|f(y) - f(x)\|} |(f(y) - f(x))^T (f(y) - f(x))| \\ &= \frac{\|f(y) - f(x)\|^2}{\|f(y) - f(x)\|} = \|f(y) - f(x)\| \end{aligned}$$

Using (4) and the preceding expression,

$$\|f(y) - f(x)\| = |a(f(y) - f(x))| \le 1 \|Df(z)(y - x)\| \le \|Df(z)\| \|y - x\|$$

where we have made use of the fact that for any linear transformation A and any vector x, $\|Ax\| \le \|A\| \|x\|$ (see Chapter 3). $\qquad\square$

4. Continuous Differentiability

We now introduce a stronger concept of differentiability that will be useful later. Let f be differentiable on an open region X – that is, we assume that the derivative $Df(x)$ exists at all points in X. We then say that f is continuously differentiable on X if its derivative is a continuous function. In this statement, we think of the derivative of f as a function Df from X to the set $L(\mathbb{R}^n, \mathbb{R}^m)$ of linear transformations from $\mathbb{R}^n$ to $\mathbb{R}^m$ equipped with the norm defined in Chapter 3.[8] With this in mind, the definition of continuity is the usual one: f is continuously differentiable if it is differentiable and any two nearby points, x and y, in its domain have as differentials linear transformations df_x and df_y, which are similar.

Definition 4.1. Continuously differentiable function. The function $f: \mathbb{R}^n \supseteq X \longrightarrow \mathbb{R}^m$ (X open) is continuously differentiable on X if it is differentiable on X and the derivative Df is a continuous function from X to $L(\mathbb{R}^n, \mathbb{R}^m)$. That is, given any x in X and an arbitrary $\varepsilon > 0$, there exists some $\delta > 0$ such that

$$\|df_x - df_y\| < \varepsilon \ \forall \ y \in B_\delta(x)$$

where the symbol $\|\cdot\|$ denotes the norm of a linear transformation.

This definition may appear a little strange, because it is difficult to visualize what we mean by continuity for a function whose value at each point is a linear mapping. The next definition and the theorem that follows it will give us a characterization of continuous differentiability in more familiar terms.

Definition 4.2. Function of class C^k. The function $f: \mathbb{R}^n \supseteq X \to \mathbb{R}^m$ (X open) is (of class) C^k in X, written $f \in C^k(X)$, if the first k partial derivatives of the component functions of f exist and are continuous on X.

By convention, a continuous function is of class C^0. If $f \in C^k$, where $k \geq 1$, we say that f is a *smooth function*, although this term is sometimes reserved for functions of class C^∞.

The following result tells us that the continuity of the first partial derivatives of the components of f is a necessary and sufficient condition for f to be continuously differentiable. Intuitively, this equivalence should not be surprising: A function is continuously differentiable if two nearby points, x and y in X, have as differentials linear functions df_x and df_y that are "close," that is, represented by similar matrices $Df(x)$ and $Df(y)$. Because the coefficients of these matrices are the partial derivatives of the components of f and, provided f is C^1, the partials are continuous functions, small changes in x will result in small changes in each of these coefficients and will therefore yield similar differentials.

Theorem 4.3. The function $f: \mathbb{R}^n \supseteq X \longrightarrow \mathbb{R}^m$ *(X open) is continuously differentiable in X if and only if it is of class* C^1 *in X.*

Proof. Let x and $x + h$ be two points in X. Under our assumptions, f is differentiable in both parts of the theorem (by assumption for the necessity part, and by Theorem 3.4 for the sufficiency implication), so df_{x+h} and df_x exist, and their difference $df_{x+h} - df_x$ is a linear transformation in $L(\mathbb{R}^n, \mathbb{R}^m)$ with matrix representation $[a_{ik}] = Df(x + h) - Df(x)$, where

$$a_{ik}(h) = f_k^i(x+h) - f_k^i(x) \tag{1}$$

Fix x and define

$$\kappa(h) = \max_{ik} |a_{ik}(h)| = \max_{ik} |f^i_k(x+h) - f^i_k(x)|$$

By Theorem 4.9 in Chapter 3, we have

$$0 \le \kappa(h) \le \|df_{x+h} - df_x\| \le \kappa(h)\sqrt{mn} \tag{2}$$

from which we obtain the equivalence

$$[\kappa(h) \to 0 \text{ as } h \to \underline{0}] \quad \text{if and only if} \quad [\|df_{x+h} - df_x\| \to 0 \text{ as } h \to \underline{0}]. \tag{3}$$

If $f \in C^1$, the continuity of the partials implies that for each i and k, $a_{ik}(h) \to 0$ as $h \to \underline{0}$ (see (1)). It follows that $\kappa(h) = \max_{ik}|a_{ik}(h)|$ also goes to zero, implying $\|df_{x+h} - df_x\| \to 0$, and hence the continuity of the derivative mapping. Conversely, the continuity of Df implies $\|df_{x+h} - df_x\| \to 0$; then $\kappa(h) \to 0$, and because $0 \le |a_{ik}(h)| \le \kappa(h)$ for all a_{ik}, we have $a_{ik}(h) \to 0$ for all i and k, that is,

$$\lim_{h \to \underline{0}} f^i_k(x+h) = f^i_k(x)$$

so the partial derivatives are indeed continuous. $\qquad\qquad\square$

Taylor's Theorem

Taylor's formula can be generalized for the case of a real-valued function of n variables. Because the notation gets rather messy, and we need only the simplest case, we shall state the following theorem for the case of a first-order approximation with a quadratic-form remainder. This result will be useful later in connection with the characterization of concavity for smooth functions and the derivation of necessary and sufficient conditions for local maxima.

Theorem 4.4. Taylor's formula for multivariate functions with second-order remainder. Let $f: \mathbb{R}^n \longrightarrow \mathbb{R}$ *be a* C^2 *function defined on an open and convex set* X. *If* x, x + h $\in$ X, *then*

$$f(x+h) = f(x) + Df(x)h + (1/2)h^T D^2 f(x + \lambda h)h \tag{1}$$

for some $\lambda \in (0, 1)$.

Problem 4.5. Prove Theorem 4.4. Hint: Apply the univariate version of Taylor's formula to the function $g(\alpha) = f(x + \alpha h)$.

The Inverse-Function Theorem

Let f be a function from $\mathbb{R}^n$ to itself. Each vector $x \in \mathbb{R}^n$ is mapped by f into another vector y in $\mathbb{R}^n$, that is

$$f(x) = y \tag{1}$$

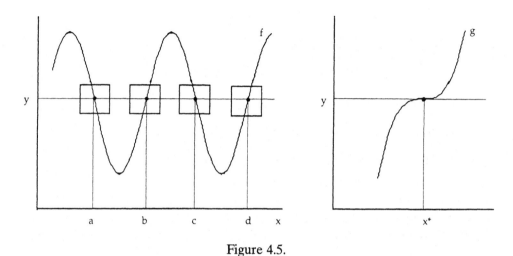

Figure 4.5.

We can also turn this expression around: Given a vector y, (1) is a system of n equations in n unknowns (the components of x). We would like to know under what conditions it is true that given a vector y, equation (1) can be solved for a value of x that is, at least locally, unique.

If f is a linear operator, (1) is equivalent to a system of the form

$$Ax = y \qquad (2)$$

where A is a square matrix. Then A is invertible if and only if its determinant is not zero, and therefore equation (2) has a unique solution $x^* = A^{-1}y$ for each given y whenever $|A| \neq 0$ – that is, provided all the equations in the system are linearly independent.

If f is not linear, the question of its invertibility is more complicated, but in many cases it is possible to determine whether or not a function is locally invertible simply by calculating the determinant of its derivative matrix. Consider first the case of a function from $\mathbb{R}$ to $\mathbb{R}$. If f is continuously differentiable on some interval I and $f'(x) \neq 0$ for all $x \in I$, then the function is monotonic and therefore one-to-one. It follows that the inverse relation f^{-1} is a well-defined function on $f(I)$. Given any y in $f(I)$, the equation $f(x) = y$ will have a unique solution, $x^* = f^{-1}(y)$.

If f is not monotonic, the inverse relation f^{-1} is not a function, and there could be several solutions to the equation $f(x) = y$, as suggested in Figure 4.5. On the other hand, these solutions will be locally unique provided f is strictly monotonic in some neighborhood of the solution. Hence, $f'(x^*) \neq 0$ and $f \in C^1$ in some open neighborhood of a solution x^* are sufficient conditions for the local invertibility of f close to x^*. If we restrict ourselves to a sufficiently small neighborhood of x^*, f^{-1} is a well-defined function under these assumptions.

We now ask if it is possible to extend this result for functions of $\mathbb{R}^n$ into itself. For this purpose it will be convenient to reinterpret the preceding discussion in terms of the invertibility of the differential of f, rather than the monotonicity of the function. If $f'(x) = a \neq 0$, then $df_x(h) = ah$ is an invertible linear function. Hence, we can rephrase our earlier conclusion by saying that a sufficient condition for a continuously differentiable function to be locally invertible in a neighborhood of a point x is that its differential at x be invertible.[9] Because the differential of a function is the best linear approximation to it, it seems reasonable to conjecture that the result is true in general, and the following theorem confirms that this is indeed the case. We may even suspect that the invertibility of its differential is necessary, as well as sufficient, for the local invertibility of a function, but the second panel of Figure 4.5 shows that this is not true: The function g is strictly monotonic and therefore globally invertible, but its derivative at the inflection point x^* is zero, and therefore its differential is not invertible.

Theorem 4.6. Inverse-function theorem. Let f: $\mathbb{R}^n \supseteq X \longrightarrow \mathbb{R}^n$ *(X open) be a continuously differentiable function, and* x^0 *a point on its domain. Assume that the determinant of the Jacobian of* f *is not zero at* x^0 *(i.e.,* $|\mathrm{D}f(x^0)| \neq 0$*). Then there exists an open neighborhood of* x^0*, U, such that*

(i) f *is one-to-one in* U; *hence the inverse relation* f^{-1} *is a well-defined function from* V = f(U) *to* U,
(ii) V = f(U) *is an open set containing* $y^0 = f(x^0)$,
(iii) *the inverse function* f^{-1} *is of class* C^1, *with derivative* $\mathrm{D}f^{-1}(y^0) = [\mathrm{D}f(x^0)]^{-1}$,
(iv) *if* f *is* C^k, *with* k > 1, *so is* f^{-1}.

A *diffeomorphism* is an invertible smooth function (C^k with $k \geq 1$) with a smooth inverse. The inverse-function theorem says that a sufficient condition for f to be locally a diffeomorphism near a point x^0 is that x^0 be a regular point of f.

Proof. Before getting into the details, which are rather complicated, let us sketch the logic of the proof. We begin by defining U as an open ball with center at x^0 and sufficiently small radius. (What we mean by this will become clear later.) To establish the local invertibility of f, we make use of an auxiliary function $\phi_y(x)$, defined for each vector y in $\mathbb{R}^n$ by

$$\phi_y(x) = x + [Df(x^0)]^{-1}[y - f(x)]$$

Observe that by construction, $y = f(x)$ if and only if x is a fixed point of $\phi_y(\ )$. Given a point x in U, let y be its image. Then it can be shown that $\phi_y(\ )$ is a contraction that maps a closed ball B with center at x into itself. By the contraction mapping theorem, for each $y \in f(U)$, $\phi_y(\ )$ has a unique fixed point in U that lies inside B. This implies that there is a unique point in U with image y (x itself); f is therefore one-to-one in U, and the restriction of the inverse relation f^{-1} to $f(U)$ is a well-defined function.

The second step is to establish the differentiability of f^{-1}. By assumption, the differential of f at x^0 is an invertible linear operator in $L(\mathbb{R}^n)$. The radius of U has been chosen small enough that df_x is invertible for all x in U. This is possible because the set $\Omega(\mathbb{R}^n)$ of invertible linear operators on $\mathbb{R}^n$ is open, as we saw in Chapter 3 (Theorem 4.14), and because f is continuously differentiable.[10]

We know, therefore, that $[Df(x)]^{-1}$ exists for all $x \in U$. Inserting this matrix into the expression that defines the derivative of the inverse function, we verify that it works, thus establishing that for $x = f^{-1}(y)$,

$$Df^{-1}(y) = \left\{ Df[f^{-1}(y)] \right\}^{-1}$$

This expression shows also that Df^{-1} is the composition of three continuous functions and is therefore continuous; that is, f^{-1} is C^1. Now for the details.

(i) f is one-to-one in U. Put $Df(x^0) = A$ (which is an invertible matrix by assumption) and define λ by

$$2\lambda \|A^{-1}\| = 1 \tag{1}$$

where, to avoid complicating the notation further, $\|A\|$ is the norm of the linear operator associated with the matrix A.

Because X is open, there exists some $\delta > 0$ such that the open ball $U = B_\delta(x^0)$ is contained in X. Further, by the continuous differentiability of f, Df is a continuous function from X to $L(\mathbb{R}^n)$, so we can choose δ in such a way that for every $x \in U$ the derivative $Df(x)$ is not very different from A; in particular, there is some $\delta > 0$ such that

$$\|Df(x) - A\| < \lambda \ \forall \ x \in U = B_\delta(x^0) \tag{2}$$

With each $y \in \mathbb{R}^n$ we associate a function $\phi_y(\ )$ defined for x in X by

$$\phi_y(x) = x + A^{-1}[y - f(x)] \tag{3}$$

and observe that $y = f(x)$ if and only if x is a fixed point of $\phi_y(\ )$.

To show that f is one-to-one in U, we have to prove that given a vector y, there exists at most one x in U such that $f(x) = y$ – or, equivalently, that for each y, $\phi_y(\ )$ has at most one fixed point in U. This will be true if $\phi_y(\ )$ is a contraction in U, as we now show.

The derivative of $\phi_y(\ )$ is

$$D\phi_y(x) = I - A^{-1}Df(x) = A^{-1}[A - Df(x)]$$

Expressions (1) and (2) and the properties of the norm in $L(\mathbb{R}^n)$ imply that for any $x \in U$,

$$\|D\phi_y(x)\| = \|A^{-1}[A - Df(x)]\| \le \|A^{-1}\|\|A - Df(x)\| < \frac{1}{2\lambda}\lambda = \frac{1}{2} \qquad (4)$$

from which we have (by Theorem 3.9) that for any x' and x'' in U,

$$\|\phi_y(x') - \phi_y(x'')\| \le \frac{1}{2}\|x' - x''\| \qquad (5)$$

establishing that the restriction of ϕ_y to U is a contraction. As U is not complete, ϕ_y may not have a fixed point in it, but it is still true that there can be no more than one such point. Hence, given y, there is at most one x in U with $f(x) = y$; f is one-to-one in U.

(ii) $f(U)$ is an open set and contains $y^0 = f(x^0)$. Put $V = f(U)$ and take an arbitrary y' in V; then $y' = f(x')$ for some $x' \in U$. Let $B = B_r[x']$ be a closed ball contained in U, with center at x' and radius r. (Observe that it is always possible to construct such a ball, because U is open.) To show that V is open, we will prove that $\|y - y'\| < \lambda r$ implies $y \in V$.

Take some y such that $\|y - y'\| < \lambda r$ and observe that by (1), $2\lambda \|A^{-1}\| = 1$,

$$\|\phi_y(x') - x'\| = \|A^{-1}(y - y')\| \le \|A^{-1}\|\|y - y'\| < \|A^{-1}\|\lambda r = r/2 \qquad (6)$$

For $x \in B$ we have, by the triangle inequality and using (5) and (6),

$$\|\phi_y(x) - x'\| \le \|\phi_y(x) - \phi_y(x')\| + \|\phi_y(x') - x'\| < (1/2)\|x - x'\| + (r/2) \le r$$

and therefore $\phi_y(x) \in B$ for $x \in B$ and y close to y'.

It follows that for an appropriate y, $\phi_y(\ )$ is a contraction that maps B into itself. Moreover, B, being a closed subset of $\mathbb{R}^n$, is complete. By the contraction mapping theorem (see Chapter 3), $\phi_y(\ )$ has a fixed point x^* in B. For this $x^* \in B = B_r[x'] \subseteq U$, $f(x^*) = y$, implying $y \in f(B) \subseteq f(U) = V$ whenever $\|y - y'\| < \lambda r$. In words, given an arbitrary point y' in V, we can construct an open ball around it that is still contained in V, that is, V is open.

(iii) The inverse function f^{-1} is differentiable, with $Df^{-1}(y^0) = [Df(x^0)]^{-1}$. Take two points y and $y + k$ in $V = f(U)$. Then there exist vectors x and $x + h$ in U such that

$$y = f(x) \quad \text{and} \quad y + k = f(x + h)$$

With $\phi_z(\ )$ defined as in (3), we have

$$\phi_z(x + h) - \phi_z(x) = h + A^{-1}[f(x) - f(x + h)] = h - A^{-1}k$$

Because $x, x + h \in U$, we have, by (5),

$$\|\phi_z(x + h) - \phi_z(x)\| = \|h - A^{-1}k\| \le (1/2)\|h\|$$

implying

$$\|h\| - \|A^{-1}k\| \le \|h - A^{-1}k\| \le (1/2)\|h\| \Rightarrow \|A^{-1}k\| \ge (1/2)\|h\|$$

and therefore, using (1),

$$\|h\| \leq 2\|A^{-1}k\| \leq 2\|A^{-1}\|\|k\| = (1/\lambda)\|k\| \tag{7}$$

Hence, if y and $y + k$ are close in V, then the distance between their preimages x and $x + h$ is also small. This expression directly implies the continuity of the inverse function f^{-1}, but we want to establish the stronger result that f^{-1} is differentiable.

Observe that (1) and (2) imply that for every x in U we have

$$\|Df(x) - A\| < \frac{1}{2\|A^{-1}\|}$$

where $A = Df(x^0)$ is by assumption invertible. By Theorem 4.14 in Chapter 4, $Df(x)$ is also invertible for every x in U; denote its inverse $[Df(x)]^{-1}$ by T. To show that f^{-1} is differentiable, we insert T in the expression that defines the derivative of f^{-1} and verify that it holds. We have

$$\begin{aligned} f^{-1}(y+k) - f^{-1}(y) - Tk &= (x+h) - x - Tk = hI - Tk \\ &= hTDf(x) - T[(y+k) - y] \\ &= -T[f(x+h) - f(x) - Df(x)h] \end{aligned}$$

from which

$$\|f^{-1}(y+k) - f^{-1}(y) - Tk\| \leq \|T\|\|f(x+h) - f(x) - Df(x)h\|$$

which, together with (7), implies

$$0 \leq \frac{\|f^{-1}(y+k) - f^{-1}(y) - Tk\|}{\|k\|} \leq \|T\| \frac{\|f(x+h) - f(x) - Df(x)h\|}{\lambda\|h\|} \tag{8}$$

Now, (7) implies that $\|h\| \to 0$ as $\|k\| \to 0$. Because f is differentiable at x and $(1/\lambda)\|T\|$ is a constant, the right-hand side of the inequality goes to zero, and therefore so does the middle term as $\|h\|$ (and hence $\|k\|$) goes to zero. In conclusion, f is differentiable, and its derivative is given by

$$Df^{-1}(y) = T = \left(Df[f^{-1}(y)]\right)^{-1} \tag{9}$$

(iv) It remains to show that f^{-1} is continuously differentiable, that is, that its derivative

$$Df^{-1}: V \to L(\mathbb{R}^n)$$

is a continuous function. By (9), we see that Df^{-1} is the composition of the following three continuous functions:

- f^{-1}, which is a differentiable and therefore continuous function from V to U, as we have just shown,
- $Df(\ )$, a continuous function (by assumption) from U to $L(\mathbb{R}^n)$, and in particular to the subset $\Omega(\mathbb{R}^n)$ of invertible operators in $L(\mathbb{R}^n)$ (because U is defined in such a way that $Df(x)$ is invertible for all x in U), and

- the inversion operator, $(\ )^{-1}:\Omega(\mathbb{R}^n) \longrightarrow \Omega(\mathbb{R}^n)$, which assigns to each invertible operator in $L(\mathbb{R}^n)$ its inverse. (This function is continuous by Theorem 4.15 in Chapter 3.)

    Hence, the composite function $Df^{-1}:U \longrightarrow \Omega(\mathbb{R}^n)$ is continuous. ☐

Problem 4.7. Let $f:\mathbb{R}^n \supseteq X \longrightarrow \mathbb{R}^n$ be a continuously differentiable function on the open set X. Show that f is locally Lipschitz on X. (See Section 6 in Chapter 2.)

5. Homogeneous Functions

A set X in $\mathbb{R}^n$ is called a *cone* if given any $x \in X$ the point λx belongs to X for any $\lambda > 0$. A function defined on a cone is said to be homogeneous of degree k if, when we multiply all its arguments by a positive real number λ, the value of the function increases in the proportion λ^k.

Definition 5.1. Homogeneous functions. A function $f:\mathbb{R}^n \supseteq X \longrightarrow \mathbb{R}$, where X is a cone, is homogeneous of degree k in X if

$$f(\lambda x) = \lambda^k f(x) \ \forall \ \lambda > 0$$

Homogeneous functions often arise naturally in economics. For example, consider the response of a consumer to an equiproportional increase in income and the prices of all goods in the market. Because this change would not change the budget set (i.e., the set of consumption bundles the agent can afford), consumption choices should not be affected. Hence, the demand function $x(p, y)$ that gives the optimal consumption bundle as a function of the vector of prices p and income y will be homogeneous of degree zero. In production theory, it often makes sense to assume that a doubling of all inputs will lead to a doubling in output. If this assumption, known as constant returns to scale, holds, the production function will be linearly homogeneous (i.e., homogeneous of degree 1).

The following theorem provides a useful characterization of homogeneous functions with continuous partial derivatives.

Theorem 5.2. Euler's theorem. Let f: $\mathbb{R}^n \supseteq X \longrightarrow \mathbb{R}$ *be a function with continuous partial derivatives defined on an open cone* X. *Then* f *is homogeneous of degree* k *in* X *if and only if*

$$\sum_{i=1}^{n} f_i(x)x_i = kf(x) \ \forall \ x \ in \ X \tag{1}$$

Proof

- Assume that f is homogeneous of degree k, and fix an arbitrary x in X. Then we have

$$f(\lambda x) = \lambda^k f(x)$$

for all $\lambda > 0$. The continuity of the partial derivatives of f guarantees the differentiability of the function. Hence, we can differentiate this expression with respect to λ. Using the chain rule, we have

$$\sum_{i=1}^n f_i(\lambda x)x_i = k\lambda^{k-1} f(x)$$

Putting $\lambda = 1$, we obtain (1).

• Conversely, suppose that (1) holds for all x. Fix an arbitrary x in X, and define the function ϕ for all $\lambda > 0$ by

$$\phi(\lambda) = f(\lambda x)$$

Then

$$\phi'(\lambda) = \sum_{i=1}^n f_i(\lambda x)x_i$$

and multiplying both sides of this expression by λ,

$$\lambda\phi'(\lambda) = \sum_{i=1}^n f_i(\lambda x)\lambda x_i = kf(\lambda x) = k\phi(\lambda) \tag{2}$$

where the second equality follows by applying (1) to the point λx.

Next, define the function F for $\lambda > 0$ by

$$F(\lambda) = \frac{\phi(\lambda)}{\lambda^k} \tag{3}$$

and observe that, using (2),

$$F'(\lambda) = \frac{\lambda^k \phi'(\lambda) - k\lambda^{k-1}\phi(\lambda)}{(\lambda^k)^2} = \frac{\lambda^{k-1}}{(\lambda^k)^2}[\lambda\phi'(\lambda) - k\phi(\lambda)] = 0$$

Hence, F is a constant function. Putting $\lambda = 1$ in (3), we have $F(1) = \phi(1)$, and therefore

$$F(\lambda) = \frac{\phi(\lambda)}{\lambda^k} = \phi(1) \Rightarrow \phi(\lambda) = \lambda^k \phi(1)$$

Finally, recalling that $\phi(\lambda) \equiv f(\lambda x)$, we have

$$f(\lambda x) = \lambda^k f(x)$$

as was to be shown.   □

Problem 5.3. Show that if f is homogeneous of degree k and "sufficiently differentiable," then its first partial derivatives are homogeneous of degree $k - 1$.

Problem 5.4

(i) Show that the Cobb-Douglas function

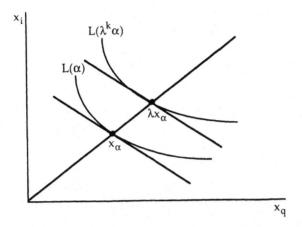

Figure 4.6. Level sets of a homogeneous function.

$$f(x) = A\prod_{i=1}^{n} x_i^{\alpha_i} \text{ is homogeneous of degree } \sum_{i=1}^{n}\alpha_i$$

(ii) Show that the constant-elasticity-of-substitution (CES) function,

$$g(x) = A\left(\sum_{i=1}^{n} \delta_i x_i^{-\rho}\right)^{-\upsilon/\rho}, \text{ where } A > 0, \ \upsilon > 0, \ \rho > -1 \text{ and } \rho \neq 0,$$

$$\delta_i > 0 \text{ for all } i, \text{ and } \sum_{i=1}^{n}\delta_i = 1$$

is homogeneous of degree v.

Homogeneous functions have some interesting geometric properties. Let X be a cone in $\mathbb{R}^n$, with $f: X \longrightarrow \mathbb{R}$ a homogeneous function of degree k, and

$$L(\alpha) = \{x \in X; \ f(x) = \alpha\}$$

the α-level set of f. Let x_α be a point in $L(\alpha)$, and consider the point λx_α (with $\lambda > 0$) obtained by moving along the ray going through the origin and x_α. Then $f(x_\alpha) = \alpha$ and by the homogeneity of $f(\ )$, we have

$$f(\lambda x_\alpha) = \lambda^k f(x_\alpha) = \lambda^k \alpha$$

Hence, $\lambda x_\alpha \in L(\lambda^k\alpha)$ if $x_\alpha \in L(\alpha)$. Conversely, if $y \in L(\lambda^k\alpha)$, then $(1/\lambda)y$ lies in $L(\alpha)$, by the same argument. Hence, the level sets of homogeneous functions are radial expansions and contractions of each other, as illustrated in Figure 4.6.

The tangent planes to the different level sets of a C^1 homogeneous function, moreover, have constant slope along each ray from the origin. To see this, let x_0 and $x_1 = \lambda x_0$ be two points lying on the same ray through the origin, and let f be C^1 and homogeneous of degree k. Using Problem 5.3, we have, for any i and q,

$$\frac{f_i(x_1)}{f_q(x_1)} = \frac{f_i(\lambda x_0)}{f_q(\lambda x_0)} = \frac{\lambda^{k-1} f_i(x_0)}{\lambda^{k-1} f_q(x_0)} = \frac{f_i(x_0)}{f_q(x_0)}$$

If f is a utility function, for example, this expression says that the marginal rate of substitution between any two goods, i and q, is constant along each ray from the origin.

A function is said to be *homothetic* if it is an increasing transformation of a homogeneous function. That is, $g(\ )$ is homothetic if it can be written in the form $g(\ ) = h[f(\ )]$, where f is homogeneous of some degree and $h: \mathbb{R} \to \mathbb{R}$ is an increasing function. Notice that, because the family of level sets of $g(\ )$ is the same as that of $f(\ )$, homothetic functions inherit the geometric properties of homogeneous functions. In particular, their level sets are radial expansions or contractions of each other, and the slope of their level sets is the same along each ray from the origin.

Bibliography

Apostol, T. 1989. *Calculus*, 2nd ed. Barcelona: Editorial Reverté.

Apostol, T. 1974. *Mathematical Analysis*, 2nd ed. Reading, MA: Addison-Wesley.

Binmore, K. 1982. *Mathematical Analysis, A Straightforward Approach.* Cambridge University Press.

Buck, R. 1978. *Advanced Calculus*, 3rd ed. New York: McGraw-Hill.

Clark, C. 1982. *Elementary Mathematical Analysis*, 2nd ed. Belmont, CA: Wadsworth.

Lang, S. 1989. *Undergraduate Analysis.* Berlin: Springer-Verlag.

Luenberger, D. 1973. *Introduction to Linear and Non-linear Programming.* Reading, MA: Addison-Wesley.

Rudin, W. 1976. *Principles of Mathematical Analysis*, 3rd ed. New York: McGraw-Hill.

Sydsæter, K. 1981. *Topics in Mathematical Analysis for Economists.* Orlando, FL: Academic Press.

Taylor, A., and Mann, W. 1983. *Advanced Calculus*, 3rd ed. New York: Wiley.

Weintraub, E. 1982. *Mathematics of Economists, An Integrated Approach.* Cambridge University Press.

Notes

1 To avoid writing out all the components of a vector when we are interested in just one of them, we will use the following notation. Let x_i be an arbitrary component of the vector x, and define the vector

$$x_{-i} = (x_1, \ldots, x_{i-1}, x_{i+1}, \ldots, x_n)$$

which contains all the components of x except for x_i. We can then write $x = (x_i, x_{-i})$.

2 As a matter of fact, we should say an affine function. A function is affine if it is the sum of a linear function and a constant.

3 In fact, we could define differentiability directly in terms of the existence of a linear mapping T_x such that

$$\lim_{\|h\| \to 0} \frac{\|f(x+h) - f(x) - T_x(h)\|}{\|h\|} = 0$$

We know, however, that given bases for $\mathbb{R}^n$ and $\mathbb{R}^m$, there exists a bijective linear function between $L(\mathbb{R}^n, \mathbb{R}^m)$ and $\mathbb{R}_{m \times n}$, so that, for all practical purposes, it makes little difference which definition we use. The one we give in the text is probably easier to visualize, but we will occasionally ask the reader to think of the derivative of f as a function $X \longrightarrow L(\mathbb{R}^n, \mathbb{R}^m)$.

4 The term "Jacobian" is sometimes used to refer to the determinant of a matrix of partial derivatives, rather than to the matrix itself. The meaning should be clear from the context.

5 This is easily verified by induction.

6 Notice what we are doing. For $n = 2$, we have

$$f(x+h) - f(x) = f(x_1 + \alpha_1, x_2 + \alpha_2) - f(x_1, x_2)$$
$$= [f(x_1 + \alpha_1, x_2 + \alpha_2) - f(x_1 + \alpha_1, x_2)] + [f(x_1 + \alpha_1, x_2) - f(x_1, x_2)]$$

We decompose the change in f from x to $x + h$ into the sum of n changes, each between two points that differ only in one coordinate. This is done so that we can use the one-dimensional mean-value theorem.

7 Here, $\|Df(x^0)\|$ is the norm of the linear transformation associated with the matrix $Df(x^0)$. Recall from Chapter 3 that if A is a linear transformation, and x a vector, then $\|Ax\| \le \|A\| \, \|x\|$.

8 Let T be a continuous linear transformation defined between two normed vector spaces X and Y. As discussed in Section 4(b) of Chapter 3, its norm is defined by $\|T\| = \sup_x \{\|Tx\|; x \in X, \|x\| \le 1\}$.

9 Another intuitive way to interpret this result is as follows. Suppose x^0 solves the system $f(x) = y$ for some value y^0 of y, and linearize the system around x^0 to get $f(x) \cong f(x^0) + Df(x^0)(x - x^0) = y$. If the equations of the linearized system are all linearly independent, then $f(x) = y$ has a locally unique solution for any y sufficiently close to y^0.

10 The inverse image of an open set under a continuous function is open. Therefore, $(Df)^{-1}(\Omega(\mathbb{R}^n))$ is open, and given a point in this set there is an open ball around it that is still contained in the set. We take U to be a subset of this ball.

Part II
Statics

5

Static Models and Comparative Statics

A great many economic models into which time does not enter explicitly can be reduced to a parameterized system of equations of the form

$$F(x; \alpha) = \underline{0} \tag{M}$$

where F is a function $F: \mathbb{R}^n \times \mathbb{R}^p \supseteq X \times \Omega \longrightarrow \mathbb{R}^m$ and typically $m = n$. We interpret α as a vector of *parameters* that summarizes the "environment" in which the system described by the model is embedded, and x as the vector of *endogenous variables* whose equilibrium values we seek. Many of the questions we ask when we analyze such a model can be formulated in terms of the properties of the solution correspondence,

$$S: \Omega \longrightarrow\!\!\!\!\longrightarrow X, \quad \text{where } S(\alpha) = \{x \in X; \, F(x; \alpha) = \underline{0}\}$$

which assigns to each vector of parameters the corresponding set of equilibrium values of the endogenous variables. In this chapter we will focus on two types of questions that arise naturally in connection with this correspondence:

(i) For a given value of α, what does the solution set of the model look like? Is it empty? If not, what is its dimension? Under this heading we have questions concerning the *existence* and *uniqueness* (local and global) of equilibrium.

(ii) How does $S(\alpha)$ change with changes in the parameters? On a practical level, we are interested in questions of *comparative statics*. That is, in what direction does the equilibrium change as a result of a change in the "environment" or in some control variable? Before we can begin to answer this question, we have to deal with the previous issue of *continuity*: Under what conditions is it true that the equilibrium moves in a continuous and therefore (at least in principle) predictable manner with changes in parameter values?

We will begin with a review of linear models. If $F(\ )$ is a linear function, then the questions we have just raised have rather simple answers in terms of rank conditions and the values of certain determinants. If $F(\ )$ is not linear, things are more complicated, but given some regularity conditions, we can use the calculus to analyze the local behavior of the model by constructing a linear approximation to it in a neighborhood of a known solution point. The basic tool for this kind of analysis is the implicit-function theorem, which will be discussed in depth in Section 2, building on the theory of differentiability for functions from $\mathbb{R}^n$ into $\mathbb{R}^m$ developed in Chapter 4. We conclude in Section 3 with a brief discussion of some results that are often used to prove the existence of solutions to nonlinear models: the intermediate-value theorem and various fixed-point theorems for functions and correspondences.

1. Linear Models

Models that can be written as linear systems of equations are particularly easy to solve and analyze. In this section we will apply some of the results on linear functions obtained in Chapter 3 to the solution of linear systems of equations.

Suppose we are given a model

$$T(x; \alpha) = T_\alpha(x) = \underline{0} \tag{M}$$

where $T : \mathbb{R}^n \times \mathbb{R}^p \supseteq X \times \Omega \longrightarrow \mathbb{R}^m$ is a linear function (and therefore so is T_α). Given bases for $\mathbb{R}^m$, $\mathbb{R}^n$, and $\mathbb{R}^p$, we can write (M) in the form

$$Ax + B\alpha = \underline{0} \tag{1}$$

where A and B are real matrices of dimensions $m \times n$ and $m \times p$, respectively. Putting $y = -B\alpha$, we can write (1) in the form

$$Ax = y \tag{2}$$

which will be more convenient when we work with fixed parameter values. We will interpret (2) as a system of m equations in n unknowns (the coordinates of x). In what follows, we will freely use the equivalence (for given bases) between matrices and linear mappings.

We saw in Chapter 3 that given a linear transformation $T : X \longrightarrow Y$, the sets

$$\ker T = T^{-1}(\underline{0}) = \{x \in X; \ T(x) = \underline{0}\} \quad \text{and}$$
$$\operatorname{im} T = T(X) = \{y \in Y; \ y = T(x) \text{ for some } x \in X\}$$

are vector subspaces of X and Y, respectively, and that their dimensions satisfy the following equality:

$$\dim(\ker T) = \dim X - \dim(\operatorname{im} T) = \dim X - \operatorname{rank} T \tag{3}$$

Thus, the kernel of T is the set of solutions to the homogeneous linear system

$$T(x) = \underline{0} \tag{H}$$

or, equivalently,

$$Ax = \underline{0} \tag{H'}$$

Let S^H denote the set of solutions to (H). We know that S^H always contains the zero vector and is a linear subspace of X. Therefore, in order to construct the "general solution" to (H) (i.e., to find all the elements of S^H), it suffices to find enough linearly independent solutions to construct a basis; that is, we need $m - \text{rank } A$ such solutions.

Next, we observe that because im T is a subspace of $\mathbb{R}^m$, the dimension of im T cannot exceed m. Hence, (3) implies

$$\dim S^H = n - \text{rank } A \geq n - m$$

That is, the dimension of the set of solutions to (H) is equal to the number of unknowns (n) minus the number of linearly independent equations (rank A); and because the second of these numbers cannot exceed the total number of equations, we have $\dim S^H \geq n - m$. Hence, if the system has more unknowns than equations $(n > m)$, we have $S^H \geq 1$, and it follows that (H) has nontrivial solutions.

We now turn to the nonhomogeneous system of linear equations

$$T(x) = y \tag{N}$$

or

$$Ax = y \tag{N'}$$

where $y \in \mathbb{R}^m$ is a known vector. Let S^N denote the solution set of (N). The following result says that S^N is an affine subspace of $\mathbb{R}^n$ parallel to S^H.

Theorem 1.1. Given a linear transformation $T: X \longrightarrow Y$, *let* x^p *be any ("particular") solution to the nonhomogeneous system of equations (N):* $T(x) = y$. *Then the set* S^N *of solutions to (N) is the set*

$$S^N = x^p + S^H = \{x^N \in X; x^N = x^p + x^H \quad \text{for some } x^H \in S^H\}$$

Proof. Let x^H be an arbitrary solution of (H). We want to show (i) that all vectors of the form $x^p + x^H$ are solutions of (N) and (ii) that only vectors of this form can solve (N), that is, every $x^N \in S^N$ can be written $x^N = x^p + x^H$ or, equivalently, that given any two solutions x^N and x^p to (N), their difference is a solution to (H). Both statements are easy to verify:

(i) If $x^p \in S^N$ and $x^H \in S^H$, then $x^p + x^H$ solves (N), because

$$T(x^p + x^H) = T(x^p) + T(x^H) = y + \underline{0} = y$$

(ii) If $x^p, x^N \in S^N$, then $x^p - x^N$ solves (H), as

$$T(x^p - x^N) = T(x^p) - T(x^N) = y - y = \underline{0} \qquad \Box$$

Hence, if the nonhomogeneous system has a solution (and it may not), S^N has the same dimension as S^H. Moreover, the first of these sets is easy to construct once we know the second: It is sufficient to find any particular solution to (N) in order to know them all, once we have the solutions to (H).

Recall that im T is the set of vectors y in $\mathbb{R}^m$ for which the system $T(x) = y$ has a solution. We also know that im T is a vector subspace of $\mathbb{R}^m$ generated by the columns of the matrix representation of T, and therefore its dimension (the rank of T) is equal to the rank of its associated matrix A, that is, the number of linearly independent equations in the system.

It follows that for a given vector y, the system $T(x) = y$ will have a solution if and only if $y \in$ im T, the space generated by the columns of the coefficient matrix. In order to obtain a more "operational" condition, observe that we can write (N) in the form

$$x_1 \begin{bmatrix} a_{11} \\ \ldots \\ a_{m1} \end{bmatrix} + \ldots + x_n \begin{bmatrix} a_{1n} \\ \ldots \\ a_{mn} \end{bmatrix} = \begin{bmatrix} y_1 \\ \ldots \\ y_m \end{bmatrix}$$

or

$$\sum_{i=1}^n x_i \operatorname{col}_i(A) = y \tag{4}$$

Looking at things this way, it is clear that a solution $x^* = (x_1^*, \ldots, x_n^*)$ of (N) exists if and only if it is possible to write y as a linear combination of column vectors of the coefficient matrix A, that is, if y is in the *column space* of A.

Next, consider the coefficient matrix $A = [\operatorname{col}_1(A), \ldots, \operatorname{col}_n(A)]$ and the matrix formed by adding to A a new column equal to the vector y, $A_y = [\operatorname{col}_1(A), \ldots, \operatorname{col}_n(A), y]$. Recall that the rank of a matrix is the number of linearly independent columns (or rows) in it. Because A_y is A augmented by a new column, the rank of A cannot exceed that of A_y. There are, then, only two possibilities:

(i) rank A = rank A_y: When we add the new column y to A, the rank of the matrix does not increase. This implies that y is a linear combination of the column vectors of A, and therefore the system has at least one solution.

(ii) rank A < rank A_y: If the rank increases when we form the augmented matrix, y must be linearly independent of the column vectors of A; that is, there are no scalars $x_1^*, \ldots, x_n^*$ such that (4) holds.

The same logic will work in reverse. If there is a solution to the system, then y can be written as a linear combination of the columns of A, and the addition of y to the coefficient matrix will not increase its rank. Hence, we have proved the following result:

Theorem 1.2. Existence of solutions for linear systems. The linear system $Ax = y$ *has (at least) one solution if and only if rank* A = *rank* A_y.

Assume that there exists a solution to (N). Given that $\dim(\ker A) = n - \text{rank } A$, this solution will be unique (i.e., S^N will have dimension zero) if and only if rank $A = n$, that is, if we have as many linearly independent equations as unknowns.[1]

Theorem 1.3. Uniqueness of solutions for linear systems. The system of m *equations in* n *unknowns,* $Ax = y$ ($x \in \mathbb{R}^n$, $y \in \mathbb{R}^m$) *has a unique solution if and only if*

$$rank\ A = n = rank\ A_y$$

Observe that we could have $m > n$, that is, more equations than unknowns, but in that case not all the equations would be linearly independent. In fact, $m - n$ of them would be redundant and would add no information to the others. Hence, we can ignore them and work with the n independent equations. If we have as many equations as unknowns, A is a square matrix, and a unique solution exists if and only if A is invertible or, equivalently, if its determinant is different from zero. In this case, the unique solution to the system is given by

$$x^* = A^{-1}y$$

and we can use *Cramer's rule* to obtain each of the components of the solution vector as the ratio of two determinants:

$$x_1^* = \frac{|A_i|}{|A|}$$

where A_i is the matrix obtained by replacing the ith column of A by the vector y (the right-hand side of the system).

A nonhomogeneous system $T(x) = y$ may have solutions for certain vectors y and no solutions for others. Clearly, $T(x) = y$ will have a solution for every $y \in \mathbb{R}^m$ if and only if im $T = T(\mathbb{R}^n) = \mathbb{R}^n$. For this, it is sufficient that the rank of T be equal to m (it cannot be larger). If, on the other hand, we have rank $T < m$, then the set of y's for which (N) has a solution is a subspace of $\mathbb{R}^m$ of dimension less than m (e.g., a straight line on the plane, or a plane in three-dimensional space). Hence, if we pick a vector y randomly, the system $Ax = y$ will have a solution only by chance, and if we start with some $y = -B\alpha$ for which there is a solution, almost any small change in the parameters will leave the system with no solutions.

Let us now reintroduce the parameters α explicitly into the model. Assume that the system

$$Ax + B\alpha = \underline{0} \qquad \text{(L.1)}$$

has n independent equations (that is, A is an $n \times n$ matrix and has full rank). Then A is invertible, and we can solve (L.1) to obtain a solution that will be unique for given parameter values:

$$x = -A^{-1}B\alpha$$

The solution function for the model is therefore

$$x^* = x(\alpha)C\alpha, \quad \text{where } C = -A^{-1}B$$

Given the matrices A and B, explicit solutions for the model can be computed using Cramer's rule or, more efficiently, some algorithm for the inversion of matrices. In any case, the solution of linear models does not pose difficulties, at least in principle.

In this case, dealing with comparative statics is easy. Because we know the solution function, we can differentiate it directly to obtain

$$\frac{\partial x_i^*}{\partial \alpha_k} = c_{ik} \qquad \text{(the } ik \text{ element of } C\text{)}$$

We can also handle discrete parameter changes quite easily. Let α' and α'' be two different parameter vectors. The corresponding equilibrium values of the endogenous variables will be given by

$$x'' = C\alpha'' \quad \text{and} \quad x' = C\alpha'$$

Hence the displacement of the equilibrium as a result of the parameter change will be

$$x'' - x' = C\alpha'' - C\alpha' = C(\alpha'' - \alpha') \Rightarrow \Delta x^* = C\Delta\alpha$$

2. Comparative Statics and the Implicit-Function Theorem

Let us now return to nonlinear models. Let F be a function $\mathbb{R}^{n+p} \supseteq X \times \Omega \longrightarrow \mathbb{R}^m$, with $X \times \Omega$ open, and consider the model

$$F(x; \alpha) = \underline{0} \qquad \text{(M)}$$

where α is a vector of parameters, and x is the vector of endogenous variables whose solution values we seek. For a given value of α, we define a function of x alone by $f_\alpha(x) = F(x; \alpha)$. Then x^* is a solution of the model for the given α if and only if it is a zero of f_α. Hence, the equilibrium or solution correspondence

$$S: \mathbb{R}^p \supseteq \Omega \longrightarrow X \subseteq \mathbb{R}^n$$

that assigns to each parameter vector α the corresponding set $S(\alpha)$ of equilibrium values of the endogenous variables is given by

$$S(\alpha) = f_\alpha^{-1}(\underline{0}) = \{x \in X; f_\alpha(x) = \underline{0}\}$$

As we have already indicated, we are interested in two types of questions: (i) For a given value of α, what does the solution set $S(\alpha)$ look like? (ii) How does it change if we change the parameters? We have seen that the answers to these questions are straightforward in the case of linear models. For nonlinear models, things are more complicated, but if we are willing to assume that F is differentiable, we can proceed by constructing a linear approximation to the model in a neighborhood of a solution point and then analyze the resulting linear model. This approach yields a tractable method for doing comparative statics and some valuable information on the local structure and dimensionality of the solution set of the model.

In what follows, we will assume that F is a C^1 function and focus on the case in which $m = n$, that is, we assume that the model (M) has as many equations as unknowns. The central result is the implicit-function theorem (IFT). This theorem gives sufficient conditions for the solution correspondence $S(\alpha)$ to be a well-defined and nicely behaved *function* in some neighborhood of a known solution point. The IFT also provides a tractable method for doing comparative statics, that is, for determining in what direction the equilibrium moves as a result of changes in the parameters of the system.

The IFT is a close relative of the inverse-function theorem. Assume that the number of equations and the number of unknowns in (M) are the same; then f_α maps $\mathbb{R}^n$ into itself, and we can apply the inverse-function theorem. Hence, if for a given value of the parameter vector α^0 the pair (x^0, α^0) satisfies (M), $F(\ )$ (and therefore f_α) is continuously differentiable, and the Jacobian of f_{α^0}, given by $|Df_{\alpha^0}(x^0)| = |D_x F(x^0, \alpha^0)|$, is not zero at x^0, then f_{α^0} is one-to-one in some neighborhood of x^0, and therefore $x^0 \in f_{\alpha^0}^{-1}(\underline{0})$ is a locally unique solution of the system $F(x; \alpha^0) = \underline{0}$.

To see what the IFT adds to this, imagine that there are changes in the parameters. For each α we obtain a new system of equations $f_\alpha(x) = \underline{0}$ and a different solution set $f_\alpha^{-1}(\underline{0})$ (possibly empty). Now, if F is a continuously differentiable function of the parameters and we restrict ourselves to a sufficiently small neighborhood of α^0, then all the f_α's will be sufficiently similar to f_{α^0} that each one of the systems $f_\alpha(x) = \underline{0}$ will have a solution close to x^0. Moreover, because each of the f_α's is locally invertible, each of these solutions will be locally unique.

(a) Derivatives of Implicit Functions and Comparative Statics

We will begin by deriving a very useful formula for doing comparative statics in differentiable models. We will then specify under what conditions the use of this formula is legitimate. Given a parameterized system of equations (M), which we can write in more detailed notation as

$$F^1(x_1, \ldots, x_n; \alpha_1, \ldots, \alpha_p) = 0$$
$$\vdots \tag{M$'$}$$
$$F^n(x_1, \ldots, x_n; \alpha_1, \ldots, \alpha_p) = 0$$

we would like to know in what direction the solution of the system $x^* = (x_1^*, \ldots, x_n^*)$ moves when there is a small change in the value of some parameter, say α_k. Suppose, for the time being, that the solution correspondence for this model is a differentiable function, that is, that we can write the equilibrium value x_i^* for each of the endogenous variables as a differentiable function of the form

$$x_i^* = x_i(\alpha) = x_i(\alpha_1, \ldots, \alpha_p)$$

We would like to determine the sign of the partial derivatives $\partial x_i^*/\partial \alpha_k$. If the model can be solved explicitly, the problem is simple. In general, however, closed forms for the solution functions of (M) will not be available, so we will have to resort to less direct methods to "extract" the properties of $x_i(\alpha)$ from those of $F(\ )$. The most straightforward approach is the following.

Substituting the solution function $x(\ )$ back into (M), we obtain the *identity*

$$F[x(\alpha), \alpha] \equiv \underline{0} \tag{1}$$

or, in more detailed notation,

$$F^i[x_1(\alpha_1, \ldots, \alpha_p), \ldots, x_n(\alpha_1, \ldots, \alpha_p); \alpha_1, \ldots, \alpha_p] \equiv 0$$
$$\text{for each } i = 1, \ldots, n \tag{1$'$}$$

We emphasize that (1) is an identity – in the sense that, unlike (M), it holds for all values of α – and in fact (1) defines the function $x(\alpha)$. Hence we can differentiate both sides of (1) with respect to any parameter and the equality will continue to hold. Differentiating (1') with respect to α_k, we have

$$\frac{dF^i}{d\alpha_k} = F^i_{x_1} \frac{\partial x_1^*}{\partial \alpha_k} + \dots + F^i_{x_n} \frac{\partial x_n^*}{\partial \alpha_k} + F^i_{\alpha_k} = 0$$

for the ith equation. Repeating the operation for each equation, we obtain the following expression for the whole system:

$$\begin{bmatrix} F^1_{x_1} \dots F^1_{x_n} \\ \dots \dots \dots \\ F^n_{x_1} \dots F^n_{x_n} \end{bmatrix} \begin{bmatrix} \dfrac{\partial x_1^*}{\partial \alpha_k} \\ \dots \\ \dfrac{\partial x_n^*}{\partial \alpha_k} \end{bmatrix} = - \begin{bmatrix} F^1_{\alpha_k} \\ \dots \\ F^n_{\alpha_k} \end{bmatrix} \tag{2}$$

If the Jacobian matrix $J = D_x F(x; \alpha)$ of first partial derivatives of F with respect to the endogenous variables is invertible (i.e., if $|J| \neq 0$), then (2) can be solved for the partial derivatives of the solution functions, $\partial x_i^*/\partial \alpha_k$. Using Cramer's rule, we have

$$\frac{\partial x_i^*}{\partial \alpha_k} = \frac{-|J_i|}{|J|} \tag{3}$$

where J_i is the matrix obtained by replacing the ith column of the Jacobian J with the vector $(F^1_{\alpha_k}, \dots, F^n_{\alpha_k})^T$ that appears on the right-hand side of (2).

The same conclusion can be obtained in much more compact form using vector notation. Differentiating (1) with respect to the parameter vector, we obtain

$$D_x F(x; \alpha) Dx(\alpha) + D_\alpha F(x; \alpha) = \underline{0}$$

from where

$$Dx(\alpha) = -[D_x F(x; \alpha)]^{-1} D_\alpha F(x; \alpha) \tag{4}$$

Equation (3) then gives us the ith component of the vector $Dx(\alpha)$.

The formula we have just derived is an extremely useful tool for the analysis of static, differentiable models. But we still have to see when it is legitimate to use it. To obtain it, we have assumed that the solution correspondence is a well-defined and differentiable function, which is not necessarily true. In the following section we will derive sufficient conditions for this to be locally true in some neighborhood of a known solution point. In particular, it suffices that F be a C^1 function and that its derivative with respect to the vector of endogenous variables, evaluated at the solution of the system, be invertible. The necessity of this second condition is apparent from (4). Before turning to this problem, we pause to observe that the procedure described earlier is equivalent to working with the linearization of (M) in some neighborhood of a given solution.

A Reinterpretation

Given a nonlinear model

$$F(x; \alpha) = \underline{0} \tag{M}$$

where F is a smooth function, and x^0 a solution of the system for given values α^0 of the parameters, we can construct a linear approximation to F in some neighborhood of (x^0, α^0):

$$F(x; \alpha) \cong F(x^0, \alpha^0) + [DF_x(x^0, \alpha^0), D_\alpha F(x^0, \alpha^0)] \begin{bmatrix} x - x^0 \\ \alpha - \alpha^0 \end{bmatrix}$$

$$= \underline{0} + D_x F(x^0, \alpha^0)(x - x^0) + D_\alpha F(x^0, \alpha^0)(\alpha - \alpha^0)$$

Hence, we can approximate (M) by the linear model

$$D_x F(x^0, \alpha^0)(x - x^0) = -D_\alpha F(x^0, \alpha^0)(\alpha - \alpha^0) \tag{L}$$

where $D_x F(x^0, \alpha^0)$ and $D_\alpha F(x^0, \alpha^0)$ are "constant" matrices. We have, then, a system of n linear equations in n unknowns (x), and if $|D_x F(x^0, \alpha^0)| \neq 0$, we can solve it to find the solution function for (L):

$$x_L^* = \phi(\alpha) = x^0 - [D_x F(x^0, \alpha^0)]^{-1} D_\alpha F(x^0, \alpha^0)(\alpha - \alpha^0)$$

Alternatively, we can use the procedure described earlier to calculate the derivative of the solution function for the original model, $x(\alpha)$. Constructing a linear approximation to this function, and using (4), we find that, close to x^0,

$$x^* \cong x^0 + Dx(\alpha^0)(\alpha - \alpha^0) = x^0 - [D_x F(x^0, \alpha^0)]^{-1} D_\alpha F(x^0, \alpha^0)(\alpha - \alpha^0) = \phi(\alpha)$$

Thus, the two approaches are equivalent: They yield the same linear approximation to the solution function for (M).

(b) The Implicit-Function Theorem

We begin the discussion of this important result by considering a simple case in which we can rely on graphical intuition. Let F be a C^1 function from $\mathbb{R}^2$ to $\mathbb{R}$, and consider the "system" formed by a single equation in one unknown and one parameter:

$$F(x; \alpha) = 0 \tag{5}$$

Graphically, the graph of F corresponds to a surface in three-dimensional space, with the values of the function measured along the vertical axis. The set of pairs (x, α) that satisfy equation (5) (the zero level set of F) corresponds to the intersection of this surface with the horizontal plane. If F satisfies certain regularity conditions, this locus will describe a curve on the plane, as illustrated in Figure 5.1.

The following question then arises: Can we interpret the curve $F(x, \alpha) = 0$ as the graph of a function $x(\alpha)$ giving the solution to (5) as a function of the parameter? We see that, in general, the answer is no: As the figure suggests, there is no guarantee that for each value of α there will exist precisely one solution to the equation $F(x, \alpha) = 0$. In the foregoing example, $x(\alpha)$ is a function on the interval $(-\infty, \alpha')$, but not on the rest of the real line, because equation (5) has two solutions in the interval (α', α''), and none for $\alpha > \alpha''$.

On the other hand, the figure also suggests that in many cases $x(\alpha)$ will

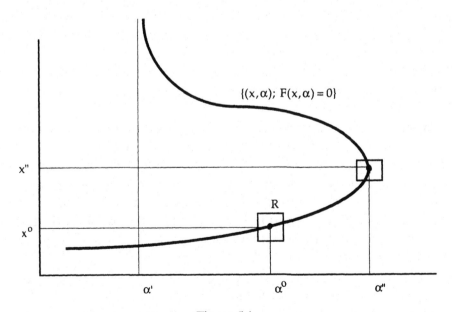

Figure 5.1.

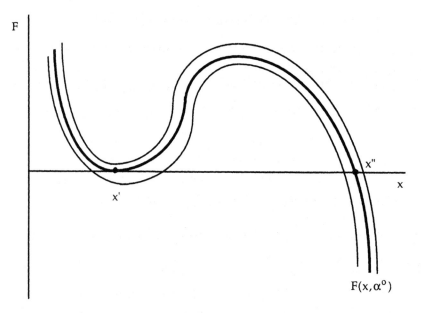

Figure 5.2.

indeed be a function locally. If we restrict ourselves to a sufficiently small rectangle R around a point (x^0, α^0) on the curve, it will be true that, for almost all points, the restriction of the curve to the rectangle is the graph of a function. The only exception in Figure 5.1 is the point (α'', x''), at which the curve is locally vertical (i.e., where $F_x(x'', \alpha'') = 0$).[2] No matter how small we draw the rectangle around this point, it will always include some values of α for which there are two solutions of the system, and others for which there is none. Hence, in this case equation (5) does not define the solution value of the endogenous variable x^* as a function of the parameter α, even locally. However, inspection of Figure 5.1 reveals that this is the only point at which we run into this problem.

Consider now the same problem from a slightly different point of view. If we fix the value of α at α^0 and plot F as a function of x, the solutions of the system correspond to the points at which the graph of $F(x, \alpha^0)$ touches the horizontal axis. Figure 5.2 suggests that two types of solutions are possible: In one case (e.g., x''), $F(\ )$ crosses the axis *transversally*, whereas in the other (e.g., x'), $F(\ )$ is only tangent to it. In the first case, the partial derivative of $F(\ )$ with respect to x will be either strictly positive or strictly negative; in the second case, we have $F_x(\ ) = 0$.

Intuitively, it is clear that the two types of equilibria will behave very differently in response to a small change in the value of the parameter. "Transversal" (or *regular*) equilibria will survive small perturbations and remain locally unique, whereas "tangency" (or *critical*) solutions will be fragile, tending to disappear with some perturbations, or to unfold into two different equilibria. Once more, we conclude that if $F_x(x, \alpha) \neq 0$ at a solution of the system, then the solution correspondence will be, at least locally, a well-defined function. On the other hand, if $F_x(x, \alpha) = 0$, we have a tangency equilibrium, and strange things may happen.

The following result formalizes the preceding discussion: If we rule out tangency equilibria, $x(\alpha)$ is locally a well-defined function and inherits the differentiability of F.

Theorem 2.1. Implicit-function theorem (simplest case). Suppose $F: \mathbb{R}^2 \longrightarrow \mathbb{R}$ *is* C^1 *on an open neighborhood* A *of a point* (x^0, α^0) *such that* $F(x^0, \alpha^0) = 0$ *and* $F_x(x^0, \alpha^0) \neq 0$. *Then there exist open intervals* I_x *and* I_α *centered at* x^0 *and* α^0, *respectively, such that the following hold:*

(i) *For each* $\alpha \subseteq I_\alpha$ *there exists a unique* $x_\alpha \in I_x$ *such that* $F(x_\alpha, \alpha) = 0$. *That is, the restriction of the zero-level curve of* F *to the rectangle* $I_x \times I_\alpha$ *defines a function*

$$x : I_\alpha \longrightarrow I_x, \text{ with } x(\alpha) = x_\alpha$$

(ii) *The function* $x(\ )$ *is differentiable, and its derivative is a continuous function given by*

$$x'(\alpha) = \frac{-F_\alpha(x, \alpha)}{F_x(x, \alpha)}$$

Although the simplest way to prove the implicit-function theorem is by applying the inverse-function theorem, we will give a direct proof for this special case of the theorem that probably will illustrate the logic of the result better than will the general proof given later.

Proof

(i) $x(\alpha)$ is a well-defined function from I_α to I_x; that is, for each α in I_α there exists a unique x_α in I_x such that $F(x_\alpha, \alpha) = 0$.

By assumption, $F_x(x^0, \alpha^0) \neq 0$; for concreteness, suppose $F_x(x^0, \alpha^0) = a > 0$. Because $F_x(x, \alpha)$ is continuous on A, there exists an open rectangular neighborhood R' of (x^0, α^0) such that for all (x, α) in R', $F_x > a/2$; that is, there exist $\eta, \delta > 0$ such that

$$\forall (x, \alpha) \in R' = B_\delta(x^0) \times B_\eta(\alpha^0), \ F_x(x, \alpha) > a/2 > 0 \tag{1}$$

(refer to Figure 5.3). That is, F is a strictly increasing function of x for given α and $(x, \alpha) \in R'$. Moreover, because F has value zero at (x^0, α^0), we have

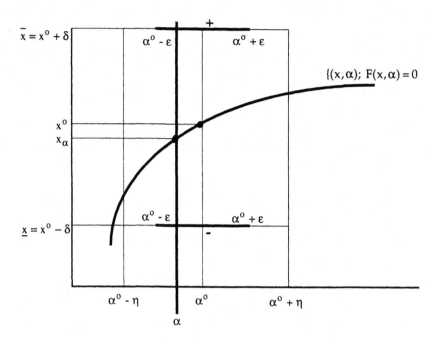

Figure 5.3.

$$F(x^0 + \delta, \alpha^0) > 0 \quad \text{and} \quad F(x^0 - \delta, \alpha^0) < 0 \qquad (2)$$

Next, fix $\bar{x} = x^0 + \delta$; then $F(\bar{x}, \alpha)$ is a continuous function of α, with $F(\bar{x}, \alpha^0) > 0$. By continuity, this inequality continues to hold for α sufficiently close to α^0; that is, there exists some $\varepsilon \in (0, \eta)$ such that $F(\bar{x}, \alpha) > 0$ for all $\alpha \in B_\varepsilon(\alpha^0)$. Similarly, if we fix $\underline{x} = x^0 - \delta$, F will be strictly negative for α sufficiently close to α^0. Hence, we can choose ε in such a way that

$$F(x^0 + \delta, \alpha) > 0 \quad \text{and} \quad F(x^0 - \delta, \alpha) < 0 \qquad \text{for all } \alpha \in B_\varepsilon(\alpha^0) \qquad (3)$$

Fix some α in $B_\varepsilon(\alpha^0)$. The function $f_\alpha(x) \equiv F(x, \alpha)$ is continuous in x, and, by (3), we have

$$f_\alpha(x^0 + \delta) > 0 \quad \text{and} \quad f_\alpha(x^0 - \delta) < 0.$$

By the intermediate-value theorem, it follows that there exists some $x_\alpha \in (x^0 - \delta, x^0 + \delta)$ such that

$$f_\alpha(x_\alpha) = F(x_\alpha, \alpha) = 0$$

Moreover, this x_α will be unique, for $f_\alpha(\ )$ is strictly increasing in $B_\delta(x^0)$ and therefore can cut the horizontal axis only once in this interval, as suggested in Figure 5.4.

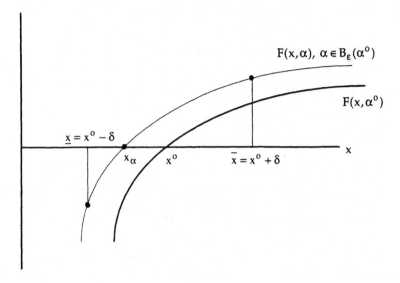

Figure 5.4.

In conclusion, we have shown that given any α in a sufficiently small neighborhood of α^0, there exists one, and only one, value of x(namely x_α) such that (x_α, α) satisfies the given equation. Hence, the solution correspondence $\alpha \longrightarrow\!\!\!\!\longrightarrow x (\alpha) = x_\alpha$ is a well-defined function from $B_\varepsilon(\alpha^0)$ to $B_\delta(x^0)$.

(ii) The function $x(\ ) : B_\varepsilon(\alpha^0) \longrightarrow B_\delta(x^0)$ is continuously differentiable.

Take two points α' and α'' in $B_\varepsilon(\alpha^0)$ and put $x' = x(\alpha')$ and $x'' = x(\alpha'')$; by construction, we have $x', x'' \in B_\delta(x^0)$ and

$$F(x', \alpha') = F(x'', \alpha'') = 0 \tag{4}$$

By the mean-value theorem, there exists some point $(x^\lambda, \alpha^\lambda)$ on the straight line segment connecting (x', α') and (x'', α'') (and therefore in $R = B_\delta(x^0) \times B_\varepsilon(\alpha^0)$) such that

$$0 = F(x', \alpha') - F(x'', \alpha'') = F_x(x^\lambda, \alpha^\lambda)(x' - x'') + F_\alpha(x^\lambda, \alpha^\lambda)(\alpha' - \alpha'') \tag{5}$$

Regrouping terms in (5),

$$x(\alpha') - x(\alpha'') = \frac{-F_\alpha(x^\lambda, \alpha^\lambda)}{F_x(x^\lambda, \alpha^\lambda)}(\alpha' - \alpha'') \tag{6}$$

and because $(x^\lambda, \alpha^\lambda) \in R'$, we have

$$F_x(x^\lambda, \alpha^\lambda) > a/2 > 0 \tag{7}$$

by (1). Moreover, $F_\alpha(x, \alpha)$ is a continuous function on the closure of R', which is a compact set, and therefore attains a maximum on this set. Hence we can write

$$F_\alpha(x^\lambda, \alpha^\lambda) \le M \equiv \max\{F_\alpha(x, \alpha); (x, \alpha) \in \mathrm{cl}\, R'\} \tag{8}$$

Expressions (6), (7), and (8) imply that

$$|x(\alpha') - x(\alpha'')| = \left|\frac{-F_\alpha(x^\lambda, \alpha^\lambda)}{F_x(x^\lambda, \alpha^\lambda)}\right| |\alpha' - \alpha''| \le \frac{2M}{a}|\alpha' - \alpha''| \tag{9}$$

where we see that $x(\ )$ is continuous, for $x(\alpha') \to x(\alpha'')$ as $\alpha' \to \alpha''$.

In fact, $x(\ )$ is not only continuous but also differentiable. To see this, recall that $(x^\lambda, \alpha^\lambda)$ lies on the straight line segment between (x', α') and (x'', α''). As $\alpha' \to \alpha''$, we have $x(\alpha') \to x(\alpha'')$, by (9), and therefore $(x', \alpha') \to (x'', \alpha'')$. Because $(x^\lambda, \alpha^\lambda)$ lies between these two points, it follows also that $(x^\lambda, \alpha^\lambda) \to (x'', \alpha'')$. Regrouping terms in (6), and taking the limits of both sides as $\alpha' \to \alpha''$, we have (making use of the differentiability of F_x and F_α)

$$x'(\alpha'') = \lim_{\alpha' \to \alpha''} \frac{x(\alpha') - x(\alpha'')}{\alpha' - \alpha''} = \lim_{\alpha' \to \alpha''} \frac{-F_\alpha(x^\lambda, \alpha^\lambda)}{F_x(x^\lambda, \alpha^\lambda)} = \frac{-F_\alpha(x'', \alpha'')}{F_x(x'', \alpha'')}$$

which establishes the differentiability of $x(\ )$ and the formula given for its value in the theorem. Finally, because $F_x(\ )$ and $F_\alpha(\ )$ are continuous functions, so is $x'(\ )$ at all points where $F_x(\ ) \ne 0$, and in particular in $B_\delta(x^0)$. $\quad\square$

We now turn to the general case of this result. Given a parameterized system of n equations in n unknowns,

$$F(x; \alpha) = \underline{0} \tag{M}$$

the implicit-function theorem gives us sufficient conditions for (M) to implicitly define a differentiable function that assigns to each α the corresponding equilibrium value of the vector of endogenous variables.

Theorem 2.2. Implicit-function theorem (general case). Let $\mathrm{F}: \mathbb{R}^{n+p} \supseteq \mathrm{X} \times \Omega \longrightarrow \mathbb{R}^n$ *be a continuously differentiable function on an open set* $\mathrm{X} \times \Omega$. *Consider the system of equations* $\mathrm{F}(x; \alpha) = \underline{0}$, *and assume that it has a solution* $\mathrm{x}^0 \in \mathrm{X}$ *for given parameter values* $\alpha^0 \in \Omega$. *If the determinant of the Jacobian of endogenous variables is not zero at* $(\mathrm{x}^0; \alpha^0)$, *that is, if*

$$|\mathrm{J}(\mathrm{x}^0; \alpha^0)| = |\mathrm{D_x F}(\mathrm{x}^0; \alpha^0)| \ne 0$$

then we have the following:

(i) There exist open sets U *in* $\mathbb{R}^{n+p}$ *and* U_α *in* $\mathbb{R}^p$, *with* $(x^0, \alpha^0) \subseteq U$ *and* $\alpha^0 \subseteq U_\alpha$, *such that for each* α *in* U_α *there exists a unique* x_α *such that*

$$(x_\alpha, \alpha) \in U \quad and \quad F(x_\alpha; \alpha) = \underline{0}$$

That is, the correspondence from U_α *to* X *defined by* $x(\alpha) = x_\alpha$ *is a well-defined function when restricted to* U.

(ii) The solution function $x(\ ) : U_\alpha \longrightarrow \mathbb{R}^n$ *is continuously differentiable, and its derivative is given by* $D_x(\alpha) = -[D_x F(x_\alpha; \alpha)]^{-1} D_\alpha F(x_\alpha; \alpha)$.

(iii) If $F(\ )$ *is* C^k, *so is* $x(\ )$.

That is, given some parameter vector α^0, suppose that x^0 solves the system (M), and the remaining assumptions of the theorem hold. Then for every α close to α^0 there exists a solution $x(\alpha)$ close to x^0 that is locally unique. Hence, $x(\alpha)$ is locally a well-defined function, and, moreover, it inherits the differentiability of F.

Proof. We will apply the inverse-function theorem to the function $G : \mathbb{R}^{n+p} \longrightarrow \mathbb{R}^{n+p}$ defined by

$$G(x; \alpha) = [F(x; \alpha), \alpha]^T \tag{1}$$

that is,

$$G^i(x; \alpha) = F^i(x; \alpha) \quad \text{for } i = 1, \ldots, n$$
$$G^{n+j}(x; \alpha) = \alpha_j \quad \text{for } j = 1, \ldots, p$$

Observe that

$$G(x^0; \alpha^0) = [F(x^0, \alpha^0), \alpha^0]^T = (\underline{0}, \alpha^0)^T \tag{2}$$

and the Jacobian of G can be written

$$DG(x; \alpha) = \begin{bmatrix} D_x F(x^0, \alpha^0) & D_\alpha F(x^0, \alpha^0) \\ \underline{0} & I \end{bmatrix}$$

where I is the identity matrix, and $\underline{0}$ a matrix of zeros. Expanding the determinant of $DG(x^0; \alpha^0)$ by cofactors, starting from the lower right-hand-side corner, we find that

$$|DG(x^0; \alpha^0)| = |D_x F(x^0; \alpha^0)| \neq 0$$

so we can apply the inverse-function theorem to G at $(x^0; \alpha^0)$.

By the inverse-function theorem, there exist open sets U and $V = G(U)$ in $\mathbb{R}^{n+p}$, with $(x^0, \alpha^0) \in U$, $(\underline{0}, \alpha^0) \in V$, and the property that G is a one-to-one function from U onto V. Hence, $G^{-1} : V \longrightarrow U$ is a well-defined function.

Because $(\underline{0}, \alpha^0) \in V$ and V is open, we have $(\underline{0}, \alpha) \in V$ for all α sufficiently close to α^0, which we write $\alpha \in U_\alpha$. Given that G is invertible, for each $\alpha \in U_\alpha$ there exists a unique point $(x_\alpha, \alpha) \in U$ such that

$$(x_\alpha, \alpha) = G^{-1}(\underline{0}, \alpha)$$

which is equivalent to

$$G(x_\alpha, \alpha) = (\underline{0}, \alpha)^T$$

and therefore implies, by definition of G,

$$F(x_\alpha, \alpha) = \underline{0}$$

In fact, we can put

$$U_\alpha = \{\alpha \in \mathbb{R}^{n+p}; (\underline{0}, \alpha) \in V\}$$

where U_α is open (in $\mathbb{R}^p$) because U is open (in $\mathbb{R}^{n+p}$). In summary, for each $\alpha \in U_\alpha$ there exists a unique solution x_α of the system such that $(x_\alpha, \alpha) \in U$. It follows that the solution correspondence is locally a function, defined on U_α by

$$x(\alpha) = x_\alpha \quad \text{such that } (x_\alpha, \alpha) \in U \quad \text{and} \quad F(x_\alpha, \alpha) = \underline{0}$$

It remains to show that this function is C^1. By the inverse function theorem, $G^{-1} : V \longrightarrow U$ is C^1, and because

$$G[x(\alpha), \alpha] = (\underline{0}, \alpha)^T \Leftrightarrow [x(\alpha), \alpha]^T = G^{-1}(\underline{0}, \alpha)$$

by definition, we have that $x(\alpha)$ is a component of a C^1 function and therefore is itself C^1 (or as smooth as G^{-1}). $\qquad \square$

Degrees of Freedom and the Regular-Value Theorem

In stating the implicit-function theorem, we have made an a priori distinction between endogenous variables and parameters. It is clear, however, that the logic of the result does not depend in any way on whether or not we choose to make this distinction. Let F, then, be a C^1 function from $\mathbb{R}^{n+p}$ to $\mathbb{R}^n$, and consider the system of n equations in $n + p$ variables, equations (M): $F(x) = \underline{0}$. If the Jacobian $DF(x)$ has rank n at a solution point x^0, then we can always find at least one partition of x into two vectors, $x = (y, z)$, with $y \in \mathbb{R}^n$ and $z \in \mathbb{R}^p$, such that the square submatrix $D_y F(y, z)$ has a nonzero determinant. By the implicit-function theorem, it follows that in some neighborhood of x^0 it is possible to solve the system for the n variables y as functions of the p variables z.

In other words, the system has p degrees of freedom: We can freely assign values to p of the variables, and the rest will then be determined by the condition $F(y, z) = \underline{0}$. This gives us some information about the local dimensionality of the set $F^{-1}(\underline{0})$ of solutions of the system.

If, in addition, $\underline{0}$ is a regular value of F, then every element x^* of $F^{-1}(\underline{0})$ is a regular point of F and therefore satisfies the assumptions of the implicit-function theorem.[3] Hence, the implicit-function theorem guarantees that the solution set always has the "right" dimension (equal to the number of unknowns minus the number of equations). The following theorem tells us that in that case, $F^{-1}(\underline{0})$ will be a geometric object with "nice" properties. To state the theorem precisely, we need some definitions.

Recall that a *diffeomorphism* is a smooth homeomorphism, that is, an invertible C^k function with $k \geq 1$ and a C^k inverse. Two sets are *diffeomorphic* if there exists a diffeomorphism that maps one onto the other, that is, if the sets are identical except for a smooth change of coordinates. A subset M of $\mathbb{R}^n$ is a *smooth manifold* of dimension k if every point in M has a neighborhood U (in $\mathbb{R}^n$) such that $U \cap M$ is diffeomorphic to an open set in $\mathbb{R}^{k}$.[4]

That is, a smooth manifold is an object that looks locally like an open set in a Euclidean space. For example, a smooth surface in $\mathbb{R}^3$ is a manifold of dimension 2, because it looks locally like a plane – in the sense that there is a smooth change of coordinates that will map any region on the surface into a neighborhood of a point on the plane (e.g., imagine that we project a neighborhood of a point in the surface onto the horizontal plane). A manifold of dimension zero is a set of isolated points. By convention, the empty set can be considered a manifold of any dimension.

The following result tells us that the inverse image of a regular value is a nice geometrical object of precisely the dimension we would expect.

Theorem 2.3. Regular-value theorem. Let $\mathrm{f}: \mathbb{R}^n \supseteq X \longrightarrow \mathbb{R}^m$, *with X open, be a C^1 function. If y is a regular value of f, then $\mathrm{f}^{-1}(\mathrm{y})$ is a smooth manifold of dimension* n − m *(in the ambient space $\mathbb{R}^n$).*

Note that $f^{-1}(y)$ may be empty, as $\varnothing$ may be considered a manifold of any dimension. For a proof of the theorem, see Guillemin and Pollack (1974, pp. 20ff.) or Milnor (1965, p. 11). At any rate, this is an almost immediate implication of the implicit-function theorem.

Intuitively, the theorem tells us that the dimension of the solution set of the system $f(x) = y$ is equal to the number of unknowns minus the number of equations in the system, provided these are linearly independent in some neighborhood of each solution point. In fact, if $m = n$, we have as many equations as unknowns, and, as we may expect, the set of solutions is a manifold of dimension zero (i.e., a set of isolated points). If $n > m$, we have more equations than unknowns, leaving us with $n - m$ degrees of freedom and a solution set of dimension $n - m$.[5]

Regular and Critical Equilibria and the Sard and Transversality-Density Theorems

An equilibrium of the model

$$F(x; \alpha) = f_\alpha(x) = \underline{0}, \quad \text{where } F: \mathbb{R}^{n+p} \supseteq X \times \Omega \to \mathbb{R}^m \qquad (X \times \Omega \text{ open}) \quad \text{(M)}$$

is a point $x^* \in f_\alpha^{-1}(\underline{0})$. An equilibrium is *critical* if it is a critical point of f_α, and *regular* otherwise. If x_α is a regular equilibrium for some α, then the assumptions of the implicit-function theorem hold at (x_α, α). Hence, regular equilibria are locally isolated and robust to small perturbations, and they change continuously with small parameter changes. Critical equilibria, on the other hand, may not behave so nicely: They may not be locally unique, and they have a tendency to disappear or unfold into several distinct equilibria with small parameter changes. The implicit-function theorem tells us that the graphical intuition developed earlier around the distinction between transversal and tangency equilibria remains valid for models with more than one endogenous variable and several parameters.

We have seen that a full-rank condition on the Jacobian of F guarantees that the solution of a system of equations has certain nice properties. Because the equilibrium of a model is determined endogenously, however, it is not legitimate simply to assume that we start out with a regular equilibrium. This suggests the following question: Is it possible to say a priori that the "probability" that we shall find ourselves at a critical equilibrium is low in some well-defined sense?

The answer is yes. We will now review two results that, loosely speaking, say that problematic (critical or tangency) equilibria are exceptions, rather than the rule, so that, in general, differentiable models will be nicely behaved. The first result, known as Sard's theorem, says that a sufficiently smooth function can have only "a few" critical values, although it may have any number of critical points. Hence, the property "being a regular point" is typical or *generic*. In some sense, therefore, it may be expected that given a system of equations $f_\alpha(x) = \underline{0}$, the zero vector will be a regular value of f_α, implying that the solution set $f_\alpha^{-1}(\underline{0})$ will contain only regular, and thus nicely behaved, equilibria. The second result (the transversality-density theorem) reinforces this conclusion: If, by chance, the zero vector turns out to be a critical value of f_α, then, under reasonable assumptions, almost any small change in any of the parameters will turn the zero vector into a regular value of the new f_α.

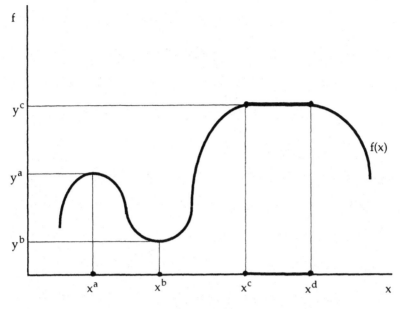

Figure 5.5.

Both theorems make use of the concept of a *set of measure zero*. Let A be a set in $\mathbb{R}^n$; we say that A has Lebesgue measure zero if given an arbitrarily small positive number ε, we can always find a countable collection of closed cubes $u_1, u_2, \ldots$ such that their union contains the set A, and the sum of their volumes (the product of the lengths of their sides) is smaller than ε.

Figure 5.5 suggests that a function may have "many" critical points, but only a few critical values. The function f has an infinite number of critical points (two isolated ones at x^a and x^b, and a continuum of them in the interval $[x^c, x^d]$), but has only three critical values, because all points in $[x^c, x^d]$ have the same image (that is, $f'(x) = 0$ on an interval implies that the function is constant in it).

Sard's theorem tells us that the figure gives the correct intuition: The property "being a regular value of a function" is generic.

Theorem 2.4. Sard's theorem. Let $f: \mathbb{R}^n \supseteq X \longrightarrow \mathbb{R}^m$ *(X open) be a C^r function with* $r > max\{0, n - m\}$, *and let* C_f *be the set of critical points of f. Then* $f(C_f)$ *has Lebesgue measure zero.*

If $n < m$, then $C_f = X$ (see note 5), and the theorem simply says that $f(X)$ has Lebesgue measure zero, implying that the equation $f(x) = y$ has no solutions for most of the vectors y in $\mathbb{R}^m$. Note that the theorem requires an assumption concerning the degree of smoothness of the function. In the

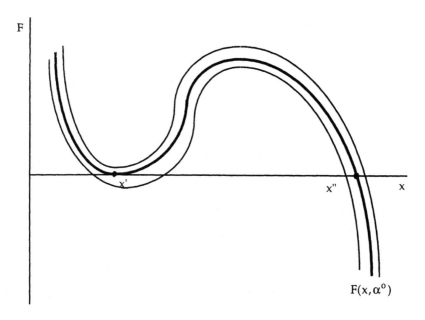

Figure 5.6.

case of greatest interest for us $(m = n)$, however, it is sufficient to have $f \in C^1$.

For parameterized functions, we have the following generalization of Sard's theorem, sometimes called the transversality-density theorem.

Theorem 2.5. Let, $F: \mathbb{R}^{n+p} \supseteq X \times \Omega \longrightarrow \mathbb{R}^m$ ($X \times \Omega$ open) be a C^r function with $r > max\{0, n - m\}$. If $y \in \mathbb{R}^m$ is a regular value of F, then the set of vectors $\alpha \in \mathbb{R}^p$ such that y is a critical value for $f_\alpha(x) = F(x; \alpha)$ has Lebesgue measure zero.

In other words, if y is a regular value for the "whole F," then it is a regular value of $f_\alpha( )$ for almost all values of α. Observe that because $DF(x; \alpha) = [D_x F(x; \alpha), D_\alpha F(x; \alpha)]$, the rank condition for a regular value is easier to satisfy for the "whole F" – that is, it is easier to be a regular point of F than one of f_α. In fact, if we have a sufficient number of parameters, it is possible to have rank $D_\alpha F(x; \alpha) = m$, which is sufficient to satisfy the assumptions of the theorem.

Figure 5.6 tries to capture the intuition of the result. For $\alpha = \alpha^0$, the function $f_{\alpha^0}( )$ has a critical value at zero. However, if F is sensitive to changes in α (and this is the intuitive meaning of the assumption of the theorem), any small perturbation will shift the graph of F in such a way that the tangency point will disappear.

In summary, because critical equilibria are problematic, we may wonder if it is possible to find some reasonable excuse for ignoring them. The answer is a qualified yes. Given some vector of parameters α, a model may have any number of critical equilibria, any number of regular equilibria, and any combination of the two. Graphical intuition, however, suggests that critical equilibria are fragile in the sense that they tend to disappear with small perturbations to the parameters. The preceding two theorems make this intuition precise: If $\underline{0}$ is a regular value of the "whole F," then it is also a regular value of f_α for almost all α, and this implies that $f_\alpha^{-1}(\underline{0})$ contains only regular equilibria. For most environments, therefore, many models will have no critical equilibria.[6]

Genericity

In many cases it is not possible to exclude completely the possibility of pathological phenomena, but it is sometimes possible to show that they are unlikely in a well-defined sense. Let X be a set, and consider some property P that elements of X may or may not have. We say that P is a *generic property* if it holds for almost all elements of this set.

There are two notions of genericity. The first, based on the concept of measure, is the one we have used here: P is generic in X if it holds for all X except possibly for a subset of measure zero. Sometimes, however, we cannot use Lebesgue measure to make precise the idea that a given set is small. This is the case, for example, in infinite-dimensional spaces. In such situations, we can resort to another notion of genericity (not as satisfactory as the first one) that is defined in topological terms.

In this second sense of the term, a property is generic in X if it holds in a subset of X that is open and dense in X. A subset D of a metric space X is *dense* in X if given any element x of X and an arbitrarily small number $\varepsilon > 0$, there exists some $y \in D$ such that $d(x, y) < \varepsilon$. That is, D is dense in X if given any point x in X there always exists some point in D arbitrarily close to x. In other words, D is dense in X if any element of X may be well approximated by some element of D.

Intuitively, a subset D of X that is both open and dense in X constitutes most of X. By the density of D, any point in X is close to some point in D. In principle, a dense subset could be a collection of isolated points (e.g., the set of rational numbers in the real line), but the requirement that D also be open eliminates that possibility. Openness also implies robustness or persistence, because small perturbations must leave us inside D.

Finally, note that genericity defined in terms of measure implies topological genericity (whenever both are defined), but the converse statement is not generally true. In fact, an open and dense subset of a Euclidean space could have arbitrarily small Lebesgue measure, although not zero.

Conclusion

The implicit-function theorem is a fundamental result for the analysis of non-linear models. On a practical level, the theorem tells us when we can use implicit differentiation to do comparative statics and gives us a formula for computing the derivatives of the solution function given the partials of F with respect to x and α. This is very helpful, because most of the models with which we work in economic theory are not specified at a sufficient level of detail to allow calculation of numerical solutions. Hence, the implicit-function theorem gives us an indispensable tool for extracting qualitative information about the solution function from qualitative assumptions incorporated into the behavioral equations of the model.

On a more basic level, the implicit-function theorem gives us sufficient conditions for the solution correspondence $S(\alpha)$ to be, at least locally, a differentiable function. This takes care of the continuity problem: Under the assumptions of the theorem, the equilibrium x^* depends continuously on the parameters, and therefore qualitative predictions concerning the effects of small changes in α are possible, at least in principle. Moreover, the conclusion that the solution correspondence is locally a continuous function also provides partial answers to the existence and uniqueness questions. It is important to emphasize, however, that such an answer has two important limitations. First, it is a conditional answer, because the theorem *assumes* the existence of a solution for some parameter vector α^0. Second, it is a local answer, as the conclusions hold only in a neighborhood of the value α^0 of the parameter vector for which a solution is known to exist. What the theorem says, therefore, is that if a solution x^0 exists for α^0 and the function F satisfies certain regularity conditions at (x^0, α^0), then locally unique solutions will also exist for parameter values close to α^0. But note that nothing is said about the existence of solutions per se.

3. Existence of Equilibrium

Nothing that we have seen thus far guarantees that the system $F(x; \alpha) = \underline{0}$ will have a solution for a given value of α. This section reviews some results that are sometimes useful in establishing the existence of equilibrium in non-linear models. The first method, based on the intermediate-value theorem, can be used only in "small" models, with two endogenous variables at most. On the other hand, it has the advantage that it is based on an obvious geometric intuition: The graph of a continuous function whose value is positive at some point and negative at another must cross the horizontal axis at some intermediate point.

For models with more than two variables, graphical methods are not, in general, very useful. In this case, fixed-point theorems are the most commonly used tools for dealing with existence problems. We will discuss a number of such results. In Chapter 8 we will see how some of them can be used to establish the existence of equilibrium in a number of important economic applications.

(a) The Intermediate-Value Theorem

We saw in Chapter 2 that a continuous function of $\mathbb{R}$ into itself maps intervals into intervals. Hence, if f takes on values y' and y'' in I, it must also take on all values in between these two numbers. The formal result, reproduced here for convenience, is the following:

Theorem 3.1. Intermediate-value theorem. Let $f: \mathbb{R} \longrightarrow \mathbb{R}$ *be a continuous function on the interval* I. *Given two points in* I, x' *and* x'', *with images* y' *and* y'', *for each number* y *between* y' *and* y'' *there exists some point* x *in* I, *lying between* x' *and* x'', *such that* $f(x) = y$.

It is easy to see how this result can be useful in establishing the existence of solutions. Let $f: \mathbb{R} \longrightarrow \mathbb{R}$ be a continuous function, and consider the equation $f(x) = 0$. If we can find two points x' and x'' such that $f(x') > 0$ and $f(x'') < 0$, then there will exist at least one point x^* lying between x' and x'' such that $f(x^*) = 0$. Figure 5.7 illustrates this geometrically obvious fact.

In many economic models, appropriate points x' and x'' can be found by asking what agents would do in "extreme situations." It is difficult to be more

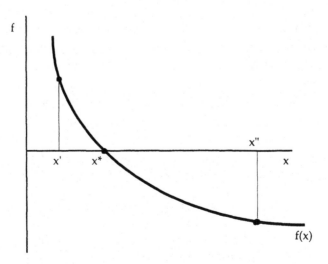

Figure 5.7. The intermediate-value theorem.

specific without a concrete example in mind, but some will turn up in the problems posed later in this chapter.

This procedure can sometimes be used to establish uniqueness. For example, if f is a strictly monotonic function, it is clear that it can cross the horizontal axis at most once. In fact, it is not necessary that f be globally monotonic. It is enough that the function be strictly monotonic in some neighborhood of any solution to the equation. If f is differentiable, that can at times be shown by evaluating $f'(x^*)$, that is, by inspecting the expression for the value of the function's derivative evaluated at an arbitrary solution point. Even if x^* is not explicitly known, the information that at such a point f has value zero may be sufficient to determine the sign of $f'(x^*)$. If $f'(x^*) > 0$ (or < 0) at all solution points, then the solution is unique, for f can cut the horizontal axis only in one direction.

For systems of two equations it is sometimes possible to use this approach repeatedly to establish existence. Suppose we are given a system of the form

$$F(x, y) = 0 \quad \text{and} \quad G(x, y) = 0 \tag{1}$$

We first consider each equation separately and see if it is possible to solve them for functions of the form

$$y = f(x) \quad \text{and} \quad y = g(x) \tag{2}$$

The slopes of these functions can be calculated by implicit differentiation, but we first have to establish existence. This can be done by the method discussed earlier. For example, if we fix $x = x^0$, then

$$F(x^0, y) = 0 \tag{3}$$

is an equation in a single unknown, and we can use the intermediate-value theorem to show that there is some y that solves (3) for the given x^0 (see Figure 5.8). Note that we may have to restrict the domain of $f(\ )$, for (3) may have solutions only for certain values of x^0. To prove that f is a well-defined function, we have to show that the solution of (3) is unique for each given x^0. This will be true, for example, if F_y is always positive or always negative, or if its sign is constant at any solution of (3).

If it is true that the two equations define functions of the form (2), the original system can be reduced to a single equation:

$$f(x) - g(x) = 0 \tag{4}$$

Graphically, we have two curves on the plane (x, y), as shown in the second panel of Figure 5.8, and we can apply the intermediate-value theorem once more. If one curve starts out above the other and ends up below, there must

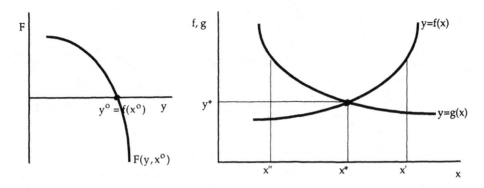

Figure 5.8.

be some point at which the two curves cross. And if we can determine that at an arbitrary intersection the slope of one is larger than that of the other, there will be at most one solution of (4).

(b) Fixed-Point Theorems

For problems in more than two dimensions, where the geometry of the plane is not very helpful, we have to resort to the more abstract methods of fixed-point theory. Two of the results of this theory most commonly used in economic analysis are the theorems due to Brouwer and Kakutani. The first one gives sufficient conditions for the existence of a fixed point of a function; the second gives similar conditions for correspondences.

A function f has a *fixed point* at x^* if the image of x^* is x^* itself, that is, if $f(x^*) = x^*$. It is easy to see the connection between equilibria and fixed points. Given a system of equations

$$f(x) = \underline{0} \tag{5}$$

define the function g by

$$g(x) = f(x) + x$$

Observe that if x^* is a fixed point of g, then

$$g(x^*) = f(x^*) + x^* = x^* \Leftrightarrow f(x^*) = \underline{0}$$

Hence, x^* solves the system (5) if and only if it is a fixed point of g.

Our first two results deal with the existence of fixed points for functions.

Theorem 3.2. Brouwer's fixed-point theorem. Let $f: X \longrightarrow X$ *be a continuous function mapping a compact and convex set X into itself. Then* f *has a fixed point in X, that is, there exists at least one* $x^* \in X$ *such that* $f(x^*) = x^*$.

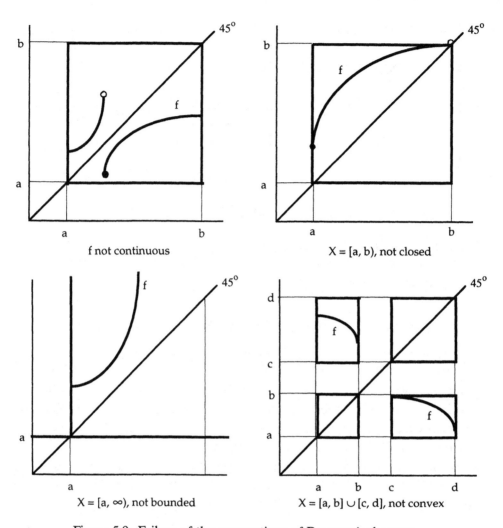

Figure 5.9. Failure of the assumptions of Brouwer's theorem.

Figure 5.9 illustrates the situation and shows that f may not have a fixed point if some of the assumptions of the theorem fail.

The standard proof of Brouwer's theorem, based on something called "simplicial topology," is a real pain in the butt; see, for example, Border (1985, ch. 2–6). For smooth functions, there exists an alternative and much nicer proof, based, surprisingly enough, on Sard's theorem. This result can then be extended to continuous functions using a theorem of Stone and Weierstrass which says that any continuous function can be uniformly approximated by a polynomial in a compact set. See Milnor (1965, pp. 13ff.) or Guillemin and Pollack (1974, pp. 65–6).

For the special case of a univariate real function, Brouwer's theorem can

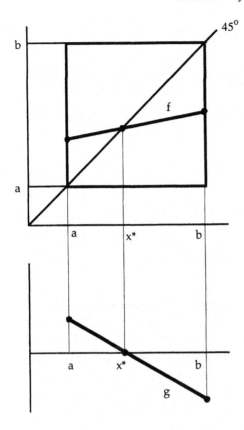

Figure 5.10. Brouwer's theorem for univariate functions.

be easily established using the intermediate-value theorem. In this case, the theorem says that a continuous function f that maps a compact interval $[a, b]$ into itself has at least one fixed point in the interval.

Consider the function g defined on $[a, b]$ by $g(x) = f(x) - x$ (Figure 5.10). Because f maps $[a, b]$ into itself, we must have

$$g(a) = f(a) - a \geq 0 \quad \text{and} \quad g(b) = f(b) - b \leq 0$$

If any of these expressions holds with equality, the fixed point is one of the end points of the interval. Otherwise, the intermediate-value theorem implies the existence of an interior zero of $g(\ )$ (i.e., a fixed point of f). In some sense, therefore, we can think of Brouwer's theorem as a generalization of the intermediate-value theorem to spaces of dimension higher than 1.

A second fixed-point theorem for functions, due to Tarsky, dispenses with the assumption of continuity, but requires that the function be nondecreasing.

Theorem 3.3. Tarsky's fixed-point theorem. Let f *be a nondecreasing function mapping the* n-*dimensional cube* $[0, 1]^n = [0, 1] \times \ldots \times [0, 1]$ *into itself. Then* f *has a fixed point.*

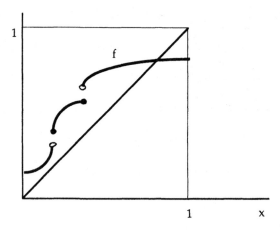

Figure 5.11. Tarsky's theorem.

Figure 5.11 illustrates the intuition behind this result in the one-dimensional case. Notice that if $f(0) = 0$, then 0 is a fixed point of f, and we are done. Otherwise, $f(0) > 0$, and $f(\ )$ starts out above the 45° line. Because the function must jump up at points of discontinuity, moreover, it cannot cross the diagonal at such points. Finally, because $f(1) \leq 1$ by assumption, the graph of f must at some point cross the diagonal.

We close this section with two fixed-point theorems for hemicontinuous correspondences.[7] For a proof and further results, the reader should refer to Border (1985, ch. 15).

Theorem 3.4. Kakutani's fixed-point theorem. Consider a correspondence Ψ from a set $X \subseteq \mathbb{R}^n$ to itself. Let X be compact and convex, and assume that Ψ is upper-hemicontinuous (or closed), as well as nonempty, compact, and convex-valued for all $x \in X$. Then Ψ has a fixed point in X, that is,

$$\exists\, x^* \in X \ s.th. \ x^* \in \Psi(x^*)$$

Theorem 3.5. Let $B \subseteq \mathbb{R}^n$ be a compact and convex set, and let $\mu : B \rightarrow\!\!\!\rightarrow B$ be a lower-hemicontinuous correspondence with closed and convex values. Then μ has a fixed point in B.

4. Problems

Problem 4.1. Given the IS-LM model

$$y = E_0 + \alpha y - \beta r + G \tag{A}$$

$$M^s/P = M_0 + \gamma y - \delta r \tag{B}$$

where y is national income, r is the interest rate, G is public expenditure, M^s/P is the money supply divided by a price index, and all the Greek letters are positive parameters.

(i) Analyze graphically the effects of increases in (a) government spending and (b) the price level on the equilibrium values of national income and the interest rate.

(ii) Write the model in matrix form. Use Cramer's rule to solve the model, writing the equilibrium values of (y, r) as functions of the parameters $(G, M^s/P, E_0,$ and $M_0)$, and show that the result is compatible with the conclusions of the graphical analysis.

Problem 4.2. The seller of a product pays a proportional tax at a flat rate θ $\in (0, 1)$. Hence, the effective price received by the seller is $(1 - \theta)P$, where P is the market price for the good. Market supply and demand are given by the differentiable functions

$$Q^d = D(P), \qquad \text{with } D'(\ ) < 0$$
$$Q^s = S((1-\theta)P), \quad \text{with } S'(\ ) > 0$$

and equilibrium requires market clearing, that is, $Q^s = Q^d$.

Analyze, graphically and analytically, the effects of a decrease in the tax rate on the quantity transacted and the equilibrium price. (Use the implicit-function theorem.)

Problem 4.3. A competitive firm chooses the quantity of labor L to be hired in order to maximize profits, taking as given the salary w and the value of a productivity parameter θ. That is, the firm solves

$$\max_{L}(\theta f(L) - wL)$$

Assume that the production function $f(\ )$ is twice continuously differentiable, increasing, and strictly concave (i.e., $f' > 0, f'' < 0$).

(i) Write the first-order condition for the firm's problem, and verify that the second-order sufficient condition for a maximum holds.

(ii) Interpret the first-order condition as an equation that implicitly defines a labor demand function of the form $L^* = L(w, \theta)$. Show, using the implicit-function theorem, that

$$\partial L^*/\partial w < 0 \quad \text{and} \quad \partial L^*/\partial \theta > 0$$

Problem 4.4. Consider an individual who lives for two periods and consumes a single good ("output"). The agent is endowed with y_1 units of output in youth, and y_2 units in old age. There exists a perfectly competitive market for output loans in which the agent may borrow or lend at an interest rate r that he takes as given. Call c_1 and c_2 his consumption levels during the first and second periods of life, and let s denote his first-period savings, $s = y_1 - c_1$ (note that s will be negative if the agent is a net borrower).

The agent's preferences are represented by a utility function of the form

$$U(c_1) + \beta U(c_2)$$

where U is a strictly increasing and strictly concave C^2 function that satisfies the following "corner" conditions:

$$U'(c) \to 0 \quad \text{as } c \to \infty \quad \text{and} \quad U'(c) \to \infty \quad \text{as } c \to 0$$

Suppose also that

$$y_1, y_2 > 0, \quad \beta \in (0, 1), \quad \text{and} \quad R \equiv 1 + r > 0$$

The individual solves the following problem:

$$\max_{c_1, c_2} \{U(c_1) + \beta U(c_2) \text{ subject to } c_1 = y_1 - s, \ c_2 = y_2 + sR\}$$

Substituting the constraints into the objective function, we obtain a maximization problem in a single decision variable, s.

(i) Write the first-order condition for this problem, and check that the second-order sufficient condition for a maximum holds.

We will interpret the first-order condition as an equation that implicitly defines a savings function of the form $s^* = s(y_1, y_2, R)$. We fix the values of (y_1, y_2) and study the behavior of s^* as a function of R.

(ii) Show that for a given value of R, the first-order condition has a unique solution s^*. (Use the intermediate-value theorem, and think of what will happen in extreme cases, e.g., if the agent decides not to eat during one of the periods.)

(iii) From (ii), we know that $s(R)$ is a well-defined function for $R > 0$. The implicit-function theorem guarantees that $s(R)$ is also differentiable. (Why? Which of our assumptions are we using here?) Substituting $s(R)$ back into the first-order condition, we have an identity. Hence, we can differentiate both sides of it with respect to R, and the equality will continue to hold. Differentiate implicitly with respect to R, and solve for $s'(R)$ in the resulting expression.

What can we say about the sign of $s'(R)$? That is, does s^* increase or decrease with the interest factor R? Does it matter whether or not the agent is a net borrower? (It should. In one of the cases you should not be able to sign the derivative. Why?)

(iv) Show that there exists some value of R (say R^0) for which the agent neither borrows nor lends, but consumes precisely his endowment each period. We say that R^0 is the agent's autarkic interest factor.

Hint: Go back to the original formulation of the agent's decision problem and think in terms of indifference curves and budget constraints in the (c_1, c_2) plane. Plot the indifference curve that goes through the endowment point (y_1, y_2). What value of R will make the agent "happy" eating precisely his endowment each period?

(v) Show that on one side of R^0 the agent is always a net saver in youth, and on the other always a net borrower. (What is the sign of $s'(R^0)$? Note that this does not imply that $s(\ )$ is always monotonic.)

Problem 4.5. Consider now an economy in which there are two different types of agents who face the decision analyzed in Problem 4.4, but may have different endowment streams, discount factors, or utility functions. To simplify, assume that there is only one agent of each type, but they both behave competitively (i.e., taking the value of R as given).

Let $s_1(R)$ and $s_2(R)$ be the savings functions for the two agents. In equilibrium, the credit market must clear (i.e., if one is a net borrower, the other must be a net lender), and aggregate savings must be zero. That is, we must have

$$Z(R) \equiv s_1(R) + s_2(R) = 0 \tag{1}$$

Show that under the assumptions of Problem 4.4 there exists at least one competitive equilibrium, that is, a value of R for which (1) holds.

Hint: Let R_1^0 and R_2^0 be the autarkic interest factors for the two agents. Without loss of generality, we can assume that $R_1^0 > R_2^0$. What happens when $R = R_1^0, R_2^0$? Use the intermediate-value theorem.

Bibliography

Apostol, T. 1974. *Mathematical Analysis*, 2nd ed. Reading, MA: Addison-Wesley.

Border, K. 1985. *Fixed Point Theorems with Applications to Economics and Game Theory.* Cambridge University Press.

Buck, R. 1978. *Advanced Calculus*, 3rd ed. New York: McGraw-Hill.

Chow, S., and Pollack, A. 1982. *Methods of Bifurcation Theory.* Berlin: Springer-Verlag.

Guillemin, V., and Pollack, A. 1974. *Differential Topology.* Englewood Cliffs, NJ: Prentice-Hall.

Hadley, G. 1961. *Linear Algebra.* Reading, MA: Addison-Wesley.

Luenberger, D. 1973. *Introduction to Linear and Non-Linear Programming.* Reading, MA: Addison-Wesley.

Mas-Colell, A. 1985. *The Theory of General Economic Equilibrium: A Differentiable Approach.* Cambridge University Press.

Mas-Colell, A., Whinston, M., and Green, J. 1995. *Microeconomic Theory.* Oxford University Press.

Milnor, J. 1965. *Topology from a Differentiable Viewpoint.* University Press of Virginia.

Rudin, W. 1976. *Principles of Mathematical Analysis,* 3rd ed. New York: McGraw-Hill.

Samuelson, P. 1985. *Foundations of Economic Analysis*. Harvard University Press.
Silberberg, E. 1978. *The Structure of Economics, a Mathematical Analysis*. New York: McGraw-Hill.
Strang, G. 1980. *Linear Algebra and Its Applications*. New York: Academic Press.
Sydsæter, K. 1981. *Topics in Mathematical Analysis for Economists*. Orlando, FL: Academic Press.

Notes

1 If the system had two solutions, say x' and x'', then it would have an infinite number of them, for every linear combination of the form $(1 - \lambda)x' + \lambda x''$ would also be a solution (the reader should verify that this is true). But then we would have an affine subspace of dimension at least 1.

2 Differentiating implicitly $F[x(\alpha), \alpha] = 0$, we see that $F_x(\ )x'(\alpha) + F_\alpha(\ ) = 0$, from where $x'(\alpha) = -F_\alpha(\ )/F_x(\ )$. Hence, the curve $x(\alpha)$ will have infinite slope whenever $F_x(\ ) = 0$.

3 See Chapter 4 for a definition of the regular value of a function.

4 To simplify, we think of a manifold as embedded in a larger ambient space, $\mathbb{R}^n$, but a more general definition could be given in which this need not be the case.

5 The third possible case may seem a little strange at first sight. Recall that y is a regular value of f if rank $Df(x) = m$ for all x in $f^{-1}(y)$. Because $Df(x)$ is an $m \times n$ matrix, its maximum rank is $\min\{m, n\}$. Hence, if $m > n$, every point in $f^{-1}(y)$ is a critical point, and the only regular values are those points that are not in the range of the function. For each of these points, $f^{-1}(y)$ is the empty set. Because, as we will see later, "most" of the values of f are regular, the theorem implies that the normal situation in this case is for the system $f(x) = y$ not to have any solutions. Because we have more equations than unknowns, this is precisely what we should expect.

6 On the other hand, if we consider "paths" of possible environments, these paths typically will cross values of α for which $\underline{0}$ is a critical value of f_α. If the environment changes slowly over time, we can imagine the equilibrium of the system $x(\alpha)$ changing along with it. Most of the time, the change will be smooth, with small changes in the environment yielding small displacements of the equilibrium. At some points, however, the system may undergo drastic changes. Such phenomena are known as *bifurcations* or *catastrophes*.

7 See Section 11 of Chapter 2 for the definitions of upper hemicontinuity and lower hemicontinuity.

6

Convex Sets and Concave Functions

Convexity conditions play a crucial role in optimization. In the context of economic theory, moreover, convexity often appears as a sensible restriction on preferences or technology. Thus the convexity of preferences can be interpreted as capturing consumers' preference for variety, and the convexity of production sets is closely related to the existence of nonincreasing returns to scale.

This chapter contains an introduction to the theory of convex sets and concave and quasiconcave functions. Much of this material will be useful in connection with the theory of optimization developed in Chapters 7 and 12. In Chapter 8 we will discuss the roles that these concepts play in some basic economic models.

1. Convex Sets and Separation Theorems in $\mathbb{R}^n$

Definition 1.1. Convex set. A set X in $\mathbb{R}^n$ (or, more generally, in a vector space over the real field) is convex if given any two points x' and x'' in X, the point

$$x^\lambda = (1 - \lambda)x' + \lambda x''$$

is also in X for every $\lambda \in [0, 1]$.

A vector of the form $x^\lambda = (1 - \lambda)x' + \lambda x''$, with $\lambda \in [0, 1]$, is called a *convex combination* of x' and x''. The set of all convex combinations of x' and x'' is the straight line segment connecting these two points. This line segment is sometimes denoted by $L(x', x'')$ or $[x', x'']$, or by $(x', x'']$, for example, if we want to exclude one of the end points. The points x' and x'' are the *end points* of the segment, and points x^λ, with $0 < \lambda < 1$, are said to be *interior* to the segment. A set X is convex if given any two points x' and x'' in it, X contains the line segment that joins them.

A convex set with a nonempty interior is sometimes called a *convex body*.

229

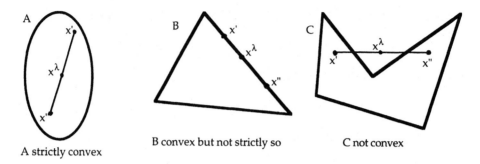

Figure 6.1. Convex and nonconvex sets.

A convex body X is said to be *strictly convex* if the line segment connecting any two points x' and x'' in X lies in the interior of X, except possibly for its end points, that is, if

$$\forall x', x'' \in X \text{ and } \forall \lambda \in (0,1), \ x^\lambda = (1-\lambda)x' + \lambda x'' \in \text{int } X$$

We now list some useful results concerning convex sets.

Theorem 1.2. Any intersection of convex sets is convex.

Problem 1.3. Prove Theorem 1.2.

Theorem 1.4. Let X and Y be convex sets in $\mathbb{R}^n$, and let α be a real number. Then the sets

$$\alpha X = \{z \in \mathbb{R}^n; \ z = \alpha x \text{ for some } x \in X\}$$

and

$$X + Y = \{z \in \mathbb{R}^n; \ z = x + y \text{ for some } x \in X \text{ and } y \in Y\}$$

are convex.

This result implies that any linear combination $\alpha X + \beta Y$ of convex sets is convex. It is also easy to show by induction that sums or linear combinations involving arbitrary numbers of convex sets are also convex.

Proof. We can prove both parts at the same time by showing that given any convex sets X and Y in $\mathbb{R}^n$ (or, more generally, in a vector space over the real field) and two arbitrary scalars α and β, the set

$$Z = \alpha X + \beta Y = \{z \in \mathbb{R}^n; \ z = \alpha x + \beta y \text{ for some } x \in X \text{ and } y \in Y\}$$

is also convex.

Take two arbitrary points z' and z'' in $Z = \alpha X + \beta Y$. By the definition of Z there exist points x', x'' in X and y', y'' in Y such that

$$z' = \alpha x' + \beta y' \quad \text{and} \quad z'' = \alpha x'' + \beta y'' \tag{1}$$

Using (1), an arbitrary convex combination of z' and z'' can be written

$$\begin{aligned} z^\lambda &= \lambda z' + (1 - \lambda) z'' = \lambda(\alpha x' + \beta y') + (1 - \lambda)(\alpha x'' + \beta y'') \\ &= \alpha[\lambda x' + (1 - \lambda)x''] + \beta[\lambda y' + (1 - \lambda)y''] \in \alpha X + \beta Y \end{aligned} \tag{2}$$

By the convexity of X and Y, $\lambda x' + (1 - \lambda)x'' \in X$, and $\lambda y' + (1 - \lambda)y'' \in Y$. Hence, $z^\lambda \in \alpha X + \beta Y$, which establishes the convexity of Z. $\qquad\square$

(a) Convex Combinations and Convex Hull

The concept of convex combinations can be extended to sets of more than two vectors.

Definition 1.5. Convex combination. A point y in $\mathbb{R}^n$ is said to be a *convex combination* of the vectors $x_1, \ldots, x_m \in \mathbb{R}^n$ if it can be written in the form

$$y = \sum_{i=1}^m \lambda_i x_i \tag{1}$$

with

$$\lambda_i \in [0, 1] \quad \text{for all } i \quad \text{and} \quad \sum_{i=1}^m \lambda_i = 1 \tag{2}$$

Hence, a convex combination is an affine combination with the additional requirement that $\lambda_i \geq 0$. (Notice that this, in turn, implies $\lambda_i \in [0, 1]$, because the sum of the λ_i's cannot exceed 1.)

We can now give an equivalent characterization of convexity in terms of (generalized) convex combinations.

Theorem 1.6. A set X *is convex if and only if every convex combination of points of* X *lies in* X.

Problem 1.7. Prove Theorem 1.6. Hint: To establish necessity, use the modified induction principle discussed in Problem 2.8 of Chapter 1.

We are sometimes interested in extending a set X so that it becomes convex by adding as few points to it as possible. The resulting set is called the convex hull of X.

Definition 1.8. Convex hull. Let X be a set in $\mathbb{R}^n$. The smallest convex set that contains X is called the convex hull of X and is denoted by conv X.

Clearly, there is at least one convex set that contains X, namely, $\mathbb{R}^n$ itself. If there are more, conv X is the intersection of all such sets. An alternative characterization is given by the following result.

Theorem 1.9. *The convex hull of* X *is the set of all convex combinations of elements of* X, *that is,*

$$conv\ X = \left\{ y = \sum_{i=1}^{m} \lambda_i x_i;\ for\ some\ m, \right.$$

$$\left. with\ x_i \in X,\ \lambda_i \in [0,\ 1]\ for\ all\ i,\ and\ \sum_{i=1}^{m} \lambda_i = 1 \right\} \tag{1}$$

Proof. Let

$$Y = \left\{ y = \sum_{i=1}^{m} \lambda_i x_i;\ for\ some\ m,\ with\ x_i \in X, \right.$$

$$\left. \lambda_i \in [0,1]\ for\ all\ i,\ and\ \sum_{i=1}^{m} \lambda_i = 1 \right\}$$

Clearly Y contains X, for any x in X can be written as a trivial convex combination with itself.

Next, we show that Y is a convex set. Let y_1 and y_2,

$$y_1 = \sum_{i=1}^{m} \lambda_i x_i \quad and \quad y_2 = \sum_{k=1}^{n} \mu_k x_k$$

with

$$\lambda_i, \mu_k \in [0,1] \quad for\ all\ i\ and\ k \quad and \quad \sum_{k=1}^{n} \mu_k = \sum_{i=1}^{m} \lambda_i = 1$$

be arbitrary points of Y, and take some $\alpha \in [0, 1]$. Then

$$y^\lambda = (1-\alpha)y_1 + \alpha y_2 = (1-\alpha)\left(\sum_{i=1}^{m} \lambda_i x_i\right) + \alpha\left(\sum_{k=1}^{n} \mu_k x_k\right)$$

$$= \sum_{i=1}^{m} (1-\alpha)\lambda_i x_i + \sum_{k=1}^{n} \alpha\mu_k x_k \tag{2}$$

Notice that

$$(1-\alpha)\lambda_i \in [0,1] \quad for\ each\ i, \qquad \alpha\mu_k \in [0,1] \quad for\ each\ k$$

and

$$\sum_{i=1}^{m} (1-\alpha)\lambda_i + \sum_{k=1}^{n} \alpha\mu_k = (1-\alpha)\sum_{i=1}^{m} \lambda_i + \alpha\sum_{k=1}^{n} \mu_k = (1-\alpha)+\alpha = 1$$

Thus, (2) shows that y^λ is a convex combination of points in X, and it follows that $y^\lambda \in Y$, which is therefore a convex set.

Hence Y is a convex set that contains X. Moreover, any convex set that contains X must include all convex combinations of points in X (by Theorem 1.6) and must therefore contain Y. It follows that Y is the smallest convex set containing X (i.e., $Y = $ conv X). □

Theorem 1.9 tells us that any point in the convex hull of X can be written as a convex combination of a finite number of points of X, but it does not tell us how many such points are required. The following result says that if X is a set in an n-dimensional vector space, this convex combination can be constructed with, at most, $n + 1$ points of X.

Theorem 1.10. Caratheodory. Let X *be a set in* $\mathbb{R}^n$. *If* y *is a convex combination of points of* X, *then* y *is a convex combination of* n + 1 *or fewer points of* X.

Proof. Let

$$y = \sum_{i=1}^{m} \lambda_i x_i \tag{1}$$

with $x_i \in X$, $\lambda_i \in [0, 1]$ for all i, and $\sum_{i=1}^{m} \lambda_i = 1$. We will show that if $m > n + 1$, then y can be written as a convex combination of $m - 1$ points of X. By applying this result repeatedly, the theorem follows.

If any λ_i in (1) is zero, then y is a convex combination of $m - 1$ or fewer points of X, and we are done. Otherwise, $\lambda_i > 0$ for all i.

Assume $m > n + 1$. Then $m - 1 > n$ (the dimension of the vector space in which we are working), and it follows that any collection of $m - 1$ vectors is linearly dependent. In particular, the $m - 1$ vectors $\{x_2 - x_1, x_3 - x_1, \ldots, x_m - x_1\}$ are linearly dependent (see Chapter 3). Thus, there exist scalars $\alpha_2, \ldots, \alpha_m$, not all zero, such that

$$\sum_{i=2}^{m} \alpha_i (x_i - x_1) = \underline{0} \tag{2}$$

Letting

$$\alpha_1 = -\sum_{i=2}^{m} \alpha_i$$

we have

$$\sum_{i=1}^{m} \alpha_i = 0 \tag{3}$$

and

$$\sum_{i=1}^{m} \alpha_i x_i = -\left(\sum_{i=2}^{m} \alpha_i\right) x_1 + \sum_{i=2}^{m} \alpha_i x_i = \sum_{i=2}^{m} \alpha_i (x_i - x_1) = \underline{0} \tag{4}$$

By subtracting an appropriate multiple of (4) from (1), we can obtain y as a convex combination of $m - 1$ or fewer points of X.

Define γ and β_i by[1]

$$\frac{1}{\gamma} = \max_i \frac{\alpha_i}{\lambda_i} = \frac{\alpha_r}{\lambda_r} \quad \text{for some } r \tag{5}$$

and

$$\beta_i = \lambda_i - \gamma \alpha_i \tag{6}$$

and observe that $\gamma = \lambda_r / \alpha_r \leq \lambda_i / \alpha_i$ for all i. It then follows that

$$\beta_i = \lambda_i - \gamma\alpha_i = \lambda_i - \frac{\lambda_r}{\alpha_r}\alpha_i \geq 0 \quad \text{and} \quad \beta_r = 0 \tag{7}$$

Using (7) and (6) we have

$$\sum_{i\neq r}^{m}\beta_i = \sum_{i=1}^{m}\beta_i = \sum_{i=1}^{m}\lambda_i - \gamma\sum_{i=1}^{m}\alpha_i = \sum_{i=1}^{m}\lambda_i - 0 = 1$$

by (3), and

$$y = \sum_{i=1}^{m}\lambda_i x_i = \sum_{i=1}^{m}\beta_i x_i + \gamma\sum_{i=1}^{m}\alpha_i x_i = \sum_{i\neq r}^{m}\beta_i x_i + 0$$

by (4). Hence, y is a convex combination of $m-1$ points of X. This establishes the result. $\qquad\qquad\square$

(b) Topological Properties of Convex Sets

Convexity implies some interesting topological properties. A convex set, for example, is clearly arcwise-connected and therefore connected. In this section we collect some less obvious results.

Theorem 1.11. Let X be a convex set in $\mathbb{R}^n$ (or, more generally, in a normed vector space). Then both its closure and its interior are convex sets.

Proof. We prove only the second part of the theorem, leaving the first as an exercise. Given two interior points of X, x and y, let $z = (1-\lambda)x + \lambda y$ for some $\lambda \in (0,1)$. We will show that z is an interior point of X.

Given some $\delta > 0$, let z' be an arbitrary point in $B_\delta(z)$. Then $z' = z + h$, where $\|h\| < \delta$, and we can write

$$z' = z + h = (1-\lambda)x + \lambda y + (1-\lambda)h + \lambda h = (1-\lambda)(x+h) + \lambda(y+h)$$

where $x + h \in B_\delta(x)$ and $y + h \in B_\delta(y)$. Hence, for any δ we have

$$B_\delta(z) \subseteq (1-\lambda)B_\delta(x) + \lambda B_\delta(y) \tag{1}$$

Now, because x and y are interior points of X, there exists some $\varepsilon > 0$ such that $B_\varepsilon(x)$ and $B_\varepsilon(y)$ are both contained in X. Then, by (1) and the convexity of X, we have

$$B_\varepsilon(z) \subseteq (1-\lambda)B_\varepsilon(x) + \lambda B_\varepsilon(y) \subseteq X$$

because any point in $B_\varepsilon(z)$ is a linear combination of two points in X, one in $B_\varepsilon(x)$ and the other in $B_\varepsilon(y)$. This shows that z is an interior point of X. $\qquad\qquad\square$

Problem 1.12. Show that the closure of a convex set is convex.

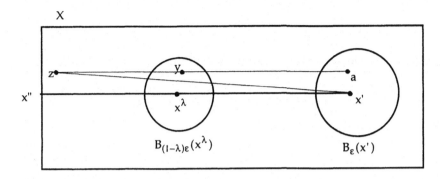

Figure 6.2.

Theorem 1.13. Let X *be a convex set with a nonempty interior, with* x′ *an interior point of* X *and* x″ *any closure point of* X. *Then every point of the segment* [x′, x″], *except possibly for* x″, *is an interior point of* X.

Proof. Because x' is an interior point of X, there exists some $\varepsilon > 0$ such that $B_\varepsilon(x') \subseteq X$. Consider an arbitrary point $x^\lambda = (1 - \lambda)x' + \lambda x''$, with $\lambda \in [0, 1)$. To show that x^λ is an interior point of X, we shall verify that the open ball with center at x' and radius $(1 - \lambda)\varepsilon$ is contained in X. In particular, let y be an arbitrary point in $B_{(1-\lambda)\varepsilon}(x^\lambda)$; we will prove that y belongs to X by showing that it can be written as a convex combination of two points in X, one close to x', and the other close to x''.

Because $y \in B_{(1-\lambda)\varepsilon}(x^\lambda)$,

$$\|y - x^\lambda\| < (1 - \lambda)\varepsilon \tag{1}$$

and because x'' is a closure point of X (i.e., any open ball around x'' contains at least one point of X), there is a point $z \in X$ sufficiently close to x'' that the segment $[z, x']$ passes close to y. In particular, we can choose $z \in X$ such that

$$\|z - x''\| < \frac{1}{\lambda}((1 - \lambda)\varepsilon - \|y - x^\lambda\|) \tag{2}$$

Hence, by the triangle inequality and (2),

$$\begin{aligned}
\|y - [(1 - \lambda)x' + \lambda z]\| &= \|y - [(1 - \lambda)x' + \lambda z + \lambda x'' - \lambda x'']\| \\
&= \|(y - x^\lambda) + \lambda(x'' - z)\| \leq \|y - x^\lambda\| + \lambda\|x'' - z\| \\
&< \|y - x^\lambda\| + ((1 - \lambda)\varepsilon - \|y - x^\lambda\|) = (1 - \lambda)\varepsilon \tag{3}
\end{aligned}$$

Next, consider the line segment through z and y, and let us extend it toward x'. If we want y to be of the form $y = (1 - \lambda)a + \lambda z$, then a must be the point

$$a = \frac{1}{1-\lambda}(y - \lambda z)$$

Dividing both sides of (3) by $(1 - \lambda)$, we obtain

$$\left\| \frac{1}{1-\lambda}(y - \lambda z) - x' \right\| = \|a - x''\| < \varepsilon \tag{4}$$

This expression shows that the "new" end point of the segment through z and y lies inside $B_\varepsilon(x')$ and is therefore a point of X, as is z. Hence, $y = (1 - \lambda)a + \lambda z$ is a convex combination of points in X, and by the convexity of this set, we conclude that $y \in Z$, which proves the theorem, for y is an arbitrary point in $B_{(1-\lambda)\varepsilon}(x^\lambda)$.   □

Problem 1.14. Using Theorem 1.13, show that given a convex set X and an interior point x of X, any ray emanating from x contains at most one boundary point of X.   □

Theorem 1.15. Let X be a convex set with a nonempty interior. Then *cl* X = *cl(int* X).

Proof. Because int $X \subseteq X$, it follows immediately that cl(int X) $\subseteq$ cl X. Conversely, let x be an interior point of X. Then for any closure point c of X, with $c \neq x,$[2] the line segment $[x, c)$ is contained in int X, by Theorem 1.13. Hence, there are points in int X arbitrarily close to c, and it follows that $c \in$ cl(int X). Because c was an arbitrary closure point of X, moreover, we have cl $X \subseteq$ cl(int X).   □

Theorem 1.16. Let X be a convex set with a nonempty interior. Then *bdy(cl* X) = *bdy* X.

Proof

(i) bdy $X \subseteq$ bdy(cl X). Let a be a boundary point (and therefore a closure point) of X, and suppose that a is not a boundary point of cl X. Then, because $a \in$ cl X, a must be an interior point of cl X, and it follows that there exists some $\varepsilon > 0$ such that $B_\varepsilon(a) \subseteq$ cl X. Because int X is nonempty by assumption, Theorem 1.15 implies that cl $X =$ cl(int X), and we have

$$B_\varepsilon(a) \subseteq \text{cl(int } X)$$

It follows that $B_\varepsilon(a)$ contains at least one interior point of X, say b.

Let $c = 2a - b$. Then $c - a = a - b$ and $\|c - a\| = \|a - b\| < \varepsilon$, implying that $c \in B_\varepsilon(a) \subseteq$ cl X. Moreover, notice that

$$a = \frac{1}{2}b + \frac{1}{2}c$$

so a lies on the line segment $[b, c)$, where b is an interior point of X and c is a closure point of the same set. Because X is convex, it follows, by Theorem 1.13, that a must be an interior point of X, which contradicts the assumption that a is a boundary point of this set.

(ii) bdy(cl X) $\subseteq$ bdy X. Let a be a boundary point of cl X. Then for each $\varepsilon > 0$, $B_\varepsilon(a)$ contains a point not in the closure of X and therefore not in X. Similarly, $B_\varepsilon(a)$ contains at least a closure point of X, say b, and because b must have points of X arbitrarily close, $B_\varepsilon(a)$ also contains a point of X. Formally, let

$$\delta = \frac{\varepsilon - \|a - b\|}{2} > 0$$

Then $B_\delta(b) \subseteq B_\varepsilon(a)$, and because b is a closure point of X, $B_\delta(b)$ must contain a point of X that also lies in $B_\varepsilon(a)$. Hence, we conclude that a is a boundary point of X. (Notice that we did not need convexity or a nonempty interior to establish this part of the theorem.)   □

Problem 1.17. Let X be a convex set with a nonempty interior. Show that int(cl X) = int X.

(c) Relative Interior and Boundary of a Convex Set

A circle in $\mathbb{R}^3$ is an example of a convex set with an empty interior. If we restrict ourselves to the plane that contains it, however, the same circle now has a nonempty interior. More generally, we may want to consider the relative interior of a convex set X in $\mathbb{R}^n$, defined as its interior relative to the smallest affine subspace of $\mathbb{R}^n$ that contains X. We begin by showing that such a subspace always exists. But first we need to introduce the concept of "hyperplane."

Definition 1.18. Hyperplane. A hyperplane in $\mathbb{R}^n$ is the $(n-1)$-dimensional affine subspace[3] of $\mathbb{R}^n$ formed by all the n-vectors that satisfy a linear equation in n unknowns. A vector $p \neq 0$ in $\mathbb{R}^n$ and a scalar α define the hyperplane $H(p, \alpha)$ given by

$$H(p, \alpha) = \left\{ x = (x^1, \ldots, x^n) \in \mathbb{R}^n; \; px = \sum_{i=1}^{n} p_i x^i = \alpha \right\}$$

Given any two vectors x' and x'' in $H(p, \alpha)$, $px' = \alpha = px''$. It follows that for any scalar λ (not necessarily between 0 and 1), we have

$$px^\lambda = p[(1-\lambda)x' + \lambda x''] = (1-\lambda)px' + \lambda px'' = (1-\lambda)\alpha + \lambda\alpha = \alpha \qquad (1)$$

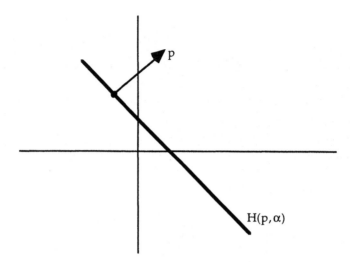

Figure 6.3. A hyperplane and its normal.

If we restrict ourselves to values of λ between 0 and 1, this expression shows that $H(p, \alpha)$ is a convex set. More generally, (1) establishes that $H(p, \alpha)$ is an affine subspace of $\mathbb{R}^n$, that is, a set of the form $H(p, \alpha) = x^0 + L$, where x^0 is an arbitrary vector in $\mathbb{R}^n$, and L is a linear subspace of $\mathbb{R}^n$. We define the *dimension of a hyperplane* $H(p, \alpha)$, or, more generally, of an affine subspace H, to be the dimension of the vector subspace L "parallel" to H.

Notice that any two vectors x' and x'' in $H(p, \alpha)$ satisfy $p(x' - x'') = 0$. Hence, p is orthogonal to any line segment in $H(p, \alpha)$. The vector p is sometimes called the *normal* to the hyperplane $H(p, \alpha)$.

We can now show that a convex set in $\mathbb{R}^n$ is contained in a hyperplane if and only if it has an empty interior.

Theorem 1.19. *Let* X *be a convex set in* $\mathbb{R}^n$. *Then there exists a hyperplane* H *that contains* X *if and only if int* X $= \emptyset$.

Proof

(i) A convex set with an empty interior is contained in a hyperplane. We will prove the contrapositive statement: If no such hyperplane exists, then X has a nonempty interior.

Assume that X does not lie on a hyperplane. Then we can find $n + 1$ points of X, say $x_0, x_1, \ldots, x_n$, that are contained in no hyperplane. We will now show that the vectors

$$y_i = x_i - x_0 \quad \text{for } i = 1, \ldots, n$$

are linearly independent. (Again, we prove the contrapositive.) Suppose $y_1, \ldots, y_n$ are linearly dependent. Then there exist scalars $p_1, \ldots, p_n$, not all zero, such that

$$\sum_{i=1}^{n} p_i y_i = \underline{0}$$

that is, there exists a vector $p = (p_1, \ldots, p_n) \neq \underline{0}$ such that

$$p y_i = p(x_i - x_0) = \underline{0}$$

Hence, all vectors $x_0, x_1, \ldots, x_n$ solve the equation $px = \beta$ (with $\beta = px_0$) and therefore lie on a hyperplane. Because that is not the case by assumption, it follows that $y_1, \ldots, y_n$ are linearly independent and therefore span $\mathbb{R}^n$.

Now, because X is a convex set, every point z of the form

$$z = \sum_{i=0}^{n} \lambda_i x_i, \quad \text{with } \lambda_i \in [0,1] \text{ for each } i = 0, \ldots, n \text{ and } \sum_{i=0}^{n} \lambda_i = 1 \quad (1)$$

lies in X. Notice that we can rewrite (1) as follows:

$$z = \lambda_0 x_0 + \sum_{i=1}^{n} \lambda_i x_i = \left(\lambda_0 + \sum_{i=1}^{n} \lambda_i \right) x_0 + \sum_{i=1}^{n} \lambda_i (x_i - x_0) = x_0 + \sum_{i=1}^{n} \lambda_i y_i$$

Hence, every point z of the form

$$z = x_0 + \sum_{i=1}^{n} \lambda_i y_i, \quad \text{with } \lambda_i \in [0,1] \text{ for each } i = 1, \ldots, n \text{ and } \sum_{i=1}^{n} \lambda_i \leq 1 \quad (2)$$

lies in X. Fix one such point,

$$\hat{z} = x_0 + \sum_{i=1}^{n} \hat{\lambda}_i y_i \in X, \quad \text{with } \hat{\lambda}_i \in [0,1] \text{ for each } i = 1, \ldots, n \text{ and } \sum_{i=1}^{n} \hat{\lambda}_i < 1$$

Next, consider points $\tilde{z}$ near $\hat{z}$. Because $y_1, \ldots, y_n$ is a basis for $\mathbb{R}^n$, every such point has a representation of the form

$$\tilde{z} - x_0 = \sum_{i=1}^{n} \beta_i y_i$$

with each β_i close to $\hat{\lambda}_i$. Hence, for all such points sufficiently close to $\hat{z}$, we have $\beta_i \in [0, 1)$ for each i, and $\sum_{i=1}^{n} \beta_i < 1$, and it follows that $\tilde{z} \in X$. This shows that X contains a ball with center at $\hat{z}$ and sufficiently small radius. Hence, $\hat{z}$ is an interior point of X, and int $X \neq \emptyset$, as was to be shown.

(ii) We will show that a set X in $\mathbb{R}^n$ with a nonempty interior is not contained in any hyperplane of $\mathbb{R}^n$. Let x be an interior point of X. Then there exists some number $2\varepsilon > 0$ such that $B_{2\varepsilon}(x) \subseteq X$. In particular, the n points of the form $x + \varepsilon e_i$, where $e_i = (0, \ldots, 1, 0, \ldots, 0)$ is the ith unit vector, lie in X. Now consider a hyperplane $H(p, \alpha)$ going through x (i.e., such that $px = \alpha$). If this hyperplane contains all the points $x + \varepsilon e_i$, we have

$$p(x + \varepsilon e_i) = px + \varepsilon p e_i = \alpha + \varepsilon p_i = \alpha$$

and therefore $p_i = 0$ for all i, and $p = \underline{0}$. It follows that there is no hyperplane in $\mathbb{R}^n$ that contains $B_{2\varepsilon}(x)$, and hence no hyperplane containing X. $\square$

Because $\mathbb{R}^n$ is itself an affine space (of dimension n), the theorem shows that every convex set X in $\mathbb{R}^n$ can be contained in an affine space. If X has an empty interior, this space is a hyperplane of dimension at most $n - 1$, but it may be of a smaller dimension. Because the intersection of affine sub-spaces of $\mathbb{R}^n$ is itself an affine subspace, we can define the *affine hull* of a set X in $\mathbb{R}^n$ as the intersection of all the affine subspaces of $\mathbb{R}^n$ that contain X. The dimension of the set X is then defined as the dimension of its affine hull.

It is clear that the affine hull of X, aff X, is the smallest affine subspace of $\mathbb{R}^n$ that contains X. It can be shown that aff X is the set of all affine combinations of elements of X. For the case where X is a circle in $\mathbb{R}^3$, for example, aff X is formed by taking all lines going through two points in X and extending them outside the set, so as to recover the plane on which the circle lies.

We can now define the relative interior of a convex set X, rint X, as its interior relative to its affine hull.

Definition 1.20. Relative interior point and relative interior of a set. Let X be a set in $\mathbb{R}^n$. A point x is a relative interior point of X if there exists some $\varepsilon > 0$ such that $B_\varepsilon(x) \cap$ aff $X \subseteq X$. The set of all relative interior points of X is called the relative interior of X, denoted by rint X.

It can be shown that the relative interior of a nonempty convex set is never empty.[4] Hence, the relative interior of a convex set is generally larger than its interior. If int $X \neq \emptyset$, however, we have aff $X = \mathbb{R}^n$, and it follows that rint $X = $ int X. Hence, we have rint $X = $ int X if and only if int $X \neq \emptyset$.

It must be noted that the relative interior of a set does not inherit the usual properties of the interior of a set. For example, $A \subseteq B$ implies int $A \subseteq$ int B, but the analogous expression need not hold for their relative interiors. As an illustration, consider a triangle in $\mathbb{R}^3$ and one of its sides. Then the affine hull of the triangle is a plane that contains it, and that of its side is a straight line. The relative interiors of these two sets (the interior of the triangle relative to the plane, and an open interval in the line) are disjoint.

Because aff X is a closed set (its complement is open), the closure of X is contained in aff X, and it follows that the "relative closure" of X is simply the closure of X. The set rbdy $X = $ cl $X \sim$ rint X is called the *relative boundary* of X. Because the closure of X is also its relative closure, rbdy X is actually the boundary of X relative to aff X.

If we confine ourselves to the affine hull of a convex set, the proofs of many of the results in the preceding section can be easily adapted to the case of the relative interior. We have, in particular, the following theorem. See Bronsted (1983) or Bazaraa and Shetty (1976) for details.

Theorem 1.21. Let X be a convex set in $\mathbb{R}^n$. Then

(i) *for any* $x_i \in$ *rint* X *and any* $x_c \in$ *cl* X *(with* $x_i \neq x_c$*), the half-open line segment* $[x_i, x_c)$ *lies in rint* X*,*

(ii) *rint* X *is convex,*
(iii) *cl* X = *cl(rint* X*),*
(iv) *rint* X = *rint(cl* X*),*
(v) *rbdy* X = *rbdy(cl* X*) = rbdy(rint* X*)*

Problem 1.22. Show that a point x_i in a convex set X is a relative interior point of X if and only if either of the two following (equivalent) conditions holds:

(i) For any line L in aff X, with $x_i \in L$, there exist points x' and x'' in $L \cap$ aff X such that $x_i \in (x', x'')$.
(ii) For any point $x' \in X$, with $x' \neq x_i$, there is a point $x'' \in X$ such that $x_i \in (x', x'')$. That is, the segment $[x', y]$ in X can be extended beyond x_i without leaving the set.

Problem 1.23. Let X be a convex set in $\mathbb{R}^n$, with int(cl X) $\neq \emptyset$. Show that int X is nonempty. Hint: Consider the affine hull of X, and prove the contrapositive.

(d) Separation Theorems

A hyperplane $H(p, \alpha)$ divides $\mathbb{R}^n$ into two regions, with all points z "on one side" of $H(p, \alpha)$ satisfying $pz \geq \alpha$, and all those on the other satisfying the reverse inequality. We say that two sets X and Y are *separated* by a hyperplane $H(p, \alpha)$ if they lie on different sides of $H(p, \alpha)$. More formally, we say that a hyperplane $H(p, \alpha)$ separates two sets X and Y in $\mathbb{R}^n$ if for all x in X and all y in Y we have $px \leq \alpha \leq py$. If this expression holds with strict inequalities, we say that X and Y are *strictly separated* by $H(p, \alpha)$.

A hyperplane $H(p, \alpha)$ is a *supporting hyperplane* for a set X if it contains a point on the boundary of X and the whole set lies on the same side of $H(p, \alpha)$. Equivalently, $H(p, \alpha)$ supports X if either

$$\alpha = \inf\{px; \, x \in X\} \quad \text{or} \quad \alpha = \sup\{px; \, x \in X\}$$

Intuition suggests that a convex set in $\mathbb{R}^n$ will have a supporting hyperplane through each point on its boundary. It also suggests that given two disjoint convex sets in $\mathbb{R}^n$, we should be able to find a hyperplane that separates them. The following theorems establish that both statements are true.

Theorem 1.24. *Let* X *be a nonempty closed and convex subset of* $\mathbb{R}^n$*, and* z $\notin$ X *a point outside* X*.*

(i) *There exists a point* x^0 *in* X *and a hyperplane* H(p, α) *through* x^0 *that supports* X *and separates it from {z}. That is,* H(p, α) *is such that* [5]

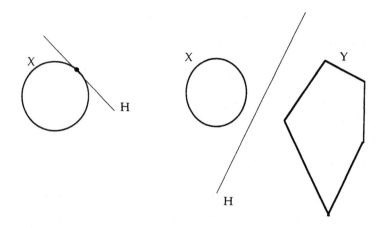

Figure 6.4. Supporting and separating hyperplanes.

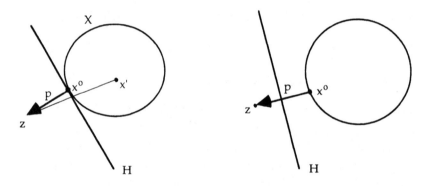

Figure 6.5.

$$pz < \alpha = px^0 = inf\{px; \; x \in X\}$$

(ii) There exists a second hyperplane H(p, β) that separates X and z strictly. That is,

$$pz < \beta < px \; \forall \, x \in X$$

Proof. We begin by showing that there is a point x^0 in X that minimizes the distance between z and X. Pick any point x' in X, and define the set

$$B = \{x \in X; \; d(z, x) \le d(z, x')\}$$

where $d(\;)$ is the Euclidean metric. Because $B = B_{d(z,x')}[z] \cap X$ is a closed and bounded set in $\mathbb{R}^n$ and $d(\cdot, z)$ is a continuous function, the extreme-value theorem guarantees the existence of a solution for the problem

$$\min\{d(x, z); \; x \in B\}$$

Call x^0 the point in B (and hence in X) that solves this problem.

(i) To prove the first part of the theorem, let

$$p = x^0 - z \quad \text{and} \quad \alpha = px^0$$

Then $H(p, \alpha)$ is the hyperplane through x^0 that is orthogonal to the line segment connecting x^0 and z. We claim that this is the desired hyperplane, that is, that

$$pz < \alpha = px^0 = \inf\{px; \ x \in X\}$$

First, we have

$$pz = px^0 + pz - px^0 = px^0 + p(z - x^0) = px^0 - pp = \alpha - \|p\|^2 < \alpha$$

so z lies below $H(p, \alpha)$.

To show that X lies above the hyperplane, we proceed by contradiction. Suppose there is a point y in X such that $py < \alpha$, and let

$$x^\lambda = (1 - \lambda)x^0 + \lambda y \quad \text{for } \lambda \in (0, 1)$$

Then $x^\lambda \in X$, by the convexity of X, and a straightforward computation yields[6]

$$\|z - x^0\|^2 - \|z - x^\lambda\|^2 = -\lambda\left(2p(y - x^0) + \lambda\|y - x^0\|^2\right) \tag{1}$$

Now, by construction $\alpha = px^0$, and by assumption $py < \alpha$, implying that $p(y - x^0) < 0$. This last inequality and (1) imply that

$$\|z - x^0\|^2 > \|z - x^\lambda\|^2$$

for small $\lambda > 0$. Hence, some $x^\lambda \in X$ is strictly closer to z than x^0 – which is impossible, because x^0 is defined as the element of X that minimizes the distance $d(x, z) = \|z - x\|$. Hence, we have a contradiction.

(ii) The proof of the second part is almost identical (with the same p), except that we now choose β so that $H(p, \beta)$ goes through the midpoint of the segment connecting z and x^0. □

The next theorem dispenses with the condition that X be closed.

Theorem 1.25. *Let* X *be a nonempty and convex (but not necessarily closed) set in* $\mathbb{R}^n$.

(i) *If* $z \notin$ X *is a point outside of this set, then there exists a hyperplane* H(p, α) *through* z *that separates* {z} *and* X, *that is,* pz = α ≤ px *for all* x ∈ X.

(ii) *If* x^0 *is a boundary point of* X, *then there exists at least one supporting hyperplane for* X *that goes through* x^0 *(supporting-hyperplane theorem).*

Proof

(i) We consider two cases: If $z \notin \text{cl } X$, then we can apply the preceding theorem, because the closure of X is a closed convex set that contains X. The other possibility is that z belongs to the closure of X, but not to X itself. Then z is a boundary point of X and either an interior point or a boundary point of cl X.

We will show that the first possibility leads to a contradiction. Suppose z is an interior point of cl X. Then int(cl X) is not empty, and by Problem 1.23, neither is int X. But then we have, by Theorem 1.16, that bdy(cl X) = bdy X. Hence, because z is a boundary point of X, it is also a boundary point of cl X, contradicting our assumption that $z \in$ int(cl X).

Hence z is a boundary point of cl X, and it follows that because any open ball around z contains at least one point in (cl $X)^c$, we can find a sequence $\{z_n\}$ with $z_n \notin$ cl X and $\{z_n\} \to z$.

Now, because $z_n \notin$ cl X, and cl X is a closed convex set (by Theorem 1.11), we can find (by Theorem 1.24), a sequence of vectors $\{q_n\}$ such that for each n,

$$q_n z_n < q_n x \ \forall \ x \in \text{cl } X \tag{1}$$

Next, define

$$p_n = \frac{1}{\|q_n\|} q_n$$

and observe that this normalization does not affect the inequality in (1). Thus, we have, for each n,

$$p_n z_n < p_n x \ \forall \ x \in \text{cl } X \tag{2}$$

Because $\|p_n\| \leq 1$, the sequence $\{p_n\}$ is bounded and therefore has a convergent subsequence $\{p_{n_k}\}$, by the Bolzano-Weierstrass theorem. Call p the limit of this subsequence. Taking limits as $k \to \infty$, (2) yields

$$pz \leq px \ \forall \ x \in \text{cl } X$$

and therefore for all x in X. Hence, $H(p, pz)$ is the desired hyperplane.

(ii) Let x^0 be a boundary point of X. If $x^0 \notin X$, then (i) applies. But even if $x^0 \in X$, the proof is identical, once we observe that, by the same argument as in (i), a boundary point of X is also a boundary point of cl X. Hence, any open ball around x^0 contains points of (cl $X)^c$, and we can construct a sequence $\{z_n\}$ as before. $\qquad \square$

Theorem 1.26. Separating-hyperplane theorem (Minkowski). *Let* X *and* Y *be disjoint and nonempty convex sets in* $\mathbb{R}^n$. *Then there exists a hyperplane* H(p, α) *that separates* X *and* Y.

Proof. By Theorem 1.4, the set

$$Z = X - Y = X + (-1)Y$$

is convex. Moreover, because $X \cap Y = \emptyset$, we have $\underline{0} \notin Z$. (Because X and Y have no common elements, for any $x \in X$ and any $y \in Y$ we have $x \neq y$, and therefore $z = x - y \neq \underline{0}$ for any z in Z.)

By the preceding theorem, there is a vector p in $\mathbb{R}^n$ that separates Z and $\{\underline{0}\}$, that is, such that

$$p\underline{0} = 0 \le pz \quad \text{for every } z \text{ in } Z$$

Equivalently, for any $x \in X$ and any $y \in Y$, we have

$$0 \le pz = p(x - y) \Rightarrow py \le px$$

The set of real numbers of the form $\{py; y \in Y\}$ is bounded above (by any px) and therefore has a supremum, which we call α. By the properties of the supremum,

$$py \le \alpha \le px$$

for $x \in X$ and $y \in Y$. Thus, $H(p, \alpha)$ separates X and Y. $\qquad\qquad$ $\square$

2. Concave Functions

Concavity and quasiconcavity are important concepts in mathematical programming. As a preview, the reader should recall the conditions for a local maximum of a univariate real function. The first-order condition $f'(x) = 0$ is necessary but not sufficient for a local maximum. It tells us that the tangent to f must be horizontal at x, which is certainly true at a local maximum, but also at a local minimum. To separate maxima from minima we use a second set of (sufficient) conditions that are often stated in terms of second derivatives. For a univariate function, $f''(x) < 0$ tells us that f is concave in a neighborhood of x. Intuitively, the curvature of the function is such that a horizontal tangent must signal a "peak" rather than a "valley." Moreover, if f is globally concave, then there can be only one "peak" and no "valleys." Hence, once we find an x^* such that $f'(x^*) = 0$, we have found the global maximum of the function.

In short, the second-order conditions for unconstrained maximization amount to checking the concavity of f in the neighborhood of a critical point. And if the function is globally concave, a local maximum is a global maximum. A similar situation arises in connection with more complicated programming problems, except that then we also have to worry about the curvature of the constraint functions.

In what follows, we consider functions of the form $f: \mathbb{R}^n \supseteq X \longrightarrow \mathbb{R}$, where X is a convex set in $\mathbb{R}^n$. Given any two points x' and x'' in X, any convex combination x^λ of x' and x'' will also lie in the domain of the function. We can therefore compare $f(x^\lambda)$ with the corresponding convex combination of $f(x')$ and $f(x'')$, $(1 - \lambda)f(x') + \lambda f(x'')$, which traces out the chord through the points $(x', f(x'))$ and $(x'', f(x''))$ on the graph of f. If the chord lies always below the function, we say that f is concave. If it lies always above the function, f is convex.

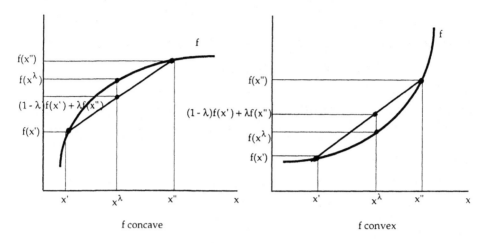

f concave   f convex

Figure 6.6. Concave and convex functions.

Definition 2.1. Concave function. The function $f: \mathbb{R}^n \supseteq X \longrightarrow \mathbb{R}$, where X is a convex set, is concave if given any two points x' and x'' in X we have

$$(1-\lambda)f(x')+\lambda f(x'') \leq f[(1-\lambda)x'+\lambda x''] \equiv f(x^\lambda) \ \forall \ \lambda \in [0,1]$$

and it is strictly concave if the inequality holds strictly for $\lambda \in (0, 1)$, that is, if

$$\forall x', x'' \in X \text{ and } \lambda \in (0,1), \ (1-\lambda)f(x')+\lambda f(x'') < f[(1-\lambda)x'+\lambda x''] \equiv f(x^\lambda)$$

Reversing the direction of the inequalities, we obtain the definitions of convexity and strict convexity.

(a) Some Characterizations

Given a function $f: \mathbb{R}^n \supseteq X \longrightarrow \mathbb{R}$, its *hypograph* is the set of points (y, x) lying on or below the graph of the function:

$$\text{hyp } f = \{(y,x) \in \mathbb{R}^{n+1}; \ x \in X \text{ and } y \leq f(x)\}$$

Similarly, the *epigraph* of f is defined as

$$\text{epi } f = \{(y, x) \in \mathbb{R}^{n+1}; \ x \in X \text{ and } y \geq f(x)\}$$

The following result gives a characterization of concave functions in terms of the convexity of their hypographs. A similar characterization of convex functions can be given in terms of the epigraph.

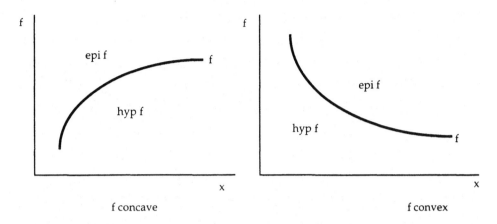

Figure 6.7.

Theorem 2.2. The function $f: \mathbb{R}^n \supseteq X \longrightarrow \mathbb{R}$ *is concave if and only if its hypograph is a convex set. The function* f *is convex if and only if its epigraph is convex.*

Proof

- f concave $\Rightarrow$ hyp f convex

   Let f be a concave function, and take two arbitrary points (x', y') and (x'', y'') in hyp f. Then $y' \le f(x')$ and $y'' \le f(x')$, and for any $\lambda \in [0, 1]$,

$$y^\lambda = (1-\lambda)y' + \lambda y'' \le (1-\lambda)f(x') + \lambda f(x'') \le f[(1-\lambda)x' + \lambda x''] \equiv f(x^\lambda) \quad (1)$$

where the second inequality holds by the concavity of f. From (1), $y^\lambda \le f(x^\lambda)$, implying that the point

$$(x^\lambda, y^\lambda) = [(1-\lambda)x' + \lambda x'', (1-\lambda)y' + \lambda y''] = (1-\lambda)(x', y') + \lambda(x'', y'')$$

lies in hyp f. Because (x', y') and (x'', y'') are arbitrary points of hyp f, this set is convex. Figure 6.8 illustrates the argument.
- hyp f convex $\Rightarrow f$ concave

   Given any two points x' and x'' in the domain of f, the points $(x', f(x'))$ and $(x'', f(x''))$ lie in hyp f. By the convexity of this set, so does the point

$$(1-\lambda)(x', f(x')) + \lambda(x'', f(x'')) = ((1-\lambda)x' + \lambda x'', (1-\lambda)f(x') + \lambda f(x''))$$

Hence,

$$(1-\lambda)f(x') + \lambda f(x'') \le f[(1-\lambda)x' + \lambda x'']$$

and because x' and x'' are arbitrary, we conclude that f is concave. $\qquad \square$

Definition 2.3. Superdifferential. Let $f: \mathbb{R}^n \supseteq X \longrightarrow \mathbb{R}$ be a function, and x^0 a point in its domain. If there exists a vector q^0 in $\mathbb{R}^n$ such that

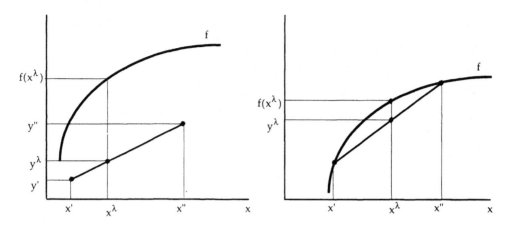

Figure 6.8.

$$f(x) \le f(x^0) + q^0(x - x^0) \qquad (1)$$

for all x in X, we say that f is superdifferentiable at x^0 and call the vector q^0 a supergradient of f. The set of all supergradients of f at x^0 is called the superdifferential of f at x^0, denoted by $\partial f(x^0)$.

If f is a concave function defined on a convex set in $\mathbb{R}^n$, then hyp f is a convex set in $\mathbb{R}^{n+1}$, and $(x, f(x))$ is a point on its boundary. By Theorem 1.25, hyp f has a supporting hyperplane through each point on the graph of f, and the function itself lies below the supporting hyperplane. Hence, concave functions are superdifferentiable.

The following theorem shows that the result we have just anticipated and its converse are both true, giving us another characterization of concavity. Notice that the supergradient of a concave function need not be unique: If the function has a kink, it will have several supporting hyperplanes, as shown in Figure 6.9.

Theorem 2.4. Let f *be a real-valued function defined on an open and convex set* X *in* $\mathbb{R}^n$. *Then* f *is concave if and only if it is superdifferentiable everywhere in its domain, that is, if given any* x^0 *in* X, *there exists a vector* q^0 *in* $\mathbb{R}^n$ *such that*

$$f(x) \le f(x^0) + q^0(x - x^0) \qquad (1)$$

for all x *in* X.

Proof

(i) f concave on an open set $\Rightarrow f$ superdifferentiable

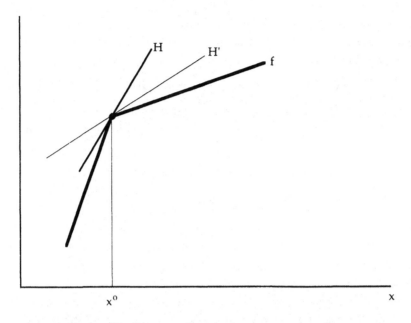

Figure 6.9. Supergradients of a concave function.

Let f be a concave function defined on an open and convex set X in $\mathbb{R}^n$. Then hyp f is a convex set in $\mathbb{R}^{n+1}$, and for any given x^0 in X, $(f(x^0), x^0)$ is a point on the boundary of this set. By Theorem 1.25, hyp f has a supporting hyperplane $H[(p_0, p), \alpha]$ through $(f(x^0), x^0)$. That is, there exists a nonzero vector $(p_0, p) \in \mathbb{R}^{n+1}$ (with $p_0 \in \mathbb{R}$ and $p \in \mathbb{R}^n$) such that

$$p_0 f(x^0) + px^0 = \alpha \tag{1}$$

and hyp f lies entirely on one side of H. For concreteness, suppose that

$$p_0 y + px \leq \alpha \ \forall \ (y, x) \in \text{hyp } f \tag{2}$$

(If the reverse inequality holds, the proof goes through with the obvious changes.) Combining (1) and (2),

$$p_0[y - f(x^0)] + p(x - x^0) \leq 0 \ \forall \ (y, x) \in \text{hyp } f \tag{3}$$

We begin by determining the sign of p_0. The point $(f(x^0) - \gamma, x^0)$ lies in hyp f for any $\gamma > 0$. By (3),

$$p_0[f(x^0) - \gamma - f(x^0)] + p(x^0 - x^0) \leq 0 \Rightarrow -\gamma p_0 \leq 0 \Rightarrow p_0 \geq 0$$

so p_0 is a nonnegative number. Next, we show that in fact p_0 must be strictly positive. We proceed by contradiction: Suppose $p_0 = 0$, then (3) implies that

$$p(x - x^0) \leq 0 \ \forall \ x \in X \tag{4}$$

If $p_0 = 0$, at least one of the components of p, say p_k, must be different from zero. Consider a point x', with

$$x'_k = x^0_k + \varepsilon p_k \quad \text{and} \quad x'_i = x^0_i \quad \text{for } i \neq k$$

Because X is an open set, we can choose $\varepsilon > 0$ small enough that x' lies in X. By (4), it follows that

$$p(x' - x^0) = p_k(x^0_k + \varepsilon p_k - x^0_k) + \sum\nolimits^n_{i \neq k} p_i(x^0_i - x^0_i) = \varepsilon p^2_k \leq 0$$

which is impossible, because $\varepsilon > 0$. Hence, we conclude that $p_0 > 0$.

Finally, given an arbitrary point $x \in X$, the point $(f(x), x)$ lies in hyp f. By (3),

$$p_0[f(x) - f(x^0)] + p(x - x^0) \leq 0$$

Dividing through by $p_0 > 0$ and rearranging,

$$f(x) \leq f(x^0) + \frac{-1}{p_0} p(x - x^0)$$

Putting $q^0 = (-1/p_0)p$, we obtain the desired result.

(ii) f superdifferentiable on $X \Rightarrow f$ concave

Fix two arbitrary points x and x^0 in X, and let $x^\lambda = (1 - \lambda)x^0 + \lambda x$ for some $\lambda \in (0, 1)$. Because X is a convex set, $x^\lambda \in X$, and, by assumption, there exists a vector $q^\lambda \in \mathbb{R}^n$ such that

$$f(x) \leq f(x^\lambda) + q^\lambda(x - x^\lambda) \tag{5}$$

$$f(x^0) \leq f(x^\lambda) + q^\lambda(x^0 - x^\lambda) \tag{6}$$

Multiplying these two inequalities by λ and $(1 - \lambda) > 0$, respectively, and adding them,

$$\begin{array}{l} \lambda f(x) \leq \lambda f(x^\lambda) + \lambda q^\lambda(x - x^\lambda) \\ \underline{(1 - \lambda)f(x^0) \leq (1 - \lambda)f(x^\lambda) + (1 - \lambda)q^\lambda(x^0 - x^\lambda)} \\ (1 - \lambda)f(x^0) + \lambda f(x) \leq f(x^\lambda) + q^\lambda[\lambda(x - x^\lambda) + (1 - \lambda)(x^0 - x^\lambda)] \end{array} \tag{7}$$

Now consider the expression inside brackets; we have

$$\lambda(x - x^\lambda) + (1 - \lambda)(x^0 - x^\lambda) = \lambda x + (1 - \lambda)x^0 - x^\lambda = \underline{0}$$

Hence, (7) reduces to

$$(1 - \lambda)f(x^0) + \lambda f(x) \leq f(x^\lambda)$$

which shows that f is concave. $\square$

Given a function $f: \mathbb{R}^n \supseteq X \longrightarrow \mathbb{R}$ and two points in its domain, x' and x'', we define the univariate function $\phi: \mathbb{R} \longrightarrow \mathbb{R}$ by

$$\phi(\lambda) = f[(1 - \lambda)x' + \lambda x''] = f[x' + \lambda(x'' - x')]$$

for fixed x' and x''. Our next theorem says that f is concave if and only if ϕ is always concave. Because working with a univariate function is often easier, this result often provides a convenient way to establish the concavity of a multivariate function.

Theorem 2.5. The function $f:\mathbb{R}^n \supseteq X \longrightarrow \mathbb{R}$, *where* X *is a convex set, is concave if and only if the function* $\phi(\lambda) = f[(1 - \lambda)x' + \lambda x'']$ *is concave for any two points* x′ *and* x″ *in the domain of* f.

Problem 2.6. Prove Theorem 2.5.

(b) *Properties of Concave Functions*

We now establish some useful properties of concave functions.

Theorem 2.7. Let $f:\mathbb{R}^n \supseteq X \longrightarrow \mathbb{R}$ *be a concave function. For any* $\alpha \in \mathbb{R}$, *the upper contour set of* f,

$$U_\alpha = \{x \in X;\ f(x) \geq \alpha\}$$

is either empty or convex. Similarly, if f *is convex, then the lower contour set,*

$$L_\alpha = \{x \in X;\ f(x) \leq \alpha\}$$

is convex whenever it is not empty.

The converse statement is not true. As we will see, the weaker property of quasiconcavity is sufficient to guarantee the convexity of the upper contour sets.

Proof. Let x′ and x″ be any two points in U_α, that is, with $f(x') \geq \alpha$ and $f(x'') \geq \alpha$. By the concavity of f,

$$f(x^\lambda) \geq (1 - \lambda)f(x') + \lambda f(x'') \geq \alpha$$

for any $\lambda \in [0, 1]$. Hence,

$$x^\lambda = (1 - \lambda)x' + \lambda x'' \in U_\alpha \quad \text{for any } \lambda \in [0, 1]$$

and U_α is therefore a convex set, as illustrated in Figure 6.10. $\square$

The results that follow show that certain transformations of concave functions are also concave.

Theorem 2.8. Let $f:\mathbb{R}^n \supseteq X \longrightarrow \mathbb{R}$ *be a concave function and* $g:\mathbb{R} \longrightarrow \mathbb{R}$ *an increasing and concave function defined on an interval* I *containing* f(X). *Then the function* g[f(x)] *is concave.*

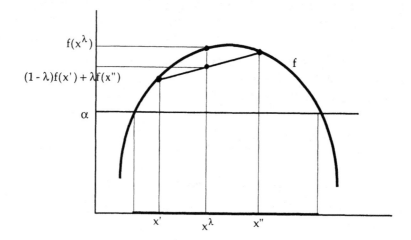

Figure 6.10. Concavity implies convexity of the upper contour sets.

Problem 2.9. Prove Theorem 2.8.

Theorem 2.10. Let f and g be concave functions $\mathbb{R}^n \supseteq X \longrightarrow \mathbb{R}$. Given arbitrary scalars α and $\beta \geq 0$, the function $h = \alpha f + \beta g$ is concave.

Problem 2.11. Prove Theorem 2.10.

Theorem 2.12. Let $\{f^s; s \in S\}$ be a (possibly infinite) family of concave functions $\mathbb{R}^n \supseteq X \longrightarrow \mathbb{R}$, all of which are bounded below. Then the function f defined on X by

$$f(x) = inf\{f^s(x); \ s \in S\}$$

is concave.

Problem 2.13. Prove Theorem 2.12. Hint: Use Theorem 2.2.

Figure 6.11 illustrates the intuition behind Theorem 2.12.

An interesting property of a concave function is that it is continuous everywhere in the interior of its domain.

Theorem 2.14. Let f be a concave function defined on an open set X in $\mathbb{R}^n$. Then f is continuous on X.

Figure 6.12 illustrates why this is true. Concavity requires that the chord through any two points on the graph of the function lie below the function itself. If the domain of the function is open, this will be impossible if the

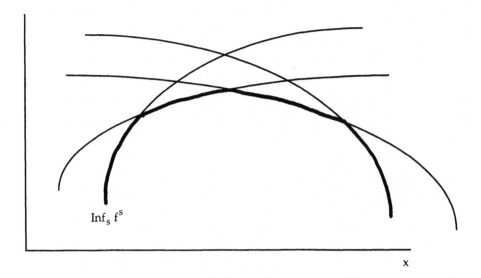

Figure 6.11.

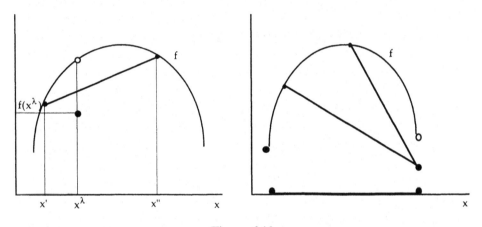

Figure 6.12.

function is discontinuous. If X is not open, discontinuities are possible, but only at points on the boundary of X.

Proof. Pick some x^0 in X. Because X is open, there is some $\delta > 0$ small enough that the cube with side 2δ,

$$C = \{x \in \mathbb{R}^n; \; x_i^0 - \delta \leq x_i \leq x_i^0 + \delta\}$$

is still contained in X. Let V be the set of the 2^n vertices of C, and put

$$\alpha = \min\{f(x); \; x \in V\}$$

The set $U_\alpha = \{x \in X; f(x) \geq \alpha\}$ is convex, by Theorem 2.7. Moreover, $V \subseteq U_\alpha$ by construction, and because C is the convex hull of V (i.e., the smallest convex set containing V), we also have $C \subseteq U_\alpha$, that is,

$$f(x) \geq \alpha \; \forall \, x \in C \tag{1}$$

Let x be an arbitrary point in the ball $B_\delta(x^0)$ (which is contained in C), and let $x^0 + u$ and $x^0 - u$ be the points where the line through x and x^0 intersects the boundary of $B_\delta(x^0)$, as shown in Figure 6.13. We can write x as a convex combination of x^0 and $x^0 + u$, and x^0 as a convex combination of x and $x^0 - u$. Because x lies on the straight line through x^0 and $x^0 + u$, we have $x = x^0 + \lambda u$ for some λ, and in particular,

$$x - x^0 = \lambda u \Rightarrow \lambda = \frac{\|x - x^0\|}{\|u\|} = \frac{\|x - x^0\|}{\delta} \tag{2}$$

Now,

$$x = x^0 + \lambda u \Rightarrow x = \lambda(x^0 + u) + (1 - \lambda)x^0 \tag{3}$$

and

$$x^0 = x - \lambda u \Rightarrow (1 + \lambda)x^0 = x - \lambda u + \lambda x^0 = x + \lambda(x^0 - u)$$

from where

$$x^0 = \frac{1}{1 + \lambda} x + \frac{\lambda}{1 + \lambda}(x^0 - u) \tag{4}$$

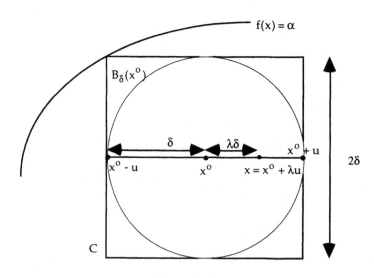

Figure 6.13.

Using (3) and (4), the concavity of f on X, and the fact that (1) holds for all points in these expressions, we have

$$(3) \Rightarrow f(x) \geq \lambda f(x^0 + u) + (1 - \lambda) f(x^0) \geq \lambda \alpha + (1 - \lambda) f(x^0)$$

implying

$$f(x) - f(x^0) \geq -\lambda [f(x^0) - \alpha] \tag{5}$$

and

$$(4) \Rightarrow f(x^0) \geq \frac{1}{1 + \lambda} f(x) + \frac{\lambda}{1 + \lambda} f(x^0 - u) \geq \frac{1}{1 + \lambda} [f(x) + \lambda \alpha]$$

from where

$$(1 + \lambda) f(x^0) \geq f(x) + \lambda \alpha \Rightarrow f(x) - f(x^0) \leq \lambda [f(x^0) - \alpha] \tag{6}$$

Combining (5) and (6) and using (2), we have

$$|f(x) - f(x^0)| \leq \lambda [f(x^0) - \alpha] = \frac{\|x - x^0\|}{\delta} [f(x^0) - \alpha]$$

Given any $\varepsilon > 0$, we have $|f(x) - f(x^0)| < \varepsilon$ for all x close enough to x^0. In particular, it is enough to choose x so that

$$\|x - x^0\| < \frac{\delta \varepsilon}{f(x^0) - \alpha}$$

In other words, f is continuous at x^0, and because this is just an arbitrary point of X, f is continuous on X. $\qquad \square$

Let $f : \mathbb{R}^n \supseteq X \longrightarrow \mathbb{R}$ be a concave function. Fix a point x in its domain and a direction vector h in $\mathbb{R}^n$, and consider moving away from x in the direction of h, as illustrated in Figure 6.14 (i.e., we consider points of the form $x + \alpha h$). The following result says that the slope of the chord through the points $(x, f(x))$ and $(x + \alpha h, f(x + \alpha h))$ decreases as we move to the right.

Theorem 2.15. Let $f : \mathbb{R}^n \supseteq X \longrightarrow \mathbb{R}$ *be a concave function defined on an open and convex set* X. *Then the ratio* $(f(x + \alpha h) - f(x))/\alpha$, *where* $h \in \mathbb{R}^n$ *is a (weakly) decreasing function of* α.

Proof. Fix $x \in X$, and let h be an arbitrary vector in $\mathbb{R}^n$. Consider first the case where $\alpha > 0$. Because X is open, $x + \alpha h \in X$ for sufficiently small but strictly positive α. We will establish the desired result by showing that

$$\frac{f(x + \alpha h) - f(x)}{\alpha} \leq \frac{f(x + \mu h) - f(x)}{\mu}$$

for any positive number μ smaller than or equal to α.

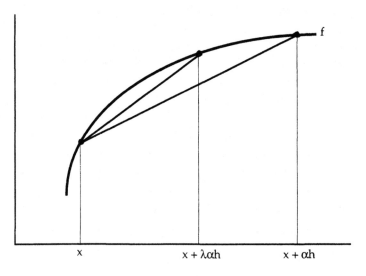

Figure 6.14.

Put $\mu = \lambda\alpha$ for $\lambda \in (0, 1)$, and observe that we can write

$$x + \mu h = x + \lambda\alpha h = x + \lambda x - \lambda x + \lambda\alpha h = (1 - \lambda)x + \lambda(x + \alpha h)$$

Now, the concavity of f implies that

$$f(x + \mu h) = f[(1 - \lambda)x + \lambda(x + \alpha h)] \geq (1 - \lambda)f(x) + \lambda f(x + \alpha h)$$

and, upon rearranging,

$$f(x + \mu h) - f(x) \geq \lambda[f(x + \alpha h) - f(x)]$$

Finally, because $\lambda = \mu/\alpha > 0$, we obtain the desired result:

$$\frac{f(x + \mu h) - f(x)}{\mu} \geq \frac{f(x + \alpha h) - f(x)}{\lambda}$$

If $\alpha < 0$, then the last inequality is reversed, but then $\mu \geq \alpha$, so the function is still increasing.   □

This result has some interesting implications. Notice that the limit of the difference quotient $(f(x + \alpha h) - f(x))/\alpha$ as α approaches zero from above is the one-sided directional derivative of f at x in the direction of h: $Df(x; h^+)$ (or $Df(x; h^-)$ if $\alpha \to 0$ from below.) As we know from Chapter 2 (Section 6), monotonic functions defined on an open interval always have one-sided limits. Hence, concave functions have one-sided directional derivatives (and, in particular, one-sided partial derivatives) at all interior points of their domains.

The supergradients of a concave function can be related to its one-sided partial derivatives. Let f be a concave function defined on an open set X, and consider moving away from a point $x \in X$ in the direction h. If q is a supergradient of f at x, then

$$f(x + \alpha h) \le f(x) + q(\alpha h)$$

for any α such that $x + \alpha h \in X$. Rearranging this expression,

$$\frac{f(x + \alpha h) - f(x)}{\alpha} \le qh \quad \text{for } \alpha > 0$$

$$\frac{f(x + \alpha h) - f(x)}{\alpha} \ge qh \quad \text{for } \alpha < 0$$

Taking the limits of these expressions as α goes to zero from above and from below, we obtain

$$Df(x; h^+) \le qh \le Df(x; h^-)$$

Finally, taking h to be the ith coordinate vector in $\mathbb{R}^n$, e^i, we arrive at

$$f_i(x^+) \le q_i \le f_i(x^-) \quad \text{for each } i = 1, \dots, n$$

Hence, the components of the supergradient of f at x are bounded by the function's left- and right-hand partial derivatives. If f is differentiable, the two one-sided partials coincide, and the unique supergradient is the derivative of f at x. Conversely, it can be shown that if f has a unique supergradient at a point x, then it is differentiable at x.

Furthermore, it can be shown that *a concave function is differentiable* (and in fact continuously differentiable) *almost everywhere in the interior of its domain* (i.e., at all points except possibly for a set of measure zero) (Rockafellar, 1970, p. 246).

We are sometimes interested in determining whether or not a given concave function is differentiable at a specific point. The following result, due to Benveniste and Scheinkman (1982), is sometimes useful in this situation.

Theorem 2.16. Let X *be a convex subset of* $\mathbb{R}^n$, *and* $V: X \longrightarrow \mathbb{R}$ *a concave function. Let* $x^0 \in int$ X, *and suppose there exists some* $\varepsilon > 0$ *and a concave and differentiable function* $W: X \longrightarrow \mathbb{R}$ *such that*

$$W(x) \le V(x) \; \forall \, x \in B_\varepsilon(x^0) \quad and \quad W(x^0) = V(x^0) \qquad (1)$$

Then V *is differentiable at* x^0, *and*

$$DV(x^0) = DW(x^0)$$

Proof. Because V is concave, it is superdifferentiable, and any supergradient q of V at x^0 satisfies

$$V(x) \leq V(x^0) + q(x - x^0)$$

for any x in $B_\varepsilon(x^0)$. Rearranging this expression and using (1),

$$W(x) - W(x^0) \leq V(x) - V(x^0) \leq q(x - x^0)$$

so q is also a supergradient of W at x^0. Because W is differentiable, moreover, q is unique, and because any concave function with a unique supergradient at an interior point of its domain is differentiable, V is differentiable at x^0, with $DV(x^0) = q = DW(x^0)$.   ☐

(c) Concavity for Smooth Functions

We will now establish some characterizations of concavity for C^1 and C^2 functions that will be useful in our development of nonlinear programming in the following chapter. In this section we will assume that f is a smooth, real-valued function defined on an open and convex set X in $\mathbb{R}^n$. Openness is required so that we can assume that f is differentiable at all points in X.

If f is a smooth concave function, its graph lies everywhere below the tangent hyperplane defined by its derivative, and vice versa, a C^1 function that lies everywhere below its tangent hyperplane is concave. The following theorem shows that a slight strengthening of this statement yields a characterization of strictly concave C^1 functions.

Theorem 2.17. Let $f: \mathbb{R}^n \supseteq X \longrightarrow \mathbb{R}$ *be a* C^1 *function defined on an open and convex set* X. *Then* f *is concave if and only if given any two points* x^0 *and* x *in* X, *we have*

$$f(x) \leq f(x^0) + Df(x^0)(x - x^0)$$

Moreover, f *is strictly concave if and only if the inequality holds strictly, that is, if and only if*

$$f(x) < f(x^0) + Df(x^0)(x - x^0)$$

for all pairs of distinct points x^0 *and* x *in* X.

Proof

- f concave $\Rightarrow f(x) \leq f(x^0) + Df(x^0)(x - x^0) \ \forall \ x, x^0 \in X$
  Fix x and x^0 in X and write

$$x^\lambda = (1 - \lambda)x^0 + \lambda x = x^0 + \lambda(x - x^0)$$

with $\lambda \in (0, 1)$. By the concavity of f, we have:

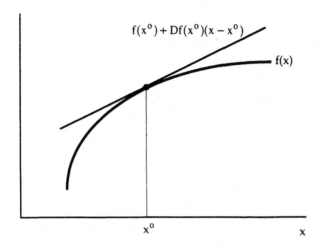

Figure 6.15. A C^1 concave function.

$$(1 - \lambda)f(x^0) + \lambda f(x) \leq f[x^0 + \lambda(x - x^0)] \tag{1}$$

from where, rearranging,

$$f(x) - f(x^0) \leq \frac{f[x^0 + \lambda(x - x^0)] - f(x^0)}{\lambda} \tag{2}$$

When we take the limit of this expression as $\lambda \to 0$, the inequality is preserved. Moreover, the limit of the right-hand side is precisely the directional derivative of f in the direction $x - x^0$. Because f is C^1, the limit exists and is equal to $Df(x^0)$ $(x - x^0)$ (see Chapter 4). Hence, (2) implies

$$f(x) - f(x^0) \leq Df(x^0)(x - x^0)$$

- Next, suppose f is strictly concave. Then (2) holds with strict inequality, that is,

$$f(x) - f(x^0) < \frac{f[x^0 + \lambda(x - x^0)] - f(x^0)}{\lambda} = \frac{f(x^\lambda) - f(x^0)}{\lambda} \tag{3}$$

for $\lambda \in (0, 1)$. Moreover, the concavity of f implies, as we have just shown, that

$$f(x^\lambda) - f(x^0) \leq Df(x^0)(x^\lambda - x^0)$$

Substituting this expression into (3) and observing that

$$\frac{1}{\lambda}(x^\lambda - x^0) = \frac{1}{\lambda}[x^0 + \lambda(x - x^0) - x^0] = x - x^0$$

we obtain the desired result:

$$f(x) - f(x^0) < \frac{f(x^\lambda) - f(x^0)}{\lambda} \leq \frac{Df(x^0)(x^\lambda - x^0)}{\lambda} = Df(x^0)(x - x^0)$$

- For the sufficiency part of the theorem, a straightforward adaptation of the proof of Theorem 2.3 will work. □

Theorem 2.18. Let $f: \mathbb{R}^n \supseteq X \longrightarrow \mathbb{R}$ *be a* C^2 *function defined on an open and convex set* X. *Then* f *is concave if and only if the Hessian matrix of second partial derivatives* $D^2f(x)$ *is negative semidefinite for any* x *in* X; *that is,*

$$\forall x \in X \text{ and } \forall h \in \mathbb{R}^n, \ h^{\mathrm{T}}D^2f(x)h \leq 0$$

Moreover, if the Hessian is negative definite (i.e., if $h^{\mathrm{T}}D^2f(x)h < 0$ *for all* $x \in X$ *and all* $h \neq \underline{0}$ *in* $\mathbb{R}^n$*), then* f *is strictly concave.*

Note that the negative definiteness of the Hessian is sufficient but not necessary for the strict concavity of *f*.

Proof

- *f* concave $\Rightarrow D^2f(x)$ negative semidefinite for all $x \in X$

  Fix some point x in X and an arbitrary direction vector $h \in \mathbb{R}^n$. Because X is open, there exists some $\delta > 0$ such that $x + \alpha h \in X$ for all $\alpha \in I = (-\delta, \delta)$. Define a function g from I to $\mathbb{R}$ by

$$g(\alpha) = f(x + \alpha h) - f(x) - \alpha Df(x)h \tag{1}$$

Observe that g is C^2, with $g(0) = 0$, and that, by the preceding theorem and the concavity of f,

$$f(x + \alpha h) \leq f(x) + Df(x)(\alpha h) \quad \text{for any } \alpha \in I$$

which implies that $g(\alpha) \leq 0$ for all α in I. Hence, g is a C^2 univariate function with an interior maximum at 0 and must therefore satisfy the necessary conditions $g'(0) = 0$ and $g''(0) \leq 0$. Differentiating (1) with respect to α,

$$g'(\alpha) = Df(x + \alpha h)h - Df(x)h$$
$$g''(\alpha) = h^T D^2 f(x + \alpha h)h$$

Thus, $g''(0) \leq 0$ becomes

$$g''(0) = h^T D^2 f(x)h \leq 0$$

Because h is an arbitrary vector in $\mathbb{R}^n$, we conclude that $D^2f(x)$ is negative semidefinite for any x in X.

- $D^2f(x)$ negative semidefinite for all $x \in X \Rightarrow f$ concave

  Because f is C^2, it is C^1, and, by Theorem 2.17, it is enough to show that

$$h^T D^2 f(x)h \leq 0 \quad \text{for any } x \text{ in } X \text{ and all } h \in \mathbb{R}^n \tag{1}$$

$$\Rightarrow f(x + h) \leq f(x) + Df(x)h \tag{2}$$

Assume that (1) holds, and pick two points x and $x + h$ in X. By Taylor's theorem, we have, for some $\alpha \in (0, 1)$,

$$f(x + h) - f(x) - Df(x)h = \frac{1}{2}h^T D^2 f(x + \alpha h)h \tag{3}$$

where $x + \alpha h \in (x, x + h) \subseteq X$. Now, $D^2 f(x + \alpha h)$ is negative semidefinite by assumption, implying that the right-hand side of the preceding expression is non-positive and therefore that

$$f(x + h) \leq f(x) + Df(x)h \tag{4}$$

which is the desired result.

- If $D^2 f(x)$ is negative definite for all x, then (4) holds with strict inequality, and f is strictly concave, by Theorem 2.17. □

The negative definiteness or semidefiniteness of the Hessian can be checked using the appropriate principal-minors test (see the appendix to this chapter). Hence, $D^2 f(x)$ is negative definite, and f is strictly concave if the leading principal minors alternate in sign, with $f_{11} < 0$, that is, if

$$(-1)^r \begin{vmatrix} f_{11} & \cdots & f_{1r} \\ \cdots & \cdots & \cdots \\ f_{r1} & \cdots & f_{rr} \end{vmatrix} > 0 \quad \text{for } r = 1, 2, \ldots, n$$

and strictly convex if $D^2 f(x)$ is positive definite, which requires that all leading principal minors be positive, that is,

$$\begin{vmatrix} f_{11} & \cdots & f_{1r} \\ \cdots & \cdots & \cdots \\ f_{r1} & \cdots & f_{rr} \end{vmatrix} > 0 \quad \text{for } r = 1, 2, \ldots, n$$

3. Quasiconcave Functions

Definition 3.1. Quasiconcavity. Let $f : \mathbb{R}^n \supseteq X \longrightarrow \mathbb{R}$ be a real-valued function defined on a convex set X. We say that f is quasiconcave if for all x' and x'' in X and all $\lambda \in [0, 1]$ we have

$$f[(1 - \lambda)x' + \lambda x''] \geq \min\{f(x'), f(x'')\}$$

We say that f is strictly quasiconcave if for all x' and x'' in X and all $\lambda \in (0, 1)$ we have

$$f[(1 - \lambda)x' + \lambda x''] > \min\{f(x'), f(x'')\}$$

Given two points x' and x'' in X, suppose that $f(x') \geq f(x'')$. Then quasiconcavity requires that as we move along the line segment from the "low point," x'', to the "high point," x', the value of f never falls below $f(x'')$. Figure 6.16 shows an example of a quasiconcave function.

The following result shows that quasiconcavity is equivalent to the convexity of the upper contour sets. The proof is left as an exercise.

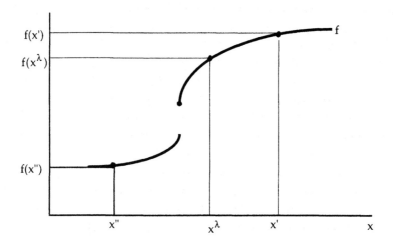

Figure 6.16. A quasiconcave function.

Theorem 3.2. Let f *be a real-valued function defined on a convex set* $X \subseteq$ $\mathbb{R}^n$. *Then* f *is quasiconcave if and only if the upper contour sets of* f *are all convex, that is, if for any* $\alpha \in \mathbb{R}$ *the set*

$$U_\alpha = \{x \in X;\ f(x) \geq \alpha\}$$

is convex.

Problem 3.3. Prove Theorem 3.2.

A direct implication of this result is that concavity implies quasiconcavity. It is also easy to show that strict concavity implies strict quasiconcavity, but the converse statements are not true. Hence, quasiconcavity is a weaker property than concavity, and quasiconcave functions need not inherit some of the useful properties of concave functions. For example, a quasiconcave function, unlike a concave one, may have discontinuities at interior points of its domain, and a nonnegative linear combination of quasiconcave functions may not be quasiconcave. The following theorem shows, however, that quasiconcavity is preserved under increasing (and not necessarily concave) transformations.

Theorem 3.4. Let f *be a quasiconcave function defined on a convex set* $X \subseteq$ $\mathbb{R}^n$, *and let* $g:\mathbb{R} \longrightarrow \mathbb{R}$ *be a weakly increasing function defined on an interval* I *that contains* f(X). *Then the composite function* g[f(x)] *is quasiconcave in* X.

Problem 3.5. Prove Theorem 3.4.

Problem 3.6. Show that the Cobb-Douglas function

$$f(x) = A \prod_{i=1}^{n} x_i^{\alpha_i}, \quad \text{where } \alpha_i > 0 \; \forall \, i$$

is quasiconcave for $x \gg \underline{0}$. Hint: Consider ln $f(x)$, and use Theorems 2.18 and 3.4.

We will now obtain a characterization of quasiconcavity for C^1 functions that resembles its analogue for smooth concave functions.

Theorem 3.7. Let f be a real-valued C^1 function defined on an open and convex set $X \subseteq \mathbb{R}^n$. Then f is quasiconcave in X if and only if for every x′ and x″ in X we have

$$\mathrm{f}(\mathrm{x}'') \le \mathrm{f}(\mathrm{x}') \Rightarrow \mathrm{Df}(\mathrm{x}'')(\mathrm{x}' - \mathrm{x}'') \ge 0$$

If, moreover,

$$\mathrm{x}' \ne \mathrm{x}'' \quad and \quad \mathrm{f}(\mathrm{x}'') \le \mathrm{f}(\mathrm{x}') \Rightarrow \mathrm{Df}(\mathrm{x}'')(\mathrm{x}' - \mathrm{x}'') > 0$$

then f is strictly quasiconcave, but the converse statement is not necessarily true.

Proof. Given x' and x'' in X and $\lambda \in [0, 1]$, define

$$g(\lambda) = f[x'' + \lambda(x' - x'')]$$

Because f is C^1, g is differentiable, and

$$g'(\lambda) = Df[x'' + \lambda(x' - x'')](x' - x'')$$

(i) Assume that f is quasiconcave and $f(x') \ge f(x'')$. Then

$$g(\lambda) = f[x'' + \lambda(x' - x'')] \ge f(x'') = g(0) \; \forall \; \lambda \in [0, 1] \qquad (1)$$

Hence, g is weakly increasing at zero, with

$$g'(0) = Df(x'')(x' - x'') \ge 0$$

If f is strictly quasiconcave, (1) holds with strict inequality, and g is strictly increasing at zero – but note that this does not imply $g'(0) > 0$ (e.g., $f(x) = x^3$ is strictly increasing at 0, even though $f'(0) = 0$).

(ii) Assume that $f(x') \ge f(x'')$ implies $Df(x'')(x' - x'') \ge 0$ for any x' and x'' in X. We want to show that this implies the quasiconcavity of f, that is,

$$g(\lambda) = f[x'' + \lambda(x' - x'')] \ge f(x'') = g(0) \; \forall \; \lambda \in [0, 1]$$

Assume that this is not true. That is, suppose that there exists some $\lambda^0 \in (0, 1)$ such that $g(\lambda^0) < g(0)$. Because $g(1) = f(x') \ge f(x'') = g(0)$, we can choose λ^0 such that $g'(\lambda^0) > 0$ (if $g'(\lambda) < 0$ for all λ such that $g(\lambda) < g(0)$, then we cannot have

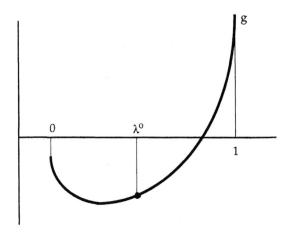

Figure 6.17.

$g(1) \geq g(0)$ as suggested in Figure 6.17). We will show that the existence of such a λ^0 leads to a contradiction.

Put $x^0 = x'' + \lambda^0(x' - x'')$. Because

$$f(x'') = g(0) > g(\lambda^0) = f(x^0)$$

and x^0 is in X, we have, by assumption,

$$Df(x^0)(x'' - x^0) = Df(x^0)(-\lambda^0)(x' - x'') \geq 0$$

and hence

$$Df(x^0)(x' - x'') \leq 0$$

On the other hand,

$$g'(\lambda^0) = Df(x^0)(x' - x'') > 0$$

by assumption, which contradicts the foregoing expression. Hence, there can be no $\lambda^0 \in (0, 1)$ such that $g(\lambda^0) < g(0)$, and we conclude that f is quasiconcave. The same logic will work for the case of strict quasiconcavity. ☐

Let f be a C^1 quasiconcave function, and x' and x'' two points in its domain, with $f(x'') \leq f(x')$. The preceding theorem says that the directional derivative of f at the "lower" point, x'', in the direction of the "higher" point, x', is nonnegative. Roughly speaking, the derivative gives us the correct signal about the direction of change of the function, which is quite helpful when looking for a maximum. Notice, however, that plain quasiconcavity is compatible with a zero directional derivative at x'' even if $f(x'') < f(x')$. Hence, a zero gradient could send the wrong signal that x'' is a candidate for a maximum. Strict quasiconcavity rules out this possibility, as does *pseudoconcavity*, a concept we now define.

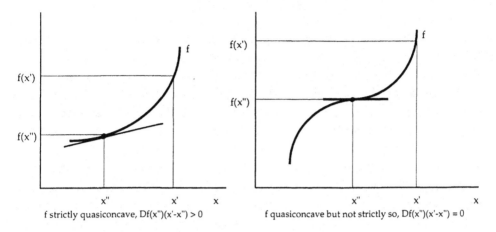

f strictly quasiconcave, Df(x'')(x'-x'') > 0   f quasiconcave but not strictly so, Df(x'')(x'-x'') = 0

Figure 6.18.

Definition 3.8. Pseudoconcavity. A C^1 function f is pseudoconcave in a set X if given any two points x' and x'' in X we have that

$$f(x') > f(x'') \Rightarrow Df(x'')(x' - x'') > 0$$

Note that strict quasiconcavity implies pseudoconcavity, but quasiconcavity does not, as illustrated in Figure 6.18. The following problem shows that nonstationarity is also sufficient to guarantee the pseudoconcavity of a quasiconcave function.

Problem 3.9. A C^1 function that has no critical points (i.e., such that $Df(x)$ $\neq \underline{0}$ for all x) is said to be *nonstationary*. Show that a nonstationary C^1 quasiconcave function is pseudoconcave.

Hint: Let x' and x'' be any two points in the domain of f such that $f(x') >$ $f(x'')$. Define the point $\hat{x}$ by $\hat{x}_1 = x'_1 - \varepsilon$, and $\hat{x}_i = x'_i$ for $i = 2, \ldots, n$, and show that for $\varepsilon > 0$ and sufficiently small, $Df(x'')(\hat{x} - x'') < 0$, which contradicts the quasiconcavity of f.

Problem 3.10. Suppose $f : \mathbb{R}^n_{++} \longrightarrow \mathbb{R}$ is C^1, homogeneous of degree 1, and positive-valued. Show that f is concave if and only if it is quasiconcave.

Hint: Concavity always implies quasiconcavity. To prove the other part of the theorem, let x' and x'' be two points in $\mathbb{R}^n_{++}$. Because $f \geq 0$, we can define λ by $\lambda = f(x')/f(x'')$ and $\lambda > 0$. Because f is homogeneous of degree 1, we have

$$f(\lambda x'') = \lambda f(x'') = f(x') \tag{1}$$

and quasiconcavity therefore implies that

$$Df(\lambda x'')(x' - \lambda x'') \geq 0 \qquad (2)$$

Exploiting the properties of homogeneous functions, show that (1) implies $Df(x'')(x' - x'') \geq f(x') - f(x'')$ and therefore the concavity of f. □

The following theorem gives some useful second-derivative characterizations of quasiconcavity. For a proof and further results, see Arrow and Enthoven (1961) and Crouzeix and Ferland (1982).

Theorem 3.11. Let $f: \mathbb{R}^n \supseteq X \longrightarrow \mathbb{R}$ *be a C^2 function defined on an open and convex set* $X \subseteq \mathbb{R}^n$, *and let* $\overline{H}_r$ *be the leading principal minor of the bordered Hessian of* f, *given by*

$$\overline{H}_r = \begin{vmatrix} 0 & f_1 & \cdots & f_r \\ f_1 & f_{11} & \cdots & f_{1r} \\ \cdots & \cdots & \cdots & \cdots \\ f_r & f_{r1} & \cdots & f_{rr} \end{vmatrix}$$

  (i) *A necessary condition for the quasiconcavity of* f *is that*

$$(-1)^r \overline{H}_r \geq 0 \ \forall \, r = 1, \ldots, n \ and \ \forall \, x \in X$$

  (ii) *A sufficient condition for* f *to be quasiconcave is that*

$$(-1)^r \overline{H}_r > 0 \ \forall \, r = 1, \ldots, n \ and \ \forall \, x \in \mathbb{R}_+^n$$

(iii) *If* $X \subseteq \mathbb{R}_{++}^n$, *if* f *is monotonically increasing, and if*

$$(-1)^r \overline{H}_r > 0 \ \forall \, r = 1, \ldots, n \ and \ \forall \, x \in X$$

  then f *is strictly quasiconcave.*

The following problem asks the reader to give a direct proof for a special case of Theorem 3.11.

Problem 3.12. Let $f: \mathbb{R}^2 \supseteq X \longrightarrow \mathbb{R}$ *be a C^2 function defined on an open and convex set* $X \subseteq \mathbb{R}^n$, *with* $f_x(x, y) > 0$ *and* $f_y(x, y) > 0$ *for all* (x, y) *in* X. *Show that* $f(x, y)$ *is quasiconcave in* X *if and only if*

$$|B| = \begin{vmatrix} 0 & f_x & f_y \\ f_x & f_{xx} & f_{xy} \\ f_y & f_{xy} & f_{yy} \end{vmatrix} > 0 \ \forall \, x \in X$$

Hint: Use the characterization of quasiconcavity in terms of the convexity of upper contour sets (Theorem 3.2). Apply the implicit-function theorem to an arbitrary level set of $f(x, y)$ to define a function $y = g(x)$, compute the second derivative of this function, and use Theorem 2.2.

Concavifiable functions

As we will see in Chapter 7, the solutions of maximization problems involving concave (objective and constraint) functions are particularly easy to characterize. These nice results can be easily extended to a larger class of functions by observing that a monotonically increasing tranformation preserves the set of maximizers and, more generally, the family of upper contour sets of a given function. It follows that whenever the function of interest can be transformed into a concave function by a monotonically increasing transformation, we are back, effectively, to the relatively simple problem of maximizing a concave function. Functions that have this convenient property are said to be *concavifiable*.

Definition 3.13. Concavifiable function. Let $f : \mathbb{R}^n \supseteq X \longrightarrow \mathbb{R}$ be a function defined on a convex set $X \subseteq \mathbb{R}^n$. We say that f is concavifiable in X if there exists a C^1 and strictly increasing function $h : \mathbb{R} \supseteq A \longrightarrow \mathbb{R}$ defined on a set A that contains $f(X)$ such that $g(x) = h[f(x)]$ is a concave function.

Because concave functions have convex upper contour sets, and increasing transformations preserve the family of such sets, a necessary condition for concavifiability is that the given function be quasiconcave. This is not sufficient, however, as shown in Problem 3.15. The following result shows that a sufficient condition for a smooth quasiconcave function to be concavifiable in a compact set is that its partial derivatives be strictly positive in the set.

Theorem 3.14. A sufficient condition for concavifiability. Let $f : \mathbb{R}^n \supseteq X \longrightarrow \mathbb{R}$ be a C^2 quasiconcave function defined on an open and convex set $X \subseteq \mathbb{R}^n$. Suppose $f_i(x) > 0$ for all x in X. Then the restriction of f to any compact and convex subset C of X is concavifiable. In particular, there exists some number $\beta > 0$ such that the function $g : X \supseteq C \longrightarrow \mathbb{R}$ defined by $g(x) = -e^{-\beta f(x)}$ is concave.

Proof. We shall prove the result for the case of a univariate function. The idea is the same in the general case, but checking the sign (definiteness) of the second derivative is a bit more complicated.

Differentiating the function $g(x) = -e^{-\beta f(x)}$, we see that

$$g'(x) = \beta f'(x)e^{-\beta f(x)}$$

and

$$g''(x) = \beta[-f'(x)\beta f'(x)e^{-\beta f(x)} + e^{-\beta f(x)}f''(x)] = \beta e^{-\beta f(x)}[f'(x)]^2 \left(\frac{f''(x)}{[f'(x)]^2} - \beta \right)$$

Let C be a convex and compact subset of X. Because f is C^2, $f''(x)/[f'(x)]^2$) is a continuous function, and therefore it attains a maximum in C, by the extreme-value theorem. Call this maximum μ. If we choose β to be positive and larger than μ, then we have $g''(x) < 0$ for all x in C, and it follows that $g(\ )$ is concave, by Theorem 2.18. $\qquad\square$

Problem 3.15. Show that the function $f(x) = x^3$ cannot be concavified in any set that has zero as an interior point. Hint: Use Theorem 2.17.

Appendix: Quadratic Forms

Definition A.1. Quadratic form. A quadratic form is a function $Q: \mathbb{R}^n \longrightarrow \mathbb{R}$ of the form

$$Q(x) = x^T A x = \sum_{i=1}^{n} \sum_{k=1}^{n} a_{ik} x_i x_k$$

where $A = [a_{ik}]$ is a symmetric square matrix with real entries, $x \in \mathbb{R}^n$ is a column vector, and x^T is its transpose.

Definition A.2. Definite quadratic form. A quadratic form $Q(x) = x^T A x$ (or its associated matrix A) is

- positive definite if $Q(x) = x^T A x > 0$ for all $x \in \mathbb{R}^n$ other than the zero vector,
- positive semidefinite if $Q(x) = x^T A x \geq 0$ for all $x \in \mathbb{R}^n$,
- negative definite if $Q(x) = x^T A x < 0$ for all $x \in \mathbb{R}^n$, with $x \neq \underline{0}$,
- negative semidefinite if $Q(x) = x^T A x \leq 0$ for all $x \in \mathbb{R}^n$,
- indefinite if it is neither positive nor negative semidefinite, that is, if there exist vectors x and z in $\mathbb{R}^n$ such that $x^T A x < 0$ and $z^T A z > 0$.

The next theorem gives necessary and sufficient conditions for the positive or negative definiteness of a matrix in terms of its eigenvalues.

Theorem A.3. Given a quadratic form $Q(x) = x^T A x$, *let* $\lambda_1, \ldots, \lambda_n$ *be the eigenvalues of* A *(which will be real numbers, because* A *is symmetric). Then* $Q(x)$ *is*

- *positive definite if and only if all eigenvalues of* A *are strictly positive (i.e.,* $\lambda_i > 0$ $\forall$ i),
- *positive semidefinite if and only if* $\lambda_i \geq 0$ $\forall$ i = 1, . . . , n,
- *negative definite if and only if* $\lambda_i < 0$ $\forall$ i = 1, . . . , n,
- *negative semidefinite if and only if* $\lambda_i \leq 0$ $\forall$ i = 1, . . . , n.

Proof. We show only that $Q(x)$ is positive definite if and only if $\lambda_i > 0$ $\forall$ $i = 1, \ldots, n$. The rest of the theorem follows by exactly the same logic.

- Necessity: $[x^T A x > 0 \; \forall \; x \in \mathbb{R}^n, x \neq \underline{0}] \Rightarrow [\lambda_i > 0 \; \forall \; i = 1, \ldots, n]$

  Let x_i be the normalized eigenvector of A (i.e., with norm 1) associated with the eigenvalue λ_i. By definition,

$$Ax_i = \lambda_i x_i \tag{1}$$

Premultiplying (1) by x_i^T, we have

$$0 < x_i^T A x_i = \lambda_i x_i^T x_i = \lambda_i \tag{2}$$

where the inequality holds by the assumption that A is positive definite, and the last equality holds because $x_i^T x_i = \|x_i\|_E = 1$ by assumption.

- Sufficiency: $[\lambda_i > 0 \; \forall \; i = 1, \ldots, n] \Rightarrow [x^T A x > 0 \; \forall \; x \in \mathbb{R}^n, x \neq \underline{0}]$

  Because A is a symmetric real matrix, it has a full set of linearly independent (actually orthogonal) eigenvectors. Hence the matrix E, with the normalized eigenvectors as columns, is invertible and satisfies[7]

$$E^T A E = \Lambda$$

where Λ is the diagonal matrix with the eigenvalues of A (λ_i) along its principal diagonal.

Putting $y = E^{-1} x$, we can write $Q(\;)$ in the form

$$Q(x) = x^T A x = y^T E^T A E y = y^T \Lambda y = \sum_{i=1}^n \lambda_i y_i^2 \tag{3}$$

Hence, a quadratic form can always be written as the weighted sum of squares of a transformed vector y, with the eigenvalues of A as weights.

From (3) it is clear that if all the eigenvalues are positive, $Q(x)$ is positive, whatever the value of x (or y), as long as $x \neq \underline{0}$ ($\Rightarrow y \neq \underline{0}$). □

An alternative test of sign definiteness for quadratic forms uses the concepts of principal minor and leading principal minor of a matrix. If A is an $n \times n$ matrix, and we eliminate $n - k$ rows and the corresponding columns of A, we obtain a submatrix of dimension $k \times k$. The determinant of this submatrix is called a *principal minor* of order k of A. The *leading principal minors* of A are the principal minors obtained by keeping the first k rows and columns of A. Hence, the leading principal minor of order k of the matrix A, denoted d_k, is the determinant of the square $k \times k$ matrix A_k, formed by the first k columns and rows of A:

$$d_k = \det A_k = \begin{vmatrix} a_{11} & \cdots\cdots & a_{1k} \\ \cdots & \cdots\cdots & \cdots \\ a_{k1} & \cdots\cdots & a_{kk} \end{vmatrix}$$

Theorem A.4. The quadratic form $Q(x) = x^T A x$ *is positive definite if and only if all the leading principal minors of* A *(d_i; $i = 1, \ldots, n$) are positive, and negative definite if and only if (iff) their signs alternate with* $d_1 < 0$. *That is,*

- $Q(x)$ *is positive definite iff* $d_1 > 0, d_2 > 0, \ldots, d_n = |A| > 0,$
- $Q(x)$ *is negative definite iff* $d_1 < 0, d_2 > 0, d_3 < 0, \ldots.$

Moreover, Q is positive semidefinite if and only if all *the principal minors of A are nonnegative.*

Note that we can determine whether a quadratic form is positive or negative definite by checking the signs of only the leading principal minors, but we have to check all the principal minors to see if it is positive semidefinite. To test for negative semidefiniteness, observe that A is negative semidefinite if and only if $-A$ is positive semidefinite.

Proof. We prove only the necessity of the leading-principal-minor condition for sign definiteness.

- Consider first the case of positive definiteness. We want to show that

$$[x^T A x > 0 \; \forall \, x \in \mathbb{R}^n, \; x \neq \underline{0}] \Rightarrow [d_i > 0 \; \forall \, i = 1, \ldots, n]$$

  If A is positive definite, then $x^T A x > 0$ for any $x \neq \underline{0}$. Consider vectors whose first elements are nonzero and whose last $n - r$ elements are all zero: $x = (x_r, \underline{0})$. The corresponding quadratic form is

$$Q(x) = x^T A x = [x_r, \underline{0}] \begin{bmatrix} A_r & * \\ * & * \end{bmatrix} \begin{bmatrix} x_r \\ \underline{0} \end{bmatrix} = x_r^T A_r x_r > 0 \tag{1}$$

  where the "*" terms represent the last $n - r$ columns and rows of A, which will be wiped out by the zero subvector of x. Because the original form is assumed to be positive definite, we have $x_r^T A_r x_r > 0$, and this new "smaller" form is also positive definite. By Theorem A.3, this implies that the eigenvalues of the matrix A_r are all positive, and hence its determinant $|A_r| = d_r$ (which is the leading principal minor of order r of A) is also positive.[8] If A is positive definite, regardless of how many zeros we put in x, $Q(x) > 0$, so $|A_r| > 0$ for all $r = 1, \ldots, n$. Positive definiteness requires that all leading principal minors be positive.
- To derive conditions for negative definiteness, note that

$$[x^T A x > 0 \; \forall \, x \in \mathbb{R}^n, \; x \neq \underline{0}] \Leftrightarrow [-x^T A x = x^T(-A)x < 0 \; \forall \, x \in \mathbb{R}^n, \; x \neq \underline{0}]$$

so A is positive definite if and only if $-A$ is negative definite, and vice versa. Moreover,

$$|-A| = (-1)^n |A| \qquad \text{(where } n \text{ is the order of the square matrix } A\text{)}$$

Hence, A will be negative semidefinite if and only if $-A$ is positive definite, requiring

$$|-A_i| = (-1)^n |A_i| = (-1)^n d_i > 0 \; \forall \, i = 1, \ldots, n \Leftrightarrow d_1 < 0, d_2 > 0, d_3 < 0, \ldots.$$

For a proof of the sufficiency part of the theorem, see Hadley (1973, p. 261).   □

A useful property of positive definite (semidefinite) matrices is that their diagonal elements must be positive (nonnegative). To see this, consider the vector $e_i = (0, \ldots, 0, 1, 0, \ldots, 0)^T$, whose components are all zero except the ith, which is a 1. Note that the quadratic form

$$Q(e_i) = e_i^T A e_i = \sum_{i=1}^{n} \sum_{i=1}^{n} a_{ik} x_i x_k = a_{ii}$$

gives us back the ith diagonal element of the A matrix. Hence, if $Q(x) > 0$ for all x, we must have, in particular, $Q(e_i) = a_{ii} > 0$. Clearly, a similar property holds for negative definite or semidefinite matrices.

A quadratic form is positive definite if its value exceeds zero when evaluated at any nonzero vector $x \in \mathbb{R}^n$. In some cases we are interested only in whether a given quadratic form is positive or negative when evaluated at a particular set of vectors, for example, those that satisfy a certain system of linear equations.

Consider a quadratic form $Q(x) = x^T A x$, with $x \in \mathbb{R}^n$, and a system of m linear equations $Bx = \underline{0}$, where B is an $m \times n$ matrix (with $m < n$) of rank m (i.e., we assume that all equations are linearly independent, otherwise we eliminate the redundant ones). We form the bordered matrix

$$\overline{A} = \begin{bmatrix} 0_{m \times m} & B \\ B^T & A \end{bmatrix}$$

and consider its leading principal minor of order r:

$$|\overline{A}_r| = \begin{bmatrix} 0_{m \times m} & B_{mr} \\ B_{mr}^T & A_r \end{bmatrix}$$

where A_r is the square matrix formed by the first r columns and rows of A, and B_{mr} is the $m \times r$ matrix formed by keeping all the m rows of B and its first r columns. The following result gives us necessary and sufficient conditions for the positive or negative definiteness of A subject to the constraints $Bx = \underline{0}$ in terms of the signs of the determinants $|\overline{A}_r|$.

Theorem A.5. Sign definiteness under constraints. The quadratic form $Q(x)$ $= x^T Ax$ *is positive definite under the constraints* $Bx = \underline{0}$, *if and only if the last* $n - m$ *leading principal minors of the bordered matrix* $\overline{A}$ *are all of the same sign as* $(-1)^m$. *That is, if* m *is even (odd), then all the last* $n - m$ *leading principal minors are positive (negative). This can be written*

$$(-1)^m |\overline{A}_r| > 0 \quad for\ r = m + 1, \ldots, n$$

Moreover, Q *is negative definite if and only if the last* $n - m$ *leading principal minors of the bordered matrix* $\overline{A}$ *alternate in sign, with the first equal to* $(-1)^{m+1}$. *That is,*

$$(-1)^r |\overline{A}_r| > 0 \quad for\ r = m + 1, \ldots, n$$

Notice that as the number of constraints increases, we have to evaluate fewer determinants. This is not surprising, because an increase in the number of constraints reduces the size of the set of vectors for which we have to determine the sign of Q.

Bibliography

Arrow, K., and Enthoven, A. 1961. Quasi-Concave Programming. *Econometrica* 29:779–800.

Bazaraa, M., and Shetty, C. 1976. *Foundations of Optimization*. Lecture Notes in Economics and Mathematical Systems, no. 122. Berlin: Springer-Verlag.

Beavis, B., and Dobbs, I. 1990. *Optimization and Stability Theory for Economic Analysis*. Cambridge University Press.

Benveniste, L., and Scheinkman, J. 1982. Duality Theory for Dynamic Optimizing Models in Economics: The Continuous Time Case. *Journal of Economic Theory* 30:1–19.

Bronsted, A. 1983. *An Introduction to Convex Polytopes*. Berlin: Springer-Verlag.

Crouzeix, J. P., and Ferland, J. 1982. Criteria for Quasi-Convexity and Pseudo-Convexity: Relationships and Comparisons. *Mathematical Programming* 23:193–205.

Green, J., and Heller, W. 1987. Mathematical Analysis and Convexity with Applications to Economics. In: *Handbook of Mathematical Economics*, vol. 1, ed. K. Arrow and M. Intriligator, Amsterdam: North Holland.

Hadley, G. 1973. *Linear Algebra*. Reading, MA: Addison-Wesley.

Lancaster, K. 1968. *Mathematical Economics*. New York: Macmillan.

Madden, P. 1986. *Concavity and Optimization in Microeconomics*. London: Basil Blackwell.

Mangasarian, O. 1982. *Nonlinear Programming*. Malabar, FL: Krieger.

Michel, P. 1984. *Cours de Mathématiques pour Economistes*. Paris: Economica.

Nikaido, H. 1968. *Convex Structures and Economic Theory*. New York: Academic Press.

Nikaido, H. 1972. *Introduction to Sets and Mappings in Modern Economics*. Amsterdam: North Holland.

Rockafellar, R. T. 1970. *Convex Analysis*. Princeton University Press.

Simon, C., and Blume, L. 1994. *Mathematics for Economists*. New York: Norton.

Sydsæter, K. 1984. *Topics in Mathematical Analysis for Economists*. Orlando, FL: Academic Press.

Sydsæter, K., and Hammond, P. 1995. *Mathematics for Economic Analysis*. Englewood Cliffs, NJ: Prentice-Hall.

Takayama, A. 1987. *Mathematical Economics*, 2nd ed. Cambridge University Press.

Notes

1 Recall that $\lambda_i > 0$, but there is no guarantee that $\alpha_i > 0$ for all i.

2 If X has no closure points different from x, then cl $X = \{x\} \subseteq$ int X, and because int $X \subseteq$ cl X, we have int $X =$ cl X, a contradiction, except if $X = \mathbb{R}^n$.

3 See Section 1 of Chapter 3.

4 If X consists of a single point, x, then its affine hull consists also of a single point (has dimension zero), and int $X = x$. See Bazaraa and Shetty (1976) or Bronsted (1983) for a proof of these results.

5 The direction of the inequalities in the statement of the theorem does not matter. Notice that in order to reverse them, it suffices to take $H(-p, -\alpha)$.

6 Note that

$$(z - x^\lambda) = z - [(1 - \lambda)x^0 + \lambda y] = z - [x^0 + \lambda(y - x^0)] = -p - \lambda(y - x^0) \quad \text{and} \quad (z - x^0) = -p$$

Hence,

$$\begin{aligned}
\|z - x^\lambda\|^2 &= (z - x^\lambda)^T (z - x^\lambda) = [p + \lambda(y - x^0)]^T [p + \lambda(y - x^0)] \\
&= \|p\|^2 + 2\lambda p(y - x^0) + \lambda^2 \|y - x^0\|^2
\end{aligned}$$

and

$$\|z - x^0\|^2 - \|z - x^\lambda\|^2 = -\lambda \left(2p(y - x^0) + \lambda \|y - x^0\|^2 \right)$$

7 See the discussion of eigenvalues, eigenvectors, and diagonalization of a square matrix in Chapter 4.

8 The product of the eigenvalues of a matrix is equal to its determinant.

7

Static Optimization

One purpose in using economic models is to make predictions concerning the behavior of individuals and groups in certain situations of interest. Clearly, this is possible only if their behavior exhibits some sort of regularity. In economic theory, it is typically assumed that the source of such regularity is the rationality of the agents involved – an axiom that is generally understood to mean that

(i) economic agents have well-specified and consistent preferences over the set of possible results of their actions, and,

(ii) given those preferences, they choose their actions so as to obtain the best result among those available.

The postulate of rationality naturally leads us to model the behavior of economic agents as the outcome of a constrained optimization problem. This approach imposes a unifying structure on any model of the behavior of a single agent and provides us a method for reducing situations of economic interest to tractable mathematical problems. This chapter deals with the "technology" for analyzing such problems (i.e., the theory of nonlinear programming or constrained optimization).

1. Nonlinear Programming

The term "mathematical programming" or "nonlinear programming" (NLP) refers to a set of mathematical methods for characterizing the solutions to constrained optimization problems. In general terms, the basic programming problem can be written

$$\max_x \{f(x; \alpha); \ x \in C(\alpha)\} \tag{P}$$

That is, given some value of α, we seek the value of x that will maximize the function $f(\cdot; \alpha)$ within the set $C(\alpha)$. In this expression,

- $x = (x_1, \ldots, x_n) \in X \subseteq \mathbb{R}^n$ is a vector of decision variables or *choice variables*,
- $\alpha = (\alpha_1, \ldots, \alpha_p) \in \Omega \subseteq \mathbb{R}^p$ is a vector of *parameters* whose values we take as given,
- $C(\alpha) \subseteq X$, the *constraint set* or *feasible set*, is the set of all feasible values of x for given values of the parameters α, and
- f is a real-valued function $f: \mathbb{R}^{n+p} \supseteq X \times \Omega \longrightarrow \mathbb{R}$, known as the *objective function*.

For our purposes, the following interpretation will often be appropriate. Let Ω be the set of all possible "environments" in which an agent may find himself, each described by a value of the parameter vector α, and let X be the set of all actions that may conceivably be available to him. Given a value of α, the agent will find his choices restricted to some subset C of X (e.g., the budget set, in consumer theory). Changes in the parameters will result in changes in the feasible set, as described by the *constraint correspondence*, $C: \Omega \twoheadrightarrow X$.

The function $f: X \times \Omega \longrightarrow \mathbb{R}$ is the agent's *objective function*; $f(x; \alpha)$ gives his payoff when he faces environment α and chooses action x. A rational agent will choose an optimal plan, defined as one that will maximize the value of the objective function over the constraint set for the given value of the parameter vector. The set of optimal actions is described by the *decision rule* or best-response correspondence $S(\alpha)$,

$$S: \Omega \twoheadrightarrow X, \quad \text{where } S(\alpha) = \arg\max_x \{f(x; \alpha); \ x \in C(\alpha)\}$$

That is, $S(\alpha)$ is the set whose elements x^* are the optimal solutions of (P). If the solution to (P) is unique for each value of α, the best-response correspondence becomes a function, and we write $x^* = x(\alpha)$.

The payoff accruing to an optimizing agent is given by the (*maximum-*) *value function*, $V: \Omega \longrightarrow \mathbb{R}$, defined by

$$V(\alpha) = \max_x \{f(x; \alpha); \ x \in C(\alpha)\} = f(x^*, \alpha), \quad \text{where } x^* \in S(\alpha)$$

Given a value of the parameter vector, $V(\ )$ yields the highest attainable payoff. Clearly, $V(\ )$ is identically equal to the value of the objective function $f(\ )$ evaluated at an optimal solution x^* for the given α.

In most economic applications we are interested in the comparative statics and other properties of the decision rule $S(\alpha) = \arg\max_x \{f(x; \alpha); x \in C(\alpha)\}$. That is, we would like to know how the behavior of an agent varies in response to changes in his environment (the prices he faces, his income, etc.). Mathematically, the question is how the solution to the problem (P) changes with the parameters α. The problem should be familiar from an earlier chapter, but the "form" of the model looks different. The main task of this section is to show how, given certain differentiability assumptions, (P) can be reduced to an equivalent system of equations that can be analyzed by the methods developed in Chapter 5. This is what "characterizing the solution to (P)" means.

We will consider three versions of the programming problem that differ in terms of the way in which the feasible set is described:

- *Convex constraint set.* C is a convex subset of $\mathbb{R}^n$; as special cases, we have the case of unconstrained maximization, where C is the whole of $\mathbb{R}^n$, and maximization subject to nonnegativity constraints, where the feasible set is the nonnegative orthant of $\mathbb{R}^n$.
- *Lagrange problem.* The constraint set is defined by a set of equality constraints:

$$C(\alpha) = \{x \in X; \; g(x; \alpha) = \underline{0}\}$$

- *Kuhn-Tucker problem.* The constraint set is defined by a set of inequality constraints:

$$C(\alpha) = \{x \in X; \; g(x; \alpha) \geq \underline{0}\}$$

We will start with the simplest case and then proceed by manipulating each new problem in order to reduce it to one we already know how to handle. For the most part, we will assume that the objective and constraint functions are either once or twice continuously differentiable. This will allow us to use the calculus and obtain results stated in terms of first and second derivatives.

The results we seek in this section are necessary and sufficient conditions for a solution to the constrained optimization problem (P). First-order necessary conditions allow us to identify potential maximizers as the solutions of a system of equations involving first derivatives. These equations are obtained from the observation that, starting from an optimal solution x^*, any sufficiently small movement that keeps us inside the feasible set cannot increase the value of the objective function. If the relevant functions are sufficiently smooth, this translates into some generalization of the zero-derivative rule for a local maximum of a univariate real-valued function. Sufficient conditions are then used to identify the true optimal solutions within the set of candidates, or to ensure that this set cannot contain minimizers or other "false signals." Essentially, sufficient conditions tell us that if the function has a certain curvature (either locally or globally) around a point that satisfies the necessary conditions, then this point must be a (local or global) solution to the programming problem.

Once we have characterized the solutions of (P) in terms of a system of necessary conditions, the comparative-statics problem can be approached using the techniques of Chapter 5. Moreover, the fact that the system we shall be working with comes from an optimization problem will allow us to be more specific about the properties of the solution functions than we could be earlier. This will be discussed in detail in a later section.

(a) Convex Constraint Set

Consider the problem

$$\max_{x}\{f(x);\ x \in C\} \tag{P.C}$$

where C is a convex set in $\mathbb{R}^n$, and $f: \mathbb{R}^n \supseteq X \longrightarrow \mathbb{R}$ is a C^2 function. We are omitting the parameters, because for the time being we are interested only in the solution to (P.C) for a fixed value of α.

We are familiar with a special case of this problem. If $C = \mathbb{R}^n$, then a necessary condition for x^* to be a maximizer of f is that $Df(x^*) = \underline{0}$. In the more general case, however, this condition is neither necessary nor sufficient for a maximum. Figure 7.1 shows an example. Notice that $f'(b) = f'(c) = 0$, but neither b nor c maximizes f on $C = [a, b]$. On the other hand, f achieves its maximum on this interval at the point a, but $f'(a) \neq 0$.

The figure suggests that if the solution to the programming problem happens to be on the boundary of the feasible set, then one or more of the partial derivatives of the objective function may not be zero at the optimum. On the other hand, it must be true that as we move away from an optimum in a feasible direction, the value of the function will decrease. Hence, directional derivatives in feasible directions must be nonpositive. We now state this result formally.

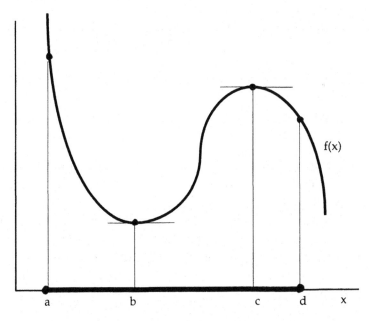

Figure 7.1. A zero derivative is neither necessary nor sufficient for a maximum.

Definition 1.1. Feasible direction. Consider the problem (P.C): $\max_x\{f(x);$ $x \in C\}$, where C is a convex set. Take a point x in C and a direction vector h in $\mathbb{R}^n$. We say that h is a feasible direction from x if there exists some $\delta > 0$ such that

$$x + \alpha h \in C \,\, \forall \, \alpha \in (0, \delta)$$

that is, if any sufficiently small movement away from x in the direction of h leaves us inside the feasible set.

Theorem 1.2. First-order necessary conditions for a maximum. Assume that f *is* C^1*, and let* x* *be an optimal solution of (P.C); then*

$$Df(x^*)h \le 0$$

for every direction vector h $\in \mathbb{R}^n$ *feasible from* x*.

Proof. Let x^* be an optimal solution of (P.C), and h an arbitrary direction vector feasible from x^*. Then there exists some $\delta > 0$ (which may depend on h) such that $x^* + \alpha h \in C$ for all $\alpha \in (0, \delta)$. Because any feasible movement away from x^* reduces the value of the function, we have

$$f(x^* + \alpha h) \le f(x^*)$$

for all α such that $x^* + \alpha h \in C$. Rearranging and dividing by $\alpha > 0$,

$$\frac{f(x^* + \alpha h) - f(x^*)}{\alpha} \le 0 \tag{1}$$

and taking the limit of this expression as $\alpha \to 0$,

$$\lim_{\alpha \to 0} \frac{f(x^* + \alpha h) - f(x^*)}{\alpha} = Df(x^*; h) = Df(x^*)h \le 0$$

That is, the limit of the ratio on the left-hand side of (1) is the (one-sided) directional derivative of f in the direction of h evaluated at x^*. Because f is C^1, the directional derivative exists and can be written as the scalar product of the derivative and the direction vector (see Chapter 4). $\qquad \square$

If C is an open set, all its points are by definition interior, and given any x in C, all directions are feasible from it. In this case the inequality $Df(x^*)h \le 0$ can hold for all h only if all first partial derivatives of f are zero at x^*. Otherwise, it is possible to increase the value of the function by moving in the direction of (or opposite to) the coordinate vector corresponding to the nonzero partial. For example, suppose $f_k(x^*) > 0$ and $f_i(x^*) = 0$ for all $i \ne k$, and choose a direction vector h, with $h_k > 0$ and $h_i = 0$ for all $i \ne k$. Then

$$Df(x^*)h = \sum_{i=1}^n f_i(x^*)h_i = f_k(x^*)h_k > 0$$

which contradicts Theorem 1.2. Hence, all partials must be zero at an optimum, and we have the following.

Corollary 1.3. Maximization in an open set. Assume that f *is a* C^1 *function and the constraint set* C *is open, and let* x* *be an optimal solution to (P.C). Then*

$$Df(x^*)h = \underline{0} \qquad (i.e., \ \partial f(x^*)/\partial x_i = 0 \ \forall \ i = 1, \ldots, n)$$

Another special case of the convex-constraint-set problem is that in which $C = \mathbb{R}_+^n$ (i.e., where we maximize f subject to the constraint that the choice variables be nonnegative). An argument similar to that used to establish Corollary 1.3 yields the following result.

Corollary 1.4. Maximization with nonnegativity constraints. If $C = \mathbb{R}_+^n$ *and* x* *is an optimal solution of (P.C), then for each* $i = 1, \ldots, n$ *we have*

$$\frac{\partial f(x^*)}{\partial x_i} \leq 0 \quad \text{with equality if} \ x_i^* > 0$$

$$x_i^* \geq 0 \quad \text{with equality if} \ \frac{\partial f(x_{-i}^*, 0)}{\partial x_i} < 0$$

Problem 1.5. Second-order necessary conditions. Let $f : \mathbb{R}^n \longrightarrow \mathbb{R}$ be a C^2 function. Show that if f achieves a local maximum at x^*, then the Hessian of f at x^* is negative semidefinite, that is,

$$h^T D^2 f(x^*) h \leq 0 \ \forall \ h \in \mathbb{R}^n$$

The following theorem shows that if f satisfies certain concavity conditions, a point that satisfies the first-order necessary conditions (FONCs) is indeed an optimal solution.

Theorem 1.6. Sufficient conditions for a global maximum. Let f *be a* C^1 *pseudoconcave function. If* $x^* \in C$, *and for every direction* $h \in \mathbb{R}^n$ *feasible from* x* *we have* $Df(x^*)h \leq 0$, *then* x* *is an optimal solution of (P.C).*

Proof. We will prove the contrapositive statement. Assume that C is convex and f is pseudoconcave, and fix some point $x^0 \in C$. We will show that if x^0 is not an optimal solution to (P.C), then it does not satisfy the first-order condition $Df(x^0)h \leq 0$ for all feasible directions $h \in \mathbb{R}^n$.

Suppose x^0 is not optimal. Then there exists some point $x \in C$ such that $f(x) > f(x^0)$. By the pseudoconcavity of f, $f(x) > f(x^0)$ implies

$$Df(x^0)(x - x^0) > 0$$

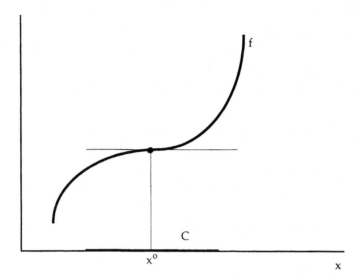

Figure 7.2. A false signal.

where $(x - x^0)$ is a feasible direction vector from x^0, by the convexity of C. Hence, x^0 does not satisfy the first-order conditions.   □

Recall that both concavity and strict quasiconcavity (or quasiconcavity and nonstationarity) imply pseudoconcavity. Hence, any of these conditions will be sufficient for a point that satisfies the necessary conditions to be an optimal solution. On the other hand, quasiconcavity alone will not do. As we mentioned in Chapter 6, quasiconcavity allows "false signals." Figure 7.2 illustrates the problem: f is quasiconcave, and the point x^0 satisfies the first-order condition, but does not maximize f in C.

The following problems provide alternative sufficient conditions for global maxima.

Problem 1.7. Let $f : \mathbb{R}^n \longrightarrow \mathbb{R}$ be a C^1 concave function. Show that if x^* is a critical point of f, then it is a global maximizer of f.

Problem 1.8. Let $f : \mathbb{R}^n \longrightarrow \mathbb{R}$ be a concave function. Show that if x^* is a local maximizer of f, then it is also a global maximizer. Hint: Proceed by contradiction.

The following theorem gives sufficient conditions for a stationary point x^* of f to be a strict local maximizer in an open set. That is, $f(x^*) > f(x)$ for all x in some open ball with center at x^*. Notice that what the theorem requires is essentially the strict concavity of f in some neighborhood of x^*.[1] A point that satisfies the conditions of this theorem is said to be a *regular maximizer* of f in C.

Theorem 1.9. Sufficient conditions for a strict local maximum. Let f be a C^2 *function, with* C *an open and convex set, and* x* *a point in* C *such that* $Df(x^*) = \underline{0}$. *If the Hessian matrix at* x*, $D^2f(x^*)$, *is negative definite, then* f *achieves a strict local maximum at* x*.

Proof. Let h be an arbitrary direction vector in $\mathbb{R}^n$. By the convexity and openness of C there exists some $\delta > 0$ such that $x^* + \alpha h \in C$ for all $\alpha \in (0, \delta)$. Fixing some α in this interval, both x^* and $x^* + \alpha h$ lie in C, and we can use Taylor's formula to write

$$f(x^* + \alpha h) - f(x^*) = Df(x^*)(\alpha h) + \frac{1}{2}(\alpha h)^T D^2 f(x^* + \lambda_\alpha \alpha h)(\alpha h) \qquad (1)$$

for some $\lambda_\alpha \in (0, 1)$. Moreover, because x^* is by assumption a stationary point, we have $Df(x^*) = \underline{0}$, and (1) reduces to

$$f(x^* + \alpha h) - f(x^*) = \frac{\alpha^2}{2} h^T D^2 f(x^* + \lambda_\alpha \alpha h) h \qquad (2)$$

Now, for the given h the quadratic form on the right-hand side of (2) can be shown to be a continuous function of α, say $Q(\alpha)$, at $\alpha = 0$ (see Problem 1.10). By assumption, moreover, $D^2f(x^*)$ is negative definite, implying that

$$Q(0) = h^T D^2 f(x^*) h < 0$$

Hence, it follows by continuity that $Q(\ )$ will preserve its sign for sufficiently small α; that is, there exists some $\gamma > 0$ such that

$$Q(\alpha) = h^T D^2 f(x^* + \lambda_\alpha \alpha h) h < 0 \qquad (3)$$

for all $\alpha < \gamma$. Finally, (2) and (3) imply that

$$f(x^*) > f(x^* + \alpha h) \ \forall \ \alpha < \gamma$$

Because h is arbitrary, any sufficiently small movement away from x^* reduces the value of the objective function. Hence, f has a strict local maximum at x^*. $\qquad \square$

We saw in the appendix to Chapter 6 that a matrix A is negative definite if and only if its leading principal minors alternate in sign, with the first one negative. As we will see later, this information will be very useful when we turn to the comparative statics of optimization models.

Problem 1.10. Let $A = [a_{ik}]$ be an $n \times n$ matrix, and consider the quadratic form $h^T A h = \Sigma_i \Sigma_k h_i a_{ik} h_k$. Using the Cauchy-Schwarz inequality, show that

$$\left| h^T A h \right| \le \sqrt{\sum_i \sum_k a_{ik}^2} \, \|h\|^2$$

where $\| \cdot \|$ is the Euclidean norm. Using this result, verify that the function $Q(\alpha)$ in the proof of Theorem 1.9 is continuous at zero (provided f is C^2) by showing that $|Q(\alpha) - Q(0)| \to 0$ as $\alpha \to 0$.

Notice that whereas Theorem 1.9 implies the local uniqueness of the maximizer, Theorem 1.6 allows for the existence of multiple optimal solutions. We close this section with a sufficient condition for the global uniqueness of the optimal solution to (P.C).

Theorem 1.11. Global uniqueness. Let x* *be an optimal solution of (P.C), with C convex. If* f *is strictly quasiconcave, then* x* *is the unique optimal solution to the problem.*

Proof. By contradiction. Suppose that there exist two optimal solutions x' and x'' in C. Then $f(x') = f(x'') = M$, and by the strict quasiconcavity of f, we have, for any $\lambda \in (0, 1)$,

$$f[(1-\lambda)x' + \lambda x''] > \min\{f(x'), f(x'')\} = M$$

where $x^\lambda = (1 - \lambda)x' + \lambda x''$ is a feasible point, by the convexity of C. Because $f(x^\lambda) > f(x') = f(x'')$, neither x' nor x'' can be an optimal solution to begin with. $\square$

Problem 1.12. Derivation of factor demand functions. Consider a competitive firm that produces a single output y using two inputs x_1 and x_2. The firm's production technology is described by a Cobb-Douglas function

$$y = f(x_1, x_2) = x_1^\alpha x_2^\beta, \quad \text{where } \beta + \alpha < 1, \ \beta > 0, \text{ and } \alpha > 0$$

Taking as given the price of its output p and input prices w_1 and w_2, the firm maximizes its profits, given by

$$\Pi(x_1, x_2) = px_1^\alpha x_2^\beta - w_1 x_1 - w_2 x_2$$

Write the first-order conditions for the firm's problem, and check that sufficient conditions for a maximum are satisfied. Using the first-order conditions, solve for the firm's factor demands, giving the optimal input levels x_i^* as functions of input and output prices.

(b) Equality Constraints: The Lagrange Problem

Consider the problem

$$\max_x \{f(x) \text{ s.t. } g(x) = \underline{0}\} \tag{P.L}$$

where $f: \mathbb{R}^n \supseteq X \longrightarrow \mathbb{R}$ and $g: \mathbb{R}^n \supseteq X \longrightarrow \mathbb{R}^c$ are C^2 functions, and "s.t." means "subject to." We will refer to the components of $g = (g^1, \ldots, g^c)^T$ as the *constraint functions* and assume that $c \leq n$ (i.e., that we have fewer constraints than choice variables).

We will start by giving an intuitive interpretation of the method of Lagrange multipliers. Consider a simple version of (P.L) with only two decision variables and one constraint:

$$\max_{x_1,x_2}\{f(x_1, x_2);\ g(x_1, x_2) = c\} \tag{P.L'}$$

Instead of directly forcing the agent to respect the constraint, imagine that we allow him to choose the values of the instruments x_1 and x_2 freely, but make him pay a fine λ "per unit violation" of the restriction. The agent's payoff, net of the penalty, is given by the Lagrangian function:

$$\pounds(x_1, x_2, \lambda) = f(x_1, x_2) - \lambda[c - g(x_1, x_2)] \tag{1}$$

The agent then maximizes (1), taking λ as given. The first-order conditions for this problem are

$$\frac{\partial \pounds(x_1, x_2, \lambda)}{\partial x_1} = \frac{\partial f}{\partial x_1} + \lambda \frac{\partial g}{\partial x_1} = 0 \Rightarrow \frac{\partial f(x^*)}{\partial x_1} = -\lambda \frac{\partial g(x^*)}{\partial x_1} \tag{L.1}$$

$$\frac{\partial \pounds(x_1, x_2, \lambda)}{\partial x_2} = \frac{\partial f}{\partial x_2} + \lambda \frac{\partial g}{\partial x_2} = 0 \Rightarrow \frac{\partial f(x^*)}{\partial x_2} = -\lambda \frac{\partial g(x^*)}{\partial x_2} \tag{L.2}$$

Given an arbitrary λ, there is no guarantee that the solutions of this system of equations will be optimal solutions of the original problem. But if we pick the correct penalty λ^*, the agent will choose to respect the constraint even if in principle he is free not to, and then the artificial problem we have constructed will give us the correct answers. Thus, λ^* must be such that the constraint holds. Hence, in addition to (L.1) and (L.2), the optimal solution $(x_1^*, x_2^*, \lambda^*)$ must satisfy the feasibility condition, which can be conveniently written in the form

$$\frac{\partial \pounds(x_1, x_2, \lambda)}{\partial \lambda} = g(x_1, x_2) - c = 0 \tag{F}$$

We have, then, a system of three equations that can be solved for the optimal values of the instruments (x_1^*, x_2^*) and the Lagrange multiplier λ^*. Notice that these equations are the conditions that define a stationary point of the Lagrangian. The optimal solution $(x_1^*, x_2^*, \lambda^*)$, however, is likely to be a saddle point rather than a maximizer of $\pounds(\ )$: Whereas x^* does maximize $\pounds(x, \lambda^*)$, it will not be true in general that λ^* maximizes $\pounds(x^*, \lambda)$.

Although a formal discussion of the topic will have to wait until we establish the envelope theorem, it should be noted that λ^* often contains useful information about the effect of the constraint. In a possible economic inter-

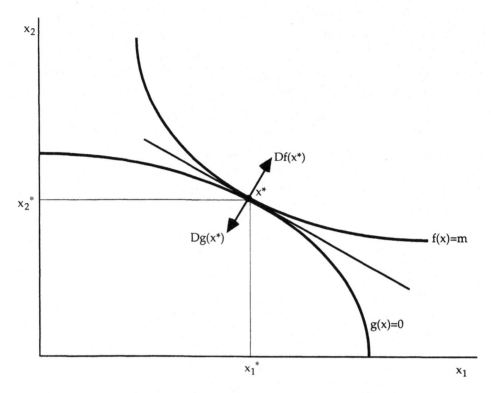

Figure 7.3. Optimal solution of a Lagrange problem.

pretation, c denotes the available stock of a certain resource, and the objective function measures something like the profit obtained through an activity that uses the resource as an input. Then the multiplier gives the maximum increase in profit that could be obtained if we had one more unit of the input – and hence the maximum amount that a rational decision-maker would be willing to pay for one additional unit of it. This is clearly a good measure of the marginal value of the resource, and it justifies the interpretation of the multiplier as a "shadow price."

Graphically, the feasible set of (P.L′) is a curve on the (x_1, x_2) plane, and the optimal solution to the problem is the point x^* on this curve that lies on the highest possible level set of f. Given certain convexity assumptions, x^* will be a tangency point of the two level curves, as shown in Figure 7.3. The existence of a common tangent to both curves implies that the gradients of f and g (both perpendicular to the tangent) lie on the same straight line. This allows us to write one of them as the product of the other and a scalar. That is, there exists a number $-\lambda^*$ such that

$$Df(x^*) = -\lambda^* Dg(x^*)$$

which is another way of writing (L.1) and (L.2). Clearly, x^* also satisfies the constraint $g(x_1, x_2) = c$. Hence, the graphical argument also suggests that the constrained maximizer of f will be characterized by the conditions discussed earlier.

The necessary conditions for the general Lagrange problem

$$\max_x \{f(x);\, g(x) = \underline{0}\} \tag{P.L}$$

can be obtained in a similar way. Introducing a column vector of Lagrange multipliers $\lambda = (\lambda_1, \ldots, \lambda_c)^T$, one for each constraint, we write the Lagrangian

$$\pounds(x, \lambda) = f(x) + \lambda^T g(x)$$

Differentiating $\pounds(\ )$ with respect to x and λ, we obtain the first-order conditions

$$D_x \pounds(x, \lambda) = Df(x) + \lambda^T Dg(x) = \underline{0} \tag{L}$$

$$D_\lambda \pounds(x, \lambda) = g(x) = \underline{0} \tag{F}$$

This is a system of $m + c$ equations in the $m + c$ unknowns (x, λ) whose solution set contains the optimal solution to the programming problem, x^*, and the "correct" values of the multipliers, λ^*. The c equations in (F) are simply the constraints of the original problem, and (L) tells us that the gradient of the objective function f can be written as a linear combination of the gradients of the constraint functions, all evaluated at an optimal solution.

Theorem 1.13. Lagrange. Let x* *be an optimal solution of*

$$\max_x \{f(x);\, g(x) = \underline{0}\} \tag{P.L}$$

where f *and* g *are* C^1 *functions, and rank* $Dg(x^*) = c \le n$. *Then there exist unique Lagrange multipliers* $\lambda^* \in \mathbb{R}^c$ *such that*

$$Df(x^*) + \lambda^{*T} Dg(x^*) = \underline{0}$$

The logic of the proof is very simple, even though the notation gets messy. We want to show that given certain assumptions, there is some vector $\lambda^* \in \mathbb{R}^c$ with certain properties, so we go ahead and construct such an object. A simple way to illustrate what we are doing is to consider the simplest possible case. Assume that we have n constraints, and rank $Dg(x^*) = n$. Then $Dg(x^*)$ is an invertible square matrix, and finding a vector $\lambda^* \in \mathbb{R}^n$ that satisfies the Lagrange condition

$$Df(x^*) + \lambda^T Dg(x^*) = \underline{0} \tag{L}$$

is easy: We can solve (L) explicitly to get

$$\lambda^{*T} = -Df(x^*)[Dg(x^*)]^{-1}$$

Under these assumptions, however, the maximization problem is trivial, because the feasible set reduces, at least locally, to a unique point that is therefore also optimal.

In the general case, the invertibility of $Dg(x^*)$ is not guaranteed, but we will show that it contains an invertible submatrix that can be used in exactly the same way. We begin by partitioning the vector x into two components:

$$x = (x_\alpha, x_\beta), \quad \text{with} \quad x_\alpha = (x_1, \dots, x_c) \quad \text{and} \quad x_\beta = (x_{c+1}, \dots, x_n)$$

In this notation, we can write the constraints $g(x_\alpha, x_\beta) = \underline{0}$ and partition the derivative of the constraint function in the corresponding manner, with

$$Dg(x^*) = [D_\alpha g(x^*), D_\beta g(x^*)]$$

Now, by the assumption that rank $Dg(x^*) = c$, $Dg(x^*)$ has c linearly independent columns. Without loss of generality, we can relabel the x_i's in such a way that the square submatrix $D_\alpha g(x^*)$ has full rank and is therefore invertible. Partitioning the relevant vectors and matrices appropriately, (L) can be written

$$\begin{bmatrix} D_\alpha f(x^*) \\ D_\beta f(x^*) \end{bmatrix} + \begin{bmatrix} \lambda^{*T} D_\alpha g(x^*) \\ \lambda^{*T} D_\beta g(x^*) \end{bmatrix} = \begin{bmatrix} \underline{0} \\ \underline{0} \end{bmatrix}$$

Because $D_\alpha g(x^*)$ is invertible, we can solve the first c equations of the system for a unique value of λ^*:

$$D_\alpha f(x^*) + \lambda^{*T} D_\alpha g(x^*) = \underline{0}$$

$$\Rightarrow \lambda^{*T} = -D_\alpha g(x^*)[D_\alpha g(x^*)]^{-1} \tag{1}$$

It only remains to show that the vector λ^* also satisfies the remaining equations of the system:

$$D_\beta f(x^*) + \lambda^{*T} D_\beta g(x^*) = \underline{0} \tag{2}$$

To establish that (2) holds, we start from the observation that if x^* is an optimal solution of (P.L), then any small feasible movement away from it will reduce the value of the objective function. The complication, relative to the simpler problems we have considered so far, is that we now have to make sure that we consider only movements that do not violate the constraint equations. One way to do this is to apply the implicit-function theorem (IFT) to "solve" the system of constraint equations, $g(x_\alpha, x_\beta) = \underline{0}$, for some of the choice variables as a function of the rest. Then we substitute this function into f to "eliminate" the constraints. This procedure allows us to transform the Lagrange problem into an equivalent problem of maximization in an open set. Direct computation using the first-order conditions for this modified problem shows that condition (2) holds.

Proof

(i) We apply the IFT to the system of constraint equations. Let $x^* = (x_\alpha^*, x_\beta^*)$ be an optimal solution of (P.L). Because x^* is feasible by definition, $g(x_\alpha^*, x_\beta^*) = \underline{0}$ and $|D_\alpha g(x_\alpha^*, x_\beta^*)| \neq 0$ by the rank assumption. Hence, x^* satisfies the conditions of the IFT, and it follows that for any given value of x_β in some neighborhood of x_β^*, there exists a unique value of x_α close to x_α^* and locally unique such that $g(x_\alpha, x_\beta) = 0$. Formally, there exists a C^1 function,

$$h : U_\beta \longrightarrow U_\alpha, \quad \text{with } h(x_\beta) = x_\alpha \text{ s.th. } g(x_\alpha, x_\beta) = \underline{0}$$

where U_α and U_β are open balls centered at x_α^* and x_β^*. The derivative of h can be easily calculated by implicit differentiation:

$$g[h(x_\beta), x_\beta] \equiv \underline{0} \Rightarrow D_\alpha g(x) Dh(x_\beta) + D_\beta g(x) = \underline{0}$$
$$\Rightarrow Dh(x_\beta) = -[D_\alpha g(x)]^{-1} D_\beta g(x) \tag{3}$$

The usefulness of the function $h(\ )$ lies in the fact that it allows us to avoid explicit consideration of the constraints. Given a value of x_β, $h(\ )$ gives us a value of x_α such that (x_α, x_β) is feasible.

(ii) We now use $h(\ )$ to transform (P.L) into an equivalent problem of maximization in an open and convex set. Define the function $F : U_\beta \longrightarrow \mathbb{R}$ by

$$F(x_\beta) = f[h(x_\beta), x_\beta]$$

Now, if $x^* = (x_\alpha^*, x_\beta^*)$ is an optimal solution of (P.L), then x_β^* will be a solution of

$$\max_{x_\beta} \{ F(x_\beta); \ x_\beta \in U_\beta \} \tag{P.U}$$

and therefore will satisfy the first-order condition

$$DF(x_\beta^*) = \underline{0} \tag{4}$$

Using (1)–(4), we can now establish the desired result by direct computation:

$$\underline{0} = DF(x_\beta^*) = Df[h(x_\beta^*), x_\beta^*] = D_\alpha f(x^*) Dh(x_\beta^*) + D_\beta f(x_\beta^*) \quad \text{[by (3)]}$$
$$= -D_\alpha f(x^*)[D_\alpha g(x^*)]^{-1} D_\beta g(x^*) + D_\beta f(x^*) \quad \text{[by (1)]}$$
$$= \lambda^{*T} D_\beta g(x^*) + D_\beta f(x^*) = \underline{0}$$

Hence, equation (2) holds, which proves the theorem. □

One of the assumptions of the Lagrange theorem is that the rank of the matrix of first partial derivatives of the constraint functions, evaluated at the

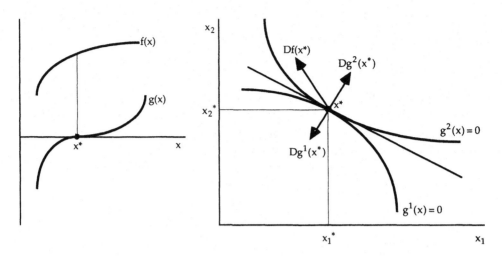

Figure 7.4. Failure of the constraint qualification.

optimal solution, is equal to the number of constraints, c. This condition is sometimes called a *constraint qualification*. To understand its role, observe that the Lagrange condition can be written

$$Df(x^*) = -\lambda^T Dg(x^*) = -\sum_{j=1}^{n} \lambda_j Dg^j(x^*) \tag{L}$$

Thus, (L) requires that we be able to write the gradient of f as a linear combination of the gradients of the constraint functions. If the constraint qualification fails, we may find that we do not have enough linearly independent constraint gradients for (L) to hold.

Figure 7.4 illustrates the geometry of the problem for a couple of trivial examples. In each case, x^* clearly maximizes f subject to $g(x) = \underline{0}$, because it is the only point in the feasible set. However, the Lagrange condition $Df(x^*) + \lambda^T Dg(x^*) = \underline{0}$ does not hold in either case. In the first panel of the figure we have $Df(x^*) > 0$ and $Dg(x^*) = 0$, so there is no number such that $Df(x^*) = -\lambda Dg(x^*)$. In the second, the zero level curves of the two constraints are tangent at the optimum. As a result, the gradients of the constraint functions lie on the same straight line and therefore do not span the (x_1, x_2) plane. Hence, $Df(x^*)$ cannot be written as a linear combination of $Dg^1(x^*)$ and $Dg^2(x^*)$, unless, by chance, it lies on the same straight line.

The following theorem gives sufficient conditions for a point that satisfies the Lagrange condition to be an optimal solution of (P.L). Before stating the result, we should observe that there is no loss of generality in assuming that the Lagrange multipliers are nonnegative, because we can always reverse their signs by rewriting one or more of the constraints in the form $-g^j(x) = 0$. For example, assume that all multipliers are nonnegative, except for one, $\lambda_j < 0$. When we multiply the corresponding constraint by -1, we reverse the signs of the partial derivatives of the constraint function and therefore the sign of the determinant of the matrix $J = D_\alpha g(x)$.[2] Now, the Lagrange multipliers are the solution to

$$\lambda^{*T} D_\alpha g(x^*) = -D_\alpha f(x^*)$$

and, by Cramer's rule, λ_j is given by

$$\lambda_j = \frac{|J_j|}{|J|}$$

where J_j is the matrix obtained by replacing the jth column of J, given by $D_\alpha g^j(x^*)$, with the right-hand-side vector, $-D_\alpha f(x^*)$. Hence, multiplication of the constraint by -1 reverses the sign of the corresponding multiplier.

With this in mind, the theorem says that if there is some way to write the Lagrangian so that the restrictions are quasiconcave and the multipliers are nonnegative, then a feasible point that satisfies the Lagrange condition is an optimum.

Theorem 1.14. Sufficient conditions for a global maximum. Let f *be pseudo-concave, and all* $g^j(x)$ *quasiconcave. If* (x^*, λ^*) *satisfy the Lagrange condition,* $Df(x^*) + \lambda^{*T} Dg(x^*) = \underline{0}$, *with* x^* *feasible and* $\lambda^* \geq \underline{0}$, *then* x^* *is an optimal solution to the Lagrange problem (P.L).*

Problem 1.15. Prove Theorem 1.14. Hint: Follow the proof of Theorem 1.6.

We now give a second set of sufficient conditions that, although only local in character, often are quite useful in economic applications. A point that satisfies the conditions of the theorem is said to be a *regular maximizer* of *f* subject to the constraints.

Theorem 1.16. Sufficient conditions for a strict local maximum. Let x^* *be a feasible point satisfying the Lagrange condition for some* λ^*. *Assume that the matrix of second partial derivatives of the Lagrangian function with respect to the choice variables* x, *evaluated at* (x^*, λ^*),

$$D_x^2 \pounds(x^*, \lambda^*) = D^2 f(x^*) + \lambda^{*T} D^2 g(x^*)$$

is negative definite subject to the constraints $Dg(x^*)h = \underline{0}$, *that is,*

$$h^T D_x^2 \pounds(x^*, \lambda^*)h < 0 \; \forall h \in \mathbb{R}^n \; s.th. \; Dg(x^*)h = \underline{0}$$

Then x^* *is a strict local maximizer of* f *subject to* $g(x) = \underline{0}$.

Proof. Let h be a direction vector in $\mathbb{R}^n$, and consider a feasible point $x^* + \alpha h$, where $\alpha > 0$. Using Taylor's formula, we can write

$$£(x^* + \alpha h, \lambda^*) - £(x^*, \lambda^*) = D_x £(x^*, \lambda^*)(\alpha h) + \frac{\alpha^2}{2} h^T D_x^2 £(x^* + \theta_\alpha \alpha h, \lambda^*) h \tag{1}$$

for some $\theta_\alpha \in (0, 1)$. Writing out (1) in more detail, we have

$$f(x^* + \alpha h) + \lambda^{*T} g(x^* + \alpha h) - f(x^*) - \lambda^{*T} g(x^*)$$

$$= [Df(x^*) + \lambda^{*T} Dg(x^*)](\alpha h) + \frac{1}{2} \alpha^2 h^T D_x^2 £(x^* + \theta_\alpha \alpha h) h \tag{2}$$

Observing that

- by assumption both x^* and $x^* + \alpha h$ are feasible, that is, $g(x^*) = g(x^* + \alpha h) = \underline{0}$, and
- x^* satisfies the Lagrange condition, $Df(x^*) + \lambda^{*T} Dg(x^*) = \underline{0}$,

equation (2) reduces to

$$f(x^* + \alpha h) - f(x^*) = \frac{\alpha^2}{2} h^T D_x^2 £(x^* + \theta_\alpha \alpha h) h \tag{3}$$

We will show that if x^* is not a strict local maximizer, then $D_{xx}^2 £(x^*, \lambda^*)$ cannot be negative definite subject to $Dg(x^*)h = \underline{0}$.

Suppose x^* is not a strict local maximizer, and consider a decreasing sequence of real numbers $\delta_k > 0$ convergent to zero. For each δ_k there exists a feasible point $x^{\delta_k} \in B_{\delta_k}(x^*)$ such that $f(x^{\delta_k}) \geq f(x^*)$. We can write the vectors x^{δ_k} in the form

$$x^{\delta_k} = x^* + \alpha_k h^k$$

where h^k is a normalized direction vector (with unit norm). Now, $\{x^{\delta_k}\} \to x^*$ by construction, implying that $\{\alpha_k\} \to 0$. Applying the Bolzano-Weierstrass theorem component by component to the bounded sequence $\{h^k\}$, we see that this sequence has a convergent subsequence (see Problem 3.12 in Chapter 2). For simplicity of notation, assume that $\{h^k\}$ itself converges to some h. Then we have, for each $x^* + \alpha_k h^k$, the following:

- By feasibility, we have

$$\frac{1}{\alpha_k}[g(x^* + \alpha_k h^k) - g(x^*)] = \underline{0}$$

and taking the limit of this expression as $k \to \infty$,

$$Dg(x^*)h = \underline{0} \tag{4}$$

- Using (3) and the assumption that $f(x^{\delta_k}) \geq f(x^*)$,

$$\frac{\alpha_k^2}{2} h^{kT} D_x^2 \pounds(x^* + \theta_k \alpha_k h) h^k = f(x^* + \alpha_k h^k) - f(x^*) \geq 0$$

Dividing by α_k^2 and taking the limit of the resulting expression as $k \to \infty$, the inequality is preserved. Hence, there exists a vector h, with $Dg(x^*)h = \underline{0}$, and such that

$$h^T D_x^2 \pounds(x^*, \lambda^*) h \geq 0 \tag{5}$$

It follows that $D_{xx}^2 \pounds(\ )$ is negative definite subject to the linearized constraints, and this establishes the desired result. $\qquad\square$

Problem 1.17. Solve the problem

$$\max_{x,y,z} 2x - 2y + z \text{ s.t. } x^2 + y^2 + z^2 = 9$$

by the method of Lagrange multipliers. Use the sufficient second-order conditions for a strict maximum to determine which of the two solutions to the system of first-order conditions yields a maximum. Verify that this is correct by comparing the values of the objective function in both cases.

(c) Inequality Constraints: The Kuhn-Tucker Problem

In this section we consider problems of the form

$$\max_{x} \{ f(x); \, g(x) \geq \underline{0} \} \tag{P.K-T}$$

where $f: \mathbb{R}^n \supseteq X \longrightarrow \mathbb{R}$ and $g: \mathbb{R}^n \supseteq X \longrightarrow \mathbb{R}^c$ are C^2 functions. The only difference from the Lagrange problem is that the constraints are now written as weak inequalities, rather than equalities.

An inequality constraint, $g^i(x) \geq 0$, is *binding* or active at a feasible point x^o if it holds with equality $(g^i(x^0) = 0)$, and not binding or inactive if it holds with strict inequality. Intuitively, it is clear that only active constraints matter and that inactive ones have no effect on the local properties of an optimal solution. Hence, if we knew from the beginning which restrictions would be binding at an optimum, the Kuhn-Tucker problem would reduce to a Lagrange problem in which we would take the active constraints as equalities and ignore the rest.

As in the Lagrange case, a good recipe for remembering the first-order conditions consists in introducing a vector λ of multipliers, one for each constraint, and writing the Lagrangian

$$\pounds(x, \lambda) = f(x) + \lambda^T g(x)$$

Next, we proceed *as if* we wanted to maximize $\pounds(x, \lambda)$ with respect to x (without constraints) and minimize it with respect to λ subject to the non-negativity constraints $\lambda \geq \underline{0}$. This yields the following conditions:

$$D_x \pounds(x, \lambda) = Df(x) + \lambda^T Dg(x) = \underline{0} \qquad \text{(L)}$$

$$D_{\lambda_j} \pounds(x, \lambda) = g^j(x) \geq 0 \quad \text{and} \quad g^j(x) = 0 \quad \text{if } \lambda_j > 0$$
$$\lambda_j \geq 0 \quad \text{and} \quad \lambda_j = 0 \quad \text{if } g^j(x) > 0 \qquad \text{(C-S)}$$

or, equivalently,

$$\lambda_j \geq 0, \quad g^j(x) \geq 0, \quad \text{and} \quad \lambda_j g^j(x) = 0 \quad \text{for each } j = 1, \ldots, c \qquad \text{(C-S')}$$

That is, either the constraint is binding ($g^j(x) = 0$) or the associated multiplier is zero, or both. Moreover, if the multiplier is strictly positive, the constraint must be binding, and if the constraint is not binding, the multiplier must be zero.

The *complementary slackness conditions* (C-S) have a very intuitive economic interpretation. Let us return to our informal interpretation of the multipliers as shadow prices that measure the implicit cost, in terms of forgone profit, of resource-availability constraints. In this context, it is clear that if a constraint is not binding (we have more than we need of the resource), a further increase in the available quantity will not increase profit. On the other hand, if the multiplier is positive, an increase in the stock will increase profit. Clearly, this can be the case only if we did not have enough of the resource to begin with, that is, if the constraint is binding. In short, if we already have too much of something, any additional amount will be useless. And if we do not have enough, we should be willing to pay a positive price in order to get a bit more.

In what follows, we will adopt the following notational convention. We will renumber the constraint functions, $g^j(x)$, $j = 1, \ldots, c$, in such a way that the binding constraints come first. That is, if x^* is a feasible point, we arrange the constraints so that

$$g^j(x^*) = 0 \quad \text{for } j = 1, 2, \ldots, B \qquad \text{(binding constraints)}$$
$$g^j(x^*) > 0 \quad \text{for } j = B+1, \ldots, c \qquad \text{(nonbinding constraints)}$$

and define

$$g^b(x^*) = \left[g^1(x^*), \ldots, g^B(x^*) \right]^T = \text{vector of constraints active at } x^*$$
$$g^n(x^*) = \left[g^{B+1}(x^*), \ldots, g^C(x^*) \right]^T = \text{vector of constraints inactive at } x^*$$

We can therefore partition the vector of constraints as

$$g(x^*) = \begin{bmatrix} g^b(x^*) \\ g^n(x^*) \end{bmatrix}$$

and partition the vector of multipliers in a corresponding way

$$\lambda^T = \left(\lambda_b, \lambda_n \right)^T$$

Using this notation, the Lagrange condition

$$Df(x) + \lambda^T Dg(x) = \underline{0}$$

can be written

$$Df(x) + (\lambda_b, \lambda_n)\begin{bmatrix} Dg^b(x) \\ Dg^n(x) \end{bmatrix} = Df(x) + \lambda_b^T Dg^b(x) + \lambda_n^T Dg^n(x) = \underline{0} \qquad (1)$$

With this in mind, the condition

$$\text{rank } Dg^b(x) = B$$

can be interpreted almost exactly as in the Lagrange case, except that it now applies only to the constraints that are binding at an optimal solution of the problem.

Theorem 1.18. Kuhn-Tucker. Let x* *be an optimal solution to the Kuhn-Tucker problem*

$$\max_{x}\{f(x); \ g(x) \geq \underline{0}\} \qquad \text{(P.K-T)}$$

where f *and* g *are* C^1, *and rank* $Dg^b(x^*) = B \leq n$. *Then there exist nonnegative Lagrange multipliers* $\lambda^* \in \mathbb{R}^c_+$ *such that* (x*, λ*) *satisfy the following conditions:*

$$Df(x^*) + \lambda^{*T} Dg(x^*) = \underline{0} \qquad \text{(L)}$$

$$\forall j = 1, \ldots, c, \quad g^j(x) \geq 0 \quad \text{and} \quad g^j(x) = 0 \quad \text{if } \lambda_j > 0 \qquad \text{(C-S)}$$

and

$$\lambda_j \geq 0 \quad \text{and} \quad \lambda_j = 0 \quad \text{if } g^j(x) > 0$$

Proof. We partition the vector of choice variables,

$$x = (x_\alpha, x_\beta), \quad \text{with } x_\alpha = (x_1, \ldots, x_B) \quad \text{and} \quad x_\beta = (x_{B+1}, \ldots, x_n)$$

and the matrix $Dg^b(x)$ correspondingly,

$$Dg^b(x) = [D_\alpha g^b(x), D_\beta g^b(x)]$$

Relabeling the x_i's, if necessary, so that the $B \times B$ matrix $D_\alpha g^b(x)$ will have rank B (and therefore will be invertible), we can write the Lagrange condition (1) in the form

$$\begin{bmatrix} D_\alpha f(x) \\ D_\beta f(x) \end{bmatrix} + \begin{bmatrix} \lambda_b^T D_\alpha g^b(x) \\ \lambda_b^T D_\beta g^b(x) \end{bmatrix} + \lambda_n^T Dg^n(x) = \underline{0} \qquad (2)$$

We now define the multipliers as follows. First, we set to zero the multipliers associated with the inactive constraints,

$$\lambda_n^* = \underline{0}$$

Then the first B equations of (2) reduce to

$$D_\alpha f(x^*) + \lambda_b^T D_\alpha g^b(x^*) = \underline{0}$$

which we solve for

$$\lambda_b^{*T} = -D_\alpha f(x^*) \left[D_\alpha g^b(x^*) \right]^{-1} \tag{3}$$

It remains to show that the remaining equations in (2) hold for these values of the multipliers and that the multipliers are all nonnegative, that is,

$$D_\beta f(x^*) + \lambda_b^{*T} D_\beta g^b(x^*) = \underline{0} \quad \text{and} \quad \lambda_b^* \geq \underline{0} \tag{4}$$

The proof proceeds, as in the case of the Lagrange theorem, by showing that an optimal solution of the original problem will also solve a related but simpler maximization. Using the first-order conditions for this problem, we will establish (4).

(i) To eliminate the inequality constraints, we introduce a vector of slack variables, one for each constraint:

$$z = (z_1, \dots, z_c)^T = (z_b, z_n)^T$$

where $z_b \in \mathbb{R}^B$ and $z_n \in \mathbb{R}^{c-B}$ are the vectors of slack variables associated respectively with the binding and nonbinding constraints.

The original constraints, $g(x) \geq 0$, can then be written

$$g(x) - z = \underline{0} \quad \text{and} \quad z \geq \underline{0}$$

Moreover, if we restrict the value of x to a sufficiently small neighborhood of x^*, the continuity of the constraint functions implies that those constraints that are not binding at x^* will continue to be inactive in this region. That is, there exists some $\varepsilon > 0$ such that for all $x \in B_\varepsilon(x^*)$ we have

$$g^j(x) > 0 \; \forall \; j = B+1, \dots, c \quad \text{(or, equivalently, } z_n \gg \underline{0})$$

As long as we stay in this region, therefore, we can ignore the inactive constraints and focus on the active ones. These can be rewritten in the form

$$G(x, z_b) = g^b(x) - I z_b = \underline{0} \quad \text{and} \quad z_b \geq \underline{0} \tag{5}$$

where I is the $b \times b$ identity matrix.

Now, if x^* solves the Kuhn-Tucker problem

$$\max_x \{ f(x); \, g(x) \geq \underline{0} \} \tag{P.K-T}$$

the preceding discussion implies that it will also solve the problem

$$\max_x \{f(x);\ G(x, z_b) = \underline{0},\ z_b \geq \underline{0},\ x \in B_\varepsilon(x^*)\} \tag{P'}$$

(ii) Next, we apply the implicit-function theorem (IFT) to (5) in order to eliminate the binding constraints. We know that $x^* = (x_\alpha^*, x_\beta^*)$ satisfies (5) with $z_b^* = \underline{0}$ (that is, there is no slack for the active constraints at the optimum). Differentiating $G(\ )$ with respect to x_α, we have

$$D_\alpha G(x^*, z_b^*) = D_\alpha G(x^*, \underline{0}) = D_\alpha g^b(x^*)$$

By the rank assumption (constraint qualification), this is an invertible matrix. Hence, the assumptions of the IFT hold at $(x^*, z_b^*) = (x_\alpha^*, x_\beta^*, \underline{0})$ and the system (5) of active constraints implicitly defines x_α as a function $h(\ )$ of (x_β, z_b). That is, there exists a function

$$h : U_{\beta,z} \to U_\alpha, \quad \text{with } h(x_\beta, z_b) = x_\alpha \text{ s.th. } G[h(x_\beta, z_b), x_\beta, z_b] = \underline{0}$$

where U_α and $U_{\beta,z}$ are open balls centered respectively at x_α^* and $(x_\beta^*, \underline{0})$. The function $h(\ )$ assigns to each pair (x_β, z_b) the value of x_α that satisfies the constraints of (P').

Implicit differentiation of the identity

$$G[h(x_\beta, z_b), x_\beta, z_b] = g^b[h(x_\beta, z_b), x_\beta] - Iz_b \equiv \underline{0}$$

gives

$$D_\alpha g^b(x^*) D_\beta h(x_\beta^*, z_b^*) + D_\beta g^b(x^*) = \underline{0}$$

from where

$$D_\beta h(x_\beta^*, \underline{0}) = -[D_\alpha g^b(x^*)]^{-1} D_\beta g^b(x^*) \tag{6}$$

and

$$D_\alpha g^b(x^*) D_z h(x_\beta^*, z_b^*) - I = \underline{0}$$

implying

$$D_z h(x_\beta^*, \underline{0}) = [D_\alpha g^b(x^*)]^{-1} \tag{7}$$

We now define the function $F : U_{\beta,z} \longrightarrow \mathbb{R}$ by

$$F(x_\beta, z_b) = f[h(x_\beta, z_b), x_\beta]$$

and observe that the pair $(x_\beta^*, z_b^*) = (x_\beta^*, \underline{0})$ will be an optimal solution to the problem

$$\max_{x_\beta, z_b} \{F(x_\beta, z_b);\ z_b \geq \underline{0},\ (x_\beta, z_b) \in U_{\beta,z}\} \tag{P''}$$

and therefore will satisfy the first-order conditions

$$D_\beta F(x_\beta^*, z_b^*) = \underline{0} \quad \text{and} \quad D_z F(x_\beta^*, z_b^*) \leq \underline{0} \tag{8}$$

That is, for each $i = 1, \ldots, B$,

$$D_{z_i} F(x^*_\beta, z^*_b) \le 0 \quad \text{and} = 0 \quad \text{if } z_i > 0$$

$$z_i \ge 0 \quad \text{and} \quad = 0 \quad \text{if } D_{z_i} F(x^*_\beta, z^*_b) < 0$$

Using (8), we have

$$\underline{0} = D_\beta F(x^*_\beta, z^*_b) = D_\beta f[h(x^*_\beta, z^*_b), x^*_\beta] = D_\alpha f(x^*) D_\beta h(x^*_\beta, z^*_b) + D_\beta f(x^*)$$

$$= -D_\alpha f(x^*)[D_\alpha g^b(x^*)]^{-1} D_\beta g^b(x^*) + D_\beta f(x^*) \qquad [\text{by (6)}]$$

$$= \lambda^{*T}_b D_\beta g^b(x^*) + D_\beta f(x^*) = \underline{0} \qquad [\text{by (3)}]$$

which is one of the things we wanted to show.

Finally, the condition $D_z F(x^*_\beta, z^*_b) \le \underline{0}$ will guarantee the nonnegativity of the multipliers. Using the second part of (8),

$$\underline{0} \ge D_z F(x^*_\beta, z^*_b) = D_z f[h(x^*_\beta, z^*_b), x^*_\beta] = D_\alpha f(x^*) D_z h(x^*_\beta, z^*_b)$$

$$= D_\alpha f(x^*)[D_\alpha g^b(x^*)]^{-1} = -\lambda^{*T}_b \qquad [\text{by (7)}]$$

that is, $\lambda^{*T}_b \ge \underline{0}$.   □

Theorem 1.19. Sufficient conditions for a global maximum. Given the problem (P.K-T), assume that the objective function f( ) is pseudoconcave and that the constraint functions g^j( ) are all quasiconcave. Let (x*, λ*) be a pair of vectors that satisfy the necessary conditions given in the Kuhn-Tucker theorem (i.e., the Lagrange and complementary slackness conditions). Then x* is an optimal solution of (P.K-T).

The proof is the same as that for the corresponding theorem for the Lagrange problem, after observing that $\lambda^{*T}_n g^n(x^*) = \underline{0}$ by construction.

Theorem 1.20. Uniqueness. Let x* be an optimal solution of (P.K-T). If f is strictly quasiconcave and the constraint functions g^j( ) are all quasiconcave, then x* is the only optimal solution of (P.K-T).

Proof. This result follows from Theorem 1.11 (uniqueness for the convex-constraint-set problem), after observing that the feasible set $\{x; g(x) \ge 0\}$ is (the intersection of convex sets and therefore) convex by the quasiconcavity of the constraint functions.   □

Problem 1.21. Integral objective and constraint functions. Let $f: \mathbb{R}^{n+1} \longrightarrow \mathbb{R}$ and $g: \mathbb{R}^{n+1} \longrightarrow \mathbb{R}$ be C^1 functions, and consider the problem

$$\max_{x(s), s \in [a,b]} \left\{ \int_a^b f[x(s), s] \, ds \text{ s.t. } \int_a^b g[x(s), s] \, ds \ge 0 \right\} \qquad (\text{P.I})$$

This problem differs from the ones we have considered so far in that instead of choosing a finite set of decision variables, we must now choose an infinite number of them. In other words, the object of choice is no longer a vector in $\mathbb{R}^n$ but a continuum of them, as described by a function $x(s):$ $[a, b] \longrightarrow \mathbb{R}^n$, which, for each possible value of the state variable s, gives us the choice of the instruments x.

Using earlier results, we will derive necessary and sufficient conditions for an optimal solution of (P.I) that will closely resemble those applicable to a standard Kuhn-Tucker problem.

(i) The argument used to derive the first-order conditions for an optimum should be familiar by now. Let $x^*(s)$ be an optimal solution function for (P.I), and let us consider a feasible *variation* from this function. In particular, we will consider a two-parameter family of functions of the form

$$\tilde{x}(s) = x^*(s) + \alpha y(s) + \beta z(s)$$

where $y(s)$ and $z(s)$ are arbitrary functions from $\mathbb{R}$ to $\mathbb{R}^n$, and the parameters α and β will be chosen so that, given $y(\ )$ and $z(\ )$, the constraint holds. Now, consider the problem

$$\max_{\alpha, \beta} \{ F(\alpha, \beta) \} = \int_a^b f[\tilde{x}(s), s]\, ds \text{ s.t. } G(\alpha, \beta) = \int_a^b g[\tilde{x}(s), s]\, ds \geq 0 \qquad \text{(P.I')}$$

This problem is clearly related to the original one. Because $x^*(s)$ is optimal for (P.I), we know that the solution of the transformed problem involves setting α and β equal to zero. The reformulation is useful, however, in that we can use already familiar techniques to obtain necessary conditions for an optimum.

In particular, introduce a multiplier λ, define the function

$$\pounds(\alpha, \beta, \lambda) = \int_a^b \pounds_s[\tilde{x}(s), \lambda, s]\, ds = \int_a^b f[\tilde{x}(s), s] + \lambda g[\tilde{x}(s), s]\, ds$$

and use the Kuhn-Tucker theorem to derive the following first-order conditions:

$$D_x \pounds_s[x^*(s), \lambda, s] = D_x f[x^*(s), s] + \lambda D_x g[x^*(s), s] = \underline{0} \qquad \text{(K-T)}$$

$$\int_a^b g[x^*(s), s]\, ds \geq 0, \quad \text{and} \quad \int_a^b g[x^*(s), s]\, ds = 0, \quad \text{if } \lambda > 0$$

$$\lambda \geq 0, \quad \text{and} \quad \lambda = 0 \quad \text{if } \int_a^b g[x^*(s), s]\, ds > 0 \qquad \text{(C-S)}$$

Notice that (K-T) must hold separately for each $s \in [a, b]$. On the other hand, there is a unique multiplier λ that does not depend on s.

(ii) Assume that $f(x, s)$ and $g(x, s)$ are concave in x for each s, and let $x^*(s)$ be a choice function that satisfies the first-order conditions for the problem. Show that $x^*(s)$ solves (P.I).

(d) Concave Programming without Differentiability

Although the differentiability of the objective and constraint functions is a convenient assumption, the essence of many of the previous results goes through without it, as shown in the following theorems.

Theorem 1.22.   Let x* *be an optimal solution for the problem*

$$\max_{x}\{f(x);\ g(x) \geq \underline{0}\}\tag{P.K-T}$$

where $f : \mathbb{R}^n \supseteq X \longrightarrow \mathbb{R}$ *and each of the components of g,* $g^j : \mathbb{R}^n \supseteq X \longrightarrow$ $\mathbb{R}$, $j = 1, \ldots, c$, *are concave functions. Suppose further that there exists a point* $x' \in \mathbb{R}^n$ *such that* $g(x') \gg \underline{0}$. *Then there exists a vector of nonnegative multipliers* $\lambda^* \in \mathbb{R}^c_+$ *such that*

$$f(x^*) + \lambda^{*\mathrm{T}} g(x^*) \geq f(x) + \lambda^{*\mathrm{T}} g(x) \ \forall\, x$$
$$\lambda^*_j g^j(x^*) = 0 \quad \text{for each } j = 1, \ldots, c$$

The assumption that there exists a point x' in $\mathbb{R}^n$ such that $g^j(x') > 0$ for all j is known as Slater's constraint qualification, or *Slater's condition*, and it requires that the constraint set have a nonempty interior. The first necessary condition says that x^* maximizes the Lagrangian function $\pounds(x, \lambda^*) = f(x) + \lambda^{*T} g(x)$ given the "correct" value of the multipliers. When f and g are C^1, this reduces to the usual Lagrange condition.

Proof. Let x^* be an optimal solution of (P.K-T), and assume that the constraint qualification holds. We shall show that there exist nonnegative multipliers $\lambda_1, \ldots, \lambda_c$ with the required properties.
   Define the set Y by

$$Y = \{y = (y_0, y_1, \ldots, y_C) \in \mathbb{R}^{c+1};\ y_0 \leq f(x) \text{ and } y_j \leq g^j(x) \text{ for some } x\}\tag{1}$$

(i) Claim: Y is a convex set. Given two arbitrary points y' and y'' in Y, let x' and x'' be points that "work" for y' and y'' in the sense that they satisfy the inequalities in (1). To establish the convexity of Y, we will show that for any $\lambda \in (0, 1)$, the point $x^\lambda = (1 - \lambda)x' + \lambda x''$ works for $y^\lambda = (1 - \lambda)y' + \lambda y''$.
   By the concavity of f and each of the components of g, we have

$$y_0^\lambda = (1-\lambda)y_0' + \lambda y_0'' \leq (1-\lambda)f(x') + \lambda f(x'') \leq f(x^\lambda)$$
$$y_j^\lambda = (1-\lambda)y_j' + \lambda y_j'' \leq (1-\lambda)g^j(x') + \lambda g^j(x'') \leq g^j(x^\lambda) \quad \text{for each } j = 1, \ldots, c$$

Hence, $y^\lambda \in Y$, as we have found an x that works for it.

(ii) Claim: $y^* = (f(x^*), \underline{0}) \in \partial Y$. That is, the vector formed by the maximum value of the objective function and the zero vector in $\mathbb{R}^c$ belongs to the boundary of the set Y.
   We proceed by contradiction. Suppose y^* is not a boundary point of Y. Then (because it does belong to the set) y^* must be an interior point of Y. Hence, there exists some $\varepsilon > 0$ such that $B_\varepsilon(y^*) \subseteq Y$. That is, starting from $y^* = (f(x^*),$ $\underline{0})$, we can move a bit in any direction without leaving Y. In particular, we can increase the first component of y^* a little and still remain in Y. Hence, there exists some vector $\mu \in B_\varepsilon(y^*) \subseteq Y$ such that

$$\mu_0 > f(x^*) \quad \text{and} \quad \mu_j \geq 0 \; \forall \; j = 1, \ldots, c$$

But then, because $\mu \in Y$, there exists some vector $\hat{x}$ that "works" for it, that is, such that

$$f(\hat{x}) \geq \mu_0 > f(x^*) \quad \text{and} \quad g^j(\hat{x}) \geq \mu_j \geq 0 \; \forall \; j$$

Notice that $\hat{x}$ is a feasible point, with the property that $f(\hat{x}) > f(x^*)$. Because x^* maximizes f, this is impossible, and we have arrived at a contradiction.

(iii) By the supporting-hyperplane theorem (Theorem 1.25 in Chapter 6), Y has a supporting hyperplane through the point y^*, that is, there exists a vector $p \neq \underline{0}$ in $\mathbb{R}^{c+1}$ such that

$$py^* = p_0 f(x^*) + \sum_{j=1}^{c} p_j 0 \leq p_0 y_0 + \sum_{j=1}^{c} p_j y_j \quad \text{for every } y \text{ in } Y \qquad (2)$$

(iv) Claim: $p_j \leq 0$ for all $j = 0, \ldots, c$. Notice that if $y \in Y$, then any point of the form $y - c$, where c is a vector with nonnegative components, belongs to Y. To establish the claim, we proceed by contradiction. Suppose $p_j > 0$ for some j, and choose c_j so that $p_j - c_j$ is a large negative number. Clearly, we can always choose c_j large enough that

$$p_0 f(x^*) \leq p_0(y_0 - c_0) + \sum_{j=1}^{c} p_j(y_j - c_j)$$

does not hold.

(v) Clearly, $(f(x), g(x)) \in Y$ for any x. Hence, (2) implies

$$p_0 f(x^*) \leq p_0 f(x) + \sum_{j=1}^{c} p_j g^j(x) \quad \text{for any } x \qquad (3)$$

(vi) Claim: $p_0 < 0$. By contradiction with the Slater condition. Suppose $p_0 = 0$ (we already know it cannot be strictly positive). Then, by (3),

$$\sum_{j=1}^{c} p_j g^j(x) \geq 0 \; \forall \; x \qquad (4)$$

We will now show that this contradicts the Slater condition. Notice that because $p_j \leq 0$ for all j, and not all the p_j's can be zero, there is at least one k such that $p_k < 0$. Next, let x' be a point such that $g^j(x') > 0$ for all j (this point exists by the Slater condition). Then (4) cannot hold for x' (because $p_k g^k(x') < 0$ and $p_j g^j(x') \leq 0$ for all $j \neq k$, the sum of these terms must be strictly negative).

(vii) Define λ^* by

$$\lambda_0^* = 1 \quad \text{and} \quad \lambda_j^* = \frac{p_j}{p_0} \geq 0 \quad \text{for } j = 1, \ldots, c$$

Then, dividing both sides of (3) by $p_0 < 0$ (which reverses the inequality), we obtain

$$f(x^*) \geq f(x) + \sum_{j=1}^{c} \lambda_j^* g^j(x) \quad \text{for any } x \qquad (5)$$

Moreover, with $x = x^*$, (5) implies that

$$\sum\nolimits_{j=1}^{c} \lambda_j^* g^j(x^*) \leq 0$$

and in fact

$$\sum\nolimits_{j=1}^{c} \lambda_j^* g^j(x^*) = 0 \tag{6}$$

because $g^j(x^*) \geq 0$ and $\lambda_j^* \geq 0$ for all j. For the same reason, each one of the terms of this sum must be nonnegative (i.e., $\lambda_j^* g^j(x^*) \geq 0 \; \forall j$), but if any of them is strictly positive, the equality in (6) cannot hold. Hence, it must be that

$$\lambda_j^* g^j(x) = 0 \; \forall j$$

Using (5) and (6), we can now write

$$\pounds(x^*, \lambda^*) = f(x^*) + \lambda^{*T} g(x^*) \geq f(x) + \lambda^{*T} g(x) = \pounds(x, \lambda^*)$$

for any x. That is, x^* maximizes $\pounds(x, \lambda^*)$. ☐

Theorem 1.23. *Consider the problem (P.K-T): $\max_x \{f(x); \; g(x) \geq 0\}$. Assume that there exist vectors $x^* \in \mathbb{R}^n$ and $\lambda^* \in \mathbb{R}_+^c$ such that x^* is feasible (i.e., $g(x^*) \geq 0$), and*

$$f(x^*) + \lambda^{*T} g(x^*) \geq f(x) + \lambda^{*T} g(x) \; \forall \, x \tag{1}$$

$$\lambda_j^* g^j(x^*) = 0 \quad \text{for each } j = 1, \ldots, c \tag{2}$$

Then x^* is an optimal solution to (P.K-T).

Notice that nothing is said about the concavity of the objective and constraint functions, or about a constraint qualification.

Proof. We want to show that x^* maximizes f subject to the constraints $g(x) \geq \underline{0}$. By assumption, x^* is feasible. By (1),

$$f(x^*) + \lambda^{*T} g(x^*) \geq f(x) + \lambda^{*T} g(x)$$

for all x, but because $\lambda^{*T} g(x^*) = 0$, by (2), we have

$$f(x^*) \geq f(x) + \lambda^{*T} g(x)$$

for any x. Finally, because $g(x) \geq \underline{0}$ for all feasible points and $\lambda^* \geq \underline{0}$, we have $\lambda^{*T} g(x) \geq 0$ for all feasible x, and therefore

$$f(x^*) \geq f(x)$$

for all x with $g(x) \geq \underline{0}$; that is, x^* solves (P.K-T). ☐

2. Comparative Statics and Value Functions

Let us now reintroduce the parameters into the analysis and consider the following family of nonlinear programming problems:

$$\max_{x \in C(\alpha)} f(x, \alpha) \qquad (P.\alpha)$$

For given values of the parameters α^0, we can solve $(P.\alpha)$ for the optimal values x^* of the choice variables (assuming a solution exists). A change in α can then be expected to lead to a new optimal solution. Solving the problem for each value of the parameters, we construct its solution correspondence,

$$S(\alpha) = \arg \max_{x \in C(\alpha)} f(\alpha, x)$$

and substituting $S(\ )$ into the objective function, we obtain the problem's value function:

$$V(\alpha) = \max_{x \in C(\alpha)} f(\alpha, x) = f(x^*, \alpha), \quad \text{where } x^* \in S(\alpha)$$

Notice that $V(\ )$ is always a well-defined function (i.e., it is single-valued even if $S(\alpha)$ is not) because all maximizers x in $S(\alpha)$ yield the same value of the objective function by definition. In fact, $S(\ )$ and $V(\ )$ are related by the following expression:

$$S(\alpha) = \arg \max_{x \in C(\alpha)} f(\alpha, x) = \{x \in C(\alpha); f(x, \alpha) = V(\alpha)\}$$

In the first part of this section we will establish an important theorem that gives sufficient conditions for the solution of $(P.\alpha)$ to change continuously with the parameters. We will then strengthen these conditions in order to ensure that the solution correspondence $S(\alpha)$ is (at least locally) a well-defined and smooth function $x^* = x(\alpha)$, and we shall develop a method for analyzing the comparative-statics properties of this function. In the remainder of the section, we will review some useful results on value functions.

(a) The Theorem of the Maximum

Theorem 2.1. Berge's theorem of the maximum. Given sets $X \subseteq \mathbb{R}^n$ *and* $\Omega \subseteq \mathbb{R}^P$, *let* $f : X \times \Omega \longrightarrow \mathbb{R}$ *be a continuous function, and* $C : \Omega \rightarrow\!\!\!\rightarrow X$ *a compact-valued and continuous correspondence, and consider the parameterized maximization problem*

$$\max_{x \in C(\alpha)} f(x, \alpha) \qquad (P.\alpha)$$

Then the value function

$$V(\alpha) = \max_{x \in C(\alpha)} f(x, \alpha) \qquad (1)$$

is continuous, and the solution correspondence $S : \Omega \rightarrow\!\!\!\rightarrow X,$

$$S(\alpha) = arg\max_{x \in C(\alpha)} = \{x \in C(\alpha);\ f(x, \alpha) = V(\alpha)\} \tag{2}$$

is nonempty, compact-valued, and upper-hemicontinuous (uhc).

Proof. Fix some $\alpha \in \Omega$. By assumption, the set $C(\alpha)$ is nonempty and compact, and $f(\cdot, \alpha)$ is continuous. By the extreme-value theorem (Theorem 8.22 in Chapter 2), $f(\ )$ achieves a maximum in the set $C(\alpha)$, and $S(\alpha)$ is nonempty. Moreover, because $S(\alpha)$ is a subset of the compact set $C(\alpha)$, it is bounded. We will now show that it is also closed and therefore compact itself (by Theorem 8.14 in Chapter 2).

Consider a convergent sequence of maximizers for the given α, $\{x_n\}$, with $x_n \in S(\alpha)$, and let x be the limit of this sequence. We want to show that $x \in S(\alpha)$, that is, that $S(\alpha)$ is closed (see Theorem 4.13 in Chapter 2). Now, because $C(\alpha)$ is closed by assumption, and $\{x_n\}$ is contained in it, it follows that $x \in C(\alpha)$ (i.e., that x is feasible). Notice also that $V(\alpha) = f(x_n, \alpha)$ for all x_n, because all x_n are maximizers. Because $f(\ )$ is continuous, it follows that $f(x, \alpha) = \lim_{n\to\infty} f(x_n, \alpha) = V(\alpha)$ (i.e., that x is also a maximizer). Hence, $x \in S(\alpha)$, as was to be shown, and we conclude that $S(\alpha)$ is compact.

Next, we show that S is upper-hemicontinuous (uhc). Because S has just been shown to be compact-valued, we can use the sequential characterization of upper hemicontinuity (Theorem 11.2 in Chapter 2). Fix α, let $\{\alpha_n\}$ be an arbitrary sequence with limit α, and choose a companion sequence $\{x_n\}$ with $x_n \in S(\alpha_n) \subseteq C(\alpha_n)$ for each n. To establish that S is uhc, we have to show that $\{x_n\}$ has a convergent subsequence with limit in $S(\alpha)$.

Because $C(\ )$ is uhc, there exists a subsequence $\{x_{n_k} \in S(\alpha_{n_k}) \subseteq C(\alpha_{n_k})\}$ converging to some point $x \in C(\alpha)$. Next, let z be an arbitrary point in $C(\alpha)$. Because $C(\ )$ is also lhc, $\{\alpha_{n_k}\}$ has a companion sequence $\{z_{n_k};\ z_{n_k} \in C(\alpha_{n_k})\}$ that converges to z (by Theorem 11.3 in Chapter 2). Now, because x_{n_k} is optimal for α_{n_k}, whereas z_{n_k} is only assured to be feasible, we have $f(x_{n_k}, \alpha_{n_k}) \geq f(z_{n_k}, \alpha_{n_k})$ for each k. Taking limits of both sides of this inequality, the continuity of $f(\ )$ implies that $f(x, \alpha) \geq f(z, \alpha)$. Because z was an arbitrary feasible point, it follows that x is a maximizer of f in $C(\alpha)$ (i.e., that $x \in S(\alpha)$). Hence, $S(\ )$ is uhc.

Finally, we show that the value function is continuous. For this, we can use the fact that the composition of two uhc correspondences is uhc (Theorem 11.13 in Chapter 2). Notice that $V(\ )$ can be written in the form

$$V(\alpha) = \max_{x \in C(\alpha)} f(x, \alpha) = f(S(\alpha), \alpha)$$

where $S(\alpha)$ is the set of maximizers for α. Hence, $V(\ )$ is the composition of a continuous function $f(\ )$ and a uhc correspondence $S(\ )$. Because a continuous function can be considered a uhc (single-valued) correspondence, it follows that $V(\ )$ is uhc. But we also know that $V(\ )$ is single-valued, and this implies that it is a continuous function. $\qquad\qquad\qquad\qquad\qquad\qquad\square$

The maximum theorem says that the set of maximizers and the value of the problem change continuously with the parameters provided the objective function is continuous and the constraint correspondence is compact-valued and continuous. Of these conditions, the one most difficult to check is the last. Our next result shows that the constraint correspondence in standard Kuhn-Tucker problems is continuous under certain assumptions. The strategy of the proof can be adapted to establish the continuity of correspondences in some other cases of interest.

Theorem 2.2. Given sets $\mathrm{X} \subseteq \mathbb{R}^n$ *and* $\Omega \subseteq \mathbb{R}^P$, *where* X *is convex, let* $g^i(x, \alpha):\times \Omega \longrightarrow \mathbb{R}$ *be a continuous function that is concave in* x *for given* α *for all* $i = 1, \ldots, c$, *and define the correspondence* $\mathrm{C}: \Omega \rightarrow\rightarrow \mathrm{X}$ *by*

$$C(\alpha) = \{x \in \mathrm{X};\ g^i(x, \alpha) \geq 0\ \forall\, i = 1, \ldots, c\}$$

Let $C(\alpha^0)$ *be compact, and assume that there exists some point* $x' \in C(\alpha^0)$ *such that* $g^i(x', \alpha^0) > 0$ *for all* i; *then* $C(\ )$ *is continuous at* α^0.

In the proof of Theorem 2.2 we will make use of the following two lemmas. We will prove both of them under the assumption that there is a single constraint $(c = 1)$ and leave the extension to the general case as an exercise.

Lemma 2.3. Under the assumptions of Theorem 2.2, the set

$$C_\varepsilon(\alpha^0) = \{x \in \mathrm{X};\ g^i(x, \alpha^0) + \varepsilon \geq 0 \text{ for } i = 1, \ldots, c\}$$

is compact for all $\varepsilon > 0$.

Proof. Assume there is a single constraint of the form $g(x, \alpha) \geq 0$, and fix some arbitrary $\varepsilon > 0$. Then $C_\varepsilon(\alpha^0)$ is a closed set because it is the inverse image of the closed set $[-\varepsilon, \infty)$ under the continuous function $g(\cdot, \alpha^0)$. To show that $C_\varepsilon(\alpha^0)$ is bounded (and therefore compact), we will proceed by contradiction.

Suppose $C_\varepsilon(\alpha^0)$ is unbounded. Then there exists a sequence $\{x_n\}$, with $x_n \in C_\varepsilon(\alpha^0)$ for all n (i.e., with $g(x_n, \alpha^0) \geq -\varepsilon$), such that $\{\|x_n\|\} \to \infty$. We know that there exists some $x' \in C(\alpha^0)$ such that $g(x', \alpha^0) = m > 0$. Observe that there exists some $\lambda \in (0, 1)$ such that

$$(1 - \lambda)m - \lambda\varepsilon > 0 \tag{1}$$

(it is enough to choose $0 < \lambda < m/(m + \varepsilon) < 1$). We will use this λ together with x' and $\{x_n\}$ to construct a sequence $\{y_n\}$ of points in $C(\alpha^0)$ that diverges to infinity in norm, contradicting the assumed boundedness of $C(\alpha^0)$.

Let

$$y_n = (1-\lambda)x' + \lambda x_n$$

Then, by the concavity of $g(\ )$ in x, and using (1), we have

$$g(y_n, \alpha^0) = g((1-\lambda)x' + \lambda x_n, \alpha^0) \geq (1-\lambda)g(x', \alpha^0) + \lambda g(x_n, \alpha^0)$$
$$\geq (1-\lambda)m - \lambda\varepsilon > 0$$

Hence $y_n \in C(\alpha^0)$ for all n. On the other hand,

$$\|y_n\| = \|(1-\lambda)x' + \lambda x_n\| \to \infty \quad \text{as } n \to \infty$$

because $\{\|x_n\|\} \to \infty$. This establishes that $C(\alpha^0)$ is unbounded, contradicting our assumptions. $\square$

Lemma 2.4. Under the assumptions of Theorem 2.2, for every $\varepsilon > 0$ there exists some $\delta > 0$ such that $C(\alpha) \subseteq C_\varepsilon(\alpha^0)$ for all $\alpha \in B_\delta(\alpha^0)$.

Proof. By contradiction. Suppose the result does not hold; then there exists some $\varepsilon > 0$, a parameter sequence $\{\alpha_n\} \to \alpha^0$, and a companion sequence $\{x_n\}$, with $x_n \in C(\alpha_n)$ and $x_n \notin C_\varepsilon(\alpha^0)$ for all n. We have, then,

$$g(x_n, \alpha_n) \geq 0 \tag{1}$$

and

$$g(x_n, \alpha^0) < -\varepsilon \tag{2}$$

for all n. On the other hand, we know that there exists some point x' such that

$$g(x', \alpha^0) > 0 \tag{3}$$

and this implies, by the continuity of $g(x, \cdot)$ and the fact that $\{\alpha_n\} \to \alpha^0$, that there exists some N such that

$$g(x', \alpha_n) > 0 \; \forall \, n > N \tag{4}$$

Using the continuity of $g(\cdot, \alpha^0)$, (2) and (3) imply that for each n there exists some point y_n of the form

$$y_n = (1-\lambda_n)x' + \lambda_n x_n, \quad \text{with } \lambda_n \in (0,1) \tag{5}$$

such that

$$g(y_n, \alpha^0) = -\varepsilon \tag{6}$$

Hence $y_n \in C_\varepsilon(\alpha^0)$ for all n. Moreover, the concavity of $g(\ )$ in x implies that

$$g(y_n, \alpha_n) = g((1-\lambda_n)x' + \lambda_n x_n, \alpha_n) \geq (1-\lambda_n)g(x', \alpha_n) + \lambda_n g(x_n, \alpha_n) > 0 \tag{7}$$

for all $n > N$, and it follows that

$$y_n \in C(\alpha_n) \, \forall \, n > N$$

Now, because $\{y_n\}$ is contained in $C_\varepsilon(\alpha^0)$ and this set is compact by Lemma 2.3, it follows (by Theorem 8.5 in Chapter 2) that this sequence has a convergent subsequence $\{y_{n_k}\}$, with limit y in $C_\varepsilon(\alpha^0)$.

Finally, consider the limit of this subsequence. By (6) and the continuity of $g(\ )$, we have

$$g(y, \alpha^0) = \lim_{k \to \infty} g(y_{n_k}, \alpha^0) = -\varepsilon$$

On the other hand, (7) implies that

$$g(y, \alpha^0) = \lim_{k \to \infty} g(y_{n_k}, \alpha) \geq 0$$

which contradicts the previous statement. □

Proof of Theorem 2.2

- *Upper hemicontinuity*: Fix some $\varepsilon > 0$. By Lemmas 2.3 and 2.4 there exists some $\delta > 0$ such that $C(\alpha)$ is contained in the compact set $C_\varepsilon(\alpha^0)$ for all $\alpha \in B_\delta(\alpha^0)$. Thus, $C(\alpha)$ is bounded for all $\alpha \in B_\delta(\alpha^0)$. Moreover, these sets are all closed, because they are inverse images of the closed set $[0, \infty) \times \ldots \times [0, \infty)$ under a continuous function. Hence, $C(\alpha)$ is compact for each $\alpha \in B_\delta(\alpha^0)$.

  Because the correspondence $C(\ )$ is compact-valued in $B_\delta(\alpha^0)$, to establish its upper hemicontinuity at α^0 it suffices (by Theorem 11.2 in Chapter 2) to show that given any sequence $\{\alpha_n\}$ in $B_\delta(\alpha^0)$ converging to α^0, every companion sequence $\{x_n\}$, with $x_n \in C(\alpha_n)$ for each n, has a convergent subsequence with limit in $C(\alpha^0)$.

  Let $\{\alpha_n\} \to \alpha^0$ be contained in $B_\delta(\alpha^0)$, and consider an arbitrary companion sequence $\{x_n\}$, with $x_n \in C(\alpha_n)$ for each n (i.e., $g^i(x_n, \alpha_n) \geq 0$ for all i and n). Because $C(\alpha_n) \subseteq C_\varepsilon(\alpha^0)$ for all n, $\{x_n\}$ is contained in the compact set $C_\varepsilon(\alpha^0)$ and therefore contains a convergent subsequence $\{x_{n_k}\}$, with limit x in $C_\varepsilon(\alpha^0)$. Hence $\{(x_{n_k}, \alpha_{n_k})\} \to (x, \alpha^0)$, and by the continuity of $g^i(\ )$ it follows that

$$g^i(x, \alpha^0) = \lim_{k \to \infty} g^i(x_{nk}, \alpha_{nk}) \geq 0$$

  for all i. This implies that $x \in C(\alpha^0)$, as was to be shown.

- *Lower hemicontinuity*. We will prove the result under the assumption that there is a single constraint (i.e., $c = 1$). The extension to the general case is straightforward.

  Let $\{\alpha_n\} \to \alpha^0$, and consider an arbitrary point $x \in C(\alpha^0)$. We want to show that there exists a companion sequence $\{x_n; x_n \in C(\alpha_n)\}$ that converges to x. Notice that because we are concerned only with the limit of this sequence, we can define a finite number of its initial terms arbitrarily.

  We will consider two cases in turn.

- Case (i): $g(x, \alpha^0) > 0$. Because $g(\ )$ is continuous, there exists some $\varepsilon > 0$ such that

$$g(y, \alpha) > 0 \ \forall \ (y, \alpha) \in B_\varepsilon(x, \alpha^0) \tag{1}$$

Consider the sequence $\{(x, \alpha_n)\}$. Because $\{(x, \alpha_n)\} \to (x, \alpha^0)$, there exists some N such that $(x, \alpha_n) \in B_\varepsilon(x, \alpha^0)$ for all $n \geq N$. By (1), this implies that

$$g(x, \alpha_n) > 0 \ \forall \ n \geq N$$

(i.e., that $x \in C(\alpha_n)$ for all $n \geq N$). Hence, we can construct the sequence $\{x_n\}$ as follows:

$$x_n = \begin{cases} x & \text{if } n \geq N \\ \text{an arbitrary } y_n \in C(\alpha_n) & \text{if } n < N \end{cases}$$

Notice that by construction $\{x_n\} \to x$ and $x_n \in C(\alpha_n)$ for all n, as we wanted to show.

- Case (ii): $g(x, \alpha^0) = 0$. We know that there exists some x' such that $g(x', \alpha^0) > 0$ and that $g(\ )$ is concave in x for given α.

  Hence, the set

$$C(\alpha^0) = \{x \in X; \ g(x, \alpha^0) \geq 0\}$$

is convex, and it follows that the line segment $[x, x']$ is contained in $C(\alpha^0)$. Moreover, for any point in (x, x'),

$$x^\lambda = (1 - \lambda)x + \lambda x', \quad \text{with } \lambda \in (0, 1) \tag{1}$$

the concavity of $g(\cdot, \alpha^0)$ implies that

$$g(x^\lambda, \alpha^0) \geq (1 - \lambda)g(x, \alpha^0) + \lambda g(x', \alpha^0) > 0 \tag{2}$$

Consider a sequence of points of the form (1), $\{y_k\} \subseteq (x, x')$, such that

$$\|y_k - x\| < 1/k$$

for each positive integer k. (To obtain such a sequence, it is enough to choose $0 < \lambda_k < 1/(k\|x' - x\|)$ in (1).) Observe that by construction $\{y_k\} \to x$ and that $g(y_k, \alpha^0) > 0$, by (2). This last expression implies (by the continuity of $g(y_k, \cdot)$ and the fact that $\{\alpha_n\} \to \alpha^0$) that for each given k there exists some positive integer n_k such that

$$g(y_k, \alpha_n) > 0 \ \forall \ n \geq n_k \tag{3}$$

Notice, moreover, that we can choose n_k as large as we want and that, in particular, we can choose it so that $n_k > n_{k-1}$ for all k.

We will now construct the desired sequence $\{x_n\}$ as follows: For $n < n_1$, let x_n be some arbitrary point in $C(\alpha_n)$; for $n_1 \leq n < n_2$, put $x_n = y_1$, and, in general, for $n_k \leq n < n_{k+1}$ let $x_n = y_k$. Because $x_n \in C(\alpha_n)$ by construction (see (3)), it only remains to show that $\{x_n\} \to x$.

Fix some arbitrary $\varepsilon > 0$. Then there exists some integer M such that $1/M < \varepsilon$. We will show that for all $n > n_M$ we have $\|x_n - x\| < \varepsilon$. Let $n > n_M$; then n lies between n_k and n_{k+1} for some $k > M$.
Hence,

$$x_n = y_k \quad \text{and} \quad \|x_n - x\| = \|y_k - x\| < 1/k < 1/M < \varepsilon$$

which establishes the theorem. $\qquad\qquad\qquad\qquad\qquad\qquad\qquad\qquad\qquad\qquad \Box$

Problem 2.5. Extend the proof of Lemmas 2.3 and 2.4 to the case of several constraints.

Problem 2.6. We will give an alternative proof of the lower hemicontinuity of $C(\ )$ under the assumptions of Theorem 2.2.

(i) Assume first that there is a single constraint. We will construct a sequence $\{x_n\}$ of the form

$$x_n = \begin{cases} x & \text{if } x \in C(\alpha_n), \text{ i.e., if } g(x, \alpha_n) \geq 0 \\ x_n \in C(\alpha_n) \text{ s.th. } g(x_n, \alpha_n) = 0 & \text{if } g(x, \alpha_n) < 0 \end{cases} \qquad (1)$$

for n larger than some N, and set x_n equal to an arbitrary point in $C(\alpha_n)$ for $n \leq N$. To set N, recall that by assumption there exists a point $x' \in C(\alpha)$ such that $g(\alpha, x') > 0$. Because $\{\alpha_n\} \to \alpha$ and $g(\ )$ is continuous in α for given x, there is some N such that $g(x', \alpha_n) > 0$ for all $n > N$. Use the continuity of $g(\cdot, \alpha_n)$ to show that for $n > N$ we can choose $x_n = (1 - \lambda_n)x + \lambda_n x'$ for some $\lambda_n \in (0, 1)$ whenever $g(x, \alpha_n) < 0$.

(ii) To complete the proof we have to show that $\{x_n\} \to x$. Suppose first that there exists some integer M such that $g(x, \alpha_n) > 0$ for all $n > M$. Then, according to (1), we have $x_n = x$ for all $n > M$, and the sequence clearly converges to the desired point. If this is not the case, then $\{\alpha_n\}$ must have a subsequence $\{\alpha_{n_k}\}$ with the property that $g(x, \alpha_{n_k}) < 0$ for all n_k, and because $g(\ )$ is continuous and $\{\alpha_{n_k}\} \to \alpha$, we have:

$$\lim_{n_k \to \infty} g(x, \alpha_{n_k}) = g(x, \alpha) \leq 0$$

Because $x \in C(\alpha)$ implies $g(x, \alpha) \geq 0$, moreover, it must be the case that

$$g(x, \alpha) = 0 \qquad (2)$$

To show that $\{x_n = (1 - \lambda_n)x + \lambda_n x'\} \to x$, consider the sequence $\{\lambda_n\}$, and notice that $\{x_n\} \to x$ if and only if $\{\lambda_n\} \to 0$. Assume that $\{\lambda_n\} \not\to 0$, and use the concavity of $g(\ )$ in x to obtain a contradiction.

(iii) Extend the proof to the case of several constraint functions. $\qquad\qquad \Box$

The following problems show that the upper hemicontinuity of $C(\alpha)$ can be established under other sets of assumptions.

Problem 2.7. Given sets $X \subseteq \mathbb{R}^n$ and $\Omega \subseteq \mathbb{R}^P$, let $g^i(x, \alpha) : X \times \Omega \longrightarrow \mathbb{R}$ be a continuous function for all $I = 1, \ldots, c$, and define the correspondence $C : \Omega \longrightarrow\!\!\!\longrightarrow X$ by

$$C(\alpha) = \{x \in X; \ \|x\| \leq B \text{ and } g^i(x, \alpha) \geq 0 \ \forall i = 1, \ldots, c\}$$

Show that $C(\ )$ is uhc at each α.

One of the crucial steps in the proof that the correspondence defined in Problem 2.7 is uhc is establishing that given an arbitrary sequence of parameters $\{\alpha_n\} \to \alpha$, any companion sequence of feasible choices $\{x_n\}$, with $x_n \in C(\alpha_n)$ for each n, has a convergent subsequence. The desired result then follows easily by the continuity of the constraint functions $g^i(\ )$. In the preceding problem, the existence of such a convergent subsequence was guaranteed by the assumption that the constraint set was contained within a "fixed" bounded set for all parameter values. The following problem shows how this assumption can be relaxed, at the expense of introducing additional assumptions on the constraint functions.

Problem 2.8. Given sets $X \subseteq \mathbb{R}^n$ and $\Omega \subseteq \mathbb{R}^P$, with $X \times \Omega$ convex, let $g^i(x, \alpha) : X \times \Omega \longrightarrow \mathbb{R}$ be a continuous and concave function (in (x, α)) for all $i = 1, \ldots, c$, and define the correspondence $C : \Omega \longrightarrow\!\!\!\longrightarrow X$ by

$$C(\alpha) = \{x \in X; \ g^i(x, \alpha) \geq 0 \ \forall i = 1, \ldots, c\}$$

Fix a value α^0 of the parameter vector and assume that $C(\alpha^0)$ is bounded. Let $\{\alpha_n\}$ be an arbitrary sequence converging to α^0, and consider a companion sequence $\{x_n\}$ with $x_n \in C(\alpha_n)$ for each n. Show that $\{x_n\}$ is bounded.

Hint: By contradiction. Suppose $\{x_n\}$ is unbounded. Then it has a subsequence that diverges to infinity in norm. To simplify the notation, assume that the sequence itself diverges in norm (i.e., that $\{\|x_n\|\} \to \infty$). Consider the sequence $\{X_n\} = \{(x_n, \alpha_n)\}$. Because $\{\|x_n\|\} \to \infty$, it follows that $\{\|X_n\|\} \to \infty$.

Construct a new sequence $\{Y_n\}$ by "projecting" $\{X_n\}$ onto the boundary of a ball in $X \times \Omega$ whose interior contains the set $C(\alpha^0) \times \{\alpha^0\}$. The resulting sequence will be bounded and will therefore have a convergent subsequence. Take the limit of this subsequence and seek a contradiction.

Problem 2.9. For each α and each $\varepsilon > 0$, define the set $\underline{C}_\varepsilon(\alpha)$ by

$$\underline{C}_\varepsilon(\alpha) = \{x \in X; \ g^i(x, \alpha) - \varepsilon \geq 0 \ \forall i = 1, \ldots, c\}$$

Show that, under the assumptions of Theorem 2.2, for every $\varepsilon > 0$ there exists some $\delta > 0$ such that $C(\alpha) \supseteq \underline{C}_\varepsilon(\alpha^0)$ for all $\alpha \in B_\delta(\alpha^0)$.

Notice that if ε is sufficiently large, $\underline{C}_\varepsilon(\alpha)$ will be empty, but the result still holds, because the empty set is a subset of every set by convention.

(b) Comparative Statics of Smooth Optimization Problems

We are often interested in determining how the behavior of an agent will vary in response to changes in some of the parameters that describe his "environment." For example, how would a change in the price of a certain good affect its demand by an optimizing consumer? Mathematically the problem reduces to that of determining the signs of the partial derivatives of the decision function,

$$x(\alpha) = \arg \max_{x \in C(\alpha)} f(x, \alpha)$$

with respect to the parameters $\partial x_i^*/\partial \alpha_k$).

In this section we discuss the traditional method of approaching this problem. Our assumptions will ensure that $x(\ )$ is a differentiable function defined implicitly as the solution to a system of equations – the first-order necessary conditions (FONCs) for the problem. Hence, the method discussed in Chapter 5 can be applied. After checking that the conditions of the implicit-function theorem (IFT) hold, we differentiate the first-order conditions implicitly with respect to the parameters, solve for the partials of interest, and try to sign them with the help of the sufficient conditions for an optimum.

In order for this method to be applicable, we need to impose the following assumptions on the optimization problem:

(i) $f(\ )$ and $g(\ )$ are C^2 functions. Because we need to differentiate the FONCs, which involve first derivatives of f and g, these functions must be C^2 for $x(\ )$ to be C^1.

(ii) The solution to the programming problem is a regular maximum (i.e., it satisfies the sufficient conditions for a strict local maximum). This assumption ensures that the matrix obtained by differentiating the system of FONCs with respect to the choice variables x will be invertible, thus allowing us to use the IFT, and it will also be helpful when it comes to signing the comparative-statics partials.

Consider the unconstrained maximization problem

$$\max_x f(x, \alpha) \tag{P}$$

where f is a C^2 function of n variables, and fix the vector of parameters at α^0. Then the first-order condition for a maximum,

$$D_x f(x, \alpha^0) = \underline{0} \tag{1}$$

is a system of n equations in the unknown optimal values of the n instruments. Assume that x^0 is a regular maximizer of f for α^0, that is, a solution of (1) such that the Hessian matrix of f evaluated at (x^0, α^0), $H = D_x^2 f(x^0, \alpha^0)$, is negative definite. Then

$$D_x f(x^0, \alpha^0) = \underline{0} \quad \text{and} \quad |H| = |D_x[D_x f(x^0, \alpha^0)]| = |D_x^2 f(x^0, \alpha^0)| \neq 0$$

That is, the conditions of the IFT hold at (x^0, α^0).[3] Hence, the solution mapping for the maximization problem, $x^* = x(\alpha)$, is locally a well-defined and smooth function. Substituting $x(\ )$ into the first-order conditions, we obtain the identity

$$D_x f[x(\alpha), \alpha] \equiv \underline{0} \tag{2}$$

Differentiating with respect to α,

$$D_x^2 f(x^0, \alpha^0) Dx(\alpha^0) + D_{x\alpha} f(x^0, \alpha^0) = \underline{0}$$

and solving for $D_x(\alpha^0)$,

$$Dx(\alpha^0) = -[D_x^2 f(x^0, \alpha^0)]^{-1} D_{x\alpha} f(x^0, \alpha^0)$$

Finally, using Cramer's rule,

$$\frac{\partial x_i^*}{\partial \alpha_k} = -\frac{|H_i|}{|H|}$$

where $|H_i|$ is the determinant of the matrix obtained by replacing the ith column of the Hessian with the kth column of $D_{x\alpha} f(x^0, \alpha^0)$, that is, the partials of the form $(\partial^2 f(x^0, \alpha^0)/\partial x_j \partial \alpha_k)$ for $j = 1, \ldots, n$. Notice that the sign of $|H|$ will be determined by the assumption that the Hessian is negative definite, so we only have to worry about the sign of $|H_i|$.[4]

A similar procedure will work for the parameterized Lagrange problem

$$\max_x \{f(x, \alpha); \ g(x, \alpha) = \underline{0}\} \tag{P.L}$$

where f and g are C^2 functions. When $\alpha = \alpha^0$, the Lagrangian for this problem is

$$\pounds(x, \lambda; \alpha^0) = f(x, \alpha^0) + \lambda^T g(x, \alpha^0)$$

The first-order conditions for a maximum give us a system of $n + c$ equations in the unknowns (x, λ):

$$D_x \pounds(x, \lambda; \alpha^0) = D_x f(x, \alpha^0) + \lambda^T D_x g(x, \alpha^0) = \underline{0}$$
$$D_\lambda \pounds(x, \lambda; \alpha^0) = g(x, \alpha^0) = \underline{0} \tag{1}$$

Assume that x^0 is a regular maximum of $f(x, \alpha^0)$ subject to $g(x, \alpha^0) = \underline{0}$. Then (1) holds at x^0, and

$$h^T D_x^2 \pounds(x^0, \lambda^0; \alpha^0) h < 0 \; \forall \; h \in \mathbb{R}^n \text{ s.th. } D_x g(x^0, \alpha^0) h = \underline{0}$$

implying that

$$|\overline{H}| = \begin{vmatrix} D_x^2 \pounds(x^0, \lambda^0; \alpha^0) & D_x g(x^0, \alpha^0)^T \\ D_x g(x^0, \alpha^0) & 0 \end{vmatrix} \neq 0$$

Now, the bordered Hessian $|\overline{H}|$ is the same as the Jacobian of endogenous variables of the system (1). We can therefore apply the IFT to the system of first-order conditions to obtain

$$\frac{\partial x_i^*}{\partial \alpha_k} = -\frac{|\overline{H}_i|}{|\overline{H}|}$$

where the sign of $|\overline{H}|$ is known.

For the Kuhn-Tucker problem, we have one additional complication. At an optimal solution for α^0, some of the constraints will be active, and others inactive. Now, if a small change in α does not change the set of binding constraints, we can proceed as in the Lagrange case, working with the active constraints and ignoring the inactive ones. At certain points, however, a small perturbation of the constraints may cause some previously active constraint to become inactive, or vice versa, giving rise to a "change of regime." At such transition points, the solution mapping $x(\alpha)$ may not be differentiable. Hence, we have to be a bit more careful and consider all the possibilities that may arise in different regimes.

Problem 2.10. An agent consumes two goods, x_1 and x_2, with prices p_1 and p_2, respectively. Her utility function is of the form $U(x_1, x_2) = \alpha(x_1^\alpha + x_2^\alpha)$, with $\alpha < 1$. Verify that $U(\;)$ is strictly concave. Derive the demand function of the agent. In what direction does the demand for good 1 change if there is an increase in the price of good 2?

Problem 2.11. A competitive firm maximizes profits, $\Pi(x) = pf(x) - wx$, taking as given the price of its output p and the vector $w \in \mathbb{R}^n$ of factor prices. Assume that the production function f is C^2 and strictly concave, with positive but diminishing marginal products ($f_i > 0, f_{ii} < 0, i = 1, \ldots, n$).

Write the first-order conditions for the firm's problem, and apply the IFT to the resulting system to show that the demand for each factor is a decreasing function of its price (i.e., that $\partial x_i^* / \partial w_i < 0$).

(c) *Value Functions and Envelope Theorems*

The value function $V:\Omega \longrightarrow \mathbb{R}$ for a maximization problem gives the maximum attainable value of the objective function for each value of the parameters:

$$V(\alpha) = \max_x \{f(x; \alpha); \; x \in C(\alpha)\} = f(x^*, \alpha), \quad \text{where } x^* \in S(\alpha)$$

As an illustration, consider the value function for an unconstrained maximization problem and refer to Figure 7.5. For each particular value of x, we can plot f as a function of the parameters alone. This yields a family of curves, some of which are shown in Figure 7.5. Graphically, the maximum-value function corresponds to the upper "envelope" of this family of curves.

Functions of this type are commonly found in economic theory. In general terms, it is clear that the maximum payoff available to a rational agent is a function of the "environment" she faces, as summarized by the vector of parameters α. An example of a maximum-value function that we will encounter later is the indirect utility function

$$\Psi(p, y) = \max_x \{U(x) \text{ s.t. } px \le y\} = U[x(p, y)]$$

which gives the maximum utility attainable by a consumer as a function of the prices (p) she faces and her income (y). Clearly, this is the utility obtained by consuming the optimal bundle, as given by the demand function $x(p, y)$.

In this section we will review some properties of value or envelope functions that play an important role in microeconomic theory. Then we will

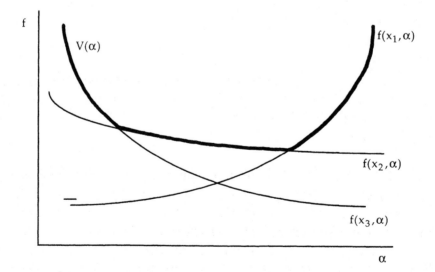

Figure 7.5. A maximum-value function.

establish some results that will allow us to relate the derivatives of the value function to those of the underlying objective and constraint functions. These so-called *envelope theorems* provide a convenient way to establish some important relationships in microeconomic theory (e.g., Roy's identity, Shephard's lemma). These results, in turn, can be used to derive some basic comparative-statics results concering demand and supply functions from the curvature properties of the value function. Somewhat surprisingly, this rather roundabout approach to comparative statics often turns out to be more convenient than the traditional route via the IFT and implicit differentiation of the first-order conditions.

We begin with two results that provide sufficient conditions for the concavity or convexity of the value function.

Theorem 2.12. Concavity of the value function. Consider the following problem and the associated value function:

$$V(\alpha) = \max_{x} \{f(x; \alpha); \ g(x; \alpha) \geq \underline{0}\}$$

Suppose the objective function f *is concave in* (x, α), *(i.e., in both parameters and decision variables) and that all the constraint functions* $g^j(\ )$, j = 1, . . . , c, *are quasiconcave. Then* V( ) *is concave.*

Proof. Take two arbitrary values of the parameter vector, α' and α'', and let $x' = x(\alpha')$ and $x'' = x(\alpha'')$ be the corresponding optimal choices of x. To establish the concavity of $V(\ )$ we need to show that

$$(1-\lambda)V(\alpha') + \lambda V(\alpha'') \leq V[(1-\lambda)\alpha' + \lambda\alpha'']$$

for any $\lambda \in (0, 1)$.

Consider now the pair $(x^\lambda, \alpha^\lambda)$ defined by

$$x^\lambda = (1-\lambda)x' + \lambda x'' \quad \text{and} \quad \alpha^\lambda = (1-\lambda)\alpha' + \lambda\alpha''$$

and observe that, in principle, $x^\lambda \neq x(\alpha^\lambda)$, that is, x^λ is not necessarily optimal for α^λ.

We begin by showing that x^λ is feasible for α^λ. Because x' and x'' are (optimal and therefore necessarily) feasible for α' and α'', we have, for each j,

$$g^j(x', \alpha') \geq 0 \quad \text{and} \quad g^j(x'', \alpha'') \geq 0 \tag{1}$$

By the quasiconcavity of g^j and (1), we have

$$g^j(x^\lambda, \alpha^\lambda) \geq \min\{g^j(x', \alpha'), g^j(x'', \alpha'')\} \geq 0$$

so x^λ is feasible for α^λ.

Next, consider the following chain of inequalities:

$$V(\alpha^\lambda) = f[x(\alpha^\lambda), \alpha^\lambda] \geq f(x^\lambda, \alpha^\lambda) \geq (1-\lambda)f[x(\alpha'), \alpha'] + \lambda f[x(\alpha''), \alpha'']$$
$$= (1-\lambda)V(\alpha') + \lambda V(\alpha'')$$

The first inequality holds by the observation that x^λ is not necessarily optimal for α^λ, and the second holds by the concavity of f. The equalities are all true by definition.   □

Unfortunately, the objective and constraint functions we find in consumer and producer theory are typically not concave jointly in decision variables and parameters. The next theorem, requiring weaker assumptions, will be more useful in applications.

Theorem 2.13. Convexity of the value function. Consider the following problem and the associated value function:

$$V(\alpha) = \max_x \{f(x; \alpha); \ g(x) \geq \underline{0}\}$$

where $\alpha \in \Omega$, a convex set. (Note that the parameters do not enter the constraint function.) If the objective function is convex in the parameters α for any given x, then $V(\ )$ is convex.

Problem 2.14. Prove Theorem 2.13.

We now consider the effect of a parameter change on the maximum payoff attainable by an optimizing agent. For a start, assume that the agent maximizes $f(x; \alpha^0)$ with no constraints, and suppose that the assumptions of the preceding section hold. Then the decision rule for the problem is a well-defined and differentiable function $x(\alpha)$ in some neighborhood of α^0, and substituting this function into $f(\ )$, we obtain the value function

$$V(\alpha) \equiv f[x(\alpha), \alpha]$$

Differentiating with respect to α,

$$DV(\alpha^0) = D_x f(x^0; \alpha^0)Dx(\alpha^0) + D_\alpha f(x^0, \alpha^0)$$

That is, a small change in the value of the parameter vector will affect the value of f in two ways: directly, because f is a function of α, and indirectly, through the induced change in the optimal values of the choice variables. On the other hand, the first-order conditions for the problem, $D_x f(x^0; \alpha^0) = \underline{0}$, ensure that the marginal gain from small changes in the values of the instruments will be zero when we start from an optimum. Hence, (1) reduces to

$$DV(\alpha^0) = D_\alpha f(x^0, \alpha^0)$$

that is, we need consider only the direct effect. We have proved the following result.

Theorem 2.15. Envelope theorem for unconstrained maximization. Let f(x, α) be a C² function, and let x⁰ be regular maximum of f for α⁰. Then

$$V(\alpha) = \max_x f(x; \alpha) = f[x(\alpha), \alpha]$$

is differentiable at α⁰, and DV(α⁰) = Dₐf(x⁰, α⁰).

We now show that a similar result holds for the Lagrange problem. The only difference is that in order to take into account the effect on the constraints of the parameter change, we have to differentiate the Lagrangian, rather than just the objective function, with respect to the parameters.

Theorem 2.16. Envelope theorem for the Lagrange problem. Let

$$V(\alpha) = \max_x \{f(x; \alpha);\ g(x, \alpha) = \underline{0}\}$$

where f and g are C². If x⁰ is a regular solution of this problem for α⁰ (i.e., satisfies the sufficient second-order conditions for a strict local maximum), then V is differentiable at α⁰, and

$$DV(\alpha^0) = D_\alpha \pounds(x^0, \alpha^0) = D_\alpha f(x^0, \alpha^0) + \lambda^{0\mathrm{T}} D_\alpha g(x^0, \alpha^0)$$

Proof. Differentiating the Lagrangian function

$$\pounds(x^0, \alpha^0) = f(x^0, \alpha^0) + \lambda^T g(x^0, \alpha^0) \tag{1}$$

we obtain the first-order conditions for the problem:

$$D_x \pounds(x, \alpha^0) = D_x f(x, \alpha^0) + \lambda^T D_x g(x, \alpha^0) = \underline{0} \tag{2}$$

$$D_\lambda \pounds(x, \alpha^0) = g(x, \alpha^0) = \underline{0} \tag{3}$$

Under the assumptions of the theorem, the decision rule for the problem is a well-defined and differentiable function. Substituting it into the objective function, we recover the value function

$$V(\alpha) \equiv f[x(\alpha), \alpha]$$

Differentiating $V(\ )$ with respect to the parameters, and using (2),

$$DV(\alpha^0) = D_\alpha f(x^0, \alpha^0) + D_x f(x^0; \alpha^0) Dx(\alpha^0)$$
$$= D_\alpha f(x^0, \alpha^0) - \lambda^T D_x g(x^0, \alpha^0) Dx(\alpha^0) \tag{4}$$

Substituting the decision rule into (3) and differentiating with respect to α,

$$D_x g(x^0, \alpha^0) Dx(\alpha^0) + D_\alpha g(x^0, \alpha^0) = \underline{0} \tag{5}$$

Using this expression, (4) reduces to

$$DV(\alpha^0) = D_\alpha f(x^0, \alpha^0) + \lambda^T D_\alpha f(x^0, \alpha^0) \qquad \qquad \square$$

As noted in the preceding section, the decision rule for a Kuhn-Tucker problem may not be differentiable at points at which a regime change takes place. The same is true of the value function.

To conclude this section, we will use the envelope theorem to provide a rigorous basis for the intuitive interpretation of the Lagrange multipliers as *shadow prices* of the constraints advanced in Section 1(b). Consider a version of the Lagrange problem in which the constraints are of the form $g^j(x) + \gamma_j = 0$ for $j = 1, \ldots, c$.

$$V(\gamma) = \max_x \{ f(x); \; g(x) + \gamma = \underline{0} \} \tag{P.γ}$$

By the envelope theorem, we have $DV(\gamma^0) = \lambda^0$, where λ^0 is the vector of Lagrange multipliers for the problem. Thus the Lagrange multiplier λ_j^0 tells us how the maximum value of the program (given by the value function V) changes with the corresponding constraint constant γ_j. In other words, the multipliers measure the "sensitivity" of the value function to changes in the constraint constants.

3. Problems and Applications

Problem 3.1. An agent lives for two periods and has an endowment of one unit of a homogeneous consumption good in the first period, and γ units in the second period. His utility function is given by

$$\ln c_1 + \ln c_2$$

where c_i is consumption in period i. The agent can store any feasible quantity of his first-period endowment for consumption at a later time and can get an interest-free loan of up to β units of the good (i.e., $s \geq -\beta$, and $R = 1$).

(i) Calculate the agent's saving function, ignoring the constraint $s \geq -\beta$.
(ii) For what combinations of parameter values will the constraint be binding? In what regions of the (β, γ) plane will we have an interior solution and a corner solution? Write the agent's savings function, taking into account the constraint.
(iii) Write the maximum-value function for the problem as a function of γ, $V(\gamma)$. Verify that $V(\gamma)$ is continuous at the point at which there is a regime change (i.e., as we go from an interior solution to one in which the constraint is binding). Is the value function differentiable at this point?

(a) Profit Maximization by a Competitive Firm

Consider the problem faced by a competitive firm that produces a single output y using a vector of inputs x. The firm takes as given input and output prices (w, p) and maximizes profits, $py - wx$, subject to the feasibility constraint $y \leq f(x)$, where f is a concave production function that describes the firm's technology. We will require, moreover, that input and output be nonnegative and assume that the input vector x is bounded (e.g., by the overall factor supplies available in the economy). Hence, $\|x\| \leq B$ for some real number B (or, if you prefer, $x \leq e$, where e is the vector of factor endowments). Finally, we will assume that $p > 0$ and $w > \underline{0}$ (i.e., input prices are nonnegative, and at least some of them are strictly positive).

The firm's problem can be written

$$\pi(p, w) = \max_{x, y}\{py - wx \text{ s.t. } y \leq f(x), (x, y) \geq \underline{0}, \text{ and } \|x\| \leq B\} \qquad \text{(P)}$$

and the problem's value function, $\pi(p, w)$, is the firm's *profit function*. To simplify notation, let $z = (y, -x)$ and $q = (p, w)$. Then profit is simply qz.

Under our assumptions, qz is a continuous function defined on a compact set. Hence, (P) always has a solution. We will now study some properties of the solution and value functions for the firm's problem under some additional assumptions.

Problem 3.2. Show that if f is strictly concave, then (P) has a unique solution for a given price vector q.

Hint: By contradiction, assume that there are two distinct optimal production plans, z' and z'', and show that we can construct a feasible plan that will yield a strictly larger profit.

Problem 3.3. Under the assumptions of Problem 3.2, the firm's production plans (i.e., its output level and factor demands) are well-defined functions of the price vector q. We will show that these functions are continuous.

Fix a vector q^0 of prices, and consider a sequence of price vectors $\{q_n\}$ convergent to q^0 and the corresponding sequence of optimal production plans $\{z_n\}$, with $z_n = z(q_n)$ for each n. We want to show that $\{z_n\}$ converges to $z(q^0) = z'$. To establish this result, we will proceed by contradiction. Suppose that $\{z_n\}$ does not converge to z'.

(i) Then $\{z_n\}$ has a convergent subsequence $\{z_{n_k}\}$, with limit z^0 different from z'. Explain why this is true.

(ii) Let $\{q_{n_k}\}$ be the price subsequence corresponding to $\{z_{n_k}\}$. We have that

$$\{q_{n_k}\} \to q^0 \quad \text{and} \quad \{z_{n_k}\} \to z^0 \neq z' = z(q^0)$$

Show that we arrive at the following contradiction: Given any price vector q_{n_k} sufficiently close to q^0, z' is strictly better than the optimal plan $\{z_{n_k}\}$. Hint: Use the fact that qz is a continuous function.

Under assumptions that guarantee the differentiability of the solution function for the firm's problem, we have shown in Problem 2.10 that the supply is increasing in output price, and the demand for each factor is decreasing in its price. The following problem shows that comparative-statics results can sometimes be obtained without differentiability assumptions.

Problem 3.4. Consider two price vectors q_1 and q_0 and the corresponding optimal production plans z_1 and z_0. Because z_1 is feasible but not necessarily optimal for q_0, it must yield a lower profit than z_0 at this price vector. Using this observation, show that for any i, $\Delta q_i \Delta z_i \geq 0$ (e.g., for the first component of these vectors we have $\Delta p \Delta y \geq 0$, i.e., an increase in the price of output must yield an increase in supply).

Problem 3.5. Show that the profit function $\pi(q)$ is convex. Can you give an economic interpretation of this property?

Problem 3.6. If the profit function is differentiable, the envelope theorem implies that $D\pi(q) = z(q)$, that is, the derivative of the profit function at a point is simply the optimal production plan (this is Hotelling's lemma). We will show that the profit function is differentiable whenever $f(\ )$ is strictly concave.

Fix a price vector q, and consider the behavior of the profit function as we move away from this point. Using the fact that $\pi(q) = qz(q)$, show that for any change h in the price vector,

$$\pi(q+h) \geq \pi(q) + hz(q) \tag{1}$$

$$\pi(q) \geq \pi(q+h) - hz(q+h) \tag{2}$$

Using (1) and (2), show that

$$h[z(q+h) - z(q)] \geq \pi(q+h) - \pi(q) - hz(q) \geq 0 \tag{3}$$

Using this expression, show that π is differentiable at q and $D\pi(q) = z(q)$.

The next problem illustrates how the envelope theorem and the properties of the value function can sometimes be used to obtain comparative-statics results.

Problem 3.7. Suppose the profit function is C^2. Using the convexity of $\pi(q)$ and the fact that $D\pi(q) = z(q)$, show once more that factor demand functions are downward-sloping.

(b) Implicit Contracts

Consider the situation faced by a firm and a large number of workers who are "associated" with it. The firm's production technology is of the form

$$y = xf(L)$$

where L is the level of labor input, and x is an exogenous productivity shock. We will assume that the production function $f(\ )$ is strictly increasing and strictly concave and that the productivity shock may be either high or low ($x \in \{x_H, x_L\}$, where $x_H > x_L$), with probabilities q_H, q_L ($q_H + q_L = 1$).

For simplicity, we will assume that there is a continuum of unit measure of identical workers, that is, an infinite number of workers, each of them represented by a point in the interval $(0, 1)$. Each worker is endowed with a unit of divisible time that he can spend at work or in leisure. His utility is given by

$$W(c, 1 - h) = U(c) + V(1 - h)$$

where c is consumption ($=$ income), $1 - h$ is leisure, and the functions $U(\ )$ and $V(\ )$ are strictly increasing and strictly concave.

Before the productivity shock is realized, the firm and its workers negotiate a contract. Notice that there is no reason that the contract should specify wage and employment levels that are independent of the value of x. In fact, both workers and firms will find it advantageous to build some flexibility into the contract (to allow them to take advantage of good production opportunities or to share risks optimally among them), and they can do so by conditioning payments and labor hours on contingencies observable by all parties involved. Hence, if the realization of the productivity shock is freely observable by both workers and firms, a contract will be a state-contingent schedule $C(x)$ specifying, for each possible state of nature x, the fraction of the labor force that will be employed (n), the number of "hours" each employed individual will work (h), and the compensation to be paid to each employed worker (c^e) and laid-off worker (c^u). Hence,

$$C(x_i) = [c^e(x_i), h(x_i), n(x_i), c^u(x_i)] \quad \text{for} \quad i = H, L$$

(To simplify the notation, we will use $h(x_i) = h_i$, etc.) We will further assume that if layoffs are called for (i.e., if $n_i < 1$ in some state), the workers to be fired will be selected by lot, so that, ex ante, each worker faces the same probability $1 - n_i$ of being laid off in state i.

It seems reasonable to assume that rational firms and workers should agree on a Pareto-efficient contract (i.e., that they would not settle for a contract if there were some feasible alternative that would make one of the parties better off without making the other worse off). Assuming that the firm is risk-neutral, that is, cares only about expected profits (e.g., because it is owned by well-diversified investors), any such contract can be characterized as the solution to the following problem:

$$\max E\pi = \sum_i q_i[x_i f(n_i h_i) - n_i c_i^e - (1 - n_i)c_i^u] \tag{P}$$

subject to

$$EW = \sum_i q_i\{n_i[U(c_i^e) + V(1 - h_i)] + (1 - n_i)[U(c_i^u) + V(1)]\} \geq W_0$$

for some given W_0. That is, we maximize expected profits subject to the constraint that workers' expected utility not fall below some given level. (If there is a competitive market in the background, we can interpret W_0, the reservation utility of the representative worker, as the utility level guaranteed by the equilibrium contract available in the market, and we can think of (P) as the problem faced by a manager who wants to maximize expected profit subject to the constraint that his contract offer must be acceptable to workers who would otherwise go elsewhere.) Alternatively, we could maximize workers' expected utility subject to the constraint that expected profits not fall below some minimum level, and we would get exactly the same results.

Problem 3.8. Show that the optimal contract involves no layoffs (i.e., $n_i = 1$ for all i).

Hint: Suppose we have a contract that specifies some layoffs in certain states of nature. Then workers face a lottery between working and being laid off in each of these states, and, being risk-averse, they do not like it. Show that it is possible to construct another contract with no layoffs that will yield the same profit in each state and will be strictly preferred by workers. A contract featuring slightly lower pay will be acceptable to workers and strictly preferred by firms. Does the argument rely in any way on the firm's risk neutrality?

The preceding result allows us to simplify the optimal-contract problem. Because workers are employed in all states with probability 1, there is no loss of generality in specifying a contract simply as $C(x) = [c(x), h(x)]$. The optimal-contract problem, then, can be written

$$\max E\pi = \sum_i q_i[x_i f(h_i) - c_i] \tag{P$'$}$$

subject to $EW = \Sigma_i q_i\{U(c_i) + V(1 - h_i)\} \geq W_0$.

Problem 3.9. We will now investigate some properties of the optimal contract.

  (i) Write the first-order conditions for (P′), and show that they imply the following conditions:

$$c_H = c_L \qquad\qquad\qquad\qquad \text{(efficient risk-sharing)}$$

$$x_i f'(h_i) = \frac{V'(1-h_i)}{U'(c_i)} \quad \text{for each} \quad i = H, L \qquad \text{(efficient hours)}$$

  Interpret these two conditions.

 (ii) Show that $h_H \geq h_L$ (i.e., more hours are worked when productivity is high). Hint: Suppose that $h_L > h_H$, and seek a contradiction using the first-order conditions.

(iii) Show that $h_H > h_L$. (By contradiction again, suppose $h_H = h_L$.)

So far, we have assumed that the realization of the productivity shock can be freely observed by both parties. If this is not so, the contract design problem becomes more complicated, and the need to provide incentives to avoid cheating by the party with private information generates distortions that prevent implementation of the first-best contract we have just characterized.

For example, suppose that the shock x can be observed only by the firm. (This may reflect, for example, the fact that firms have better information about market conditions than their workers.) Then, hours and compensation cannot be made contingent directly on the realization of x, but only on the firm's announcement of the state (x_a). In this situation, however, the firm may find it advantageous to lie in some states. To prevent this, the contract problem will have to incorporate additional constraints designed to force the firm to tell the truth.

We will now explore the form these constraints must take. Given a contract $C(x) = [c(x_i), h(x_i); i = H, L]$, let $\Pi(x_a \mid x_i)$ be the firm's profit when the true state is x_i and x_a is announced (so h_a and c_a are implemented). Then

$$\Pi(x_a|x_i) = x_i f(h_a) - c_a$$

and the optimal strategy for the firm is to announce the state x_a that will maximize $\Pi(x_a \mid x_i)$. Notice that, given an arbitrary contract, there is no guarantee that the optimal announcement is the true state.

Problem 3.10. Show that under the first-best contract characterized in Problem 3.9, the firm has an incentive to lie in one of the states. Which one? Why?

This result implies that the first-best contract is not implementable when there is private information. The second-best-contract problem (which characterizes the best feasible contract under the circumstances) must incorporate additional constraints to prevent cheating by the firm. This is achieved by making truth-telling the profit-maximizing strategy in all states. Hence, we require

$$\Pi(x_i \mid x_i) \geq \Pi(x_a \mid x_i) \, \forall \, i \quad \text{and} \quad \forall \, a \tag{IC}$$

This type of constraint is often called an *incentive compatibility* (or *truth-telling*) *constraint*, for it ensures that the party with private information will have an incentive to reveal it truthfully in all states.

The optimal-contract problem with imperfect information can be written

$$\max_{c,h} E\Pi(x) = \sum_i q_i [x_i f(h_i) - c_i] \tag{P''}$$

subject to

$$\sum_i q_i [U(c_i) + V(1 - h_i)] \geq W_0$$

$$\Pi(x_L \mid x_L) = x_L f(h_L) - c_L \geq x_L f(h_H) - c_H = \Pi(x_H \mid x_L) \tag{IC.L}$$

$$\Pi(x_H \mid x_H) = x_H f(h_H) - c_H \geq x_H f(h_L) - c_L = \Pi(x_L \mid x_H) \tag{IC.H}$$

The following problems explore the implications of the additional constraints and the nature of the distortions they induce. Notice that in our case the incentive compatibility constraints must make it unprofitable for the firm to announce a high state when productivity is actually low. To achieve this, such a strategy must be penalized in some way. One obvious way to do this is to force the firm to pay a higher wage when it announces the high state. This, however, involves an efficiency cost, for full insurance can no longer be offered. As we will see, however, this is not the only inefficiency implied by the incentive constraints.

Problem 3.11. Show that the incentive compatibility constraints, by themselves, imply that $c_H \geq c_L$ and $h_H \geq h_L$. Hint: Rearrange, and add the two incentive compatibility constraints.

Problem 3.12. Write the first-order conditions for (P''). Use them and the preceding results in the following:

(i) Show that $c_H > c_L$ and $h_H > h_L$ Hint: Suppose not. Then two of the first-order conditions imply $\lambda_L = \lambda_H$; use this and the other first-order conditions to obtain a contradiction, $x_L > x_H$.

(ii) Show that both incentive constraints cannot be binding at the same time. (If they are, $h_H = h_L$, contradicting the previous result.)

Hence, precisely one incentive compatibility constraint must be binding. Why?

(iii) Show that the active incentive compatibility constraint is the one corresponding to the low-productivity state.

Notice that, by (i), we have $c_H > c_L$, so the second-best contract does not provide complete insurance for workers.

(iv) Show that the employment level is also distorted, but only in one state, (That is, for the given c_i, compare the employment level in each state with the one that would be implied by the efficient-hours condition, $x_i f'(h_i) = V'(1 - h_i)/U'(c_i)$.

Bibliography

Arrow, K., and Hahn, F. 1971. *General Competitive Analysis*. San Francisco: Holden-Day.

Azariadis, C. 1975. Implicit Contracts and Underemployment Equilibria. *Journal of Political Economy* 83:1183–202.

Baily, M. 1974. Wages and Unemployment with Uncertain Demand. *Review of Economic Studies* 41:37–50.

Beavis, B., and Dobbs, I. 1990. *Optimization and Stability Theory for Economic Analysis*. Cambridge University Press.

Berge, C. 1966. *Espace Topologiques. Fonctions Multivoques*. Paris: Dunod.

Binmore, K. 1982. *Mathematical Analysis, a Straightforward Approach*, 2nd ed. Cambridge University Press.

Cooper, R. 1987. *Wage and Employment Patterns in Labor Contracts*: *Micro-foundations and Macro-economic Implications*. London: Harwood.

Dixit, A. 1990. *Optimization in Economic Theory*, 2nd ed. Oxford University Press.

de la Fuente, A., and Naranjo, M. T. Continuity of the Constraint Correspondence in Parameterized Kuhn-Tucwer problems with Concave Constraints. Forthcoming in Economics Letters.

Hastenes, M. 1975. *Optimization Theory, the Finite Dimensional Case*. New York: Wiley.

Intriligator, M. 1971. *Mathematical Optimization and Economic Theory*. Englewood Cliffs, NJ: Prentice-Hall.

Luenberger, D. 1973. *Introduction to Linear and Nonlinear Programming*. Reading, MA: Addison-Wesley.

Madden, P. 1986. *Concavity and Optimization in Microeconomics*. London: Basil Blackwell.

Mangasarian, O. 1982. *Nonlinear Programming*. Malabar, FL: Krieger.

Silberberg, E. 1978. *The Structure of Economics*: *A Mathematical Analysis*. New York: McGraw-Hill.

Simmons, G. 1972. *Differential Equations with Applications and Historical Notes*. New York: McGraw-Hill.

Stiglitz, J. 1984. Theories of Wage Rigidity. NBER working paper no. 1442.

Stokey, N., and Lucas, R. 1989. *Recursive Methods in Economic Dynamics*. Harvard University Press.

Sydsaeter, K. 1981. *Topics in Mathematical Analysis for Economists*. Orlando, FL: Academic Press.

Takayama, A. 1985. *Mathematical Economics*, 2nd ed. Cambridge University Press.

Vives, X. 1996. *Static Oligopoly Pricing: Old Ideas and New Tools*. Barcelona: Instituto de Análisis Económico.
Varian, H. 1984. *Microeconomic Analysis*. New York: Norton.

Notes

1 In fact, it is a bit stronger. Recall that negative definiteness of the Hessian is sufficient but not necessary for concavity.

2 It can be shown that when we multiply a row of a matrix by a constant, the determinant of the resulting matrix is equal to the constant times the determinant of the original matrix.

3 Notice that the Jacobian of endogenous variables of the system of first-order conditions, $D_x^2 f(x^0, \alpha^0)$ is precisely the determinant of the Hessian whose negative definiteness we are assuming. From the appendix to Chapter 6, the negative definiteness of this matrix implies that its determinant will not be zero. In particular, we have that $(-1)^n |H| > 0$, where n is the dimension of the Hessian matrix.

4 Notice that, in principle, there is no guarantee that $\partial x_i^*/\partial \alpha_k$ will have a "constant sign" for all values of the parameters. Clearly, restrictions on the sign of the cross-partials $D_{x\alpha}f(x, \alpha)$ can be used to guarantee "monotone comparative statics." More general conditions, not requiring differentiability, have been established for programming problems in lattices. The interested reader is referred to the discussion of supermodularity by Vives (1996, ch. 2).

8

Some Applications to Microeconomics

The first part of this book has covered most of the mathematical tools required for analysis of static economic models. In this chapter we will discuss some applications of this material to a number of microeconomic models. Our goal will not be to provide a comprehensive treatment of a set of topics generally covered in the standard first-year graduate sequence in microeconomics, but only to illustrate the usefulness of the techniques we have developed and to introduce the reader to the general logic of model-building in economic theory.

We began Chapter 7 with the observation that the "postulate of rationality" – the assumption that individuals have well-defined and consistent preferences and act accordingly – is central in (neoclassical) economics as a source of regularity in individual behavior that makes prediction possible, at least in principle. We then claimed that this postulate led naturally to the modeling of individual decision-making as the outcome of a constrained optimization problem, and we devoted a fair amount of time to studying the "technology" required for solving such problems. Section 1 of this chapter backtracks a little. We consider a standard consumer and discuss how his preferences can be represented by a binary relation and how this relation can be used to construct a utility function. Section 2 then analyzes the behavior of this consumer when he faces market-determined prices for the commodities he wants to purchase with his (exogenously given) income.

The first half of the chapter focuses on modeling the behavior of a single agent under a set of restrictions imposed on him by his environment. To understand the determination of most economic magnitudes, however, we have to go one step beyond such single-agent models and ask what will come out of the interactions of a number of (rational) decision-makers. This takes us to the concept of *equilibrium*. Given an "economic game" played by a set of agents, many outcomes are possible in principle. The heart of an economic theory is a concept of equilibrium, a criterion that allows us to select a subset of these outcomes that can be considered to be more plausible, in some reasonable sense.

"Equilibrium" literally means "equal weight," from the condition for balancing a bar on a pivot. The etymology of the word, then, suggests a balance of forces inside the system that results in a state of rest unless some outside force prompts a change. This interpretation carries over to economic models, where an equilibrium typically corresponds to a situation in which no agent has an incentive to change his behavior. The other key idea associated with economic equilibrium is that of the compatibility of the actions of individually optimizing agents.

These two basic strands of the notion of equilibrium can be made operational in many different ways and with varying degrees of "strength." In this chapter we will review some of the standard concepts of equilibrium in economic theory. In Section 3 we consider an exchange economy populated by a large number of price-taking rational consumers who interact with each other through competitive markets, and we establish the existence and some welfare properties of a Walrasian equilibrium in this setting. In Section 4 we introduce some of the basic notions of the theory of games and discuss the concept of Nash equilibrium. Finally, Section 5 will ask the reader to work through some useful models of imperfect competition.

In all cases, our approach will be the same. Given an economic system composed of a set of agents who interact with each other in a specified way (a "game," for short), we will characterize the set of likely outcomes by considering two "subproblems" in turn:

(i) *The individual decision problem.* Assume that we have a game with well-defined rules, and consider an individual player. Given the particular game, there will be things that the agent controls and things he does not control. As we have already argued, it seems natural to model the behavior of a rational player as a constrained optimization problem. Hence, we will assume that each agent behaves as if he maximizes his objective or payoff function by his choices of the variables he controls, subject to whatever constraints are imposed on him by the rules of the game, and taking as given the things he cannot control. This problem yields as a solution a decision rule specifying the best action for the agent as a function (correspondence) of the things he takes as parameters.

(ii) *The equilibrium problem.* We still have to check that the optimal responses of the different players are consistent with each other and the overall resources of the system. Whereas the requirement of feasibility is generally straightforward, we have a considerable amount of latitude in specifying what degree of consistency we require among the actions of the players. For example, in a competitive equilibrium, "consistency" translates into market clearing, the requirement that each agent be able to sell or buy as much as he wants of each good at the market price. An alternative notion of equilibrium, however, would allow for the possibility of rationing (i.e., for the existence of quantity constraints that might prevent agents from buying or selling their desired quantities).

It is important to emphasize that these two "problems" are very closely interrelated. Until we know what kind of game is being played, we cannot say which behaviors are rational, nor can we even write down the individual's problem, because we do not know what he controls, what he must take as given, and what constraints he faces. Similarly, unless we know how individual players are behaving, it is impossible to write down a meaningful equilibrium condition. Hence, the two problems must be written down and solved simultaneously. On the other hand, thinking in terms of these two separate problems is often a useful way to approach the question of what will come out of the interactions of a group of rational individuals.

1. Consumer Preferences and Utility

This section discusses the representation of preferences by binary relations and numerical functions. The reader may want to refer to Chapter 1 for some background material on binary relations and ordered sets. Section (a) introduces the concept of preference relation and discusses some properties that such relations are commonly assumed to possess. In particular, the "consistent preferences" half of the postulate of rationality is typically embodied in the assumption that a preference relation is a complete preordering. The other half ("consistent behavior") translates into the assumption that agents choose undominated elements of the set of feasible alternatives. Additional assumptions commonly made concerning preference relations capture ideas like the desirability of commodities and the taste for diversification, or they may be imposed for technical convenience.

Section (b) shows that a preference preorder can be conveniently represented by a numerical function, provided that certain regularity conditions are satisfied. In Section (c) we strengthen these conditions to obtain a differentiable utility function. The resulting model of individual behavior can be analyzed using the methods developed in Chapter 7. This will be the subject of Section 2.

(a) Preference Relations

Let X be a set, and consider an agent who must choose one of its elements. The most natural way to represent her preferences over such objects is probably in terms of a binary relation. Intuitively, we can imagine selecting two elements at a time from the given set and asking the agent which one she prefers. Such a questionnaire would yield a pairwise ranking of alternatives that could be used, under certain assumptions, to construct an exhaustive list of possible options ranked by their desirability. We can then imagine her as figuring out which elements are feasible and then choosing the one that is closest to the top of the list.

More formally, our experiment of repeatedly confronting the agent with a choice between two elements of X can be used to construct a binary relation "$\geq$" in $X \times X$. This relation will be the set of all pairs (x, y) of elements of X such that x is weakly preferred to y by the agent (written $x \geq y$). A relation of this kind is called a *preference relation*.

In principle, then, there is no problem in representing preferences over elements of an arbitrary set by a binary relation "$\geq$". The next question is what kinds of properties we may reasonably assume "$\geq$" to possess. This section reviews a number of assumptions commonly made about preferences and explores their meaning. Roughly, such assumptions come in two different types. Some are meant to capture the idea of rational behavior, and the rest are technical assumptions made so that it is possible to construct models that can be analyzed using standard mathematical techniques. In particular, it is convenient to make assumptions that will ensure that preferences can be represented by a continuous or differentiable quasiconcave numerical function. We shall see in the next section how such a representation can be constructed.

Returning to the preference relation, it is clear that "$\geq$" will be reflexive, as any agent should be indifferent between x and itself (i.e., $x \geq x$). Next, if the agent is "rational," we may expect that her preferences will be "consistent." One way to formalize this is to assume transitivity, that is, if x is preferred to y, and y to z, then x is preferred to z. Notice that if this were not true, the agent might be unable to make up her mind about which element of the set she preferred (she could "cycle" from x to y, from y to z, and then back to x), and the decision problem would not have a solution.[1] Hence, the "consistent preferences" part of the postulate of rationality will be formalized by requiring that "$\geq$" be reflexive and transitive – that is, the preference relation will always be assumed to be a *preordering*.

Like any preordering, a preference relation can be decomposed into its symmetric and asymmetric components by defining the following two subrelations:

$$x > y \quad \text{if and only if } x \geq y \text{ and } y \ngeq x$$

$$x \sim y \quad \text{if and only if } x \geq y \text{ and } y \geq x$$

(where $y \ngeq x$ means "not $y \geq x$"). We shall refer to "$>$" as the *strict preference relation* ($x > y$ means that x is strictly preferred to y), and to "$\sim$" as the *indifference relation* ($x \sim y$ means that the agent is indifferent between x and y).

A further assumption that is often made is that the preference preordering is *complete,* that is, that given any two elements x and y of X, the agent can compare them and know whether she strictly prefers one of the elements or is indifferent between them. This looks innocuous enough, but it implicitly requires some strong assumptions about the information available to the agent. In particular, it presupposes that she knows exactly what alternatives are open to her – and that her knowledge of what each alternative entails is precise enough that she can always tell which is better.

These assumptions have been criticized as being too strong, and weaker alternatives do exist in the literature. For many purposes, however, they seem reasonable enough. We will take the following axiom as the first half of the postulate of rationality and see where it takes us.

Axiom 1.1. The preference relation "$\geq$" defined on the choice set X *is a complete preordering. This requires*

(i) *reflexivity:* $\forall x \in X, x \geq x,$
(ii) *transitivity:* $\forall x, y, z \in X, [x \geq y$ *and* $y \geq z] \Rightarrow x \geq z,$ *and*
(iii) *completeness:* $\forall x, y \in X,$ *either* $x \geq y$ *or* $y \geq x$ *or both.*

Intuitively, if this axiom holds, we can picture the agent as having a complete listing of the elements of X ranked by their desirability. If we restrict her choices to some subset of X, all she has to do is choose the element of this subset that is closest to the top of the list. That she behaves in this way will complete our description of what we mean by rationality. We formalize this as follows:

Axiom 1.2. Let X *be the choice set, and* C *the subset of* X *that contains the alternatives available to an agent with a complete preference preordering "$\geq$" defined over* X. *The agent chooses a largest element* x* *of* C. *That is, if* x* *is chosen, there is no* $y \in$ C *such that* $y > x^*$.

So far we have made no assumptions about the choice set X. It is convenient, however, to impose additional structure on this set. For many purposes, assuming that X is a normed vector space is sufficient. This allows us to say, for example, that two alternatives, x and y, are similar or close to each other. Once a notion of distance (a metric or, more generally, a topology) is defined on X, it seems reasonable to require that similar alternatives not be too far from each other in the consumer's preference ranking. This leads to the following regularity condition.

Definition 1.3. Continuity. Let (X, d) be a metric space. We say that the preferences represented by the preorder "$\geq$" are continuous if for any x in X, the sets

$$B(x) = \{y \in X : y \geq x\} \quad \text{and} \quad W(x) = \{y \in X : y \leq x\}$$

are closed in (X, d).

Here $B(x)$ is the set of points of X that are weakly preferred to x by the agent, and $W(x)$ is the set of points that are weakly worse than x given the consumer's preferences. Requiring them to be closed means, for example, that if we consider a convergent sequence $\{y_n\} \to y$ of points all of which are weakly better than x, then the limit of the sequence, y, is also weakly better than x. It is easy to see that this condition is equivalent to the requirement that the set "$\geq$" be closed in $X \times X$. Alternatively, the complement of $W(x)$, that is, the set of alternatives that are strictly preferred to x, is open. Hence, if y is strictly preferred to x, any other alternative y' that is sufficiently close to y (in terms of the distance function $d(\ )$) will also be strictly preferred to x.

It is apparent that at this level of generality, the axioms of rationality do not buy us much. Our two axioms amount to the assumptions (i) that agents have consistent preferences over all available choices and (ii) that they act accordingly. That is, people do what they like best – provided they can. To get any predictions out of this structure, we clearly have to be more specific about agents' preferences and about the constraints they face. In general this can be done only with a more specific situation in mind, but we can list two further assumptions that are useful in many situations. The first one is that people prefer more to less. Hence, we introduce a new concept that roughly captures the "greediness" that economists often assume of their "agents."

Definition 1.4. (Strong) monotonicity. Let the choice space X be a subset of $\mathbb{R}^n$. Preferences are said to be (strongly) monotonic if

$$x > y \Rightarrow x \succ y$$

In the context of standard consumer theory this means that given two bundles x and y that are identical except for the fact that x has more of some good, the consumer always prefers x. To some extent this is a matter of definition: If a good is undesirable (a "bad"), we may consider the negative of its quantity as a good, and the axiom holds. Weaker versions of monotonicity are often used and suffice for most purposes. The idea, however, is the same: Assumptions of this type often capture the view that agents pursue their own self-interest. This may be thought of as specializing rationality to selfish behavior, but it need not be so: There is nothing in the model that rules out altruistic preferences.

Given continuity and some sort of monotonicity (possibly weaker than we are assuming), there is an interesting connection between the topological and order properties of X. In particular, the indifference subrelation

$$I = \{(x, y) \in X \times X; \, x \sim y\}$$

turns out to be the topological boundary of "$\succeq$," thought of as a subset of $X \times X$. The strict preference relation "$>$" is therefore the interior of "$\succeq$". This result will be useful later in connection with the concept of smooth preferences.

Problem 1.5. Let "$\succeq$" be a continuous and monotonic preference preorder defined on a subset X of $\mathbb{R}^n$. Show that $\partial \succeq = I \equiv \{(x, y) \in X \times X; \, x \sim y\}$.

The last assumption we introduce is that preferences are convex, in the sense that convex combinations of alternatives are preferred to "pure" choices. In many cases this can be interpreted as capturing a taste for variety or diversification.

Definition 1.6. Convexity. Let the choice space X be a convex subset of $\mathbb{R}^n$. Preferences are said to be convex if

$$x \succeq y \Rightarrow \lambda x + (1 - \lambda) y \succeq y \, \forall \, \lambda \in (0, 1)$$

A stronger version of this property (strict convexity) requires that

$$x \succeq y \text{ and } x \neq y \Rightarrow \lambda x + (1 - \lambda) y > y \, \forall \, \lambda \in (0, 1)$$

Notice that in the definitions of monotonicity and convexity we have required X to be a subset of a finite-dimensional Euclidean space. Although more general choice spaces are often used, this is quite adequate for our purposes in this section.

Problem 1.7. Let "$\succeq$" be a convex preference preorder defined on a convex set X. Show that the better-than sets induced by these preferences,

$$B(y) = \{x \in X; \, x \succeq y\}$$

are convex.

We close this section with a theorem which shows that it is possible to obtain some results working directly with preference preorderings. On the other hand, this probably is not the easiest way to proceed. The following section will show that it is possible to represent a preference preordering by a real-valued function. Once this is done, we can use more standard mathematical techniques to analyze models of individual choice.

Theorem 1.8. Let X *be a subset of* $\mathbb{R}^n$. *Let* C, *the feasible subset of* X, *be compact and nonempty. Suppose the preference relation "$\succeq$" is a complete and continuous preorder. Then the set of largest elements*

$$x(\succeq, C) = \{x \in C : x \succeq y \; \forall y \in C\}$$

is nonempty. If "$\succeq$" is strictly convex and C *is a convex set, then* $x(\succeq, C)$ *contains a single element.*

Proof. For each x, let $B(x, C) = B(x) \cap C = \{y \in C : y \succeq x\}$ be the set containing all feasible alternatives that are weakly better than x. Because $B(x, C)$ is the intersection of two closed sets, it is closed itself. Let $x_1, \ldots, x_n$ be a finite collection of elements of C. Without loss of generality we can assume that $x_1 \succeq x_i$ for all $i = 2, \ldots, n$. Hence, $x_1 \in \cap_{i=1}^n B(x_i, C)$, and it follows that the collection of sets $\{B(x, C); x \in C\}$ has the finite-intersection property (i.e., any finite subcollection has a nonempty intersection). By assumption, C is compact, so every collection of closed sets with the finite-intersection property has a nonempty intersection (by Theorem 8.13 in Chapter 2). In particular, $\cap_{x \in C} B(x, C) \neq \emptyset$, and because this set must be contained in $x(\succeq, C)$, the latter is nonempty.

Finally, assume that preferences are strictly convex, and suppose we have two distinct maximizers, x and x'. Then $x \sim x'$, and by the assumption that preferences are strictly convex, any convex combination $\lambda x + (1 - \lambda)x'$, with $\lambda \in (0, 1)$, is preferred to both x and x'. If C is convex, moreover, such combinations are feasible. But then x and x' cannot be maximizers, and we have reached a contradiction. $\qquad\square$

(b) Representation by a Utility Function

Definition 1.9. A real-valued function $U^i : X^i \longrightarrow \mathbb{R}$ is said to represent a preference preordering $\{\succeq_i\}$ defined on the choice set X^i of agent i if

$$\forall x, y \in X^i, \; x \succeq_i y \Leftrightarrow U^i(x) \geq U^i(y)$$

That is, U^i represents $\{\succeq_i\}$ if and only if, given any two alternatives, the function $U^i(\ )$ assigns a larger value to the one that is preferred by the agent. We refer to the function $U^i(\ )$ as the payoff, objective, or *utility function* for agent i. The subindex i is used in the definition to emphasize that different agents typically will have different preferences, even over a common set of alternatives; from here on, it will be omitted.

A utility function provides a convenient tool for modeling the behavior of a rational agent. Its advantage over the more primitive representation of preferences discussed in the preceding section stems primarily from the fact that functions are generally easier to manipulate than preorders. In particular, there is a well-developed theory of maximization for real-valued functions that can be applied to choice problems once preferences are represented by utility functions.

It is clear that given a numerical function U defined on X we can work back to a preference preorder. The converse statement is harder to prove and requires some restrictions on X and "$\succeq_i$." A number of representation theorems are available in the literature. We will state without proof a fairly general theorem due to Debreu and then prove a weaker result using monotonicity to simplify the proof.

Theorem 1.10. Representation of preferences by a numerical function (1). A continuous preference preorder {≥} defined on a convex subset X *of a separable normed vector space can be represented by a continuous real-valued function.*

In fact, the theorem holds for separable topological spaces. A topological space Y is separable if it contains a countable subset C whose closure is Y itself (i.e., $\bar{C} = Y$). Any Euclidean space E is separable, for example, because the set of vectors with rational coordinates is countable and dense in E. Convexity of X can be replaced with connectedness. The assumption of connectedness, in turn, can be dispensed with if we assume that X is a perfectly separable topological space (i.e., if it contains a countable class $\mathbb{O}$ of open sets such that every open set in X is the union of sets in the class $\mathbb{O}$). A separable metric space is perfectly separable. For proofs and further discussion of these results, see Debreu (1983b, pp. 105ff.).

It is easy to see that the utility function that represents a preference preorder is not uniquely defined. Any monotonically increasing transformation $\varphi(\ )$ of $U(\ )$ will represent exactly the same preferences, because with $\varphi(\ )$ strictly increasing, we have

$$U(x) \geq U(y) \quad \text{if and only if} \quad \varphi[U(x)] \geq \varphi[U(y)]$$

for all $x, y \in X$. Hence, we say that $U(\ )$ is an *ordinal* (as opposed to cardinal) utility function. That is, the sign of the difference $U(x) - U(y)$ is important because it tells us which outcome is preferred – but the value of this difference is meaningless, as it will change with any nontrivial increasing transformation $\varphi(\ )$.

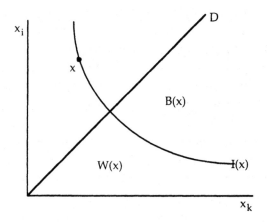

Figure 8.1. A well-behaved indifference map.

Theorem 1.11. Representation theorem (2). Let $X = \mathbb{R}^n_+ = \{x \in \mathbb{R}^n; x_i \geq 0 \;\forall$ $i = 1, \ldots, n\}$, and assume that the preference relation "$\gtrsim$" defined on X is a complete preordering, continuous and strictly monotone. Then "$\gtrsim$" can be represented by a real-valued, continuous, and increasing payoff function $U: X \longrightarrow \mathbb{R}$. If preferences are convex, U is quasiconcave.

To see how a utility function can be constructed, it is useful to think of representing the preference preorder "$\gtrsim$" in terms of its indifference sets. We have seen that a preference preordering can be decomposed into a symmetric part and an asymmetric part. The symmetric part is the indifference relation $\{\sim\}$. It is easy to see that $\{\sim\}$ is an equivalence relation. It follows that the indifference sets

$$I(x) = \{y \in X; y \sim x\}$$

form a partition of X. That is, each x in X belongs to precisely one such set. If preferences are continuous and monotonic, we get a picture familiar from basic courses in microeconomics: The indifference sets are indeed indifference "curves" (i.e., connected sets), and each such curve is the common boundary between the (closed) better-than and worse-than sets, $B(x)$ and $W(x)$.

If the picture is "correct," then we can construct a utility function by assigning a number to each indifference curve. For example, if each indifference curve intersects the 45° line (labeled D in Figure 8.1) exactly once, we can assign to all the x's on a given indifference curve the distance from their intersection with the diagonal to the origin (we will do something like that later). Intuitively speaking, for this approach to work we need to have the "right number" of "nice" indifference curves. The proof of the following lemma should clarify what we mean by this.

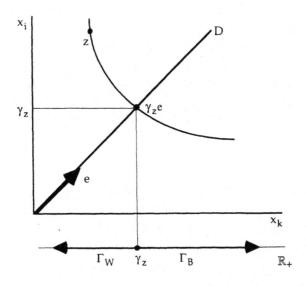

Figure 8.2.

Lemma 1.12. Let "$\succeq$" be a continuous and strictly monotone preorder defined on $X = \mathbb{R}^n_+$*. Then, given any* $z \in X$*, the indifference set* $I(z) = \{x \in X;$ $x \sim z\}$ *intersects the "diagonal line"* $D = \{x \in \mathbb{R}^n_+; x_1 = \ldots = x_n\}$ *precisely once.*

Proof. The set D of bundles with the same amounts of each commodity (the "diagonal line") can be described by

$$D = \left\{ x \in \mathbb{R}^n_+; \ x = \gamma e \text{ for some } \gamma \in \mathbb{R}_+ \right\}$$

where $e = \underline{1} = (1, 1, \ldots, 1)$. Hence, there is a one-to-one correspondence between D and $\mathbb{R}_+$. Fix some arbitrary bundle z in X, and consider the subsets of $\mathbb{R}_+$ corresponding to bundles in D that are respectively weakly better and weakly worse than z:

$$\Gamma_B = \{\gamma \in \mathbb{R}_+; \ \gamma e \succeq z\} \quad \text{and} \quad \Gamma_w = \{\gamma \in \mathbb{R}_+; \ \gamma e \preceq z\}$$

(refer to Figure 8.2). By strong monotonicity, both of these sets are non-empty. (For example, all γ such that $\gamma > \max_i z_i$ are in Γ_B, and all those with $\gamma < \min_i z_i$ are in Γ_w). Moreover, the assumed completeness of the preference preorder implies that Γ_B and Γ_w must add up to $\mathbb{R}_+$ (i.e., $\mathbb{R}_+ = \Gamma_B \cup \Gamma_w$), for any bundle γe must satisfy either $\gamma e \succeq z$ or $\gamma e \preceq z$ (or both).

Next, we show that continuity implies that both Γ_B and Γ_w are closed sets. Let $\{\gamma_n\}$ be a convergent sequence of nonnegative real numbers with limit γ, and assume that $\gamma_n \in \Gamma_B$ for all n. Then $\{x_n; x_n = \gamma_n e\}$ is a sequence of bundles contained in $B(z)$ that converges to γe. Because the set $B(z)$ is closed, by the continuity of preferences, the limit of $\{x_n\}$ lies in $B(z)$. That is, $\gamma e \succeq z \in$

$B(z)$, which implies that $\gamma \in \Gamma_B$ and therefore the closedness of Γ_B. A similar argument will work for Γ_w.

Finally, because $\mathbb{R}_+ = (0, \infty)$ is connected (i.e., has no "holes"),[2] and we have $\mathbb{R}_+ = \Gamma_B \cup \Gamma_w$, with both Γ_B and Γ_w closed, it follows that these sets must have at least one point in common (otherwise they would be separated, and that would contradict the connectedness of $\mathbb{R}_+$). Hence, there exists some γ_z such that $\gamma_z e \sim z$. By strong monotonicity, this point of intersection between $I(z)$ and D is unique, for $\gamma e > \gamma_z e$ implies $\gamma e > \gamma_z e \sim z$, and $\gamma < \gamma_z$ implies $\gamma e < z$. $\qquad \square$

With this result, the proof of the representation theorem is easy. Given some x in X, we look for the point where the indifference surface $I(x)$ intersects the diagonal line $D = \{x \in \mathbb{R}^n; x = \gamma e, \text{with } \gamma \in \mathbb{R}\}$ and assign to x the number γ_x corresponding to this point. Because we have just shown that this number exists and is unique, we have in fact defined a function $U: \mathbb{R}^n \longrightarrow \mathbb{R}$, with $U(x) = \gamma_x$, where γ_x is such that $\gamma_x e \sim x$.

We will now show that $U(\ )$ does represent the given preferences and is increasing. Take two bundles x and y, with $x \geq y$. By construction, we have

$$U(x) = \gamma_x, \quad \text{where } \gamma_x e \sim x \quad \text{and} \quad U(y) = \gamma_y, \quad \text{where } \gamma_y e \sim y$$

Hence,

$$\gamma_x e \sim x \geq y \sim \gamma_y e$$

and by monotonicity $U(x) = \gamma_x \geq \gamma_y = U(y)$ (for otherwise $\gamma_x e$ would be dominated by $\gamma_y e$ and could not be preferred to it). Hence, $U(\ )$ does represent "$\geq$." Moreover, $U(\ )$ is an increasing function, for if $x \geq y$, then $x \geq y$ by monotonicity, and we have just shown that this implies that $U(x) \geq U(y)$.

Next, we shall show that U is continuous. For this, it is sufficient to show that the inverse image of any closed interval is closed. But note that given any two positive real numbers γ_y and γ_z,

$$U^{-1}[\gamma_y, \gamma_z] = \{x \in \mathbb{R}^n; U(\gamma_y e) \leq U(x) \leq U(\gamma_z e)\}$$
$$= \{x \in \mathbb{R}^n; \gamma_y e \leq x \leq \gamma_z e\} = B(\gamma_y e) \cap W(\gamma_z e)$$

Hence, $U^{-1}[\gamma_x, \gamma_y]$ is the intersection of two sets, a better-than set and a worse-than set, that are closed, by the continuity of preferences. It follows that $U^{-1}[\gamma_x, \gamma_y]$ is closed, which establishes the continuity of $U(\ )$. Finally, if preferences are convex, the upper contour sets of this function, $\{x \in X; U(x) \geq \alpha\}$, are convex sets, because

$$\{x \in X; U(x) \geq \alpha\} = \{x \in X; x \geq \alpha e\} = B(\alpha e)$$

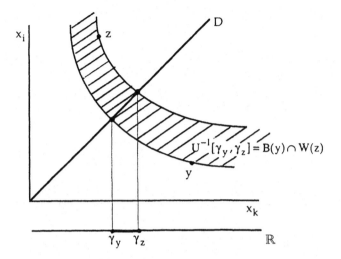

Figure 8.3. Continuity of the utility function.

and the better-than set $B(\alpha e)$ is convex, by Problem 1.7. This implies that $U(\ )$ is quasiconcave (by Theorem 3.2 in Chapter 6). □

The following problem shows that under our assumptions, indifference sets are indeed nicely behaved indifference curves, with no holes in them.

Problem 1.13. Let "≥" be a continuous and strictly monotone preference preorder defined on $X = \mathbb{R}_+^n$, and let z be an arbitrary point in X. We will show that the indifference set $I(z)$ is connected.

A standard way to show that a set A is connected is by showing that the set is homeomorphic to another one B that is known to be connected – that is, by establishing that there exists an invertible continuous function $h(\ )$ with a continuous inverse that maps A onto B. Then $A = h^{-1}(B)$ is the continuous image of a connected set and therefore is connected itself (by Theorem 9.3 in Chapter 2).

In this case, let B be the open unit simplex

$$\Delta = \{z \in \mathbb{R}_{++}^n;\ ze = 1\}$$

where $e = \underline{1}$ and $\mathbb{R}_{++}^n = \{x \in \mathbb{R}^n;\ x_i > 0\ \forall\ i = 1, \ldots, n\}$. Given an indifference set $I(z)$, we "project" it onto Δ by following a ray through the origin from each point x in I until it intersects the simplex (Figure 8.4). Hence, the function $h(\ )$ is of the form

$$h(x) = \frac{1}{xe} x = \frac{1}{\sum_{i=1}^{n} x_i} x$$

Show that $h(\ )$ is a homeomorphism.

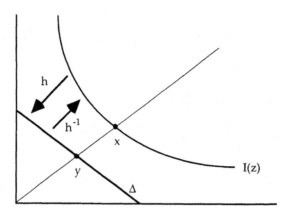

Figure 8.4.

Hint: The only potentially difficult part is establishing the continuity of $h^{-1}(\ )$. Use the sequential characterization of continuity and seek a contradiction. In particular, fix some arbitrary y^0 in Δ and assume that $\{y_n\} \to y^0$, but $\{x_n = h^{-1}(y_n)\}$ does not converge to $x^0 = h^{-1}(y^0)$. Notice that because y and $x = h^{-1}(y)$ lie on the same ray through the origin for any y in Δ, we can write

$$x_n = h^{-1}(y_n) = \lambda_n y_n \quad \text{and} \quad x^0 = h^{-1}(y^0) = \lambda^0 y^0$$

for some positive real numbers λ_n and λ^0. Observe that $\{\lambda_n\}$ is a sequence of real numbers bounded below by zero. Consider two possibilities in turn: (i) $\{\lambda_n\}$ is bounded above, and (ii) $\{\lambda_n\}$ is not bounded above. Then seek a contradiction.

(c) Smooth Preferences

This short section shows that, given some additional conditions, a preference relation "$\geq$" can be represented by a twice continuously differentiable utility function. This is a very convenient result, because it allows us to use calculus techniques both to characterize the solutions to the optimization problems that agents are supposed to solve and to do comparative statics.

Intuitively, differentiability is obtained by strengthening the continuity assumption with the requirement that the indifferent sets be smooth surfaces in X or, more formally, that the indifference relation be a smooth manifold in $X \times X$.

Definition 1.14. Smooth preferences. Let X be an open subset of $\mathbb{R}^n$. A monotone preference relation "$\geq$" defined on X is said to be of class C^k ($k \geq 0$) if the indifference subrelation

$$I = \{(x, y) \in X \times X; \ x \sim y\}$$

is a C^k manifold.

Recall that a manifold is a set that is locally diffeomorphic to an open set in a Euclidean space. If the diffeomorphism in the definition is of class C^k, we have a C^k manifold. If $k \geq 1$, we speak of smooth manifolds and smooth preferences. (A function is of class C^0 if it is continuous.)

Theorem 1.15. Let X *be an open subset of* $\mathbb{R}^n$. *A strictly monotone preference preorder "$\succeq$" defined on* X *can be represented by a* C^k *utility function with no critical points if and only if it is itself of class* C^k *(i.e., if the indifference relation* I *is a* C^k *manifold).*

Proof. We prove only the easy part: If "$\succeq$" can be represented by a smooth utility function U with no critical points, then I must be a smooth manifold. To see this, define $v: X \times X \longrightarrow \mathbb{R}$ by

$$v(x, y) = U(x) - U(y)$$

By assumption, $U(\ )$ has no critical points, so $DU(x) \neq \underline{0}$, and this in turn implies $Dv(x, y) = [DU(x), -DU(y)] \neq \underline{0}$. Hence $v(\ )$ has no critical points, and therefore the set

$$I = v^{-1}(\underline{0}) = \{(x, y) \in X \times X; \ U(x) = U(y)\}$$

is the inverse image of a regular value of v. By the regular-value theorem (Theorem 2.3 in Chapter 5), I is a smooth manifold.

The converse can be found in Mas-Colell (1985, pp. 64–6). In fact, he proves a more general result: The theorem holds for locally nonsatiated preferences with connected indifferent sets. Because strong monotonicity trivially implies local nonsatiation and, by Problem 1.13, connectedness of the indifference sets, the theorem follows as stated. $\square$

We conclude with the observation that given an appropriate topology on the space of continuous preference relations, the set of smooth preference relations is dense in this space. Intuitively, this means that any continuous preference relation can be approximated "fairly well" by a smooth one – and hence that the assumption of a differentiable utility function is not unreasonable, at least as a first approximation.

2. Consumer Theory

Consider an agent (whom we will call the consumer) who has preferences defined over the set $\mathbb{R}_+^G$ of possible consumption bundles, $x = (x^1, \ldots, x^G)$, where we interpret $x^i \geq 0$ as the amount of good i consumed by the agent. We assume that these preferences can be represented by a continuous, increasing, and quasiconcave utility function $U: \mathbb{R}^G_+ \longrightarrow \mathbb{R}$. Given income y and a vector of commodity prices $p \in \mathbb{R}^G_+$, the set of feasible consumption bundles is described by the budget correspondence,

$$B(p,y) = \{x \in \mathbb{R}^G_+; \, px \leq y\}$$

which gives, for each price-income pair, the set of bundles whose cost $px = \sum_{i=1}^G p_i x_i$ does not exceed the available income, $y \geq 0$. The consumer will be assumed to maximize utility subject to the constraint imposed by the budget correspondence.

(a) *Utility Maximization and Ordinary Demand Functions*

Under the preceding assumptions, the problem faced by the consumer can be written

$$V(p, y) = \max_{x \in B(p,y)} U(x) \qquad\qquad \text{(C.U)}$$

where $B(p, y) = \{x \in \mathbb{R}^G_+; \, y - px \geq 0\}$. The maximum-value function for the consumer's problem, $V(p, y)$, called the indirect utility function, gives the maximum utility attainable by a consumer who faces income y and prices p. The solution of the problem is given by a Marshallian or ordinary demand correspondence,

$$x(p, y) = \arg \max_{x \in B(p,y)} U(x)$$

which gives for each pair (p, y) the set of optimal consumption bundles. If this correspondence is single-valued, we speak of a demand function. Notice that the indirect utility function and the demand correspondence are related by the expression

$$V(p, y) = U(x(p, y))$$

because the maximum attainable utility is the utility provided by any optimal consumption bundle.

In this section we will analyze the properties of the demand correspondence and the indirect utility function. We start with a result that gives sufficient conditions for the continuity of the budget correspondence[3] (i.e., for the set of feasible options to change continuously with changes in the parameters p and y).

Theorem 2.1. Continuity of the budget correspondence. Let $B: \mathbb{R}_+^{G+1} \to\to \mathbb{R}_+^G$ *be defined by* $B(p, y) = \{x \in \mathbb{R}_+^G; px \le y\}$. *Then* B *is continuous at any point* (p, y), *with* $p \gg \underline{0}$ *and* y > 0.

Proof. Notice that the constraint function is linear and therefore concave in *x* for given *p* and *y*. Hence, we can apply Theorem 2.2 in Chapter 7, and it suffices to show that $B(p, y)$ is compact and contains an interior point, which is clearly the case under the given assumptions. □

Problem 2.2. Give a direct proof of the continuity of the budget correspondence. Hint: Use the sequential characterizations of upper hemicontinuity and lower hemicontinuity. For upper hemicontinuity, consider a sequence $x_n \in B(p_n, y_n)$ converging to a point $(p, y) \gg \underline{0}$. Show that it is bounded, and apply the Bolzano-Weierstrass theorem. For lower hemicontinuity, construct the sequence as in Problem 2.6 in Chapter 7.

Given the preceding result, we can now use the theorem of the maximum to guarantee the upper hemicontinuity of the demand correspondence and the continuity of the indirect utility function. In addition to these two results, the following theorem establishes some other useful properties of these mappings.

Theorem 2.3. Properties of the demand correspondence and the indirect utility function. Let the utility function $U: \mathbb{R}_+^G \to \mathbb{R}$ *be continuous, increasing, and quasiconcave. Then for each price–income pair* (p, y), *with* $p \gg \underline{0}$ *and* y > 0, *there exists at least one solution to the consumer problem* (C.U). *Moreover, the demand correspondence* x(p, y) *is uhc and homogeneous of degree zero, in the sense that if* $z \in x(p, y)$, *then* $z \in x(\mu p, \mu y)$ *for any* $\mu > 0$. *The indirect utility function* V(p, y) *is continuous, quasiconvex, homogeneous of degree zero in* (p, y), *increasing in income, and decreasing in prices.*

If, in addition, U( ) *is strictly increasing, then the budget constraint holds with equality, that is,* px = y *for any* $x \in x(p, y)$ *(the "adding-up" property). If* U( ) *is strictly quasiconcave, then* x(p, y) *is a (single-valued) function and continuous.*

Proof

- Existence of a solution and uniqueness, given strict quasiconcavity. If $p \gg \underline{0}$ and y > 0, the budget set $B(p, y) = \{x \in \mathbb{R}_+^G; px \le y\}$ is a nonempty compact and convex set. Hence the existence of a solution to the consumer problem follows by the extreme-value theorem (Theorem 8.22 in Chapter 2). Given strict quasiconcavity, the solution will be unique, by Theorem 1.11 in Chapter 7.

- Continuity of $V(p, y)$ and $x(p, y)$. Because $B(p, y)$ is compact-valued and continuous for any (p, y), with $p \gg \underline{0}$ and $y > 0$, the theorem of the maximum (Theorem 2.1 in Chapter 7) guarantees the continuity of $V(p, y)$ and the upper hemicontinuity of $x(p, y)$. Because a uhc single-valued correspondence is a continuous function (see Section 11 of Chapter 2), moreover, $x(p, y)$ is a continuous function whenever U is strictly quasiconcave.

- Adding up. We will now show that any optimal consumption bundle exhausts the available income when $U(\ )$ is strictly increasing. Suppose this is not the case, that is, that there exists some bundle $z \in x(p, y)$ with $pz < y$. Then there is some consumption bundle that dominates z and is still feasible (i.e., there exists a point $z' > z$ such that $pz' < y$). Because $U(\ )$ is strictly increasing by assumption, we then have $U(z') > U(z)$, which contradicts the assumption that z is a maximizer.

- Homogeneity of $x(p, y)$ and $V(p, y)$. Notice that any equiproportionate changes in prices and income do not change the budget set. That is, if $px \leq y$, then $(\mu p)x = \mu(px) \leq \mu y$ for any $\mu > 0$. Hence, $B(p, y) = B(\mu p, \mu y)$ for any $\mu > 0$, and the feasible set does not change with μ. Because prices and income do not enter the objective function $U(\ )$, the consumption choice will not be affected when we multiply all prices and income by the same positive factor, and neither will utility be affected. Hence, this property extends also to the indirect utility function. Notice that $V(p, y) = U(x(p, y))$, where $x(p, y)$ is any optimal consumption bundle. Thus, we can write

$$V(\mu p, \mu y) = U[x(\mu p, \mu y)] = U[x(p, y)] = V(p, y) \quad \text{for any } \mu > 0$$

- $V(\ )$ is increasing in y and nonincreasing in prices. Take y' and y'', with $y'' > y'$. Then clearly

$$B(p, y'') \supseteq B(p, y')$$

That is, the budget set is (strictly) larger with the higher income. Let $x' \in x(p, y')$ be an optimal consumption bundle for income y'. Then x' is still feasible, but not necessarily optimal for income y'', so certainly $V(p, y'') \geq V(p, y')$. In fact, the inequality is strict when $U(\ )$ is strictly increasing, for then $px' = y' < y''$, so we can find some point $x'' > x'$ that is feasible for income y''. Then $V(p, y'') \geq U(x'') > U(x') = V(p, y')$. Thus, we conclude that $V(\ )$ is strictly increasing in income when $U(\ )$ is strictly increasing. A similar argument will establish monotonicity in prices.

- Quasiconvexity of $V(p, y)$. Given a real number v, the lower contour set of $V(\ )$ is the set

$$L_v = \{(p, y); \ V(p, y) \leq v\}$$

To establish the quasiconvexity of $V(\ )$, we have to show that L_v is a convex set for any given v. Let (p', y') and (p'', y'') be two arbitrary points in L_v, that is, with $V(p', y') \leq v$ and $V(p'', y'') \leq v$, and let

$$(p^\lambda, y^\lambda) = ((1 - \lambda)p' + \lambda p'', (1 - \lambda)y' + \lambda y'') \quad \text{for } \lambda \in (0, 1)$$

We want to show that $(p^\lambda, y^\lambda) \in L_v$, that is, that $V(p^\lambda, y^\lambda) \le v$. Notice that it is sufficient to show that for any point x that is feasible for (p^λ, y^λ) (i.e., such that $p^\lambda x \le y^\lambda$), we have $U(x) \le v$, because $V(p^\lambda, y^\lambda)$ is the value of one such point.

First, notice that $p^\lambda x \le y^\lambda$ implies

$$p^\lambda x = [(1-\lambda)p' + \lambda p'']x = (1-\lambda)p'x + \lambda p''x \le (1-\lambda)y' + \lambda y'' = y^\lambda$$

Now, because

$$(1-\lambda)p'x + \lambda p''x \le (1-\lambda)y' + \lambda y''$$

it must be true that either $p'x \le y'$ or $p''x \le y''$ or both. If the first inequality holds, then x is feasible, but not necessarily optimal for (p', y'), and we have $U(x) \le V(p', y') \le v$. Otherwise, $p''x \le y''$ implies $U(x) \le V(p'', y'') \le v$, by the same argument. In either case, $U(x) \le v$, and the result follows. $\qquad\square$

Problem 2.4. Show that if $U(\ )$ is homothetic, then demand is linear in income, that is, $x(p, y) = yx(p, 1)$.

Hint: Recall that a function is said to be homothetic if it is a monotonically increasing transformation of a homogeneous function.

Let us now strengthen our continuity assumptions and require that $U(\ )$ be a twice continuously differentiable function. In this case, both the demand and indirect utility mappings are differentiable functions, and we can obtain some further results. In particular, we assume that $U(\ )$ is a C^2, strictly quasiconcave, and strictly increasing function that satisfies the second-order sufficient condition for strict quasiconcavity in terms of the bordered Hessian given in Theorem 3.11 in Chapter 6. These assumptions will allow us to use the techniques developed in Chapter 5 and apply the implicit-function theorem to analyze the comparative-statics properties of the ordinary demand functions.

Because we know that the budget constraint will hold as an equality when $U(\ )$ is strictly increasing, we can rewrite (C.U) as a Lagrange problem:

$$\max_x\{U(x) \text{ s.t. } y - px = 0\} \qquad \text{(C.U')}$$

where we are implicitly assuming that we have identified a priori those G goods that will be consumed in positive amounts, and we exclude the rest. Differentiating the Lagrangian for the problem,

$$\pounds(x, \lambda; p, y) = U(x) + \lambda(y - px)$$

yields the first-order conditions

$$\frac{\partial \pounds}{\partial x_i} = \frac{\partial U}{\partial x_i} - \lambda p_i = 0 \Rightarrow \lambda = \frac{U_i(x)}{p_i} \quad \forall \, i = 1, \dots, G \tag{1}$$

$$\frac{\partial \pounds}{\partial \lambda} = y - px = 0 \tag{2}$$

where $U_i(\;)$ denotes the partial derivative of $U(\;)$ with respect to its ith argument. Given our assumptions, these conditions will characterize a unique optimal solution x^*. Notice that optimality requires

$$\frac{U_k(x)}{p_k} = \lambda = \frac{U_i(x)}{p_i} \Leftrightarrow \frac{p_i}{p_k} = \frac{U_i(x^*)}{U_k(x^*)}$$

This is the familiar condition requiring that the marginal utility of the last dollar spent on each good must be the same for all of them or, equivalently, that the marginal rate of substitution between any two goods i and k must be equal to the ratio of their prices.

Equations (1) and (2) constitute a system of $G+1$ equations in $G+1$ unknowns that we would like to solve for the ordinary demand functions, $x_i^* = x_i(p, y)$ for $i = 1, \dots, G$, and the multiplier, $\lambda^* = \lambda(p, y)$. In some simple cases it is possible to solve (1) and (2) explicitly for x^* and λ^*. In general, however, such closed-form solutions are not available, and we have to resort to the implicit-function theorem (IFT) to do comparative statics. To apply this theorem, rewrite the first-order conditions in the form

$$F^i(x, \lambda; p) = U_i(x) - \lambda p_i = 0 \quad \text{for each } i = 1, \dots, G \tag{3}$$

$$F^{G+1}(x, \lambda; p) = y - px = 0 \tag{4}$$

and observe that the Jacobian of endogenous variables of this system is given by

$$|J| = |D_{(x,\lambda)} F(x, \lambda; p)| = \begin{vmatrix} U_{11} & \cdots & U_{1G} & -p_1 \\ \cdots & \cdots & \cdots & \cdots \\ U_{G1} & \cdots & U_{GG} & -p_G \\ -p_1 & \cdots & -p_G & 0 \end{vmatrix}$$

Using the first-order conditions $(U_i = \lambda p_i)$, and factoring things out, this determinant can be written in terms of the bordered Hessian of the utility function,

$$|J| = (-1/\lambda)^{2n} \begin{vmatrix} U_{11} & \cdots & U_{1G} & U_1 \\ \cdots & \cdots & \cdots & \cdots \\ U_{G1} & \cdots & U_{GG} & U_G \\ U_1 & \cdots & U_G & 0 \end{vmatrix}$$

which is nonzero by our assumptions on $U(\ )$. Hence, the sufficient conditions for a strict local maximum hold (see Theorem 1.16 in Chapter 7), and the solution to the system of first-order conditions is a regular solution of the consumer's problem. This guarantees that we can use the IFT to compute the partial derivatives of the ordinary demand functions. In particular, we have

$$\frac{\partial x_i(p, y)}{\partial p_k} = \frac{|J_{ik}|}{|J|}$$

where J_{ik} is the matrix obtained by replacing the ith column of the Jacobian J with the vector $(D_{p_k}F(x, \lambda; p))^T$.

Unfortunately, it turns out that the sign of $|J_{ik}|$ cannot be determined unambiguously even when $i = k$. Hence, it is not necessarily true that demands are decreasing in their own price or increasing in income. The one restriction on individual behavior we get from utility maximization is the one given in the following result.

Theorem 2.5. Slutsky. Assume that U$(\ )$ *is* C^2 *and satisfies the sufficient second-order conditions for a local maximum. Then the Slutsky matrix* $[s_{ik}]$, *with*

$$s_{ik} = \frac{\partial x_i(p, y)}{\partial p_k} + x_k(p, y)\frac{\partial x_i(p, y)}{d_y} \tag{5}$$

is symmetric and negative semidefinite.

A proof of this theorem (which can also be established by direct computation using the IFT) and a discussion of its meaning will be given later. For the time being, we just note that the symmetry of the Slutsky matrix requires that

$$s_{ik} = s_{ki} \Rightarrow \frac{\partial x_i(p, y)}{\partial p_k} + x_k(p, y)\frac{\partial x_i(p, y)}{\partial y} = \frac{\partial x_k(p, y)}{\partial p_i} + x_i(p, y)\frac{\partial x_k(p, y)}{\partial y} \tag{6}$$

and its negative definiteness implies that the elements in its principal diagonal will be nonpositive, that is,

$$s_{ii} = \frac{\partial x_i(p, y)}{\partial p_i} + x_i(p, y)\frac{\partial x_i(p, y)}{\partial y} \le 0 \tag{7}$$

This last property can be used to establish what Samuelson calls the "fundamental theorem of demand theory": If a good is not inferior, its ordinary demand curve is downward-sloping. This follows immediately from (7) and the definition of inferior good. If a good is not inferior, then the income effect is positive, that is, $\partial x_i(p, y)/\partial y \geq 0$, and (7) implies

$$\frac{\partial x_i(p, y)}{\partial p_i} \leq -x_i(p, y)\frac{\partial x_i(p, y)}{\partial y} \leq 0$$

On the other hand, inferior goods may have upward-sloping demands (these are the so-called Giffen goods) if the income effect is negative and strong enough to outweigh the substitution effect.

These results completely exhaust the implications of demand theory. It can be shown that given a set of homogeneous demand functions that add up to income and satisfy the Slutsky conditions, it is possible to "integrate" the demands back to a well-behaved utility function. Hence, we can go not only from utility to demand, but from demand to utility as well. The two sets of properties (those of $U(\ )$ and those of $x(\ )$) are fully equivalent, and this implies that there are no more implications to be had from utility maximization. Note that our results are rather weak: Maximization of a quasi-concave utility function does not impose too many restrictions on ordinary demand functions.

The following problem asks the reader to verify that there exists a simple relationship between the indirect utility function and Marshallian demand. In applied demand analysis it is sometimes more convenient to start out with some specification of the indirect utility function that has reasonable properties and then derive the demand functions from it – rather than starting with the direct utility function.

Problem 2.6. Roy's identity. Assume that the indirect utility function is differentiable. Show that then

$$x_i(p, y) = \frac{-\partial V(p, y)/\partial p_i}{\partial V(p, y)/\partial y}$$

Problem 2.7. Consider the following indirect utility function:

$$V(p, y) = \frac{y - \sum_k p_k b_k}{\prod_k p_k^{a_k}}, \quad \text{where } \sum_k a_k = 1$$

Use Roy's identity to find the ordinary demand functions.

(b) Expenditure Minimization and Compensated Demand

In this section we approach the consumer's decision problem from a slightly different perspective. Rather than taking income as given, we fix an arbitrary utility level u (i.e., an indifference curve) and solve for the consumption bundle x^* that will minimize the expenditure (cost) needed to put the consumer on this particular indifference curve. That is, we will solve the problem

$$\min_{x}\{px;\ U(x) \geq u\} \qquad \text{(C.E)}$$

If we write the solution to this expenditure-minimization problem as a function of the parameters, we obtain the optimal consumption bundle as a function $h(p, u)$ of prices and the required utility level

$$h(p, u) = \arg \min_{x}\{px;\ U(x) \geq u\}$$

The resulting mapping (with u rather than y as an argument) is known as a compensated or Hicksian demand function or correspondence, because it allows us, by holding utility constant, to abstract from income effects, thus isolating the pure substitution effect of price changes on consumption behavior. The (minimum) value function for the expenditure-minimization problem,

$$E(p, u) = \min_{x}\{px;\ U(x) \geq u\} = ph(p, u)$$

is known as the expenditure function and gives the minimum expenditure necessary to achieve a desired level of utility u. As usual, we can recover $E(p, u)$ by substituting the optimal solution of the problem (i.e., the Hicksian demands, $h(\ )$) back into the objective function.

In this section we investigate the properties of the compensated demands and the expenditure function. In the next section we will discuss the relationship between the two formulations of the consumer problem and relate the properties of compensated and ordinary demands to each other, proving, in particular, the Slutsky theorem.

Theorem 2.8. Properties of the compensated demand correspondence and the expenditure function. Let the utility function $U : \mathbb{R}_+^G \longrightarrow \mathbb{R}$ *be continuous, strictly increasing, and quasiconcave, and consider the problem*

$$E(p, u) \min_{x}\{px;\ U(x) \geq u\} \qquad \text{(C.E)}$$

Let $\underline{u} = U(\underline{0})$ *and* $(\bar{u}) = sup\{U(x); x \in \mathbb{R}_+^n\} \leq \infty$. *Then for each* $p \gg \underline{0}$ *and* $u \in (\underline{u}, \bar{u})$, *there exists at least one solution to the consumer problem (C.E), and $h(p, u)$ is uhc in this set. Moreover, the compensated demand correspondence $h(p, u)$ is homogeneous of degree 0 in p (in the sense that $h(p, u) = h(\mu p, \mu y)$ for any $\mu > 0$), and the solution of the problem leaves no excess utility, meaning that for any $x \in h(p, u)$ we have $U(x) = u$. If $U(\ )$ is strictly quasiconcave, then $h(p, u)$ is a (single-valued) function and is continuous.*

The expenditure function $E(p, u)$ *is a continuous function, concave and increasing in prices, strictly increasing in* u, *and homogeneous of degree 1 in prices.*

Proof

- Existence of solutions and uniqueness, given strict quasiconcavity. The feasible set $\Gamma(u) = \{x \in \mathbb{R}_{+}^{G}; U(x) \geq u\} = U^{-1}[u, \infty)$ is closed, by the continuity of $U(\ )$, but is unbounded and therefore not compact. It is not difficult, however, to "compactify" it. Given $p \gg \underline{0}$ and $u \in (\underline{u}, \bar{u})$, choose a bundle $\bar{x}$ such that $U(\bar{x}) > u$. Such a bundle exists, by the assumption that $u \in (\underline{u}, \bar{u})$. Then $\bar{x}$ is feasible for u, but not necessarily optimal, and this implies that for any $x \in h(p, u)$ we have $px \leq p\bar{x}$. Hence the solution to (C.E) will lie in the compact set

$$\bar{\Gamma}(p, u) = \{x \in \mathbb{R}_{+}^{G}; U(x) \geq u \text{ and } px \leq p\bar{x}\}$$

Because $U(\ )$ is continuous, the extreme-value theorem guarantees the existence of a solution to (C.E). Moreover, because $U(\ )$ is quasiconcave, $\bar{\Gamma}(p, u)$ is the intersection of two convex sets and therefore is convex itself. If $U(\ )$ is strictly quasiconcave, it follows (by Theorem 1.11 in Chapter 7) that the solution is unique.

- $e(p, u)$ is strictly increasing in u. By contradiction. Suppose $e(p, u) = ph(p, u)$ is not strictly increasing in u. Then there exist utility levels u' and u'', with $u'' > u' > U(\underline{0})$, and corresponding optimal consumption bundles x' and x'', with $x' \in h(p, u')$ and $x'' \in h(p, u'')$, such that $0 < px'' \leq px'$. By the no-excess-utility property, moreover, we have $U(x'') = u'' > u' = U(x')$. Consider now a consumption bundle of the form $z = \lambda x''$, with $\lambda \in (0, 1)$. By the continuity of $U(\ )$, we can choose λ close enough to unity that $U(\lambda x'') > u' = U(x')$, and because $\lambda < 1$ we have $p(\lambda x'') = \lambda(px'') < px'' \leq px'$. This contradicts the assumption that x' solves (C.E) with required utility u', for we have found a bundle $\lambda x''$ that is strictly cheaper than x' and yields greater utility.

- $e(p, u)$ is increasing in p. Fix some u, let p' and p'' be arbitrary price vectors, with $p'' > p'$, and let x'' be optimal for (p'', u). Then x'' is feasible for (p', u) because $U(x'') \geq u$, but it does not necessarily minimize expenditure; hence,

$$e(p'', u) = p''x'' \geq p'x'' \geq e(p', u)$$

- Continuity. First we will show that $h(p, u)$ is compact-valued. As we have shown, $h(p, u)$ is contained in the compact set $\bar{\Gamma}(p, u)$ and therefore is bounded. To see that it is closed, let $m = e(p, u) = px \equiv P(x)$ for some x. Then $\{m\}$ is a closed set in $\mathbb{R}$, and $h(p, u) = P^{-1}(\{m\}) \cap U^{-1}[u, \infty)$ is the intersection of two closed sets, by the continuity of the utility function and the inner product $P(\ )$. Hence, $h(\ )$ is compact-valued, and we can use the sequential characterization of upper hemicontinuity given in Theorem 11.2 in Chapter 2.

  Thus, we have to show that given any sequence $\{(p_n, u_n)\}$ converging to (p, u), with $p \gg \underline{0}$ and $u \in (\underline{u}, \bar{u})$, every companion sequence of demands $\{x_n\}$, with $x_n \in h(p_n, u_n)$ has a convergent subsequence with limit in $h(p, u)$.

We will show that the sequence $\{x_n\}$ is bounded. Let $z \gg \underline{0}$ be such that $U(z) > u$. Because $\{u_n\} \to u$, we can assume that (possibly after deleting some initial terms of the sequence)

$$U(z) \geq u_n \ \forall \, n \tag{1}$$

Then z is feasible, but not necessarily optimal for all (u_n, p_n), and we have

$$p_n z \geq e(p_n, u_n) = p_n x_n$$

where the last equality holds because $x_n \in h(p_n, u_n)$. Hence, expenditure in the ith good is bounded by $p_n z$ (i.e., $p_n^i x_n^i \leq p_n z$). Because $\{p_n\} \to p$ (which implies that $\{p_n^i\} \to p^i$ for all i), moreover, we will have

$$p_n^i > p^i / 2 \quad \text{and} \quad p_n z \leq pz + 1$$

for n sufficiently large. Hence,

$$x_n^i \leq \frac{p_n z}{p_n^i} \leq \frac{pz + 1}{p^i / 2}$$

for all i and sufficiently large n.

Because $\{x_n\}$ is bounded, it contains a convergent subsequence, say $\{x_{n_k}\}$, with limit $\tilde{x}$. Because $x_{n_k} \in h(p_{n_k}, u_{n_k})$, we have $U(x_{n_k}) \geq u_{n_k}$ for all k, and the continuity of $U(\ )$ implies that $U(\tilde{x}) \geq u$. Hence $\tilde{x}$ is feasible for (p, u).

To establish that $\tilde{x}$ is also optimal, that is, that $\tilde{x} \in h(p, u)$, we proceed by contradiction. Suppose $\tilde{x} \notin h(p, u)$; then there exists some feasible x that costs less than $\tilde{x}$. That is, there exists some x such that

$$px < p\tilde{x} \tag{2}$$

$$U(x) \geq u \tag{3}$$

Next, we construct a sequence $\{z_{n_k}\}$ as follows:

$$z_{n_k} = \begin{cases} x & \text{if } u_{n_k} < u \\ z_{n_k} \in [z, x] \text{ s.th. } U(z_{n_k}) = u_{n_k} & \text{otherwise} \end{cases}$$

Notice that the required $z_{n_k} \in [z, x]$, with $U(z_{n_k}) = u_{n_k}$ exists whenever $u_{n_k} \geq u$, by the continuity of $U(\ )$ and the fact that $U(z) \geq u_{n_k} \geq u = U(x)$. Observe also that z_{n_k} is feasible for (p_{n_k}, u_{n_k}), by construction, but not necessarily optimal. Hence

$$p_{n_k} z_{n_k} \geq e(p_{n_k}, z_{n_k}) = p_{n_k} x_{n_k} \tag{4}$$

because $x_{n_k} \in h(p_{n_k}, u_{n_k})$. On the other hand, it can be shown that $\{z_{n_k}\} \to x$ (see Problem 2.10). Hence, taking limits of both sides of (4), and recalling that $\{x_{n_k}\} \to \tilde{x}$, we have

$$px \geq p\tilde{x} \tag{5}$$

which contradicts (2). This establishes the desired result.   □

Problem 2.9. To complete the proof of Theorem 2.8, show that under the given assumptions, we have the following:

  (i) Compensated demand is homogeneous of degree 0 in prices, and the expenditure function is homogeneous of degree 1 in p.
 (ii) The solution to the expenditure-minimization problem yields no excess utility. Hint: By contradiction. Show that if the result does not hold, then we can construct a bundle that will yield the required level of utility and will cost less than the optimum.
(iii) The expenditure function is concave in prices. Give an intuitive interpretation of this fact.

Problem 2.10. Show that the sequence $\{z_{n_k}\}$ constructed in the last part of the proof of Theorem 2.8 converges to x.

  Hint: Notice that we can choose z so that $z \gg x$, use the strict monotonicity of the utility function and the fact that $U(x) \geq u$, and seek a contradiction.

If we assume that $U(\ )$ is C^2 and strictly quasiconcave, then $h(p, u)$ is a differentiable function, and we can apply the implicit-function theorem to the first-order conditions of the expenditure-minimization problem to study the comparative statics of compensated demands. In this particular case, however, an indirect approach turns out to be much more convenient. The first step is based on the observation that by the linearity of the objective function there is a simple relationship between the expenditure function and the compensated demands.

Theorem 2.11. Shephard's lemma. Assume that U$(\ )$ *is* C^1. *Then the expenditure function is differentiable, and*

$$D_p E(p, u) = h(p, u); \quad i.e., \quad \frac{\partial E(p, u)}{\partial p_i} = h_i(p, u) \, \forall \, i$$

Proof. By the no-excess-utility property, (C.E) can be written as a standard Lagrange problem (with a single equality constraint). Shephard's lemma then follows immediately by the envelope theorem (Theorem 2.16 in Chapter 7). The Lagrangian for the expenditure-minimization problem is

$$\pounds(x, \lambda; p, u) = \sum_{i=1}^{G} p_i x_i + \lambda[U(x) - u]$$

Hence the envelope theorem yields

$$\frac{\partial E(p, u)}{\partial p_i} = \frac{\partial \pounds(x^*, \lambda^*; p, u)}{\partial p_i} = x_i^* = h_i(p, u) \qquad \square$$

Using this result, it is easy to derive some important properties of the compensated demand functions from the concavity of the expenditure function. The crucial observation is that by Shephard's lemma, the second partials of the expenditure function are the first partials of the Hicksian demands. That is,

$$\frac{\partial^2 E(p, u)}{\partial p_i \partial p_k} = \frac{\partial h_i(p, u)}{\partial p_k}$$

whenever $E(\ )$ is twice differentiable.

Theorem 2.12. *Comparative statics of compensated demand. Assume that the expenditure function is* C^2. *Then*

(i) *the compensated demand functions are decreasing in their own price, that is,* $\partial h_i(p, u)/\partial p_i \le 0$ *for all* i, *and*
(ii) *they satisfy the condition* $\partial h_i(p, u)/\partial p_k = \partial h_k(p, u)/\partial p_i$ *for all* i *and* k.

Proof

- By the concavity of the expenditure function in prices, the Hessian matrix of second derivatives of $E(\ )$ with respect to prices is negative semidefinite (by Theorem 2.18 in Chapter 6). Because all diagonal elements of a negative semidefinite matrix must be nonnegative (see the appendix to Chapter 6), we have, by Shephard's lemma,

$$\frac{\partial h_i(p, u)}{\partial p_i} = \frac{\partial^2 E(p, u)}{\partial p_i^2} \le 0 \ \forall i = 1, \dots, G$$

- If $E(p, u)$ is C^2, we have, by Young's (Schwarz's) theorem (Theorem 2.6 in Chapter 4), that the matrix of second partials is symmetric (the order of differentiation does not matter); hence,

$$\frac{\partial^2 E(p, u)}{\partial p_i \partial p_k} = \frac{\partial^2 E(p, u)}{\partial p_k \partial p_i}$$

and by Shephard's lemma this implies

$$\frac{\partial h_i(p,u)}{\partial p_k} = \frac{\partial h_k(p,u)}{\partial p_i} \qquad \square$$

The first part of the theorem says that the compensated demand functions are "downward-sloping." The reason for this should be intuitively clear. The sign of the derivative $\partial h_i(p, u)/\partial p_i$ tells us how a consumer will adjust his purchases of good i in response to an increase in its price when he also receives an income transfer that allows him to stay on the original indifference curve. By holding utility constant, the compensated demand function isolates the pure substitution effect of a price change. Barring income effects, an increase in the price of a good can only make it less attractive relative to other goods, thereby reducing its consumption. The condition given in the second part of the theorem is equivalent, as we will soon see, to the Slutsky symmetry condition asserted in Theorem 2.5.

(c) Relationship between Compensated and Ordinary Demands: The Slutsky Equation

We have analyzed the consumer's decision problem from two slightly different perspectives. In Section (a) we fixed the allowable expenditure and looked for the highest attainable indifference curve. In Section (b) we selected an arbitrary indifference curve and looked for the lowest iso-expenditure line compatible with it. It is intuitively clear that, provided we are careful to identify the correct indifference curve and expenditure levels, the two problems yield the same optimal bundle (Figure 8.5). The following result makes this equivalence more precise.

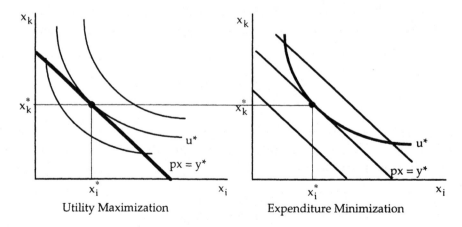

Figure 8.5. Equivalence between utility maximization and expenditure minimization.

Theorem 2.13. Equivalence between utility maximization and expenditure minimization. Let $U: \mathbb{R}_+^G \longrightarrow \mathbb{R}$ *be a strictly increasing and continuous utility function, and fix some* $p \gg \underline{0}$.

(i) *If* x_u *solves (C.U) when income is* $y > 0$, *then* x_u *solves (C.E) when the required utility is* $U(x_u)$. *Moreover, the minimized expenditure level for the latter problem is* y.

(ii) *If* x_e *solves (C.E) when the required utility level is* $u \in (\underline{u}, \bar{u})$, *then* x_e *solves (C.U) when income is* px_e. *Moreover, the maximized utility level in the second problem is* u.

Problem 2.14. Prove Theorem 2.13. Hint: By contradiction. Assume that x solves one of the problems, but not the other, and show that then it cannot solve the first one either.

Theorem 2.13 allows us to write the following identity:

$$h(p, u) \equiv x^* \equiv x(p, y) \tag{8}$$

where y is the minimum level of expenditure needed to reach the indifference curve indexed by u – and u is the maximum utility attainable with expenditure y. More explicitly, we have

$$h[p, V(p, y)] \equiv x(p, y) \tag{9}$$

$$x[p, E(p, u)] \equiv h(p, u) \tag{10}$$

Focusing on the *i*th component of (10),

$$h_i(p, u) \equiv x_i[p, E(p, u)] \tag{10'}$$

and differentiating this expression with respect to an arbitrary price p_k, we have

$$\frac{\partial h_i(p, u)}{\partial p_k} = \frac{\partial x_i(p, y)}{\partial p_k} + \frac{\partial x_i(p, y)}{\partial y} \frac{\partial E(p, u)}{\partial p_k} \tag{11}$$

By Shephard's lemma and (8), moreover,

$$\frac{\partial E(p, u)}{\partial p_k} = h_k(p, u) = x_k(p, y)$$

Substituting this expression into (11), we obtain an equation that relates the partial derivatives of the compensated and ordinary demand functions:

$$\frac{\partial h_i(p, u)}{\partial p_k} = \frac{\partial x_i(p, y)}{\partial p_k} + x_k(p, y) \frac{\partial x_i(p, y)}{\partial y} \tag{12}$$

This identity is known as the *Slutsky equation.*

Comparing (12) with equation (5) in Section (a), we see that the Slutsky terms s_{ik} are in fact the partial derivatives of compensated demand with respect to prices. By Theorem 2.11 we know that

$$s_{ik} = \frac{\partial h_i(p,u)}{\partial p_k} = \frac{\partial h_k(p,u)}{\partial p_i} = s_{ki}$$

and

$$s_{ii} = \frac{\partial h_i(p,u)}{\partial p_i} \leq 0$$

as asserted in Theorem 2.5. Hence, the properties we attributed in Section (a) to the Slutsky matrix have been derived in Section (b) from the concavity in prices of the expenditure function, using Shephard's lemma.

The Slutsky equation allows us to decompose the effect on demand of a price change into a substitution effect and an income effect. Solving (12) for $\partial x_i(p,y)/\partial p_k$, we get

$$\frac{\partial x_i(p,y)}{\partial p_k} = \frac{\partial h_i(p,u)}{\partial p_k} - x_k(p,y*)\frac{\partial x_i(p,y)}{\partial y} \tag{13}$$

which we can interpret as follows:

$$\begin{array}{c} \text{total effect of} \\ \text{a price change} \end{array} = \begin{array}{c} \text{substitution} \\ \text{effect} \end{array} + \begin{array}{c} \text{income effect, weighted by the importance} \\ \text{of the good whose price has changed} \end{array}$$

It seems natural to weight the income effect by the consumption of the good whose price has changed. If the expenditure on this particular good is small (e.g., salt), even a large price change will have little effect on the consumer's real income. Finally, consider the decomposition of the effect of a change in a good's own price on its demand:

$$\frac{\partial x_i(p,y)}{\partial p_i} = \frac{\partial h_i(p,u)}{\partial p_i} - x_i(p,y*)\frac{\partial x_i(p,y)}{\partial y} \tag{14}$$

By Theorem 2.12, the substitution effect is negative. If the good is normal, $\partial x_i(\ )/\partial y$ is positive, and the income and substitution effects work in the same direction, implying that $\partial x_i(\ )/\partial p_i \leq 0$. This is the "fundamental law of demand."

3. Walrasian General Equilibrium in a Pure Exchange Economy

In this section we develop the standard theory of general competitive equilibrium in the context of a pure exchange economy. The adjective "general" indicates that we explicitly model the interdependence among the different sectors in the economy, as opposed to a partial-equilibrium analysis, where we might focus on a specific market in isolation. The words "competitive" and "Walrasian"[4] indicate reliance on a specific concept of equilibrium which assumes that markets are "perfectly competitive" in a sense to be made precise later.

The economy we study will be populated by a large number of consumers characterized by a well-behaved utility function and endowed with an initial vector of commodity holdings. Each of these consumers will take prices as given and will trade with other agents through a complete set of competitive markets. However, there will be no firms. Ignoring production will simplify matters considerably, while still allowing us to study the basic problem of how markets coordinate the actions of individual economic agents.

We assume that

(i) consumers are rational agents who maximize their utility, taking prices as exogenously given, and constrained only by the requirement that the market value of one's consumption bundle not exceed that of one's endowment, and

(ii) these individuals interact with each other only through a complete set of competitive markets in which prices are determined in such a way that supply always equals demand.

That is, in the Walrasian view, the consistency requirement that we have to impose on individual actions in order to speak of an equilibrium takes the form of market clearing. Notice that individuals are constrained only by prices precisely because markets clear (otherwise some sort of rationing would arise). Individual agents do not feel constrained by the actions of others in any specific way, because they can sell or buy any quantity of any good at the market price. This allows us to formulate and solve the individual's optimization problem as if he were free to choose independently of all other agents. On the other hand, this is not strictly true, as it is the interaction of all agents that determines market prices.

Before we can begin to investigate how prices are determined, we need to define some basic concepts.

Definition 3.1. Exchange economy and allocation. An exchange economy is a couple

$$\xi = (U, e) = \{(U^i, e^i); \ i = 1, \ldots, n\}$$

where U^i is a function $\mathbb{R}^G_+ \longrightarrow \mathbb{R}$, and $e^i = (e^i_1, \ldots, e^i_G)$ is a vector in $\mathbb{R}^G_+$. We interpret $U^i(\ )$ as the utility function of agent i, and e^i as his endowment vector (i.e., as his initial holdings of commodities).

An allocation $x = (x^1, \ldots, x^n) \in \mathbb{R}^{nG}_+$ is a vector that describes the amount of each commodity consumed by each of the n agents in the economy. An allocation is *feasible* if the total consumption of each commodity does not exceed its total endowment (i.e., if $\sum_{i=1}^{n} x^i \leq \sum_{i=1}^{n} e^i$).

Definition 3.2. Competitive or Walrasian equilibrium. A Walrasian equilibrium is a price-allocation pair (p^*, x^*) such that when all agents maximize utility, taking p^* as given, markets clear and agents receive the (feasible) allocation $x^* = (x^{1*}, \ldots, x^{n*})$.

This definition suggests the following procedure for finding an equilibrium. First, we derive the individual demand functions or correspondences as the solution mappings for the optimization problems faced by the individual traders. Then we aggregate over agents to obtain the total demand for the economy. Finally, we impose market clearing; that is, we require that supply equal demand in the markets for all goods.

This procedure yields a system of G equations (the market-clearing conditions) in G unknowns (the equilibrium prices of the goods). We can exploit the fact that we know how the system is constructed (from individual optimization and an overall equilibrium condition) to establish certain properties of the equilibrium mapping. The basic questions are still the ones we discussed in Chapter 5: First, we need to establish that a solution to the system (i.e., a competitive equilibrium) exists under certain conditions. Then we can ask whether or not the solution is unique, how it varies with changes in the parameters of the model (endowments), and whether or not it has any desirable welfare properties.

Some of these issues will be discussed in detail in the remainder of this section. Section (a) derives some properties of aggregate demand, making use of earlier results on consumer behavior. In Section (b), we provide sufficient conditions for the existence of equilibrium. Finally, Section (c) investigates the welfare properties of competitive equilibrium.

(a) Aggregate Demand

The optimization problem faced by the traders in our exchange economy is almost identical with the one analyzed in Section 2. The only difference is that income is now given by the market value of the endowment vector e^i. Hence, the demand correspondence for agent i is now given by

$$x^i(p, pe^i) = \arg \max_{x^i} \{ (U^i(x^i) \text{ s.t. } px^i \leq pe^i) \}$$

It is easy to check that this change does not alter the properties of individual demand correspondences. The following theorem lists some of these properties and derives an additional one (the unboundedness of demand as some prices go to zero).

Theorem 3.3. Properties of the demand correspondence. Let the utility function $U^i: \mathbb{R}_+^G \longrightarrow \mathbb{R}$ be continuous, strictly increasing, and quasiconcave. Then

(i) *the demand correspondence $x^i(p, pe^i)$, is uhc in p for any $p \gg \underline{0}$,*

(ii) *compact- and convex-valued for any $p \gg \underline{0}$, and*

(iii) *homogeneous of degree 0, in the sense that if $x \in x(p, pe^i)$ then $x \in x(\mu p, \mu p e^i)$ for all $\mu > 0$.*

(iv) *The budget constraint holds with equality, that is, $pz^i = pe^i$ for any $z^i \in x^i(p, pe^i)$ (the "adding-up" property).*

(v) *If $U(\ )$ is strictly quasiconcave, then $x^i(p, pe^i)$ is a (single-valued) function of prices and is continuous.*

(vi) *Let $\{p_n\}$ be a convergent price sequence, with $p_n \gg \underline{0}$ for all n, and assume that its limit p has some zero component (i.e., $p_g = 0$ for some good g) and satisfies $pe^i > 0$. Then the corresponding sequence of demand vectors tends to infinity, in the following sense. Let*

$$m_n = \inf\{\|x\|; \ x \in x^i(p_n, p_n e^i)\}$$

then $\{m_n\} \to \infty$ as $n \to \infty$.

Proof. The results follow immediately from Theorem 2.3, except for (ii) and (vi). To see that $x^i(p, pe^i)$ is a convex and compact set, notice that

$$x^i(p, pe^i) = B(p, pe^i) \cap \left\{ z \in \mathbb{R}_+^G; \ U^i(z) \geq u_i \equiv \max_{x \in B(p, pe^i)} U^i(x) \right\}$$
$$= B(p, pe^i) \cap U_i^{-1}[u_i, \infty] \tag{1}$$

is the intersection of two convex sets, the budget set $B(p, pe^i)$ and an upper contour set of the quasiconcave function $U^i(\cdot)$, and therefore it is convex itself. Similarly, the last expression in (1) shows that $x^i(p, pe^i)$ is a closed subset of the compact set $B(p, pe^i)$ and therefore is compact itself (by Theorem 8.14 in Chapter 2). Hence, $x^i(p, pe^i)$ is a convex- and compact-valued correspondence.

To establish the boundary property (vi), we proceed by contradiction. Fix some p, with some component $p_g = 0$, and consider a sequence $\{p_n\} \to p$, with $p_n \gg \underline{0}$ for all n. First, observe that the consumer's problem has no solution when some price is zero. Because utility is strictly increasing in all goods, there can be no best consumption bundle, because given any bundle, an alternative that includes more of the free good will be strictly preferred and will always be feasible. Hence, $x^i(p, pe^i) = \varnothing$.

Suppose now that the desired result is not true. Then there is a bounded set $B \subseteq \mathbb{R}_+^G$ and a subsequence $\{p_{n_k}\}$ of $\{p_n\}$ such that

$$x^i(p_{n_k}, p_{n_k}e^i) \cap B \neq \varnothing$$

for all n_k. Let $z_k \in x^i(p_{n_k}, p_{n_k}e^i) \cap B$ for each k. Then the sequence $\{z_k\}$ is bounded and therefore contains a convergent subsequence, say $\{z_{k_q}\}$, with limit z. We will show that $z \in x^i(p, pe^i)$. This contradicts the fact that $x^i(p, pe^i) = \varnothing$ and establishes the result.

To conclude the proof, we need to show that $z \in x^i(p, pe^i)$, that is, that for every y in $B(p, pe^i)$ we have $U(z) \geq U(y)$. First, notice that because $z_{k_q} \in x^i(p_{n_{k_q}}, p_{n_{k_q}}e^i)$, we have $p_{n_{k_q}}z_{k_q} \leq p_{n_{k_q}}e^i$ for all q. Taking limits of this expression, we see that $pz \leq pe^i$, that is, $z \in B(p, pe^i)$. Hence z is feasible for (p, e^i).

We now consider two cases:

(i) Assume that y is such that $py < pe^i$. Then we have $p_{n_{k_q}}y < p_{n_{k_q}}e^i$ for k_q large enough. Hence y is feasible for $(p_{n_{k_q}}, e^i)$ and because $z_{k_q} \in x^i(p_{n_{k_q}}, p_{n_{k_q}}e^i)$ is optimal, it follows that $U(z_{k_q}) \geq U(y)$ for all sufficiently large k_q. Taking limits of this inequality, it follows, by the continuity of $U(\ )$, that $U(z) \geq U(y)$.

(ii) Alternatively, y is such that $py = pe^i > 0$. Then we can find a sequence $\{y_k\}$ converging to y such that $py_k < pe^i$. By case (i) we have $U(z) \geq U(y_k)$ for all k, which implies, by the continuity of $U(\ )$, that $U(z) \geq U(y)$. This concludes the proof of the theorem. $\square$

Once we have derived the individual demand functions, the next step is to aggregate them to obtain the "global" demand for all agents. Because all consumers face the same prices, the total quantity of each commodity demanded or supplied at a given price vector is simply the sum of the quantities each individual wants to buy or sell at that price. Hence, we define the *aggregate demand* correspondence by summing over the n agents,

$$x(p, e) = \sum_{i=1}^{n} x^i(p, pe^i) \tag{1}$$

and the *aggregate excess-demand* correspondence by

$$Z(p, e) = \sum_{i=1}^{n} [x^i(p, pe^i) - e^i] = x(p, e) - \sum_{i=1}^{n} e^i \tag{2}$$

where e is the nG vector $e = (e^1, \ldots, e^n)$. Notice that, in general, both $x(\ )$ and $Z(\ )$ will depend not only on total resources but also on the distribution of wealth in the economy.

The aggregate demand correspondence inherits some (but not all) of the properties of individual demand. By Theorem 11.11 in Chapter 2 and Theorem 1.4 in Chapter 6, $x(\ )$ and $Z(\ )$ inherit the upper hemicontinuity and compact- and convex-valuedness of individual demands. It is clear that the unboundedness of individual demand as some price converges to zero carries over to the aggregate. It is also easy to see that aggregation preserves the homogeneity of degree 0 in prices. We know that for each agent i,

$$x^i(\mu p, \mu p e^i) = x^i(p, p e^i) \; \forall \; \mu > 0$$

Summing over agents, we have

$$x(\mu p, e) = \sum_{i=1}^{n} x^i(\mu p, \mu p e^i) = \sum_{i=1}^{n} x^i(p, p e^i) = x(p, e)$$

for all $\mu > 0$, so $x(\ )$ is homogeneous of degree 0. Similarly, we know that all the individual budget constraints hold with equality. Hence,

$$p x^i(p, p e^i) = p e^i$$

for each i, and, summing over all consumers,

$$\sum_{i=1}^{n} p x^i(p, p e^i) = \sum_{i=1}^{n} p e^i$$

This expression implies that the value of the aggregate excess-demand vector must be zero, that is,

$$p \sum_{i=1}^{n} [x^i(p, p e^i) - e^i] = p Z(p, e) = 0 \qquad \text{(W)}$$

an equality often referred to as *Walras's law*. We summarize these results in the following theorem.

Theorem 3.4. Properties of aggregate demand. Suppose $U^i : \mathbb{R}^G_+ \longrightarrow \mathbb{R}$ *is quasiconcave, strictly increasing, and continuous for all agents. Then the aggregate excess-demand correspondence*

$$Z(p, e) = \sum_{i=1}^{n} [x^i(p, p e^i) - e^i] = x(p, e) - \sum_{i=1}^{n} e^i$$

is homogeneous of degree 0 in prices, nonempty, compact- and convex-valued, and uhc in prices for given $e > \underline{0}$ *and* $p \gg \underline{0}$, *and it satisfies Walras's law:*

$$p Z(p, e) = 0 \qquad \text{(W)}$$

Moreover, given any sequence $\{p_n\}$, *with* $p_n \gg \underline{0}$ *for all* n, *that converges to a price vector* p, *with* $p e^i > \underline{0}$ *for some* i *and some component equal to zero, the sequence* $\{Z(p_n, e)\}$ *is unbounded. Finally, if* $U^i(\ )$ *is strictly quasiconcave for all agents, then* $Z(\ )$ *is a continuous (single-valued) function.*

Two implications of this result will be useful later. First, notice that Walras's law implies that if all markets except one clear, then the last one must necessarily clear as well. Hence, we need to worry about market clearing for only $G - 1$ goods. Second, the homogeneity of degree 0 of $Z(\ )$ in prices means that only relative prices matter. Formally, this allows us to normalize prices and worry about only $G - 1$ of them. Among all the possible normalizations, two are very commonly used:

(i) Set the price of one of the goods (called the "numeraire") to 1. The price vector is then of the form $p = (p_1, p_2, \ldots, p_{G-1}, 1)$.

(ii) Assume that the price vector belongs to the unit simplex in $\mathbb{R}_+^G$ (i.e., that prices satisfy the relation $\Sigma_{i=1}^G p_g = 1$).

It should be noted that our results concerning the properties of the Slutsky matrix for individual demand functions do not, in general, survive aggregation. Because these conditions (together with the properties that aggregate demand does inherit) are, as we have seen, equivalent to utility maximization, it follows that the aggregate demand function is not, generally speaking, *utility-generated*. That is, most economies do not behave as if we had a single "representative agent" making all consumption decisions. On the other hand, the aggregate excess-demand function will share the properties of individual demands in some special cases. It can be shown that a necessary and sufficient condition for the aggregate excess-demand function to be utility-generated, and hence independent of the distribution of wealth, is that preferences be homothetic and identical for all agents in the economy. The sufficiency part of this result is easily established using the result given in Problem 2.4. With identical and constant marginal propensities to consume in each good, any redistribution of resources will have no effect on aggregate spending patterns. Hence, the aggregate demand function does not depend on the distribution of wealth.

(b) Existence of Competitive Equilibrium

We have defined a competitive equilibrium as a price-allocation pair (p^*, x^*) such that when all agents optimize, taking p^* as given, the markets for all goods clear, and agents receive the allocation x^*. Because the aggregate demand mapping already embodies the assumption that consumers optimize, taking prices as given, to establish the existence of an equilibrium it is sufficient to show that there exists some price vector $p^* > \underline{0}$ that generates a zero aggregate excess demand. If aggregate demand is single-valued, this condition reduces to a system of equations of the form

$$Z(p, e) = \underline{0} \qquad \text{(W.E)}$$

which can (hopefully) be solved for p^*, the equilibrium price vector, for a given vector of endowments. We can then determine the equilibrium allocation by using the individual demand functions to see how much of each commodity will be consumed by each trader at equilibrium prices p^*, that is, $x^* = x(p^*, e)$.[5] If aggregate demand is not single-valued, equilibrium will require the existence of some price vector such that the resulting aggregate excess-demand set will contain the zero vector. That is, the equilibrium condition will be of the form

$$\underline{0} \in Z(p, e) \qquad \text{(W.E')}$$

We will focus for the time being on the simpler case in which $Z(\ )$ is a single-valued function. Verifying that a solution of the system (W.E) does exist, at least under some circumstances, is an important test of the consistency of the model we have developed in this section. The mathematical problem we face is that of determining whether or not a given system of equations has a solution. The economic question behind it is whether or not there exist prices that will clear all markets simultaneously, or, to put it slightly differently, whether or not it is possible for all the agents in the model to optimize simultaneously without "running into each other."

As a first check, we start by counting equations and unknowns. We have G of each (G unknown prices and as many equations, one for each market), so things seem to be O.K. at first sight. On closer inspection, two complications arise, but they just happen to cancel out. The first one is that we have a redundant price. By the homogeneity of degree 0 of the excess-demand function, only relative prices matter, so there are only $G - 1$ prices to be determined. Fortunately, we also have a redundant equation, because Walras's law implies that if $G - 1$ markets clear, the Gth market will automatically clear as well. Hence, the equality of equations and unknowns has been preserved, but this is neither a necessary condition nor a sufficient condition for the system to have a solution.

To proceed further we will analyze a simple example in some detail. We will consider a two-good economy described by an aggregate excess-demand function, with the properties given in Theorem 3.4, and establish the existence of equilibrium for such an economy in two slightly different ways. The first will be more natural, but the second will turn out to be easier to extend to the general case.

Let us normalize the price vector $p = (p_1, p_2)$ so that prices lie on the unit simplex (i.e., so that $p_1 + p_2 = 1$). Abusing notation, we can write the aggregate excess-demand function in the form

$$Z(p_1) = [Z_1(p_1), Z_2(p_1)] \equiv [Z_1(p_1, 1 - p_1), Z_2(p_1, 1 - p_1)] = Z(p)$$

Walras's law then requires that

$$p_1 Z_1(p_1) + (1 - p_1) Z_2(p_1) = 0 \qquad (1)$$

for all p_1. By the unboundedness of excess demand as prices go to zero, we know that

$$Z_1(p_1) \to \infty \ \text{ as } p_1 \to 0 \quad \text{and} \quad Z_2(p_1) \to \infty \ \text{ as } p_2 = 1 - p_1 \to 0 \qquad (2)$$

Fix some $B > 0$, and observe that, by (2), there exist numbers ε and δ in the interval $(0, 1)$, with $\varepsilon < 1 - \delta$, such that

$$Z_1(p_1) \geq B > 0 \; \forall \; p_1 \in (0, \varepsilon) \tag{3}$$

$$Z_2(p_1) \geq B \; \forall \; p_1 \in (1 - \delta, 1) \tag{4}$$

Using Walras's law and (4), we have

$$0 = (1 - \delta)Z_1(1 - \delta) + \delta Z_2(1 - \delta) \geq (1 - \delta)Z_1(1 - \delta) + \delta B$$

from where

$$Z_1(1 - \delta) \leq \frac{-\delta B}{1 - \delta} < 0 \tag{5}$$

Using (3) and (5), the intermediate-value theorem implies that there exists some price $p_1^* \in (\varepsilon, 1 - \delta)$ such that $Z_1(p_1^*) = 0$. Hence, $p_1^* Z_1(p_1^*) = 0$, and Walras's law implies that

$$0 + (1 - p_1^*)Z_2(p_1^*) = 0 \Rightarrow Z_2(p_1^*) = 0$$

Hence, there exists an equilibrium for this economy, that is, a price vector $p^* = (p_1^*, p_2^*) = (p_1^*, 1 - p_1^*) > \underline{0}$ that clears both markets simultaneously.

The main problem in extending this argument to the general case is that we cannot rely on the intermediate-value theorem when we work with an arbitrary number of commodities. A strategy that avoids this difficulty involves transforming the problem in such a way that we can use either the Brouwer or the Kakutani fixed-point theorem (see Section 3(b) in Chapter 5). Both of these theorems, however, apply to continuous functions (or hemi-continuous correspondences) that map a compact and convex set into itself. Hence, it will be difficult to work with the aggregate excess-demand correspondence, because $Z : \Delta \rightarrow\rightarrow \mathbb{R}_+^{nG}$ maps the open unit simplex

$$\Delta = \left\{ p \in \mathbb{R}_{++}^G ; \; \sum_{g=1}^{G} p_g = 1 \right\}$$

into an unbounded set; recall that $Z(\;)$ is not defined when one of the prices is zero, and it becomes unbounded as we approach such a point. There is, however, a workable alternative that involves constructing an appropriate mapping of the price simplex into itself and then invoking a fixed-point theorem.

Let us see how this can be done in our simple example, where it is easy to sidestep some of the difficulties that arise in the general case. The idea will be to construct a continuous function $F : \Delta \longrightarrow \Delta$ that can be loosely interpreted as a set of instructions for a hypothetical *auctioneer* to adjust prices iteratively until an equilibrium is attained. We can then picture the auctioneer calling out price vectors and asking each agent how much of each commodity he is willing to purchase/sell at those prices, adding up the quantities over agents, and determining the excess demand in each case. The price-adjustment function will be constructed so that excess demand will lead to an increase in the good's price, and excess supply to a reduction. Clearly, a fixed point of this mapping will be an equilibrium price vector, for a price vector requiring no further adjustment will be one that makes supply equal to demand in all markets.

This description may be misleading, in that it invites us to picture a process of adjustment over time, eventually converging to equilibrium as eager consumers bid up the prices of scarce commodities and suppliers lower the prices of those goods they cannot sell. In fact, nothing of this sort is implied. We are not claiming that the *tâtonnement* process described by the function $F(\ )$ will eventually converge to an equilibrium, but only that there exists some p^* such that if it is, by chance, called out by the auctioneer, no further adjustment will be needed.

One price-adjustment rule that will work in our example is the following. We define the function $F: \Delta \longrightarrow \Delta$ by

$$q_1 = F_1(p_1) = \frac{p_1 + \max\{0, Z_1(p_1)\}}{p_1 + \max\{0, Z_1(p_1)\} + (1 - p_1) + \max\{0, Z_2(p_1)\}}$$

$$q_2 = F_2(p_1) = 1 - F_1(p_1) = \frac{p_2 + \max\{0, Z_2(p_1)\}}{p_1 + \max\{0, Z_1(p_1)\} + p_2 + \max\{0, Z_2(p_1)\}} \quad (6)$$

Notice that $F(\ )$ maps a price vector $p = (p_1, p_2)$ in the open unit simplex into another vector q in the same set. The numerator of each fraction in (6) instructs us to form each new price as follows. First, set

$$p'_g = p_g + \max[0, Z_g(p)]$$

That is, if excess demand is negative (i.e., if there is an excess supply) or zero, we leave the price as it is, and if there is an excess demand for good g, we increase its price by adding the excess demand to the old price. Division by the expression in the denominator (which is the sum of all the adjusted prices) then renormalizes these prices to "bring them back" into the unit simplex.

Figure 8.6 illustrates the functioning of the price-adjustment scheme. We start with an arbitrary price vector p and suppose that it yields an excess demand for good 1, $Z_1(p) > 0$; then, by Walras's law, $Z_2(p) < 0$. The auctioneer's rule, $F(\ )$, tells us to add $Z_1(p)$ to p_1 and leave p_2 as it is. This gives us a new price vector p', with $p_1' = p_1 + Z_1(p)$. However, p' is not in the unit simplex. The normalization in $F(p)$ amounts to selecting point q in the figure, which does lie on the unit simplex. The net effect, when we consider the final change in normalized prices ($p \to q$), is to decrease p_2 in response to the

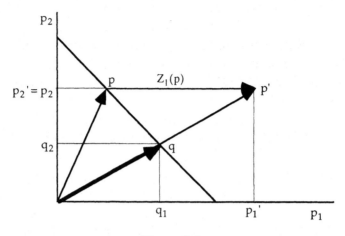

Figure 8.6.

original situation of excess supply and to increase p_1 in response to the excess demand for good 1.

It is easy to show (see Problem 3.5) that a fixed point of $F(\ )$ is an equilibrium price vector for our two-good economy. Hence, proving the existence of equilibrium for our economy reduce to the problem of showing that the function $F(\ )$ has a fixed point. Notice that $F(\ )$ maps the *open* unit simplex Δ into itself (i.e., we are requiring both prices to be strictly positive, because $Z(\ )$ is not defined otherwise). Because Δ is not a compact set, we cannot use Brouwer's fixed-point theorem. It is easy, however, to establish the existence of a fixed point using the intermediate-value theorem.

Observe that $F_1(p_1)$ will have a fixed point if and only if the equation $F_1(p_1) - p_1 = 0$ has a solution. The function $F_1(\ )$ is continuous on the interval $(0, 1)$, because the continuity of each $Z_g(\ )$ implies that of $\max\{0, Z_g(p)\}$, and the denominator of $F_1(\ )$ never vanishes. Using (3) and (4), we have, moreover,

$$F_1(\varepsilon) - \varepsilon = \frac{\varepsilon + \max\{0, Z_1(\varepsilon)\}}{\varepsilon + \max\{0, Z_1(\varepsilon)\} + (1-\varepsilon) + \max\{0, Z_2(\varepsilon)\}} - \varepsilon$$

$$= \frac{\varepsilon + Z_1(\varepsilon)}{\varepsilon + Z_1(\varepsilon) + (1-\varepsilon)} - \varepsilon = \frac{(1-\varepsilon)Z_1(\varepsilon)}{1 + Z_1(\varepsilon)} > 0$$

and

$$F_1(1-\delta) - (1-\delta) = \frac{(1-\delta) + \max\{0, Z_1(1-\delta)\}}{(1-\delta) + \max\{0, Z_1(1-\delta)\} + \delta + \max\{0, Z_2(1-\delta)\}} - (1-\delta)$$

$$= \frac{(1-\delta)}{1 + Z_2(1-\delta)} - (1-\delta) < 0$$

By the intermediate-value theorem, there exists some point $p_1^* \in (\varepsilon, 1 - \delta)$ such that $p_1^* = F_1(p_1^*)$. This, in turn, implies that

$$p_2^* = 1 - p_1^* = 1 - F_1(p_1^*) = F_2(p_1^*)$$

so $p^* = (p_1^*, p_2^*)$ is a fixed point of $F(\ )$ and therefore a competitive-equilibrium price vector for our two-good economy.

Problem 3.5. Define a mapping $F: \Delta \longrightarrow \Delta$ by

$$F(p) = \frac{p_1 + \max[0, Z_1(p)] + \ldots + p_G + \max[0, Z_G(p)]}{\displaystyle\sum_{g=1}^{G} (p_g + \max[0, Z_g(p)])}$$

where $Z(p) = Z_1(p), \ldots, Z_G(p)$ is an aggregate-excess-demand function satisfying Walras's law, $pZ(p) = 0$ for all p. Show that any fixed point of $F(\ )$ is a competitive-equilibrium price vector. That is, if $p^* = F(p^*) > \underline{0}$, then

$$Z_g(p^*) \leq 0 \; \forall g \quad \text{and} \quad Z_g(p^*) = 0 \quad \text{whenever } p_g^* > 0$$

Notice that we allow for the possibility of free goods. A good may be in excess supply in equilibrium ($Z_g(p^*) < 0$), but then its price must be zero.

If we are willing to assume that the excess-demand function $Z(p)$ is continuous on the closed price simplex, the preceding argument can be extended to establish the existence of competitive equilibrium in economies with strictly convex preferences. Unfortunately, this assumption is not reasonable in view of the fact that aggregate demand becomes unbounded in the boundary of this set (i.e., for price vectors with some component equal to zero). We will now prove an existence theorem that does not require such an unreasonable assumption. The idea behind the proof is essentially the same as before, but we have to be careful to avoid "boundary problems." The first step involves defining a correspondence $\mu(\ )$ that does essentially the same thing as the function $F(\ )$ we introduced earlier and using Kakutani's fixed-point theorem to establish the following result.

Lemma 3.6. Let S be a closed and convex subset of the open unit simplex,

$$\Delta = \left\{ p \in \mathbb{R}_{++}^{G} ; \; \sum\nolimits_{g=1}^{G} p_g = 1 \right\}$$

Let $f: S \longrightarrow \mathbb{R}^{G}$ *be a continuous function with the property that*

$$pf(p) \leq 0 \; \forall p \in S$$

Then there exists some $p^* \in S$ *such that*

$$pf(p^*) \le 0 \ \forall p \in S$$

Proof. Define the correspondence $\mu: S \twoheadrightarrow S$ by[6]

$$\mu(p) = \arg\max_{q \in S} qf(p) \tag{1}$$

Because $f(\ )$ is a continuous function, and S a compact set, $f(\ )$ is bounded in the set. It follows that for given p, $qf(p)$ is a continuous function of q, and it attains a maximum in the compact set S. Hence $\mu(p)$ is nonempty. Moreover, $\mu(\ )$ is convex-valued, because $\mu(p)$ is the set of maximizers of a quasiconcave function, and it is compact-valued and uhc by the theorem of the maximum, because $qf(p)$ is continuous and the constraint set is compact and "constant" and therefore a trivially continuous correspondence.

Thus, we see that the correspondence $\mu(\ )$ satisfies the conditions of Kakutani's fixed-point theorem (Theorem 3.4 in Chapter 5). Therefore, there exists some point $p^* \in S$ such that

$$p^* \in \mu(p^*) = \arg\max_{q \in S} qf(p^*)$$

This implies that

$$p^* f(p^*) \ge pf(p^*)$$

for any $p \in S$. But because $pf(p) \le 0$ for all $p \in S$, we have $p^* f(p^*) \le 0$, and it follows that p^* is such that

$$pf(p^*) \le 0 \ \forall p \in S \qquad \square$$

Notice that in a pure exchange economy with strictly convex preferences (and the other properties we have assumed), the excess-demand mapping will be a function that satisfies the conditions of Lemma 3.6 for any compact subset of the open unit simplex. To establish the existence of equilibrium for such an economy, we apply Lemma 3.6 to a sequence $\{S_n\}$ of sets converging to the closed unit simplex and show that the limit of the resulting sequence $\{p_n^*\}$ clears all markets.

Theorem 3.7. Existence of competitive equilibrium in an economy with strictly convex preferences. Let $Z(\ )$ *be the excess-demand function characterizing a pure exchange economy with strictly convex preferences. Assume that* $Z(\ )$ *is continuous for all* $p \gg 0$, *that it satisfies Walras's law,*

$$pZ(p) = 0 \tag{W}$$

and that we have the following boundary condition: Given any sequence $\{p_n\}$, *with* $p_n \gg 0$ *for all* n, *that converges to a price vector* p, *with* $pe^i > 0$ *for some* i, *and some component equal to zero, the sequence {Z(p_n, e)} is unbounded. Then there exists a price vector* p* $\in \Delta$, *with* p* $\gg \underline{0}$, *such that* Z(p*) = $\underline{0}$.

Proof. Consider the increasing sequence of sets $\{S_n\}$, with

$$S_n = \{p \in \Delta;\ p_g \geq 1/n\ \forall\ g = 1, \ldots, G\}$$

for $n \geq G$, and notice that $\cup_n S_n = \bar{\Delta}$. Because the excess-demand function $Z(\ )$ is continuous in each S_n and satisfies Walras's law, Lemma 3.6 implies that for each n there exists some vector p_n^* such that

$$pZ(p_n^*) \leq 0\ \forall\ p \in S_n \tag{1}$$

Because the sequence $\{p_n^*\}$ is contained in the compact set $\bar{\Delta}$, it has a convergent subsequence with limit in $\bar{\Delta}$. To simplify the notation, suppose that $\{p_n^*\}$ itself converges, and let $p^* \in \bar{\Delta}$ be its limit. Next, consider the sequence $\{Z(p_n^*)\}$. This sequence will be bounded, because (i) $\{Z(p_n^*)\}$ is bounded below (e.g., by $\Sigma_{i=1}^n e^i$) because excess supply cannot be unbounded, and (ii) $pZ(p_n^*) \leq 0$ for all n and an arbitrary $p \gg \underline{0}$ in some S_n, by (1), which implies that $Z(p_n^*)$ is also bounded above. Hence, $\{Z(p_n^*)\}$ will also have a convergent subsequence, and we can assume without loss of generality that the sequence itself converges to some point z^*. The boundedness of $\{Z(p_n^*)\}$ also implies that $p^* \gg \underline{0}$, for if $\{p_n^*\}$ converged to a price vector with some component equal to zero, $\{Z(p_n^*)\}$ would be unbounded, by the boundary condition. Using this fact and the continuity of $Z(\ )$ in the interior of the price simplex, we conclude that

$$z^* = \lim_{n \to \infty} Z(p_n^*) = Z(p^*) \tag{2}$$

Next, we show that $pz^* \leq 0$ for all $p \in \bar{\Delta}$. If p lies in the interior of $\bar{\Delta}$ (i.e., if $p \gg \underline{0}$), then $p \in S_n$ for all sufficiently large n, and (1) implies $pZ(p_n^*) \leq 0$ for all such n. Taking limits of this expression as $n \to \infty$, we conclude that $pz^* \leq 0$. If p is a boundary point of $\bar{\Delta}$, we can find a sequence $\{q_n\} \to p$, with $q_n \in S_n$. By (1), $q_n Z(p_n^*) \leq 0$, and, taking limits, $pz^* \leq 0$ also in this case.

Now, $pZ(p^*) = pz^* \leq 0$ for all $p \in \bar{\Delta}$ implies that $Z(p^*) \leq \underline{0}$ (e.g., letting $p = (1, 0, \ldots, 0)$, we see that $Z_1(p^*) \leq 0$, and so on). By Walras's law, moreover, we have $p^*Z(p^*) = 0$, with $p^* \gg \underline{0}$. From this we conclude that $Z(p^*) = \underline{0}$, for if $Z(p^*)$ has any strictly negative components, then $p^*Z(p^*) = \Sigma_{g=1}^G p_g^* Z_g(p^*) < 0$, contradicting Walras's law. $\qquad\square$

The foregoing result can be easily extended to the case in which preferences are convex, but not strictly so. Problem 3.8 asks the reader to extend Lemma 3.6 to the case of a bounded and uhc correspondence. Given this result, the proof of the existence theorem goes through essentially unchanged when $Z(\ )$ is a uhc correspondence.

Problem 3.8. Let S be a closed and convex subset of the open unit simplex in $\mathbb{R}^G$, and $\phi: S \twoheadrightarrow \mathbb{R}^G$ a uhc and convex-valued correspondence with the following properties:

(i) $\phi(\ )$ is bounded i.e., there exists a bounded set B in $\mathbb{R}^G$ such that $\phi(p) \subseteq B$ for all $p \in S$), and
(ii) for all $p \in S$ we have $pz \leq 0$ for every $z \in \phi(p)$.

Show that there exists some $p^* \in S$ and $z^* \in \phi(p^*)$ such that

$$pz^* \leq 0 \ \forall \, p \in S$$

Hint: Adapt the proof of Lemma 3.6. Define the correspondence $\mu(\ )$ on B, and consider the product correspondence $\mu(z) \times \phi(p)$.

(c) *Welfare Properties of Competitive Equilibrium*

Having established the existence of competitive equilibrium, we can now investigate its welfare properties. After introducing an appropriate concept of social optimality, known as Pareto efficiency, we will prove two important results on the relationship between Pareto efficiency and competitive equilibrium.

Consider the problem of a hypothetical social planner who must decide between two feasible allocations. Early approaches to this problem assumed that individual utilities could be added to obtain a meaningful measure of social welfare. The planner's problem was then reduced to the maximization of social utility. On the other hand, we have seen that in modern consumer theory, utility is an ordinal concept and cannot be meaningfully added across agents. This makes social-welfare comparisons difficult, for given any two feasible allocations, it is very likely that at least some agents will disagree about which is better. If individual preferences cannot be quantified and weighted somehow, there is no way of answering the question of which state is to be preferred.

In this context, the efficiency criterion proposed by Pareto provides not so much a solution as a way to sidestep the problem. Given two allocations x and y, we say that x is *Pareto-superior* to y if and only if nobody prefers y to x and at least one agent strictly prefers x to y. An allocation x is said to be *Pareto-efficient* (*-optimal*) if there is no other feasible allocation that is Pareto-superior to it. In this way, we avoid the need to make interpersonal utility comparisons. The catch, of course, is that we can make welfare judgments only in cases in which there is no disagreement. To see how restrictive this is, observe that if there is a single dissenting individual who prefers y to x against the unanimous opinion of all others, then x and y are not comparable in the Pareto sense. Notice also that an allocation that gives all resources in the economy to a single agent is Pareto-optimal, because presumably he would object to any attempt to confiscate his wealth.

More formally, we have the following definitions.

Definition 3.9. Pareto dominance and Pareto optimality.

(i) An allocation $x = (x^1, \ldots, x^n)$ *Pareto-dominates* another allocation $y = (y^1, \ldots, y^n)$ if

$$\forall i = 1, \ldots, n, x^i \succeq_i y^i \quad \text{and} \quad \exists k \text{ s.th. } x^k \succ_k y^k$$

(ii) A feasible allocation $x = (x^1, \ldots, x^n)$ is *Pareto-optimal* if there exists no feasible allocation y that Pareto-dominates it.

That is, an allocation is Pareto-optimal if the available resources cannot be redistributed in a way that would make some agents better off without making others worse off.

The following theorems establish that there is a close connection between competitive equilibrium and Pareto optimality.

Theorem 3.10. First welfare theorem. Consider a competitive exchange economy with strictly monotonic preferences. Then any competitive-equilibrium allocation is Pareto-optimal.

Strict monotonicity can be replaced by a weaker non-satiation assumption. On the other hand, some of the implicit assumptions of the theorem should perhaps be made explicit. They include the absence of externalities, asymmetric information, and market power, and the existence of a complete set of markets. Notice that the theorem does not require convexity of preferences. Equilibrium may not exist without convexity, but if it does, it is Pareto-optimal.

A superficial reading of the theorem may skip over the implicit assumptions and conclude that competitive markets are "superior" and that government intervention can only create inefficiencies. A more careful conclusion is that in the absence of some quite common complications, we can expect competitive markets (if they work as they are supposed to) to yield outcomes that are efficient in Pareto's (rather restrictive) sense of the word. The set of (implicit) assumptions of the theorem, moreover, gives us a convenient list of where to look for possible inefficiencies.

Proof. The proof proceeds by contradiction. Let $x = (x^1, \ldots, x^n) \in x(p, e)$ be an allocation corresponding to the equilibrium price vector p, and let $z = (z^1, \ldots, z^n)$ be a feasible allocation that Pareto-dominates x, that is, such that (i) $z^i \geq_i x^i$ for all agents i, and (ii) there exists at least one agent k such that $z^k >_k x^k$. Because z is feasible by assumption, we have

$$\sum_{i=1}^{n} z^i \leq \sum_{i=1}^{n} e^i \tag{1}$$

where e^i is the endowment vector of the ith agent.

We will show that z cannot be a feasible allocation. By definition, the equilibrium allocation x maximizes the utility of each agent subject to the budget constraint. By the strict monotonicity of preferences (or some weaker nonsatiation assumption), the budget constraint will hold with equality for each agent (i.e., $px^i = pe^i$ for all i). Next, observe that if z^i was preferred, but x^i was chosen, it must be that z^i was "too expensive." Moreover, because for some agents z^k was strictly preferred to x^k, it must be that the first bundle was strictly too expensive. That is,

$$pz^i \geq pe^i \; \forall \; i \quad \text{and} \quad pz^k > pe^k \quad \text{for some } k \tag{2}$$

Adding up over all agents, we obtain

$$\sum_{i=1}^{n} pz^i > \sum_{i=1}^{n} pe^i \Rightarrow p\sum_{i=1}^{n} z^i > p\sum_{i=1}^{n} e^i$$

Because $p \gg \underline{0}$, this implies that

$$\sum_{i=1}^{n} z^i > \sum_{i=1}^{n} e^i$$

which contradicts (1). Hence, any allocation that is weakly preferred to a competitive equilibrium by all agents and is strictly preferred by some cannot be feasible. □

Our second result says that if preferences are convex, any Pareto-optimal allocation can be supported as a competitive equilibrium given an appropriate redistribution of endowments. The implicit assumptions are the same as for the previous theorem.

Theorem 3.11. Second welfare theorem. Let $x \in \mathbb{R}_+^{nG}$ be a Pareto-optimal allocation for a pure exchange economy. Assume that preferences are convex, continuous, and strictly monotonic. Then there exists a price vector $p \in \mathbb{R}_+^{G}$ such that (p, x) is a competitive equilibrium for the economy, with initial endowments $e^i = x^i$ for all i.[7]

Proof.

(i) We observe that if x^* is Pareto optimal, then there is no way to redistribute initial resources so as to make everybody better off.

Given the Pareto-optimal allocation $x = (x^1, \ldots, x^n)$, define for each agent i the set

$$P_i(x^i) = \{ y^i \in \mathbb{R}^G_+ ; y^i >_i x^i \}$$

of bundles that are strictly preferred to x^i. Summing over all consumers, we obtain the set

$$P(x) = \sum_{i=1}^n P_i(x^i) = \left\{ z; z = \sum_{i=1}^n y^i, \text{ with } y^i \in P_i(x^i) \, \forall \, i \right\}$$

of total-resource vectors that would allow us to make all agents strictly better off than under the allocation x. Let

$$E = \sum_{i=1}^n x^i = \sum_{i=1}^n e^i \tag{1}$$

(where the equality follows by the monotonicity of preferences)[8] denote the total resources of the economy (the aggregate-endowment vector). Because x is Pareto-optimal, there is no redistribution of E that would make all the agents better off. Hence, $E \notin P(x)$.

(ii) We shall use a separating-hyperplane theorem to establish the existence of a vector p that will be a candidate for an equilibrium price vector.

Each $P_i(x^i)$ is a convex set, by the convexity of preferences. This implies that $P(x)$ is convex, because it is the sum of convex sets (Theorem 1.4 in Chapter 6). Because $E \notin P(x)$, we can apply a separating-hyperplane theorem (Theorem 1.25 in Chapter 6) to conclude that there is a nonzero vector p in $\mathbb{R}^G$ such that

$$pE \leq pz \, \forall \, z \in P(x) \tag{2}$$

Interpreting p as a price vector, (2) says that the value of the resources needed to make all agents better off (weakly) exceeds the value of the resources available in this economy, both valued at prices p.

We still have to show that p can be interpreted as a price vector and that it will support the allocation x as a competitive equilibrium.

(iii) We will show that $p \geq \underline{0}$, that is, that p can be interpreted as a vector of (non-negative) prices.

Let u_g be the gth unit vector in $\mathbb{R}^G$ (i.e., u_g has a 1 in the gth coordinate, and 0's in all others). By monotonicity, adding one unit to the total available amount of any commodity will allow us to make all agents better off (e.g., by assigning each agents $1/n$ extra unit of the good). Hence, $E + u_g \in P(x)$ for all g, and it follows by (2) that the value of $E + u_g$ exceeds that of E. That is,

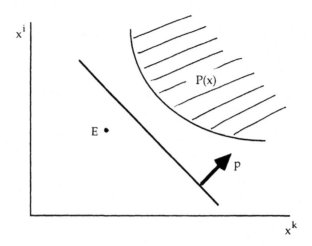

Figure 8.7.

$$pE \le p(E + u_g) \ \forall \ g = 1, \dots, G$$

from where

$$p(E + u_g) - pE = pu_g = p_g \ge 0 \ \forall \ g$$

(iv) We will show that any bundle strictly preferred to x^i costs strictly more than x^i at prices p (i.e., that $z^i >_i x^i$ implies $pz^i > px^i$). This proves the theorem, because it means that any bundle z^i strictly preferred to x^i would not be affordable for the agent at prices p. In an economy with endowments $e^i = x^i$, no trade would take place at those prices, and we would have an autarkic equilibrium, with each agent consuming his endowment.

Let k be an arbitrary agent, and z^k a consumption bundle such that $z^k >_k x^k$. Then the allocation $(x^1, \dots, x^{k-1}, z^k, x^{k+1}, \dots, x^n)$ differs from x only in agent k's consumption, but contains enough resources to allow us to make all agents better off than under x. Starting from this allocation, we will construct a new allocation $\bar{x}$ by taking a little bit of each good away from agent k and allocating it to the other agents in equal shares. That is,

$$\bar{x}^k = z^k - \varepsilon \underline{1}$$

$$\bar{x}^i = x^i + \frac{\varepsilon}{n-1} \underline{1} \ \forall \ i \ne k$$

where $\underline{1}$ is a vector of 1's, and ε is a positive real number. Because $z^k >_k x^k$, the continuity of preferences implies that we can choose ε small enough that agent k still will prefer his new bundle to x^k. Notice also that for any $\varepsilon > 0$, the rest of the agents will always prefer the new allocation to x^i, by the strict monotonicity of preferences. Hence, there is some $\varepsilon > 0$ such that

$$\bar{x}^k = z^k - \varepsilon \underline{1} >_k x^k \quad \text{and} \quad \bar{x}^i = x^i + \frac{\varepsilon}{n-1}\underline{1} >_i x^i \ \forall \, i \neq k$$

Because $\bar{x}$ is strictly preferred to x by all agents (by construction), we have $\sum_{i=1}^n \bar{x}^i \in P(x)$. By (1) and (2), this implies that

$$p\left(\sum_{i=1}^n \bar{x}^i\right) \geq pE = \sum_{i=1}^n px^i$$

Expanding this expression and canceling out identical terms,

$$p\left(z^k - \varepsilon\underline{1} + \sum_{i \neq k}[x^i + (\varepsilon/n-1)\underline{1}]\right) \geq p\left(x^k + \sum_{i \neq k} x^i\right) \Rightarrow pz^k \geq px^k$$

Because k was arbitrary, a similar result holds for all agents, that is,

$$z^i >_i x^i \Rightarrow pz^i \geq pz^i \ \forall \, i \tag{3}$$

Finally, we show that the inequality in (3) is a strict inequality. We proceed by contradiction. Suppose $z^i >_i x^i$ and $pz^i = px^i$. By the continuity of preferences, we can find some scalar $\lambda < 1$ such that $\lambda z^i >_i x^i$. Because λz^i has strictly less of all commodities than z^i, it is cheaper than z^i, and we have $\lambda pz^i < pz^i = px^i$. This, however, contradicts (3), for λz^i is strictly preferred to x^i and strictly cheaper. $\qquad\square$

This theorem has been used to argue that efficiency and fairness can be separated. The market mechanism guarantees efficient outcomes, but it is "ethically neutral." To achieve fairness, however we may want to define it, all we have to do is redistribute (in a lump-sum manner) wealth in some equitable way and then let the market operate freely. This version of the idea that we can have our cake and eat it too has sometimes been called *market socialism*.

One implication of the second welfare theorem that can sometimes be of practical interest is that competitive equilibria can be characterized as the solutions of appropriate planning problems. In many cases it is easier to solve these problems than to find the equilibrium allocations by equating supply and demand. In a two-agent economy, for example, we can trace out the *contract curve* (the set of Pareto-efficient allocations) by solving the problem

$$\max_{x_1, x_2} U_1(x_1) \text{ subject to } U_2(x_2) \geq u_2$$

and an appropriate feasibility condition, where we treat u_2 as a parameter. By assigning different values to u_2, we trace out the entire contract curve.

The first-order conditions for the problem give us a characterization of the set of Pareto-efficient allocations. Because the equilibrium allocations will be in this set, we may be able to infer some of their qualitative properties without actually solving for them. If we have more than two agents, the following generalization of the foregoing problem will work:

$$\max_{x}\left\{\sum_i \lambda_i U_i(x_i) \text{ s.t. feasibility and } \sum_i \lambda_i = 1\right\}$$

That is, we maximize a weighted average of the utilities of the agents. By changing the weights λ_i, we can trace out the multidimensional analogue of the contract curve.

Problem 3.12. Consider an island economy populated by a representative individual who lives for two periods and has preferences described by the utility function

$$U(c, x) = \ln c + \beta \ln x \tag{1}$$

where c and x are first- and second-period consumptions. In period 1, the individual has an endowment of e units of a homogeneous consumption/capital good. He consumes part of it and uses the rest (k) as input for a production technology of the form $y = k^{\alpha}$, with $\alpha < 1$. Hence, the consumption-possibilities schedule for the economy is of the form

$$x \le k^{\alpha} = (e - c)^{\alpha} \tag{2}$$

(i) Draw the consumption-possibilities frontier and indifference curves on the (x, c) plane. Where is the optimum? Solve the planning problem

$$\max_{c, x}\left\{\ln c + \beta \ln x \text{ subject to } (e - c)^{\alpha} - x \ge 0\right\} \tag{P.1}$$

Write the first-order conditions. Is the constraint binding? Why? Or why not? Solve for the optimal values of c and $k = e - c$. (Don't worry about the second-order conditions. They hold.)

(ii) Next, consider a competitive version of the same economy. The agent now owns all the shares of a competitive firm that has access to the same technology as before, and he can lend part of his endowment to the firm, which maximizes profits, taking as given the market interest factor $R = 1 + r$ (capital depreciates completely upon use), and then distributes its profits to the shareholder. We shall verify that the competitive allocation coincides with the planning optimum.

Solve the firm's profit-maximization problem,

$$\max_{k} \pi = k^{\alpha} - Rk \tag{P.F}$$

and write the firm's maximized profit as a function of k.

Next, write the first-order conditions for the household's utility-maximization problem,

$$\max_s v(s) = \ln(e-s) + \beta\ln(sR+\pi) \tag{P.H}$$

(the agent takes as given both the market interest rate and the firm's profits), and solve for the optimal levels of saving and consumption.

Finally, in equilibrium the desired savings of the household must be the same as the desired level of capital input by the firm (i.e., $s = k$). Solve for the equilibrium values of saving/investment and consumption. They should be the same as in the first part of the problem. □

4. Games in Normal Form and Nash Equilibrium

The model analyzed in the preceding section assumed that the actions taken by each of our competitive consumers affected other agents only through the impersonal channel of market prices, which determined each agent's consumption opportunities. In many situations of interest, the interdependence between the agents involved is much more direct, with individual actions having a perceptible effect on others' payoffs. In this section we will develop a rather general framework for analysis of games involving a set of rational agents and an appropriate concept of equilibrium due to Nash. Our main purpose is not to provide a systematic introduction to game theory, but to introduce a rather general conceptual framework that will be appropriate for thinking about the "equilibrium problem" in models in which agents interact strategically.

The word "game" evokes a situation in which a number of players engage in some sort of competition, behaving in accordance with certain rules. The actions of the players (along with an element of chance, in most cases) jointly determine the outcome of the game, from which the players derive some sort of payoff, monetary or otherwise. To describe such a game, we need to specify the actions or strategies available to each player and his preferences concerning the outcome of the game. Formally, we have the following definition:

Definition 4.1. Game in normal form. A game in normal form is an n-tuple of the form

$$\Gamma = \{(U_i, A_i),\ i = 1, \dots, n\}$$

where A_i is a nonempty set, known as the action space or *strategy space* for player i, and U_i is a real-valued function, $U_i : A_1 \times A_2 \times \dots \times A_n \longrightarrow \mathbb{R}$, known as the *payoff function* for agent i.

That is, we have a set $N = \{1, \ldots, n\}$ of players; each one of them is described by his preferences, represented by a payoff function $U_i(\ )$, and by his set A_i of available actions. We typically identify the set A_i of actions available to the ith agent with a subset of $\mathbb{R}^m$. An element a_i of A_i is called an *action* or *strategy* for agent i. The Cartesian product $A = A_1 \times A_2 \times \ldots \times A_n$ is the *action space* of the game. An element a of A, called an *action* or *strategy profile*, is a vector $a = (a_1, \ldots, a_n)$ in $\mathbb{R}^{mn}$ that specifies the strategies chosen by the different players. The actions of all players jointly determine the result of the game and the payoff to each agent, $U_i(a) = U_i(a_1, \ldots, a_n)$, which depends not only on his actions but also on those of all the other agents. For convenience, we will sometimes partition an action profile into two components:

$$a = (a_i; a_{-i}), \quad \text{where } a_{-i} = (a_1, \ldots, a_{i-1}, a_{i+1}, \ldots, a_n)$$

Thus, a_{-i} provides us a compact way to refer to "everybody else's" actions.

We now introduce a concept of equilibrium for games in normal form that requires both individual rationality and mutual compatibility among the choices of the different agents.

Definition 4.2. Nash equilibrium. An action profile $a^* = (a_1^*, \ldots, a_n^*)$ is a Nash equilibrium if it is feasible (i.e., $a \in A$) and if each player's action is a best response to the joint actions of all the other players. That is,

$$a_i^* \in \arg \max_{a_i \in A_i} U_i(a_i; a_{-i}^*) \, \forall \, i = 1, \ldots, n \tag{N}$$

That is, given that other agents play a_{-i}^*, there is no incentive for the ith player to deviate unilaterally from the equilibrium profile a^*.

Notice that this definition subsumes both the individual-decision problem and the equilibrium problem. We require that each player i behave as if he is solving a constrained optimization problem, given by (N), in which the actions of the other agents are taken as given. But (N) says more than that: It tells us that this must be true for all agents simultaneously, or that the actions of all the agents are mutually best responses to one another. Loosely, in equilibrium, all agents optimize at the same time.

To establish the existence of Nash equilibrium, it will be convenient to "separate" the two subproblems. We will first describe the behavior of each individual agent through a best-response mapping and then impose a consistency requirement on their joint choices. In this manner, establishing the existence of Nash equilibrium will be reduced to the familiar mathematical problem of showing that a given correspondence has a fixed point.

An action a_i^* is said to be a *best response* by player i to actions a_{-i} by the other players if it maximizes agent i's payoff, given a_{-i}. By considering an agent's best response to all possible combinations of actions of his rivals, we can construct his *best-response mapping*, $\Phi_i: A_{-i} \rightarrow\rightarrow A_i$, with

$$\Psi_i(a_{-i}) = \arg \max_{a_i \in A_i} U_i(a_i; a_{-i})$$

Notice that $\Psi_i( )$ is analogous to a demand correspondence, except that we now get the set of optimal choices for agent i as a function of the other agents' actions, rather than prices.

Taking the Cartesian product of the best-response mappings for the individual players, we obtain the *best-response mapping for the game*, $\Psi: A \rightarrow\rightarrow A$, defined by

$$\Psi(a) = \Psi_1(a_{-1}) \times \Psi_2(a_{-2}) \times \ldots \times \Psi_n(a_{-n})$$

We can now redefine a Nash equilibrium as a fixed point of the correspondence $\Psi( )$. Notice that if $a^* \in \Psi(a^*)$, then we have

$$a_i^* \in \Psi_i(a_{-i}^*) = \arg \max_{a_i \in A_i} U_i(a_i; a_{-i}^*) \quad \text{or} \quad U(a_i^*; a_{-i}^*) \geq U(a_i; a_{-i}^*) \, \forall \, a_i \in A_i$$

and for all $i = 1, 2, \ldots, n$. Hence, a^* is indeed a Nash equilibrium (i.e., an action profile such that each player's action is a best response to the actions of the other players).

The proof of the following theorem is now straightforward. It suffices to verify that the best-response mapping for the game satisfies the conditions of Kakutani's fixed-point theorem.

Theorem 4.3. Existence of Nash equilibrium. Let $\Gamma = \{(U_i, A_i), i = 1, \ldots, n\}$ be a game in normal form, and assume that

(i) *the action space for each player A_i is a nonempty, compact, and convex subset of $\mathbb{R}^m$, and*

(ii) *the payoff functions $U_i: A \longrightarrow \mathbb{R}$ are continuous and quasiconcave in a_i for given a_{-i}.*

Then the game Γ has at least one Nash equilibrium. That is, there exists some $a^* \in A$ such that $a^* \in \Psi(a^*)$.

Proof. We have seen that we can define a Nash equilibrium as a fixed point of the best-response correspondence for the game, $\Psi( )$. Hence, all we have to do is show that $\Psi( )$ satisfies the conditions for Kakutani's theorem, namely, that $\Psi( )$ is uhc, nonempty, and compact- and convex-valued, and that A is compact and convex.

First, notice that $A = A_1 \times A_2 \times \ldots \times A_n$ is compact and convex because it is the Cartesian product of compact and convex sets. Next, consider the best-response correspondence for agent i,

$$\Psi_i(a_{-i}) = \arg \max_{a_i \in A_i} U_i(a_i; a_{-i})$$

Because A_i is a compact set, and $U_i(\ )$ a continuous function, $\Psi_i(a_{-i})$ is non-empty by the extreme-value theorem. Moreover,

$$\Psi_i(a_{-i}) = A_i \cap \left\{ b_i;\ U_i(b_i; a_{-i}) \geq \max_{a_i \in A_i} U_i(a_i; a_{-i}) \right\}$$

is the intersection of two convex sets, A_i and an upper contour set of the quasiconcave function $U_i(\cdot; a_{-i})$, and is therefore convex itself. Hence, $\Psi_i(\ )$ is convex-valued. Finally, $\Psi_i(\ )$ is uhc and compact-valued, by the theorem of the maximum (because the constraint correspondence is compact-valued and "constant" and therefore continuous).

The correspondence $\Psi(a)$ is defined as the Cartesian product of the individual best-response mappings and therefore inherits the required properties from them. Hence, the conditions of Kakutani's theorem are satisfied, and it follows that $\Psi(\ )$ has a fixed point a^* in A. □

Debreu (1983a) has proved an extension of Nash's theorem for the case in which the action space for each player is given by a continuous and convex-valued correspondence $A_i = \Gamma_i(a_{-i})$ of the actions of the other players. This result can be used to establish the existence of competitive equilibrium in an economy like the one analyzed in Section 3. For this, we consider a game played by $n + 1$ agents: our n price-taking consumers and a fictional agent we will call the Walrasian auctioneer. Traders choose consumption bundles in order to maximize their utility within their budget sets, taking prices as given. The auctioneer is assumed to set prices so as to maximize the value of excess demand pZ, taking the actions of all traders (i.e., the vector Z) as given. It is easy to show that the equilibrium for this game is a competitive equilibrium in the sense defined in Section 3.

Problem 4.4. Cournot duopoly. Two firms compete in the market for a homogeneous good. The inverse demand function, which gives the price that consumers are willing to pay as a function of the total output of the good, is of the form

$$P(q_1 + q_2) = \theta - q_1 - q_2 \tag{1}$$

where $\theta > 0$ is a given parameter, and q_i is the level of output of the ith firm.

Each firm maximizes its profits, taking as given the function (1) and the output level of its competitor. For example, firm 1 solves

$$\max_{q_1} P(q_1 + q_2)q_1 - c_1 q_1 \tag{2}$$

where c_1 is its (constant) marginal cost, treating q_2 as a given constant.

(i) Solve firm 1's problem for its reaction function, that is, a function of the form $q_1 = \phi_1(q_2; c_1, \theta)$ that will give the optimal level of output as a function of its rival's output and the parameters (c_1, θ).

(ii) Firm 2's reaction function will have the same form as the one you have just derived. In a Nash equilibrium, each firm maximizes its profit, taking as given the other's output level. To find the equilibrium, we solve the system

$$q_1^* = \phi_1(q_2^*; c_1, \theta), \qquad q_2^* = \phi_2(q_1^*; c_2, \theta) \tag{3}$$

Draw the two reaction functions (their intersection corresponds to the equilibrium). Solve (3) explicitly to obtain the solution mapping for the model,

$$q^* = (q_1^*, q_2^*) = \Psi(\theta, c_1, c_2)$$

What conditions must be imposed on the parameters for the system to have an interior solution (i.e., one in which both firms produce)? Analyze, graphically and analytically, the effect of changes in θ and c_1 on equilibrium output levels.

(iii) Compute the equilibrium price and industry output and the equilibrium profit of each firm.

Problem 4.5. Stackelberg duopoly. We will now analyze a market much like the one described in the preceding problem, but in which the timing of actions is slightly different. Instead of assuming that both firms move simultaneously, we now assume that firm 1 moves first. This gives firm 1 a strategic advantage: Because it knows how its rival will behave, it can maximize its own profits, taking as given firm 2's reaction function. Firm 2 then observes firm 1's output choice and behaves accordingly. Solve for the equilibrium of this game, and compare it to the Cournot equilibrium analyzed in Problem 4.4.

5. Some Useful Models of Imperfect Competition

In this section we ask the reader to work through the details of two simple models of general equilibrium with imperfect competition. The first model, which builds on the work of Dixit and Stiglitz (1977) and Ethier (1982), formalizes the idea that increasing specialization, as measured by the number of differentiated intermediate goods available, yields efficiency gains that appear as external economies to firms. Different versions of this model have been used by Romer (1987) and Grossman and Helpman (1991), among other authors, as building blocks for models in which growth is fueled by endogenous investment in research-and-development (R&D) activities that lead to the development of new product varieties. In Chapter 13 we will analyze one such *endogenous growth model.*

The second model, based on the work of Dixit and Norman (1980, ch. 9), analyzes a two-good economy in which one sector is imperfectly competitive because of the existence of fixed entry costs. The equilibrium involves two sources of inefficiency: Excess entry leads to the duplication of production facilities and high unit costs, and the existence of market power in one sector distorts relative prices and hence consumer choices. Because in this context an increase in market size will mitigate both types of distortions, the model can be used to illustrate some of the potential advantages of economic integration.

(a) *Increasing Returns to Specialization in a Dixit-Stiglitz Model of Monopolistic Competition*

Economists have long argued that an increase in the degree of specialization can increase efficiency. This idea, which goes back to Smith (1961), Marshall (1961), and Young (1928), has recently been revived in both the trade and growth literatures. To formalize it, we shall now develop a version of the Dixit-Stiglitz-Ethier model of monopolistic competition in which there are fixed setup costs in the production of (differentiated) intermediate goods.

Consider an economy in which there are two types of goods, a homogeneous consumption good and a continuum of measure n of differentiated intermediate products $x(s)$, with $0 \leq s \leq n$. The final good (Y) is produced in a competitive industry by assembling intermediate inputs using a constant-elasticity-of-substitution production function,[9]

$$Y = \left(\int_0^n x_s^\alpha \, ds \right)^{1/\alpha}, \quad \text{where } 0 < \alpha < 1 \tag{1}$$

and the differentiated components are produced by identical monopolistically competitive firms using labor (L) as an input and a production technology that involves constant marginal costs and decreasing average costs due to a fixed setup cost (c) measured in labor units:

$$L_s = x_s + c \tag{2}$$

where L_s is the amount of labor required to produce x_s units of any intermediate good.

Let us start by observing that the foregoing specification of technology captures Smith's idea that there are increasing returns to specialization. To see this, let L_x be the total amount of "variable labor" employed in the production of components. Because all components enter symmetrically in the production function for final goods and are themselves produced using the same technology, final output will be produced using the same quantity of each input, given by $x = L_x/n$. Substituting this expression into (1), final output is given by

$$\cdot \quad Y = \left(\int_0^n x^\alpha ds \right)^{1/\alpha} = n^{1/\alpha} x = n^{(1/\alpha)-1} L_x \tag{3}$$

Hence, if the elasticity of substitution among components is low enough (in particular, if $\alpha < 1$), final output will be an increasing function of the number of component varieties for a given amount of (variable) labor input.

It remains to determine the equilibrium number of product varieties. In this section we assume that entry is limited by a fixed setup cost, but in a later chapter we will want to allow n to grow over time as a result of R&D investment. Hence, it will be convenient to start by characterizing a "pseudoequilibrium" in which the number of product varieties (n) and the total "variable labor" (L_x) are taken as given. Profit levels and wage rates in such a situation will then give us an indication of the incentive either to directly set up production of a new component or, in a more dynamic context, to invest in R&D.

Problems 5.1 and 5.2 ask the reader to characterize the optimal behaviors of component producers and final-goods producers.

Problem 5.1. Consider first the behavior of final-goods producers. Although firm size is indeterminate with constant returns and perfect competition, each firm minimizes the cost of producing its desired level of output y, taking as given the prices $\mathbf{p} = \{p(s); 0 \le s \le n\}$ of the different inputs $x(s)$. That is, each firm solves

$$\min_{x_s; s \in [0, n]} \int_0^n p_s x_s \, ds \text{ s.t. } y = \left(\int_0^n x_s^\alpha \, ds \right)^{1/\alpha}$$

Using the first-order conditions for this problem, derive the conditional demand for intermediate goods as a function of final output and input prices and the firm's unit-cost function (see Problem 1.21 in Chapter 7). Verify that after aggregating over all final producers, the market demand function is of the form

$$x_s(\mathbf{p}, Y) = \phi p_s^{-\varepsilon}, \quad \text{where } \phi = \frac{Y}{\left(\int_0^n p_t^{1-\varepsilon} \, dt \right)^{1/\alpha}} \tag{4}$$

and Y is the aggregate output of final goods, with unit costs being given by

$$c(\mathbf{p}) = \left(\int_0^n p_s^{1-\varepsilon} \, ds \right)^{1/(1-\varepsilon)} \tag{5}$$

Problem 5.2. Taking the market demand schedule (4), the wage rate (w), and the prices set by its competitors as given, each component producer maximizes operating profits, given by

$$\Pi_s = p_s x_s - w x_s = \phi\left(p_s^{1-\varepsilon} - w p_s^{-\varepsilon}\right) \qquad (6)$$

Solve this problem for the firm's optimal output level and the implied level of profits.

To characterize the equilibrium, let us take as given, for the moment, the number of component varieties n and the total amount of "variable labor" employed in the intermediate sector, L_x, and consider a symmetric equilibrium in which all component producers set the same price (p) and produce the same output (x). Problem 5.3 asks the reader to solve for profits and wages in such a "pseudoequilibrium."

Problem 5.3. In equilibrium, free entry will ensure that profits will be zero in the perfectly competitive final-goods sector. Hence, the price of final output, which we will normalize to 1, must be equal to its unit cost. Using this condition, together with previous results, show that equilibrium wages and profits are given by

$$\pi = \frac{(1-\alpha)Y}{n} \quad \text{and} \quad w = \frac{\alpha Y}{n l_x} \qquad (7)$$

where $l_x = L_x/n$ is "variable employment" in a representative component producer. Hence, output is divided between wages and profits. Profits per firm decrease with the number of competitors n and with the difficulty of substituting one input for another, measured by α.

We can now solve for the equilibrium number of product varieties in a free-entry equilibrium.

Problem 5.4. We have assumed that anybody willing to pay a fixed cost of c units of labor can set up shop and start producing a new component variety. Compute the total demand for labor, and set it equal to the fixed labor supply L. Using this condition and the assumption of free entry into the sector, solve for the equilibrium number of firms n^* as a function of L and c, and use (3) to derive a reduced-form aggregate-production function giving output per capita as a function of the same variables. Verify that this function exhibits increasing returns to labor when $\alpha < 1$.

(b) Fixed Costs, Market Power, and Excess Entry
in a Cournot Model

Consider an economy populated by L identical individuals, with preferences over two consumption goods described by a utility function of the form

$$U(c, x) = \alpha \ln x + (1 - \alpha) \ln y \tag{1}$$

We take good y as the numeraire and normalize its price to 1. Agents are endowed with a unit of labor time each, and they own shares in firms. They maximize (1) subject to the budget constraint

$$px + y = I \tag{2}$$

where I denotes total (wage plus other) income, and p is the price of good x. It is easily shown that the assumed preferences imply constant expenditure shares equal to each good's (normalized) weight in the utility function. Hence, consumer optimization implies

$$px = \alpha I \quad \text{and} \quad y = (1 - \alpha)I \tag{3}$$

We assume that labor is the only factor of production and that the production technologies for x and y are of the form

$$L_x = x + c \quad \text{and} \quad L_y = y \tag{4}$$

where L_x denotes the amount of labor required to produce x units of the good, and c is a fixed setup cost (in labor units). Hence, marginal costs are constant and equal for the two commodities, but good x is produced at decreasing average cost.

The planning optimum for this economy is easily characterized. To minimize fixed costs, all production of good x should take place in a single plant. The remaining labor $(L - c)$ should be allocated to the production of the two goods in proportion to their weights in the utility function. The first-best per-capita consumption-and-production bundle (FB) corresponds, as shown in Figure 8.8, to a point of tangency between an indifference curve of the representative consumer and a per-capita production-possibilities frontier (PPF) with unit slope (because the marginal costs of both goods are the same).

This allocation, however, will not be attained in equilibrium. Notice that the existence of fixed costs implies that the x sector cannot be competitive. We will assume that firms in this sector compete in a Cournot fashion, taking as given the quantities produced by their rivals, and that free entry drives equilibrium profits to zero. Noncompetitive producers will charge prices in

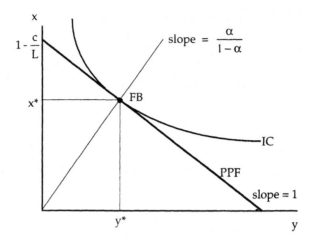

Figure 8.8. Optimal allocation.

excess of marginal costs, implying that equilibrium x production will be sub-optimally low. Free entry will, of course, limit the equilibrium markup, but it also will generate a second inefficiency, as any increase in the number of firms will involve a fixed cost that will reduce overall production possi-bilities. Problem 5.5 asks the reader to solve for a symmetric free-entry equilibrium. Problem 5.6 then compares this equilibrium with the planning optimum characterized earlier and analyzes the effect of an increase in market size.

Problem 5.5. Consider a free-entry equilibrium in which sector y is com-petitive, and x producers compete à la Cournot. Zero profits in the com-petitive sector imply that the salary will be equal to the price of y, which we have normalized to 1. Let us focus on the market for x and characterize a symmetric Cournot equilibrium. Aggregating over consumers, the total demand for x can be written

$$X = \frac{\alpha Q}{p}$$

where $Q = LI$ is aggregate income. Inverting this function, and assuming that there are $n + 1$ producers in this sector, we can write the inverse demand schedule perceived by a representative producer i in the form

$$p(x_i) = \frac{\alpha Q}{nx_{-i} + x_i}$$

(5)

where x_i denotes his own output level, and x_{-i} that of an arbitrary competitor.

Producer i maximizes profits,

$$\Pi_i = p(x_i)x_i - x_i - c = \frac{\alpha Q x_i}{n x_{-i} + x_i} - x_i - c$$

taking as given the salary ($w = 1$), aggregate income Q, and the outputs of his n competitors (x_{-i}). Using the first-order conditions for this problem, derive a reaction function giving optimal output for the ith producer as a function of those of his rivals. In a symmetric equilibrium, all firms will choose the same output level. Set $x_i = x_{-i} \equiv x$, and find (i) the equilibrium level of output, (ii) the equilibrium price of good x, and (iii) the equilibrium level of firm profits – all written as functions of aggregate income and the number of firms in the sector.

Now, in a free-entry equilibrium profits are zero, and it follows that aggregate income is given by

$$Q = Lw = L \tag{10}$$

Using this last expression and setting $\pi = 0$, find (i) the equilibrium number of x producers (ignoring integer constraints), (ii) the equilibrium price of good x, (iii) total x output, (iv) total fixed costs, and (v) total y output – all written as functions of "market size," measured by αL, and the fixed cost c.

Problem 5.6. Using a diagram similar to Figure 8.8, compare the equilibrium per-capita allocation and the social optimum, illustrating the two sources of inefficiency we have identified. Using your results from Problem 5.5, discuss how things change as "market size" (measured by L) increases.

Bibliography

Arrow, K. 1983a. Economic Equilibrium. In: *Collected Papers of Kenneth J. Arrow. Vol. 2: General Equilibrium.* Harvard University Press.

Arrow, K. 1983b. An Extension of the Basic Theorems of Classical Welfare Economics. In: *Collected Papers of Kenneth J. Arrow. Vol. 2: General Equilibrium.* Harvard University Press.

Arrow, K. 1983c. General Economic Equilibrium: Purpose, Analytic Techniques, Collective Choice. In: *Collected Papers of Kenneth J. Arrow. Vol. 2: General Equilibrium.* Harvard University Press.

Arrow, K. 1989. Economic Theory and the Hypothesis of Rationality. In: *The New Palgrave: Utility and Probability*, ed. J. Eatwell, M. Milgate, and P. Newman. New York: Norton.

Arrow, K., and Debreu, G. 1983. Existence of an Equilibrium for a Competitive Economy. In: *Collected Papers of Kenneth J. Arrow. Vol. 2: General Equilibrium.* Harvard University Press.

Arrow, K., and Hahn, F. 1971. *General Competitive Analysis. Advanced Textbooks in Economics*, Vol. 12, ed. C. Bliss, and M. Intriligator. Amsterdam: North Holland.

Blad, M., and Keiding, H. 1990. *Microeconomics. Institutions, Equilibrium and Optimality.* Amsterdam: North Holland.

Border, K. 1989. *Fixed Point Theorems with Applications to Economics and Game Theory*. Cambridge University Press.

Deaton, A., and Muellbauer, J. 1986. *Economics and Consumer Behaviour*. Cambridge University Press.

Debreu, G. 1959. *Theory of Value. An Axiomatic Analysis of Economic Equilibrium*. Cowles Foundation Monographs, no. 17. New Haven, CT: Cowles.

Debreu, G. 1976. Economic Theory in the Mathematical Mode. *American Economic Review* 66:280–7.

Debreu, G. 1982. Existence of Competitive Equilibrium. In: *Handbook of Mathematical Economics*, Vol. 2, ed. K. Arrow and M. Intriligator, pp. 697–743. Amsterdam: North Holland.

Debreu, G. 1983a. A Social Equilibrium Existence Theorem. In: *Mathematical Economics: Twenty Papers of Gerard Debreu*, Econometric Society Monographs, no. 4. Cambridge University Press. (Originally published 1952.)

Debreu, G. 1983b. Representation of a Preference Ordering by a Numerical Function. In: *Mathematical Economics: Twenty Papers of Gerard Debreu*, Econometric Society Monographs, no. 4. Cambridge University Press. (Originally published 1954.)

Dixit, A., and Norman, V. 1980. *Theory of International Trade*. Cambridge University Press.

Dixit, A., and Stiglitz, J. 1977. Monopolistic Competition and Optimum Product Diversity. *American Economic Review* 67:297–308.

Ethier, W. 1982. National and International Returns to Scale in the Modern Theory of International Trade. *American Economic Review* 72:389–405.

Fishburn, P. 1989. Representation of Preferences. In: *The New Palgrave: Utility and Probability*, ed. J. Eatwell, M. Milgate, and P. Newman. New York: Norton.

Friedman, J. 1986. *Game Theory with Applications to Economics*. Oxford University Press.

Grossman, G., and Helpman, E. 1991. *Innovation and Growth in the Global Economy*. Massachusetts Institute of Technology Press.

Hildenbrand, W. 1974. *Core and Equilibria of a Large Economy*. Princeton University Press.

Hildenbrand, W., and Kirman, A. 1976. *Introduction to Equilibrium Analysis. Variations on Themes by Edgeworth and Walras*. Amsterdam: North Holland.

Krepps, D. 1990. *A Course in Microeconomic Theory*. Princeton University Press.

Malinvaud, E. 1985. *Lectures on Microeconomic Theory*. Amsterdam: North Holland.

Marshall, A. 1961. *Principles of Economics*, 9th ed., with annotations by C. Guillebaud. London: Macmillan.

Mas-Colell, A. 1985. *The Theory of General Economic Equilibrium: A Differentiable Approach*. Econometric Society Monographs, no. 9. Cambridge University Press.

Mas-Colell, A., Whinston, M., and Green, J. 1995. *Microeconomic Theory*. Oxford University Press.

Nash, J. 1950. Equilibrium Points in *N*-Person Games. *Proceedings of the National Academy of Sciences, USA* 36:48–9.

Nikaido, H. 1972. *Introduction to Sets and Mappings in Modern Economics*. Amsterdam: North Holland.

Romer, P. 1987. Growth Based on Increasing Returns due to Specialization. *American Economic Review, Papers and Proceedings* 77:56–62.

Sen, A. 1989. Rational Behaviour. In: *The New Palgrave: Utility and Probability*, ed. J. Eatwell, M. Milgate, and P. Newman. New York: Norton.

Smith, A. 1961. *The Wealth of Nations*. London: University Paperbacks. (Originally published 1776.)

Varian, H. 1984. *Microeconomic Analysis*, 2nd ed. New York: Norton.

Young, A. 1928. Increasing Returns and Economic Progress. *Economic Journal* 38:527–42.

Notes

1 For many purposes, we can make do with a weaker property, called acyclicity. This requires that the strict preference relation contain no cycles, i.e., that there exist no collection $x_1, \ldots, x_n$ of alternatives such that $x_1 > x_2 > \ldots > x_n$ and $x_n > x_1$. This is both necessary and sufficient for the existence of a nonempty set of undominated alternatives in any finite collection of objects.

2 See Section 9 of Chapter 2 for a discussion of connectedness and some useful results.

3 The reader should refer to Section 11 of Chapter 2 and Section 2(a) of Chapter 7 for a discussion of the continuity of correspondences and the theorem of the maximum.

4 After Léon Walras, the first author who tried to develop a rigorous theory of general equilibrium for a competitive economy.

5 In fact, this has to be generalized a bit. We observe that some goods (e.g., air) are free ($p_g = 0$), and this is compatible with their being in excess supply. To account for this, we can write the equilibrium condition as

$$p \geq \underline{0}, \quad Z_g(p) \leq 0 \quad \text{and} \quad Z_g(p) = 0 \quad \text{if } p_g > 0 \qquad \text{(W.E}')$$

We will ignore this complication from now on.

6 Notice that if we interpret $f(p)$ as an excess-demand function, the adjustment rule $\mu(\ )$ instructs us to find a price vector q that will maximize the value of the excess-demand vector $f(p)$. This involves setting $p_g = 0$ for all g, such that $f_g(p) < 0$ and it entails "high" prices for those goods with a positive excess demand. Notice that if $f(p) = \underline{0}$, then any price vector q will do, because then $qf(p) = 0$ for all q. Hence, if $f(p) = \underline{0}$, we have $p \in \mu(p)$, and p will be a fixed point of $\mu(\ )$.

7 This may sound a bit funny, particularly after you look at the proof and see that no trade takes place in equilibrium. Notice, however, that we could replace the condition that the endowment itself be x^i by the assumption that the endowment vector for agent i has the same value as x^i at equilibrium prices and that these endowment vectors are collectively feasible. The equilibrium would then generally involve some exchange.

8 If the sum of individual consumptions were strictly less than the total endowment of resources, we could increase the consumption of all agents, making them strictly better off.

9 The additive functional in (1) was introduced by Dixit and Stiglitz (1977) as a utility function. Ethier (1982) reinterpreted it as a production function.

Part III

Dynamics

9

Dynamical Systems. I: Basic Concepts and Scalar Systems

In many applications in economics and other disciplines we are interested in the evolution of certain systems over time. Suppose the state of the system of interest at a given point in time can be described by a dated vector of real numbers, $x_t \in \mathbb{R}^n$, which we call the *state vector*. To give a precise description of the evolution of x_t, we introduce a vector-valued function

$$\phi: \mathbb{R}^{n+1+p} \supseteq X \times \mathbb{R} \times \Omega \longrightarrow \mathbb{R}^n, \quad \text{with } x_t = \phi(x_0, t; \alpha)$$

that gives the value of the state vector at time t as a function of its initial value, $x_0 \in \mathbb{R}^n$ and a vector of parameters $\alpha \in \mathbb{R}^p$ that describes the environment in which the system is embedded. Such a function is called a *transition function* or *flow*. Notice that $\phi(\ )$ fully describes the behavior of the system: For given initial conditions x_0 and fixed parameter values α, we obtain the time path of the system by giving values to t; and by changing x_0 and α we can determine how this path varies with changes in initial conditions or parameters.

In most cases the flow of a dynamical system is not given to us directly. Instead, we start from a parameterized system of difference or differential equations and must "solve it" to construct its flow. In this chapter and those that follow we will review some of the basic elements of the theory of difference and differential equations and some applications to economics. To abbreviate, we will refer to dynamical systems described by systems of differential equations as "continuous" or "continuous-time" systems (CS), and to those described by systems of difference equations as "discrete" or "discrete-time" systems (DS). When it is not necessary to distinguish between them, we will speak simply of dynamical systems (S).

1. Difference and Differential Equations: Basic Concepts

An ordinary *differential equation* is an equation of the form

$$x^{(m)}(t) = F[t, x(t), \dot{x}(t), \ddot{x}(t), \dots, x^{(m-1)}(t); \alpha] \tag{1}$$

where $x(t) = [x_1(t), x_2(t), \dots, x_n(t)]$ is a vector-valued function of a real variable that we will interpret as time; $\dot{x}(t) = (dx_1(t)/dt, dx_2(t)/dt, \dots, dx_n(t)/dt)$ is the first derivative of $x(t)$ with respect to time, with $\ddot{x}(t)$ its second derivative and $x^{(m)}$ its mth derivative; $\alpha \in \Omega \subseteq \mathbb{R}^p$ is a vector of parameters; and $F(\ )$ is a function $\mathbb{R}^{1+n(m-1)+p} \longrightarrow \mathbb{R}^n$ that we will typically assume to be at least C^1.

Observe that (1) is a functional equation, that is, an equation in which the unknown is a function $x(t)$, rather than a number or a vector. Solving (1) means finding those functions $x(t)$ that, together with their derivatives $\dot{x}, \dots, x^{(m)}$, will satisfy the equation for given values of the parameters.

In a system of differential equations, time is a continuous variable, that is, t can take any real value. In many cases, however, it is convenient to restrict t to integer values that correspond to some natural period (e.g., a year). In this case, we work with *difference equations*, that is, equations of the form

$$x_{t+m} = G[t, x_t, x_{t+1}, x_{t+2}, \dots, x_{t+m-1}; \alpha] \tag{2}$$

where $x_s \in \mathbb{R}^n$ denotes the state of the system in period s. Like (1), equation (2) is a functional equation, because the unknown is once more a function of t that must satisfy certain properties. On the other hand, given that t is a discrete variable, the solution to (2) will be a sequence rather than a differentiable function of t.

A differential equation is *linear* if $F(\ )$ is linear in $x(t)$ and its derivatives, but not necessarily in t or α. Similarly, a difference equation is linear if $G(\ )$ is a linear function of $x_t, x_{t+1}, x_{t+2}, \dots, x_{t+m-1}$. A dynamical system is *autonomous* if t does not appear as an independent argument of $F(\ )$ or $G(\ )$, but enters only through $x(t)$. As we will see later, linear systems are much easier to analyze than nonlinear ones. Because explicit solutions for nonlinear systems cannot be found, except in special cases, we have to settle for qualitative results or numerical solutions for specific functional forms. In the case of autonomous systems of one or two dimensions, qualitative results are easily obtained by graphical methods. For higher-dimensional systems, we have to rely on linear approximations to obtain local results for nonlinear systems.

The *order* of a differential equation is the order of the highest derivative of $x(t)$ that appears in it; the order of a difference equation is equal to the difference between the highest and lowest time subscripts that appear in the equation. Hence, both (1) and (2) are of order m.

It is easy to see that any system of difference or differential equations can be reduced to an equivalent first-order system by introducing additional equations and variables. For example, given the second-order differential equation

$$\ddot{x} = a\dot{x} + bx$$

we can define a new variable $y = \dot{x}$ and rewrite the equation in the form of a system of two first-order equations:

$$\dot{x} = y \quad \text{and} \quad \dot{y} = ay + bx$$

Hence, we can restrict ourselves, with no loss of generality, to the study of first-order systems of the form

$$\dot{x} = f(x, t; \alpha) \qquad \qquad (\text{CS}(t, \alpha))$$

or

$$x_{t+1} = g(x_t, t; \alpha) \qquad \qquad (\text{DS}(t, \alpha))$$

where we indicate in parentheses the arguments of $f(\ )$ or $g(\ )$ other than x.

(a) Geometrical Interpretation

In order to visualize the kind of information contained in a system of equations of the form (CS) or (DS) and to understand what it means to solve such a system, it will be convenient to think of the equations (CS) and (DS) as descriptions of the motion of a particle in n-dimensional space. If we interpret x_t as the position of the particle at time t, the difference equation $x_{t+1} = g(x_t, t; \alpha)$ tells us that a particle that is in position x_t at time t will be at the point x_{t+1} one period later. Subtracting x_t from both sides of the equation, we obtain the vector

$$\Delta x_t = x_{t+1} - x_t = g(x_t, t; \alpha) - x_t$$

Graphically, Δx_t can be represented as an arrow that takes us from the current position of the particle to its next position, as shown in Figure 9.1. Once in x_{t+1}, we can construct a new arrow, $\Delta x_{t+1} = g(x_{t+1}, t+1) - x_{t+1}$, follow it to x_{t+2}, and so on.

In summary, a difference equation describes the motion of a particle step by step. If we specify an initial time and position and follow the arrows of motion, we can reconstruct the *trajectory* or *orbit* of the system, obtaining a sequence $\{x_t\}$ that is a *particular solution* to the system. Of course, if we choose a different initial time or position, or if we change the values of the parameters, the same system will generate a different trajectory in the state space X. Hence, the difference equation $(\text{DS}(t, \alpha))$ will in general have an infinite number of solutions, indexed by the system's initial time and position and by the parameter vector.

Although it is perhaps easier to visualize the behavior of a discrete-time system, it is often more convenient or more natural to work in continuous time. The analogy with the motion of a particle in space remains valid for systems of differential equations, the only difference being that the particle now moves smoothly rather than in discrete jumps. In fact, a differential

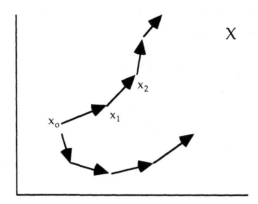

Figure 9.1. Solution trajectories of a discrete system.

equation is simply the limiting case of a difference equation as the length of the period between jumps goes to zero. In the preceding discussion we arbitrarily set the length of the period to 1, but more generally, we can set it to h. Then the change in x between two consecutive periods is given by $\Delta x_t = x_{t+h} - x_t$. Dividing Δx_t by h and taking the limit as $h \to 0$, we obtain the time derivative $\dot{x}(t)$, which can be interpreted as a velocity vector.

Hence, the system $(CS(t, \alpha))$, $\dot{x} = f(x, t; \alpha)$, assigns to each point $x \in X$ an arrow (which we imagine "attached" to x) whose direction is the instantaneous direction of motion (i.e., the tangent to the body's trajectory at the given point) and whose length is proportional to the speed of movement. In this context, f (or g) is sometimes referred to as a *vector field*.

Solving the differential equation (CS) means reconstructing the set of functions $\varphi(t)$ that describe trajectories in state space that are compatible with the given set of velocity vectors. The idea is the same as in the discrete case, with the difference that the orbits of the system will now be smooth curves (differentiable functions of time) rather than discrete sets of points (sequences). Like $(DS(t, \alpha))$, the continuous system $(CS(t, \alpha))$ will in general have an infinite number of solutions, for the particle's trajectory will depend on its initial position and the time at which it is set in motion, as well as on the values of the parameters.

(b) Initial- and Boundary-Value Problems

As already indicated, a dynamical system $(S(t))$ will in general have an infinite number of solutions, corresponding to the different trajectories that the state vector may follow in state space depending on its initial position and the time at which the system is set in motion. The set of all such "par-

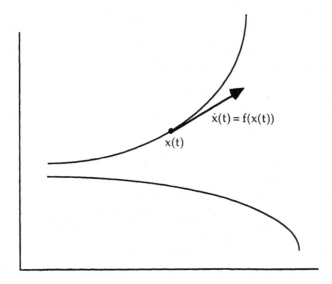

Figure 9.2. Solution trajectories of a continuous system.

ticular" solutions of the system, $\phi(t, x^0, t_0)$, is sometimes called its *general solution*. In certain cases it is relatively easy to first construct the general solution and then select the particular solution in which we are interested. This process is referred to as *definitizing the solution* of the system. One way to choose an appropriate particular solution is by imposing an *initial condition*, that is, a condition of the form

$$x(0) = x^0 \qquad\qquad (\text{C}(x^0, 0))$$

requiring that the system start out at time zero from some given position x^0. A system of difference or differential equations and an initial condition together define an *initial-value problem*, and the solution to this problem is a particular solution of the system.

Imposing an initial condition (in the strict sense of the word) is not the only way to definitize the solution of a dynamical system. More generally, we can use side or *boundary conditions* of the type

$$x(t_0) = x^0 \qquad\qquad (\text{C}(x^0, t_0))$$

to specify that the state vector x must take on a given value x^0 at some point in time $t_0 \in [0, +\infty]$ that need not be equal to zero. We will denote the *boundary-value problem* defined by a dynamical system $(\text{S}(t, \alpha))$, and the side condition $(\text{C}(x^0, t_0))$ by $(\text{P}(x^0, t_0, \alpha))$. We will show later that although the dynamical system $(\text{S}(t, \alpha))$ will in general have an infinite number of solutions, the boundary-value problem $(\text{P}(x^0, t_0, \alpha))$ will have precisely one solution, provided the function $f(\ )$ or $g(\ )$ satisfies certain reasonable conditions.

In the mathematical literature on dynamical systems, the distinction between initial and boundary conditions is seldom made. To return to our interpretation of a dynamical system as the law of motion of a particle in space, the trajectory of the particle is fully determined once we specify that it must go through some point x^0 at a given time t_0. For this purpose, it is irrelevant whether x^0 is the initial position of the particle when it is set in motion "at the beginning of time," its final destination, or any other point in the trajectory.

In many economic applications, however, the difference between initial conditions per se and other types of boundary conditions is important. We often have natural initial conditions associated with variables like the capital stock whose initial values (today) are predetermined by what has happened in the past. On the other hand, there are economic variables, such as asset prices, that are able to "jump" instantaneously and for which there are no obvious initial conditions. In such cases, the choice of an appropriate boundary condition must be made on economic grounds rather than mathematical grounds, and often it will reflect important assumptions concerning the formation of expectations and the choice of equilibrium concept. We will return to this question in Chapter 11 and deal with it in the context of a specific example that will allow for a more precise discussion.

(c) Some Definitions

In this section we will formalize some of the concepts we have just introduced. Consider, for concreteness, a continuous-time system

$$\dot{x} = f(x, \alpha, t) \qquad (\text{CS}(t, \alpha))$$

where the function $f(\ )$ maps some set $X \times \Omega \times I$ in $\mathbb{R}^{n+p+1}$ into $X \subseteq \mathbb{R}^n$, and I is an interval in the real line.

A (*particular*) *solution* of $(\text{CS}(t, \alpha))$ is a differentiable function $\varphi(t)$: $J_\varphi \longrightarrow X$, defined on some interval $J_\varphi \subseteq I$ called its *interval of definition*, and taking values in X, that together with its derivative satisfies the differential equation $(\text{CS}(t, \alpha))$ in J_φ, that is, such that

$$\varphi'(t) = f[\varphi(t), \alpha, t] \; \forall \, t \in J_\varphi$$

It is important to distinguish between a solution function $\varphi(t)$ and the trajectory it describes in state space. Given a solution $\varphi(t)$ of the differential equation (CS) defined on the interval J_φ, we define the *orbit* of (CS) induced by φ as the set

$$\gamma(\varphi) = \varphi(J_\varphi) = \{x \in X; \, x = \varphi(t) \text{ for some } t \in J_\varphi\}$$

Given a solution $\varphi(t)$ of $(\text{CS}(t, \alpha))$, fix some $t_0 \in J_\varphi$, and let $x^0 = \varphi(t_0)$. It is then clear that $\varphi(t)$ is a solution of the boundary-value problem

$$\dot{x} = f(x, \alpha, t), \qquad x(t_0) = x^0 \qquad (\text{PC}(x^0, t_0, \alpha))$$

Conversely, we will show later that under appropriate assumptions on $f(\ )$, the problem $(\text{PC}(x^0, t_0, \alpha))$ has precisely one solution defined on a maximal interval $J_m(x^0, t_0, \alpha)$ that depends on the initial data of the problem and the parameter vector. Clearly, this solution is also a solution of the differential equation $(\text{CS}(t, \alpha))$. Hence, we can identify the set of solutions of $(\text{CS}(t, \alpha))$ with the solutions of the family of boundary-value problems $(\text{PC}(x^0, t_0, \alpha))$, where we now regard x^0, t_0, and α as "variables." Because any change in these data will generally yield a different solution of $(\text{CS}(t, \alpha))$, we can define a mapping $\phi(t; x^0, t_0, \alpha)$ by setting, for each t in $J_m(x^0, t_0, \alpha)$,

$$\phi(t; x^0, t_0, \alpha) \equiv \varphi(t)$$

where $\varphi(\ )$ is the unique maximal solution of the differential equation $(\text{CS}(t, \alpha))$ satisfying the boundary condition $\varphi(t_0) = x^0$. The resulting function, $\varphi(t; x^0, t_0, \alpha)$, is called the *flow* of the system $(\text{CS}(t, \alpha))$, or the flow of the vector field $f(x, \alpha, t)$.

By the uniqueness of solutions to boundary-value problems, we can define the *orbit* of the system $(\text{CS}(t, \alpha))$ through the point (x^0, t_0) as the orbit induced by the corresponding solution function, $\varphi(t) = \phi(t; x^0, t_0, \alpha)$. Hence,

$$\gamma(x^0, t_0) = \gamma[\phi(t; x^0, t_0, \alpha)] = \varphi(J_m(x^0, t_0, \alpha))$$
$$= \{x \in X; \ x = \varphi(t) \text{ for some } t \in J_m(x^0, t_0, \alpha)\}$$

It will be convenient at times to distinguish between the positive and negative orbits through a point. Given a point (x^0, t_0), let $J_m(x^0, t_0, \alpha) = (a, b)$ be the maximal interval of definition of the solution through (x^0, t_0), given by the function $\varphi(t) = \phi(t; x^0, t_0, \alpha)$. Then $t_0 \in J_m(x^0, t_0, \alpha)$, and we define the *positive orbit* through (x^0, t_0) by

$$\gamma^+(x^0, t_0) = \varphi([t_0, b)) = \{x \in X; \ x = \varphi(t) \text{ for some } t \in [t_0, b) \subseteq J_m(x^0, t_0, \alpha)\}$$

and the negative orbit through the same point by

$$\gamma^-(x^0, t_0) = \varphi((a, t_0]) = \{x \in X; \ x = \varphi(t) \text{ for some } t \in (a, t_0] \subseteq J_m(x^0, t_0, \alpha)\}$$

Similar concepts can be defined in an analogous way for the discrete system

$$x_{t+1} = g(x_t, t; \alpha) \qquad (\text{DS}(t, \alpha))$$

where the function $g(\ )$ maps some set $X \times I \times \Omega$ in $\mathbb{R}^{n+1+p}$ into $X \subseteq \mathbb{R}^n$. We now assume that I is a set of consecutive integers (we will sometimes refer to such a set as an "interval" for short). A solution of $(\text{DS}(t, \alpha))$ is a sequence (i.e., a function $\varphi(t): J_\varphi \longrightarrow X$) defined on some "interval" of integers

$J_\varphi \subseteq I$ called its "interval" or *set of definition*. This function takes values in X and satisfies the difference equation (DS(t, α)) in J_φ, that is,

$$\varphi(t+1) = g[\varphi(t), t; \alpha] \ \forall \ t \in J_\varphi$$

As in the continuous case, each solution of the difference equation (DS(t, α)) can be identified with the solution of an appropriate boundary-value problem, and the flow of the system can be defined in the same way as before (at least for all $t \geq t_0$, as discussed later). The orbits of the system through any given point (x^0, t_0) are also defined in a similar way. Notice, however, that orbits will now be discrete sets of points, rather than differentiable curves in state space.

(d) Existence, Uniqueness, and Other Properties of Solutions

We will now establish the existence, uniqueness, and other important properties of the solutions to discrete-time boundary-value problems of the form (PD(x^0, t_0, α)). We will also state a theorem that gives similar results for continuous-time systems. The proof of this result, which requires a lot more work than its discrete-time analogue, will be left for Section 6, where we will analyze in some detail the properties of solutions of differential equations.

Consider the boundary-value problem

$$x_{t+1} = g(x_t, t; \alpha), \qquad x(t_0) = x^0 \qquad \text{(PD(x^0, t_0, α))}$$

where the function $g(\ )$ maps some set $X \times I \times \Omega$ in $\mathbb{R}^{n+1+p}$ into $X \subseteq \mathbb{R}^n$, I is an "interval" containing t_0, and x^0 is a point in X. For convenience, we set $t_0 = 0$ in the following, but the same procedure could be followed for an arbitrary value of t_0.

The construction of the solution to this problem poses no conceptual difficulty. Intuitively, to recover the system's trajectory it is enough to "follow the arrows" starting from the initial position. Analytically, we can construct the solution sequence $\varphi(t) = \varphi_t(x^0, t_0, \alpha)$ iteratively by setting $\varphi(0) = x^0$ and then using $g(\ )$ to define $\varphi(t)$ recursively by $\varphi(t+1) = g[\varphi(t), t; \alpha]$. That is,

$$\phi_0(x^0, 0, \alpha) = x^0$$
$$\phi_1(x^0, 0, \alpha) = g(x^0, \alpha, 0) = g[\phi_0(x^0, 0, \alpha), 0, \alpha]$$
$$\phi_2(x^0, 0, \alpha) = g[\phi_1(x^0, 0, \alpha), 1, \alpha]$$
$$\vdots$$
$$\phi_t(x^0, 0, \alpha) = g[\phi_{t-1}(x^0, 0, \alpha), t-1, \alpha] \qquad (1)$$

If $g(\ )$ is continuous (or C^k), the function $\phi_t(x^0, t_0, \alpha)$ constructed in (1) is defined as the composition of continuous (C^k) functions and is therefore continuous (C^k) itself in (x^0, α).

Notice that if $g(\cdot, \alpha)$ is defined in the whole space $\mathbb{R}^{n+1}$, this process can be continued indefinitely, and a solution exists for each $t \geq t_0 = 0$. If $X \times I$ is not the entire space, on the other hand, the solution may cease to exist at some point if $g(\cdot, \alpha)$ maps (x_t, t) into some point $(x_{t+1}, t+1)$ outside the domain of $g(\cdot, \alpha)$. Hence, the solution sequence $\varphi(t) = \phi_t(x^0, 0, \alpha)$ will in general be defined on some maximal set of consecutive integers $J_\varphi \subseteq I$ containing zero.

We observe also that the solution sequence $\varphi(t)$ is uniquely defined for $t \geq 0$ (for given x^0 and α) provided that $g(\cdot, \alpha)$ is a well-defined function. Under this assumption, any other solution sequence $\Psi(t)$ starting from x^0 at time zero will adopt exactly the same values and can be continued to the same interval as $\varphi(t)$. Uniqueness does not necessarily survive, however, when we try to extend the solution sequence to negative values of t (or, more generally, for $t < t_0$).

To construct such an extension, we define the functions $h_t(\ )$ by $h_t(x) = g(x, t; \alpha)$ for $t < 0$ and construct the sequence $\phi_t(x^0, 0, \alpha)$ recursively by starting with $\phi_0(x^0, 0, \alpha) = x^0$ and then setting

$$\phi_t(x^0, 0, \alpha) = h_t^{-1}(\phi_{t+1}(x^0, 0, \alpha))$$

for each $t = -1, -2, \ldots$. As before, $\phi_t(\cdot)$ may fail to exist after some point. There is no guarantee, moreover, that $h_t(\ )$ will be invertible for all t, so the inverse mapping $h_t^{-1}(\ )$ may well be a correspondence. In this case, the solution to $(PD(x^0, 0, \alpha))$ will not be unique for $t < 0$. On the other hand, if $h_t(\ )$ is a homeomorphism for all t (i.e., a continuous function with a continuous inverse), then the solution sequence will be unique, and $\phi_t(\ )$ will be a continuous function of (x^0, α) also for $t < 0$.

We summarize the discussion in the following theorem.

Theorem 1.1. *Existence and uniqueness of solutions for discrete systems and dependence on initial conditions and parameters. Let* $g{:}X \times I \times \Omega \supseteq \mathbb{R}^{n+p+1} \longrightarrow \mathbb{R}^n$ *be a well-defined function, and* I *a set of consecutive integers. Then the boundary-value problem*

$$x_{t+1} = g(x_t, \alpha, t), \qquad x(t_0) = x^0 \qquad (PD(x^0, t_0, \alpha))$$

has a solution sequence $\varphi(t) = \phi_t(x^0, t_0, \alpha)$ *for each* $(x^0, t_0, \alpha) \in X \times I \times \Omega$. *This solution is defined on a maximal set* $J_m(x^0, t_0, \alpha) \subseteq I$ *containing* t_0 *that depends on the initial data and the parameters of the problem. Moreover, the solution is unique for all* $t \geq t_0$, *in the sense that if* $\Psi(t)$ *is a solution sequence of* $(PD(x^0, t_0, \alpha))$ *defined on some set* J_Ψ, *then* $J_\Psi \subseteq J_m(x^0, t_0, \alpha)$, *and* $\Psi(t) = \varphi(t)$ *for all* $t \in J_\Psi$ *with* $t \geq t_0$.

Moreover, if g( ) is continuous (C^k) in (x_t, α), then for each $t \in J_m(x^0, t_0, \alpha)$, *with* $t \geq t_0$, *the function* $\phi_t(x^0, t_0, \alpha)$ *is continuous (C^k) in (x^0, α). If, in addition,* $h_t(x) = g(x, t; \alpha)$ *is invertible and has a continuous (C^k) inverse for all* t, *then the solution is unique in all of* $J_m(x^0, t_0, \alpha)$ *and* $\phi_t(x^0, t_0, \alpha)$ *is continuous (C^k) in (x^0, α) for all* t *in* $J_m(x^0, t_0, \alpha)$.

With continuous-time systems, things are not so simple. However, it is still possible to obtain similar results with slightly stronger assumptions. In Section 6 we will prove a version of the following result.

Theorem 1.2. Existence and uniqueness of solutions for continuous-time systems and dependence on initial conditions and parameters. Let $f: X \times I \times \Omega \supseteq \mathbb{R}^{n+p+1} \longrightarrow \mathbb{R}^n$ *be C^1 on the set* $X \times I \times \Omega$, *where X and Ω are open sets, and I is an open interval in the real line. Then the boundary-value problem*

$$\dot{x} = f(x, \alpha, t), \qquad x(t_0) = x^0 \qquad\qquad (PC(x^0, t_0, \alpha))$$

has a unique solution $\varphi(t) = \phi(t, x^0, t_0, \alpha)$ *for each* $(x^0, t_0, \alpha) \in X \times I \times \Omega$ *defined on a maximal open interval* $J_m(x^0, t_0, \alpha) \subseteq I$ *containing t_0 that depends on the initial data and parameters of the problem. That is, if* $\Psi(t)$ *is a solution of* $(PC(x^0, t_0, \alpha))$ *defined on some interval* J_Ψ, *then* $J_\Psi \subseteq J_m(x^0, t_0, \alpha)$ *and* $\Psi(t) = \varphi(t)$ *for all* $t \in J_\Psi$. *Moreover, the flow of the system,* $\phi(t, x^0, t_0, \alpha)$, *is* C^1.

One convenient implication of the uniqueness of solutions for boundary-value problems is that the solutions of differential or difference equations cannot cross, in the sense that two different solution trajectories cannot go through the same point at the same time and then "separate." The following result makes this precise.

Theorem 1.3. Let f be C^1 on the set $X \times I$, *where X is an open set, and I an open interval in the real line. Let* $\phi(t, t_0, x^0)$ *be the flow of the system (CS(t)),* $\dot{x} = f(x, t)$. *Then for each* $(x^0, t_0) \in X \times I$ *and every* $s \in J_m(x^0, t_0)$ *we have* $J_m[\phi(s, t_0, x^0), s] = J_m(x^0, t_0)$, *and*

$$\phi(t, t_0, x^0) = \phi[t, s, \phi(s, t_0, x^0)] \qquad\qquad (2)$$

for all $t \in J_m(x^0, t_0)$.

Let $\varphi(t) = \phi(t, t_0, x^0)$ and $\Psi(t) = \phi(t, s, x^s)$ be two solutions of the system (SC(t)) indexed by two arbitrary points in their graphs (t_0, x^0) and (s, x^s). The theorem says that if the two graphs have a point in common, that is, if $\varphi(t)$ goes through x^s at the same time that $\Psi(t)$ does, then the two solutions are the same in the sense that their maximal intervals of definition coincide, and so do their values for any t in this interval. Equivalently, the result says that if we follow the solution $\phi(t, t_0, x^0)$ to some point $(s, x^s = \phi(s, t_0, x^0))$ and then stop, and then solve the boundary-value problem with initial data (s, x^s) and follow its solution, then we stay on the same path we would follow if we did not stop.

A similar result holds for discrete systems whenever the flow is a well-defined function. In particular, equation (2) will hold for all $t, s \in J_m(x^0, t_0)$ and greater than t_0, implying that solutions that at some point come together cannot separate later on. Notice that equation (2) may not hold for $s, t < t_0$, for it is possible that $g( )$ may map two distinct points into the same one. Hence, different solution sequences may "converge" at some point if $g( )$ is not invertible, but they can never "diverge" once they have coincided.

Proof. Let $\varphi(t) = \phi(t, t_0, x^0)$ be the unique maximal solution of $(CS(t))$ going through the point (t_0, x^0). Fix some arbitrary s in $J_m(x^0, t_0)$ and let

$$\varphi(s) = \phi(s, t_0, x^0) = x^s \in X$$

Clearly, $\varphi(t)$ is a solution of the boundary-value problem $(PC(s, x^s))$. Let

$$\Psi(t) = \phi(t, s, x^s)$$

be the maximal solution of this problem defined on the maximal interval $J_m(s, x^s)$. Then, by the uniqueness of solutions (Theorem 1.2), we have $J_m(x^0, t_0) \subseteq J_m(s, x^s)$ and

$$\varphi(t) = \Psi(t) \ \forall \ t \in J_m(x^0, t_0) \tag{1}$$

Moreover, because $\Psi(t)$ is defined at t_0, we have

$$\Psi(t_0) = \varphi(t_0) = x^0$$

so $\Psi( )$ also goes through the point (t_0, x^0). Because $\varphi( )$ is the maximal solution through this point, Theorem 1.2 implies that $J_m(s, x^s) \subseteq J_m(x^0, t_0)$, so in fact $J_m(s, x^s) = J_m(x^0, t_0)$.

Using (1) and the definition of x^s, we now have

$$\phi(t, t_0, x^0) = \varphi(t) = \Psi(t) = \phi(t, s, x^s) = \phi[t, s, \phi(s, t_0, x^0)]$$

for all t in $J_m(x^0, t_0) = J_m(s, x^s)$. $\qquad\square$

2. Autonomous Systems

A dynamical system is said to be autonomous if time does not enter the function $f( )$ or $g( )$ as a separate argument, that is, if the system is of the form

$$\dot{x} = f(x) \tag{CS}$$

or

$$x_{t+1} = g(x_t) \tag{DS}$$

In this section we will analyze some important properties of autonomous systems and introduce some concepts that will play important roles in the rest of the chapter.

(a) The Flow of an Autonomous System

We have seen that the uniqueness of solutions for boundary-value problems implies that the solutions of differential or difference equations cannot cross, in the sense that two different solution trajectories cannot go through the same point at the same time and then separate. It is still possible, however, that different solutions may cross a given point at different times and then follow different trajectories. The reason, of course, is that in the general specification of a dynamical system,

$$\dot{x} = f(x,t) \tag{CS(t)}$$

or

$$x_{t+1} = g(x_t, t) \tag{DS(t)}$$

the vector field f or g can be a function of t. Graphically, the arrow of motion $\dot{x}$ or Δx associated with a point x in the state space can change with time. Hence, the direction of motion of the system depends not only on its current position but also on time.

In the case of the autonomous system

$$\dot{x} = f(x) \tag{CS}$$

or

$$x_{t+1} = g(x_t) \tag{DS}$$

however, each point x in X has attached to it a unique, time-invariant arrow, and therefore all particles that at some time reach point x follow exactly the same trajectory in X (from then on, in the case of a discrete system; always, in the case of a continuous system) whenever the assumptions of the corresponding existence and uniqueness theorem are satisfied.

That is, given an autonomous system (S), the solutions satisfying the boundary conditions

$$x(t_0) = x^0 \quad \text{and} \quad x(t_1) = x^0, \quad \text{with } t_0 \neq t_1$$

have the same orbit if (S) is a continuous system, and the same positive orbit if (S) is discrete. Hence, solution trajectories never cross. If X is some subset of the real line or the plane, the set of all trajectories can be shown in a figure

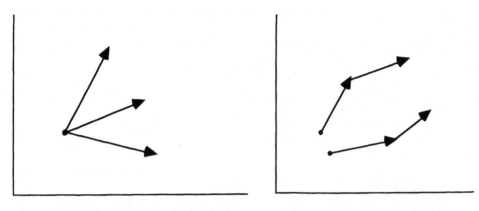

Non-autonomous system: several trajectories may go through the same point (at different times).

Autonomous system: only one solution trajectory can go through each point in X.

Figure 9.3. Autonomous versus nonautonomous systems.

called a *phase diagram*, using arrows to indicate the directions of motion. This device is a very useful tool for analysis of the dynamics of low-dimensional autonomous systems (Figure 9.3).

In the remainder of this section we will formally establish this no-crossing property and investigate some other properties of the flow of autonomous systems that are closely related to it.

We start with the discrete case,

$$x_{t+1} = g(x_t) \tag{DS}$$

Analytically, the flow of (DS) can be obtained by the repeated composition of the time map $g(\ )$ with itself. Letting $\phi_0(x^0) \equiv x^0$ indicate the position of the system at time zero, we define $\phi_t(x^0)$ recursively by

$$\phi_{t+1}(x^0) = g(\phi_t(x^0)) = g[g^t(x^0)] \equiv g^{t+1}(x^0) \tag{1}$$

where $g^n(\ )$ denotes the nth iteration of $g(\ )$ (and not its nth power). Hence, the flow of (DS) can be written

$$\phi_t(x^0) = g^t(x^0) \quad \text{for } t > 0$$

and, by the associativity of the composition of functions, we obtain $g^{t+s}(x^0) = g^t(g^s(x^0))$ or

$$\phi_{t+s}(x^0) = \phi_t[\phi_s(x^0)] = \phi_s[\phi_t(x^0)] \tag{2}$$

for all integers $t, s \geq 0$ whenever s, t, and $t + s$ lie on the maximal interval of definition of the solution through $x^0, J_m(x^0)$. If $g(\ )$ is invertible, the same procedure will work backward, with $g^{-n}(\ )$ now denoting the n-fold composition of the inverse function $g^{-1}(\ )$ with itself, and then equation (1) holds also for nonpositive integers.

Using equation (2), we can now establish the no-crossing property. Given a point z in X, let $\phi_t(x^0)$ and $\phi_t(y^0)$ be two solutions of (DS) going through z at different times, say s and $r \geq 0$. Then

$$\phi_s(x^0) = z = \phi_r(y^0)$$

and for any $t \geq 0$ in $J_m(z)$ we have, using (2),

$$\phi_{s+t}(x^0) = \phi_t[\phi_s(x^0)] = \phi_t(z) \quad \text{and} \quad \phi_{r+t}(y^0) = \phi_t[\phi_r(y^0)] = \phi_t(z)$$

Hence, we have that $s + t$ and $r + t \in J_m(z)$, and

$$\phi_{s+t}(x^0) = \phi_{r+t}(y^0) \tag{3}$$

for all $t \geq 0$ in $J_m(z)$. If two solutions $\phi_t(x^0)$ and $\phi_t(y^0)$ go through a common point z, then they coincide thereafter. Equivalently, we can say that the position of a particle that goes through a given point z depends only on the time spanned since it reached this point, not on the time at which it attained it.

We will now show that a similar property holds for the flows of the continuous-time autonomous system

$$\dot{x} = f(x) \tag{CS}$$

Lemma 2.1. Let $\varphi(t)$ be a solution of the autonomous system (CS) defined on the maximal interval J_φ. Then $\varphi(t + r)$ is also a solution of (CS) for any constant r and any $t + r \in J_\varphi$.

To understand this deceptively simple result, it is probably best to see why it fails to hold in the case of a nonautonomous system. Let $\varphi(\ )$ be a solution of the nonautonomous system

$$\dot{x} = f(x, t) \tag{CS(t)}$$

Then, by definition,

$$\varphi'(s) = f[\varphi(s), s]$$

for all s in $J_\varphi = (a, b)$. Given some fixed constant r, define a new function

$$\Psi(t) = \varphi(t + r)$$

for all t such that $t + r \in J_\varphi = (a, b)$, that is, for t in $J_\varphi - r = (a - r, b - r) = J_\Psi$. Then

$$\Psi'(t) = \varphi'(t + r) = f[\varphi(t + r), t + r] = f[\Psi(t), t + r] \tag{4}$$

so, in general, $\Psi(t)$ is not a solution of (CS(t)) except when $r = 0$. In the special case of the autonomous system (CS), however, time is not an argument of $f(\ )$, and (4) becomes

$$\Psi'(t) = \varphi'(t + r) = f[\varphi(t + r)] = f[\Psi(t)]$$

so $\Psi(t) = \varphi(t + r)$ is indeed a solution of (CS) under the assumptions of the lemma.

Notice that $\varphi(t)$ and $\Psi(t)$ are different solutions of (CS), but they describe the same orbit or solution curve in state space.

Theorem 2.2. *Assume that* f *is* C^1 *in some open set* $X \subseteq R^n$, *and let* $\phi(t, t_0, x^0)$ *be the flow of the autonomous system (CS). Then, for each* (t_0, x^0) *in* $X \times R$ *we have* $J_m(x^0, 0) = J_m(x^0, t_0) - t_0$ *and*

$$\phi(t, t_0, x^0) = \phi(t - t_0, 0, x^0) \tag{5}$$

for every $t \in J_m(x^0, t_0)$, *or, equivalently, for every* $t - t_0 \in J_m(x^0, 0)$.

Proof. Let $\varphi(s) = \phi(s, t_0, x^0)$ be the maximal solution of the boundary-value problem $(PS(t_0, x^0))$ defined on the maximal interval $J_m(x^0, t_0) = (a, b)$, and $\Psi(s) = \phi(s, 0, x^0)$ the maximal solution of $(PS(0, x^0))$ defined on the maximal interval $J_m(x^0, 0) = (c, d)$.

Define the function $\varphi_0(s)$ on $(a - t_0, b - t_0) = J_m(x^0, t_0) - t_0$ by

$$\varphi_0(s) = \varphi(s + t_0) = \phi(s + t_0, t_0, x^0) \tag{1}$$

(notice that if $s \in J_m(x^0, t_0) - t_0$, then $a - t_0 < s < b - t_0$, and therefore $a < s + t_0 < b$, so $s + t_0 \in J_m(x^0, t_0)$; because $\varphi(s + t_0)$ is defined for $s + t_0 \in J_m(x^0, t_0)$, $\varphi_0(s)$ is defined on $J_m(x^0, t_0) - t_0$). By Lemma 2.1, $\varphi_0(s) \equiv \varphi(s + t_0)$ is a solution of the autonomous system (CS). Moreover,

$$\varphi_0(0) = \varphi(t_0) = x^0$$

so $\varphi_0(s)$ is a solution of the boundary-value problem $(PS(0, x^0))$, just like $\Psi(s)$. Because $\Psi(s)$ is the maximal solution of this problem, Theorem 1.2 implies that $(a - t_0, b - t_0) = \{J_m(x^0, t_0) - t_0\} \subseteq J_m(x^0, 0)$ and

$$\Psi_0(s) = \Psi(s) \equiv \phi(s, 0, x^0) \tag{2}$$

for all $s \in (a - t_0, b - t_0) \subseteq J_m(x^0, 0)$.

Similarly, define $\Psi_0(s)$ on $(c + t_0, d + t_0) = \{J_m(x^0, 0) + t_0\}$ by

$$\varphi_0(s) = \Psi(s - t_0) = \phi(s - t_0, 0, x^0) \tag{3}$$

and observe that $\Psi_0(s)$ is a solution of $(PC(t_0, x^0))$, because

$$\Psi_0(t_0) = \Psi(0) = \phi(0, 0, x^0) = x^0$$

Because $\varphi(s)$ is the maximal solution for this problem, it follows by Theorem 1.2 that $(c + t_0, d + t_0) = \{J_m(x^0, 0) + t_0\} \subseteq J_m(x^0, t_0)$ and

$$\Psi_0(s) = \varphi(s) = \phi(s, t_0, x^0) \tag{4}$$

for all $s \in (c + t_0, d + t_0) \subseteq J_m(x^0, t_0)$.

Notice that we have shown that

$$J_m(x^0, t_0) - t_0 = J_m(x^0, 0)$$

Using (1) and (2), we have

$$\phi(s + t_0, t_0, x^0) \equiv \varphi_0(s) = \Psi(s) \equiv \phi(s, 0, x^0) \tag{5}$$

for all $s \in \{J_m(x^0, t_0) - t_0\} = J_m(x^0, 0)$. Letting $t = s + t_0$, we have, finally,

$$\phi(t, t_0, x^0) = \phi(t - t_0, 0, x^0)$$

for all $t \in J_m(x^0, t_0)$. $\qquad\square$

Theorem 2.2 says that the position at time t of an autonomous system depends only on its initial position and the time spanned since the system was set in motion, not on the initial time itself. One convenient implication of the theorem is that we can "normalize" t_0 to zero and omit the second argument of the flow. When we do this, of course, we have to normalize the maximal interval of existence accordingly. Hence, letting $s = t - t_0$, we can rewrite the flow in terms of the normalized time, s, as

$$\phi(t, t_0, x^0) = \phi(t - t_0, 0, x^0) = \phi(s, 0, x^0) \tag{6}$$

and then $\phi(s, 0, x^0)$ is defined for all s in $J_m(x^0, 0) = J_m(x^0, t_0) - t_0$ (i.e., for all $t = s + t_0$ in $J_m(x^0, t_0)$). In most of what follows we will take advantage of this normalization. Except when we need to make explicit reference to the initial time, we will assume that it is equal to zero and write the flow of an autonomous system in the form $\phi(t, x^0)$, denoting the maximal interval of definition of the solution starting (at time zero) from x^0 by $J_m(x^0)$.

Theorem 2.3. Assume that f *is* C^1 *in some open set* $X \subseteq \mathbb{R}^n$, *and let* $\phi(t, x^0)$ *be the flow of the autonomous system (CS). Let* $s \in J_m(x^0)$. *Then*

$$J_m[\phi(s, x^0)] = J_m(x^0) - s$$

and

$$\phi(r + s, x^0) = \phi[r, \phi(s, x^0)] \tag{7}$$

for any $r \in J_m[\phi(s, x^0)]$, *or, equivalently, for any* $r + s \in J_m(x^0)$.

Proof. Reverting to our former notation for the flow, equation (7) means

$$\phi(r + s, 0, x^0) = \phi[r, 0, \phi(s, 0, x^0)] \tag{1}$$

But notice that

$$\phi(r, 0, \phi(s, 0, x^0)) = \phi[r + s, s, \phi(s, 0, x^0)] = \phi(r + s, 0, x^0) \tag{2}$$

where the first equality follows by Theorem 2.2 (use the formula $\phi(t - t_0, 0, x^0) = \phi(t, t_0, x^0)$, with $t_0 = s$, $t = r + s$, and $x^0 = \phi(s, 0, x^0)$), and the second follows from Theorem 1.3 (use the formula $\phi[t, s, \phi(s, t_0, x^0)] = \phi(t, t_0, x^0)$, with $t = r + s$ and $t_0 = 0$). Hence, (1) holds, and, eliminating the zero arguments, this equality reduces to the desired expression.

Observe also that Theorems 1.3 and 2.2 guarantee that each side is defined if the other is defined. We have, in particular, that if $s \in J_m(x^0)$, then

$$J_m[\phi(s, 0, x^0), 0] = J_m[\phi(s, 0, x^0), s] - s = J_m(x^0, 0) - s \qquad (3)$$

where, as before, the first equality follows by Theorem 2.2 (using $J_m(x^0, 0) = J_m(x^0, t_0) - t_0$, with $t_0 = s$ and $x^0 = \phi(s, 0, x^0)$), and the second follows from Theorem 1.3 (using $J_m[\phi(s, t_0, x^0), s] = J_m(x^0, t_0)$, with $t_0 = 0$). Assume that the right-hand side of (1) is defined, that is, that $s \in J_m(x^0)$ and $r \in J_m[\phi(s, 0, x^0), 0]$. Then we have, by (3), that

$$r \in J_m[\phi(s, 0, x^0), 0] = J_m(x^0, 0) - s$$

so

$$s + r \in J_m(x^0, 0)$$

and the left-hand side of (1) is defined. Conversely, if s, $s + r \in J_m(x^0, 0)$, then, by (3),

$$r \in J_m(x^0, 0) - s = J_m[\phi(s, 0, x^0), 0]$$

so the right-hand side of (1) is defined. $\qquad\qquad\square$

It is now easy to show that any two solutions of an autonomous system that cross the same point in phase space (possibly at different times) define the same orbit. The argument is the same as in the discrete case. Let z be a point in X, and $\phi(t, x^0)$ and $\phi(t, y^0)$ two solutions of (CS) going through z at different times, say

$$\phi(s, x^0) = z = \phi(r, y^0)$$

Then, for any t in $J_m(z) = J_m[\phi(s, x^0)] = J_m(x^0) - s = J_m(x^0) - r$ we have

$$\phi(s + t, x^0) = \phi[t, \phi(s, x^0)] = \phi(t, z) \quad \text{and} \quad \phi(r + t, y^0) = \phi[t, \phi(r, y^0)] = \phi(t, z)$$

Hence,

$$\phi(s + t, x^0) = \phi(r + t, y^0) \qquad (8)$$

for all t with $s + t$, $r + t \in J_m(z)$. Notice that we do not require t to be a positive number. Hence, if the orbits of the two solutions $\phi(t, x^0)$ and $\phi(t, y^0)$ have a point in common, the two orbits are the same.

(b) Asymptotic Behavior

Given a dynamical system, we are often interested in determining what happens to its solution as $t \to \infty$ (provided, of course, the solution is defined for all $t \geq 0$). If the solution trajectory approaches some simple configuration (e.g., a single point or a closed curve), we can think of this point or set of points as a long-run equilibrium.

For studying the asymptotic behavior of dynamical systems, we need some definitions. In what follows, $\phi(t, x^0)$ is the flow of a (continuous or discrete) dynamical system.

Definition 2.4. Positive or ω limit point and limit set. A point $y \in X$ is an ω limit point of the orbit $\gamma(x^0)$ if there exists a sequence of real numbers $\{t_n\} \to \infty$ such that $\{\phi(t_n, x^0)\} \to y$ as $n \to \infty$. That is, y is a positive limit point of $\gamma(x^0)$ if, given any $\varepsilon > 0$, there exists some positive integer n_ε such that $\|y - \phi(t_n, x^0)\| < \varepsilon$ for all $n > n_\varepsilon$.

The set of all positive limit points of $\gamma(x^0)$ is the *positive limit set* of the orbit, denoted by $\omega(x^0)$. The concepts of negative (or α) limit set and limit point can be defined in the same way by reversing the direction of time.

Intuitively, the positive limit set of an orbit is the set of points to which the orbit tends as $t \to \infty$. For example, a closed orbit or cycle is its own positive limit set, and also that of any other orbit that approaches it asymptotically. This example shows why the definition of limit point must be formulated in terms of a sequence of t's even if we work in continuous time. Assume that the solution $\phi(t, x^0)$ describes a spiral trajectory $\gamma(x^0)$ that approaches a closed orbit Γ, as illustrated in Figure 9.4. Because the solution keeps circling around, we cannot say that any one point $y \in \Gamma$ is the limit of $\phi(t, x^0)$ as $t \to \infty$. However, the figure shows that it is possible to choose a sequence $\{t_n\}$ of points in time such that $\{\phi(t_n, x^0)\} \to y$ as $n \to \infty$.

Some subsets of the state space X have the property that any orbit that enters them never leaves (with time running forward, backward, or both). Such a set is said to be invariant under the flow of the system.

Definition 2.5. Invariant set. A set S in X is positively invariant under the flow of a system if, given any x^0 in S, the positive orbit through x^0, $\gamma^+(x^0)$, is contained in S. Equivalently, S is positively invariant if for all $t \geq 0$ we have $\phi(t, S) \subseteq S$. Similarly, S is negatively invariant if $\phi(t, S) \subseteq S$ for $t \leq 0$, and invariant if it is both positively and negatively invariant.

Intuitively, a set S is (i) positively invariant if any trajectory that enters the set remains in it, (ii) negatively invariant if any orbit that contains a point

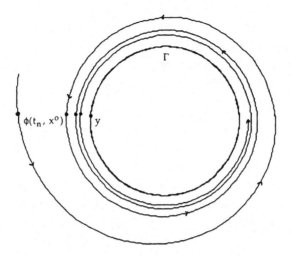

Figure 9.4. A limit cycle.

of S must have started in S, and (iii) invariant if both things are true at the same time.

(c) Steady States and Stability

Consider a discrete-time autonomous system

$$x_{t+1} = g(x_t) \qquad \text{(DS)}$$

where g is a continuous function, and let $\{x_t\}$ be a solution sequence for the system. If $\{x_t\}$ converges to a point x^* as $t \to \infty$, the continuity of $g(\ )$ implies that x^* itself must be a solution of (DS); that is, if $g(\ )$ is a continuous function, we have

$$x^* = \lim_{t \to \infty} x_{t+1} = \lim_{t \to \infty} g(x_t) = g\left(\lim_{t \to \infty} x_t\right) = g(x^*)$$

Hence, constant solutions play a special role in analyses of the asymptotic behavior of autonomous systems.

Problem 2.6. Show that this is true also for the continuous-time system (CS), $\dot{x} = f(x)$. That is, if

$$\lim_{t \to \infty} \phi(t, x^0) = x^*$$

then x^* must be a constant solution of (CS) (i.e., $f(x^*) = \underline{0}$.) Hint: Use Theorem 2.3.

Definition 2.7. Steady or stationary state (fixed point, rest point, or equilibrium). A stationary state of a dynamical system is a constant solution of the system. In the case of a discrete system, $x_{t+1} = g(x_t)$, a point $\bar{x} \in X$ is a steady state if it is a fixed point of $g(\ )$, that is, if $\bar{x} = g(\bar{x})$. For the continuous system $\dot{x} = f(x)$, a steady state is a point $\bar{x} \in X$ such that $f(\bar{x}) = \underline{0}$ (i.e., a zero of $f(\ )$).

A steady state or equilibrium of a dynamical system is a rest point of the system, a value $\bar{x}$ of the state vector that, if ever reached, will be preserved forever unless the system is disturbed in some way. In economic applications, a steady state often can be interpreted as a long-run equilibrium.

Given a steady state $\bar{x}$, the question of its *stability* naturally arises. Consider a system that is initially at rest at an equilibrium point $\bar{x}$, and imagine that it suffers some shock that causes a small deviation from the rest point. What will happen to the system? Will it return to the equilibrium point, or at least remain close to it, or will it get farther and farther away from it over time?

Definition 2.8. Stability. Let $\bar{x}$ be an isolated steady state of the system (CS), $\dot{x} = f(x)$. We say that $\bar{x}$ is a stable equilibrium of (CS) if, given any $\varepsilon > 0$, there exists some real number $\delta \in (0, \varepsilon]$ such that

$$\|x(t_0) - \bar{x}\| < \delta \quad \text{for some } t_0 \Rightarrow \|x(t) - \bar{x}\| < \varepsilon \; \forall \; t \geq t_0$$

That is, take a ball of arbitrarily small radius ε centered at $\bar{x}$. If $\bar{x}$ is stable, we can find some δ (possibly smaller than ε) such that any solution $x(t)$ that at some point enters the ball of radius δ around $\bar{x}$ remains within the ball of radius ε. Figure 9.5 illustrates the definition.

Definition 2.9. Asymptotic stability. A steady state $\bar{x}$ is asymptotically stable if it is stable, and, moreover, δ can be chosen (in the preceding definition) in such a way that for any solution $x(t)$ that enters $B_\delta(\bar{x})$ at some point we have $\lim_{t \to \infty} x(t) = \bar{x}$.

That is, trajectories that get sufficiently close to $\bar{x}$ not only remain nearby but also converge to $\bar{x}$ as $t \to \infty$. (Observe that $x(t)$ cannot reach $\bar{x}$ in finite time, only asymptotically. Otherwise, the uniqueness of solutions would be violated.)

The largest region such that any solution that enters it converges to $\bar{x}$ is called the *basin of attraction* of $\bar{x}$. If the basin of attraction is the whole of the state space, that is, if $x(t) \to \bar{x}$ for every initial position x^0, we say that $\bar{x}$ is globally asymptotically stable.

An equilibrium that is not stable is *unstable*. In particular, there exists some $\varepsilon > 0$ and some solution that, while passing arbitrarily close to the steady state, does not remain within the ball of radius ε centered at $\bar{x}$.

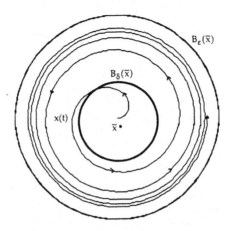

Figure 9.5. A stable steady state.

3. Autonomous Differential Equations

In this section and the next we will study autonomous systems in one dimension, that is, dynamical systems defined by a single autonomous difference or differential equation. For the case of linear systems, we will show how to compute explicit solutions. For nonlinear systems, we will introduce a simple graphical device that can be used to study the qualitative properties of solutions and establish some results that relate the local behavior of a nonlinear system near a steady state $\bar{x}$ to that of the linear system defined by its derivative at $\bar{x}$. In this section we deal with continuous-time systems, leaving the discrete-time case for Section 4.

Consider the first-order differential equation (CS), $\dot{x} = f(x)$, where $f : \mathbb{R} \supseteq X \longrightarrow \mathbb{R}$ is a C^1 function. In the first part of this section we will show how to construct the general solution of this equation when $f(\ )$ is a linear (affine) function. Part (b) deals with nonlinear equations.

(a) Linear Equations with Constant Coefficients

To construct the general solution of the first-order linear equation with constant coefficients, we start with the simplest case, that of the homogeneous equation

$$\dot{x} = ax \tag{CH}$$

where a is a real number, and $x(\ )$ a function from $\mathbb{R}$ to itself. This equation can be solved analytically by the method of *separation of variables*. Rearranging terms in (CH), we can write

$$\frac{dx}{dt} = ax \Rightarrow \frac{dx}{x} = a\,dt$$

and integrating both sides of this expression,

$$\int \frac{dx}{x} = \int a\,dt \Rightarrow \ln x = at + c_1$$

where c_1 is an arbitrary constant of integration. Taking antilogs, we arrive at

$$x(t) = ce^{at} \tag{1}$$

where $c = e^{c_1}$ is also an arbitrary constant. This shows that the solution of (CH) must be a function of the form (1). Moreover, any function of this form is a solution of (CH), as we see by differentiating the function given in (1):

$$\dot{x}(t) = cae^{at} = ax(t)$$

Hence, we have found the *general solution* of (CH), a family of exponential functions parameterized by an arbitrary constant c:

$$x^h(t, c) = ce^{at} \tag{2}$$

We now turn to the more general case of the nonhomogeneous equation

$$\dot{x} = ax + b \tag{CN}$$

where b is a constant. We will solve (CN) by reducing it to a homogeneous equation through a simple change of variables. We define a new variable, y, as the deviation of the state variable, x, from its steady-state value, $\bar{x} = -b/a$.[1] Because $\bar{x}$ is a constant and $y = x - \bar{x}$, we have $\dot{y} = \dot{x}$. The original system can then be rewritten in terms of y and $\dot{y}$:

$$\dot{x} = ax + b \Rightarrow \dot{y} = ax + b = a\left(x + \frac{b}{a}\right) = a(x - \bar{x}) = ay$$

Notice that by rewriting the equation in terms of deviations from the steady state we have reduced it to the homogeneous equation $\dot{y} = ay$, with solution $y(t, c) = ce^{at}$. It is now easy to recover the general solution of the original system; because $x(t) = y(t) + \bar{x}$, we have

$$x^g(t, c) = \bar{x} + ce^{at} \tag{G.S}$$

Let us rewrite the general solution of (CN) in a slightly different way that may throw some light on the meaning of the arbitrary constant c. Evaluating the general solution at time zero, we have

$$x(0) = \bar{x} + ce^{a0} \Rightarrow c = x(0) - \bar{x}$$

Thus, c corresponds to the initial deviation of the state variable from its steady-state value. Substituting this expression back into (G.S), we can write the general solution in the form

$$x(t, x^0) = \bar{x} + [x(0) - \bar{x}]e^{at} \tag{G.S$'$}$$

which gives the value of x at time t as a function of time and the system's initial position. It is clear from this expression that specifying a value of c is equivalent to choosing an initial position for the system. Notice, however, that the value of $x(0)$ remains unknown until we specify a boundary condition.[2]

The conditions for the stability or instability of the steady state can be easily determined using either form of the general solution. Rearranging (G.S'), for example, we can write

$$x(t, x^0) - \bar{x} = [x(0) - \bar{x}]e^{at}$$

This expression shows that the stability of $\bar{x}$ depends on the value of the coefficient a. If a is positive, any initial deviation from the steady state will grow over time and approach infinity as $t \to \infty$. Hence, the system displays explosive behavior, except when it happens to start out at the steady state ($c = 0$ or $x(0) = \bar{x}$). On the other hand, if $a < 0$, the deviation shrinks over time and goes to zero as $t \to \infty$. Thus, the steady state of the system is asymptotically stable. Figure 9.6 shows the system's trajectory in each case.

We summarize the results of this section in the following theorem.

Theorem 3.1. The first-order linear equation (CN), $\dot{x} = ax + b$ ($a \neq 0$), has a unique steady state $\bar{x} = -b/a$ that is asymptotically stable if $a < 0$, and unstable if $a > 0$. The general solution of (CN) is of the form $x^g(t, c) = \bar{x} + ce^{at}$, where c is an arbitrary constant to be definitized by choice of an appropriate boundary condition.

Problem 3.2. When $a = 0$, the nonhomogeneous system is of the form $\dot{x} = b$. Using the method of separation of variables, find the general solution of this equation.

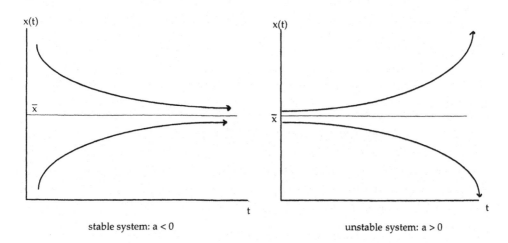

stable system: $a < 0$ unstable system: $a > 0$

Figure 9.6. Solution trajectories of stable and unstable linear systems.

Problem 3.3. There is no particular reason that we should choose to index the solutions of a system by their values at time zero. Rewrite the general solution of the system (CN) as a function of $x(s)$, the value of x at some arbitrary time s.

(b) Nonlinear Autonomous Equations

When we drop the assumption of linearity, closed-form solutions of differential equations are no longer available, except in special cases. When the system is of dimension 1, however, it is easy to study the qualitative properties of its solutions with the help of a simple graphical device. To construct the *phase diagram* of the nonlinear equation

$$\dot{x} = f(x) \qquad \text{(CS)}$$

we begin by plotting the function $f(\ )$ that gives the time derivative $\dot{x}$ as a function of x. The graph of this function is sometimes called the *phase line*. Notice that the intersections of the phase line with the horizontal axis correspond to the steady states of the system. The steady states, moreover, divide the horizontal axis into a number of intervals. The next step involves checking whether the function $f(\ )$ lies above or below the axis in each of these regions. If $\dot{x} = f(x) > 0$ in a given interval (i.e., if the phase line lies above the axis), then x increases over time in this interval – a fact that can conveniently be indicated by an "arrow of motion" pointing to the right (Figure 9.7). Similarly, if $f(\ )$ lies below the axis, the derivative of x with respect to time is negative. Hence, the variable decreases over time, and the arrow that describes the motion of x points to the left.

Once we have constructed the phase diagram, it is easy to determine the system's trajectory from any given initial point $x(0)$. The idea is simply to follow the arrows of motion from $x(0)$ to the closest steady state, provided there is one in the direction of motion of x. Otherwise, x is always increasing or always decreasing. For example, in Figure 9.7 we have the following:

(i) Any trajectory that starts from an initial point below $\bar{x}_1$, or lying on the interval between $\bar{x}_1$ and $\bar{x}_2$, converges to $\bar{x}_1$ as t goes to infinity.
(ii) If the starting value of x is larger than $\bar{x}_2$, the solution converges to $\bar{x}_3$.

The phase diagram can also be used to determine whether or not each of the steady states is stable. If the phase line cuts the horizontal axis from above at $\bar{x}$, then $\bar{x}$ is a stable equilibrium, for the arrows of motion of the system point toward the steady state from both sides. That is, if for all x in some neighborhood of a steady state $\bar{x}$ we have

$$x < \bar{x} \Rightarrow \dot{x} > 0 \quad \text{and} \quad x > \bar{x} \Rightarrow \dot{x} < 0$$

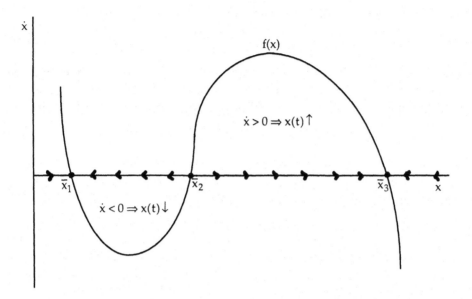

Figure 9.7. Phase diagram for a scalar continuous system.

then $\bar{x}$ is asymptotically stable: If $x(t) < \bar{x}$, then $\dot{x}(t) > 0$, and therefore x increases over time, getting closer to $\bar{x}$. Moreover, because $\dot{x}$ is strictly positive as long as $x < \bar{x}$, the trajectory cannot stop before reaching the stationary point. Similarly, if for all x in some open neighborhood of a stationary point $\bar{x}$ we have

$$x < \bar{x} \Rightarrow \dot{x} < 0 \quad \text{or} \quad x > \bar{x} \Rightarrow \dot{x} > 0$$

then $\bar{x}$ is unstable, for trajectories that start close to the steady state tend to move away from it, at least from one side. Thus, if the phase line cuts the horizontal axis from below, the steady state is unstable, as suggested by Figure 9.7 (compare $\bar{x}_1$ and $\bar{x}_2$).

In summary, we have the following lemma.

Lemma 3.4. A stationary state $\bar{x}$ of the scalar equation $\dot{x} = f(x)$ is stable if and only if there exists some $\delta > 0$ such that for all $x \in B_\delta(\bar{x})$ we have

$$(x - \bar{x})f(x) < 0$$

and unstable if there exists some $\delta > 0$ such that

$$(x - \bar{x})f(x) > 0$$

for all x in $(\bar{x} - \delta, \bar{x})$ or $(\bar{x}, \bar{x} + \delta)$.

Using this result, it is easy to obtain sufficient conditions for the asymptotic stability or instability of a stationary state $\bar{x}$ of a nonlinear equation in terms of the derivative of $f(\ )$ at $\bar{x}$. Notice that in order to determine whether or not $\bar{x}$ is stable, it is enough to know in what direction f cuts the horizontal axis at this point. If the phase line cuts the horizontal axis transversally, the derivative will tell us. On the other hand, because a zero derivative at the steady state gives no information about the direction of the crossing, nothing can be said about the stability of the system without additional information. We have, then, the following theorem.

Theorem 3.5. Local stability by linearization. Assume that f *is* C^1, *and let* $\bar{x}$ *be a stationary solution of the equation (CS),* $\dot{x} = f(x)$, *with* $f'(\bar{x}) \neq 0$. *Then* $\bar{x}$ *is asymptotically stable if* $f'(\bar{x}) < 0$, *and unstable if* $f'(\bar{x}) > 0$.

Proof. We start by rewriting the original system (1), $\dot{x} = f(x)$, in deviations from the steady state. Putting $h = x - \bar{x}$, equation (1) yields (2), $\dot{h} = \dot{x} = f(\bar{x} + h)$. Next, let $\varphi(h)$ be the error committed when we approximate $f(\ )$ by its differential at $\bar{x}$, that is,

$$\varphi(h) = f(\bar{x} + h) - f'(\bar{x})h, \quad \text{with } \varphi'(h) = f'(\bar{x} + h) - f'(\bar{x})$$

and observe that $\varphi(0) = 0$ and $\varphi'(0) = 0$ and that $\varphi(\ )$ inherits the continuous differentiability of $f(\ )$. Thus, we can write (2) in the form

$$\dot{h} = f'(\bar{x})h + \varphi(h) \tag{3}$$

that is, as the sum of a linear system and a perturbation term that, by the differentiability of $f(\ )$, will be "small" close to $\bar{x}$.

Fix some positive ε such that $\varepsilon < |f'(\bar{x})|$. By the continuous differentiability of $f(\ )$, there exists some $\delta > 0$ such that $|\varphi'(s)| = |f'(\bar{x} + s) - f'(\bar{x})| < \varepsilon$ for all $s \in B_\delta(0)$. Using the identity

$$\varphi(h) = \varphi(0) + \int_0^h \varphi'(s)\, ds = \int_0^h \varphi'(s)\, ds$$

we have

$$|\varphi(h)| = \left| \int_0^h \varphi'(s)\, ds \right| \leq \int_0^h |\varphi'(s)|\, ds \leq \varepsilon |h| < |f'(\bar{x})h|$$

for all h, with $|h| < \delta$. It follows from this expression and from (3) that for h sufficiently close to zero, the sign of $\dot{h}$ (and hence that of $\dot{x}$) is determined by the linear term $f'(\bar{x})h = f'(\bar{x})(x - \bar{x})$ and does not depend on the signs of the higher-order terms in the Taylor-series expansion of $f(\ )$, which are captured by the remainder $\varphi(h)$.

Using Lemma 3.2, we see that (2), and hence (1), are stable if and only if $f'(\bar{x}) < 0$. Notice that $f'(\bar{x}) < 0$ implies that h and $\dot{h}$ (and hence $\dot{x}$) have opposite signs. For example, if h is positive (x is above its steady-state value), then

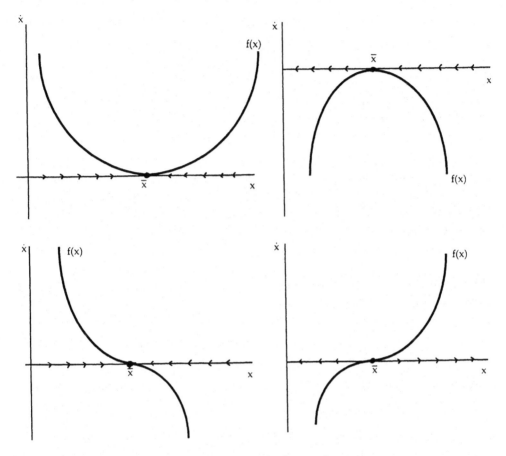

Figure 9.8. Nonhyperbolic steady states.

$\dot{x}$ is negative (x decreases with time). Hence, a strictly negative derivative implies local stability, and by a similar argument, a strictly positive derivative implies that the steady state is unstable.

In conclusion, under the assumptions of the theorem, the original system and its linearization yield the same sign for $\dot{x}$ in some neighborhood of a given stationary point. Hence, we can infer the local stability properties of the original system from those of its linear approximation.   □

A stationary state $\bar{x}$ is said to be *hyperbolic* if $f'(\bar{x}) \neq 0$, and nonhyperbolic if $f'(\bar{x}) = 0$. The theorem says that linearization (i.e., the approximation of a nonlinear system by the linear system given by its derivative at a steady state) works well around hyperbolic equilibria. Figure 9.8 shows why hyperbolicity is needed: A zero derivative gives no information concerning the way in which the phase line crosses the horizontal axis, and therefore no information concerning stability.

(c) A Note on Comparative Dynamics

Consider a parameterized dynamical system

$$\dot{x} = f(x, \alpha) \qquad \qquad (\text{CS}(\alpha))$$

where $f(\ )$ is a C^1 function. As we will show in Section 6, a solution $x(t, \alpha)$ of this system is a differentiable function of t and α. In this section we will show how to compute the partial derivative of the solution function $x(t, \alpha)$ with respect to the parameter α.

The procedure is similar to the one we followed in Chapter 5 to analyze the comparative statics of the solutions to parameterized systems of static equations. Notice that the solution function $x(t, \alpha)$ satisfies identically the original system, that is,

$$\dot{x}(t, \alpha) \equiv f[x(t, \alpha), \alpha] \qquad (1)$$

Because this is an identity, we can differentiate both sides of (1) with respect to the parameter vector, α, obtaining

$$\frac{\partial \dot{x}(t, \alpha)}{\partial \alpha} = f_x[x(t, \alpha), \alpha]x_\alpha + f_\alpha[x(t, \alpha), \alpha] \qquad (2)$$

Assume further that the order of differentiation can be inverted in the expression on the left-hand side of (2), so that

$$\frac{\partial \dot{x}(t, \alpha)}{\partial \alpha} \equiv \frac{\partial^2 x(t, \alpha)}{\partial t \partial \alpha} = \frac{\partial^2 x(t, \alpha)}{\partial \alpha \partial t} \equiv \dot{x}_\alpha$$

Then equation (2) yields the differential equation

$$\dot{x}_\alpha = f_x(\ )x_\alpha + f_\alpha(\ ) \qquad (3)$$

where $f_x(\ )$ and $f_\alpha(\ )$ are evaluated along the solution trajectory, $x(t, \alpha)$. Hence, the derivative of interest, x_α, satisfies a linear differential equation. The solution of this equation will give us the trajectory of $x_\alpha(t)$, that is, the derivative of x with respect to the parameter at each point in the solution trajectory.

In general, it is difficult to solve (3) along an arbitrary solution trajectory, but there is a special case that can be easily handled. This is the case in which we are initially in a steady state, for then (3) is evaluated along a constant trajectory and is therefore an autonomous linear equation. In this case, the general solution of (3) is of the form

$$x_\alpha(t) = x_\alpha(\infty) + [x_\alpha(0) - x_\alpha(\infty)]e^{f_x t} = x_\alpha(0)e^{f_x t} + x_\alpha(\infty)(1 - e^{f_x t}) \qquad (4)$$

where f_x is a constant and $x_\alpha(\infty)$ is the solution of

$$\dot{x}_\alpha = 0 \Rightarrow x_\alpha(\infty) = \frac{-f_\alpha(\ )}{f_x(\ )} = \frac{\partial \bar{x}}{\partial \alpha}$$

Notice that $x_\alpha(\infty)$ is also the comparative-statics partial derivative of x across steady states and can therefore be interpreted as the long-run effect of the parameter change when the system converges to a new steady state. Hence, equation (4) tells us that the impact of the parameter change at time t can be written as a weighted average of its immediate or impact effect, $x_\alpha(0)$, and its long-run effect, $x_\alpha(\infty)$.

It remains to determine the appropriate initial condition for equation (4), and this typically requires thinking about the economics of the problem. For example, if x is a predetermined variable, the impact effect will be zero. If x is a free variable, however, in some cases we can jump directly to the new steady state, that is, $x_\alpha(0) = x_\alpha(\infty)$. (The reader should refer to Chapter 11 for a discussion of some of these issues in the context of a specific model.)

4. Autonomous Difference Equations

We now turn to the scalar system in discrete time (DS), $x_{t+1} = g(x_t)$, where $g: \mathbb{R} \supseteq X \longrightarrow \mathbb{R}$ is a C^1 function. The discussion closely parallels that of the preceding section. We will first show how the solution can be obtained in the linear case. We shall then discuss two methods, one of them graphical and the other analytic, that can be used to obtain information about the qualitative properties of the solutions of nonlinear equations.

(a) Linear Equations with Constant Coefficients

The homogeneous equation

$$x_{t+1} = ax_t \tag{DH}$$

where $a, x \in \mathbb{R}$, can be solved by iteration. Because (DH) holds for all periods, we have

$$x_t = ax_{t-1}, \qquad x_{t-1} = ax_{t-2}$$

and so on. Starting at time t, and substituting recursively, we have

$$x_t = ax_{t-1} = a(ax_{t-2}) = a^2 x_{t-2} = a^2(ax_{t-3}) = a^3 x_{t-3} = \ldots = a^t x_0$$

Because the initial value of the state variable, x_0, remains undetermined in the absence of a boundary condition, what this expression says is that all solutions of (DH) must be functions of the form $x_t = ca^t$, where c is an arbitrary constant. Moreover, it is easy to see that any function of the form $x_t = ca^t$ (where t is an integer) satisfies (DH):

$$x_t = ca^t = a(ca^{t-1}) = ax_{t-1}$$

Thus, we have identified the general solution of the homogeneous equation (DH), which we write

$$x_t^h(c) = ca^t$$

As in the continuous-time case, the general solution of the nonhomogeneous equation,

$$x_{t+1} = ax_t + b \qquad\qquad (\text{DN})$$

is readily obtained through a change of variable that reduces (DN) to a homogeneous equation in deviations from the steady state, $\bar{x} = b/(1-a)$.[3] Subtracting $\bar{x}$ from both sides of (DN),

$$x_{t+1} - \bar{x} = ax_t + b - \frac{b}{1-a} = ax_t - \frac{ba}{1-a} \Rightarrow x_{t+1} - \bar{x} = a(x_t - \bar{x})$$

Thinking of $x_t - \bar{x}$ as a single variable, we now have a homogeneous equation whose solution is given by

$$x_t - \bar{x} = ca^t$$

Rearranging terms, the general solution of the nonhomogeneous equation can be written

$$x_t^g(c) = \bar{x} + ca^t = \bar{x} + x_t^h(c) \qquad\qquad (\text{GS})$$

where $x_t^h(c) = ca^t$ (the so-called *complementary function*) is the general solution of the homogeneous equation $x_{t+1} = ax_t$.

Evaluating (GS) at time zero, we can solve for c as a function of the initial value of the state variable:[4]

$$x_0 = \bar{x} + ca^0 \Rightarrow c = x_0 - \bar{x}$$

Substituting this expression into (GS), we get an alternative form of the general solution:

$$x_t^g(x_0) = \bar{x} + (x_0 - \bar{x})a^t \qquad\qquad (\text{GS}')$$

This expression says that the deviation of x from its steady-state value $\bar{x}$ at time t depends on the initial deviation, the time spanned since the system was set in motion, and the value of a. If x_t starts out at the steady state ($x_0 = \bar{x}$), the term $(x_0 - \bar{x})a^t$ is always zero, and the system remains at the rest point forever.

If, on the other hand, $x_0 \neq \bar{x}$, then the system is not initially at rest. What happens then will depend on the absolute value of a. If $|a| < 1$, the term $(x_0 - \bar{x})a^t$ approaches zero: The initial deviation decreases over time, and the system gradually returns to its stationary state, which is therefore asymptotically stable. If $|a| > 1$, we have $|(x_0 - \bar{x})a^t| \to \pm\infty$ as $t \to \infty$, and the steady state is unstable. Hence the stability of the unique steady state of the system depends on the absolute value of the coefficient a.

Finally, the sign of a determines whether the path of the system is monotonic or oscillatory. If $a > 0$, the term ca^t has the same sign for all t, and the system converges or diverges monotonically. If $a < 0$, on the other hand, a^t is positive or negative as t is even or odd, and the system jumps from one side of $\bar{x}$ to the other each period. We summarize in the following theorem.

Theorem 4.1. *The first-order linear equation (DN), $x_{t+1} = ax_t + b$ ($a \neq 1$), has a unique steady state $\bar{x} = b/(1 - a)$ that is asymptotically stable if $|a| < 1$, and unstable if $|a| > 1$. The general solution of (N) is of the form $x_t^g(c) = \bar{x} + ca^t$, where c is an arbitrary constant to be definitized by choice of an appropriate boundary condition.*

(b) Nonlinear Equations

We now consider the case of the nonlinear equation

$$x_{t+1} = g(x_t) \tag{DS}$$

where $g: \mathbb{R} \supseteq X \longrightarrow \mathbb{R}$. The first part of this section deals with the construction of the phase diagram of (DS), and the second introduces the method of linearization.

(i) Phase Diagrams

To analyze the behavior of difference equations in a single variable we can use a graphical procedure very similar to the one we discussed in the preceding section for the case of differential equations. To construct the phase diagram of the discrete-time system (DS), we plot the function $g(\ )$ in the (x_t, x_{t+1}) plane along with a 45° line going through the origin. The phase line (the graph of $g(\ )$) now gives us next period's value of x as a function of its current value, and the 45° line can be used to project the value of x from one axis to the other. Combining the two lines, it is easy to reconstruct the time path of x. Given an initial value x_0, we use the graph of $g(\ )$ to obtain the value of x at time 1 ($x_{t+1} = x_1 = g(x_0)$). Using the 45° line, we then project x_1 to the horizontal axis, use $g(\ )$ again to find the next value of x, and so on, as illustrated in Figure 9.9.

The steady states of the system now correspond to the intersections of the phase line and the 45° line. At any such point we have $x_{t+1} = g(x_t) = x_t$, implying that x remains constant over time ($\Delta x_t = x_{t+1} - x_t = 0$). To determine the

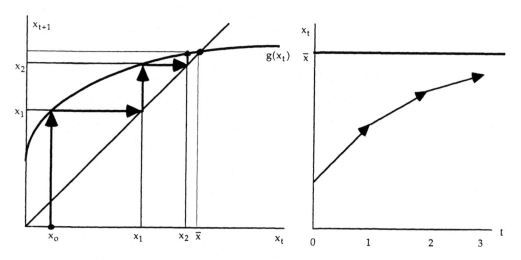

Figure 9.9. Phase diagram for a discrete-time system.

direction of the arrows of motion, observe that in those regions in which the phase line lies above the 45° line we have

$$x_{t+1} = g(x_t) > x_t \quad \text{or} \quad \Delta x_t = x_{t+1} - x_t = g(x_t) - x_t > 0$$

Hence, x_t increases over time, and the arrows of motion along the horizontal axis point to the right. When the phase line lies below the 45° line, on the other hand, we have $x_{t+1} = g(x_t) < x_t$, so x_t decreases over time, and the arrows of motion point to the left.

The procedure is very similar to the one we used in the case of a differential equation, but there are some differences between the two types of systems. In particular, the fact that the variable x now moves in discrete jumps makes it necessary to be a bit careful when it comes to analyzing the stability of the steady states and allows the emergence of some phenomena, such as cyclical behavior patterns, that cannot arise in the case of differential equations in a single variable.

The notion of stability of a steady state is the same as for continuous-time systems. A steady state $\bar{x}$ of (DS) is stable if any solution trajectory that starts sufficiently close to $\bar{x}$ converges to this point, and unstable if there exist trajectories that start arbitrarily close to $\bar{x}$ and eventually get far from it. The only problem is that in the case of a discrete-time system, it is not always possible to determine whether or not a given steady state is stable by checking the direction of the arrows of motion in a neighborhood of this point. In particular, when the phase line is downward-sloping over some interval, x can "jump" from one side of the steady state to the other, and it is possible for a steady state to be unstable even though all the arrows of motion point toward it.

This problem does not arise when the phase line is always upward-sloping. To see this, assume that $g(\ )$ is differentiable. By the mean-value theorem, we can write

$$g(x_{t+1}) = g(x_t) + g'(x^0)(x_{t+1} - x_t)$$

where x^0 is some point lying on the line segment that joins x_t and x_{t+1}. Subtracting x_{t+1} from both sides of this expression, and recalling that $x_{t+1} = g(x_t)$, we have

$$g(x_{t+1}) - x_{t+1} = g(x_t) + g'(x^0)(x_{t+1} - x_t) - x_{t+1} = g'(x^0)[g(x_t) - x_t]$$

If $g(\ )$ is always increasing, we have $g'(x^0) > 0$ for any t, and it follows that the terms $[g(x_{t+1}) - x_{t+1}]$ and $[g(x_t) - x_t]$ must have the same sign. That is, $g(x_t) > x_t$ implies $g(x_{t+1}) > x_{t+1}$, and $g(x_t) < x_t$ implies $g(x_{t+1}) < x_{t+1}$. Hence, if the phase line is above the 45° line at time t, it will also lie above it at $t+1$. This implies that the trajectories of x cannot "cross" a steady state. Thus, the problems mentioned earlier cannot arise when $g(\ )$ is always increasing.

In conclusion, when the function $g(\ )$ is increasing, we can determine the stability of the steady states by checking the directions of the arrows of motion, just as in the case of a continuous-time system. When this is not the case, we need to be more careful. As an illustration, Figure 9.10 shows the different situations that can arise in the case of a linear equation of the form $x_{t+1} = ax_t + b$.

(ii) Linearization

Given the nonlinear equation

$$x_{t+1} = g(x_t) \tag{DS}$$

where g is a C^1 function, we can use Taylor's formula to construct a linear approximation to (DS) in some neighborhood of a fixed point $\bar{x}$:

$$x_{t+1} \cong g(\bar{x}) + g'(\bar{x})(x_t - \bar{x}) \tag{L}$$

Intuitively, it may be expected that the linear equation (L), called the linearization of (DS), will be a "good approximation" to the nonlinear equation (DS) whenever x is close to $\bar{x}$. As we will soon see, this is true in most cases. As a result, the method of linearization allows us to obtain information concerning the local behavior of a nonlinear system by studying the linear approximation given by its derivative at the steady state.

The following result says, in particular, that provided $|g'(\bar{x})| \neq 1$, the nonlinear system (DS) is (locally) stable if and only if its linearization is stable.

Theorem 4.2. Local stability by linearization. Let g *be a* C^1 *function. A fixed point* $\bar{x}$ *of the equation (DS),* $x_{t+1} = g(x_t)$, *is asymptotically stable if* $|g'(\bar{x})| < 1$, *and unstable if* $|g'(\bar{x})| > 1$.

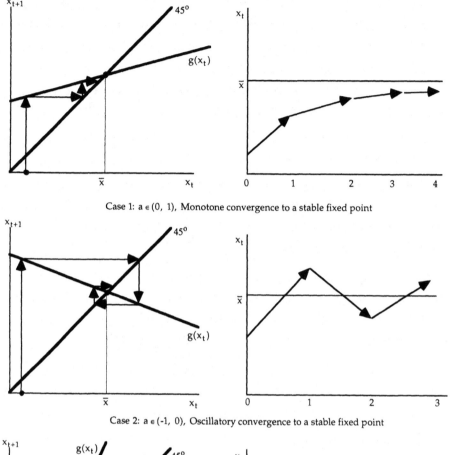

Case 1: $a \in (0, 1)$, Monotone convergence to a stable fixed point

Case 2: $a \in (-1, 0)$, Oscillatory convergence to a stable fixed point

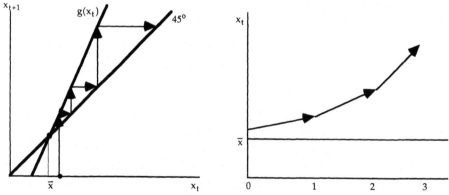

Case 3: $a > 1$, Unstable fixed point, monotone divergence

Figure 9.10. Phase diagrams and trajectories of x for linear equations.

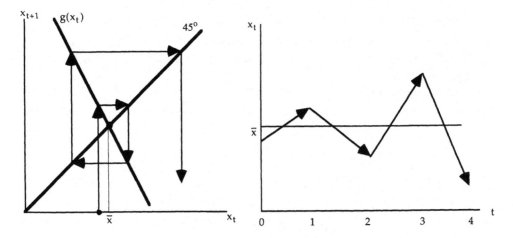

Case 4: a < -1, Unstable fixed point, oscillatory divergence

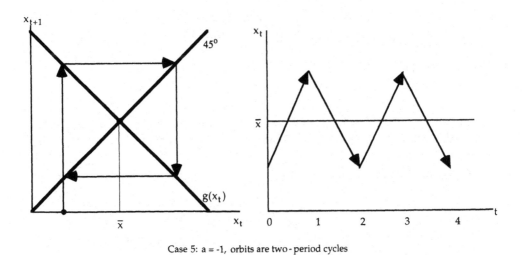

Case 5: a = -1, orbits are two-period cycles

Figure 9.10. *Continued*

Proof. We can assume, with no loss of generality, that the fixed point $\bar{x}$ is at the origin, that is, $g(0) = 0$. (Otherwise, we simply translate the origin to the point $(\bar{x}, g(\bar{x}))$ by an appropriate coordinate change.) For any given $\varepsilon > 0$, we define m_ε and M_ε by

$$m_\varepsilon \equiv \min\{|g'(x)|;\ |x| \le \varepsilon\} \quad \text{and} \quad M_\varepsilon \equiv \max\{|g'(x)|;\ |x| \le \varepsilon\}$$

To prove each part of the theorem we will make use of the following identity:

$$g(x) = g(0) + \int_0^x g'(s)\,ds = \int_0^x g'(s)\,ds \tag{1}$$

(i) Condition for local stability. Assume that $|g'(0)| < 1$. By the continuity of $g'(\ )$, we can find some $\varepsilon > 0$ such that $M_\varepsilon < 1$. Fix such an ε, and let x be an arbitrary point in $B_\varepsilon(0)$. Then we have $|g'(x)| \leq M_\varepsilon < 1$. We will use this fact to show that the positive orbit through x converges to the steady state $\bar{x} = 0$ (i.e., that $g^n(x) \to 0$ as $n \to \infty$).

Using the identity (1), we have

$$|g(x)| = \left| \int_0^x g'(s)\, ds \right| \leq \int_0^x |g'(s)|\, ds \leq M_\varepsilon |x| < |x| \tag{2}$$

(because $|x| \leq \varepsilon$). Hence $g(x)$ also lies in $B_\varepsilon(0)$. Next, consider the second iteration of g, $g^2(x) = g[g(x)]$. By the chain rule, we have

$$\frac{dg^2(x)}{dx} = g'[g(x)]g'(x) \leq M_\varepsilon M_\varepsilon = M_\varepsilon^2$$

where the inequality follows from the fact that both x and $g(x)$ lie in $B_\varepsilon(0)$.

By the same argument, we see that

$$|g^2(x)| = \left| \int_0^x \frac{dg^2(s)}{ds}\, ds \right| \leq M_\varepsilon^2 |x|$$

and so on, yielding

$$|g^n(x)| \leq M_\varepsilon^n |x|$$

Finally, because $M_\varepsilon < 1$, $M_\varepsilon^n \to 0$ as $n \to \infty$. It follows that for every $x \in B_\varepsilon(0)$, $g^n(x) \to 0$ as $n \to \infty$. That is, the fixed point $\bar{x} = 0$ is asymptotically stable when $|g'(0)| < 1$.

(ii) Condition for local instability. Given any $\varepsilon > 0$ and any x in $B_\varepsilon(0)$, observe that[5]

$$|g(x)| = \left| \int_0^x g'(s)\, ds \right| \geq m_\varepsilon |x|$$

Assume that $|g'(0)| > 1$. Then we can choose $\varepsilon > 0$ and arbitrarily small in such a way that $m_\varepsilon > 1 + \gamma$, where $\gamma > 0$. Fix some $\varepsilon > 0$ with this property, and let x be any point of $B_\varepsilon(0)$, with $x \neq 0$ (i.e., any point different from the steady state). To show that the positive orbit through x must eventually leave $B_\varepsilon(0)$, we will proceed by contradiction. Assume that $g^n(x) \in B_\varepsilon(0)$ for all n. Then we have

$$\frac{dg^2(x)}{dx} = g'[g(x)]g'(x) \geq m_\varepsilon^2$$

and

$$|g^2(x)| = \left| \int_0^x \frac{dg^2(x)}{dx}\, ds \right| \geq m_\varepsilon^2 |x| > (1 + \gamma)^2 |x|$$

By the same argument, we obtain

$$|g^n(x)| \geq m_\varepsilon^n |x| > (1 + \gamma)^n |x|$$

whenever $g^{n-1}(x) \in B_\varepsilon(0)$. Because $(1 + \gamma)^n|x| \to \infty$ as $n \to \infty$ (as $x \neq 0$), and ε is a fixed number, we arrive at a contradiction, for if $|g^n(x)| \to \infty$, then it cannot stay within $B_\varepsilon(0)$ for all time. Hence the origin is an unstable fixed point, as the orbit through a point x arbitrarily close to it must eventually leave $B_\varepsilon(0)$, although it could remain within a larger ball. □

Notice that the theorem says nothing about the stability or instability of those fixed points at which the derivative $g'(\bar{x})$ is equal to 1 in absolute value. Such steady states are said to be nonhyperbolic, and all the rest are *hyperbolic*. As in the case of differential equations, the derivative does not give us sufficient information to determine whether or not a nonhyperbolic equilibrium is stable. Figure 9.11 illustrates the point: Both systems have derivative 1 at the steady state, but each of them is stable from a different side, and unstable from the other.

Problem 4.3. Comparative dynamics for discrete systems. Let $x(t, \alpha)$ be the solution function of the parameterized discrete system (DS(α)), $x_{t+1} = g(x_t, \alpha)$, where $g(\ )$ is a C^1 function. Proceeding as in Section 3(c), show that the partial derivative of the solution function with respect to the parameter

$$x_\alpha(t, \alpha) = \frac{\partial x(t, \alpha)}{\partial \alpha}$$

satisfies a linear difference equation. Write the solution of this equation for the special case where $x(t, \alpha)$ is a steady-state solution of (DS(α)).

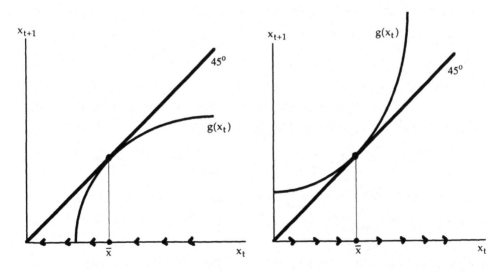

Figure 9.11. Nonhyperbolic steady states of a discrete system.

5. Solution of Nonautonomous Linear Equations

We want to compute the solution of the first-order, nonautonomous linear equation

$$\dot{x}(t) = a(t)x(t) + b(t) \tag{1}$$

where the coefficients a and b are continuous functions of time.

Rewrite (1) in the form

$$\dot{x}(t) - a(t)x(t) = b(t) \tag{2}$$

and consider the function

$$e^{-\alpha(t)}, \quad \text{with } \alpha(t) = \int_0^t a(s)\, ds \tag{3}$$

where

$$\frac{de^{-\alpha(t)}}{dt} = -e^{-\alpha(t)}a(t) \tag{4}$$

Multiplying both sides of (2) by $e^{-\alpha(t)}$,

$$e^{-\alpha(t)}[\dot{x}(t) - a(t)x(t)] = b(t)e^{-\alpha(t)} \tag{5}$$

Notice that we have defined $e^{-\alpha(t)}$ in such a way that the left-hand side of (5) is the derivative of the product $e^{-\alpha(t)}x(t)$, for

$$\frac{d}{dt}\left(e^{-\alpha(t)}x(t)\right) = e^{-\alpha(t)}\dot{x}(t) - x(t)a(t)e^{-\alpha(t)}$$

Hence, we can write (5) in the form

$$\frac{d}{dt}\left(e^{-\alpha(t)}x(t)\right) = b(t)e^{-\alpha(t)} \tag{6}$$

We will use this expression to derive two (equivalent) forms of the general solution of equation (1). To derive the first form, we integrate both sides of (6) "backward" between zero and s, obtaining

$$\int_0^s \frac{d}{dt}\left(e^{-\alpha(t)}x(t)\right) dt = \int_0^s b(t)e^{-\alpha(t)}\, dt \Rightarrow e^{-\alpha(t)}x(t)\big|_0^s = \int_0^s b(t)e^{-\alpha(t)}\, dt$$

$$\Rightarrow e^{-\alpha(s)}x(s) - 1x(0) = \int_0^s b(t)e^{-\alpha(t)}\, dt$$

$$\Rightarrow x(s) = x(0)e^{\alpha(s)} + \int_0^s b(t)e^{\alpha(s)-\alpha(t)}\, dt \tag{7}$$

This expression, sometimes called the *backward solution* of equation (1), gives us the value of $x(s)$ in terms of its initial value $x(0)$ and a weighted sum of the past values of the forcing term, $b(t)$. This form of the solution is particularly convenient when the system has a natural initial condition, that is, when $x(0)$ is a predetermined constant. Otherwise the second form of the general solution (the so-called forward solution) may be more useful.

To derive the *forward solution*, we integrate both sides of (6) forward between s and infinity,

$$\int_s^\infty \frac{d}{dt}\left(x(t)e^{-\alpha(t)}\right)dt = \int_s^\infty b(t)e^{-\alpha(t)}\,dt$$

obtaining

$$\lim_{t\to\infty} x(t)e^{-\alpha(t)} - x(s)e^{-\alpha(s)} = \int_s^\infty b(t)e^{-\alpha(t)}\,dt$$

or

$$x(s) = e^{\alpha(s)}\lim_{t\to\infty} x(t)e^{-\alpha(t)} - \int_s^\infty b(t)e^{\alpha(s)-\alpha(t)}\,dt \tag{8}$$

provided the required limits exist.

Define the *fundamental solution* of (1), denoted by $F(s)$, by

$$F(s) = -\int_s^\infty b(t)e^{\alpha(s)-\alpha(t)}\,dt \tag{9}$$

and assume that this integral converges for all s. Using the backward solution (7), and taking limits as $t \to \infty$, we have

$$\lim_{t\to\infty} x(t)e^{-\alpha(t)} = x(0) + \lim_{t\to\infty}\int_0^t b(u)e^{-\alpha(u)}\,du = x(0) + \int_0^\infty b(u)e^{-\alpha(u)}\,du$$
$$= x(0) - F(0) \tag{10}$$

Hence, this limit exists by the assumption that $F(\ )$ converges, and substituting (9) and (10) into (8) we can write the forward solution in the form

$$x(s) = [x(0) - F(0)]e^{\alpha(s)} + F(s) \tag{11}$$

We sometimes refer to the first term on the right-hand side of (11) as the *bubble term* of the forward solution of (1).[6]

The following problem asks the reader to work out the forward and backward solutions of a discrete-time system.

Problem 5.1. Consider the first-order difference equation

$$x_t = ax_{t-1} + b_{t-1} \tag{1}$$

Iterating (1) backward and forward, derive the discrete-time analogues of equations (7) and (11).

6. Solutions of Continuous-Time Systems

In Section 1(d) we stated a theorem on the existence, uniqueness, and other properties of the solutions of continuous-time systems. In this section we will prove this result. As the reader will soon discover, things are considerably more complicated than in the discrete-time case.

Let $f(\ )$ be a function mapping some subset $D = X \times \Omega \times I$ of $\mathbb{R}^{n+p+1}$ into $\mathbb{R}^n$. We will investigate the existence, uniqueness, and other properties of the solution to the continuous-time boundary-value problem

$$\dot{x} = f(x, \alpha, t), \qquad x(t_0) = x^0 \qquad \text{(PC(x^0, t_0, α))}$$

We will start in Section (a) by establishing the local existence and uniqueness of solutions to (PC) under suitable conditions on the function $f(\ )$ and its domain. Section (b) will show that under essentially the same assumptions, unique "global" solutions of (PC) can be constructed by pasting together local solutions. Finally, in Section (c) we will investigate the continuity of the flow $\phi(t, x^0, t_0, \alpha)$ in initial conditions and parameters.

A few technical comments probably are in order before we start. Notice that under our assumptions, both the vector field $f(x, t)$ and any of its solutions $\phi(t)$ are vector-valued functions,

$$f(x, t) = \left(f^1(x, t), \dots, f^n(x, t) \right) \quad \text{and} \quad \phi(t) = \left(\phi^1(t), \dots, \phi^n(t) \right)$$

Hence, the integral of $f(\ )$ should be understood to be a vector of the form

$$\int_{t_0}^t f[\phi(s), s]\, ds = \left(\int_{t_0}^t f^1[\phi(s), s]\, ds, \dots, \int_{t_0}^t f^n[\phi(s), s]\, ds \right) \qquad (1)$$

In a similar way, we could allow $f(\ )$ and $\phi(\ )$ to be matrix-valued, and then the integral in (1) would be interpreted as a matrix in which each entry would be an ordinary integral.

To aid intuition and to simplify the exposition somewhat, most of the proofs in this section will be written for the special case of a one-dimensional system with a single parameter (i.e., under the additional assumption that x and α are real numbers). In many of these proofs we will make use of the important inequality

$$\left| \int_a^b g(s)\, ds \right| \leq \int_a^b |g(s)|\, ds \qquad (2)$$

where $g(\ ):[a, b] \longrightarrow \mathbb{R}$ is a real-valued function of one variable. This inequality is derived by taking the limit of a similar "discrete" inequality for

Riemann sums. We will also make use of the concepts of Lipschitz function and the norm of a linear operator, which were introduced in Chapters 2 and 3, respectively.

The extension of the proofs to the general case of a vector-valued function is generally straightforward. For such an extension it is sometimes useful to keep in mind that all norms in $\mathbb{R}^n$ are equivalent (see Section 10 of Chapter 2). Hence, we can choose the most convenient norm, and in many cases this turns out to be not the Euclidean norm, but the $\|\cdot\|_1$ norm, defined for each $x \in \mathbb{R}^n$ by

$$\|x\|_1 = \sum_{i=1}^{n} |x_i|$$

where $|x_i|$ is the absolute value of the ith component of x. If $g(s)$ is now a vector-valued function, we have, using (2) and omitting the subscript of the norm symbol,

$$\left\| \int_a^b g(s)\, ds \right\| = \sum_{i=1}^{n} \left| \int_a^b g^i(s)\, ds \right| \leq \sum_{i=1}^{n} \left(\int_a^b |g^i(s)|\, ds \right) = \int_a^b \left(\sum_{i=1}^{n} |g^i(s)| \right) ds = \int_a^b \|g(s)\|\, ds$$

Hence, inequality (2) will now be replaced by

$$\left\| \int_a^b g(s)\, ds \right\| \leq \int_a^b \|g(s)\|\, ds \tag{3}$$

(a) Local Existence and Uniqueness

In this section and the next we will establish some properties of the solutions of (PC) for given parameter values. Hence, we suppress the parameter vector α and consider a boundary-value problem of the form

$$\dot{x} = f(x, t), \qquad x(t_0) = x^0 \tag{PC(x^0, t_0)}$$

where $f(\ )$ is a function mapping a set in $\mathbb{R}^{n+1}$ into $\mathbb{R}^n$. We will make various assumptions about the properties of $f(\ )$ in some set of the form $D = X \times I$, where I is some interval of the real line, but allow for the possibility that $f(\ )$ may be defined on a larger set where it may not satisfy the required properties. We say that a differentiable function $\phi(t)$ defined on some interval $J \subseteq I$ containing t_0 is a solution of (PC(x^0, t_0)) in D if

(i) $\phi(t_0) = x^0$,

(ii) the graph of $\phi(t)$ is contained in D, that is,

$$\{(\phi(t), t) \in \mathbb{R}^{n+1};\ t \in J\} \subseteq D$$

and

(iii) $\phi'(t) = f(\phi(t), t)$ for all $t \in J$,

where the derivative in (iii) will be understood to be the appropriate one-sided derivative if t is an end point of J.

To investigate the existence of local solutions to $(PC(x^0, t_0))$, we start with the observation that the given boundary-value problem can be transformed into an equivalent integral equation that turns out to be easier to work with. This equivalence result will later be used repeatedly.

Lemma 6.1. Let f(x, t) *be continuous in* $D = X \times I$. *The function* $\phi : J \longrightarrow \mathbb{R}^n$ *(where* $J \subseteq I$ *is an interval containing* t_0*) is a solution of the boundary-value problem* $(PC(x^0, t_0))$ *if and only if it is a continuous solution of the integral equation*

$$\phi(t) = x^0 + \int_{t_0}^t f[\phi(s), s] ds \; \forall \, t \in J \qquad (PI(x^0, t^0))$$

The proof of the lemma is very simple. If $\phi(\;)$ is a solution of $(PC(x^0, t_0))$ defined in J, then it satisfies

$$\phi'(s) = f[\phi(s), s] \; \forall \, s \in J$$

Integrating both sides of this expression from t_0 to an arbitrary t in J, we obtain

$$\int_{t_0}^t f[\phi(s), s] \, ds = \int_{t_0}^t \phi'(s) \, ds = \phi(t) - \phi(t_0)$$

by the fundamental theorem of calculus. Imposing the initial condition $\phi(t_0) = x^0$, we see that $\phi(\;)$ satisfies the integral equation $(PI(x^0, t_0))$.

On the other hand, if $\phi(\;)$ is a continuous solution of $(PI(x^0, t_0))$, then it is also differentiable, because the function under the integral is continuous. Differentiating both sides of $(PI(x^0, t_0))$ with respect to t, we obtain, by Leibniz's rule, (see p. 654)

$$\phi'(t) = f[\phi(t), t]$$

for any t in J. Moreover, putting $t = t_0$ in $(PI(x^0, t_0))$, we see that $\phi(t_0) = x^0$. Hence, $\phi(t)$ is indeed a solution of the boundary-value problem $(PC(x^0, t_0))$. Notice, incidentally, that because $f(\;)$ is continuous, this last expression implies that $\phi(t)$ is C^1, because $\phi'(t)$ is the composition of two continuous functions.

We can now return to the question of the local existence and uniqueness of solutions to $(PC(x^0, t_0))$. By Lemma 6.1, the problem reduces to that of establishing the existence and uniqueness of a continuous solution to the integral equation $(PI(x^0, t_0))$. We will exploit this equivalence to construct a sequence of increasingly better approximations to the solution of $(PI(x^0, t_0))$ following Picard's *method of successive approximations*. Then we will apply the contraction mapping theorem to conclude that this sequence converges to a function that is the unique solution of the problem.

We start out with what is probably a very poor approximation to $\phi(\ )$: We guess that the solution function is constant at its only known value, that is,

$$\phi_0(t) = x^0 \quad \text{for all } t \text{ in some subinterval } J \text{ of } I \text{ containing } t_0.$$

Next, we insert this function on the right-hand side of the integral equation and use the result as a second, and hopefully better, approximation to the solution:

$$\phi_1(t) = x^0 + \int_{t_0}^t f[\phi_0(s), s]\, ds \quad \text{for each } t \in J$$

(Refer to Figure 9.12) Repeating this procedure, we construct recursively a sequence of functions $\{\phi_n\}$, with

$$\phi_{n+1}(t) = x^0 + \int_{t_0}^t f[\phi_n(s), s]\, ds \quad \text{for each } t \in J$$

Intuitively, each new term of the sequence $\{\phi_n\}$ should be a better approximation to the solution of $(\mathrm{PI}(x^0, t_0))$ than the previous term. Hence, it can be expected that the sequence will converge to the exact solution for some appropriate interval J. We will now see that this is indeed the case.

Theorem 6.2. Local existence and uniqueness of solutions (Picard). Let f(x, t) *be a continuous function defined on the closed box*

$$\mathrm{B}(x^0, t_0) = \mathrm{B}_{x^0} \times \mathrm{I}_0 = \{(x, t);\ |t - t_0| \le a,\ \|x - x^0\| \le b\}$$

Assume that f(x, t) *is Lipschitz in* x *on* B, *that is, that there exists a positive constant* K *such that*

$$\|f(x_1, t) - f(x_2, t)\| \le K\|x_1 - x_2\| \ \forall\ (x_1, t) \text{ and } (x_2, t) \text{ in } \mathrm{B}(x^0, t_0)$$

Then there exists some number r $\le$ a *such that the boundary-value problem*

$$\dot{x} = f(x, t), \qquad x(t_0) = x^0 \qquad\qquad (PC(x^0, t_0))$$

has a unique solution $\phi(t)$ *defined on the interval* J = $[t_0 - r, t_0 + r]$, *with* $\phi(t) \in \mathrm{B}_{x^0}$ *for all* t $\in$ J.

Observe that the theorem requires continuity and a Lipschitz condition. If f is C^1, it is continuous and locally Lipschitz (Problem 4.7 in Chapter 4), so it is always possible to find a sufficiently small region B around (x^0, t_0) in which the assumptions of the theorem hold.

The proof makes use of the fact that the space $C(J)$ of continuous real-valued functions $g(\ )$ defined on a compact interval J is a complete metric space, with the sup metric defined for $g \in C(J)$ by $\|g\| = \sup\{|g(t)|;\ t \in J\}$.

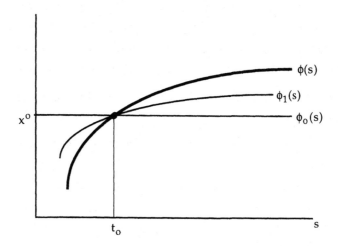

Figure 9.12. Successive approximations to the solution function.

(Notice that because $g(\ )$ is continuous and J is compact, $g(\ )$ is bounded on J. The completeness of $C(J)$ then follows by Theorem 7.12 in Chapter 2.)

Proof. As noted earlier, we will prove the result for the scalar case. Hence, B_{x^0} is a compact interval in the real line, and the norms can be replaced by absolute values in the Lipschitz condition.

Because $f(\ )$ is continuous on the compact set $B = B(x^0, t_0)$, it is bounded; that is, there exists some $M > 0$ such that

$$|f(x,t)| \le M \ \forall \ (x,t) \in B \tag{1}$$

Choose r so that

$$0 < r < \min\left\{a, \frac{1}{K}, \frac{b}{M}\right\} \tag{2}$$

We have to verify that this r will work.

Consider the space $C(J)$ of continuous real-valued functions defined on the interval $J = [t_0 - r, t_0 + r]$, and define the operator $T : C(J) \longrightarrow C(J)$ by

$$T\varphi(t) = x^0 + \int_{t_0}^{t} f[\varphi(s), s]\,ds \quad \text{for } t \in J = [t_0 - r, t^0 + r] \tag{3}$$

Using this operator, the successive approximations of Picard are given by the sequence of functions $\{\phi_n\}$ in $C(J)$ defined for each $t \in J$ by

$$\phi_0(t) = x^0 \quad \text{and} \quad \phi_{n+1}(t) = T\phi_n(t) \quad \text{for } n = 1, 2, \ldots$$

Observe that a function ϕ is a solution of the integral equation $(PI(x^0, t_0))$ in Lemma 6.1 if and only if it is a fixed point of T (i.e., if it solves $T\phi = \phi$). To establish the existence and uniqueness of such a function, we will show that T is a contraction that maps a complete space into itself. Given this result, the contraction mapping theorem (Theorem 7.16 in Chapter 2) ensures that T has a unique fixed point ϕ that is a continuous solution of the integral equation $(\text{PI}(x^0, t_0))$ and therefore of the initial-value problem $(\text{PC}(x^0, t_0))$, by Lemma 6.1. Moreover, the sequence of approximations $\{\phi_n\}$ converges to ϕ, so iteration of T can be used to approximate the solution to any desired level of accuracy. To prove this result, we rely on the completeness of $C(J)$ and on the fact that a closed subset of a complete metric space is itself complete (Theorem 7.9 in Chapter 2).

- Claim (i): The set of continuous real-valued functions φ defined on J, with the property that $|\varphi(t) - \phi_0(t)| \leq Mr$ for all $t \in J = [t_0 - r, t_0 + r]$, is complete.

  Observe that this subset of $C(J)$ corresponds to the closed ball $B_{Mr}[\phi_0]$ in $C(J)$ equipped with the sup norm. Because a closed subset of a complete metric space is complete, $B_{Mr}[\phi_0]$ is complete.

  Notice that if $\varphi(t) \in B_{Mr}[\phi_0]$, then we have $|\varphi(t) - x^0| \leq Mr < Mb/M = b$, by (2). Hence, $\varphi(t) \in B_{x^0}$ for all t in J, and $(\varphi(t), t)$ lies inside the box $B(x^0, t_0)$ for all $t \in J$. This allows us to apply the Lipschitz condition to $f(\varphi(t), t)$.

- Claim (ii): T maps $B_{Mr}[\phi_0]$ into itself.

  That is, given any suitable function φ "close to" ϕ_0, T yields another function $T\varphi$ that also is not far from ϕ_0. To show that this is true, note that for each t in $J = [t_0 - r, t_0 + r]$ we have, using the boundedness of $f( )$,

$$|T\varphi(t) - \phi_0(t)| = \left| x^0 + \int_{t_0}^t f[\varphi(s), s]\, ds - x^0 \right|$$
$$= \left| \int_{t_0}^t f[\varphi(s), s]\, ds \right| \leq \int_{t_0}^t |f[\varphi(s), s]|\, ds \leq M|t - t_0| \leq Mr$$

Hence, Mr is an upper bound of $|T\varphi(t) - \phi_0(t)|$ in J, implying that

$$\|T\varphi - \phi_0\| = \sup\{|T\varphi(t) - \phi_0(t)|;\ t \in J\} \leq Mr$$

that is, $T\varphi \in B_{Mr}[\phi_0]$.

- Claim (iii): T is a contraction on $C(J)$, that is, for all $\varphi_1, \varphi_2 \in C(J)$, $\|T\varphi_1 - T\varphi_2\| < \|\varphi_1 - \varphi_2\|$.

  Given any two functions $\varphi_1( )$ and $\varphi_2( )$ in $C(J)$, we have, for any given t in $J = [t_0 - r, t_0 + r]$

$$|T\varphi_1(t) - T\varphi_2(t)| = \left| \int_{t_0}^t (f[\varphi_1(s), s] - f[\varphi_2(s), s])\, ds \right|$$
$$\leq \int_{t_0}^t |f[\varphi_1(s), s] - f[\varphi_2(s), s]|\, ds$$
$$\leq \int_{t_0}^t K|\varphi_1(s) - \varphi_2(s)|\, ds \qquad \text{(by the Lipschitz condition)}$$
$$\leq K\int_{t_0}^t \sup_{s \in J}|\varphi_1(s) - \varphi_2(s)|\, ds = K\int_{t_0}^t \|\varphi_1 - \varphi_2\|\, ds$$
$$= K|t - t_0|\,\|\varphi_1 - \varphi_2\| < \|\varphi_1 - \varphi_2\|$$

because with t in $[t_0 - r, t_0 + r]$ we have $|t - t_0| \leq r$ and, by (2), $Kr < 1$. Now, this inequality holds for all t in the interval of interest, so $\|\varphi_1 - \varphi_2\|$ is an upper bound of $|T\varphi_1(t) - T\varphi_2(t)|$ for any t in J, and it follows that the sup remum over $t \in J$ cannot exceed $\|\varphi_1 - \varphi_2\|$, implying $\|T\varphi_1 - T\varphi_2\| < \|\varphi_1 - \varphi_2\|$.

Hence, T is a contraction from a complete space of continuous functions to itself. By the contraction mapping theorem, T has a unique fixed point in $B_{Mr}[\phi_0]$ that we will call ϕ. This function is continuous and solves $T\phi = \phi$, the integral equation from which we started, and therefore the initial-value problem $(PC(x^0, t_0))$. Because $\phi \in B_{Mr}[\phi_0]$, moreover, $\phi(J)$ is contained in B_{x^0}, as established in (i).   □

Example 6.3 and Problem 6.4 will show that the solution may not be unique when $f(\ )$ is not a Lipschitz function.

Example 6.3. Consider the initial-value problem

$$\dot{x} = f(x) = 3x^{2/3}, \qquad x(0) = 0 \tag{P}$$

We will solve the differential equation by the method of *separation of variables* and then impose the initial condition. Notice that (making improper but convenient use of the notation) we can rewrite the equation $\dot{x} = 3x^{2/3}$ in the form

$$\frac{dx}{dt} = 3x^{2/3}$$

and, rearranging terms,

$$dt = \frac{x^{-2/3}}{3} dx$$

Integrating both sides of the preceding expression, we have

$$\int dt = \int \frac{x^{-2/3}}{3} dx \Rightarrow c + t = x^{1/3}$$

where c is an arbitrary constant of integration. Hence, the functions of the form

$$x(t) = (c + t)^3 \tag{S}$$

are solutions of the given differential equation (as can be easily checked by differentiating (S)). To select the member of this family that solves (P), we impose the initial condition $x(0) = 0$. When $t = 0$ and $x = 0$, we have

$$0 = (c + 0)^3 \Rightarrow c = 0$$

Substituting this expression in (S), one solution of the initial-value problem (P) is the function

$$x(t) = t^3$$

Notice, however, that the function $y(t) = 0$ for all t is also a solution of the initial-value problem, for $y(0) = 0$, and $y(t)$ satisfies the differential equation, as

$$0 = \frac{dy}{dt} = 3y(t)^{2/3} = 0$$

Notice that the function $f(x) = 3x^{2/3}$ is not differentiable at zero, because $f'(x) = 2/(x^{1/3}) \to \infty$ as $x \to 0$. $\qquad\qquad\square$

Problem 6.4. Show that the function $f(x) = 3x^{2/3}$ is not Lipschitz in any neighborhood of zero.

Problem 6.5. Continuous dependence on initial conditions and parameters. Let $f(x, \alpha, t)$ be a continuous function defined on the set $B = B_x \times B_\alpha \times I$, where B_x, B_α, and $I = [-a, a]$ are closed intervals in the real line. Assume further that $f(\ )$ is Lipschitz in (x, α) on B, that is, that there exists some positive constant K such that

$$|f(y, \beta, t) - f(x, \alpha, t)| \leq K \|(y, \beta) - (x, \alpha)\| \ \forall \ (y, \beta, t) \text{ and } (x, \alpha, t) \text{ in } B \quad (\mathrm{L})$$

Show the following:

(i) For each (x^0, α) in the interior of $B_x \times B_\alpha$, the initial-value problem

$$\dot{x} = f(x, \alpha, t), \qquad x(0) = x^0 \qquad\qquad (\mathrm{PC}(x^0, 0, \alpha))$$

has a unique solution defined on a closed interval $J(x^0) \subseteq I$ containing zero.

(ii) The function $\phi_t(x^0, \alpha)$ that gives the solution to $(\mathrm{PC}(x^0, 0, \alpha))$ as a function of initial conditions and parameters is continuous. Hint: Restrict yourself to a sufficiently small region around (x^0, α), and use Theorem 7.18 in Chapter 2.

(b) Maximal Solutions

Assume that $f(x, t)$ is continuous and locally Lipschitz in some open region $D = X \times I$ in $\mathbb{R}^{n+1}$ containing (x^0, t_0), and consider the initial-value problem

$$\dot{x} = f(x, t), \qquad x(0) = x^0 \qquad\qquad (\mathrm{PC}(x^0, t_0))$$

By Theorem 6.2 we know that $(\mathrm{PC}(x^0, 0))$ has a unique solution defined on some (possibly small) closed interval around zero, $J_0 = [-r(x^0), r(x^0)]$. In this section we will show that this solution can be uniquely extended in D to some *maximal interval of existence* $J_m(x^0, D)$, and we shall investigate the properties of the resulting *maximal* or *global solution* as it approaches the end points of its interval of definition. The global solution will be constructed by pasting together local solutions of appropriate boundary problems. We will use the uniqueness of the local solutions to establish the uniqueness of the global solution and show that this "collation" process can be continued until the graph of the global solution approaches the boundary of the set D.

Throughout most of the remainder of this section we will make the following assumption.

Assumption 6.6. The function $f(x, t)$ is continuous and locally Lipschitz in x on some region $D = X \times I$ in $\mathbb{R}^{n+1}$, where X is an open set in $\mathbb{R}^n$, and I is an open interval on the real line.

Notice that if $f(\ )$ is C^1 on D, then this assumption holds. Hence, all our results extend automatically to the case where f is C^1.

The first step will be to establish that any two solutions of the boundary-value problem $(\mathrm{PC}(x^0, t_0))$ coincide in the intersection of their domains. Figure 9.13 illustrates the intuition behind this result: If two solutions of $(\mathrm{PC}(x^0, t_0))$, say $\phi(t)$ and $\varphi(t)$, "separate" at some point (x^1, t_1), then the uniqueness of the solutions of $(\mathrm{PC}(x^1, t_1))$ is violated.

Lemma 6.7. Assume that f(x, t) *satisfies Assumption 6.6 in the open region* $\mathrm{D} = \mathrm{X} \times \mathrm{I}$ *in* $\mathbb{R}^{n+1}$, *and consider the initial-value problem*

$$\dot{\mathrm{x}} = \mathrm{f}(\mathrm{x}, \mathrm{t}), \qquad \mathrm{x}(\mathrm{t}_0) = \mathrm{x}^0, \quad \text{with } (\mathrm{x}^0, \mathrm{t}_0) \in \mathrm{D} \qquad (PC(\mathrm{x}^0, \mathrm{t}_0))$$

Let $\phi(\mathrm{t})$ *and* $\varphi(\mathrm{t})$ *be solutions of* $(PC(\mathrm{x}^0, t_0))$ *defined on subintervals* J_ϕ *and* J_φ *of I, respectively, with the property that* $\phi(\mathrm{t}) \in \mathrm{X}$ *for all* $\mathrm{t} \in \mathrm{J}_\phi$ *and* $\varphi(\mathrm{t}) \in \mathrm{X}$ *for all* $\mathrm{t} \in \mathrm{J}_\varphi$. *Then* $\phi(\mathrm{t})$ *and* $\varphi(\mathrm{t})$ *coincide in the intersection of their domains, that is,* $\phi(\mathrm{t}) = \varphi(\mathrm{t})$ *for all* $\mathrm{t} \in \mathrm{J} = \mathrm{J}_\phi \cap \mathrm{J}_\varphi$.

Problem 6.8. Prove Lemma 6.7. Hint: By the local-existence and uniqueness theorem (Theorem 6.2) we know that $\phi(t)$ and $\varphi(t)$ coincide over some interval containing t_0. Let J_m be the largest subinterval of J over which the two solutions coincide. To show that $J_m = J$, assume that J_m is strictly contained in J, and seek a contradiction.

We can now return to the problem posed at the beginning of this section. Assume that $f(x, t)$ is continuous and locally Lipschitz in some open region $D = X \times I$ in $\mathbb{R}^{n+1}$ containing (x^0, t_0). Then we can find some closed box $B(x^0, t_0) \subseteq D$ around (x^0, t_0) such that $f(\ )$ is bounded and Lipschitz in $B(x^0, t_0)$, and it follows by the local existence and uniqueness theorem (Theorem 6.2) that there exists some $r_0 = r(x^0) > 0$ such that the initial-value problem $(\mathrm{PC}(x^0, t_0))$ has a unique solution $\phi^0(t)$ defined on an interval $J_0 = [t_0 - r_0, t_0 + r_0]$, with the property that its graph, $(J_0, \phi^0(J_0))$, is contained in $B(x^0, t_0) \subseteq D$.

We will now see how this solution can be extended to the right. (A similar argument will yield the *continuation* of the solution to the left.) Let $t_1 = t_0 + r_0$ and $x^1 = \phi^0(t_1)$, and consider the initial-value problem

$$\dot{x} = f(x, t), \qquad x(t_1) = x^1 \qquad (PC(x^1, t_1))$$

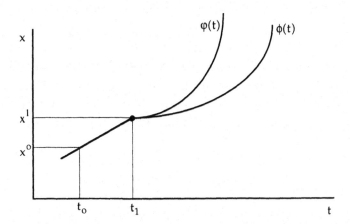

Figure 9.13. Local uniqueness implies global uniqueness.

Because $(x^1, t_1) = (\phi^0(t_1), t_1) \in D$, and D is open, the conditions of the local existence and uniqueness theorem are again satisfied in a suitable box around (x^1, t_1), and it follows that there exists some positive r_1 such that $(\text{PC}(x^1, t_1))$ has a unique solution $\phi^1(t)$ defined on the interval $J_1 = [t_1 - r_1, t_1 + r_1]$.

Now, because $\phi^0(t)$ is also a solution of $(\text{PC}(x^1, t_1))$, it follows by Lemma 6.7 that $\phi^0(t) = \phi^1(t)$ for $t \in J_0 \cap J_1$. Define now the function $\phi(t)$ on $J_0 \cup J_1$ by

$$\phi(t) = \begin{cases} \phi^0(t) & \text{for } t \in J_0 \\ \phi^1(t) & \text{for } t \in J_1 \sim J_0 \end{cases}$$

Notice that $\phi(t)$ is a continuous function, because both $\phi^0(t)$ and $\phi^1(t)$ are continuous, and they coincide over their intersection. Moreover, $\phi(t)$ is a solution of $(\text{PC}(x^0, t_0))$ because it satisfies the integral equation $(\text{PI}(x^0, t_0))$ in Lemma 6.1. This is certainly the case in $J_0 = [0, t_1]$, but also in $J_1 \sim J_0 = (t_1, t_1 + r_1]$, because for any t in this interval we have

$$\phi(t) = \phi^1(t) = x^1 + \int_{t_0}^{t} f(\phi^1(s), s)\, ds = \phi^0(t_1) + \int_{t_1}^{t} f(\phi^1(s), s)\, ds$$

$$= x^0 + \int_{t_0}^{t_1} f(\phi^0(s), s)\, ds + \int_{t_1}^{t} f(\phi^1(s), s)\, ds$$

$$= x^0 + \int_{t_0}^{t_1} f(\phi(s), s)\, ds + \int_{t_1}^{t} f(\phi(s), s)\, ds = x^0 + \int_{t_0}^{t} f(\phi(s), s)\, ds$$

where we have made use of the fact that $\phi^0(t)$ is a solution of $(\text{PC}(x^0, t_0))$ in J_0, and $\phi^1(t)$ is a solution of $(\text{PC}(x^1, t_1))$ in J_1. Hence, we have extended the solution to $(\text{PC}(x^0, t_0))$ beyond its original domain J_0. The extension is also unique in the set $J_0 \cup J_1$, because Lemma 6.7 implies that any other solution defined over any subset of $J_0 \cup J_1$ must coincide with $\phi(t)$ over the intersection of their domains.

Notice that because the right end point of the graph of the extended solution $(\phi^1(t_1 + r_1), t_1 + r_1)$ still lies in the open set D, the continuation process can be repeated in a similar way starting from this point. In fact, because the extended solution obtained in this manner never leaves the open set D, the continuation process can be repeated an infinite number of times. Hence, the maximal solution $\phi(\ )$ obtained as the limit of this process will be defined in the union of an infinite number of partially overlapping closed intervals J_n constructed as illustrated earlier. The resulting set,

$$J_m\left(x^0, t_0\right) = \bigcup_{n \geq 0} J_n \subseteq I$$

is called the *maximal interval of existence* of the solution to $(PC(x^0, t_0))$ in D, because it is the largest interval of definition of a solution of $(PC(x^0, t_0))$ whose graph is contained in D. Notice that the infinite union of partially overlapping closed intervals will itself be an interval, but not necessarily a closed one. In fact, $J_m(x^0, t_0)$ must be an open interval, for if $J_m(x^0, t_0) = [a, b]$, then $(\phi(b), b)$ lies in the open set D, and it follows by an already familiar argument that the solution $\phi(\ )$ can be extended within D to a larger interval $[a, b + r]$, thereby contradicting the fact that $[a, b]$ is the maximal interval of existence.

We summarize the preceding discussion in the following theorem.

Theorem 6.9. Let $f(x, t)$ satisfy Assumption 6.6 *(continuity and existence of a local Lipschitz constant) in the open region* $D = X \times I$ *in* $\mathbb{R}^{n+1}$ *containing* (x^0, t_0). *Then the boundary-value problem* $(PC(x^0, t_0))$ *has a unique maximal solution* $\phi(t)$ *in* D *defined on the open maximal interval* $J_m(x^0, t_0) = (a, b) \subseteq I$. *That is, if* $\varphi(t)$ *is any solution of* $(PC(x^0, t_0))$ *in* D *defined on some interval* J_φ, *then* $J_\varphi \subseteq J_m(x^0, t_0)$ *and* $\varphi(t) = \phi(t)$ *for all* $t \in J_\varphi$.

We will now investigate the behavior of solutions as they approach the end points of their intervals of definition. The following example shows that the maximal interval of existence depends, in general, on the initial conditions of the problem and need not be the entire real line, even when $f(\ )$ is nicely behaved in the whole of $\mathbb{R}^{n+1}$.

Example 6.10. Consider the initial-value problem

$$\dot{x} = x^2, \qquad x(0) = x^0 \tag{P}$$

As in Example 6.3, we will solve the differential equation by the method of separation of variables and then impose the initial condition. Rearranging terms in the equation $dx/dt = x^2$, we have

$$dt = x^{-2}\, dx$$

Integrating both sides of this expression,

$$\int dt = \int x^{-2}\, dx \Rightarrow -x^{-1} = c + t$$

where c is an arbitrary constant of integration. Hence, the solutions of the equation are of the form

$$x(t) = \frac{-1}{c+t} \tag{S}$$

To select the member of this family that solves (P), we impose the initial condition $x(0) = x^0$. When $t = 0$ and $x = x^0$, we have

$$x^0 = \frac{-1}{c+0} \Rightarrow c = -1/x^0$$

Substituting this condition into (S), the solution of the initial-value problem is given by the function

$$x(t) = \frac{1}{(1/x^0) - t}$$

Notice that $x(t) \to \infty$ as $t \to 1/x^0$. Hence, the solution to (P) is defined on $(-\infty, 1/x^0)$. □

The example also illustrates how solutions to $(PC(x^0, t_0))$ may fail to exist for finite t. When the conditions of the local existence and uniqueness theorem are satisfied, a solution $\phi(t)$ cannot mysteriously "evaporate." It may, however, "explode" in finite time. If the set D in which $f(\ )$ is well behaved is not the whole of $\mathbb{R}^{n+1}$, the solution can also fail to exist by leaving this set. The following theorems give some more precise results about the limiting behavior of the maximal solutions of $(PC(x^0, t_0))$.

Lemma 6.11. Assume that $f(x, t)$ *is bounded in some region* $D = X \times I$ *in* $\mathbb{R}^{n+1}$, *and consider the initial-value problem*

$$\dot{x} = f(x, t), \qquad x(t_0) = x^0, \quad \text{with } (x^0, t_0) \in D \qquad (PC(x^0, t_0))$$

Let $\phi(t)$ *be a solution of* $(PC(x^0, t_0))$ *defined on a finite interval* $(a, b) \subseteq I$ *containing* t_0, *with the property that* $\phi(t) \in X$ *for all* $t \in (a, b)$. *Then the limits*

$$\lim_{t \to a^+} \phi(t) \quad \text{and} \quad \lim_{t \to b^-} \phi(t)$$

exist.

Proof. Let t_1 and t_2 be two arbitrary points in (a, b), with $t_1 < t_2$. By Lemma 6.1, we have

$$\phi(t_1) = x^0 + \int_{t_0}^{t_1} f(\phi(s), s)\, ds \quad \text{and} \quad \phi(t_2) = x^0 + \int_{t_0}^{t_2} f(\phi(s), s)\, ds$$

Hence,

$$\phi(t_2) - \phi(t_1) = \int_{t_1}^{t_2} f(\phi(s), s)\, ds \tag{1}$$

Because $(\phi(s), s) \in D$ for all $s \in [t_1, t_2]$, and $f(\ )$ is bounded in D, there is some positive constant M such that $|f(\phi(s), s)| \le M$. Hence, (1) implies that

$$|\phi(t_2) - \phi(t_1)| \le M|t_2 - t_1| \tag{2}$$

Now, as $t_1, t_2 \to b$ from below, we have $|t_2 - t_1| \to 0$, implying that $|\phi(t_2) - \phi(t_1)| \to 0$. This, in turn, implies, by the completeness[7] of $\mathbb{R}$ (or $\mathbb{R}^n$ in the general case), that $\phi(t)$ converges to some limit as $t \to b^-$. A similar argument shows that $\phi(t)$ has a limit as $t \to a^+$. $\qquad\square$

Using this result, we will now show that if a solution $\phi(t)$ is not defined on the entire interval I, then it leaves any compact subset of X. This implies that as t approaches the right end point of the maximal interval of definition, the solution either tends to the boundary of the domain or "explodes" to infinity, or both. If I is the entire real line, and $X = \mathbb{R}^n$, then the theorem says that if the right end point of the maximal interval of definition is finite (i.e., if $b < \infty$), then $\phi(t)$ goes to infinity in finite time. (Notice that if the system is autonomous, then we can assume that I is the entire real line by defining $f(x, t) = f(x)$ for all t.)

Theorem 6.12. Let f(x, t) *satisfy Assumption 6.6 in the open region* $D = X \times I$ *in* $\mathbb{R}^{n+1}$ *containing* (x^0, t_0). *Let* $\phi(t)$ *be the maximal solution of* $(PC(x^0, t_0))$ *in* D, *defined on the maximal interval* $J_m(x^0, t_0) = (a, b)$. *Assume that* $b \in int$ I. *Then, given any compact set* $K \subseteq X$, *there exists some* $t \in (t_0, b)$ *such that* $\phi(t) \notin K$. *Similarly, if* $a \in int$ I, *then* $\phi(t) \notin K$ *for some* $t \in (b, t_0)$.

Proof. By contradiction. Let $K \subseteq X$ be compact, and assume that $\phi(t) \in K$ for all t in (a, b). Because f is continuous on the compact set $K \times [0, b]$, it is bounded in this set. By Lemma 6.11, $\phi(t)$ has a limit as $t \to b^-$. Let

$$x^1 = \lim_{t \to b^-} \phi(t)$$

be this limit, and define the function $\varphi(t)$ in $(a, b]$ by

$$\varphi(t) = \begin{cases} \phi(t) & \text{for } t \in (a, b) \\ x^1 & \text{for } t = b \end{cases}$$

Then $\varphi(t)$ is continuous in $(a, b]$ (from the left at b) and solves $(PC(x^0, t_0))$ in this interval (by Lemma 2.1), because $\varphi(t) = \phi(t)$ solves $(PC(x^0, t_0))$ in (a, b) and

$$\varphi(b) = \lim_{t \to b^-} \phi(t) = x^0 + \lim_{t \to b^-} \int_0^t f(\phi(s), s) \, ds$$

$$= x^0 + \int_0^b f(\phi(s), s) \, ds = x^0 + \int_0^b f(\varphi(s), s)$$

Notice also that because K is compact, with $\varphi(t)$ continuous and $\varphi(t) \in K$ for all t in (a, b), then $x^1 = \varphi(b)$ (is a closure point of K and therefore) lies also in $K \subseteq X$. Hence, $(\varphi(b), b) \in D$, and it follows that $\varphi(t)$ is a solution of (PC(x^0, t_0)) in D defined on $(a, b]$. This contradicts the fact that (a, b) is the maximal interval of existence of the solution of (PC(x^0, t_0)) in D. $\qquad \square$

Corollary 6.13. Under the hypotheses of Theorem 6.12, if $b \in int$ I *and* $\lim_{t \to b^-} \phi(t)$ *exists, then*

$$x^1 = \lim_{t \to b^-} \phi(t) \in bdy \ X$$

Proof. Assume that $b \in int \ I$. Let $\varphi(t)$ be the (continuous) extension of $\phi(t)$ to the interval $(a, b]$ defined in the proof of Theorem 6.12. Then the set

$$K = \varphi[0, b] = \{x \in P^v; \ x = \varphi(t) \text{ for some } t \in [0, b]\}$$

is compact, because it is the continuous image of a compact interval. Assume that $\varphi(b) = x^1 \in X$. Then, because $\varphi[0, b) = \phi[0, b)$ is certainly contained in X, we have $K \subseteq X$, and it follows by Theorem 6.12 that there is some $t \in (0, b)$ such that $\varphi(t) \notin K$. This contradicts the definition of K, so $x^1 \notin X$. But because $\varphi(t) \in X$ for all t in $[0, b)$, it follows by the continuity of $\varphi(\ )$ that $x^1 = \varphi(b)$ is a closure point of X. Hence, $x^1 \in cl \ X \sim X = bdy \ X$. $\qquad \square$

The contrapositive of Theorem 6.12 says that if there exists a compact set K in X such that the maximal solution $\phi(t)$ stays within K for all t in $[0, b)$, then b is the right end point of I. A similar argument at the other end point yields the following result.

Corollary 6.14. Under the hypotheses of Theorem 6.12, if there exists a compact set K *in* X *such that the maximal solution* $\phi(t)$ *stays within* K *for all* t *in* $J_m(x^0, t_0) = (a, b)$, *then* $J_m(x^0, t_0) = I$.

Of course, if $I = \mathbb{R}$, or the system is autonomous, this implies that any solution that stays within a compact subset of X is defined for all t.

Using Theorem 6.12, it is easy to show that if f is a linear function of x, that is, if $f(x, t) = A(t)x$, where the function $A(t)$ is continuous on the interval I containing t_0, then the boundary-value problem (PC(x^0, t_0)) has a unique solution defined on the entire interval I. Problem 6.15 asks the reader to prove this result for the special case of a scalar system.

Problem 6.15. Let $c(t)$ be a continuous real-valued function defined on an open interval $I = (\alpha, \beta)$ containing t_0. Consider the initial-value problem defined by the linear system $\dot{x} = c(t)x$ and the initial condition $x(t_0) = x^0 \in \mathbb{R}$. Show that the solution to this problem is defined on the whole of I.

Hint: By contradiction, using Theorem 6.12 and Gronwall's lemma (the following Lemma 6.16).

(c) Dependence on Initial Conditions and Parameters

In this section we will investigate the dependence on initial conditions of the solutions of the family of boundary-value problems

$$\dot{x} = f(x, t), \qquad x(t_0) = x^0 \qquad (\text{PC}(x^0, t_0))$$

where we now regard the initial data (x^0, t_0) as variables. As usual, we assume that $f(x, t)$ is continuous and locally Lipschitz in some open region $D = X \times I$ in $\mathbb{R}^{n+1}$, where I is an open interval (Assumption 6.6). Then Theorem 6.9 assures us that for each (x^0, t_0) in D the boundary-value problem $(\text{PC}(x^0, t_0))$ has a unique solution in D. Hence, we can define the *flow* of $f(\ )$ as the function $\phi(t, x^0, t_0): E \to X$ defined on the set

$$E = \{(t, x^0, t_0) \in I \times X \times I; \ t \in J_m(x^0, t_0)\} \subseteq D \times I$$

such that for each fixed (x^0, t_0), the function $\phi(\cdot, x^0, t_0)$ defined in $J_m(x^0, t_0)$ is a solution of $(\text{PC}(x^0, t_0))$. Because $\phi(\cdot, x^0, t_0)$ is a solution of $(\text{PC}(x^0, t_0))$, we know already that $\phi(\ )$ is C^1 in its first argument. We will now show that under our maintained assumptions, E is an open set, and $\phi(t, x^0, t_0)$ is a continuous function of all its arguments. In fact, if $f(\ )$ is C^k in D, then so is $\phi(\ )$. Roughly speaking, then, the flow of a continuous system is as smooth as the vector field itself.

In most of what follows, we will work with a fixed t_0, suppress the third argument of the flow, writing it $\phi(t, x^0)$, and concentrate on the dependence of the solution on the initial position x^0. All our results can be easily extended to (x^0, t_0).

We will first establish a useful lemma. Using this result, it will then be easy to obtain a bound on the distances between solutions of $(\text{PC}(x^0, t_0))$ that start from different initial values.

Lemma 6.16. Gronwall's lemma. Let $u(t) \geq 0$ *be a continuous real-valued function defined on the interval* $[t_0, t_1]$. *Assume that there exist positive constants* C *and* K *such that*

$$0 \leq u(t) \leq C + K \int_{t_0}^{t} u(s) \, ds$$

for all $t \in [t_0, t_1]$. *Then we have*

$$u(t) \le Ce^{K\|t-t_0\|} \ \forall \ t \in [t_0, t_1]$$

Proof. For each $t \in [t_0, t_1]$, let

$$U(t) = C + K \int_{t_0}^{t} u(s) \, ds > 0$$

Then $u(t) \le U(t)$ by assumption. Differentiating $U(\ )$, we have

$$U'(t) = Ku(t)$$

Hence,

$$\frac{d \ln U(t)}{dt} = \frac{U'(t)}{U(t)} = \frac{Ku(t)}{U(t)} \le \frac{KU(t)}{U(t)} = K$$

Integrating both sides of this expression between t_0 and t,

$$\ln U(t) - \ln U(t_0) \le K|t - t_0| \Rightarrow \ln U(t) \le \ln U(t_0) + K|t - t_0|$$

Taking exponentials and observing that $U(t_0) = C$, we obtain the desired inequality

$$U(t) \le U(t_0)e^{K|t-t_0|} = Ce^{K|t-t_0|} \qquad \square$$

Lemma 6.17. *Let* f(x, t) *satisfy Assumption 6.6 in the open set* $D = X \times I$ *in* $\mathbb{R}^{n+1}$. *Assume that* f( ) *is Lipschitz in* x *on* D, *with Lipschitz constant* K. *Given two points* (t_0, x^0) *and* (t_0, y^0) *in* D, *let* $\phi(t, y^0)$ *and* $\phi(t, x^0)$ *be the unique solutions in* D *of the system* (CS(t)), $\dot{x} = f(x, t)$, *going through these points, defined respectively in the maximal intervals* $J_m(x^0)$ *and* $J_m(y^0) \subseteq I$. *Then, for each* $t \in J_m(x^0) \cap J_m(y^0)$ *we have*

$$|\phi(t, y^0) - \phi(t, x^0)| \le \|y^0 - x^0\| e^{K|t-t_0|} \qquad (4)$$

Problem 6.18. Prove Lemma 6.17. Hint: Consider the scalar case and apply Gronwall's lemma to the function $\varphi(t) = |\phi(t, y^0) - \phi(t, x^0)|$.

The preceding lemma almost implies the continuity of $\phi(t, x^0)$ in x^0 for given t when $f(\ )$ is (globally) Lipschitz on D. If we fix some t in $J_m(x^0)$ and let $\|y^0 - x^0\|$ go to zero, inequality (4) implies that $\|\phi(t, y^0) - \phi(t, x^0)\| \to 0$ – provided that $\phi(t, y^0)$ is defined for all y^0 sufficiently close to x^0. Our next result takes care of this loose end by showing that for any $t \in J_m(x^0)$, $\phi(s, y^0)$ is defined in $[0, t]$ for all y^0 sufficiently close to x^0. The proof of the theorem also shows that the graphs of the two solutions $\phi(t, y^0)$ and $\phi(t, x^0)$ in $[a, b]$ stay within a compact subset of D. Hence, the inequality in Lemma 6.17 continues to hold for some K, and $\phi(\ )$ is continuous in x^0 for given t provided that $f(\ )$ is locally Lipschitz (because, by Theorem 8.25 in Chapter 2, a function that is locally Lipschitz on a set D is Lipschitz on any compact subset of D).

Theorem 6.19. Let f(x, t) *satisfy Assumption 6.6 in the open set* $D = X \times I$ *in* $\mathbb{R}^{n+1}$. *Given some point* (x^0, t_0) *in D, let the unique solution* $\phi(t, x^0)$ *of* $(PC(x^0, t_0))$ *be defined on a closed interval* $[a, b] \subseteq J_m(x^0)$. *Then there exists some* $\delta > 0$ *and a positive constant* K *such that for all* $y^0 \in B_\delta(x^0)$ *the initial-value problem* $(PC(y^0, t_0))$ *has a unique solution* $\phi(t, y^0)$ *defined on* $[a, b]$ *that satisfies*

$$\left| \phi(t, y^0) - \phi(t, x^0) \right| \le \left| y^0 - x^0 \right| e^{K|t - t_0|}$$

for all t *in* $[a, b]$.

Proof. Because $[a, b]$ is compact and $\phi(t, x^0)$ is a continuous function of t, the set

$$A = \phi([a, b], x^0) = \left\{ x \in X; \ x = \phi(t, x^0) \text{ for some } t \in [a, b] \right\}$$

is a compact subset of X. Because X is open, moreover, there exists some $\varepsilon > 0$ such that the compact set

$$B = \bigcup_{x \in A} B_\varepsilon[x] = \left\{ z \in \mathbb{R}^n; \ \|z - \phi(t, x^0)\| \le \varepsilon \text{ for some } t \in [a, b] \right\}$$

is a subset of X. Moreover, because $f(\ )$ is Lipschitz in x on the open set D, and $C = B \times [a, b]$ is a compact subset of D, it follows by Theorem 8.25 in Chapter 2 that $f(\ )$ is Lipschitz on C, that is, that there exists a positive constant K such that

$$|f(y, t) - f(x, t)| \le K|y - x| \tag{1}$$

for all (y, t) and (x, t) in C.

Choose some $\delta > 0$ such that

$$\delta \le \min\left\{ \varepsilon, \varepsilon e^{-K(b-a)} \right\} \tag{2}$$

and let y^0 be a point in $B_\delta(x^0)$. Because $(y^0, t_0) \in D$, Theorem 6.9 guarantees the existence of a unique solution $\phi(t, y^0)$ going through this point and defined on some maximal interval of existence $J_m(y^0) = (\alpha, \beta) \subseteq I$ containing t_0. We will show that $[a, b] \subseteq (\alpha, \beta)$ and that $\phi(t, y^0)$ satisfies the desired inequality. We start by establishing the following fact:

(i) Claim: If $\phi(t, y^0)$ is defined in $[a, b]$, then $\phi(t, y^0) \in B$ for all $t \in [a, b]$.

Assume that $\phi(t, y^0)$ is defined in $[a, b]$, and observe that because $\phi(t_0, y^0) = y^0 \in B_\delta(x^0) \subseteq B_\varepsilon(x^0) \subseteq B$, we have $\phi(t, y^0) \in B$ for all t in some interval containing t_0. We assume that $\phi(t, y^0)$ leaves B at some point in $[a, b]$ to the right of t_0 and thus obtain a contradiction (a similar argument will work in the other case). Under this assumption (by the continuity of $\phi(\ )$ in t) there exists some $t^* \in (t_0, b)$ such that $\phi(t, y^0) \in B$ for $t \in [t_0, t^*]$, and $\phi(t^*, y^0) \in$ bdy B.

Now, because $\phi(t, y^0) \in B$ for all t in $[t_0, t^*] \subseteq [a, b]$, the graph of $\phi(t, y^0)$ in $[t_0, t^*]$ is contained in the compact set $C = B \times [a, b]$, and it follows that K is a Lipschitz constant for $f(\ )$ in this region. By Lemma 6.17, this implies that

$$|\phi(t, y^0) - \phi(t, x^0)| \le |y^0 - x^0| e^{K(t-t_0)} \tag{3}$$

for all $t \in [t_0, t^*]$. Using (2), this inequality implies, with $t = t^* \in [a, b]$, that

$$|\phi(t^*, y^0) - \phi(t^*, x^0)| \le |y^0 - x^0| e^{K(t^*-t_0)} < \delta e^{K(b-a)} < \varepsilon \tag{4}$$

because $y^0 \in B_\delta(x^0)$. Because $\phi(t^*, x^0) \in A$, it follows that $\phi(t^*, y^0)$ is an interior point of B (see the definitions of the two sets). This is a contradiction, because $\phi(t^*, y^0)$ is a boundary point of B. Hence $\phi(t, y^0) \in B$ for all $t \in [a, b]$.

(ii) By the same argument, it follows that if $\beta \le b$, then $\phi(t, y^0) \in B$ for all $t \in [t_0, \beta)$. If $\beta \le b$, then the point t^* in (i), with $\phi(t^*, y^0) \in$ bdy B, must lie in (t_0, β), but then (4) holds (because $t^* < \beta \le b$), and $\phi(t^*, y^0)$ is also an interior point of B, which is again a contradiction.

(iii) Next, we show that $[a, b] \subseteq (\alpha, \beta) = J_m(y^0)$, so that indeed $\phi(t, y^0)$ is defined on the entire interval $[a, b]$ on which we know $\phi(t, x^0)$ to be defined. We assume that $\beta \le b$ and obtain a contradiction. Under this assumption we have $\phi(t, y^0) \in B$ for all $t \in [t_0, \beta)$, by (ii). But notice that if $\beta \le b$, then $[t_0, \beta] \subseteq [t_0, b]$, where b is an interior point of the (open) interval $J_m(x^0)$ and therefore is an interior point of I. Hence, β is also an interior point of I. But then Theorem 6.12 implies that $\phi(t, y^0)$ must leave any compact subset of X and, in particular, that there exists some $t \in (t_0, \beta)$ such that $\phi(t, y^0) \notin B$, which contradicts (ii). Hence, it must be that $b < \beta$.

A similar argument can be used to establish that if $\alpha \ge a$, then $\phi(t, y) \in B$ for all $t \in (\alpha, t_0]$ and that this also leads to a contradiction. Hence $a > \alpha$, and we conclude that $[a, b]$ is contained in (α, β), the maximal interval of existence of $\phi(t, y^0)$. Thus $\phi(t, y^0)$ is defined in the entire interval $[a, b]$, as claimed.

(iv) Once we have shown that $\phi(t, y)$ is defined in the entire interval $[a, b]$, (i) implies that $\phi(t, y^0) \in B$ for all t in $[a, b]$. Hence, the graph of $\phi(t, y^0)$ in $[a, b]$ is contained in the compact set $C = B \times [a, b]$, and it follows that K is a Lipschitz constant for f in this region. Lemma 6.17 then gives

$$|\phi(t, y^0) - \phi(t, x^0)| \le |y^0 - x^0| e^{K|t-t_0|}$$

for all $t \in [a, b]$. $\qquad\square$

Using this result, it is now easy to establish the continuity of the flow.

Theorem 6.20. Continuity of the flow. Assume that f(x, t) *satisfies Assumption 6.6 (continuity and existence of a local Lipschitz constant) in some open region* $D = X \times I$ *in* $\mathbb{R}^{n+1}$. *Then the flow of the continuous system (CS(t)),* $\phi(t, x^0) : E \longrightarrow X$, *is a continuous function, and its domain of definition*

$$E = \{(t, x) \in I \times X; \ t \in J_m(x)\} \subseteq D$$

is an open set.

Proof

- Openness of E. Let (s, x^0) be an arbitrary point of E. We want to show that any point (t, x) sufficiently close to (s, x^0) lies in E, that is, that $t \in J_m(x)$ for any such point.

  Assume that $(s, x^0) \in E$ and, for concreteness, that $s > t_0$. Then $s \in J_m(x^0)$, and it follows that the solution $\phi(t, x^0)$ of the initial-value problem $(PC(x^0, t_0))$ is defined on $[t_0, s]$. Because $J_m(x^0)$ is open, s is an interior point of $J_m(x^0)$, and it follows that $\phi(t, x^0)$ can be extended to the interval $[t_0, s + \varepsilon]$ for some $\varepsilon > 0$. Hence $\phi(t, x^0)$ is defined on the closed interval $[s - \varepsilon, s + \varepsilon]$.

  It then follows by Theorem 6.18 that there exists some $\delta > 0$ such that for any $y^0 \in B_\delta(x^0)$ the solution $\phi(t, y^0)$ of $(PC(y^0, t_0))$ is defined for all t in $[s - \varepsilon, s + \varepsilon]$. Hence, $(s - \varepsilon, s + \varepsilon) \times B_\delta(x^0) \subseteq E$, and it follows that E is open in D.

- Continuity of $\phi(\ )$. Given some point $(s, x^0) \in E$, let ε and δ be as in the first part of the proof, and choose some μ, with $0 < \mu < \min\{\varepsilon, \delta\}$. Consider a point (t, y^0) such that $t \in (s - \mu, s + \mu)$ and $y^0 \in B_\mu(x^0)$. Then $(t, y^0) \in E$, so $\phi(t, y^0)$ is defined and satisfies

$$\left|\phi(t, y^0) - \phi(s, x^0)\right| \le \left|\phi(t, y^0) - \phi(t, x^0)\right| + \left|\phi(t, x^0) - \phi(s, x^0)\right|$$

  by the triangle inequality. Consider the limit of the right-hand side of this expression as $(t, y^0) \to (s, x^0)$. By the continuity of $\phi(\ )$ in x for given t, the first term goes to zero as $y^0 \to x^0$. Similarly, the second term goes to zero, by the continuity of $\phi(\ )$ in t for given x. Hence, $\phi(t, y^0) \to \phi(s, x^0)$ as $(t, y^0) \to (s, x^0)$, which establishes the continuity of $\phi(t, x)$ at an arbitrary point (s, x^0) in E, and therefore in the whole set. $\square$

Continuity of the Flow of Parameterized Systems

Let us now introduce the parameters explicitly into the analysis (while still maintaining a fixed t_0) and consider the family of parameterized boundary-value problems

$$\dot{x} = f(x, t, \alpha), \qquad x(t_0) = x^0 \qquad\qquad (PC(x^0, t_0, \alpha))$$

where $f(\ )$ will now be assumed to be continuous and locally Lipschitz in x on some region $D \times \Omega = X \times I \times \Omega$ in $\mathbb{R}^{n+1+p}$, with X an open set in $\mathbb{R}^n$, I an open interval in $\mathbb{R}$, and Ω an open set in $\mathbb{R}^p$. For a given value of α we have a nonparameterized system of the type we have studied in this section, and our previous results ensure the existence of a unique and continuous maximal solution of the boundary-value problem. This solution, however, will generally change with the parameters, as will its maximal interval of existence in D. Hence, we will denote the solution of $(\mathrm{PC}(x^0, t_0, \alpha))$ by $\phi(t, x^0, \alpha)$, and its maximal interval of definition by $J_m(x^0, \alpha)$. Proceeding as before, we can now define the flow of the system as the function $\phi(t, x^0, \alpha): E \longrightarrow X$ defined on the set

$$E = \{(t, x^0, \alpha) \in I \times X \times \Omega; \ t \in J_m(x^0, \alpha)\} \subseteq D \times \Omega \tag{5}$$

such that for each fixed (x^0, α), the function $\phi(\cdot, x^0, \alpha)$ defined in $J_m(x^0, \alpha)$ is the unique maximal solution of $(\mathrm{PC}(x^0, t_0, \alpha))$.

We will use a simple transformation to show that all our previous results on the properties of the flow of nonparameterized systems extend to the present case. Define the vector y and the function $F(\ )$ by

$$y = (x, \alpha) \quad \text{and} \quad F(y, t) = (f(x, t, \alpha), \underline{0})$$

and consider the initial-value problem

$$\dot{y} = F(y, t), \qquad y(0) = y^0 = (x^0, \alpha) \tag{P.y}$$

Notice that (P.y) is simply the system

$$(\dot{x} = f(x, t, \alpha), \dot{\alpha} = 0)$$

with the initial condition

$$(x(0) = x^0, \alpha(0) = \alpha)$$

(i.e., we treat the parameters as additional state variables but set their derivatives to zero so that they remain constant over time).

Then the flow of F is a function of the form

$$\Phi(t, y^0) = (\phi(t, x^0, \alpha), \alpha)$$

where $\phi(t, x^0, \alpha)$ is the flow of f. Because (P.y) is a nonparameterized system, our previous results guarantee that its flow will be nicely behaved provided that F is continuous and locally Lipschitz in y. And because $\phi(t, x^0, \alpha)$ is just a component of $\Phi(t, y^0)$, this function will be continuous. Hence, we have the following result.

Theorem 6.21. Continuity of the flow of a parameterized system. Assume that f(x, α, t) *is continuous and locally Lipschitz in* (x, α) *on some region* D × Ω = X × I × Ω *in* $\mathbb{R}^{n+p+1}$, *with X an open set in* $\mathbb{R}^n$, *I an open interval in* $\mathbb{R}$, *and* Ω *an open set in* $\mathbb{R}^p$. *Then the flow of the continuous system* (CS(α, t)), ϕ(t, x⁰, α):E ⟶ X, *is a continuous function, and its domain of definition*

$$\mathrm{E} = \{(t, x^0, \alpha) \in I \times X \times \Omega; \ t \in J_m(x^0, \alpha)\} \subseteq D \times \Omega$$

is an open set.

Differentiability of the Flow

Our final result in this section shows that if $f(\ )$ is a C^1 function in D, then so is the flow $\phi(t, x^0, \alpha)$ in the set E defined in Theorem 6.21. By the discussion in the preceding section, it is sufficient to consider the case of a nonparameterized system, because any results on the dependence on initial conditions extend automatically to the parameters, provided $f(\ )$ is as smooth in α as in x.

We have already seen that $\phi(\ )$ is a continuously differentiable function of t for given x^0. Hence, it suffices to show that $D_x\phi(t, x^0)$ exists and is a continuous function of (t, x^0). Assuming for now that $D_x\phi(t, x^0)$ is defined, we can begin by guessing what this derivative must look like. Consider the initial-value problem

$$\dot{x} = f(x, t), \qquad x(t_0) = x^0 \qquad\qquad (PC(x^0, t_0))$$

where $f(\ )$ is C^1, and let $\phi(t, x^0)$ be its maximal solution defined on the interval $J_m(x^0, t_0)$. Substituting the solution function back into the differential equation and using D_t and D_x to indicate partial derivatives with respect to t and x, respectively, we have the identity

$$D_t\phi(t, x^0) \equiv f[\phi(t, x^0), t]$$

Differentiating both sides of this identity with respect to x^0, we have

$$D_x D_t\phi(t, x^0) = D_x f[\phi(t, x^0), t]D_x\phi(t, x^0)$$

If we assume further that the order of differentiation can be inverted in the term in the left-hand side of this expression, we have

$$D_t D_x\phi(t, x^0) = D_x f[\phi(t, x^0), t]D_x\phi(t, x^0) \qquad\qquad (6)$$

Hence $D_x\phi(t, x^0)$ satisfies a linear differential equation. This can be better brought out by letting

$$z(t, x^0) = D_x\phi(t, x^0) \quad \text{and} \quad A(t, x^0) = D_x f[\phi(t, x^0), t]$$

and rewriting (6) in the form

$$\dot{z} = A(t, x^0)z \qquad\qquad (7)$$

Notice, moreover, that at time t_0 the solution must go through the given initial condition. Hence, $\phi(t_0, x^0) = x^0$, and therefore

$$z(t_0) = D_x\phi(t_0, x^0) = \mathbf{I} \qquad\qquad (8)$$

where $\mathbf{I}$ is the identity matrix. Hence, our candidate for $D_x\phi(t, x^0)$ is the unique solution $z(t)$ of a boundary-value problem involving a parameterized linear system. By Problem 6.15, the solution $z(t, x^0)$ to this linear problem is defined whenever $A(t, x^0)$ is defined, that is, on the whole interval $J_m(x^0, t_0)$, and by Theorem 6.21, $z(t, x^0)$ is continuous in t and x^0. Hence, $D_x\phi(t, x^0) = z(t, x^0)$ is continuous, and it follows that $\phi(\ )$ is a continuously differentiable function of x^0.

Notice that in the general case, where f maps $\mathbb{R}^n$ into $\mathbb{R}^n$, $z = D_x\phi(\ )$ is an $n \times n$ matrix. This poses no particular problem, because we can think of z as a vector in $\mathbb{R}^{n \times n}$. Alternatively, we can bring (7) back to a more familiar dimension by working with the differential of $\phi(\ )$, rather than with its derivative. Let h be an arbitrary vector in $\mathbb{R}^n$, and define $y \in \mathbb{R}^n$ by $y = zh$. Then $\dot{y} = \dot{z}h = Azh = Ay$, and we obtain a linear system in n variables. Notice that now the initial condition will be $y(t_0) = z(t_0)h = \mathbf{I}h = h$.

We will now show that the solution of the *variational problem* (7) is indeed the derivative of the flow with respect to x^0. To simplify things somewhat, we will consider the case of the autonomous system (CS), $\dot{x} = f(x)$.

Theorem 6.22. Differentiability of the flow. *Let* $f(x, \alpha)$ *be* C^1 *in the open set* $X \times \Omega$ *in* $\mathbb{R}^{n+p}$, *and let*

$$E = \{(t, x^0, \alpha) \in \mathbb{R} \times X \times \Omega; \ t \in J_m(x^0, \alpha)\}$$

Then the flow of $f(\ )$, $\phi(t, x^0, \alpha):E \longrightarrow X$, *is a* C^1 *function.*

Proof. We will later make use of the following fact. Let $f(\ )$ be a C^1 function; then we have

$$f(y) - f(x) = Df(x)(y - x) + R(y, x) \tag{1}$$

by Taylor's theorem, where

$$\frac{R(y, x)}{|y - x|} \to 0 \quad \text{as} \quad y \to x$$

This means that given any $\varepsilon > 0$, there exists some $\delta > 0$ such that

$$|R(y, x)| \le \varepsilon |y - x| \tag{2}$$

for all y such that $|y - x| \le \delta$. Notice that, in general, the value of δ will depend on x. If we restrict x to a compact set C, however, given any ε we can find a δ that will work for all x in C (by the same argument as in the proof of Theorem 8.24 in Chapter 2). Hence, $R(y, x)/|y - x| \to 0$ as $y \to x$ *uniformly* for x in the compact set C.

As noted, it suffices to consider the case of the nonparameterized system (CS), $\dot{x} = f(x)$. Letting $t_0 = 0$ for convenience, let $\phi(t, x^0)$ and $\phi(t, x^0 + h)$ be the maximal solutions of (CS) going through the points x^0 and $x^0 + h$, respectively, at time zero. Let $J_m(x^0)$ be the (maximal) interval of definition of the first of these functions, and fix some compact interval $J_b = [0, b]$ contained in $J_m(x^0)$. Let $z(t)$ be the solution of the variational problem

$$\dot{z} = D_x\phi(t, x^0)z, \qquad z(0) = \frac{\partial\phi(0, x^0)}{\partial x^0} = \frac{\partial x^0}{\partial x^0} = 1 \qquad \text{(PV)}$$

As noted in the discussion prior to the statement of the theorem, $z(t)$ will be defined on the entire set $J_m(x^0)$ and therefore in all of J_b.

By Lemma 6.1, we have, for each $t \in J_b$,

$$\phi(t, x^0) = x^0 + \int_0^t f(\phi(s, x^0))\, ds$$

$$\phi(t, x^0 + h) = x^0 + h + \int_0^t f(\phi(s, x^0 + h))\, ds$$

$$z(t) = 1 + \int_0^t Df(x_s)z(s)\, ds \qquad (3)$$

where, for short, we write $Df(x_s)$ for $Df(\phi(s, x^0))$. Using these expressions, we have

$$g(t) \equiv |\phi(t, x^0 + h) - \phi(t, x^0) - z(t)h|$$

$$= \left|\int_0^t [f(\phi(s, x^0 + h)) - f(\phi(s, x^0)) - Df(x_s)z(s)h]\, ds\right|$$

$$\leq \int_0^t |f(\phi(s, x^0 + h)) - f(\phi(s, x^0)) - Df(x_s)z(s)h|\, ds$$

$$= \int_0^t |Df(x_s)[\phi(s, x^0 + h) - \phi(s, x^0) - z(s)h]|\, ds$$

$$+ \int_0^t |R(\phi(s, x^0 + h), \phi(s, x^0))|\, ds \qquad (4)$$

for each $t \in J_b$, where the last equality follows by applying Taylor's theorem to $f(\phi(s, x^0 + h)) - f(\phi(s, x^0))$ (see equation (1)), and $R(\cdot, \cdot)$ is the Taylor remainder.

Now, let

$$N = \max\{\|Df(x_s)\|;\ s \in J_b\}$$

where $\|\cdot\|$ denotes the norm of the linear operator Df (in fact, this could be replaced by the absolute value, because we are in the scalar case), and N exists because J_b is a compact set and $\|Df(x_s)\| = \|Df(\phi(s, x^0))\|$ is a continuous function of s (because $f(\ )$ is C^1 and $\phi(\ )$ is continuous). We have, then,

$$\int_0^t |Df(x_s)[\phi(s, x^0 + h) - \phi(s, x^0) - z(s)h]|\, ds$$

$$\leq \int_0^t \|Df(x_s)\|\,|\phi(s, x^0 + h) - \phi(s, x^0) - z(s)h|\, ds$$

$$\leq N\int_0^t |\phi(s, x^0 + h) - \phi(s, x^0) - z(s)h|\, ds \leq N\int_0^t g(s)\, ds \qquad (5)$$

Substituting this expression in (4), and recalling the definition of $g(\ )$,

$$g(t) \leq N\int_0^t g(s)\, ds + \int_0^t |R(\phi(s, x^0 + h), \phi(s, x^0))|\, ds \qquad (6)$$

for all $t \in J_b$.

To apply Gronwall's lemma to $g(\ )$, we need to show that the integral of the Taylor error terms is bounded. Fix some arbitrary $\varepsilon > 0$ and observe that the set $\phi(J_b, x^0)$ is compact because it is the continuous image of a compact interval. Hence,

$$\frac{R[\phi(s, x^0), \phi(s, x^0 + h)]}{|\phi(s, x^0 + h) - \phi(s, x^0)|} \to 0 \quad \text{as } |\phi(s, x^0 + h) - \phi(s, x^0)| \to 0$$

uniformly for $\phi(s, x^0)$ in the compact set $\phi(J_b, x^0)$ (i.e., for all $s \in J_b$). Hence, there is some number $\delta_{0\varepsilon}$ (valid for all $s \in J_b$) such that

$$|R[\phi(s, x^0), \phi(s, x^0 + h)]| \le \varepsilon |\phi(s, x^0 + h) - \phi(s, x^0)| \quad \text{when}$$
$$|\phi(s, x^0 + h) - \phi(s, x^0)| \le \delta_{0\varepsilon} \text{ and } s \in J_b \tag{7}$$

Now, by Theorem 6.19 there exists some $\delta_{1\varepsilon} > 0$ and some positive constant K such that for all h, with $|h| < \delta_{1\varepsilon}$, we have

$$|\phi(s, x^0 + h) - \phi(s, x^0)| \le |h| e^{Ks} \le |h| e^{Kb} < \delta_{1\varepsilon} e^{Kb}$$

for all $s \in J_b$. Clearly, we can choose $\delta_{1\varepsilon}$ small enough that

$$|\phi(s, x^0 + h) - \phi(s, x^0)| \le |h| e^{Kb} < \delta_{0\varepsilon} \tag{8}$$

Assume now that $|h| < \delta_{1\varepsilon}$. Then, by (8), we have $|\phi(s, x^0 + h) - \phi(s, x^0)| < \delta_{0\varepsilon}$, so it follows by (7) and (8) that

$$|R[\phi(s, x^0), \phi(s, x^0 + h)]| \le \varepsilon |\phi(s, x^0 + h) - \phi(s, x^0)| \le \varepsilon |h| e^{Kb}$$

for all $s \in J_b$. Integrating this expression between zero and $t \in J_b$,

$$\int_0^t |R(\phi(s, x^0 + h), \phi(s, x^0))| \, ds \le \int_0^t \varepsilon |h| e^{Kb} \, ds = \varepsilon t |h| e^{Kb} \le \varepsilon b |h| e^{Kb}$$

Substituting this expression into (6),

$$g(t) \le N \int_0^t g(s) \, ds + \varepsilon b |h| e^{Kb} \tag{9}$$

Gronwall's lemma now yields

$$g(t) \le \varepsilon b |h| e^{Kb} e^{Nt} \le \varepsilon b |h| e^{(K+N)b} \tag{10}$$

for any $t \in J_b$. Dividing through by $|h|$ and recalling the definition of $g(t)$ in (4), we have

$$\frac{g(t)}{|h|} = \frac{|\phi(t, x^0 + h) - \phi(t, x^0) - z(t)h|}{|h|} \le \varepsilon b e^{(K+N)b}$$

for all $t \in J_b$. Because ε is an arbitrary positive number, it follows that

$$\lim_{|h| \to 0} \frac{|\phi(t, x^0 + h) - \phi(t, x^0) - z(t)h|}{|h|} = 0$$

uniformly for $t \in J_b$. Hence, we have shown that, as claimed,[8] the solution of the variational problem (PV) is the partial derivative of the flow, that is,

$$z(t, x^0) = D_x \phi(t, x^0)$$

Because $z(t, x^0)$ is a continuous function defined on the entire interval J_b, moreover, so is $D_x \phi(t, x^0)$, and this implies that $\phi(\ )$ is C^1 on $J_b = [0, b]$. Because b is an arbitrary point of $J_m(x^0)$, finally, we conclude that $\phi(\ )$ is C^1 on its entire domain. $\qquad \square$

Our next result shows that the flow is as smooth as the vector field $f(\ )$.

Theorem 6.23. Let $f(x, \alpha)$ *be* C^r *(with* $1 \le r \le \infty$*) in the open set* $D \times \Omega$ *in* $\mathbb{R}^{n+p}$. *Then the flow of* $f(\ )$, $\phi(t, x^0, \alpha) : E \longrightarrow X$, *is a* C^r *function.*

Proof. As before, it suffices to consider the case of the nonparameterized system (CS), $\dot{x} = f(x)$. We proceed by induction on r. By the preceding theorem, the result holds for $r = 1$. Assume now that f is C^r and that if F is a C^{r-1} function, then the flow of the system $\dot{y} = F(y)$ is C^{r-1}. Consider the system formed by (CS) and its variational equation

$$\dot{z} = Df(x)z \qquad \qquad \text{(V)}$$

Letting $y = (x, z)$ and $F(y) = F(x, z) = (f(x), Df(x)z)$, this system can be written

$$\dot{y} = F(y) \qquad \qquad \text{(P.}y)$$

Notice that F is a C^{r-1} function, because its first component, $f(\ )$, is C^r in x, and its second component, $Df(x)z$, is C^{r-1} in x and linear (and therefore C^∞) in z. It follows (by the induction assumption) that the flow of F, $\Phi(t, y)$, is C^{r-1}. But notice that $\Phi(\ )$ is of the form

$$\Phi(t, y^0) = \Phi(t, x^0, z^0) = (\phi(t, x^0), D_x\phi(t, x^0))$$

because the second component of (P.y) is the variational equation of (CS). Hence, $D_x\phi(t, x^0)$ is C^{r-1}, and it follows that $\phi(t, x^0)$ is C^r in x. Moreover, $D_t\phi(t, x^0)$ is C^{r-1}, because

$$D_t\phi(t, x^0) = f(\phi(t, x^0))$$

and both $f(\ )$ and $\phi(t, x)$ are C^{r-1} or better. Hence, $\phi(t, x^0)$ is C^r, because both of its partial derivatives are C^{r-1}. This proves the theorem. $\qquad \square$

Bibliography

Arnold, V. 1990. *Ordinary Differential Equations.* Massachusetts Institute of Technology Press.

Arrowsmith, D., and Place, C. 1990. *An Introduction to Dynamical Systems.* Cambridge University Press.

Azariadis, C., and de la Fuente, A. 1993. Discrete Dynamical Systems. Part I. In: *Intertemporal Macroeconomics,* pp. 1–170. Oxford: Blackwell.

Boyce, W., and DiPrima, R. 1977. *Elementary Differential Equations,* 3rd ed. New York: Wiley.

Brauer, F., and Nohel, J. 1969. *The Qualitative Theory of Ordinary Differential Equations, An Introduction.* New York: Dover.

Guzmán, M. 1980. *Ecuaciones Diferenciales Ordinarias. Teoría de Estabilidad y Control.* Madrid: Alhambra.

Hale, J., and Koçak, H. 1991. *Dynamics and Bifurcations.* Berlin: Springer-Verlag.

Hirsch, M., and Smale, S. 1974. *Differential Equations, Dynamical Systems and Linear Algebra.* San Diego: Academic Press.

Lang, S. 1983. *Undergraduate Analysis. Undergraduate Texts in Mathematics.* Berlin: Springer-Verlag.

Lelong-Ferrand, J., and Aurnadies, J. M. 1977. *Cours de Mathématiques. Tome 4: Equations Différentielles, Integrales Multiples.* Paris: Dunod Université.

Obstfeld, M. 1980. Primer on Differential Equations. Mimeograph, Department of Economics, Columbia University.

Oniki, H. 1973. Comparative Dynamics (Sensitivity Analysis) in Optimal Control Theory. *Journal of Economic Theory* 6(3):265–83.

Perko, L. 1991. *Differential Equations and Dynamical Systems. Texts in Applied Mathematics,* no. 7. Berlin: Springer-Verlag.

Simmons, G. 1972. *Differential Equations with Applications and Historical Notes.* New York: McGraw-Hill.

Sotomayor, J. 1979. *Lições de Equações Diferenciais Ordinárias.* Rio de Janeiro: Instituto de Matemática Pura e Aplicada.

Sydsaeter, K. 1981 *Topics in Mathematical Analysis for Economists.* San Diego: Academic Press.

Wiggins, S. 1990. *Introduction to Applied Nonlinear Dynamical Systems and Chaos. Texts in Applied Mathematics,* no. 2. Berlin: Springer-Verlag.

Notes

1 To find the steady state of the system, we set $\dot{x} = 0$ in (N) and solve for x.

2 All that we have done has been to reindex the family of solutions of (N) by $x(0)$, instead of c, but we still have to specify which trajectory of the system we want. This can be done by choosing the value of $x(0)$ directly (i.e., by imposing an initial condition in the strict sense of the term) or by specifying some other type of boundary condition, in which case we have to solve for the value of $x(0)$. See Chapter 11 for some examples.

3 To find the steady state of (ND), we suppress the time subindices and solve for x:

$$(1-a)x = b \Rightarrow \bar{x} = \frac{b}{1-a} \quad \text{provided } a \neq 1$$

4 This can be done for an arbitrary time s. When $t = s$, we have $x_s = \bar{x} + ca^s$. Solving for c and substituting in (GS), we obtain $x_t = \bar{x} + (x_s - \bar{x})a^{t-s}$. If x_s is known, this expression gives the particular solution that goes through this point at time s. Otherwise, x_s is undetermined, and we just have another equivalent form of the general solution.

5 Notice that

if $g'(s)$ changes sign in the interval, then $m_\varepsilon = 0$, and therefore $|g(x)| \geq 0 = m_\varepsilon |x|$

if $g'(s) > 0$ everywhere in the interval, then $|g(x)| = \int_0^x g'(s)\, ds \geq m_\varepsilon |x|$, and

if $g'(s) < 0$ everywhere in the interval, then $|g(x)| = \int_0^x -g'(s)\, ds \geq m_\varepsilon |x|$.

6 In Section 2 of Chapter 11 we will make use of the forward solution for an equation that describes the evolution of the price of a share of stock. The reason for the terms "fundamental solution" and "bubble term" will then become clear.

7 Think of t_1 and t_2 as terms of a sequence $\{t_n\}$ converging to b. Then (2) implies that $\{\phi(t_n)\}$ is Cauchy, and convergence follows by completeness.

8 See the definition of "derivative" in Section 3 of Chapter 4.

10

Dynamical Systems. II: Higher Dimensions

In this chapter we will study dynamical systems of dimension 2 or higher, that is, those defined by systems of two or more differential equations in several variables. Sections 1–3 will deal with linear systems. In the remainder of the chapter we will discuss some techniques for analyzing nonlinear autonomous systems.

1. Some General Results on Linear Systems

Our discussion of linear systems will concentrate on the solution of systems with constant coefficients. We begin, however, by listing some important results of the general theory of linear dynamical systems that will be useful later. Consider a first-order homogeneous system of the form

$$\dot{x} = A(t)x \qquad \text{(CH)}$$

where the coefficients of the $n \times n$ matrix A can be arbitrary functions of time defined on some interval of the real line. The discussion will be in terms of continuous-time systems, but it is easily shown that the results also hold for discrete systems.

Our first result concerns the algebraic structure of the space of solutions of (CH).

Theorem 1.1. The set

$$S^H = \{x(t), t \in I; \dot{x}(t) = A(t)x(t) \, \forall \, t \in I\}$$

of solutions of (CH) is a vector space of dimension n.

A set $F = \{x^1(t), \ldots, x^n(t)\}$ of n linearly independent solutions of (CH),[1] that is, a basis of S^H, is called a *fundamental set of solutions* of (CH), and the matrix

$$\Psi(t) = [x^1(t), \ldots, x^n(t)]$$

is a *fundamental matrix* for the system.

Because S^H is a vector space and F is a basis for it, given an arbitrary solution $y(t)$ of (CH), we can write it precisely in one way as a linear combination of $x^1(t), \ldots, x^n(t)$; that is, there exist unique scalars $c_1, \ldots, c_n$ such that

$$y(t) = \sum_{i=1}^{n} c_i x^i(t) \tag{1}$$

Assigning different values to the vector $c = (c_1, \ldots, c_n)$, we can recover all the solutions of the system. Hence, we can think of (1) as the general solution of (CH). Notice that in order to construct the general solution of the system it suffices to find a fundamental set of solutions, that is, a family of n linearly independent solutions of (CH).

Once we have found a fundamental set of solutions of (CH), the solution of any initial-value problem can be easily obtained. The most compact way to write such solution is in terms of a fundamental matrix. As we have seen, the general solution of (CH) can be written

$$x^g(t) = \sum_{i=1}^{n} c_i x^i(t) = \Psi(t)c$$

Next, suppose we are given the boundary condition

$$x(t_0) = x^0$$

In order to find the value of c that corresponds to this boundary condition, we observe that the solution we seek satisfies

$$x(t_0) = \Psi(t_0)c = x^0$$

Solving this equation for c,

$$c = [\Psi(t_0)]^{-1} x^0$$

and substituting the result in the general solution, we obtain the solution of the given boundary-value problem:

$$x(t) = \Psi(t)[\Psi(t_0)]^{-1} x^0$$

Next we turn to the nonhomogeneous first-order system

$$\dot{x} = A(t)x + b(t) \tag{CN}$$

and consider its solution space:

$$S^N = \{x(t), t \in I; \dot{x}(t) = A(t)x(t) + b(t) \ \forall \ t \in I\}$$

It is easy to show that S^N is an affine space of dimension n "parallel" to S^H. That is, S^N is a translation of S^H, and the translation factor is an arbitrary particular solution $x^P(t)$ of (CN). Hence, the general solution of the nonho-

mogeneous continuous system (CN) is the sum of the general solution of
the homogeneous system (CH) and an arbitrary particular solution of (CN).
We can therefore write

$$x^N(t) = x^H(t) + x^P(t)$$

where the general solution of the homogeneous system, $x^H(t)$, is sometimes
called the *complementary function*.

2. Solution of Linear Systems with Constant Coefficients

In this section we will study linear systems with constant coefficients, that is,
systems of the form

$$\dot{x} = Ax + b \Leftrightarrow \begin{bmatrix} \dot{x}_1 \\ \dots \\ \dot{x}_n \end{bmatrix} = \begin{bmatrix} a_{11} & \dots\dots & a_{1n} \\ \dots & \dots\dots & \dots \\ a_{n1} & \dots\dots & a_{nn} \end{bmatrix} \begin{bmatrix} x_1 \\ \dots \\ x_n \end{bmatrix} + \begin{bmatrix} b_1 \\ \dots \\ b_n \end{bmatrix} \qquad \text{(CN)}$$

in continuous time, or

$$x_{t+1} = Ax_t + b \Leftrightarrow \begin{bmatrix} x_{t+1}^1 \\ \dots \\ x_{t+1}^n \end{bmatrix} = \begin{bmatrix} a_{11} & \dots\dots & a_{1n} \\ \dots & \dots\dots & \dots \\ a_{n1} & \dots\dots & a_{nn} \end{bmatrix} \begin{bmatrix} x_t^1 \\ \dots \\ x_t^n \end{bmatrix} + \begin{bmatrix} b_1 \\ \dots \\ b_n \end{bmatrix} \qquad \text{(DN)}$$

in discrete time.

We have seen that the general solution of a nonhomogeneous system can
be written as the sum of the general solution of the corresponding homogeneous system and any particular solution of the nonhomogeneous system.
Hence, we start by solving the homogeneous system

$$\dot{x} = Ax \qquad \text{(CH)}$$

or

$$x_{t+1} = Ax_t \qquad \text{(DH)}$$

Having done this, the general solution of the nonhomogeneous system is
easily completed by computing its stationary solution or steady state.

In the following section we will develop a solution procedure for homogeneous systems that will allow us to exploit our knowledge of the general
solution to the scalar linear equation. The method works by reducing (CH)
or (DH) to an equivalent diagonal or uncoupled system through an appropriate change of variables. A diagonal system is simply a set of independent
first-order linear equations that we already know how to solve. Given its
solution, it is easy to recover that of the original system by applying the
inverse of the diagonalizing transformation. In Sections 2(b) and 2(c) we will
discuss the complications that arise when the coefficient matrix A has
complex eigenvalues or cannot be diagonalized. In the remainder of Section

2 we will analyze the nonhomogeneous case and discuss the stability of linear systems.

(a) Solution by Diagonalization

Consider the discrete-time homogeneous system

$$x_{t+1} = Ax_t \tag{DH}$$

where A is an $n \times n$ matrix of real numbers, and x is a vector in $\mathbb{R}^n$. For concreteness, we will often work with the two-dimensional or "planar" system:

$$\begin{bmatrix} x_{t+1}^1 \\ x_{t+1}^2 \end{bmatrix} = \begin{bmatrix} a_{11} & a_{12} \\ a_{21} & a_{22} \end{bmatrix} \begin{bmatrix} x_t^1 \\ x_t^2 \end{bmatrix} \tag{DH2}$$

Notice that there is a special case of (DH2) that we already know how to solve. If A is a diagonal matrix, that is, if $a_{12} = a_{21} = 0$, then (DH2) is simply a set of two independent equations in one variable,

$$x_{t+1}^1 = a_{11}x_t^1 \quad \text{and} \quad x_{t+1}^2 = a_{22}x_t^2$$

and their general solutions are of the form

$$x_t^1 = c_1 a_{11}^t \quad \text{and} \quad x_t^2 = c_2 a_{22}^t$$

where c_1 and c_2 are arbitrary constants.

In the general case, A is not a diagonal matrix. In many cases, however, we can find a change of coordinates that will diagonalize or "uncouple" the system. In particular, recall from Chapter 3 that if A has no repeated eigenvalues, then its eigenvectors $e_1, \ldots, e_n$ are all linearly independent, and the matrix $E = [e_1, \ldots, e_n]$ can be used to diagonalize A. That is, $E^{-1}AE = \Lambda$, where $\Lambda = \text{diag}(\lambda_1, \ldots, \lambda_n)$ is the matrix with the eigenvalues of A in the principal, diagonal, and zeros elsewhere.

Using this result, we can now derive a formula for the general solution of (DH) when the coefficient matrix A has no repeated eigenvalues. Premultiplying both sides of

$$x_{t+1} = Ax_t \tag{DH}$$

by the inverse of the matrix of eigenvectors, E (observe that $EE^{-1} = I$),

$$E^{-1}x_{t+1} = E^{-1}A(EE^{-1})x_t = (E^{-1}AE)(E^{-1}x_t)$$

Using the fact that $E^{-1}AE = \Lambda$, we have

$$E^{-1}x_{t+1} = \Lambda(E^{-1}x_t)$$

Finally, defining the transformed variables

$$y_t = E^{-1}x_t$$

we can rewrite the equation in the form

$$y_{t+1} = \Lambda y_t$$

In this way, we obtain a diagonal or uncoupled system in the transformed variables y_t whose coefficients are the eigenvalues of the coefficient matrix of the original system. The general solution of this system, denoted by y_t^h, is easy to calculate, as we will soon see. Given $y_t^h(c)$, we can recover the general solution of the original system simply by applying the inverse of the diagonalizing transformation, that is, by premultiplying y_t^h by the matrix formed by the eigenvectors of A:

$$x_t^h = E y_t^h$$

For example, the planar system

$$\begin{bmatrix} x_{t+1}^1 \\ x_{t+1}^2 \end{bmatrix} = \begin{bmatrix} a_{11} & a_{12} \\ a_{21} & a_{22} \end{bmatrix} \begin{bmatrix} x_t^1 \\ x_t^2 \end{bmatrix} \tag{DH2}$$

reduces, after diagonalization, to two independent equations,

$$y_{t+1}^1 = \lambda_1 y_t^1 \quad \text{and} \quad y_{t+1}^2 = \lambda_2 y_t^2 \tag{1}$$

where

$$y = (y^1, y^2) = E^{-1} x$$

The general solution of (1) can be written

$$y_t^h(c) = \begin{bmatrix} y_t^1 \\ y_t^2 \end{bmatrix} = \begin{bmatrix} c_1 \lambda_1^t \\ c_2 \lambda_2^t \end{bmatrix} \tag{2}$$

in terms of the transformed variables, and

$$\begin{bmatrix} x_t^1 \\ x_t^2 \end{bmatrix} = x_t^h(c) = E y_t^h(c) = \begin{bmatrix} e_{11} & e_{21} \\ e_{12} & e_{22} \end{bmatrix} \begin{bmatrix} c_1 \lambda_1^t \\ c_2 \lambda_2^t \end{bmatrix} = \begin{bmatrix} c_1 e_{11} \lambda_1^t + c_2 e_{21} \lambda_2^t \\ c_1 e_{12} \lambda_1^t + c_2 e_{22} \lambda_2^t \end{bmatrix}$$

in terms of the original variables. As usual, $c = (c_1, c_2)^T$ is a vector of arbitrary constants, and the choice of a value for c is equivalent to the specification of a boundary condition.

The generalization for systems of arbitrary dimension n is straightforward. The general solution of $y_{t+1} = \Lambda y_t$ is of the form

$$y_t = \Lambda^t c$$

where $\Lambda^t = \text{diag}(\lambda_1^t, \ldots, \lambda_n^t)$, and c is a column vector of arbitrary constants. Premultiplying by E, the general solution of the original system is given by

$$x_t^h(c) = E y_t^h(c) = E \Lambda^t c \tag{3}$$

Operating in (3), the general solution can be written as shown in the following theorem, which summarizes our results.

Theorem 2.1. Let A *be a real* n × n *matrix with no repeated eigenvalues. Then the jth component of the general solution of the system* $x_{t+1} = Ax_t$ *can be written*

$$x_{jt}^h(c) = \sum_{i=1}^{n} c_i e_{ij} \lambda_i^t$$

where e_{ij} *is the jth component of the eigenvector* e_i *associated with the eigenvalue* λ_i.

Proceeding in a similar fashion, we obtain an analogous result for the homogeneous linear system in continuous time,

$$\dot{x} = Ax \qquad \text{(CH)}$$

The general solution of (CH) is of the form

$$x^h(t; c) = Ee^{\Lambda t}c \qquad (4)$$

where

$$e^{\Lambda t} = \begin{bmatrix} \exp(\lambda_1 t) & \cdots & 0 \\ \cdots & \cdots & \cdots \\ 0 & \cdots & \exp(\lambda_n t) \end{bmatrix}$$

Theorem 2.2. Let A *be a real* n × n *matrix with no repeated eigenvalues. Then the jth component of the general solution of the system (CH),* $\dot{x} = Ax$, *can be written*

$$x_j^h(t; c) = \sum_{i=1}^{n} c_i e_{ij} \exp(\lambda_i t)$$

where e_{ij} *is the jth component of the eigenvector* e_i *associated with the eigenvalue* λ_i.

Problem 2.3 will ask the reader to derive this result using a diagonalization procedure. But first we give an alternative proof of the theorem that may be instructive.

Proof. We seek solutions of the system (CH), $\dot{x} = Ax$, of the form

$$x(t) = e^{\alpha t}z \qquad (1)$$

where z is a vector, and α a scalar. For a function of the form (1) to be a solution of the system, we will have to impose certain restrictions on z and α. In particular, we want (1) to satisfy equation (CH), that is,

$$[\dot{x}(t) =] \alpha e^{\alpha t}z = e^{\alpha t}Az [= Ax(t)]$$

Dividing both sides by $e^{\alpha} \neq 0$ and rearranging, we have

$$(A - \alpha I)z = \underline{0}$$

where I is the identity matrix. Observe that this is precisely the condition that must be satisfied by the eigenvalues and eigenvectors of A. Hence, the vector-valued function $x(t) = ze^{\alpha t}$ is a solution of (CH) if α is an eigenvalue of A and z is a corresponding eigenvector. Occasionally we will refer to solutions of this form as *elementary solutions* of (CH).

Hence, the functions of the form

$$x^i(t) = \left[x_1^i(t), \ldots, x_n^i(t)\right]^T = \exp(\lambda_i t)e_i \qquad (2)$$

are solutions of (CH). Moreover, we have assumed that the eigenvalues λ_1, $\ldots$, λ_n are all distinct. Because this guarantees the linear independence of the eigenvectors, the functions $\{x^i(t); i = 1, \ldots, n\}$ are linearly independent and therefore constitute a fundamental set of solutions. Thus, we can write the general solution of (CH) in the form given in the theorem,

$$x^h(t; c) = \sum_{i=1}^n c_i \exp(\lambda_i t)e_i \qquad \square$$

Problem 2.3. Derive equation (4) by diagonalizing the coefficient matrix of (CH).

(b) Imaginary Eigenvalues

Let A be a real matrix with no repeated eigenvalues. We have just seen that the functions of the form $x^i(t) = \exp(\lambda_i t)e_i$ form a basis for the solution space of the homogeneous system

$$\dot{x} = Ax \qquad \text{(CH)}$$

Hence, the general solution of (CH) can be written in the form

$$x^h(t; c) = \sum_{i=1}^n c_i \exp(\lambda_i t)e_i \qquad \text{(G.S)}$$

If A has only real eigenvalues, its eigenvectors will have real components, and by assigning real values to the constants c_i in (G.S), we can obtain all the real-valued solutions of the system. If the system has some complex roots, (G.S) remains valid, but its usefulness is limited, as this expression now describes a family of complex-valued functions. Although all these functions are indeed solutions of the system, typically we are interested only in those that are real-valued. Hence, we would like to construct a different basis for the solution space, one that will allow us to recover the real solutions of the system by assigning real values to the arbitrary constants.

This turns out to be fairly easy to do. If A is a matrix with real entries, its complex eigenvalues and eigenvectors come in conjugate pairs, and, therefore, so do the functions $x^i(t) = \exp(\lambda_i t)e_i$ that are still solutions of (1). That is, if $x^i(t) = u(t) + iv(t)$ is a solution of (CH), then so is the function

$x^j(t) = u(t) - iv(t)$. It is possible to show, moreover, that the real functions $u(t)$ and $v(t)$ are themselves solutions of (CH) and that they can be used, together with any real-valued elementary solutions of the system, $\exp(\lambda_i t)e_i$, to form a real-valued basis for the solution space of the system.

For the sake of concreteness, let us assume that the first two eigenvalues of the coefficient matrix, λ_1 and λ_2, are complex, and the rest, $\lambda_3, \ldots, \lambda_m$, are real numbers. If A has only real coefficients, then λ_1 and λ_2 are conjugates, that is,

$$\lambda_1 = \alpha + i\mu \quad \text{and} \quad \lambda_2 = \alpha - i\mu$$

and the same is true of the corresponding eigenvectors, which can be written

$$e_1 = d + if \quad \text{and} \quad e_2 = d - if$$

where d and f are vectors in $\mathbb{R}^n$. The corresponding elementary solutions are the functions

$$x^1(t) = \exp(\lambda_1 t)e_1 \quad \text{and} \quad x^2(t) = \exp(\lambda_2 t)e_2$$

Let us rewrite $x^1(t)$ in a more convenient form.[2] We have

$$\begin{aligned} x^1(t) &= \exp(\lambda_1 t)e_1 = e^{(\alpha+i\mu)t}(d+if) = e^{\alpha t}(\cos\mu t + i\sin\mu t)(d+if) \\ &= e^{\alpha t}\{d\cos\mu t + if\cos\mu t + id\sin\mu t + i^2 f\sin\mu t\} \\ &= e^{\alpha t}(d\cos\mu t - f\sin\mu t) + ie^{\alpha t}(f\cos\mu t + d\sin\mu t) \end{aligned}$$

Proceeding in the same way,

$$x^2(t) = \exp(\lambda_2 t)e_2 = e^{\alpha t}(d\cos\mu t - f\sin\mu t) - ie^{\alpha t}(f\cos\mu t + d\sin\mu t)$$

We now define the functions

$$u(t) = e^{\alpha t}(d\cos\mu t - f\sin\mu t) \quad \text{and} \quad v(t) = e^{\alpha t}(f\cos\mu t + d\sin\mu t)$$

and write the elementary solutions in the form

$$x^1(t) = u(t) + iv(t) \quad \text{and} \quad x^2(t) = u(t) - iv(t)$$

We know that any linear combination of solutions of (CH) is also a solution of (CH). Therefore,

$$\begin{aligned} y(t; \kappa_1, \kappa_2) &= \kappa_1 x^1(t) + \kappa_2 x^2(t) = \kappa_1[u(t) + iv(t)] + \kappa_2[u(t) - iv(t)] \\ &= (\kappa_1 + \kappa_2)u(t) + i(\kappa_1 - \kappa_2)v(t) \end{aligned}$$

is also a solution for any (complex) scalars κ_1 and κ_2. In particular, we can put

$$y(t; 1/2, 1/2) = u(t) \quad \text{and} \quad y(t; -i/2, i/2) = v(t)$$

to conclude that $u(t)$ and $v(t)$ are also solutions of (CH). Moreover, it can be shown that $u(\ )$ and $v(\ )$ are linearly independent of each other and the other elementary solutions. Hence, instead of $x^1(t)$ and $x^2(t)$, we can use $u(t)$ and $v(t)$ to complete the fundamental set of solutions. Then we can write the general solution of the system in the form

$$x^h(t;c) = c_1 u(t) + c_2 v(t) + \sum_{i=3}^{n} c_i \exp(\lambda_i t) e_i$$
$$= c_1 e^{\alpha t}(d \cos \mu t - f \sin \mu t) + c_2 e^{\alpha t}(f \cos \mu t + d \sin \mu t) + \sum_{i=3}^{n} c_i \exp(\lambda_i t) e_i$$
$$(5)$$

For the case of the discrete system $x_{t+1} = A x_t$, a similar procedure can be used. Assume that the first eigenvalues λ_1 and λ_2 of the coefficient matrix are complex,

$$\lambda_1 = \alpha + i\mu = r(\cos \theta + i \sin \theta), \qquad \lambda_2 = \alpha - i\mu = r(\cos \theta - i \sin \theta)$$

where r is the common modulus of λ_1 and λ_2, θ is the angle formed by the vector λ_1 in the complex plane and the horizontal axis (see Section 7 of Chapter 1), and the rest, $\lambda_3, \ldots, \lambda_n$, are real. Then the general solution can be written in terms of a real basis, as follows:

$$x_t^h(c) = c_1 u(t) + c_2 v(t) + \sum_{i=3}^{n} c_i \lambda_i^t e_i$$
$$= c_1 r^t(d \cos \theta t - f \sin \theta t) + c_2 r^t(f \cos \theta t + d \sin \theta t) + \sum_{i=3}^{n} c_i \lambda_i^t e_i \quad (6)$$

Problem 2.4. Derive equation (6).

(c) Repeated Eigenvalues

We now consider what happens when the coefficient matrix of the homogeneous linear system has some repeated eigenvalues. If ξ is an eigenvalue of multiplicity m (i.e., it is repeated m times), then associated with it there is a set of up to m (but possibly fewer) linearly independent eigenvectors. If we cannot find a full set of m linearly independent characteristic vectors, the coefficient matrix will not be diagonalizable, and the procedure we have used thus far will not work.

From a slightly different perspective, the problem is that we may not have enough linearly independent elementary solutions of the form $\exp(\lambda_i t) e_i$ to complete a basis of the solution space. To complete a fundamental set of solutions, we will have to search for functions of a different form. It turns out that the additional solutions we need can be found among a family of functions of a relatively simple form, each containing the product of a polynomial in t and an exponential.

In particular, assume that the coefficient matrix A has k distinct roots $\mu_1, \ldots, \mu_k$, with multiplicities $m_1, \ldots, m_k$, respectively. Then the solutions of the system (CH), $\dot{x} = Ax$, will be of the form

$$x(t) = \sum_{i=1}^{k} P_i(t)\exp(\mu_i t) = \sum_{i=1}^{k}\sum_{j=1}^{m_i} p_{ij}t^{j-1}\exp(\mu_i t) \tag{7}$$

where $P_i(t)$ is a polynomial in t of order $k-1$ (with vector-valued coefficients). We observe, however, that not all functions of the form (7) are solutions of (CH). Additional restrictions must be placed on the coefficients p_{ij} in order for $x(t)$ to be a solution of the system, as shown in the following problem.

Problem 2.5. Given the linear system (CH), $\dot{x} = Ax$, assume that there is one eigenvalue ξ of multiplicity 2 ($\lambda_1 = \lambda_2 = \xi$), and the rest of the eigenvalues $\lambda_3, \ldots, \lambda_n$ of A are all different from each other. Associated with the repeated eigenvalue we have two elementary solutions:

$$x^1(t) = \exp(\lambda_1 t)e_1 = e^{\xi t}e_1 \quad \text{and} \quad x^2(t) = \exp(\lambda_2 t)e_2 = e^{\xi t}e_2$$

Clearly, if e_1 and e_2 are linearly independent eigenvectors associated with ξ, the elementary solutions $x^1(t)$ and $x^2(t)$ are also independent from each other and from the rest of the elementary solutions $x^3(t), \ldots, x^n(t)$. Hence the set of elementary solutions is still a basis for the solution space of the homogeneous system, and we can write the general solution as before:

$$x^g(t) = c_1 x^1(t) + \ldots + c_n x^n(t) \tag{G.S}$$

If e_1 and e_2 are linearly dependent, however, so are $x^1(t)$ and $x^2(t)$, and we do not have enough independent elementary solutions to span the solution space. To complete a basis for the solution space that will allow us to write the general solution, we need to find an additional solution to (CH) that will be linearly independent from the elementary solutions. We will seek a solution of the form

$$\phi(t) = (a + bt)e^{\xi t} = ae^{\xi t} + bte^{\xi t} \tag{1}$$

that is, the product of a polynomial of order 1 (1 less than the multiplicity of ξ) in t and the exponential term in the eigenvalue ξ. What restrictions must be placed on the vectors a and b so that $\phi(t)$ will indeed be a solution of the system, that is, will satisfy the equation $\phi'(t) = A\phi(t)$? Write the general solution of the system.

(d) Nonhomogeneous Systems and Stability Conditions

We now turn to nonhomogeneous linear systems of the form

$$\dot{x} = Ax + b \tag{CN}$$

or

$$x_{t+1} = Ax_t + b \qquad \text{(DN)}$$

We have seen that the general solution of such a system can be written

$$x^N(t) = x^H(t) + x^P(t) \qquad \text{(G.S)}$$

where the complementary function $x^H(t)$ is the general solution of the corresponding homogeneous system, and $x^P(t)$ is an arbitrary particular solution of the nonhomogeneous system.

In the preceding sections we have shown how to compute $x^H(t)$. Hence, it suffices to find one particular solution of (CN) or (DN) to be able to write its general solution. An obvious choice is the stationary solution of the system, $\bar{x}$, whenever it exists. To find it, in the discrete case we put $x_{t+1} = x_t$, eliminating the time subscripts, and solve for x to obtain

$$x = Ax + b \Rightarrow (A - I)x = -b$$
$$\Rightarrow \bar{x} = -(A - I)^{-1}b \qquad (8)$$

whenever $A - I$ is invertible. In the continuous case, we set $\dot{x}$ to zero:

$$\dot{x} = Ax + b = \underline{0} \Rightarrow Ax = -b$$
$$\Rightarrow \bar{x} = -A^{-1}b \qquad (9)$$

provided A is invertible.[3]

Using the results from the preceding section, we can write the general solutions of the given systems directly.[4] Then the conditions for stability or instability follow immediately by inspection.

Theorem 2.6. Let A *be a real* $n \times n$ *matrix with no repeated eigenvalues, all different from zero. Then the general solution of the system (CN),* $\dot{x} = Ax + b$, *is given by*

$$x^g(t; c) = \bar{x} + \sum_{i=1}^{n} c_i exp(\lambda_i t)e_i \qquad \text{(G.S.C)}$$

where $\bar{x} = -A^{-1}b$ *is the unique stationary state of the system,* $c_1, \ldots, c_n$ *are arbitrary constants to be definitized by choice of a boundary condition,* λ_i *is the ith characteristic root of the coefficient matrix* A, *and* e_i *is the corresponding characteristic vector.*

Given (G.S), it is easily determined whether the steady state $\bar{x}$ is stable or unstable. Suppose first that all roots of the system are real numbers. Then the jth component of the general solution is given by

$$x_j^g(t; c) = \bar{x}_j + \sum_{i=1}^{n} c_i e_{ij} exp(\lambda_i t) \qquad (10)$$

The stability of the steady state depends on the signs of the system's eigenvalues. If all roots are negative, then all terms of the form $exp(\lambda_i t)$ go to zero as $t \to \infty$, and the solution converges asymptotically to the steady state $\bar{x}$ for any value of the constants c_i – that is, from any initial position. On the other hand, if any of the roots of the system are strictly positive, the corresponding exponential terms $\exp(\lambda_i t)$ go to infinity as $t \to \infty$. Hence the system is unstable and diverges from the steady state, unless we "kill" the explosive roots by assigning a zero value to the corresponding constants.

If any of the characteristic roots are complex, the general solution can be written in the form derived in the preceding section. In particular, if $\lambda_1 = \alpha + i\mu$ and $\lambda_2 = \alpha - i\mu$ are the only complex eigenvalues, with eigenvectors $e_1 = d + if$ and $e_2 = d - if$, we have

$$x^g(t; c) = \bar{x} + c_1 e^{\alpha t}(d \cos \mu t - f \sin \mu t) + c_2 e^{\alpha t}(f \cos \mu t + d \sin \mu t)$$

$$+ \sum_{i=3}^{n} c_i \exp(\lambda_i t) e_i \tag{11}$$

This expression shows that the crucial determinants of the stability of the steady state are the signs of the real parts of the eigenvalues of the system, α. The existence of a nonzero imaginary component μ introduces a cyclical element into the solution through the functions $\sin \mu t$ and $\cos \mu t$, but what determines the convergence or divergence of the system is the behavior of the term $e^{\alpha t}$. Observe also that if the eigenvalues of A are all pure imaginary numbers, the solutions of the system are cyclical and describe closed trajectories around the steady state.

Finally, if the system has repeated roots, the general solution is of the form

$$x(t) = \sum_{i=1}^{k} P_i(t) \exp(\mu_i t) = \sum_{i=1}^{k} \sum_{j=1}^{m_i} p_{ij} t^{j-1} \exp(\mu_i t) \tag{12}$$

This expression implies that even with repeated roots, the stability of the system depends on the signs of the real parts of its eigenvalues. If μ_i is real and negative, for example, the terms of the form $te^{\mu t}$ also tend to zero as $t \to \infty$, because the exponential term prevails. By L'Hôpital's rule, we have

$$\lim_{t \to \infty} te^{\mu t} = \lim_{t \to \infty} \frac{t}{e^{-\mu t}} = \lim_{t \to \infty} \frac{1}{-\mu e^{-\mu t}} \sim \frac{1}{\infty} = 0$$

In summary, the stability of the continuous-time autonomous linear system depends on the signs of the real parts of the eigenvalues of its coefficient matrix. We summarize as follows:

Theorem 2.7. Let A be a real n × n matrix with nonzero eigenvalues. Then the unique steady state of the system (CS), $\bar{x} = -A^{-1}b$, is (globally) asymptotically stable if and only if all the eigenvalues of the coefficient matrix A have strictly negative real parts, and it is unstable if at least one of the eigenvalues is strictly positive.

A steady state that satisfies the conditions of the theorem (i.e., has nonzero characteristic roots) is said to be *hyperbolic*.

For discrete-time systems, we have a very similar situation.

Theorem 2.8. Let A *be a real* $n \times n$ *matrix with eigenvalues all distinct and different from* $1.$[5] *Then the general solution of the system (DN),* $x_{t+1} = Ax_t + b,$ *is given by*

$$x_t^g(c) = \bar{x} + \sum\nolimits_{i=1}^{n} c_i \lambda_i^t e_i \qquad \text{(G.S.D)}$$

where $\bar{x} = -(A - I)^{-1}b$ *is the unique steady state of the system,* $c_1, \ldots, c_n$ *are arbitrary constants whose values will be determined by the choice of an appropriate boundary condition,* λ_i *is the ith eigenvalue of* A, *and* e_i *is the corresponding eigenvector.*

This expression shows that what determines the convergence or divergence of the system is whether or not the absolute values of its roots are smaller than 1. If we have complex roots, we have

$$x_t^g(c) = c_1 r^t (d \cos\theta t - f \sin\theta t) + c_2 r^t (f \cos\theta t + d \sin\theta t) + \sum\nolimits_{i=3}^{n} c_i \lambda_i^t e_i$$

where we observe that the stability of the system depends on the value of r, the modulus of its complex roots. In the case of systems with repeated roots, the situation is similar to the one that arises in continuous-time systems. We have, then, the following:

Theorem 2.9. Let A *be a real* $n \times n$ *matrix whose eigenvalues all have moduli different from 1. Then the unique steady state of the system (DN), given by* $\bar{x} = -(A - I)^{-1}b,$ *is (globally) asymptotically stable if and only if all the eigenvalues of the coefficient matrix* A *have moduli strictly smaller than 1, and unstable if at least one eigenvalue has modulus strictly larger than 1.*

A Class of Nonautonomous Systems

The diagonalization procedure discussed in Section 2(a) can be extended to deal with nonautonomous systems of the form

$$\dot{x} = Ax + b(t) \quad \text{or} \quad x_{t+1} = Ax_t + b_t \qquad (13)$$

where the coefficient matrix A is constant, but the forcing term b is a function of time.

Assume that A is diagonalizable, and consider, for concreteness, the discrete case. Proceeding as before, we premultiply both sides of (13) by the inverse of the eigenvector matrix, E^{-1}, to get

$$E^{-1}x_{t+1} = E^{-1}A(EE^{-1})x_t + E^{-1}b_t = \Lambda E^{-1}x_t + E^{-1}b_t$$

If we now define the transformed variables

$$y_t = E^{-1}x_t \quad \text{and} \quad d_t = E^{-1}b_t$$

we can rewrite the earlier expression as

$$y_{t+1} = \Lambda y_t + d_t$$

Because $\Lambda = \text{diag}(\lambda_1, \ldots, \lambda_n)$ is diagonal, the transformed system reduces to a set of independent equations of the form

$$y_{t+1}^i = \lambda_i y_t^i + d_t^i$$

Following the procedure discussed in Section 5 of Chapter 9, we can solve each of these equations separately. To recover the solution of the original system, it suffices to apply the inverse of the original transformation, that is, to use the relation $x_t = Ey_t$.

(e) Stable and Unstable Spaces

We have seen that the stability of a linear system depends on the values of its characteristic roots. In the case of the continuous-time system $\dot{x} = Ax + b$, for example, if all the eigenvalues of A have negative real parts, the solution converges asymptotically to the stationary state $\bar{x}$ from any initial position. In this case, we say that $\bar{x}$ is a *sink*. If all the characteristic roots of A have positive real parts, the system is "completely unstable" and "explodes" from any initial position other than the steady state itself. In this case, we speak of a *source*. The situation is similar in the case of discrete-time systems, except that now we are concerned with the moduli of the eigenvalues, rather than with the signs of their real parts.

When the system has roots with positive real parts and roots with negative real parts (or roots inside and roots outside the unit circle in the complex plane, in the discrete-time case), we say that its steady state is a *saddle point*. A saddle point is an unstable equilibrium, according to the definition given in Chapter 9, for there exist solution trajectories that, starting arbitrarily close to the steady state, get arbitrarily far from it as time passes. There are, however, other trajectories that converge asymptotically to the steady state. In fact, there is a possibly large region of the state space with the property that any trajectory originating in it converges to the steady state. This region is what we call the *stable space* or stable manifold of the system.

Suppose, for concreteness, that we have a homogeneous system in continuous time, (CH), $\dot{x} = Ax$, with n distinct eigenvalues, all real and different from zero. Partition the eigenvalues of A, $\{\lambda_i;\ i = 1, \ldots, n\}$, into two sets, S and U, with $i \in S$ if $\lambda_i < 0$ and $i \in U$ if $\lambda_i > 0$, and write the general solution of the system in the form

$$x^g(t; c_u, c_s) = \sum_{i=1}^{n} c_i \exp(\lambda_i t) e_i = \sum_{i \in S} c_i \exp(\lambda_i t) e_i + \sum_{i \in U} c_i \exp(\lambda_i t) e_i$$
(14)

where, as usual, $c = (c_1, \ldots, c_n)^T$ is a vector of arbitrary constants. Clearly, if we set the constants c_u corresponding to the unstable roots equal to zero, then, the solution of the system, which reduces to

$$x^g(t; \underline{0}\ c_s) = \sum_{i \in S} c_i \exp(\lambda_i t) e_i$$

converges to the steady state $\bar{x} = \underline{0}$ for any value of the vector c_s.

Setting some of the arbitrary constants equal to zero is equivalent to choosing a subset of the state space $\mathbb{R}^n$. We will show that the subset of $\mathbb{R}^n$ corresponding to the boundary condition $c_u = \underline{0}$ is the subspace of $\mathbb{R}^n$ spanned by the eigenvectors associated with the stable roots. Recall that the absence of repeated roots guarantees the linear independence of the eigenvectors of the coefficient matrix A. Hence, under our assumptions, A has a full set of n linearly independent eigenvectors, $e = \{e_i \in \mathbb{R}^n; i = 1, \ldots, n\}$, and this family of vectors is a basis for the state space $\mathbb{R}^n$. Let x^0 be the initial position of the system at time zero. Because e is a basis of $\mathbb{R}^n$, the vector x^0 can be written in precisely one way as a linear combination of the eigenvalues of A. That is, there exist real numbers $\beta_1, \ldots, \beta_n$, not all zero, such that

$$x^0 = \sum_{i=1}^{n} \beta_i e_i$$
(15)

Moreover, evaluating the general solution of the system at time zero,

$$x^g(0, c) = \sum_{i=1}^{n} c_i \exp(\lambda_i 0) e_i = \sum_{i=1}^{n} c_i e_i = x^0$$
(16)

and combining (15) and (16),

$$\sum_{i=1}^{0} (c_i - \beta_i) e_i = \underline{0}$$
(17)

Finally, by the linear independence of the eigenvectors, (17) implies that

$$c_i = \beta_i \ \forall\, i = 1, \ldots, n$$

That is, the arbitrary constants c_i in the general solution correspond to the coordinates of the system's initial position in the coordinate system defined by the eigenvectors of the coefficient matrix.

Now, the convergent space of the system is the set of points for which $c_u = \underline{0}$, that is, the set of n-vectors that can be written as linear combinations of the stable eigenvectors, or the subspace of $\mathbb{R}^n$ generated by $\{e_i \in \mathbb{R}^n; i \in S\}$. Call this set $W^s(\underline{0})$, where $\underline{0}$ is the steady state of the given homogeneous system. Given any point x^0 in $W^s(\underline{0})$, the particular solution of the system through this point is given by

$$x(t; x^0) = \sum_{i \in S} \beta_i \exp(\lambda_i t) e_i$$

Hence, $x(t; x^0) \to \underline{0}$ as $t \to \infty$. Moreover, $W^s(\underline{0})$ is invariant under the flow of the system, for if x^0 is a linear combination of the stable eigenvectors, so is $x(t; x^0)$ for any t. Similarly, if $y^0 = \sum_{i \in U} \gamma_i e_i$ is a point in the unstable subspace of the system $W^u(\underline{0}) = \text{span}\{e_i; i \in U\}$, the solution through y^0 is given by

$$x(t; y^0) = \sum_{i \in U} \gamma_i \exp(\lambda_i t) e_i$$

and we have

$$\|x(t; y^0)\| \to \infty \quad \text{as } t \to \infty \quad \text{and} \quad x(t; y^0) \to \underline{0} \quad \text{as } t \to -\infty$$

So far, we have assumed that all the characteristic roots of the system are real-valued, but the situation is not very different if some eigenvalues are complex. Suppose A has n distinct but possibly complex roots,

$$\lambda_i = \alpha_j + i\mu_j \qquad (j = 1, \ldots, n)$$

with corresponding eigenvectors

$$e_j = u_j + iv_j$$

(Recall that complex eigenvalues and eigenvectors come in conjugate pairs. Hence, if $\mu_k \neq 0$ for some k, then $\bar{\lambda}_k = \alpha_k - i\mu_k$ is also an eigenvalue, and its corresponding eigenvector is of the form $\bar{e}_k = u_k - iv_k$.) For each pair of complex eigenvalues, we can replace the eigenvectors e_k and $\bar{e}_k$ by the real vectors u_k and v_k and proceed as before. Hence, the stable and unstable subspaces of the homogeneous system $\dot{x} = Ax$ are now given by

$$W^s(\underline{0}) = \text{span}\{u_j, v_j; \alpha_j < 0\} \quad \text{and} \quad W^u(\underline{0}) = \text{span}\{u_j, v_j; \alpha_j > 0\} \quad (18)$$

Finally, in the case of the nonhomogeneous system $\dot{x} = Ax + b$, with steady state $\bar{x}$, the stable and unstable spaces $W^s(\bar{x})$ and $W^u(\bar{x})$ are obtained by "displacing" the stable and unstable subspaces of the homogeneous system so that they "go through" the steady state $\bar{x}$. That is, $W^s(\bar{x})$ and $W^u(\bar{x})$ are the affine (rather than linear) subspaces of $\mathbb{R}^n$ given by

$$W^s(\bar{x}) = \bar{x} + W^s(\underline{0}) \quad \text{and} \quad W^u(\bar{x}) = \bar{x} + W^u(\underline{0}) \tag{19}$$

We summarize the discussion in the following theorem.

Theorem 2.10. Stable and unstable manifold for linear systems. Consider the linear system $\dot{x} = Ax + b$, with steady state $\bar{x}$, and suppose that A has no repeated roots. Then the sets $W^s(\bar{x})$ and $W^u(\bar{x})$ defined in (19) are invariant under the flow of the system. Moreover, given any point x^0 in $W^s(\bar{x})$, the solution of the system through this point, $x(t; x^0)$, converges to $\bar{x}$ as $t \to \infty$. Given any point y^0 in $W^u(\bar{x})$, the corresponding solution, $x(t; y^0)$, satisfies

$$\|x(t; y^0)\| \to \infty \quad \text{as } t \to \infty \quad \text{and} \quad x(t; y^0) \to \bar{x} \quad \text{as } t \to -\infty$$

A similar result holds for discrete-time systems. In this case, however, the stable (unstable) space is defined by the eigenvectors corresponding to eigenvalues inside (outside) the unit circle in the complex plane, that is,

$$W^s(\underline{0}) = \operatorname{span}\{u_j, v_j; |\lambda_j| < 1\} \quad \text{and} \quad W^u(\underline{0}) = \operatorname{span}\{u_j, v_j; |\lambda_j| > 1\} \quad (20)$$

(f) Linear Systems on the Plane

In this section we analyze in detail the dynamics of autonomous linear systems in the plane, that is, systems of the form

$$\dot{x} = Ax + b \tag{CS2}$$

or

$$x_{t+1} = Ax_t + b \tag{DS2}$$

where A is a real 2×2 matrix.

Practically all the information we need to describe the dynamics of (CS2) or (DS2) is summarized by the eigenvalues of the coefficient matrix A. Depending on whether the characteristic roots of A are real or complex, have positive or negative real parts, or lie inside or outside the unit circle in the complex plane, the steady state of the system will be stable or unstable, and the solution trajectories will behave differently. We will examine the different possibilities that can arise in the continuous- and discrete-time cases. To summarize our results, we will construct two figures (one for discrete systems and the other for continuous systems) drawn on a Cartesian plane, with det A on the vertical axis and tr A on the horizontal axis. For each type of system we will divide this plane into a number of regions, each corresponding to a different type of steady state.

Recall from Chapter 3 (Section 6) that the eigenvalues of A (λ_1 and λ_2) satisfy the relations

$$\operatorname{tr} A = \lambda_1 + \lambda_2 \tag{21}$$

$$\det A = \lambda_1 \lambda_2 \tag{22}$$

and are the solutions of the characteristic equation

$$p(\lambda) = |A - \lambda \mathbb{I}| = \lambda^2 - (\operatorname{tr} A)\lambda + \det A = 0 \tag{23}$$

Hence, by the quadratic formula, λ_1 and λ_2 are given by

$$\lambda_1, \lambda_2 = \frac{\operatorname{tr} \pm \sqrt{\operatorname{tr}^2 - 4\det}}{2} \tag{24}$$

Equation (24) shows that the eigenvalues of A are real or complex depending on the sign of the discriminant of the characteristic equation,

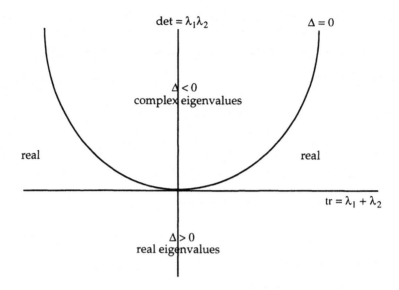

Figure 10.1. Regions of real and complex eigenvalues.

$$\Delta = \text{tr}^2 - 4\det$$

Setting Δ equal to zero and solving for the determinant,

$$\Delta = \text{tr}^2 - 4\det = 0 \Rightarrow \det = \text{tr}^2/4 \tag{25}$$

we obtain the equation for a parabola with a minimum at the origin. This curve divides the plane into two regions, as shown in Figure 10.1. In the region above the parabola we have $\Delta < 0$, that is, $\text{tr}^2 < 4\det$, indicating that the roots of the system are complex numbers, whereas the region below the curve corresponds to the case of real eigenvalues ($\Delta > 0$).

Equation (24) also shows that complex eigenvalues come in conjugate pairs. Hence, if $\lambda_1 = \alpha + i\mu$ is an eigenvalue, then so is $\lambda_2 = \alpha - i\mu$, and equations (21) and (22) imply that

$$\text{tr } A = \lambda_1 + \lambda_2 = (\alpha + i\mu) + (\alpha - i\mu) = 2\alpha \tag{26}$$

$$\det A = \lambda_1 \lambda_2 = (\alpha + i\mu) + (\alpha - i\mu) = \alpha^2 + i\mu\alpha - i\mu\alpha - i^2\mu^2 = \alpha^2 + \mu^2 = |\lambda_1|^2 = |\lambda_2|^2 \tag{27}$$

Hence, when the eigenvalues are complex, the trace of the coefficient matrix is equal to twice the (common) real part of the eigenvalues, and the determinant is the square of their (common) modulus.

(i) Continuous Time

Consider the planar system in continuous time,

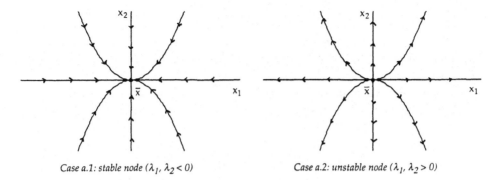

Case a.1: stable node $(\lambda_1, \lambda_2 < 0)$　　　　Case a.2: unstable node $(\lambda_1, \lambda_2 > 0)$

Figure 10.2. Nodes.

$$\dot{x} = Ax + b \tag{CS2}$$

and recall the general discussion of stability in Section 2(d).

Suppose first that $\Delta = \mathrm{tr}^2 - 4\det > 0$ (i.e., we are in the region below the parabola). Then the characteristic roots of the system are real numbers, and its general solution can be written

$$x_1^g(t, c) = \bar{x}_1 + c_1 e_{11}\exp(\lambda_1 t) + c_2 e_{21}\exp(\lambda_2 t)$$

$$x_2^g(t, c) = \bar{x}_2 + c_1 e_{12}\exp(\lambda_1 t) + c_2 e_{22}\exp(\lambda_2 t)$$

The stability of the system depends on the signs of the eigenvalues. The possible cases are the following.

• Case (a). Real roots of the same sign: nodes

If $\det A = \lambda_1 \lambda_2 > 0$, then both roots are real numbers with the same sign. In this case, the steady state $\bar{x}$ is called a *node*, because all the trajectories point directly "into" or "out of" the steady state. Given that the eigenvalues of A must have the same sign, the sign of the trace of this matrix will tell us whether the system is stable or unstable. If $\mathrm{tr}\, A = \lambda_1 + \lambda_2 < 0$, both eigenvalues are negative, and all trajectories converge smoothly to the steady state, yielding an (asymptotically) stable node. If the trace is positive, so are both eigenvalues, and the node is unstable, as illustrated in Figure 10.2.

A similar situation arises if $(\mathrm{tr}\, A)^2 - 4(\det A) = 0$. Then the system has a repeated real root ($\lambda_1 = \lambda_2 = \xi$), and its general solution is of the form

$$x_1^g(t, c) = \bar{x}_1 + c_1 e_{11}\exp(\xi t) + c_2 b_1 t \exp(\xi t)$$

$$x_2^g(t, c) = \bar{x}_2 + c_1 e_{12}\exp(\xi t) + c_2 b_2 t \exp(\xi t)$$

where $e_1 = (e_{11}, e_{12})^T$ is an eigenvector of A associated with the repeated root, and $b = (b_1, b_2)^T$ is a 2-vector. Note that the solution trajectories converge if $\xi < 0$, and diverge when $\xi > 0$.

- Case (b). Real roots of different signs: saddle points

    If $\det A = \lambda_1 \lambda_2 < 0$, the roots of the system are real numbers, of opposite signs, and the steady state is a *saddle point*. As we saw in Section 2(e), in this case the solutions of the system converge from some initial positions and diverge from others.

    For concreteness, suppose that $\lambda_1 > 0$ and $\lambda_2 < 0$, and consider the general solution of the system:

$$x_1^g(t,c) = \bar{x}_1 + c_1 e_{11} \exp(\lambda_1 t) + c_2 e_{21} \exp(\lambda_2 t)$$

$$x_2^g(t,c) = \bar{x}_2 + c_1 e_{12} \exp(\lambda_1 t) + c_2 e_{22} \exp(\lambda_2 t)$$

It is clear that if $c_1 \neq 0$, the system's behavior will ultimately be dominated by its positive root $\lambda_1 > 0$. As $t \to \infty$, $|c_1 \exp(\lambda_1 t)| \to \infty$, and the system displays explosive behavior, moving farther and farther from the steady state as time passes. On the other hand, if we impose the boundary condition $c_1 = 0$, the system's behavior is determined by its negative root alone, and it converges to the steady state $\bar{x}$ as $t \to \infty$.

Note that in order to "kill off" the explosive root we have to assign a value of zero to one of the arbitrary constants, c_1, while the other remains "free." We have seen that assigning values to the two constants is equivalent to picking an initial point for the system, and that assigning a value to only one of them is equivalent to selecting a subspace of the phase plane. Hence, the system will converge to the steady state if and only if it starts out from a point in some subset of the (x_1, x_2) plane characterized by the condition that the arbitrary constant associated with the explosive root is equal to zero.

To see what the stable subspace looks like, set $c_1 = 0$ in the general solution to get

$$x_1(t) - \bar{x}_1 = c_2 e_{21} \exp(\lambda_2 t)$$

$$x_2(t) - \bar{x}_2 = c_2 e_{22} \exp(\lambda_2 t) \tag{28}$$

Using the second equation to eliminate $c_2 \exp(\lambda_2 t)$ from the first one,

$$[x_1(t) - \bar{x}_1] = \frac{e_{21}}{e_{22}} [x_2(t) - \bar{x}_2]$$

$$\Rightarrow x_1(t) = \bar{x}_1 + \frac{e_{21}}{e_{22}} [x_2(t) - \bar{x}_2] \tag{29}$$

which is the equation of the straight line labeled S in Figure 10.3. This line, known as the *saddle path*, is the convergent subspace of the (x_1, x_2) plane. If the system does not start out from a point on S, it will embark on an explosive path, as shown in the figure.

Notice that the slope of the saddle path is determined by the eigenvector e_2 associated with the stable root $\lambda_2 < 0$. If we take the steady state as its origin, the stable eigenvector points in the direction of the saddle path. The other eigenvector (associated with $\lambda_1 > 0$) also defines an interesting direction in the state plane,

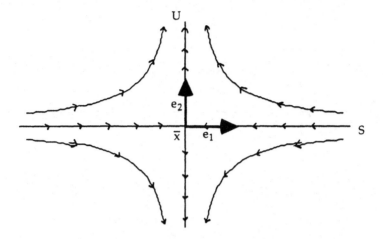

Figure 10.3. Case (b): saddle point ($\lambda_1 > 0$, $\lambda_2 < 0$).

that of a divergent path, the "anti–saddle path" or unstable subspace, labeled U in the figure. (Note that the two eigenvectors need not be orthogonal to each other.)

- Case (c). Complex roots: spiral points

Next, suppose that the discriminant $\Delta = \text{tr}^2 - 4\det$ is negative. Then the eigenvalues of the system are complex numbers, $\lambda_1 = \alpha + i\mu$ and $\lambda_2 = \alpha - i\mu$, and, following the discussion in Section 2(b), the general solution can be written

$$x^g(t, c) = \bar{x} + c_1 u(t) + c_2 v(t) \tag{30}$$

where

$$u(t) = e^{\alpha t}(d \cos \mu t - f \sin \mu t) \quad \text{and} \quad v(t) = e^{\alpha t}(f \cos \mu t + d \sin \mu t)$$

When the characteristic roots of the system are complex, the steady state is said to be a spiral point, because the circular functions $\sin \mu t$ and $\cos \mu t$ in the solution induce a spiral-like pattern in the orbits of the system. As nodes, spiral points can be either stable or unstable. This can be determined by checking the sign of the trace, which in this case reduces to

$$\text{tr } A = \lambda_1 + \lambda_2 = \alpha + i\mu + \alpha - i\mu = 2\alpha$$

Hence, if tr $A < 0$, the eigenvalues have a negative real part α, and (30) describes a family of spiral trajectories converging to the steady state $\bar{x}$; if tr $A > 0$, then $\alpha > 0$, and the spirals diverge away from $\bar{x}$.

- Case (d). Pure imaginary roots: centers

If tr $A = 0$ and det $A > 0$, the discriminant is negative, and the eigenvalues of the system are pure imaginary numbers with a zero real part α. Hence, the scale factor $e^{\alpha t}$ that multiplies the circular functions $u(t)$ and $v(t)$ in the general solu-

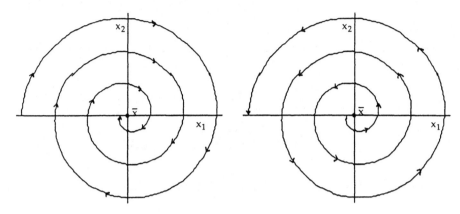

Case c.1: stable spiral point ($\alpha < 0$) Case c.2: unstable spiral point ($\alpha > 0$)

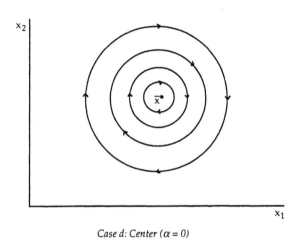

Case d: Center ($\alpha = 0$)

Figure 10.4. Spiral points and centers.

tion (30) becomes a constant, and the trajectories of the system are closed curves around a steady state that is called a center. This is the only case in which the continuous linear system (CS2), $\dot{x} = Ax + b$, has cyclical solutions. Note that a center is stable, because nearby solutions remain nearby, but not asymptotically so, because they do not converge to the steady state.

• Summary

We have seen that the nature and stability of the steady state of the 2×2 autonomous linear system depend on the values of its characteristic roots, given by

$$\lambda_1, \lambda_2 = \frac{\text{tr} \pm \sqrt{\text{tr}^2 - 4\text{det}}}{2} \tag{24}$$

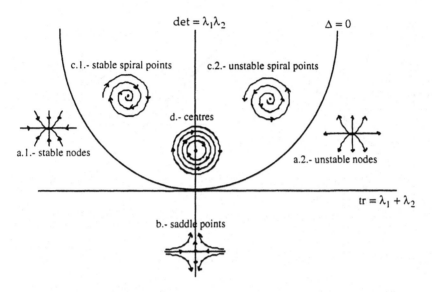

Figure 10.5. Stability map for continuous linear systems in the plane.

By keeping in mind (24) and

$$\text{tr } A = \lambda_1 + \lambda_2 \tag{21}$$

$$\det A = \lambda_1 \lambda_2 \tag{22}$$

it is easy to determine the nature of the system's steady state and orbits just by looking at the coefficient matrix. In particular, we have seen the following:

(i) If $\det A = \lambda_1 \lambda_2 < 0$, the eigenvalues of the system are real numbers of opposite signs; hence, we have a saddle point.

(ii) If $\det A = \lambda_1 \lambda_2 > 0$, the roots are either complex numbers or real numbers of the same sign. In this case there are two possibilities:

  (a) If $\text{tr } A = \lambda_1 + \lambda_2 < 0$, the two eigenvalues are negative (if real) or have negative real parts; in either case the system is stable.

  (b) If $\text{tr } A = \lambda_1 + \lambda_2 > 0$, both roots are positive or have positive real parts; in both cases, the system is unstable.

(ii) Discrete Time

In the discrete-time case, stability is determined by the moduli of the eigenvalues of the coefficient matrix. When the characteristic roots of the system are real, the question reduces to whether or not they fall inside the interval $(-1, 1)$. A convenient way to determine when this is the case is based on the following observation.

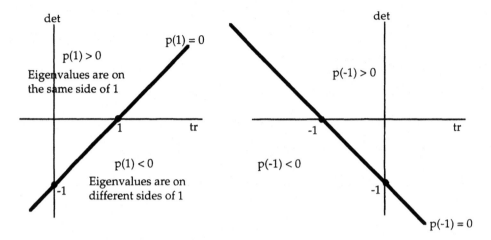

Figure 10.6.

Let λ_1 and λ_2 be the eigenvalues of A. We can factor the characteristic polynomial of the matrix and write it in the form

$$p(\lambda) = (\lambda - \lambda_1)(\lambda - \lambda_2)$$

Suppose for the time being that both eigenvalues are real, and imagine that we want to determine whether or not both of them fall on the same side of a given constant a. Evaluating $p(\ )$ at a, we have

$$p(a) = (a - \lambda_1)(a - \lambda_2)$$

Clearly, $p(a) > 0$ if and only if the two factors on the right-hand side have the same sign, that is, if λ_1 and λ_2 fall on the same side of a.

In our case, we are interested in determining whether or not the (real) eigenvalues of A fall on the same sides of 1 and -1. Thus, we will draw the lines $p(1) = 0$ and $p(-1) = 0$. Recalling that

$$p(\lambda) = \lambda^2 - (\text{tr } A)\lambda + \det A$$

we have

$$p(1) = 1 - \text{tr} + \det \geq 0$$
$$\Rightarrow \det \geq \text{tr} - 1 \tag{31}$$

Hence, the set of points in the (tr, det) plane that satisfies $p(1) = 0$ is a straight line through the points $(0, -1)$ and $(1, 0)$ that divides the plane into two regions, as shown in Figure 10.6. In the region above the line, we have $p(1) > 0$, indicating that both roots lie on the same side of 1, whereas the opposite inequality holds in the region below the $p(1) = 0$ line, indicating that the eigenvalues fall on opposite sides of 1 on the real line.

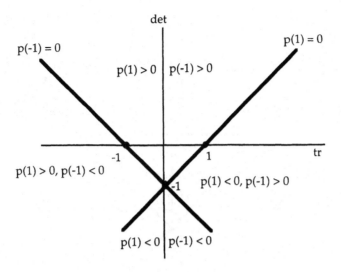

Figure 10.7.

Similarly, we have

$$p(-1) = 1 + \mathrm{tr} + \det \geq 0$$
$$\Rightarrow \det \geq -1 - \mathrm{tr} \tag{32}$$

The line $p(-1) = 0$ goes through the points $(-1, 0)$ and $(0, -1)$. In the region above the line, we have $p(-1) > 0$, and both roots are on the same side of -1. Combining the two graphs, the plane is divided into four regions, as shown in Figure 10.7.

Next, we add to this graph the line

$$\Delta = \mathrm{tr}^2 - 4\det = 0$$
$$\Rightarrow \det = \frac{\mathrm{tr}^2}{4} \tag{33}$$

As we know, points above the parabola described by (33) correspond to systems with complex eigenvalues. It is easy to check that the line $\Delta = 0$ is tangent to $p(-1) = 0$ at the point $(-2, 1)$ and to $p(1) = 0$ at $(2, 1)$. The parabola is therefore entirely contained in the "upper quadrant" of the plane, as partitioned by the two straight lines.

Figure 10.8 shows that the plane can be divided into eight regions by the three reference lines described earlier and a horizontal line at $\det = 1$. For each of these regions, we can now determine the stability type of the steady state.

First, we concentrate on the regions of the plane that correspond to real eigenvalues (1, 2, 3, 4, 7, and 8). The steady state is a sink if both roots are

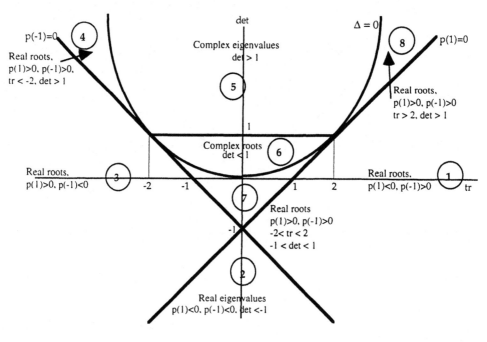

Figure 10.8.

in the interval $(-1, 1)$, a source if neither eigenvalue falls in this region, and a saddle point if one root is within this interval and the other is not. Taking each region in turn, we have the following:

Region 1: $p(1) < 0$ and $p(-1) > 0$. The two eigenvalues fall on the same side of -1 and on different sides of 1. The only possibility is shown here: There is one eigenvalue in $(-1, 1)$, and the other is larger than 1. The steady state is a saddle point.

Region 2: $p(1) < 0$ and $p(-1) < 0$. The steady state is a source.

Region 3: $p(1) > 0$ and $p(-1) < 0$. The steady state is a saddle point.

Region 4: $p(1) > 0$ and $p(-1) > 0$. The two eigenvalues are on the same sides of 1 and -1. Moreover, we have $\det > 0$, so both eigenvalues have the same sign, and $\mathrm{tr} < -2$, so they are both negative. Hence, both roots are smaller than -1. The steady state is a source.

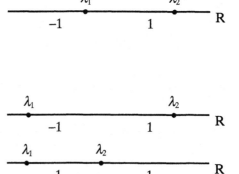

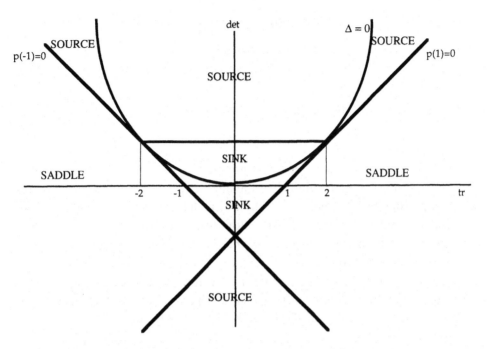

Figure 10.9. Stability map for the discrete planar system.

Region 8: $p(1) > 0$ and $p(-1) > 0$. Now $\det > 0$ and $\text{tr} > 2$, so the two roots are positive and fall on the same sides of both 1 and -1. Hence, they must be larger than 1, and the steady state is a source.

Region 7: $p(1) > 0$ and $p(-1) > 0$. Now we have $-2 < \text{tr} < 2$ and $-1 < \det < 1$. Both eigenvalues must lie in $(-1, 1)$, and we have a sink.

In regions 5 and 6, the eigenvalues are complex numbers,

$$\lambda_1 = \alpha + i\mu \quad \text{and} \quad \lambda_2 = \alpha - i\mu$$

Recalling that

$$\text{tr } A = \lambda_1 + \lambda_2 = 2\alpha$$

$$\det A = \lambda_1 \lambda_2 = \alpha^2 + \mu^2 = |\lambda_1|^2 = |\lambda_2|^2$$

it is easy to determine the stability of the system. In region 5, we have $\det > 1$, implying that $|\lambda_1| = |\lambda_2| > 1$. Hence, the steady state is a source, whereas in region 6 the opposite inequality holds, indicating that we have a sink. Our conclusions are summarized in Figure 10.9.

3. Autonomous Nonlinear Systems

In this section we will study autonomous nonlinear systems of the form

$$\dot{x} = f(x) \tag{CS}$$

or

$$x_{t+1} = g(x_t) \tag{DS}$$

where $f, g : \mathbb{R}^n \supseteq X \longrightarrow \mathbb{R}^n$ are C^1 functions. Because explicit solutions for nonlinear systems are, in general, not available, we will have to rely on more indirect methods to analyze the behavior of such systems. We start by developing a graphical method that will allow us to obtain qualitative information about the behavior of planar dynamical systems and present it in a convenient and intuitive manner. We then show that a considerable amount of information regarding the behavior of a nonlinear system near an equilibrium can be obtained by studying its linearization, that is, the linear system defined by the derivative of $f(\ )$ or $g(\ )$ at the steady state.

(a) Phase Diagrams for Planar Systems

In Chapter 9 we introduced the phase diagram as a useful tool for studying nonlinear systems in one dimension. In this section we will see that this technique can be extended to the case of dynamical systems in two variables. The basic idea is the same in both cases: We project onto the state space the graphs of the solutions of the system as a way to visualize their behavior. In two dimensions, the result is a diagram showing the system's trajectories on the plane.

Given a system of differential equations in the plane,

$$\dot{x} = f(x, y) \tag{1}$$

$$\dot{y} = g(x, y) \tag{2}$$

where f and g are C^1 functions, the first step is to set $\dot{x}$ and $\dot{y}$ equal to zero in (1) and (2) to obtain the equations of the *phase lines*:

$$\dot{x} = 0 \Rightarrow f(x, y) = 0 \tag{3}$$

$$\dot{y} = 0 \Rightarrow g(x, y) = 0 \tag{4}$$

Each of these equations describes a curve in the (x, y) plane.[6]

Consider these lines one at a time. The phase line $\dot{x} = 0$ divides the (x, y) plane into two regions. In one of them, we have $\dot{x} > 0$, indicating that x increases over time $(x\uparrow)$, whereas in the other, $\dot{x} < 0$, and x decreases over

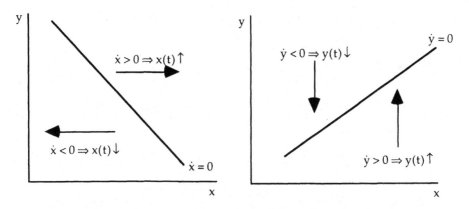

Figure 10.10. Phase lines and arrows of motion.

time. To determine which is which (if it is not obvious from inspection of the equations), we can evaluate either of the derivatives[7]

$$\frac{\partial \dot{x}}{\partial x} = \frac{\partial f(x, y)}{\partial x} \qquad \frac{\partial \dot{x}}{\partial y} = \frac{\partial f(x, y)}{\partial y}$$

at a convenient point in the $\dot{x} = 0$ line (typically at the steady state). For example, suppose that $\partial \dot{x} / \partial x > 0$, as assumed in Figure 10.10. This tells us that, starting from the $\dot{x} = 0$ line, a small movement to the right will increase the value of $\dot{x}$, making it strictly positive. Hence, $\dot{x} > 0$ in the region to the right of the phase line. We indicate this in the graph through a horizontal "arrow of motion" pointing to the right along the x axis.

Doing the same thing with the $\dot{y} = 0$ phase line, we obtain the second panel of Figure 10.10. The next step is to combine the two phase lines into a single diagram. Intersections of the phase lines correspond to steady states of the system (at such points, we have $\dot{x} = 0$ and $\dot{y} = 0$, so both variables remain constant over time). The (x, y) plane is now divided into a number of regions by the phase lines (four if they intersect only once). Combining the information summarized by the two panels of Figure 10.10, we can draw, for each region of the plane, a set of arrows of motion describing the direction of motion of the system along each of the axes, as shown in Figure 10.11.

The pattern of the arrows of motion will give us valuable information about the behavior of the system. In this case, for example, they suggest the existence of a convergent saddle path through the upper and lower quadrants. Arrows alone are not enough, however, to provide a complete description of the trajectories of the system. We may, for example, find configurations that are compatible with a closed cycle or a (convergent or divergent) spiral path; hence, we may need further information to determine the actual pattern of the solution trajectories.

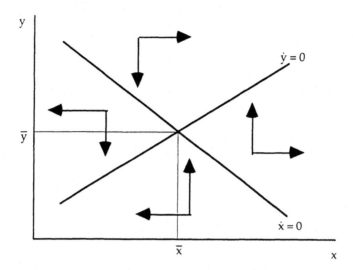

Figure 10.11. Phase diagram.

For the case of discrete-time systems, the procedure is very similar. Given a system of the form

$$x_{t+1} = f(x_t, y_t) \quad \text{or} \quad \Delta x_t = x_{t+1} - x_t = f(x_t, y_t) - x_t \tag{5}$$

$$y_{t+1} = g(x_t, y_t) \quad \text{or} \quad \Delta y_t = y_{t+1} - y_t = g(x_t, y_t) - y_t \tag{6}$$

we obtain the phase lines by setting Δx_t and Δy_t equal to zero (i.e., by deleting the time subscripts and setting $x_{t+1} = x_t = x$):

$$\Delta x_t = 0 \Rightarrow x = f(x, y)$$

$$\Delta y_t = 0 \Rightarrow y = g(x, y)$$

As in the continuous case, the $\Delta x_t = 0$ phase line divides the phase plane into two regions. In one of them, $\Delta x_t > 0$, and x increases over time, whereas in the other, $\Delta x_t < 0$, and x decreases. To determine the pattern of the arrows of motion in each region, we differentiate (5) with respect to one of the variables and evaluate one of the derivatives

$$\frac{\partial \Delta x_t}{\partial x_t} = \frac{\partial f(x_t, y_t)}{\partial x_t} - 1 \quad \text{or} \quad \frac{\partial \Delta x_t}{\partial y_t} = \frac{\partial f(x_t, y_t)}{\partial y_t}$$

at a convenient point in the $\Delta x_t = 0$ line. We then proceed as discussed earlier.

Although phase diagrams can be extremely useful tools, they do not yield sufficient information to analyze all aspects of interest in a system's behavior, and they can be used to study systems in only one or two dimensions. In the remainder of this section, we will review some results that yield more precise (but only local) information about the behavior of nonlinear systems of any dimension. The basic idea is to approximate a nonlinear system in the neighborhood of a steady state by the linear system defined by its derivative. As we will see, the local behaviors of the two systems are very similar in most cases.

(b) Local Analysis by Linearization

Let $f: \mathbb{R}^n \supseteq X \longrightarrow \mathbb{R}^n$ be a C^1 function, and x^0 a point in its domain. As we saw in Chapter 4, we can write

$$f(x) = f(x^0) + Df(x^0)(x - x^0) + E_f(x - x^0) \tag{7}$$

and the differentiability of f implies that the error term $E_f(x - x^0)$ will be small for x close to x^0, in the sense that

$$\lim_{x \to x^0} \frac{\|E_f(x - x^0)\|}{\|x - x^0\|} = 0 \tag{8}$$

With this in mind, consider a nonlinear autonomous system of the form

$$\dot{x} = f(x) \tag{NC}$$

or

$$x_{t+1} = g(x_t) \tag{ND}$$

where $f, g : \mathbb{R}^n \supseteq X \longrightarrow \mathbb{R}^n$ are C^1 functions, and let $\bar{x}$ be a steady state of (N). Then the linear system[8]

$$\dot{x} = Df(\bar{x})(x - \bar{x}) \tag{LC}$$

or

$$x_{t+1} = \bar{x} + Dg(\bar{x})(x_t - \bar{x}) \tag{LD}$$

can be expected to be a reasonable approximation to (N) around the equilibrium point $\bar{x}$, for the only difference between the two systems is the error term $E_f(x - \bar{x})$. Because expression (8) guarantees that this term will be small in the neighborhood of $\bar{x}$, we can expect it to have little influence on the behavior of the system. For a large class of systems this is indeed the case, and as a result we can obtain a fair amount of information about the behavior of the nonlinear system (N) near an equilibrium by studying its linearization (i.e., the linear system defined by the derivative of f or g at the steady state).

To make this result more precise, we need to introduce some additional concepts. Two systems are topologically equivalent if they have similar orbit structures. More formally, two systems are topologically equivalent if their solution trajectories are the same after a continuous "change of coordinates."

Definition 3.1. Topological or flow equivalence. Given two dynamical systems *f* and *g*, we say that they are topologically equivalent if there exists a homeomorphism *h* (a continuous change of coordinates) that maps *f* orbits into *g* orbits while preserving the sense of direction in time.

The concept of flow equivalence allows us to make precise the idea that two systems behave "very similarly." The central result of this section says that most nonlinear systems are topologically equivalent to their linearizations near an equilibrium point. There are, however, some exceptions. Equilibria for which linearization is guaranteed to work well are said to be hyperbolic.

Definition 3.2. Hyperbolic equilibrium. Let $\bar{x}$ be a steady state of the nonlinear system (N), $\dot{x} = f(x)$ [or $x_{t+1} = g(x_t)$]. We say that $\bar{x}$ is a hyperbolic equilibrium if the derivative of f evaluated at $\bar{x}$, $Df(\bar{x})$, has no eigenvalues with zero real parts [$Dg(\bar{x})$ has no eigenvalues with moduli equal to 1].

Theorem 3.3. Grobman-Hartman. Let $\bar{x}$ be a hyperbolic equilibrium of (NC), $\dot{x} = f(x)$. Then there is a neighborhood U of $\bar{x}$ such that (NC) is topologically equivalent to the linear system

$$\dot{x} = Df(\bar{x})(x - \bar{x}) \tag{LC}$$

in U. Similarly, given the discrete system (ND), $x_{t+1} = g(x_t)$, if $\bar{x}$ is hyperbolic and $Dg(\bar{x})$ is invertible, then there is a neighborhood U of $\bar{x}$ such that (ND) is topologically equivalent to the linear system

$$x_{t+1} = \bar{x} + Dg(\bar{x})(x_t - \bar{x}) \tag{LD}$$

Hence, linearization works well around hyperbolic equilibria.[9] In the discrete case, we require $g(\ )$ to be locally invertible, so that the negative orbit is defined.

Our next two results provide more precise information about the behavior of the nonlinear system. The first theorem tells us that around hyperbolic equilibria, the stability type of the equilibrium is the same for the nonlinear system and for its linearization. The second one says that if the linearized system has a saddle point, so does the nonlinear system. Moreover, the nonlinear system has a saddle path of the same dimension as and tangent to the stable space of the linearized system at the steady state.

Theorem 3.4. Local stability for nonlinear systems. Consider the system (NC), $\dot{x} = f(x)$, where $f : \mathbb{R}^n \supseteq X \longrightarrow \mathbb{R}^n$ is a C^1 function, and let $\bar{x}$ be an equilibrium point of (NC). Then we have the following:

- *If all eigenvalues of* Df ($\bar{x}$) *have strictly negative real parts, then* $\bar{x}$ *is asymptotically stable.*
- *If at least one eigenvalue of* Df($\bar{x}$) *has a positive real part, then* $\bar{x}$ *is (locally) unstable.*
- *If at least one eigenvalue of* Df($\bar{x}$) *has a zero real part, and all other eigenvalues have negative real parts, then the equilibrium* $\bar{x}$ *may be stable, asymptotically stable, or unstable.*

Similarly, let $\bar{x}$ *be a steady state of the discrete system (ND),* $x_{t+1} = g(x_t)$. *Then we have the following:*

- *If all eigenvalues of* Dg($\bar{x}$) *have moduli strictly less than 1,* $\bar{x}$ *is asymptotically stable (a sink).*
- *If at least one eigenvalue has modulus greater than 1, then* $\bar{x}$ *is unstable (a source).*
- *If the eigenvalues of the Jacobian are all inside the unit circle, but at least one is on the boundary (has modulus 1), then* $\bar{x}$ *may be stable, asymptotically stable, or unstable.*

Theorem 3.5. Stable manifold. Let $\bar{x}$ *be a steady state of the system (NC),* $\dot{x} = f(x)$ *[or (ND),* $x_{t+1} = g(x_t)$*], where* f, g $: \mathbb{R}^n \longrightarrow \mathbb{R}^n$ *is a* C^1 *function. Suppose the matrix* Df($\bar{x}$) *[Dg($\bar{x}$)] has* k *eigenvalues with negative real parts [inside the unit circle in the complex plane] and* n $-$ k *eigenvalues with positive real parts [outside the unit circle]. Then there exists a* k*-dimensional differentiable manifold* S, *tangent to the stable space of the linearization of (NC) [(ND)] at* $\bar{x}$, *that is invariant under the flow of the system and such that for any* x^0 *in* S, *the solution through* x^0 *converges to the steady state, that is,*

$$\lim_{t \to -\infty} x(t, x^0) = \bar{x}$$

Similarly, there is an (n $-$ k)*-dimensional differentiable manifold* U, *tangent to the unstable space of the linearized system at* $\bar{x}$, *that is invariant under the flow of (N). For any point* y^0 *in* U, *moreover,*

$$\lim_{t \to -\infty} x(t, x^0) = \bar{x}$$

The proofs of these results would take us too far afield. The interested reader can consult Perko (1991, ch. 2) and Ruelle (1989) and the references cited therein.

4. Problems

Problem 4.1. Polar coordinates. When working with planar systems it is sometimes convenient to work in polar coordinates. Consider a point with Cartesian (ordinary) coordinates (x, y). Its polar coordinates are (r, θ), where r is the Euclidean distance from the origin to the point (x, y), and θ

is the angle formed by the line segment going from the origin to the point (x, y) and the horizontal axis. Hence, r and θ are defined by

$$r^2 = x^2 + y^2 \tag{1}$$

$$\theta = \arctan(y/x) \tag{2}$$

and θ is such that

$$\cos\theta = x/r \quad \text{and} \quad \sin\theta = y/r \tag{3}$$

Differentiating (1) and (2) implicitly with respect to time, show that

$$r\dot{r} = x\dot{x} + y\dot{y} \tag{4}$$

$$r^2\dot{\theta} = x\dot{y} - y\dot{x} \tag{5}$$

Hint: Recall that if $y = \arctan u$, then $y' = u'/(1 + u^2)$.
To rewrite a system of the form

$$\dot{x} = f(x, y), \qquad \dot{y} = g(x, y) \tag{6}$$

in polar coordinates, we substitute (6) into (4) and (5) and see whether or not the resulting expressions can be written entirely in terms of r and θ. If this can be done, and the resulting system can be solved explicitly, the solution functions for the original system, $x(t)$ and $y(t)$, can be recovered using the following relation, derived from (3):

$$x = r\cos\theta \quad \text{and} \quad y = r\sin\theta \tag{7}$$

Problem 4.2. Let A be a 2×2 real matrix with complex eigenvalues λ_1, $\lambda_2 = \alpha \pm i\mu$ and corresponding complex eigenvectors $e_1, e_2 = u \pm iv$. It can be shown that the real vectors u and v are linearly independent, so the matrix $P = [u, v]$ is invertible.

(i) Show that

$$P^{-1}AP = R = \begin{bmatrix} \alpha & -\mu \\ \mu & \alpha \end{bmatrix} \tag{8}$$

Equation (8) shows that if A has complex eigenvalues, then the planar system $\dot{z} = Az$ can be written (after a coordinate change) in the form

$$\begin{bmatrix} \dot{x} \\ \dot{y} \end{bmatrix} = \begin{bmatrix} \alpha & -\mu \\ \mu & \alpha \end{bmatrix} \begin{bmatrix} x \\ y \end{bmatrix}$$

or, equivalently,

$$\dot{x} = \alpha x - \mu y \tag{9}$$

$$\dot{y} = \mu x - \alpha y \qquad (10)$$

(Think of using P, rather than the eigenvector matrix E, to "diagonalize" A. The resulting matrix is not diagonal, but, as we will soon see, is quite convenient.)

(ii) Rewrite the system (9)–(10) in polar coordinates and solve it, leaving the solution $(r(t), \theta(t))$ as a function of the initial values $r(0)$ and $\theta(0)$.

(iii) Using the trigonometric identities

$$\sin(a+b) = (\sin a)(\cos b) + (\cos a)(\sin b) \qquad (11)$$

$$\cos(a+b) = (\cos a)(\cos b) - (\sin a)(\sin b) \qquad (12)$$

recover the solution $(x(t), y(t))$ of the original system, written as a function of the initial values $x(0)$ and $y(0)$.

Problem 4.3. Consider the following system of differential equations:

$$\dot{x} = f(x, y) = y + x(c - x^2 - y^2) \qquad (17)$$

$$\dot{y} = g(x, y) = -x + y(c - x^2 - y^2) \qquad (18)$$

(i) Show that the point $(0, 0)$ is the only steady state of the system for any value of c.

(ii) Linearize the system around the steady state and compute its eigenvalues. What can we say about the stability and type of the steady state? (There are three possible cases, depending on the value of c.)

(iii) Show that the original system can be written in polar coordinates as

$$\dot{r} = r(c - r^2) \qquad (19)$$

$$\dot{\theta} = -1 \qquad (20)$$

Using these expressions, describe the behavior of the system, and compare the results with those obtained in (ii). Linearization should give accurate local results in two cases, but we can now "see" more things. What happens in the third case?

Bibliography

Arnold, V. 1990. *Ordinary Differential Equations*. Massachusetts Institute of Technology Press.

Arrowsmith, D., and Place, C. 1990. *An Introduction to Dynamical Systems*. Cambridge University Press.

Azariadis, C., and de la Fuente, A. 1993. Discrete Dynamical Systems. Part I. In: *Intertemporal Macroeconomics*, pp. 1–170. Oxford: Blackwell.

Beavis, B., and Dobbs, I. 1990. *Optimization and Stability Theory for Economic Analysis*. Cambridge University Press.

Beltrami, E. 1987. *Mathematics for Dynamic Modelling*. Orlando, FL: Academic Press.

Boyce, W., and DiPrima, R. 1977. *Elementary Differential Equations*, 3rd ed. New York: Wiley.

Brauer, F., and Nohel, J. 1969. *The Qualitative Theory of Ordinary Differential Equations, An Introduction*. New York: Dover.

Brock, W., and Malliaris, A. 1989. *Differential Equations, Stability and Chaos in Dynamic Economics*. Amsterdam: North Holland.

Coddington, E. 1961. *An Introduction to Ordinary Differential Equations*. Englewood Cliffs, NJ: Prentice-Hall.

Guckenheimer, J., and Holmes, P. 1983. *Nonlinear Oscillations, Dynamical Systems, and Bifurcations of Vector Fields*. Berlin: Springer-Verlag.

Guzmán, M. 1980. *Ecuaciones Diferenciales Ordinarias. Teoría de Estabilidad y Control*. Madrid: Alhambra.

Hale, J., and Koçak, H. 1991. *Dynamics and Bifurcations*. Berlin: Springer-Verlag.

Hirsch, M., and Smale, S. 1974. *Differential Equations, Dynamical Systems and Linear Algebra*. New York: Academic Press.

Lelong-Ferrand, J., and Aurnadies, J. M. 1977. *Cours de Mathématiques. Tome 4: Equations Différentielles, Integrales Multiples*. Paris: Dunod Université.

Luenberger, D. 1979. *Introduction to Dynamic Systems*. New York: Wiley.

Obstfeld, M. 1980. Primer on Differential Equations. Mimeograph, Department of Economics, Columbia University.

Perko, L. 1991. *Differential Equations and Dynamical Systems*. Berlin: Springer-Verlag.

Ruelle, D. 1989. *Elements of Differentiable Dynamics and Bifurcation Theory*. Orlando, FL: Academic Press.

Sanchez, D. 1968. *Ordinary Differential Equations and Stability Theory: An Introduction*. San Francisco: Freeman.

Simmons, G. 1972. *Differential Equations with Applications and Historical Notes*. New York: McGraw-Hill.

Sydsaeter, K. 1981. *Topics in Mathematical Analysis for Economists*. Orlando, FL: Academic Press.

Tu, P. 1994. *Dynamical Systems. An Introduction with Applications in Economics and Biology*. Berlin: Springer-Verlag.

Notes

1 Note that each solution $x^i(t)$ is a vector-valued function.

2 By Euler's formula: $e^{i\theta} = \cos\theta + i\sin\theta$. See Section 7 of Chapter 1.

3 That is, provided $\det A \neq 0$. Because the determinant is equal to the product of the eigenvalues, what we need is that A have no zero roots.

4 We can also transform the given systems into equivalent homogeneous ones, simply by rewriting them in deviations from the steady state. That was what we did in our discussion of scalar systems in Chapter 9.

5 The characteristic roots of the matrix $B = A - I$ are the solutions of the system $\det(B - \lambda I) = \det[A - (\lambda + 1)I] = 0$, and those of A solve $\det(A - \lambda I) = 0$. Hence, the characteristic values of the two matrices satisfy the relation $\lambda_B + 1 = \lambda_A$. For B to be invertible (thus guaranteeing the existence of a unique steady state), we need its determinant to be different from zero, or, equivalently, its eigenvalues all to be different from zero. But $\lambda_B \neq 0$ is equivalent to $\lambda_A \neq 1$; hence the assumptions of the theorem.

6 If equation (3) or (4) cannot be solved explicitly, we can use the implicit-function theorem to determine the slopes of the curves they define.

7 Either one will do, as long as we are careful with how we interpret the sign of the derivative. Essentially, what we are doing is checking the sign of $\dot{x}$ at an arbitrary point in one of the subplanes into which the phase line divides the plane. All the points in a given subplane should yield the same sign for $\dot{x}$; but note that "below" and "to the right"

of an upward-sloping line are one and the same thing, so in the preceding graph it does not matter whether we check at A ($\partial\dot{x}/\partial x$) or at B ($\partial\dot{x}/\partial y$).

It may be easy to remember that $\partial\dot{x}_i/\partial x_i > 0$ implies that the arrow of motion for x_i points away from the corresponding ($\dot{x}_i = 0$) phase line. An increase in x_i makes $\dot{x}_i$ positive, and hence causes x_i to increase even more.

8 To get (L) from (7), notice that $f(\bar{x}) = \underline{0}$ and $g(\bar{x}) = \bar{x}$ by definition of steady state.

9 It can be shown that "most" equilibria are hyperbolic. Intuitively, nonhyperbolicity is a fragile property, for the following reason. Note that the real parts of the eigenvalues of $Df(\bar{x})$ are continuous functions of the entries of the Jacobian matrix. If a given eigenvalue has a zero real part, any small change in the values of these entries will make it nonzero, turning the equilibrium into a hyperbolic steady state.

11

Dynamical Systems. III: Some Applications

This chapter discusses some examples of dynamic economic models in order to illustrate the use in economic theory of some of the techniques and results discussed earlier.

We will first study in detail the dynamics of an IS-LM model with adaptive expectations and sticky prices. This exercise will illustrate the construction of phase diagrams and the use of a system's eigenvalues to determine its stability properties. We will then turn to a simple perfect-foresight model that illustrates how the choice of boundary conditions embodies important economic assumptions. A similar issue arises in regard to Dornbusch's celebrated overshooting model, which will be discussed next. The last part of the chapter contains an introduction to neoclassical growth theory and a discussion of some techniques that are useful in dealing with nonlinear systems.

1. A Dynamic IS-LM Model

Introductory texts in macroeconomics often rely on Keynesian-style static IS-LM models like the one we analyzed in Chapter 5 (Problem 4.1). A simple version of this model can be written as follows:

$$y = \beta y - \gamma r \qquad \text{(IS)} \qquad (1)$$

$$m = \kappa y - \alpha(r + \pi^e) \qquad \text{(LM)} \qquad (2)$$

where the Greek letters are positive parameters, y is the log of real output, r is the real interest rate, π^e is the expected rate of inflation, and $m = \ln(M/P)$ is the logarithm of real money balances, that is, the nominal money supply (M) divided by the price level (P). Equation (1), often called the *IS schedule*, can be interpreted as an equilibrium condition for the goods market. It says that the demand for output, which is an increasing function of income and a decreasing function of the interest rate, should be equal to the supply of output. Equation (2), the *LM schedule*, is an equilibrium condition for the money market. It requires that the demand for real balances, which is

494

increasing in income and decreasing in the nominal interest rate $(r + \pi^e)$, be equal to the real money supply.

If we take the real money supply and the expected rate of inflation as given, equations (1) and (2) can be solved for the equilibrium values of income and the interest rate (y^* and r^*) as functions of m and π^e. It is easy to check that

$$y^* = y(m, \pi^e) = \frac{m + \alpha\pi^e}{c}, \quad \text{where } c \equiv \kappa + \frac{\alpha(1-\beta)}{\gamma} > 0 \qquad (3)$$

$$r^* = r(m, \pi^e) = \frac{-(m + \alpha\pi^e)}{d}, \quad \text{where } d \equiv \alpha + \frac{\kappa\gamma}{1-\beta} > 0 \qquad (4)$$

To turn the preceding model into a dynamic model, we make some simple assumptions about the evolution of the money supply, the formation of expectations, and price dynamics. First, we assume that the nominal money supply M grows over time at a constant rate μ. Hence:

$$\frac{\dot{M}}{M} = \mu \qquad (5)$$

Second, we assume that actual inflation at each point in time ($\pi = \dot{P}/P$) is a function of expected inflation and the difference between current output and a "natural" rate of output $\bar{y}$. Hence, if demand is very high, and that pushes the economy to operate at more than normal capacity, prices will rise faster than expected, as described by the following *Phillips relation*:[1]

$$\left(\frac{\dot{P}}{P}\right)\pi = \pi^e + \theta(y - \bar{y}) \qquad (6)$$

Finally, we assume that expectations are adaptive, with inflation forecasts updated each period by a fraction of the current forecast error:

$$\dot{\pi}^e = \delta(\pi - \pi^e) \qquad (7)$$

To analyze the dynamics of the model, we reduce the preceding equations to a system of differential equations in m and π^e. To obtain the law of motion describing expected inflation, we substitute (6) into (7) and use (3) to get

$$\dot{\pi}^e = \delta\theta[y(m, \pi^e) - \bar{y}] = \delta\theta\left(\frac{m + \alpha\pi^e}{c} - \bar{y}\right) = \frac{\delta\theta\alpha}{c}\pi^e + \frac{\delta\theta}{c}m - \delta\theta\bar{y} \quad (\text{L}.\pi^e)$$

To get the second equation that we need, notice that by definition $m = \ln(M/P) = \ln M - \ln P$. Differentiating this expression with respect to time, we have

$$\dot{m} = \frac{\dot{M}}{M} - \frac{\dot{P}}{P} = \mu - \pi$$

Substituting (6) into this last expression, and using (3), we obtain

$$\dot{m} = \mu - \pi^e - \theta(y - \bar{y}) = \mu - \pi^e + \theta\bar{y} - \theta\frac{m + \alpha\pi^e}{c} = -\left(1 + \frac{\theta\alpha}{c}\right)\pi^e - \frac{\theta}{c}m + \mu + \theta\bar{y}$$

$$\text{(L.}m)$$

Hence, the model reduces to a system of two linear and autonomous differential equations.[2] We will construct its phase diagram and compute the eigenvalues of the coefficient matrix to check the stability of the steady state.

In what follows, we treat π^e and P (and therefore $m = M/P$) as predetermined variables. That is, we assume that the time paths of actual prices and expected inflation are continuous and therefore do not display sudden jumps. Economically, we are saying that both prices and expectations respond with some sluggishness to changing circumstances. This assumption, common in old-fashioned Keynesian-type models, is not necessarily the most reasonable one that can be made. In later sections we will study other models in which prices are allowed to adjust instantaneously, even if this involves a discrete jump in their level.

(a) *Phase Diagram and Stability Analysis*

The evolution of our model economy is described by a first-order system of differential equations:

$$\dot{\pi}^e = \delta\theta\left(\frac{m + \alpha\pi^e}{c} - \bar{y}\right) = \frac{\delta\theta\alpha}{c}\pi^e + \frac{\delta\theta}{c}m - \delta\theta\bar{y} \qquad \text{(L.}\pi^e)$$

$$\dot{m} = \mu - \pi^e + \theta\left(\bar{y} - \frac{m + \alpha\pi^e}{c}\right) = -\left(1 + \frac{\theta\alpha}{c}\right)\pi^e - \frac{\theta}{c}m + \mu + \theta\bar{y} \qquad \text{(L.}m)$$

As a first step in our analysis of this system we compute its steady state and construct its phase diagram. Setting $\dot{\pi}^e = 0$ and $\dot{m} = 0$ in the laws of motion describing expected inflation and the real money supply, we obtain the equations of the phase lines:

$$\dot{\pi}^e = 0 \Rightarrow \frac{m + \alpha\pi^e}{c} = \bar{y} \Rightarrow m = c\bar{y} - \alpha\pi^e \qquad \text{(P.}\pi^e)$$

$$\dot{m} = 0 \Rightarrow \pi^e = \mu + \theta\left(\bar{y} - \frac{m + \alpha\pi^e}{c}\right) \qquad \text{(P.}m)$$

This system of equations can be solved for the steady-state values of m and π^e. Using (P.π^e) in (P.m), we see that

$$\bar{\pi}^e = \mu \qquad (8)$$

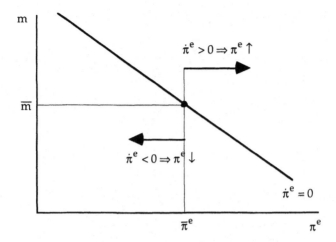

Figure 11.1. The $\dot{\pi}^e = 0$ phase line.

Next, substituting (8) into (P.π^e),

$$\overline{m} = c\overline{y} - \alpha\mu \tag{9}$$

Given $\overline{m}$ and $\overline{\pi}^e$, we can use (3) and (4) to solve for the steady-state values of output and the interest rate:

$$y^*(\overline{m}, \overline{\pi}^e) = \frac{\overline{m} + \alpha\overline{\pi}^e}{c} = \frac{c\overline{y} - \alpha\mu + \alpha\mu}{c} = \overline{y}$$

$$r(\overline{m}, \overline{\pi}^e) = \frac{-(\overline{m} + \alpha\overline{\pi}^e)}{d} = \frac{-(c\overline{y} - \alpha\mu + \alpha\mu)}{d} = -(c/d)\overline{y}$$

We can think of the steady state as a long-run equilibrium position. In such an equilibrium, both anticipated inflation and actual inflation (see equation (7)) are equal to the rate of money creation μ, and because there are no inflationary surprises, output is at its natural rate. The equilibrium money supply is positively related to (the natural rate of) output and negatively related to μ – because monetary growth induces inflation, which lowers the demand for real balances.

Turning now to the dynamics of the model, the next step is to plot each of the phase lines with the corresponding arrows of motion. From

$$m = c\overline{y} - \alpha\pi^e \tag{P.π^e}$$

we see that the $\dot{\pi}^e = 0$ phase line defines a downward-sloping function in the (π^e, m) plane, as shown in Figure 11.1. This line divides the plane into two regions: one in which $\dot{\pi}^e > 0$ (i.e., expected inflation increases over time), and a second one in which the reverse is true. To determine which is which, consider the following experiment: Imagine that, starting out from a point in the

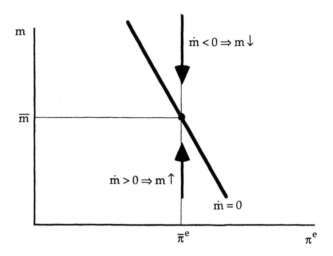

Figure 11.2. The $\dot{m} = 0$ phase line.

$\dot{\pi}^e = 0$ phase line (say the steady state), we increase the value of m slightly and see what happens to the value of $\dot{\pi}^e$. More formally, we use $(L.\pi^e)$ to compute the derivative of $\dot{\pi}^e$ with respect to m, and (if this derivative is not a constant) we evaluate it at the starting point:

$$\frac{\partial \dot{\pi}^e}{\partial m} = \delta\theta/c > 0$$

Because the derivative is positive and the initial value of $\dot{\pi}^e$ was zero, we conclude that moving "north" of the phase line puts us in the region in which $\dot{\pi}^e > 0$. Hence, π^e increases over time in the region above the phase line, and the corresponding arrows of motion along the π^e axis point to the right.[3]

For the $\dot{m} = 0$ phase line we proceed in similar fashion (Figure 11.2). Solving for m as a function of π^e in $(P.m)$, we see that the phase line is downward-sloping:

$$m = \frac{c}{\theta}(\mu + \theta\bar{y}) - \frac{c}{\theta}\left(1 + \frac{\theta\alpha}{c}\right)\pi^e \tag{10}$$

Differentiating $(L.m)$, we see that the partial derivative of $\dot{m}$ with respect to m,

$$\frac{\partial \dot{m}}{\partial m} = -(\theta/c) < 0$$

is negative. Thus, $\dot{m}$ decreases (from an initial value of zero at the steady state) and becomes negative as we move into the region above the phase line. Hence, m decreases over time in this area of the phase plane, and we indicate this fact with an arrow of motion pointing down along the m axis.

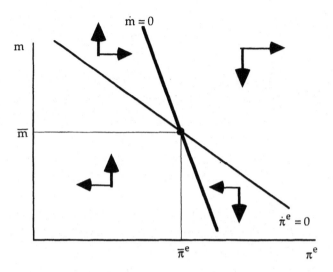

Figure 11.3. Phase diagram.

Combining the two phase lines and the corresponding arrows of motion, we can now construct the phase diagram. Because both lines are downward-sloping, the first step is to determine which is steeper. Using (P.*m*) and (10), we see that

$$\left|\left(\frac{dm}{d\pi^e}\right)_\pi\right| = \alpha < (c/\theta) + \alpha = \left|\left(\frac{dm}{d\pi^e}\right)_m\right|$$

so the phase line (P.*m*), $\dot{m} = 0$, is steeper, as shown in Figure 11.3. Notice that the pattern of arrows of motion is compatible with (convergent or divergent) spiral trajectories or with a saddle path, depending on the values of the parameters. To be more precise, we have to look at the eigenvalues of the system.

To determine the local stability properties of the steady state, we compute the eigenvalues of the coefficient matrix of the system,

$$A = \begin{bmatrix} -\dfrac{\theta}{c} & -\left(1 + \dfrac{\alpha\theta}{c}\right) \\ \dfrac{\delta\theta}{c} & \dfrac{\alpha\delta\theta}{c} \end{bmatrix}$$

As we saw in Chapter 3 (Section 6), the characteristic roots of *A* are given by

$$\lambda_1, \lambda_2 = \frac{\text{tr} \pm \sqrt{\text{tr}^2 - 4\det}}{2}$$

where

$$\operatorname{tr} A = \lambda_1 + \lambda_2 = -\frac{\theta}{c} + \frac{\alpha\delta\theta}{c} = \frac{\theta}{c}(\alpha\delta - 1)$$

$$\det A = \lambda_1\lambda_2 = -\frac{\theta}{c}\frac{\alpha\delta\theta}{c} + \left(1 + \frac{\theta\alpha}{c}\right)\frac{\delta\theta}{c} = -\frac{\alpha\delta\theta^2}{c^2} + \frac{\delta\theta}{c} + \frac{\alpha\delta\theta^2}{c^2} = \frac{\delta\theta}{c} > 0$$

Hence, the determinant of the coefficient matrix is positive, and the trace may be either positive or negative depending on parameter values. Similarly, the discriminant $\Delta = \operatorname{tr}^2 - 4\det$ may be either positive or negative, and as a result the eigenvalues of the system may be either real numbers or complex numbers.

Suppose first that the eigenvalues are real numbers (i.e., that $\Delta > 0$). In that case the positive sign of the determinant (which, as we know, is equal to the product of the eigenvalues) implies that λ_1 and λ_2 have the same sign. The stability of the system then depends on the sign of the trace (whose value is equal to the sum of the eigenvalues). In particular, the steady state will be stable if

$$\operatorname{tr} A = \lambda_1 + \lambda_2 < 0 \Leftrightarrow \delta < 1/\alpha$$

as both eigenvalues will then be negative real numbers.[4]

If the discriminant is negative, on the other hand, the eigenvalues of the system will be complex conjugates of the form $\lambda_1 = a + ib$ and $\lambda_2 = a - ib$. Hence,

$$\operatorname{tr} = \lambda_1 + \lambda_2 = 2a$$

so the sign of the real parts of the eigenvalues is the same as the sign of the trace. If $\delta < 1/\alpha$, the trace and therefore the real parts of the eigenvalues are negative, and the system is stable.

Hence, the stability condition is the same in both cases and depends crucially on the size of the expectations adjustment parameter δ. This parameter tells us how quickly expectations are revised in response to forecast errors. If δ is small, there is an element of sluggishness built into the model. Inflationary expectations take a while to catch up with actual inflation. They do eventually catch up, however, and equilibrium is restored, but this may take some time. Thus, with low δ, the model is stable and slow to adjust. If, on the other hand, δ is "too large," the model becomes unstable, because price expectations "overreact," and because expected inflation becomes a component of actual inflation, there is no way to restore equilibrium.

In the remainder of this section we will assume that parameter values are such that the eigenvalues are both real and negative. This gives us a "well-behaved system" that converges asymptotically to the steady state without cyclical oscillations.

(b) Effects of Monetary Policy

We can now use the phase diagram and the stability assumption we have just made to analyze the response of the system to a change in the value of one of its parameters. In particular, we focus on the effect of a once-and-for-all change in the rate of money creation μ.

Assume that we are initially at the steady state S_0 that corresponds to a constant rate of monetary growth μ_0. Next, imagine that the government increases the rate of growth of the nominal money supply from μ_0 to μ_1 and promises never to change it again, and people believe it. What happens?

Because we have assumed the system is stable, it will converge asymptotically to a new steady state S_1 that corresponds to the new value of μ. There are two different questions to consider: First, we have to see what happens to the steady state when the parameter changes. This is an exercise in comparative statics. Second, we would like to determine the path the system follows from its initial position (the steady state associated with μ_0) to the new long-run equilibrium.

Let us start with the long-run effects of the proposed policy change. Recall that the steady state of the system lies at the intersection of the phase lines

$$m = \frac{c}{\theta}(\mu + \theta \bar{y}) - \frac{c}{\theta}\left(1 + \frac{\theta \alpha}{c}\right)\pi^e \qquad (\text{P}.m)$$

$$m = c\bar{y} - \alpha \pi^e \qquad (\text{P}.\pi^e)$$

Inspection of these equations shows that an increase in μ shifts the $\dot{m} = 0$ phase line upward, but has no effect on the $\dot{\pi}^e = 0$ locus. The new steady state S_1 will therefore lie to the southeast of the old one, as illustrated in Figure 11.4. Hence, the long-run effect of an increase in the rate of money growth is to increase expected inflation and reduce real money holdings.

Recalling equation (8), $\bar{\pi}^e = \mu$, we see that an increase in the rate of monetary growth leads in the long run to a proportional increase in the rate of expected (and actual) inflation and to a reduction in the stock of real balances. We also know that

$$y^*(\bar{m}, \bar{\pi}^e) = \bar{y} \quad \text{and} \quad r^*(\bar{m}, \bar{\pi}^e) = -(c/d)\bar{y}$$

so steady-state output and real interest rates are independent of monetary policy. Hence, monetary policy is neutral in the long run, because it has no effect on output[5] or interest rates. Its only effect is a proportional increase in the rate of inflation that reduces the demand for real balances.

In the short run, however, a change in the rate of money creation will have real effects. Figure 11.5 describes the transition to the new long-run equilibrium. At time zero, the system is at point S_0. This point is the steady state

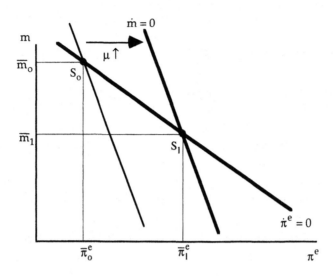

Figure 11.4. Long-run effect of an increase in the rate of money creation.

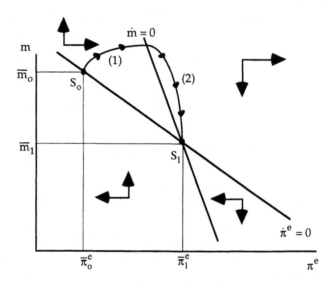

Figure 11.5. Adjustment to an increase in the rate of money creation.

corresponding to μ_0, but it is no longer a steady state when the increase in the rate of money creation shifts the $\dot{m} = 0$ phase line to the right. Under the new policy, the arrows of motion of the system point to the northeast at S_0. Hence, money balances and expected inflation increase along the first part of the adjustment trajectory, labeled (1) in Figure 11.5. Eventually, however, the system enters into a different quadrant in which the arrows of motion point to the southeast, the segment of the system's trajectory labeled

(2). During this second stage of the adjustment process, expected inflation continues to increase, but real money holdings now decrease, eventually falling below their initial value.

Given the trajectories of π^e and m, we can derive the time paths of output and the real interest rate. We have seen that

$$y^*(m, \pi^e) = \frac{m + \alpha\pi^e}{c} \quad \text{and} \quad r^*(m, \pi^e) = -\frac{m + \alpha\pi^e}{d}$$

where c and d are positive numbers. In part (1) of the adjustment trajectory, both m and π^e are increasing, so y^* is rising, and r^* is falling. This is the standard Keynesian result concerning the expansionary effects of a loosening of monetary policy. These responses, however, are reversed later, with both income and the real interest rate returning to their original levels in the new steady state S_1.

2. An Introduction to Perfect-Foresight Models

In Chapters 9 and 10 we warned the reader that the selection of appropriate boundary conditions often is not as straightforward in economic models as in the case of physical systems. In this section we study two examples that will serve to illustrate this point and to introduce the reader to the logic of *perfect-foresight models*. The first is a simple model of stock prices based on the no-arbitrage principle, and the second is a model of exchange-rate determination. In both cases we seek the equilibrium path of some asset price. Because this variable is not tied down by previous history, we have to rely on economic considerations to determine which of the infinitely many solutions of a certain dynamical system should be considered the equilibrium trajectory.

(a) A Model of Stock Prices

Suppose investors in financial markets have a choice between two assets: government bonds, which pay a fixed interest rate r, and shares of stock, which pay a constant stream of dividends d. We take r and d as given and develop a model of the evolution of share prices (v).

To derive the asset-pricing equation, we start out from the postulate that no obvious profit opportunities should remain unexploited in equilibrium. The instantaneous return earned by an agent who invests v dollars in bonds is rv. Alternatively, if he buys a share of stock, his expected return is the sum of the dividend d and the expected increase in the value of the share $\dot{v}_e = dv_e/dt$. In equilibrium, the expected returns on the two assets must be the same, yielding the condition

$$rv = d + \dot{v}_e \qquad (1)$$

If this condition did not hold, we could not be in equilibrium, because no investor would want to hold the asset with the lower return. Prices would have to adjust until somebody was willing to hold all existing assets.

It remains to specify how expectations are formed. We will consider two possibilities. The first is that agents have *adaptive expectations*, formed in accordance with the equation

$$\dot{v}_e = \alpha(v - v_e) \qquad (2)$$

That is, if the actual price of the share v exceeds its expected price v_e, agents revise their expectations upward. The size of the correction depends on the "forecast error" and on the value of the parameter α, which can be interpreted as a measure of the speed of learning. To ensure that the model behaves sensibly, we assume that $0 < \alpha < r$. The second possibility is that agents have perfect foresight (i.e., that they forecast share prices correctly). In this case, $v_e(t) = v(t)$ for all t (and hence $\dot{v}_e = \dot{v}$).

In what follows, we refer to the present value of the stream of dividends,

$$v^* = \int_0^\infty d e^{-rt} dt = \frac{d}{r}$$

as the *fundamental value* of the stock.

(i) Adaptive Expectations

In this section we will assume that expectations are adaptive. Under this assumption, the evolutions of actual and expected share prices are described by equations (1) and (2). To solve the model, we start by finding the time path of expected share prices. Solving for v in (1),

$$v = \frac{d}{r} + \frac{\dot{v}_e}{r} \qquad (3)$$

and substituting this expression in (2), we obtain a differential equation in v_e:

$$\dot{v}_e = \alpha v - \alpha v_e = \alpha\left(\frac{d}{r} + \frac{\dot{v}_e}{r}\right) - \alpha v_e \Rightarrow \dot{v}_e\left(1 - \frac{\alpha}{r}\right) = -\alpha v_e + \frac{\alpha d}{r}$$

$$\Rightarrow \dot{v}_e = -\gamma v_e + \frac{\alpha d}{r - \alpha}, \quad \text{where} \quad \gamma \equiv \frac{\alpha r}{r - \alpha} \qquad (4)$$

Setting $\dot{v}_e = 0$ in (4), we can solve for the steady-state value of v_e:

$$\frac{\alpha r}{r - \alpha} v_e = \frac{\alpha d}{r - \alpha}$$

$$\Rightarrow \bar{v}_e = v^* = \frac{d}{r} \qquad (5)$$

The solution of (4) is then given by

$$v_e(t) = v^* + [v_e(0) - v^*]e^{-\gamma t} \tag{5}$$

Under the assumption that $\alpha < r$, we have $\gamma > 0$, and the system is stable. Any initial discrepancy between the expected share price and its *fundamental value* decreases over time and disappears asymptotically. In the long run, the expected price of a share of stock is equal to the present value of its dividends.

Next, we solve for the time path of v. Substituting

$$\dot{v}_e = \alpha(v - v_e) \tag{2}$$

in (3), we have

$$v = v^* + \frac{\alpha}{r}(v - v_e) \Rightarrow v\left(1 - \frac{\alpha}{r}\right) = v^* - \frac{\alpha}{r}v_e$$

Substituting equation (5) into this expression and solving for v, we obtain, after some algebra,

$$v(t) = v^* - \frac{\alpha}{r - \alpha}[v_e(0) - v^*]e^{-\gamma t} \tag{6}$$

Under our assumptions, $e^{-\gamma t} \to 0$ as $t \to \infty$. Hence, asymptotically, the market price of the stock also converges to its fundamental value v^*.

The long-run predictions of the model are both intuitive and reasonable: In the steady state, the market price of the share is equal to the discounted value of its dividend stream, and expectations are correct ($\bar{v} = \bar{v}_e = v^*$). This is no longer the case in the short run, as we will soon see. During the transition to the steady state, actual and expected prices need not be equal, and both can deviate from the stock's fundamental value. Comparing (5) and (6), we see, moreover, that $v(t)$ and $v_e(t)$ lie on opposite sides of v^* and must be moving in opposite directions (Figure 11.6). That is, when actual prices are "too high" relative to the fundamental value, the expected price is below v^*, and when share prices are rising, expected share prices are falling.

Another disturbing feature of the model is that the forecast error is predictable. Combining (5) and (6), we can solve explicitly for the time path of the forecast error,

$$v_e(t) - v(t) = (v^* + [v_e(0) - v^*]e^{-\gamma t}) - \left(v^* - \frac{\alpha}{r - \alpha}[v_e(0) - v^*]e^{-\gamma t}\right)$$

$$= \frac{r}{r - \alpha}[v_e(0) - v^*]e^{-\gamma t} \tag{7}$$

Setting $t = 0$ in equation (7),

$$v_e(0) - v(0) = \frac{r}{r - \alpha}[v_e(0) - v^*]$$

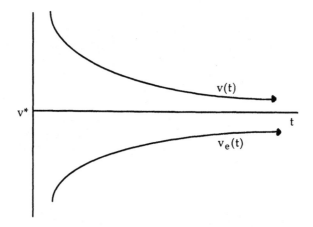

Figure 11.6. Time paths of actual and expected stock prices with adaptive expectations.

we obtain a relation between the actual and expected prices of the stock at time zero:

$$\frac{r-\alpha}{r}v(0)+\frac{\alpha}{r}v_e(0) = v^* \tag{8}$$

Notice that equations (1) and (2) describe the time paths of v and v_e, but do not tie down their initial values. For both equations to hold simultaneously, these initial values must satisfy condition (8), but what does this mean? If we take the initial expected price as given, then (8) gives the equilibrium price of the stock at time zero. Alternatively, if we take $v(0)$ as given, we can solve (8) for $v_e(0)$, but it is hard to see why agents would choose to make just such a forecast. In any event, if initial expected prices are correct $(v_e(0) = v(0))$, then both actual and expected prices must be equal to the fundamental value of the stock v^*; but if the expected price at time zero is different from v^*, the initial equilibrium price must be on the opposite side of v^*, and the forecast error disappears only gradually.

Perhaps the most unsatisfactory implication of the model we have just developed is that (except when $v_e(0) = v(0) = v^*$) agents commit, each period, a perfectly predictable forecast error that costs them money. As a result, an agent who knows the structure of the model will have an incentive to deviate from the predicted behavior, thereby invalidating the theory. For example, if you know that expected prices tomorrow will be below market prices, you can write a contract today offering to buy tomorrow at the expected price. If expectations are formed as we have assumed, somebody will be willing to buy such a contract – but when tomorrow comes you will immediately be able to resell the stock at a profit. Hence, the predictable discrepancy between actual and expected prices involves an opportunity for quick profits. Agents would have an incentive to compute the actual trajectory of prices, but the model assumes that they do not do so (i.e., that they form expectations according to (2)).

This is hard to reconcile with the hypothesis that individuals are rational and maximize utility or wealth. In the context of a model as simple as the present one, without uncertainty or asymmetric information, the easiest way to model the idea that individuals are rational is to assume that they know the model and all the relevant data, such as the time path of dividends. But then each agent could compute the solution, just as we have done, and it makes little sense to assume that forecast errors would be eliminated only gradually when it would be possible (and profitable) to avoid them completely.

(ii) Perfect Foresight

In conclusion, in a world without uncertainty, adaptive expectations are not consistent with the assumption of rationality. The theory works only as long as agents do not understand what is happening. To avoid this problem, we will postulate that agents form expectations that are consistent with the structure of the model. In particular, we assume that the agents know the model and use it, along with all the relevant information they have, to predict the evolution of share prices. Because there is no stochastic element in the model, the time path of prices will be correctly anticipated. Hence, we replace equation (2) with the assumption of perfect foresight:

$$v_e(t) = v(t) \, \forall \, t \tag{9}$$

Let us see where this assumption takes us. Given (9), $\dot{v}_e = \dot{v}$ for all t, and the equation describing the time path of asset prices becomes

$$rv = d + \dot{v}$$
$$\Rightarrow \dot{v} = rv - d \tag{10}$$

Like equation (4), equation (10) has a unique stationary solution,

$$v^* = d/r$$

in which share prices reflect the discounted value of the dividend stream. The dynamics of the two systems are, however, very different. In particular, whereas (4) is stable, the stationary state of (10) is unstable, because $r > 0$. The general solution of (10) is given by

$$v^g(t, c) = v^* + ce^{rt} = v^* + [v(0) - v^*]e^{rt} \tag{11}$$

where we emphasize that assigning a value to the arbitrary constant c is equivalent to choosing an initial value for the share price.

At first sight, this does not look very promising. Because the "bubble term" ce^{rt} goes to plus or minus infinity as $t \to \infty$, equation (11) predicts that share prices will explode, except in the case in which $v(0) = v^*$. If we take the initial value of v as given, then the model predicts an unreasonable-looking path of share prices, except by chance. This difficulty, common in asset-pricing models, almost led to the abandonment of perfect-foresight models. However, researchers like Sargent and Wallace (1973) and Calvo (1977) soon realized that taking initial asset prices as given was not always the most reasonable alternative. Because asset prices are free to move, and even "jump" at each point in time, at least half the problem is determining their initial value.

In more general terms, the important point is that it is not always legitimate from the point of view of economic theory to take the initial value of a variable as a parameter fixed by previous history. The choice of an appropriate boundary condition often requires a little thought about the economics of the problem. What equation (10) says is that the solution of the model must be one of the family of functions described by $v^g(t, c)$. The economic problem is that of determining which of these trajectories corresponds to an equilibrium. The answer then determines the appropriate boundary condition and therefore the initial value of v.

For the sake of the argument, let us take an arbitrary value of $v(0)$ as given. The instability of the system implies that if the initial price is incorrect (in the sense of not reflecting the fundamental value of the asset), then things can only get worse. To see why, let us return to (10) and rewrite it in the form

$$\frac{\dot{v}+d}{v}=r \quad \text{or} \quad \dot{v}=rv-d=r(v-v^*) \tag{12}$$

Suppose that $v(0) > v^*$ (i.e., that share prices are higher than what would be reasonable in terms of the present value of the underlying dividend flow). Then, in order for (12) to hold, the price of the share must be increasing at a rate such that the capital gains are just enough to make up for a dividend that is low relative to the price. Today's price increase, on the other hand, makes tomorrow's price even less reasonable, and therefore requires an even higher rate of appreciation in the future.

It is not clear what mechanism would make tomorrow's share prices rise by enough to justify, ex post, today's unreasonably high price. In fact, the only sensible way to interpret such an explosive path of share prices is as a "bubble" in which unreasonable expectations become self-fulfilling. Although such phenomena are not unknown, it may be reasonable to rule out such behavior under "normal" circumstances. This leaves us with only the constant solution ($c = 0$) given by the fundamental value of the asset, in which share prices accurately reflect the present value of dividends. In equilibrium, the value of the share, v, jumps immediately to v^* and remains constant forever – unless the system is disturbed in some way.

It is worth noting that the assumption of perfect foresight eliminates the inconsistency we found in the adaptive expectations model. An individual who knows the structure of the economy and knows that all other agents use an adaptive forecasting rule has every incentive to deviate from the predicted behavior (i.e., to forecast prices correctly, and get rich along the way). But because the same is true of each and every agent, the model cannot be correct. With perfect foresight, by contrast, everybody uses the correct model to predict prices, and nobody has an incentive to behave differently. Although the ability to predict prices exactly does not generate extraordinary returns, any other alternative will lose money, on average.

Next, we will see how the model can be used to analyze the response of share prices to a change in the tax rate on dividends. The exercise will also serve to check the "reasonableness" of the model.

Assume that dividends are taxed at a flat rate τ that remains constant over time. Then equation (10) becomes

$$\dot{v} = rv - (1 - \tau)d \qquad (13)$$

where $(1 - \tau)d$ is the net-of-tax dividend. The general solution of this equation is given by

$$v^g(t, c; \tau) = v^*(\tau) + ce^{rt} = v^*(\tau) + [v(0) - v^*(\tau)]e^{rt}$$

where the stationary solution

$$v^*(\tau) = \frac{(1 - \tau)d}{r}$$

now reflects the present value of *after-tax* dividends.

The policy change we will analyze involves an increase in the tax rate from τ_0 to some higher value τ_1. To start, let us suppose that the tax increase is unexpected and that the agents believe that the new rate will remain in effect forever. As shown in Figure 11.7, the change in the tax parameter shifts the phase line upward, yielding a new stationary solution

$$v^*(\tau_1) = \frac{(1 - \tau_1)d}{r} < \frac{(1 - \tau_0)d}{r} = v^*(\tau_0)$$

If we rule out explosive paths, the value of v jumps down immediately after the policy change to its new fundamental value $v^*(\tau_1)$. The model predicts, reasonably enough, that a tax increase will result in an immediate drop in prices equal to the reduction in the present value of the after-tax dividend stream.

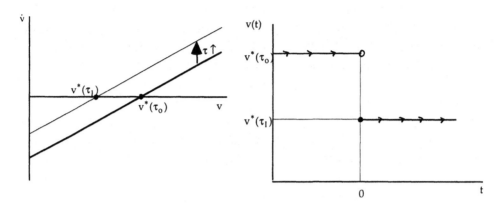

Figure 11.7. Response of stock prices to an unanticipated increase in dividend taxes.

Next, imagine that today (at time zero) the government announces (and everybody believes it) that the tax rate will be raised to τ_1 at some time T in the future and will remain constant thereafter. To determine the equilibrium path of the system following the announcement, we work backward in time. If we rule out explosive paths, at time T the system must be at the new fundamental solution $v^*(\tau_1)$. For $t < T$, the initial tax rate (τ_0) still applies, and the system must therefore obey the "old" law of motion:

$$\dot{v} = rv - (1 - \tau_0)d \tag{14}$$

Hence, the equilibrium path of the system during the transition period $[0, T)$ must be one of the family of functions described by the general solution of the "old" system:

$$v^g(t, c; \tau_0) = v^*(\tau_0) + ce^{rt} = v^*(\tau_0) + [v(0) - v^*(\tau_0)]e^{rt} \tag{15}$$

The equilibrium solution is the one that puts us at the new fundamental price $v^*(\tau_1)$ precisely at the time T at which the policy change takes effect. Formally, the appropriate boundary condition is

$$v(T; \tau_0) = v^*(\tau_1) \Rightarrow v^*(\tau_0) + [v(0) - v^*(\tau_0)]e^{rT} = v^*(\tau_1)$$

Notice that the only unknown in this expression is the price of the stock at time zero (i.e., at the moment of the announcement). Solving for $v(0)$,

$$v(0) = v^*(\tau_0) - [v^*(\tau_0) - v^*(\tau_1)]e^{-rT} \tag{16}$$

the initial drop in share prices is given by

$$v^*(\tau_0) - v(0) = [v^*(\tau_0) - v^*(\tau_1)]e^{-rT} \tag{17}$$

Substituting this expression into the general solution, we obtain the trajectory of stock prices during the transition to the new steady state:

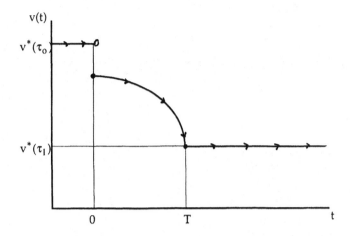

Figure 11.8. Response of stock prices to an anticipated increase in dividend taxes.

$$v(t) = v^*(\tau_0) - [v^*(\tau_0) - v^*(\tau_1)]e^{r(t-T)} \qquad (18)$$

Hence, stock prices fall immediately as a result of the announcement, and they continue to fall until they reach the new fundamental price precisely at the time of the tax change. Observe also that the size of the immediate capital loss is equal to the discounted value (at time zero) of the change in the stock's fundamental value. In some sense, this is what we should expect.

Figure 11.8 displays the time path of share prices. During the transition period, prices follow what looks like (but is not) an explosive path of the "old" system. In fact, the equilibrium path is the only solution of the system that yields a continuous trajectory from time zero on and ends up at the new fundamental value of the stock at time T. This continuity property has an intuitive economic interpretation: If share prices were to remain constant at $v^*(\tau_0)$ until the time of the actual policy change, agents would be anticipating a capital loss of $v^*(\tau_0) - v^*(\tau_1)$ at time T. To avoid such loss, each agent would try to sell his shares just an instant before T. Hence, prices would fall, pushing $v(T - \varepsilon)$ below $v^*(\tau_0)$. In fact, the adjustment must start even earlier, for the same logic implies that the price cannot be $v^*(\tau_0)$ at time $T - 2\varepsilon$ if agents anticipate a capital loss at $T - \varepsilon$, and so on. In fact, there cannot be an equilibrium in which agents anticipate a rate of return on the stock lower than r at any point in the future. Hence, the full burden of the adjustment must fall on the initial shareholders, who, taken by surprise by the announcement, cannot do anything to avoid a capital loss.

Problem 2.1 asks the reader to verify that the solution trajectory we have just derived can be obtained directly by solving a nonautonomous version of the stock-pricing equation.

Problem 2.1. When the tax rate on dividends varies over time, our stock-pricing equation can be written in the form

$$\dot{v} = rv - b(t) \tag{1}$$

where

$$b(t) = (1 - \tau_t)d$$

Equation (1) is a nonautonomous linear equation of the type we studied in Section 5 of Chapter 9. Its solution can be written in the ("forward") form

$$v(t) = [v(0) - F(0)]e^{rt} + F(t) \tag{2}$$

where

$$F(t) = \int_t^\infty b(s)e^{r(t-s)}ds \tag{3}$$

the *fundamental solution* of (1), is the discounted value of the stream of future after-tax dividends, and $[v(0) - F(0)]e^{rt}$ is a *bubble term* capturing possible deviations from the fundamental value of the stock. By the same logic as in our earlier discussion, we will rule out bubbles and assume that $v(t) = F(t)$ for all t. Hence, the value of the stock at each point in time will be given by (3). We will now show that this fundamental solution gives the same time path of stock prices in response to a preannounced future increase in dividend taxes as the procedure we followed earlier.

(i) Show that

$$\int_t^b e^{r(t-s)}ds = \frac{1}{r}\left(1 - e^{r(t-b)}\right) \tag{4}$$

(ii) As before, assume that an announcement is made at time zero that dividend taxes will increase at time T from τ_0 to τ_1. Then

$$\begin{aligned} b(t) &= (1 - \tau_0)d \quad \text{for } t \in [0, T) \\ &= (1 - \tau_1)d \quad \text{for } t \in [T, \infty) \end{aligned} \tag{5}$$

Using (3) and (4), compute the trajectory of stock prices following the announcement.

Problem 2.2. Cagan's model with perfect foresight. Consider the following specification of equilibrium in the money market:

$$m(t) - p(t) = -\lambda\pi(t), \quad \text{with } \lambda > 0 \tag{1}$$

where m is the log of the nominal money supply, p is the log of the price level, and $\pi = \dot{p}$ is the (both actual and expected) inflation rate (i.e., we are assuming perfect foresight). If we are willing to assume away real-side complications (e.g., assume that output is fixed at the natural rate), then the full equilibrium of the economy is determined by this equation.

Assume that the nominal money supply grows at a constant rate $\dot{m} = \mu$. Differentiating (1) with respect to time, we can obtain a differential equation in the inflation rate,

$$\mu - \pi = \dot{m} - \dot{p} = -\lambda\dot{\pi}$$
$$\Rightarrow \dot{\pi} = \theta(\pi - \mu), \quad \text{where } \theta \equiv 1/\lambda \qquad (2)$$

(i) Find the steady state of this equation, and write its general solution.

(ii) Assume that μ remains constant forever. From an economic point of view, which is the most reasonable particular solution of this equation? Why?

(iii) Assume that we are at time zero and that μ has always been constant at some value μ_0. Suddenly the government announces that at some time T in the future the rate of money creation will increase to $\mu_1 > \mu_0$ and will remain constant forever thereafter (and people believe the announcement). Describe the evolution of the inflation rate following the announcement and your reasons for selecting this particular adjustment path. Write the particular solution corresponding to this behavior, and use it to solve for the jump in the price level at the time of the announcement. What factors determine the size of this jump?

(b) Dornbusch's Overshooting Model

The model we study in this section is an open-economy IS-LM model with perfect foresight and sticky output prices. It is designed to study how price rigidity in goods markets affects the short-run responses of exchange rates to policy shifts and other exogenous disturbances. Because the focus is on short-run dynamics, we assume that the level of output is fixed. We will find that the sticky-price assumption yields a model that mimics the observed tendency of exchange rates to exhibit considerably more volatility than the underlying "fundamentals."

As in Section 1, Greek letters will denote positive parameters, and variables denoted by lowercase letters will be the natural logarithms of the corresponding variables denoted by uppercase letters. Asterisks will be used to denote foreign variables. For example, $p = \ln P$ is the log of the domestic price level, and hence $\dot{p} = \dot{P}/P$ is the domestic rate of inflation. We will use s to denote (the log of) the nominal exchange rate, defined as the price of one unit of foreign money in domestic currency units. Hence, an increase in s represents a loss of value of the home currency, and $\dot{s}$ is its rate of depreciation.

Starting with the market for domestic output, the basic equations of the model are the following. Output supply is fixed at some constant, exogenous level

$$y^s = y \tag{1}$$

Demand for domestic output, on the other hand, depends positively on the ratio of foreign to domestic output prices expressed in a common currency unit $(s + p^* - p)$. Aggregate demand is also positively related to government expenditures g and negatively related to the real interest rate $R - \dot{p}$, where R is the nominal interest rate, and $\dot{p}$ is the (actual and expected) rate of inflation:

$$y^d = \delta(s + p^* - p) - \sigma(R - \dot{p}) + g \tag{2}$$

If demand exceeds supply, inventories are drawn down, and prices increase in proportion to excess demand, as described by the following "Phillips curve":

$$\dot{p} = \alpha(y^d - y) \tag{3}$$

The last two equations of the model,

$$m - p = \phi y - \lambda R \tag{4}$$

$$R = R^* + \dot{s} \tag{5}$$

are asset-market equilibrium conditions. Equation (4) is a standard LM schedule, relating the demand for real balances $(m - p)$ to income and the nominal interest rate, and (5) is an *uncovered interest parity* relation, telling us that the interest-rate differential between domestic and foreign bonds must be just enough to offset the depreciation $(\dot{s})$ of the domestic currency.

We will make the standard "small-economy" assumption and treat the world interest rate R^* as an exogenous constant. To simplify things, we will also assume that the nominal money supply (m), government expenditures (g), and the foreign price level (p^*) remain constant over time. This leaves us with three time-dependent state variables: s, p, and R.

Working with equations (2)–(5), it is easy to solve for the steady state of the model. Setting $\dot{s}$ equal to zero in (5), we have

$$\bar{R} = R^* \tag{ss.R}$$

That is, the domestic interest rate must be equal to the world rate in a long-run equilibrium, for otherwise the domestic currency would have to appreciate or depreciate in order to compensate investors for the interest-rate differential between domestic and foreign bonds.

Using $\bar{R} = R^*$, we can solve (4) for the steady-state price level:

$$(4) \Rightarrow m - \bar{p} = \phi y - \lambda R^*$$
$$\Rightarrow \bar{p} = m - \phi y + \lambda R^* \tag{ss.p}$$

Setting $\dot{p} = 0$ in equation (3), we obtain $y^d = y$. Using this expression, equation (2) can be solved for the steady-state exchange rate:

$$(2) \Rightarrow y = \delta(\bar{s} + p^* - \bar{p}) - \sigma(R^* - 0) + g$$
$$\Rightarrow \bar{s} = \bar{p} - p^* + (1/\delta)(y + \sigma R^* - g) \tag{ss.s}$$

The steady-state exchange rate depends on the relative price levels of the two countries, $\bar{p} - p^*$, but notice that there is an additional term. From equation (2), δ is the real-exchange-rate elasticity of the demand for domestic output. If domestic and foreign goods were perfect substitutes, we would have $\delta \to \infty$ and (ss.s) would reduce to $\bar{s} = \bar{p} - p^*$, which would be the (long-run) purchasing-power-parity relation (one unit of domestic currency buys the same output in both countries).

Equations (1)–(5) can be reduced to a system of two differential equations in p and s that summarize, respectively, the behaviors of asset markets and goods markets. First, we solve (4) for R,

$$R = \frac{\phi y - m + p}{\lambda} \tag{6}$$

and substitute the result into (5) to get the law of motion describing the evolution of the exchange rate,

$$\dot{s} = R - R^* = \frac{\phi y - m + p}{\lambda} - R^* \tag{L.s}$$

Next, substituting (2) into (3),

$$\dot{p} = \alpha[\delta(s + p^* - p) - \sigma(R - \dot{p}) + g - y]$$

and solving for $\dot{p}$, we have

$$\dot{p} = \frac{\alpha}{1 - \alpha\sigma}[\delta(s + p^* - p) - \sigma R + g - y] \tag{7}$$

Finally, we substitute (6) into (7) to get

$$\dot{p} = \frac{\alpha}{1 - \alpha\sigma}\left(\delta(s + p^* - p) - \sigma\frac{\phi y - m + p}{\lambda} + g - y\right) \tag{8}$$

and, grouping terms,

$$\dot{p} = \frac{\alpha}{1 - \alpha\sigma}\left(\delta(s + p^*) - [\delta + (\sigma/\lambda)]p - \sigma\frac{\phi y - m}{\lambda} + g - y\right) \tag{L.p}$$

The next two problems ask the reader to investigate the dynamic behavior of this system of differential equations and to identify the solution trajectory that corresponds to the equilibrium of the model. The first step is to construct the phase diagram.

Problem 2.3. Construct the phase diagram for the system (L.*s*)–(L.*p*). Assume that $1 - \alpha\sigma > 0$. What does this assumption mean?

Next, the reader is asked to verify that the steady state of the system is a saddle point. As we saw in Chapter 10, this implies that the system converges to the steady state provided its initial position lies on a straight line through this point, called the convergent subspace of the system or saddle path. For a given initial value of the domestic price level (which we take to be a pre-determined variable) there is a unique value of the exchange rate that will put us on this convergent trajectory. Because any other solution of the system would "explode," generating a rather unreasonable trajectory of domestic prices and exchange rates, we will take the saddle path as the equilibrium solution of the model. The reader is asked to solve explicitly for the appropiate particular solution of the dynamical system.

Problem 2.4. Solution of Dornbusch's model.

(i) Compute the eigenvalues and eigenvectors of the system (L.*s*)–(L.*p*), and verify that the steady state is a saddle point.
(ii) Write the general solution of the system. Find the particular solution of the system that corresponds to the saddle path, and discuss the equilibrium trajectory of the system from an arbitrary initial price level. Find the equation that describes the saddle path, and show that it has negative slope.

We will now use the model to analyze the effects of different monetary-policy and fiscal-policy measures on price levels and exchange rates. The first two policy changes are unanticipated changes in government expenditures and in the money supply. To analyze their impact, the reader can proceed essentially as we have done in previous exercises of a similar nature. The first step is to determine the effect of the policy change on the steady state of the system. Then we select the solution of the system that, given the initial price level, will take us eventually to the new steady state. This solution is required to be continuous at all points, except possibly at time zero, when the exchange rate (which is assumed to be a "free variable") is allowed to jump as required in order to put us on the convergent trajectory.

Problem 2.5. Assume that the economy is initially (at time zero) at the steady state $S_0 = (\bar{p}_0, \bar{s}_0)$ corresponding to values m_0 and g_0 of the money supply and government expenditures.

(i) Suppose the government announces an immediate and unanticipated permanent increase in its expenditure level on domestic goods to $g_1 > g_0$. Discuss the impact on the steady state of the system, and describe the adjustment trajectory from the initial position to the new equilibrium.

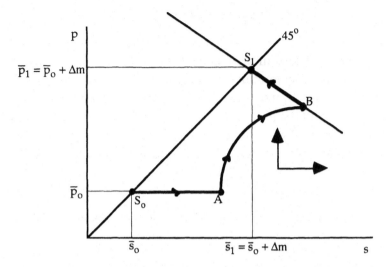

Figure 11.9. Adjustment to an anticipated increase in the money supply.

(ii) Analyze the effect of an immediate, unanticipated, and permanent increase in the nominal money supply to $m_1 > m_0$. It will be seen that the exchange rate temporarily "overshoots" its new long-run equilibrium value. Explain in what sense this is true, and discuss the economic mechanism that generates this result. What determines the degree of overshooting?

The final policy experiment we will consider is a preannounced future increase in the money supply. The logic of the analysis is still the same. We want to identify a trajectory that will eventually take us to a new steady state and that will be continuous at all points, except possibly at the time of the announcement. In constructing such a path, the reader should keep in mind that the system must obey the "old" law of motion (corresponding to the initial parameter values) until the policy change actually takes place.

Problem 2.6. As before, assume that the economy is initially (at time zero) at the steady state $S_0 = (\bar{p}_0, \bar{s}_0)$ corresponding to a value m_0 of the money supply. Now imagine that at time zero the government announces that at some time T in the future the money supply will be permanently increased from the current level of m_0 to $m_1 = m_0 + \Delta m$. The change in the steady state will be as in the preceding problem, with the long-run equilibrium levels of p and m increasing proportionately to Δm. The adjustment path is sketched in Figure 11.9. Explain how this path is constructed, and explain how you would go about finding the coordinates of points A and B in Figure 11.9 using the general solution of the system (derived earlier) and appropriate boundary conditions.

3. Neoclassical Growth Models

This section reviews some simple models of growth in a one-sector neo-classical economy. These models have become the standard framework for much work in macroeconomics, as well as in growth theory. We begin by setting down some common assumptions concerning the technology and characterizing equilibrium factor prices in a one-sector neoclassical setting. We then develop Solow's classic model (1956) and an extension of it due to Diamond (1965) that endogenizes the savings behavior of finitely-lived individuals.

(a) Technology and Factor Prices in a Neoclassical World

The predictions of a growth model regarding the time path of output and the evolution of the international distribution of income depend, essentially, on its technological assumptions concerning the existence of constant or increasing returns to scale in capital and the nature and determinants of technical progress. In this section we will review the central technological assumptions of the basic neoclassical models. Some of their implications will be explored later within the framework of the Solow model.

Consider a world with two factors and a single good. Capital (K) and labor (L) are used to produce a homogeneous output that can be consumed directly or used as capital in the production process. We will assume that the technology can be described by an aggregate production function

$$Y = F(K, L) \tag{1}$$

where Y is aggregate output. We will typically assume that $F(\ )$ is a smooth and concave function that exhibits constant returns to scale and positive and decreasing marginal products (F_K, $F_L > 0$, and F_{KK}, $F_{LL} < 0$). In most cases, we will also assume that both capital and labor are essential for production ($F(0, L) = F(K, 0) = 0$) and that the following Inada conditions hold:

$$F_K \to 0 \quad \text{as } K \to \infty, \qquad F_K \to \infty \quad \text{as } K \to 0,$$
$$F_L \to 0 \quad \text{as } L \to \infty, \qquad F_L \to \infty \quad \text{as } L \to 0 \tag{2}$$

We will often use as an example the Cobb-Douglas specification

$$Y = AK^\alpha L^\beta \tag{3}$$

where A is an index of "total factor productivity" that summarizes the current state of technical know-how. The coefficients α and β measure the elasticity of output with respect to the stocks of the two factors: If the stock of capital increases by 1%, holding the labor force constant, national output will increase by α%.

Before discussing the neoclassical specification of the production function, we need to introduce the notion of *returns to scale*. We will say that the production function $F(\ )$ exhibits increasing returns to scale (in K and L) if increases in the stocks of both factors in the same proportion yield a more-than-proportional increase in output, that is, if for all $\lambda > 1$ we have

$$F(\lambda K, \lambda L) > \lambda F(K, L)$$

Similarly, $F(\ )$ exhibits constant returns when $F(\lambda K, \lambda L) = \lambda F(K, L)$, and decreasing returns when $F(\lambda K, \lambda L) < \lambda F(K, L)$ for all $\lambda > 1$. In the case of a Cobb-Douglas function, we have

$$F(\lambda K, \lambda L) = A(\lambda K)^{\alpha}(\lambda L)^{\beta} = \lambda^{\alpha+\beta} A K^{\alpha} L^{\beta} = \lambda^{\alpha+\beta} F(K, L)$$

Hence, $F(\ )$ presents increasing returns if and only if $\alpha + \beta > 1$, decreasing returns if and only if $\alpha + \beta < 1$, and constant returns when $\beta = 1 - \alpha$.

In the simplest version of the neoclassical model, technology exhibits constant returns in K and L. This hypothesis is usually justified in part by a replication argument: If the stocks of all inputs were to double, we could simply replicate all productive processes at the existing scale, thus ensuring that output would also double. If K and L are the only relevant factors, this argument implies that the technology would present nondecreasing returns, but it does not rule out, in principle, the possibility of strictly increasing returns, for we might be able to increase efficiency by expanding the scale of certain processes. The neoclassical literature, however, has tended to ignore this possibility, largely because increasing returns are difficult to reconcile with the traditional assumption of perfect competition and therefore tend to make modeling more complicated.[6]

The assumption of constant returns to scale turns out to be very convenient. One of the main reasons is that it allows us to write factor prices in a competitive equilibrium as simple functions of a single state variable, the capital/labor ratio in the economy. To see this, let us start by introducing a per-capita production function. Exploiting the linear homogeneity of the production function, and letting $\lambda = 1/L$, we can write

$$F(K/L, 1) = (1/L)F(K, L) \Rightarrow Y = F(K, L) = LF(K/L, 1)$$
$$\Rightarrow Y/L = F(K/L, 1)$$

Thus, per-capita output is a function of the capital stock per worker. Letting Z and Q denote the capital stock and output per worker, respectively ($Z = K/L$ and $Q = Y/L$), we define the per-capita production function by

$$Q = f(Z) \equiv F(K/L, 1) \tag{4}$$

The relationship between the per-capita and aggregate production functions is therefore given by

$$F(K, L) \equiv Lf(Z) = Lf(K/L)$$

Differentiating this expression with respect to K and L, the corresponding marginal products can be written as functions of Z:

$$F_K(K, L) = Lf'(Z)(1/L) = f'(Z)$$
$$F_L(K, L) = Lf'(Z)(-K/L^2) + f(Z) = f(Z) - f'(Z)Z$$

Finally, using the homogeneity of degree zero of the partial derivatives of $F(\ )$,[7] we have

$$f'(Z) = F_K(K, L) = F_1(K/L, 1)$$

from where

$$f''(Z) = F_{11}(K/L, 1) < 0$$

Thus, under the standard assumption that the marginal product of capital falls with K, the per-capita production function is an increasing and concave function of capital intensity.

Consider now an economy endowed with a constant-returns technology in which all agents behave competitively. Firms maximize profits, taking factor prices as given. Workers have no utility for leisure and therefore supply their entire endowment of labor time at the market-determined wage rate. The economy is always in competitive equilibrium, with full employment of labor, and factor prices are given by the corresponding marginal products.

A competitive firm hires labor at the market-determined wage w and rents capital at a net rental rate r – meaning that it must return to lenders $1 + r$ units of output (principal plus interest) per unit of borrowed capital. If capital depreciates at a rate δ, the gross rental rate of capital is $\rho = r + \delta$, and profits are given by

$$F(K, L) - wL - \rho K$$

Using the per-capita production function, total profits can be written as the product of profits per worker and the size of the labor force. The firm's problem,

$$\max_{Z, L} L[f(Z) - \rho Z - w] \tag{P}$$

can be approached in two steps. First, Z will be chosen to maximize profits per worker, yielding the necessary condition

$$f'(Z) = \rho$$

which defines the optimal capital/labor ratio Z as a function of the rental rate. The linearity of the objective function in L implies that the optimal choice of scale depends on factor prices in a discontinuous way. If w and ρ are such that maximum profits per worker are negative, the optimal decision is to shut down ($L = 0$) in order to minimize losses. If profits per worker are positive, however, the thing to do is to set $L = \infty$. This choice, however, is incompatible with equilibrium. If there is free entry into the industry, new firms will come in until profits are eliminated, that is, until

$$w = f(Z) - \rho Z = f(Z) - Zf'(Z) \equiv w(Z)$$

Now, with zero profits per worker, the size of individual firms is indeterminate (they are indifferent among sizes, because they earn zero profits anyway). Equilibrium factor prices, however, are easily determined. If we take as given the aggregate stock of capital K and the size of the labor force L, then the aggregate capital/labor ratio $Z = K/L$ is determined, and because in equilibrium all firms (facing the same technology and factor prices) use inputs in the same proportion, equilibrium factor prices can be conveniently written as simple functions of Z:

$$\rho = f'(Z) \quad \text{and} \quad w = w(Z) = f(Z) - Zf'(Z) \tag{5}$$

In some models, factor productivity increases over time as a result of technological progress. A common way to model this process is to write the production function in the form

$$Y_t = F(B_t K_t, A_t L_t) \tag{6}$$

where A_t and B_t are indices of labor productivity and capital productivity. If we define Z as the capital/labor ratio in "effective units,"

$$Z = BK/AL$$

we can proceed as before. Output per efficiency unit of labor is now given by

$$f(Z) \equiv F(BK/AL, 1)$$

and total output is

$$Y = F(BK, AL) = ALf(Z)$$

In a competitive equilibrium, the wage is

$$w(Z) = f(Z) - Zf'(Z)$$

per efficiency unit of labor, or $W(Z) = Aw(Z)$ per worker, and the rental rate is $f'(Z)$ per efficiency unit, or $Bf'(Z)$ per physical unit of capital.

(b) The Solow Model

In this section we will study a simple model of a dynamic economy developed by Solow (1956) in one of the papers that marked the beginning of modern growth theory.[8]

Suppose technology is described by a neoclassical production function $Y = F(K, AL)$, with constant returns to scale and labor-augmenting technical progress at a constant exogenous rate $g = \dot{A}/A$. We assume that a constant fraction s of the current flow of output is invested at each point in time. If capital depreciates at a constant rate δ, the evolution of the capital stock over time is described by the equation

$$\dot{K} = sY - \delta K = sALf(Z) - \delta K \tag{7}$$

where $\dot{K} = dK/dt$ can be interpreted as the increase in the aggregate stock of capital during a period of time of infinitesimal length, and $Z = K/AL$ is the capital/labor ratio in efficiency units. Dividing both sides of (7) by K,

$$\frac{\dot{K}}{K} = s\frac{f(Z)}{Z} - \delta \tag{8}$$

we see that the growth rate of the aggregate capital stock ($\dot{K}/K$) is the difference between investment per unit of capital and the rate of depreciation. If investment exceeds depreciation, K increases over time, and vice versa. Given that $Z = K/AL$, we can take logs of both sides of this expression,

$$\ln Z = \ln K - \ln A - \ln L$$

and differentiate with respect to time, obtaining

$$\frac{\dot{Z}}{Z} = \frac{\dot{K}}{K} - \frac{\dot{L}}{L} - \frac{\dot{A}}{A} = \frac{\dot{K}}{K} - (n + g)$$

where $\dot{L}/L = n$ is the (constant) rate of population growth. That is, the rate of growth of the stock of capital per effective unit of labor is the difference between the rates of growth of the aggregate capital stock and the labor force, measured in efficiency units. Substituting (8) into the foregoing expression, we arrive at

$$\frac{\dot{Z}}{Z} = \frac{\dot{K}}{K} - \frac{\dot{L}}{L} - \frac{\dot{A}}{A} = \frac{sLAf(Z) - \delta K}{K} - (n + g) = s\frac{f(Z)}{Z} - (\delta + n + g) \tag{9}$$

Equation (9) shows that, given a constant investment ratio, the rate of growth of Z depends crucially on the behavior of the average product of capital $f(Z)/Z$, which is itself a function of the capital/labor ratio. What can we say about the shape of this function? Recall that $f(Z) = F(Z, 1)$, where $F(\ )$ is linearly homogeneous in both its arguments. Hence, for any $\lambda > 1$, we have

$$f(\lambda Z) = F(\lambda Z, 1) < F(\lambda Z, \lambda) = \lambda f(Z)$$

whenever $F(\ )$ is strictly increasing in its second argument. Constant returns in capital and labor imply diminishing returns in capital alone and therefore in the per-capita production function. As we combine more and more capital with a unit of labor, output increases less than proportionately. Dividing both sides of the foregoing expression by Z and rearranging, we see that

$$\frac{f(\lambda Z)}{\lambda Z} < \frac{f(Z)}{Z}$$

for any $\lambda > 1$. Hence, the average product of capital decreases with Z.

An important implication of this feature of the technology is that the growth rate will tend to fall as investment flows into decreasingly productive activities. Plotting both terms from the right-hand side of (9) as functions of Z, the rate of growth of Z ($\dot{Z}/Z$) is given by the vertical distance between these lines, as shown in Figure 11.10. The negative slope of $sf(Z)/Z$ therefore implies that the growth rate of Z (and therefore that of income per efficiency unit of labor) will be a decreasing function of capital intensity. Moreover, if the productivity of investment falls sufficiently that $sf(Z)/Z$ drops below the horizontal line $n + g + \delta$, growth (in output per efficiency unit of labor) will eventually stop. This condition will be satisfied whenever[9]

$$\lim_{Z \to \infty} \frac{f(Z)}{Z} = \lim_{Z \to \infty} f'(Z) = f'(\infty) < n + g + \delta \tag{10}$$

This outcome, however, does not necessarily follow from the linear homogeneity of the aggregate production function, and thus it requires stronger assumptions. For example, if we assume a linear technology, $F(K, AL) = aK + bAL$, we have $f(Z)/Z = a + (b/Z)$, and growth will continue indefinitely, provided that $a > n + g + \delta$. Hence, constant returns per se do not rule out the possibility of sustained growth in output per efficiency unit of labor. One common assumption that does imply (10) is the Inada condition, $f'(\infty) = 0$, which implies that labor is an essential factor in production ($F(K, 0) = 0$). Observe that by the homogeneity of $F(\ )$ we can write

$$\frac{f(Z)}{Z} = \frac{1}{Z}F(Z, 1) = F(1, 1/Z)$$

and taking limits,

$$f'(\infty) = \lim_{Z \to \infty} \frac{f(Z)}{Z} = \lim_{Z \to \infty} F(1, 1/Z) = F(1, 0)$$

In short, the problem is that labor is fixed in supply and is essential. If capital increases without bound, "labor per machine" goes to zero, driving down the productivity of capital to the point where it can no longer reproduce itself.

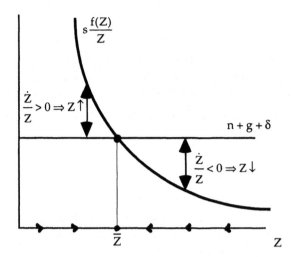

Figure 11.10. Dynamics of the Solow model under strongly decreasing returns.

Figure 11.10 shows the dynamics of the Solow model under the standard assumption of strongly decreasing returns implied by the Inada condition. The decreasing function $sf(Z)/Z$ intersects the horizontal line $\delta + n + g$ at the point $\overline{Z}$ that solves the equation $\dot{Z}/Z = 0$. The negative slope of the curve also implies that Z converges toward its stationary value $\overline{Z}$. As the figure shows, $\dot{Z}/Z$ is positive (i.e., Z is increasing over time) when the stock of capital per worker is low (and therefore the return on investment is high), and negative when Z is "high" (higher than $\overline{Z}$), for in this case the low return on investment implies that saving will not be enough to cover depreciation and equip newborn workers with the preexisting average stock of capital.

In the long run the system converges to a stationary equilibrium in which the capital/labor ratio Z is constant. Output per worker along such a *balanced-growth path* is given by

$$\overline{Q}_t = A_t f(\overline{Z}) \tag{11}$$

Taking logarithms of this expression, and using the fact that A grows exponentially over time at a constant rate g (i.e., $A_t = A_o e^{gt}$), we have

$$\ln \overline{Q}_t = \ln \left(A_o f(\overline{Z}) \right) + gt$$

Hence, the time path of the system is as shown in Figure 11.11. An economy that starts out with a capital/labor ratio below its steady-state value will initially grow at a rate exceeding g, but will gradually approach the balanced-growth path given by (8). Asymptotically, output per worker grows at the (exogenous) rate of technical progress, g.

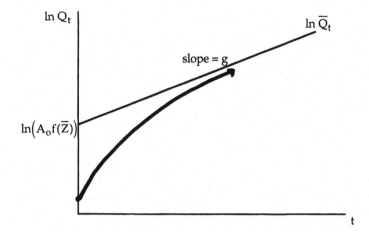

Figure 11.11. Time path of output in the Solow model.

This result has some strong implications. First, notice that in the absence of technological progress ($g = 0$), growth in per capita income eventually stops. Standard neoclassical assumptions allow for "extensive" growth: If capital and labor grow at the same rate, output will increase proportionately. However, the technological assumptions we have made severely limit the possibility of growth in income per capita, for the technology exhibits strongly decreasing returns in the only reproducible factor, K, whose marginal product falls to zero in the limit.

Second, the model predicts that policy changes will have only *level effects*. That is, changes in economic policy (or other parameters of the model) can affect the level of the path of output, but will have no effect on its long-run growth rate, which is determined only by the exogenous rate of technical progress. As an example, Figures 11.12 and 11.13 illustrate the effect of an increase in the investment ratio. A higher s shifts the curve $sf(Z)/Z$ upward, yielding a higher steady-state capital/labor ratio. This, in turn, shifts the intercept of the balanced-growth trajectory upward, but does not change its slope. During the transition period, higher investment does yield a temporarily higher growth rate, but this effect disappears gradually over time as the economy approaches its new balanced-growth path. Thinking in cross-sectional terms, the model implies that in the long run, countries that invest more (or have lower rates of population growth) will have higher income levels but the same growth rates as those that invest less (or have faster-growing populations). On the other hand, countries that are similar in these respects will eventually end up with the same per capita income, even if they start out with very different endowments of capital per worker.

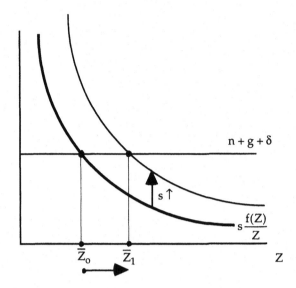

Figure 11.12. Effect of an increase in the investment rate on steady-state capital intensity.

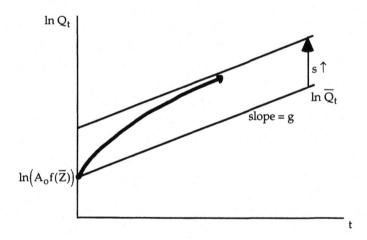

Figure 11.13. Time path of output following an increase in the investment rate.

Problem 3.1. The Solow model with a Cobb-Douglas production function. Assume that the aggregate production function is Cobb-Douglas, with labor-augmenting technical progress

$$Y = K^{\alpha}(AL)^{1-\alpha} \tag{1}$$

with $\dot{A}/A = g$. Write the intensive-production function $f(Z)$, giving output per efficiency unit of labor as a function of the capital/labor ratio in efficiency units, $Z = K/AL$. Derive the law of motion for Z under Solow's assumptions, and solve explicitly for the steady state of the system. What factors determine a country's long-term level of income?

Problem 3.2. Suppose the production function is of the form (1): $Y_t = (B_t K_t)^\alpha (A_t L_t)^{1-\alpha}$, with both capital- and labor-augmenting technical progress at rates $\dot{B}/B = g_B$ and $\dot{A}/A = g_A$. Derive the equation of motion for the capital/labor ratio in effective units, $Z = BK/AL$, under the assumptions of the Solow model. Show that the system has a balanced-growth path (i.e., a constant-Z solution) if and only if $g_B = 0$ (i.e., if technical progress is only labor-augmenting).

(c) An Overlapping-Generations Model (Diamond)

Although Solow's model is extremely simple, at the time it was written it brought real progress. The reason is that, unlike static formulations of the Keynesian type, it explicitly brought out the role of investment in increasing the economy's productive capacity and highlighted the trade-off between present consumption and future consumption. One obvious limitation of the model, however, is its assumption of an exogenous savings rate. Back in the 1950s, that was seen as a perfectly reasonable simplification. Since then, however, economists have come to insist that the behavior of agents should be derived from some sort of optimization problem. To remedy this shortcoming, the Solow-Swan model was soon extended by authors who derived savings behavior from the maximization of lifetime utility. Two specifications have become standard in the literature. The main difference between them is their demographic structure. One of them, first developed by Cass (1965) and Koopmans (1965), building on earlier work by Ramsey (1928), features a representative household that lives forever; the other, due to Diamond (1965), assumes, rather more sensibly, finite lifetimes. In this section we will study the second of these models, which is simpler in some ways, leaving the Cass-Koopmans model for a later chapter.

An interesting feature of the Diamond (1965) model is its demographic structure. The economy is populated by successive generations of finitely-lived workers. In the simplest version of the model, agents live for two periods and "have children" at the end of the first one. At any given point in time, then, members of two generations coexist on the earth (hence the name *overlapping generations*) and interact with each other and with firms through competitive markets for labor and output/capital. Young agents sell their labor, eat part of the proceeds, and save the rest for old age by lending unconsumed output to firms for use as capital in the next period's production. Old individuals do not work, but simply consume their savings, including interest earnings. Firms hire labor and borrow capital to produce output using a constant-returns-to-scale production technology.

(i) Household Behavior

The utility of an agent born in period t (belonging to the tth generation) is an increasing function of consumption in the first and second periods of his life (c and x, respectively):

$$U_t = U(c_t, x_{t+1}) \tag{1}$$

We will assume that U is strictly increasing in both arguments, smooth, and strictly quasiconcave. Having no taste for leisure, households sell their entire endowment of labor time (one unit in youth) in the labor market in exchange for a real wage of w_t units of output. Part of this income goes to current consumption, c_t, and the rest (s_t) is lent to firms for use as capital in next period's production at an interest rate r_{t+1}. Old agents, therefore, have a total wealth of $s_t R_{t+1} = s_t(1 + r_{t+1})$ units of output and, not caring about their children, consume all of it.

Households, then, maximize (1) subject to the constraints

$$w_t = c_t + s_t \quad \text{and} \quad s_t R_{t+1} = x_{t+1}$$

For future reference, it will be convenient to study a slightly more general version of this problem. We will allow for the possibility that agents may have some income in the second period of their lives and solve

$$\max_{c,x}\{U(c, x)\,\text{s.t.}\ y_1 = c + s \text{ and } x = y_2 + sR\} \tag{P}$$

where y_1 and y_2 denote first- and second-period incomes, respectively. We will make the following assumptions:

$$U_c, U_x > 0 \tag{A.1}$$

$$U_{cc}, U_{xx} < 0 \quad \text{and} \quad U_{cx} = U_{xc} \geq 0 \tag{A.2}$$

$$U_c(c, x) \to \infty \quad \text{as } c \to 0 \quad \text{and} \quad U_x(c, x) \to \infty \quad \text{as } x \to 0 \tag{A.3}$$

Assumption (A.2) is plausible and allows us easily to sign certain partial derivatives of interest. We will show later that it can be replaced by the assumption that consumption is a normal good in both periods. The third assumption is made to avoid the possibility of corner solutions. Because the marginal utility of consumption in either period goes to infinity as consumption approaches zero, agents will consume positive amounts in both periods whenever they have any income at all. Hence, the natural nonnegativity constraints on c and x will not be binding at an optimum and can be ignored in the formulation of the problem.

Substituting the constraints into the utility function $U(\ )$, we can rewrite (P) as

$$\max_{s} U(y_1 - s, y_2 + sR) \tag{P$'$}$$

Differentiating U with respect to s, we obtain the first-order condition

$$\frac{\partial U}{\partial s} = U_c(y_1 - s, y_2 + sR)(-1) + U_x(y_1 - s, y_2 + sR)R = 0 \Rightarrow R = \frac{U_c(c, x)}{U_x(c, x)} \tag{2}$$

As usual, the agent sets the marginal rate of substitution between present consumption and future consumption (i.e., the rate at which he would be willing to trade present consumption for future consumption) equal to the rate at which he can do so, which is given by the interest factor. Because U is a concave function of s, equation (2) does characterize an optimum.

The solution to this problem gives us the optimal level of savings as a function of first- and second-period incomes and the interest factor, that is, a savings function of the form

$$s^* = s(y_1, y_2, R)$$

which conveniently describes the optimal behavior of the household. The following proposition summarizes the properties of the function $s(\ )$.

Proposition 3.3. Properties of the savings function. Consider the function

$$s(y_1, y_2, R) = arg \max_{s} U(y_1 - s, y_2 + sR)$$

Under the assumption that (i) first- and second-period consumptions are normal goods (i.e., the demand for them is increasing in income), or (ii) U_{cc}, $U_{xx} < 0$ and $U_{cx} \geq 0$, we have that

$$\frac{\partial s^*}{\partial y_1} \in (0, 1), \quad \frac{\partial s^*}{\partial y_2} < 0, \quad and \quad \frac{\partial s^*}{\partial R} > 0 \quad for\ s^* \leq 0$$

If, in addition, c and x are strict substitutes (i.e., if an increase in the relative price of one, measured by the interest factor, leads to an increase in the demand for the other), then

$$\frac{\partial s^*}{\partial R} > 0$$

also for net savers (s > 0).

Problem 3.4. Prove Proposition 3.3.

To conclude, note that the problem faced by a worker in Diamond's model is exactly the one in the proposition, with

$$y_1 = w_t, \quad y_2 = 0, \quad \text{and} \quad R = R_{t+1}$$

Hence, we can write the savings function

$$s^* = s(w_t, R_{t+1})$$

and under the assumptions of Proposition 3.3 we can sign the partial derivatives $s_W(\ )$ and $s_R(\ )$.

(ii) Equilibrium and Dynamics

We will assume that population grows at a constant rate n (i.e., $L_{t+1} = (1 + n)L_t$) and that capital depreciates at a rate δ. Each period young agents sell their labor, eat part of the proceeds, and lend the remainder to firms. Older workers simply consume their savings. Firms are of the standard neoclassical variety. In equilibrium, factor prices are equal to their marginal products, and factor markets clear. Hence (see Section 3(a)),

$$w_t = w(Z_t) = f(Z_t) - Z_t f'(Z_t) \quad \text{and}$$
$$R_{t+1} = 1 + r_{t+1} = 1 + \rho_{t+1} - \delta = f'(Z_{t+1}) + (1 - \delta)$$

Labor-market clearing means simply that all young workers are employed. Capital-market clearing requires that next period's capital stock be equal to current savings by the young:[10]

$$K_{t+1} = L_t s_t \tag{3}$$

Dividing both sides of this expression by $L_{t+1} = (1 + n)L_t$, and letting $Z = K/L$, we have[11]

$$\frac{K_{t+1}}{L_{t+1}} = \frac{L_t s_t}{(1+n)L_t}$$
$$\Rightarrow (1+n)Z_{t+1} = s_t \tag{4}$$

Substituting the savings function, evaluated at equilibrium factor prices, into (4), we arrive finally at

$$(1+n)Z_{t+1} = s[w(Z_t), f'(Z_{t+1}) + (1 - \delta)] \tag{5}$$

To simplify the exposition somewhat, in the remainder of this section we will assume that the population is constant ($n = 0$) and that capital depreciates completely upon use ($\delta = 1$). With these assumptions, equation (5) reduces to

$$Z_{t+1} = s[w(Z_t), f'(Z_{t+1})] \tag{6}$$

Equation (6) implicitly defines a function of the form $Z_{t+1} = \phi(Z_t)$, that is, a first-order difference equation (notice that Z_{t+1} appears on both sides of this expression).

Without knowing the specific forms of $U(\ )$ and $f(\ )$ we cannot solve for $\phi(\ )$ explicitly, but we can get some qualitative information about it. We are particularly interested in two questions. The first has to do with the existence of steady states for the dynamical system described by (6). Second, if steady states exist, we would like to determine under what conditions they are stable. To answer these questions, we need some information about the properties of $\phi(\ )$. Steady states of the system are just fixed points of ϕ, and their stability depends on the value of $\phi'(Z)$.

Differentiating (6) implicitly with respect to Z_t, we obtain the slope of the phase line, $\phi'(Z_t) = dZ_{t+1}/dZ_t$:

$$\frac{dZ_{t+1}}{dZ_t} = s_w(\ )w'(Z_t) + s_R(\ )f''(Z_{t+1})\frac{dZ_{t+1}}{dZ_t}$$

$$\Rightarrow \phi'(Z_t) = \frac{dZ_{t+1}}{dZ_t} = \frac{s_W(\ )w'(Z_t)}{1 - s_R(\ )f''(Z_{t+1})} \tag{7}$$

Notice that the denominator of this expression is always positive. Because $f''(\ ) < 0$, the whole expression will be positive provided that $s_R(\ ) > 0$ or $s_R(\ ) < 0$ and is "small" in absolute value. To determine whether or not a given steady state $\overline{Z}$ is stable, we only have to check whether or not $|\phi'(\overline{Z})|$ is smaller than 1. There is, however, no guarantee of stability, or even of the existence of any interior steady states.

The function $\phi(\ )$ summarizes the effect of the capital stock on savings, as mediated by both preferences and technology through separate interest and wage channels. Standard assumptions are not sufficient to ensure that (6) will be as well-behaved as the Solow model we analyzed in the preceding section. They are, however, sufficient to show that $\phi(0) = 0$ and $\phi(Z) < Z$ for sufficiently large Z. Hence, $\phi(\ )$ goes through the origin and eventually falls below the 45° line, making indefinitely sustained growth impossible. The origin is always a steady state, but the system may have no interior steady states, or any odd number of them, with alternating stability properties, as suggested in Figure 11.14.

Clearly, a sufficient condition for the existence of a nontrivial steady state is that $\phi'(0) > 1$, and a sufficient condition for uniqueness is that, in addition, $\phi(\ )$ be concave. The following proposition summarizes the key properties of the model.

Proposition 3.5. Existence of steady states in the Diamond model. Assume that the intensive production function f($\ $) *is concave, with* f(0) = 0 *and*

$$f'(Z) \to 0 \quad as \quad Z \to \infty \quad and \quad f'(Z) \to \infty \quad as \quad Z \to 0$$

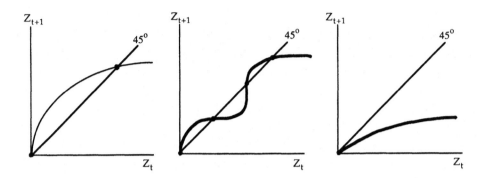

Figure 11.14. Possible phase diagrams for the Diamond model.

Then $\phi(0) = 0$, and for Z_t sufficiently large, $Z_{t+1}/Z_t = \phi(Z_t)/Z_t < 1$. Hence, 0 is always a steady state of the system, and indefinite growth is not possible. Moreover, if

$$\lim_{Z \to 0} \phi'(Z) > 1$$

then there exists at least one additional steady state with $Z > 0$. If this last condition is satisfied and ϕ is increasing and concave, there is a unique nontrivial and globally stable steady state.[12]

Proof

- First, we note that $Z = 0$ is always a steady state for the system, that is, $\phi(0) = 0$. With *zero* capital, no production is possible ($f(0) = 0$), and hence $w(0) = 0$. With zero wages, no savings are possible [$s(0, R) = 0$], and therefore there can be no capital accumulation.

- Next, we show that $(Z_{t+1}/Z_t) \to 0$ as $Z_t \to \infty$. It follows that for sufficiently large Z we have $Z_{t+1}/Z_t = \phi(Z_t)/Z_t < 1 \Rightarrow Z_{t+1} = \phi(Z_t) < Z_t$, and hence the graph of ϕ is below the 45° line. This implies that capital accumulation cannot continue forever, for if Z is large enough, it must be decreasing.

  To derive this result, note that

$$0 \le \frac{Z_{t+1}}{Z_t} = \frac{s(w_t, R_{t+1})}{Z_t} \le \frac{w(Z_t)}{Z_t} = \frac{f(Z_t)}{Z_t} - f'(Z_t) \le \frac{f(Z_t)}{Z_t}$$

Taking limits as $Z \to \infty$, we have, by L'Hôpital's rule,

$$0 \le \lim_{Z \to \infty} \frac{Z_{t+1}}{Z_t} \le \lim_{Z \to \infty} \frac{f(Z_t)}{Z_t} = \lim_{Z \to \infty} f'(Z) = 0$$

whenever $f(\ )$ is unbounded; otherwise, we can omit the penultimate term in the foregoing expression, and the inequalities will still hold.

- The function ϕ, then, goes through the origin and is below the 45° line for Z large enough. Clearly, whether or not additional steady states (with $Z > 0$) exist will depend on the slope of ϕ at the origin. There are two possibilities: If the slope of

ϕ is greater than 1 at the origin, then ϕ starts above the 45° line; because it must eventually end up below it, continuity implies that it must cross it an odd number of times, and at least one additional steady state exists. On the other hand, if ϕ starts below the 45° line, we will have an even number of such equilibria, possibly zero. Note that because $\phi(0) = 0$,

$$\lim_{Z \to 0} \phi'(Z) = \lim_{Z \to 0} \frac{\phi(Z)}{Z} \le \lim_{Z \to 0} \frac{w(Z)}{Z} = \lim_{Z \to 0} w'(Z)$$

so a necessary condition for $\phi'(0) > 1$ is $w'(0) > 1$. The last part of the proposition is obvious. $\qquad \square$

Example 3.6. Cobb-Douglas technology and log preferences. Assume that the population grows at a constant rate n, and the production and utility functions are of the form

$$U(c, x) = \beta \ln c + (1 - \beta) \ln x, \quad \text{where } \beta \in (0, 1) \tag{U}$$

$$F(K, L) = K^\alpha L^{1-\alpha}, \quad \text{where } \alpha \in (0, 1) \tag{P}$$

Under these assumptions we have

$$w = (1 - \alpha) Z^\alpha, \quad R = \alpha Z^{\alpha - 1}, \quad \text{and} \quad s(w, R) = (1 - \beta) w$$

and the law of motion for the stock of capital per worker is given by

$$(1 + n) Z_{t+1} = (1 - \beta)(1 - \alpha) Z_t^\alpha$$

$$\Rightarrow Z_{t+1} = \phi(Z_t) = \frac{(1 - \beta)(1 - \alpha)}{(1 + n)} Z_t^\alpha \tag{L.Z}$$

Note that

$$\phi'(Z_t) = \frac{(1 - \beta)(1 - \alpha)}{(1 + n)} \alpha Z_t^{\alpha - 1} > 0 \quad \text{and}$$

$$\phi''(Z_t) = \frac{(1 - \beta)(1 - \alpha)}{(1 + n)} \alpha(\alpha - 1) Z_t^{\alpha - 2} < 0$$

Thus, the phase line goes through the origin and is monotonically increasing and strictly concave. Notice also that $\phi'(Z) \to \infty$ as $Z \to 0$, and $\phi'(Z) \to 0$ as $Z \to \infty$. Hence, the phase line $\phi(\ )$ starts out above the 45° line, but eventually becomes flatter and must therefore eventually go below it. This implies the existence of an interior steady state, $\overline{Z} > 0$. In fact, we can solve for $\overline{Z}$ explicitly. Eliminating the time subscripts in (L.Z),

$$\phi(Z) = Z \Rightarrow Z = \frac{(1 - \beta)(1 - \alpha)}{(1 + n)} Z^\alpha$$

which holds for $Z = 0$. For $Z \ne 0$, we can divide through by Z^α to get

$$Z^{1-\alpha} = \frac{(1 - \beta)(1 - \alpha)}{(1 + n)} \Rightarrow \overline{Z} = \left(\frac{(1 - \beta)(1 - \alpha)}{(1 + n)} \right)^{1/(1-\alpha)} > 0$$

Because $\phi'(0) > 1$, the steady state at the origin is an unstable node. To check the stability of $\overline{Z}$, note that

$$\phi'(\overline{Z}) = \frac{(1-\beta)(1-\alpha)}{(1+n)}\alpha\overline{Z}^{\alpha-1} = \frac{(1-\beta)(1-\alpha)}{(1+n)}\alpha\left(\frac{(1-\beta)(1-\alpha)}{(1+n)}\right)^{-1} = \alpha \in (0,1)$$

so the interior steady state is a stable node.   □

4. Some Useful Techniques

Nonlinear differential equations often lack closed-form solutions. Whereas it is often possible to analyze the qualitative behavior of such systems, it is more difficult to get accurate quantitative predictions by analytical methods. As we will see in the first part of this section, one possibility is to linearize the system around a steady state and work with the linearized model. The resulting approximation, although valid only locally (in a neighborhood of a steady state), is often quite useful, both in theoretical studies and in empirical work. An alternative, which also allows us to deal with systems whose behavior is difficult to characterize with analytical methods, is to use a computer package to solve the system numerically. In the second part of this section we will solve the Solow model using *Mathematica*. In Chapter 13 we will see how to deal with more complicated systems.

(a) Linearization and Derivation of a Convergence Equation

We have seen that in the Solow model the growth rate of the stock of capital per efficiency unit of labor is given by

$$\frac{\dot{Z}}{Z} = \frac{\dot{K}}{K} - \frac{\dot{L}}{L} - \frac{\dot{A}}{A} = s\frac{f(Z)}{Z} - (\delta + n + g) \tag{1}$$

where $Z = K/AL$. If all countries have access to the same technology (i.e., if A is the same for all of them) and all share the same rates of depreciation (δ) and technical progress (g), and if the production function exhibits decreasing returns to capital, this equation implies that the rate of capital accumulation per worker (and therefore the rate of growth of income per capita, Q) will be a decreasing function of Z (and hence of Q) and population growth (n), and an increasing function of the investment rate (s).

To test these hypotheses, we can try to estimate equation (1), after assuming some specific functional form for the production function. As it stands, however, this equation is not very suitable for empirical work. The main difficulty is that it is written in terms of a variable (the stock of capital per efficiency unit of labor) for which we do not have very good data.[13] In this section we will construct an approximation to (1) that will be useful in empirical work, following the procedure developed by Barro and Sala-i-Martin (1990) and Mankiw, Romer, and Weil (1992). The equation we will obtain can be seen as a reduced form of the Solow model, or simply as a convenient way of estimating the production function using flow data.

Suppose the production function is Cobb-Douglas. Then equation (1) becomes

$$\frac{\dot{Z}}{Z} = sZ^{\alpha-1} - (\delta + n + g) \tag{2}$$

To construct a suitable approximation to this equation, we start by introducing a new variable,

$$z = \ln Z$$

and observing that

$$\dot{z} = \frac{\dot{Z}}{Z} \quad \text{and} \quad Z = e^{z}$$

Hence, we can rewrite (1) in the form

$$\dot{z} = se^{z(\alpha-1)} - (\delta + g + n) \equiv \phi(z) \tag{3}$$

Notice that the steady-state value of z satisfies

$$se^{z(\alpha-1)} = (\delta + g + n)$$

$$\Rightarrow \bar{z} = \frac{1}{1-\alpha} \ln \frac{s}{\delta + g + n} \tag{4}$$

and the derivative of $\phi(\ )$ at the steady state is given by

$$\phi'(\bar{z}) = (\alpha - 1)se^{z(\alpha-1)} = -(1-\alpha)(\delta + g + n) < 0$$

Hence, the log-linearized system

$$\dot{z} = -\lambda(z - \bar{z}), \quad \text{where } \lambda = (1-\alpha)(\delta + g + n) \tag{5}$$

is stable, like the original one, provided that $\alpha < 1$ (see Problem 3.1).

Because equation (5) is a first-order linear differential equation, we can write its solution immediately. If we consider the period from t to $t + h$, the final value of z (z_{t+h}) is given by a weighted average of its initial (z_t) and stationary ($\bar{z}$) values, with weights determined by the coefficient λ and the duration of the period h:

$$z_{t+h} = \bar{z} + (z_t - \bar{z})e^{-\lambda h} = z_t e^{-\lambda h} + \bar{z}(1 - e^{-\lambda h}) \tag{6}$$

Equation (6) implies a relationship between the rate of income growth over the period and its initial level, as well as other variables. To make this relation explicit, recall that output per worker is given by $Q = AZ^{\alpha}$. Taking logarithms of both sides of this expression,

$$q = a + \alpha z \Rightarrow \alpha z = q - a \tag{7}$$

and substituting (6) into (7) evaluated at time $t + h$,

$$q_{t+h} = a_{t+h} + \alpha z_{t+h} = a_{t+h} + (q_t - a_t)e^{-\lambda h} + (1 - e^{-\lambda h})\alpha \bar{z}$$

Subtracting initial income q_t from both sides, dividing through by h, and using the fact that $a_{t+h} = a_t + gh$, we obtain

$$\frac{q_{t+h} - q_t}{h} = g + \frac{1 - e^{-\lambda h}}{h}[\alpha \bar{z} - (q_t - a_t)]$$

$$= g + \frac{1 - e^{-\lambda h}}{h}\left(\frac{\alpha}{1-\alpha}\ln\frac{s}{\delta + g + n} - (q_t - a_t)\right) \tag{8}$$

This *convergence equation* relates the growth of per-capita income over the period to the initial level of income per capita, the determinants of the steady state, the rate of technical progress, and the inital value of the technological index. In particular, equation (8) tells us that the rate of growth over a given period is equal to the rate of technical progress, g, plus a transitional factor that depends on the difference between current output per efficiency unit of labor $(q - a)$ and the steady-state value of this variable, $\alpha \bar{z}$. For a given value of the steady state, the transitional component of growth decreases with initial income and increases with a, because technical progress reduces the stock of capital per efficiency unit of labor.

The empirical implementation of equation (8) does not raise any special difficulties. Given time-series data on output per capita or per worker, investment, and population or labor-force growth, the equation can be estimated using cross-section or panel data at the national or regional level. This specification allows us to estimate the rate of convergence and to recover (given values for some parameters) the coefficient of capital in the production function.[14]

Problem 4.1. Measuring the speed of convergence. The "eigenvalue" λ of the log-linearized system provides a measure of the speed of convergence of an economy toward its steady state. Show that the half-life of the system described by equation (5) (defined as the time H at which half the original deviation of z from its steady-state value has been eliminated)[15] is given by

$$H = \frac{\ln 2}{\lambda}$$

Notice that H is inversely proportional to λ.

Problem 4.2. Determinants of long-run income dispersion. Assume that the evolution of income per capita in a given country can be described by the equation

$$y_{i,t+1} = x_i + (1-\beta)y_{i,t} + \varepsilon_{it} \quad \text{or} \quad \Delta y_{i,t} = x_i - \beta y_{i,t} + \varepsilon_{it} \tag{1}$$

where $y_{i,t} = \ln(Q_{it}/Q_t)$ denotes the logarithm of income per capita in country i in period t (Q_{it}) normalized by the sample mean of the same variable (Q_t), and $\Delta y_{i,t} = y_{i,t+1} - y_{i,t}$ is approximately equal to the growth rate of per-capita income in country i, measured in deviations from the average growth rate in the sample. In this expression, ε_{it} is a random disturbance, with zero mean and variance, σ_ε^2, independent and identically distributed over time and across countries and uncorrelated with $y_{i,t}$ and x_i. The term x_i, which summarizes the "fundamental" determinants of growth in territory i, is constant over time and is distributed across countries, with zero mean and variance σ_x^2. (This equation can be interpreted as a linear approximation to the convergence equation we have just derived, with x_i summarizing the effect of the rates of investment and population growth in country i.)

Taking the expected values for both sides of (1), given initial income $y_{i,0}$, we obtain a nonstochastic equation in expected income $y_{i,t}^e$:

$$y_{i,t+1}^e = x_i + (1-\beta)y_{i,t}^e, \quad \text{with } y_{i,0}^e = y_{i,0} \tag{2}$$

The solution of (2) is of the form

$$y_{i,t}^e = y_i^* + \left(y_{i,0} - y_i^*\right)(1-\beta)^t \tag{3}$$

where

$$y_i^* = \frac{x_i}{\beta}$$

is the steady-state value of y_{it}. Equation (3) shows that the stability of the system depends on the value of the slope coefficient β. If $\beta \in (0, 1)$, the term $(1-\beta)^t$ goes to zero as $t \to \infty$. The system is therefore stable, and the expected income for each nation converges monotonically to its steady state y_i^* at a rate determined by β. Hence, we can interpret y_i^* as the expected (relative) income level of country i in a long-run equilibrium.

We want to use equation (1) to investigate the determinants of income inequality across countries in the long run. Let σ_t^2 denote the sample variance of y_{it}, and $c_t = Ex_i y_{it}$ the covariance between current income and country fundamentals, and observe that if the number of countries is large, the sample variance and covariance will be approximately equal to their population values. Using (1), derive a system of difference equations in σ_t^2 and c_t, discuss its stability properties, and compute its steady state. What determines the degree of income inequality in the long run, measured by the steady-state value of σ_t^2?

Hint: Take the variance for both sides of (1), and notice that $c_{t+1} = Ex_i y_{i,t+1}$.

(b) Solving the Solow Model with **Mathematica**

It is easy to see that the law of motion for the capital/labor ratio in the Solow
model with a Cobb-Douglas production function is given by

$$\dot{Z} = sZ^{\alpha} - (\delta + n + g)Z$$

(see Problem 3.1). This equation is a nonlinear differential equation that
does not have a closed-form solution. In this section we will show how equations such as this one can be solved numerically using *Mathematica*, a computer program that has a built-in routine for such computations.

Because *Mathematica* does not have Greek letters, we will start by rewriting our equation in the form

$$\dot{Z} = F(z, s, a, d, g, n) = sz^{a} - (d + n + g)z \tag{9}$$

The first step is to define the function $F(\ )$. For this, we type (the text in bold-
face letters is what we type in; the stuff in italics is the computer's output):

In[1] :=
F[z_,s_,a_,d_,g_,n_]:=s*(z^a)−(d+g+n)*z

followed by "enter" or "shift-return." (A normal "return" puts you on a new
line, but it does not tell the computer to execute the command.) This tells
the computer to define a function called **F** with the arguments specified
inside the square brackets. Notice that each argument is followed by the
symbol "_", arguments are separated by commas, and the definition of the
function must be preceded by the symbol ":=".

Next, we assign values to the parameters and compute the steady-state
value of z using the formula

$$\overline{Z} = \left(\frac{s}{\delta + n + g} \right)^{1/(1-\alpha)}$$

derived in Problem 3.1. In order to illustrate how the value of α (a) affects
the speed of convergence to the steady state, we will repeat the exercise with
two different values of a (**a1** = 0.69 and **a2** = 0.33). Notice that we use "="
to assign values to parameters. The program returns the steady states corresponding to the two values of a. (To prevent the computer from repeating all the parameter values, we use a semicolon at the end of each line.)

In[2] :=
a1=0.69; a2=0.33;
d=0.03; g=0.02;
s=0.25; n=0.01;
zs1=(s/(d+g+n))^(1/(1−a1))
zs2=(s/(d+g+n))^(1/(1−a2))

```
Out[ 5]=
    99.8432
Out[ 6]=
    8.41507
```

The next statement asks the computer to solve equation (9) numerically, together with an initial condition which specifies that the initial value of z is equal to one-half the corresponding steady state. Notice that a separate statement is needed to compute the solution for each set of parameter values. Prior to executing **NDSolve**, we must assign values to all the parameters,[16] so that the only unspecified argument of $F(\ )$ is the variable whose time path we seek (z). We must also specify that this variable is a function of time by writing it **z[t]** (or **z[s]** ....) on both sides of the equation, which are separated by two equal signs (==). The list of equations to be solved goes inside curly brackets separated by commas (the initial condition is also considered an equation). After the list of equations, we specify that the "unknown" is z, and then (also in curly brackets) we indicate that the dependent variable (i.e., "time") is t and that we want the solution evaluated for all t between 0 and 100. Finally, the first side of each statement assigns a name (**sol1** and **sol2**) to each "solution function."

```
In[ 7] :=
  sol1=NDSolve[{z'[t]==F[z[t], s, a1, d, g, n],
     z[0]==zs1/2}, z, {t, 0, 100}]
  sol2=NDSolve[{z'[t]==F[z[t], s, a2, d, g, n],
     z[0]==zs2/2}, z, {t, 0, 100}]
Out[ 7]=
  {{z -> InterpolatingFunction[{0., 100.}, <>]}}
Out[ 8]=
  {{z -> InterpolatingFunction[{0., 100.}, <>]}}
```

Out[7] and *Out*[8] inform us that the commands have been executed successfully (otherwise you will get an error message) and the solution path of z has been placed into what *Mathematica* calls *InterpolatingFunctions*. The next step is to put the solution functions in a usable form. For this, we evaluate the generic solution function **z[t]** using each of the solution rules (**sol1** and **sol2**) to obtain two new functions, **pz1[t]** and **pz2[t]**, that can be manipulated as ordinary functions.

```
In[ 9] :=
  pz1[t_]:=z[t]/.sol1
  pz2[t_]:=z[t]/.sol2
```

Finally, we can use the **Plot** command to display the time path of z. The following statement asks *Mathematica* to plot **pz1[t]** and (the constant) **zs1** as functions of t, with this variable taking values between 0 and 100.

$In[11]:=$
    Plot[{pz1[t],zs1},{t, 0, 100}]
$Out[11]=$
    -Graphics-

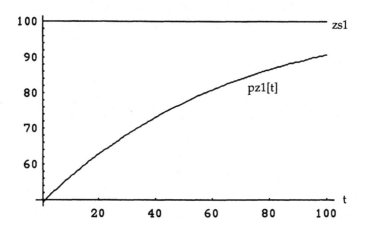

In[12] repeats the experiment with the lower value of α. Notice that in this case convergence toward the steady state is much faster.

$In[12]:=$
    Plot[{pz2[t],zs2},{t, 0, 100}]
$Out[12]=$
    -Graphics-

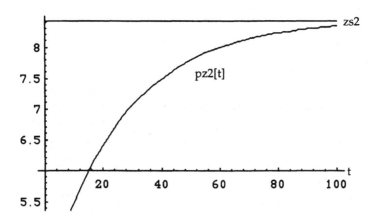

5. Problems

Problem 5.1. Homogeneous output is produced using two types of capital (private and public), K and P, according to a technology of the form

$$Y_t = K_t^\alpha P_t^\beta \quad \text{where} \quad \alpha + \beta < 1 \tag{1}$$

Both types of capital depreciate completely upon use. In each period, the government taxes income at a rate τ and invests the proceeds in public capital for the next period. Agents save a fixed fraction s of their after-tax income and invest it in private capital. Hence,

$$K_{t+1} = s(1 - \tau)Y_t \tag{2}$$

and

$$P_{t+1} = \tau Y_t \tag{3}$$

Using (1)–(3), derive a single difference equation in Y that describes the evolution of income. Call this equation (4). Solve for the steady-state value of Y, and show that the system is stable. How does steady-state income vary with s and τ? What value of τ should the government choose if it wants to maximize steady-state output?

Problem 5.2. Consider an economy endowed with an aggregate production function of the form

$$Y = K^\alpha (LH)^{1-\alpha} \tag{1}$$

where K is the aggregate stock of physical capital, L is employment in goods production, and H is the average stock of human capital. "Pure knowledge," A, increases over time at a constant exogenous rate g, that is,

$$A_{t+1} = (1+g)A_t \tag{2}$$

Pure knowledge and teacher's time and human capital are combined to "produce" the next generation's human capital according to

$$H_{t+1} = (\tau H_t)^\gamma A_t^{1-\gamma} \tag{3}$$

where τ is the fraction of the population employed as teachers, a variable chosen by the government.

Suppose that population is constant, and normalize it to 1 (so that the labor force is $L = 1 - \tau$), and suppose that capital depreciates completely upon use and that agents save a constant fraction s of their income. Then the law of motion for the capital stock is of the form

$$K_{t+1} = sK_t^\alpha H_t^{1-\alpha}(1 - \tau)^{1-\alpha} \tag{4}$$

(i) Define

$$Z = K/A \quad \text{and} \quad E = H/A$$

Using the previous expressions, derive a system of difference equations in Z and E that will describe the evolution of the economy.

(ii) Solve for the steady-state values of Z and E, and compute the steady-state value of $Q = Y/A$.

(iii) Find the value of τ that will maximize steady-state Q.

(iv) Let $z = \ln Z$ and $e = \ln E$. The system derived in (i) should be linear in e and z. Working with the system in logs, compute its eigenvalues, and discuss the stability of its steady state.

(v) Draw the phase diagram for the system.

Problem 5.3. A model of learning by doing. Starting from the Solow model with exogenous technical progress, we will develop a simple model of endogenous growth and examine some of its implications. Assume that the production function is of the form

$$Y = K^{\alpha}(AL)^{1-\alpha}$$

Then output per worker is given by

$$Q = AZ^{\alpha} \tag{1}$$

where A is an index of technical efficiency, and $Z = K/AL$ is the capital/labor ratio in efficiency units. Given a constant investment coefficient s, the growth rate of Z is given by the following equation:

$$\frac{\dot{Z}}{Z} = sZ^{\alpha-1} - (\delta + n + g_A) \tag{2}$$

where n is the rate of population growth, and $g_A = \dot{A}/A$ is the rate of technical progress.

Instead of assuming that g_A is a given constant, we will now assume that the rate of technical progress g_A reflects the accumulation of knowledge with productive experience. In particular, we assume that the instantaneous increase of A is proportional to output per worker, that is,

$$\dot{A} = \gamma Q = \gamma A Z^{\alpha} \tag{3}$$

where the coefficient γ measures the speed of learning.

(i) Show that under these assumptions the law of motion of the capital/labor ratio is of the form

$$\dot{Z} = (s - \gamma Z)Z^{\alpha} - (\delta + n)Z \tag{5}$$

(ii) Construct the phase diagram for the system, and discuss the stability of its steady state. What is the growth rate of income per worker along the steady-state path?

(iii) Analyze the impact of an increase in the investment rate on the steady state and on the time path of the system. Things are now quite different from what they were in the Solow model with exogenous technical progress. In what sense?

(iv) Consider two countries that are identical except for their investment rates. Discuss the predictions of the current model and the Solow model with exogenous technical progress concerning the evolution of the relative income levels of the two countries.

Problem 5.4. An extended Solow model with human capital (Mankiw et al., 1992). Suppose the aggregate production function is of the form

$$Y = K^{\alpha} E^{\gamma} (AL)^{1-\alpha-\gamma} = ALZ^{\alpha} H^{\gamma} \qquad (1)$$

where K and E are the aggregate stocks of physical capital and human capital, L is the size of the labor force, and A is a productivity index that summarizes the current state of technical knowledge. The normalized variables $Z = K/AL$ and $H = E/AL$ denote the stocks of physical capital and human capital per efficiency unit of labor.

We postulate constant rates of population growth and exogenous technical progress ($\dot{L}/L = n$ and $\dot{A}/A = g$) and assume that the fractions of gross domestic product (GDP) devoted to investment in physical capital and human capital (s_k and s_h) remain constant over time. Under these assumptions, the accumulation of productive factors is described by the system

$$\dot{K} = s_k Y - \delta K \quad \text{and} \quad \dot{E} = s_h Y - \delta E \qquad (2)$$

where the depreciation rate δ is assumed to be the same for both types of capital. Using the fact that $\dot{Z}/Z = \dot{K}/K - n - g$, and $\dot{H}/H = (\dot{E}/E) - n - g$, the laws of motion for the stocks of physical capital and human capital can be rewritten in terms of the normalized variables,

$$\frac{\dot{Z}}{Z} = s_k Z^{\alpha-1} H^{\gamma} - (\delta + g + n) \qquad (3)$$

$$\frac{\dot{H}}{H} = s_h Z^{\alpha} H^{\gamma-1} - (\delta + g + n) \qquad (4)$$

(i) Find the steady-state values of Z, H, and output per efficiency unit of labor, $P = Y/AL$.

(ii) We will now construct a log-linear approximation to the system and use it to derive a convergence equation similar to the one obtained in Section 4(a) Letting $z = \ln Z$ and $h = \ln H$ (from where $Z = e^z$ and $H = e^h$), rewrite the system (3)–(4) in terms of z and h. Show that the linear approximation to the transformed system around the steady state is given by

$$\dot{z} = -(1-\alpha)(\delta+g+n)\tilde{z} + \gamma(\delta+g+n)\tilde{h} \qquad (11)$$

$$\dot{h} = \alpha(\delta+g+n)\tilde{z} - (1-\beta)(\delta+g+n)\tilde{h} \qquad (12)$$

where $\tilde{x} = x - \bar{x}$ denotes the current deviation of variable x from its steady-state value. Discuss the stability of the system (11)–(12) (and hence that of the original system).

(iii) Using the system (11)–(12) and the fact that $p = \alpha z + \gamma h$, derive a linear differential equation in p that describes the approximate behavior of this variable, and solve it. Rewriting the solution in terms of output per worker $q = p + a$, derive a convergence equation of the form

$$\frac{q_{t+d} - q_t}{d} = g + \frac{1 - e^{-\lambda d}}{d}[p_t - (q_t - a_t)]$$

where d is the duration of the period, and $\lambda = (1 - \alpha - \gamma)(\delta + g + n)$.

Problem 5.5. Diamond's model with variable labor supply. In the basic Diamond model, leisure does not enter the utility function of households. As a result, each worker supplies inelastically his or her endowment of labor time, and the level of employment is constant (on a per-capita basis). We will now relax this assumption.

To simplify things, we assume that the rate of population growth is zero ($n = 0$) and that individuals work in youth and consume only in old age. Young workers, on the other hand, enjoy their leisure and must therefore seek an optimal trade-off between the disutility of working and the need for income. The utility function of a representative worker is given by

$$U(x_{t+1}, L_t) = \frac{x_{t+1}^{1-\gamma}}{1-\gamma} - L_t$$

where $\gamma \in (0, 1)$, L is labor time supplied in youth, and x is old-age consumption. The per-capita production function is

$$y = \sqrt{kL}$$

(i) Because consumption takes place only in old age, workers save their entire labor income wL and consume their savings plus interest earnings ($w_t L_t R_{t+1}$) in the second period of their lives. They solve, then,

$$\max_{x,L} \left\{ U = \frac{x^{1-\gamma}}{1-\gamma} - L \text{ s.t. } x = wLR \right\}$$

Solve this problem for the agent's labor supply (L^s) and savings functions.

(ii) Firms maximize profits per worker, that is,

$$\max_{k,L} \pi_t = y_t - R_t k_t - w_t L_t = (k_t L_t)^{1/2} - R_t k_t - w_t L_t$$

Write the first-order conditions for this problem, solve for w and R as functions of (k/L), and derive the firm's labor demand function.

(iii) In equilibrium, agents optimize, and labor and capital markets clear. Because population is constant, market clearing requires, in per-capita terms,

$$L_t^s = L_t^d \tag{5}$$

$$s_t = k_{t+1} \tag{6}$$

Show that the conditions for market clearing and individual optimization can be reduced to the following system of first-order difference equations in k and R:

$$k_{t+1} = R_t k_t \tag{A}$$

$$R_{t+1}^{1-\gamma} = 4k_t^{\gamma} R_t^{1+\gamma} \tag{B}$$

Hint: The idea is to eliminate w and L from the foregoing equations. Use the first-order conditions for the firm's problem to show that

$$w_t = 1/4\, R_t \tag{7}$$

$$w_t L_t = k_t R_t \tag{8}$$

and substitute the savings function into the market-clearing condition to get (A). Next, use the market-clearing and optimization conditions together with (7) to obtain (B).

(iv) We have been able, then, to reduce the model to a system of two first-order difference equations that describe the sequence of competitive equilibria in this economy. Note that if we take logs, the system becomes linear. Defining

$$\kappa = \ln k \quad \text{and} \quad \rho = \ln R$$

we can rewrite (A) and (B) as

$$\kappa_{t+1} = \rho_t + \kappa_t \tag{A$'$}$$

$$(1-\gamma)\rho_{t+1} = \ln 4 + \gamma\kappa_t + (1+\gamma)\rho_t \tag{B$'$}$$

Construct the phase diagram of the system, compute its solution, and analyze its dynamics. What would be a reasonable initial condition for this model?

Problem 5.6. Social security in Diamond's model. Consider a Diamond economy like the one analyzed in Example 3.6. Population grows at a constant rate n, preferences are of the form

$$U(c, x) = \beta \ln c + (1 - \beta) \ln x \tag{U}$$

with $\beta \in (0, 1)$, and the production function is Cobb-Douglas,

$$Y = K^{\alpha} L^{1-\alpha} \tag{P}$$

with $\alpha \in (0, 1)$.

We assume that wages are taxed at a proportional rate τ and that proceeds are used to finance a balanced pay-as-you go social-security scheme. Hence, first-period after-tax income for an agent born at time t is given by

$$y_1 = (1 - \tau)w_t$$

and his second-period retirement subsidy is equal to

$$y_2 = \tau(1+n)w_{t+1}$$

(because there are $1+n$ young agents for each old agent).

   (i) Maximize $U(c,x)$ subject to the appropriate budget constraint, and solve for
       the agent's savings function $s^* = s(y_1, y_2, R)$ and his indirect utility function
       $v(w_t, w_{t+1}, R_{t+1}, \tau)$. Taking factor prices as given, when is the agent's welfare an
       increasing function of the social-security tax rate?
  (ii) Derive the law of motion for the capital/labor ratio, $Z = K/L$, and compute
       the steady-state values of Z and factor prices as functions of τ. Call these
       functions

$$\overline{Z} = Z_s(\tau), \quad \overline{w} = w_s(\tau), \quad \text{and} \quad \overline{R} = R_s(\tau)$$

       Under what conditions is it true that $1 + n > R_s(0)$?
 (iii) What are the effects of an increase in τ on steady-state Z and factor prices?
       Compute the following derivatives evaluated at $\tau = 0$:

$$\frac{Z'_s(\tau)}{Z_s(\tau)}, \quad \frac{w'_s(\tau)}{w_s(\tau)}, \quad \text{and} \quad \frac{R'_s(\tau)}{w_s(\tau)}$$

  (iv) One of the advantages of working with a model in which indiviudal prefer-
       ences are clearly specified is that this gives us a natural criterion for evaluat-
       ing the desirability of possible policy alternatives. Using your previous results,
       and considering only its effects on steady-state welfare, when will it be a good
       idea to introduce a social-security scheme? To answer this question, compute
       the derivative of a representative individual's (maximized) welfare with respect
       to τ, taking into account both the direct effects of the tax and its indirect effects
       through the induced change in steady-state factor prices, and evaluate it at
       $\tau = 0$.

       Hint: Leave everything in terms of $z'_s(0)$.

Bibliography

Azariadis, C. 1993. *Intertemporal Macroeconomics*. Oxford: Blackwell.
Barro, R., and Sala-i-Martin, X. 1990. Economic Growth and Convergence across
    the United States. NBER working paper no. 3419.
Barro, R., and Sala-i-Martin, X. 1992. Convergence. *Journal of Political Economy*
    100(2):223–51.
Blanchard, O., and Fischer, S. 1989. *Lectures on Macroeconomics*. Massachusetts
    Institute of Technology Press.
Cagan, P. 1956. The Monetary Dynamics of Hyperinflation. In: *Studies in the
    Quantity Theory of Money*, ed. M. Friedman. University of Chicago Press.
Calvo, G. 1977. The Stability of Models of Money and Perfect Foresight: A
    Comment. *Econometrica* 45:1737–9.
Cass, D. 1965. Optimum Growth in an Aggregative Model of Capital
    Accumulation. *Review of Economic Studies* 32:223–40.

de la Fuente, A. 1992. Histoire d'A: Crecimiento y Progreso Técnico. *Investigaciones Económicas* 16(3):331–91.

Galor, O., and Ryder, H. 1989. On the existence of equilibrium in an overlapping generations model with productive capital. *Journal of Economic Theory* 49:360–75.

Diamond, P. 1965. National Debt in a Neoclassical Growth Model. *American Economic Review* 55:1126–50.

Dornbusch, R. 1976. Expectations and Exchange Rate Dynamics. *Journal of Political Economy* 84:1161–76.

Koopmans, T. 1965. On the Concept of Optimal Economic Growth. In: *The Econometric Approach to Development Planning*. Chicago: Rand McNally.

Mankiw, G., Romer, D., and Weil, D. 1992. A Contribution to the Empirics of Economic Growth. *Quarterly Journal of Economics* 107(2):407–37.

Obstfeld, M. 1980. Anticipated Disturbances in a Perfect Foresight Model. Mimeograph, Department of Economics, Columbia University.

Ramsey, F. 1928. A Mathematical Theory of Savings. *Economic Journal* 38:543–59.

Sargent, T., and Wallace, N. 1973. The Stability of Models of Money and Growth with Pefect Foresight. *Econometrica* 45:1043–8.

Solow, R. 1956. A Contribution to the Theory of Economic Growth. *Quarterly Journal of Economics* 70:65–94.

Solow, R. 1970. *Growth Theory: An Exposition*. Oxford University Press.

Swan, T. W. 1956. Economic Growth and Capital Accumulation. *The Economic Record* 32:334–61.

Wolfram, S. 1991. *Mathematica. A System for Doing Mathematics by Computer*, 2nd ed. Reading, MA: Addison-Wesley.

Notes

1 Solving (6) for the level of output, we can reinterpret this relation as a "Lucas" aggregate supply function,

$$y = \bar{y} + (1/\theta)(\pi - \pi^e)$$

saying that output supply will be above its natural rate whenever inflation exceeds expectations. One possible mechanism behind this relation works through the impact of unanticipated inflation on perceived real wages. When inflation is higher than workers realize, they may overestimate their real wage, and this may induce them to supply more labor than they would otherwise.

2 Note how we have arranged things so that the model becomes autonomous. Instead of working with price levels, we are working with inflation rates. In a steady state, therefore, it is not prices, but rather inflation, that remains constant. Second, the driving force behind inflation will be the growth of the nominal money supply. If we allowed the rate of monetary growth to change over time, we would have a nonautonomous system. To simplify things, we assume that μ is constant. Then we can analyze the effect of a change in monetary policy by looking at the impact of a once-and-for-all change in μ.

3 Notice that we would get the same answer if we moved east, rather than north, from the steady state. Hence, we could have used $\partial \dot{\pi}^e/\partial \pi^e$ instead of $\partial \dot{\pi}^e/\partial m$.

4 See Section 2(d) of Chapter 10 for a discussion of the conditions for the stability of linear systems with constant coefficients.

5 This is more an assumption than a result. Our original equations already embody the natural-rate hypothesis.

6 A simple way to see this is the following. Suppose the production function is homogeneous of degree h, where h is not necessarily equal to 1. Then, by Euler's theorem,

$$KF_K(K, L) + LF_L(K, L) = hF(K, L) \tag{1}$$

Suppose $h = 1$ (i.e., we have constant returns to scale) and there is perfect competition. Then factor prices are given by the corresponding marginal products, and equation (1) says that when capital and labor are paid their equilibrium prices, total output is just exhausted. If $h > 1$, however (i.e., when we have increasing returns), factors cannot be paid their marginal product, because the required amount is larger than total output.

7 It can be shown that if F is homogeneous of degree 1, then its partial derivatives are homogeneous of degree 0, that is, for any $\lambda > 0$, $F_K(K, L) = F_K(\lambda K, \lambda L)$, and similarly for F_L. See Chapter 4.

8 A similar model with a Cobb-Douglas technology was proposed simultaneously by Swan (1956). Hence, we sometimes speak of the Solow-Swan model.

9 The first equality in this expression follows by L'Hôpital's rule whenever $f(\ )$ is unbounded.

10 Notice that firms return undepreciated capital to the old workers after production takes place. Because the old "eat everything," the young have to start from scratch each period.

11 Technical progress can be handled in the same way as population growth. Let g be the rate of labor-augmenting technical progress, i.e., $A_{t+1} = (1 + g)A_t$, and define $Z = K/AL$. Then we have

$$\frac{K_{t+1}}{A_{t+1}L_{t+1}} = \frac{L_t s_t}{(1+n)(1+g)A_t L_t} \Rightarrow (1+n)(1+g)Z_{t+1} = \frac{s[A_t w(Z_t), f'(Z_{t+1}) + (1-\delta)]}{A_t}$$

where $Aw(Z)$ is the salary per worker. Notice, however, that this equation will not, in general, have a constant-Z solution. If preferences are homothetic, however, the savings function is of the form $s(y, R) = s(R)y$, and the previous expression simplifies to

$$(1+n)(1+g)Z_{t+1} = s[f'(Z_{t+1}) + (1-\delta)]w(Z_t)$$

which does have a steady state.

12 It is shown in the proof that $\phi'(0) > 1$ requires that $w'(0) > 1$. Galor and Ryder (1989) have shown that this condition is stronger than the Inada condition $f'(0) = \infty$. Hence, the Inada condition is not sufficient to guarantee the existence of a nontrivial steady state.

13 Because Z is a function of A, which is not observable, it may instead be better to work with the growth rate of the capital stock per worker. Although data on this variable are indeed available for some countries, their quality is in general rather poor, and the available figures may not be fully comparable across countries. Hence, it may be better to use a transformation of (1) that will allow us to work directly with (more reliable) data on investment flows, rather than with capital stocks.

14 See Barro and Sala-i-Martin (1990, 1992) and Mankiw, Romer, and Weil (1992) for empirical applications of this methodology.

15 Because z is in logs, this is approximately the deviation from the steady state in percentage terms.

16 This can also be done inside the function. Thus we could replace the statement in *In[7]* by

```
soll=NDSolve[{z'[t]==F[z[t], 0.25, 0.69, 0.03, 0.02,
0.01],z[0]==zs1/2}, z,{t, 0, 100}]
```

12

An Introduction to Dynamic Optimization

This chapter contains an introduction to dynamic optimization. In Section 1 we develop some basic elements of dynamic programming that are then used in Section 2 in an informal derivation of the maximum principle. Applications will be discussed in Chapter 13.

1. Dynamic Programming

Consider a system, economic or otherwise, whose evolution over time can be at least partially controlled by the actions of a decision-maker. At each point in time s, the state of the system can be described by a dated vector of real variables, $x_s \in \mathbb{R}^n$, which we call the *state vector*. In each period the decision-maker chooses a vector of *control* or *decision variables, $u_s \in \mathbb{R}^m$. Together, the current state of the system and the choices of controls determine the value of the state vector for the following period according to the (possibly time-dependent) law of motion

$$x_{s+1} = m_s(x_s, u_s) \tag{1}$$

Thus, different choices of the control variables will yield different time paths of the system. It will be assumed that the decision-maker has preferences defined over such time paths that can be summarized by a time-additive *return* or *objective function*

$$W_t = \sum_{s=t}^{T-1} f_s(x_s, u_s) \tag{2}$$

For simplicity, we will take as given the planning horizon and the initial and terminal values of the state vector. Thus, we consider the problem faced by a planner who inherits at time t a predetermined state vector x_t, cares only about what happens between times t and T ($\leq \infty$), and is obliged to leave the state vector with value x_T at the end of the planning period. The agent can also be constrained by further restrictions on the state and control vectors, which we will write $(x_s, u_s) \in C_s$ for each s.

Given the initial state of the system, x_t, and a sequence $\mathbf{u}_{t,T-1} = \{u_s; s = t, t+1, \ldots, T-1\}$ of control variables, the evolution of the state vector is determined by the law of motion (1). Thus, x_t and $\mathbf{u}_{t,T-1}$ induce a sequence of states $\mathbf{x}_{t+1,T} = \{x_s; s = t+1, \ldots, T\}$. We will write $\mathbf{z}_{t,T} = \{\mathbf{u}_{t,T-1} \cup \mathbf{x}_{t+1,T}\}$ and say that a such sequence is *admissible* if both states and controls are feasible at all times and the terminal value of the state vector is equal to the required value, x_T. The set of all sequences $\mathbf{z}_{t,T}$ admissible from a given initial state vector x_t will be denoted by $\Phi(x_t)$, or by $\Phi(x_t, x_T)$ when we also want to make explicit the terminal constraint on the state. When we want to indicate explicitly the initial and terminal conditions on this sequence, we will write $\mathbf{z}(\mathbf{u}_{t,T-1}, x_t, x_T)$, and we will denote the portion of $\mathbf{z}_{t,T}$ between points a and b in time by $\mathbf{z}(\mathbf{u}_{t,T-1}, x_t, x_T)|_a^b$.

In this notation the decision-maker's objective function can be written

$$W(\mathbf{z}_{t,T}, t, T-1) = \sum_{s=t}^{T-1} f_s(x_s, u_s) \tag{2'}$$

Notice that $W(\ )$ is given by the sum of the instantaneous or period return functions $\{f_s\}$, where each f_s is a function only of time and the current state and control vectors and does not depend on either past or future values of x or u.

(a) The Principle of Optimality and Bellman's Equation

The problem the agent faces is that of choosing the time path of the control variables so as to maximize the objective function W_t subject to the law of motion (1) and appropriate feasibility constraints, taking as given the planning horizon (t, T) and the initial and terminal values of the state vector. We will denote by $V(\ )$ the *value function* for the planner's problem (i.e., the maximum attainable value of the objective function). Clearly, $V(\ )$ will be a function of the parameters of the maximization problem (the initial and terminal times and state vectors) and is equal to the objective function evaluated at the optimal control path and the induced state sequence, assuming they exist. Formally, the problem can be written

$$V(x_t, t; x_T, T) = \max_{\mathbf{u}_{t,T-1}} \{W[\mathbf{z}(\mathbf{u}_{t,T-1}, x_t, x_T), t, T-1]$$

$$= \sum_{s=t}^{T-1} f_s(x_s, u_s) \text{ s.t. } x_{s+1} = m_s(x_s, u_s), t, T, x_t,$$

$$\text{and } x_T \text{ given, } (x_s, u_s) \in C_s \subseteq \mathbb{R}^{n+m} \text{ for each } s\} \quad \text{(DP)}$$

If T is finite (which may not be the case), (DP) can be solved by the standard methods for dealing with constrained optimization problems (i.e., by applying the Lagrange or Kuhn-Tucker theorems). The structure of the problem, moreover, permits some important simplifications and will also allow us to deal with infinite-horizon problems (to which the standard theorems do not apply). The features that make things easier are the additive separability of the objective function and the simple structure of the law of motion – the fact that for each s, f_s (the period return function) and m_s (the law of motion) depend only on s and on the current values of the state and control variables, but not on their past or future values, and that the total return is simply the sum of the period return functions.

This property has the following implication. Let $\mathbf{z}_{t,T} = \mathbf{z}(\mathbf{u}_{t,T-1}, x_t, x_T)$ be an admissible sequence of controls and induced states between end points x_t and x_T, and let a and b be positive integers, with $t \le a < b \le T-1$. Then we can write the return function in the form

$$W(\mathbf{z}_{t,T}, t, T-1) = W\left(\mathbf{z}_{t,T}\big|_t^{a-1}, t, a-1\right) + W\left(\mathbf{z}_{t,T}\big|_a^{b-1}, a, b-1\right) + W\left(\mathbf{z}_{t,T}\big|_b^{T-1}, b, T-1\right)$$

That is, the total payoff associated with a state–control sequence over the whole planning horizon is simply the sum of the payoffs associated with different portions of the sequence over the corresponding subperiods. Using this additivity property, it is easy to establish the following result, which gives an important property of the optimal solution of (DP).

Theorem 1.1. The principle of optimality. Let $z_{t,T}^* = \mathbf{z}(\mathbf{u}_{t,T-1}^*, x_t, x_T) = \{u_s^*,$ *$x_{s+1}^*\}$ be the optimal solution of (DP) between given end points* (x_t, t) *and* $(x_T,$ *$T)$. Given arbitrary points* a *and* b, *with* $t \le a < b \le T-1$, *let* x_a^* *and* x_b^* *be the corresponding terms of the optimal state sequence* $\{x_s^*\}$. *Then the optimal solution to*

$$V(x_a^*, a; x_b^*, b) = \max_{u_{a,b-1}} \left\{ W(\mathbf{z}_{a,b-1}, a, b-1) = \sum_{s=a}^{b-1} f_s(x_s, u_s) \right.$$

$$\text{s.t. } x_{s+1} = m_s(x_s, u_s),\ a,\ b,\ x_b^*,\ and\ x_a^*\ given,$$

$$\left. (x_s, u_s) \in C_s \subseteq \mathbb{R}^{n+m}\ for\ each\ s \right\} \qquad (DP.ab)$$

is given by $z_{t,T}^*\big|_a^{b-1}$.

Roughly speaking, the theorem says that each portion of the optimal plan is optimal on its own right. More precisely, any portion of an optimal trajectory is an optimal trajectory for an appropriate subproblem of (DP) in which we constrain the end-point values of the state vector to be equal to the corresponding terms of the optimal state sequence for the whole problem.

Proof. We proceed by contradiction. Let $\Phi(x_a^*, x_b^*)$ be the set of feasible trajectories $\mathbf{z}_{a,b-1}$ between end points (x_a^*, a) and (x_b^*, b). This set is not empty, as it contains at least the relevant portion of the optimal sequence for the whole problem, $\mathbf{z}_{t,T-1}^* |_a^b$, which exists by assumption. Now suppose that $\mathbf{z}_{t,T-1}^* |_a^{b-1}$ is not optimal for the subperiod from a to b. Then there exists a feasible sequence between these end points, $\mathbf{z}_{a,b-1}'$, such that $W(\mathbf{z}_{a,b-1}') > W(\mathbf{z}_{t,T-1}^* |_a^{b-1})$. By the time-additivity of the objective function,

$$W\!\left(\mathbf{z}_{t,T}^* \Big|_t^{a-1}\right) + W(\mathbf{z}_{a,b-1}') + W\!\left(\mathbf{z}_{t,T}^* \Big|_b^{T-1}\right) > W\!\left(\mathbf{z}_{t,T}^* \Big|_t^{T-1}\right)$$

Hence, we have found a sequence $\mathbf{z}_{t,T-1}^* |_t^{a-1} \cup \mathbf{z}_{a,b-1}' \cup \mathbf{z}_{t,T-1}^* |_b^{T-1}$ that yields a higher return than $\mathbf{z}_{t,T-1}^*$. Moreover, because this sequence is feasible by construction, we have reached a contradiction: $\mathbf{z}_{t,T-1}^*$ cannot be an optimal solution for the "whole" problem. $\square$

Problem 1.2. A violation of the principle of optimality. Consider an agent who lives three periods and maximizes a utility function of the form

$$V_1 = U_1 + \alpha U_2 + \beta U_3$$

where utility in period i, U_i, is a function of current and (expected) future consumption, that is,

$$U_1(c_1, c_2, c_3) = \ln(c_1 c_2 c_3), \quad U_2(c_2, c_3) = \ln(c_2 c_3), \quad \text{and} \quad U_3(c_3) = \ln c_3$$

and the budget constraint is of the form

$$A_{t+1} = A_t - c_t \qquad (A_1 \text{ given, and } A_4 = 0)$$

where A is wealth.

Notice that the return function is additive, but not separable over periods, as the period-1 utility, for example, depends on (expected) consumption at times 2 and 3. Hence, the assumptions of Theorem 1.1 do not hold, and, as we will see, the principle of optimality fails.

(i) Compute the optimal consumption plan from the perspective of time 1, $c^1 = (c_1^1, c_2^1, c_3^1)$.

(ii) Next, consider what happens as the agent begins to implement this plan. At time 1, he consumes c_1^1, receives utility U_1, and has leftover wealth $A_2 = A_1 - c_1^1$. He then faces the problem of maximizing utility over the remainder of his life,

$$\max V_2 = \alpha U_2 + \beta U_3$$

subject to $c_2 + c_3 = A_2$. Compute the new optimal plan, $c^2 = (c_2^2, c_3^2)$, and compare it with the last portion of c^1. Has the consumer changed his mind? How and why? Does the Bellman equation (discussed later) hold? $\square$

The principle of optimality has an important implication, sometimes called *time consistency:* Suppose we compute the optimal path from the beginning of the planning period and start moving along it. After a while, we stop and recalculate the optimal solution from the current time and state. The principle of optimality tells us that the solution of this new problem will be the remainder of the original optimal plan. Hence, the decision-maker will not be tempted to "change his mind."

This property allows us to approach the problem sequentially, leaving for tomorrow decisions about future controls, thus breaking up the original dynamic problem into a sequence of static subproblems. To make this precise, consider one particular decomposition of the problem, that into (i) today's choice of controls and (ii) all the rest of the plan. By the additivity of the objective function, we can write

$$V(x_t, t; x_T, T) = \max_{\mathbf{u}_{t,T-1}} W[\mathbf{z}(\mathbf{u}_{t,T-1}, x_t, x_T), t, T-1]$$

$$= \max_{u_t, \mathbf{u}_{t+1,T-1}} \{ f_t(u_t, x_t) + W[\mathbf{z}(\mathbf{u}_{t+1,T-1}, x_{t+1}, x_T), t+1, T-1] \}$$

where the maximization is subject to the usual constraints and, in particular, $x_{t+1} = m_t(x_t, u_t)$. The structure of the problem allows us to approach the choice of the current (u_t) and future ($\mathbf{u}_{t+1,T-1}$) controls sequentially. Notice that states and controls dated $t+1$ or higher do not affect the current return, given by $f_t(u_t, x_t)$, and that the current state and control vectors (x_t, u_t) affect future returns only through their effects on tomorrow's state, x_{t+1}. Thus, we can solve the problem in two steps: Given any choice of the current control, tomorrow we will face the problem of choosing $\mathbf{u}_{t+1,T-1}$ so as to maximize $W[\mathbf{z}(\mathbf{u}_{t+1,T-1}, x_{t+1}, x_t), t+1, T-1]$, taking as given the state x_{t+1} resulting from today's decision – a problem identical with today's except for the initial state and time. Having solved this problem, today's decision reduces to choosing u_t, taking into account both its direct contribution to the current return and its indirect contribution to future payoffs through its effect on tomorrow's state. The principle of optimality assures us that this stepwise or sequential maximization process will yield the same result as simultaneous determination of the whole control path. Thus, we can write

$$V(x_t, t; x_T, T) = \max_{u_t, \mathbf{u}_{t+1,T-1}} \{ f_t(u_t, x_t) + W[\mathbf{z}(\mathbf{u}_{t+1,T-1}, x_{t+1}, x_T), t+1, T-1] \}$$

$$= \max_{u_t} \Big\{ f_t(u_t, x_t) + \max_{\mathbf{u}_{t+1,T-1}} \{ W[\mathbf{z}(\mathbf{u}_{t+1,T-1}, x_{t+1}, x_T), t+1, T-1] \}$$

$$\text{s.t. } x_{t+1} = m_t(x_t, u_t) \Big\}$$

Finally, observe that the payoff resulting from the inside maximization is given by the value function corresponding to "tomorrow's problem." Thus,

$$\max_{u_t}\Big\{f_t(u_t, x_t)+ \max_{u_{t+1,T-1}}\{W[\mathbf{z}(\mathbf{u}_{t+1,T-1}, x_{t+1}, x_T), t+1, T-1]\}\ \text{s.t.}\ x_{t+1} = m_t(x_t, u_t)\Big\}$$

$$= \max_{u_t}\{f_t(u_t, x_t)+V(x_{t+1}, t+1; x_T, T)\ \text{s.t.}\ x_{t+1} = m_t(x_t, u_t)\}$$

and we arrive at *Bellman's equation,*

$$V(x_t, t; x_T, T) = \max_{u_t}\{f_t(u_t, x_t)+V(x_{t+1}, t+1; x_T, T)\ \text{s.t.}\ x_{t+1} = m_t(x_t, u_t)\} \quad \text{(BE)}$$

This expression formally characterizes the optimal choice of the current control vector as the solution of a static optimization problem in which the future consequences of current actions are summarized by incorporating tomorrow's value function into today's objective function. The solution to the static maximization problem in (BE) yields a *policy function* that gives the optimal value of the current control, u_t^*, as a function $g_t(x_t)$ of time and the current state. Tomorrow's state is then given by $x_{t+1} = m_t[g_t(x_t), x_t]$, and a solution to a similar problem (with x_{t+1} now given) then yields tomorrow's optimal control. (Notice that time enters both the value and policy functions as a separate argument, reflecting the fact that periods may differ in factors other than the state vector.)

The recursive relation given by (BE) is useful in that it allows us to conceptually transform a dynamic choice problem into a sequence of static problems we already know how to handle, at least in principle. But notice that the maximization in Bellman's equation is not really a standard problem in at least one sense: The value function $V(\ )$ appears both inside and outside the maximization operator (although with different arguments) and therefore is not a known function. In fact, (BE) is a functional equation – an equation in the unknown function $V(\ )$. Hence, the reformulation of the original problem does not really solve it, nor put it in a form we can solve directly. The Bellman equation, however, does provide the basis for an alternative approach to the problem that will indeed lead to an operational solution method. In the sections that follow we will consider two cases: finite-horizon problems, and infinite-horizon problems with some additional restrictions.

(i) Solution of Finite-Horizon Problems through Backward Induction

Dynamic programming problems over a finite planning horizon do not present any conceptual difficulties. The value and policy functions can be obtained by starting from the end and working backward. The optimal control sequence can then be computed by applying the sequence of policy functions, $g_1, \ldots, g_{T-1}$, to the initial state vector.

One period before the end of the planning period the problem reduces to choosing the last control, taking as given the terminal value of the state. Omitting some of the arguments of the value function, we can write

$$V(x_{T-1}, T-1) = \max_{u_{T-1}}\{f_{T-1}(u_{T-1}, x_{T-1}) \text{ s.t. } m_{T-1}(x_{T-1}, u_{T-1}) = x_T \text{ given}\}$$

Notice that at this stage there is no unknown value function inside the max operator; hence, $V(x_{T-1}, T-1)$ is well defined by the foregoing expression, and for a fully specified problem its computation is, in principle, straightforward. On the other hand, the value of x_{T-1} is not known at this point, but this does not matter, for we are interested in the whole function $V(\cdot, T-1)$, rather than its value for a specific state vector.

This procedure will also work for a class of problems more general than those we have considered thus far. In particular, we can abandon the assumption of a predetermined terminal state vector and let the agent choose x_T taking into account its contribution to his payoff, given by a *scrap* or *salvage* value function $S(x_T)$.[1] In this case, the last-stage maximization becomes

$$V(x_{T-1}, T-1) = \max_{u_{T-1}}\{f_{T-1}(u_{T-1}, x_{T-1}) + S(x_T) \text{ s.t. } x_T = m_{T-1}(x_{T-1}, u_{T-1})\}$$

In any case, the solution of the last-period problem yields a policy function that gives the optimal value of the last control as a function of the state at the beginning of the period: $u^*_{T-1} = g_{T-1}(x_{T-1})$. As for the value function, the value of the argument is not known at this stage, but what we want is the function itself.

Given $V(x_{T-1}, T-1)$, we can go back one step and compute the value function for the previous period,

$$V(x_{T-2}, T-2) = \max_{u_{T-2}}\{f_{T-2}(u_{T-2}, x_{T-2}) + V(x_{T-1}, T-1)$$
$$\text{s.t. } x_{T-1} = m_{T-2}(x_{T-2}, u_{T-2})\}$$

obtaining also the corresponding policy function, $u^*_{T-2} = g_{T-2}(x_{T-2})$. Proceeding in this manner, we eventually reach the initial period and solve

$$V(x_t, t) = \max_{u_t}\{f_t(u_t, x_t) + V(x_{t+1}, t+1; x_T, T) \text{ s.t. } x_{t+1} = m_t(x_t, u_t)\}$$

to obtain the value function for the original problem and the first policy function, $g_t(\cdot)$. At this point, the initial value of the state, x_t, is a given quantity, and the whole sequence of policy functions $\{g_s; s = t, t+1, \ldots, T-1\}$ is also known. Hence, we can recover the optimal sequence of instruments, given by $u^*_s = g_s(x_s)$, and the induced sequence of states, $x_{s+1} = m_s(x_s, u^*_s)$.

(ii) Discounting and Stationarity

It should be clear that the foregoing solution algorithm cannot be used when the planning horizon is infinite, for there is no terminal date from which to work backward. As we will see, however, certain kinds of infinite-horizon problems can be dealt with and in many cases are easier to solve than finite-horizon problems. In this section we introduce some notation and impose some additional structure on the dynamic programming problem before briefly discussing a particular class of infinite-horizon problems that will be analyzed in greater detail later.

Discounting. In many situations, payoffs accruing at different points in time are valued differently by the decision-maker. Typically, those that are realized further into the future are valued less than those that accrue immediately. Although our earlier specification of a time-dependent period return function $f_s(x_s, u_s)$ implicitly allows for this possibility, it will be convenient to bring it out explicitly by introducing a sequence of period-specific weights. In particular, we will assume that the period return function at time s is of the form $f_s(x_s, u_s) = \alpha_s F_s(x_s, u_s)$, where the discount factor α_s is a nonnegative real number, and consider an agent who faces a problem of the form

$$V(x_0, 0) = \max_{u_{0,T-1}} \sum_{s=0}^{T-1} \alpha_s F_s(x_s, u_s)$$

subject to the usual constraints. We will interpret $F_s(\ )$ as the payoff that accrues at time s, valued from the perspective of time s itself, and $f_s(\ )$ $= \alpha_s F_s(\ )$ as the same payoff "discounted back" to the beginning of the planning period at time zero. Thus, multiplication of the current payoff $F_s(\ )$ by α_s brings it back to time-zero units, and division of the discounted payoff $f_s(\ )$ by the same factor brings it forward to time-s units. Because first-period returns need no discounting, we set α_0 equal to 1.

As time passes and the agent gets to period t, he faces the subproblem of maximizing the remainder of the objective function,

$$V(x_t, t) = \max_{u_{t,T-1}} \sum_{s=t}^{T-1} \alpha_s F_s(x_s, u_s)$$

Notice that the value function in this expression gives the maximum attainable payoff evaluated from the perspective of time zero, because each period return is multiplied by the corresponding discount factor. When maximizing over the subperiod starting at t, however, it is often more convenient to make "current" valuations (as of time t). Thus, we define the current value function by

$$V^c(x_t, t) = \frac{V(x_t, t)}{\alpha_t} = \max_{u_{t,T-1}} \sum_{s=t}^{T-1} \frac{\alpha_s}{\alpha_t} F_s(x_s, u_s)$$

As usual, successive subproblems are linked by the Bellman equation:

$$V(x_t, t) = \max_{u_t}\{\alpha_t F_t(x_t, u_t) + V(x_{t+1}, t+1)\}$$

To rewrite this equation in terms of current values, we divide both sides of this expression by α_t, obtaining

$$V^c(x_t, t) = \max_{u_t}\{F_t(x_t, u_t) + \beta_t V^c(x_{t+1}, t+1)\}$$

where the one-period discount factor, $\beta_t = \alpha_{t+1}/\alpha_t$, discounts values from $t+1$ to t (multiplying by α_{t+1} brings them back to zero, dividing by α_t takes them back up to t). The interpretation of this expression is almost exactly the same as that of the undiscounted version of the Bellman equation: Given tomorrow's state, x_{t+1}, $V^c(x_{t+1}, t+1)$ gives the maximum attainable payoff in "tomorrow's utility units." To bring it back to "today's units," we multiply $V^c(\ )$ by β_t. The optimal policy is then to choose u_t so as to maximize the sum of today's period return and the discounted value of tomorrow's current value function.

Infinite Horizon, Stationary Problem. In many problems of interest it can be assumed that the period return function, the law of motion, the one-period discount factor, and the feasible set C to which states and controls must belong are all time-invariant, that is,

$$F_s = F, \qquad m_s = m, \qquad C_s = C, \qquad \beta_s = \beta \qquad (\forall\, s)$$

This assumption allows some further simplifications of the problem. Notice that with a constant β, we have $\alpha_{s+1} = \beta\alpha_s$. This equation, together with the assumption that $\alpha_0 = 1$, implies that the discount factor must be of the form $\alpha_s = \beta^s$. Thus, the subproblem starting at time t can be written

$$V^c(x_t, t) = \max_{u_t, T-1}\sum_{s=t}^{T-1}\mathbf{b}^{s-t}F(x_s, u_s)$$

In the finite-horizon case, t is still a separate argument of the current value function, as subproblems that start at different dates differ from each other not only in the initial value of the state vector but also in the time remaining until the end of the planning period. If the planning horizon is infinite, however, this is no longer the case, and all subproblems are identical. Thus, for infinite-horizon stationary problems, the current value function is a function of the initial state alone, $V^c(x_t)$, and the Bellman equation becomes

$$V^c(x_t) = \max_{u_t}\{F(x_t, u_t) + \beta V^c(x_{t+1})\}$$

It follows that the policy function, $u_t^* = g(x_t)$, is also time-invariant. This is an important simplification, because we now have to find only one such function, rather than $T - t$ of them.

As noted earlier, the backward-induction algorithm cannot be used to solve infinite-horizon problems. The following observation, however, provides the basis for a way to deal with such problems, as we will see later. Given a function $v(\ )$ from $\mathbb{R}^n$ to $\mathbb{R}$, we can define an operator T mapping the space of such functions into itself:

$$Tv(x) = \max_u \{F(x,u) + \beta v(y) \text{ s.t. } y = m(x,u), (x,u) \in C\}$$

The Bellman equation can then be written $V^c = TV^c$. Hence, a function V solves Bellman's equation if and only if it is a fixed point of the operator T. Under certain assumptions, the contraction mapping theorem can be used to establish the existence and uniqueness of a solution to Bellman's equation and to determine some properties of interest of such a function.

(iii) Uncertainty

Dynamic programming is particularly useful when dealing with problems that involve uncertainty in a dynamic setting. Provided we ignore some technical problems, the previous discussion can be easily extended to deal with stochastic problems.

Imagine that instead of a deterministic law of motion we have a stochastic law: x_t and u_t no longer determine the value of x_{t+1}, but only its probability distribution, described by a distribution function of the form $G(x_{t+1}; x_t, u_t)$, where

$$G(y; x_t, u_t) = \text{pr}(x_{t+1} \le y \mid x_t, u_t)$$

Agents now maximize expected utility. At time t, they choose u_t, not knowing for certain the value of next period's state. Whatever x_{t+1} turns out to be, they will optimize from tomorrow on, obtaining a value of $V^c(x_{t+1}, t+1)$. From today's perspective, then, u_t must be chosen so as to maximize the sum of the current return and the discounted value of the expectation of $V^c(x_{t+1}, t+1)$, computed using $G(\ )$. Hence, the Bellman equation becomes

$$V^c(x_t, t) = \max_{u_t} \{F_t(u_t, x_t) + \beta_t \int V^c(x_{t+1}, t+1) \, dG(x_{t+1}; x_t, u_t)\}$$

(b) Some Results for Stationary Discounted Problems

In this section we will analyze in greater detail a class of infinite-horizon problems. Given a predetermined state vector x_t, a decision-maker faces the problem of maximizing the objective function

$$W_t(\mathbf{z}_{t,\infty}) = \sum_{s=t}^{\infty} \beta^{s-t} F(x_s, u_s)$$

with $\beta \in (0, 1)$, over the set of feasible sequences $\mathbf{z}_{t,\infty} = \{u_s, x_{s+1}\} \in \Phi(x_t)$, where $x_{s+1} = m(x_s, u_s)$. We will assume that the series W_t converges (although possibly to plus or minus infinity) for all feasible sequences $\mathbf{z}_{t,\infty}$ and that the feasibility constraints are of the form

$$u_s \in \Gamma(x_s)$$

where Γ is a correspondence mapping points in $\mathbb{R}^n$ into sets in $\mathbb{R}^m$. The problem faced by the agent can then be written

$$V^c(x_t) = \max_{\mathbf{u}_{t,\infty}} \left\{ \sum_{s=t}^{\infty} \beta^{s-t} F(x_s, u_s) \right.$$

$$\left. \text{s.t. } x_{s+1} = m(x_s, u_s), \; u_s \in \Gamma(x_s), \; x_t \text{ given} \right\} \qquad (DP.\infty)$$

and the current value function $V^c(x_t)$ gives the maximum attainable value of the objective function whenever the problem has a solution. We know from our previous discussion that if the value function does exist, then it satisfies the Bellman equation:

$$V^c(x) = \max_{u \in \Gamma(x)} \{ F(x, u) + \beta V^c(y) \text{ s.t. } y = m(x, u) \} \qquad (BE)$$

The converse of this statement, however, is not necessarily true. The Bellman equation may have several solutions, and only one of them can be the value function for the programming problem. Hence, we need to establish conditions under which we can be sure that a given solution of (BE) is the value function we seek.

Theorem 1.3. Let the function $v:\mathbb{R}^n \longrightarrow \mathbb{R}$ *solve the Bellman equation (BE) and satisfy the boundedness condition*

$$\lim_{n \to \infty} \beta^n v(x_n) = 0 \qquad (0)$$

for any sequence $\{x_n\}$ *feasible from the initial state* x_t. *Suppose, moreover, that there exists a sequence* $z_{t,\infty}^* = x_t \cup \{u_s^*, x_{s+1}^*\}$, *where* u_s^* *solves*

$$v(x_s) = \max_{u_s \in \Gamma(x_s)} \{ F(x_s, u_s) + \beta v[m(x_s, u_s)] \} \qquad (BE.s)$$

for each s and $x_{s+1}^* = m(x_s^*, u_s^*)$. *Then v is the current value function for the programming problem, and* $\mathbf{z}_{t,\infty}^*$ *solves (DP.∞)* .

Proof. To show that $v(\;)$ is the value function for the programming problem, we need to show that for any given initial state x_t,

(i) $v(x_t) \geq W_t(\mathbf{z}_{t,\infty})$ for any sequence $\mathbf{z}_{t,\infty} \in \Phi(x_t)$, and
(ii) there exists a sequence $\mathbf{z}_{t,\infty}^* \in \Phi(x_t)$ such that $W_t(\mathbf{z}_{\lambda,\infty}^*) = v(x_t)$.

That is, $v(x_t)$ is an upper bound for the value of the problem over the set of feasible sequences, and there is a feasible sequence that attains this value.

Let $\mathbf{z}_{t,\infty} = x_t \cup \{u_s, x_{s+1}; s \geq t\}$ be an arbitrary sequence feasible from x_t. Then, by (BE.s),

$$v(x_t) = \max_{u_t \in \Gamma(x_t)} \{F(x_t, u_t) + \beta v(x_{t+1})\} \geq F(x_t, u_t) + \beta v(x_{t+1})$$

$$\geq F(x_t, u_t) + \beta[F(x_{t+1}, u_{t+1}) + \beta v(x_{t+2})]$$

$$\geq \ldots \geq \sum_{s=t}^{t+n} \beta^{s-t} F(x_s, u_s) + \beta^{n+1} v(x_{t+n+1}) \tag{3}$$

Taking the limit of this expression as $n \to \infty$, and using the boundedness condition (0),

$$v(x_t) \geq W_t(\mathbf{z}_{t,\infty}) + \lim_{n \to \infty} \beta^{n+1} v(x_{n+1}) = W_t(\mathbf{z}_{t,\infty})$$

for any feasible sequence $\mathbf{z}_{t,\infty}$. Hence, $v(x_t)$ is an upper bound for the value of the problem. Moreover, the sequence $\mathbf{z}_{t,\infty}^* = x_t \cup \{u_s^*, x_{s+1}^*\}$ of solutions to (BE.s) attains this value. Notice that by definition,

$$v(x_s^*) = \max_{u_s \in \Gamma(x_s)} \{F(x_s^*, u_s) + \beta v[m(x_s^*, u_s)]\} = F(x_s^*, u_s^*) + \beta v(x_{s+1}^*)$$

Hence, all the weak inequalities in (3) hold as equalities, and we conclude that

$$v(x_t^*) = W_t(\mathbf{z}_{t,\infty}^*)$$

which proves the theorem. $\qquad\qquad\square$

Theorem 1.3 says that if we can find a bounded solution to the Bellman equation, the original problem reduces to a sequence of static maximizations. There is, however, no assurance that such a solution will exist in all cases. Our next task is to identify conditions under which the Bellman equation has a unique bounded solution. The discussion relies heavily on the reader's familiarity with the concepts of a complete metric space and the contraction mapping theorem (for a review of this material, see Section 7 of Chapter 2).

We define the operator T mapping real-valued functions into real-valued functions by

$$Tv(x) = \max_{u \in \Gamma(x)} \{F(x, u) + \beta v[m(x, u)]\}$$

Then the Bellman equation can be written in the form

$$V(x) = TV(x) \tag{BE$'$}$$

Thus, we see that finding a solution to the Bellman equation is equivalent to finding a fixed point of the operator T. If we can show that under appropriate assumptions, T is a contraction mapping a complete metric space into itself, we can invoke the contraction mapping theorem to establish the existence and uniqueness of an appropriate solution to (BE).

We recall from Chapter 2 (see Theorem 7.12) that the space $C(X)$ of bounded, continuous real-valued functions defined on a set X in $\mathbb{R}^n$ is a complete metric space under the sup norm, defined by

$$\|f\|_s = \sup\{|f(x)|;\ x \in X\}$$

Next we will check that under certain continuity and boundedness restrictions on the objective function, the law of motion, and the constraint correspondence, the operator T maps $C(X)$ into itself (i.e., T maps continuous bounded functions into continuous bounded functions) and that T is a contraction. By the contraction mapping theorem, it follows that (BE′) has a unique bounded solution in $C(X)$ that, by Theorem 1.3, is the value function we are seeking.

In what follows, we will make the following assumption.

Assumption 1.4. Continuity. The period return function F is bounded and continuous, the law of motion m is continuous, the constraint correspondence Γ is continuous,[2] and the set $\Gamma(x)$ is nonempty and compact for each x.

Under these conditions we can establish the following result.

Theorem 1.5. Suppose that Assumption 1.4 holds. Then T *is an operator mapping continuous bounded functions into continuous bounded functions. Moreover* T : C(X) $\longrightarrow$ C(X) *is a contraction and therefore has a unique fixed point* V *in* C(X). *This* V *is the value function for the corresponding dynamic programming problem.*

Moreover, under Assumption 1.4, the solution function for the maximization in (BE) is the policy correspondence g( ) *for the programming problem, giving the set of optimal values of the control* u *as a function of the state, and* g( ) *is nonempty and uhc.*

Proof

- Let $v \in C(X)$. Under our assumptions, the maximization problem that defines the operator T,

$$Tv(x) = \max_{u \in \Gamma(x)}\{F(x, u) + \beta v[m(x, u)]\}$$

is, for each x, that of maximizing a continuous function on a compact set. Hence, by the extreme-value theorem, a maximum exists, and Tv is well defined. Because both v and F are bounded, Tv is also bounded; and because F and v are continuous and the constraint correspondence is continuous and compact-valued, the theorem of the maximum (Theorem 2.1 in Chapter 7) guarantees the continuity of Tv. Hence, T maps $C(X)$ into itself. Moreover, by the theorem of the maximum, the solution mapping for this maximization (i.e., the policy function $g(x)$), is a nonempty and uhc correspondence.

- To establish that T is a contraction, we make use of Blackwell's sufficient conditions (see Theorem 7.19 in Chapter 2). We have to show that T satisfies

   (i) monotonicity: $\forall f, g \in C(X), f(x) \leq g(x) \ \forall X \Rightarrow Tf(x) \leq Tg(x)$, and
   (ii) discounting: $\exists \beta \in (0, 1)$ s.th. $\forall f \in C(X), x \in X, a \geq 0: T[f(x) + a] \leq Tf(x) + \beta a$.

First, suppose that $w(y) \leq v(y)$ for all y in X. Then for each (x, u), $w[m(x, u)] \leq v[m(x, u)]$, and therefore

$$Tv(x) = \max_{u \in \Gamma(x)} \{F(x, u) + \beta v[m(x, u)]\} \geq \max_{u \in \Gamma(x)} \{F(x, u) + \beta w[m(x, u)]\} = Tw(x)$$

Thus, T is monotone. Next, note that for any positive constant a, we have

$$T[v(x) + a] = \max_{u \in \Gamma(x)} \{F(x, u) + \beta \{v[m(x, u)] + a\}\}$$
$$= \max_{u \in \Gamma(x)} \{F(x, u) + \beta v[m(x, u)]\} + \beta a = Tv(x) + \beta a$$

Hence, T discounts. Because it satisfies both of Blackwell's conditions, T is a contraction.

- Because T is a contraction on a complete metric space, it follows directly from the contraction mapping theorem (Theorem 7.15 in Chapter 2) that it has a unique fixed point V.

- By Theorem 1.3, the bounded continuous function V is the value function for the corresponding dynamic programming problem. Moreover, the solution mapping for the maximum problem in the Bellman equation is the optimal policy correspondence.   □

It also follows from the contraction mapping theorem that if, starting with an arbitrary continuous and bounded function V_o, we define a sequence $\{V_n\}$ of functions by

$$V_{n-1} = TV_n$$

this sequence converges to the value function V. This fact can sometimes be used to find the value function.

Knowing when the Bellman equation has a unique bounded solution (i.e., when the value function is well defined) is an important first step, but one that is of little practical help. To go further we need to establish conditions under which V will have certain desirable properties.

In the remainder of this section we will use the foregoing results relating the value function with the bounded solution of the Bellman equation to show that under reasonable restrictions on the period objective function F and the constraints, the value function is strictly increasing and strictly concave, and the policy correspondence is a continuous function. For this, we will rely on the following result: Recall that if (X, d) is a complete metric space and Y is a closed subset of X, then (Y, d) is also a complete metric space (Theorem 7.9 in Chapter 2). Now suppose that $T : X \longrightarrow X$ is a contraction in X and, moreover, that T maps Y into itself. Then T is also a contraction in Y, and it follows that the unique fixed point of T on X must be in Y. A slight twist on this result yields the following theorem.

Theorem 1.6. Let (X, d) be a complete metric space, and let $T : X \longrightarrow X$ be a contraction with fixed point $v \in X$. Further, let Y be a closed subset of X, and assume that T maps points in Y into some subset Z of Y (i.e., $T : Y \longrightarrow Z$). Then the unique fixed point v of T in X will be in Z.

Problem 1.7. Prove Theorem 1.6.

We will show that the set $ND(X)$ of nondecreasing bounded and continuous functions is a closed subset of $C(X)$ and that the operator T in the Bellman equation maps nondecreasing functions into strictly increasing functions. It follows by Theorem 1.6 that the value function V must be strictly increasing. A similar argument will allow us to establish strict concavity.

Lemma 1.8. Consider the normed vector space $[C(X), \|\cdot\|_s]$, where $C(X)$ is the set of bounded continuous functions $f : \mathbb{R}^n \supseteq X \longrightarrow \mathbb{R}$, with the sup norm $\|f\|_s = \sup\{|f(x)|; x \in X\}$. Let $ND(X)$ be the set of nondecreasing bounded and continuous functions on X. Then $ND(X)$ is a closed subset of $C(X)$.

Recall that a function $f : X \longrightarrow \mathbb{R}$ is said to be nondecreasing if

$$\forall x_0, x_1 \in X, \ x_1 > x_0 \Rightarrow f(x_1) \geq f(x_0)$$

and strictly increasing if

$$\forall x_0, x_1 \in X, \ x_1 > x_0 \Rightarrow f(x_1) > f(x_0)$$

Proof. Let $\{f_n\}$ be a sequence of nondecreasing continuous functions convergent (in the sup norm and hence pointwise) to a function f (which is bounded and continuous, by the completeness of $C(X)$). To establish that $ND(X)$ is a closed subset of $C(X)$, it suffices to show that f is nondecreasing. Let x_0 and x_1 be arbitrary points in X such that $x_1 > x_0$, and consider the sequence of real numbers $\{f_n(x_1) - f_n(x_0)\}$. Because $\{f_n\} \to f$, $\{f_n(x_1) - f_n(x_0)\}$ converges to $f(x_1) - f(x_0)$, and because f_n is nondecreasing, $f_n(x_1) - f_n(x_0) \geq 0$ for all n. Hence, we have a convergent sequence of nonnegative real numbers, and it follows that the limit of the sequence, $f(x_1) - f(x_0)$, is nonnegative. This establishes that the limit function $f(\ )$ is also nondecreasing.   □

Assumption 1.9. Monotonicity. Assume that $F(\ )$ is strictly increasing in x, $m(\ )$ is increasing in x, and the constraint correspondence $\Gamma(\ )$ is increasing in the sense that

$$x_1 \geq x_0 \Rightarrow \Gamma(x_1) \supseteq \Gamma(x_0)$$

Lemma 1.10. Let $\mathrm{T} : C(X) \longrightarrow C(X)$ *be the operator defined by*

$$\mathrm{T}v(x) = \max_{u \in \Gamma(x)}\{F(x, u) + \beta v[m(x, u)]\}$$

and assume that Assumption 1.9 (monotonicity) holds. Then T *maps nondecreasing functions into strictly increasing functions.*

Problem 1.11. Prove Lemma 1.10.

Combining these two lemmas with Theorem 1.6, the following result is immediate.

Theorem 1.12. Suppose that Assumptions 1.4 and 1.9 (continuity and monotonicity) hold. Then the value function V *is strictly increasing in the state* x.

To summarize, we know that under the continuity assumption the Bellman equation has a unique continuous and bounded solution V that is the value function for the corresponding programming problem. This function can be characterized as a fixed point of an appropriately defined operator $T : C(X) \longrightarrow C(X)$. We have shown that the set of nondecreasing bounded and continuous functions $ND(X)$ is a closed subset of $C(X)$ and that under Assumption 1.9, T maps nondecreasing functions into strictly increasing functions. It follows that the value function must be strictly increasing. Intuitively, our assumptions ensure that an "increase" in the state is strictly desirable because it strictly increases the current return and does not reduce future opportunities.

We will now develop a very similar argument to show that under certain conditions, V is strictly concave. Recall that a function f is said to be (weakly) concave if

$$\forall x_0, x_1 \in X, \ \lambda \in [0,1], \ (1-\lambda)f(x_0) + \lambda f(x_1) \leq f[(1-\lambda)x_0 + \lambda x_1]$$

and strictly concave if

$$\forall\, x_0, x_1 \in X,\ \lambda \in (0,1),\ (1-\lambda)f(x_0)+\lambda f(x_1) < f[(1-\lambda)x_0 + \lambda x_1]$$

Lemma 1.13. *Consider the normed vector space* $[C(X),\ \|\cdot\|_s]$, *where* $\|\cdot\|_s$ *is the sup norm, and assume* X *is a convex set. The set of (weakly) concave functions in* $C(X)$ *is a closed subset of* $C(X)$.

Problem 1.14. Prove Lemma 1.13.

Assumption 1.15. Concavity. Assume that F is strictly concave, m is concave, for each x the constraint set $\Gamma(x)$ is convex, and the constraint correspondence Γ is convex in the sense that

$$\forall\, x_0, x_1 \in X,\ \lambda \in [0,1],\ u_0 \in \Gamma(x_0), u_1 \in \Gamma(x_1)$$
$$\Rightarrow (1-\lambda)u_0 + \lambda u_1 \in \Gamma[(1-\lambda)x_0 + \lambda x_1]$$

Lemma 1.16. *Let* $T : C(X) \longrightarrow C(X)$ *be the operator defined by*

$$Tv(x) = \max_{u \in \Gamma(x)}\{F(x,u)+\beta v[m(x,u)]\}$$

and assume that the concavity and monotonicity assumptions hold. Then T *maps weakly concave functions into strictly concave functions.*

Problem 1.17. Prove Lemma 1.16.

Using Lemmas 1.13 and 1.16 and Theorem 1.6, it follows that under the continuity, monotonicity, and concavity assumptions, the value function V is strictly concave.

Theorem 1.18. *Suppose the continuity, monotonicity, and concavity assumptions hold. Then the value function* V *is strictly concave and strictly increasing, and the policy correspondence* $g(\ )$ *is a continuous function.*

Proof. The first part of the theorem is immediate. Moreover, we know by the maximum theorem and Theorem 1.5 that the optimal policy correspondence is uhc. Because any single-valued uhc correspondence is a continuous function (see Section 11 of Chapter 2), we need only establish that the solution u^* to the maximization in the Bellman equation is unique, but this follows immediately by the strict concavity of F, the concavity of $m(\ )$, and the concavity and monotonicity of V, all of which ensure that the objective function for the problem is strictly concave (in (x, u) and therefore in u alone). $\qquad\square$

Differentiability of the Value Function. The maximization in the Bellman equation is a static optimization problem that looks like an ordinary Lagrange or Kuhn-Tucker problem. Hence, one is tempted to write the Lagrangean function and differentiate it with respect to u to obtain a set of first-order conditions and then proceed in the usual way (by applying the implicit-function theorem or differentiating implicitly the first-order conditions) to establish the comparative-statics properties of the optimal policy function. This approach, however, presupposes that all the functions involved are twice differentiable, an assumption that generally is not valid.

The basic problem arises because the value function for the problem, $V(\ )$, appears also inside the maximization operator. Whereas we are free to make whatever assumptions we want about $m(\ )$ and $F(\ )$, the differentiability of $V(\ )$ must be established rather than directly assumed.[3] It can be shown that $V(\ )$ will be (once or twice) differentiable for a certain class of problems, but not in general.[4] As a result, the standard approach to studying the comparative-statics properties of maximization systems is not generally available for the case of dynamic programming problems.

2. Optimal Control

We now switch from discrete time to continuous time and develop the basic elements of optimal control theory. A central result of this section is a set of necessary conditions for an optimum in a certain class of dynamic optimization problems, the so-called maximum principle of Pontryagin. We will derive the maximum principle from a dynamic programming formulation. Roughly, we start with a discrete-time problem, apply the dynamic programming techniques discussed earlier, and consider what happens in the limit as the length of the period goes to zero.

The continuous-time analogue of the problem studied in the preceding section can be written

$$V^c(x_0, 0) = \max_{u(t), 0 \le t \le T} \left\{ W_0\left(u(t)|_{t=0}^T, x(t)|_{t=0}^T\right) = \int_0^T \alpha(t) F[u(t), x(t), t]\, dt \right.$$

$$+ \alpha(T) S[x(T)] \text{ s.t. } x(0) = x_0 \text{ given,}$$

$$\left. \text{and } \dot{x}(t) = m[u(t), x(t), t] \right\} \tag{P.0}$$

where, as before, x is the state vector, and u the vector of control variables. The salvage or scrap function $S(\ )$ is used to allow for the possibility that we may place some value on the state at the end of the planning horizon T (which may or may not be finite). We will assume that the discount factor corresponding to period t is of the form

$$\alpha(t) = \exp\left(-\int_0^t \rho(s)\, ds\right)$$

which reduces to the more familiar $e^{-\rho t}$ whenever the discount rate ρ is constant over time.[5] The notation $x(t)$ indicates that the state is a function of time. For convenience, we will often replace this functional notation by the subscript notation x_t to indicate dependence on time, or omit the t's when they are not particularly needed. We will often treat x and u as if they were single variables, but the reader should keep in mind that they are vectors.

The problem is similar to the one analyzed in Section 1 except that the planner now must choose a control trajectory (i.e., a function of time, $u(t)$, defined for $t \in [0, T]$, that describes the values of the instruments at each point in time), rather than a control sequence $\{u_t\}_{t=0}^{T-1}$. Given a control path $u^0(t)|_{t=0}^T$, the corresponding trajectory of the state vector, $x^0(t)|_{t=0}^T$, is determined by the law of motion, $\dot{x}_t = m(u, x, t)$, and the initial condition $x(0) = x_0$. Evaluating W_0, we obtain the value of the given trajectories, $W_0(u^0(t)|_{t=0}^T, x^0(t)|_{t=0}^T)$. Our goal is to characterize the time paths of u and x that will yield the largest possible value for the objective function. This will be achieved by transforming the dynamic maximization problem (P.0) into a combination of two more familiar problems: a static maximization at each point in time, and a system of ordinary differential equations.

(a) The Maximum Principle

We begin with an intuitive discussion of the logic of the maximum principle. At each point in time t the planner finds herself with some predetermined value of the state x_t and must choose a control vector u_t that will determine both the immediate payoff $F_t(\ )$ and the rate of change of the state variables $\dot{x}_t$.[6] Current decisions, therefore, have two effects on total value: an immediate one through $F_t(\ )$, and an indirect one through the induced change in x. Clearly, a control chosen to maximize just the current return is unlikely to be optimal. We need some way to take into account the effects of current decisions on future opportunities. Intuitively, the maximum principle achieves this by attaching a price to the *stocks* of state variables.

The idea is to introduce a modified objective function that will add to the immediate return the value of the change in the state vector due to current decisions. To this end, we introduce a new set of variables q_t, one for each component of the state vector. These variables, known as multipliers or *costate variables*, can be interpreted as the prices associated with the state variables. The modified objective function, known as the *current-value Hamiltonian*, is then defined as

$$H_t^c = H^c(u_t, x_t, q_t, t) \equiv F_t(u_t, x_t) + q_t m_t(u_t, x_t) = F_t(\ ) + q_t \dot{x}_t$$

The first component of the Hamiltonian is $F_t(u_t, x_t)$, the current flow return (utility, profit) to the decision-maker. The second term, $q_t \dot{x}_t$, measures the increase in value due to the change in the state variables. Thus, we can think of H^c as the sum of the immediate payoff from (x, u) plus the value of the future gains to accrue from the "investment in the future" represented by the change in the state variable.

In view of the foregoing discussion, it seems plausible that, given the correct shadow prices, maximization of the Hamiltonian will yield the optimal choice of instruments at each point in time. If H^c is a differentiable function of u, a necessary condition for an optimum is

$$\frac{\partial H_t^c}{\partial u_t} = 0 \Rightarrow \frac{\partial F_t(u_t, x_t)}{\partial u_t} + q_t \frac{\partial m_t(u_t, x_t)}{\partial u_t} = 0$$

That is, the decision-maker must balance immediate gains from a higher u against the value loss stemming from the reduction of future opportunities that the correspondingly lower future x entails.

The procedure is in some ways analogous to the method of Lagrange multipliers used to solve static optimization problems with side constraints. In both cases, the idea is to reduce a more complicated problem to an unconstrained maximization by introducing a set of prices to give the decision-maker the right incentives. As in the Lagrange case, this leaves us with the problem of making sure the shadow prices are set correctly (i.e., that they truly reflect the marginal contribution of the state variables to the agent's total payoff). One way to ensure this is simply to define the multipliers as the partial derivatives of the value function with respect to the corresponding state variables,

$$q_t \equiv \frac{\partial V^c(x, t)}{\partial x_t}$$

As we will see, this implies that the evolution of the costate variables over time is described by the system

$$-\frac{\partial H_t^c}{\partial x_t} = \dot{q}_t - \rho_t q_t \tag{1}$$

The law of motion for the shadow prices can be interpreted as a no-arbitrage or asset-valuation equation. Observe that the derivative of the Hamiltonian with respect to the state variables,

$$\frac{\partial H_t^c}{\partial x_t} = \frac{\partial F_t(u_t, x_t)}{\partial x_t} + q_t \frac{\partial m_t(u_t, x_t)}{\partial x_t}$$

measures the marginal yield of the "asset" x, given by the sum of its current marginal return $\partial F_t/\partial x_t$ and its contribution to the increase in the stock of x valued at its shadow price q. Rearranging (1), we obtain

$$\frac{\partial H_t^c/\partial x_t + \dot{q}_t}{q_t} = \rho_t \qquad (2)$$

The left-hand side of this expression is the instantaneous rate of return on the asset x, given by the ratio of its total return (the sum of its "dividend" $\partial H_t^c/\partial x_t$ and capital gains $\dot{q}_t$) to its current price q_t. The right-hand side is the instantaneous discount rate (the "utility interest rate"). Equation (2) requires that the marginal yield on "asset x" be equal to the required rate of return, ρ_t, signaling the impossibility of further gains from a change in asset holdings. This ensures that the asset is correctly valued.

We can now give a more formal statement of the result. We seek to characterize the solution to the problem

$$V^c(x_0, 0) = \max_{u(t), 0 \le t \le T} \left\{ W_0\left(u(t)|_{t=0}^T, x(t)|_{t=0}^T\right) = \int_0^T \alpha(t) F[u(t), x(t), t]\, dt \right.$$
$$\left. + \alpha(T) S[x(T)] \text{ s.t. } x(0) = x_0 \text{ given, } \dot{x}(t) = m[u(t), x(t), t] \right\} \qquad \text{(P.0)}$$

We will assume that the functions $F(u, x, t)$ and $m(u, x, t)$ are continuously differentiable with respect to the state vector x. Control trajectories $u(t)$ will be required to be piecewise-continuous functions of time, with at most a finite number of discontinuities in any bounded interval, and to have both right- and left-hand-side limits at any points of discontinuity. Under these assumptions, necessary conditions for an optimum are given by the following theorem.

Theorem 2.1. Pontryagin's maximum principle. Let u*(t), *with* t ∈ *[0, T], be the time path of the control vector that solves the problem* (P.0). *Then there exist continuous functions of time* q(t) *such that for each* t ∈ *[0, T],*

(i) *the control maximizes the current-value Hamiltonian,*

$$u_t^* = arg\ \max_u H^c(u, x, q, t) = arg\ \max_u \{F(x, u, t) + qm(x, u, t)\}$$

(ii) *the law of motion of the state vector holds,*

$$\dot{x}(t) = m[u^*(t), x(t), t] \qquad (3)$$

(iii) *and the functions* q(t) *satisfy the differential equations*

$$-\frac{\partial H_t^c}{\partial x_t} = \dot{q}_t - \rho_t q_t \qquad (4)$$

Given an admissible control path, $m[u(t), x(t), t]$ is a piecewise-continuous function of time. Thus the state trajectory, given by

$$x(t) = x(0) + \int_0^t m[u(s), x(s), s] \, ds$$

is continuous and piecewise-differentiable. The same is true of the time paths of the costate variables $q(t)$. The time derivatives of both $q(t)$ and $x(t)$ may be discontinuous at points of discontinuity of the controls. At such points, however, (3) and (4) will still hold for both left and right time derivatives.

We will now give a heuristic derivation of this result based on a dynamic programming approach. To simplify things a bit, we consider the case in which the discount rate is constant over time,

$$V^c(x_0, 0) = \max_{u(t); 0 \le t \le T} \left\{ \int_0^T e^{-\rho t} F[u(t), x(t), t] \, dt + e^{-\rho T} S[x(T)] \right.$$

$$\text{s.t. } x(0) = x_0 \text{ given, } \dot{x}(t) = m[u(t), x(t), t] \Big\} \tag{P.1}$$

and assume that the value function and the time paths of the controls are differentiable functions (as they will be in most applications we are likely to encounter). We begin by constructing a convenient discrete-time analogue of (P.1). Time is now measured in discrete periods of length h, and the one-period discount rate is of the form $\beta(h) = e^{-\rho h}$. At the beginning of the period starting at t, the planner chooses the value of the control u_t, which remains constant over the interval $[t, t + h)$. The function $F_t(u_t, x_t)$ now measures the instantaneous flow of value, and the total return from (u_t, x_t) over a period of length h is given by $hF_t(u_t, x_t)$ in current-value terms. The state and control vectors determine next period's state in accordance with the law of motion, $x_{t+h} = x_t + hm_t(x_t, u_t)$. The planner, then, solves

$$V^c(x_0, 0) = \max_{u_{0, T-1}} \left\{ \sum_{t=0}^{T-1} \beta(h)^t \, hF_t(x_t, u_t) + \beta(h)^T S(x_T) \right.$$

$$\text{s.t. } x_{t+h} = x_t + hm_t(x_t, u_t), \, x_0 \text{ given} \Big\}$$

The Bellman equation for this problem can be written

$$V^c(x_t, t) = \max_{u_t} \{ hF_t(x_t, u_t) + \beta(h)V^c[x_t + hm_t(x_t, u_t), t + h] \} \tag{5}$$

If the value function is differentiable, the first-order condition for the maximization in (5) is given by

$$h\frac{\partial F_t(u_t, x_t)}{\partial u_t} + \beta(h)\frac{\partial V^c(x_{t+h}, t + h)}{\partial x_{t+h}} \frac{\partial x_{t+h}}{\partial u_t} = 0$$

which describes the optimal trade-off between current and future values. Recalling that the multiplier is defined as the partial derivative of the value function with respect to the state, $q_t \equiv \partial V^c(x, t)/\partial x_t$, and using the law of motion to calculate $\partial x_{t+h}/\partial u_t$, we obtain

$$h\frac{\partial F_t(u_t, x_t)}{\partial u_t} + \beta(h)q_{t+h}h\frac{\partial m_t(u_t, x_t)}{\partial u_t} = 0$$

Dividing by h and taking limits as h goes to zero, we arrive at the necessary condition for the control to maximize the Hamiltonian,

$$\frac{\partial H_t^c}{\partial u_t} = \frac{\partial F_t(u_t, x_t)}{\partial u_t} + q_t\frac{\partial m_t(u_t, x_t)}{\partial u_t} = 0$$

Next, we compute the partial derivative that defines the costate variable. Using the envelope theorem in (5), and operating as before,

$$q_t = \frac{\partial V^c(x_t, t)}{\partial x_t} = h\frac{\partial F_t(u_t, x_t)}{\partial x_t} + \beta(h)\frac{\partial V^c(x_{t+h}, t+h)}{\partial x_{t+h}}\frac{\partial x_{t+h}}{\partial x_t}$$

$$= h\frac{\partial F_t(u_t, x_t)}{\partial x_t} + \beta(h)q_{t+h}\left(1 + h\frac{\partial m_t(x_t, u_t)}{\partial x_t}\right)$$

Subtracting βq_t from both sides of this expression,

$$[1 - \beta(h)]q_t = h\frac{\partial F_t(u_t, x_t)}{\partial x_t} + \beta(h)(q_{t+h} - q_t) + \beta(h)q_{t+h}h\frac{\partial m_t(x_t, u_t)}{\partial x_t}$$

dividing by h,

$$\frac{1 - \beta(h)}{h}q_t = \frac{\partial F_t(u_t, x_t)}{\partial x_t} + \beta(h)q_{t+h}\frac{\partial m_t(x_t, u_t)}{\partial x_t} + \beta(h)\frac{q_{t+h} - q_t}{h}$$

and taking the limit as h goes to zero, we obtain the equation of motion for the costate variables:

$$\rho q_t = \frac{\partial F_t(u_t, x_t)}{\partial x_t} + q_t\frac{\partial m_t(u_t, x_t)}{\partial x_t} + \dot{q}_t \Leftrightarrow -\frac{\partial H_t^c}{\partial x_t} = \dot{q}_t - \rho q_t \qquad \square$$

The maximum principle allows us to transform the original dynamic optimization problem into a combination of two more familiar problems. The maximization of the current-value Hamiltonian at each point in time yields a policy function,

$$u_t^* = g(x_t, q_t, t) = \arg\max_u\{H^c(u, x, q, t) = F(x, u, t) + qm(x, u, t)\} \qquad (6)$$

giving the optimal control as a function of the contemporaneous values of the state and costate vectors and time.[7] Substituting this function into the other necessary conditions, we eliminate u_t and obtain a system of differential equations in the state and costate variables:

$$\dot{x}(t) = m[g(x_t, q_t, t), x_t, t] \tag{7}$$

$$\dot{q}_t - \rho_t q_t = -\frac{\partial H_t^c[g(x_t, q_t, t), q_t, x_t, t]}{\partial x_t} \tag{8}$$

The solution of the dynamic optimization problem will then be one of the solutions of this system that satisfy the initial condition $x(0) = x_0$ given. Notice, however, that if the state vector is of dimension n, then (7)–(8) is a system of $2n$ equations in as many variables, and we have only n initial conditions (corresponding to the initial values of the state variables). To determine which of the solutions of the dynamical system solves the original problem, we need some additional conditions, as discussed in the following section.

(b) Transversality and Sufficient Conditions

The additional restrictions needed to identify the optimal path often take the form of terminal conditions on the multipliers, sometimes called *transversality conditions*. The simplest case is that of the finite-horizon problem with a scrap function, that is, maximization of

$$\int_0^T \alpha(t)F[u(t), x(t), t]\, dt + \alpha(T)S[x(T)]$$

subject to the usual conditions. Notice that the current value function at the end of the planning horizon is now simply

$$V^c(x_T, T) = S(x_T)$$

Because the costate vector is defined as the derivative of the value function with respect to the state, the appropriate terminal condition is

$$q_T = DS(x_T)$$

In many cases of interest there is no scrap function, but it may be natural to impose some restrictions on the terminal value of the state vector. A finitely-lived consumer, for example, (see footnote 5) may not derive any utility from leaving a bequest to his children, but it seems reasonable to require his terminal wealth to be nonnegative or, equivalently, to impose the constraint that the discounted value of his consumption stream should not exceed the present value of his lifetime income. In this case, the objective function reduces to

$$\int_0^T \alpha(t) F[u(t), x(t), t]\, dt$$

but we have as an additional constraint the nonnegativity condition $x_T \geq 0$. To derive the appropriate transversality condition, let us go back to the artificial discrete-time problem we used to derive the maximum principle,

$$V^c(x_0, 0) = \max_{u_{0,T-1}} \left\{ \sum_{t=0}^{T-1} \beta(h)^t h F_t(x_t, u_t) \text{ s.t. } x_{t+h} = x_t + h m_t(x_t, u_t),\, x_0 \text{ given},\, x_T \geq 0 \right\}$$

and consider the subproblem corresponding to the choice of the last control, u_{T-h},

$$V^c(x_{T-h}, T - h) = \max_{u_{T-h}} \{ h F_{T-h}(x_{T-h}, u_{T-h}) \text{ s.t. } x_T = x_{T-h} + h m_{T-h}(x_{T-h}, u_{T-h}) \geq 0 \}$$

This is an ordinary Kuhn-Tucker problem. Forming the Lagrangian,

$$\pounds = h F_{T-h}(x_{T-h}, u_{T-h}) + \lambda [x_{T-h} + h m_{T-h}(x_{T-h}, u_{T-h})]$$

the necessary conditions for the optimal choice of u_{T-h} can be written

$$\frac{\partial \pounds}{\partial u_{T-h}} = 0 \Rightarrow \frac{\partial F_{T-h}(x_{T-h}, u_{T-h})}{\partial u_{T-h}} + \lambda \frac{\partial m_{T-h}(x_{T-h}, u_{T-h})}{\partial u_{T-h}} = 0$$

$$x_T \geq 0, \quad \text{with equality if } \lambda > 0$$

$$\lambda \geq 0, \quad \text{with equality if } x_T > 0$$

Moreover, the envelope theorem yields

$$q_{T-h} = \frac{\partial V^c(x_{T-h}, T - h)}{\partial x_{T-h}} = \frac{\partial \pounds}{\partial x_{T-h}}$$

$$= h \frac{\partial F_{T-h}(x_{T-h}, u_{T-h})}{\partial x_{T-h}} + \lambda \left(1 + h \frac{\partial m_{T-h}(x_{T-h}, u_{T-h})}{\partial x_{T-h}} \right)$$

Taking the limit of this expression as $h \to 0$, we obtain $q_T = \lambda$. Hence, the last two necessary conditions can be written

$$x_T \geq 0, \quad q_T \geq 0, \quad \text{and} \quad q_T x_T = 0 \tag{T.1}$$

Thus the transversality condition is essentially the complementary slackness condition for a Kuhn-Tucker problem. It says that if we are going to "leave something at the end," that something must be worthless, and if it is not worthless, then we will leave nothing. In any case, the value of the terminal state, $q_T x_T$, must be zero.

As an illustration, consider once more the problem of a nonaltruistic consumer who maximizes the discounted value of lifetime utility subject to a flow budget constraint and the restriction that terminal wealth be nonnegative:

$$\max \int_0^T e^{-\rho t} U(c_t) \, dt \text{ s.t. } \dot{a}_t = r_t a_t + y_t - c_t \text{ and } a_T \geq 0$$

It is easily shown that in this problem the current-value multiplier is the marginal utility of consumption, $q_t = U'(c_t)$. The transversality condition now requires that terminal wealth be positive only if the agent is satiated, that is, if $q_T = U'(c_T) = 0$, and that a_T be zero whenever the marginal utility of terminal consumption is strictly positive.

The following proposition gives the necessary conditions for an optimal solution of the finite-horizon problem with nonnegativity terminal constraints on the states. The maximum principle still holds.

Theorem 2.2. Maximum principle and transversality conditions, finite horizon. Let $u^*(t)$, $t \in [0, T]$, *be the time path of the control vector that solves the problem*

$$V^c(x_0, 0) = \max_{u(t); 0 \leq t \leq T} \left\{ \int_0^T \alpha(t) F[u(t), x(t), t] \, dt \text{ s.t. } x_T \geq 0, \right.$$

$$\left. x(0) = x_0 \text{ given, } \dot{x}(t) = m[u(t), x(t), t] \right\} \tag{P.0}$$

where $\alpha(t) = exp(-\int_0^t \rho(s) \, ds)$. *Then there exist costate variables* $q(t)$, *continuous functions of time, such that for each* t,

  (i) *the control maximizes the current-value Hamiltonian,*

$$u_t^* = arg \max_u H^c(u, x, q, t) = arg \max_u \{F(x, u, t) + qm(x, u, t)\}$$

  (ii) *the law of motion of the state vector holds,*

$$\dot{x}(t) = m[u^*(t), x(t), t]$$

  (iii) *the functions* $q(t)$ *satisfy the differential equations*

$$-\frac{\partial H_t^c}{\partial x_t} = \dot{q}_t - \rho_t q_t$$

  (iv) *and the transversality conditions*

$$q_T \geq 0 \quad and \quad q_T x_T = 0 \tag{T.1}$$

The conditions we have derived thus far are necessary conditions for an optimum. To be certain that they characterize a maximum, we need sufficient or "second-order" conditions, which, as in the case of static optimization problems, often take the form of concavity assumptions.

Theorem 2.3. Sufficient conditions for an optimal path. Assume that the maximized Hamiltonian,

$$\tilde{H}(x, q, t) = \max_u \{H^c(x, u, q) = F_t(x, u, t) + q_t m_t(x, u)\}$$

is a concave function of x *for given* q *and* t*. Then any policy satisfying the necessary conditions specified in Theorem 2.2 (i.e., the Pontryagin and transversality conditions) is optimal for the finite-horizon problem with terminal constraint* $x_T \geq 0$.

Observe that $\tilde{H}$ will be concave in x provided that $F(\ )$ and $m(\ )$ are concave in (x, u), but weaker conditions will suffice.

Proof. Let u_t^* be a policy satisfying the necessary conditions for a solution to the control problem, and (x_t^*, q_t^*) the corresponding paths of the state and costate vectors. Let u_t be any other feasible policy, and x_t the corresponding path of the state. We will show that the time path (u_t^*, x_t^*) yields a greater value than any other feasible trajectory.

For any given (q, x), we have (omitting the time subscripts)

$$\tilde{H}(x, q) = \max_u H^c(x, u, q) = H^c(u^0, x, q) \geq H^c(u, x, q) \quad \text{for any } u \quad (1)$$

where u^0 is the optimal choice of instruments given (q, x). By the assumption that $\tilde{H}(x, q)$ is concave in x for given q (and t), we can write

$$\tilde{H}(x, q^*) \leq \tilde{H}(x^*, q^*) + D_x\tilde{H}(x^*, q^*)(x - x^*) \quad (2)$$

for any x. From (1), moreover,

$$\tilde{H}(x, q^*) \geq H^c(u, x, q^*) \quad \text{for any } u, \quad \text{and} \quad \tilde{H}(x^*, q^*) = H^c(x^*, u^*, q^*) \quad (3)$$

Using (3), (2) implies

$$H^c(u, x, q^*) \leq H^c(x^*, u^*, q^*) + D_x\tilde{H}(x^*, q^*)(x - x^*) \quad (3)$$

from where

$$F(u^*, x^*) - F(u, x) \geq q^*(\dot{x} - \dot{x}^*) - D_x\tilde{H}(x^*, q^*)(x - x^*) \quad (4)$$

Next, using the envelope theorem in (1) and the necessary conditions for an optimal path,

$$-D_x\tilde{H}(x^*, q^*) = -D_xH^c(x^*, q^*, u^*) = \dot{q} - \rho q$$

Substituting this expression into (4) and multiplying both sides by the discount factor $\alpha(t)$,

$$\alpha(t)[F(u^*, x^*) - F(u, x)] \geq \alpha(t)q^*(\dot{x} - \dot{x}^*) + \alpha(t)(\dot{q} - \rho q)(x - x^*) \quad (5)$$

We observe that the expression on the right-hand side of (5) is the derivative of $\alpha(t)q_t(x_t - x_t^*)$ with respect to time.[8] Integrating both sides of the inequality from $t = 0$ to T,

$$\int_0^T \alpha(t)[F_t(u^*, x^*) - F(u, x)]\, dt \geq \int_0^T \frac{d}{dt}\left(\alpha(t)q_t^*\left(x_t - x_t^*\right)\right) dt$$

$$= \alpha(T)q_T^*\left(x_T - x_T^*\right) - \alpha(0)q_0^*\left(x_0 - x_0^*\right) \quad (6)$$

The last term in this expression vanishes, as the given initial value of the state must be the same for any feasible trajectory. Using the transversality conditions

$$q_T^* \geq 0 \quad \text{and} \quad q_T^* x_T^* = 0 \quad (\text{T.1})$$

and the terminal constraint $x_T \geq 0$, (6) implies the desired result:

$$\int_0^T \alpha(t)[F_t(u^*, x^*) - F(u, x)]\, dt \geq \alpha(T)q_T^* x_T \geq 0$$

That is, the path $[x^*(t), u^*(t)]$ that satisfies the Pontryagin and transversality conditions provides a greater return than any other feasible trajectory and is therefore optimal.   □

Infinite Horizon

It is often convenient (and not a bad approximation) to assume that the planning horizon is infinite. Infinite-horizon problems, however, pose some new problems. First, the objective functional, now given by the improper integral

$$\int_0^\infty \alpha(t)F[u(t), x(t), t]\, dt = \lim_{T \to \infty} \int_0^T \alpha(t)F[u(t), x(t), t]\, dt$$

may not converge. Even if it does, moreover, there is no guarantee that an optimal control path will exist. If it does exist, however, the necessary conditions derived earlier are still valid. The one exception to this has to do with the transversality conditions, which can no longer be derived from a terminal condition on x. On the other hand, the proof of the sufficiency theorem (Theorem 2.3) will still go through provided that we replace (T.1) with

$$\lim_{t \to \infty} \alpha(t)q_t \geq 0 \quad \text{and} \quad \lim_{t \to \infty} \alpha(t)q_t x_t = 0 \quad (\text{T.2})$$

Thus, the transversality conditions may no longer be necessary for an optimum, but they still have a role as sufficient conditions. That is, they may not hold, but if they do hold for a given path $u^*(t)$, and if the maximized Hamiltonian is concave in x, then that path is optimal.

The transversality conditions at infinity (T.2) can be seen as natural extensions of those for the finite-horizon problem. Recall that (T.1) can be interpreted as the complementary slackness condition associated with a nonnegativity restriction on the terminal state. It tells us that the current value of the terminal state, evaluated using its shadow price, must be zero (i.e., that nothing valuable should be left at the end of the planning period). Because we no longer have a terminal date, we can make no such argument. However, the condition that the value of the state be asymptotically non-negative still makes sense in many cases. For example, in the consumer optimization problem that we have been using as an illustration, such a con-straint is equivalent to the requirement that the discounted value of the agent's consumption not exceed the present value of her income. Intuitively speaking, (T.2) can be used to impose this type of constraint. The main change from the finite-horizon case is that now we must consider the dis-counted value of the state, $\alpha(t)q_t x_t$, whereas in the finite-horizon case it made no difference whether we worked in current or in discounted value terms. We summarize in the following.

Theorem 2.4. Maximum principle and sufficient conditions, infinite horizon. Let $u^*(t)$, $t \in [0, T]$, *be the time path of the control vectors that solves the problem*

$$V^c(x_0, 0) = \max_{u(t); 0 \le t \le \infty} \left\{ \int_0^\infty \alpha(t) F[u(t), x(t), t] \, dt \; s.t. \right.$$

$$\left. x(0) = x_0 \; given, \; \dot{x}(t) = m[u(t), x(t), t] \right\} \tag{P.0}$$

where $\alpha(t) = exp(-\int_0^t \rho(s) \, ds)$. *Then there exist continuous functions of time,* $q(t)$, *such that for each* t,

  (i) *the control maximizes the current-value Hamiltonian,* $u_t^* = arg \, max_u \, H^c(u, x, q, t)$,
  (ii) *the law of motion of the state vector holds,* $\dot{x}(t) = m[u^*(t), x(t), t]$, *and*
  (iii) *the functions* $q(t)$ *satisfy the differential equations* $-\partial H_t^c / \partial x_t = \dot{q}_t - \rho_t q_t$.

Moreover, if the maximized Hamiltonian,

$$\tilde{H}(x, q, t) = \max_u \{ H^c(x, u, q) = F_t(x, u, t) + q_t m_t(x, u) \}$$

is a concave function of x for given q and t, then any policy satisfying the Pontryagin conditions and the transversality conditions at infinity,

$$\lim_{t \to \infty} \alpha(t) q_t \geq 0 \quad \text{and} \quad \lim_{t \to \infty} \alpha(t) q_t x_t = 0 \qquad \text{(T.2)}$$

is optimal.

In some cases of interest, the sufficient conditions allow us to identify the optimal path with the stable manifold leading to a saddle-point steady state. For example, in the case of a stationary problem with a constant discount rate ρ and time-invariant instantaneous return function $F(x, u)$ and law of motion $m(x, u)$, the maximum principle yields an autonomous system of differential equations

$$\dot{x}_t = m[g(x_t, q_t), x_t]$$

$$\dot{q}_t - \rho q_t = -\frac{\partial H_t^c[g(x_t, q_t), q_t, x_t]}{\partial x_t}$$

in which time does not enter as a separate argument in any of the transition equations. This system often has a steady state and solution trajectories leading to it. The following proposition shows that if we can find a path (x_t, q_t) that satisfies the necessary conditions and converges to a steady state, then, under certain conditions, that path is optimal.

Theorem 2.5. Sufficient conditions for an optimum. Let x*(t), u*(t), *and* q*(t) *be a path satisfying the necessary conditions for a stationary, infinite-horizon control problem, as given in Theorem 2.3, with* $\alpha(t) = e^{-\rho t}$, $\rho > 0$. *Suppose further that the concavity assumption of the sufficiency part of the theorem holds. Then, if* x*(t) *and* q*(t) *converge to a steady state* (x^s, q^s), *with* x^s, q^s $\geq$ *0, they constitute an optimal path.*

Proof. Because $x^*(t)$ and $q^*(t)$ converge to finite limits, and $e^{-\rho t} \to 0$ as $t \to \infty$, the transversality conditions

$$\lim_{t \to \infty} e^{-\rho t} q_t \geq 0 \quad \text{and} \quad \lim_{t \to \infty} e^{-\rho t} q_t x_t = 0 \qquad \text{(T.2)}$$

are satisfied. Optimality follows by the first sufficiency theorem. $\square$

This result is particularly useful when the Pontryagin conditions give rise to an autonomous system that has a unique saddle-point equilibrium, because then the unique convergent path leading to the steady state will be the optimal one.

(c) Constraints Involving State and Control Variables

In many cases, control problems involve additional complications in the form of constraints that limit the choice of the decision or control variables

u to a set that generally depends on the contemporaneous values of the state variables x. The procedure for dealing with this problem involves the introduction of a Lagrange function, similar to the one used in static programming problems. The necessary conditions for an optimum can then be rewritten in terms of the partial derivatives of the Lagrangian (sometimes called the augmented Hamiltonian), rather than the Hamiltonian.

To illustrate the procedure for solving such problems, we return to the finite-horizon problem of Section 2(a), to which we add some additional side constraints. The problem is now

$$V^c(x_0, 0) = \max_{u(t);0 \le t \le T} \left\{ \int_0^T \alpha(t) F[u(t), x(t), t] \, dt \text{ s.t. } x_T \ge 0, \; x(0) = x_0 \text{ given}, \right.$$

$$C[x(t), u(t), t] \ge 0, \dot{x}(t) = m[u(t), x(t), t] \Big\} \tag{P.C}$$

where $\alpha(t) = \exp(-\int_0^t \rho(s) \, ds)$.

The same logic as before can be used to show that at any given time t the optimal policy u^* will maximize the corresponding Hamiltonian. Of course, the maximization is now subject to the additional side constraints. Thus $u^*(t)$ now solves

$$\max_u \{ H^c(u, x, q, t) \text{ s.t. } C[x(t), u(t), t] \ge 0 \} \tag{1}$$

Subject to the standard constraint qualification, we can apply the Kuhn-Tucker theorem to characterize the solution to this problem. In particular, if u^* solves (1), there will exist Lagrange multipliers λ^* such that

$$\lambda^* \ge 0 \quad \text{and} \quad \lambda^{*T} C(x, u^*, t) = 0 \tag{2}$$

Moreover, if we define the Lagrangian function by

$$\pounds_t^c = H^c(u, x, q, t) + \lambda C[x(t), u(t), t] = F(u, x, t) + qm(x, u, t) + \lambda C(x, u, t) \tag{3}$$

the necessary conditions for the maximization problem in (1) will include

$$\frac{\partial \pounds_t^c}{\partial x_t} = 0 \tag{4}$$

Similarly, the equation of motion for the costate variables can be written in terms of the partial derivatives of the Lagrangian. In particular, we have now

$$-\frac{\partial \pounds_t^c}{\partial x_t} = \dot{q}_t - \rho_t q_t \tag{5}$$

For other versions of the control problem, the necessary conditions can be similarly amended to involve partial derivatives of the Lagrangian function. (In particular, the necessary conditions are the same for the infinite-horizon case.) Moreover, our previous results concerning the transversality conditions and sufficient conditions for an optimum still hold as stated. Note, however, that certain conditions may have to be imposed on the constraint functions $C(\ )$ to ensure the concavity of the maximized Hamiltonian required in the sufficiency theorem.

Bibliography

Araujo, A. 1991. The Once but not Twice Differentiability of the Policy Function. *Econometrica* 59(5):1383–93.

Araujo. A., and Scheinkman, J. 1983. Maximum Principle and Transversality Conditions for Concave Infinite-Horizon Economic Models. *Journal of Economic Theory* 27:1–16.

Arrow, K. 1968. Applications of Control Theory to Economic Growth. In: *Mathematics of Decision Sciences, Part 2*, pp. 85–119. Providence, RI: American Mathematical Society.

Arrow, K., and Kurz, M. 1970. Methods of Optimization over Time. In: *Public Investment, the Rate of Return, and Optimal Fiscal Policy*. Baltimore: Johns Hopkins University Press.

Beavis, B., and Dobbs, I. 1990. *Optimization and Stability Theory for Economic Analysis*. Cambridge University Press.

Benveniste, L., and Scheinkman, J. 1982. Duality Theory for Dynamic Optimizing Models in Economics: the Continuous Time Case. *Journal of Economic Theory* 30:1–19.

Dixit, A. 1990. *Optimization in Economic Theory*, 2nd ed. Oxford University Press.

Dorfman, R. 1969. An Economic Interpretation of Optimal Control Theory. *American Economic Review* 59:817–31.

Intriligator, M. 1981. *Mathematical Optimization and Economic Theory*. Englewood Cliffs, NJ: Prentice-Hall.

Kamien, M., and Schwartz, N. 1981. *Dynamic Optimization: The Calculus of Variations and Optimal Control in Economics and Management*. Amsterdam: North Holland.

Léonard, D., and Van Long, N. 1992. *Optimal Control Theory and Static Optimization in Economics*. Cambridge University Press.

Santos, M. 1995. Smoothness of the Policy Function in Discrete Time Economic Models. *Econometrica* 59(5):1365–82.

Sargent, T. 1987. *Dynamic Macroeconomic Theoory*. Harvard University Press.

Stokey, N., and Lucas. R. 1989. *Recursive Methods in Economic Dynamics*. Harvard University Press.

Takayama, A. 1987. *Mathematical Economics*. Cambridge University Press.

Notes

1 For example, if x_T is leftover wealth at the time of death, $S(x_T)$ captures the utility the agent obtains by leaving a bequest to his or her children. More generally, $S(\ )$ assigns a valuation to the final state vector.

2 Continuity for correspondences was defined in Section 11 of Chapter 2. Intuitively, the idea is the same as for the continuity of functions: Γ is continuous if the set $\Gamma(x)$ does not change very much with small changes of x.

3 Theorem 2.15 in Chapter 6 can sometimes be used to establish the differentiability of the value function. See Section 2 of Chapter 13 for an example.

4 See, for example, Araujo (1991) and Santos (1995).

5 In certain cases of interest the instantaneous discount rate ρ cannot be assumed to be constant over time. For example, if the control problem is that faced by a firm that attempts to maximize the present value of a stream of cash flows, future receipts will be discounted at the market rate of interest, which is likely to vary from period to period. This gives rise to a discount factor of the form given in the text.

6 It may be useful to have a concrete example in mind. Consider the problem of an individual who wants to maximize the discounted value of lifetime utility from consumption plus the utility of the bequest he leaves to his children at death:

$$\int_0^T e^{-\rho t} U(c_t)\, dt + e^{-\rho t} S(a_T)$$

The state variable a now represents the consumer's current asset holdings. The agent takes as given his initial wealth (a_0) and the time paths of income (y_t) and interest rates (r_t). The law for motion for the state variable is the flow budget constraint:

$$\dot{a}_t = r_t a_t + y_t - c_t$$

7 In some cases it turns out to be more convenient to use the first-order conditions for the maximization of the Hamiltonian to solve for the costate variable as a function of the control and then use this expression to get rid of q in the system of differential equations. We will see some examples in Chapter 13.

8 Observe that $\alpha'(t) = -\alpha(t)\rho_t$; then

$$\frac{d}{dt}\Big(\alpha(t)q_t\big(x_t - x_t^*\big)\Big) = \alpha(t)q_t\big(\dot{x} - \dot{x}^*\big) + \big[\alpha(t)\dot{q} - \alpha(t)\rho_t q_t\big]\big(x_t - x_t^*\big)$$

13

Some Applications of Dynamic Optimization

In this chapter we will review some applications of dynamic optimization to economics. In Section 1 we develop two models of search to illustrate the use of dynamic programming in a stochastic setting. Section 2 analyzes the decision problem faced by a social planner who maximizes the utility of an infinitely-lived representative agent in a one-good neoclassical economy. In Section 3 we study the optimal investment policy of a competitive firm when the installation of capital is costly. Finally, in Section 4 we develop the Cass-Koopmans model of a dynamic competitive economy and use it to analyze the welfare cost of factor taxes. Section 5 concludes with a series of problems.

1. Search Models

Search theory provides a simple and yet interesting application of dynamic programming to economics. In the basic search model, wage offers drawn from a given distribution arrive at fixed or random intervals, and an agent simply decides whether to accept one of them and become employed or reject them and continue searching for a better opportunity. We have, then, a very simple problem in stochastic dynamic programming: The control is simply a take-it-or-leave-it decision, and the distribution of the state variables (the offers) is time-invariant and does not depend on either the state or the control.

The first part of this section introduces the basic "microeconomic" model of job search. In addition to its interest as an application of dynamic programming, this model provides a useful counterpoint to the neoclassical model of a competitive labor market. In the latter model, transactions are assumed to take place instantaneously and at no cost, and wages are set so that the market clears continuously. Hence, there is no room for unemployment. In the search model, on the other hand, it may be optimal for an agent to remain temporarily unemployed in order to wait for a better opportunity than those available today. Hence, the search model provides a useful framework for analyzing how rational agents will respond to changes in the level or duration of unemployment benefits, the abundance and riskiness of employment offers, and many other questions that can hardly be addressed within the neoclassical model.

The search model, however, does not necessarily require a departure from the spirit of the neoclassical model. Notice, in particular, that the unemployment that naturally arises in any search model is frictional in nature and essentially voluntary. Hence, the explicit modeling of the process of job search may well yield nothing more than a model with a natural rate of unemployment. On the other hand, it is relatively easy to incorporate additional features into a search model that add a strong Keynesian flavor to it. If we are willing to assume that an increase in the level of aggregate activity makes it easier for potential trading partners to locate each other, we have a participation externality that generates inefficiency and the possibility of multiple equilibria, thus opening the door for public intervention to improve things. A "macro" model with these features will be developed in the second part of the section.

(a) *The Basic Model of Job Search*

Consider an infinitely-lived, risk-neutral worker who maximizes (the expectation of) the discounted value of lifetime income,

$$E\left\{\sum_{t=0}^{\infty}\beta^{t}y_{t}\right\}$$

where income at time t, y_t, is equal to the wage rate (x) for employed workers and to a government-provided benefit (b) for the unemployed. Unemployed workers also receive one employment offer each period. All jobs are permanent and pay the same wage each period. Wages, however, may differ across jobs. Hence, x is a (nonnegative) random variable that we assume to be drawn from a time-invariant distribution described by a cumulative distribution function (cdf) $F(\ )$, where $F(w) = \text{pr}(x \leq w)$.

A worker who has just received an offer has two options: One is to accept the job and work forever at the specified wage x;[1] the other is to reject the offer and wait for a better one to arrive. We will denote the value of the first option (accepting and being employed at wage x) by $W_a(x)$, and that of the second (rejecting the offer and remaining unemployed) by W_r. Clearly, $W_a(x)$, the present value of lifetime earnings on a job paying salary x, is an increasing function of x given by

$$W_a(x) = \sum_{t=0}^{\infty}\beta^{t}x = \frac{x}{1-\beta} \tag{1}$$

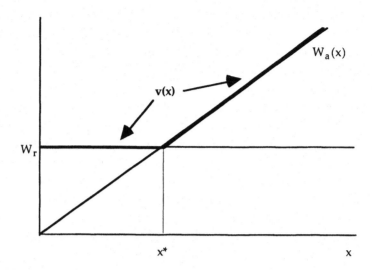

Figure 13.1. Value function and reservation wage for the search problem.

On the other hand, W_r is not a function of x: The expected present value of lifetime earnings for an unemployed worker is independent of the wage offer he has just rejected.

A rational worker will choose the action that will yield the larger value. Thus, the expected value of lifetime income for an agent who has just received an offer x is given by the value function

$$v(x) = \max[W_a(x,), W_r] \qquad (2)$$

and he accepts the offer if and only if $W_a(x) \geq W_r$ (i.e., if the value of being employed at the offered wage exceeds the value of being unemployed). As illustrated in Figure 13.1, the optimal decision strategy takes the form of a reservation-wage rule. Because $W_a(x)$ is increasing in the salary, and W_r is independent of it, a job will be accepted if and only if it pays a wage that is higher than some critical value x^*. This critical or *reservation wage* is defined as the value of x that makes the agent indifferent between taking the job and remaining unemployed, that is, x^* solves $W_a(x^*) = W_r$.

It remains, of course, to determine the reservation wage x^* or, equivalently, the value of being unemployed, W_r. As a first step, consider the situation of a worker who is currently unemployed (i.e., who has just rejected an offer): His income today is the unemployment benefit b; tomorrow he will receive a new offer, x, and will accept it or reject it depending on whether or not its value exceeds W_r. Hence, his current value one period hence (from tomorrow's perspective) will be given by $v(x) = \max[W_a(x), W_r]$. As of today, however, the realization of x is not known, so we can only work with the expected value of $v(x)$. Moreover, because this value will accrue tomorrow, we have to discount it by one period. Formally, then, the value of being unemployed is defined recursively by

$$W_r = b + \beta E\{\max[W_a(x), W_r]\} \tag{3}$$

We can now characterize the reservation salary. By definition, x^* is the value of x that makes the agent indifferent between accepting and rejecting the offer. Hence, x^* satisfies

$$W_a(x^*) \equiv \frac{x^*}{1-\beta} = W_r$$

and therefore

$$x^* = (1-\beta)W_r \tag{4}$$

Substituting (3) into (4),

$$x^* = W_r - \beta W_r = b + \beta E\{\max[W_a(x), W_r]\} - \beta W_r$$

Bringing the (constant) last term into the expectation and the max operator, we obtain

$$x^* = b + \beta E\{\max[W_a(x) - W_r, 0]\} \tag{5}$$

an equation that can be solved for x^*. This expression can be simplified as follows. We begin by writing out the expectation,

$$x^* = b + \beta \int_0^\infty \max[W_a(x) - W_r, 0] \, dF(x) \tag{6}$$

and observing that the resulting integral can be broken up into two parts:

$$\int_0^\infty \max[W_a - W_r, 0] \, dF = \int_0^{x^*} \max[W_a - W_r, 0] \, dF + \int_{x^*}^\infty \max[W_a - W_r, 0] \, dF$$

Notice that over the first interval of integration we have $x \leq x^*$, implying that $W_a(x) \leq W_r$; thus, $\max[W_a(x) - W_r, 0] = 0$ for $x \in (0, x^*]$, and the first integral vanishes. For $x \in (x^*, \infty)$, on the other hand, we have $W_a(x) \geq W_r$, implying $\max[W_a(x) - W_r, 0] = W_a(x) - W_r$. Hence, (6) reduces to

$$x^* = b + \beta \int_{x^*}^\infty [W_a(x) - W_r] \, dF(x)$$

Finally, recalling that $W_r = x^*/(1 - \beta)$ and $W_a(x) = x/(1 - \beta)$, we arrive at the *fundamental reservation-wage equation*,

$$x^* = b + \frac{\beta}{1-\beta} \int_{x^*}^\infty (x - x^*) \, dF(x) \tag{R}$$

which implicitly defines the reservation wage x^* as a function of the parameters of the model and the distribution of wage offers. This equation can be used to study the comparative statics of the reservation wage, as we will show later using an extension of this model.

Continuous-Time and Stochastic-Offer Arrivals

One of the crucial determinants of how selective a worker can afford to be in regard to wage offers is the availability of job opportunities. The model in the preceding section, which assumes that the worker receives an offer every period, ignores this aspect of the problem. We will now relax this restrictive assumption and extend the model to incorporate a measure of the "scarcity" of work opportunities through a parameter that reflects the rate of arrival of job offers. We will also illustrate how to go from discrete time to continuous time – a formulation that, although less intuitive when it comes to the derivation of the valuation equations, turns out to be more convenient in many cases.

We will make two changes with respect to the earlier model. The first will be to parameterize the length of the period. We will assume that all periods have the same duration h and reinterpret the wage and the unemployment benefit as rates per unit of time. Thus, an unemployed worker's income during a period is now bh, and an employed worker earns xh. We will also assume that the one-period discount factor is a function $\beta(h)$ of the length of the period. To go from discrete time to continuous time, we will take limits as the length of the period goes to zero.

Second, we will now model the arrival of wage offers as a stochastic process. We will assume that an unemployed worker has probability λh of receiving an offer during the current period. In the limit, as h goes to zero, offer arrivals follow a Poisson process with parameter λ, which can be interpreted as the instantaneous probability of receiving an offer.

The solution procedure is similar to that used earlier. The value of accepting a job that pays salary x per unit of time is given by

$$W_a(x) = \sum_{t=0}^{\infty} \beta(h)^t xh = \frac{xh}{1 - \beta(h)} \tag{1}$$

and the value of rejecting it, W_r, is still independent of x. The reservation wage x^* is the salary that makes the agent indifferent between accepting and rejecting employment and therefore satisfies

$$W_a(x^*) = W_r$$
$$\Rightarrow x^* = \frac{1 - \beta(h)}{h} W_r \tag{2}$$

To characterize W_r, consider the prospects of an unemployed worker, which are now slightly more complicated by the fact that he no longer knows when the next offer will arrive. During the current period, his only income is the unemployment benefit bh. Next period, he will receive an offer with probability λh, and no offer otherwise (with probability $1 - \lambda h$).

In the second case, his value next period will again be W_r. In the first case, his payoff next period will be given by $v(x) = \max[W_a(x), W_r]$, but because the realization of x is not known today, we have to compute the expected return. Finally, all values accruing tomorrow must be discounted by one period. Hence, the expected value of being currently unemployed is given by

$$W_r = bh + \beta(h)\{\lambda h E \max[W_a(x), W_r] + (1 - \lambda h)W_r\} \tag{3}$$

The next step is to manipulate this expression so that we can substitute it into the right-hand side of (2). Subtracting $\beta(h)W_r$ from both sides of (3),

$$[1 - \beta(h)]W_r = bh + \beta(h)E\{\lambda h \max[W_a(x), W_r] - \lambda h W_r\}$$
$$= bh + \beta(h)\lambda h E\{E \max[W_a(x) - W_r, 0]\}$$

and dividing by h,

$$\frac{1 - \beta(h)}{h}W_r = b + \beta(h)\lambda E\{\max[W_a(x) - W_r, 0]\} \tag{4}$$

Substituting (4) into (3) and simplifying, we could obtain a reservation-wage equation very similar to the one in the preceding section. Instead, let us go to continuous time. For this, let the discount factor be of the form $\beta(h) = e^{-\rho h}$. Then we have (using L'Hôpital's rule in the second expression)

$$\lim_{h \to \infty} \beta(h) = 1 \quad \text{and} \quad \lim_{h \to 0} \frac{1 - \beta(h)}{h} = \rho \tag{5}$$

Taking limits as $h \to 0$, (1) yields $W_a(x) = x/\rho$, (2) becomes

$$x^* = \rho W_r \tag{2'}$$

and (4) implies[2]

$$\rho W_r = b + \lambda E\{\max[W_a(x) - W_r, 0]\} \tag{4'}$$

Substituting (4') into (2') and proceeding as in the preceding section, we obtain the reservation-wage equation:

$$x^* = \rho W_r = b + \lambda \int_0^\infty \max[W_a(x) - W_r, 0]\, dF(x)$$

Now, if $x < x^*$, the agent rejects the offer, that is, $W_a(x) < W_r$, and therefore $\max[W_a(x) - W_r, 0] = 0$. On the other hand, if $x > x^*$, then $W_a(x) > W_r$, and therefore $\max[W_a(x) - W_r, 0] = W_a(x) - W_r$. Hence, we can break up the domain of integration into two parts, $(0, x^*)$ and (x^*, ∞), and observing that the integral over the first interval vanishes, we have

$$x^* = b + \lambda \int_{x^*}^\infty [W_a(x) - W_r]\, dF(x)$$

Finally, substituting $W_r = x^*/(\rho)$ and $W_a(x) = x/(\rho)$ in this expression, we obtain the fundamental reservation-wage equation:

$$x^* = b + \frac{\lambda}{\rho} \int_{x^*}^{\infty} (x - x^*)\, dF(x) \qquad\qquad \text{(R)}$$

This equation has an intuitive interpretation. Rearrange it to get

$$x^* - b = \frac{\lambda}{\rho} \int_{x^*}^{\infty} (x - x^*)\, dF(x)$$

Then the left-hand side measures the immediate opportunity cost of rejecting an offer, and the right-hand side gives the present value of the expected gain from continued search. The reservation wage, by definition, equates the two quantities.

It is straightforward to do comparative statics using this expression. Write

$$H(x^*; b, \lambda, \rho) = x^* - b - \frac{\lambda}{\rho} \int_{x^*}^{\infty} (x - x^*)\, dF(x) = 0$$

and compute the partial derivatives of $H(\ ):$[3]

$$H_{x^*} = 1 - \frac{\lambda}{\rho}\left(\int_{x^*}^{\infty} (-1)\, dF(x) - (x^* - x^*)F'(x^*) \right)$$

$$= 1 + \frac{\lambda}{\rho} \int_{x^*}^{\infty} dF(x) = 1 + \frac{\lambda}{\rho}[1 - F(x^*)] > 0$$

$$H_b = -1 < 0$$

$$H_{\lambda} = -\frac{1}{\rho} \int_{x^*}^{\infty} (x - x^*)\, dF(x) < 0$$

$$H_{\rho} = \frac{\lambda}{\rho^2} \int_{x^*}^{\infty} (x - x^*)\, dF(x) > 0$$

By the implicit-function theorem,

$$\frac{\partial x^*}{\partial b} = -\frac{H_b}{H_{x^*}} > 0, \quad \frac{\partial x^*}{\partial \lambda} = -\frac{H_{\lambda}}{H_{x^*}} > 0, \quad \text{and} \quad \frac{\partial x^*}{\partial \rho} = -\frac{H_{\rho}}{H_{x^*}} < 0$$

That is, an increase in the unemployment benefit leads to an increase in the reservation salary, as workers can now afford to wait longer for a better offer (an increase in b reduces the opportunity cost of rejecting any offer). An increase in λ means that jobs become less scarce, and it has a similar effect (the expected cost of rejecting an offer is now lower because the expected delay until a new one arrives is shorter). Finally, an increase in ρ means that future benefits are discounted at a higher rate (agents are less patient); because the expected benefits of continued search will accrue in the future, waiting becomes less attractive, and the reservation wage decreases.

(b) A Search-Based Macro Model

Standard neoclassical models implicitly rely on the Walrasian auctioneer to perform two crucial tasks. One is setting prices so that markets will clear continuously. The second can be called trade coordination: The auctioneer is assumed to provide clearing services that will make it unnecessary for the parties to a transaction to physically locate each other, thus simplifying the task of matching desired quantities. In short, these models assume that the allocation of resources is a costless and frictionless process. One implication of this assumption, if we take it literally, is that there is no room for involuntary unemployment. Extensions of the neoclassical model can generate fluctuations in employment levels as agents adjust their labor supply in response to price or productivity shocks, but the labor market must clear continuously, like any other market.

Search models do away with the trade-coordination function of the auctioneer and explicitly model the fact that many transactions must take place between individuals who must first find each other. Trade thus becomes a costly and time-consuming process. Applied to labor markets, this kind of model leads to the emergence of frictional unemployment, for agents will be inactive during some of the time that they wait for an acceptable job.

Moreover, this view of the process of resource allocation naturally suggests an important externality associated with the exchange technology: It seems likely that the greater the number of people who want to trade at any given time, the easier it will be for each of them to locate a suitable partner. Loosely speaking, because an increase in the level of economic activity makes it easier for the parties to an exchange to find each other, individual decisions have external effects over the opportunities available to other agents. One result of this phenomenon is that the equilibrium will not be Pareto-optimal, as agents will fail to take into account the external effects of their actions. Another implication is the possibility of multiple equilibria, as either pessimistic or optimistic expectations tend to become self-fulfilling. Thus, there is a role for government policy, both in correcting for externalities and in helping the economy select a good equilibrium. Policy may be useful as a device for improving coordination between agents in a way the market cannot achieve because of the presence of external effects.

The search model has served as a framework for some contributions to a literature which shows that macro models with "Keynesian" properties can be built from solid micro foundations. The remainder of this section develops one such model, due to Diamond (1982) and Diamond and Fudenberg (1989), in which an agent must first search for production opportunities and then locate a trading partner before consumption can take place. The model illustrates how, in the presence of a plausible participation externality, a suboptimally low level of economic activity may arise as a result of the difficulty of coordinating exchange in an economy with many agents.

Diamond's Search Model

Imagine a tropical island inhabited by infinitely-lived natives who walk around the beaches looking for coconut trees (production opportunities). Having found a tree, an agent must decide whether or not to climb it. If he does, he comes down with a coconut, but he is not finished yet: An ancient taboo forbids the consumption of one's own coconuts. Hence, the agent must find another native with whom to trade coconuts (one for one) before eating.[4] Having done this, he continues to search for additional production opportunities.

All trees have exactly one piece of fruit, but they may differ in height (production cost). Consumption of a coconut yields utility y. Production costs (the disutility of climbing) are proportional to the height of the tree, which is a nonnegative random variable, c, bounded below by $\underline{c}$ and drawn from a known distribution with cdf $G(\ )$. That is, $G(x) = \mathrm{pr}(c \leq x)$, and $G(\underline{c}) = 0$. Agents maximize the expected value of discounted lifetime utility,

$$V = E\sum\nolimits_{t=0}^{\infty} e^{-pt_i}U_{t_i}, \quad \text{where} \quad U_{t_i} = y_{t_i} - c_{t_i}$$

Notice that although time is continuous, production and consumption take place at discrete intervals. At a given time t_i, the agent may be engaged in production (climbing a tree), in which case his instantaneous utility is $-c$, in eating (with utility y), or in doing neither, in which case his instantaneous utility is zero.

An agent who is not engaged in production or consumption may be in either of two states. We will say that he is unemployed if he is looking for a production opportunity and that he is employed if he is carrying a coconut and is looking for someone with whom to trade. The arrivals of production opportunities and trading partners follow Poisson processes, with parameters that are taken as given by each individual agent. We will denote by a the instantaneous probability of finding a tree, and by $b(e)$ the instantaneous probability of finding a trading partner.

A crucial assumption of the model is that b is an increasing function of the aggregate employment rate e. That is, the larger the number of people who are walking around with coconuts in their hands, the easier it will be for them to bump into each other. We will assume that

$$b(0) = 0, \quad b'(e) > 0, \quad \text{and} \quad b''(e) < 0$$

Thus, an individual's decision to produce has a positive spillover effect on other agents' trading opportunities. When making production decisions, agents will not take this factor into account. As a result, the equilibrium level of activity will be suboptimally low. As we will see, the externality is also at the root of the possibility of multiple equilibria, for it makes both optimism and pessimism potentially self-fulfilling. For example, if most agents believe that trading will be easy, they will have an incentive to climb even relatively high trees. If they all do, then finding a trading partner will indeed be easy, thus validating ex post their initial optimism.

Production Decisions. The only decision that an agent has to take in the model is whether or not to climb a tree he has just run into. As in the job-search model, the decision rule takes the form of a reservation level: Agents will accept all of those production opportunities whose cost is smaller than some critical level $c*$ (i.e., natives will climb all sufficiently low trees).

To characterize the reservation cost, we will proceed as before, beginning with a discrete-time version of the model and then taking limits as the duration of the period, h, goes to zero. In what follows, then, the relevant transition probabilities will be ah and bh for one period, and the one-period discount factor will be given by $\beta(h) = e^{-\rho h}$.

Denote by $W_e(e)$ the expected lifetime utility of an employed worker when the employment rate is equal to e, and by $W_u(e)$ the value of being unemployed given e,[5] and consider the situation of an employed worker at time t. With probability $b(e_t)h$ he will find a trading partner during the current period, consume his coconut (earning utility y), and then become unemployed. With probability $1 - b(e_t)h$ he will be unable to consume and will remain employed. Thus, his expected payoff is given by

$$W_e(e_t) = bh[y + \beta(h)W_u(e_{t+h})] + (1 - bh)\beta(h)W_e(e_{t+h})$$

where we have taken into account the fact that from this period to the next (which starts at $t + h$) the employment rate may change, altering the expected values of both employed and unemployed agents. Subtracting $\beta(h)W_e(e_t)$ from both sides of the foregoing expression and dividing both sides by h, we obtain

$$[1 - \beta(h)]W_e(e_t) = bhy + \beta(h)[bhW_u(e_{t+h}) + (1 - bh)W_e(e_{t+h}) - W_e(e_t)]$$
$$= bhy + \beta(h)[bh[W_u(e_{t+h})] - W_e(e_{t+h})] + [W_u(e_{t+h}) - W_e(e_t)]$$
$$\Rightarrow \frac{1 - \beta(h)}{h}W_e(e_t) = by + \beta(h)\left(b[W_u(e_{t+h}) - W_e(e_{t+h})] + \frac{W_e(e_{t+h}) - W_e(e_t)}{h}\right)$$

Taking the limit on both sides of this expression as h goes to zero,

$$\rho W_e(e_t) = by + b[W_u(e_t) - W_e(e_t)] + \frac{dW_e(e_t)}{dt}$$

or, assuming that $W_e(\cdot)$ is a differentiable function,

$$\rho W_e(e_t) = by + b[W_u(e_t) - W_e(e_t)] + W_e'(e_t)\dot{e}_t \qquad (1)$$

where $\dot{e}$ denotes the derivative of the employment rate with respect to time.

This expression is similar to the asset-valuation equations of earlier sections, but contains an additional term, $W_e'(e_t)\dot{e}_t$, that captures a new source of "capital gains" (or losses) not present in the previous model: the possibility that changes in the state variable e will affect the asset's value.

In a similar way, it is easy to show that the expected utility of an unemployed worker satisfies

$$\rho W_u(e_t) = a\int_{\underline{c}}^{c^*} [W_e(e_t) - W_u(e_t) - c]\,dG(c) + W_u'(e_t)\dot{e}_t \qquad (2)$$

where c^* is the reservation cost of production (the maximum acceptable tree height). An unemployed worker finds a production opportunity with instantaneous probability a. If the opportunity is good enough (i.e., if $c \leq c^*$), he takes it, pays the cost c, and changes status from unemployed to employed. Thus, the net gain in value is given by $(W_e - W_u - c)$ if c is low enough, and by zero otherwise (as for $c > c^*$, the agent ignores the tree and remains unemployed). Ex ante, the realization of c is not known, so we have to calculate the expected value of this quantity. Using the argument illustrated in the preceding section, it is easy to see that this expectation can be written as the average gain over the interval of acceptable opportunities $(\underline{c}, c^*)$.

The reservation cost is the value of c that makes the agent indifferent between accepting and rejecting a production opportunity. Hence, the net gain from climbing a tree of height c^* is zero or, equivalently,

$$W_e(e_t) - W_u(e_t) = c^* \Rightarrow \rho c^* = \rho[W_e(e) - W_u(e)] \qquad (3)$$

Substituting (1) and (2) into (3),

$$\rho c^* = \rho W_e(e) - \rho W_u(e)$$

$$= by + b[W_u(e) - W_e(e)] + W_e'(e)\dot{e} - a\int_{\underline{c}}^{c^*} [W_e(e) - W_u(e) - c]\,dG(c) - W_u'(e)\dot{e}$$

$$\Rightarrow \rho c^* = by - bc^* + W_e'(e)\dot{e} - a\int_{\underline{c}}^{c^*} [W_e(e) - W_u(e) - c]\,dG(c) - W_u'(e)\dot{e} \qquad (4)$$

To simplify this expression, notice that (i) differentiating (3) with respect to time, $\dot{c}^* = W_e'(e)\dot{e} - W_u'(e)\dot{e}$, and (ii)

$$\int_{\underline{c}}^{c^*} [W_e(e) - W_u(e) - c]\,dG(c) = [W_e(e) - W_u(e)]g(c^*)$$

$$- \int_{\underline{c}}^{c^*} c\,dG(c) = c^*G(c^*) - \int_{\underline{c}}^{c^*} c\,dG(c)$$

because $W_e(e)$ and $W_u(e)$ are not functions of c.

Substituting these expressions into (4), we obtain a necessary condition for the optimal willingness to produce along a path:

$$\rho c^* = b(e)(y - c^*) - ac^* G(c^*) + a \int_{\underline{c}}^{c^*} c \, dG(c) + \dot{c}^*$$

Solving this equation for $\dot{c}^*$ as a function of c^* and e, we obtain the law of motion for c^* along an individually rational trajectory:

$$\dot{c}^* = [\rho + b(e) + aG(c^*)]c^* - b(e)y - a \int_{\underline{c}}^{c^*} c \, dG(c) \equiv B(e, c^*) \tag{5}$$

From the point of view of each agent, the time path of e is exogenous, but in equilibrium e is also determined by individual choices. Given the matching technology described by $b(\ )$ and the rate of arrival of production opportunities, a, the instantaneous rate of change of employment is the difference between the flows into and out of employment. At each point in time, a fraction e of the population is employed. The probability that each employed agent will run into a trading partner and become unemployed after eating is $b(e)$. Thus the fraction of the population that becomes unemployed during the "period" is $eb(e)$. The remaining fraction $1 - e$ of the agents are unemployed. Each of them finds a tree with probability a and climbs it, thus becoming employed, provided that $c \leq c^*$, that is with probability $G(c^*) = \text{pr}(c \leq c^*)$. Thus, the instantaneous flow into employment is $(1 - e)aG(c^*)$, and the rate of change in employment is given by

$$\dot{e} = aG(c^*)(1 - e) - b(e)e \equiv A(e, c^*) \tag{6}$$

Dynamics. We now have a system of differential equations in e and c^* that describe the evolution of the economy over time. To analyze its behavior, we begin by constructing the phase diagram. Setting $\dot{e} = 0$, we obtain

$$\dot{e} = A(e, c^*) \equiv aG(c^*)(1 - e) - b(e)e = 0 \tag{7}$$

Equation (7) implicitly defines a function of the form $e = e(c^*)$ that gives the stationary level of employment as a function of the reservation cost c^*. Because a higher c^* means that agents are willing to accept more production opportunities and therefore tend to become employed faster, the stationary level of employment increases with c^*, yielding an upward-sloping phase line. Formally, we compute the partial derivatives of A,

$$A_e = -aG(c^*) - [b'(e)e + b(e)] < 0 \quad \text{and} \quad A_c = aG'(c^*)(1 - e) > 0$$

and apply the implicit-function theorem to calculate the derivative of $e(c^*)$:

$$e'(c^*) = -\frac{A_c}{A_e} > 0$$

To plot the function $e(c^*)$, notice further that if $c^* \leq \underline{c}$, then $G(c^*) = 0$, and therefore $e = 0$; that is, if nobody is climbing coconut trees (the reservation height is below that of the shortest tree), the only sustainable employment

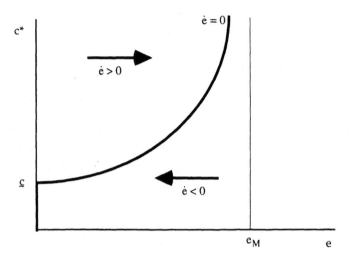

Figure 13.2. The $\dot{e} = 0$ phase line.

rate is zero. Second, as c^* increases without bound, we have $G(c^*) \to 1$ (natives come closer to climbing all trees), and the stationary level of employment approaches a maximum value, e_M, which solves $a(1 - e) - b(e)e = 0$. Hence, the $\dot{e} = 0$ phase line looks as shown in Figure 13.2. Its first portion coincides with the vertical axis ($e = 0$ for all $c \leq c^*$), and the function has a vertical asymptote at e_M.

It remains to determine the direction of the arrows of motion along the e axis. Notice that

$$\dot{e} \geq 0 \quad \text{if and only if} \quad G(c^*) \geq \frac{b(e)e}{a(1-e)}$$

and because G is an increasing function, this is true for "high" values of c^*. Thus, for points in the state space that lie above the phase line, the arrows of motion along the e axis point to the right, as shown in Figure 13.2. Alternatively, notice that

$$\frac{\partial \dot{e}}{\partial c^*} = A_C = aG'(c^*)(1-e) > 0$$

So, starting from the $\dot{e} = 0$ locus, a small increase in c^* (which takes us above the phase line) puts us in the region where the level of employment is rising over time.

To plot the second phase line we proceed in a similar way. Setting $\dot{c}^* = 0$ in (5), we obtain

$$\dot{c}^* = B(c^*, e) = [\rho + b(e) + aG(c^*)]c^* - b(e)y - a\int_{\underline{c}}^{c^*} c \, dG(c) = 0 \qquad (8)$$

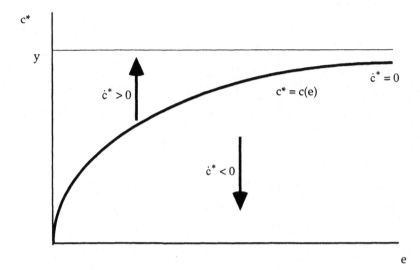

Figure 13.3. The $\dot{c}^* = 0$ phase line.

an equation that implicitly defines a function of the form $c^* = c(e)$ giving the reservation cost c^* as a function of e when the latter is constant (or when agents expect it to be constant). Taking the partial derivatives of $B(\ )$,

$$B_e = b'(e)(c^* - y) < 0$$
$$B_c = [\rho + b(e) + aG(c^*)] + ac^* G'(c^*) - ac^* G'(c^*) = \rho + b(e) + aG(c^*) > 0$$

we find that

$$c'(e) = -\frac{B_e}{B_c} = \frac{b'(e)(y - c^*)}{\rho + b(e) + aG(c^*)} > 0$$

That is, in a stationary environment, the reservation cost increases with the employment rate, provided that $b'(\ ) > 0$. When e is high, agents do not have to wait long for partners with whom to trade. Thus, they find it worthwhile to climb even relatively high trees, rather than waiting for a better opportunity, for doing so does not imply a large delay, on average.

Observe that $c^* < y$, for no agent will accept a production opportunity whose net return is negative (the cost of climbing exceeds the value of the coconut). Also, the phase line goes through the origin, $c(0) = 0$, for it is never worthwhile to expend effort to get a coconut when there is nobody around with whom to exchange it.[6] Finally, the arrows of motion along the c^* axis point upward in the region above the $\dot{c}^* = 0$ line, as $\partial \dot{c}^*/\partial e = B_e < 0$ (Figure 13.3).

Combining the preceding two figures, we obtain the phase diagram shown

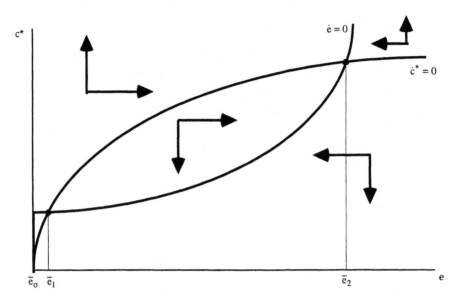

Figure 13.4. Phase diagram.

in Figure 13.4. Notice that there is always a steady state at the origin: If no production is undertaken, nobody will be employed, and if nobody is employed, it would never pay one to become employed and produce, because one would never find a trading partner.

In some cases, this may be the only long-run equilibrium. But if the phase lines cross outside the origin, they must do so at least twice, for the $\dot{c}^* = 0$ locus is bounded above by y, and the $\dot{e} = 0$ curve has a vertical asymptote at e_M. Notice that the existence of trading externalities is crucial for the existence of multiple steady states. The $\dot{e} = 0$ phase line is always upward-sloping (as natives become willing to climb higher trees, they become employed faster, raising the stationary employment level). The $\dot{c}^* = 0$ locus, on the other hand, becomes a horizontal line if the rate of arrival of trading opportunities is independent of the employment rate, that is, if $b'(e) = 0$. In this case, the system has a unique interior steady state.

The stability properties of each steady state can be determined from the eigenvalues of the corresponding Jacobian matrix (the coefficient matrix for the linearization of the system around each steady state). Given the Jacobian

$$J = \begin{bmatrix} A_e & A_{c^*} \\ B_e & B_{c^*} \end{bmatrix}$$

the corresponding eigenvalues satisfy

$$\lambda_1 \lambda_2 = \det J = A_e B_{c^*} - A_{c^*} B_e$$

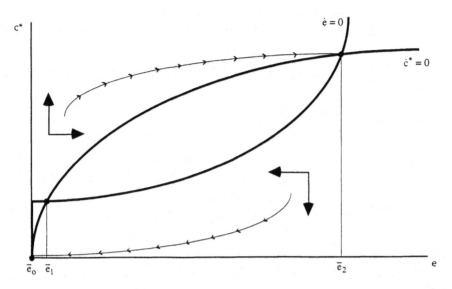

Figure 13.5. Convergent trajectories.

If $\det J < 0$, the eigenvalues are real numbers of opposite signs, and the steady state is a saddle point. We can relate the sign of $\det J$ to the relative slopes of the phase lines. Observe that

$$\det J < 0 \Leftrightarrow -\frac{B_e}{B_{c^*}} < -\frac{A_e}{A_{c^*}} \Leftrightarrow c'(e) < \frac{1}{e'(c^*)}$$

Hence, a steady state is a saddle point if and only if it corresponds to a point where the $\dot{e} = 0$ phase line is steeper and cuts the $\dot{c}^* = 0$ locus from below.

In the phase diagram shown in Figure 13.4 there are therefore two saddle points: the equilibrium at the origin, and the steady state with the highest level of activity. Figure 13.5 shows the saddle-path trajectories leading to these equilibria, which are also the possible equilibrium paths of the system.[7] The figure shows that, at least for certain initial values of the predetermined state variable e, there are two equilibrium trajectories, one leading to the high-activity steady state, and the other leading to the "shutdown" equilibrium at the origin.

There are, then, two "natural rates" or long-run equilibria, one clearly superior to the other, and, in many cases, two equilibrium paths, each leading to one of these steady states. We therefore face a *coordination problem* – which of the paths will be taken will depend on the ability of agents to coordinate their actions on the good equilibrium. As noted earlier, we can think of the problem in terms of the tendency for optimistic or pessimistic expectations to become self-fulfilling. In some sense, the problem is one of coordinating beliefs. This raises the possibility that the assumption of rational expectations may not be sufficient to fully close the model: Even if agents know the structure of the model and can compute the equilibrium paths, there is uncertainty concerning the actual path of the economy, for agents cannot know for sure which equilibrium will be selected.

2. Optimal Growth in Discrete Time

Consider an economy populated by a constant number of identical infinitely-lived agents. There is a single good that can be consumed directly or used as capital in production. The preferences of a representative individual are described by a utility function of the form

$$\sum_{t=0}^{\infty} \beta^t U(c_t) \tag{1}$$

where $\beta \in (0, 1)$ is the rate of time discount, a measure of the agent's "impatience," c_t is consumption at time t, and the period utility function $U(\ )$ is a strictly increasing and strictly concave C^2 function. All agents are endowed with one unit of labor time each period.

Production of the single good requires both labor (L) and capital (K). The production technology is described by a strictly concave production function,

$$Y = F(K, L)$$

where we interpret Y as gross output (i.e., new production plus undepreciated capital).[8] We assume that $F(\ )$ is C^2 and is strictly increasing and exhibits constant returns to scale (i.e., is homogeneous of degree 1). Thus, if both inputs are changed by the same factor λ, output changes also by a factor of λ, and we have

$$F(\lambda K, \lambda L) = \lambda F(K, L) \tag{2}$$

This property of the production function allows a convenient normalization. In (2), let $\lambda = 1/L$, and note that

$$F(K/L,\ L/L) = (1/L)F(K, L) \Rightarrow F(K, L) = LF(K/L, 1)$$

If we write k for the per-capita capital stock (K/L) and define the per-capita production function by

$$f(k) \equiv F(k, 1) \tag{3}$$

we can write total output as

$$Y = Lf(k)$$

and per-capita output $y = Y/L$ as a function of the average capital stock per worker,

$$y = f(k) \tag{4}$$

Imagine that this economy is regulated by a benevolent, all-powerful social planner who makes production, consumption, and investment decisions so as to maximize the lifetime utility of the representative individual. The planner chooses a sequence $\{c_t, k_{t+1}\}_{t=0}^{\infty}$ of consumption levels and capital stocks so as to maximize the utility function (1), taking as given the production technology, and subject to a resource-availability constraint. Working in per-capita terms, the initial capital stock k_0 is given, and at each point in time, consumption and investment must satisfy the constraint

$$f(k_t) = c_t + k_{t+1} \tag{5}$$

That is, current output per capita, including undepreciated capital, $f(k_t)$, can be either consumed today or used for tomorrow's production.

At any given point in time t, the initial capital stock k_t describes completely the state of the system and determines the economy's consumption possibilities for the current period and all future time. Given k_t, the planner's immediate concern is to choose current consumption. Alternatively, because $k_{t+1} + c_t$ must add up to current output, we can think of the planner as choosing an investment level k_{t+1}. Hence, the planner's problem can be written

$$V(k_0) = \max_{\{k_{t+1}\}_{t=0}^{\infty}} \left\{ \sum_{t=0}^{\infty} \beta^t U[f(k_t) - k_{t+1}] \text{ s.t. } 0 \le k_{t+1} \le f(k_t),\ k_0 \text{ given} \right\} \tag{P}$$

The constraint says that next period's capital stock cannot be negative and cannot exceed current gross output. To rule out corner solutions, we will assume that both the production function and the period utility function satisfy the following conditions:

$$f(0) = 0, \quad f'(0) = \infty, \quad f'(\infty) = 0, \quad U'(0) = \infty, \quad \text{and} \quad U'(\infty) = 0 \tag{6}$$

Following our discussion in Chapter 12, the (current) value function for the planner's problem satisfies the Bellman equation,

$$V(k_t) = \max_{k_{t+1}} \{ U[f(k_t) - k_{t+1}] + \beta V(k_{t+1}) \text{ s.t } 0 \le k_{t+1} \le f(k_t) \} \tag{BE.P}$$

Under our assumptions regarding preferences and technology, all but one of the conditions that would guarantee the existence and uniqueness of a bounded, continuous, strictly increasing and strictly concave solution to (BE.P) are satisfied. In particular, recall that Theorem 1.5 in Chapter 12 required the period return function to be bounded. In the current context, however, the period utility function $U(\ )$ and the production function may very well be unbounded. There is, however, a simple way to sidestep the problem by restricting ourselves to a bounded subset of the domain of $f(\ )$.

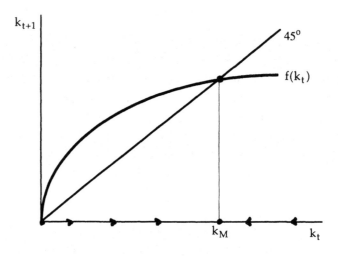

Figure 13.6.

Imagine, for a moment, that consumption is zero in all periods. Then the evolution of the capital stock is described by the difference equation

$$k_{t+1} = f(k_t) \tag{7}$$

It is easy to show (see the discussion of the Solow model in Chapter 11) that under our assumptions, the phase diagram for this equation is as shown in Figure 13.6, with a unique and globally stable steady state, k_M. Hence, even if all output is invested each period, there is a maximum sustainable per-capita capital stock. We can therefore restrict ourselves to values of k in the interval $[0, k_M]$. Because $U[f(k)]$ is certainly bounded in this set, we can apply Theorems 1.5 and 1.18 in Chapter 12 to obtain the following result.

Proposition 2.1. The Bellman equation (BE.P) has a unique continuous and bounded solution V. This function is the value function for the planner's problem (P) and is strictly increasing and strictly concave. Moreover, the policy correspondence g( ) giving next period's optimal capital stock as a function of today's state k_t is a well-defined and continuous function.

Given this result, we can establish some important properties of the policy function by studying the maximization inside the Bellman equation. We begin by using Theorem 2.15 in Chapter 6 to show that $V( )$ is differentiable. This will allow us to use the first-order condition for the maximization in (BE.P) to characterize the optimal investment decision.

Proposition 2.2. The value function for the planner's problem, V( ), is differentiable, with

$$V'(k_t) = U'[f(k_t) - k_{t+1}]f'(k_t)$$

Proof. Fix some k_t^0 in $(0, k_M)$, and let k_{t+1}^0 be a solution of the problem

$$V(k_t^0) = \max_{k_{t+1}}\{U[f(k_t^0) - k_{t+1}] + \beta V(k_{t+1}) \text{ s.t. } 0 \le k_{t+1} \le f(k_t^0)\} \quad \text{(BE.P)}$$

Next, define the function

$$W(k_t) = U[f(k_t) - k_{t+1}^0] + \beta V(k_{t+1}^0)$$

for k_t within some ε-ball with center at k_t^0, $B_\varepsilon(k_t^0)$. Under assumption (6), k_{t+1}^0 will be an interior solution of this problem, that is, $0 < k_{t+1}^0 < f(k_t^0)$. By the continuity of f, ε can be chosen small enough that $f(k_t) > k_{t+1}^0$ for all $k_t \in B_\varepsilon(k_t^0)$, that is, so that k_{t+1}^0 is still feasible for all $k_t \in B_\varepsilon(k_t^0)$. On the other hand, k_{t+1}^0 is not necessarily optimal for an arbitrary k_t in $B_\varepsilon(k_t^0)$. Hence,

$$W(k_t) = U[f(k_t) - k_{t+1}^0] + \beta V(k_{t+1}^0) \le \max_{k_{t+1}}\{U[f(k_t) - k_{t+1}] + \beta V(k_{t+1})\} = V(k_t)$$

for all $k_t \in B_\varepsilon(k_t^0)$, and

$$W(k_t^0) = V(k_t^0)$$

because k_{t+1}^0 is optimal for k_t^0. Moreover, $W(\ )$ is a differentiable function of k_t, because $U(\ )$ and $f(\ )$ are differentiable, and $V(k_{t+1}^0)$ is just a constant. Hence, by Theorem 2.15 in Chapter 6, $V(\ )$ is differentiable at k_t^0, and

$$V'(k_t^0) = W'(k_t^0) = U'[f(k_t^0) - k_{t+1}^0]f'(k_t^0) \qquad \square$$

Because $V(\ )$ is differentiable, an interior solution of the maximization inside the Bellman equation is characterized by the first-order condition

$$U'[f(k_t) - k_{t+1}] = \beta V'(k_{t+1}) \tag{8}$$

which implicitly defines the policy function

$$k_{t+1}^* = g(k_t)$$

Without additional restrictions there will be no guarantee that V will be twice differentiable. Hence, we cannot differentiate (8) again to establish the comparative-statics properties of the function $g(\ )$. As we will see, however, equation (8) and the concavity of the value function provide sufficient information to establish some important properties of the policy function and the optimal sequence of capital stocks.

In some cases it will be useful to rewrite (8) in an alternative way. By Proposition 2.2, applied at time $t + 1$, we have that

$$V'(k_{t+1}) = U'[f(k_{t+1}) - k_{t+2}]f'(k_{t+1}) = U'(c_{t+1})f'(k_{t+1}) \tag{9}$$

Substituting (9) into (8), we obtain the so-called *Euler equation*,

$$U'[f(k_t) - k_{t+1}] = \beta U'[f(k_{t+1}) - k_{t+2}]f'(k_{t+1}) \tag{10}$$

or, reintroducing consumption explicitly,

$$U'(c_t) = \beta U'(c_{t+1}) f'(k_{t+1}) \tag{10'}$$

To interpret this equation, consider reducing period-t consumption by one unit in order to invest it and increase consumption at $t + 1$. On the one hand, there is a utility loss of $U'(c_t)$ in period t. On the other, an additional unit of investment will allow consumption to be higher by $f'(k_{t+1})$ units next period, yielding a utility gain of $U'(c_{t+1})f'(k_{t+1})$. Because this utility gain comes one period later, however, we must discount it by β. The Euler equation says that along an optimal path, today's loss and tomorrow's gain must be equal, for otherwise a feasible rearrangement of the consumption/investment plan would increase its total value, implying that the original plan could not have been optimal. Hence, along an optimal trajectory, the planner must be indifferent, at the margin, between using an additional unit of output for current consumption or for investment.

There are now two different ways to proceed. One is to work directly with the first-order condition (8); the other is to analyze the two-equation system formed by the Euler equation (10') and the constraint (5), reinterpreted as the law of motion for the capital stock,

$$k_{t+1} = f(k_t) - c_t \tag{5'}$$

We will work through the first approach and let the reader explore the second approach through a series of problems.

(a) Properties of the Policy Function and the Optimal Capital Sequence

Given the policy function $g(\ )$, the optimal time path for the capital stock is the solution of the difference equation $k_{t+1} = g(k_t)$. We know that the optimal sequence, $\{k_t^*\}$, must satisfy the first-order condition (8) and the Euler equation (10) and that the value function $V(\ )$ is strictly concave and increasing. In this section, we will use this information to establish some properties of $g(\ )$ and $\{k_t^*\}$.

We begin by characterizing the steady state of the system. Setting $k_t = k_{t+1} = k_{t+2} \equiv k$ in the Euler equation (10), we obtain

$$U'[f(k) - k] = \beta U'[f(k) - k] f'(k)$$
$$\Rightarrow f'(k) = 1/\beta \tag{11}$$

an equation that implicitly defines the steady-state capital stock $\bar{k}$ as a function of the discount rate β.[9] Because $f(\ )$ is strictly concave, the marginal product of capital, $f'(k)$, is a strictly decreasing function of the capital stock, implying that equation (11) has at most one solution. The assumptions that $f'(0) = \infty$ and $f'(\infty) = 0$, moreover, ensure the existence of a positive solution,

$\bar{k}$. Moreover, we have $\bar{k} \le k_M$, as $\bar{k}$ cannot be larger than the maximum sustainable capital stock described earlier.

Next, we show that the policy function $g(\ )$ is an increasing function of k_t. This result is then used to establish that the optimal sequence of capital stocks $\{k_t^*\}_{t=0}^{\infty}$ is monotonic and converges asymptotically to the steady state for any given initial stock $k_0 > 0$.

Proposition 2.3. *The policy function* $k_{t+1}^* = g(k_t)$ *is increasing in* k_t.

Proof. By contradiction. Suppose $g(\ )$ is not increasing everywhere. Then there exist capital stocks k' and k'' such that $k'' > k'$ and

$$g(k'') < g(k') \tag{1}$$

Because $V(\ )$ is concave, moreover, $V'(\ )$ is decreasing, and (1) implies

$$V'[g(k'')] > V'[g(k')] \tag{2}$$

By the first-order condition

$$U'[f(k_t) - k_{t+1}] = \beta V'(k_{t+1}) \tag{8}$$

inequality (2) implies

$$U'[f(k'') - g(k'')] > U'[f(k') - g(k')]$$

Now, Because $U(\ )$ is strictly concave by assumption, the foregoing expression implies that

$$f(k'') - g(k'') < f(k') - g(k') \Rightarrow g(k'') - g(k') > f(k'') - f(k') > 0$$

where the last inequality holds because $f(\ )$ is increasing. But then $g(k'') > g(k')$, which contradicts (1). $\qquad\square$

Proposition 2.4. *The optimal capital sequence* $\{k_t^*\}$, *defined recursively by* $k_{t+1}^* = g(k_t^*)$, *with* k_0 *given, is monotonic.*

Proof. Suppose $k_1^* > k_0$. Because $g(\ )$ is increasing, we have

$$k_2^* = g(k_1^*) \ge g(k_0) = k_1^*$$

which implies, in turn,

$$k_3^* = g(k_2^*) \ge g(k_1^*) = k_2^*$$

and so forth. Similarly, if $k_1^* < k_0$, then

$$k_2^* = g(k_1^*) \le g(k_0) = k_1^*$$

and so on. $\qquad\square$

Proposition 2.5. If the initial capital stock k_0 is above the steady state $\bar{k}$, then $\{k_t^*\}$ decreases monotonically; if $k_0 < \bar{k}$, then $\{k_{t+1}^*\}$ increases monotonically.

Proof. Because $V(\ )$ is strictly concave, $V'(\ )$ is strictly decreasing. Hence

$$k'' > k' \Rightarrow V'(k'') < V'(k') \tag{1}$$

Consider two successive capital stocks, k_t^* and k_{t+1}^*, where $k_{t+1}^* = g(k_t^*)$. By (1), $k_t^* - k_{t+1}^*$ and $V'(k_t^*) - V'(k_{t+1}^*)$ will have opposite signs, that is,

$$(k_t^* - k_{t+1}^*)[V'(k_t^*) - V'(k_{t+1}^*)] \le 0 \qquad (= 0 \text{ at the steady state}) \tag{2}$$

By equations (8) and (9), we have

$$(8) \Rightarrow V'(k_{t+1}^*) = (1/\beta)U'[f(k_t^*) - k_{t+1}^*]$$
$$(9) \Rightarrow V'(k_t^*) = U'[f(k_t^*) - k_{t+1}^*]f'(k_t^*)$$

Substituting these expressions in (2),

$$(k_t^* - k_{t+1}^*)\{U'[f(k_t^*) - k_{t+1}^*]f'(k_t^*) - (1/\beta)U'[f(k_t^*) - k_{t+1}^*]\} \le 0$$

and, dividing by $U'(\ ) > 0$,

$$(k_t^* - k_{t+1}^*)[f'(k_t^*) - (1/\beta)] \le 0 \tag{3}$$

Recall that at the steady state, $f'(\bar{k}) = 1/\beta$, and $f'(\ )$ is decreasing, by the concavity of $f(\ )$. Hence,

- if $k_t^* < \bar{k}$, we have $f'(k_t^*) > (1/\beta)$, and (3) implies that $k_t^* \le k_{t+1}^*$, that is, $\{k_t^*\}$ is increasing, and
- if $k_t^* > \bar{k}$, we have $f'(k_t^*) < (1/\beta)$, and (3) implies that $k_t^* \ge k_{t+1}^*$, that is, $\{k_t^*\}$ is decreasing. □

Proposition 2.6. The optimal capital sequence $\{k_t^*\}$ converges (monotonically) to the steady-state capital stock $\bar{k}$ for any initial $k_0 > 0$.

Proof. Note that $\{k_t^*\}$ is monotonic and bounded (above by k_M, below by zero or, alternatively, by k_0 and $\bar{k}$). Because every monotonic bounded sequence converges, $\{k_t^*\}$ has a limit that we will call k^*. By the continuity of the policy function $g(\ )$, k^* must be a fixed point of $g(\ )$, for

$$k^* = \lim_{t \to \infty} k_{t+1}^* = \lim_{t \to \infty} g(k_t) = g\left(\lim_{t \to \infty} k_t\right) = g(k^*)$$

Hence, k^* is a steady state. Because there is a unique steady state $\bar{k}$, we conclude that $\{k_t^*\} \to \bar{k}$. □

(b) The Euler Equation and Dynamics

In the preceding section we found it convenient to solve the resource constraint for c and work only with the capital stock. Using the concavity of the value function and the first-order condition for the maximization in the Bellman equation, we have established that the optimal capital sequence $\{k_t^*\}$ converges monotonically to the steady state of the system. We can then use the constraint again to infer the optimal path of consumption over time. We now illustrate a second and probably more instructive approach to analyzing the dynamics of the optimal-growth model. The basic idea is to treat the system formed by the Euler equation and the transition law for the capital stock,

$$U'(c_t) = \beta U'(c_{t+1})f'(k_{t+1}) \tag{11}$$

$$k_{t+1} = f(k_t) - c_t \tag{12}$$

as an ordinary system of difference equations and study its dynamics in the standard way. Thus, we first solve for the steady state; then we construct a phase diagram and compute the eigenvalues of the Jacobian matrix at the steady state to check for stability.

Setting $c_t = c_{t+1} \equiv c$ and $k_t = k_{t+1} \equiv k$ in (11) and (12), we get

$$(11) \Rightarrow U'(c) = \beta U'(c)f'(k) \Rightarrow \beta f'(k) = 1 \tag{13}$$

$$(12) \Rightarrow c = f(k) - k \tag{14}$$

As we have seen, equation (13) has a unique solution $\bar{k}$. Given $\bar{k}$, equation (14) can be solved for steady-state consumption $\bar{c}$.

The system (11)–(12) is not quite in the "standard form." In particular, we would like to have each variable (k_{t+1} and c_{t+1}) as a function of the lagged values k_t and c_t. To this end, we solve (12) for k_{t+1}, substitute the result into (11), and apply the implicit-function theorem to the resulting equation to obtain a function $\phi(\ )$ giving c_{t+1} as a function of k_t and c_t. This yields the system

$$k_{t+1} = f(k_t) - c_t \equiv \varphi(k_t, c_t) \tag{15}$$

$$U'(c_t) = \beta U'(c_{t+1})f'[f(k_t) - c_t] \Leftrightarrow c_{t+1} = \phi(k_t, c_t) \tag{16}$$

Problem 2.7. Apply the implicit-function theorem to compute the partial derivatives of the function $\phi(k_t, c_t)$ defined implicitly by equation (16), and determine their sign.

Problem 2.8. Setting $c_t = c_{t+1} = c$ and $k_t = k_{t+1} = k$ in (15) and (16), draw the phase lines $\Delta k_t = 0$ and $\Delta c_t = 0$. To complete the phase diagram, determine the directions of motion along the c and k axes in each of the four regions into which the state plane (c, x) is divided by the phase lines.

Problem 2.9. The phase diagram you have just drawn should suggest that the steady state is a saddle point. Check that this is true by showing that the

606 Some Applications of Dynamic Optimization

eigenvalues of the Jacobian matrix for the system are positive real numbers lying on opposite sides of 1.

The phase diagram we have constructed shows the orbits of the system (15)–(16), but only one of these trajectories corresponds to the solution of the original planning problem. These two equations can be thought of as the first-order conditions for an optimum, but they are not sufficient to fully characterize the optimal path.

Out of all the solutions of (15)–(16), we want to identify the one that corresponds to the solution of the programming problem. To select one particular solution, we need two boundary conditions to pin down one point in the phase plane through which the system will have to go. The initial value of the capital stock should be taken as given; this yields one initial condition, $k(t = 0) = k_0$, a given constant, specifying that the system starts out from some point on a vertical line through k_0 in the phase plane. On the other hand, there is no natural initial condition for the free variable c, so we need another way to identify the optimal path.

It turns out that the optimal consumption/investment plan is the one described by the saddle-path trajectory. An intuitive way to see this is by examining the phase diagram for the system after adding to it a feasibility bound requiring that consumption not exceed current output, that is, $c \leq f(k)$. Inspection of this figure suggests that all trajectories other than the saddle path eventually run into either the k axis or the feasibility bound, where present consumption exhausts output, leaving nothing for next period. In either case, consumption becomes zero and remains so thereafter. It is clear that such paths cannot be optimal, leaving us with only the saddle path.

A more formal way to identify the optimal path is through a so-called *transversality condition*. In some sense, the problem is the same as in a static maximization problem: The first-order conditions (the Euler equations here) identify possible candidates for a maximum, but they are also satisfied by points that are not maxima. To find an optimum, we need an additional criterion, some sort of second-order condition relating to the concavity of the objective function at the candidate point. The transversality condition plays a similar role in the present context, and as we will see, the sufficiency proof relies heavily on the concavity of the objective function.

An alternative way to think of the transversality condition is as a terminal condition for the system of difference equations. Consider first a finite-horizon version of the planning problem we are studying. In that case k_{T+1} is the capital stock to be left "at the end of time"; it is clear that the optimal thing to do is to leave nothing, so $k_{T+1} = 0$, providing us with a second boundary condition to identify the particular solution of (15)–(16) that solves the planner's problem. As we saw in Chapter 12, in the infinite-horizon case the transversality condition can be interpreted in a somewhat similar way, as the requirement that as $t \to \infty$ the suitably discounted value of the capital stock should go to zero. Intuitively, we want to prevent the planner from accumulating too much capital at the expense of deferring consumption forever.

Proposition 2.10. Transversality condition. Let $s^* = k_0 \cup \{c_t^*, k_{t+1}^*\}_{t=0}^{\infty}$ *be a solution sequence of the system (15)–(16). If this sequence satisfies the transversality condition*

$$\lim_{T \to \infty} \beta^T U'(c_T) f'(k_T) k_T = 0 \tag{T}$$

then it solves the planner's problem.

Proof. Let $s^* = k_0 \cup \{c_t^*, k_{t+1}^*\}$ be a sequence satisfying the conditions of the proposition, and $s = k_0 \cup \{c_t, k_{t+1}\}$ an arbitrary feasible sequence. To establish that s^* is optimal, we show that

$$d = W_0(s^*) - W_0(s) = \sum_{t=0}^{\infty} \beta^t [U(c_t^*) - U(c_t)] \geq 0$$

That is, the total "utility value" of the candidate sequence s^* is at least as large as that of any feasible sequence.

To show this, it will be convenient to solve the resource constraint for c,

$$k_{t+1} = f(k_t) - c_t \Rightarrow c_t = f(k_t) - k_{t+1}$$

and write the period utility function as

$$U(k_t, k_{t+1}) = U[f(k_t) - k_{t+1}]$$

It is easy to show that the function $U(k_t, k_{t+1})$ is concave. Moreover, we have

$$U_1(k_t, k_{t+1}) = U'[f(k_t) - k_{t+1}] f'(k_t) > 0 \tag{1}$$

$$U_2(k_t, k_{t+1}) = -U'[f(k_t) - k_{t+1}] < 0 \tag{2}$$

In this notation the Euler equation can be written

$$U'[f(k_t) - k_{t+1}] = \beta U'[f(k_{t+1}) - k_{t+2}] f'(k_{t+1})$$
$$\Rightarrow U_2(k_t, k_{t+1}) + \beta U_1(k_{t+1}, k_{t+2}) = 0 \tag{3}$$

Next, write d in the form

$$d = W_0(s^*) - W_0(s) = \lim_{T \to \infty} \sum_{t=0}^{T} \beta^t \{U(k_t^*, k_{t+1}^*) - U(k_t, k_{t+1})\}$$

and observe that, by the concavity of $U(k_t, k_{t+1})$,

$$U(k_t, k_{t+1}) \leq U(k_t^*, k_{t+1}^*) + U_1(k_t^*, k_{t+1}^*)(k_t - k_t^*) + U_2(k_t^*, k_{t+1}^*)(k_{t+1} - k_{t+1}^*)$$

or, rearranging,

$$U(k_t^*, k_{t+1}^*) - U(k_t, k_{t+1}) \geq U_1(k_t^*, k_{t+1}^*)(k_t^* - k_t) + U_2(k_t^*, k_{t+1}^*)(k_{t+1}^* - k_{t+1}) \quad (4)$$

Hence, we have

$$d = \lim_{T \to \infty} \sum_{t=0}^{T} \beta^t \{ U(k_t^*, k_{t+1}^*) - U(k_t, k_{t+1}) \}$$

$$\geq \lim_{T \to \infty} \sum_{t=0}^{T} \beta^t \{ U_1(k_t^*, k_{t+1}^*)(k_t^* - k_t) + U_2(k_t^*, k_{t+1}^*)(k_{t+1}^* - k_{t+1}) \}$$

$$= \beta^0 \{ U_1(k_0^*, k_1^*)(k_0^* - k_0) + U_2(k_0^*, k_1^*)(k_1^* - k_1) \}$$

$$+ \beta \{ U_1(k_1^*, k_2^*)(k_1^* - k_1) + U_2(k_1^*, k_2^*)(k_2^* - k_2) \} + \ldots +$$

$$\beta^t \{ U_1(k_t^*, k_{t+1}^*)(k_t^* - k_t) + U_2(k_t^*, k_{t+1}^*)(k_{t+1}^* - k_{t+1}) \}$$

$$+ \beta^{t+1} \{ U_1(k_{t+1}^*, k_{t+2}^*)(k_{t+1}^* - k_{t+1}) + U_2(k_{t+1}^*, k_{t+2}^*)(k_{t+2}^* - k_{t+2}) \} + \ldots$$

Observe that the initial capital stock is given and thus is the same in both s and s^*; hence $k_0^* - k_0 = 0$, and the first term in the sum vanishes. The remaining terms can be rearranged to give

$$d = \lim_{T \to \infty} \left\{ \sum_{t=1}^{T} \beta^{t-1} \{ [U_2(k_{t+1}^*, k_t^*) + \beta U_1(k_t^*, k_{t+1}^*)](k_t^* - k_t) \} \right.$$
$$\left. + \beta^T U_2(k_T^*, k_{T+1}^*)(k_{T+1}^* - k_{T+1}) \right\} \quad (5)$$

Next, recall that s^* is assumed to satisfy the Euler equation

$$U_2(k_t^*, k_{t+1}^*) + \beta U_1(k_{t+1}^*, k_{t+2}^*) = 0 \quad (3)$$

Hence the terms in the summation vanish, and we have

$$d = W_0(s^*) - W_0(s) \geq \lim_{T \to \infty} \beta^T U_2(k_T^*, k_{T+1}^*)(k_{T+1}^* - k_{T+1})$$

Moreover, we have $k_{T+1} \geq 0$, by the feasibility constraint, and $U_2(\ ) < 0$, by (2). Hence, the product $U_2(k_T^*, k_{T+1}^*)(-k_{T+1})$ is positive, and we have, using the Euler equation,

$$d = W_0(s^*) - W_0(s) \geq \lim_{T \to \infty} \beta^T U_2(k_T^*, k_{T+1}^*) k_{t+1}^*$$

$$= \lim_{T \to \infty} \beta^{T+1} U_1(k_{T+1}^*, k_{T+2}^*) k_{T+1}^* = -\lim_{T \to \infty} \beta^{T+1} U'(c_{T+1}^*) f'(k_{T+1}^*) k_{T+1}^* = 0$$

where the next-to-last equality follows from (1), and the last limit is zero, by the transversality condition (T).

In conclusion, we have shown that

$$d = W_0(s^*) - W_0(s) \geq 0$$

Because the sequence s^* that satisfies both the Euler equation and the transversality condition must yield a greater value than any other feasible sequence, it must be optimal. □

Problem 2.11. Show that the function $U(k_t, k_{t+1})$ defined in the proof of Proposition 2.10 is concave.

To conclude, it is easy to verify that the saddle-path solution satisfies the transversality condition (T) and is therefore optimal. For this solution, both c_t and k_t converge to finite values c and k. Hence, k, $U'(c)$, and $f'(k)$ are just finite constants, and

$$\lim_{T \to \infty} \beta^T U'(c) f'(k) k = 0$$

because $\beta \in (0, 1)$. Along explosive paths, however, either k or c will become zero. In that case, $f'(k) \to \infty$ or $U'(c) \to \infty$, so (T) may not hold.

3. Investment with Installation Costs

In the standard static model the firm is assumed to maximize current profits, defined as the difference between output and contemporaneous factor payments. Letting K and L denote labor and capital inputs, and w and R the wage and the rental rate of capital in units of output, the firm's problem can be written

$$\max_{K,L} F(K, L) - wL - RK \tag{1}$$

The solution functions for this problem are factor demands giving optimal input levels as functions of factor prices:

$$K^* = K(w, r) \quad \text{and} \quad L^* = L(w, r)$$

This formulation assumes that the firm can rent inputs in "spot markets" and put them to work immediately and at no cost. This clearly unrealistic assumption may lead, at best, to a theory of the determination of the optimal capital stock, but it has no implications (or very naive ones) for the optimal investment policy.

In practice, capital is typically purchased, rather than rented, and its installation may involve considerable delays and adjustment costs. Thus, a firm's stock of "installed capital" becomes a sluggish state variable, and investment decisions must be made taking into account their effect on the entire time path of profits, rather than on a period-by-period basis.

The first part of this section analyzes the optimal investment policy for a competitive firm when the installation of capital is costly. In the second part, we go from partial to general equilibrium and study the time paths of investment and share prices in a small open economy and their responses to changes in tax policy.

(a) A Model of Investment with Installation Costs

Consider a competitive firm with access to a constant-returns technology $F(K, L)$. The firm hires labor in spot markets at a constant wage rate w and may devote part of its output to productive investment I. The installation of new capital involves a cost. In particular, an investment expenditure of I units of output yields $\Psi(I, K) < I$ units of new productive capital when the already-installed stock is K. If capital depreciates at a constant rate δ, the instantaneous rate of change of the firm's stock of installed capital is given by

$$\dot{K}_t = \Psi(I_t, K_t) - \delta K_t \tag{1}$$

Profits, defined as output minus wage payments, are taxed at a constant rate τ, and investment is subsidized at a rate c. Thus, the firm's instantaneous net cash flow is given by

$$\Pi_t = (1 - \tau)[F(K_t, L_t) - wL_t] - (1 - c)I_t$$

We will assume that net cash flows are distributed as dividends among the firm's owners each period and that the stock market values the firm correctly (i.e., that the value of its stock is the discounted value of the dividend stream),

$$\int_0^\infty e^{-rt} \Pi_t dt \tag{2}$$

where r is the market rate of interest (assumed constant). In these circumstances, all shareholders will agree that the firm should maximize (2). The firm's problem can therefore be written[10]

$$V(K_0) = \max_{\substack{I(t), L(t), \\ 0 \le t \le \infty}} \left\{ \int_0^\infty e^{-rt}((1 - \tau)[F(K_t, L_t) - wL_t] - (1 - c)I_t) \, dt \right.$$

$$\left. \text{s.t. } \dot{K}_t = \Psi(I_t, K_t) - \delta K_t, \, K_0 \text{ given} \right\} \tag{P}$$

We will assume that $F(\ )$ and $\Psi(\ )$ exhibit constant returns to scale and are increasing and concave functions that are twice continuously differentiable, with

$$F_{KK}, F_{LL} < 0, \qquad F_{KL} > 0, \qquad F_L(K, 0) = \infty$$

$$\Psi_{KK}, \Psi_{II}, \Psi_{KI} < 0, \quad \Psi(I, K) \le I, \quad \text{and} \quad \Psi(0, K) = 0 \, \forall K$$

Thus, the installation function is concave in I for given K and goes through the origin. More investment leads to faster capital accumulation, but at a decreasing rate, and the marginal productivity of capital in installation (Ψ_K) is positive, but decreases with both K and I. In principle, we allow investment to be negative; that is, capital can be disinstalled and "eaten," but only at a loss ($\Psi < I$ implies that we lose some capital when we disinstall it).

The state variable is the stock of installed capital K, and the decision variables are the investment rate and the level of employment at each point in time. Necessary conditions for an optimal solution of (P) can be obtained by applying the maximum principle. Following the procedure developed in Section 2 of Chapter 12, we begin by introducing a (current-value) costate variable or multiplier, q_t, and forming the current-value Hamiltonian,

$$H_t^c = (1-\tau)[F(K_t, L_t) - wL_t] - (1-c)I_t + q_t[\Psi(I_t, K_t) - \delta K_t]$$

The shadow price of installed capital, q, is the derivative of the value of the firm, V, with respect to K, that is, the increase in the firm's (stock-market) value that would result from an additional unit of installed capital. The last term in H^c, $q\dot{K}$, is the current value of the contemporaneous increase in K. The Hamiltonian, defined as the sum of $q\dot{K}$ and the firm's current dividend, measures the total flow of (current and discounted future) benefits arising from today's decisions. Thus, the control variables L and I should be chosen to maximize H_t^c, yielding the following conditions:

$$\frac{\partial H_t^C}{\partial L_t} = 0 \Rightarrow (1-\tau)[F_L(K, L) - w] = 0$$
$$\Rightarrow F_L(K, L) = w \tag{3}$$

$$\frac{\partial H_t^C}{\partial I_t} = 0 \Rightarrow -(1-c) + q\Psi_I(I, K) = 0$$
$$\Rightarrow 1 - c = q\Psi_I(I, K) \tag{4}$$

The equation of motion for the costate variable q is given by

$$\dot{q}_t - rq_t = -\frac{\partial H_t^C}{\partial K_t}$$
$$\Rightarrow \dot{q} = q[r + \delta - \Psi_K(I, K)] - (1-\tau)F_K(K, L) \tag{5}$$

Maximization of H^c with respect to L yields a familiar condition: Because employment decisions can be made on a period-by-period basis, the marginal product of labor should be set equal to the wage, exactly as in the static model. Equation (4) requires that the net cost (after subsidies) of one unit of newly purchased capital equal its marginal contribution to the firm's value, obtained by multiplying the resulting increase in installed capital (Ψ_I) by its shadow price q. Both conditions are in agreement with the general proposition that additional units of an input should be purchased as long as each yields a marginal benefit that exceeds its cost.

Equations (3) and (4) define policy functions giving the optimal choices of instruments ($I*$ and $L*$) as functions of the state and costate variables and the wage rate. To write these functions in a convenient form, we will exploit the homogeneity of degree 0 and the monotonicity of the first partial derivatives of the production and installation functions.[11] Equation (3) can be written

$$F_L(K, L) = F_L(K/L, 1) = w$$

Inverting $F_L(\cdot, 1)$, we can solve for the optimal capital/labor ratio as a function of the wage and write

$$L* = \frac{K}{\Phi(w)}, \quad \text{where} \quad \Phi = F_L^{-1}(\cdot, 1) \tag{6}$$

showing that the optimal employment level increases with the stock of capital and decreases with the wage. Similarly, equation (4) can be written

$$\frac{1-c}{q} = \Psi_I(I/K, 1)$$

and, letting $\beta(\ ) = \Psi_I^{-1}(\cdot, 1)$, we see that the optimal level of investment is an increasing function of K and q:[12]

$$I* = \beta\left(\frac{1-c}{q}\right)K, \quad \text{with} \quad \frac{\partial \beta[(1-c)/q]}{\partial q} = \beta'(\ )\frac{-(1-c)}{q^2} = \frac{1}{\Psi_{II}}\frac{-(1-c)}{q^2} > 0 \tag{7}$$

Finally, we turn to the law of motion for the multiplier. Rearranging equation (5), we obtain

$$r = \frac{\dot{q} + (1-\tau)F_K(\ )}{q} + \Psi_K(\ ) - \delta \tag{8}$$

To interpret this expression, think of an investor who has a choice between two assets: a bond that pays the market rate of interest, r, and "stock certificates," each of which entitles the holder to ownership of one unit of the firm's capital and the corresponding dividends. The right-hand side of this expression gives the rate of return on installed capital if we price it at its shadow value.[13] Equation (8), which requires that the returns on the two assets be the same, can therefore be interpreted as an equilibrium condition, for nobody will hold capital if there is another riskless asset that will yield a higher return.

In fact, the no-arbitrage interpretation of the law of motion for the multipliers can be taken quite literally in the present model, for it turns out that q will indeed correspond to the market valuation of a unit of installed capital. Recall that q is the marginal contribution of an additional unit of capital to the firm's market value; in principle, this need not coincide with the market price, which should reflect the average value. With constant returns to scale in both production and installation, however, "average" q and "marginal" q coincide, as we will presently show, implying that we can indeed interpret q as the market price of a unit of installed capital,[14] equation (8) as a no-arbitrage condition, and the current-value Hamiltonian as the objective function for a manager who seeks to maximize the current market valuation of his firm.

Proposition 3.1. Assume that the installation and production functions (Ψ and F) exhibit constant returns to scale (homogeneity of degree 1) and that the transversality condition

$$lim_{t \to \infty} e^{-rt} q_t x_t = 0$$

holds. Then average q and marginal q coincide (i.e., $V^c(K) = qK$).

Proof. The value of the firm at time s is given by

$$V^c(K_s) = \int_s^\infty e^{-r(t-s)} \left((1-\tau)[F(K_t^*, L_t^*) - wL_t^*] - (1-c)I_t^* \right) dt \qquad (9)$$

where the asterisks indicate the optimal values of the instruments, as characterized earlier, and K_t^* is the optimal path of the capital stock, the solution to

$$\dot{K}_t = \Psi(I_t^*, K_t) - \delta K_t \qquad (K_0 \text{ given})$$

Exploiting the homogeneity of the installation and production functions, we can rewrite (9) in a convenient way. Notice the following:

- Euler's theorem and the equality of the wage and the marginal product of labor imply that current profits will be equal to the product of the stock of capital and its marginal product:

$$F(K, L) = KF_K + LF_L = KF_K + Lw$$
$$\Rightarrow F(K, L) - wL = KF_K \qquad (10)$$

- Similarly, by the linear homogeneity of the installation function, we have

$$\Psi(I, K) = I\Psi_I + K\Psi_K \Rightarrow I\Psi_I = \Psi(I, K) - K\Psi_K$$

Substituting this expression in the condition for the optimal investment level, equation (4), $(1 - c) = q\Psi_I(I, K)$, we have

$$(1-c)I = q[\Psi(I, K) - K\Psi_K] \qquad (11)$$

Substituting (10) and (11) into (9), the value of the firm is given by

$$V^c(K_s) = \int_s^\infty e^{-r(t-s)}\{(1-\tau)KF_K - q[\Psi(I,K) - K\Psi_K]\}\,dt$$

$$= \int_s^\infty e^{-r(t-s)}\{(1-\tau)KF_K - q(\dot{K} + \delta K - K\Psi_K)\}\,dt$$

$$= \int_s^\infty e^{-r(t-s)}\{K[(1-\tau)F_K - q(\delta - \Psi_K)] - q\dot{K}\}\,dt$$

$$= \int_s^\infty e^{-r(t-s)}\{K(rq - \dot{q}) - q\dot{K}\}\,dt$$

where the second equality follows by the law of motion for the capital stock ($\Psi(I, K) = \dot{K} + \delta K$), and the last follows by the transition equation for the costate variables.[15] Observing that

$$\dot{q}K + q\dot{K} = \frac{d(qK)}{dt}$$

we have

$$V^C(K_s) = re^{rs}\int_s^\infty e^{-rt}q_t K_t\,dt - e^{rs}\int_s^\infty e^{-rt}\frac{d(qK)}{dt}\,dt$$

Integrating the second integral by parts, we arrive at

$$V^C(k_s) = re^{rs}\int_s^\infty e^{-rt}q_t K_t\,dt - e^{rs}\left([e^{-rt}q_t K_t]_s^\infty + r\int_s^\infty e^{-rt}q_t K_t\,dt\right)$$

$$= -e^{rs}[e^{-rt}q_t K_t]_s^\infty = -e^{rs}\left(\lim_{t\to\infty} e^{-rt}q_t K_t - e^{-rs}q_s K_s\right) = q_s K_s$$

where the limit vanishes, by the transversality condition. $\qquad\square$

Phase Diagram and Dynamics. Substituting the policy functions (6) and (7) into the transition equations for the state and costate variables,

$$\dot{K}_t = \Psi(I_t^*, K_t) - \delta K_t$$

$$\dot{q}_t = q_t[r + \delta - \Psi_K(I_t^*, K_t)] - (1-\tau)F_K(K_t, L_t^*)$$

we obtain a system of differential equations in (q, K):

$$\dot{K}_t = \Psi\left(\beta\left(\frac{1-c}{qt}\right), 1\right)K_t - \delta K_t \tag{12}$$

$$\dot{q}_t = q_t\left(r + \delta - \Psi_K\left(\beta\left(\frac{1-c}{q_t}\right), 1\right)\right) - (1-\tau)F_K(\Phi(w), 1) \tag{13}$$

where we have once more made use of the homogeneity of $\Psi(\ )$, $F_K(\ )$, and $\Psi_K(\ )$.

Setting $\dot{K} = 0$, the equation of the first phase line is implicitly defined by the condition that gross investment per unit of capital be equal to the rate of depreciation,

$$\Psi\left(\beta\left(\frac{1-c}{q}\right), 1\right) = \delta \tag{14}$$

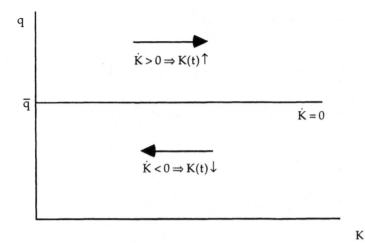

Figure 13.7. The $\dot{K} = 0$ phase line.

Because the left-hand side of this equation is a monotonic function of q, there is at most one value of q that satisfies this equation. We will assume that $\Psi(\ )$ is such that equation (14) has a solution, and we call it $\bar{q}$.[16] This solution value of q corresponds to the lowest "share price" at which it becomes profitable to invest enough to offset depreciation. From (12),

$$\frac{\partial \dot{K}}{\partial q} = \Psi_I(\ ) \frac{\partial \beta}{\partial q} K > 0$$

so K increases over time whenever $q > \bar{q}$, as indicated by the arrows of motion shown in Figure 13.7.

The second phase line ($\dot{q} = 0$) is defined by the condition that the rate of return on installed capital in the absence of capital gains be equal to the interest rate, that is,

$$r = \frac{(1 - \tau) F_K(\Phi(w), 1)}{q} + \Psi_K\left(\beta\left(\frac{1-c}{q}\right), 1\right) - \delta \tag{15}$$

As K does not enter into this equation, and the right-hand side is a decreasing function of q, (15) also yields a horizontal phase line at a constant value of q, say q^*. Differentiating (13) with respect to q,

$$\left.\frac{\partial \dot{q}}{\partial q}\right|_{\dot{q}=0}^{0} = [r + \delta - \Psi_K(\beta(\ ), 1)] - q \Psi_{KI}(\beta(\ ), 1) \frac{\partial \beta}{\partial q}$$

$$= \frac{(1 - \tau) F_K(\Phi(w), 1)}{q} - q \Psi_{KI}(\beta(\ ), 1) \frac{\partial \beta}{\partial q} > 0 \tag{16}$$

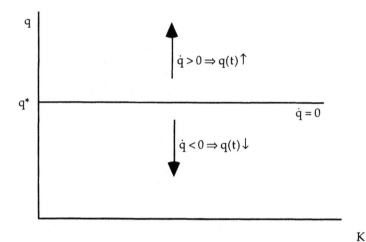

Figure 13.8. The $\dot{q} = 0$ phase line.

(provided that $\Psi_{KI} < 0$), we see that the arrows of motion along the q axis point away from the phase line, as shown in Figure 13.8. Intuitively, if q is "too high" relative to the underlying stream of dividends, people will hold capital only if they expect it to appreciate over time.

Assuming that $q^* > \bar{q}$ (i.e., that the sustainable stationary price of capital induces investment in excess of depreciation), and combining the two phase lines, we obtain the phase diagram shown in Figure 13.9. The system has no steady states, and all paths are explosive in some sense. The closest thing to a saddle path is the horizontal trajectory along the $\dot{q} = 0$ phase line, with constant q and unbounded capital accumulation at a constant rate given by

$$\frac{\dot{K}}{K} = \Psi\left(\beta\left(\frac{1-c}{q^*}\right), 1\right) - \delta \equiv g \tag{17}$$

If $g < r$, the transversality condition

$$\lim_{t \to \infty} e^{-rt} q^* K_t = 0$$

holds, and this is indeed the optimal path, by Theorem 2.3 in Chapter 12. Using (15) and (17) and the homogeneity of the installation function,

$$g - r = \Psi\left(\beta\left(\frac{1-c}{q^*}\right), 1\right) - \delta - \frac{(1-\tau)F_K(\Phi(w), 1)}{q^*} - \Psi_K\left(\beta\left(\frac{1-c}{q^*}\right), 1\right) + \delta$$

$$= \Psi(\beta^*, 1) - \Psi_K(\beta^*, 1) - \frac{(1-\tau)F_K(\Phi(w), 1)}{q^*}$$

$$= \Psi_I(\beta^*, 1)\beta^* - \frac{(1-\tau)F_K(\Phi(w), 1)}{q^*} = \frac{(1-c)\beta^* - (1-\tau)F_K(\Phi(w), 1)}{q^*}$$

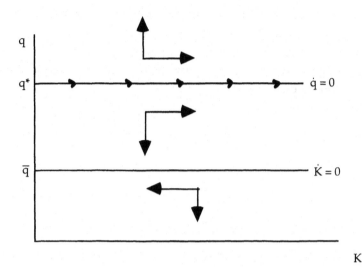

Figure 13.9. Phase diagram.

where the last equality follows from the necessary condition for optimal investment, equation (4). Because $\beta^* = I^*/K$, we have $g < r$ whenever $(1 - c)I^* < (1 - \tau)F_K(\ )K$, that is, whenever the firm pays positive dividends.

In conclusion, given constant returns to scale in both production and installation and constant factor prices, a competitive firm will grow over time at a steady rate while maintaining a constant shadow price of installed capital equal to the present value of the (constant) stream of dividends per unit of capital. It is clear, however, that this situation cannot persist in equilibrium, where the factor demands of firms are unlikely to be made compatible with the factor supply decisions of households at constant input prices. In particular, capital accumulation is unlikely to continue at a constant rate forever. With a constant population, for example, the increase in the stock of capital per worker will drive down the marginal product of capital and increase the equilibrium wage rate. Both changes will reduce the profitability of investment and eventually bring it to a stop.

(b) Capital Accumulation and Share Prices in a Small Open Economy

We will now construct the simplest possible general-equilibrium extension of the investment model developed in the first part of this section. We consider a small open economy with constant population. Wages will now be determined endogenously and will indeed rise with capital accumulation, putting a limit to it. The interest rate, however, will be determined in world capital markets and can therefore be taken as a given constant. Thus, capital will flow in from abroad if domestic investment is sufficiently productive, and we can solve the model for the equilibrium paths of q and K without taking explicitly into account the behavior of households.

Because firms behave exactly as in the preceding section, the Pontryagin conditions obtained earlier still apply:

$$\dot{K}_t = \Psi(I_t^*, K_t) - \delta K_t \tag{1}$$

$$\dot{q}_t = q_t[r + \delta - \Psi_K(I_t^*, K_t)] - (1 - \tau)F_K(K_t, L_t^*) \tag{5}$$

$$I^* = \beta\left(\frac{1-c}{q}\right)K \tag{7}$$

$$F_L(K_t, L_t^*) = w_t \tag{3'}$$

The only thing that changes is that the wage is no longer exogenous. Normalizing the size of the population to 1, we can write the labor-market-clearing condition

$$L_t^* = 1 \tag{18}$$

and interpret equation (3′) as giving the equilibrium wage as a function of (K, L), rather than as the demand for labor as a function of the wage. Aside from this, the model remains the same. Substituting (7) and (18) into (1) and (5), we obtain a system of two differential equations in (K, q):

$$\dot{K}_t = \Psi\left(\beta\left(\frac{1-c}{q_t}\right), 1\right)K_t - \delta k_t \equiv \varphi(q_t, K_t) \tag{19}$$

$$\dot{q}_t = q_t\left(r + \delta - \Psi_K\left(\beta\left(\frac{1-c}{q_t}\right), 1\right)\right) - (1 - \tau)F_K(K, 1) \equiv \phi(q_t, K_t) \tag{20}$$

Equation (19) still yields a horizontal $\dot{K} = 0$ line at the value of q that makes optimal investment equal to depreciation, $\bar{q}$. On the other hand, the $\dot{q} = 0$ phase line is no longer horizontal; it is now defined implicitly by

$$q\left(r + \delta - \Psi_K\left(\beta\left(\frac{1-c}{q}\right), 1\right)\right) = (1 - \tau)F_K(K, 1)$$

It is easy to check that the left-hand side of this expression is an increasing function of q and that the right-hand side decreases with K. Thus, an increase in K lowers the stationary value of q to reflect the declining marginal productivity of capital. The $\dot{q} = 0$ locus is therefore downward-sloping, and under plausible assumptions the system has a steady state. It is still true, however, that $\partial \dot{q}/\partial q|_{\dot{q}=0} > 0$, so the vertical lines of motion point away from the phase line. The phase diagram and arrows of motion are shown in Figure 13.10.

The Jacobian of the system (19)–(20), evaluated at the steady state, is given by[17]

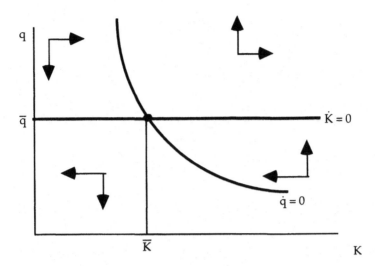

Figure 13.10. Phase diagram.

$$J = \begin{bmatrix} \varphi_K & \varphi_q \\ \phi_k & \phi_q \end{bmatrix} = \begin{bmatrix} 0 & \Psi_I \dfrac{\partial \beta(\ )}{\partial q} K \\ (-(1-\tau)F_{KK}(K,1)) & r \end{bmatrix}$$

Recalling that the product of the system's eigenvalues is equal to the determinant of J,

$$\lambda_1 \lambda_2 = \det J = \Psi_I \frac{\partial \beta(\ )}{\partial q} K(1-\tau)F_{KK}(K,1) < 0$$

we see that the steady state is a saddle point, as suggested by the pattern of the arrows of motion in the phase diagram (Figure 13.10). It is easy to see that the transversality condition for the firm's problem is satisfied along the convergent trajectory (Figure 13.11). Because the Hamiltonian is concave in K, the convergent path is compatible with firm optimization and is therefore the equilibrium trajectory of the system. Given an initial K below the steady state, $\overline{K}$, the market price of installed capital decreases as capital accumulation reduces the marginal return on investment.

Changes in Tax Policy. We will now use the model to analyze the responses of investment and asset prices to a change in tax policy. Imagine that there is an unanticipated and permanent increase in the corporate tax rate τ. The first step is to see how this policy change affects the steady state of the system. Because τ does not enter into the law of motion for the capital stock, given by equation (19), a change in τ leaves the $\dot{K} = 0$ phase line unchanged.

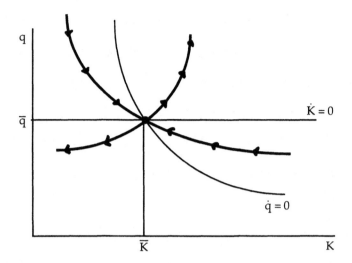

Figure 13.11. Convergent trajectory.

That is, the value of q that induces replacement investment is independent of the tax rate. Taxes, however, do enter into the other transition equation,

$$\dot{q}_t = q_t \left(r + \delta - \Psi_K \left(\beta \left(\frac{1-c}{q_t} \right), 1 \right) \right) - (1-\tau) F_K(K,1) \equiv \phi(q_t, K_t) \qquad (20)$$

and do, therefore, affect the position of the $\dot{q}=0$ locus. Setting $\dot{q}=0$, (20) yields

$$q \left(r + \delta - \Psi_K \left(\beta \left(\frac{1-c}{q} \right), 1 \right) \right) = (1-\tau) F_K(K,1)$$

Because the left-hand side of this expression is an increasing function of q, an increase in τ, which reduces the value of the right-hand side, yields a lower value of q for any given K. Thus, an increase in the corporate tax rate shifts the $\dot{q}=0$ locus down, as, given K, the sustainable price of capital must fall in response to a reduction in after-tax dividends.

In summary, the tax increase reduces the steady-state capital stock, but has no effect on the steady-state value of q. To study the transition, refer to Figure 13.12 and suppose that just prior to the policy change the economy was at the steady state corresponding to the old tax rate, $E(0)$. After the change, the new steady state is $E(1)$, and the equilibrium path of the new system is the stable manifold leading to the new stationary equilibrium SS'. At the time of the change, therefore, the economy must jump from the initial position to the new equilibrium path, and because the initial capital stock is predetermined, the whole burden of the adjustment falls on share prices, which experience a sudden drop. Initially, the higher tax rate reduces

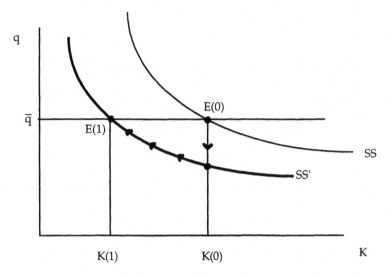

Figure 13.12. Effect of an unanticipated tax increase.

the stream of dividends accruing to the owners of the firm. As the capital stock declines, however, the marginal product of capital rises, and eventually q goes back to the original level, which supports only replacement investment.

Finally, we analyze the response of the system to an anticipated tax increase. At time zero (i.e., today), the government announces that at some time T in the future the corporate tax rate will be permanently increased. Eventually, the economy must reach the same steady state we have just described, but what is the adjustment trajectory? We know that the transition path

(i) asymptotically reaches the new steady state,
(ii) must obey at each instant the laws of motion for the system corresponding to the tax policy currently in effect (i.e., until the policy change actually takes place, the motion of the system must be consistent with the phase diagram for the original tax rate), and
(iii) must be continuous everywhere, except possibly at time zero.[18]

Using these three properties, we can reconstruct the adjustment trajectory by working backward (Figure 13.13). At time T, we must be on the saddle path leading to the new steady state. From 0 to T, we must be on what looks like an explosive trajectory of the old system. This trajectory must take us to the saddle path of the new system at precisely the time of the policy change. Following it backward, we can determine the value of q at time zero and calculate the immediate drop in prices.

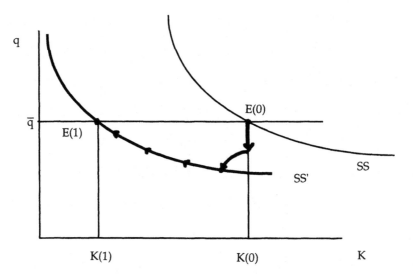

Figure 13.13. Effect of an anticipated tax increase.

4. The Cass-Koopmans Model and Some Applications

Perhaps the most commonly used model in the growth literature, and in much of macroeconomics as well, is that developed by Cass (1965) and Koopmans (1965), building on earlier work by Ramsey (1928). In this section we will develop a version of this model and use it to discuss some techniques that will be useful in policy analysis when we don't have closed-form solutions.

(a) Optimal Consumption for an Infinitely-Lived Household

Imagine a neoclassical economy populated by a number of identical agents (or altruistic families) who live forever. The preferences of each (identical) individual are summarized by a time-separable utility function of the form[19]

$$\int_0^\infty \frac{C_t^{1-\sigma}}{1-\sigma} e^{-\rho t} \, dt \tag{1}$$

where $\sigma > 0$ is the inverse of the intertemporal elasticity of substitution, C is consumption, and ρ is the rate of time discount. At each point in time, the agent faces the flow budget constraint

$$\dot{a}_t = a_t r_t + y_t - C_t \tag{2}$$

That is, the instantaneous change in the stock of real assets held by the household ($\dot{a}_t$) is equal to the difference between the current flow of earnings (interest on existing assets, ar, plus other income, y) and current consumption. The agent chooses time paths of consumption and asset holdings so as to maximize (1) subject to (2), taking as given initial wealth, a_0, and the time paths of interest rates and noninterest income.

To obtain the necessary conditions for a solution to this problem, we will use the maximum principle. The current-value Hamiltonian for the problem is

$$H_t^c = \frac{C_t^{1-\sigma}}{1-\sigma} + \lambda_t(a_t r_t + y_t - C_t)$$

The costate variable, λ_t, can be interpreted as the shadow price of wealth (in utility units), and H_t^c gives the current flow of utility plus the increase in the "utility value" of the stock of assets that results from the current consumption/saving decision. The Pontryagin conditions are given by

$$\frac{\partial H^C}{\partial C} = C^{-\sigma} - \lambda = 0 \tag{3}$$

$$-\frac{\partial H^C}{\partial a} = -\lambda r = \dot{\lambda} - \rho\lambda \tag{4}$$

$$\Rightarrow \frac{\dot{\lambda}}{\lambda} = \rho - r_t \tag{4'}$$

Equation (3) says that the agent balances the benefits of current consumption against its opportunity cost in terms of forgone future consumption. Equation (4) can be interpreted as saying that the total return on savings (r plus the rate of "capital gains," $\dot{\lambda}/\lambda$) is equal to the "interest rate" ρ at which the agent discounts future utility flows; hence, there will be no gain or loss (in utility terms) from holding one more unit of capital rather than consuming it.

Equations (3) and (4) can be consolidated into a single differential equation describing the time path of consumption. Taking logs of both sides of (3) and differentiating with respect to time, we have

$$\ln C = (-1/\sigma)\ln \lambda \Rightarrow \frac{\dot{C}}{C} = -\frac{1}{\sigma}\frac{\dot{\lambda}}{\lambda}$$

and substituting (4') into this last expression,

$$\frac{\dot{C}}{C} = \frac{1}{\sigma}(r - \rho) \tag{5}$$

Along an optimal path, the growth rate of per-capita consumption is equal to the product of the intertemporal elasticity of substitution and the difference between the interest rate and the rate of intertemporal discount. We can think of ρ as measuring the agent's impatience, and of r as the reward for postponing consumption. Hence, less impatient agents will be more willing to defer consumption and will tend to save more, and consequently their consumption will increase at a faster rate. This tendency will be stronger if the elasticity of substitution $(1/\sigma)$ is high (i.e., if future consumption is a good substitute for current consumption).

Equations (2) and (5), together with the initial asset holdings of the household and the transversality condition,

$$\lim_{t\to\infty} a_t e^{-\rho t} \geq 0 \quad \text{and} \quad \lim_{t\to\infty} a_t \lambda_t e^{-\rho t} = 0 \tag{6}$$

characterize the optimal paths of consumption and asset holdings for the household for given paths of income and the interest rate.

Integrating the law of motion for consumption (5) and the flow budget constraint (2), we obtain[20]

$$C_t = C_0 e^{\beta(t)}, \quad \text{with} \quad \beta(t) = \frac{1}{\sigma}\int_0^t (r_s - \rho)\, ds \tag{7}$$

$$a_t e^{-R(t)} = a_0 + \int_0^t e^{-R(s)}(y_s - C_s)\, ds, \quad \text{with} \quad R(t) = \int_0^t r_s\, ds \tag{8}$$

Equation (8) says that the present value (discounted to time zero) of household assets at time t is equal to initial assets plus the discounted value of accumulated savings.

The transversality condition (6) imposes a nonnegativity restriction on the asymptotic value of household assets. In the absence of this constraint, the optimal behavior of the household would involve unbounded borrowing and consumption. To understand the role of this condition, rearrange (8) and take limits as $t \to \infty$ to obtain

$$\lim_{t\to\infty} a_t e^{-\rho t} = \lim_{t\to\infty}\left(a_0 + \int_0^t e^{-R(s)}(y_s - C_s)\, ds\right)e^{R(t)-\rho t} \tag{9}$$

The first part of the transversality condition requires that the limit in this expression be nonnegative. For this inequality to hold, the limit of the term inside the parentheses must be greater than zero, that is,

$$\left(a_0 + \int_0^\infty e^{-R(s)} y_s\, ds\right) - \int_0^\infty e^{-R(s)} C_s\, ds \equiv (a_0 + Y_0) - PVC_0 \geq 0$$

where Y_0 and PVC_0 denote the present value, as of time zero, of the income and consumption streams, respectively. Hence, the first part of (6) requires that the discounted value of consumption not exceed total wealth,

$$PVC_0 \equiv \int_0^\infty e^{-R(s)} C_s\, ds \leq a_0 + Y_0$$

In fact, this expression will hold as an equality, for the utility function we have chosen implies that the agent will never be satiated. Given that $\lambda_t = C_t^{-\sigma}$, we can use (9) and (7) to write the second half of the transversality condition in the form

$$\lim_{t\to\infty} a_t \lambda_t e^{-\rho t} = \lim_{t\to\infty}\left(a_0 + \int_0^t e^{-R(s)}(y_s - C_s)\, ds\right)e^{R(t)-\rho t} C_0^{-\sigma} e^{-\sigma\beta(t)} = 0 \tag{10}$$

Now, notice that

$$-\sigma\beta(t) = -\int_0^t (r_s - \rho)\,ds = pt - R(t)$$

so the exponential terms in (10) cancel out, and we end up with

$$\left(a_0 + \int_0^\infty e^{-R(s)} y_s\,ds\right) - \int_0^\infty e^{-R(s)} C_s\,ds \equiv (a_0 + Y_0) - \mathrm{PV}C_0 = 0 \qquad (11)$$

which can be interpreted as the present-value form of the budget constraint.

Finally, we can solve for the initial consumption level. Substituting (7) into (11),

$$\int_0^\infty e^{-R(s)} C_s\,ds = \int_0^\infty e^{\beta(s)-R(s)} C_0\,ds = a_0 + Y_0$$

from where

$$C_0 = \frac{a_0 + Y_0}{\int_0^\infty e^{\beta(s)-R(s)}\,ds} \qquad (12)$$

Notice that this is a fairly complicated function. Current consumption is a linear function of total wealth, but it depends on the whole time path of income and interest rates. A change in interest rates will affect the propensity to consume out of current wealth (the direction of the effect depends on whether or not $\sigma < 1$), but also the discounted value of the income stream (Y_0).

(b) Equilibrium and Dynamics in a Model with Taxes on Factor Income

So far, we have focused on the behavior of individual agents, taking as given the time path of wages and the interest rate. In equilibrium, the equations derived in the preceding section continue to hold, but they must be evaluated at equilibrium factor prices. We will now derive these and introduce a couple of policy parameters.

We will assume that the technology is described by a constant-returns-to-scale neoclassical production function with labor-augmenting exogenous technical change, that is,

$$Y = F(K, AL) = ALf(Z), \quad \text{where} \quad Z = K/AL \text{ and } f(Z) \equiv F(Z, 1) \qquad (11)$$

$$\frac{\dot{A}}{A} = g \qquad (12)$$

Firms rent capital and labor services in competitive markets at equilibrium prices given by the net marginal products of capital and labor,

$$r = f'(Z) - \delta \qquad (13)$$

$$w = w(Z) = f(Z) = f'(Z)Z \tag{14}$$

where w is the salary per efficiency unit of labor. In equilibrium, factor markets must clear. We will assume that population is constant, and normalize it to 1, and that each agent is endowed with one unit of labor "per instant." Because they have no taste for leisure, agents supply their entire endowment of time inelastically, and labor-market clearing requires $L_t = 1$ for all t.

The government taxes labor and net capital incomes at proportional rates τ_w and τ_r, makes a lump-sum transfer P to each individual, and destines X units of output (per capita) to public consumption. We will assume that the government must run a balanced budget at each point in time and that tax rates, transfers, and public-consumption expenditures per efficiency unit of labor ($x = X/A$ and $p = P/A$) are constant over time. Hence, the government's budget constraint can be written

$$\tau_r[f'(Z) - \delta]Z + \tau_w w(Z) = x + p \tag{15}$$

where the left-hand side is total tax revenue per efficiency unit of labor, and the right-hand side gives total expenditure. Given constant values of $x + p$ and τ_r, equation (15) can be solved for the value of τ_w that will preserve budget balance for each value of Z.

Substituting (13) into (5) (where r should be interpreted as the net-of-tax interest rate), the law of motion for consumption becomes

$$\frac{\dot{C}}{C} = \frac{1}{\sigma}\{(1 - \tau_r)[f'(Z) - \delta] - \rho\} \tag{16}$$

In equilibrium, the representative agent's non-interest income after tax is given by

$$y = (1 - \tau_w)Aw(Z) + Ap \tag{17}$$

and his real asset holdings must be equal to the stock of capital per worker (there are no other assets). Hence $a = K = AZ$, and the flow budget constraint given by equation (2) becomes

$$\dot{K} = (1 - \tau_r)[f'(Z) - \delta]AZ + (1 - \tau_w)Aw(Z) + pA - C$$
$$= A[f'(Z)Z + w(Z)] - \delta K - C - A\{\tau_r[f'(Z) - \delta]Z + \tau_w w(Z) - p\}$$

Using equations (14) and (15), the growth rate of the capital stock is given by

$$\frac{\dot{K}}{K} = \frac{f(Z)}{Z} - \delta - \frac{C/A}{Z} - \frac{x}{Z} \tag{18}$$

In the presence of exogenous technical change, productivity increases without bound, and so does consumption per capita. Hence, the system as it stands will not have a steady state. It is convenient to define a new variable,

$$c = \frac{C}{A} \tag{19}$$

to rewrite the system in a way that will admit a constant solution. Taking logs of (19) and differentiating with respect to time,

$$\frac{\dot{c}}{c} = \frac{\dot{C}}{C} - g$$

Substituting (16) into this expression,

$$\frac{\dot{c}}{c} = \frac{1}{\sigma} \{(1 - \tau_r)[f'(Z) - \delta] - \rho\} - g \tag{20}$$

Similarly, $\dot{Z}/Z = \dot{K}/K - g$, so (18) yields

$$\frac{\dot{Z}}{Z} = \frac{f(Z)}{Z} - \delta - \frac{c}{Z} - \frac{x}{Z} - g$$

from where

$$\dot{Z} = f(Z) - (g + \delta)Z - c - x \tag{21}$$

We have reduced the model to a system of two autonomous equations in Z and c:

$$\dot{c} = \left(\frac{1}{\sigma} \{(1 - \tau_r)[f'(Z) - \delta] - \rho\} - g \right) c_t \equiv \phi(c, Z; \tau_r) \tag{20}$$

$$\dot{Z} = f(Z) - (g + \delta)Z - c - x \equiv \varphi(c, Z) \tag{21}$$

Equation (21) is a resource constraint; it says that the instantaneous change in the capital/labor ratio is equal to net output per efficiency unit of labor (after depreciation, taxes, and current consumption) minus the amount required to equip new efficiency units of labor with the prevailing average stock of capital (gZ). Equation (20) is the condition for the optimal allocation of consumption over time evaluated at equilibrium factor prices.

From (20) and (21) we see that

$$\dot{Z} \geq 0 \Leftrightarrow c \leq f(Z) - (g + \delta)Z - x \equiv c_s(Z) \tag{22}$$

$$\dot{c} \geq 0 \Leftrightarrow f'(Z) \geq \frac{g\sigma + \rho}{1 - \tau_r} + \delta \tag{23}$$

The phase diagram is shown in Figure 13.14, under the assumptions that x is small enough that the two phase lines cross in the positive quadrant and $f(0) = 0, f'(0) = \infty$, and $f'(\infty) = 0$. These conditions are sufficient to guarantee the existence of a unique nontrivial steady state (Z^*, c^*).

The direction of the arrows of motion suggests that the steady state is a saddle point. To verify this, we compute the determinant of the Jacobian matrix of the system evaluated at the steady state:

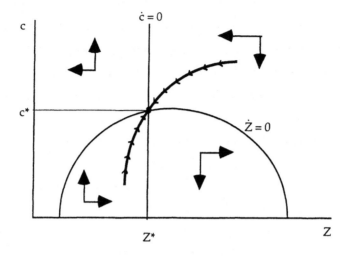

Figure 13.14. Phase diagram and convergent trajectory.

$$J = \begin{bmatrix} \phi_c & \phi_z \\ \varphi_c & \varphi_z \end{bmatrix} = \begin{bmatrix} 0 & \dfrac{c^*}{\sigma}(1-\tau_r)f''(Z^*) \\ -1 & f'(Z^*)-g-\delta \end{bmatrix} \qquad (24)$$

Because

$$\det J = \lambda_1 \lambda_2 = \frac{c^*}{\sigma}(1-\tau_r)f''(Z^*) < 0$$

the eigenvalues of the system are real numbers of opposite signs, and the steady state is indeed a saddle. Using the transversality condition for the household problem, it can be shown that the equilibrium path for this economy is the unique solution to the system (20)–(21) that satisfies the initial condition $Z(0) = Z_0$ (a given constant) and converges to the steady state.

Let $\lambda < 0$ denote the stable root of the system. For future reference, we will compute the eigenvector $\underline{e} = (e_1, e_2)$ associated with this root. As the reader will recall, $\underline{e}$ is "tangent" to the saddle path at the steady state. Normalizing the second component of $\underline{e}$ to 1, the stable eigenvector satisfies $J\underline{e} = \lambda\underline{e}$, and therefore

$$-e_1 + \varphi_z = \lambda$$

Hence, the slope of the stable manifold at the steady state is given by

$$e_1 = \varphi_z - \lambda \qquad (25)$$

where, using (23) and (24),

$$\varphi_z = f'(Z^*) - g - \delta = \frac{g\sigma + \rho}{1 - \tau_r} - g \qquad (26)$$

Note. The equilibrium trajectory of the system approaches a steady state in which c is constant and $C_t = cA_t = cA_0e^{gt}$ grows at a constant rate equal to the rate of technical progress. In such an equilibrium, the utility of a representative individual, given by

$$\int_0^\infty \frac{C_t^{1-\sigma}}{1-\sigma}e^{-\rho t}\,dt = \frac{(A_0c)^{1-\sigma}}{1-\sigma}\int_0^\infty e^{[(1-\sigma)g-\rho]t}\,dt \tag{27}$$

will be unbounded whenever $(1-\sigma)g - \rho > 0$. In fact, in this case the problem cannot be solved by the methods we developed in Chapter 12. To avoid such problems, we will assume that g is low enough that (27) converges, that is,

$$(1-\sigma)g - \rho < 0 \tag{28}$$

We will refer to this assumption as the *boundedness condition.*

Problem 4.1. A social planner maximizes the utility of the representative individual,

$$\int_0^\infty \frac{C_t^{1-\sigma}}{1-\sigma}e^{-\rho t}\,dt$$

subject to the resource constraint

$$\dot{K}_t = F(K_t, A_t) - \delta K_t - C_t, \quad \text{with} \quad \frac{\dot{A}}{A} = g$$

List the necessary conditions for this problem, and show that they reduce to equations (20) and (21) whenever there are no taxes or subsidies. Hence, under these conditions, the competitive equilibrium will be a social optimum.

(c) The Welfare Cost of Factor Taxes

We will now study the effects of a tax change. The specific experiment we will analyze is the following: Suppose the economy is initially at the steady state corresponding to the given values of the different tax parameters. Without previous announcement, the government changes the tax rate on interest income from the initial value τ_{r0} to a new one τ_{r1}, keeping total expenditure per efficiency unit of labor $(x + p)$ constant, and adjusting the tax rate on wage income as needed to preserve budget balance at each point in time.

The first step is to determine the effects of the policy change on the steady-state values of income and consumption, given by the solution of the system

$$\dot{Z} = 0 \Leftrightarrow c = f(Z) - (g+\delta)Z - x \equiv c_s(Z) \tag{22'}$$

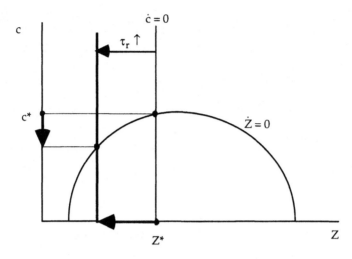

Figure 13.15. Long-run effect of an increase in capital income taxes.

$$\dot{c} = 0 \Leftrightarrow f'(Z) = \frac{g\sigma + \rho}{1 - \tau_r} + \delta \tag{23'}$$

With x fixed, the position of the $\dot{Z} = 0$ phase line does not depend on the value of τ_r. From (23'), however, it is clear that an increase in τ_r reduces the stationary value of the capital/labor ratio and shifts the $\dot{c} = 0$ phase line to the left, as shown in Figure 13.15. The effect on consumption depends on the slope of the $\dot{Z} = 0$ phase line at the steady state, given by

$$c_s'(Z^*) = \varphi_z = f'(Z^*) - (g + \delta) = \frac{g\sigma + \rho}{1 - \tau_r} - g$$

Hence, $c_s'(Z^*) > 0$, provided that $g(1 - \sigma) - \rho < g\tau_r$. The boundedness condition (28) ensures that the left-hand side of this expression is negative. Hence, for any nonnegative tax rate on interest income, an increase in this parameter will reduce steady-state consumption. The reason should be clear from the law of motion for consumption, equation (20): An increase in τ_r discourages accumulation by reducing the net return on savings. In the long run, therefore, the capital stock is a decreasing function of τ_r.

Problem 4.2. Assuming a Cobb-Douglas production function (i.e., $f(Z) = Z^\alpha$), solve for the steady-state savings rate as a function of τ_r and the other parameters of the model.

Welfare comparisons across steady states are straightforward. Because steady-state utility, given by

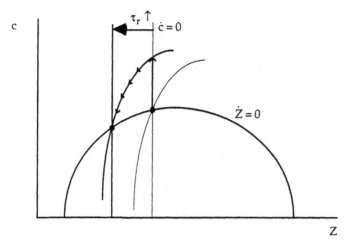

Figure 13.16. Transition path following an increase in capital income taxes.

$$v_s(c^*) = \int_0^\infty \frac{(c^*A_t)^{1-\sigma}}{1-\sigma}e^{-\rho t}\,dt = \frac{(A_0c^*)^{1-\sigma}}{1-\sigma}\int_0^\infty e^{[(1-\sigma)g-\rho]t}\,dt$$

$$= \frac{(A_0c^*)^{1-\sigma}}{1-\sigma}\frac{1}{\rho-(1-\sigma)g} \tag{29}$$

is an increasing function of steady-state consumption, increases in τ_r will reduce welfare.

Once we take into account the transition from one steady state to another, the effect of capital income taxes on welfare is no longer so obvious. To see why, consider the transition path shown in Figure 13.16. The impact effect of the tax change is a jump in consumption that takes us to the new saddle path. The saddle lies above the $\dot{Z}=0$ line and therefore above the initial steady state. The reduction in the incentive to save causes agents to increase their consumption. This behavior, of course, leads to a reduction in the capital stock and, in the long run, to lower consumption as well. During part of the transition, however, consumption exceeds its old steady-state level, and therefore so does the current flow of utility.

To calculate the net welfare change, we have to evaluate the utility function along the whole adjustment path. The idea is simple. We define a function that gives the utility of the representative individual as a function of the policy parameter:

$$V(\tau_r) = \int_0^\infty \frac{C_t(\tau_r)^{1-\sigma}}{1-\sigma}e^{-\rho t}\,dt$$

where $C_t(\tau_r) = A_t c_t(\tau_r)$ is consumption along the equilibrium solution of the system

$$\dot{c} = \left(\frac{1}{\sigma}\{(1 - \tau_r)[f'(Z) - \delta] - \rho\} - g\right)c_t \equiv \phi(c, Z; \tau_r) \tag{20}$$

$$\dot{Z} = f(Z) - (g + \delta)Z - c - x \equiv \varphi(c, Z) \tag{21}$$

corresponding to the given value of the policy parameter. Our objective is to evaluate the derivative $V'(\tau_r)$ starting from a steady state.

The most difficult part of the problem is to characterize the solution function of the system in a way that will be precise enough to allow us to compute derivatives. We begin by observing that we can think of the saddle path of the system as the graph of a *policy function,*

$$c = p(Z, \tau_r)$$

that gives the equilibrium value of consumption as a function of the current value of the state variable Z and the tax parameter. Notice that we have some information on the properties of this function at the steady state. In particular, we know that the slope of the saddle at the steady state is negative and is given by the slope of the stable eigenvector and that a tax increase will shift the saddle path upward. Using subscripts to denote partial derivatives, we have, then,

$$p_z = e_1 = \varphi_z - \lambda = f'(Z^*) - g - \delta - \lambda = \frac{g\sigma + \rho}{1 - \tau_r} - g - \lambda < 0 \quad \text{and} \quad p_\tau > 0 \tag{30}$$

Next, substituting the policy function into the law of motion for Z given in equation (21), the equilibrium dynamics of the system can be characterized by a single differential equation that describes the evolution of the state variable along the stable manifold:

$$\dot{Z} = \varphi(c, Z) = \varphi[p(Z, \tau_r), Z] \equiv \Psi(Z, \tau_r) \tag{31}$$

Notice that this equation has a unique steady state that coincides with the steady-state value of Z for the original system. This steady state is stable; in fact, the "eigenvalue" of this equation is the stable eigenvalue of the full system, because, using (24) and (30),

$$\Psi_Z(Z^*, \tau_r) = \varphi_c p_z + \varphi_z = -p_z + \varphi_z = -\varphi_z + \lambda + \varphi_z = \lambda < 0$$

The solution of (31) yields the equilibrium value of Z as a function of time and the tax parameter $Z_t(\tau_r)$. Finally, substituting this function into the policy function, we obtain the time path of c:

$$c_t(\tau_r) = p[Z_t(\tau_r), \tau_r] \tag{32}$$

To calculate the change in welfare, we need to compute the effect of the policy change on the whole time path of consumption. Using (32), the marginal change in consumption at time t is given by

$$\frac{dc_t(\tau_r)}{d\tau_r} = p_z(\ )\frac{dZ_t(\tau_r)}{d\tau_r} + p_\tau(\ ) \tag{33}$$

Evaluating this expression will be easier than it might seem, at least when we start from a steady state. In that case, $p_z(Z^*, \tau_r)$ and $p_\tau(Z^*, \tau_r)$ are constants of known sign, and $dZ_t(\tau_r)/d\tau_r = Z_\tau(t, \tau_r)$ is, as we shall presently see, easily computed using the method discussed in Section 3(c) of Chapter 9.

To compute $Z_\tau(t, \tau_r)$, notice that the solution function of (31), $Z_t(\tau_r) = Z(t, \tau_r)$, must satisfy identically the original equation,

$$\dot{Z}(t, \tau_r) \equiv \varphi[p(Z(t, \tau_r), \tau_r), Z(t, \tau_r)]$$

Differentiating both sides of this identity with respect to τ_r (and assuming that all the functions involved are sufficiently smooth), we can write

$$\dot{Z}_\tau = \frac{dZ_\tau}{dt} = \varphi_c(\ )[p_z(\ )Z_\tau(\ ) + p_\tau(\ )] + \varphi_z(\ )Z_\tau(\ )$$
$$= [\varphi_c(\ )p_z(\ ) + \varphi_z(\ )]Z_\tau(\ ) + \varphi_c(\ )p_\tau(\ )$$

Hence, Z_τ satisfies a linear differential equation. When we start from a steady state, moreover, the coefficients of this equation are constant, and we can write, using (24) and (30),

$$\dot{Z}_\tau = [-1(\varphi_z - \lambda) + \varphi_z]Z_\tau - p_\tau = \lambda Z_\tau - p_\tau \tag{34}$$

The general solution of this autonomous linear equation is given by

$$Z_\tau(t) = e^{\lambda t}Z_\tau(0) + (1 - e^{\lambda t})Z_\tau(\infty)$$

where, because the capital stock is a predetermined variable, $Z_\tau(0)$, the impact effect of the tax change on the stock of capital is equal to zero. Because $\lambda < 0$, the steady state of this equation is stable, and Z_τ converges asymptotically to its stationary value, given by

$$Z_\tau(\infty) = \frac{p_\tau(Z^*, \tau_r)}{\lambda} < 0 \tag{35}$$

which is also the derivative of the steady-state value of Z with respect to the tax parameter.[21] Hence, the equilibrium time path of Z_τ is given by

$$Z_\tau(t) = (1 - e^{\lambda t})Z_\tau(\infty) = (1 - e^{\lambda t})\frac{p_\tau(Z^*, \tau_r)}{\lambda} \quad \left(= \frac{dZ_t(\tau_r)}{d\tau_r} \right) \tag{36}$$

That is, following a small tax change, Z falls gradually toward its new steady-state value at an exponential rate given by the stable root of the original system.

Substituting (36) into (33), we can now compute the derivative of the time path of consumption with respect to the tax parameter:

$$\frac{dc_t(\tau_r)}{d\tau_r} = p_z \frac{dZ_t(\tau_r)}{d\tau_r} + p_\tau = p_z(1-e^{\lambda t})\frac{p_\tau(Z^*,\tau_r)}{\lambda} + p_\tau = p_\tau\left((1-e^{\lambda t})\frac{p_z}{\lambda}+1\right)$$

(37)

Notice that

$$\frac{dc_0(\tau_r)}{d\tau_r} = p_\tau > 0$$

$$\frac{dc_\infty(\tau_r)}{d\tau_r} = p_\tau\left(\frac{p_z}{\lambda}+1\right) = p_\tau\frac{p_z+\lambda}{\lambda} = \frac{p_\tau\varphi_z}{\lambda} < 0$$

Hence, the derivative of $c_t(\tau_r)$ at time zero – the impact effect of the policy change – is equal to the upward shift in the saddle path, and its long-run effect is the decrease in steady-state consumption. As we already knew, consumption increases at first and then decreases.

Now that we have calculated the change in consumption at each point in time, it remains only to evaluate the derivative of the utility function with respect to the policy parameter. We have

$$V(\tau_r) = \int_0^\infty \frac{C_t(\tau_r)^{1-\sigma}}{1-\sigma}e^{-\rho t}\,dt = \int_0^\infty \frac{(A_t c_t)^{1-\sigma}}{1-\sigma}e^{-\rho t}\,dt$$

$$= \int_0^\infty \frac{(A_0 e^{gt})^{1-\sigma}}{1-\sigma}[c_t(\tau_r)]^{1-\sigma}e^{-\rho t}\,dt = \frac{A_0^{1-\sigma}}{1-\sigma}\int_0^\infty e^{[(1-\sigma)g-\rho]t}c_t(\tau_r)^{1-\sigma}\,dt$$

Differentiating with respect to τ_r, evaluating the result at a steady state, and using (37) and (30), $(p_z + \lambda = \varphi_z)$, we have

$$V'(\tau_r) = A_0^{1-\sigma}\int_0^\infty e^{[(1-\sigma)g-\rho]t}c_t^{-\sigma}\frac{dc_t(\tau_r)}{d\tau_r}\,dt$$

$$= A_0^{1-\sigma}(c^*)^{-\sigma}\int_0^\infty e^{[(1-\sigma)g-\rho]t}p_\tau\left((1-e^{\lambda t})\frac{p_z}{\lambda}+1\right)dt$$

$$= A_0^{1-\sigma}(c^*)^{-\sigma}p_\tau\int_0^\infty e^{[(1-\sigma)g-\rho]t}\left(\frac{p_z+\lambda}{\lambda}-e^{\lambda t}\frac{p_z}{\lambda}\right)dt$$

$$= A_0^{1-\sigma}(c^*)^{-\sigma}p_\tau\left(\int_0^\infty e^{[(1-\sigma)g-\rho]t}\frac{p_z+\lambda}{\lambda}\,dt - \int_0^\infty e^{[(1-\sigma)g-\rho]t}e^{\lambda t}\frac{p_z}{\lambda}\,dt\right)$$

$$= A_0^{1-\sigma}(c^*)^{-\sigma}p_\tau\left(\frac{p_z+\lambda}{\lambda[\rho-(1-\sigma)g]}-\frac{p_z}{\lambda[\rho-(1-\sigma)g-\lambda]}\right)$$

$$= A_0^{1-\sigma}(c^*)^{-\sigma}\frac{p_\tau}{\lambda}\left(\frac{p_z+\lambda}{\rho-(1-\sigma)g}-\frac{p_z}{\rho-(1-\sigma)g-\lambda}\right)$$

To simplify this expression, notice that, using (30), $p_z = (g\sigma+\rho)/(1-\tau_r)-g-\lambda$,

$$\frac{p_z + \lambda}{\rho - (1-\sigma)g} - \frac{p_z}{\rho - (1-\sigma)g - \lambda} = \frac{(p_z + \lambda)[\rho - (1-\sigma)g - \lambda] - p_z[\rho - (1-\sigma)g]}{[\rho - (1-\sigma)g][\rho - (1-\sigma)g - \lambda]}$$

$$= \frac{\lambda[\rho - (1-\sigma)g - \lambda - p_z]}{[\rho - (1-\sigma)g][\rho - (1-\sigma)g - \lambda]} = \lambda \frac{\rho + g\sigma - (g\sigma + \rho)/(1 - \tau_r)}{[\rho - (1-\sigma)g][\rho - (1-\sigma)g - \lambda]}$$

$$= \frac{-\lambda \tau_r (g\sigma + \rho)}{[\rho - (1-\sigma)g][\rho - (1-\sigma)g - \lambda](1 - \tau_r)}$$

Hence,

$$V'(\tau_r) = A_0^{1-\sigma}(c^*)^{-\sigma} p_\tau \frac{-\tau_r(g\sigma + \rho)}{[\rho - (1-\sigma)g][\rho - (1-\sigma)g - \lambda](1 - \tau_r)}$$

Recall that $p_\tau > 0$, $\lambda < 0$, and that $\rho - (1 - \sigma)g > 0$ by the boundedness condition (28). Hence,

$$V'(\tau_r) < 0 \quad \text{iff} \quad \tau_r > 0$$

and it follows that setting τ_r equal to zero is the optimal policy: Increasing tax rates on capital will decrease welfare if the tax rate is positive and increase welfare if the tax rate is negative.

Problem 4.3. One limitation of the approach we have followed is that it assumes that the economy is initially at a steady state. Otherwise the coefficients of the variational equation (the law of motion for Z_t) would change over time, and that would make it difficult to evaluate $V'(\tau_r)$. It is still possible (and in fact much easier) to show that a zero tax on capital income is optimal by showing that when $\tau_r = 0$, the equilibrium path for the economy solves a closely related planning problem.

Consider, in particular, the problem faced by a social planner, similar to the one described in Problem 2.1, who maximizes the utility of the representative agent subject to the standard resource constraint and the additional restriction that he must "throw away" an amount of output equal to xA at each point in time. Write the planning problem, derive the necessary conditions for an optimum, and verify that they reduce to equations (20) and (21) when $\tau_r = 0$ in this system.

Numerical Solution: The Time-Elimination Method

The analysis of the preceding section can be used to provide (for specific parameter values and functional forms) a quantitative estimate of the welfare gain associated with a marginal policy change. To evaluate the impact of "large" policy changes, however, we need to resort to numerical methods.

In principle, this poses no problem. We saw in Chapter 11 that there are computer packages that can be used to solve systems of differential equations numerically. The model we have developed in this section, however, presents one additional difficulty that we did not have to face in the case of the Solow model. The problem is that in the present model the boundary conditions that allow us to pick the particular solution of interest are not in a very convenient form. Whereas in the Solow model we had a single predetermined variable, in the Cass-Koopmans model consumption is a "free variable" without a predetermined initial value. As we have seen, the equilibrium trajectory of the model is the only time path that, from the given initial value of Z, approaches the steady state as $t \to \infty$. Computer programs, however, do not let us specify asymptotic boundary conditions directly, so we need to find an indirect way to impose them.

One possibility is to use a trial-and-error "shooting" method. Given Z_0, we can guess an initial value of c, have the computer solve the problem, and follow the solution path. If this path "explodes," we adjust the original guess accordingly and repeat the experiment until we find a solution that seems to approach the steady state. This method is quite time-consuming and not very accurate.

Fortunately, there is a better alternative, sometimes called the time-elimination method.[22] The idea is to eliminate time from the original laws of motion to obtain a differential equation with Z (rather than t) as the independent variable. The solutions of this single equation will correspond to the solution trajectories of the original system in the (c, Z) phase plane (rather than to the time paths of c and Z). Using an easy-to-impose boundary condition (instead of an asymptotic one), we can find the policy function that gives the equilibrium value of c as a function of Z (i.e., find the saddle path). Then we proceed as before: Substituting the policy function into the law of motion for Z, we eliminate c and obtain a single differential equation in Z (with time as the independent variable) that can be solved for the equilibrium time path of Z. Finally, evaluating the policy function along this trajectory, we obtain the equilibrium time path of c. We can then evaluate the utility function along the solution path to determine the change in welfare.

The procedure, in somewhat greater detail, is as follows. We seek the "saddle-path" solution of a system of the form

$$\frac{dc}{dt} = \phi(c, Z) \tag{38}$$

$$\frac{dZ}{dt} = \varphi(c, Z) \tag{39}$$

"Dividing" (38) by (39), we "eliminate time" from the system and obtain a single differential equation,

$$\frac{dc}{dZ} = \frac{dc/dt}{dZ/dt} = \frac{\phi(c,Z)}{\varphi(c,Z)} \equiv \psi(c,Z) \tag{40}$$

whose solution gives us the value of c as a function of Z, $c(Z)$. Intuitively, $\psi(c, Z)$ gives us, for each point in the phase plane (c, Z), the slope of the solution trajectory of (38)–(39) that goes through this point. Solving (40) means using this information to reconstruct the family of curves in the phase plane that correspond to the solution trajectories of the original system. We are interested in one specific member of this family of curves, the one that goes through the steady state (c^*, Z^*). To select it, we only have to impose the boundary condition $c(Z^*) = c^*$.

Before we can ask the computer to solve (40), we have to deal with one minor complication. Notice that the function $\psi(c, Z)$ is not well defined at the steady state, for $\psi(c^*, Z^*) = 0/0$. We know, however, that the slope of the saddle path at the steady state is equal to the slope of the eigenvector associated with the stable (negative) eigenvalue of the linearized system, e_{i1}/e_{i2}. Hence, we need to extend (40) and define

$$\psi(c,Z) = e_{i1}/e_{i2}, \quad \text{when} \quad (c,Z) = (c^*, Z^*)$$
$$= \frac{\phi(c,Z)}{\varphi(c,Z)} \quad \text{otherwise} \tag{41}$$

Now we can ask the computer to solve the problem

$$\frac{dc}{dZ} = \psi(c,Z), \quad \text{together with the boundary condition } c(Z^*) = c^*$$

for the policy function $c = c(Z)$. Substituting this function into the law of motion for Z, we obtain an ordinary differential equation in Z,

$$\dot{Z} = \varphi[c(Z), Z] \tag{42}$$

which describes the motion of the predetermined state variable along the saddle path. Solving equation (42) together with the natural initial condition on Z ($Z(0) = Z_0$ given), we obtain the solution path of Z, $Z(t)$, which can then be substituted into the policy function to recover the time path of c,

$$c(t) = c[Z(t)]$$

To apply the method, of course, we need to choose explicit functional forms and assign specific values to the parameters. Under the assumption that the production function is Cobb-Douglas ($Y = K^\alpha (AL)^{1-\alpha}$), equations (20) and (21) become

$$\dot{c} = \frac{c}{\sigma}\{(1 - \tau_r)[\alpha Z^{\alpha-1} - \delta] - \rho\} - gc \equiv \phi(c, Z) \tag{43}$$

$$\dot{Z} = Z^{\alpha} - (\delta + g)Z - x - c \equiv \varphi(c, Z) \tag{44}$$

and the steady-state values of c and Z are given by

$$\dot{c} = 0 \Leftrightarrow Z^* = \left(\frac{g\sigma + \rho}{\alpha(1 - \tau_r)} + \frac{\delta}{\alpha} \right)^{1/(\alpha-1)}$$

$$\dot{Z} = 0 \Leftrightarrow c^* = Z^{*\alpha} - (\delta + g)Z^* - x$$

The next subsection contains a *Mathematica* program that carries out the computations we have just outlined. After solving the system numerically for two different values of the parameters, τ_{r_0} and τ_{r_1}, we evaluate the utility function of the representative individual in each case and compute the welfare gain in consumption-equivalent terms. For this, we will use a procedure that is useful to evaluate the welfare effects of discrete policy changes. We introduce an auxiliary parameter, η, in the utility function, defined now by

$$V(\tau_r, \eta) = \int_0^{\infty} \frac{[(1 + \eta)C_t(\tau_r)]^{1-\sigma}}{1 - \sigma} e^{-\rho t} dt$$

Notice that an increase in η has the same effect on welfare as a proportional increase in consumption in all periods. Hence, the solution $\eta(\tau_{r_0}, \tau_{r_1})$ of the equation

$$V(\tau_{r_0}, \eta) = V(\tau_{r_1}, 0)$$

can be interpreted as the proportional variation in consumption equivalent, in terms of welfare, to a change in policy from τ_{r_0} to τ_{r_1}.

Numerical Solution and Welfare Analysis with Mathematica

We will now write a *Mathematica* program to compute numerically the solution trajectory of the growth model developed earlier and analyze the welfare impact of change in a tax parameter.

We begin by assigning values to the parameters and computing the steady-state values of Z (**zss0** and **zss1**) and c for two different values of the tax rate on interest income (**tr0** and **tr1**). (Note: A semicolon after a command suppresses "feedback output"; without it, the computer prints out the value of the calculation or the value assigned to the parameter. Hence, *Out[11]=* *5.33363* gives the value of **zss0**, for example. When you are writing a program, it may be a good idea not to use semicolons, so that you can check the results of intermediate calculations).

```
In[1]:=
  sigma=2; alfa=0.33; d=0.02; ro=0.03;
  g=0.02; tr0=0.20; tr1=0.15;
```

```
In[10]:=
  zss0=((d/alfa)+(((g*sigma)+ro)/(alfa*
    (1-tr0))))∧(1/(alfa-1))
  x=0.10*(zss0∧alfa);
  css0=(zss0∧alfa)-(d+g)*zss0-x;
  zss1=((d/alfa)+(((g*sigma)+ro)/(alfa*
    (1-tr1))))∧(1/(alfa-1))
  css1=(zss1∧alfa)-(d+g)*zss1-x;
Out[11]=
  5.33363
Out[14]=
  5.73887
```

We set x (public consumption per efficiency unit of labor) to 10% of steady-state output per efficiency unit of labor to make sure that the assigned value is not "unreasonable."

The next step is to define the laws of motion for consumption (given by the function **fc[ ]**) and the capital/labor ratio (**fz[ ]**). Differentiating these functions with respect to z and c, and evaluating the resulting function at the steady state, we construct the Jacobian of the linearized system (**Jac**) and compute its eigenvalues and eigenvectors.

```
In[16]:=
  fc[c_,z_,tr_]:=((alfa*(z∧(alfa-1))-d)*(1-
    tr1)-ro)*(c/sigma)-g*c;
  fz[c_,z_,tr_]:=(z∧alfa)-(d+g)*z-x-c;
```

To calculate the Jacobian, we first define an "empty matrix," **Jac**, and give names to its entries. To compute each one of them, we proceed in two steps. First, we compute the symbolic derivative of the law of motion with respect to each of the state variables (using the command **D[function[ ]**, with respect to]) and then evaluate this expression at the steady state.

```
In[19]:=
  Jac={{jcc,jcz},{jzc,jzz}}
Out[20]=
  {{jcc, jcz},  {jzc, jzz}}
In[21]:=
  jcc0=D[fc[c,z,tr1],c];
  jcc=jcc0/.{c->css1,z->zss1};
  jcz0=D[fc[c,z,tr1],z];
  jcz=jcz0/.{c->css1,z->zss1};
  jzc0=D[fz[c,z,tr1],c];
  jzc=jzc0/.{c->css1,z->zss1};
```

```
jzz0=D[fz[c,z,tr1],z];
jzz=jzz0/.{c->css1,z->zss1};
```

Finally, we ask the computer to print out the Jacobian in matrix form and to compute its eigenvalues and eigenvectors. (Notice that the first entry of the Jacobian should be zero, it is almost zero, but not quite). The function **N[ ]** asks the computer to use the numerical values of the entries of the Jacobian matrix to perform the actual calculations.

```
In[29]:=
  MatrixForm[Jac]
  {l1,l2}=Eigenvalues[N[Jac]]
  {eig1,eig2}=Eigenvectors[N[Jac]]
Out[30]//MatrixForm=
  3.46945 10⁻¹⁸   -0.00699145
  -1               0.0623529
Out[31]=
  {0.120414, -0.0580615}
Out[32]=
  {{0.0579639, -0.998319}, {-0.119551, -0.992828}}
```

As expected, one of the eigenvalues of the system is positive, and the other negative. The eigenvector corresponding to the stable root is the second one. Because of the way we have arranged the elements of the Jacobian (with $\dot{c}$ on top of $\dot{Z}$, and the derivatives with respect to c before the ones with respect to Z), the c coordinate of the eigenvalue is listed first, and the slope of the saddle path at the steady state (in a Cartesian plane with c in the vertical axis) is given by the ratio of the first to the second coordinate of the second eigenvector. To select each coordinate of this vector, we use subindices inside double brackets, as shown next.

The following statement defines the function we have called $\psi(c, Z)$ in the text (**gc[ ]** in the program). Next, we solve the differential equation

$$\frac{dc}{dz} = \psi(c, Z)$$

together with the boundary condition $c(Z^*) = c^*$, to obtain the "policy function" or saddle path, denoted by **pfc[z]**, and we ask the computer to plot it, together with the two steady-state values of c.

```
In[33]:=
gc[c_,z_]:=If[z==zss1,eig2[[1]]/eig2[[2]],
   fc[c,z,tr1]/fz[c,z,tr1]];
```

```
In[35]:=
  AccuracyGoal->Infinity;
  MaxSteps->700;
  mxz=Max[zss0,zss1]*1.1;
  mnz=Min[zss0,zss1]*0.9;
In[40]:=
  sol=NDSolve[{c'[z]== gc[c[z],z],c[zss1]==
    css1},c,{z,mnz,mxz}]
Out[40]=
  {{c -> InterpolatingFunction[{4.80027,
    6.31276}, <>]}}
In[41]:=
  pfc[z_]:=c[z]/.sol
  Plot[{pfc[z],css0,css1},{z,zss0,zss1}]
Out[42]=
  -Graphics-
```

To find the time path of z, we substitute the policy function into the law of motion for z and solve the resulting "ordinary" differential equation in z, together with an initial condition that specifies that we start from the value of z corresponding to the "old steady state." We call the solution function **cpath[t]**. Next, we recover the time path of z, denoted by **zpath[t]**, and plot both time paths (for time = 0–100) to visualize the adjustment path from one steady state to the next.

```
In[43]:=
  solz=NDSolve[{z'[t]==
    fz[pfc[z[t]],z[t],tr1],z[0]== zss0},z,{t,0,100}]
Out[44]=
  {{z -> InterpolatingFunction[{0., 100.}, <>]}}
```

```
In[45]:=
  zpath[t_]:=z[t]/.solz
  cpath[t_]:=pfc[zpath[t]]
  Plot[{zpath[t],zss0,zss1},{t,0,100}]
  Plot[{cpath[t],css0,css1},{t,0,100}]
Out[47]=
  -Graphics-
```

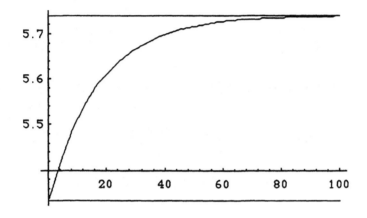

```
Out[48]=
  -Graphics-
```

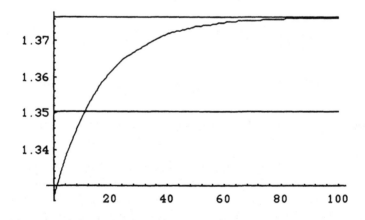

The last step is to calculate the welfare change due to the policy experiment. We begin by defining a function, **Vs[ ]**, that gives us steady-state utility. (It does not matter that we get a negative number; we should with $\sigma > 1$. What matters is that marginal utility is positive.) Then, **Vs[css0]** gives the equilibrium utility that would have obtained if the economy had stayed in the path corresponding to the old policy, and **Vs[css1]** the utility we obtain if we have moved immediately to the new steady state.

```
In[49]:=
  Vs[c_]:=(c^(1-sigma))/((1-sigma)*(ro-
    (1-sigma)*g));
  Vs[css0]
  Vs[css1]
Out[52]=
  -14.8107
Out[53]=
  -14.5278
```

As expected, steady-state utility is higher with the lower tax rate on interest income. We still have to take into account the transition, however. To approximate total utility, we integrate numerically the utility function (evaluated along the new equilibrium path) between $t = 0$ and $t = 100$ and add to it the discounted value of the average of **Vs[css1]** and **Vs[ ]** evaluated at the consumption level obtained at the end of the 100 years. (We cannot integrate the utility function numerically over an infinite time path, but after 100 years we will be very close to the new steady state, and with a reasonable discount rate it does not matter much what happens that far in the future anyway.) As expected, utility is higher under the new policy, even when we take into account the transition.

```
In[54]:=
  V1=(1/(1-sigma))*NIntegrate[Evaluate[(cpath[t]^
    (1-sigma))*Exp[((1-sigma)*g-ro)*t]],{t,0,100}]
    +Exp[-100*ro]*(1/2)*(Vs[css1]+Vs[cpath[100]]))
Out[57]=
  {{-14.6773}}
```

Finally, we compute the consumption equivalent of the welfare gain from the change in tax policy, denoted by eta, which turns out to be around 0.9%.

```
In[59]:=
  eta=(1/(1-sigma))*Log[V1*(1-sigma)*(ro-(1-
    sigma)*g)]-Log[css0]
Out[59]=
  {{0.00904369}}
```

5. Problems

In this section we will ask the reader to work through a number of problems that make use of the material developed in this chapter.

(a) An Efficiency-Wage Model

Efficiency-wage theories are attempts to explain the emergence of wage rigidities that can generate unemployment in an equilibrium context. The key feature of these models is that labor productivity depends partly on the wage rate. Knowing this, firms set wages and employment levels so as to maximize profits. Because increasing wages increases output, firms may find it optimal to pay a wage that is above the market-clearing level. Hence, unemployment may arise in equilibrium.

The difficult part, of course, is explaining why the wage can have an impact on productivity. Several mechanisms have been explored in the literature. Some of them rely on informational asymmetries, others on turnover costs, and the rest on sociological factors. The following problem develops a "shirking" model of efficiency wages due to Shapiro and Stiglitz (1984). In this model, labor productivity depends on the level of (costly) effort exerted by workers, a variable that can be monitored only imperfectly by firms. In particular, workers who do not exert effort will be caught, with some probability $q < 1$. Hence, all workers who are not caught shirking will have to be paid the same wage. If detected shirkers go unpunished, pay will be independent of effort, and workers will find it optimal to shirk.

One possible way to avoid this outcome is by firing detected shirkers. Notice, however, that this will work only as long as job losses are costly. To achieve this, a firm can resort to raising its wage offer above the market-clearing level, so that its workers will value their jobs and will not shirk. If all firms are alike, all of them will act in the same way, and the equilibrium wage will be above the market-clearing level. Hence, the equilibrium involves unemployment, which serves as a discipline device: Workers who are fired will not be rehired immediately and therefore will incur a cost. To prevent this, they refrain from shirking. This unemployment, moreover, is involuntary: Workers would prefer to work even at a wage below the current one, but firms will not reduce wages and hire them because at the lower wage, workers' promises not to shirk would not be credible.

Consider an economy populated by N identical and risk-neutral workers, with a separable instantaneous utility function $U(w, E) = w - E$, where w is the instantaneous wage rate (assumed to be constant over time), and E the level of effort. Workers maximize

$$\int_0^\infty (w - E)e^{-\rho t}dt \qquad (1)$$

by choice of their effort level. For simplicity we will assume that effort can take only one of two values: zero and some positive level x. If a worker shirks (exerts zero effort), there is an instantaneous probability $q \in \varepsilon\ (0, 1)$ that he will be caught and fired. Whether or not he shirks, there is a probability b of separation due to other factors. Unemployed workers are paid unemployment benefits at a rate w_u and are assumed to find new jobs with instantaneous probability a, which we will take as given for now. The parameters b and q are taken as exogenous in the model and are constant over time.

Problem 5.1.

(i) Let $V_e(s)$ be the expected lifetime utility of an employed worker who shirks, $V_e(n)$ the expected lifetime utility of an employed non-shirker, and V_u the expected lifetime utility of an unemployed worker. Write the valuation equations defining $V_e(s)$ and $V_e(n)$, and explain their meaning.

Hint: If it helps, consider the analogous discrete-time problem with periods of length h and take the limit as $h \to 0$.

(ii) An employed worker will choose not to shirk if $V_e(n) \geq V_e(s)$. Show that this "no-shirking" condition implies that $V_e(s) \geq V_u$, so that workers prefer to be employed, and use it to solve for the minimum wage w_m at which workers will find it optimal not to shirk. What factors determine w_m?

Let L be the effective labor force employed by the representative firm, defined as the number of non-shirkers it employs (for simplicity, we assume that workers who shirk contribute nothing to output). The firm maximizes profit $f(L) - wL$ subject to the constraint that (because it can detect shirking only imperfectly and ex post) it must pay the same wage to all workers. To produce at all, then, the firm needs to set a wage that will induce its workers not to shirk. It follows that in equilibrium, $w \geq w_m$, so workers do not shirk, and the expected lifetime utility of an employed worker, V_e, is given by $V_e(n)$.

To maximize profit, the representative firm will pay the minimum non-shirking wage w_m and then set the level of employment so that the marginal product of labor will be equal to the wage. Hence, the firm's labor demand function is implicitly given by

$$f'(L) = w_m \tag{8}$$

Problem 5.2. We will now characterize a stationary equilibrium of the model.

(i) Let w_u be the unemployment benefit. Derive the expected lifetime utility of an unemployed worker, V_u, as a function of w_u and the value of an employed worker, V_e.

(ii) Using the expressions for V_e ($= V_e(n)$) and V_u derived earlier, solve for V_e and V_u as functions of a and the parameters of the model. Rewrite the no-shirking condition, replacing V_u by its equilibrium value. How do unemployment benefits and the probability of finding employment affect the minimum non-shirking wage?

(iii) Let N be the given labor supply. In a steady-state equilibrium, the flow into unemployment and the flow out of it must be equal. Using this condition, solve for the probability of finding employment, a, as a function of b, L, and N, and substitute the result into the no-shirking condition. Interpret the resulting condition. The equilibrium wage and unemployment levels are determined by the intersection of the non-shirking condition and the labor demand schedule $f'(L) = w_m$. Draw both functions in the (w, L) plane, and verify that the equilibrium involves an excess supply of labor.

(b) Unemployment in a Matching Model

This section is based on Pissarides (1990). Consider an economy in which workers and firms look for each other. The population is a continuum of measure 1 of homogeneous, risk-neutral workers. Let u be the unemployment rate (the fraction of the population that is unemployed), and v the vacancy rate (the number of open but vacant jobs available as a fraction of the population). The instantaneous rate of matching between unemployed workers and vacant jobs is given by a matching function of the form

$$x = u^\alpha v^{1-\alpha} = v\theta^{-\alpha}, \quad \text{where } \theta = v/u \tag{1}$$

Hence, the instantaneous probability that an open vacancy will be filled is given by

$$\frac{x}{v} = \theta^{-\alpha} \tag{2}$$

and the instantaneous probability that an unemployed worker will find a job is

$$\frac{x}{u} = \theta^{1-\alpha} \tag{3}$$

Each firm consists of a single job that can be either filled or vacant. When a worker and a firm meet, they form a match. An occupied job produces a flow of output at a constant rate y and has an instantaneous probability s of disappearing because of "structural shocks." An open vacancy has a cost c per instant of time. An unemployed worker earns unemployment benefits at an instantaneous rate b. The wage, w, is set through a bargaining process described later.

Problem 5.3.

(i) Derive an expression that describes the evolution of the unemployment rate over time as a function of the instantaneous rate of separation (s) and the probability of finding employment, $\theta^{1-\alpha}$. Set $\dot{u} = 0$ and solve for the steady-state unemployment rate as a function of the rates of flow into and out of unemployment (assuming θ is constant).

(ii) Let V be the value of a vacancy, J the value of a filled job, and r the discount rate. Taking into account the relevant transition probabilities and the flows of costs and benefits for an occupied job and a vacant job, write the valuation equations for these two assets, J and V. Explain their meaning. Using the two asset-valuation equations (subtract one from the other), derive an expression for $J - V$ as a function of y, c, w, r, and the relevant transition probabilities.

(iii) Let E and U be the "values" of an employed worker and an unemployed worker, respectively. Write and explain the corresponding asset-valuation equations, and derive an expression for $E - U$.

Wages are set through a centralized bargaining process between a union and firms. The equilibrium wage is the one given by the Nash bargaining solution, that is, the value of w that solves

$$\max_{w}(E - U)^{\beta}(J - V)^{1-\beta}$$

where β is an index of workers' bargaining power.

Problem 5.4. Using the results of Problem 5.3, solve for the equilibrium wage.

Problem 5.5. In equilibrium, new firms enter until the value of a vacant job drops to zero, that is, until $V = 0$.

(i) Using the valuation equations for V and J, show that

$$\frac{y - w}{r + s} = c\theta^{\alpha} \tag{13}$$

(ii) Using equation (13), along with the expression for the equilibrium wage obtained in Problem 5.4 and the formula for the steady-state unemployment rate obtained in Problem 5.3, solve for the equilibrium values of u, w, and θ. Draw a diagram in the (u, θ) plane illustrating the determination of equilibrium.

(iii) What are the effects on the equilibrium unemployment rate of an increase in workers' bargaining power (β), an increase in the unemployment benefit (b), and an increase in the probability of structural shocks (s)?

(c) The Behavior of the Savings Rate in the Cass-Koopmans Model

Consider an infinitely-lived dynasty whose size increases over time at a constant rate n. The objective function is now of the form

$$\int_{0}^{\infty} \frac{C^{1-\sigma}}{1-\sigma} L_{t} e^{-\rho t} dt \tag{1}$$

where $L_{t} = L_{0}e^{nt}$ is the size of the dynasty, and C is per-capita consumption. The household maximizes (1) subject to the budget constraint

$$\dot{K} = K^\alpha (AL)^{1-\alpha} - LC - \delta K \tag{2}$$

where δ is the rate of depreciation, and A grows at a constant rate g. We will assume that the condition

$$g\sigma + \rho > n + g \tag{3}$$

holds, in order to guarantee the boundedness of (1). Following the same procedure as before, it is easy to show that the necessary conditions for household optimization yield the following system of equations:

$$\frac{\dot{c}}{c} = \frac{1}{\sigma} \{\alpha Z^{\alpha-1} - (\rho + \delta)\} - g \tag{4}$$

$$\frac{\dot{Z}}{Z} = Z^{\alpha-1} - \frac{c}{Z} - (n + g + \delta) \tag{5}$$

where $c = C/A$ and $Z = K/AL$.

Following Barro and Sala-i-Martin (1995), we will analyze the behavior of the savings rate in this model. The first step will be to rewrite it in terms of the consumption ratio and the interest factor.

Problem 5.6. Define the variables

$$X = \frac{c}{Z^\alpha} \quad \text{and} \quad R = Z^{\alpha-1} \tag{6}$$

(i) Rewrite the system (4)–(5) in terms of X and R. Solve for the steady-state values of X and Z.
(ii) Construct the log-linearization of the system obtained in (i). Compute the eigenvalues of its coefficient matrix, and show that the steady state is a saddle point. Compute the eigenvector associated with the negative eigenvalue, and relate the slope of the saddle path to the size of the negative eigenvalue. Does anything look familiar?

Problem 5.7. Next, we will consider a special case. Assume that the following restriction on the parameters holds:

$$\rho + \delta + g\sigma = \alpha\sigma(\delta + n + g) \tag{12}$$

Construct the phase diagram for the system, and compute its negative eigenvalue and the associated eigenvector.

Problem 5.8. Let us now return to the general case of the model. Define the parameter μ by

$$1 + \mu \equiv \frac{\rho + \delta + g\sigma}{\alpha\sigma(\delta + n + g)} \tag{18}$$

and notice that if $\mu = 0$, then we are in Problem 5.7. Write the negative eigenvalue of the system and the corresponding eigenvector as functions of μ, and relate the slope of the saddle path to the sign of μ. Draw the phase diagram of the system for $\mu > 0$ and $\mu < 0$.

(d) Productive Government Spending in a Model of Endogenous Growth

As in Barro (1990), a representative agent with the usual preferences

$$\int_0^\infty \frac{c^{1-\sigma}}{1-\sigma} e^{-\rho t} dt \tag{1}$$

is endowed with an initial amount of capital k_0 and with a production technology of the form

$$y = k^{1-\alpha} p^\alpha \qquad (0 < \alpha < 1) \tag{2}$$

where p are government-provided public services. Income is taxed at a constant proportional rate τ. Assuming there is no depreciation, the agent's flow budget constraint can be written

$$\dot{k} = (1-\tau) k^{1-\alpha} p^\alpha - c \tag{3}$$

Problem 5.9.

(i) Taking as given the time path of p, write the necessary conditions for a solution to the consumer's problem. Derive an equation describing the evolution of consumption over time.

(ii) Assume that $p = \tau y$, that is, that all tax revenue is used to finance public services. Substituting the production function in this last expression, solve for p as a function of τ and k. Substitute the result into the flow budget constraint and the transition equation for consumption. Call γ the growth rate of consumption, $\dot{c}/c$, obtained from this step, and let β be the coefficient of k in the law of motion for k (both γ and β are functions of τ and other parameters). Notice that β can be written as a simple function of γ.

(iii) Observe that consumption grows at a constant exponential rate. Hence, once we determine its initial level, we have characterized its entire path. Integrating the flow budget constraint and imposing the transversality condition, we obtain

$$k_0 = \int_0^\infty c_t e^{-\beta t} dt \tag{9}$$

Use this expression to solve for c_0.

Problem 5.10.

(i) Substitute the equilibrium path of consumption into the agent's objective function to obtain utility as a function of γ (or τ), $U(\gamma)$. What condition must we impose in order to guarantee that utility is bounded? Assume this condition holds.

(ii) Find the optimal value of τ.

Hint: Differentiate $U(\gamma)$. Can you sign the derivative? Proceed accordingly. Does the result "look right"? Why or why not?

(e) A Model of Endogenous R&D

Let us return to the product-variety model developed in Section 5(a) of Chapter 8. As the reader will recall, we had a two-sector economy in which labor was used to produce differentiated components that were then assembled into a homogeneous consumption good. In equilibrium, final output was proportional to ("variable") employment in goods production and was an increasing function of the existing number of component varieties. More specifically, output per worker was given by the (reduced-form) per-capita production function

$$Q = n^{(1-\alpha)/\alpha} \frac{L_x}{L} \tag{1}$$

where L_x was total employment in goods production, L was the (constant) size of the labor force, and the parameter $\alpha < 1$ measured the substitutability of components in the production of final goods.

The previous version of the model was static. The equilibrium number of component varieties was determined by a zero-profit condition and a fixed entry cost: Firms entered the market until their operating profits were just enough to pay for the cost of a given amount of labor required to set up production. Let us now consider a dynamic version of the same economy in which the entry charge must be paid only once and will be interpreted as the cost of designing a new intermediate product.[23] More specifically, we will assume that blueprints for new components are developed in an R&D sector that takes labor as an input. We will also assume that the amount of labor required to produce a blueprint for a new product is inversely proportional to the stock of accumulated technical knowledge, summarized by the number of preexisting varieties of intermediate products.[24] Hence, the rate of introduction of new products is given by

$$\frac{\dot{n}}{n} = aL_n = a(L - L_x) \tag{2}$$

where na is the number of blueprints that can be produced with a unit of labor, and $L_n = (L - L_x)$ is total employment in R&D. Equation (2) then implies that (if the fraction of the labor force employed in R&D remains constant over time, as will indeed be the case in equilibrium) output growth is driven exclusively by the increase in efficiency that results from the introduction of new product varieties. The rate of technical progress will be determined by the level of employment in research activities. Our main task in this section will be to show how this variable is determined.

Problem 5.11. It will be convenient in what follows to work with the growth rate of per-capita consumption, denoted by g. Assuming that the level of employment in goods production, L_x, remains constant over time, solve for L_x as a function of g. Keep an eye out for scale effects, that is, reasons why a larger economy (as measured by the size of the labor force, L) may be able to grow faster.

Our task is to determine how available resources are allocated between goods production and research. Loosely speaking, the equilibrium level of R&D employment (i.e., the value of g) will be determined by the requirement that the savings decisions of consumers must be compatible with the investment decisions of producers. Because researchers must be paid out of somebody's savings, factor prices must adjust so that in equilibrium consumers will be willing to finance the volume of investment that producers want to undertake.

We will characterize the equilibrium value of g in terms of two relations between the interest rate and the growth rate, one implied by consumer intertemporal maximization, and the other summarizing equilibrium in the production sector of the economy. Let us start with the consumption side of the model. For a change, households will be assumed to maximize the function

$$U = \int_0^\infty \frac{C_t^{1-\sigma}}{1-\sigma} e^{-\rho t} dt \tag{4}$$

where C_t is consumption of the composite final good at time t, subject to a standard budget constraint. The solution of this problem yields the familiar condition for the optimal allocation of consumption over time,

$$g = \frac{\dot{C}}{C} = \frac{r-\rho}{\sigma}$$
$$\Rightarrow r = \rho + \sigma g \tag{SS}$$

where r is the market interest rate. Hence, consumer optimization implies a positive relationship between the growth rate of consumption and the interest rate (both at the individual level and at the aggregate level): High growth implies deferral of consumption to liberate resources for investment, and a high interest rate is required in order to provide consumers the incentive to postpone consumption. To put it in a slightly different way, if we want consumers to accept a steeper consumption profile (i.e., to trade more current consumption for future consumption), we have to give them an incentive, by making future consumption relatively cheaper.

To derive the second relation between g and r, we need to think about the incentive to do research. It will be convenient to imagine that innovation takes place in a separate R&D sector. Agents, in their role as suppliers of labor, have a choice between taking a "regular job" in industry at wage w or entering the research sector. In the latter case, we will think of them as starting a new company for each blueprint they produce and selling its shares at the going price (v) in the stock market. In equilibrium, employment levels and earnings in the research and production sectors must be such that, at the margin, no agent has an incentive to switch sectors. If research and manufacturing are to coexist in equilibrium, net earnings per unit of labor must be the same in the two sectors. That is, the equilibrium wage (w) must be equal to the market value of the blueprints that can be produced with one unit of labor (an):

$$w = anv \tag{5}$$

Finally, the stock-market value of a firm in the intermediate sector will be equal to the discounted value of its flow of future profits, that is,

$$v_t = \int_t^\infty \pi_{t+s} e^{-rs} ds \tag{6}$$

Problem 5.12. Using equations (5) and (6), together with the expressions for equilibrium factor prices derived in Section 5(a) of Chapter 8, derive the following relationship between the interest rate and the growth rate of consumption:

$$r = \frac{a(1-\alpha)}{\alpha} L - \frac{\alpha}{1-\alpha} g \tag{II}$$

Interpret this condition.

Putting the II and SS schedules together, we can solve for the equilibrium values of the interest rate and the rate of growth. When the interest rate is low, R&D investment is attractive, but saving is not, whereas at high interest rates we have the opposite situation. Savings and investment decisions will be compatible only at the interest rate given by the intersection of the SS and II schedules, as shown in Figure 13.17.

Problem 5.13. Solve for the equilibrium values of g and the fraction of the labor force employed in research (L_n/L). Discuss the determinants of the equilibrium growth rate and the impact on both variables of an increase in the size of the labor force, L. Consider also the effects of "merging" two isolated economies into a larger, integrated one. Does anything change? To

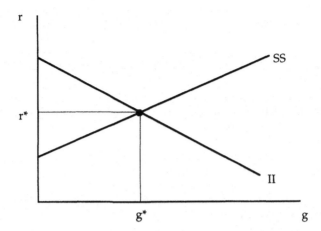

Figure 13.17. Determination of the equilibrium growth rate.

what extent is the answer to this question sensitive to the details of the specification we have used?

Bibliography

Abel, A. 1981. Dynamic Effects of Permanent and Temporary Tax Policies in a *q* Model of Investment. *Journal of Monetary Economics* 9:353–73.

Abel, A., and Blanchard, O. 1983. An Intertemporal Equilibrium Model of Saving and Investment. *Econometrica* 51(3):675–92.

Arrow, K. 1968. Applications of Control Theory to Economic Growth. In: *Mathematics of Decision Sciences, Part 2*, pp. 85–119. Providence, RI: American Mathematical Society.

Barro, R. 1990. Government Spending in a Simple Model of Endogenous Growth. *Journal of Political Economy* 98(5, pt.2):S103–25.

Barro, R., and Sala-i-Martin, X. 1995. *Economic Growth*. New York: McGraw-Hill.

Blanchard, O., and Fischer, S. 1989. *Lectures on Macroeconomics*. Massachusetts Institute of Technology Press.

Cass, D. 1965. Optimum Growth in an Aggregative Model of Capital Accumulation. *Review of Economic Studies* 32:223–40.

Diamond, P. 1982. Aggregate Demand Management in Search Equilibrium. *Journal of Political Economy* 90:881–94.

Diamond, P. 1984. *A Search-Equilibrium Approach to the Micro Foundations of Macroeconomics*. Massachusetts Institute of Technology Press.

Diamond, P., and Fudenberg, D. 1989. Rational Expectations Business Cycles in Search Equilibrium. *Journal of Political Economy* 97(3):606–20.

Grossman, G., and Helpman, E. 1991. *Innovation and Growth in the Global Economy*. Massachusetts Institute of Technology Press.

Hayashi, F. 1982. Tobin's Marginal *q* and Average *q*: A Neoclassical Interpretation. *Econometrica* 50(1):213–24.

Koopmans, T. 1965. On the Concept of Optimal Economic Growth. In: *The Econometric Approach to Development Planning*. Chicago: Rand McNally.

Lucas, R. 1990. Supply-Side Economics: An Analytical Review. *Oxford Economic Papers* 42:293–316.

Mortensen, D. 1986. Job Search and Labor Market Analysis. In: *Handbook of Labor Economics*, vol. 2, ed. O. Ashenfelter and R. Layard, pp. 849–919. Amsterdam: Elsevier.

Mulligan, C., and Sala-i-Martin, X. 1991. A Note on the Time-Elimination Method for Solving Recursive Dynamic Economic Models. NBER technical working paper no. 116.

Pissarides, C. 1990. *Equilibrium Unemployment Theory*. London: Blackwell.

Ramsey, F. 1928. A Mathematical Theory of Savings. *Economic Journal* 38:543–59.

Romer, P. 1990. Endogenous Technological Change. *Journal of Political Economy* (October):S71–S102.

Sargent, T. 1987. *Dynamic Macroeconomic Theory*. Harvard University Press.

Shapiro, C., and Stiglitz, J. 1989. Equilibrium Unemployment as a Worker Discipline Device. *American Economic Review* 74:433–44.

Simmons, G. 1972. *Differential Equations with Applications and Historical Notes*. New York: McGraw-Hill.

Stokey, N., and Lucas, R. 1989. *Recursive Methods in Economic Dynamics*. Harvard University Press.

Tobin, J. 1969. A General Equilibrium Approach to Monetary Theory. *Journal of Money, Credit and Banking* 1:15–29.

Wolfram, S. 1991. *Mathematica. A System for Doing Mathematics by Computer*. Reading, MA: Addison-Wesley.

Notes

1　It can be shown that, given our assumptions, it will never be optimal for the worker to quit a job he has already accepted in order to look for a better job. To avoid complications, we will simply assume that he is not allowed to quit.

2　As usual, this expression can be interpreted directly as an asset-valuation equation. "Being unemployed" can be thought of as an asset that will pay a direct instantaneous dividend, b, and with instantaneous probability λ will yield the opportunity for a capital gain $W_a(x) - W_r$, because of a change in status from unemployed to employed. Because this change will take place only when the offer is accepted, we take the maximum of this quantity and zero, and because x is not known, we compute the expectation. Finally, the expected return of the asset, measured as a fraction of its value, must be equal to the discount rate ρ.

3　In computing H_x^*, we make use of the following result, known as Leibniz's rule. Consider the function $(x) = \int_{a(x)}^{b(x)} F(x, s)\, ds$. Then

$$\phi'(x) = \int_{a(x)}^{b(x)} \frac{\partial F(x,s)}{\partial x} ds + b'(x)F[x, b(x)] - a'(x)F[x, a(x)]$$

4　This assumption captures the fact that in a modern economy, people seldom consume much of what they produce. Hence, consumption requires trade, as well as production.

5　The aggregate employment rate determines the probability of an "employed" worker finding a trading partner during the period, given by $b(e)$: The larger e is, the faster the agent can expect to be able to eat. Thus, the value of being employed increases with e. The value of being unemployed depends partly on the value of being employed and therefore is also a function of e.

6　From (8)

$$c^* = \frac{b(e)y + a\int_{\underline{c}}^{c^*} c\, dG(c)}{\rho + b(e) + aG(c^*)} \le \frac{b(e)y + ac^* G(c^*)}{\rho + b(e) + aG(c^*)}$$

and, rearranging terms,

$$c* \leq \frac{b(e)y}{\rho + b(e)} \leq y$$

When $e = 0$, $c*$ is the solution to,

$$c* \leq \frac{a\int_{\underline{c}}^{c*} c\, dG(c)}{\rho + aG(c*)} \tag{1}$$

Now, $c* = 0$ is clearly one solution of this equation. To show that there are no others, notice that

$$\frac{a\int_{\underline{c}}^{c*} c\, dG(c)}{\rho + aG(c*)} \leq \phi(c*) \equiv \frac{ac*G(c*)}{\rho + aG(c*)}$$

and observe that $\phi(c*) = 0$ for $c* \leq \underline{c}$ and

$$\phi(c*) = \frac{c*}{1 + (\rho/aG(c*))} < c* \quad \text{for} \quad c* > \underline{c}$$

Thus, the functions on the two sides of (1) cross only at the origin.

7 Other paths will eventually violate either some feasibility condition or the transversality condition for the agent's optimization problem, which requires $c*$ to be bounded and strictly positive for $b(e) > 0$.

8 That is, if net output is given by $G(K, L)$, and δ is the rate of depreciation of the capital stock, we have $F(K, L) = G(K, L) + (1 - \delta)K$.

9 Observe that the steady-state capital stock depends only on the production function and the rate of time preference, not at all on the form of the period utility function.

10 We are assuming that the firm does not use debt financing. In the absence of taxes, however, the capital structure of the firm makes no difference. To see this, assume the firm borrows b dollars at time zero, uses them to increase the current dividend, and then pays interest forever on the debt. The net gain to shareholders from the operation is $b - br/r = 0$. When we consider taxes, things get messier.

Notice also that there is no guarantee that dividends will be positive every period. Negative dividends would amount to stockholders buying additional shares of the firm in order to provide funds to carry out current investment plans.

11 Recall that the first partial derivatives of a linearly homogeneous function $g(x, y)$ are homogeneous of degree 0. This implies that the partial derivative is a function only of the ratio of the two arguments, e.g., $g_x(x, y) = g_x(x/y, 1)$. For a discussion of homogeneous functions, see Section 5 of Chapter 4.

12 In a well-known paper, Tobin (1969) anticipated this result. He conjectured that the firm should continue to invest as long as what he called "marginal q" (the marginal contribution of a unit of installed capital to the market value of the firm, divided by the price of investment goods) exceeded 1.

13 This rate of return is the sum of two terms: The first is the ratio of capital gains and the current dividend, net of taxes, to the asset's price, and the second captures depreciation and the fact that installed capital reduces installation costs.

14 Another useful aspect of this result is that it makes the theory potentially testable, as the firm's market value is an observable quantity, and K can, in principle, be computed from accounting information.

15 That is, $\dot{q} = q[r + \delta - \Psi_K(I, K)] - (1-u)F_K(K, L) \Rightarrow (1-u)F_K(K, L) - q(\delta - \Psi_K) = rq - \dot{q}$.

16 This requires only that $\Psi(\beta(\cdot), 1) > \delta$ as $q \to \infty$, which seems reasonable enough.

17 First, note that

$$\varphi_K(\ ) = \Psi\left(\beta\left(\frac{1-c}{q}\right), 1\right) - \delta = 0$$

at a steady state, and

$$\phi_q = \frac{\partial \dot{q}}{\partial q} = [r + \delta - \Psi_K(\beta(\ ), 1)] - q\Psi_{KI}(\beta(\ ), 1))\frac{\partial \beta}{\partial q} = [r + \delta - \Psi_{KI}(\beta(\ ), 1)] + \Psi_{KI}(\beta(\ ), 1))\frac{1-c}{q\Psi_{II}}$$

where the second equality makes use of the fact that $\partial \beta[(1 - c)/q]/\partial q = -(1 - c)/\Psi_{II}q^2$. Next, because the installation function is homogeneous of degree 1, its partials are homogeneous of degree 0, implying

$$\Psi_{II} I + \Psi_{IK} K = 0 \Rightarrow (\Psi_{IK}/\Psi_{II}) = -(I/K)$$

Thus, we can write

$$\frac{\partial \dot{q}}{\partial q} = [r + \delta - \Psi_K(\beta(\ ), 1)] - \frac{(1-c)I}{qK} = [r + \delta - \Psi_K(\beta(\ ), 1)] - \Psi_I(I/K, 1)\frac{I}{K}$$

making use of the condition for optimal investment, $(1 - c)/q = \Psi_I(I/K, 1)$. By the linear homogeneity of the installation function, $\Psi_I(I/K, 1)(I/K) + \Psi_K(I/K, 1) = \Psi(I/K, 1)$, implying

$$\left.\frac{\partial \dot{q}}{\partial q}\right|_{ss} = r + \delta - \Psi(\beta(\ ), 1) = r$$

because at a steady state, $\Psi(\beta(\ ), 1) = \delta$.

18 With perfect foresight, future discontinuities in the time path of asset prices are incompatible with equilibrium. If such discontinuities existed, agents would anticipate very large capital gains or losses at some point in the future and would act now to take advantage of them or avoid them. These actions, however, would bring the price change to the present. At the time of the announcement, for example, agents will know that stock prices will fall at time T, if not sooner. To avoid such losses, agents will dump their stock holdings now, causing an immediate drop in the "stock price" q. Thus the trajectory must be continuous, except possibly at the time of the announcement, when surprised stockholders will be unable to avoid unexpected capital losses. See Section 2 in Chapter 11.

19 The reader should check that this is the only functional form for which the model has a balanced growth path when there is technical progress.

20 See Section 5 of Chapter 9 for a discussion of the solution of nonautonomous linear differential equations.

21 Observe that this steady-state derivative can also be computed using (22′) and (23′). The resulting expression can be used, together with (35), to solve for $p_\tau(Z^*, \tau_r)$.

22 See Mulligan and Sala-i-Martin (1991), Simmons (1972), or some other textbook on differential equations.

23 This section draws on the work of Grossman and Helpman (1991) and Romer (1990).

24 Without this assumption, innovation would eventually stop with a fixed population, because of a market-saturation effect; as we know, profit is a decreasing function of the number of existing competitors.

Appendix

Solutions to the Problems

Chapter 1

Problem 2.2. Prove the following equivalence (X is the universal set):

$$P \subseteq Q \Leftrightarrow (\sim P) \cup Q = X$$

$$X = (\sim P) \cup Q \Leftrightarrow X \cap (\sim Q) = [(\sim P) \cup Q] \cap (\sim Q)$$

$$\Leftrightarrow X \sim Q = [(\sim P) \cap (\sim Q)] \cup [Q \cap (\sim Q)]$$

$$\Leftrightarrow X \sim Q = \sim(P \cup Q) \cup \varnothing$$

$$\Leftrightarrow \sim Q = \sim(P \cup Q)$$

$$\Leftrightarrow Q = P \cup Q \Leftrightarrow P \subseteq Q \qquad \square$$

See Figure A.1.1.

Problem 2.3. Prove the second of De Morgan's laws: Let $\mathbb{A} = \{A_i; i \in I\}$ be a family of sets in X. Then $\sim(\cap_i A_i) = \cup_i(\sim A_i)$.

$$x \in \sim(\cap_i A_i) \Leftrightarrow x \notin \cap_i A_i \Leftrightarrow \neg \, (\forall i \in I, \, x \in A_i)$$

$$\Leftrightarrow \exists i \in I \text{ s.th. } x \notin A_i \Leftrightarrow \exists i \in I \text{ s.th. } x \in \sim A_i$$

$$\Leftrightarrow x \in \cup_i(\sim A_i) \qquad \square$$

Problem 2.8. The following modification of the induction principle is sometimes useful: Let P be a property that natural numbers (or positive integers) may or may not have. If

(i) $P(0)$ holds and
(ii) if P holds for all integers $k = 0, 1, \ldots, n - 1$, then it also holds for n.

Then P holds for all natural numbers. Prove this result.

Let S be the set of nonnegative integers for which $P(n)$ is false. Assume that S is not empty. Then, by the well-ordering principle, this set has a smallest element we will call n_0. By (i), $n_0 \neq 0$, and because n_0 is the least element of S, $P(k)$ holds for all $0 \leq k < n_0$. By (ii), $P(n_0)$ is true, implying that $n_0 \notin S$, a contradiction. $\square$

Problem 2.9. Use the modified induction principle to prove that any integer larger than 1 is either a prime number (it has no integer divisors other than 1) or the product of prime numbers.

The result holds trivially for 2. Assume that it holds for every integer k where $1 < k < n$. We have to show that this implies that the result holds also for every k

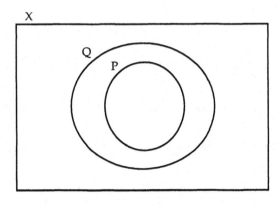

Figure A1.1.

with $1 < k < n + 1$. There are two possibilities: (i) n is prime, in which case there is no problem, or (ii) n is not a prime number. But if n is not prime, it has a divisor $d < n$, and we have $n = dc$, where c is also between 1 and n. Hence, $1 < c, d < n$, so both numbers are, by hypothesis, either prime or products of primes, and therefore so is $n = dc$. $\quad\square$

Problem 4.4. Explain why inclusion works only in one direction in the second part of Theorem 4.3, but in both directions in the first part.

(i) Give an example in which $\cap_{i \in I} f(A_i)$ is strictly larger than $f(\cap_{i \in I} A_i)$.
(ii) Prove that if f is one-to-one, then $\cap_{i \in I} f(A_i) = f(\cap_{i \in I} A_i)$.

The proof that $f(\cap_{i \in I} A_i) \subseteq \cap_{i \in I} f(A_i)$ goes as follows:

$$y \in f(\cap_{i \in I} A_i) \Leftrightarrow \exists\, x \in \cap_{i \in I} A_i \text{ s.th. } f(x) = y$$
$$\Rightarrow \forall\, i \in I, \exists\, x_i \in A_i \text{ s.th. } f(x_i) = y \quad (\text{e.g., } x_i = x\ \forall\, i)$$
$$\Leftrightarrow \forall\, i \in I,\, y \in f(A_i) \Leftrightarrow y \in \cap_{i \in I} f(A_i)$$

The second implication is the only one that goes only in one direction. If there exists some x that belongs to all the A_i's simultaneously and has a certain property, it must be true that each A_i contains at least one element (the given x) with the desired property. But the converse is not necessarily true: Even if each A_i contains an appropriate x_i, it does not follow that any of these points will lie in the intersection of the A_i's, as each of the x_i's may be different, and it is possible that for each i we might have $x_i \in A_i \cap (\sim A_k)$ for some $k \neq i$.

However, if the function is one-to-one, then y has a unique inverse image, implying that all the x_i's are the same. In this case, the converse implication also holds.

The proof of $f^{-1}(\cap_{i \in I} B_i) = \cap_{i \in I} f^{-1}(B_i)$, on the other hand, is of the form

$$x \in f^{-1}(\cap_{i \in I} B_i) \Leftrightarrow f(x) \in \cap_{i \in I} B_i$$
$$\Leftrightarrow \forall\, i \in I,\, f(x) \in B_i$$
$$\Leftrightarrow \forall\, i \in I,\, x \in f^{-1}(B_i)$$
$$\Leftrightarrow x \in \cap_{i \in I} f^{-1}(B_i)$$

In this case, all the implications go in both directions. In particular, because $f(x)$ is a single element (which is not generally the case for inverse images), if $f(x) \in B_i$ for all i, then $f(x) \in \cap_{i \in I} B_i$, and vice versa.

Consider the function $f(x) = x^2$, defined on the interval $[-1, 1]$. (See Fig. A.1.1.2 on p. 661). Then we have

$$f([-1, 0] \cap [0, 1]) = f(0) = 0 \quad \text{and} \quad f([-1, 0]) \cap f([0, 1]) = [0, 1] \quad\square$$

Problem 4.5. Given a function $f : X \longrightarrow Y$, two subsets of X, A_1 and A_2, and two subsets of Y, B_1 and B_2, show that

(i) $f^{-1}(\sim B_1) = \sim f^{-1}(B_1)$,
(ii) $f^{-1}(B_1 \sim B_2) = f^{-1}(B_1) \sim f^{-1}(B_2)$, and
(iii) if f is bijective, then

$$f(\sim A_1) = \sim f(A_1) \quad \text{and} \quad f(A_1 \sim A_2) = f(A_1) \sim f(A_2)$$

What can we say if f is not bijective?

(i) $x \in f^{-1}(\sim B_1) \Leftrightarrow f(x) \notin B_1 \Leftrightarrow x \notin f^{-1}(B_1) \Leftrightarrow x \in \sim f^{-1}(B_1)$
(ii) $f^{-1}(B_1 \sim B_2) = f^{-1}[B_1 \cap (\sim B_2)] = f^{-1}(B_1) \cap f^{-1}(\sim B_2) = f^{-1}(B_1) \cap [\sim f^{-1}(B_2)] = f^{-1}(B_1) \sim f^{-1}(B_2)$
(iii) $y \in f(\sim A_1) \Leftrightarrow \exists\, x_0 \in (\sim A_1) \text{ s.th. } y = f(x_0) \text{ (if } f \text{ is one-to-one)} \Rightarrow y \in \sim f(A_1)$

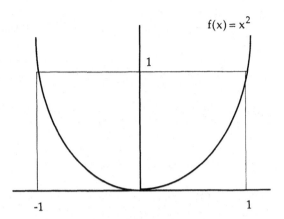

$$f(x) = x^2$$

1

-1   1

Figure A1.2.

If f is one-to-one, x_0 is the only inverse image of y (i.e., there is no other x with y as an image). Hence, for every $x \in A_1, f(x) \neq y$, and it follows that $y \in {\sim}f(A_1)$. Notice, however, that the argument requires that f be one-to-one. If that were not so, y could have several preimages, and then it could be an element of both $f({\sim}A_1)$ and $f(A_1)$.

$$y \in {\sim}f(A_1) \Leftrightarrow \nexists\ x \in A_1 \text{ s.th. } y = f(x) \text{ (if } f \text{ is "onto")}$$
$$\Rightarrow \exists\ x \in {\sim}A_1 \text{ s.th. } y = f(x) \Leftrightarrow y \in f({\sim}A_1)$$

If f is onto, each y will have some preimage; if it does not belong to A_1, it will lie in ${\sim}A_1$, implying that $y \in f({\sim}A_1)$. If y is not onto, however, y may have no preimage.

If f is bijective, we have, using Problem 4.4 and condition (iii),

$$f(A_1 \sim A_2) = f[A_1 \cap ({\sim}A_2)] = f(A_1) \cap f({\sim}A_2)$$
$$= f(A_1) \cap ({\sim}f(A_2)) = f(A_1) \sim f(A_2)$$

If f is not bijective, we have $f(A_1) \cap f({\sim}A_2) \supseteq f[A_1 \cap ({\sim}A_2)] = f(A_1 \sim A_2)$. □

Problem 4.6. Let f be a function from X to Y, with A a subset of X, and B a subset of Y. Then

$$f[f^{-1}(B)] \subseteq B \quad \text{and} \quad A \subseteq f^{-1}[f(A)]$$

When are the two sets not equal to each other?

Some elements of B may not have preimages. Hence, when we "go" to $f^{-1}(B)$ and "come back," we may lose some elements. Similarly, there are elements of $f(A)$ that may have preimages outside A; hence, when we go to $f(A)$ and come back, we may pick up some additional elements. □

Problem 5.3. Let "$*$" be a law of internal composition on X that satisfies the associative property and is endowed with an identity element. Prove that if x and y have symmetric elements x^s and y^s, then the symmetric element of $x * y$ is $y^s * x^s$.

$$(x * y) * (y^s * x^s) = x * (y * y^s) * x^s = x * e * x^s = x * x^s = e$$ □

Problem 5.4. Let X be an arbitrary set, and $\{G, *\}$ a group. Show that the set of functions of X into G, endowed with the operation defined by the composition of images, that is,

$$\forall\, x \in X,\ (f * g)(x) = f(x) * g(x)$$

is a group.

Given that $f(x)$ and $g(x)$ are elements of G, so is their composition, implying that the set of functions from X to G is closed under "$*$." For the same reason, this set inherits the associative property from $\{G, *\}$. The identity element is the function given by $e(x) = e$ for all x in G, and the symmetric element of a function f is the function f^s, defined by $f^s(x) = [f(x)]^s$ for each x in G. $\qquad\square$

Problem 5.5. Show that the intersection of subgroups of G is a subgroup of G.

Let $\{G_i; G_i \subseteq G, i \in I\}$ be a family of subsets of G such that $\{G_i, *\}$ is a group for each i. Because "$*$" is associative in G, it will remain so for any subset of G, including $\cap_i G_i$. By assumption, each $\{G_i, *\}$ is a subgroup, implying that the identity element e belongs to each and all the G_i's and therefore to $\cap_i G_i$. Next, because each G_i is closed under "$*$," if we take two points, x and y, in $\cap_i G_i$ we will have $x * y \in G_i$ for all i, implying that $x * y \in \cap_i G_i$. Finally, every x in G_i has a symmetric element x^s in G_i; thus, if $x \in G_i$ for all i, so does x^s, and it is therefore true that every x in $\cap_i G_i$ has a symmetric element also in $\cap_i G_i$. $\qquad\square$

Problem 5.9. Prove Theorem 5.8: Let V be a vector space over a field F, and let S be a nonempty subset of V. Then S is a vector subspace of V if and only if

$$\forall\, \alpha, \beta \in F \text{ and } \forall\, x, y \in S, \text{ we have } \alpha x + \beta y \in S \tag{1}$$

Clearly, S inherits those manipulative properties of vector addition and multiplication by a scalar that hold in all V. With $\alpha = \beta = 1$, equation (1) implies that S is closed under vector addition, and also (with $\beta = 0$) that the product of any element of S and a scalar is an element of S. With $\alpha = \beta = 0$, we have $0x + 0y = \underline{0} + \underline{0} = \underline{0} \in S$, and $\alpha = -1$ and $\beta = 0$ imply $(-1)x + 0y = -x + \underline{0} = -x \in S$, from which we conclude that the symmetric element of x is also in S. $\qquad\square$

Problem 6.1. Show that there is no rational number $a = p/q$ (where p and q are integers with no common divisors) such that $a^2 = 2$.

Assume this is not true, that is, $p^2/q^2 = 2$. Then $p^2 = 2q^2$, and p^2 is an even number. Because the square of an odd integer is odd [if $z = (2n + 1)$, then $z^2 = 4n^2 + 2n + 1 = 2(2n^2 + n) + 1$, also odd], it must be that p itself is even, and therefore we have $p = 2k$ for some integer k. But then

$$p^2 = 2q^2 \Rightarrow 4k^2 = 2q^2 \Rightarrow q^2 = 2k^2$$

and q is also even. Hence, 2 is a common divisor of p and q, which contradicts our assumptions. $\qquad\square$

Problem 6.5. Let $x, y,$ and z be arbitrary real numbers. Using the order axioms, show that the following statements are true:

(i) $(x \le y \text{ and } x' \le y') \Rightarrow x + x' \le y + y'$
(ii) $x \le y \Rightarrow -y \le -x$

(i) $x \le y \Rightarrow x + x' \le y + x'$, and $x' \le y' \Rightarrow x' + y \le y' + y$, from where $x + x' \le y + x' \le y' + y$.
(ii) Add $-x - y$ to both sides. $\qquad\square$

Problem 6.11. Prove Theorem 6.10: The set $\mathbb{N}$ of the natural numbers is not bounded above (i.e., for any $x \in \mathbb{R}$, there exists a natural number n such that $n > x$).

If the result is false, there exists a real number x that is an upper bound of $\mathbb{N}$. Then, by the supremum property, $\mathbb{N}$ has a supremum, u. Because u is the least upper bound of $\mathbb{N}$, $u - 1$ is not an upper bound, and there exists a positive integer k such that $k > u - 1$. Therefore, $u < k + 1$, but because $k + 1$ is a positive integer, this contradicts the fact that u is an upper bound of $\mathbb{N}$. □

Problem 6.13. Let A and B be nonempty sets of real numbers, both of them bounded above, and let C be the set

$$C = \{c = a + b;\ a \in A,\ b \in B\}$$

Show that C has a supremum that is given by

$$\sup C = \sup A + \sup B$$

Let $a^* = \sup A$ and $b^* = \sup B$. For each $c \in C$, we have $c = a + b$, where $a \in A$ and $b \in B$. Because $a \leq a^*$ and $b \leq b^*$, we have

$$\forall c \in C,\ c = a + b \leq a^* + b^* \tag{1}$$

implying that $a^* + b^*$ is an upper bound of C. Hence C is bounded above, and by the supremum property it has a supremum we will call c^*, with the property that $c^* \leq a^* + b^*$. It remains to prove the reverse inequality to show that $c^* = b^* + a^*$.

Fix an arbitrary $\varepsilon > 0$. Because no number smaller than the supremum is an upper bound, there exist numbers $a \in A$ and $b \in B$ such that

$$a > a^* - \varepsilon \quad \text{and} \quad b > b^* - \varepsilon$$

Adding these inequalities,

$$a^* + b^* - 2\varepsilon < a + b = c \leq c^*$$

and given that this must hold for any $\varepsilon > 0$, we conclude that $a^* + b^* \leq c^*$ by Theorem 2.4. □

Problem 6.14. Show that a nonempty set S of real numbers is an interval if and only if whenever x and y are in S, any real number z such that $x < z < y$ lies also in S.

The first part is obvious by the definition of interval. Conversely, let S be a set with the desired property, and define

$a = \inf S$ (or $a = -\infty$ if S is not bounded below),
$b = \sup S$ (or $b = \infty^*$ if S is not bounded above).

We will show that $(a, b) \subseteq S \subseteq [a, b]$, where we interpret (a, b) as the empty set if $a = b$. Clearly, if this chain of inclusions can be established, S can only be an interval.

First, notice that $S \subseteq [a, b]$ follows by the definition of a and b. It remains to show that $(a, b) \subseteq S$. For this, let z be an arbitrary point in (a, b). Then $z > a$, and by the definition of a there exists a point x in S with $x < z$ (otherwise z would be a lower bound for S, and a could not be the infimum). Similarly, $z < b$, and this implies that there exists a point y in S with $y > z$. Hence we have $x < z < y$, where both x and y are in S, and it follows that $z \in S$. Because z was an arbitrary point of (a, b), we have shown that $(a, b) \subseteq S$. □

Problem 6.15. Show that if $a \geq 0$, then $|x| \leq a$ if and only if $-a \leq x \leq a$.

Because $|x| = x$ or $|x| = -x$, we have $-|x| \leq x \leq |x|$. If we assume $|x| \leq a$, we have $-a \leq -|x| \leq x \leq |x| \leq a$. Conversely, if $-a \leq x \leq a$, then

if $x \geq 0$, then $|x| = x \leq a$, and
if $x < 0$, then $|x| = -x \leq a$ (because $x \leq y \Rightarrow -y \leq -x$),

so, in any event, $|x| \leq a$. $\qquad\square$

Problem 6.17. Given real numbers x_i, $i = 1, 2, \ldots, n$, show the following:

(i) $|\Sigma_{i=1}^n x_i| \leq \Sigma_{i=1}^n |x_i|$
(ii) $|a - c| \leq |a - b| + |b - c|$

(i) We know that the result holds for $n = 2$, because it then reduces to the triangle inequality. Assume that the result holds for n; then it will also hold for $n + 1$, because

$$\left|\sum_{i=1}^{n+1} x_i\right| = \left|\left(\sum_{i=1}^n x_i\right) + x_{n+1}\right| \leq \left|\sum_{i=1}^n x_i\right| + |x_{n+1}| \leq \sum_{i=1}^n |x_i| + |x_{n+1}| = \sum_{i=1}^{n+1} |x_i|$$

where the first inequality holds by the triangle inequality, and the second by the assumption that the property holds for n.

(ii) Let $x = a - b$ and $y = b - c$ in the triangle inequality, $|x + y| \leq |x| + |y|$. $\qquad\square$

Chapter 2

Problem 1.7. The Cauchy-Schwarz-Bunyakovsky inequality. Let f and g be continuous functions $[a, b] \longrightarrow \mathbb{R}$. Adapt the proof of the Cauchy-Schwarz inequality to establish the following analogue for integrals:

$$\left(\int_a^b f(x)g(x)\, dx\right)^2 \leq \left(\int_a^b [f(x)]^2\, dx\right)\left(\int_a^b [g(x)]^2\, dx\right)$$

Identical with the one in the text, with $\lambda = \int_a^b f(x)g(x)\, dx / \int_a^b [g(x)]^2\, dx$. $\qquad\square$

Problem 1.8. An alternative to the Euclidean norm in $\mathbb{R}^n$ is given by the sup norm, defined for any $x \in \mathbb{R}^n$ by the absolute value of its largest component:

$$\|x\|_s = \max_i\{|x^i|;\ i = 1, 2, \ldots, n\}$$

Show that $\|\cdot\|_s : \mathbb{R}^n \longrightarrow \mathbb{R}$ is a norm.

The only thing that is not obvious is that $\|\cdot\|_s$ satisfies the triangle inequality. To show that it does, we use the triangle inequality for real numbers. Given three points x, y, and z in $\mathbb{R}^n$, we have, for each $i = 1, \ldots, n$,

$$|x^i - z^i| = |(x^i - y^i) + (y^i - z^i)| \leq |x^i - y^i| + |y^i - z^i| \leq \|x - y\|_s + \|y - z\|_s$$

Therefore,

$$\|x - z\|_s \leq \|x - y\|_s + \|y - z\|_s \qquad\square$$

Problem 1.9. Show that $\|\cdot\|_s$ and the Euclidean norm $\|\cdot\|_E$ are Lipschitz-equivalent norms by proving that for any n-vector x, $\|x\|_s \leq \|x\|_E \leq \sqrt{n}\|x\|_s$.

$$\|x\|_S = \max_i |x^i| = \max_i \sqrt{(x^i)^2} \leq \sqrt{\sum_{k=1}^n (x^k)^2} = \|x\|_E$$

$$\|x\|_E = \sqrt{\sum_{k=1}^{n} (x^k)^2} \le \sqrt{n(\max_i |x^i|)^2} = \sqrt{n} \max_i |x^i| = \sqrt{n}\|x\|_E \qquad \square$$

Problem 1.11. Show that d_π is a metric.

Let $z = (x, y)$, $z' = (x', y')$, and $z'' = (x'', y'')$ be arbitrary points in $X \times Y$, and let d_π be defined by

$$[d_\pi(z, z')]^2 = [d_1(x, x')]^2 + [d_2(y, y')]^2 \qquad (1')$$

We want to check that the triangle inequality holds for d_π, i.e., that

$$d_\pi(z, z'') \le d_\pi(z, z') + d_\pi(z', z'') \qquad (2)$$

or, equivalently, that

$$[d_\pi(z, z'')]^2 \le [d_\pi(z, z') + d_\pi(z', z'')]^2 = [d_\pi(z, z')]^2 + [d_\pi(z', z'')]^2 + 2d_\pi(z, z')d_\pi(z', z'') \qquad (2')$$

Because the triangle inequality holds for both d_1 and d_2, we have

$$\begin{aligned}
[d_\pi(z, z'')]^2 &= [d_1(x, x'')]^2 + [d_2(y, y'')]^2 \\
&\le [d_1(x, x') + d_1(x', x'')]^2 + [d_2(y, y') + d_2(y', y'')]^2 \\
&= [d_1(x, x')^2 + d_2(y, y')^2] + [d_1(x', x'')^2 + d_2(y', y'')^2] \\
&\quad + 2[d_1(x, x')d_1(x', x'') + d_2(y, y')d_2(y', y'')] \\
&= d_\pi(z, z')^2 + d_\pi(z', z'')^2 + 2[d_1(x, x')d_1(x', x'') + d_2(y, y')d_2(y', y'')]
\end{aligned} \qquad (3)$$

Applying the Cauchy-Schwarz inequality to the expression within brackets in the last term of (3), we have

$$\begin{aligned}
d_1(x, x')&d_1(x', x'') + d_2(y, y')d_2(y', y'') \\
&\le \sqrt{d_1(x, x')^2 + d_2(y, y')^2} \sqrt{d_1(x', x'')^2 + d_2(y', y'')^2} \\
&= d_\pi(z, z')d_\pi(z', z'')
\end{aligned} \qquad (4)$$

Using (4) in (3), we obtain the desired result:

$$[d_\pi(z, z'')]^2 \le d_\pi(z, z')^2 + d_\pi(z', z'')^2 + 2d_\pi(z, z')d_\pi(z', z'') = [d_\pi(z, z') + d_\pi(z', z'')]^2$$

$$\square$$

Problem 1.13. Prove that the union of any finite collection of bounded sets is bounded. (Prove it for two sets; the result then follows by induction.)

Let S_1 and S_2 be bounded sets in a metric space (X, d), and let x_1 and x_2 in X and m_1 and m_2 in $\mathbb{R}$ be such that $d(x_i, s_i) \le m_i$ for all $s_i \in S_i$. (These numbers exist by the boundedness of S_1 and S_2.) Let $x = x_1$, and $m = \max\{m_1, m_2 + d(x_1, x_2)\}$. Then for every $s \in S_1 \cup S_2$, either

(i) $s \in S_1$ and $d(s, x) = d(s, x_1) \le m_1 \le m$, or
(ii) $s \in S_2$ and $d(s, x) = d(s, x_1) \le d(s, x_2) + d(x_2, x_1) \le m_2 + d(x_1, x_2) \le m$.

Hence, $S_1 \cup S_2$ is contained in $B_m(x)$. $\qquad \square$

Problem 1.14. Using the triangle inequality, show that for any x, y, and z in a normed vector space, the following are true:

(i) $\|x - y\| \ge \|x\| - \|y\|$ and   (ii) $\|x - z\| \le \|x - y\| + \|y - z\|$

(i) $\|x\| = \|(x - y) + y\| \le \|x - y\| + \|y\| \Rightarrow \|x - y\| \ge \|x\| - \|y\|$

(ii) $\|x - z\| = \|(x - y) + (y - z)\| \le \|x - y\| + \|y - z\|$ □

Problem 1.15. Show that the set of bounded real sequences is a metric space, with the norm defined by $d(x, y) = \sup_n |x_n - y_n|$.

Once more, we only need to check the triangle inequality:

$$d(x, z) = \sup_n |x_n - z_n| = \sup_n |(x_n - y_n) + (y_n - z_n)| \le \sup_n \{|x_n - y_n| + |y_n - z_n|\}$$

$$\le \sup_n |x_n - y_n| + \sup_n |y_n - z_n| = d(x, y) + d(y, z)$$

The first inequality holds by the triangle inequality for real numbers, and the second holds because taking separate suprema for $|x_n - y_n|$ and $|y_n - z_n|$ may allow us to do better, but never worse, than taking a single supremum for the sum. □

Problem 1.16. Let (X_2, d_2) be a metric space, X_1 a set, and $f: X_1 \longrightarrow X_2$ a one-to-one function. Define a function $d_1(\ )$ by

$$d_1(x, y) = d_2[f(x), f(y)] \ \forall \ x, y \in X_1$$

Show that (X_1, d_1) is a metric space.

First, $d_1(x, y) = d_2[f(x), f(y)] \ge 0$, with equality if and only if $f(x) = f(y)$. Because f is one-to-one, $f(x) = f(y)$ if and only if $x = y$.

$$d_1(x, y) = d_2[f(x), f(y)] = d_2[f(y), f(x)] = d_1(y, x)$$

$$d_1(x, z) = d_2[f(x), f(z)] \le d_2[f(x), f(y)] + d_2[f(y), f(z)] = d_1(x, y) + d_1(y, z)$$ □

Problem 1.17. Give an example of two sets A and B in a metric space such that $A \cap B = \varnothing$, but $d(A, B) = 0$.

The intervals (a, b) and (b, c), with $a < b < c$, in the real line with the usual metric. □

Problem 1.18. Prove that the set $C[a, b]$ of continuous real functions defined on the interval $[a, b]$ is a metric space when the distance between two functions f and g is defined by

$$d(f, g) = \sup_{x \in [a,b]} |f(x) - g(x)|$$

We verify that the triangle inequality holds:

$$d(f, h) = \sup_{x \in [a,b]} |f(x) - h(x)| = \sup_{x \in [a,b]} \|[f(x) - g(x)] + [g(x) - h(x)]\|$$

$$\le \sup_{x \in [a,b]} \{|f(x) - g(x)| + |g(x) - h(x)|\} \le \sup_{x \in [a,b]} |f(x) - g(x)| + \sup_{x \in [a,b]} |g(x) - h(x)|$$

$$= d(f, g) + d(g, h)$$
□

Problem 1.19. Show that the following inequality holds for any $x \in \mathbb{R}^n$:
$\|x\|_E \le \Sigma_{i=1}^n |x_i|$.

Assume that $n = 2$. Then we have

$$(|x_1| + |x_2|)^2 = |x_1|^2 + |x_2|^2 + 2|x_1||x_2| \ge |x_1|^2 + |x_2|^2 = x_1^2 + x_2^2$$

and taking the square root of this expression,

$$|x_1| + |x_2| \ge \sqrt{x_1^2 + x_2^2} = \|x\|_E$$

as desired.

For $n > 2$, we proceed by induction. Let $x \in \mathbb{R}^{n+1}$, partition $x = (y, z)$ with $y \in \mathbb{R}^n$ and $z = x_{n+1} \in \mathbb{R}$, and assume that

$$\|y\|_E = \sqrt{\sum_{i=1}^n y_i^2} \leq \sum_{i=1}^n |y_i| \tag{1}$$

Then we have

$$\|x\|_E^2 = \sum_{i=1}^{n+1} x_i^2 = \sum_{i=1}^n y_i^2 + z^2 = \|y\|_E^2 + |z|^2 \leq \|y\|_E^2 + |z|^2 + 2|z|\|y\|_E = (|z| + \|y\|_E)^2$$

Taking the square root of this expression, using (1), and recalling that $z = x_{n+1}$, we have

$$\|x\|_E \leq \|y\|_E + |z| \leq \sum_{i=1}^n |y_i| + |z| = \sum_{i=1}^n |x_i| + |x_{n+1}| = \sum_{i=1}^{n+1} |x_i|$$

which is the desired result. $\qquad\square$

Problem 2.2. Using the formal definition of limit, show that

   (i) $\displaystyle\lim_{n \to \infty} \frac{1}{n} = 0,$ (ii) $\displaystyle\lim_{n \to \infty} \frac{1}{\sqrt{n}} = 0,$ (iii) $\displaystyle\lim_{n \to \infty} \frac{n^2 + 2}{3n^2 + 4} = \frac{1}{3}$

Imagine you are given some arbitrarily small ε. You must produce a positive integer N such that. . . .

  (i) Fix some arbitrary $\varepsilon > 0$. We want to find some $N(\varepsilon)$ such that for all $n > N(\varepsilon)$,

$$\left|\frac{1}{n} - 0\right| = \frac{1}{n} < \varepsilon$$

Clearly, this inequality holds for $n > 1/\varepsilon$, so it is sufficient to choose $N(\varepsilon) = 1/\varepsilon$.
  (ii) In the same manner,

$$\left|\frac{1}{\sqrt{n}} - 0\right| = \frac{1}{\sqrt{n}} < \varepsilon \Leftrightarrow n > \frac{1}{\varepsilon^2}, \text{ so } N(\varepsilon) = \frac{1}{\varepsilon^2}$$

(iii)

$$\left|\frac{n^2 + 2}{3n^2 + 4} - \frac{1}{3}\right| = \frac{n^2 + 2}{3n^2 + 4} - \frac{1}{3} = \frac{3(n^2 + 2) - (3n^2 + 4)}{3(3n^2 + 4)} = \frac{2}{3(3n^2 + 4)} < \varepsilon$$

$$\Leftrightarrow 3n^2 + 4 > \frac{2}{3\varepsilon} \Leftrightarrow n^2 > \frac{2}{9\varepsilon} - \frac{4}{3} \Leftrightarrow n > \sqrt{\frac{2}{9\varepsilon} - \frac{4}{3}}$$

(For ε sufficiently small, the right-hand side is positive; otherwise the penultimate inequality is always true.) $\qquad\square$

Problem 2.4. Let $\{x_n\}$ be a convergent sequence with limit x. Show that every subsequence of $\{x_n\}$ converges to x.
    Assume $\{x_n\} \to x$, and let $p(k)$ be a strictly increasing function from $\mathbb{N}$ to $\mathbb{N}$. We want to show that any subsequence $\{x_{p(k)}\}$ of $\{x_n\}$ converges to x. Because $\{x_n\} \to x$, we have

$$\forall \varepsilon > 0, \ \exists N(\varepsilon) \text{ s.th. } n > N(\varepsilon) \Rightarrow d(x_n, x) < \varepsilon$$

Because $p(\ )$ is strictly increasing, $p(n) > n$ for all n (by induction). Hence, given some $\varepsilon > 0$, $n > N(\varepsilon)$ implies $p(n) > N(\varepsilon)$, and therefore

$$d(x_{p(n)}, x) < \varepsilon$$

The result is intuitively obvious: If all x_n with $n > N(\varepsilon)$ are within a distance ε of x, the same is true for all $x_{p(n)}$, provided that $p(n) > N(\varepsilon)$, for, since $p(\ )$ is increasing, these terms are "farther along" in the sequence. $\square$

Problem 3.4. We want to show that every real sequence $\{x_n\}$ contained in $[a, b]$ has a subsequence that converges to a point x in the interval. Because $\{x_n\}$ is bounded, the Bolzano-Weierstrass theorem ensures that it does indeed have a convergent subsequence. Assume that the limit of this subsequence lies outside $[a, b]$ (e.g., $x > b$). Show that this leads to a contradiction. (First, draw a picture.)

Intuitively, if $x > b$, then when x_n gets sufficiently close to x the sequence must leave the interval. Formally, assume $\{x_n\} \rightarrow x > b$. Then there exists some N such that

$$k > N \Rightarrow |x - x_n| = x - x_n < x - b$$

But then $x_n > b$ for all $n > N$, which contradicts the assumption that $x_n \leq b$ for all n. $\square$

Problem 3.9. Prove Theorem 3.8: Let $\{x_n\}$ be a sequence of positive real numbers. Then $\{x_n\} \rightarrow \infty$ if and only if $\{1/x_n\} \rightarrow 0$.

To show that $\{1/x_n\} \rightarrow 0$, fix some arbitrary $\varepsilon > 0$. Because $\{x_n\} \rightarrow \infty$, we know that there exists some N such that $n > N \Rightarrow x_n > 1/\varepsilon$. Thus, $0 < 1/x_n < \varepsilon$ for all $n > N$. For the converse, the same argument will work in reverse. $\square$

Problem 3.11. Convergence in product spaces. Let (X, d_1) and (Y, d_2) be metric spaces, and consider the product space $(Z = X \times Y, d_\pi)$, with the *product metric* d_π defined by

$$d_\pi(z, z') = d_\pi[(x, y), (x', y')] = \sqrt{[d_1(x, x')]^2 + [d_2(y, y')]^2} \tag{1}$$

Show that the sequence $\{z_n\} = \{(x_n, y_n)\}$ converges to $z = (x, y)$ in $(X \times Y, d_\pi)$ if and only if $\{x_n\}$ converges to x in (X, d) and $\{y_n\}$ converges to y in (Y, d).

- ($\rightarrow$) First, assume $\{z_n\} \rightarrow z$, and fix some $\varepsilon > 0$. Because $\{z_n\} \rightarrow z$, there exists some N such that $d_\pi(z_n, z) < \varepsilon$ for all $n > N$. That is,

$$n > N \Rightarrow d_\pi(z_n, z) = \sqrt{[d_1(x_n, x)]^2 + [d_2(y_n, y)]^2} < \varepsilon$$

Now observe that

$$d_1(x_n, x) = \sqrt{[d_1(x_n, x)]^2} \leq \sqrt{[d_1(x_n, x)]^2 + [d_2(y_n, y)]^2} = d_\pi(z_n, z)$$

and by a similar argument, $d_2(y_n, y) \leq d_\pi(z_n, z)$. Hence, for $n > N$ we have

$$d_1(x_n, x) < \varepsilon \quad \text{and} \quad d_2(y_n, y) < \varepsilon$$

That is, the component sequences $\{x_n\}$ and $\{y_n\}$ converge to x and y, respectively, in the original spaces.

- ($\leftarrow$) Now assume $\{x_n\} \rightarrow x$ in (X, d_1) and $\{y_n\} \rightarrow y$ in (Y, d_2), and fix some $\varepsilon > 0$. By the convergence of these sequences, there exist positive integers N_1 and N_2 such that

$$n > N_1 \Rightarrow d_1(x_n, x) < \varepsilon/\sqrt{2} \quad \text{and} \quad n > N_2 \Rightarrow d_2(y_n, y) < \varepsilon/\sqrt{2} \tag{1}$$

If we now define $N = \max\{N_1, N_2\}$, (1) holds for both sequences, provided that $n > N$. We have, then,

$$d_\pi(z_n, z) = \sqrt{[d_1(x_n, x)]^2 + [d_2(y_n, y)]^2} < \sqrt{2\varepsilon^2/2} = \varepsilon \ \forall \ n > N$$

Hence, $\{z_n\} \rightarrow z$ in $(X \times Y, d_\pi)$, as was to be shown. $\square$

Problem 3.12. Show that every bounded sequence in $\mathbb{E}^m$ contains at least one convergent subsequence.

For simplicity, we will work in $\mathbb{E}^2$. Let $\{x_n\} = \{(y_n, z_n)\}$ be a bounded sequence of 2-vectors. Then the first component sequence $\{y_n\}$ is a bounded sequence of real numbers, and it follows by the Bolzano-Weierstrass theorem (Theorem 3.3) that this sequence has a convergent subsequence, say $\{y_{n_k}\}$ with limit y. Consider now the corresponding subsequence of the second component sequence, $\{z_{n_k}\}$. Because this is also a bounded sequence of real numbers, it too has a convergent subsequence, say $\{z_{n_{k_q}}\}$ with limit z. Going back to the first component sequence, the corresponding subsequence $\{y_{n_{k_q}}\}$ is still convergent to y (because any subsequence of a convergent sequence is itself convergent). By Theorem 3.10, the subsequence $\{x_{n_{k_q}}\} = \{(y_{n_{k_q}}, z_{n_{k_q}})\}$ of the original sequence converges to (x, y). The argument can proceed in the same manner for vectors of any finite dimension. $\qquad\square$

Problem 3.14. Prove the Bernoulli inequality by induction: For each positive integer n and any $x \geq -1$, $(1+x)^n \geq 1 + nx$. Where in the proof do you need the assumption that $x \geq -1$?

For $n = 1$, the inequality holds trivially. Now suppose $(1+x)^n \geq 1 + nx$ and $1 + x \geq 0$; then we can multiply both sides of the first inequality by $1 + x$ without reversing its direction, and we get

$$(1+x)^{n+1} = (1+x)^n(1+x) \geq (1+nx)(1+x) = 1+(n+1)x+nx^2 \geq 1+(n+1)x \qquad\square$$

Problem 3.15. Prove Theorem 3.13: Let a be a real number, and consider the sequence $\{a^n\}$. As $n \to \infty$, we have the following: (i) If $|a| < 1$, then $\{a^n\} \to 0$. (ii) If $a > 1$, then $\{a^n\} \to \infty$. (iii) If $a \leq -1$, then $\{a^n\}$ diverges.

Assume $|a| < 1$. If $a = 0$, then the result is immediate; otherwise we can write $|a| = 1/(1+x)$ for some $x > 0$. By the Bernoulli inequality, $(1+x)^n \geq 1 + nx > nx$, and hence

$$|a^n - 0| = |a^n| = \frac{1}{(1+x)^n} < \frac{1}{nx}$$

Finally, fix some $\varepsilon > 0$, and observe that

$$|a^n| < \frac{1}{nx} < \varepsilon \quad \text{provided that } n > \frac{1}{\varepsilon x}$$

If $a > 1$, we can write $a = 1 + x$ for some $x > 0$. Then

$$a^n = (1+x)^n \geq 1 + nx > nx$$

Given any $B > 0$, we have $a^n > nx > B$ for all $n > B/x$. $\qquad\square$

Problem 3.19. Consider the sequence $\{a^n; n = 0, 1, \ldots\}$, where $0 < a < 1$, and define S_N as before. Verify that $(1-a)S_N = 1 - a^{N+1}$. Use this to show that $\Sigma_{n=0}^{\infty} a^n = 1/(1-a)$.

Notice that

$$(1-a)S_N = (1+a+a^2+\ldots+a^N) - (a+a^2+\ldots+a^N+a^{N+1}) = 1 - a^{N+1}$$

Hence,

$$S_N = \frac{1-a^{N+1}}{1-a}$$

Taking limits as $N \to \infty$,

$$\sum_{n=0}^{\infty} a^n = \lim_{N \to \infty} \frac{1 - a^{N+1}}{1 - a} = \frac{1}{1 - a}$$ □

Problem 3.20. Given the function

$$f(x) = \frac{x^2 + 2}{2x}$$ (1)

define a sequence $\{x_n\}$ of rational numbers by

$$x_1 = 1 \quad \text{and} \quad x_{n+1} = f(x_n) \; \forall \; n > 1$$ (2)

We have, then,

$$x_2 = 1.5, \qquad x_3 = 1.417\ldots$$ (3)

(i) Prove that if $\{x_n\}$ converges, then its limit is $x = \sqrt{2}$. (Complete the following expression: $x = \lim_{n \to \infty} x_{n+1} = \lim_{n \to \infty} f(x_n) = \ldots$)
   We have

$$x = \lim_{n \to \infty} x_{n+1} = \lim_{n \to \infty} f(x_n) = \lim_{n \to \infty} \frac{x_n^2 + 2}{2x_n} = \frac{x^2 + 2}{2x}$$

from which

$$2x^2 = x^2 + 2 \Rightarrow x^2 = 2 \Rightarrow x = \sqrt{2}$$

(ii) Prove that for $n \geq 2$ we have $x_n \geq \sqrt{2}$. (Show that $f(x) \geq \sqrt{2}$ using $a^2 + b^2 \geq 2ab$. Why?)

$$(a - b)^2 = a^2 + b^2 - 2ab \geq 0 \Rightarrow a^2 + b^2 \geq 2ab$$

Using this, we have

$$f(x) = \frac{x^2 + 2}{2x} = \frac{x^2 + (\sqrt{2})^2}{2x} \geq \frac{2\sqrt{2}x}{2x} = \sqrt{2}$$

(iii) Calculate the value of $(x_{n+1} - x_n)$ as a function of x_n and x_{n-1}. Use the resulting expression to prove that for $n \geq 2$, $\{x_n\}$ is decreasing (by induction).
   By the analogue of Theorem 3.1 for decreasing sequences bounded below, $\{x_n\}$ converges to a real number. Hence, there is a real number x such that $x^2 = 2$.

$$x_{n+1} - x_n = f(x_n) - f(x_{n-1}) = \frac{x_n^2 + 2}{2x_n} - \frac{x_{n-1}^2 + 2}{2x_{n-1}} = \frac{x_{n-1}(x_n^2 + 2) - x_n(x_{n-1}^2 + 2)}{2x_n x_{n-1}}$$

$$= \frac{x_{n-1}x_n^2 + 2x_{n-1} - x_n x_{n-1}^2 - 2x_n}{2x_n x_{n-1}} = \frac{(x_{n-1}x_n)(x_n - x_{n-1}) - 2(x_n - x_{n-1})}{2x_n x_{n-1}}$$

$$= (x_n - x_{n-1})\left(\frac{1}{2} - \frac{1}{x_n x_{n-1}}\right)$$

Because $x_n \geq \sqrt{2}$ for $n \geq 2$, we have

$$\left(\frac{1}{2} - \frac{1}{x_n x_{n-1}}\right) > 0 \quad \text{for } n > 2$$

and therefore

$$\text{sign}(x_{n+1} - x_n) = \text{sign}(x_n - x_{n-1})$$

Because $x_3 - x_2 = 1.417 - 1.5 < 0$, the sequence is decreasing. □

Problem 4.4. Prove Theorem 4.3: (i) $\varnothing$ and X are closed in X. (ii) The intersection of an arbitrary collection of closed sets is closed. (iii) The union of a finite family of closed sets is closed.

(i) Because X is open, its complement $\varnothing$ is closed, and vice versa.
(ii) and (iii) The proof is almost immediate using De Morgan's laws:

$$\sim(\cup_i A_i) = \cap_i(\sim A_i) \quad \text{and} \quad \sim(\cap_i A_i) = \cup_i(\sim A_i)$$

Consider the union of a finite number of closed sets, $\cup_{i=1}^n C_i$. By definition, the complement of each C_i is open, and therefore so is the intersection

$$\bigcap_{i=1}^n (\sim C_i) = \sim\left(\bigcup_{i=1}^n C_i\right)$$

Hence its complement, $\cup_{i=1}^n C_i$, is closed. A similar argument can be used to prove (iii). □

Problem 4.7. Prove that $\partial A = \text{cl } A \cap \text{cl}(\sim A)$.

Pick an arbitrary boundary point of A, $x \in \partial A$. By definition, any open ball around x interesects both A and $\sim A$. Hence, a boundary point of A is a closure point of both A and $\sim A$, and it follows that $\text{cl } A \cap \text{cl}(\sim A) \supseteq \partial A$.

Let y be an arbitrary point in $\text{cl } A \cap \text{cl}(\sim A)$. Because y is a closure point of both A and $\sim A$, we have, by definition, that for any $\varepsilon > 0$,

$$B_\varepsilon(x) \cap A \neq \varnothing \quad \text{and} \quad B_\varepsilon(x) \cap (\sim A) \neq \varnothing$$

Thus, any point y in $\text{cl } A \cap \text{cl}(\sim A)$ is a boundary point of A, that is, $\partial A \supseteq \text{cl } A \cap \text{cl}(\sim A)$. □

Problem 4.9. Prove parts (iii) and (iv) of Theorem 4.8:

(iii) $\text{cl } A$ is the smallest closed set that contains A.
(iv) A is closed if and only if $A = \text{cl } A$.

First, we show that $\text{cl } A$ is closed. It is obvious from the definitions that the interior, exterior, and boundary of a set are disjoint sets, and

$$\text{int } A \cup \text{ext } A \cup \partial A = X, \qquad \text{cl } A = \text{int } A \cup \partial A, \qquad \text{ext } A = \text{int}(\sim A)$$

Hence,

$$\text{cl } A = \sim(\text{ext } A) = \sim(\text{int } \sim A), \quad \text{and so} \quad \sim(\text{cl } A) = \text{int}(\sim A)$$

and because int is open, so is $\sim(\text{cl } A)$.

Next, we show that $\text{cl } A$ is the smallest closed set that contains A. Let B be a closed set containing A. Then $\sim B$ is open, and because $B \supseteq A$, we have $\sim A \supseteq \sim B$, that is, $\sim B$ is an open set contained in $\sim A$. Now, $\text{int}(\sim A)$ is the largest open subset of $\sim A$; it follows that $\text{int}(\sim A) \supseteq \sim B$. Moreover, we know that $\text{int}(\sim A) = \sim(\text{cl } A)$, from where $\sim(\text{cl } A) \supseteq \sim B$; this, in turn, implies $B \supseteq \text{cl } A$. Hence, any closed set B that contains A also contains $\text{cl } A$.

Given this, it is obvious that if A is closed, the smallest closed set that contains A is A itself. And if $A = \text{cl } A$, then A is closed, because $\text{cl } A$ is closed. □

Problem 4.14. Show that in a metric space the closed ball $B_r[x]$ is a closed set. (Take a limit point a of $B_r[x]$ and consider an arbitrary sequence $\{x_n\}$ in $B_r[x]$ with limit a. Use the triangle inequality to show that a must be in $B_r[x]$.)

Let a be an arbitrary limit point of $B_r[x]$. We will show that $a \in B_r[x]$. By the definition of limit point, there exists a sequence $\{y_n\}$ in $B_r[x]$ that converges to a. Because $y_n \in B_r[x]$, we have $d(y_n, x) \le r$ for all n. Using the triangle inequality,

$$d(a, x) \le d(a, y_n) + d(y_n, x) \le d(a, y_n) + r$$

Because $\{y_n\} \to a$, $d(a, y_n) \to 0$, and, taking limits, $d(a, x) \le r$, i.e., $a \in B_r[x]$. Hence, $B_r[x]$ contains all its limit points and is therefore closed. $\qquad\square$

Problem 4.15. Let B be a nonempty set of real numbers bounded above. Let $s = \sup B$. Show that $s \in \bar{B}$. Notice that this implies that $s \in B$ if B is closed.

If $s \in B$, then $s \in \bar{B}$. Suppose $s \notin B$. Then for every $\varepsilon > 0$ there exists some point $x \in B$ such that $s - \varepsilon < x < s$, for otherwise $s - \varepsilon$ would be an upper bound of B smaller than s, and s could not be the supremum. Thus, s is a limit point of B, and therefore $s \in \bar{B}$. $\qquad\square$

Problem 4.16. Let A be a set in a metric space (X, d). Show that if A is closed and $x \notin A$, then $d(x, A) > 0$.

We will prove the contrapositive statement: Let A be a closed set, and x a point such that $d(x, A) = 0$. Then $x \in A$. Because $d(x, A) = 0$, for any given $\varepsilon > 0$ there exists some point $a \in A$ such that $d(x, a) < \varepsilon$. That is, $B_\varepsilon(x) \cap A \ne \varnothing$ for every $\varepsilon > 0$. Hence, either $x \in A$ (if $x = a$) or x is a limit point of A (otherwise). Because A is closed (and therefore contains all its limit points), $x \in A$ in any event. $\qquad\square$

Problem 5.6. Use the definition of the limit of a function to show that if

$$\lim_{x \to x^0} f(x) = a \quad \text{and} \quad \lim_{x \to x^0} g(x) = b$$

then $\lim_{x \to x^0}[f(x) + g(x)] = a + b$. Prove the same result using the analogous theorem for limits of sequences.

(i) Direct proof: Fix some $\varepsilon > 0$. Because f has limit a and g has limit b as $x \to x^0$, we can find positive numbers δ_f and δ_g such that

$$|f(x) - a| < \varepsilon/2 \quad \text{whenever } |x - x^0| < \delta_f \quad \text{and}$$

$$|g(x) - b| < \varepsilon/2 \quad \text{whenever } |x - x^0| < \delta_g$$

Put $\delta = \min\{\delta_f, \delta_g\}$. Then for all x such that $|x - x^0| < \delta$, we have

$$|[f(x) + g(x)] - (a + b)| = |[f(x) - a] + [g(x) - b]| \le |f(x) - a| + |g(x) - b| < \varepsilon$$

which shows that $\lim_{x \to x^0}[f(x) + g(x)] = a + b$.

(ii) Because $\lim_{x \to x^0} f(x) = a$ and $\lim_{x \to x^0} g(x) = b$, we must have $\{f(x_n)\} \to a$ and $\{g(x_n)\} \to b$ for any sequence $\{x_n\}$ with $\{x_n\} \to x^0$ and $x_n \ne x^0$ for all n (Theorem 5.2, necessity). By Theorem 3.6, $\{f(x_n) + g(x_n)\} \to a + b$ for any such sequence, implying

$$\lim_{x \to x^0}[f(x) + g(x)] = a + b$$

by Theorem 5.2 (sufficiency). $\qquad\square$

Problem 6.2. Preservation of sign. Let f be a continuous function from a metric space (X, d) to $\mathbb{R}$, with the usual metric. Prove (directly) that the set $\{x \in X; f(x) > 0\}$ is open. Intuitively, this result says that a continuous function that is strictly positive (or negative) at a point will maintain its sign within a sufficiently small ball around the original point.

Let x be such that $f(x) > 0$. By the continuity of f, for every $\varepsilon > 0$ there exists some $\delta > 0$ such that

$$|f(y) - f(x)| < \varepsilon \; \forall \; y \in B_\delta(x)$$

In particular, if we choose $\varepsilon = f(x)/2$, continuity ensures that we can find some $\delta > 0$ such that for $y \in B_\delta(x)$

$$f(x) - f(y) < f(x)/2 \Rightarrow f(y) > f(x)/2 > 0$$

Hence, $f^{-1}(0, \infty)$ is open.

The robustness of the sign of a continuous real-valued function to small perturbations of its arguments is a property we will use quite often. □

Problem 6.5. Let $f: \mathbb{R} \longrightarrow \mathbb{R}$ be the function defined by $f(x) = 1$ for x rational and by $f(x) = 0$ for x irrational. Show that f is discontinuous everywhere. (Recall that any interval in the real line contains both rational and irrational numbers.)

Choose an arbitrary point x^0 in $\mathbb{R}$, and let $\varepsilon \le 1$. Then, for any $\delta > 0$, the interval $(x^0 - \delta, x^0 + \delta)$ contains both rational and irrational numbers and, in particular, some x of the type opposite to x^0. For this x, we have $|f(x^0) - f(x)| = 1 \ge \varepsilon$. □

Problem 6.6. Given a function $f: \mathbb{R} \longrightarrow \mathbb{R}$, define $g: \mathbb{R} \longrightarrow \mathbb{R}^2$ by $g(x) = (x, f(x))$. Use the sequential characterization of continuity to show that if f is continuous at some point x^0, then so is g.

Consider an arbitrary sequence $\{x_n\}$ convergent to x^0. Because f is continuous, $\{f(x_n)\} \to f(x^0)$. But then

$$\{g(x_n)\} = \{(x_n, f(x_n))\} \to (x, f(x^0)) = g(x^0)$$

so g is continuous at x^0. □

Problem 6.7. Consider the finite-dimensional Euclidean space E^n. For any $k \in \{1, 2, \ldots, n\}$, the kth projection mapping, $p_k: \mathbb{R}^n \longrightarrow \mathbb{R}$, is defined for $x = (x_1, \ldots, x_n)$ by $p_k(x) = x_k$. Show that $p_k(\;)$ is a continuous function.

Let $x = (x_1, \ldots, x_n)$ and $y = (y_1, \ldots, y_n)$ be points in $\mathbb{R}^n$. For each $k = 1, \ldots, n$ we have

$$|p_k(y) - p_k(x)| = |x_k - y_k| = \sqrt{(x_k - y_k)^2} \le \sqrt{\sum_{i=1}^n (x_i - y_i)^2} = d_E(x, y) \qquad (1)$$

To establish continuity, we have to show that for any given $\varepsilon > 0$, there exists a $\delta > 0$ such that $d_E(x, y) < \delta$ implies $|p_k(y) - p_k(x)| < \varepsilon$. By (1), it is enough to take $\delta = \varepsilon$. □

Problem 6.8. Show that in any normed vector space $(X, \|\cdot\|)$ the norm is a continuous function from X to $\mathbb{R}$.

We know (Problem 1.14) that $\|x - y\| \ge \|x\| - \|y\|$. Reversing the roles of x and y, we have $\|x - y\| = \|y - x\| \ge \|y\| - \|x\|$, and therefore $\|\|x\| - \|y\|\| \le \|x - y\|$. Using the same argument as in the preceding problem, continuity follows directly. □

Problem 6.9. Prove that if f is a continuous function, then for any set A, $f(\text{cl } A) \subseteq \text{cl}[f(A)]$.

We want to show that if $y \in f(\text{cl } A)$, then it also belongs to $\text{cl } f(A)$, that is, for any $\varepsilon > 0$, $B_\varepsilon(y) \cap f(A) \ne \varnothing$. Take an arbitrary $y \in f(\text{cl } A)$ and fix some $\varepsilon > 0$. Because $y \in f(\text{cl } A)$, we have $y = f(x)$ for some $x \in \text{cl } A$, that is,

$$\forall \; \delta > 0, \; B_\delta(x) \cap A \ne \varnothing \qquad (1)$$

By the continuity of f, we can choose some $\delta(\varepsilon)$ such that $f[B_{\delta(\varepsilon)}(x)] \subseteq B_\varepsilon(f(x))$. Because (1) continues to hold for this $\delta(\varepsilon)$, $B_{\delta(\varepsilon)}(x) \cap A$ is not empty, and therefore neither is its image, $f[B_{\delta(\varepsilon)}(x) \cap A]$. Using Theorem 4.3 in Chapter 1,

$$f[B_{\delta(\varepsilon)}(x) \cap A] \subseteq f[B_{\delta(\varepsilon)}(x)] \cap f(A) \subseteq B_\varepsilon(f(x)) \cap f(A)$$

so $B_\varepsilon(f(x)) \cap f(A) \neq \emptyset$, which is what we wanted to show. □

Problem 6.11. Let f and g be functions $\mathbb{R} \longrightarrow \mathbb{R}$, and assume that f is continuous at y^0 and that $g(x) \to y^0$ as $x \to \infty$. Show that $\lim_{x\to\infty} f[g(x)] = f(y^0)$.

Fix an arbitrary $\varepsilon > 0$. By the continuity of f at y^0, there exists some $\delta_\varepsilon > 0$ such that

$$|f(y) - f(y^0)| < \varepsilon \; \forall \; y \text{ s.th. } |y - y^0| < \delta_\varepsilon \tag{1}$$

Because $g(x) \to y^0$ as $x \to \infty$, we can find some number $B(\delta_\varepsilon)$ such that

$$|g(x) - y^0| < \delta_\varepsilon \; \forall \; x > B(\delta_\varepsilon)$$

For any $x > B(\delta_\varepsilon)$ we have, then, $|g(x) - y^0| < \delta_\varepsilon$, and therefore $|f[g(x)] - f(y^0)| < \varepsilon$, by (1). That is, $f[g(x)] \to f(y^0)$ as $x \to \infty$. □

Problem 6.15. Using Theorem 6.13, prove Theorem 6.14: Let (X, d) and (Y, ρ) be metric spaces, and f a function $X \longrightarrow Y$. Then f is continuous if and only if for every set A open in (Y, ρ) the set $f^{-1}(A)$ is open in (X, d).

Let A be an arbitrary open set in Y, and f a continuous function. Then A^c is closed, and by the continuity of f, so is $f^{-1}(A^c)$. But then the complement of this set, $\sim f^{-1}(A^c) = f^{-1}(A)$, is open (see Problem 4.5 in Chapter 1). Conversely, let f be a function such that $f^{-1}(A)$ is open for every set A open in Y, and consider an arbitrary closed set B. The complement of B, B^c, is open, and, by assumption, this implies that $f^{-1}(B^c)$ is open. But then $\sim f^{-1}(B^c) = f^{-1}(B)$ is closed. Because B is arbitrary, f is continuous, by Theorem 6.13. □

Problem 6.16. Let (X, d) be a metric space, and $(Y, \|\cdot\|)$ a normed vector space with zero vector $\underline{0}$. Given a continuous function $f: X \longrightarrow Y$, adapt the proof of the characterization of continuity in terms of the inverse images of closed sets to show that the set $f^{-1}(\underline{0})$ is closed.

We shall show that if f is continuous, then $f^{-1}(\underline{0})$ is closed in (X, d), by verifying that it contains all its limit points. Let x be an arbitrary limit point of $f^{-1}(\underline{0})$; then there exists a sequence $\{x_n\}$ in $f^{-1}(\underline{0})$ that converges to x. Because f is continuous, the sequence $\{f(x_n)\}$ converges to $f(x)$. By construction, $f(x_n) = \underline{0}$ for all n, and therefore $\{f(x_n)\} \to \underline{0}$. Thus, $f(x) = \underline{0}$, i.e., $x \in f^{-1}(\underline{0})$. □

Problem 6.19. Show that a Lipschitz function is uniformly continuous (and therefore continuous).

Let X and Y be normed spaces, and $f: X \longrightarrow Y$ a function with Lipschitz constant K on some subset E of X. We want to show that f is uniformly continuous on E, that is, that for all $x, y \in E$ and for any $\varepsilon > 0$ there exists some number $\delta(\varepsilon) > 0$, independent of x, such that

$$\|y - x\| < \delta(\varepsilon) \Rightarrow \|f(y) - f(x)\| < \varepsilon$$

Fix some arbitrary $\varepsilon > 0$ and let

$$\delta(\varepsilon) = \varepsilon/K$$

Then for any y such that

$$\|y - x\| < \delta(\varepsilon) = \varepsilon/K \tag{1}$$

we have

$$\|f(y) - f(x)\| \leq K\|y - x\| < \varepsilon$$

where the first inequality holds by the definition of Lipschitz function, and the second follows from (1). Because $\delta(\varepsilon)$ is independent of x, we have shown that f is uniformly continuous on E. ☐

Problem 6.25. We will now give an alternative proof for the intermediate-value theorem. Let f be a real function of one variable defined and continuous on an interval $[a, b]$. Assume that $f(a) < 0 < f(b)$. To show that there exists some point c in (a, b) such that $f(c) = 0$, we construct two sequences $\{l_n\}$ and $\{u_n\}$ in the following way:

1. Put $l_1 = a$ and $u_1 = b$.
2. For each n, let $m_n = (l_n + u_n)/2$ and evaluate f at m_n. Then

   (a) if $f(m_n) > 0$, put $l_{n+1} = l_n$ and $u_{n+1} = m_n$,
   (b) if $f(m_n) < 0$, put $l_{n+1} = m_n$ and $u_{n+1} = u_n$, and
   (c) if $f(m_n) = 0$, stop.

(i) Prove that $\{l_n\}$ and $\{u_n\}$ converge, and call their limits c' and c'': $\{l_n\}$ is an increasing sequence bounded above by b, and $\{u_n\}$ a decreasing sequence bounded below by a. Hence, both converge: $\{l_n\} \to c'$ and $\{u_n\} \to c''$, and therefore $\{u_n - l_n\} \to c'' - c'$.

(ii) We will now show that $\{u_n - l_n\} \to 0$, implying $c' = c'' \equiv c$. If $f(m_n) > 0$, then $u_{n+1} - l_{n+1} = m_n - l_n$, and if $f(m_n) < 0$, then $u_{n+1} - l_{n+1} = u_n - m_n$. In either case, $u_{n+1} - l_{n+1} = (u_n - l_n)/2$, and iterating, we get

$$0 \le u_{n+1} - l_{n+1} = \frac{u_n - l_n}{2} = \frac{u_{n-1} - l_{n-1}}{4} = \ldots = \frac{b - a}{2^n}$$

Taking limits, $(b - a)/2^n \to 0$ as $n \to \infty$, and therefore $\{u_n - l_n\} \to 0$.

(iii) It remains to show that $f(c) = 0$. By continuity, both $\{f(l_n)\}$ and $\{f(u_n)\}$ converge to $f(c)$. But $f(l_n) \le 0$ for all n, so $\lim_{n\to\infty} f(l_n) = f(c) \ge 0$, and $f(u_n) \le 0$ for all n, so $\lim_{n\to\infty} f(u_n) = f(c) \ge 0$. It follows that $f(c) = 0$. ☐

Problem 7.6. Prove Theorem 7.5: Any Cauchy sequence is bounded.

Let $\{x_n\}$ be a Cauchy sequence. Then

$$\forall \varepsilon > 0, \ \exists N(\varepsilon) \text{ s.th. } m, n > N(\varepsilon) \Rightarrow d(x_m, x_n) < \varepsilon$$

Because this holds for all ε, it will hold for $\varepsilon = 1$; hence, for all $m, n > N(1)$, we have $d(x_m, x_n) < 1$, and all the terms of the sequence of order higher than $N(1)$ fit inside an open ball of radius 1. The number of terms of the sequence that lie outside the ball is finite, and therefore these points must also lie within a ball of finite radius. Hence the sequence is bounded. ☐

Problem 7.7. Prove that the sequence $\{x_n\}$, defined in Problem 3.20, is Cauchy.

We have

$$|x_{n+1} - x_n| = |x_n - x_{n-1}| \left(\frac{1}{2} - \frac{1}{x_n x_{n-1}} \right)$$

Because the sequence is decreasing and $x_2 = 3/2$, for $n \ge 3$ we have

$$0 < \left(\frac{1}{2} - \frac{1}{x_n x_{n-1}} \right) < \left(\frac{1}{2} - \frac{4}{9} \right) = \frac{1}{18}$$

and therefore

$$|x_{n+1} - x_n| < (1/18)|x_n - x_{n-1}|$$

From now on, we can use the same argument as in the proof of the contraction mapping theorem. □

Problem 7.17. Let (X, d) be a complete metric space, and $T: X \longrightarrow X$ a function whose nth iteration T^n is a contraction. Show that T has a unique fixed point.

If T^n is a contraction, there exists some $\beta \in (0, 1)$ such that

$$d(T^n x, T^n y) \le \beta d(x, y) \ \forall \ x, y \in X \tag{1}$$

and by the contraction mapping theorem, T^n has a unique fixed point that we will call $x*$. Now, $T^n x* = x*$, and, using (1),

$$d(Tx*, x*) = d[T(T^n x*), T^n x*] = d[T^n(Tx*), T^n x*] \le \beta d(Tx*, x*)$$

Because $\beta < 1$, we must have $d(Tx*, x*) = 0$, and therefore $Tx* = x*$, that is, $x*$ is a fixed point of T. Moreover, any fixed point of T is a fixed point of T^n. It follows that T has a unique fixed point, for if it had more than one, so would T^n, and we know that is not the case. □

Problem 8.17. Show that a compact set in a metric space is complete.

Let A be a compact set, and let $\{x_n\}$ be an arbitrary Cauchy sequence in A. To establish completeness, we need to show that $\{x_n\}$ converges to some point in A. Now, by the sequential compactness of A, $\{x_n\}$ has a convergent subsequence with limit x in A. That x must be the limit of the entire sequence follows by Theorem 7.8. □

Problem 8.18. Let A be a compact set, and let $\{A_n\}$ be a "decreasing sequence" of nonempty closed subsets of A such that $A_n \subseteq A_{n+1}$. Show that $\cup_{n=1}^{\infty} A_n$ is not empty.

Let $\{x_n\}$ be a sequence constructed by taking a point in each A_n, i.e., $x_n \in A_n \subseteq A$. Because A is compact, $\{x_n\}$ has a convergent subsequence $\{x_{n_k}\}$ with limit x in A. Consider the subsequences $\{x_n^q\}$ of $\{x_n\}$, with $\{x_n^q\} = \{x_n; n \ge q\}$. Each such subsequence is contained in A_q and has a convergent subsequence (the appropriate portion of $\{x_{n_k}\}$) with limit x. Hence, x is a limit point of A_q for each q. But because A_q is closed by assumption, we have $x \in A_q$ for all q, i.e., $x \in \cap_{n=1}^{\infty} A_n$.

Problem 8.23. Give an alternative proof for Theorem 8.21 (the continuous image of a compact set is compact) using directly the definition of compactness.

Let $\{U_i; i \in I\}$ be an open cover of $f(C)$. Because f is continuous, each of the sets $f^{-1}(U_i)$ is open. The collection $\{f^{-1}(U_i); i \in I\}$ is an open cover of C. (Why?) Because C is compact, there is a finite subcollection, say $\{f^{-1}(U_k); k = 1, \ldots, n\}$, that still covers C, that is,

$$C \subseteq f^{-1}(U_1) \cup \ldots \cup f^{-1}(U_n)$$

Hence,

$$f(C) \subseteq f[f^{-1}(U_1) \cup \ldots \cup f^{-1}(U_n)] = f[f^{-1}(U_1)] \cup \ldots \cup f[f^{-1}(U_n)] \subseteq U_1 \cup \ldots \cup U_n$$

and we have found a finite subcover for $f(C)$, which is therefore compact. (We are using Theorem 4.3 and Problem 4.5 in Chapter 1.) □

Problem 8.26. Compactness of the product space. Let (X, d_1) and (Y, d_2) be metric spaces, and consider the product space $(Z = X \times Y, d_\pi)$, with the *product metric* d_π defined by

$$d_\pi(z, z') = d_\pi[(x, y), (x', y')] = \sqrt{[d_1(x, x')]^2 + [d_2(y, y')]^2} \tag{1}$$

Show that the product space $(Z = X \times Y, d_\pi)$ is compact if and only if both (X, d_1) and (Y, d_2) are compact.

We will make use of the sequential characterization of compactness (see Definition 8.4 and Theorems 8.5 and 8.11) and of Problem 3.11 (on convergence in product spaces).

First, assume that $(Z = X \times Y, d_\pi)$ is (sequentially) compact, and let $\{x_n\}$ and $\{y_n\}$ be arbitrary sequences in X and Y, respectively. We want to show that each of these sequences has a subsequence that converges to a point in the relevant set. By the sequential compactness of the product space, the sequence $\{(x_n, y_n)\}$ has a convergent subsequence $\{(x_{n_k}, y_{n_k})\}$ with limit $(x, y) \in X \times Y$. By Problem 3.11 we have that $\{x_{n_k}\} \to x \in X$ and $\{y_{n_k}\} \to y \in Y$, so both (X, d_1) and (Y, d_2) are sequentially compact and therefore compact.

Conversely, assume that (X, d_1) and (Y, d_2) are sequentially compact, and let $\{(x_n, y_n)\}$ be an arbitrary sequence in $X \times Y$. By the sequential compactness of (X, d_1), the first "component sequence" $\{x_n\}$ has a convergent subsequence $\{x_{n_k}\}$ with limit $x \in X$. Consider now the corresponding subsequence of the second component sequence, $\{y_{n_k}\}$. By the sequential compactness of (Y, d_2), this sequence has a convergent subsequence $\{y_{n_{k_q}}\}$ with limit $y \in Y$. Moreover, the corresponding first component subsequence $\{x_{n_{k_q}}\}$ still converges to $x \in X$. By Problem 3.11, the subsequence $\{(x_{n_{k_q}}, y_{n_{k_q}})\}$ converges to $(x, y) \in X \times Y$, which establishes the (sequential) compactness of the product space. $\qquad \square$

Problem 10.4. Prove Theorem 10.3: Let X be a nonempty set, and d_1 and d_2 two metrics defined on it. Then a necessary and sufficient condition for d_1 and d_2 to be topologically equivalent is the following: A subset A of X is d_1-open if and only if it is d_2-open.

- ($\leftarrow$) Assume that the metrics d_1 and d_2 generate the same open sets in X, and let (Y, ρ) be a metric space. Recall that by Theorem 6.14 a function $f : X \longrightarrow Y$ is continuous if and only if the inverse image of any open set is open. Because the open sets are the same in both cases, any (d_1, ρ)-continuous function is (d_2, ρ)-continuous, and vice versa. By Theorem 10.2, this implies that d_1 and d_2 are topologically equivalent.
- ($\rightarrow$) Assume that d_1 and d_2 are topologically equivalent metrics. Then, by Theorem 10.2, they preserve continuity, and it follows that the identity mapping $I : X \longrightarrow X$, with $I(x) = x$, being (d_1, d_1)-continuous, is also (d_1, d_2)-continuous. Now let A be a d_2-open set; by Theorem 6.14, the set $I^{-1}(A)$ is d_1-open. But then $I^{-1}(A) = A$ is also d_1-open. A similar argument will work in the opposite direction. $\qquad \square$

Problem 10.6. Prove Theorem 10.5: Lipschitz equivalence implies topological equivalence.

Let $\{x_n\}$ be a d_1-convergent sequence with limit x. Given that d_1 and d_2 are Lipschitz-equivalent, we want to show that $\{x_n\}$ converges to x in (X, d_2). Fix some $\varepsilon > 0$. Then, by the d_1-convergence of $\{x_n\}$, there exists some integer N such that

$$d_1(x_n, x) \le \varepsilon / M \ \forall \, n > N \tag{2}$$

Combining the Lipschitz condition (equation (1) in the theorem) and (2), we have

$$d_2(x_n, x) \le M d_1(x_n, x) \le \varepsilon \, \forall \, n > N$$

which shows that $\{x_n\}$ converges to x in (X, d_2). $\qquad \square$

Problem 11.5. Show that a closed correspondence is closed-valued.

Consider a sequence of points $\{y_n\}$ in $\Psi(x)$ converging to some point y in Y. We want to show that y lies in $\Psi(x)$ (in principle, it could be outside this set). Take a "constant" sequence $\{x_n\}$, with $x_n = x$ for all n, and notice that $\{y_n\}$ is a companion sequence of $\{x_n\}$. Clearly, $\{x_n\}$ converges to x, and because the correspondence is closed and $\{y_n\} \to y$, we have also that $y \in \Psi(x)$, which is what we wanted to show.   □

Problem 11.8. Prove Theorem 11.7: Let the correspondence $\Psi: X \to\to Y$ be compact-valued and uhc, and let $\Gamma: X \to\to Y$ be closed, and assume that $\Psi(x) \cap \Gamma(x) \neq \emptyset$. Then the intersection correspondence $\Psi \cap \Gamma$, defined by $(\Psi \cap \Gamma)(x) = \Psi(x) \cap \Gamma(x)$, is compact-valued and uhc.

The set $\Psi(x) \cap \Gamma(x)$ is compact because it is a closed subset of a compact set (Theorem 8.12). Let $\{x_n\}$ be a sequence converging to x, and $\{y_n\}$ an arbitrary companion sequence with $y_n \in \Psi(x_n) \cap \Gamma(x_n)$ for each n. To establish the desired result we have to show that $\{y_n\}$ has a convergent subsequence with limit in $\Psi(x) \cap \Gamma(x)$.

Because Ψ is by assumption compact-valued and uhc, $\{y_n\}$ does have a convergent subsequence $\{y_{n_k}\}$ with limit y in $\Psi(x)$. Consider now the sequence $\{x_{n_k}, y_{n_k}\}$. By construction, this sequence is contained in G_Γ, the graph of Γ, and converges to (x, y). Because G_Γ is closed by assumption, we know further that $(x, y) \in G_\Gamma$, i.e., that $y \in \Gamma(x)$. Hence, $y \in \Psi(x) \cap \Gamma(x)$, as was to be shown.   □

Problem 11.10. Prove Theorem 11.9: Let the correspondence $\Psi: X \to\to Y$ be compact-valued and uhc. Then the image under Ψ of a compact set C, $\Psi(C) = \cup_{x \in C} \Psi(x)$, is compact.

Using the sequential characterization of compactness (Theorem 8.11), it is enough to show that every sequence $\{y_n\}$ contained in $\Psi(C)$ has a convergent subsequence with limit in $\Psi(C)$. Let $\{y_n\}$ be an arbitrary sequence in $\Psi(C)$. Then for each y_n there exists some $x_n \in C$ such that $y_n \in \Psi(x_n)$. Because C is compact, $\{x_n\}$ contains a convergent subsequence $\{x_{n_k}\}$ with limit x in C. Because Ψ is uhc and compact-valued, by Theorem 11.2 (sequential characterization of uhc) the sequence $\{y_{n_k}\}$ has a convergent subsequence with limit in $\Psi(x)$ and hence in $\Psi(C)$.   □

Problem 11.12. Prove Theorem 11.11: Let the correspondences $\Psi_i: X \to\to Y$, with $i = 1, \ldots, n$, be compact-valued and uhc at x. Then the sum correspondence Ψ, defined by $\Psi(x) = \Sigma_{i=1}^n \Psi_i(x)$ for each x, is compact-valued and uhc at x.

Let $\{x_n\}$ be an arbitrary sequence converging to x, and consider a companion sequence $\{y_n\}$, with $y_n \in \Sigma_{i=1}^n \Psi_i(x_n)$ for each n. Notice that each y_n is of the form

$$y_n = \sum_{i=1}^n y_n^i, \text{ with } y_n^i \in \Psi_i(x_n)$$

By Theorem 11.2, each sequence $\{y_n^i\}$ has a convergent subsequence $\{y_{n_{k_j}}^i\}$, with limit y^i in $\Psi_i(x)$. By Theorem 3.10 (equivalence of convergence and coordinate-wise convergence), it follows that $\{y_n\}$ has a convergent subsequence $\{y_{n_k}\}$, with limit $\Sigma_{i=1}^n y^i \in \Sigma_{i=1}^n \Psi_i(x)$.   □

Problem 11.15. Prove Theorem 11.14: Let $\Gamma^i: X \to\to Y$, with $i = 1, \ldots, n$, be compact-valued and uhc correspondences. Then the product correspondence $\Gamma(\ )$, with $\Gamma(x) = \Gamma^1(x) \times \ldots \times \Gamma^n(x)$ for each x in X, is compact-valued and uhc.

Fix an arbitrary x in X. Then the set $\Gamma(x)$ is compact because it is the Cartesian product of compact sets (Problem 8.26). Hence, $\Gamma(\ )$ is compact-valued, and in order to establish its upper hemicontinuity it is sufficient to show that given any sequence $\{x_n\}$ converging to x, every "companion sequence" $\{y_n\}$, with $y_n \in \Gamma(x_n)$ for all n, has a convergent subsequence $\{y_{n_k}\}$ with limit in $\Gamma(x)$.

To simplify a bit, suppose $n = 2$. Then $y_n \in \Gamma(x_n)$ will be of the form (y_n^1, y_n^2), with $y_n^1 \in \Gamma^1(x_n)$ and $y_n^2 \in \Gamma^2(x_n)$. By the upper hemicontinuity of $\Gamma^1(\ )$, the sequence $\{y_n^1\}$ has a convergent subsequence $\{y_{n_k}^1\}$, with limit $y^1 \in \Gamma^1(x)$. Consider now the corresponding second component sequence, $\{y_{n_k}^2\}$. By the upper hemicontinuity of $\Gamma^2(\ )$, this sequence has a subsequence $\{y_{n_{k_q}}^2\}$ converging to a point y^2 in $\Gamma^2(x)$. Hence, the subsequence $\{y_{n_{k_q}}\} = \{(y_{n_{k_q}}^1, y_{n_{k_q}}^2)\}$ converges to a point $y = (y^1, y^2) \in \Gamma^1(x) \times \Gamma^2(x) = \Gamma(x)$. This proves the result. $\square$

Chapter 3

Problem 1.6. Prove Theorem 1.5: Let V be a vector space of dimension n. Then any linearly independent family of n vectors in V, $\mathrm{v} = \{v_1, \ldots, v_n\}$, is a basis for V.

We want to show that $\mathrm{v} = \{v_1, \ldots, v_n\}$ spans V, that is, that each $x \in V$ can be written as a linear combination of the vectors in v. By Theorem 1.4, $\{v_1, \ldots, v_n, x\}$ is a linearly dependent family for any x; therefore, there exist scalars $\alpha_1, \ldots, \alpha_{n+1}$ not all zero such that

$$\sum\nolimits_{i=1}^n \alpha_i v_i + \alpha_{n+1} x = \underline{0}$$

where, moreover, $\alpha_{n+1} \neq 0$ (otherwise, the v_i's could not be linearly independent). Hence, we can solve for x and write it as a linear combination of the elements of v:

$$x = \sum\nolimits_{i=1}^n \frac{-\alpha_i}{\alpha_{n+1}} v_i \qquad\qquad \square$$

Problem 1.8. Prove the following result: Let X be a finite-dimensional normed linear space with basis $\{v_1, \ldots, v_m\}$ over the real field. A sequence $\{x_n\}$ in X, with $x_n = \sum_{i=1}^m \alpha_i^n v_i$ (α_i^n real), converges to $x = \sum_{i=1}^m \alpha_i v_i$ if and only if each coordinate sequence $\{\alpha_i^n\}$ converges to α_i for each $i = 1, \ldots, m$.

It is sufficient to consider the case in which $x = \underline{0}$.

(i) Show that if $\{\alpha_i^n\} \to 0$ for all i, then $\{x_n\} \to \underline{0}$.

Suppose that each coordinate sequence $\{\alpha_i^n\}$ converges to zero, and fix some $\varepsilon > 0$. For each i, there exists some integer N_i such that

$$|\alpha_i^n| < \frac{\varepsilon}{\sum_{i=1}^m \|v_i\|} \quad \forall\, n > N_i \tag{1}$$

Putting $N = \max_i N_i$, (1) holds for all $n > N$ and all $i = 1, \ldots, m$. Now, by the triangle inequality and the defining properties of the norm,

$$\|x_n\| = \left\| \sum\nolimits_{i=1}^m \alpha_i^n v_i \right\| \leq \sum\nolimits_{i=1}^m |\alpha_i^n|\, \|v_i\| \leq \frac{\varepsilon}{\sum_{i=1}^m \|v_i\|} \left(\sum\nolimits_{i=1}^m \|v_i\| \right) = \varepsilon$$

for all $n > N$, that is, $\{x_n\} \to \underline{0}$.

(ii) To prove the converse implication, suppose that $\{x_n\} \to \underline{0}$, but for some k the coordinate sequence $\{\alpha_k^n\}$ does not converge to 0. Then there exists a subsequence of $\{x_n\}$ (for convenience of notation, still referred to as $\{x_n\}$) and some $r > 0$ such that $|\alpha_k^n| > r$ for all n. For each $n \in \mathbb{N}$, write

$$M_n = \max_i \{|\alpha_i^n|;\ 1 \leq i \leq m\}$$

and consider the sequence $\{y_n\}$, with $y_n = x_n/M_n)$. We will show that $\{y_n\} \to \underline{0}$. Because $M_n > r$ for all $n \in \mathbb{N}$, we have

$$0 \le \|y_n\| = \frac{1}{M_n} \|x_n\| < \frac{1}{r} \|x_n\|$$

and therefore $\|y_n\| \to 0$.

(iii) Use the Bolzano-Weierstrass theorem to show that from $\{y_n\}$ we can choose a subsequence that converges coordinate-wise, but to a nonzero element. By the first part of the theorem, we have a contradiction.

Observe that for each n, the coordinates of y_n lie between -1 and $+1$, and at least one of them is equal to -1 or $+1$. The coordinate sequences $\{\alpha_i^n\}$ are therefore all bounded, and at least one of them has a convergent subsequence whose terms are all equal to $+1$ or -1 (there are infinite numbers of $+1$'s or -1's or both to allocate among a finite number of coordinate sequences, so at least one contains an infinite number of one of these). For convenience, suppose this is the first coordinate sequence $\{\alpha_1^n\}$, and call the constant subsequence $\{\alpha_1^{q_1(k)}\}$.

Consider the corresponding subsequence of $\{y_n\}$, $\{y_{q_1(k)}\}$, and its second coordinate sequence, $\{\alpha_2^{q_1(k)}\}$. By the Bolzano-Weierstrass theorem (B-W), this bounded real sequence has a convergent subsequence that we call $\{\alpha_2^{q_2(k)}\}$. Note that the corresponding first coordinate subsequence, $\{\alpha_1^{q_2(k)}\}$, still converges (any subsequence of a convergent sequence converges). Next, consider the corresponding subsequence of $\{y_n\}$, $\{y_{q_2(k)}\}$, and its third coordinate sequence, $\{\alpha_3^{q_2(k)}\}$. By B-W, it too has a convergent subsequence, say $\{\alpha_3^{q_3(k)}\}$, and $\{\alpha_1^{q_3(k)}\}$ and $\{\alpha_2^{q_3(k)}\}$ still converge. Continuing in this way for each of the m coordinate sequences, we construct a subsequence $\{y_{q_m(k)}\}$ whose coordinate sequences $\{\alpha_i^{q_m(k)}\}$ are all convergent, but at least one of them (the first one) does not have limit zero. Hence, the coordinate-wise limit is not the zero vector, and by the first part of the theorem it follows that $\{y_{n_k}\} \not\to \underline{0}$, which contradicts (ii).   □

Problem 1.9. Using the foregoing result and the completeness of $\mathbb{R}$, we will show that every finite-dimensional normed vector space over $\mathbb{R}$ is complete.

(i) First, show that if $\{x_n\}$ is Cauchy, then every coordinate sequence $\{\alpha_i^n\}$ is Cauchy. (Prove the contrapositive statement: If some coordinate sequence $\{\alpha_k^n\}$ is not Cauchy, then neither is $\{x_n\}$. Use the result in Problem 1.8.)

(ii) Using (i), Problem 1.8 again, and the completeness of $\mathbb{R}$, show that the desired result holds.

(i) Let X be a normed vector space with a basis $\{v_1, \ldots, v_m\}$. Let $\{x_n\}$ be a sequence in X. Write it $x_n = \Sigma_{i=1}^m \alpha_i^n v_i$ (α_i^n real), and suppose that some coordinate sequence $\{\alpha_k^n\}$ is not Cauchy. We will show that $\{x_n\}$ cannot be Cauchy. If $\{\alpha_k^n\}$ is not Cauchy, then there exists some $r > 0$ such that for each $q \in \mathbb{N}$, there exist $m_q, n_q > q$ such that

$$\left| \alpha_k^{m_q} - \alpha_k^{n_q} \right| > r$$

Hence, the subsequence $\{\alpha_k^{m_q} - \alpha_k^{n_q}\}$ does not converge to zero. But then, by Problem 1.8, the subsequence $\{x_{m_q} - x_{n_q}\}$ does not converge to the zero vector, implying that $\{x_n\}$ is not Cauchy.

(ii) Let $\{x_n\}$ be a Cauchy sequence in X. From part (i), each coordinate sequence $\{\alpha_i^n\}$ is a Cauchy sequence of real numbers, and by the completeness of $\mathbb{R}$, each converges to some real limit, say α_i. By Problem 1.8, $\{x_n\}$ converges to $x = \Sigma_{i=1}^m \alpha_i v_i$.   □

Problem 2.2. Show that for any linear function T, $T(\underline{0}) = \underline{0}$.
Because $0x = \underline{0}$ for any vector x, we have, by the linearity of T, that $T(\underline{0}) = T(0x)$
$= 0T(x) = \underline{0}$. $\qquad\square$

Problem 2.4. Show that the composition of two linear functions is linear.
   Let $R: X \longrightarrow Y$ and $S: Y \longrightarrow Z$ be linear mappings, and let $T = S \circ R$ be their
composition. Given any two vectors x and y in X and arbitrary scalars α and β,
we have, exploiting the linearity of S and T,

$$T(\alpha x + \beta y) = S[R(ax + \beta y)] = S[\alpha R(x) + \beta R(y)] = \alpha S[R(x)] + \beta S[R(y)] = \alpha T(x) + \beta T(y)$$
$\qquad\square$

Problem 2.8. Prove Theorem 2.7: Given a linear transformation $T: X \longrightarrow Y$,
ker T is a vector subspace of X.
   Let x_1 and x_2 be two vectors in ker T, that is, such that $T(x_1) = T(x_2) = \underline{0}$. Given
any scalars α and β, we have, by the linearity of T,

$$T(\alpha x_1 + \beta x_2) = \alpha T(x_1) + \beta T(x_2) = \alpha \underline{0} + \beta \underline{0} = \underline{0}$$

Hence, $\alpha x_1 + \beta x_2 \in$ ker T. $\qquad\square$

Problem 2.12. Prove Theorem 2.11: Let $T \in L(X, Y)$ be an invertible linear
function. Then the inverse map $T^{-1}: Y \longrightarrow X$ is linear; that is, $T^{-1} \in L(Y, X)$.
   Let y and y' be two arbitrary points in Y. Because T is invertible, there exist
points x and x' in X such that

$$y = T(x), \qquad x = T^{-1}(y), \qquad y' = T(x'), \qquad x' = T^{-1}(y') \qquad (1)$$

Then, using the linearity of T, the definition of inverse, and (1), we have

$$T^{-1}(\alpha y + \beta y') = T^{-1}[\alpha T(x) + \beta T(x')] = T^{-1}[T(\alpha x + \beta x')]$$
$$= \alpha x + \beta x' = \alpha T^{-1}(y) + \beta T^{-1}(y')$$

which shows that T^{-1} is linear. $\qquad\square$

Problem 2.14. Prove Theorem 2.13: A linear transformation $T: X \longrightarrow Y$ is one-
to-one if and only if $T(x) = \underline{0} \Rightarrow x = \underline{0}$, that is, if ker $T = \{\underline{0}\}$.
   Recall that for any linear mapping T we have $T(\underline{0}) = \underline{0}$ (Problem 2.2). If ker
$T \neq \{\underline{0}\}$, then there is at least one other element $x \neq \underline{0}$ in the kernel, and it follows
that T is not one-to-one, because it maps two different vectors into the zero vector.
   Conversely, suppose ker $T = \{\underline{0}\}$, and let x and x' be two distinct elements of X.
Then $x - x' \neq \underline{0}$, implying $x - x' \notin$ ker T, and therefore $T(x - x') \neq \underline{0}$. But then, by
the linearity of T,

$$T(x) - T(x') = T(x - x') \neq \underline{0}$$

from where $T(x) \neq T(x')$. $\qquad\square$

Problem 4.4. We will prove the following theorem: Given normed linear spaces X
and Y and a linear function $T: X \longrightarrow Y$, the inverse function T^{-1} exists and is a
continuous linear mapping on $T(X)$ if and only if there exists some $m > 0$ such
that $m\|x\| \leq \|Tx\|$.

   (i) Using Theorem 2.13, show that if there exists some $m > 0$ such that
       $m\|x\| \leq \|Tx\|$, then T is one-to-one (and therefore invertible on $T(X)$).
  (ii) Use Theorem 4.3 to show that T^{-1} is continuous on $T(X)$.
 (iii) Using Theorem 4.3, show that if T^{-1} is continuous on $T(X)$, then there exists
       some $m > 0$ such that $m\|x\| \leq \|Tx\|$.

(i) If $x \neq \underline{0}$, then $\|x\| > 0$ and $\|Tx\| \geq m\|x\| > 0$, so $Tx \neq \underline{0}$, implying that T is one-to-one (Theorem 2.13). Hence, T^{-1} is defined on $T(X)$ and is linear (Problem 2.12).

(ii) To show that T^{-1} is continuous on $T(X)$, write $x = T^{-1}(y)$. For any y in $T(X)$, we have

$$m\|x\| = m\|T^{-1}(y)\| = m\|x\| \leq \|Tx\| = \|y\| \Rightarrow \|T^{-1}(y)\| \leq \frac{\|y\|}{m} \ \forall \ y \in T(X)$$

Hence, T^{-1} is bounded and therefore continuous (by Theorem 4.3).

(iii) Conversely, if T^{-1} is continuous on $T(X)$, then by Theorem 4.3 there exists some $M > 0$ such that

$$\|T^{-1}(y)\| \leq M\|y\| \ \forall \ y \in T(X)$$

Now, $y = Tx$, so

$$\|T^{-1}(Tx)\| \leq M\|Tx\| \Rightarrow \frac{\|x\|}{M} \leq \|Tx\| \ \forall \ x \in X$$

and the result follows with $m = 1/M$. $\qquad\square$

Problem 5.1. Show that the matrix P that represents a coordinate change is invertible.

Let x be an arbitrary vector in V, with coordinate vector $\alpha = (\alpha_1, \ldots, \alpha_n)^T$ in basis a, and $\beta = (\beta_1, \ldots, \beta_n)^T$ in basis b. We have seen that there is a matrix P such that $\alpha = P\beta$. By the same argument, there is also a matrix Z such that $\beta = Z\alpha$. Hence,

$$\alpha = P\beta = PZ\alpha$$

for any vector with (arbitrary coordinates) α. Hence, $PZ = \mathbf{I}$, and by the same argument $ZP = \mathbf{I}$. Hence, $Z = P^{-1}$, and P is invertible. $\qquad\square$

Problem 5.3. Show that similar matrices have the same determinant.

$$|B| = |P^{-1}AP| = |P^{-1}||A||P| = |A||P^{-1}||P| = |A|, \text{ because } P^{-1}P = \mathbf{I}, \ |P^{-1}||P| = |\mathbf{I}| = 1 \qquad\square$$

Problem 6.2. Show that the eigenspace of A corresponding to an eigenvalue λ is a vector space.

Let x and y be any two vectors in the eigenspace of A corresponding to λ. Then $Ax = \lambda x$, $Ay = \lambda y$, and we have, for any scalars α and β,

$$A(\alpha x + \beta y) = \alpha(Ax) + \beta(Ay) = \alpha(\lambda x) + \beta(\lambda y) = \lambda(\alpha x + \beta y)$$

so $\alpha x + \beta y$ lies in the eigenspace of A, which is therefore a vector (sub-) space. $\square$

Problem 6.3. Show that if λ is an eigenvalue of A, then (i) λ^n is an eigenvalue of A^n, and (ii) λ^{-1} is an eigenvalue of A^{-1}.

(i) We proceed by induction. First, consider the case where $n = 2$. Let λ be an eigenvalue of A, and x an eigenvector belonging to it; then $Ax = \lambda x$, and

$$A^2x = A(Ax) = A(\lambda x) = \lambda(Ax) = \lambda(\lambda x) = \lambda^2 x$$

so λ^2 is indeed an eigenvalue of A^2, and x an eigenvector. Next, suppose that λ^n is an eigenvalue of A^n, and x an eigenvector belonging to it (i.e., $A^n x = \lambda_x^n$). Then

$$A^{n+1}x = A^n Ax = A^n(\lambda x) = \lambda(A^n x) = \lambda(\lambda^n x) = \lambda^{n+1}x$$

(ii) Observe that $Ax = \lambda x$ implies $x = \mathbf{I}x = A^{-1}Ax = A^{-1}\lambda x$, and therefore $A^{-1}x = \lambda^{-1}x$. □

Problem 6.4. Find the eigenvalues and eigenvectors of the matrix

$$A = \begin{bmatrix} 3 & -2 & 0 \\ -2 & 3 & 0 \\ 0 & 0 & 5 \end{bmatrix}$$

The characteristic equation of A is of the form

$$|A - \lambda\mathbf{I}| = \det\begin{bmatrix} 3-\lambda & -2 & 0 \\ -2 & 3-\lambda & 0 \\ 0 & 0 & 5-\lambda \end{bmatrix} = (3-\lambda)^2(5-\lambda) - 4(5-\lambda)$$

$$= (5-\lambda)(5 - 6\lambda + \lambda^2) = 0$$

Hence, $\lambda_1 = 5$, and

$$\lambda_2, \lambda_3 = \frac{6 \pm \sqrt{36 - 20}}{2} = 5, 1$$

We have one repeated eigenvalue (5) and a second eigenvalue (1) with multiplicity 1.

By definition, $e = (e_1, e_2, e_3)^T$ is an eigenvector of A belonging to the eigenvalue λ if it is a nonzero solution of the equation

$$(A - \lambda\mathbf{I})e = \underline{0} \Leftrightarrow \begin{bmatrix} 3-\lambda & -2 & 0 \\ -2 & 3-\lambda & 0 \\ 0 & 0 & 5-\lambda \end{bmatrix}\begin{bmatrix} e_1 \\ e_2 \\ e_3 \end{bmatrix} = \begin{bmatrix} 0 \\ 0 \\ 0 \end{bmatrix}$$

With $\lambda = 1$, we have the system

$$2e_1 - 2e_2 = 0, \qquad -2e_1 + 2e_2 = 0, \qquad 4e_3 = 0$$

Clearly, the first and second equations are not linearly independent. This leaves us with an undetermined system of two equations in three unknowns, and we have

$$e_3 = 0 \quad \text{and} \quad e_1 = e_2 = r$$

where r is an arbitrary number different from zero. Hence, the eigenvectors of A corresponding to the eigenvalue $\lambda = 1$ are the nonzero vectors of the form

$$e = \begin{bmatrix} e_1 \\ e_2 \\ e_3 \end{bmatrix} = \begin{bmatrix} r \\ r \\ 0 \end{bmatrix} = r\begin{bmatrix} 1 \\ 1 \\ 0 \end{bmatrix}, \quad \text{with } r \neq 0$$

□

Chapter 4

Problem 1.2. Let f and g be functions $\mathbb{R} \longrightarrow \mathbb{R}$, and assume that they are both differentiable at the point x^0. Using the elementary properties of limits and the continuity of f and g at x, show that the product function p, defined by $p(x) = f(x)g(x)$, is differentiable at x^0 and that

$$p'(x^0) = f(x^0)g'(x^0) + f'(x^0)g(x^0)$$

Observe that

$$f(x)g(x) - f(x^0)g(x^0) = f(x)g(x) - f(x^0)g(x) + f(x^0)g(x) - f(x^0)g(x^0)$$
$$= g(x)\left[f(x) - f(x^0)\right] + f(x^0)\left[g(x) - g(x^0)\right]$$

Taking the limit of this expression as x approaches x^0,

$$\lim_{x \to x^0} \frac{f(x)g(x) - f(x^0)g(x^0)}{x - x^0} = \left(\lim_{x \to x^0} g(x)\right)\left(\lim_{x \to x^0} \frac{f(x) - f(x^0)}{x - x^0}\right) + f(x^0)\left(\lim_{x \to x^0} \frac{g(x) - g(x^0)}{x - x^0}\right)$$
$$= g(x^0)f'(x^0) + f(x^0)g'(x^0) \qquad \square$$

Problem 1.3. Let $f(x) = x^n$. Show by induction that $f'(x) = nx^{n-1}$.

Let $f(x) = x^2$. Then

$$f'(x) = \lim_{h \to 0} \frac{f(x+h) - f(x)}{h} = \lim_{h \to 0} \frac{(x+h)^2 - x^2}{h} = \lim_{h \to 0} (2x + h) = 2x$$

Next, suppose that $dx^n/dx = nx^{n-1}$; we want to show that then $dx^{n+1}/dx = (n+1)x^n$. Observe that

$$(x+h)^{n+1} - x^{n+1} = (x+h)^n(x+h) - x^n x = x\left[(x+h)^n - x^n\right] + h(x+h)^n$$

Hence,

$$\frac{x^{n+1}}{dx} = \lim_{h \to 0} \frac{(x+h)^{n+1} - x^{n+1}}{h} = \lim_{h \to 0} \frac{x\left[(x+h)^n - x^n\right] + h(x+h)^n}{h}$$
$$= x\left(\lim_{h \to 0} \frac{(x+h)^n - x^n}{h}\right) + \lim_{h \to 0}(x+h)^n = x\frac{dx^n}{dx} + x^n = xnx^{n-1} + x^n = (n+1)x^n \qquad \square$$

Problem 1.8. Let $f: \mathbb{R} \longrightarrow \mathbb{R}$ be a differentiable function on an interval I. Show that (i) if $f'(x) = 0$ for each $x \in I$, then f is constant on the interval, and (ii) if $f'(x) > 0$ on (a, b), then f is strictly increasing on I.

Let x and y, with $x < y$, be two arbitrary points in I. We will use the mean-value theorem to show that $f(x) = f(y)$ (or $f(y) > f(x)$). Because x and y are arbitrary, the desired result follows.

By the mean-value theorem, there exists some point $z \in (x, y) \subseteq I$ such that

$$f'(z) = \frac{f(y) - f(x)}{y - x}$$

In (i), $f'(z) = 0$, implying that $f(y) = f(x)$. In (ii), $f'(z) > 0$, implying that $f(y) > f(x)$. $\qquad \square$

Problem 1.10. A sufficient condition for a local maximum. Let $f: \mathbb{R} \longrightarrow \mathbb{R}$ be twice differentiable on some interval containing x^0. Assume, moreover, that $f'(x^0) = 0$, $f''(x^0) < 0$, and f'' is continuous at x^0. Use Problem 1.8 to show that x^0 is a local maximizer of f.

Because $f''(x^0) < 0$ and f'' is continuous, f'' is negative on some interval I containing x^0 (by the sign-preservation property of continuous functions, see Problem 6.2 in Chapter 2). By Problem 1.8, a negative second derivative implies a decreasing first derivative. Thus, $f'(x) > 0$ for x to the left of x^0 in the interval I, and $f'(x) < 0$ for x to the right of x^0 in the same interval. By Problem 1.8 again, $f(\ )$ decreases to the left of x^0 and increases to its right, which proves the result.   □

Problem 1.11. Let $f: \mathbb{R} \longrightarrow \mathbb{R}$ be $m + 1$ times differentiable on an interval around the point x^0. Assume that for some $m > 1$, $f^{(m)}(x^0)$ is the first nonzero derivative of f at x^0, that is,

$$f'(x^0) = f''(x^0) = f^{(3)}(x^0) = \ldots = f^{(m-1)}(x^0) = 0 \quad \text{and} \quad f^{(m)}(x^0) \neq 0$$

Use Taylor's theorem to show that

(i) if m is even and $f^{(m)}(x^0) < 0$, then f has a local maximum at x^0,
(ii) if m is even and $f^{(m)}(x^0) > 0$, then f has a local minimum at x^0,
(iii) if m is odd, then f has neither a local maximum nor a local minimum at x^0.

To simplify the notation, suppose $x^0 = 0$. By assumption, $f^{(m)}$ is differentiable and therefore continuous at $x^0 = 0$; hence, by the sign-preservation property of continuous functions, there exists some open interval I around 0 in which $f^{(m)}$ does not change sign.

Next, by Taylor's theorem, we have, for each x in I,

$$f(x) = f(0) + \sum_{k=1}^{m-1} \frac{f^{(k)}(0)}{k!} x^k + \frac{f^{(m)}(\lambda x)}{m!} x^m = f(0) + \frac{f^{(m)}(\lambda x)}{m!} x^m$$

where $\lambda \in (0, 1)$, and therefore $\lambda x \in I$. Hence, for any $x \in I$, we have

$$f(x) - f(0) = \frac{f^{(m)}(\lambda x)}{m!} x^m$$

where the sign of $f^{(m)}(\lambda x)$ is the same as that of $f^{(m)}(0)$. Consider the sign of the right-hand side of this expression. If m is even, $x^m > 0$ for all $x \in I$ and different from zero. If $f^{(m)}(0) < 0$, we have $f^{(m)}(\lambda x) < 0$, and therefore $f(x) - f(0) < 0$ for all x in I distinct from zero, implying that x is a local maximizer of f. By a similar argument, the rest of the cases follow.   □

Problem 1.12. Cauchy's mean-value theorem. Prove the following result: Let f and $g: [a, b] \longrightarrow \mathbb{R}$ be differentiable on (a, b), and suppose that $g'(x) \neq 0$ for all x in (a, b). Then there is a point z in (a, b) such that

$$\frac{f(b) - f(a)}{g(b) - g(a)} = \frac{f'(z)}{g'(z)}$$

Define $\phi(\ )$ by

$$\phi(x) = [g(b) - g(a)]f(x) - [f(b) - f(a)]g(x)$$

and observe that $\phi(\ )$ is differentiable, with $\phi(a) = g(b)f(a) - f(b)g(a) = \phi(b)$. Applying Rolle's theorem to $\phi(\ )$, there exists some point z in (a, b) such that

$$\phi'(z) = [g(b) - g(a)]f'(z) - [f(b) - f(a)]g'(z) = 0 \tag{1}$$

By assumption, $g'(z) \neq 0$. Moreover, $g(a) - g(b) \neq 0$, for otherwise Rolle's theorem applied to $g(\ )$ would show that $g'(x) = 0$ for some x in (a, b), and that would contradict our assumption. Hence, we can divide by these two terms and rearrange (1) to get

$$\frac{f(b) - f(a)}{g(b) - g(a)} = \frac{f'(z)}{g'(z)}$$

     □

Problem 1.13. L'Hôpital's rule. Suppose f and g are continuous real-valued functions defined and differentiable on some open interval containing the point a and such that $f(a) = g(a) = 0$. Show that if $f'(x)/g'(x)$ tends to a limit as $x \to a$, so does $f(x)/g(x)$, and

$$\lim_{x \to a} \frac{f(x)}{g(x)} = \lim_{x \to a} \frac{f'(x)}{g'(x)}$$

Assume that $f'(x)/g'(x) \to L$ as $x \to a$, and fix some arbitrary $\varepsilon > 0$. Then there exists some $\delta > 0$ such that

$$\left| \frac{f'(x)}{g'(x)} - L \right| < \varepsilon \ \forall \ x \in B_\delta(a) = (a - \delta, a + \delta) \tag{1}$$

Choose some x in $(a, a + \delta)$ and apply the Cauchy mean-value theorem to f and g in the interval $[a, x]$ to show that there exists some number z in (a, x) such that

$$\frac{f'(z)}{g'(z)} = \frac{f(x) - f(a)}{g(x) - g(a)} = \frac{f(x)}{g(x)}$$

Because $z \in (a, x) \subseteq (a - \delta, a + \delta)$, we have, by (1),

$$\left| \frac{f(x)}{g(x)} - L \right| = \left| \frac{f'(z)}{g'(z)} - L \right| < \varepsilon$$

Because x was an arbitrary point of $(a, a + \delta)$, we have shown that

$$\left| \frac{f(x)}{g(x)} - L \right| < \varepsilon$$

for all $x \in (a, a + \delta)$, and because ε was arbitrary, this establishes that $f(x)/g(x) \to L$ as x approaches a from above. A similar argument then yields that $f(x)/g(x) \to L$ as $x \to a^-$, and the result follows. $\qquad\qquad\square$

Problem 2.2. Let $f(x_1, x_2) = x_1 x_2$, $u = (3/5, 4/5)$, and $x^0 = (1, 2)$. Compute $Df(x^0; u)$ directly by taking the appropriate limits, and verify that the result is the same if you use the formula $Df(x^0; u) = \nabla f(x^0) u$.

$$Df(x; u) = \lim_{\alpha \to 0} \frac{f(x + \alpha u) - f(x)}{\alpha} = \lim_{\alpha \to 0} \frac{\left(x_1 + \dfrac{3\alpha}{5}\right)\left(x_2 + \dfrac{4\alpha}{5}\right) - x_{21} x_2}{\alpha}$$

$$= \lim_{\alpha \to 0} \left(\frac{4x_1}{5} + \frac{3x_2}{5} + \frac{12\alpha}{25} \right) = \frac{4x_1}{5} + \frac{3x_2}{5}$$

Therefore,

$$Df(x^0; u) = \frac{4}{5} + \frac{6}{5} = 2$$

On the other hand,

$$Df(x^0; u) = \nabla f(x^0) u = \left[\frac{\partial f(x^0)}{\partial x_1}, \frac{\partial f(x^0)}{\partial x_1} \right] \begin{bmatrix} u_1 \\ u_2 \end{bmatrix} = (x_2^0, x_1^0) \begin{bmatrix} u_1 \\ u_2 \end{bmatrix}$$

$$= (2, 1)(3/5, 4/5)^T = 2 \qquad\qquad\square$$

Problem 2.4. Given the functions
$$y = f(x_1, x_2) = \sin(x_1 x_2 + x_2^2), \qquad y = f(x_1, x_2) = x_1^2 x_2 + x_2^3 \ln x_1,$$
$$y = f(x_1, x_2) = \ln(x_2 + e_1^x x_2)$$
compute, for each of them, the partial derivatives $\partial y / \partial x_1$ and $\partial y / \partial x_2$.

$$y = \sin(x_1 x_2 + x_2^2), \qquad \frac{\partial y}{\partial x_1} = \cos(x_1 x_2 + x_2^2) x_2, \qquad \frac{\partial y}{\partial x_2} = \cos(x_1 x_2 + x_2^2)(x_1 + 2x_2)$$

$$y = x_1^2 x_2 + x_2^3 \ln x_1, \qquad \frac{\partial y}{\partial x_1} = 2x_1 x_2 + \frac{x_2^3}{x_1}, \qquad \frac{\partial y}{\partial x_2} = x_1^2 + 3x_2^2 \ln x_1$$

$$y = \ln(x_2 + x_2 e^{x_1}), \qquad \frac{\partial y}{\partial x_1} = \frac{x_2 e^{x_1}}{x_2 + x_2 e^{x_1}}, \qquad \frac{\partial y}{\partial x_2} = \frac{1 + e^{x_1}}{x_2 + x_2 e^{x_1}} \qquad \square$$

Problem 2.5. Find the points where all the partial derivatives of the function
$$f(x_1, x_2) = x_1^4 x_2 - x_1^2 x_2^3$$
are zero.

We have to solve the following system of equations:

$$\frac{\partial f(x)}{\partial x_1} = 4x_1^3 x_2 - 2x_1 x_2^3 = 2x_1 x_2 (2x_1^2 - x_2^2) = 0 \tag{1}$$

$$\frac{\partial f(x)}{\partial x_2} = x_1^4 - 3x_1^2 x_2^2 = x_1^2(x_1^2 - 3x_2^2) = 0 \tag{2}$$

Therefore,

(i) if $x_1 = 0$, then $\partial f(x)/\partial x_1 = \partial f(x)/\partial x_2 = 0$ for all x_2, and
(ii) if $x_1 \neq 0$, then
   (a) $\partial f(x)/\partial x_1 = 0$ if $x_2 = 0$ or $2x_1^2 - x_2^2 = 0$, and
   (b) $\partial f(x)/\partial x_2 = 0$ if $x_1^2 - 3x_2^2 = 0$

so we have to consider two cases:

• If $x_2 = 0$, then (b) reduces to $x_1^2 = 0$.
• The other possibility is to have

$$2x_1^2 = x_2^2 \quad \text{and} \quad x_1^2 = 3x_2^2$$

at the same time. Substituting the first expression into the second, $x_1^2 = 3(2x_1^2)$, which holds only if $x_1 = 0$, so there are no other solutions. $\square$

Problem 3.6. Let $w = f(x, y, z) = xy^2 z$, where
$$x = r + 2s + t, \qquad y = 2r + 3s + t, \qquad z = 3r + s + t$$
Use the chain rule to calculate $\partial w / \partial r$, $\partial w / \partial s$, and $\partial w / \partial t$.

We have

$$\frac{\partial w}{\partial x} = y^2 z, \qquad \frac{\partial x}{\partial r} = 1, \qquad \frac{\partial y}{\partial r} = 2, \qquad \frac{\partial z}{\partial r} = 3$$

$$\frac{\partial w}{\partial y} = 2xyz, \qquad \frac{\partial x}{\partial s} = 2, \qquad \frac{\partial y}{\partial s} = 3, \qquad \frac{\partial z}{\partial s} = 1$$

$$\frac{\partial w}{\partial z} = xy^2, \qquad \frac{\partial x}{\partial t} = -1, \qquad \frac{\partial y}{\partial t} = 1, \qquad \frac{\partial z}{\partial t} = 1$$

Hence,

$$\frac{\partial w}{\partial s} = \frac{\partial w}{\partial x}\frac{\partial x}{\partial s} + \frac{\partial w}{\partial y}\frac{\partial y}{\partial s} + \frac{\partial w}{\partial z}\frac{\partial z}{\partial s} = 2(y^2 z) + 3(2xyz) + 1(xy^2)$$

$$= 2(2r + 3s + t)^2(3r + s + t) + 6(r + 2s + t)(2r + 3s + t)(3r + s + t)$$

$$+ 1(r + 2s + t)(2r + 3s + t)^2, \quad \text{etc.} \qquad \square$$

Problem 3.8. Prove the following theorem: Let $f: \mathbb{R}^n \longrightarrow \mathbb{R}^m$ be differentiable on an open subset X of $\mathbb{R}^n$, and let x and y be two points in X such that $L(x, y)$ is contained in X. Then for each vector a in $\mathbb{R}^m$ there exists a vector z in $L(x, y)$ such that

$$a[f(y) - f(x)] = a[Df(z)(y - x)] \tag{2}$$

Put $h = y - x$. As X is open and contains $L(x, y)$, there exists some $\delta > 0$ such that $x + \lambda h \in X$ for $\lambda \in (-\delta, 1 + \delta)$. Fix an arbitrary vector $a = (a_1, \ldots, a_m) \in \mathbb{R}^m$, and define a real-valued function ϕ_a on the interval $(-\delta, 1 + \delta)$ by

$$\phi_a(\lambda) = af(x + \lambda h) = \sum_{i=1}^{m} a_i f^i(x + \lambda h)$$

By construction, $\phi_a(\ )$ is differentiable on $(-\delta, 1 + \delta)$, with derivative

$$\phi_a'(\lambda) = \sum_{i=1}^{m} a_i \left[\sum_{k=1}^{n} f_k^i(x + \lambda h)h_k \right] = \sum_{i=1}^{m} a_i [Df^i(x + \lambda h)h] = a[Df(x + \lambda h)h]$$

Applying the mean-value theorem for univariate real functions to $\phi_a(\ )$, we have

$$\phi_a(1) - \phi_a(0) = \phi_a'(\theta) \quad \text{for some } \theta \in (0, 1)$$

which is equivalent to

$$a[f(y) - f(x)] = [\phi_a(1) - \phi_a(0) = \phi_a'(\theta)] = a[Df(x + \theta h)h]$$

Putting

$$z = x + \theta h$$

we obtain the desired result. Note that the value of z depends on the chosen vector a. $\qquad \square$

Problem 4.5. Prove Theorem 4.4: Let $f: \mathbb{R}^n \longrightarrow \mathbb{R}$ be a C^2 function defined on an open and convex set X. If $x, x + h \in X$, then

$$f(x + h) = f(x) + Df(x)h + (1/2)h^T D^2 f(x + \lambda h)h \tag{1}$$

for some $\lambda \in (0, 1)$.

We apply the univariate version of Taylor's formula to the function g defined by

$$g(\alpha) = f(x + \alpha h)$$

Observe that because X is open and convex and both x and $x + h$ are in X, there exists some $\delta > 0$ such that $x + \alpha h \in X$ for $\alpha \in (-\delta, 1 + \delta)$ and such that g is twice continuously differentiable on this interval. By Taylor's theorem for univariate real functions, we have

$$f(x + h) - f(x) = g(1) - g(0) = \sum_{k=1}^{n-1} \frac{g^{(k)}(0)}{k!} + \frac{g^{(n)}(\lambda)}{n!} \tag{2}$$

for some $\lambda \in (0, 1)$. Computing the derivatives of g, we can generalize the univariate result for any n. To obtain a formula with quadratic remainder, we set $n = 2$ and observe that

$$g'(\alpha) = \sum_{k=1}^{n} f_k(x + \alpha h)h_k = Df(x + \alpha h)h$$

$$g''(\alpha) = \sum_{k=1}^{n} h_k \left(\sum_{j=1}^{n} f_{kj}(x + \alpha h)h_j\right) = h^T D^2 f(x + \alpha h)h$$

Substituting these expressions in (2), we obtain the desired result:

$$f(x + h) - f(x) = Df(x)h + (1/2)h^T D^2 f(x + \lambda h)h \quad \text{for some } \lambda \in (0, 1) \qquad \square$$

Problem 4.7. Let $f\colon \mathbb{R}^n \supseteq X \longrightarrow \mathbb{R}^n$ be a continuously differentiable function on the open set X. Show that f is locally Lipschitz on X.

Recall that the function f is said to be locally Lipschitz on the set X if for each point x_0 in X there exists some $\varepsilon_0 > 0$ and some $K_0 > 0$ such that $B_{\varepsilon_0}(x_0) \subseteq X$, and for all x and y in $B_{\varepsilon_0}(x_0)$,

$$\|f(x) - f(y)\| \le K_0\|x - y\| \tag{1}$$

Let x_0 be an arbitrary point in X. Because X is open, there exists some $\varepsilon_0 > 0$ such that $B_{2\varepsilon_0}(x_0) \subseteq X$. Because f is continuously differentiable and the norm is a continuous function, the function $X \longrightarrow \mathbb{R}$ defined by $\|Df(x)\|$ is continuous, and it therefore achieves a maximum on the compact set $B_{\varepsilon_0}[x_0] \subseteq X$. Let K_0 be this maximum, that is,

$$K_0 = \max\{\|Df(x)\|; \ x \in B_{\varepsilon_0}[x_0]\}$$

Let x and y be two arbitrary points in $B_{\varepsilon_0}(x_0)$. Because $B_{\varepsilon_0}(x_0)$ is a convex set, it contains the line segment $L(x, y)$. By Theorem 3.9, there exists a vector z in $L(x, y) \subseteq B_{\varepsilon_0}(x_0)$ such that

$$\|f(y) - f(x)\| \le \|Df(z)\|\|y - x\| \tag{2}$$

Now, because $z \in L(x, y) \subseteq B_{\varepsilon_0}(x_0)$, we have

$$\|Df(z)\| \le K_0 \tag{3}$$

and using (3) in (2),

$$\|f(y) - f(x)\| \le \|Df(z)\|\|y - x\| \le K_0\|y - x\|$$

Because x and y are arbitrary, K_0 is a Lipschitz constant for f on $B_{\varepsilon_0}(x_0)$, which is the desired result. $\qquad \square$

Problem 5.3. Show that if f is homogeneous of degree k and is "sufficiently differentiable," then its first partial derivatives are homogeneous of degree $k - 1$.

By the homogeneity of f, $f(\lambda x) = \lambda^k f(x)$ for all $\lambda > 0$. Keeping λ fixed, differentiate this expression with respect to x_i, obtaining

$$\lambda f_i(\lambda x) = \lambda^k f_i(x)$$

Dividing through by λ, we obtain the desired result. $\qquad \square$

Problem 5.4

(i) Show that the Cobb-Douglas function $f(x) = A\Pi_{i=1}^{n} x_i^{\alpha_i}$ is homogeneous of degree $\Sigma_{i=1}^{n}\alpha_i$.

(ii) Show that the CES function $g(x) = A(\Sigma_{i=1}^{n}\delta_i x_i^{-\rho})^{-v/\rho}$, where $A > 0$, $v > 0$, $\rho > -1$ and $\rho \ne 0$, $\delta_i > 0$ for all i, and $\Sigma_{i=1}^{n}\delta_i = 1$, is homogeneous of degree v.

$$f(\lambda x) = A\prod_{i=1}^{n}(\lambda x_i)^{\alpha_i} = A\left(\prod_{i=1}^{n}\lambda^{\alpha_i}\right)\left(\prod_{i=1}^{n}x_i^{\alpha_i}\right) = \lambda^{\Sigma_i \alpha_i} f(x)$$

$$g(\lambda x) = A\left(\sum_{i=1}^{n}\delta_i(\lambda x_i)^{-\rho}\right)^{-v/\rho} = A\left(\lambda^{-\rho}\sum_{i=1}^{n}\delta_i x_i^{-\rho}\right)^{-v/\rho} = A\lambda^{v}\left(\sum_{i=1}^{n}\delta_i x_i^{-\rho}\right)^{-v/\rho} = \lambda^{v}g(x)$$

□

Chapter 5

Problem 4.1. Given the IS-LM model

$$y = E_0 + \alpha y - \beta r + G \tag{A}$$
$$M^s/P = M_0 + \gamma y - \delta r \tag{B}$$

where y is national income, r is the interest rate, G is public expenditure, M^s/P is the money supply divided by a price index, and all the Greek letters are positive parameters.

(i) Analyze graphically the effects of increases in (a) government spending and (b) the price level on the equilibrium values of national income and the interest rate.
(ii) Write the model in matrix form. Use Cramer's rule to solve the model, writing the equilibrium values of (y, r) as functions of the parameters $(G, M^s/P, E_0,$ and $M_0)$, and show that the result is compatible with the conclusions of the graphical analysis.

• $G\uparrow \Rightarrow IS$ shifts to the right. For any given level of r, planned expenditure (y) increases, as can be seen in equation (A). Hence, the equilibrium level of national income increases, and so does the interest rate (Figure A5.1).
• $P\uparrow \Rightarrow (M^s/P)\downarrow \Rightarrow$ the real money supply decreases, so LM shifts up (for any given y, the interest rate must increase in order to preserve the equality of money demand and supply, now reduced). Equilibrium income falls, and the interest rate increases.

Analytically, rewriting (A) and (B) with the endogenous variables (y, r) on one side and the parameters on the other, we have

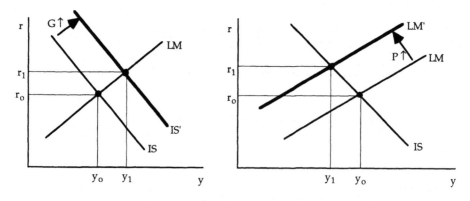

Figure A5.1. Effects of increases in G and M.

$$(1-\alpha)y + \beta r = E_0 + G \tag{A'}$$

$$\gamma y - \delta r = (M^s/P) - M_0 \tag{B'}$$

or, in matrix form,

$$\begin{bmatrix} 1-\alpha & \beta \\ \gamma & -\delta \end{bmatrix} \begin{bmatrix} y \\ r \end{bmatrix} = \begin{bmatrix} E_0 + G \\ (M^s/P) - M_0 \end{bmatrix} \Leftrightarrow Ax = d$$

Using Cramer's rule, we can solve for the equilibrium values of the endogenous variables. For each x_i, we have

$$x_i^* = \frac{|A_i|}{|A|}$$

where A_i is obtained by replacing the ith column of the coefficient matrix A by the vector on the right-hand side of the equation. Using this formula,

$$y^* = \frac{|A_y|}{|A|} = \frac{\begin{vmatrix} E_0 + G & \beta \\ (M^s/P) - M_0 & -\delta \end{vmatrix}}{\begin{vmatrix} 1-\alpha & \beta \\ \gamma & -\delta \end{vmatrix}} = \frac{\delta(G + E_0) + \beta[(M^s/P) - M_0]}{(1-\alpha)\delta + \beta\gamma}$$

from where

$$\frac{\partial y^*}{\partial G} = \frac{\delta}{(1-\alpha)\delta + \beta\gamma} > 0 \quad \text{and} \quad \frac{\partial y^*}{\partial P} = \frac{\partial y^*}{\partial (M^s/P)} \frac{\partial (M^s/P)}{\partial P} = \frac{\beta}{(1-\alpha)\delta + \beta\gamma} \frac{-M^s}{P^2} < 0$$

Similarly,

$$r^* = \frac{|A_r|}{|A|} = \frac{\begin{vmatrix} (1-\alpha) & G + E_0 \\ \gamma & (M^s/P) - M_0 \end{vmatrix}}{\begin{vmatrix} 1-\alpha & \beta \\ \gamma & -\delta \end{vmatrix}} = \frac{\gamma(G + E_0) - (1-\alpha)[(M^s/P) - M_0]}{(1-\alpha)\delta + \beta\gamma}$$

implying

$$\frac{\partial r^*}{\partial G} = \frac{\gamma}{(1-\alpha)\delta + \beta\gamma} > 0 \quad \text{and} \quad \frac{\partial r^*}{\partial P} = \frac{\partial r^*}{\partial (M^s/P)} \frac{\partial (M^s/P)}{\partial P} = \frac{-(1-\alpha)}{(1-\alpha)\delta + \beta\gamma} \frac{-M^s}{P^2} > 0$$

The signs of the partials give the same comparative-statics results as the graphical analysis. $\square$

Problem 4.2. The seller of a product pays a proportional tax at a flat rate $\theta \in (0, 1)$. Hence, the effective price received by the seller is $(1 - \theta)P$, where P is the market price for the good. Market supply and demand are given by the differentiable functions

$$Q^d = D(P), \qquad \text{with } D'(\ ) < 0$$

$$Q^s = S((1-\theta)P), \quad \text{with } S'(\ ) > 0$$

and equilibrium requires market clearing, that is, $Q^s = Q^d$.

Analyze, graphically and analytically, the effects of a decrease in the tax rate on the quantity transacted and the equilibrium price.

Market clearing requires

$$S((1-\theta)P) = D(P) \tag{1}$$

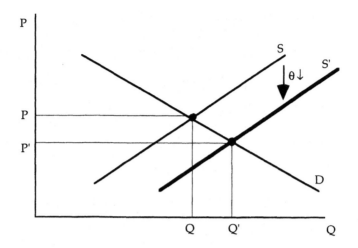

Figure A5.2. Effect of a tax reduction.

This equation implicitly defines the equilibrium price as a function $P^* = P(\theta)$ of the parameter θ. Substituting the solution function $P(\ )$ back into (1), we have the identity

$$S[(1-\theta)P(\theta)] \equiv D[P(\theta)] \tag{2}$$

Differentiating with respect to the parameter and solving for $P'(\theta)$,

$$S'(\ )[(1-\theta)P'(\theta)-P] = D'(\ )P'(\theta) \Rightarrow P'(\theta) = \frac{-PS'(\ )}{D'(\ )-(1-\theta)S'(\ )} = \frac{(-)}{(-)} > 0$$

Next, the quantity transacted in equilibrium is given by $Q^* = D[P(\theta)]$, and therefore

$$\frac{dQ^*}{d\theta} = D'(P^*)P'(\theta) < 0$$

Graphically, a reduction in the tax rate increases the effective price received by sellers for any given market price; these are therefore willing to sell any given quantity at a lower market price. Hence, the supply curve shifts down. The equilibrium price falls, and the equilibrium quantity increases, as shown in Figure A5.2.   □

Problem 4.3. A competitive firm chooses the quantity of labor L to be hired in order to maximize profits, taking as given the salary w and the value of a productivity parameter θ. That is, the firm solves

$$\max_{L}(\theta f(L) - wL)$$

Assume that the production function $f(\ )$ is twice continuously differentiable, increasing, and strictly concave (i.e., $f' > 0, f'' < 0$).

(i) Write the first-order condition for the firm's problem, and verify that the second-order sufficient condition for a maximum holds.
(ii) Interpret the first-order condition as an equation that implicitly defines a labor demand function of the form $L^* = L(w, \theta)$. Show, using the implicit-function theorem, that

$$\partial L^*/\partial w < 0 \quad \text{and} \quad \partial L^*/\partial \theta > 0$$

Putting

$$\pi(L) = \theta f(L) - wL$$

we have

$$\pi'(L) = \theta f'(L) - w \quad \text{and} \quad \pi''(L) = \theta f''(L) < 0$$

Therefore, $\pi(L)$ is strictly concave, and the first-order condition $\pi'(L) = 0$ characterizes a maximum. Write the first-order condition in the form

$$F(L; w, \theta) = \theta f'(L) - W = 0$$

and observe that

$$F_L = \theta f''(L) < 0, \quad F_W = -1 < 0, \quad \text{and} \quad F_\theta = f'(L) > 0$$

By the implicit-function theorem, the derivatives of the solution function $L^* = L(w, \theta)$ are given by

$$\frac{\partial L^*}{\partial w} = \frac{-F_W}{F_L} = -\frac{(-)}{(-)} < 0 \quad \text{and} \quad \frac{\partial L^*}{\partial \theta} = \frac{-F_\theta}{F_L} = -\frac{(+)}{(-)} > 0$$

Hence, the demand for labor decreases with the wage rate, and increases with the productivity parameter θ. $\qquad\qquad\square$

Problem 4.4. Consider an individual who lives for two periods and consumes a single good ("output"). The agent is endowed with y_1 units of output in youth, and y_2 units in old age. There exists a perfectly competitive market for output loans in which the agent may borrow or lend at an interest rate r that he takes as given. Call c_1 and c_2 his consumption levels during the first and second periods of life, and let s denote his first-period savings, $s = y_1 - c_1$ (note that s will be negative if the agent is a net borrower).

The agent's preferences are represented by a utility function of the form

$$U(c_1) + \beta U(c_2)$$

where U is a strictly increasing and strictly concave C^2 function that satisfies the following "corner" conditions:

$$U'(c) \to 0 \quad \text{as } c \to \infty \quad \text{and} \quad U'(c) \to \infty \quad \text{as } c \to 0$$

Suppose also that

$$y_1, y_2 > 0, \quad \beta \in (0, 1), \quad \text{and} \quad R \equiv 1 + r > 0$$

The individual solves the following problem:

$$\max_{c_1, c_2} \{ U(c_1) + \beta U(c_2) \text{ subject to } c_1 = y_1 - s, \ c_2 = y_2 + sR \}$$

Substituting the constraints into the objective function, we obtain a maximization problem in a single decision variable, s.

(i) Write the first-order condition for this problem and check that the second-order sufficient condition for a maximum holds.

Substituting the constraints into the objective function, the agent solves

$$\max_s v(s) = U(y_1 - s) + \beta U(y_2 + sR)$$

The first-order condition for this problem is

$$v'(s) = -U'(y_1 - s) + \beta U'(y_2 + sR)R = 0 \tag{1}$$

Differentiating again,

$$v''(s) = U''(y_1 - s) + \beta U''(y_2 + sR)R^2 < 0$$

we see that the second-order condition holds by the strict concavity of $U(\ )$.

We will interpret the first-order condition as an equation that implicitly defines a savings function of the form $s^* = s(y_1, y_2, R)$. We fix the values of (y_1, y_2) and study the behavior of s^* as a function of R.

(ii) Show that for a given value of R, the first-order condition has a unique solution s^*. (Use the intermediate-value theorem, and think of what will happen in extreme cases, e.g., if the agent decides not to eat during one of the periods.)

Fix (y_1, y_2, R), with $0 < R < \infty$, and write the first-order condition in the form

$$F(s) = \beta R U'(y_2 + sR) - U'(y_1 - s) = \beta R U'(c_2) - U'(c_1) = 0 \qquad (1')$$

To apply the intermediate-value theorem, we will use the assumption that $U'(c) \to \infty$ as $c \to 0$, that is, the marginal utility of consumption goes to infinity as consumption approaches zero.

If the consumer does not eat during the first period ($c_1 = 0$ and $s = y_1$), then (abusing the notation somewhat)

$$F(y_1) = \beta R U'(y_2 + y_1 R) - U'(0) = -\infty$$

On the other hand, if the consumer is willing to eat nothing during the second period, he can borrow an amount $s = -y_2/R$ in the first period, and we have

$$F(-y_2/R) = \beta R U'(0) - U'(y_1 + (y_2/R)) = +\infty$$

Hence, taking s'' close to y_1 and s' close to $-y_2/R$, and using the continuity of $U'(\ )$, we can invoke the intermediate-value theorem to conclude that there exists a solution s^* of $(1')$ for any bounded $R > 0$ (Figure A5.3).

Moreover, we know that $F(\ )$ is a monotonic function, because

$$F'(s) = \beta R^2 U''(y_2 + sR) + U''(y_1 - s) < 0 \qquad (2)$$

Hence, the intersection is unique, and it follows that for each R there exists a unique optimal level of savings.

(iii) From (ii), we know that $s(R)$ is a well-defined function for $R > 0$. The implicit-function theorem guarantees that $s(R)$ is also differentiable. (Why? Which of our assumptions are we using here?) Substituting $s(R)$ back into the first-order condition, we have an identity. Hence, we can differentiate both sides of it with respect to R, and the equality will continue to hold. Differentiate implicitly with respect to R, and solve for $s'(R)$ in the resulting expression.

What can we say about the sign of $s'(R)$? That is, does s^* increase or decrease with the interest factor R? Does it matter whether or not the agent is a net borrower? (It should. In one of the cases you should not be able to sign the derivative. Why?)

Expression (2) guarantees that we can apply the implicit-function theorem. Substituting the solution function $s^* = s(R)$ in the first-order condition, we obtain the identity

$$\beta R U'[y_2 + s(R)R] \equiv U'[y_1 - s(R)] \qquad (3)$$

Differentiating with respect to R,

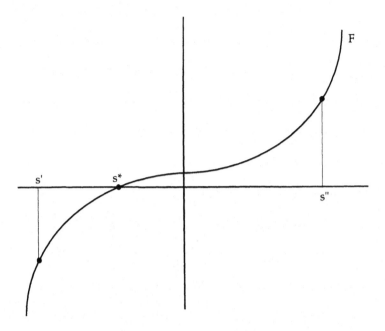

Figure A5.3. Existence and uniqueness of the optimal level of savings.

$$\beta\{U'(c_2) + RU''(c_2)[s'(R)R + s^*]\} = -U''(c_1)s'(R)$$

and solving for $s'(R)$,

$$s'(R) = \frac{\beta U'(c_2) + \beta R U''(c_2)s^*}{U''(c_1) + \beta R^2 U''(c_2)}$$

The denominator is negative, but the sign of the numerator is ambiguous, because s^* may be positive or negative. We have

$$\text{sign } s'(R) = \text{sign}[\beta U'(c_2) + \beta R U''(c_2)s^*] = (+) + (-)\text{sign}(s^*)$$

Hence we have the following:

- If $s^* \leq 0$, then $s'(R) > 0$. That is, if the agent is a net borrower, then an increase in the interest rate makes him borrow less. In this case, the income and substitution effects of the change in R work in the same direction. An increase in R (which can be interpreted as the premium the market pays for postponing consumption) makes consumption in the second period relatively cheaper, which tends to reduce the agent's borrowing. Moreover, the same increase in R makes the agent (who is a net debtor) poorer. In response, the agent will tend to reduce his level of consumption in both periods, thus increasing his savings (or, rather, reducing the amount of his dissaving).
- If $s^* > 0$, then the sign of $s'(R)$ may be positive or negative. Now the substitution and income effects work in opposite directions. As before, the change in the relative prices of current consumption and future consumption tends to favor the second alternative (and hence induces higher savings). On the other hand, because the agent is now a net saver, the increase in the interest rate makes him richer, pushing his consumption level up in both periods and lowering savings. The net result of these two effects is uncertain.

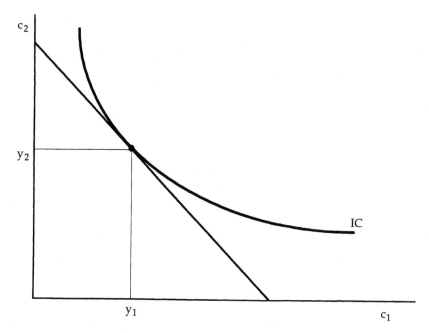

Figure A5.4. Determination of the autarkic interest factor.

(iv) Show that there exists some value of R (say R^0) for which the agent neither borrows nor lends, but consumes precisely his endowment each period. We say that R^0 is the agent's autarkic interest factor.

(Go back to the original formulation of the agent's decision problem and think in terms of indifference curves and budget constraints in the (c_1, c_2) plane. Plot the indifference curve that goes through the endowment point (y_1, y_2). What value of R will make the agent "happy" eating precisely his endowment each period?)

Let us return to the original formulation of the problem:

$$\max_{c_1,c_2}\{U(c_1)+\beta U(c_2) \text{ s.t. } c_1 = y_1 - s,\ c_2 = y_2 + sR\}$$

Solving for s in one of the constraints, and substituting the result in the other, we can consolidate the two restrictions into a single lifetime budget constraint:

$$c_2 + c_1 R = y_2 + y_1 R \tag{4}$$

That is, the future value of lifetime consumption is equal to the future value of total income. Plotting the budget constraint (4) and the indifference curves on the plane (c_1, c_2), the optimal solution corresponds to a tangency point, as shown in Figure A5.4.

Observe that for given values of (y_1, y_2), changes in R make the budget line rotate about the point (y_1, y_2), which is always feasible (you can always eat your endowment during each period). Hence, for the agent to decide to remain at this point, it is enough to rotate the budget line until it is tangent to the indifference curve through (y_1, y_2). Because the slope of the budget line is $-R$, we need $R^0 = -$slope of IC at (y_1, y_2).

An indifference curve is the locus of all combinations (c_1, c_2) that yield the same utility level u_0; hence the equation of an indifference curve is

$$U(c_1) + \beta U(c_2) = u_0$$

Differentiating implicitly with respect to c_1,

$$U'(c_1) + \beta U'(c_2)\frac{dc_2}{dc_1} = 0 \Rightarrow \left.\frac{dc_2}{dc_1}\right|_{IC} = \frac{-U'(c_1)}{\beta U'(c_2)}$$

and therefore, evaluating this expression at the endowment point,

$$R^0 = \frac{U'(y_1)}{\beta U'(y_2)}$$

(v) Show that on one side of R^0 the agent is always a net saver in youth, and on the other always a net borrower. (What is the sign of $s'(R^0)$? Note that this does not imply that $s(\ )$ is always monotonic.)

  We have seen before that if $s^* \leq 0$, then $s'(R) > 0$. In particular, if $R = R^0$, then $s^* = 0$, and therefore $s'(R^0) > 0$. Hence, the savings function $s(R)$ crosses the horizontal axis with strictly positive slope and therefore can cross it only once. Although $s(\ )$ may very well not be monotonic in the region in which it is positive, it is true that

- if $R < R^0$, the agent is a net borrower ($s^* < 0$), and
- if $R > R^0$, he is a net saver ($s^* > 0$). $\qquad\square$

Problem 4.5. Consider now an economy in which there are two different types of agents who face the decision analyzed in Problem 4.4, but may have different endowment streams, discount factors, or utility functions. To simplify, assume that there is only one agent of each type, but they both behave competitively (i.e., taking the value of R as given).

  Let $s_1(R)$ and $s_2(R)$ be the savings functions for the two agents. In equilibrium, the credit market must clear (i.e., if one is a net borrower, the other must be a net lender), and aggregate savings must be zero. That is, we must have

$$Z(R) \equiv s_1(R) + s_2(R) = 0 \qquad (1)$$

  Show that under the assumptions of Problem 4.4 there exists at least one competitive equilibrium, that is, a value of R for which (1) holds. (Let R_1^0 and R_2^0 be the autarkic interest factors for the two agents. Without loss of generality, we can assume that $R_1^0 > R_2^0$. What happens when $R = R_1^0, R_2^0$?)

  If $R = R'' > R_1^0$, both agents want to save, and therefore $Z(R'') > 0$. With $R = R' < R_2^0$, both want to borrow, and $Z(R') < 0$. By the intermediate-value theorem, there exists at least one $R^* \in (R', R'')$ such that $Z(R^*) = 0$. That is, there exists at least one equilibrium interest rate (Figure A5.5).

Chapter 6

Problem 1.3. Prove Theorem 1.2: Any intersection of convex sets is convex.

  Let $\{X_i\}$ be a collection of convex sets, and consider two points in their intersection: x' and $x'' \in \cap_i X_i$. Because x' and x'' belong to each of the X_i's, and these are convex sets, we have, for any $\lambda \in [0, 1]$, that

$$x^\lambda = (1 - \lambda)x' + \lambda x'' \in X_i \ \forall$$

implying that $x^\lambda \in \cap_i X_i$, as was to be shown. $\qquad\square$

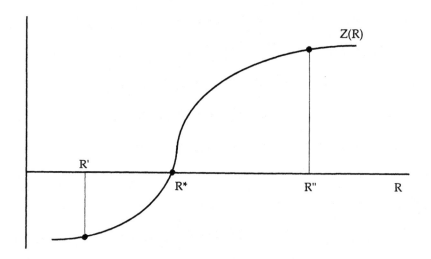

Figure A5.5. Existence of an equilibrium interest factor.

Problem 1.7. Prove Theorem 1.6: A set X is convex if and only if every convex combination of points of X lies in X.

The sufficiency result is obvious. If any convex combination of points in X lies in X, then, in particular, any convex combination of two points of X lies in X, which establishes the convexity of the set.

To prove the necessity part, observe first that the convexity of X implies that any convex combination of two points of X lies in X. We will now assume that this property holds for all convex combinations involving k or fewer points of X and show that the result follows for the case of $k + 1$ points.

Consider a convex combination of $k + 1$ points of X, $x_1, \ldots, x_{k+1}$,

$$y = \sum_{i=1}^{k+1} \lambda_i x_i \tag{1}$$

with $\lambda_i \in [0, 1]$ for all i and $\Sigma_{i=1}^{k+1} \lambda_i = 1$. We want to show that $y \in X$. If $\lambda_{k+1} = 1$, then $\Sigma_{i=1}^{k} \lambda_i = 0$, and because all λ_i's are nonnegative, it must be that $\lambda_i = 0$ for all $i = 1, \ldots, k$. Hence, $y = x_{k+1} \in X$, and we are done. Otherwise, $\lambda_{k+1} < 1$, and

$$\sum_{i=1}^{k} \lambda_i = 1 - \lambda_{k+1} > 0 \tag{2}$$

We can then write (1) in the form

$$y = \sum_{i=1}^{k} \lambda_i x_i + \lambda_{k+1} x_{k+1} = \left(\sum_{i=1}^{k} \lambda_i \right) \left(\sum_{i=1}^{k} \frac{\lambda_i}{\sum_{j=1}^{k} \lambda_j} x_i \right) + \lambda_{k+1} x_{k+1} \tag{3}$$

Now, because

$$\sum_{i=1}^{k} \frac{\lambda_i}{\sum_{j=1}^{k} \lambda_j} = 1$$

the point

$$z = \sum_{i=1}^{k} \frac{\lambda_i}{\sum_{j=1}^{k} \lambda_j} x_i \tag{4}$$

is a convex combination of k points of X and therefore lies in X (by assumption). Using (2) and (4), equation (3) reduces to

$$y = (1 - \lambda_{k+1})z + \lambda_{k+1}x_{k+1} \tag{5}$$

Hence, y is a linear combination of two points in X, and it follows (again by assumption) that $y \in X$. This concludes the proof.   □

Problem 1.12. Show that the closure of a convex set is convex.

Let X be a convex set. Given two points x and y in cl X, let $z = \lambda x + (1 - \lambda)y$ for some $\lambda \in (0, 1)$. We will show that z is a closure point of X, that is, that for any $\varepsilon > 0$ the ball $B_\varepsilon(z)$ contains at least one point of X.

Fix an arbitrary $\varepsilon > 0$. Because x and y are both closure points of X, $B_\varepsilon(x) \cap X$ and $B_\varepsilon(y) \cap X$ are both nonempty. Take two points, $x' \in B_\varepsilon(x) \cap X$ and $y' \in B_\varepsilon(y) \cap X$, and define

$$z' = \lambda x' + (1 - \lambda)y'$$

Then $z' \in X$, by the convexity of X. Moreover, $z' \in B_\varepsilon(z)$, for

$$\|z - z'\| = \|\lambda x + (1 - \lambda)y - \lambda x' - (1 - \lambda)y'\| = \|\lambda(x - x') + (1 - \lambda)(y - y')\|$$
$$\leq \lambda\|x - x'\| + (1 - \lambda)\|y - y'\| < \varepsilon$$

Hence, $B_\varepsilon(z) \cap X$ is nonempty for any $\varepsilon > 0$, establishing that any linear combination of closure points of X is also a closure point of X.   □

Problem 1.14. Using Theorem 1.13, show that given a convex set X and an interior point x of X, any ray emanating from x contains at most one boundary point of X.

Suppose there are two boundary points of X on this ray, say y and z, with z farther away from x than y. Then $y \in [x, z)$, and because x is an interior point and z a closure point of X, y is an interior point of X, by Theorem 1.13, contrary to our assumption.   □

Problem 1.17. Let X be a convex set with a nonempty interior. Show that int(cl X) = int X.

Because $X \subseteq$ cl X, it follows immediately that int $X \subseteq$ int(cl X) without any further assumptions. Conversely, suppose X is convex, with a nonempty interior, and let x be an interior point of cl X. Then x is not a boundary point of cl X, so by Theorem 1.16 it is not a boundary point of X either. But x is a closure point of X, and because cl X = int $X \cup$ bdy X, it must be an interior point.   □

Problem 1.22. Show that a point x_i in a convex set X is a relative interior point of X if and only if either or both of the two following (equivalent) conditions hold:

(i) For any line L in aff X, with $x_i \in L$, there exist points x' and x'' in $L \cap$ aff X such that $x_i \in (x', x'')$.
(ii) For any point $x' \in X$, with $x' \neq x_i$, there is a point $x'' \in X$ such that $x_i \in (x', x'')$. That is, the segment $[x', y]$ in X can be extended beyond x_i without leaving the set.

It is obvious that $x_i \in$ rint X implies (i) (because X contains a ball in aff X around x_i) and that (i) implies (ii). We show that (ii) implies that x_i is a relative interior point. We know that rint X is not empty, so there exists some point $y \in$ rint X. If $y = x_i$, there is nothing further to prove. Otherwise there exists a point z in X such that $x_i \in (y, z)$, by (ii). But then $x_i \in$ rint X, by part (i) of Theorem 1.20.   □

Problem 1.23. Let X be a convex set in $\mathbb{R}^n$, with $\text{int(cl } X) \neq \varnothing$. Show that int X is nonempty.

We prove the contrapositive statement. Suppose int X is empty. Then, by Theorem 1.19, the affine hull of X is contained in an $(n-1)$-dimensional hyperplane H. Because H is a closed set that contains X, it also contains cl X. And because H has an empty interior, so does cl X. Hence, $\text{int(cl } X)$ is empty whenever int X is empty. □

Problem 2.6. Prove Theorem 2.5: Given a function $f: \mathbb{R}^n \supseteq X \longrightarrow \mathbb{R}$, where X is a convex set, define for each pair of points x' and x'' in X the function ϕ by

$$\phi(\lambda) = f[\lambda x' + (1-\lambda)x'']$$

Then f is concave if and only if $\phi(\ )$ is concave for all x' and x'' in X.

- First assume that ϕ is concave, and fix two arbitrary points x' and x'' in X. Then for each $\lambda \in [0, 1]$, we have

$$\phi(\lambda) = \phi[\lambda 1 + (1-\lambda)0] \geq \lambda\phi(1) + (1-\lambda)\phi(0)$$

but then

$$\phi(\lambda) = f[\lambda x' + (1-\lambda)x''] \geq \lambda f(x') + (1-\lambda)f(x'') = \lambda\phi(1) + (1-\lambda)\phi(0)$$

for all $\lambda \in [0, 1]$. That is, $f(\ )$ is concave.
- Assume that f is concave, and fix two arbitrary points x' and x'' in X. We have to show that for any $\mu_1, \mu_2 \in \mathbb{R}$ and all $\lambda \in [0, 1]$,

$$\phi(\lambda\mu_1 + (1-\lambda)\mu_2) \geq \lambda\phi(\mu_1) + (1-\lambda)\phi(\mu_2) \tag{1}$$

To verify that this expression holds by the concavity of f, put

$$y^1 = \mu_1 x' + (1-\mu_1)x''$$
$$y^2 = \mu_2 x' + (1-\mu_2)x''$$
$$t = \lambda\mu_1 + (1-\lambda)\mu_2$$

Then

$$\phi(\mu_1) = f[\mu_1 x' + (1-\mu_1)x''] = f(y^1)$$
$$\phi(\mu_2) = f[\mu_2 x' + (1-\mu_2)x''] = f(y^2)$$
$$\phi[\lambda\mu_1 + (1-\lambda)\mu_2] = \phi(t) = f[tx' + (1-t)x'']$$

but notice that

$$\begin{aligned} tx' + (1-t)x'' &= [\lambda\mu_1 + (1-\lambda)\mu_2]x' + [1 - \lambda\mu_1 - (1-\lambda)\mu_2]x'' \\ &= \lambda\mu_1 x' + (1-\lambda)\mu_2 x' + (1-\lambda+\lambda)x'' - \lambda\mu_1 x'' - (1-\lambda)\mu_2 x'' \\ &= \lambda[\mu_1 x' + x'' - \mu_1 x''] + (1-\lambda)[\mu_2 x' + x'' - \mu_2 x''] \\ &= \lambda[\mu_1 x' + (1-\mu_1)x''] + (1-\lambda)[\mu_2 x' + (1-\mu_2)x''] \\ &= \lambda y^1 + (1-\lambda)y^2 \end{aligned}$$

Hence, (1) becomes

$$f[\lambda y^1 + (1-\lambda)y^2] \geq \lambda f(y^1) + (1-\lambda)f(y^2)$$

which holds by the concavity of f. □

Problem 2.9. Prove Theorem 2.8: Let $f: \mathbb{R}^n \supseteq X \longrightarrow \mathbb{R}$ be a concave function and $g: \mathbb{R} \longrightarrow \mathbb{R}$ an increasing and concave function defined on an interval I containing $f(X)$. Then the function $g[f(x)]$ is concave.

Because f is concave on X, we have

$$(1-\lambda)f(x')+\lambda f(x'') \le f[(1-\lambda)x'+\lambda x''] \equiv f(x^\lambda)$$

$$\text{for any } x' \text{ and } x'' \text{ in } X \text{ and any } \lambda \in [0,1] \tag{1}$$

Using the facts that g is nondecreasing and concave, we have

$$g[f(x^\lambda)] \ge g[(1-\lambda)f(x')+\lambda f(x'')] \ge (1-\lambda)g[f(x')]+\lambda g[f(x'')]$$

which shows that $g[f(x)]$ is concave. $\qquad\square$

Problem 2.11. Prove Theorem 2.10: Let f and g be concave functions $\mathbb{R}^n \supseteq X \longrightarrow \mathbb{R}$. Given arbitrary scalars α and $\beta \ge 0$, the function $h = \alpha f + \beta g$ is concave.

Take any two points x' and x'' in X. By the concavity of f and g, we have

$$h(x^\lambda) = \alpha f(x^\lambda)+\beta g(x^\lambda) \ge \alpha[(1-\lambda)f(x')+\lambda f(x'')]+\beta[(1-\lambda)g(x')+\lambda g(x'')]$$

$$= (1-\lambda)[\alpha f(x')+\beta g(x')]+\lambda[\alpha f(x')+\beta g(x')] = (1-\lambda)h(x')+\lambda h(x'')$$

for any $\lambda \in [0,1]$, which establishes the concavity of h. $\qquad\square$

Problem 2.13. Prove Theorem 2.12: Let $\{f^s; s \in S\}$ be a (possibly infinite) family of concave functions $\mathbb{R}^n \supseteq X \longrightarrow \mathbb{R}$, all of which are bounded below. Then the function f defined on X by $f(x) = \inf_{s \in S} f^s(x)$ is concave.

Because each f^i is concave, its hypograph

$$\text{hyp } f^i = \{(y,x) \in \mathbb{R}^{n+1}; x \in X, y \le f^i(x)\}$$

is a convex set. Now, the hypograph of $f = \inf_{i \in I} f^i$ is the intersection of the hypographs of all the f^i's, because $y \le f(x)$ if and only if $y \le f^i(x)$ for all i. By the preceding result, hyp f is a convex set, and by Theorem 1.2, f is concave. $\qquad\square$

Problem 3.3. Prove Theorem 3.2: Let $f: \mathbb{R}^n \supseteq X \longrightarrow \mathbb{R}$ be a real-valued function defined on a convex set $X \subseteq \mathbb{R}^n$. Then f is quasiconcave if and only if the upper contour sets of f are all convex, that is, if for any $\alpha \in \mathbb{R}$ the set $U_\alpha = \{x \in X; f(x) \ge \alpha\}$ is convex.

- Assume U_α is convex for all α. Given any two points x' and x'' in X, put $m = \min\{f(x'), f(x'')\}$. By assumption, $U_m = \{x \in X; f(x) \ge m\}$ is convex, so $(1-\lambda)x'+\lambda x'' \in U_m$ for all $\lambda \in (0,1)$, but this means that

$$f[(1-\lambda)x'+\lambda x''] \ge m = \min\{f(x'), f(x'')\} \qquad \text{(i.e., } f \text{ is quasiconcave)}$$

- Let f be quasiconcave, and fix some arbitrary real number α. If U_α is empty or consists of a single point, then it is convex by definition. Otherwise, choose x' and x'' in U_α. Then $f(x') \ge \alpha$ and $f(x'') \ge \alpha$, and the quasiconcavity of f implies that for any $\lambda \in (0,1)$,

$$f[(1-\lambda)x'+\lambda x''] \ge \min\{f(x'), f(x'')\} \ge \alpha$$

Hence, for any x' and x'' in U_α,

$$(1-\lambda)x'+\lambda x'' \in U_\alpha$$

which says that U_α is a convex set. $\qquad\square$

Problem 3.5. Prove Theorem 3.4: Let $f: \mathbb{R}^n \supseteq X \longrightarrow \mathbb{R}$ be a quasiconcave function defined on a convex set $X \subseteq \mathbb{R}^n$, and let $g: \mathbb{R} \longrightarrow \mathbb{R}$ be a weakly increasing function defined on an interval I that contains $f(X)$. Then the composite function $g[f(x)]$ is quasiconcave in X.

By the quasiconcavity of f in X we have, for any two points x' and x'' in X,

$$f(x') \ge f(x'') \Rightarrow f[(1-\lambda)x'+\lambda x''] \ge f(x'') \ \forall \ \lambda \in (0,1)$$

Because g is nondecreasing, it does not reverse rankings, that is,

$$f(x') \geq f(x'') \Leftrightarrow g[f(x')] \geq g[f(x'')]$$

Now, $f(x') \geq f(x'')$ implies $f[(1 - \lambda)x' + \lambda x''] \geq f(x'')$, and this in turn implies that

$$g[f[(1 - \lambda)x' + \lambda x'']] \geq g[f(x'')] \, \forall \, \lambda \in (0, 1)$$

so $g(f)$ is quasiconcave. $\qquad\qquad\qquad\qquad\qquad\qquad\qquad\qquad\qquad\qquad\square$

Problem 3.6. Show that the Cobb-Douglas function

$$f(x) = A \prod_{i=1}^{n} x_i^{\alpha_i}, \quad \text{where } \alpha_i > 0 \, \forall \, i$$

is quasiconcave for $x \gg \underline{0}$.

Consider the function

$$g(x) = \ln f(x) = \ln A + \sum_{i=1}^{n} \alpha_i \ln x_i$$

Then

$$g_i(x) = \frac{\alpha_i}{x_i}, \quad g_{ii}(x) = \frac{-\alpha_i}{x_i^2}, \quad \text{and} \quad g_{ik}(x) = 0 \quad \text{for } k \neq i$$

Hence, the Hessian of g, $D^2 g(x)$, is a diagonal matrix with entries of the form $-\alpha_i / x_i^2 < 0$, and its leading principal minors are of the form

$$d_1 = \frac{-\alpha_1}{x_1^2} < 0, \qquad d_2 = \frac{\alpha_1 \alpha_2}{x_1^2 x_2^2} > 0, \qquad d_3 = \frac{-\alpha_1 \alpha_2 \alpha_3}{x_1^2 x_2^2 x_3^2} < 0, \dots.$$

Thus, g is (strictly) concave, by Theorems 2.18 and A.4, and $f(x) = e^{g(x)}$ is a monotonically increasing transformation of a concave function and therefore quasiconcave, by Theorem 3.4. $\qquad\qquad\qquad\qquad\qquad\qquad\qquad\qquad\square$

Problem 3.9. A C^1 function that has no critical points (i.e., such that $Df(x) \neq \underline{0}$ for all x) is said to be nonstationary. Show that a nonstationary C^1 quasiconcave function is pseudoconcave.

Let x' and x'' be any two points in the domain of f such that $f(x') > f(x'')$. We will show that if

$$Df(x'')(x' - x'') \leq 0 \qquad\qquad\qquad\qquad\qquad\qquad\qquad\qquad (1)$$

then we arrive at a contradiction. By the nonstationarity of f, at least one of the components of $Df(x'')$ is nonzero. For concreteness, suppose that $f_1(x'') > 0$, and define the point $\hat{x}$ by

$$\hat{x}_1 = x_1' - \varepsilon \quad \text{and} \quad \hat{x}_i = x_i' \quad \text{for } i = 2, \dots, n$$

For $\varepsilon > 0$ and sufficiently small, we have, by continuity, that $f(\hat{x}) > f(x'')$, but, using expression (1),

$$Df(x'')(\hat{x} - x'') = f_1(x'')(\hat{x}_1 - x_1'') + \sum_{i=2}^{n} f_i(x'')(\hat{x}_i - x_i'')$$

$$= f_1(x'')(x_1' - x_1'' - \varepsilon) + \sum_{i=2}^{n} f_i(x'')(x_i' - x_i'')$$

$$= -\varepsilon f_1(x'') + \sum_{i=1}^{n} f_i(x'')(x_i' - x_i'')$$

$$= -\varepsilon f_1(x'') + Df(x'')(x' - x'') \leq -\varepsilon f_1(x'') + 0 < 0$$

(using assumption (1)). Hence, $f(\hat{x}) > f(x'')$, but $Df(x'') \, (\hat{x} - x'') < 0$, which contradicts the quasiconcavity of f. $\qquad\qquad\qquad\qquad\qquad\qquad\qquad\qquad\square$

Problem 3.10. Suppose $f: \mathbb{R}^n_{++} \longrightarrow \mathbb{R}$ is C^1, homogeneous of degree 1, and positive-valued. Show that f is concave if and only if it is quasiconcave.

Concavity always implies quasiconcavity. To prove the other part of the theorem, let x' and x'' be two points in $\mathbb{R}^n_{++}$. Because $f \geq 0$, we can define λ by $\lambda = f(x')/f(x'')$ and $\lambda > 0$. Because f is homogeneous of degree 1, we have

$$f(\lambda x'') = \lambda f(x'') = f(x') \tag{1}$$

and quasiconcavity therefore implies that

$$Df(\lambda x'')(x' - \lambda x'') \geq 0 \tag{2}$$

Exploiting the properties of homogeneous functions, we will show that (1) implies $Df(x'')(x' - x'') \geq f(x') - f(x'')$ and therefore the concavity of f.

First, notice that because f is homogeneous of degree 1, its partial derivatives are homogeneous of degree 0. Hence,

$$Df(\lambda x'') = Df(x'') \tag{3}$$

Moreover, by Euler's theorem,

$$Df(x'')x'' = f(x'') \tag{4}$$

Using (1), (3), (4), and the definition of λ, expression (2) can be rewritten in the form

$$Df(\lambda x'')(x' - \lambda x'') = Df(x'')(x' - \lambda x'') = Df(x'')x' - \lambda f(x'') = Df(x'')x' - f(x') \geq 0$$

from where

$$Df(x'')x' \geq f(x') \tag{5}$$

Finally, subtracting (4) from (5),

$$Df(x'')(x' - x'') \geq f(x') - f(x'')$$

Because x' and x'' are arbitrary points in the positive orthant, f is concave in this set. $\square$

Problem 3.12. Let $f: \mathbb{R}^2 \supseteq X \longrightarrow \mathbb{R}$ be a C^2 function defined on an open and convex set $X \subseteq \mathbb{R}^n$, with $f_x(x, y) > 0$ and $f_y(x, y) > 0$ for all (x, y) in X. Show that $f(x, y)$ is quasiconcave in X if and only if

$$|B| = \begin{vmatrix} 0 & f_x & f_y \\ f_x & f_{xx} & f_{xy} \\ f_y & f_{xy} & f_{yy} \end{vmatrix} > 0 \; \forall \, x \in X$$

First, notice that

$$|B| = \begin{vmatrix} 0 & f_x & f_y \\ f_x & f_{xx} & f_{xy} \\ f_y & f_{xy} & f_{yy} \end{vmatrix} = 0 + (-1)^{2+1} f_x \begin{vmatrix} f_x & f_y \\ f_{xy} & f_{yy} \end{vmatrix} + (-1)^{3+1} f_y \begin{vmatrix} f_x & f_y \\ f_{xx} & f_{xy} \end{vmatrix}$$

$$= -f_x(f_x f_{yy} - f_y f_{xy}) + f_y(f_x f_{xy} - f_y f_{xx}) = 2 f_{xy} f_x f_y - f_x^2 f_{yy} - f_y^2 f_{xx}$$

Now, recall that the function f is quasiconcave if and only if its upper contour sets, $U_\alpha = \{(x, y) \in X; f(x, y) \geq \alpha\}$, are convex. Applying the implicit-function theorem to the equation $f(x, y) = \alpha$, we obtain a function $y = g(x)$, whose graph coincides with the α level set of f. Because the function $f(\;)$ is increasing, $y \geq g(x)$ implies that (x, y) lies in U_α, and vice versa. Hence, the level set U_α is precisely the epigraph of the function $g(\;)$. By Theorem 2.2, epi $g = U_\alpha$ is convex if and only if $g(\ )$ is a convex function. Because $g(\ )$ is twice differentiable under our assumptions, we can check its concavity by computing its second derivative.

Substituting the function $y = g(x)$ into the equation of the level set, we obtain the identity $f(x, g(x)) = \alpha$. Differentiating with respect to x,

$$f_x(x, g(x)) + f_y(x, g(x))g'(x) = 0$$

from where

$$g'(x) = \frac{-f_x(x, g(x))}{f_y(x, g(x))} \tag{1}$$

Differentiating this expression again,

$$\begin{aligned} g''(x) &= \frac{-f_y[f_{xx} + f_{xy}g'(x)] + f_x[f_{xy} + f_{yy}g'(x)]}{f_y^2} \\ &= \frac{-f_y f_{xx} + f_y f_{xy}(f_x/f_y) + f_x f_{xy} - f_x f_{yy}(f_x/f_y)}{f_y^2} \\ &= \frac{-f_y f_{xx} + f_{xy}f_x + f_x f_{xy} - f_x f_{yy}(f_x/f_y)}{f_y^2}\frac{f_y}{f_y} \\ &= \frac{-f_y^2 f_{xx} + 2f_{xy}f_x f_y - f_x^2 f_{yy}}{f_y^3} = \frac{|B|}{f_y^3} \end{aligned} \tag{2}$$

Because $f_y > 0$, $g''(x)$ has the same sign as $|B|$. Hence, $g(\ )$ is convex (and f is therefore quasiconcave) if and only if $|B| > 0$. □

Problem 3.15. Show that the function $f(x) = x^3$ cannot be concavified in any set that has zero as an interior point.

Let h be a C^1 and strictly increasing function, and define the function $g(\ )$ on some interval $I = (-2a, 2a)$, with $a > 0$, by $g(x) = h(x^3)$. We will show that for any such function, there exist two points in I, x and x_0, such that

$$g(x) > g(x_0) + g'(x_0)(x - x_0) \tag{1}$$

(This inequality implies that $g(\ )$ is not concave, by Theorem 2.17.)

In particular, let $x^0 = 0$ and $x = a$. Then

$$g'(x_0) = 3x^3 h'(x_0) = 0$$

and (1) becomes

$$g(a) = h(a^3) > h(0) + 0a = h(0)$$

Because $a^3 > 0$ and $h(\ )$ is strictly increasing, this inequality holds. □

Chapter 7

Problem 1.5. Let $f: \mathbb{R}^n \longrightarrow \mathbb{R}$ be a C^2 function. Show that if f achieves a local maximum at x^*, then the Hessian of f at x^* is negative semidefinite, that is,

$$h^T D^2 f(x^*)h \leq 0 \ \forall h \in \mathbb{R}^n$$

Fix an arbitrary $h \in \mathbb{R}^n$. For any given $\alpha > 0$ we can use Taylor's theorem to write

$$f(x^* + \alpha h) - f(x^*) = Df(x^*)(\alpha h) + \frac{\alpha^2}{2}\Delta x^T D^2 f(x^* + \lambda_\alpha \alpha h)h \tag{1}$$

for some $\lambda_\alpha \in (0, 1)$. If x^* is a local maximizer, we have $Df(x^*) = \underline{0}$, and (1) reduces to

$$f(x^* + \alpha h) - f(x^*) = \frac{\alpha^2}{2} h^T D^2 f(x^* + \lambda_\alpha \alpha h) h \tag{2}$$

Moreover, it must be true that for any sufficiently small α we have

$$f(x^* + \alpha h) \le f(x^*)$$

Hence,

$$\frac{\alpha^2}{2} h^T D^2 f(x^* + \lambda_\alpha \alpha h) h \le 0$$

for any sufficiently small α. Taking limits as $\alpha \to 0$, we obtain the desired result. $\square$

Problem 1.7. Let $f: \mathbb{R}^n \longrightarrow \mathbb{R}$ be a C^1 concave function. Show that if x^* is a critical point of f, then it is a global maximizer of f.

Let x^* be a critical point of $f(\ )$, and consider an arbitrary point x in $\mathbb{R}^n$. By the concavity of f, we have

$$f(x) \le f(x^*) + Df(x^*)(x - x^*) \tag{1}$$

Because x^* is a critical point, $Df(x^*) = \underline{0}$, and (1) reduces to

$$f(x^*) \ge f(x)$$

Because x is an arbitrary point in $\mathbb{R}^n$, x^* is a global maximizer of $f(\ )$. $\square$

Problem 1.8. Let $f: \mathbb{R}^n \longrightarrow \mathbb{R}$ be a concave function. Show that if x^* is a local maximizer of f, then it is also a global maximizer.

By contradiction. Assume that f attains a global maximum at $x' \ne x^*$. Then $f(x') > f(x^*)$, and the concavity of $f(\ )$ implies

$$f(x^\lambda) = f[(1 - \lambda)x' + \lambda x^*] \ge (1 - \lambda)f(x') + \lambda f(x^*) > f(x^*) \; \forall \lambda \in (0, 1)$$

Now, for any given $\varepsilon > 0$ we can choose λ small enough that $x^\lambda = (1 - \lambda)x' + \lambda x^* \in B_\varepsilon(x^*)$, and we still have that $f(x^\lambda) > f(x^*)$. Hence, x^* cannot be a local maximizer. $\square$

Problem 1.10. Let $A = [a_{ik}]$ be an $n \times n$ matrix, and consider the quadratic form $h^T A h = \Sigma_i \Sigma_k h_i a_{ik} h_k$. Using the Cauchy-Schwarz inequality, show that

$$|h^T A h| \le \sqrt{\sum_i \sum_k a_{ik}^2} \; \|h\|^2$$

where $\|\cdot\|$ is the Euclidean norm. Using this result, verify that the function $Q(\alpha)$ in the proof of Theorem 1.9 is continuous at zero (provided f is C^2) by showing that $|Q(\alpha) - Q(0)| \to 0$ as $\alpha \to 0$.

Let α_i and β_i, $i = 1, \ldots, n$, be real numbers; then, by the Cauchy-Schwarz inequality (taking roots of both sides), we have

$$\left| \sum_{i=1}^n \alpha_i \beta_i \right| \le \sqrt{\sum_{i=1}^n \alpha_i^2} \; \sqrt{\sum_{i=1}^n \beta_i^2}$$

Using this inequality twice, and the triangle inequality, we can write

$$|h^T A h| = \left| \sum_i h_i \left(\sum_k a_{ik} h_k \right) \right| \le \left| \sum_i h_i \left(\sqrt{\sum_k a_{ik}^2} \; \sqrt{\sum_k h_k^2} \right) \right|$$

$$\le \|h\| \sum_i |h_i| \sqrt{\sum_k a_{ik}^2} \le \|h\| \sqrt{\sum_i h_i^2} \; \sqrt{\sum_i \left(\sqrt{\sum_k a_{ik}^2} \right)^2}$$

$$= \|h\|^2 \sqrt{\sum_i \sum_k a_{ik}^2}$$

Next, for any fixed h we have

$$0 \le |Q(\alpha) - Q(0)| = |h^T [D^2 f(x^* + \lambda_\alpha \alpha h) - D^2 f(x^*)] h|$$

$$\le \|h\|^2 \sqrt{\sum_i \sum_k [f_{ik}(x^* + \lambda_\alpha \alpha h) - f_{ik}(x^*)]^2}$$

Because f is C^2, the partial derivatives are continuous functions. As $\alpha \to 0$, $x^* + \lambda_\alpha \alpha h \to x^*$ (because $0 \le \lambda_\alpha \alpha \le \alpha$), and by the continuity of the second partials, $|f_{ik}(x^* + \lambda_\alpha \alpha h) - f_{ik}(x^*)| \to 0$, implying that $Q(\alpha) \to Q(0)$, that is, Q is continuous at zero. $\qquad \square$

Problem 1.12. Derivation of factor demand functions. Consider a competitive firm that produces a single output y using two inputs x_1 and x_2. The firm's production technology is described by a Cobb-Douglas function

$$y = f(x_1, x_2) = x_1^\alpha x_2^\beta, \quad \text{where } \beta + \alpha < 1, \ \beta > 0, \text{ and } \alpha > 0$$

Taking as given the price of its output p and input prices w_1 and w_2, the firm maximizes its profits, given by

$$\Pi(x_1, x_2) = p x_1^\alpha x_2^\beta - w_1 x_1 - w_2 x_2$$

Write the first-order conditions for the firm's problem, and check that the sufficient conditions for a maximum are satisfied. Using the first-order conditions, solve for the firm's optimal factor demands x_i^* as functions of input and output prices.
The first-order conditions (FOCs) for the firm's problem,

$$\max_{x_1, x_2} \Pi = p x_1^\alpha x_2^\beta - w_1 x_1 - w_2 x_2$$

are given by

$$\frac{\partial \Pi}{\partial x_1} = p \alpha x_1^{\alpha-1} x_2^\beta - w_1 = 0 \tag{1}$$

$$\frac{\partial \Pi}{\partial x_2} = p \beta x_1^\alpha x_2^{\beta-1} - w_2 = 0 \tag{2}$$

To establish that (1) and (2) actually characterize a maximum rather than a minimum, we show that the production function $f(\ )$ is strictly concave provided that $\alpha + \beta < 1$, as assumed. As discussed elsewhere, $f(\ )$ will be concave provided its Hessian is negative definite. One way to check this is to show that the leading principal minors, d_1 and d_2, alternate in sign, with $d_1 < 0$ and $d_2 > 0$.
The first and second partial derivatives of $f(\ )$ are given by

$$f_1 = \alpha x_1^{\alpha-1} x_2^\beta = \frac{\alpha y}{x_1}$$

$$f_2 = \beta x_1^\alpha x_2^{\beta-1} = \frac{\beta y}{x_2}$$

$$f_{11} = \alpha(\alpha - 1) x_1^{\alpha-2} x_2^\beta = \frac{\alpha(\alpha - 1)y}{x_1^2}$$

$$f_{22} = \beta(\beta - 1) x_1^\alpha x_2^{\beta-2} = \frac{\beta(\beta - 1)y}{x_2^2}$$

$$f_{12} = f_{21} = \alpha\beta x_1^{\alpha-1} x_2^{\beta-1} = \frac{\alpha\beta y}{x_1 x_2}$$

We can now check the sign of the leading principal minors:

$$d_1 = f_{11} = \frac{\alpha(\alpha-1)y}{x_1^2} < 0$$

$$d_2 = |H| = |D^2 f(x)| = \begin{vmatrix} f_{11} & f_{12} \\ f_{21} & f_{22} \end{vmatrix} = f_{11}f_{22} - f_{12}f_{21} = \frac{\alpha\beta(1-\alpha-\beta)y^2}{x_1^2 x_2^2} > 0$$

provided $\alpha + \beta < 1$.

Hence, the production function is concave, and this implies that the objective function

$$\Pi = pf(x_1, x_2) - w_1 x_1 - w_2 x_2$$

is also concave (why?), which guarantees that the FOCs characterize a maximum.

To derive the input demand functions we need to solve the FOCs for x_1 and x_2 as functions of input and output prices. From (1) and (2) we have

$$\frac{p\alpha y}{x_1} = w_1 \tag{3}$$

$$\frac{p\beta y}{x_2} = w_2 \tag{4}$$

Dividing (3) by (4),

$$\frac{w_1}{w_2} = \frac{\alpha x_2}{\beta x_1} \Rightarrow x_2 = \frac{\beta w_1 x_1}{\alpha w_2} \tag{5}$$

Substituting (5) back into (1),

$$w_1 = p\alpha x_1^{\alpha-1} x_2^\beta = p\alpha x_1^{\alpha-1} \frac{(\beta w_1 x_1)^\beta}{(\alpha w_2)^\beta} = p\alpha^{1-\beta} w_1^\beta w_2^{-\beta} \beta^\beta x_1^{\alpha+\beta-1}$$

$$\Rightarrow x_1^* = x_1(p, w_1, w_2) = \left(\frac{p\alpha^{1-\beta}\beta^\beta w_1^\beta}{w_2^\beta} \right)^{1/(1-\alpha-\beta)}$$

which is the demand for x_1. The demand for the other input can be obtained in the same way. $\qquad\square$

Problem 1.15. Prove Theorem 1.14: Let $f(\ )$ be pseudoconcave, and all $g^i(x)$ quasiconcave. If (x^*, λ^*) satisfy the Lagrange condition, $Df(x^*) + \lambda^{*T} Dg(x^*) = \underline{0}$, with x^* feasible and $\lambda^* \geq \underline{0}$, then x^* is an optimal solution to the Lagrange problem (P.L).

Assume that f is pseudoconcave, the constraint functions are all quasiconcave, and $\lambda^* \geq \underline{0}$. We will show that if x^* is not optimal, then it cannot satisfy the Lagrange condition.

Suppose x^* is not an optimal solution of (P.L). Then there exists some feasible $x \neq x^*$ such that $f(x) > f(x^*)$. By the pseudoconcavity of f,

$$f(x) > f(x^*) \Rightarrow Df(x^*)(x-x^*) > 0 \tag{1}$$

Because x and x^* are both feasible, $g^i(x) = g^i(x^*) = 0$ for all $j = 1, \ldots, c$. By the quasiconcavity of the constraint functions, this implies

$$Dg^j(x^*)(x-x^*) \geq 0 \ \forall \ j \Rightarrow Dg(x^*)(x-x^*) \geq \underline{0} \tag{2}$$

Now we form the expression that appears in the Lagrange condition and evaluate it at x^*. From (1) and (2) we have, for any $\lambda^* \geq \underline{0}$,

$$0 < Df(x^*)(x - x^*) + \lambda^{*T} Dg(x^*)(x - x^*) = [Df(x^*) + \lambda^{*T} Dg(x^*)](x - x^*)$$

from where

$$Df(x^*) + \lambda^{*T} Dg(x^*) \neq \underline{0}$$

Hence, the Lagrange condition does not hold at x^*.   □

Problem 1.17. Solve the problem $\max_{x,y,z}\{2x - 2y + z \text{ s.t. } x^2 + y^2 + z^2 = 9\}$ by the method of Lagrange multipliers. Use the sufficient second-order conditions for a strict maximum to determine which of the two solutions to the system of first-order conditions yields a maximum. Verify that this is correct by comparing the values of the objective function in both cases.

The Lagrangian is

$$\pounds = 2x - 2y + z + \lambda[x^2 + y^2 + z^2 - 9]$$

Differentiating $\pounds$ with respect to the choice variables and the multiplier, we obtain the first-order necessary conditions for the problem:

$$\frac{\partial \pounds}{\partial x} = 2 + 2\lambda x = 0 \Rightarrow x = \frac{-1}{\lambda} \tag{1}$$

$$\frac{\partial \pounds}{\partial y} = -2 + 2\lambda y = 0 \Rightarrow y = \frac{1}{\lambda} \tag{2}$$

$$\frac{\partial \pounds}{\partial z} = 1 + 2\lambda z = 0 \Rightarrow z = \frac{-1}{2\lambda} \tag{3}$$

$$\frac{\partial \pounds}{\partial \lambda} = 0 \Rightarrow x^2 + y^2 + z^2 = 9 \tag{4}$$

Substituting (1)–(3) into (4),

$$\left(\frac{1}{\lambda^2} + \frac{1}{\lambda^2} + \frac{1}{4\lambda^2}\right) = \frac{9}{4\lambda^2} = 9 \Rightarrow \lambda = \pm\frac{1}{2}$$

Hence, we have two candidate solutions:

$$\lambda_1 = \frac{1}{2}, \quad x_1 = -2, \quad y_1 = 2, \quad z_1 = -1 \tag{i}$$

$$\lambda_2 = -\frac{1}{2}, \quad x_2 = 2, \quad y_2 = -2, \quad z_2 = 1 \tag{ii}$$

Substituting them into the objective function,

$$f(x_1, y_1, z_1) = -4 - 4 - 1 = -9 \quad \text{and} \quad f(x_2, y_2, z_2) = 4 + 4 + 1 = 9$$

so the second point is the maximizer we seek.

To apply Theorem 1.16 (sufficient conditions for a strict local maximum), we have to check the leading principal minors of the bordered Hessian:

$$H = \begin{bmatrix} 0 & g_x & g_y & g_z \\ g_x & \pounds_{xx} & \pounds_{xy} & \pounds_{xz} \\ g_y & \pounds_{yx} & \pounds_{yy} & \pounds_{yz} \\ g_z & \pounds_{zx} & \pounds_{zy} & \pounds_{zz} \end{bmatrix} = \begin{bmatrix} 0 & 2x & 2y & 2z \\ 2x & 2\lambda & 0 & 0 \\ 2y & 0 & 2\lambda & 0 \\ 2z & 0 & 0 & 2\lambda \end{bmatrix}$$

For a maximum, we need this matrix to be negative definite subject to the constraints $Dg(x^*)h = 0$. This requires that the last three principal minors of H alternate in sign, with $(-1)^r H_r > 0$ for $r = 1, 2, 3$.

Now

$$(-1)|H_1| = -\begin{vmatrix} 0 & 2x \\ 2x & 2\lambda \end{vmatrix} = 4x^2 > 0$$

$$(-1)^2|H_2| = \begin{vmatrix} 0 & 2x & 2y \\ 2x & 2\lambda & 0 \\ 2y & 0 & 2\lambda \end{vmatrix} = -8\lambda y^2 - 8\lambda x^2 = -8\lambda(x^2 + y^2) > 0, \quad \text{with } \lambda_2 = -\frac{1}{2}$$

$$(-1)^3|H_3| = -\left((-1)^3 2x \begin{vmatrix} 2x & 2y & 2z \\ 0 & 2\lambda & 0 \\ 0 & 0 & 2\lambda \end{vmatrix} + (-1)^4 2y \begin{vmatrix} 2x & 2y & 2z \\ 2\lambda & 0 & 0 \\ 0 & 0 & 2\lambda \end{vmatrix} + (-1)^5 2z \begin{vmatrix} 2x & 2y & 2z \\ 2\lambda & 0 & 0 \\ 0 & 2\lambda & 0 \end{vmatrix} \right)$$

$$= -\{(-1)2x(8x\lambda^2) + 2y(-8y\lambda^2) - 2z(8z\lambda^2)\} = 16\lambda^2(x^2 + y^2 + z^2) > 0$$

□

Problem 1.21. **Integral objective and constraint functions.** Let $f: \mathbb{R}^{n+1} \longrightarrow \mathbb{R}$ and $g: \mathbb{R}^{n+1} \longrightarrow \mathbb{R}$ be C^1 functions, and consider the problem

$$\max_{x(s),\, s \in [a,b]} \left\{ \int_a^b f[x(s), s]\, ds \text{ s.t. } \int_a^b g[x(s), s]\, ds \geq 0 \right\} \tag{P.I}$$

(i) Let $x^*(s)$ be an optimal solution function for (P.I), and let us consider a feasible *variation* from this function. In particular, we will consider a two-parameter family of functions of the form

$$\tilde{x}(s) = x^*(s) + \alpha y(s) + \beta z(s)$$

where $y(s)$ and $z(s)$ are arbitrary functions from $\mathbb{R}$ to $\mathbb{R}^n$, and the parameters α and β will be chosen so that, given $y(\ )$ and $z(\ )$, the constraint holds.

Now consider the problem

$$\max_{\alpha,\, \beta} \left\{ F(\alpha, \beta) = \int_a^b f[\tilde{x}(s), s]\, ds \text{ subject to } G(\alpha, \beta) = \int_a^b g[\tilde{x}(s), s]\, ds \geq 0 \right\} \quad \text{(P.I}')$$

and observe that the solution of the transformed problem involves setting α and β equal to zero. Introducing a multiplier λ, we define the Lagrangian

$$\pounds(\alpha, \beta, \lambda) = \int_a^b \pounds_s[\tilde{x}(s), \lambda, s]\, ds = \int_a^b (f[\tilde{x}(s), s] + \lambda g[\tilde{x}(s), s])\, ds$$

Use the Kuhn-Tucker theorem to derive the following first-order conditions:

$$D_x \pounds_s[x^*(s), \lambda, s] = D_x f[x^*(s), s] + \lambda D_x g[x^*(s), s] = \underline{0} \tag{K-T}$$

$$\int_a^b g[x^*(s), s]\, ds \geq 0 \quad \text{and} \quad \int_a^b g[x^*(s), s]\, ds = 0 \quad \text{if } \lambda > 0$$

$$\lambda \geq 0 \quad \text{and} \quad \lambda = 0 \quad \text{if } \int_a^b g[x^*(s), s]\, ds > 0 \tag{C-S}$$

Applying the Kuhn-Tucker theorem to (P.I$'$) and evaluating the resulting conditions at $\alpha = \beta = 0$, we have

$$D_\alpha \pounds(\alpha, \beta, \lambda) = \int_a^b D_x \pounds_s (x_s^*, \lambda, s) y(s)\, ds$$

$$= \int_a^b [D_x f(x_s^*, s) + \lambda D_x g(x_s^*, s)] y(s)\, ds = 0 \tag{1}$$

$$D_\beta \pounds(\alpha, \beta, \lambda) = \int_a^b D_x \pounds_s (x_s^*, \lambda, s) z(s)\, ds$$

$$= \int_a^b [D_x f(x_s^*, s) + \lambda D_x g(x_s^*, s)] z(s)\, ds = 0 \tag{2}$$

$$\int_a^b g(x_s^*, s)\, ds \geq 0 \quad \text{and} \quad \int_a^b g(x_s^*, s)\, ds = 0 \quad \text{if} \quad \lambda > 0$$

$$\lambda \geq 0 \quad \text{and} \quad \lambda = 0 \quad \text{if} \quad \int_a^b g(x_s^*, s)\, ds > 0 \tag{C-S}$$

Notice, moreover, that (1) and (2) must hold for any functions $y(s)$ and $z(s)$. This implies that the terms inside the brackets must be zero for each s.

(ii) Assume that $f(x, s)$ and $g(x, s)$ are concave in x for each s, and let $x^*(s)$ be a choice function that satisfies the first-order conditions for the problem. Show that $x^*(s)$ solves (P.I).

Let x_s be an arbitrary feasible choice function. By the concavity of $f(\ )$ and $g(\ )$, we have, for each s,

$$f_s(x_s) \leq f_s(x_s^*) + D_x f_s(x_s^*)(x_s - x_s^*) \Rightarrow f_s(x_s^*) - f_s(x_s) \geq -D_x f_s(x_s^*)(x_s - x_s^*) \tag{3}$$

$$g_s(x_s) \leq g_s(x_s^*) + D_x g_s(x_s^*)(x_s - x_s^*) \Rightarrow D_x g_s(x_s^*)(x_s - x_s^*) \geq g_s(x_s) - g_s(x_s^*) \tag{4}$$

Integrating (3) between a and b, and using (4) and (K-T), we have

$$\int_a^b [f_s(x_s^*) - f_s(x_s)]\, ds \geq -\int_a^b D_x f_s(x_s^*)(x_s - x_s^*)\, ds = \lambda \int_a^b D_x g_s(x_s^*)(x_s - x_s^*)\, ds$$

$$\geq \lambda \int_a^b [g_s(x_s) - g_s(x_s^*)]\, ds = \lambda \int_a^b g_s(x_s)\, ds - \lambda \int_a^b g_s(x_s^*)\, ds = \lambda \int_a^b g_s(x_s)\, ds - 0 \geq 0$$

Notice that $\lambda \int_a^b g_s(x_s^*)\, ds = 0$, by (C-S), and that the last inequality follows because $\lambda \geq 0$, by (C-S), and $\int_a^b g_s(x_s)\, ds \geq 0$, by the feasibility of x_s. Hence we conclude that

$$\int_a^b f_s(x_s^*)\, ds \geq \int_a^b f_s(x_s)\, ds$$

for any feasible but otherwise arbitrary choice function x_s. This establishes the desired result. □

Problem 2.5. Extend the proof of Lemmas 2.3 and 2.4 to the case of several constraints.

• *Lemma 2.3:* We know that there exists some $x' \in C(\alpha^0)$ such that $g^i(x', \alpha^0) = m_i > 0$ for each i. Let $m = \min_i\{m_i\}$, and choose λ so that

$$(1 - \lambda)m - \lambda\varepsilon > 0 \tag{1}$$

Construct the sequence $\{y_n\}$ as before, with

$$y_n = (1 - \lambda)x' + \lambda x_n$$

and use the concavity of $g^i(\ )$ in x to establish that

$$g^i(y_n, \alpha^0) \geq (1 - \lambda)g^i(x', \alpha^0) + \lambda g^i(x_n, \alpha^0) \geq (1 - \lambda)m_i - \lambda\varepsilon \geq (1 - \lambda)m - \lambda\varepsilon > 0$$

for all $i = 1, \ldots, c$. Hence $y_n \in C(\alpha^0)$ for all n, and the rest of the argument is as before.

• *Lemma 2.4:* Conditions (1)–(3) in the proof of Lemma 2.4 now become

$$g^i(x_n, \alpha_n) \geq 0 \tag{1'}$$

$$g^i(x_n, \alpha^0) < -\varepsilon \tag{2'}$$

$$g^i(x', \alpha^0) > 0 \tag{3'}$$

for all n and all $i = 1, \ldots, c$. As before, (3') implies that there exists some N such that

$$g^i(x', \alpha_n) > 0 \; \forall i \quad \text{and} \quad \forall n > N \tag{4'}$$

Define the function

$$g(x) = \min_i g^i(x, \alpha^0)$$

and observe that $g(\ )$ is continuous and concave, by the continuity of the $g^i(\ )$'s and their concavity in x, and that (2) and (3) imply that

$$g(x_n) < -\varepsilon \; \forall \, n \text{ and } g(x') > 0 \tag{5}$$

Using this expression, the continuity of $g(\ )$ implies that for each n there is a point y_n of the form

$$y_n = (1 - \lambda_n)x' + \lambda_n x_n, \quad \text{with } \lambda_n \in (0, 1) \tag{6}$$

such that

$$g(y_n) = \min_i g^i(y_n, \alpha^0) = -\varepsilon$$

Hence,

$$g^i(y_n, \alpha^0) \geq -\varepsilon \; \forall \, i = 1, \ldots, c \tag{7}$$

which implies that $y_n \in C_\varepsilon(\alpha^0)$ for all n, and for each n there exists some $j_n \in \{1, \ldots, c\}$ such that

$$g^{j_n}(y_n, \alpha^0) = -\varepsilon$$

Because we have only a finite number of constraints, moreover, at least one of the i's will be repeated an infinite number of times in the sequence $\{j_n\}$. Hence, there exists some $j \in \{1, \ldots, c\}$ and a subsequence $\{y_{n_k}\}$ of $\{y_n\}$ with the property that

$$g^j(y_{n_k}, \alpha^0) = -\varepsilon \; \forall \, n_k \tag{8}$$

Consider next the subsequence $\{(y_{n_k}, \alpha_{n_k})\}$. The concavity of $g^i(\ )$ in x implies that

$$g^i(y_{n_k}, \alpha_{n_k}) = g^i((1 - \lambda_{n_k})x' + \lambda_{n_k} x_{n_k}, \alpha_{n_k}) \geq (1 - \lambda_{n_k})g^i(x', \alpha_{n_k}) + \lambda_{n_k} g^i(x_{n_k}, \alpha_{n_k}) > 0 \tag{9}$$

for all i and all $n_k > N$, and it follows that

$$y_{n_k} \in C(\alpha_{n_k}) \; \forall \, n_k > N$$

Now, because $\{y_{n_k}\}$ is contained in $C_\varepsilon(\alpha^0)$ and this set is compact, by Lemma 2.3, it follows (by Theorem 8.5 in Chapter 2) that this sequence has a convergent subsequence $\{y_{n_{k_q}}\}$ with limit y in $C_\varepsilon(\alpha^0)$.

   Finally, consider the limit of this subsequence. By (8) and the continuity of $g^j(\ )$, we have

$$g^i(y, \alpha^0) = \lim_{q \to \infty} g(y_{n_{k_q}}, \alpha^0) = -\varepsilon$$

On the other hand, (9) implies that

$$g^i(y, \alpha^0) = \lim_{q \to \infty} g(y_{n_{k_q}}, \alpha_{n_{k_q}}) \geq 0 \; \forall \, i \text{ (including } j)$$

which contradicts the previous statement. $\qquad\qquad\square$

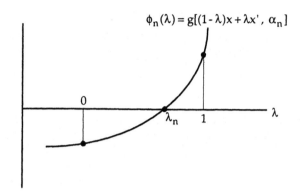

Figure A7.1.

Problem 2.6. We will give an alternative proof of the lower hemicontinuity of $C(\ )$ under the assumptions of Theorem 2.2.

- *One constraint:* Let $\{\alpha_n\} \to \alpha$, and consider an arbitrary point $x \in C(\alpha)$. We want to show that there exists a companion sequence $\{x_n; x_n \in C(\alpha_n)\}$ that converges to x.

  We will construct a sequence $\{x_n\}$ of the form

$$
x_n = \begin{cases} x & \text{if } x \in C(\alpha_n) \quad \text{i.e., if } g(x, \alpha_n) \geq 0 \\ x_n \in C(\alpha_n) \text{ s.th. } g(x_n, \alpha_n) = 0 & \text{if } g(x, \alpha_n) < 0 \end{cases} \tag{1}
$$

for n larger than some N, and set x_n equal to an arbitrary point in $C(\alpha_n)$ for $n \leq N$. To set N, recall that by assumption there exists a point $x' \in C(\alpha)$ such that $g(\alpha, x') > 0$. Because $\{\alpha_n\} \to \alpha$ and $g(\ )$ is continuous in α for given x, there is some N such that $g(x', \alpha_n) > 0$ for all $n > N$. We will now show that for $n > N$ we can construct a sequence of the form (1).

  Given some x, suppose $g(x, \alpha_n) < 0$ for $n > N$. For each such n define the function $\phi_n : [0, 1] \longrightarrow \mathbb{R}$ by

$$
\phi_n(\lambda) = g[(1 - \lambda)x + \lambda x', \alpha_n]
$$

and observe that this function is continuous (because it is the composition of two continuous functions) and satisfies

$$
\phi_n(1) = g(x', \alpha_n) > 0 \quad \text{and} \quad \phi_n(0) = g(x, \alpha_n) < 0
$$

By the intermediate-value theorem (Theorem 6.24 in Chapter 2), for each n there exists a number $\lambda_n \in [0, 1]$ such that $\phi_n(\lambda_n) = 0$ (Figure A7.1). Hence, we can put

$$
x_n = (1 - \lambda_n)x + \lambda_n x'
$$

in (1) whenever $g(x, \alpha_n) < 0$, for then $g(x_n, \alpha_n) = 0$, and this implies that $x_n \in C(\alpha_n)$.

  To complete the proof, we have to show that $\{x_n\} \to x$. Suppose first that there exists some integer M such that $g(x, \alpha_n) > 0$ for all $n > M$. Then, according to (1), we have $x_n = x$ for all $n > M$, and the sequence clearly converges to the desired point. If this is not the case, then $\{\alpha_n\}$ must have a subsequence $\{\alpha_{n_k}\}$ with the property that $g(x, \alpha_{n_k}) < 0$ for all n_k, and because $g(\ )$ is continuous and $\{\alpha_{n_k}\} \to \alpha$, we have

$$
\lim_{n_k \to \infty} g(x, \alpha_{n_k}) = g(x, \alpha) \leq 0
$$

Because $x \in C(\alpha)$ implies $g(x, \alpha) \geq 0$, moreover, it must be the case that

$$g(x, \alpha) = 0 \tag{2}$$

To show that $\{x_n = (1 - \lambda_n)x + \lambda_n x'\} \to x$, consider the sequence $\{\lambda_n\}$, and notice that $\{x_n\} \to x$ if and only if $\{\lambda_n\} \to 0$. We will assume that $\{\lambda_n\} \nrightarrow 0$ and obtain a contradiction. If $\{\lambda_n\} \nrightarrow 0$, then there exists some $\varepsilon > 0$ and a subsequence $\{\lambda_{n_p}\}$ of $\{\lambda_n\}$ such that $\lambda_{n_p} > \varepsilon$ for all n_p. Because $\{\lambda_{n_p}\}$ is a bounded sequence of real numbers, it will contain a convergent subsequence, say $\{\lambda_{n_{p_q}}\}$, with limit $\mu \geq \varepsilon > 0$. Using the concavity of $g(\ )$ in x, we can then write

$$0 = g(x_{n_{p_q}}, \alpha_{n_{p_q}}) = g[(1 - \lambda_{n_{p_q}})x + \lambda_{n_{p_q}}x', \alpha_{n_{p_q}}] \geq (1 - \lambda_{n_{p_q}})g(x, \alpha_{n_{p_q}}) + \lambda_{n_{p_q}}g(x', \alpha_{n_{p_q}}) \tag{3}$$

where the first equality holds by the definition of $x_{n_{p_q}}$. Taking limits of this expression and using (2), we have

$$(1 - \mu)g(x, \alpha) + \mu g(x', \alpha) = 0 + \mu g(x', \alpha) \leq 0$$

which is a contradiction, because both μ and $g(x', \alpha)$ are strictly positive.

- *Several constraints*: We will prove the result for $c = 2$, and the general case will then follow by induction on c. Notice that we can write $C(\alpha) = C^1(\alpha) \cap C^2(\alpha)$, where

$$C^i(\alpha) = \{x \in \mathbb{R}^m; \ g^i(\alpha, x) \geq 0\}$$

Let $\{\alpha_n\} \to \alpha$, and consider an arbitrary point $x \in C(\alpha) = C^1(\alpha) \cap C^2(\alpha)$. We want to show that there exists a companion sequence $\{x_n; x_n \in C(\alpha_n) = C^1(\alpha_n) \cap C^2(\alpha_n)\}$ that converges to x. Proceeding as in the proof of the preceding theorem, we can construct two sequences $\{x_n^1; x_n^1 \in C^1(\alpha_n)\}$ and $\{x_n^2; x_n^2 \in C^2(\alpha_n)\}$ that both converge to x. (See the proof of Theorem 2.2 for the construction of these sequences.) We will use these two sequences to construct a sequence $\{x_n\}$ contained in $C(\alpha) = C^1(\alpha) \cap C^2(\alpha)$ with limit x.

Recall that x_n^i is of the form $(1 - \lambda_n^i)x + \lambda_n^i x'$, with $\lambda_n^i \in [0, 1]$, and refer to Figure A7.2. Notice that both x_n^1 and x_n^2 lie on the line segment $[x, x']$, and consider the intersections of this segment with $C^1(\alpha_n)$, $C^2(\alpha_n)$, and $C(\alpha_n)$. By the concavity of g^i in x for given α, both $C^1(\alpha_n)$ and $C^2(\alpha_n)$ are convex sets, and therefore so is $C(\alpha_n) = C^1(\alpha_n) \cap C^2(\alpha_n)$. Moreover, we have $x_n^1 \in C^1(\alpha_n)$ and $x_n^2 \in C^2(\alpha_n)$ by construction, and $x' \in C^1(\alpha_n) \cap C^2(\alpha_n)$, for n sufficiently large, by the continuity of $g^1(\ )$ and $g^2(\ )$ and the fact that $g^i(x', \alpha) > 0$ for $i = 1, 2$ (and $\{\alpha_n\} \to \alpha$). By the convexity of $C^i(\alpha_n)$, the line segment $[x_n^i, x']$ is contained in $C^i(\alpha_n)$, because both of its end points lie on this set, and the segment $[x_n^1, x'] \cap [x_n^2, x']$ is contained in the intersection $C(\alpha_n)$.

Using these facts, we can now construct a sequence $\{x_n\}$, with $x_n \in C(\alpha_n)$ and converging to x. Let $\lambda_n = \max\{\lambda_n^1, \lambda_n^2\}$, put $x_n = (1 - \lambda_n)x + \lambda_n x'$, and notice that $[x_n^1, x'] \cap [x_n^2, x'] = [x_n, x'] \subseteq C(\alpha_n)$. Hence $x_n \in C(\alpha_n)$ for each n. It remains to show that $\{x_n\} \to x$.

For this, define the function $g(\ )$ by $g(x, \alpha) = \min\{g^1(x, \alpha), g^2(x, \alpha)\}$, and observe that this function is concave in x and continuous (by the concavity and continuity of the g^i's). Next, notice that if there exists some N such that $g(x, \alpha_n) > 0$ (i.e., $g^1(x, \alpha_n) > 0$ and $g^2(x, \alpha_n) > 0$) for all $n > N$, then we have $x_n = x$ for all $n > N$, and the sequence converges trivially to the desired point. If this is not the case, we can proceed exactly as before, exploiting the concavity in x of $g(x, \alpha)$ to obtain a contradiction if $\{x_n\} \nrightarrow x$. $\square$

Problem 2.7. Given sets $X \subseteq \mathbb{R}^n$ and $\Omega \subseteq \mathbb{R}^p$, let $g^i(x, \alpha): X \times \Omega \longrightarrow \mathbb{R}$ be a continuous function for all $i = 1, \ldots, c$, and define the correspondence $C: \Omega \longrightarrow\!\!\!\rightarrow X$ by

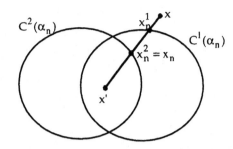

Figure A7.2. Construction of $\{x_n\}$.

$$C(\alpha) = \{x \in X; \ \|x\| \leq B \text{ and } g^i(x, \alpha) \geq 0 \ \forall \ i = 1, \ldots, c\}$$

Show that $C(\ )$ is uhc at each α.

- First, we show that $C(\alpha)$ is compact-valued (i.e., that the set $C(\alpha)$. is compact for each α). Fix an arbitrary α in Ω. Because $C(\alpha)$ is contained in a ball of radius B, it is bounded. To establish that it is also closed (and therefore compact), observe that $C(\alpha)$ is defined as the intersection of closed sets, namely, a closed ball and sets of the form $\{x \in X; \ g^i(x, \alpha) \geq 0\}$ that are inverse images of a closed set under a continuous function.

- Because the correspondence $C(\ )$ is compact-valued, to establish its upper hemicontinuity at α it suffices to show that given any sequence $\{\alpha_n\}$ converging to α, every companion sequence $\{x_n\}$, with $x_n \in C(\alpha_n)$ for each n, has a convergent subsequence with limit in $C(\alpha)$.

  Let $\{\alpha_n\} \to \alpha$, and consider a companion sequence $\{x_n\}$, with $x_n \in C(\alpha_n)$ for each n. Because all the sets $C(\alpha_n)$ are contained within a ball of radius B, the sequence $\{x_n\}$ is bounded. By the Bolzano-Weierstrass theorem (see Problem 3.12 in Chapter 2), $\{x_n\}$ has a convergent subsequence, say $\{x_{n_k}\}$, with limit z. Because $\|x_{n_k}\| \leq B$ and $g^i(x_{n_k}, \alpha_{n_k}) \geq 0$ for all i and k, we can take limits, and, using the continuity of the Euclidean norm $\|\cdot\|$ and $g^i(\ )$, we conclude that

$$\|x\| = \lim_{k \to \infty} \|x_{n_k}\| \leq B$$

$$g^i(z, \alpha) = \lim_{k \to \infty} g^i(x_{n_k}, \alpha_{n_k}) \geq 0 \ \forall \ i = 1, \ldots, c$$

Hence, $z \in C(\alpha)$, and this establishes the desired result. $\square$

Problem 2.8. Given sets $X \subseteq \mathbb{R}^n$ and $\Omega \subseteq \mathbb{R}^P$, with $X \times \Omega$ convex, let $g^i(x, \alpha) : X \times \Omega \longrightarrow \mathbb{R}$ be a continuous and concave function (in (x, α)) for all $i = 1, \ldots, c$, and define the correspondence $C : \Omega \rightarrow\rightarrow X$ by

$$C(\alpha) = \{x \in X; \ g^i(x, \alpha) \geq 0 \ \forall \ i = 1, \ldots, c\}$$

Fix a value α^0 of the parameter vector and assume that $C(\alpha^0)$ is bounded. Let $\{\alpha_n\}$ be an arbitrary sequence converging to α^0, and consider a companion sequence $\{x_n\}$, with $x_n \in C(\alpha_n)$ for each n. Show that $\{x_n\}$ is bounded.

By contradiction. Suppose $\{x_n\}$ is unbounded. Then it has a subsequence that diverges to infinity in norm. To simplify the notation, assume that the sequence itself diverges in norm (i.e., that $\{\|x_n\|\} \to \infty$). Consider the sequence $\{X_n\} = \{(x_n, \alpha_n)\}$. Because $\{\|x_n\|\} \to \infty$, it follows that $\{\|X_n\|\} \to \infty$.

We will construct a new sequence $\{Y_n\}$ by projecting $\{X_n\}$ onto the boundary of a ball in $X \times \Omega$ that contains the set $C(\alpha^0) \times \{\alpha^0\}$. The resulting sequence will be

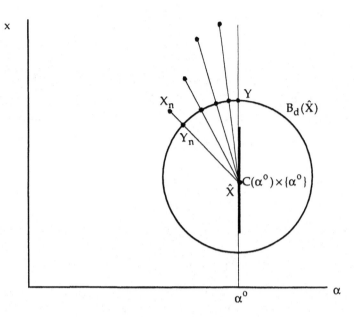

Figure A7.3. Construction of $\{Y_n\}$.

bounded and therefore will have a convergent subsequence. Taking the limit of this subsequence, we will obtain a contradiction.

Let

$$\overline{X} = (\overline{x}, \alpha^0) \in \arg \max_{x \in C(\alpha^0)} \|(x, \alpha^0)\|$$

For a fixed α, $\|(\cdot, \alpha^0)\|$ is a continuous function of x, and because $C(\alpha^0)$ is compact (bounded by assumption and closed by the continuity of $g^i(\ )$), the function achieves a maximum in the set. Let

$$M_\alpha = \|\overline{X}\| = \|(\overline{x}, \alpha^0)\|$$

be this maximum.

Fix an arbitrary $\hat{x} \in C(\alpha^0)$. Let $\hat{X} = (\hat{x}, \alpha^0)$, and observe that for any $X = (x, \alpha^0)$, with $x \in C(\alpha^0)$, we have

$$d(X, \hat{X}) \le d(X, \underline{0}) + d(\underline{0}, \hat{X}) = \|x\| + \|\hat{X}\| \le 2\|\overline{X}\| = 2M_\alpha$$

Hence the set $C(\alpha^0) \times \{\alpha^0\}$ is contained in the interior of the closed ball $B_d[\hat{X}]$, with $d = 2M_\alpha + 1$, and any point in the boundary of this ball lies outside $C(\alpha^0) \times \{\alpha^0\}$.

We will now use $\{X_n\}$ to construct a new sequence $\{Y_n\} = \{(y_n, \beta_n)\}$ that will lie in $B_d[\hat{X}]$. We proceed as follows: If $X_n \in B_d[\hat{X}]$, then we set $Y_n = X_n$. Because $\{\|X_n\|\} \to \infty$, there will be some N such that X_n lies outside $B_d[\hat{X}]$ for all $n > N$. For these points, we obtain Y_n by "projecting" X_n onto the boundary of the ball $B_d[\hat{X}]$ (Figure A7.3). For $n > N$, the terms of $\{Y_n\}$ will be of the form

$$Y_n = (y_n, \beta_n) = (1 - \lambda_n)\hat{X} + \lambda_n X_n = \hat{X} + \lambda_n(X_n - \hat{X}), \quad \text{with } \lambda_n \in [0, 1] \qquad (1)$$

We will, moreover, choose λ_n so that Y_n lies on the boundary of $B_d[\hat{X}]$. That is, we want

$$\|Y_n - \hat{X}\| = d \ \forall \ n > N \qquad (2)$$

Because $\|Y_n - \hat{X}\| = \lambda_n \|X_n - \hat{X}\|$, by (1), we need to set

$$\lambda_n = \frac{d}{\|X_n - \hat{X}\|} \tag{3}$$

Notice that $\{\lambda_n\} \to 0$. By the concavity of $g^i(\ )$, and using the fact that $\hat{X} \in C(\alpha^0)$ and $x_n \in C(\alpha_n)$, we have

$$g^i(Y_n) = g^i(y_n, \beta_n) \ge (1 - \lambda_n)g^i(\hat{X}) + \lambda_n g^i(Xn) \ge 0 \ \forall \ i = 1, \ldots, c \text{ and } \forall \ n > N \tag{4}$$

Because the sequence $\{Y_n\}$ is bounded by construction, it has a convergent subsequence $\{Y_{n_k}\} = \{(y_{n_k}, \beta_{n_k})\}$. Observe that $\{\beta_{n_k} = (1 - \lambda_{n_k})\alpha^0 + \lambda_{n_k}\alpha_{n_k}\} \to \alpha^0$, because $\{\lambda_n\} \to 0$ and $\{\alpha_n\} \to \alpha^0$. Hence, the limit of $\{Y_{n_k}\}$ is of the form $Y = (y, \alpha^0)$. By (4), and using the continuity of $g^i(\ )$, we have

$$g^i(y, \alpha^0) = \lim_{k \to \infty} g^i(y_{n_k}, \beta_{n_k}) \ge 0 \ \forall \ i = 1, \ldots, c \tag{5}$$

which implies that $y \in C(\alpha^0)$. On the other hand, using (2) and the continuity of the norm, we see that

$$\|Y - \hat{X}\| = \lim_{k \to \infty} \|Y_{n_k} - \hat{X}\| = d > 2M_\alpha$$

which implies that $Y = (y, \alpha^0)$ lies on the boundary of $B_d[\hat{X}]$ and therefore outside $C(\alpha^0) \times \{\alpha^0\}$. It follows that $y \notin C(\alpha^0)$, which contradicts our previous statement. $\square$

Problem 2.9. For each α and each $\varepsilon > 0$, define the set $\underline{C}_\varepsilon(\alpha)$ by

$$\underline{C}_\varepsilon(\alpha) = \{x \in X; \ g^i(x, \alpha) - \varepsilon \ge 0 \ \forall \ i = 1, \ldots, c\}$$

Show that, under the assumptions of Theorem 2.2, for every $\varepsilon > 0$ there exists some $\delta > 0$ such that $C(\alpha) \supseteq \underline{C}_\varepsilon(\alpha^0)$ for all $\alpha \in B_\delta(\alpha^0)$.

Notice that if ε is sufficiently large, $\underline{C}_\varepsilon(\alpha)$ will be empty, but the result still holds, because the empty set is a subset of every set, by convention.

We will prove the result under the assumption that there is a single constraint of the form $g(x, \alpha) \ge 0$. The extension to the general case is straightforward (see the solution to Problem 2.5).

We will proceed by contradiction. Suppose the result does not hold. Then, negating the statement, there exists some $\varepsilon > 0$ such that

$$\forall \delta > 0 \ \exists \ \alpha \in B_\delta(\alpha^0) \text{ s.th. } C(\alpha) \not\supseteq \underline{C}_\varepsilon(\alpha^0) \tag{1}$$

By (1) there exists a sequence $\{\alpha_n\} \to \alpha^0$ such that for each n the set $C(\alpha_n)$ does not contain $\underline{C}_\varepsilon(\alpha^0)$. Hence, for each n there exists a point $x_n \in \underline{C}_\varepsilon(\alpha^0)$ with the property that $x_n \notin C(\alpha_n)$. For the resulting sequence $\{(\alpha_n, x_n)\}$ we have:

$$x_n \in \underline{C}_\varepsilon(\alpha^0) \Rightarrow g(x_n, \alpha^0) \ge \varepsilon \ \forall \ n \tag{2}$$

$$x_n \notin C(\alpha_n) \Rightarrow g(x_n, \alpha_n) < 0 \ \forall \ n \tag{3}$$

Notice that $x_n \in \underline{C}_\varepsilon(\alpha^0) \subseteq C(\alpha^0)$ for all n. Because $C(\alpha^0)$ is compact by assumption, $\{x_n\}$ has a convergent subsequence, say $\{x_{n_k}\}$, with limit $x \in C(\alpha^0)$. Using the continuity of $g(\ )$, we have

$$g(x, \alpha^0) = \lim_{k \to \infty} g(x_{n_k}, \alpha^0) \ge \varepsilon > 0$$

by (2), and

$$g(x, \alpha^0) = \lim_{k \to \infty} g(x_{n_k}, \alpha_{n_k}) \le 0$$

by (3), contradicting the previous statement. $\square$

Problem 2.10. An agent consumes two goods, x_1 and x_2, with prices p_1 and p_2, respectively. Her utility function is of the form $U(x_1, x_2) = \alpha(x_1^\alpha + x_2^\alpha)$, with $\alpha < 1$. Verify that $U(\ )$ is strictly concave. Derive the demand function of the agent. In what direction does the demand for good 1 change if there is an increase in the price of good 2?

To obtain the first-order conditions for the agent's problem,

$$\max_{x_1, x_2} \left\{ \alpha(x_1^\alpha + x_2^\alpha) \text{ s.t. } p_1 x_1 + p_2 x_2 = y \right\}$$

we write the Lagrangian function

$$\pounds = \alpha(x_1^\alpha + x_2^\alpha) + \lambda[y - p_1 x_1 - p_2 x_2]$$

and differentiate with respect to the choice variables, obtaining

$$\frac{\partial \pounds}{\partial x_1} = \alpha^2 x_1^{\alpha-1} - \lambda p_1 = 0 \Rightarrow \lambda = \frac{\alpha^2}{p_1 x_1^{1-\alpha}} \tag{1}$$

$$\frac{\partial \pounds}{\partial x_2} = \alpha^2 x_2^{\alpha-1} - \lambda p_2 = 0 \Rightarrow \lambda = \frac{\alpha^2}{p_2 x_2^{1-\alpha}} \tag{2}$$

To check the second-order conditions we compute the second-order partial derivatives of $U(x_1, x_2) = \alpha(x_1^\alpha + x_2^\alpha)$:

$$U_1 = \alpha^2 x_1^{\alpha-1}, \qquad U_2 = \alpha^2 x_2^{\alpha-1}$$
$$U_{11} = \alpha^2(\alpha-1)x_1^{\alpha-2}, \qquad U_{22} = \alpha^2(\alpha-1)x_2^{\alpha-2}, \qquad U_{12} = U_{21} = 0$$

Hence, the Hessian matrix is

$$H = \begin{bmatrix} U_{11} & U_{12} \\ U_{21} & U_{22} \end{bmatrix} = \begin{bmatrix} \alpha^2(\alpha-1)x_1^{\alpha-2} & 0 \\ 0 & \alpha^2(\alpha-1)x_2^{\alpha-2} \end{bmatrix}$$

and the leading principal minors are given by

$$d_1 = \alpha^2(\alpha-1)x_1^{\alpha-2} < 0 \qquad \text{(because } \alpha < 1\text{)}$$
$$d_2 = \alpha^4(\alpha-1)^2 x_1^{\alpha-2} x_2^{\alpha-2} > 0$$

Hence, H is negative definite, and the sufficient conditions for a strict local maximum are satisfied.

To find the demand function, notice that, using (1) and (2),

$$\frac{\alpha^2}{p_1 x_1^{1-\alpha}} = \frac{\alpha^2}{p_2 x_2^{1-\alpha}} \Rightarrow \left(\frac{x_2}{x_1}\right)^{1-\alpha} = \frac{p_1}{p_2} \Rightarrow \frac{x_2}{x_1}\left(\frac{p_1}{p_2}\right)^{1/(1-\alpha)} \tag{3}$$

Substituting (3) into the constraint,

$$p_1 x_1 + p_2 x_1 \left(\frac{p_1}{p_2}\right)^{1/(1-\alpha)} = y$$

from where

$$x_1^* = x_1(p_1, p_2, y) = \frac{y}{p_1 + p_2\left(\dfrac{p_1}{p_2}\right)^{1/(1-\alpha)}} = \frac{y}{p_1\left(1 + \left(\dfrac{p_1}{p_2}\right)^{\alpha/(1-\alpha)}\right)}$$

The demand for the other good is almost identical, but with the roles of p_1 and p_2 reversed. Differentiating the demand for the first good with respect to p_2,

$$\frac{\partial x_1^*}{\partial p_2} = \frac{y}{p_1} \frac{-\dfrac{\alpha}{1-\alpha}\left(\dfrac{p_1}{p_2}\right)^{[\alpha/(1-\alpha)]-1} p_1 \dfrac{-1}{p_2^2}}{\left(1+\left(\dfrac{p_1}{p_2}\right)^{\alpha/(1-\alpha)}\right)^2}$$

Because $1-\alpha > 0$, the sign of this derivative is the same as the sign of α. If $\alpha > 0$, the goods are substitutes (an increase in the price of one of them induces the agent to switch to the other, increasing its demand), and if $\alpha < 0$ they are complements, as an increase in the price of either good reduces the demand for both.   □

Problem 2.11. A competitive firm maximizes profits, $\Pi(x) = pf(x) - wx$, taking as given the price of its output p and the vector $w \in \mathbb{R}^n$ of factor prices. Assume that the production function f is C^2 and strictly concave, with positive but diminishing marginal products ($f_i > 0, f_{ii} < 0, i = 1, \ldots, n$).

Write the first-order conditions for the firm's problem, and apply the implicit-function theorem (IFT) to the resulting system to show that the demand for each factor is a decreasing function of its price (i.e., that $\partial x_i^*/\partial w_i < 0$).

The first-order conditions for the firm's problem are

$$\frac{\partial \Pi(x)}{\partial x_i} = pf_i(x) - w_i = 0 \ \forall \ i = 1, \ldots, n \tag{1}$$

which is the familiar condition that the value of the marginal product of each input should be equal to its price.

In vector notation,

$$D_x\Pi(x; p, w) = pDf(x) - w = \underline{0} \Leftrightarrow F(x; w, p) = \underline{0} \tag{1'}$$

The strict concavity of f (and therefore of Π) ensures that (1') does indeed characterize a maximum, rather than a minimum. Moreover, this automatically ensures that we are dealing with a regular maximum, and the Jacobian of endogenous variables of $F(\ )$ does not vanish, as

$$|J| = |D_x F(x; w, p)| = |D_x^2\Pi(x; p, w)| = p^n |D^2 f(x)| \neq 0$$

by the strict concavity of f [f strictly concave $\Rightarrow$ Hessian negative definite $\Rightarrow$ $|D_x^2 f(x)|$ has sign $(-1)^n$, and $p > 0$].

Since the conditions of the IFT are satisfied, we can use the determinant rule to solve for the partial derivatives of the factor demand functions. For example,

$$\frac{\partial x_1(p, w)}{\partial w_1} = -\frac{|J_{11}|}{|J|}$$

where

$$|J| = |pD^2 f(\ )| = \begin{vmatrix} \dfrac{\partial^2\Pi}{\partial x_1\partial x_1} & \dfrac{\partial^2\Pi}{\partial x_1\partial x_2} & \cdots & \dfrac{\partial^2\Pi}{\partial x_1\partial x_n} \\ \dfrac{\partial^2\Pi}{\partial x_2\partial x_1} & \dfrac{\partial^2\Pi}{\partial x_2\partial x_2} & \cdots & \dfrac{\partial^2\Pi}{\partial x_2\partial x_n} \\ \cdots & \cdots & \cdots & \cdots \\ \dfrac{\partial^2\Pi}{\partial x_n\partial x_1} & \dfrac{\partial^2\Pi}{\partial x_n\partial x_2} & \cdots & \dfrac{\partial^2\Pi}{\partial x_n\partial x_n} \end{vmatrix} = \begin{vmatrix} pf_{11} & pf_{12} & \cdots & pf_{1n} \\ pf_{21} & pf_{22} & \cdots & pf_{2n} \\ \cdots & \cdots & \cdots & \cdots \\ pf_{n1} & pf_{n2} & \cdots & pf_{nn} \end{vmatrix} = p^n d_n$$

$$|J_{11}| = \begin{vmatrix} \dfrac{\partial^2 \Pi}{\partial x_1 \partial w_1} & \dfrac{\partial^2 \Pi}{\partial x_1 \partial x_2} & \cdots & \dfrac{\partial^2 \Pi}{\partial x_1 \partial x_n} \\ \dfrac{\partial^2 \Pi}{\partial x_2 \partial w_1} & \dfrac{\partial^2 \Pi}{\partial x_2 \partial x_2} & \cdots & \dfrac{\partial^2 \Pi}{\partial x_2 \partial x_n} \\ \cdots & \cdots & \cdots & \cdots \\ \dfrac{\partial^2 \Pi}{\partial x_n \partial w_1} & \dfrac{\partial^2 \Pi}{\partial x_n \partial x_2} & \cdots & \dfrac{\partial^2 \Pi}{\partial x_n \partial x_n} \end{vmatrix} = \begin{vmatrix} -1 & pf_{12} & \cdots & pf_{1n} \\ 0 & pf_{22} & \cdots & pf_{2n} \\ \cdots & \cdots & \cdots & \cdots \\ 0 & pf_{n2} & \cdots & pf_{nn} \end{vmatrix} = (-1)(-1)^{1+1} p^{n-1} d_{n-1}$$

where d_r refers to the rth leading principal minor of the Hessian of the production function $D^2 f(\ )$. By concavity, this is a negative definite matrix. Hence, its rth leading principal minor will have sign $(-1)^r$. This allows us to establish the sign of the (own price) partials of the factor demand functions. For example

$$\text{sign } \frac{\partial x_1(p, w)}{\partial w_1} = \text{sign } \frac{-|J_{11}|}{|J|} = \frac{-(-1)(-1)^{n-1}}{(-1)^n} = (-)$$

that is, the factor demand functions are downward-sloping in their own price.

In this particular case, this result can also be obtained without that much manipulation of determinants. By the IFT, we can write the optimal input vector as a function of input and output prices, $x(p, w)$. This function must satisfy the first-order necessary conditions identically, so we have

$$pDf[x(p,w)] - w \equiv \underline{0} \Leftrightarrow F[x(p,w); w, p] \equiv \underline{0} \tag{2}$$

Differentiating with respect to w, we get

$$pD^2 f(x)D_w x(p,w) - \mathbf{I} = \underline{0} \qquad \text{(where } \mathbf{I} \text{ is the identity matrix)} \tag{3}$$

which we can solve for the "substitution matrix"

$$D_w x(p,w) = \left[pD^2 f(x) \right]^{-1} \tag{4}$$

Because the substitution matrix is the inverse of the Hessian of the production function times p (and the inverse of a negative definite matrix is itself negative definite), its diagonal entries must be negative, and we conclude that

$$\frac{\partial x_i(p,w)}{\partial w_i} < 0 \tag{5}$$

Problem 2.14. Prove Theorem 2.13: Consider the following problem and the associated value function:

$$V(\alpha) = \max_x \{ f(x; \alpha); \ g(x) \geq \underline{0} \}$$

where $\alpha \in \Omega$, a convex set. (Note that the parameters do not enter the constraint function.) If the objective function is convex in the parameters α for any given x, then $V(\ )$ is convex.

As in the preceding theorem, given two arbitrary values of the parameter vector α' and α'', let $x' = x(\alpha')$ and $x'' = x(\alpha'')$ be the corresponding optimal choices of x. To establish the convexity of $V(\ )$, we need to show that for any $\lambda \in (0, 1)$ we have

$$(1 - \lambda)V(\alpha') + \lambda V(\alpha'') \geq V(\alpha^\lambda)$$

Consider the optimal choice of x for α^λ, $x(\alpha^\lambda)$, where $\alpha^\lambda = (1 - \lambda)\alpha' + \lambda\alpha'' \in \Omega$, by the convexity of Ω. Because the constraint set does not depend on the parameters, $x(\alpha^\lambda)$ is feasible but not necessarily optimal for α' or α''. Therefore,

$$f(x', \alpha') \geq f[x(a^\lambda), \alpha'] \quad \text{and} \quad f(x'', \alpha'') \geq f[x(\alpha^\lambda), \alpha'']$$

from where

$$(1-\lambda)V(\alpha') + \lambda V(\alpha'') = (1-\lambda)f(x', \alpha') + \lambda f(x'', \alpha'')$$
$$\geq (1-\lambda)f[x(\alpha^\lambda), \alpha'] + \lambda f[x(\alpha^\lambda), \alpha''] \geq f[x(\alpha^\lambda), \alpha^\lambda] = V(\alpha^\lambda)$$

where the last inequality follows from the convexity of f as a function of α. □

Problem 3.1. An agent lives for two periods and has an endowment of one unit of a homogeneous consumption good in the first period, and γ units in the second period. His utility function is given by

$$\ln c_1 + \ln c_2$$

where c_i is consumption in period i. The agent can store any feasible quantity of his first-period endowment for consumption at a later time and can get an interest-free loan of up to β units of the good (i.e., $s \geq -\beta$ and $R = 1$).

  (i) Calculate the agent's saving function, ignoring the constraint $s \geq -\beta$.
 (ii) For what combinations of parameter values will the constraint be binding? In what regions of the (β, γ) plane will we have an interior solution and a corner solution? Write the agent's saving function, taking into account the constraint.
(iii) Write the maximum-value function for the problem as a function of γ, $V(\gamma)$. Verify that $V(\gamma)$ is continuous at the point at which there is a regime change (i.e., as we go from an interior solution to one in which the constraint is binding). Is the value function differentiable at this point?

  (i) Substituting the constraints $c_1 + s = 1$ and $c_2 = s + \gamma$ into the objective function, the agent solves

$$\max_s \ f(s) = \ln(1-s) + \ln(\gamma + s)$$

The first-order condition for an optimum is

$$f'(s) = \frac{-1}{1-s} + \frac{1}{s+\gamma} = 0$$

It is easy to check that the sufficient conditions for a maximum are satisfied. Solving for s, we obtain the unconstrained saving function

$$s^* = s(\gamma) = \frac{1-\gamma}{2}$$

 (ii) If the unconstrained optimal solution obtained earlier does not violate the constraint, then it is also the constrained optimum. If the agent would like to borrow more than β and he cannot, then he will take the largest feasible loan, and we have a corner solution. Hence, the solution function for the complete problem is given by

$$s^* = s(\beta, \gamma) = \frac{1-\gamma}{2} \quad \text{if} \quad \frac{1-\gamma}{2} \geq -\beta$$

$$= -\beta \quad \text{if} \quad \frac{1-\gamma}{2} \leq -\beta$$

and the restriction will be binding if and only if

$$\frac{1-\gamma}{2} \leq -\beta \Rightarrow \gamma \geq 1 + 2\beta$$

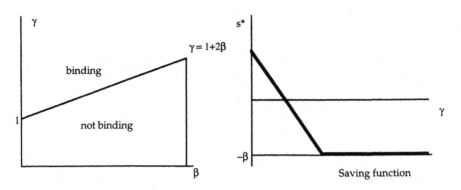

Figure A7.4.

(iii) To recover the value function, we substitute the optimal solution into the objective function:

$$V(\beta, \gamma) = \ln[1 - s(\beta, \gamma)] + \ln[\gamma + s(\beta, \gamma)]$$

Now, because $s(\beta, \gamma)$ has two different "segments," so will $V(\ )$. If the constraint is not binding, we have

$$V^n(\gamma) = \ln\left(1 - \frac{1-\gamma}{2}\right) + \ln\left(\gamma + \frac{1-\gamma}{2}\right) = 2\ln\left(\frac{1+\gamma}{2}\right)$$

and if it is binding,

$$V^b(\gamma, \beta) = \ln(1+\beta) + \ln(\gamma - \beta)$$

The "complete function" is

$$V(\gamma, \beta) = V^n(\gamma) \qquad \text{if } \gamma < 1+2\beta$$
$$= V^b(\gamma, \beta) \quad \text{if } \gamma \geq 1+2\beta$$

To verify the continuity of V, we check that its two segments have a common end point. Put $\gamma^0 = 1 + 2\beta$ (the point at which there is a regime switch) and note that

$$V^n(\gamma^0) = 2\ln\left(\frac{1+\gamma^0}{2}\right) = 2\ln(1+\beta),$$

$$V^b(\gamma^0, \beta) = \ln(1+\beta) + \ln(\gamma^0 - \beta) = 2\ln(1+\beta)$$

Hence, $V^n(\gamma^0) = V^b(\gamma^0, \beta)$, and $V(\ )$ is continuous at (γ^0, β), which is the only point at which there could be trouble.

To check whether or not $V(\ )$ is differentiable at (γ^0, β), we compute its right and left derivatives at this point,

$$\frac{dV^n(\gamma^0)}{d\gamma} = 2\frac{1/2}{(1+\gamma^0)/2} = \frac{2}{1+\gamma^0}$$

$$\frac{\partial V^n(\gamma^0, \beta)}{\partial \gamma} = \frac{1}{\gamma^0 - \beta} = \frac{1}{\gamma^0 - (\gamma^0 - 1)/2} = \frac{2}{1+\gamma^0}$$

where we have made use of the fact that $\gamma^0 = 1 + 2\beta$, implying $\beta = (\gamma^0 - 1)/2$. Because the two one-sided derivatives coincide, the value function is differentiable at this point. □

Problem 3.2. Show that if f is strictly concave, then (P) has a unique solution for a given price vector q.

Suppose there are two distinct optimal production plans $z' = (y', -x')$ and $z'' = (y'', -x'')$. Then both plans must yield the same profit, given by

$$qz' = qz'' = \pi_0 \tag{1}$$

We will show that if $z' \neq z''$ and $f(\ )$ is strictly concave, then it is possible to construct a feasible plan that will yield a profit strictly larger than π_0.

For any $\lambda \in (0, 1)$, consider the input vector

$$x^\lambda = (1 - \lambda)x' + \lambda x''$$

Because $\{x \in \mathbb{R}^n_+; \|x\| \leq B\}$ is a convex set, x^λ is an admissible input vector, and $(f(x^\lambda), x^\lambda)$ is a feasible production plan. Moreover, by the strict concavity of $f(\ )$, we have

$$f(x^\lambda) > (1 - \lambda)f(x') + \lambda f(x'') \geq (1 - \lambda)y' + \lambda y'' \tag{2}$$

where the second inequality follows by the feasibility of z' and z''. This expression implies that $(f(x^\lambda), x^\lambda)$ yields a profit strictly larger than the supposedly optimal plans,

$$pf(x^\lambda) - wx^\lambda > p[(1 - \lambda)y' + \lambda y''] - w[(1 - \lambda)x' + \lambda x''] = (1 - \lambda)qz' + \lambda qz'' = \pi_0$$

so we have reached a contradiction.   □

Problem 3.3. Under the assumptions of Problem 3.2, the firm's production plans (i.e., its output level and factor demands) are well-defined functions of the price vector q. We will show that these functions are continuous.

Fix a vector q^0 of prices, and consider a sequence of price vectors $\{q_n\}$ convergent to q^0 and the corresponding sequence of optimal production plans $\{z_n\}$, with $z_n = z(q_n)$ for each n. We want to show that $\{z_n\}$ converges to $z(q^0) = z'$. To establish this result, we shall proceed by contradiction. Suppose $\{z_n\}$ does not converge to z'.

(i) Then $\{z_n\}$ has a convergent subsequence $\{z_{n_k}\}$ with limit z^0 different from z'. Explain why this is true.

Because $\{z_n\}$ is bounded (by the second constraint), it has a convergent subsequence $\{z_{n_k}\}$ with limit z^0. Moreover, we can take z^0 different from z'. Why? Fix some $\varepsilon > 0$. Then, because $\{z_n\}$ does not converge to z', for any N there is some $n > N$ such that z_n is outside $B_\varepsilon(z')$. In this manner we can construct a subsequence of $\{z_n\}$ with the property that none of its subsequences converge to z'. But because this sequence is still bounded, it has a convergent subsequence that must therefore converge to some other point.

(ii) Let $\{q_{n_k}\}$ be the price subsequence corresponding to $\{z_{n_k}\}$. We have that

$$\{q_{n_k}\} \rightarrow q^0 \quad \text{and} \quad \{z_{n_k}\} \rightarrow z^0 \neq z' = z(q^0)$$

Show that we arrive at the following contradiction: Given any price vector q_{n_k} sufficiently close to q^0, z' is strictly better than the optimal plan $\{z_{n_k}\}$.

We will now obtain a contradiction. Because z' is optimal for q^0, but z^0 is not (but it is feasible, because feasibility does not depend on prices), we have

$$q^0z' > q^0z^0 \tag{1}$$

and therefore $d = q^0z' - q^0z^0 > 0$. Because $\{q_{n_k}\} \rightarrow q^0$, $\{z_{n_k}\} \rightarrow z^0$, and qz is a continuous function, we have that

$$\{q_{n_k} z_{n_k}\} \to q^0 z^0 \quad \text{and} \quad \{q_{n_k} z'\} \to q^0 z' \tag{2}$$

We want to show that there exists some integer K such that for all $k > K$ we have

$$q_{n_k} z' > q_{n_k} z_{n_k}$$

That is, z' is better than the optimum for q_{n_k} sufficiently close to q^0. The idea is simple: By (2) and (1), we have

$$q_{n_k} z' \sim q^0 z' > q^0 z^0 \sim q_{n_k} z_{n_k}$$

where "$\sim$" means "very close to," and this holds for sufficiently high k.

Formally,

$$q_{n_k} z' - q_{n_k} z_{n_k} = (q_{n_k} z' - q^0 z') + (q^0 z' - q^0 z^0) + (q^0 z^0 - q_{n_k} z_{n_k})$$
$$= (q_{n_k} z' - q^0 z') + d + (q^0 z^0 - q_{n_k} z_{n_k})$$

Now, $d > 0$, and by (2) there exist integers K_1 and K_2 such that the absolute values of the other two terms are smaller than $d/2$ for $k > K_i$. Hence, for $k > \max\{K_1, K_2\}$, the right-hand side is strictly positive, and the desired result follows. But this is a contradiction, for we have found a production plan z' that is better than the optimum for prices q_{n_k}. $\square$

Problem 3.4. Consider two price vectors q_1 and q_0 and the corresponding optimal production plans z_1 and z_0. Because z_1 is feasible but not necessarily optimal for q_0, it must yield a lower profit than z_0 at this price vector. Using this observation, show that for any i, $\Delta q_i \Delta z_i \geq 0$ (e.g., for the first component of these vectors we have $\Delta p \Delta y \geq 0$, i.e., an increase in the price of output must yield an increase in supply).

We have

$$q_1 z_1 \geq q_1 z_0$$
$$q_0 z_0 \geq q_0 z_1$$

Adding these two inequalities side by side,

$$q_1 z_1 + q_0 z_0 \geq q_1 z_0 + q_0 z_1$$

from where

$$q_1(z_1 - z_0) + q_0(z_0 - z_1) \geq 0$$
$$(q_1 - q_0)(z_1 - z_0) \geq 0$$

Consider changes in the price vector that affect only one component, such as

$$q_1 = (p_1, w_1) = (p_0 + \Delta p, w_0)$$

Then all terms but one in the product vanish, and we have

$$(q_1 - q_0)(z_1 - z_0) = \Delta p \Delta y \geq 0$$

so supply increases with output price. More generally,

$$\Delta q_i \Delta z_i \geq 0$$

so

$$-\Delta w_i \Delta x_i \geq 0$$

and factor demands are downward-sloping in their "own price." $\square$

Problem 3.5. Show that the profit function $\pi(q)$ is convex. Can you give an economic interpretation of this property?

Let q' and q'' be two arbitrary price vectors, and z' and z'' the corresponding optimal production plans. Define q^λ by $q^\lambda = (1 - \lambda)q' + \lambda q''$ for $\lambda \in (0, 1)$, and let $z^\lambda = z(q^\lambda)$ be the corresponding optimal production plan. By definition,

$$\pi(q^\lambda) = q^\lambda z^\lambda = (1 - \lambda)q'z^\lambda + \lambda q''z^\lambda \tag{1}$$

Observe that z^λ is feasible but not necessarily optimal for prices q' and q''; hence,

$$q'z^\lambda \leq q'z' \tag{2}$$

$$q''z^\lambda \leq q''z'' \tag{3}$$

Substituting (2) and (3) into (1), we get

$$\pi(q^\lambda) = (1 - \lambda)q'z^\lambda + \lambda q''z^\lambda \leq (1 - \lambda)q'z' + \lambda q''z'' \equiv (1 - \lambda)\pi(q') + \lambda\pi(q'')$$

so $\pi(q)$ is convex.

The convexity of the profit function can be given an intuitive economic interpretation. Suppose that an optimizing firm initially faces prices q^0 and chooses an optimal plan z^0. We force the firm to keep its production plan z^0 constant, allow the price of output to vary, and plot profit as a function of p. The resulting "no-adjustment" profit function will be a straight line. If we now allow the firm to adjust its production plan optimally as p changes, it certainly will do no worse and probably will do better. Hence, the profit function will be above the straight (no-adjustment) line. It will, however, be tangent to it at the value of p^0 for which the original z^0 is optimal (so no adjustment is needed anyway). This property of staying above their tangents characterizes convex functions. □

Problem 3.6. If the profit function is differentiable, the envelope theorem implies that $D\pi(q) = z(q)$, that is, the derivative of the profit function at a point is simply the optimal production plan (this is Hotelling's lemma). We will show that the profit function is differentiable whenever $f(\ )$ is strictly concave.

Fix a price vector q, and consider the behavior of the profit function as we move away from this point. By definition, for any change h in the price vector,

$$\pi(q + h) = (q + h)z(q + h) \geq (q + h)z(q) = qz(q) + hz(q) = \pi(q) + hz(q) \tag{1}$$

$$\pi(q) = qz(q) \geq qz(q + h) = (q + h)z(q + h) - hz(q + h) = \pi(q + h) - hz(q + h) \tag{2}$$

Rearranging these expressions,

$$\pi(q + h) - \pi(q) - hz(q) \geq 0 \quad \text{and} \quad hz(q + h) \geq \pi(q + h) - \pi(q)$$

and therefore, subtracting $hz(q)$ from the right-hand side of the second inequality, and using the first one,

$$h[z(q + h) - z(q)] \geq \pi(q + h) - \pi(q) - hz(q) \geq 0$$

Dividing through by $\|h\|$ and taking limits as $\|h\| \to 0$, we obtain the desired result: Because $z(q + h) \to z(q)$, by the continuity of $z(\ )$, and $h/(\|h\|)$ is bounded, the left-hand side goes to zero. Hence, so does the term in the middle, but this is just the definition of differentiability. □

Problem 3.7. Suppose the profit function is C^2. Using the convexity of $\pi(q)$ and the fact that $D\pi(q) = z(q)$, show once more that factor demand functions are downward-sloping.

If the profit function

$$\pi(p, w) = \max_{x,y}\{py - wx \text{ s.t. } (y, -x) \in Y\} = py(p, w) - wx(p, w)$$

is differentiable, the envelope theorem yields

$$\frac{\partial \pi(p, w)}{\partial p} = y(p, w) \quad \text{and} \quad \frac{\partial \pi(p, w)}{\partial w_j} = -x_j(p, w)$$

That is, the first partial derivative of the profit function with respect to the price of output gives us the supply schedule, and differentiation with respect to the jth-factor price yields -1 times the corresponding factor demand function.

From before, we know that $\pi(p, w)$ is convex on input and output prices; hence, if $\pi(p, w)$ is C^2 (implying that $y(p, w)$ and $x(p, w)$ are differentiable), we have the following:

By convexity, the Hessian matrix $D^2\pi(p, w)$ is positive semidefinite, which implies that its diagonal elements must be nonnegative. Hence

$$\frac{\partial^2 \pi(p, w)}{\partial p^2} = \frac{\partial y(p, w)}{\partial p} \geq 0 \qquad \text{(upward-sloping supply functions)}$$

$$\frac{\partial^2 \pi(p, w)}{\partial w_j^2} = -\frac{\partial x_j(p, w)}{\partial w_j} \geq 0 \qquad \text{(downward-sloping factor demands)} \qquad \square$$

Problem 3.8. Show that the optimal contract involves no layoffs (i.e., $n_i = 1$ for all i). Hint: Suppose we have a contract that specifies some layoffs in certain states of nature. Then workers face a lottery between working and being laid off in each of these states, and, being risk-averse, they do not like it. Show that it is possible to construct another contract with no layoffs that will yield the same profit in each state and will be strictly preferred by workers. A contract featuring slightly lower pay will be acceptable to workers and strictly preferred by firms. Does the argument rely in any way on the firm's risk neutrality?

Consider a contract C that specifies layoffs in some state of nature:

$$C(x_i) = [n_i < 1, h_i, c_i^e, c_i^u]$$

In state i, each worker faces a lottery: With probability n_i he will be employed and will get (h_i, c_i^e), and with probability $1 - n_i$ he will get $(0, c_i^u)$. His expected utility, before he knows whether or not he will be laid off, is given by

$$W_i = n_i[U(c_i^e) + V(1 - h_i)] + (1 - n_i)[U(c_i^u) + V(1)]$$

A risk-averse worker will strictly prefer another contract C' that will guarantee him, with certainty, the expected hours and the expected consumption level under C, that is, a contract with

$$n_i' = 1, \quad h_i' = n_i h_i, \quad \text{and } c_i' = n_i c_i^e + (1 - n_i)c_i^u$$

That is, by the strict concavity of U and V, we have

$$n_i U(c_i^e) + (1 - n_i)U(c_i^u) < U[n_i c_i^e + (1 - n_i)c_i^u]$$
$$n_i V(1 - h_i) + (1 - n_i)V(1) < V[n_i(1 - h_i) + (1 - n_i)1].$$

This new contract, however, will yield exactly the same profit in this state as would the previous one, for the total number of hours worked and the total wage bill will be exactly the same in the two cases. Because firms are indifferent between the two contracts and workers are strictly better off, the initial contract would not have been Pareto-optimal.

Alternatively, risk-averse workers will be willing to pay an insurance premium (work at a lower expected wage) to eliminate layoff-related uncertainty within each state. The firm can provide this service at no cost by allocating optimal work hours equally among workers and make a profit in the process.

Notice that the assumption of the firm's risk neutrality is not required for this result: Because the new contract involves exactly the same profit *in each state* as the previous one, even a risk-averse firm would be indifferent between them. Hence, the crucial assumption is the workers' risk aversion, but we have also made some implicit assumptions that are needed for the result. In particular, we have assumed that men and hours are "perfect substitutes," in the sense (i) that the only thing that matters is total hours, so that we can write the production function in the form $f(nh)$, (ii) that compensation per employed worker involves no "fixed-cost" elements, and (iii) that there are no legal obstacles to varying work hours.   □

Problem 3.9. We will now investigate some properties of the optimal contract.

(i) Write the first-order conditions for (P'), and show that they imply the following conditions:

$$c_H = c_L \qquad \qquad \text{(efficient risk-sharing)}$$

$$x_i f'(h_i) = \frac{V'(1 - h_i)}{U'(c_i)} \quad \text{for each } i = H, L \qquad \text{(efficient hours)}$$

Interpret these two conditions.

(ii) Show that $h_H \geq h_L$ (i.e., more hours are worked when productivity is high).

(iii) Show that $h_H > h_L$ (by contradiction again, suppose $h_H = h_L$).

Differentiating the Lagrangian function for (P'),

$$\pounds = \sum_i q_i [x_i f(h_i) - c_i] + \mu \Big[\sum_i q_i \{ U(c_i) + V(1 - h_i) \} - W_0 \Big]$$

we obtain the first-order necessary conditions:

$$\frac{\partial \pounds}{\partial h_i} = q_i x_i f'(h_i) - \mu q_i V'(1 - h_i) = 0 \quad \text{for each } i$$

$$\Rightarrow x_i f'(h_i) = \mu V'(1 - h_i) \tag{1}$$

$$\frac{\partial \pounds}{\partial c_i} = -q_i + \mu q_i U'(c_i) = 0 \quad \text{for each } i$$

$$\Rightarrow \mu = \frac{1}{U'(c_i)} \tag{2}$$

Notice that by (2) and the fact that $U(\ )$ is strictly increasing, the multiplier μ is strictly positive, implying that the (participation) constraint is always binding.

Substituting (2) into (1), we obtain the efficient-hours condition:

$$x_i f'(h_i) = \frac{V'(1 - h_i)}{U'(c_i)}$$

That is, efficiency in employment requires that we equate the marginal product of labor (the marginal rate of transformation of time into output) to the marginal rate of substitution between leisure and consumption for the worker.

Next, (2) implies $U'(c_H) = U'(c_L)$, and by the strict concavity of $U(\ )$ (which implies that $U'(\ )$ is strictly decreasing), consumption must be the same in both states. It is efficient for risk-neutral firms to completely insure consumption for risk-averse workers. (With a more general specification, e.g., risk-averse firms, efficient risk-sharing would require that the marginal rate of substitution of consumption across states be the same for all agents. Notice that if the workers' utility function is not separable, consumption need not be the same in all states, even with risk-neutral firms. What is equalized is only marginal utility, but this may vary with leisure.)

From the first-order conditions, we have $\mu > 0$ and

$$x_H f'(h_H) = \mu V'(1 - h_H)$$
$$x_L f'(h_L) = \mu V'(1 - h_L)$$

Subtracting the second expression from the first, we obtain

$$x_H f'(h_H) - x_L f'(h_L) = \mu[V'(1 - h_H) - V'(1 - h_L)] \tag{3}$$

To show that $h_H \geq h_L$, we proceed by contradiction. Using the concavity of U and V, we will show that (3) cannot hold if $h_L > h_H$.

If $h_L > h_H$, then, by the strict concavity of f,

$$f'(h_L) < f'(h_H)$$

and because $x_L < x_H$, the left-hand side of (3) is strictly positive:

$$x_H f'(h_H) - x_L f'(h_L) > 0$$

On the other hand, $h_L > h_H$ implies $1 - h_L < 1 - h_H$. It follows, by the decreasing marginal utility of leisure, that

$$V'(1 - h_L) > V'(1 - h_H)$$

which implies that the right-hand side of (3) is strictly negative,

$$\mu[V'(1 - h_H) - V'(1 - h_L)] < 0$$

Hence, the two sides of (3) have different signs, and the equality cannot hold. We have reached a contradiction.

Finally, we show that $h_H > h_L$. If $h_H = h_L = h$, equation (3) becomes

$$(x_H - x_L)f'(h) = \mu 0 = 0$$

implying that $x_H = x_L$, a contradiction.

Problem 3.10. Show that under the first-best contract characterized in Problem 3.9, the firm has an incentive to lie in one of the states. Which one? Why?

Under the first-best contract the firm will always announce x_H and therefore will lie in the bad state. Because compensation is the same in all states, and more hours are worked when high productivity is announced, the firm's profits will be higher if it announces x_H even when the true state is x_L. $\square$

Problem 3.11. Show that the incentive compatibility constraints, by themselves, imply that $c_H \geq c_L$ and $h_H \geq h_L$.

Rearranging the incentive compatibility constraints, we obtain

$$(IC.L) \Rightarrow c_H - c_L \geq x_L[f(h_H) - f(h_L)] \tag{1}$$
$$(IC.H) \Rightarrow x_H[f(h_H) - f(h_L)] \geq c_H - c_L \tag{2}$$

Adding these two inequalities, term by term,

$$(c_H - c_L) + x_H[f(h_H) - f(h_L)] \geq (c_H - c_L) + x_L[f(h_H) - f(h_L)]$$

from where

$$(x_H - x_L)[f(h_H) - f(h_L)] \geq 0$$

implying that

$$f(h_H) \geq f(h_L)$$

Hence, $h_H \geq h_L$, because $f(\ )$ is increasing. The second inequality, $c_H \geq c_L$, then follows by (1).   □

Problem 3.12. Write the first-order conditions for (P″). Use them and the preceding results in the following:

(i)   Show that $c_H > c_L$ and $h_H > h_L$. Hint: Suppose not. Then two of the first-order conditions imply $\lambda_L = \lambda_H$; use this and the other first-order conditions to obtain a contradiction, $x_L > x_H$.

(ii) Show that both incentive constraints cannot be binding at the same time. (If they are, $h_H = h_L$, contradicting the previous result.)
      Hence, precisely one incentive compatibility constraint must be binding. Why?

(iii) Show that the active incentive compatibility constraint is the one corresponding to the low-productivity state.

(iv) Show that the employment level is also distorted, but only in one state. That is, for the given c_i, compare the employment level in each state with the one that would be implied by the efficient-hours condition, $x_i f'(h_i) = V'(1 - h_i)/U'(c_i)$.

Differentiating the Lagrangian for (P′),

$$£ = q_L[x_L f(h_L) - c_L] + q_H[x_H f(h_H) - c_H]$$
$$+ \mu\{q_L[U(c_L) + V(1 - h_L)] + q_H[U(c_H) + V(1 - h_H)] - W_0\}$$
$$+ \lambda_L\{x_L f(h_L) - c_L - x_L f(h_H) + c_H\} + \lambda_H\{x_H f(h_H) - c_H - x_H f(h_L) + c_L\}$$

with respect to the choice variables, we obtain the first-order conditions

$$\frac{\partial £}{\partial h_L} = q_L x_L f'(h_L) - \mu q_L V'(1 - h_L) + \lambda_L x_L f'(h_L) - \lambda_H x_H f'(h_L) = 0 \qquad (\text{F.}h_L)$$

$$\frac{\partial £}{\partial h_H} = q_H x_H f'(h_H) - \mu q_H V'(1 - h_H) - \lambda_L x_L f'(h_H) + \lambda_H x_H f'(h_H) = 0 \qquad (\text{F.}h_H)$$

$$\frac{\partial £}{\partial c_L} = -q_L + \mu q_L U'(c_L) - \lambda_L + \lambda_H = 0 \qquad (\text{F.}c_L)$$

$$\frac{\partial £}{\partial c_H} = -q_H + \mu q_H U'(c_H) - \lambda_H + \lambda_L = 0 \qquad (\text{F.}c_H)$$

or, rearranging,

$$f'(h_L)[q_L x_L + \lambda_L x_L - \lambda_H x_H] = \mu q_L V'(1 - h_L) \qquad (\text{F.}h'_L)$$

$$f'(h_H)[q_H x_H - \lambda_L x_L + \lambda_H x_H] = \mu q_H V'(1 - h_H) \qquad (\text{F.}h'_H)$$

$$\mu q_L U'(c_L) = q_L + \lambda_L - \lambda_H \qquad (\text{F.}c'_L)$$

$$\mu q_H U'(c_H) = q_H + \lambda_H - \lambda_L \qquad (\text{F.}c'_H)$$

In addition, we have the incentive compatibility and participation constraints and their corresponding complementary slackness conditions:

$$x_L f(h_L) - c_L \geq x_L f(h_H) - c_H \quad \text{with equality if } \lambda_L > 0 \qquad (\text{IC.}L)$$

$$x_H f(h_H) - c_H \geq x_H f(h_L) - c_L \quad \text{with equality if } \lambda_H > 0 \qquad (\text{IC.}H)$$

$$\sum_i q_i[U(c_i) + V(1 - h_i)] \geq W_0 \quad \text{with equality if } \mu > 0 \qquad (\text{PART})$$

$\lambda_L \geq 0$ with equality if (IC.L) is not binding

$\lambda_H \geq 0$ with equality if (IC.H) is not binding

$\mu \geq 0$ with equality if (PART) is not binding

This looks like a mess, but it is not so bad. Often, the best strategy is to guess the result and then prove it by contradiction.

(i) By contradiction (recall that the desired inequality holds, at least nonstrictly, by Problem 3.11). Suppose $c_H = c_L \equiv c$ and $h_H = h_L \equiv h$. Then the first-order conditions imply

$$\left(\text{F.}c_L'\right) \Rightarrow \mu U'(c) = 1 + \frac{\lambda_L - \lambda_H}{q_L}$$

$$\left(\text{F.}c_H'\right) \Rightarrow \mu U'(c) = 1 + \frac{\lambda_H - \lambda_L}{q_H}$$

Hence,

$$\frac{\lambda_L - \lambda_H}{q_L} = \frac{\lambda_H - \lambda_L}{q_H} \Rightarrow (\lambda_H - \lambda_L)\left(\frac{1}{q_L} + \frac{1}{q_H}\right) = 0 \Rightarrow \lambda_H = \lambda_L \equiv \lambda$$

Then the other first-order conditions imply that

$$(\text{F.}h_L) \Rightarrow x_L f'(h) - \mu V'(1-h) = \frac{\lambda(x_H - x_L)f'(h)}{q_L} > 0$$

$$(\text{F.}h_H) \Rightarrow x_H f'(h) - \mu V'(1-h) = \frac{\lambda(x_L - x_H)f'(h)}{q_H} < 0$$

Subtracting the second from the first inequality,

$$(x_L - x_H)f'(h) > 0 \Rightarrow x_L > x_H$$

which is a contradiction.

(ii) Next, we show that the two incentive compatibility constraints cannot both be binding at the same time. Suppose they are. Then

$$(\text{IC.}L) \Rightarrow c_H - c_L = x_L[f(h_H) - f(h_L)]$$

$$(\text{IC.}H) \Rightarrow c_H - c_L = x_H[f(h_H) - f(h_L)]$$

and subtracting these two expressions,

$$(x_H - x_L)[f(h_H) - f(h_L)] = 0$$

which implies $h_H = h_L$, contradicting the previous claim.

(iii) Hence, at most one of the incentive constraints binds. Moreover, at least one of them does, for if it did not we would be back to the first-best contract, and we know that the firm has an incentive to lie in the bad state.

To show that this constraint is always binding at a (second-best) optimum, we proceed by contradiction. If (IC.L) doesn't bind, then (IC.H) must be binding, and we have $\lambda_L = 0$ and $\lambda_H \geq 0$. Then

$$\left(\text{F.}c_L'\right) \Rightarrow \mu U'(c_L) = 1 - \frac{\lambda_H}{q_L}$$

$$\left(\text{F.}c_H'\right) \Rightarrow \mu U'(c_H) = 1 + \frac{\lambda_H}{q_H}$$

implying $U'(c_L) \leq U'(c_H)$. Hence $c_L \geq c_H$, contradicting (i).

(iv) Hence, (IC.L) is binding, and (IC.H) is not, implying $\lambda_H = 0$, $\lambda_L \geq 0$, and

$$\left(\text{F}.h_L'\right) \Rightarrow f'(h_L)x_L(q_L + \lambda_L) = \mu q_L V'(1 - h_L)$$

$$\left(\text{F}.c_L'\right) \Rightarrow \mu q_L U'(c_L) = q_L + \lambda_L$$

Combining these two expressions, we obtain the efficient-hours condition:

$$x_L f'(h_L) = \frac{V'(1 - h_L)}{U'(c_L)}$$

Thus, employment is efficient in the low-productivity state. In the high-productivity state, however, we have

$$\left(\text{F}.c_H'\right) \Rightarrow \mu q_H U'(c_H) = q_H - \lambda_L > 0 \qquad (1)$$

$$\left(\text{F}.h_H'\right) \Rightarrow f'(h_H)(q_H x_H - \lambda_L x_L) = \mu q_H V'(1 - h_H)$$

Combining these two expressions,

$$f'(h_H)[q_H x_H - \lambda_L(x_L + x_H - x_H)] = (q_H - \lambda_L)\frac{V'(1 - h_H)}{U'(c_H)}$$

$$\Rightarrow f'(h_H)x_H(q_H - \lambda_L) + f'(h_H)\lambda_L(x_H - x_L) = (q_H - \lambda_L)\frac{V'(1 - h_H)}{U'(c_H)}$$

$$\Rightarrow x_H f'(h_H) = \frac{V'(1 - h_H)}{U'(c_H)} - f'(h_H)\frac{\lambda_L(x_H - x_L)}{q_H - \lambda_L}$$

Because $q_H - \lambda_L > 0$, by (1), we have

$$x_H f'(h_H) < \frac{V'(1 - h_H)}{U'(c_H)}$$

and, by the concavity of $f(\ )$, h_H is higher than the efficient number of hours. Hence, the second distortion induced by the incentive compatibility constraint takes the form of "overemployment" in the high-productivity state.

Different assumptions about worker and firm preferences and the nature of the private information lead to different predictions concerning the direction of the distortion generated by the incentive constraints. For example, Stiglitz (1984, pp. 19ff.) notes that if firms are more risk-averse than workers, underemployment becomes the more likely outcome. Cooper (1987, pp. 36–9) considers a model in which the stochastic state variable has to do with preferences rather than with output prices or productivity and is observed only by workers. He writes worker utility as $U(c, 1 - h, x)$ and shows that if leisure is normal and $U_{13} \geq 0$, then underemployment will result in most states. $\square$

Chapter 8

Problem 1.5. Let "$\geq$" be a continuous and monotonic preference preorder defined on a subset X of $\mathbb{R}^n$. Show that $\partial \geq = I \equiv \{(x, y) \in X \times X; x \sim y\}$.

Take some arbitrary point (x, y) in the boundary of "$\geq$." By continuity, "$\geq$" is closed and therefore contains its boundary. Hence, $(x, y) \in \geq$ (i.e., $x \geq y$). If $x > y$, continuity also implies that all points close enough to (x, y) will be in "$\geq$" (i.e.,

">" is open) and hence in "≥." This, however, would contradict the assumption that (x, y) is a boundary point of "≥". Hence, we must have $x \sim y$, and it follows that any boundary point of "≥" lies on I, i.e., that $\partial{\geq} \subseteq I$.

For the converse, take (x, y) such that $x \sim y$. By monotonicity, there exists some $y' > y$ arbitrarily close to y such that $y' > y \sim x$. Hence $(x, y') \notin {\geq}$, even though it is arbitrarily close to (x, y). Hence, (x, y) is a boundary point of "≥," which implies that $I \subseteq \partial{\geq}$, because (x, y) is an arbitrary point of I.   □

Problem 1.7. Let "≥" be a convex preference preorder defined on a convex set X. Show that the better-than sets induced by these preferences, $B(y) = \{x \in X; x \geq y\}$, are convex.

Fix an arbitrary point y in X, and consider the set $B(y) = \{x \in X; x \geq y\}$. Let x' and x'' be any two points in $B(y)$, and (relabeling them if necessary) assume that $x' \geq x''$. Then, by the convexity of preferences, we have

$$x^\lambda = (1 - \lambda)x' + \lambda x'' \geq x'' \quad \text{for any } \lambda \in (0, 1)$$

Because $x'' \in B(y)$, moreover, we have $x'' \geq y$. By transitivity,

$$(1 - \lambda)x' + \lambda x'' \geq x'' \geq y \quad \text{for any } \lambda \in (0, 1)$$

Hence, $(1 - \lambda)x' + \lambda x'' \in B(y)$, and it follows that $B(y)$ is a convex set.   □

Problem 1.13. Let "≥" be a continuous and strictly monotone preference preorder defined on $X = \mathbb{R}^n_+$, and let z be an arbitrary point in X. We will show that the indifference set $I(z)$ is connected.

A standard way to show that a set A is connected is by showing that it is homeomorphic to another set B that is known to be connected – that is, that there exists an invertible continuous function $h(\ )$ with a continuous inverse that maps A onto B. Then $A = h^{-1}(B)$ is the continuous image of a connected set and therefore is connected itself (by Theorem 9.3 in Chapter 2).

In this case, let B be the open unit simplex

$$\Delta = \{z \in \mathbb{R}^n_{++}; \ ze = 1\}$$

where $e = \underline{1}$ and $\mathbb{R}^n_{++} = \{x \in \mathbb{R}^n; x_i > 0 \ \forall \ i = 1, \ldots, n\}$. Given an indifference set $I(z)$, we "project" it onto Δ by following a ray through the origin from each point x in I until it intersects the simplex (Figure 8.4). Hence, the function $h(\ )$ is of the form

$$h(x) = \frac{1}{xe} x = \frac{1}{\sum_{i=1}^n x_i} x$$

Show that $h(\ )$ is a homeomorphism.

We have to show that the function $h: I \longrightarrow \Delta$ is a homeomorphism. It is clear that $h(\ )$ is one-to-one, for two points x and x' in I would have the same image only if they lay on the same ray through the origin; but then these two points could not be on the same indifference curve, because the "higher" one would be preferred, by the strict monotonicity of preferences. Second, $h(\ )$ maps I onto Δ (i.e., each point y in Δ has a preimage in I). This is easily seen by taking an arbitrary point y in Δ and considering the ray from the origin that goes through it. The argument in the proof of Lemma 1.12 then shows that this ray must intersect the indifference set precisely once. It is also easy to check that $h(\ )$ is a continuous function.

It only remains, then, to show that the inverse function h^{-1} is continuous. Using the sequential characterization of continuity, this means that given any y^0 in Δ and an arbitrary convergent sequence $\{y_n\}$ in Δ, with $\{y_n\} \to y^0$, the companion sequence $\{x_n\}$, with $x_n = h^{-1}(y_n) \in I$, converges to $x^0 = h^{-1}(y^0) \in I$.

We will establish this result by contradiction. Suppose that $\{y_n\} \to y^0$, but $\{x_n\}$ does not converge to $x^0 = h^{-1}(y^0)$. Notice that because y and $x = h^{-1}(y)$ lie on the same ray through the origin for any $y \in \Delta$, we can write

$$x_n = h^{-1}(y_n) = \lambda_n y_n \quad \text{for each } n \quad \text{and} \quad x^0 = h^{-1}(y^0) = \lambda^0 y^0$$

for some nonnegative real numbers λ_n and λ^0. Notice also that $\{x_n\}$ and x^0 lie on the same indifference set, $I(z)$. On the other hand, we have

$$x_n = \lambda_n y_n \not\to \lambda^0 y^0$$

but because $\{y_n\} \to y^0$, it must be that $\{\lambda_n\} \not\to \lambda^0$. Now, $\{\lambda_n\}$ is a sequence of real numbers bounded below by zero. Hence, if $\{\lambda_n\} \not\to \lambda^0$, there are only two possibilities:

(i) $\{\lambda_n\}$ is bounded above. Then $\{\lambda_n\}$ contains a convergent subsequence $\{\lambda_{n_k}\}$, with limit $\mu \neq \lambda^0$. (Because $\{\lambda_n\} \not\to \lambda^0$, there is some $\varepsilon > 0$ and a subsequence of $\{\lambda_n\}$ that lies outside $B_\varepsilon(\lambda^0)$. Because this subsequence is bounded, it contains a convergent subsequence (with limit $\mu \neq \lambda^0$), by the Bolzano-Weierstrass theorem (Theorem 3.3 in Chapter 2).

(ii) $\{\lambda_n\}$ is not bounded above. Then $\{\lambda_n\}$ contains a subsequence $\{\lambda_{n_k}\}$ with $\{\lambda_{n_k}\} \to \infty$.

We will consider each case in turn and seek a contradiction.

(i) Assume that $\{\lambda_{n_k}\} \to \mu \neq \lambda^0$. Then, because $\{y_{n_k}\} \to y^0 \in \Delta$, we have

$$x_{n_k} = h^{-1}(y_{n_k}) = \lambda_{n_k} y_{n_k} \to \mu y^0 \neq \lambda^0 y^0 = x^0 = h^{-1}(y^0)$$

Observe that $\{x_{n_k}\}$ is a convergent sequence contained in the set $I(z) = B(z) \cap W(z)$. Because both $B(z)$ and $I(z)$ are closed, by the continuity of preferences, $I(z)$ is also closed, and it follows that the limit of $\{x_{n_k}\}$, μy^0, lies in $I(z)$. Hence, we have that μy^0 and $\lambda y^0 = x^0$ lie on the same indifference curve $I(z)$ and on the same ray through the origin. Because we know that there is precisely one point of intersection between these two sets, it follows that $\mu = \lambda^0$, which contradicts the fact that $\mu \neq \lambda^0$. Hence, if $\{\lambda_n\}$ is bounded, we have $\{\lambda_n\} \to \lambda^0$, implying that $\{x_n = h^{-1}(y_n)\} \to x^0 = h^{-1}(y^0)$. Because y^0 was an arbitrary point of Δ, this establishes the continuity of $h^{-1}(\ )$.

(ii) Suppose now that $\{\lambda_{n_k}\} \to \infty$, and fix some $\varepsilon > 0$. Because $\{y_{n_k}\} \to y^0$, there is some N such that $y_{n_k} \geq y^0 - \varepsilon \underline{1}$ for all $n_k > N$. Because $\{\lambda_{n_k}\} \to \infty$, moreover, we have

$$x_{n_k} = h^{-1}(y_{n_k}) = \lambda_{n_k} y_{n_k} \geq \lambda_{n_k}(y^0 - \varepsilon \underline{1}) > \lambda^0 y^0 = h^{-1}(y^0)$$

for all n_k sufficiently large. Notice that x_{n_k} lies on the same indifference curve as $h^{-1}(y^0)$, but it also dominates the latter point, which contradicts the monotonicity of preferences. Hence, $\{\lambda_n\}$ cannot be unbounded. $\qquad\square$

Problem 2.2. Give a direct proof of the continuity of the budget correspondence. Hint: Use the sequential characterizations of upper and lower hemicontinuity. For upper hemicontinuity, consider a sequence $x_n \in B(p_n, y_n)$ converging to a point $(p, y) \gg \underline{0}$. Show that it is bounded, and apply the Bolzano-Weierstrass theorem. For lower hemicontinuity, construct the sequence as in Problem 2.6 in Chapter 7.

• Upper hemicontinuity. First, it is clear that for given (p, y) with $(p, y) \gg \underline{0}$ (i.e., all components of the vector must be strictly positive), $B(p, y)$ is a compact set.

Hence $B(\ )$ is compact-valued, and to establish its upper hemicontinuity it suffices to show that given any price–income sequence $\{(p_n, y_n)\}$ converging to $(p, y) \gg \underline{0}$, any companion sequence of feasible consumption bundles $\{x_n\}$, with $x_n \in B(p_n, y_n)$, has a convergent subsequence $\{x_{n_k}\}$ whose limit is a feasible consumption bundle $x \in B(p, y)$.

We first show that there is some integer N such that $\{x_n; n > N\}$ is bounded (which implies that the whole sequence is bounded). Let x_n^g denote the gth component of the consumption bundle x_n (i.e., the consumption of the gth good). Then, given income y_n and the price of this good p_n^g, the maximum feasible consumption of good g is bounded by y_n/p_n^g. Hence,

$$0 \le x_n^g \le y_n / p_n^g$$

Now, because $\{(p_n, y_n)\} \to (p, y) \gg \underline{0}$, there is some N such that for all $n > N$ we have

$$y_n \le y+1 \quad \text{and} \quad p_n^g \ge p^g/2 \ge p_{\min}/2, \quad \text{where } p_{\min} = \min_g p^g > 0$$

Hence, each of the components of x_n is bounded by

$$0 \le x_n^g \le \frac{2(y+1)}{p_{\min}}$$

for $n > N$. Hence, $\{x_n\}$ is a bounded sequence, and therefore it contains a convergent subsequence (by Problem 3.12 in Chapter 2). Call this convergent subsequence $\{x_{n_k}\}$, and let x be its limit. Because $x_{n_k} \in B(p_{n_k}, y_{n_k})$, we have $p_{n_k} x_{n_k} \le y_{n_k}$ for each n_k. Taking limits of both sides of the inequality as $n_k \to \infty$, we have $px \le y$. Hence, $x \in B(p, y)$, which establishes the upper hemicontinuity of $B(\ )$.

- To establish that $B(\ )$ is an lhc correspondence, we need to show that given any price–income sequence $\{(p_n, y_n)\}$ converging to $(p, y) \gg \underline{0}$ and an arbitrary point $x \in B(p, y)$, there exists a companion sequence of consumption bundles $\{x_n\}$, with $x_n \in B(p_n, y_n)$ for all n, that converges to x.

  We will construct such a sequence. Let

$$x_n = x \quad \text{if } x \in B(p_n, y_n)$$

$$x_n = \frac{y_n}{p_n x} x \quad \text{otherwise}$$

Notice that x_n is feasible for (p_n, y_n) by construction, because (whenever x is not feasible) x_n is defined as the largest fraction of the bundle x that the consumer can afford with income y_n and prices p_n. It is also clear that $\{x_n\} \to x$. If x lies in the interior of the budget set (i.e., if $px < y$), then we have $x_n = x$ for n sufficiently large. Otherwise, $y = px$, and

$$\lim_{n \to \infty} x_n = \lim_{n \to \infty} \frac{y_n}{p_n x} x = \frac{y}{px} x = x \qquad \square$$

Problem 2.4. Show that if $U(\ )$ is homothetic, then demand is linear in income, that is, $x(p, y) = yx(p, 1)$.

Recall that a function is said to be homothetic if it is a monotonically increasing transformation of a homogeneous function (Section 5 of Chapter 4). Because monotone increasing transformations of a utility function represent the same preferences, we can, without loss of generality, assume that U is homogeneous of degree k. That is,

$$\forall \lambda > 0, \ U(\lambda x) = \lambda^k U(x)$$

Let

$$x^* \in x(p, 1) = \arg \max_x \{U(x); \ px \le 1\} \tag{1}$$

so that $U(x^*) \ge U(x)$ for any bundle x whose value does not exceed 1. Now consider a consumer with income y, and observe that yx^* is feasible for this agent. Using the homogeneity of $U(\ )$, we have

$$U(yx^*) = y^k U(x^*) \ge y^k U(x) = U(yx)$$

for any bundle x whose value does not exceed 1. But note that any bundle whose value does not exceed y can be written in the form yx, where $px \le 1$. Hence yx^* is optimal, given income y, and it follows that $yx(p, 1) \subseteq x(p, y)$. The same argument in reverse yields the opposite inclusion. □

Problem 2.6. Roy's identity. Assume that the indirect utility function is differentiable. Show that then

$$x_i(p, y) = \frac{-\partial V(p, y)/\partial p_i}{\partial V(p, y)/\partial y}$$

Recall that V is defined as

$$V(p, y) = \max_x \{U(x); \ y - px = 0\}$$

The Lagrangian function for the consumer problem is

$$\pounds(x, \lambda; p, y) = U(x) + \lambda \left(y - \sum_{i=1}^{G} p_i x_i \right)$$

By the envelope theorem,

$$\frac{\partial V(p, y)}{\partial p_i} = \frac{\partial \pounds(x^*, \lambda^*)}{\partial p_i} = -\lambda^* x_i^* = -\lambda^* x_i(p, y)$$

$$\frac{\partial V(p, y)}{\partial y} = \frac{\partial \pounds(x^*, \lambda^*)}{\partial y} = \lambda^*$$

Dividing these two expressions, we get the desired result. □

Problem 2.7. Consider the following indirect utility function:

$$V(p, y) = \frac{y - \sum_k p_k b_k}{\prod_k p_k^{a_k}}, \quad \text{where } \sum_k a_k = 1$$

Use Roy's identity to find the ordinary demand functions.

$$\frac{\partial V(p, y)}{\partial p_i} = \frac{-b_i \left(\prod_k p_k^{a_k} \right) - \left(y - \sum_k p_k b_k \right) \left(a_i p_i^{a_i - 1} \prod_{k \ne i} p_k^{a_k} \right)}{\left(\prod_k p_k^{a_k} \right)^2}$$

$$= \frac{-b_i \left(\prod_k p_k^{a_k} \right) - \left(y - \sum_k p_k b_k \right) \left(a_i p_i^{-1} \prod_k p_k^{a_k} \right)}{\left(\prod_k p_k^{a_k} \right)^2} = \frac{-b_i - \left(y - \sum_k p_k b_k \right) \left(a_i p_i^{-1} \right)}{\prod_k p_k^{a_k}}$$

and

$$\frac{\partial V(p, y)}{\partial y} = \frac{1}{\prod_k p_k^{a_k}}$$

By Roy's identity, the demand for the ith good will be given by

$$x_i(p, y) = \frac{-\partial V(p, y)/\partial p_i}{\partial V(p, y)/\partial y} = b_i + a_i \frac{y - \sum_k p_k b_k}{p_i} \qquad \square$$

Problem 2.9. To complete the proof of Theorem 2.8, show that under the given assumptions, we have the following:

(i) Compensated demand is homogeneous of degree 0 in prices, and the expenditure function is homogeneous of degree 1 in p.
(ii) The solution to the expenditure-minimization problem yields no excess utility.
(iii) The expenditure function is concave in prices. Give an intuitive interpretation of this fact.

(i) *Homogeneity.* Notice that the feasible set $\{U(x) \geq u\}$ does not change with prices. Consider an arbitrary real number $\mu > 0$, and notice that minimizing px or μpx in the same set yields the same solution. Hence $h(p, u) = h(\mu p, u)$ for any $\mu > 0$, and the compensated demands are homogeneous of degree 0. Now let x^* be a point in $h(p, u)$ and therefore in $h(\mu p, u)$. Then

$$e(\mu p, u) = (\mu p)x^* = \mu(px)^* = \mu e(p, u)$$

so the expenditure function is homogeneous of degree 1.

(ii) *No excess utility.* Let x be a solution of (C.E), that is, $x \in h(p, u)$. To show that $U(x) = u$, we proceed by contradiction. Suppose this is not the case, that is, that $U(x) > u$, and consider a consumption bundle of the form $x - \varepsilon \underline{1}$, with $\varepsilon > 0$. By the continuity of $U(\ )$, we can choose ε small enough that $U(x - \varepsilon \underline{1}) > u$, and because $\varepsilon > 0$ and $p \gg \underline{0}$, we have $p(x - \varepsilon \underline{1}) < px$. Hence, x cannot be optimal, because we have found another consumption bundle that will yield the required level of utility and will cost less than x.

(iii) *Concavity of $e(p, u)$ in prices.* Let p' and p'' be two arbitrary price vectors, and define

$$p^\lambda = (1 - \lambda)p' + \lambda p'' \quad \text{for } \lambda \in [0, 1]$$

Let x^λ, x', and x'' be optimal solutions to the expenditure-minimization problem for a given u and prices p^λ, p', and p'' (i.e., $x' \in h(p', u)$, etc.). We want to show that

$$E(p^\lambda, u) \geq (1 - \lambda)E(p', u) + \lambda E(p'', u)$$

Now, by definition,

$$E(p^\lambda, u) = p^\lambda x^\lambda = (1 - \lambda)p'x^\lambda + \lambda p''x^\lambda \qquad (1)$$

Observe that x^λ is not necessarily the optimal (cost-minimizing) bundle for prices p' or p''. Hence, its value at prices other than p^λ is not necessarily the lowest one among the feasible bundles, and we have

$$p'x^\lambda \geq p'x' \qquad (2)$$
$$p''x^\lambda \geq p''x'' \qquad (3)$$

Using (2) and (3) in (1), we get

$$E(p^\lambda, u) = (1 - \lambda)p'x^\lambda + \lambda p''x^\lambda \geq (1 - \lambda)p'x' + \lambda p''x''$$
$$\equiv (1 - \lambda)E(p', u) + \lambda E(p'', u)$$

which is what we wanted to show.

The concavity of the expenditure function has a very intuitive interpretation. Hold utility and all other prices constant and plot $E(\ )$ as a function of one price. As p_i rises, minimum expenditure would increase linearly if the agent chose to always consume the same bundle. Generally, however, consumers will minimize the expenditure needed to reach a given indifference curve by rearranging purchases so as to take advantage of substitution possibilities among goods. Through this process the consumer cannot do worse than if no substitution were allowed, and will generally do better. Hence, $E(\ )$ is below the linear function described earlier, except at one point at which they are tangent; thus E is concave. □

Problem 2.10. Show that the sequence $\{z_{n_k}\}$ constructed in the last part of the proof of Theorem 2.8 converges to x.

Choose z so that $z \gg x$, and observe that each z_{n_k} is of the form

$$z_{n_k} = (1 - \lambda_k)x + \lambda_k z, \quad \text{with } \lambda_k \in [0, 1]$$

Hence $z_{n_k} \gg x$ for all $\lambda_k \in (0, 1]$, and $\{z_{n_k}\} \to x$ if and only if $\{\lambda_k\} \to 0$. We will assume that $\{\lambda_k\} \nrightarrow 0$ and obtain a contradiction.

Because $\{\lambda_k\}$ is contained in the compact interval $[0, 1]$, it contains a convergence subsequence $\{\lambda_{k_q}\}$, with limit $\mu \in [0, 1]$. Suppose $\{\lambda_k\} \nrightarrow 0$. Then $\mu > 0$, and the subsequence $\{z_{n_{k_q}}\}$ converges to

$$\hat{z} = (1 - \mu)x + \mu z \gg x$$

By the strict monotonicity of the utility function, we have $U(\hat{z}) > U(x) \geq u$. On the other hand, we have $U(z_{n_{k_q}}) = u_{n_{k_q}}$ for all q, and $\{u_{n_{k_q}}\} \to u$, implying that $U(\hat{z}) = u$, contradicting the previous statement. □

Problem 2.14. Prove Theorem 2.13: Equivalence between utility maximization and expenditure minimization.

- By contradiction. Let x_u solve (C.U), and suppose x_u does not solve (C.E) with required utility $u = U(x_u)$. Then there exists some consumption bundle that costs less than x_u and yields at least as much utility, that is, there exists some z such that $pz < px_u \leq y$ and $U(z) \geq U(x_u)$. Because z does not exhaust income y, we can find some real number $\varepsilon > 0$ such that $p(z + \varepsilon\underline{1}) < y$, and by the strict monotonicity of U we have $U(z + \varepsilon\underline{1}) > U(z) \geq U(x_u)$. Notice that this contradicts the assumption that x_u solves (C.U), for we have found a bundle $z + \varepsilon\underline{1}$ that is feasible with income y and yields greater utility than x_u. Hence, we conclude that x_u must solve (C.E) when the required utility is $U(x_u)$, and we have $e(p, U(x_u)) = px_u$. Finally, because x_u solves (C.U) and we have, from Theorem 2.3, that $px_u = y$, we conclude that $e(p, U(x_u)) = px_u = y$.

- Let x_e solve (C.E), with $u \in (\underline{u}, \bar{u})$, and observe that $u > U(\underline{0})$ implies $x_e \neq \underline{0}$, and therefore $px_e > 0$. Suppose x_e does not solve (C.U) with income px_e. Then there exists some consumption bundle that costs no more than x_e and yields greater utility, that is, there exists some z such that $U(z) > U(x_e)$ and $pz \leq px_e$. Consider a bundle $z = z - \varepsilon\underline{1}$. By the continuity of $U(\ )$ we can choose $\varepsilon > 0$ small enough that $U(z - \varepsilon\underline{1}) > U(x_e)$; moreover, $p(z - \varepsilon\underline{1}) < pz \leq px_e$ because $p > \underline{0}$. This contradicts the assumption that x_e solves (C.E), for we have found a bundle $z - \varepsilon\underline{1}$ that yields more than the required utility and costs strictly less than x_e. Hence, x_e must solve (C.U) with income px_e. Finally, because x_e solves (C.E) and we have, from Theorem 2.7, that $U(x_e) = u$, we conclude that $V(p, px_e) = U(x_e) = u$. □

Problem 3.5. Define a mapping $F: \Delta \longrightarrow \Delta$ by

$$F(p) = \frac{p_1 + \max[0, Z_1(p)], \dots, p_G + \max[0, Z_G(p)]}{\sum_{g=1}^{G}(p_g + \max[0, Z_g(p)])}$$

where $Z(p) = Z_1(p), \dots, Z_G(p)$ is an aggregate excess-demand function satisfying Walras's law, $pZ(p) = 0$ for all p. Show that any fixed point of $F(\ )$ is a competitive-equilibrium price vector. That is, if $p^* = F(p^*)$, then we have

$$Z_g(p^*) \leq 0 \; \forall \, g \quad \text{and} \quad Z_g(p^*) = 0 \quad \text{whenever } p_g^* > 0$$

Let p be a fixed point of $F(\ )$, that is, a point such that $p_g = F_g(p_g)$ for $g = 1, \dots,$ G. Substituting this expression into Walras's law, we get

$$\sum_{g=1}^{G} p_g Z_g(p) = \sum_{g=1}^{G} F_g(p) Z_g(p) = 0$$

which implies that

$$\sum_{g=1}^{G} \left\{ Z_g(p) \frac{p_g + \max[0, Z_g(p)]}{\sum_{i=1}^{G}(p_i + \max[0, Z_i(p)])} \right\}$$

$$= \sum_{g=1}^{G} \left\{ \frac{p_g Z_g(p)}{\sum_{i=1}^{G}(p_i + \max[0, Z_i(p)])} \right\} + \sum_{g=1}^{G} \left\{ \frac{Z_g(p) \max[0, Z_g(p)]}{\sum_{i=1}^{G}(p_i + \max[0, Z_i(p)])} \right\} = 0$$

Because the first term in the middle part of this expression must be zero, by Walras's law, the second term must also be equal to zero. This implies that

$$\sum_{g=1}^{G} Z_g(p) \max\{0, Z_g(p)\} = 0 \tag{1}$$

Notice that each individual term in this sum must be nonnegative. If $Z_g(p) > 0$, the term becomes $[Z_g(p)]^2 > 0$; if $Z_g(p) < 0$, on the other hand, the term becomes zero. If any of the $Z_g(p)$'s were strictly positive, the sum in (1) could not be zero, because there would be no negative terms to offset them. It follows that each of the terms must be zero, and therefore we must have $Z_g(p^*) \leq 0$ for all g.

Moreover, by Walras's law, we have

$$\sum_{g=1}^{G} p_g Z_g(p) = 0 \tag{2}$$

Now, by assumption, $p_g \geq 0$, and we have just shown that $Z_g(p) \leq 0$. Hence, (2) is a sum of nonpositive terms. As before, it can be zero only if all terms are zero; hence $p_g Z_g(p) = 0$ for all g, and it follows that

$$p_g > 0 \Rightarrow Z_g(p) = 0 \quad \text{and} \quad Z_g(p) < 0 \Rightarrow p_g = 0$$

Thus, p is indeed an equilibrium price vector, as it clears all markets, except possibly those for goods that are in excess supply when their price is zero. $\square$

Problem 3.8. Let S be a closed and convex subset of the open unit simplex in $\mathbb{R}^G$, and $\phi: S \rightarrow\rightarrow \mathbb{R}^G$ a uhc and convex-valued correspondence with the following properties:

(i) $\phi(\ )$ is bounded (i.e., there exists a bounded set B in $\mathbb{R}^G$ such that $\phi(p) \subseteq B$ for all $s \in S$), and

(ii) for all $p \in S$ we have $pz \leq 0$ for every $z \in \phi(p)$.

Show that there exists some $p^* \in S$ and $z^* \in \phi(p^*)$ such that

$$pz^* \leq 0 \; \forall \, p \in S$$

Define the correspondence $\mu: B \twoheadrightarrow S$ by

$$\mu(z) = \arg \max_{q \in S} qz \tag{1}$$

for each $z \in B$. As in the proof of Lemma 3.6, $\mu(\ )$ is nonempty, convex- and compact-valued, and uhc. Consider now the correspondence $\mu(\ ) \times \phi(\ ) : B \times S \twoheadrightarrow B \times S$. By Theorem 11.14 in Chapter 2, this mapping will be compact-valued and uhc, because it is defined as the Cartesian product of two compact-valued uhc correspondences. Because we can take the bounded set B to be convex (if it is not, consider its convex hull), the correspondence $\mu(\ ) \times \phi(\ )$ satisfies the conditions of Kakutani's fixed-point theorem.

Hence, there exists some point $(z^*, p^*) \in B \times S$ such that $z^* \in \phi(p^*)$ and

$$p^* \in \mu(z^*) = \arg \max_{q \in S} qz^*$$

This implies that

$$p^*z^* \geq pz^*$$

for any $p \in S$. But because $pz \leq 0$ for all $z \in \phi(p)$ by assumption (ii), we have $p^*z^* \leq 0$, and it follows that

$$pz^* \leq 0 \; \forall \, p \in S \qquad\qquad \square$$

Problem 3.12. Consider an island economy populated by a representative individual who lives for two periods and has preferences described by the utility function

$$U(c, x) = \ln c + \beta \ln x \tag{1}$$

where c and x are first- and second-period consumptions. In period 1, the individual has an endowment of e units of a homogeneous consumption/capital good. He consumes part of it and uses the rest (k) as input for a production technology of the form $y = k^\alpha$, with $\alpha < 1$. Hence, the consumption-possibilities schedule for the economy is of the form

$$x \leq k^\alpha = (e - c)^\alpha \tag{2}$$

(i) Draw the consumption-possibilities frontier and indifference curves on the (x, c) plane. Where is the optimum? Solve the planning problem

$$\max_{c,x} \left\{ \ln c + \beta \ln x \text{ s.t. } (e - c)^\alpha - x \geq 0 \right\} \tag{p.1}$$

Write the first-order conditions. Is the constraint binding? Why? Or why not? Solve for the optimal values of c and $k = e - c$. (Don't worry about the second-order conditions. They hold.)

(ii) Next, consider a competitive version of the same economy. The agent now owns all the shares of a competitive firm that has access to the same technology as before, and he can lend part of his endowment to the firm, which maximizes profits, taking as given the market interest factor $R = 1 + r$ (capital depreciates completely upon use), and then distributes its profits to the shareholder. We will verify that the competitive allocation coincides with the planning optimum.

Solve the firm's profit maximization problem,

$$\max_{k} \pi = k^{\alpha} - Rk \tag{P.F}$$

and write the firm's maximized profit as a function of k.

Next, write the first-order conditions for the household's utility-maximization problem,

$$\max_{s} v(s) = \ln(e - s) + \beta \ln(sR + \pi) \tag{P.H}$$

(the agent takes as given both the market interest rate and the firm's profits), and solve for the optimal levels of saving and consumption.

Finally, in equilibrium, the desired savings of the household must be the same as the desired level of capital input by the firm (i.e., $s = k$). Solve for the equilibrium values of saving/investment and consumption. They should be the same as in the first part of the problem.

(i) Differentiating the Lagrangian for the planner's problem,

$$\pounds(c, x, \lambda) = \ln c + \beta \ln x + \lambda \left[(e - c)^{\alpha} - x \right]$$

we obtain the following first-order conditions:

$$\frac{\partial \pounds(\ )}{\partial c} = \frac{1}{c} - \lambda \alpha (e - c)^{\alpha - 1} = 0 \Rightarrow \frac{1}{c} = \lambda \alpha (e - c)^{\alpha - 1} \tag{1}$$

$$\frac{\partial \pounds(\ )}{\partial x} = \frac{\beta}{x} - \lambda = 0 \Rightarrow \frac{\beta}{x} = \lambda$$

$$\frac{\partial \pounds(\ )}{\partial \lambda} = (e - c)^{\alpha} - x \geq 0 \quad \text{with equality if } \lambda > 0 \tag{2}$$

Observe that (2) implies that $\lambda > 0$ for any finite x. Hence, the constraint holds as an equality, and we have

$$x = (e - c)^{\alpha} \tag{3}$$

Substituting (2) into (1), we have

$$\frac{1}{c} = \frac{\beta}{x} \alpha (e - c)^{\alpha - 1} \quad \text{or} \quad \frac{x}{\beta c} = \alpha (e - c)^{\alpha - 1} \tag{4}$$

The left-hand side of this expression is the slope of an indifference curve for the representative consumer (i.e., the marginal rate of substitution between x and c), and the right-hand side is the slope of the production-possibilities frontier (PPF) (i.e., the marginal rate of transformation between present consumption and future consumption). Hence, equations (3) and (4) imply that the optimum (c^*, x^*) must lie at the point of tangency between an indifference curve and the PPF, as illustrated in Figure A8.1.

Substituting (3) into (4), we can solve for c:

$$\frac{(e - c)^{\alpha}}{\beta c} = \alpha (e - c)^{\alpha - 1} \Rightarrow e - c = \alpha \beta c \Rightarrow c^* = \frac{e}{1 + \alpha \beta} \tag{5}$$

(ii) In the competitive version of the economy, the first-order condition for the firm's problem is

$$\pi'(k) = \alpha k^{\alpha - 1} - R = 0 \Rightarrow R = \alpha k^{\alpha - 1} \tag{6}$$

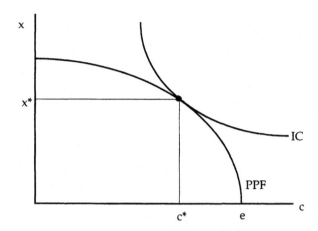

Figure A8.1. Planning optimum.

Substituting (6) into the firm's objective function, profits are given by

$$\pi(k) = k^\alpha - Rk = k^\alpha - \alpha k^{\alpha-1}k = (1-\alpha)k^\alpha \tag{7}$$

On the other hand, the consumer's problem yields

$$v'(s) = \frac{-1}{e-s} + \frac{\beta R}{sR+\pi} = 0 \Rightarrow s^* = \frac{e\beta R - \pi}{(1+\beta)R} \tag{8}$$

In equilibrium, we have $s^* = k$. Using this expression, together with (6) and (7), equation (8) yields

$$(1+\beta)Rk = e\beta R - \pi \Rightarrow (1+\beta)\alpha k^{\alpha-1}k = e\beta\alpha k^{\alpha-1} - (1-\alpha)k^\alpha \Rightarrow$$

$$[(1+\beta)\alpha + (1-\alpha)]k^\alpha = e\beta\alpha k^{\alpha-1} \Rightarrow k^* = \frac{\alpha\beta e}{1+\alpha\beta} \tag{9}$$

Using this expression, we can calculate c^*:

$$c^* = e - s^* = e - k^* = \left(1 - \frac{\alpha\beta}{1+\alpha\beta}\right)e = \frac{e}{1+\alpha\beta}$$

As expected, the result is the same as in part (i) of the problem. □

Problem 4.4. Cournot duopoly. Two firms compete in the market for a homogeneous good. The inverse demand function, which gives the price that consumers are willing to pay as a function of the total output of the good, is of the form

$$P(q_1 + q_2) = \theta - q_1 - q_2 \tag{1}$$

where $\theta > 0$ is a given parameter, and q_i is the level of output of the ith firm.

Each firm maximizes its profits, taking as given the function (1) and the output level of its competitor. For example, firm 1 solves

$$\max_{q_1} P(q_1 + q_2)q_1 - c_1 q_1 \tag{2}$$

where c_1 is its (constant) marginal cost, treating q_2 as a given constant.

(i) Solve firm 1's problem for its reaction function, that is, a function of the form $q_1 = \phi_1(q_2; c_1, \theta)$ that will give the optimal level of output as a function of its rival's output and the parameters (c_1, θ).

(ii) Firm 2's reaction function will have the same form as the one you have just derived. In a Nash equilibrium, each firm maximizes its profit, taking as given the other's output level. To find the equilibrium, we solve the system

$$q_1^* = \phi_1\left(q_2^*; c_1, \theta\right), \qquad q_2^* = \phi_2\left(q_1^*; c_2, \theta\right) \tag{3}$$

Draw the two reaction functions (their intersection corresponds to the equilibrium). Solve (3) explicitly to obtain the solution mapping for the model,

$$q^* = \left(q_1^*, q_2^*\right) = \Psi(\theta, c_1, c_2)$$

What conditions must be imposed on the parameters for the system to have an interior solution (i.e., one in which both firms produce)? Analyze, graphically and analytically, the effect of changes in θ and c_1 on equilibrium output levels.

(iii) Compute the equilibrium price and industry output and the equilibrium profit of each firm.

Firm 1 solves

$$\max_{q_1} \pi_1 = P(q_1 + q_2)q_1 - c_1 q_1 = (\theta - q_1 - q_2)q_1 - c_1 q_1 = (\theta - c_1 - q_2)q_1 - q_1^2$$

Differentiating π_1 with respect to the firm's choice variable, we obtain the first-order condition

$$\frac{\partial \pi_1}{\partial q_1} = (\theta - c_1 - q_2) - 2q_1 = 0 \tag{1}$$

Moreover,

$$\frac{\partial^2 \pi_1}{\partial q_1^2} = -2 < 0$$

so the objective function is concave, and the first-order condition characterizes a maximum. Solving (1) for q_1, firm 1's reaction function is of the form

$$q_1 = \phi_1(q_2; c_1, \theta) = \frac{\theta - c_1 - q_2}{2} \tag{2}$$

By symmetry, firm 2's reaction function will be

$$q_2 = \phi_2(q_1; c_2, \theta) = \frac{\theta - c_2 - q_1}{2} \tag{3}$$

To solve for the equilibrium, substitute (3) into (2), obtaining

$$2q_1 = \frac{2(\theta - c_1) - \theta + c_2 + q_1}{2} \Rightarrow q_1^* = \frac{\theta - 2c_1 + c_2}{3} \tag{4}$$

and

$$q_2^* = \frac{\theta - 2c_2 + c_1}{3} \tag{5}$$

Hence, q_1^* and $q_2^* \geq 0$ if

$$c_1 \leq \frac{\theta - c_2}{2} \quad \text{and} \quad c_2 \leq \frac{\theta - c_1}{2}$$

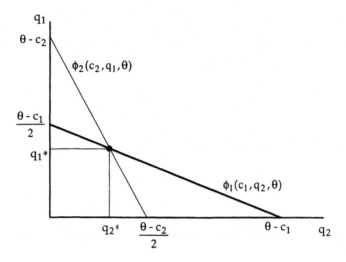

Figure A8.2. Cournot equilibrium.

From (4) and (5), it is clear that an increase in θ shifts both reaction functions upward and increases the equilibrium level of output for both firms. An increase in c_1 affects only the reaction function for firm 1, which shifts down. Hence, in the new equilibrium, the output of firm 2 increases, whereas that of firm 1 decreases.

In equilibrium industry output is given by

$$Q^* = q_1^* + q_2^* = \frac{\theta - 2c_1 + c_2}{3} + \frac{\theta - 2c_2 + c_1}{3} = \frac{2\theta - c_1 - c_2}{3}$$

and the market price is

$$P^* = P(Q^*) = \theta - Q^* = \frac{\theta + c_1 + c_2}{3}$$

Hence, equilibrium profits are given by

$$\pi_1^* = (P^* - c_1)q_1^* = \frac{\theta - 2c_1 + c_2}{3} \frac{\theta - 2c_1 + c_2}{3} = \frac{(\theta - 2c_1 + c_2)^2}{9}$$

$$\pi_2^* = (P^* - c_2)q_2^* = \frac{\theta - 2c_2 + c_1}{3} \frac{\theta - 2c_2 + c_1}{3} = \frac{(\theta - 2c_2 + c_1)^2}{9} \qquad \square$$

Problem 4.5. Stackelberg duopoly. We will now analyze a market much like the one described in the preceding problem, but in which the timing of the actions is slightly different. Instead of assuming that both firms move simultaneously, we now assume that firm 1 moves first. This gives firm 1 a strategic advantage: Because it knows how its rival will behave, it can maximize its own profits taking as given firm 2's reaction function. Firm 2 then observes firm 1's output choice and behaves accordingly. Solve for the equilibrium of this game, and compare it to the Cournot equilibrium analyzed in Problem 4.4.

Firm 1 now solves

$$\max_{q_1} \pi_1 = P(q_1 + q_2)q_1 - c_1 q_1 = (\theta - q_1 - q_2 - c_1)q_1$$

subject to firm 2's reaction function

$$q_2 = \phi_2(q_1; c_2, \theta) = \frac{\theta - c_2 - q_1}{2}$$

Substituting $\phi_2(\ )$ into firm 1's objective function,

$$\pi_1 = [\theta - q_1 - \phi_2(q_1) - c_1]q_1 = \left(\theta - q_1 - c_1 - \frac{\theta - c_2 - q_1}{2}\right)q_1 = \frac{\theta + c_2 - 2c_1}{2}q_1 - \frac{1}{2}q_1^2$$

The first-order condition for this problem,

$$\frac{\partial \pi_1}{\partial q_1} = \frac{\theta + c_2 - 2c_1}{2} - q_1 = 0$$

yields

$$q_1^* = \frac{\theta + c_2 - 2c_1}{2}$$

Substituting this expression into $\phi_2(\ )$,

$$q_2^* = \phi_2\left(q_1^*; c_2, \theta\right) = \frac{\theta - c_2 - q_1^*}{2} = \frac{\theta - 3c_2 + 2c_1}{4}$$

Hence,

$$Q^* = q_1^* + q_2^* = \frac{\theta + c_2 - 2c_1}{2} + \frac{\theta - 3c_2 + 2c_1}{4} = \frac{3\theta - 2c_1 - c_2}{4}$$

$$P^* = P(Q^*) = \theta - Q^* = \frac{\theta + 2c_1 + c_2}{4}$$

$$\pi_1^* = (P^* - c_1)q_1^* = \left(\frac{\theta + 2c_1 + c_2}{4} - c_1\right)q_1^* = \frac{(\theta + c_2 - 2c_1)^2}{8}$$

$$\pi_2^* = (P^* - c_2)q_2^* = \frac{(\theta - 3c_2 + 2c_1)^2}{16}$$

Comparing these expressions with those obtained in the preceding problem, we see that firm 1 has greater output and higher profits when it acts as a leader. □

Problem 5.1. Consider first the behavior of final-goods producers. Although firm size is indeterminate with constant returns and perfect competition, each firm minimizes the cost of producing its desired level of output y, taking as given the prices $\mathbf{p} = \{p(s); 0 \le s \le n\}$ of the different inputs $x(s)$. That is, each firm solves

$$\min_{x_s; s \in [0,n]} \int_0^n p_s x_s \, ds \text{ s.t. } y^\alpha = \int_0^n x_s^\alpha ds$$

Using the first-order conditions for this problem, derive the conditional demand for intermediate goods as a function of final output and input prices and the firm's unit-cost function (see Problem 1.21 in Chapter 7). Verify that after aggregating over all final producers, the market demand function is of the form

$$x_s(\mathbf{p}, Y) = \phi p_s^{-\varepsilon}, \quad \text{where } \phi = \frac{Y}{\left(\int_0^n p_t^{1-\varepsilon} dt\right)^{1/\alpha}} \tag{4}$$

and Y is the aggregate output of final goods, with unit costs being given by

$$c(\mathbf{p}) = \left(\int_0^n p_s^{1-\varepsilon}\, ds \right)^{1/(1-\varepsilon)} \tag{5}$$

Differentiating the Lagrangian for the firm's problem,

$$\pounds = p_s x_s + \lambda(y^\alpha - x_s^\alpha)$$

with respect to x_s, we obtain the first-order condition

$$p_s = \lambda\alpha x_s^{\alpha-1} \Rightarrow x_s = \left(\frac{\lambda\alpha}{p_s} \right)^\varepsilon, \quad \text{where } \varepsilon = \frac{1}{1-\alpha} > 1 \tag{1.1}$$

Substituting (1.1) into the production constraint, we can solve for the multiplier,

$$y^\alpha = \int_0^n x_s^\alpha\, ds = \int_0^n \left(\frac{\lambda\alpha}{p_s} \right)^{\alpha\varepsilon} ds \Rightarrow {}^1 (\lambda\alpha)^{\alpha\varepsilon} = \frac{y^\alpha}{\int_0^n p_s^{1-\varepsilon}\, ds} \tag{1.2}$$

and substituting this expression in (1.1), we obtain the conditional demand for intermediate input $x(s)$ as a function of input prices and final output,

$$x_s(\mathbf{p}, y) = (\lambda\alpha)^\varepsilon p_s^{-\varepsilon} = \frac{y p_s^{-\varepsilon}}{\left(\int_0^n p_t^{1-\varepsilon}\, dt \right)^{1/\alpha}} \tag{1.3}$$

Substituting (1.3) into the objective function, the (minimum) cost of producing output y is given by

$$C(\mathbf{p}, y) = \int_0^n p_s x_s\, ds = \int_0^n p_s \frac{y p_s^{-\varepsilon}}{\left(\int_0^n p_t^{1-\varepsilon}\, dt \right)^{1/\alpha}}\, ds = {}^2 \tag{1.4}$$

$$y \left(\int_0^n p_s^{1-\varepsilon}\, ds \right)^{1/(1-\varepsilon)} \equiv c(\mathbf{p}) y$$

Aggregating over final-goods producers, the market demand for component s is given by

$$x_s(\mathbf{p}, Y) = \phi p_s^{-\varepsilon}, \quad \text{where } \phi = \frac{Y}{\left(\int_0^n p_t^{1-\varepsilon}\, dt \right)^{1/\alpha}} \tag{1.5}$$

and Y is the aggregate output of final goods. $\qquad\square$

Problem 5.2. Taking the market demand schedule (4), the wage rate, and the prices set by its competitors as given, each component producer maximizes operating profits, given by

$$\Pi_s = p_s x_s - w x_s = \phi(p_s^{1-\varepsilon} - w p_s^{-\varepsilon}) \tag{6}$$

Solve this problem for the firm's optimal output level and the implied level of profits.

Differentiating Π_s with respect to p_s, the first-order condition for the firm's problem yields a constant-markup pricing rule,

$$(1-\varepsilon)p_s^{-\varepsilon} + w\varepsilon p_s^{-\varepsilon-1} = 0 \Rightarrow (\varepsilon-1) = w\varepsilon p_s^{-1} \Rightarrow p_s^* = \frac{\varepsilon w}{\varepsilon-1} = \frac{w}{\alpha} \tag{2.1}$$

Using (2.1) and the market demand schedule (4), we can compute optimal output,

$$x_s^* = \phi p_s^{-\varepsilon} = \phi \alpha^\varepsilon w^{-\varepsilon} \tag{2.2}$$

and the firm's operating profits,

$$\pi = (p_s - w)x_s = \frac{1-\alpha}{\alpha} w x_s^* = \frac{1-\alpha}{\alpha} \phi \alpha^\varepsilon w^{1-\varepsilon} \tag{2.3}$$

□

Problem 5.3. In equilibrium, free entry will ensure that profits will be zero in the perfectly competitive final-goods sector. Hence, the price of final output, which we will normalize to 1, must be equal to its unit cost. Using this condition, together with previous results, show that equilibrium wages and profits are given by

$$\pi = \frac{(1-\alpha)Y}{n} \quad \text{and} \quad w = \frac{\alpha Y}{nl_x} \tag{7}$$

where $l_x = L_x/n$ is "variable employment" in a representative component producer. Hence, output is divided between wages and profits. Profits per firm decrease with the number of competitors n and with the difficulty of substituting one input for another, measured by α.

In a symmetric equilibrium, all component producers set the same price (p) and produce the same output (x). Hence, each firm employs $l_x = L_x/n$ workers and produces the same quantity of components. Hence,

$$Y = \left(\int_0^n x_s^\alpha \, ds \right)^{1/\alpha} = n^{1/\alpha} x = n^{1/\alpha} l_x = n^{(1/\alpha)-1} L_x \tag{3.1}$$

where $(1/\alpha) - 1 > 0$ because $\alpha < 1$. Given the total variable employment, final output is an increasing function of the number of component varieties. Specialization improves overall efficiency.

With equal component prices, the unit cost of final output can be written

$$c(\mathbf{p}) = \left(\int_0^n p_s^{1-\varepsilon} \, ds \right)^{1/(1-\varepsilon)} = (n p^{1-\varepsilon})^{1/(1-\varepsilon)} = p n^{1/(1-\varepsilon)} \tag{3.2}$$

where it can be seen that for a given component price, the unit cost of final output decreases with the number of component varieties (because $\varepsilon > 1$). Free entry will ensure that profits will be zero in the perfectly competitive final-goods sector. Hence, the price of final output, which we will normalize to 1, must be equal to its unit cost. That is,

$$p n^{1/(1-\varepsilon)} = 1 \Rightarrow p = n^{1/(\varepsilon-1)} \tag{3.3}$$

and therefore, using (2.1) and (3.1),

$$w = \alpha p = \alpha n^{1/(\varepsilon-1)} = \alpha n^{(1/\alpha)-1} = \frac{\alpha Y}{L_x} \tag{3.4}$$

Using (3.3), we see that

$$\left(\int_0^n p_t^{1-\varepsilon} \, dt \right)^{1/\alpha} = (n p^{1-\varepsilon})^{1/\alpha} = (n n^{-1})^{1/\alpha} = 1$$

implying that

$$\phi = \frac{Y}{\left(\int_0^n p_t^{1-\varepsilon} \, dt \right)^{1/\alpha}} = Y$$

Hence, using (2.1), (2.2) ($w = \alpha p$), and (3.3),

$$x^* = \phi \alpha^\varepsilon w^{-\varepsilon} = \alpha^\varepsilon \left(\alpha n^{1/(\varepsilon-1)} \right)^{-\varepsilon} Y \Rightarrow n^{-\varepsilon/(\varepsilon-1)} Y \Rightarrow x^* = n^{-1/\alpha} Y \qquad (3.5)$$

as expected, and by (2.3),

$$\pi = \frac{1-\alpha}{\alpha} \phi \alpha^\varepsilon w^{1-\varepsilon} = \frac{1-\alpha}{\alpha} \alpha^\varepsilon \left(\alpha n^{1/(\varepsilon-1)} \right)^{1-\varepsilon} Y \Rightarrow \pi = \frac{(1-\alpha)Y}{n} \qquad (3.6)$$

□

Problem 5.4. We have assumed that anybody willing to pay a fixed cost of c units of labor can set up shop and start producing a new component variety. Compute the total demand for labor, and set it equal to the fixed labor supply L. Using this condition and the assumption of free entry into the sector, solve for the equilibrium number of firms n^* as a function of L and c, and use (3) to derive a reduced-form aggregate production function giving output per capita as a function of the same variables. Verify that this function exhibits increasing returns to labor when $\alpha < 1$.

Because production of a component variety requires c units of labor for setup, the total labor demand by a representative firm is $l_x + c$, and labor-market clearing requires

$$n(l_x + c) = L \qquad (4.1)$$

where L is the aggregate labor force. Firms will enter until total profits are zero (i.e., until operating profits are equal to entry costs). Using (3.4) and (3.6),

$$\pi = cw \Rightarrow \frac{(1-\alpha)Y}{n} = c \frac{\alpha Y}{n l_x} \qquad (4.2)$$

Solving for l_x in (4.2), the equilibrium firm size is given by

$$l_x = \frac{\alpha c}{1-\alpha} \qquad (4.3)$$

and substituting (4.3) into (4.1), the equilibrium number of firms is given by

$$nc\left(1 + \frac{\alpha}{1-\alpha}\right) = L \Rightarrow n = \frac{(1-\alpha)L}{c} \qquad (4.4)$$

Hence, the number of component varieties increases proportionately with market size, as measured by L. Total "variable labor" employed in production is

$$L_x = L - nc = L - (1-\alpha)L = \alpha L$$

Substituting this expression into (3), final output can be written as a function of the aggregate labor supply and the entry cost,

$$Y = n^{(1/\alpha)-1} L_x = \left(\frac{(1-\alpha)L}{c} \right)^{(1/\alpha)-1} \alpha L = \left(\frac{(1-\alpha)}{c} \right)^{(1/\alpha)-1} \alpha L^{1/\alpha} \qquad (4.5)$$

Notice that this function exhibits increasing returns in labor when $\alpha < 1$. If there are fixed entry costs, the size of the market limits the degree of specialization and, therefore, average productivity. Dividing (4.5) by L, we have

$$Q = \frac{Y}{L} = \left(\frac{(1-\alpha)}{c} \right)^{(1/\alpha)-1} \alpha L^{(1/\alpha)-1} \qquad (4.6)$$

All things considered, output per capita increases with L whenever $\alpha < 1$. □

Problem 5.5. Consider a free-entry equilibrium in which sector y is competitive, and x producers compete à la Cournot. Zero profits in the competitive sector imply that the salary will be equal to the price of y, which we have normalized to 1. Let us focus on the market for x and characterize a symmetric Cournot equilibrium. Aggregating over consumers, the total demand for x can be written

$$X = \frac{\alpha Q}{p}$$

where $Q = LI$ is aggregate income. Inverting this function, and assuming that there are $n + 1$ producers in this sector, we can write the inverse demand schedule perceived by a representative producer i in the form

$$p(x_i) = \frac{\alpha Q}{nx_{-i} + x_i} \tag{5}$$

where x_i denotes his own output level, and x_{-i} that of an arbitrary competitor.
   Producer i maximizes profits

$$\Pi_i = p(x_i)x_i - x_i - c = \frac{\alpha Q x_i}{nx_{-i} + x_i} - x_i - c$$

taking as given the salary ($w = 1$), aggregate income Q, and the outputs of his n competitors (x_{-i}). Using the first-order conditions for this problem, derive a reaction function giving optimal output for the ith producer as a function of those of his rivals. In a symmetric equilibrium, all firms will choose the same output level. Set $x_i = x_{-i} \equiv x$, and find (i) the equilibrium level of output, (ii) the equilibrium price of good x, and (iii) the equilibrium level of firm profits – all written as functions of aggregate income and the number of firms in the sector.
   Now, in a free-entry equilibrium, profits are zero, and it follows that aggregate income is given by

$$Q = Lw = L \tag{10}$$

Using this last expression and setting $\pi = 0$, find (i) the equilibrium number of x producers (ignoring integer constraints), (ii) the equilibrium price of good x, (iii) total x output, (iv) total fixed costs, and (v) total y output – all written as functions of "market size," measured by αL, and the fixed cost c.
   The first-order condition for the problem faced by a representative producer in the x sector,

$$\frac{\partial \Pi_i}{\partial x_i} = \alpha Q \frac{nx_{-i} + x_i - x_i}{(nx_{-i} + x_i)^2} - 1 = 0 \Rightarrow \alpha Q \frac{nx_{-i}}{(nx_{-i} + x_i)^2} = 1 \tag{6}$$

implicitly defines a reaction function giving optimal output for the ith producer as a function of those of his rivals. In a symmetric equilibrium, all firms will choose the same output level. Hence, we can set $x_i = x_{-i} \equiv x$ and solve (6) explicitly for the equilibrium level of output as a function of aggregate income and the number of firms in the sector:

$$\alpha Q \frac{nx}{(n+1)^2 x^2} = 1 \Rightarrow x = \frac{\alpha Q n}{(n+1)^2} \tag{7}$$

Not surprisingly, x is a decreasing function of the number of firms in the sector.
   Substituting (7) back into the industry demand function (5), we obtain the equilibrium price

$$p(x) = \frac{\alpha Q}{(n+1)x} = \frac{n+1}{n} \tag{8}$$

Hence, the price (or, actually, the price/wage ratio) decreases with the number of competitors. Notice that $p \to 1$ as $n \to \infty$, that is, the price approaches its competitive level (= marginal cost) as the number of firms in the industry gets very large. Finally, using (7) and (8), we see that the firm's profits are given by

$$\pi = (p-1)x - c = \frac{1}{n}\frac{\alpha Qn}{(n+1)^2} - c = \frac{\alpha Q}{(n+1)^2} - c \tag{9}$$

Now, in an equilibrium with free entry, profits are zero, and it follows that aggregate income is given by

$$Q = Lw = L \tag{10}$$

Using this last expression and setting $\pi = 0$ in (9), the equilibrium number of x producers (ignoring integer constraints) is given by

$$(n+1)^2 = \frac{\alpha L}{c} \Rightarrow 1 + n = \sqrt{\frac{\alpha L}{c}} \tag{11}$$

and is therefore an increasing function of "market size," measured by αL, and a decreasing function of the fixed cost c.

Using (10), (11), (7), and (8), we can compute the equilibrium price,

$$\frac{1}{p} = \frac{n}{n+1} = \frac{\sqrt{\frac{\alpha L}{c}} - 1}{\sqrt{\frac{\alpha L}{c}}} = 1 - \sqrt{\frac{c}{\alpha L}} \tag{12}$$

total industry output,

$$X = (1+n)x = (1+n)\frac{\alpha Qn}{(n+1)^2} = \frac{\alpha Ln}{n+1} = \alpha L\left(1 - \sqrt{\frac{c}{\alpha L}}\right) \tag{13}$$

and total fixed costs,

$$(1+n)c = \sqrt{\frac{\alpha L}{c}}\,c = \sqrt{\alpha Lc} \tag{14}$$

Finally, total y output (and consumption) is given by

$$Y = Q - pX = L - \alpha L = (1 - \alpha)L \tag{15}$$

(the reader can check that the same result is obtained, after some manipulation, by subtracting total employment in the X sector, including "fixed costs," from the aggregate labor supply). Notice that the price distortion decreases with L, as do total fixed costs per capita.

Problem 5.6. Using a diagram similar to Figure 8.8, compare the equilibrium per-capita allocation and the social optimum, illustrating the two sources of inefficiency we have identified. Using your results from Problem 5.5, discuss how things change as "market size" (measured by L) increases.

The inefficiencies due to the existence of market power and excess entry are illustrated in Figure A8.3, which compares the equilibrium (EQ) and first-best (FB) per-capita allocations. As shown in the figure, the "true" per capita social budget constraint (PPF) and that perceived by the representative consumer (BCP) are different, for two reasons. First, the existence of several ($N = n + 1$)

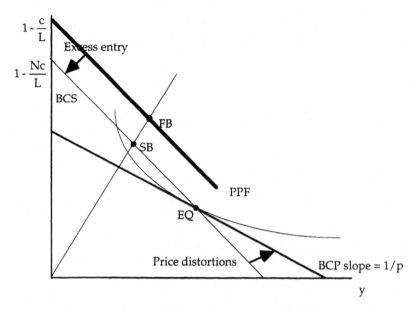

Figure A8.3. Equilibrium versus social optimum.

suppliers of x goods, with the implied duplication of fixed costs, forces the economy to produce inside its PPF, putting it on a second-best social budget constraint (BCS) with a lower vertical intercept and the same slope. Given the equilibrium number of firms, the second-best optimum would correspond to the tangency of BCS and an indifference curve (point SB). This allocation, however, will not be attained, because oligopolistic markup pricing raises the relative price of x above its social opportunity cost in terms of y. Hence, the private budget line perceived by consumers (with slope $1/p$) is flatter than the social resource constraint, and the equilibrium allocation (EQ) involves an inefficiently low level of x consumption.

Market enlargement tends to reduce both of these distortions. To see why, consider the effect of an increase in the labor force L. As shown in Problem 5.5, an increase in L leads to an increase in the number of firms, which translates into a lower markup. Moreover, because the number of firms increases less than proportionately with market size, fixed costs per capita are reduced. Hence, both average costs and markups will be smaller in a larger economy. In terms of Figure A8.3, an increase in the size of the market will shift both the social and private budget constraints outward, by reducing per-capita fixed costs, and will rotate the private budget line clockwise, bringing the relative price of x close to its social opportunity cost.

Notes

1 $1 - \varepsilon = 1 - \dfrac{1}{1 - \alpha} = \dfrac{-\alpha}{1 - \alpha} = -\alpha\varepsilon$

2 $1 - \dfrac{1}{\varepsilon} = 1 - (1 - \alpha) = \alpha$ and $1 - \dfrac{1}{\alpha} = \dfrac{\alpha - 1}{\alpha} = \dfrac{1}{1 - \varepsilon}$.

Chapter 9

Problem 2.6. Let $\phi(t, x^0)$ be the flow of the continuous-time system (CS), $\dot{x} = f(x)$. Show that if

$$\lim_{t \to \infty} \phi(t, x^0) = x*$$

then $x*$ must be a constant solution of (CS), i.e., $f(x*) = \underline{0}$.

Put $t = r + s$ for some fixed but otherwise arbitrary s. Then, using the continuity of $\phi(\ )$,

$$x* = \lim_{t \to \infty} \phi(t, x^0) = \lim_{r \to \infty} \phi(s + r, x^0) = \lim_{r \to \infty} \phi(s, \phi(r, x^0)) = \phi\left(s, \lim_{r \to \infty} \phi(r, x^0)\right) = \phi(s, x*)$$

Hence $x* = \phi(s, x*)$ for any s. This implies that $\phi(s, x*)$ is constant, i.e., $f(x*) = \underline{0}$. $\qquad\square$

Problem 3.2. When $a = 0$, the nonhomogeneous system is of the form $\dot{x} = b$. Using the method of separation of variables, find the general solution of this equation.

Rearranging the equation

$$\frac{dx}{dt} = b$$

we have

$$dx = b \, dt$$

Integrating both sides of this expression, we obtain the general solution

$$\int dx = \int b \, dt \Rightarrow x(t) = c + bt$$

Setting t equal to zero, we have $c = x(0)$. Hence, the general solution can also be written in the form

$$x(t) = x(0) + bt \qquad\qquad\square$$

Problem 3.3. Rewrite the general solution of the system (CN) as a function of $x(s)$, the value of x at some arbitrary time s.

We have seen that the general solution of the nonhomogeneous system (CN) is of the form

$$x^g(t, c) = \bar{x} + ce^{at} \qquad\qquad\qquad \text{(G.S)}$$

Because (G.S) must hold for $t = s$, we have

$$x(s) = \bar{x} + ce^{as}$$

and solving for c,

$$c = [x(s) - \bar{x}]e^{-as}$$

Substituting this expression back into (G.S), we can write the general solution in the form

$$x(t, x_s) = \bar{x} + [x(s) - \bar{x}]e^{a(t-s)} \qquad\qquad\qquad \text{(G.S')}$$
$$\square$$

Problem 4.3. Comparative dynamics for discrete systems. Let $x(t, \alpha)$ be the solution function of the parameterized discrete system $(DS(\alpha))$, $x_{t+1} = g(x_t, \alpha)$, where $g(\ )$ is a C^1 function. Proceeding as in Section 3(c), show that the partial derivative of the solution function with respect to the parameter

$$x_\alpha(t, \alpha) = \frac{\partial x(t, \alpha)}{\partial \alpha}$$

satisfies a linear difference equation. Write the solution of this equation for the special case where $x(t, \alpha)$ is a steady-state solution of $(DS(\alpha))$.

As before, the solution function $x(t, \alpha)$ satisfies identically the original system, i.e.,

$$x(t+1, \alpha) \equiv g[x(t, \alpha), \alpha] \tag{1}$$

Differentiating both sides of (1) with respect to the parameter vector α, we obtain a linear difference equation in x_α:

$$x_\alpha(t+1, \alpha) = g_x[x(t, \alpha), \alpha]x_\alpha(t, \alpha) + g_\alpha[x(t, \alpha), \alpha] \tag{2}$$

If $x(t, \alpha) = x^*$ is a steady-state solution, then the coefficients of (2) are constant, and its solution is given by

$$x_\alpha(t) = x_\alpha(\infty) + [x_\alpha(0) - x_\alpha(\infty)][g_x(x^*, \alpha)]^t \tag{3}$$

where $x_\alpha(\infty) = \partial \bar{x}/\partial \alpha$ is the solution of

$$x_\alpha = g_x(x^*, \alpha)x_\alpha + g_\alpha(x^*, \alpha) \qquad \square$$

Problem 5.1. Consider the first-order difference equation

$$x_t = ax_{t-1} + b_{t-1} \tag{1}$$

Iterating (1) backward and forward, derive the discrete-time analogues of equations (7) and (11) in the text.

Iterating (1) backward, we have

$$x_t = ax_{t-1} + b_{t-1} = a(ax_{t-2} + b_{t-2}) + b_{t-1} = a^2 x_{t-2} + ab_{t-2} + b_{t-1}$$
$$= a^2(ax_{t-3} + b_{t-3}) + ab_{t-2} + b_{t-1} = a^3 x_{t-3} + a^2 b_{t-3} + ab_{t-2} + b_{t-1} = \ldots$$
$$= a^n x_{t-n} + a^{n-1}b_{t-n} + \ldots + a^2 b_{t-3} + ab_{t-2} + b_{t-1}$$
$$= a^n x_{t-n} + \sum_{i=t-n}^{t-1} a^{t-1-i}b_i$$

after n iterations. Letting $n = t$, we have

$$x_t = a^t x_0 + \sum_{i=0}^{t-1} a^{t-1-i}b_i \tag{2}$$

which is the backward solution of the given equation.

To derive the forward solution, notice that leading (1) one period,

$$x_{t+1} = ax_t + b_t$$

and solving for x_t we have

$$x_t = (1/a)x_{t+1} - (1/a)b_t \tag{3}$$

Iterating (3) forward for n periods, we obtain

$$x_t = (1/a)x_{t+1} - (1/a)b_t = (1/a)[(1/a)x_{t+2} - (1/a)b_{t+1}] - (1/a)b_t$$
$$= (1/a)^2 x_{t+2} - (1/a)^2 b_{t+1} - (1/a)b_t$$
$$= (1/a)^2 [(1/a)x_{t+3} - (1/a)b_{t+2}] - (1/a)^2 b_{t+1} - (1/a)b_t$$
$$= (1/a)^3 x_{t+3} - (1/a)^3 b_{t+2} - (1/a)^2 b_{t+1} - (1/a)b_t = \ldots$$
$$= (1/a)^n x_{t+n} - \left[(1/a)^n b_{t+n-1} + (1/a)^{n-1} b_{t+n-2} + \ldots + (1/a)^2 b_{t+1} + (1/a)b_t \right]$$
$$= (1/a)^n x_{t+n} - (1/a)\sum_{j=t}^{t+n-1} (1/a)^{j-t} b_j \tag{4}$$

Letting $n \to \infty$, and putting $s = n + t$, the forward solution is given by

$$x_t = a^t \left(\lim_{s\to\infty}(1/a)^s x_s \right) - (1/a)\sum_{j=t}^{\infty} (1/a)^{j-t} b_j \tag{5}$$

Now define

$$F(t) = -(1/a)\sum_{j=t}^{\infty} (1/a)^{j-t} b_j \tag{6}$$

Using the backward solution (2), we have

$$(1/a)^s x_s = x_0 + (1/a)^s \sum_{i=0}^{s-1} a^{s-1-i} b_i = x_0 + (1/a)\sum_{i=0}^{s-1} a^{-i} b_i = x_0 + (1/a)\sum_{i=0}^{s-1} (1/a)^i b_i$$

and taking limits as $s \to \infty$,

$$\lim_{s\to\infty}(1/a)^s x_s = x_0 - F(0) \tag{7}$$

Substituting (6) and (7) into (5), the forward solution can be written

$$x_t = a^t[x_0 - F(0)] + F(t) \tag{8}$$

$\square$

Problem 6.4. Show that the function $f(x) = 3x^{2/3}$ is not Lipschitz in any neighborhood of zero.

Negating the definition of (locally) Lipschitz function, we have to show that given any $K > 0$ and any $\varepsilon > 0$, there exist points x and y in $B_\varepsilon(0)$ such that $|f(y) - f(x)| > K|y - x|$.

Fix some arbitrary $K > 0$ and $\varepsilon > 0$, and let $y > 0$ be a point in $B_\varepsilon(0)$. Then $x = \lambda y > 0$ is also a point in $B_\varepsilon(0)$ for any $\lambda \in [0, 1]$. We have, then,

$$|y - x| = y - x = y - \lambda y = (1 - \lambda)y$$

and

$$|f(y) - f(x)| = |3y^{2/3} - 3\lambda^{2/3} y^{2/3}| = 3(1 - \lambda^{2/3})|y^{2/3}| = 3(1 - \lambda^{2/3})y^{2/3}$$

Hence, we have $|f(y) - f(x)| > K|y - x|$ if and only if we can find a pair (λ, y) such that

$$3(1 - \lambda^{2/3})y^{2/3} > K(1 - \lambda)y \Leftrightarrow g(\lambda, y) = 3(1 - \lambda^{2/3}) - K(1 - \lambda)y^{1/3} > 0$$

Set $y^* > 0$, so that $Ky^{1/3} < 1$, i.e., $y^* < K^{-3}$. Then

$$g(\lambda, y^*) = 3(1 - \lambda^{2/3}) - K(1 - \lambda)(y^*)^{1/3} > G(\lambda) \equiv 3(1 - \lambda^{2/3}) - (1 - \lambda) > 0$$

Notice that $G(\ )$ is a continuous function of λ, with

$$G(0) = 3 - 1 = 2 > 0$$

Hence, $g(\lambda, y^*) > G(\lambda) > 0$ for λ^* strictly positive but sufficiently small, and it follows that $x^* = \lambda^* y^*$ and y^* are points in $B_\varepsilon(0)$ with the property that

$|f(y^*) - f(x^*)| > K|y^* - x^*|$. Because $K > 0$ and $\varepsilon > 0$ were arbitrary, this establishes that $f(\ )$ is not locally Lipschitz around zero. □

Problem 6.5. Continuous dependence on initial conditions and parameters. Let $f(x, \alpha, t)$ be a continuous function defined on the set $B = B_x \times B_\alpha \times I$, where B_x, B_α, and $I = [-a, a]$ are closed intervals in the real line. Assume further that $f(\ )$ is Lipschitz in (x, α) on B, i.e., that there exists some positive constant K such that

$$|f(y, \beta, t) - f(x, \alpha, t)| \leq K\|(y, \beta) - (x, \alpha)\| \ \forall \ (y, \beta, t) \text{ and } (x, \alpha, t) \text{ in } B \qquad \text{(L)}$$

Show the following:

(i) For each (x^0, α) in the interior of $B_x \times B_\alpha$, the initial-value problem

$$\dot{x} = f(x, \alpha, t), \qquad x(0) = x^0 \qquad \text{(PC}(x^0, 0, x))$$

has a unique solution defined on a closed interval $J(x^0) \subseteq I$ containing zero.

(ii) The function $\phi_t(x^0, \alpha)$ that gives the solution to (PC$(x^0, 0, \alpha)$) as a function of initial conditions and parameters is continuous.

Because f is continuous on the compact set B, it is bounded; i.e., there exists some $M > 0$ such that

$$|f(x, \alpha, t)| \leq M \ \forall \ (x, \alpha, t) \in B \qquad (1)$$

For each x in the interior of B_x, let $r(x)$ be such that

$$0 < r(x) < \min\left\{a, \frac{1}{K}, \frac{b(x)}{M}\right\} \qquad (2)$$

where $b(x) > 0$ is the distance from the interior point x to the boundary of B_x. By the same argument as in the proof of Theorem 6.2, a unique solution to (PC$(x^0, 0, \alpha)$) defined on the interval $[-r(x^0), (r(x^0)]$ exists for any given (x^0, α), with x^0 in the interior of B_x.

Now, fix some point (x^0, α^0), with $x^0 \in \text{int } B_x$ and $\alpha^0 \in \text{int } B_\alpha$. Then there is some number $\varepsilon > 0$ such that $B_{2\varepsilon}[x^0]$ is contained in the interior of B_x, and $B_\varepsilon(\alpha^0) \subseteq B_\alpha$. Let y be an arbitrary point in $B_\varepsilon[x^0]$, and observe that $b(y) > \varepsilon$. Hence, there is some number r_0 such that

$$0 < r_0 < \min\left\{a, \frac{1}{K}, \frac{\varepsilon}{M}\right\} \leq r(y) \quad \text{for any } y \in B_\varepsilon[x^0] \qquad (3)$$

and it follows that solutions to (PC$(x^0, 0, \alpha)$) starting in $B_\varepsilon[x^0]$ will be defined over the common interval $J_0 = [-r_0, r_0]$.

For each $y \in B_\varepsilon[x^0]$, let

$$B_{Mr_0}[y] = \{\varphi(t) \in C(J_0); \ \|\varphi - y\| \leq Mr_0\}$$

and define the set F by

$$F = \bigcup_{y \in B_\varepsilon[x^0]} B_{Mr_0}[y]$$

Notice that for any $\varphi(t)$ in F we have, by (3),

$$|\varphi(t) - y| \leq Mr_0 < \varepsilon$$

for some $y \in B_\varepsilon[x^0]$. Hence $\varphi(t)$ stays inside $B_{2\varepsilon}[x^0] \subseteq B_x$. Hence, $\varphi(t)$ stays inside B_x for all t in J_0, and it follows that $f[\varphi(t), \alpha, t]$ is Lipschitz. Observe that (L) implies that $f(\ )$ is Lipschitz in $x = \varphi$ for given α, because

$$\|(y, \alpha) - (x, \alpha)\| = |y - x|$$

Define now the function T on $B_\varepsilon[x^0] \times B_\varepsilon(\alpha^0) \times F$ by

$$T(y, \alpha)\varphi(t) = y + \int_0^t f[\varphi(s), s] \, ds \quad \text{for each } t \in J_0 \tag{4}$$

Then, by the argument in the proof of Theorem 6.2, $T(y, \alpha)$ is a contraction mapping a closed ball in $C(J_0)$ into itself, and it follows that $T(y, \alpha)$ has a fixed point that is the unique solution to the initial-value problem $(PC(y, 0, \alpha))$ on the interval $[-r_0, r_0]$.

We want to show that this fixed point varies continuously with (y, α). By Theorem 7.18 in Chapter 2, it is enough to show that T is a continuous function of (y, α). To establish the continuity of T in (y, α), let $\varphi(t)$ be an arbitrary function in F, and consider two points (y, α) and (x, β) in $B_\varepsilon[x^0] \times B_\varepsilon(\alpha^0)$. Because $\varphi(t)$ stays within B_x, we have

$$|f(\varphi(t), \alpha, t) - f(\varphi(t), \beta, t)| \leq K|\alpha - \beta| \ \forall \ t \text{ in } J_0$$

by (L). Hence,

$$|T(y, \alpha)\varphi(t) - T(x, \beta)\varphi(t)| = \left| y - x + \int_0^t [f[\varphi(s), \alpha, s] - f[\varphi(s), \beta, s]] \, ds \right|$$

$$\leq |y - x| + |t|K|\alpha - \beta| \leq |y - x| + r_0 K|\alpha - \beta|$$

for all t in J_0. Hence,

$$\|T(y, \alpha) - T(x, \beta)\| \leq |y - x| + r_0 K|\alpha - \beta|$$

Finally, observe that $T(y, \beta) \to T(x, \alpha)$ as $(y, \alpha) \to (x, \beta)$, which establishes the continuity of T. $\qquad \square$

Problem 6.8. Prove Lemma 6.7. By the local existence and uniqueness theorem (Theorem 6.2) we know that $\phi(t)$ and $\varphi(t)$ coincide over some interval containing t_0. Let J_m be the largest subinterval of $J = J_\phi \cap J_\varphi$ over which the two solutions coincide. To show that $J_m = J$, we assume that J_m is strictly contained in J and obtain a contradiction. If J_m is strictly contained in J, then J_m has at least one end point $t_1 \in J$ that either belongs to $J \sim J_m$ or lies in the interior of J. For concreteness, assume that t_1 is the right end point of J_m. Observe that by the continuity of $\phi(t)$ and $\varphi(t)$ in J we have

$$\phi(t_1) = \lim_{t \to t_1^-} \phi(t) = \lim_{t \to t_1^-} \varphi(t) = \varphi(t_1) \equiv x^1 \in X \qquad \text{(because } t_1 \in J\text{)}$$

Hence, t_1 is the "last point" for which $\phi(t) = \varphi(t)$, and it follows that $t_1 \in J_m$ lies in the interior of J. Notice, however, that both $\phi(t)$ and $\varphi(t)$ are solutions to the initial-value problem

$$\dot{x} = f(x, t), \qquad x(t_1) = x^1 \qquad \qquad (PC \ (x^1, t_1))$$

where $(x^1, t_1) \in D$. It follows, by the local uniqueness of solutions, that $\phi(t) = \varphi(t)$ for all t in some interval $[t_1 - r_1, t_1 + r_1]$, with $r_1 > 0$. Hence, t_1 is not the "last point" for which $\phi(t) = \varphi(t)$, and we have reached a contradiction. $\qquad \square$

Problem 6.15. Let $c(t)$ be a continuous real-valued function defined on an open interval $I = (\alpha, \beta)$ containing t_0. Consider the initial-value problem defined by the linear system $\dot{x} = c(t)x$ and the initial condition $x(t_0) = x^0 \in \mathbb{R}$. Show that the solution to this problem is defined on the whole of I.

Under our assumptions, the function $f(x, t) = c(t)x$ is clearly continuous and locally Lipschitz in the open set $\mathbb{R} \times I$. It follows by Theorem 6.9 that the given boundary-value problem will have a unique maximal solution $\phi(t)$ defined on some maximal open interval $(a, b) \subseteq I = (\alpha, \beta)$ containing t_0. We will assume that

$(a, b) \neq I$ and obtain a contradiction. Assume, for concreteness, that $b < \beta$, so that b is an interior point of I, and $c(t)$ is defined on $[t_0, b]$. Because $c(\ )$ is a continuous function, it is bounded in the compact set $[t_0, b]$. Let

$$M = \max\{|c(s)|;\ s \in [t_0, b]\}$$

and observe that for any t in $[t_0, b)$ we have

$$|\phi(t)| = \left|x^0 + \int_{t_0}^t c(s)\phi(s)\,ds\right| \leq |x^0| + \int_{t_0}^t |c(s)\phi(s)|\,ds \leq |x^0| + M\int_{t_0}^t |\phi(s)|\,ds$$

By Gronwall's lemma,

$$|\phi(t)| \leq |x^0|e^{M|t-t_0|} < |x^0|e^{M|b-t_0|}$$

Hence, the solution stays within a compact set for all t in $[t_0, b)$. Because b is an interior point of I, this contradicts Theorem 6.12. □

Problem 6.18. Prove Lemma 6.17.

Because $\phi(t, y^0)$ and $\phi(t, x^0)$ are solutions of (CS(t)) going through y^0 and x^0, respectively, at time t_0, we have

$$\phi(t, y^0) = y^0 + \int_{t_0}^t f[\phi(s, y^0), s]\,ds \quad \text{and} \quad \phi(t, x^0) = x^0 + \int_{t_0}^t f[\phi(s, x^0), s]\,ds \quad (1)$$

and because both solutions stay in X, we have $(s, \phi(s, y^0))$ and $(s, \phi(s, x^0)) \in D$ for all $s \in J_m(x^0) \cap J_m(y^0) \subseteq I$. This implies that for all such s,

$$|f[\phi(s, y^0), s] - f[\phi(s, x^0), s]| \leq |\phi(s, y^0) - \phi(s, x^0)| \quad (2)$$

by the Lipschitz condition on $f(\ )$.

Define the function $\varphi(t)$ in $J_m(x^0) \cap J_m(y^0)$ by

$$\varphi(t) = |\phi(t, y^0) - \phi(t, x^0)|$$

Then, using (1) and (2), we have

$$\varphi(t) = \left|y^0 - x^0 + \int_{t_0}^t [f[\phi(s, y^0), s] - f[\phi(s, x^0), s]]\,ds\right|$$

$$\leq |y^0 - x^0| + \int_{t_0}^t |f[\phi(s, y^0), s] - f[\phi(s, x^0), s]|\,ds$$

$$\leq |y^0 - x^0| + \int_{t_0}^t K|\phi(s, y^0) - \phi(s, x^0)|\,ds$$

$$= |y^0 - x^0| + K\int_{t_0}^t \varphi(s)\,ds$$

for all $t \in J_m(x^0) \cap J_m(y^0)$.

Hence, $\varphi(t)$ satisfies the conditions of Gronwall's lemma, and it follows that

$$|\phi(t, y^0) - \phi(t, x^0)| = \varphi(t) \leq |y^0 - x^0|e^{K|t-t_0|}$$

for all t in $J_m(x^0) \cap J_m(y^0)$, which is the desired result. □

Chapter 10

Problem 2.3. Derive the equation

$$x^h(t; c) = Ee^{\Lambda t}c, \quad \text{where } e^{\Lambda t} = \begin{bmatrix} \exp(\lambda_1 t) & \cdots & 0 \\ \cdots & \cdots & \cdots \\ 0 & \cdots & \exp(\lambda_n t) \end{bmatrix} \quad (4)$$

by diagonalizing the coefficient matrix of (CH).

Given the homogeneous continuous system

$$\dot{x} = Ax \qquad \text{(CH)}$$

we premultiply both sides by the inverse of the eigenvector matrix, E^{-1}:

$$E^{-1}\dot{x} = E^{-1}Ax$$

Noting that $EE^{-1} = I$ (the identity matrix), this is equivalent to

$$E^{-1}\dot{x} = E^{-1}AEE^{-1}x$$

Now, because $E^{-1}AE = \Lambda$, we have

$$E^{-1}\dot{x} = \Lambda E^{-1}x \qquad (1)$$

Define y by

$$y = E^{-1}x \qquad (2)$$

and observe that

$$\dot{y} = E^{-1}\dot{x} \qquad (3)$$

Using (2) and (3), the system can be written

$$\dot{y} = \Lambda y \qquad (4)$$

where $\Lambda = \text{diag}(\lambda_1, \ldots, \lambda_n)$. Because (4) is an uncoupled system, its solution is of the form

$$y(t) = e^{\Lambda t}c \qquad (5)$$

where c is a vector of arbitrary constants. To recover the solution in terms of the original variables x, we premultiply (5) by E:

$$x(t) = Ey(t) = Ee^{\Lambda t}c \qquad \Box$$

Problem 2.4. Derive the following equation:

$$x_t^h(c) = c_1 r^t (d\cos\theta t - f\sin\theta t) + c_2 r^t (f\cos\theta t + d\sin\theta t) + \sum_{i=3}^{n} c_i \lambda_i^t e_i \qquad (6)$$

Because the coefficient matrix A is a real matrix, its eigenvalues and eigenvectors come in conjugate pairs. Hence, if λ_1 and λ_2 are complex eigenvalues of A, they are of the form[1]

$$\lambda_1 = \alpha + i\mu = r(\cos\theta + i\sin\theta) = re^{i\theta}$$
$$\lambda_2 = \alpha - i\mu = r(\cos\theta - i\sin\theta) = re^{-i\theta} \qquad (1)$$

where θ is the angle formed by the vector $\lambda_1 = (\alpha, \mu)$ and the horizontal axis of the complex plane. Moreover, the corresponding eigenvectors will be given by

$$e_1 = d + if \quad \text{and} \quad e_2 = d - if \qquad (2)$$

where d and f are vectors. The elementary solutions associated with these eigenvalues are then

$$z_t^1 = \lambda_1^t e_1 \quad \text{and} \quad z_t^2 = \lambda_2^t e_2 \qquad (3)$$

Using (1) and (2), the elementary solutions can be written

$$z_t^1 = \lambda_1^t e_1 = (re^{i\theta})^t (d + if) = r^t (\cos\theta t + i\sin\theta t)(d + if)$$
$$= r^t (d\cos\theta t + id\sin\theta t + if\cos\theta t + i^2 f\sin\theta t)$$
$$= r^t (d\cos\theta t - f\sin\theta t) + ir^t (d\sin\theta t + f\cos\theta t)$$

and

$$z_t^2 = \lambda_2^t e_2 = (re^{-i\theta})^t (d - if) = r^t (\cos\theta t - i\sin\theta t)(d - if)$$
$$= r^t (d\cos\theta t - id\sin\theta t - if\cos\theta t + i^2 f\sin\theta t)$$
$$= r^t (d\cos\theta t - f\sin\theta t) - ir^t (d\sin\theta t + f\cos\theta t)$$

Hence, the elementary solutions are complex conjugates themselves. Putting

$$u_t = r^t (d\cos\theta t - f\sin\theta t) \quad \text{and} \quad v_t = r^t (d\sin\theta t + f\cos\theta t)$$

we have

$$z_t^1 = u_t + iv_t, \qquad z_t^2 = u_t - iv_t$$

By the same argument used in Section 2(*b*), it can be shown that the real functions (sequences) u_t and v_t are solutions of the system (DH), $x_{t+1} = Ax_t$. It can also be shown that these functions are linearly independent from each other and from the rest of the elementary solutions of the system. Hence, we can use them to complete a fundamental set of solutions and write the general solution of the system in the form (6). $\qquad\square$

Problem 2.5. Given the linear system (CH), $\dot{x} = Ax$, assume that there is one eigenvalue ξ of multiplicity 2 ($\lambda_1 = \lambda_2 = \xi$), and the rest of the eigenvalues $\lambda_3, \ldots,$ λ_n of A are all different from each other. Associated with the repeated eigenvalue we have two elementary solutions:

$$x^1(t) = \exp(\lambda_1 t)e_1 = e^{\xi t}e_1 \quad \text{and} \quad x^2(t) = \exp(\lambda_2 t)e_2 = e^{\xi t}e_2$$

Clearly, if e_1 and e_2 are linearly independent eigenvectors associated with ξ, the elementary solutions $x^1(t)$ and $x^2(t)$ are also independent from each other and from the rest of the elementary solutions $x^3(t), \ldots, x^n(t)$. Hence the set of elementary solutions is still a basis for the solution space of the homogeneous system, and we can write the general solution as before:

$$x^g(t) = c_1 x^1(t) + \ldots + c_n x^n(t) \tag{G.S}$$

If e_1 and e_2 are linearly dependent, however, so are $x^1(t)$ and $x^2(t)$, and we do not have enough independent elementary solutions to span the solution space. To complete a basis for the solution space that will allow us to write the general solution, we need to find an additional solution to (CH) that will be linearly independent from the elementary solutions. We will seek a solution of the form

$$\phi(t) = (a + bt)e^{\xi t} = ae^{\xi t} + bte^{\xi t} \tag{1}$$

that is, the product of a polynomial of order 1 (1 less than the multiplicity of ξ) in t and the exponential term in the eigenvalue ξ. What restrictions must be placed on the vectors a and b so that $\phi(t)$ will indeed be a solution of the system, that is, will satisfy the equation $\phi'(t) = A\phi(t)$? Write the general solution of the system.

We need to choose the vectors a and b so that $\phi(t)$ satisfies the homogeneous equation, that is, we need

$$\phi'(t) = A\phi(t) \Rightarrow \frac{d}{dt}[ae^{\xi t} + bte^{\xi t}] = A[ae^{\xi t} + bte^{\xi t}]$$
$$\Rightarrow \xi ae^{\xi t} + bt\xi e^{\xi t} + be^{\xi t} = Aae^{\xi t} + Abte^{\xi t}$$
$$\Rightarrow [\xi a + b]e^{\xi t} + \xi bte^{\xi t} = Aae^{\xi t} + Abte^{\xi t}$$

And setting the coefficients of $e^{\xi t}$ and $te^{\xi t}$ on both sides equal to each other, we get

$$(\text{for } te^{\xi t}:) \; \xi b = Ab \Rightarrow Ab - \xi b = \underline{0}$$
$$\Rightarrow (A - \xi I)b = \underline{0} \tag{2}$$

$$(\text{for } e^{\xi t}:) \; \xi a + b = Aa$$
$$\Rightarrow (A - \xi I)a = b \tag{3}$$

That is, b must be an eigenvector associated with the repeated eigenvalue (e.g., $b = e_1$), and a must satisfy the restriction given by (3) in order for $\phi(t)$ to be a solution to (1). If these conditions are satisfied, we can write the general solution to the homogeneous system with one eigenvalue of multiplicity 2 ($\lambda_1 = \lambda_2 = \xi$) and all the rest $\lambda_3, \ldots, \lambda_n$ of multiplicity 1 as

$$x^g(t) = c_1 x^1(t) + c_2 \phi(t) + c_3 x^3(t) + \ldots + c_n x^n(t)$$
$$\Rightarrow x^g(t) = c_1 e^{\xi t} e_1 + c_2 [ae^{\xi t} + te_1 e^{\xi t}] + c_3 \exp(\lambda_3 t)e_3 + \ldots + c_n \exp(\lambda_n t)e_n \tag{4}$$
$$\square$$

Problem 4.1. Polar coordinates. When working with planar systems it is sometimes convenient to work in polar coordinates. Consider a point with Cartesian (ordinary) coordinates (x, y). Its polar coordinates are (r, θ), where r is the Euclidean distance from the origin to the point (x, y), and θ is the angle formed by the line segment going from the origin to the point (x, y) and the horizontal axis. Hence, r and θ are defined by

$$r^2 = x^2 + y^2 \tag{1}$$
$$\theta = \arctan(y/x) \tag{2}$$

and θ is such that

$$\cos\theta = x/r \quad \text{and} \quad \sin\theta = y/r \tag{3}$$

Differentiating (1) and (2) implicitly with respect to time, show that

$$r\dot{r} = x\dot{x} + y\dot{y} \tag{4}$$
$$r^2\dot{\theta} = x\dot{y} - y\dot{x} \tag{5}$$

Differentiating (1) implicitly with respect to time, we have

$$2r\dot{r} = 2x\dot{x} - 2y\dot{y}$$
$$\Rightarrow r\dot{r} = x\dot{x} + y\dot{y} \tag{4}$$

Proceeding in a similar way with (2),

$$\dot{\theta} = \frac{(x\dot{y} - y\dot{x})/x^2}{1 + (y/x)^2} = \frac{(x\dot{y} - y\dot{x})/x^2}{(x^2 + y^2)/x^2} = \frac{x\dot{y} - y\dot{x}}{x^2 + y^2}$$
$$\Rightarrow r^2\dot{\theta} = x\dot{y} - y\dot{x} \tag{5}$$
$$\square$$

Problem 4.2. Let A be a 2×2 real matrix with complex eigenvalues $\lambda_1, \lambda_2 = \alpha \pm i\mu$ and corresponding complex eigenvectors $e_1, e_2 = u \pm iv$. It can be shown that the real vectors u and v are linearly independent, so the matrix $P = [u, v]$ is invertible.

(i) Show that

$$P^{-1}AP = R = \begin{bmatrix} \alpha & -\mu \\ \mu & \alpha \end{bmatrix} \tag{8}$$

Equation (8) shows that if A has complex eigenvalues, then the planar system $\dot{z} = Az$ can be written (after a coordinate change) in the form

$$\begin{bmatrix} \dot{x} \\ \dot{y} \end{bmatrix} = \begin{bmatrix} \alpha & -\mu \\ \mu & \alpha \end{bmatrix} \begin{bmatrix} x \\ y \end{bmatrix}$$

or, equivalently,

$$\dot{x} = \alpha x - \mu y \tag{9}$$

$$\dot{y} = \mu x + \alpha y \tag{10}$$

(ii) Rewrite the system (9)–(10) in polar coordinates and solve it, leaving the solution $(r(t), \theta(t))$ as a function of the initial values $r(0)$ and $\theta(0)$.

(iii) Using the trigonometric identities

$$\sin(a+b) = (\sin a)(\cos b) + (\cos a)(\sin b) \tag{11}$$

$$\cos(a+b) = (\cos a)(\cos b) - (\sin a)(\sin b) \tag{12}$$

recover the solution $(x(t), y(t))$ of the original system, written as a function of the initial values $x(0)$ and $y(0)$.

(i) Because λ_1 is an eigenvalue of A, and e_1 a corresponding eigenvector, we have $Ae_1 = \lambda_1 e_1$, that is,

$$A(u+iv) = (\alpha+i\mu)(u+iv)$$

Expanding both sides of this expression,

$$Au + iAv = \alpha u + i\alpha v + i\mu u + i^2 \mu v = (\alpha u - \mu v) + i(\alpha v + \mu u)$$

that is,

$$Au = (\alpha u - \mu v) \quad \text{and} \quad Av = (\mu u + \alpha v)$$

or, in matrix form,

$$A[u, v] = [u, v] \begin{bmatrix} \alpha & -\mu \\ \mu & \alpha \end{bmatrix} \Leftrightarrow AP = PR$$

and because P is invertible (by the fact that u and v are linearly independent), this last expression yields the desired result (premultiplying both sides by P^{-1}).

(ii) Substituting (9) and (10) into (4), we have

$$r\dot{r} = x(\alpha x - \mu y) + y(\mu x + \alpha y) = \alpha(x^2 + y^2) = \alpha r^2$$

from where

$$\dot{r} = \alpha r \tag{13}$$

Similarly, using (5),

$$r^2\dot{\theta} = x\dot{y} - y\dot{x} = x(\mu x + \alpha y) - y(\alpha x - \mu y) = \mu(x^2 + y^2) = \mu r^2$$

from where

$$\dot{\theta} = \mu \tag{14}$$

We have, then, a system of two uncoupled equations in (r, θ). The solutions of (13) and (14) are of the form

$$r(t) = r(0)e^{\alpha t} \tag{15}$$

$$\theta(t) = \theta(0) + \mu t \tag{16}$$

(iii) To recover the solution in terms of the original variables, we use equation (7) and the trigonometric identities (11) and (12). Substituting (15) and (16) into (7), and using (11) and (12),

$$x(t) = r(t)\cos\theta(t) = r(0)e^{\alpha t}\cos(\theta(0) + \mu t)$$
$$= r(0)e^{\alpha t}[\cos\theta(0)\cos\mu t - \sin\theta(0)\sin\mu t]$$
$$= r(0)e^{\alpha t}\left(\frac{x(0)}{r(0)}\cos\mu t - \frac{y(0)}{r(0)}\sin\mu t\right) = e^{\alpha t}[x(0)\cos\mu t - y(0)\sin\mu t]$$

Similarly,

$$y(t) = r(t)\sin\theta(t) = r(0)e^{\alpha t}\sin(\theta(0) + \mu t)$$
$$= r(0)e^{\alpha t}[\sin\theta(0)\cos\mu t + \cos\theta(0)\sin\mu t]$$
$$= r(0)e^{\alpha t}\left(\frac{y(0)}{r(0)}\cos\mu t + \frac{x(0)}{r(0)}\sin\mu t\right) = e^{\alpha t}[y(0)\cos\mu t + x(0)\sin\mu t] \qquad \Box$$

Problem 4.3. Consider the following system of differential equations:

$$\dot{x} = f(x, y) = y + x(c - x^2 - y^2) \tag{17}$$
$$\dot{y} = g(x, y) = -x + y(c - x^2 - y^2) \tag{18}$$

(i) Show that the point $(0, 0)$ is the only steady state of the system for any value of c.
(ii) Linearize the system around the steady state and compute its eigenvalues. What can we say about the stability and type of the steady state? (There are three possible cases, depending on the value of c.)
(iii) Show that the original system can be written in polar coordinates as

$$\dot{r} = r(c - r^2) \tag{19}$$
$$\dot{\theta} = -1 \tag{20}$$

Using these expressions, describe the behavior of the system, and compare the results with those obtained in (ii). Linearization should give accurate local results in two cases, but we can now "see" more things. What happens in the third case?

(i) The steady state $s = (\bar{x}, \bar{y})$ satisfies

$$\dot{x} = 0 \Rightarrow y + x(c - x^2 - y^2) = 0$$
$$\dot{y} = 0 \Rightarrow -x + y(c - x^2 - y^2) = 0$$

Clearly, $(0, 0)$ is a solution to this system of equations. If $x = 0$, then $y = 0$, by the first equation; similarly, if $y = 0$, then $x = 0$, by the second equation. Finally, assume $x, y \neq 0$; then we can divide the first equation by x and the second by y to get

$$-y/x = c - x^2 - y^2 \quad \text{and} \quad x/y = c - x^2 - y^2$$

from where

$$-y/x = x/y \Rightarrow x^2 = -y^2$$

which is impossible for $x, y \neq 0$. Hence $s = (0, 0)$ is the only steady state.
(ii) The partial derivatives of the functions $f(\ )$ and $g(\ )$ evaluated at the steady state are given by

$$f_x = x(-2x) + 1(c - x^2 - y^2) = 0 + c = c$$
$$f_y = 1 + x(-2y) = 1 - 0 = 1$$
$$g_x = -1 + y(-2x) = -1 + 0 = -1$$
$$g_y = 1(c - x^2 - y^2) + y(-2y) = c + 0 = c$$

Hence, the coefficient matrix of the linearized system is of the form

$$A = \begin{bmatrix} c & 1 \\ -1 & c \end{bmatrix}$$

To find the eigenvalues of A, we solve

$$|A - \lambda I| = \begin{vmatrix} c - \lambda & 1 \\ -1 & c - \lambda \end{vmatrix} = 0$$

or

$$(c - \lambda)^2 + 1 = c^2 - 2c\lambda + \lambda^2 + 1 = \lambda^2 - 2c\lambda + (1 + c^2) = 0$$

By the quadratic formula,

$$\lambda_1, \lambda_2 = \frac{2c \pm \sqrt{4c^2 - 4 - 4c^2}}{2} = c \pm i$$

Hence, the eigenvalues of the system are complex numbers. If $c < 0$, the steady state is a locally stable spiral point, and if $c > 0$, the steady state is locally unstable. If $c = 0$, the steady state is nonhyperbolic, and its stability cannot be determined without further information.

(iii) Substituting (17) and (18) into (4),

$$r\dot{r} = x\dot{x} + y\dot{y} = x[y + x(c - x^2 - y^2)] + y[-x + y(c - x^2 - y^2)]$$
$$= (x^2 + y^2)(c - x^2 - y^2) = r^2(c - r^2)$$

and simplifying,

$$\dot{r} = r(c - r^2) \tag{19}$$

Similarly, substituting (17) and (18) into (5),

$$r^2\dot{\theta} = x\dot{y} - y\dot{x} = x[-x + y(c - x^2 - y^2)] - y[y + x(c - x^2 - y^2)]$$
$$= -(x^2 + y^2) = -r^2$$

from where

$$\dot{\theta} = -1 \tag{20}$$

Hence, the original system (17)–(18) reduces in polar coordinates to a set of two independent first-order equations: The behavior of the system can be determined directly by inspection of (19) and (20). First, notice that the angle θ decreases over time. Hence, the solution trajectories rotate clockwise, forming either spirals or circles. The exact shapes of the trajectories will depend on the behavior of r, the distance from the origin. Using (20), we see that if $c \leq 0$, then we have $\dot{r} = r(c - r^2) < 0$ for all $r > 0$, and all trajectories converge to the origin, which is a stable spiral point. If $c > 0$, things are slightly more complicated. Notice that if $r = \sqrt{c}$, then $\dot{r} = 0$, and r remains constant over time. Hence, the system has a periodic orbit or cyclical solution. If $r > \sqrt{c}$, then $\dot{r} = r(c - r^2) < 0$, and if $r < \sqrt{c}$ we have $\dot{r} = r(c - r^2) > 0$.

In either case, we approach the periodic orbit. Hence, trajectories starting on either side of this closed curve converge to it as $t \to \infty$. ☐

Chapter 11

Problem 2.1. When the tax rate on dividends varies over time, our stock-pricing equation can be written in the form

$$\dot{v} = rv - b(t) \tag{1}$$

where

$$b(t) = (1 - \tau_t)d$$

Equation (1) is a nonautonomous linear equation of the type we studied in Section 5 of Chapter 9. Its solution can be written in the ("forward") form

$$v(t) = [v(0) - F(0)]e^{rt} + F(t) \tag{2}$$

where

$$F(t) = \int_t^\infty b(s)e^{r(t-s)} \, ds \tag{3}$$

the "fundamental solution" of (1), is the discounted value of the stream of future after-tax dividends, and $[v(0) - F(0)]e^{rt}$ is a "bubble term" capturing possible deviations from the fundamental value of the stock. By the same logic as in our earlier discussion, we shall rule out bubbles and assume that $v(t) = F(t)$ for all t. Hence, the value of the stock at each point in time will be given by (3). We shall now show that this fundamental solution gives the same time path of stock prices in response to a preannounced future increase in dividend taxes as the procedure we followed earlier.

(i) Show that

$$\int_t^b e^{r(t-s)} ds = \frac{1}{r}\left(1 - e^{r(t-b)}\right) \tag{4}$$

(ii) As before, assume that an announcement is made at time zero that dividend taxes will increase at time T from τ_0 to τ_1. Then

$$b(t) = (1 - \tau_0)d \quad \text{for } t \in [0, T)$$
$$= (1 - \tau_1)d \quad \text{for } t \in [T, \infty) \tag{5}$$

Using (3) and (4), compute the trajectory of stock prices following the announcement.

(i) To compute the given integral, we will make a change of variable. Let

$$u = u(s) = r(t - s)$$

Then

$$du = -r \, ds, \quad \text{so } ds = \frac{-du}{r}$$

and

$$\int_t^b e^{r(t-s)} \, ds = \frac{-1}{r} \int_{u(t)}^{u(b)} e^u \, du = \frac{-1}{r}[e^u]_{u(t)}^{u(b)}$$

$$= \frac{-1}{r}[e^{r(t-s)}]_t^b = \frac{-1}{r}(e^{r(t-b)} - e^0) = \frac{1}{r}(1 - e^{r(t-b)})$$

(ii) We will consider two possible cases. First, let $t \geq T$. Then

$$v(t) = F(t) = \int_t^\infty b(s)e^{r(t-s)} \, ds = (1-\tau_1)d\int_t^\infty e^{r(t-s)} \, ds = \frac{(1-\tau_1)d}{r} \lim_{b \to \infty}(1-e^{r(t-b)})$$

$$= \frac{(1-\tau_1)d}{r}(1-0) = \frac{(1-\tau_1)d}{r} = v^*(\tau_1)$$

so the two solution procedures agree for $t \geq T$.

Next, if $t \in [0, T)$, we have

$$v(t) = F(t) = \int_t^\infty b(s)e^{r(t-s)} \, ds = \int_t^T b(s)e^{r(t-s)} \, ds + \int_T^\infty b(s)e^{r(t-s)} \, ds$$

$$= \int_t^T (1-\tau_0)de^{r(t-s)} \, ds + \int_T^\infty (1-\tau_1)de^{r(t-s+T-T)} \, ds$$

$$= \frac{(1-\tau_0)d}{r}(1-e^{r(t-T)}) + e^{r(t-T)}\int_T^\infty (1-\tau_1)de^{r(T-s)} \, ds$$

$$= \frac{(1-\tau_0)d}{r}(1-e^{r(t-T)}) + e^{r(t-T)}\frac{(1-\tau_1)d}{r}$$

$$= v^*(\tau_0)(1-e^{r(t-T)}) + e^{r(t-T)}v^*(\tau_1)$$

$$= v^*(\tau_0) - [v^*(\tau_0) - v^*(\tau_1)]e^{r(t-T)}$$

which is equation (18) in the text. Hence, the two procedures give the same result also for the transition period. ☐

Problem 2.2. Cagan's model with perfect foresight. Consider the following specification of equilibrium in the money market:

$$m(t) - p(t) = -\lambda\pi(t), \quad \text{with } \lambda > 0 \tag{1}$$

where m is the log of the nominal money supply, p is the log of the price level, and $\pi = \dot{p}$ is the (both actual and expected) inflation rate (i.e., we are assuming perfect foresight). If we are willing to assume away real-side complications (e.g., assume that output is fixed at the natural rate), then the full equilibrium of the economy is determined by this equation.

Assume that the nominal money supply grows at a constant rate $\dot{m} = \mu$. Differentiating (1) with respect to time, we can obtain a differential equation in the inflation rate,

$$\mu - \pi = \dot{m} - \dot{p} = -\lambda\dot{\pi}$$

$$\Rightarrow \dot{\pi} = \theta(\pi - \mu), \quad \text{where } \theta \equiv 1/\lambda \tag{2}$$

(i) Find the steady state of this equation, and write its general solution.

Setting $\dot{\pi}$ equal to zero in (2) and solving for π, we see that the steady-state rate of inflation is equal to the rate of growth of the money supply ($\bar{\pi} = \mu$). As discussed in Section 3(a) of Chapter 9, the general solution of the linear equation (2) can be written

$$\pi(t) = \bar{\pi} + [\pi(0) - \bar{\pi}]e^{\theta t} \tag{3}$$

where $\pi(0)$ is the initial inflation rate.

(ii) Assume that μ remains constant forever. From an economic point of view, which is the most reasonable particular solution of this equation? Why?

Because the coefficient θ is positive, the system is unstable. Thus, if initial inflation is not equal to the rate of money growth, the inflation rate either increases or decreases without bound. With a constant rate of money growth, such an explosive, hyperinflationary (or deflationary) outcome does not seem very reasonable. Hence, we shall assume that the equilibrium of the model involves an immediate jump to the steady state.

(iii) Assume that we are at time zero and that μ has always been constant at some value μ_0. Suddenly the government announces that at some time T in the future the rate of money creation will increase to $\mu_1 > \mu_0$ and will remain constant forever thereafter (and people believe the announcement). Describe the evolution of the inflation rate following the announcement and your reasons for selecting this particular adjustment path. Write the particular solution corresponding to this behavior, and use it to solve for the jump in the price level at the time of the announcement. What factors determine the size of this jump?

At the time the policy change takes place we must be in the new steady state $\bar{\pi}_1 = \mu_1$. Hence, we must have

$$\pi(T) = \mu_1 \tag{4}$$

During the period between zero and T we must be on a solution trajectory of the old system, which is of the form (2), with $\bar{\pi} = \mu_0$:

$$\pi(t) = \mu_0 + [\pi(0) - \mu_0]e^{\theta t} \tag{5}$$

Using (4) as a boundary condition in (5), we can solve for the initial inflation rate $\pi(0)$:

$$\pi(T) = \mu_1 = \mu_0 + [\pi(0) - \mu_0]e^{\theta T}$$

from where

$$\pi(0) - \mu_0 = (\mu_1 - \mu_0)e^{-\theta T}$$

Hence, the immediate jump in the inflation rate (from its initial value of μ_0) depends on the increase in the rate of money creation, the time from the announcement until the actual policy change, and the elasticity of the demand for money. □

Problem 2.3. Construct the phase diagram for the system (L.s)–(L.p). Assume that $1 - \alpha\sigma > 0$. What does this assumption mean?

The system whose behavior we want to analyze is of the form

$$\dot{p} = \frac{\alpha}{1 - \alpha\sigma}\left(\delta(s + p^*) - [\delta + (\sigma/\lambda)]p - \sigma\frac{\phi y - m}{\lambda} + g - y\right) \tag{L.p}$$

$$\dot{s} = \frac{\phi y - m + p}{\lambda} - R^* \tag{L.s}$$

- Setting $\dot{s} = 0$ in (L.s) and solving for p, the equation of the first phase line is given by

$$\dot{s} = 0 \Rightarrow p = m - \phi y + \lambda R^* \ (= \bar{p}) \tag{P.s}$$

which is a horizontal line in phase space. Moreover,

$$\frac{\partial \dot{s}}{\partial p} = 1/\lambda > 0$$

The sign of this derivative indicates that, starting from the phase line (where $\dot{s} = 0$), a small increase in the value of p puts us in the region in which $\dot{s}$ is positive. Hence, s increases over time in the region above the phase line, and the arrows of motion along the s axis point to the right, as shown in Figure A11.1.

- Similarly, setting $\dot{p} = 0$ in (L.p), we have

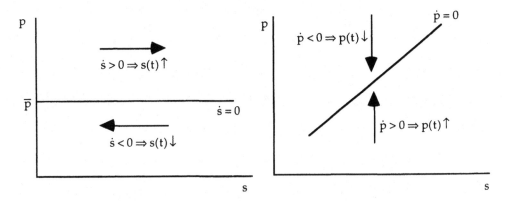

Figure A11.1. Phase lines and arrows of motion.

$$\dot{p} = 0 \Rightarrow [\delta + (\sigma/\lambda)]p = \delta(s + p^*) - \sigma\frac{\phi y - m}{\lambda} + g - y$$

$$\Rightarrow p = \frac{1}{\delta + (\sigma/\lambda)}\left(\delta(s + p^*) - \sigma\frac{\phi y - m}{\lambda} + g - y\right) \qquad (\text{P}.p)$$

Thus, the $\dot{p} = 0$ phase line is upward-sloping, with slope

$$\frac{dp}{ds} = \frac{\delta}{\delta + (\sigma/\lambda)} < 1$$

Differentiating (L.p) with respect to p, we obtain

$$\frac{\partial\dot{p}}{\partial p} = -\frac{\alpha[\delta + (\sigma/\lambda)]}{1 - \alpha\sigma}$$

In principle, the sign of this expression is ambiguous. Under the assumption that $1 - \alpha\sigma > 0$, however, the derivative is negative, and $\dot{p}$ is negative in the region above the phase line. Hence, the arrows of motion along the p axis point toward the phase line, and the output market is "stable" in the sense that prices fall if they are too high for the market to clear. Combining the two phase lines, we get the phase diagram shown in Figure A11.2.

Recall that the parameter α measures the speed of price adjustment. Hence, the assumption that

$$1 - \alpha\sigma > 0 \quad \text{or} \quad \alpha < 1/\sigma$$

requires that prices not adjust "too quickly." As we will see in the next problem, if this assumption does not hold, the system is unstable and displays "unreasonable" behavior.

Problem 2.4. Solution of Dornbusch's model.

(i) Compute the eigenvalues and eigenvectors of the system (L.s)–(L.p), and verify that the steady state is a saddle point.

  Expressing p and s in deviations from the steady state, the system (L.p)–(L.s) can be written in matrix form as

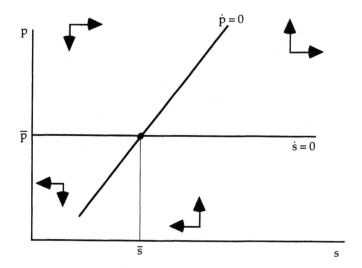

Figure A11.2. Phase diagram.

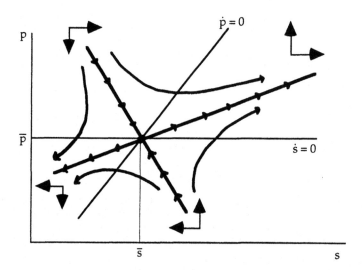

Figure A11.3. Phase diagram and saddle path.

$$\begin{bmatrix} \dot{p} \\ \dot{s} \end{bmatrix} = \begin{bmatrix} \dfrac{-\alpha[\delta + (\sigma/\lambda)]}{1 - \alpha\sigma} & \dfrac{\alpha\delta}{1 - \alpha\sigma} \\ 1/\lambda & 0 \end{bmatrix} \begin{bmatrix} p - \bar{p} \\ s - \bar{s} \end{bmatrix}$$

Observe that the determinant of the coefficient matrix,

$$|A| = \eta_1\eta_2 = 0 - \frac{\alpha\delta}{1 - \alpha\sigma}\frac{1}{\lambda} < 0$$

is negative under the assumption that $1 - \alpha\sigma > 0$. Because the determinant of the coefficient matrix is equal to the product of the eigenvalues η_1 and η_2, it follows that both roots of the system are real numbers and have different signs (say $\eta_1 > 0$ and $\eta_2 < 0$). Hence, the steady state is a saddle point. As we saw in Chapter 10, the system will converge to the steady state if its initial position lies on a straight line through this point, called the convergent subspace of the system or saddle path. There is also an anti–saddle path to which all other trajectories converge (Figure A11.3).

To write the general solution to the model we will need to find the eigenvectors of the coefficient matrix. Normalizing its second component to 1, we can write the eigenvector associated with η_i as $e_i = (x_i, 1)^T$. By definition, the eigenvector satisfies $Ae_i = \eta_i e_i$, so we have

$$\begin{bmatrix} -\alpha[\delta + (\sigma/\lambda)] & \dfrac{\alpha\delta}{1-\alpha\sigma} \\ \dfrac{1}{1-\alpha\sigma} & \\ 1/\lambda & 0 \end{bmatrix} \begin{bmatrix} x_i \\ 1 \end{bmatrix} = \begin{bmatrix} \eta_i x_i \\ \eta_i \end{bmatrix}$$

Focusing on the second equation in this system (recall that we can work with whichever one is more convenient), we have

$$(1/\lambda)x_i + 0 = \eta_i \Rightarrow x_i = \lambda\eta_i$$

Hence, the eigenvectors of the system are of the form

$$e_1 = (\lambda\eta_1, 1)^T \quad \text{and} \quad e_2 = (\lambda\eta_2, 1)^T$$

(ii) Write the general solution of the system. Find the particular solution of the system that corresponds to the saddle path, and discuss the equilibrium trajectory of the system from an arbitrary initial price level. Find the equation that describes the saddle path, and show that it has negative slope.

Because the model is linear, we can write its solution using the formulas derived in Section 2(f)(i) of Chapter 10:

$$p(t) - \bar{p} = k_1\lambda\eta_1 \exp(\eta_1 t) + k_2\lambda\eta_2 \exp(\eta_2 t)$$

$$s(t) - \bar{s} = k_1 \exp(\eta_1 t) + k_2 \exp(\eta_2 t) \tag{G.S}$$

where k_1 and k_2 are arbitrary constants to be definitized by choice of an appropriate boundary condition. We rule out explosive paths and assume that for the given value of the predetermined variable (p), the free variable (s) adjusts continuously so as to keep the system on the unique convergent path, the saddle path. To impose this assumption, we set the constant k_1 associated with the explosive root ($\eta_1 > 0$) equal to zero to obtain the particular solution

$$p(t) - \bar{p} = k_2\lambda\eta_2 \exp(\eta_2 t) \quad \text{and} \quad s(t) - \bar{s} = k_2 \exp(\eta_2 t) \tag{G.P}$$

Differentiating the first equation with respect to time, we see that

$$\dot{p}(t) = k_2\lambda\eta_2 \exp(\eta_2 t)\eta_2 = \eta_2[p(t) - \bar{p}] \qquad (\eta_2 < 0)$$

That is, the speed with which prices adjust toward their long-run equilibrium level is directly proportional to the difference between the current and steady-state values. The speed of adjustment of the system then depends on the value of η_2, a function of the parameters of the system. By solving explicitly for η_2, you will see that high elasticities will increase the absolute value of η_2 and hence the speed of the price adjustment.

From (G.P) we can obtain the equation of the saddle path. Dividing the first equation by the second, we get

$$\frac{p(t) - \bar{p}}{s(t) - \bar{s}} = \lambda\eta_2$$

$$\Rightarrow p(t) - \bar{p} = \lambda\eta_2(s(t) - \bar{s}) \tag{S.P}$$

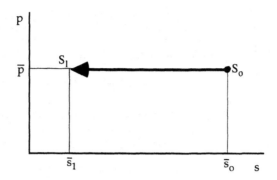

Figure A11.4. Effect of an unanticipated increase in government expenditures.

which describes a straight line in the phase plane going through the steady
state.   □

Problem 2.5. Assume that the economy is initially (at time zero) at the steady
state $S_0 = (\bar{p}_0, \bar{s}_0)$ corresponding to values m_0 and g_0 of the money supply and
government expenditures.

(i) Suppose the government announces an immediate and unanticipated
permanent increase in its expenditure level on domestic goods to $g_1 > g_0$.
Discuss the impact on the steady state of the system, and describe the
adjustment trajectory from the initial position to the new equilibrium.
Recall that the steady-state values of p and s are given by

$$\bar{p} = m - \phi y + \lambda R^* \qquad\qquad \text{(ss.}p)$$

$$\bar{s} = \bar{p} - p^* + (1/\delta)(y + \sigma R^* - g) \qquad\qquad \text{(ss.}s)$$

Hence, an increase in g has no effect on the price level and requires a
decrease in s, which can take place through an appreciation of the home
currency that deflects foreign demand away from domestic output. The
adjustment is immediate and is illustrated in Figure A11.4.

(ii) Analyze the effect of an immediate, unanticipated, and permanent increase in
the nominal money supply to $m_1 > m_0$. It will be seen that the exchange rate
temporarily "overshoots" its new long-run equilibrium value. Explain in what
sense this is true, and discuss the economic mechanism that generates this
result. What determines the degree of overshooting?
Consider the effect of a one-time surprise (permanent) increase in the
nominal money supply, from m_0 to $m_1 = m_0 + \Delta m$. We recall that the steady-
state values of the price level and the exchange rate are given by

$$\bar{p} = m - \phi y + \lambda R^* \qquad\qquad \text{(ss.}p)$$

$$\bar{s} = \bar{p} - p^* + (1/\delta)(y + \sigma R^* - g) \qquad\qquad \text{(ss.}s)$$

Using subscripts to denote the steady-state values of p and s before and after
the policy change, it is clear that

$$\bar{p}_1 - \bar{p}_0 = m_1 - m_0 = \Delta m = \bar{s}_1 - \bar{s}_0$$

Hence, the steady state shifts northeast along a straight line with slope 1. The
long-run effect of a monetary expansion is simply to increase prices and
exchange rates in the same proportion, leaving real variables unaffected. In
the short run, however, a change in the money supply will have real effects.

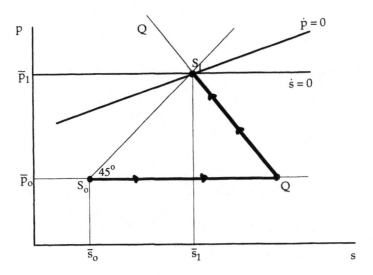

Figure A11.5. Adjustment trajectory in response to an increase in the money supply.

Assuming that we are initially at the old steady state S_0 and that the exchange rate adjusts immediately to put us on the saddle path leading to the new steady state S_1, the adjustment path is as shown in Figure A11.5. The impact effect is an immediate depreciation of the currency (s increases) with a fixed price level; then the currency appreciates slowly, and prices rise along the saddle-path trajectory of the system.

Observe that (because the saddle path is downward-sloping) s "overshoots" its new long-run equilibrium level $\bar{s}_1$. Overshooting occurs because output prices are sluggish to respond, so the full burden of the adjustment falls initially on asset prices, which are flexible. The instantaneous depreciation produces a disequilibrium in the goods market that is eliminated slowly over time as output prices adjust. Following the sudden depreciation, and with output prices given, domestic goods become cheaper relative to foreign goods, and that leads to an excess demand for them. The excess demand leads, in turn, to a gradual upward adjustment in the domestic price level through the Phillips relation.

Note also that with p predetermined, the increase in m is an increase in the real money supply and leads to a reduction in domestic interest rates. This increases demand for output and generates additional inflationary pressures. Moreover, at the lower R, the domestic currency will be held only if it is expected to appreciate in the future (otherwise, real returns on domestic bonds would be less than for foreign bonds). Such appreciation is possible only if the immediate adjustment puts s above its long-run level; hence the need for overshooting. As the adjustment proceeds, domestic prices rise, reducing the real money supply and increasing the interest rate. This, in turn, leads to an appreciation of the home currency that reverses some of the initial depreciation.

It is clear from the figure that the extent of overshooting depends on the slope of the saddle path, which is given by $\lambda \eta_2$. In general, an increase in the absolute value of $\lambda \eta_2$ makes the saddle path steeper and reduces the overshooting. To interpret this observation, note that λ is the interest

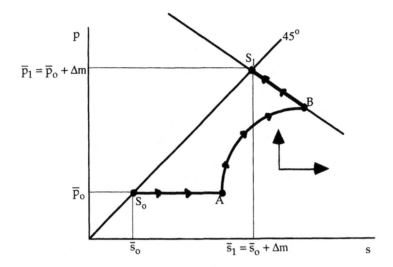

Figure A11.6. Adjustment to an anticipated increase in the money supply.

elasticity of the demand for (domestic) money balances. A high elasticity implies that a given reduction in the money stock will induce only a small decline in interest rates and hence will require only a small appreciation to compensate for it. Second, we have seen that η_2 reflects the speed of price adjustment. This brings us back to the earlier comment that overshooting arises because asset markets adjust rapidly relative to output markets. Things that speed up price adjustment (high elasticities) also reduce overshooting. □

Problem 2.6. Anticipated increase in the money supply. As before, assume that the economy is initially (at time zero) at the steady state $S_0 = (\bar{p}_0, \bar{s}_0)$ corresponding to a value m_0 of the money supply. Now imagine that at time zero the government announces that at some time T in the future the money supply will be permanently increased from the current level of m_0 to $m_1 = m_0 + \Delta m$. The change in the steady state will be as in the preceding problem, with the long-run equilibrium levels of p and m increasing proportionately by Δm. The adjustment path is sketched in Figure A11.6. Explain how this path is constructed, and explain how you would go about finding the coordinates of points A and B in the figure using the general solution of the system (derived earlier) and appropriate boundary conditions.

The logic is similar to what we used in the Cagan model. We need a continuous path, except for a possible jump at the time of the announcement. Discontinuities in the path of prices are ruled out by assumption. Discontinuities in the path of the exchange rate are possible, but only at the time of the announcement, because any future discontinuities would imply (anticipated but) unexploited profit opportunities. Moreover, the adjustment path must eventually converge to the new steady state S_1 and must obey the equations of motion of the "old" system (with $m = m_0$) for $t \in (0, T)$, and those of the "new" system (with $m = m_1$) for $t > T$.

Proceeding backward, there is only one path that will work: Because the path must converge to the steady state S_1 under the laws of motion of the "new" system, at the time of the actual policy change (T), the state vector (s, p) must be on the saddle path for the new system (point B). We must get there while obeying the laws of motion of the old system; hence the path for $(0, T)$ must be an apparently explosive path of the old system, starting from point A. At time zero there is a jump in s, with p fixed at the old level, which takes the system to point A. Notice that this initial adjustment must take the form of a depreciation of the currency (an increase in s). Otherwise, the starting position of the system would be to the left of the old steady state, and the arrows of motion of the system are such that no trajectory starting in this region would intersect the new saddle path.

To characterize the adjustment path more precisely, we need to find the points A and B. We know that the orbit segment AB must satisfy the general solution of the old system, that is,

$$p(t) - \bar{p}_0 = k_1 \lambda \eta_1 \exp(\eta_1 t) + k_2 \lambda \eta_2 \exp(\eta_2 t)$$

$$s(t) - \bar{s}_0 = k_1 \exp(\eta_1 t) + k_2 \exp(\eta_2 t) \qquad \text{(G.S}_0)$$

Now let the coordinates of B be (p_T, s_T) (because we reach this point at time T), and let those of A be (p_0, s_0). We know that B must satisfy (G.S$_0$). Hence

$$p_T - \bar{p}_0 = k_1 \lambda \eta_1 \exp(\eta_1 T) + k_2 \lambda \eta_2 \exp(\eta_2 T)$$

$$s_T - \bar{s}_0 = k_1 \exp(\eta_1 T) + k_2 \exp(\eta_2 T)$$

Moreover, B must be on the saddle path of the new system and therefore satisfies

$$p_T - \bar{p}_1 = \lambda \eta_2 (s_T - \bar{s}_1) \qquad \text{(S.P}_1)$$

Similarly, we know that A must satisfy (G.S$_0$), so we have

$$p_0 - \bar{p}_0 = k_1 \lambda \eta_1 \exp(0) + k_2 \lambda \eta_2 \exp(0) = k_1 \lambda \eta_1 + k_2 \lambda \eta_2$$

$$s_0 - \bar{s}_0 = k_1(1) + k_2(1)$$

and that in addition

$$p_0 = \bar{p}_0$$

because prices are predetermined. This gives us a system of six equations in six unknowns that can be solved for the coordinates of A and B and the two arbitrary constants k_1 and k_2. Once we know these constants, we can determine the initial exchange rate s_0. $\qquad \square$

Problem 3.1. The Solow model with a Cobb-Douglas production function. Assume that the aggregate production function is Cobb-Douglas, with labor-augmenting technical progress

$$Y = K^\alpha (AL)^{1-\alpha} \qquad (1)$$

with $\dot{A}/A = g$. Write the intensive-production function $f(Z)$, giving output per efficiency unit of labor as a function of the capital/labor ratio in efficiency units, $Z = K/AL$. Derive the law of motion for Z under Solow's assumptions, and solve explicitly for the steady state of the system. What factors determine a country's long-term level of income?

Given the production function (1), output per worker is given by

$$f(Z) = \frac{Y}{AL} = \frac{K^\alpha (AL)^{1-\alpha}}{AL} = \frac{(K/AL)^\alpha AL}{AL} = Z^\alpha$$

Substituting this expression into equation (9) in the text, the growth rate of Z is given by

$$\frac{\dot{Z}}{Z} = s\frac{f(Z)}{Z} - (\delta + n + g) = sZ^{\alpha-1} - (\delta + n + g) \tag{2}$$

Setting $\dot{Z}/Z$ equal to zero in (2), we can solve for the steady-state value of the capital/labor ratio in efficiency units:

$$sZ^{\alpha-1} = \delta + n + g \Rightarrow \overline{Z} = \left(\frac{s}{\delta + n + g}\right)^{1/(1-\alpha)}$$

Per-capita income in the steady-state path is given by

$$\overline{Q}_t = A_t\overline{Z}^{\alpha} = A_t\left(\frac{s}{\delta + n + g}\right)^{\alpha/(1-\alpha)}$$

where it can be seen that $\overline{Q}_t$ is an increasing function of the level of technical efficieny (A_t) and the investment coefficient (s) and a decreasing function of the rate of growth of the work force (n) and the rate of depreciation (δ). An increase in the rate of technical progress, g, reduces $\overline{Q}$ for a given value of A, but also increases the growth rate of income.   □

Problem 3.2. Suppose the production function is of the form (1): $Y_t = (B_tK_t)^{\alpha}(A_tL_t)^{1-\alpha}$, with both capital- and labor-augmenting technical progress at rates $\dot{B}/B = g_B$ and $\dot{A}/A = g_A$. Derive the equation of motion for the capital/labor ratio in effective units, $Z = BK/AL$, under the assumptions of the Solow model. Show that the system has a balanced-growth path (i.e., a constant-Z solution) if and only if $g_B = 0$ (i.e., if technical progress is only labor-augmenting).

Under our assumptions, the instantaneous increase in the capital stock is given by

$$\dot{K} = sY - \delta K = s(BK)^{\alpha}(AL)^{1-\alpha} - \delta K = sALZ^{\alpha} - \delta K \tag{2}$$

Given that $Z = BK/AL$, we have, taking logs of both sides of this expression,

$$\ln Z = \ln B + \ln K - \ln A - \ln L$$

and differentiating with respect to time,

$$\frac{\dot{Z}}{Z} = \frac{\dot{K}}{K} - \frac{\dot{L}}{L} + (g_B - g_A)$$

Substituting (2) into this last expression and simplifying, we arrive at

$$\frac{\dot{Z}}{Z} = \frac{\dot{K}}{K} - \frac{\dot{L}}{L} + (g_B - g_A) = \frac{sLABZ^{\alpha} - \delta K}{BK} - (n + g_A - g_B) = sBZ^{\alpha-1} - (n + \delta + g_A - g_B) \tag{3}$$

Setting $\dot{Z}/Z$ equal to zero in this expression (and introducing time subscripts), we have

$$sB_tZ_t^{\alpha-1} = n + \delta + g_A - g_B \tag{4}$$

If technical progress is purely labor-augmenting (i.e., if $g_B = 0$), then B_t is constant, and (4) has a constant-Z solution. If this is not the case, however, B changes over time, and so does the value of Z that solves (4).   □

Problem 3.4. Prove Proposition 3.3 (properties of the savings function).

To sign the partials of the savings function, we will use the implicit-function theorem. Rewriting equation (2) in the text in the form

$$F(s; y_1, y_2, R) = RU_x(y_1 - s, y_2 + sR) - U_c(y_1 - s, y_2 + sR) = 0 \qquad (3)$$

and differentiating $F(\ )$, we obtain

$$F_s = R[U_{cx}(-1) + RU_{xx}] - [U_{cc}(-1) + RU_{cx}]$$
$$= -2RU_{cx} + R^2 U_{xx} + U_{cc} < 0 \qquad (= \partial^2 U / \partial s^2)$$
$$F_{y_1} = RU_{cx} - U_{cc} > 0$$
$$F_{y_2} = RU_{xx} - U_{cx} < 0$$
$$F_R = RsU_{xx} + U_x - sU_{cx} = s(RU_{xx} - U_{cx}) + U_x \gtreqless 0$$

By the implicit-function theorem, then,

$$\frac{\partial s(\ )}{\partial y_1} = -\frac{F_{y_1}}{F_s} > 0, \qquad \frac{\partial s(\ )}{\partial y_2} = -\frac{F_{y_2}}{F_s} < 0, \qquad \frac{\partial s(\ )}{\partial R} = -\frac{F_R}{F_s} \gtreqless 0$$

That is, an increase in first-period income increases savings, as part of the new income is saved to increase second-period consumption. Similarly, an increase in second-period income induces the agent to consume more also in the first period, and savings fall. The sign of $\partial s^*/\partial R$, on the other hand, may be positive or negative. To see why, note that

$$\frac{\partial s^*}{\partial R} = -F_R / F_s = (-1/F_s)[s(RU_{xx} - U_{cx}) + U_x] = s^* \frac{\partial s^*}{\partial y_2} - \frac{U_x}{F_s} \qquad (4)$$

The first term in this expression measures the income effect and the second the substitution effect of a change in the interest factor. The substitution effect is always positive $[-(U_x/F_s) > 0]$ – an increase in R makes present consumption more expensive in terms of forgone future consumption and encourages people to defer consumption to the second period, increasing savings. The sign of the income effect depends on whether the individual is a saver or a borrower. An increase in R makes borrowers ($s \leq 0$) "poorer," forcing them to reduce consumption in both periods. As c falls, savings increase (become "less negative"). Thus income and substitution effects work in the same direction for borrowers. Net lenders, on the other hand, become "richer" when R increases. This leads to an increase in first-period (and second-period) consumption, and hence to a decline in s. The overall effect of a change in R for net savers depends, therefore, on the relative strengths of the income and substitution effects.

Similar results can be obtained by replacing

$$U_{cc}, U_{xx} < 0 \quad \text{and} \quad U_{cx} = U_{xc} \geq 0 \qquad (A.2)$$

with the assumption that c and x are both normal goods. A good is said to be normal if demand for it increases as income rises. Normality of consumption in both periods implies, therefore, that

$$\frac{\partial c^*}{\partial y_1}, \frac{\partial c^*}{\partial y_2}, \frac{\partial x^*}{\partial y_1}, \frac{\partial x^*}{\partial y_2} > 0$$

To see the implications of this assumption for the partials of the savings function, observe that the optimal consumption and savings functions must satisfy the budget constraints identically. Hence, we have

$$y_1 - c(y_1, y_2, R) \equiv s(y_1, y_2, R) \qquad (5)$$

$$x(y_1, y_2, R) \equiv y_2 + Rs(y_1, y_2, R) \qquad (6)$$

Combining these two expressions,

$$c(y_1, y_2, R) + \frac{x(y_1, y_2, R)}{R} \equiv y_1 + \frac{y_2}{R} \qquad (7)$$

Differentiating (7) with respect to y_1 we find that

$$\frac{\partial c^*}{\partial y_1} + \frac{1}{R}\frac{\partial x^*}{\partial y_1} = 1$$

It is obvious that if $\partial c^*/\partial y_1$ and $\partial x^*/\partial y_1$ are both to be positive, then $\partial c^*/\partial y_1 \in (0, 1)$. But then it must be true that $\partial s/^*\partial y_1 \in (0, 1)$ as well, because differentiating (5) with respect to y_1 we see that

$$1 - \frac{\partial c^*}{\partial y_1} = \frac{\partial s^*}{\partial y_1}$$

Similarly, (5) implies that

$$-\frac{\partial c^*}{\partial y_2} = \frac{\partial s^*}{\partial y_2}$$

so $\partial s^*/\partial y_2 < 0$ under the assumption of normality. This, in turn, implies, by (4), that $\partial s^*/\partial R > 0$ for $s \leq 0$.

Another assumption that is commonly made is that first- and second-period consumptions are substitutes. Two goods are said to be substitutes if an increase in the (relative) price of one leads to increased demand for the other. As noted, R reflects the "price" of current consumption in terms of forgone future consumption. If c and x are (strict) substitutes, an increase in R that makes x cheaper should reduce c^*. In other words, $\partial c^*/\partial R < 0$. Because (5) implies that $\partial s^*/\partial R = -\partial c^*/\partial R$, it follows that under the substitutability assumption we have $\partial s^*/\partial R > 0$, even for net lenders. $\qquad\square$

Problem 4.1. Measuring the speed of convergence. The eigenvalue λ of the log-linearized Solow model provides a measure of the speed of convergence of an economy toward its steady state. Show that the half-life of the system described by equation (5) (defined as the time H at which half the original deviation of z from its steady-state value has been eliminated) is given by

$$H = \frac{\ln 2}{\lambda}$$

To compute the half-life of the system, notice that, by definition, z_H satisfies

$$z_H - \bar{z} = \frac{z_0 - \bar{z}}{2}$$

Substituting this expression into the solution of the log-linear approximation to the law of motion for z (equation (6) in the text) evaluated at $t = H$, we have

$$(z_H - \bar{z}) = \frac{z_0 - \bar{z}}{2} = (z_0 - \bar{z})e^{-\lambda H}$$

from where

$$2 = e^{\lambda H} \Rightarrow H = \frac{\ln 2}{\lambda} \qquad\qquad \square$$

Problem 4.2. Determinants of long-run income dispersion. Assume that the evolution of income per capita in a given country can be described by the equation

$$y_{i,t+1} = x_i + (1-\beta)y_{i,t} + \varepsilon_{it} \quad \text{or} \quad \Delta y_{i,t} = x_i - \beta y_{i,t} + \varepsilon_{it} \tag{1}$$

where $y_{i,t} = \ln(Q_{it}/Q_t)$ denotes the logarithm of income per capita in country i in period t (Q_{it}) normalized by the sample mean of the same variable (Q_t), and $\Delta y_{i,t} = y_{i,t+1} - y_{i,t}$ is approximately equal to the growth rate of per-capita income in country i, measured in deviations from the average growth rate in the sample. In this expression, ε_{it} is a random disturbance, with zero mean and variance σ_ε^2, independent and identically distributed over time and across countries and uncorrelated with $y_{i,t}$ and x_i. The term x_i, which summarizes the "fundamental" determinants of growth in territory i, is constant over time and is distributed across countries, with zero mean and variance σ_x^2.

Taking the expected values for both sides of (1), given initial income $y_{i,0}$, we obtain a nonstochastic equation in expected income $y_{i,t}^e$:

$$y_{i,t+1}^e = x_i + (1-\beta)y_{i,t}^e, \quad \text{with } y_{i,0}^e = y_{i,0} \tag{2}$$

The solution of (2) is of the form

$$y_{i,t}^e = y_i^* + \left(y_{i,0} - y_i^*\right)(1-\beta)^t \tag{3}$$

where

$$y_i^* = \frac{x_i}{\beta}$$

is the steady-state value of y_{it}. Equation (3) shows that the stability of the system depends on the value of the slope coefficient β. If $\beta \in (0, 1)$, the term $(1-\beta)^t$ goes to zero as $t \to \infty$. The system is therefore stable, and the expected income of each nation converges monotonically to its steady state y_i^* at a rate determined by β. Hence, we can interpret y_i^* as the expected (relative) income level of country i in a long-run equilibrium.

We want to use equation (1) to investigate the determinants of income inequality across countries in the long run. Let σ_t^2 denote the sample variance of y_{it}, and $c_t = Ex_i y_{it}$ the covariance between current income and country fundamentals, and observe that if the number of countries is large, the sample variance and covariance will be approximately equal to their population values. Using (1), derive a system of difference equations in σ_t^2 and c_t, discuss its stability properties, and compute its steady state. What determines the degree of income inequality in the long run, measured by the steady-state value of σ_t^2?

Taking the variance of both sides of (1), we obtain

$$\sigma_{t+1}^2 = (1-\beta)^2 \sigma_t^2 + \sigma_\varepsilon^2 + \sigma_x^2 + 2(1-\beta)c_t \tag{4}$$

where $c_t = \text{cov}(y_{it}, x_i)$. Using (1) again,

$$c_{t+1} = Ex_i y_{i,t+1} = Ex_i[x_i + (1-\beta)y_{i,t} + \varepsilon_{it}] = Ex_i^2 + (1-\beta)Ex_i y_{i,t} + E\varepsilon_{it}x_i$$

from where, given that $E\varepsilon_{it}x_i = 0$ by assumption,

$$c_{t+1} = \sigma_x^2 + (1-\beta)c_t \tag{5}$$

The expected time path of the variance of income and the covariance of income and country characteristics is given by the solution of a simple system of difference equations:

$$\begin{bmatrix} \sigma_{t+1}^2 \\ c_{t+1} \end{bmatrix} = \begin{bmatrix} (1-\beta)^2 & 2(1-\beta) \\ 0 & (1-\beta) \end{bmatrix} \begin{bmatrix} \sigma_t^2 \\ c_t \end{bmatrix} + \begin{bmatrix} \sigma_x^2 + \sigma_\varepsilon^2 \\ \sigma_x^2 \end{bmatrix}$$

Because the coefficient matrix is diagonal, the eigenvalues of the system are the coefficients of the principal diagonal, $(1-\beta)^2$ and $(1-\beta)$. Hence, the system is stable if and only if the absolute value of $1 - \beta$ is smaller than 1, i.e., if equation (1) is stable.

Eliminating the time subscripts in (4) and (5) and solving for σ and c, it is easy to see that the stationary values of these variables are given by

$$\bar{\sigma}^2 = \frac{\sigma_\varepsilon^2 + \sigma_x^2 + 2(1-\beta)\bar{c}}{1-(1-\beta)^2}, \quad \text{where } \bar{c} = \frac{\sigma_x^2}{\beta} \tag{6}$$

Hence, if the system is stable and country characteristics do not change over time, the distribution of income per capita converges to a stationary distribution with a constant level of inequality. Equation (6) shows that the long-run dispersion of relative income depends on the variance of the shocks, σ_ε^2, and on the dispersion of country characteristics, summarized by σ_x^2. During the transition toward the stationary equilibrium, the value of σ_t^2 could either increase or decrease, depending on the relation between its initial and stationary values. $\square$

Problem 5.1. Homogeneous output is produced using two types of capital (private and public), K and P, according to a technology of the form

$$Y_t = K_t^\alpha P_t^\beta, \quad \text{where } \alpha + \beta < 1 \tag{1}$$

Both types of capital depreciate completely upon use. In each period, the government taxes income at a rate τ and invests the proceeds in public capital for the next period. Agents save a fixed fraction s of their after-tax income and invest it in private capital. Hence,

$$K_{t+1} = s(1-\tau)Y_t \tag{2}$$

and

$$P_{t+1} = \tau Y_t \tag{3}$$

Using (1)–(3), derive a single difference equation in Y that describes the evolution of income. Call this equation (4). Solve for the steady-state value of Y, and show that the system is stable. How does steady-state income vary with s and τ? What value of τ should the government choose if it wants to maximize steady-state output?

Using (1), (2), and (3), we have

$$Y_{t+1} = K_{t+1}^\alpha P_{t+1}^\beta = [s(1-\tau)Y_t]^\alpha [\tau Y_t]^\beta = s^\alpha (1-\tau)^\alpha \tau^\beta Y_t^{\alpha+\beta} \tag{4}$$

Eliminating the time subscripts in (4) and solving for Y,

$$Y^{1-\alpha-\beta} = s^\alpha (1-\tau)^\alpha \tau^\beta \Rightarrow \bar{Y} = s^{\alpha/(1-\alpha-\beta)} (1-\tau)^{\alpha/(1-\alpha-\beta)} \tau^{\beta/(1-\alpha-\beta)}$$

and taking logs of this expression,

$$\ln \bar{Y} \equiv \bar{y} = \frac{\alpha}{1-\alpha-\beta} \ln s + \frac{\alpha}{1-\alpha-\beta} \ln(1-\tau) + \frac{\beta}{1-\alpha-\beta} \ln \tau \tag{5}$$

Notice that the slope of the phase line at the steady state is given by

$$\frac{\partial Y_{t+1}}{\partial Y_t} = s^\alpha (1-\tau)^\alpha \tau^\beta (\alpha+\beta) \bar{Y}^{\alpha+\beta-1} = s^\alpha (1-\tau)^\alpha \tau^\beta (\alpha+\beta) s^{-\alpha} (1-\tau)^{-\alpha} \tau^{-\beta} = \alpha+\beta \in (0,1)$$

Hence, the steady state is stable.

Differentiating (5) with respect to s and τ,

$$\frac{\partial \bar{y}}{\partial s} = \frac{\alpha}{1-\alpha-\beta} \frac{1}{s} > 0$$

so steady-state output is an increasing function of the savings rate, and

$$\frac{\partial \bar{y}}{\partial \tau} = \frac{\alpha}{1-\alpha-\beta}\frac{-1}{1-\tau} + \frac{\beta}{1-\alpha-\beta}\frac{1}{\tau}$$

Notice that

$$\frac{\partial \bar{y}}{\partial \tau} \geq 0 \quad \text{if and only if} \quad \frac{\alpha}{1-\alpha-\beta}\frac{1}{1-\tau} \leq \frac{\beta}{1-\alpha-\beta}\frac{1}{\tau}$$

or, equivalently,

$$\alpha\tau \leq \beta(1-\tau) \Leftrightarrow \tau \leq \frac{\beta}{\alpha+\beta}$$

This expression shows that in order to maximize steady-state output, the government should set the tax rate equal to public capital's "relative weight" in the aggregate production function, i.e., $\tau = \beta/(\alpha+\beta)$. $\square$

Problem 5.2. Consider an economy endowed with an aggregate production function of the form

$$Y = K^{\alpha}(LH)^{1-\alpha} \tag{1}$$

where K is the aggregate stock of physical capital, L is employment in goods production, and H is the average stock of human capital. "Pure knowledge," A, increases over time at a constant exogenous rate g, that is,

$$A_{t+1} = (1+g)A_t \tag{2}$$

Pure knowledge and teacher's time and human capital are combined to "produce" the next generation's human capital according to

$$H_{t+1} = (\tau H_t)^{\gamma} A_t^{1-\gamma} \tag{3}$$

where τ is the fraction of the population employed as teachers, a variable chosen by the government.

Suppose that population is constant, and normalize it to 1 (so that the labor force is $L = 1 - \tau$), and suppose that capital depreciates completely upon use and that agents save a constant fraction s of their income. Then the law of motion for the capital stock is of the form

$$K_{t+1} = sK_t^{\alpha}H_t^{1-\alpha}(1-\tau)^{1-\alpha} \tag{4}$$

(i) Define $Z = K/A$ and $E = H/A$. Using the previous expressions, derive a system of difference equations in Z and E that will describe the evolution of the economy.

Dividing both sides of (4) by $A_{t+1} = (1 + g)A_t$, we have

$$\frac{K_{t+1}}{A_{t+1}} = \frac{s(1-\tau)^{1-\alpha}}{1+g}\frac{K_t^{\alpha}}{A_t^{\alpha}}\frac{H_t^{1-\alpha}}{A_t^{1-\alpha}}$$

from where

$$Z_{t+1} = \frac{s}{1+g}(1-\tau)^{1-\alpha}Z_t^{\alpha}E_t^{1-\alpha} \tag{5}$$

Similarly, dividing both sides of (3) by $A_{t+1} = (1 + g)A_t$,

$$\frac{H_{t+1}}{A_{t+1}} = \frac{\tau^{\gamma}}{1+g}\frac{H_t^{\gamma}}{A_t^{\gamma}}\frac{A_t^{1-\gamma}}{A_t^{1-\gamma}}$$

and hence

$$E_{t+1} = \frac{\tau^\gamma}{1+g} E_t^\gamma \tag{6}$$

(ii) Solve for the steady-state values of Z and E, and compute the steady-state value of $Q = Y/A$.

Eliminating the time subscripts in (5) and (6), we have

$$(6) \Rightarrow E = \frac{\tau^\gamma}{1+g} E^\gamma \Rightarrow \overline{E} = \left(\frac{\tau^\gamma}{1+g} \right)^{1/(1-\gamma)}$$

and

$$(5) \Rightarrow Z = \frac{s}{1+g}(1-\tau)^{1-\alpha} Z^\alpha E^{1-\alpha} \Rightarrow Z^{1-\alpha} = \frac{s}{1+g}(1-\tau)^{1-\alpha} E^{1-\alpha}$$

$$\Rightarrow \overline{Z} = \left(\frac{s}{1+g} \right)^{1/(1-\alpha)} (1-\tau)\overline{E}$$

from where

$$\overline{Z} = (1-\tau)\left(\frac{s}{1+g} \right)^{1/(1-\alpha)} \left(\frac{\tau^\gamma}{1+g} \right)^{1/(1-\gamma)}$$

Steady-state output per efficiency unit of labor, $\overline{Q}$, is given by

$$\overline{Q} = \frac{Y}{A} = \overline{Z}^\alpha (1-\tau)^{1-\alpha} \overline{E}^{1-\alpha} = (1-\tau)^{1-\alpha} \left(\frac{s}{1+g} \right)^{\alpha/(1-\alpha)} (1-\tau)^\alpha \overline{E}^\alpha \overline{E}^{1-\alpha}$$

$$\Rightarrow \overline{Q} = (1-\tau)\left(\frac{s}{1+g} \right)^{\alpha/(1-\alpha)} \overline{E} = (1-\tau)\left(\frac{s}{1+g} \right)^{\alpha/(1-\alpha)} \left(\frac{\tau^\gamma}{1+g} \right)^{1/(1-\gamma)} \tag{7}$$

(iii) Find the value of τ that will maximize steady-state Q.

To maximize $\overline{Q}$ with respect to τ, we take logarithms of (7) and, disregarding the constant terms, maximize the function

$$g(\tau) = \ln(1-\tau) + \frac{\gamma}{1-\gamma} \ln \tau$$

The first-order condition for a maximum is of the form

$$g'(\tau) = \frac{-1}{1-\tau} + \frac{\gamma}{1-\gamma}\frac{1}{\tau} = 0$$

from where

$$(1-\gamma)\tau = (1-\tau)\gamma, \quad \text{implying } \tau = \gamma$$

(iv) Let $z = \ln Z$ and $e = \ln E$. The system derived in (i) should be linear in e and z. Working with the system in logs, compute its eigenvalues, and discuss the stability of its steady state.

Taking logs of (5) and (6), the system can be written

$$z_{t+1} = \Gamma_z + \alpha z_t + (1-\alpha)e_t \tag{8}$$

$$e_{t+1} = \Gamma_e + \gamma e_t \tag{9}$$

where

$$\Gamma_z = \ln \frac{s}{1+g}(1-\tau)^{1-\alpha} \quad \text{and} \quad \Gamma_e = \ln \frac{\tau^\gamma}{1+g}$$

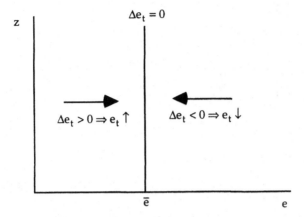

Figure A11.7. The $\Delta e_t = 0$ phase line.

Hence, the Jacobian of the coefficient matrix,

$$J = \begin{bmatrix} \gamma & 0 \\ 1-\alpha & \alpha \end{bmatrix}$$

is diagonal, and the eigenvalues of the system are $\lambda_1 = \alpha$ and $\lambda_2 = \gamma$, both positive numbers smaller than 1. The steady state is therefore stable.

(v) Draw the phase diagram for the system.

Equation (9) can be written

$$\Delta e_t = \Gamma_e - (1-\gamma)e_t$$

Setting Δe_t equal to zero in this expression, the equation of the corresponding phase line is

$$\bar{e} = \frac{\Gamma_e}{1-\gamma}$$

so the $\Delta e_t = 0$ phase line is a vertical line at $\bar{e}$. Notice that

$$\frac{d\Delta e_t}{de_t} = -(1-\gamma) < 0$$

Hence, $\Delta e_t < 0$ when $e_t > \bar{e}$, and the arrows of motion along the e axis point toward the phase line (Figure A11.7).

For the other phase line, we have

$$\Delta z_t = \Gamma_z + (1-\alpha)e_t - (1-\alpha)z_t \qquad (8')$$

from where, setting $\Delta z_t = 0$,

$$z = \frac{\Gamma_z}{1-\alpha} + e$$

(the phase line is upward-sloping), and

$$\frac{d\Delta z_t}{dz_t} = -(1-\alpha) < 0$$

Hence $\Delta z_t < 0$ in the region above the phase line, and the arrows of motion are as shown in Figure A11.8.

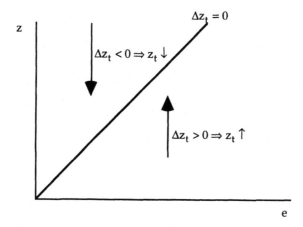

Figure A11.8. The $\Delta z_t = 0$ phase line.

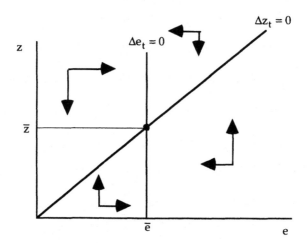

Figure A11.9. Phase diagram.

Finally, combining the two preceding graphs, we obtain the full phase diagram for the system (Figure A11.9).

Problem 5.3. A model of learning by doing. Starting from the Solow model with exogenous technical progress, we will develop a simple model of endogenous growth and examine some of its implications. Assume that the production function is of the form

$$Y = K^\alpha (AL)^{1-\alpha}$$

Then output per worker is given by

$$Q = AZ^\alpha \tag{1}$$

where A is an index of technical efficiency, and $Z = K/AL$ is the capital/labor ratio in efficiency units. Given a constant investment coefficient s, the growth rate of Z is given by the equation

$$\frac{\dot{Z}}{Z} = sZ^{\alpha-1} - (\delta + n + g_A) \tag{2}$$

where n is the rate of population growth, and $g_A = \dot{A}/A$ is the rate of technical progress.

Instead of assuming that g_A is a given constant, we will now assume that the rate of technical progress g_A reflects the accumulation of knowledge with productive experience. In particular, we assume that the instantaneous increase of A is proportional to output per worker, that is,

$$\dot{A} = \gamma Q = \gamma A Z^{\alpha} \tag{3}$$

where the coefficient γ measures the speed of learning.

(i) Show that under these assumptions the law of motion for the capital/labor ratio is of the form

$$\dot{Z} = (s - \gamma Z)Z^{\alpha} - (\delta + n)Z$$

Dividing both sides of (3) by A, the rate of technical progress is given by

$$g_A = \frac{\dot{A}}{A} = \gamma Z^{\alpha} \tag{4}$$

Substituting (4) into (2) and regrouping terms, we have

$$\dot{Z} = (s - \gamma Z)Z^{\alpha} - (\delta + n)Z \tag{5}$$

(ii) Construct the phase diagram for the system, and discuss the stability of its steady state. What is the growth rate of income per worker along the steady-state path?

To analyze the dynamics of equation (5), we will use Figure A11.10. In the upper panel we plot the functions Z^{α} and $s - \gamma Z$. The product of these two functions, which gives us the first term on the right-hand side of (5), is shown in the lower panel. Because the product $(s - \gamma Z)Z^{\alpha}$ must be equal to zero when either factor is zero, and positive when both factors are positive, the graph of this function has an inverted-U shape and cuts the horizontal axis twice, one of those cuts being at the origin.

The lower panel of the figure shows the graph of $(\delta + n)Z$, which is a straight line through the origin. By (5), the vertical distance between the curve $(s - \gamma Z)Z^{\alpha}$ and the line $(\delta + n)Z$ gives us the instantaneous increment of Z. Notice that there is a steady state, $\bar{Z}$, that corresponds to the point where the two lines cross. As in the Solow model, this steady state is stable, because Z increases when its value is larger than $\bar{Z}$, and decreases otherwise.

Hence, the economy converges in the long run to a balanced-growth path in which the value of Z is constant. Along this path, output per worker is given by

$$\bar{Q}_t = A_t \bar{Z}^{\alpha}$$

and increases, therefore, at the same rate as A. Using equation (4), the long-run rate of growth (of A and hence of output per worker) is given by

$$\bar{g}_Q = \bar{g}_A = \gamma \bar{Z}^{\alpha}$$

The value of $\bar{g}_A$ can also be determined graphically. If we draw, in the upper panel of the figure, the function γZ^{α}, the height of this curve when $Z = \bar{Z}$ gives us the long-run growth rate.

(iii) Analyze the impact of an increase in the investment rate on the steady state and on the time path of the system. Things are now quite different from

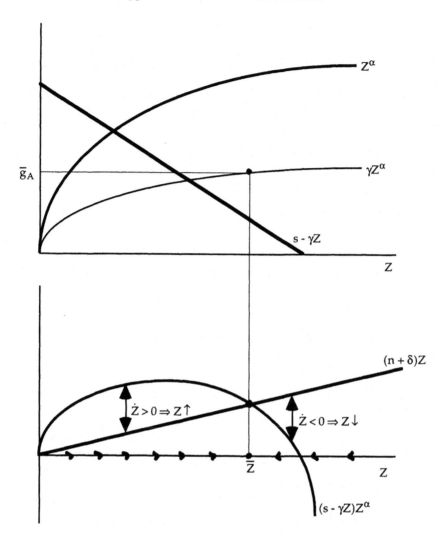

Figure A11.10. Dynamics of the learning-by-doing model.

what they were in the Solow model with exogenous technical progress. In what sense?

Consider now the effects of an increase in the investment rate. As shown in Figure A11.11, an increase in s shifts the line $(s - \gamma Z)$ upward (in the upper panel) and, therefore, also the curve $(s - \gamma Z)Z^\alpha$ in the lower panel. The new steady state involves a higher value of Z and a higher growth rate.

In this model (unlike the Solow model with exogenous technical progress), changes in economic policies can have permanent effects on the growth rate – that is, can affect not only the level of the balanced-growth path but also its slope, as shown in Figure A11.12.

(iv) Consider two countries that are identical except for their investment rates. Discuss the predictions of the current model and the Solow model with exogenous technical progress concerning the evolution of the relative income levels of the two countries.

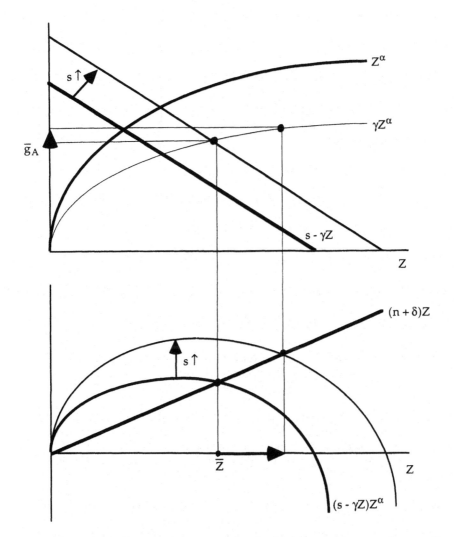

Figure A11.11. Impact of an increase in the investment rate on the steady state.

A second important difference between this model and the ones we studied in the preceding section involves their implications for convergence. To illustrate this point, consider the case of two countries that differ only in their investment coefficients s. We have seen that when technical progress is exogenous and takes place at the same rate in both countries, they converge to balanced-growth paths with the same slope, although with different heights. This implies that the ratio of the per-capita incomes of the economies eventually stabilizes at a constant value. In the present case, however, the slopes of the balanced-growth trajectories will be different. In the steady state, income per capita will grow faster in the thriftier country. This implies that with the passage of time, income differences between countries will grow without bound. Small differences in investment rates (possibly due to differences in economic policies) can generate extremely large income differentials in the long run.   □

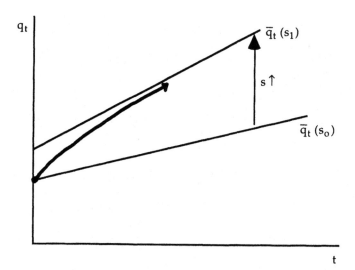

Figure A11.12. Effect of an increase in the investment rate on the path of output per worker.

Problem 5.4. An extended Solow model with human capital (Mankiw et al., 1992). Suppose the aggregate production function is of the form

$$Y = K^\alpha E^\gamma (AL)^{1-\alpha-\gamma} = ALZ^\alpha H^\gamma \tag{1}$$

where K and E are the aggregate stocks of physical capital and human capital, L is the size of the labor force, and A is a productivity index that summarizes the current state of technical knowledge. The normalized variables $Z = K/AL$ and $H = E/AL$ denote the stocks of physical capital and human capital per efficiency unit of labor.

We postulate constant rates of population growth and exogenous technical progress ($\dot{L}/L = n$ and $\dot{A}/A = g$) and assume that the fractions of GDP devoted to investment in physical capital and human capital (s_k and s_h) remain constant over time. Under these assumptions, the accumulation of productive factors is described by the system

$$\dot{K} = s_k Y - \delta K \quad \text{and} \quad \dot{E} = s_h Y - \delta E \tag{2}$$

where the depreciation rate δ is assumed to be the same for both types of capital. Using the fact that $\dot{Z}/Z = (\dot{K}/K) - n - g$, and $\dot{H}/H = (\dot{E}/E) - n - g$, the laws of motion for the stocks of physical capital and human capital can be rewritten in terms of the normalized variables,

$$\frac{\dot{Z}}{Z} = s_k Z^{\alpha-1} H^\gamma - (\delta + g + n) \tag{3}$$

$$\frac{\dot{H}}{H} = s_h Z^\alpha H^{\gamma-1} - (\delta + g + n) \tag{4}$$

(i) Find the steady-state values of Z, H, and output per efficiency unit of labor, $P = Y/AL$.

Setting $\dot{Z}$ and $\dot{H}$ equal to zero in (3) and (4), we can solve for the steady-state values of Z and H. We have

$$\dot{Z} = 0 \Rightarrow s_k Z^{\alpha-1} H^\gamma = (\delta + g + n) \tag{5}$$

$$\dot{H} = 0 \Rightarrow s_h Z^\alpha H^{\gamma-1} = (\delta + g + n) \tag{6}$$

from where

$$s_k Z^{\alpha-1} H^\gamma = s_h Z^\alpha H^{\gamma-1} \Rightarrow H = \frac{s_h}{s_k} Z$$

Substituting this last expression into (5), we see that

$$s_k Z^{\alpha-1} \left(\frac{s_h}{s^k} Z \right)^\gamma = (\delta + g + n) \Rightarrow s_k^{1-\gamma} s_h^\gamma Z^{\alpha+\gamma-1} = (\delta + g + n)$$

$$\Rightarrow \overline{Z} = \left(\frac{s_k^{1-\gamma} s_h^\gamma}{\delta + g + n} \right)^{1/(1-\alpha-\gamma)} \tag{7}$$

and

$$\overline{H} = \frac{s_h}{s_k} \overline{Z} = \left(\frac{s_k^\alpha s_h^{1-\alpha}}{\delta + g + n} \right)^{1/(1-\alpha-\gamma)} \tag{8}$$

Finally, we define output per efficiency unit of labor,

$$P = \frac{Y}{AL} = Z^\alpha H^\gamma \tag{9}$$

and compute its steady-state value:

$$\overline{P} = \overline{Z}^\alpha \overline{H}^\gamma = \left(\frac{s_k^{1-\gamma} s_h^\gamma}{\delta + g + n} \right)^{\alpha/(1-\alpha-\gamma)} \left(\frac{s_k^\alpha s_h^{1-\alpha}}{\delta + g + n} \right)^{\gamma/(1-\alpha-\gamma)}$$

$$= \left(\frac{s_k}{\delta + g + n} \right)^{\alpha/(1-\alpha-\gamma)} \left(\frac{s_h}{\delta + g + n} \right)^{\gamma/(1-\alpha-\gamma)}$$

Using lowercase letters to indicate that we are taking logarithms, this expression can be rewritten in the form

$$\overline{p} = \alpha\overline{z} + \gamma\overline{h} = \frac{\alpha}{1-\alpha-\gamma} \ln \frac{s_k}{\delta + g + n} + \frac{\gamma}{1-\alpha-\gamma} \ln \frac{s_h}{\delta + g + n} \tag{10}$$

(ii) We will now construct a log-linear approximation to the system and use it to derive a convergence equation similar to the one obtained in Section 4(a). Letting $z = \ln Z$ and $h = \ln H$ (from where $Z = e^z$ and $H = e^h$), rewrite the system (3)–(4) in terms of z and h. Show that the linear approximation to the transformed system around the steady state is given by

$$\dot{z} = -(1-\alpha)(\delta + g + n)\tilde{z} + \gamma(\delta + g + n)\tilde{h} \tag{11}$$

$$\dot{h} = \alpha(\delta + g + n)\tilde{z} - (1-\beta)(\delta + g + n)\tilde{h} \tag{12}$$

where $\tilde{x} = x - \overline{x}$ denotes the current deviation of variable x from its steady-state value. Discuss the stability of the system (11)–(12) (and hence that of the original system).

To rewrite the system in terms of the transformed variables, notice that

$$Z = e^z, \quad H = e^h, \quad \dot{z} = \frac{\dot{Z}}{Z}, \quad \text{and} \quad \dot{h} = \frac{\dot{H}}{H}$$

Using these expressions, we can rewrite (3) and (4) in the form

$$\dot{z} = s_k e^{(\alpha-1)z} e^{\gamma h} - (\delta+g+n) \equiv F(z, h) \qquad (3')$$

$$\dot{h} = s_h e^{\alpha z} e^{(\gamma-1)h} - (\delta+g+n) \equiv G(z, h) \qquad (4')$$

Setting $\dot{z}$ and $\dot{h}$ equal to zero, we see that in the steady state,

$$s_k e^{(\alpha-1)z} e^{\gamma h} = \delta+g+n = s_h e^{(\gamma-1)h} \qquad (13)$$

Next, we compute the partial derivatives of the functions $F(\ )$ and $G(\ )$ with respect to z and h, and, using (13), we evaluate them at the steady state.

$$F_z = (\alpha-1)s_k e^{(\alpha-1)z} e^{\gamma h} = -(1-\alpha)(\delta+g+n)$$

$$F_h = \gamma s_k e^{(\alpha-1)z} e^{\gamma h} = \gamma(\delta+g+n)$$

$$G_z = \alpha s_h e^{\alpha z} e^{(\gamma-1)h} = \alpha(\delta+g+n)$$

$$G_h = (\gamma-1)s_h e^{\alpha z} e^{(\gamma-1)h} = -(1-\gamma)(\delta+g+n)$$

Using Taylor's formula to approximate $F(\ )$ and $G(\ )$ around the point $(\bar{z}, \bar{h})$, and observing that

$$\tilde{p} = \alpha\tilde{z} + \gamma\tilde{h}$$

we have

$$F(z, h) \cong F_z\tilde{z} + F_h\tilde{h} = -(1-\alpha)(\delta+g+n)\tilde{z} + \gamma(\delta+g+n)\tilde{h} = (\delta+g+n)(\tilde{p}-\tilde{z})$$

$$G(z, h) \cong G_z\tilde{z} + G_h\tilde{h} = \alpha(\delta+g+n)\tilde{z} - (1-\gamma)(\delta+g+n)\tilde{h} = (\delta+g+n)(\tilde{p}-\tilde{h})$$

where $\tilde{x} = x - \bar{x}$ denotes the deviation of the variable x with respect to its steady state. Hence, the linear approximation to the system is of the form

$$\dot{z} = -(1-\alpha)(\delta+g+n)\tilde{z} + \gamma(\delta+g+n)\tilde{h} = (\delta+g+n)(\tilde{p}-\tilde{z}) \qquad (11)$$

$$\dot{h} = \alpha(\delta+g+n)\tilde{z} - (1-\gamma)(\delta+g+n)\tilde{h} = (\delta+g+n)(\tilde{p}-\tilde{h}) \qquad (12)$$

The coefficient matrix is of the form

$$A = \begin{bmatrix} -(1-\alpha)(\delta+g+n) & \gamma(\delta+g+n) \\ \alpha(\delta+g+n) & -(1-\gamma)(\delta+g+n) \end{bmatrix}$$

Hence

$$\text{tr } A = -(2-\alpha-\gamma)(\delta+g+n) < 0$$

$$\det A = (1-\alpha)(1-\gamma)(\delta+g+n)^2 - \alpha\gamma(\delta+g+n)^2$$

$$= (1-\alpha-\gamma+\alpha\gamma-\alpha\gamma)(\delta+g+n)^2 = (1-\alpha-\gamma)(\delta+g+n)^2 > 0$$

$$\Delta = \text{tr}^2 - 4\det = (2-\alpha-\gamma)^2(\delta+g+n)^2 - 4(1-\alpha-\gamma)(\delta+g+n)^2$$

$$= (\delta+g+n)^2\left\{[1+(1-\alpha-\gamma)]^2 - 4(1-\alpha-\gamma)\right\}$$

$$= (\delta+g+n)^2\left[1+2(1-\alpha-\gamma)+(1-\alpha-\gamma)^2 - 4(1-\alpha-\gamma)\right]$$

$$= (\delta+g+n)^2\left[1-2(1-\alpha-\gamma)+(1-\alpha-\gamma)^2\right]$$

$$= (\delta+g+n)^2[1-(1-\alpha-\gamma)]^2 = (\delta+g+n)^2(\alpha+\gamma)^2 > 0$$

from where

$$\lambda_1, \lambda_2 = \frac{\text{tr} \pm \sqrt{\text{tr}^2-4\det}}{2} = \frac{-(2-\alpha-\gamma)(\delta+g+n) \pm (\delta+g+n)(\alpha+\gamma)}{2}$$

$$= (\delta+g+n)\frac{(\alpha+\gamma-2) \pm (\alpha+\gamma)}{2}$$

and therefore

$$\lambda_1 = -(\delta + g + n) \quad \text{and} \quad \lambda_2 = -(1 - \alpha - \gamma)(\delta + g + n)$$

Hence, the eigenvalues are negative real numbers, and the steady state of the system is stable.

(iii) Using the system (11)–(12) and the fact that $p = \alpha z + \gamma h$, derive a linear differential equation in p that describes the approximate behavior of this variable, and solve it. Rewriting the solution in terms of output per worker, $q = p + a$, derive a convergence equation of the form

$$\frac{q_{t+d} - q_t}{d} = g + \frac{1 - e^{-\lambda d}}{d}[\bar{p} - (q_t - a_t)]$$

where d is the duration of the period, and $\lambda = (1 - \alpha - \gamma)(\delta + g + n)$.

Because $p = \alpha z + \gamma h$, we have

$$\dot{p} = \alpha \dot{z} + \gamma \dot{h} = (\delta + g + n)[\alpha(\tilde{p} - \tilde{z}) + \gamma(\tilde{p} - \tilde{h})] = (\delta + g + n)[(\alpha + \gamma)\tilde{p} - \tilde{p}]$$

or

$$\dot{p} = -\lambda \tilde{p} \tag{14}$$

where $\lambda = (1 - \alpha - \gamma)(\delta + g + n)$ and $\tilde{p} = p - \bar{p}$. If we consider the period from t to $t + d$, the final value of p is given by

$$p_{t+d} = p_t e^{-\lambda d} + \bar{p}(1 - e^{-\lambda d}) \tag{15}$$

Hence, output per efficiency unit of labor converges to its steady-state value at an exponential rate λ that depends on the degree of returns to scale in reproducible factors $(1 - \alpha - \gamma)$ and on the rates of depreciation, population growth, and technical progress.

Finally, because output per efficiency unit of labor is not observable, it will be convenient to rewrite (15) in terms of the log of output per worker, $q = p + a$. We have

$$\begin{aligned}
q_{t+d} &= p_{t+d} + a_{t+d} = p_t e^{-\lambda d} + \bar{p}(1 - e^{-\lambda d}) + a_{t+d} \\
&= (q_t - a_t)e^{-\lambda d} + \bar{p}(1 - e^{-\lambda d}) + a_t + gd \\
&= q_t e^{-\lambda d} + \bar{p}(1 - e^{-\lambda d}) + a_t(1 - e^{-\lambda d}) + gd
\end{aligned}$$

Subtracting q_t from both sides of this expression and dividing through by the length of the period, d, we arrive at the desired expression:

$$\frac{q_{t+d} - q_t}{d} = g + \frac{1 - e^{-\lambda d}}{d}[\bar{p} - (q_t - a_t)]$$

Notice that this expression is almost identical with the one we derived in Section 4(a). The only differences are that the steady state now depends also on the rate of investment in human capital and that the speed of convergence is now given by $\lambda = (1 - \alpha - \gamma)(\delta + g + n)$, rather than by $(1 - \alpha)(\delta + g + n)$. Hence, what matters for the speed of convergence is the sum of the coefficients of the reproducible factors, physical and human capital. □

Problem 5.5. Diamond's model with variable labor supply. In the basic Diamond model, leisure does not enter the utility function of households. As a result, each worker supplies inelastically his or her endowment of labor time, and the level of employment is constant (on a per-capita basis). We will now relax this assumption.

To simplify things, we assume that the rate of population growth is zero $(n = 0)$ and that individuals work in youth and consume only in old age. Young workers, on the other hand, enjoy their leisure and must therefore seek an optimal trade-off between the disutility of working and the need for income. The utility function of a representative worker is given by

$$U(x_{t+1}, L_t) = \frac{x_{t+1}^{1-\gamma}}{1-\gamma} - L_t$$

where $\gamma \in (0, 1)$, L is labor time supplied in youth, and x is old-age consumption. The per-capita production function is

$$y = \sqrt{kL}$$

(i) Because consumption takes place only in old age, workers save their entire labor income wL and consume their savings plus interest earnings $(w_t L_t R_{t+1})$ in the second period of their lives. They solve, then

$$\max_{x,L}\left\{ U = \frac{x^{1-\gamma}}{1-\gamma} - L \text{ subject to } x = wLR \right\}$$

Solve this problem for the agent's labor supply (L^s) and savings functions. Substituting the constraint into the objective function, we get

$$\max_L U = \frac{1}{1-\gamma}(wLR)^{1-\gamma} - L$$

from where

$$\frac{\partial U}{\partial L} = (wLR)^{-\gamma} wR - 1 = 0$$

$$\Rightarrow L^s = (w_t R_{t+1})^{(1-\gamma)/\gamma} \tag{1}$$

which is the labor supply function. The savings function is therefore of the form

$$s_t = s(w_t, R_{t+1}) = wL^s = w_t(w_t R_{t+1})^{(1-\gamma)/\gamma} \tag{2}$$

(ii) Firms maximize profits per worker, that is,

$$\max_{k,L} \pi_t = y_t - R_t k_t - w_t L_t = (k_t L_t)^{1/2} - R_t k_t - w_t L_t$$

Write the first-order conditions for this problem, solve for w and R as functions of (k/L), and derive the firm's labor demand function. The first-order conditions for the firm's problem are

$$\frac{\partial \pi}{\partial L} = (1/2)(kL)^{-1/2} k - w = 0$$

$$\Rightarrow 2w_t = (k_t/L_t)^{1/2} \tag{3}$$

$$\frac{\partial \pi}{\partial k} = (1/2)(kL)^{-1/2} L - R = 0$$

$$\Rightarrow 2R_t = (L_t/k_t)^{1/2} \tag{4}$$

These two equations can be interpreted as defining the firm's labor and capital demands (k_t^d, L_t^d) or, alternatively, as defining factor prices as functions of input use.

(iii) In equilibrium, agents optimize, and labor and capital markets clear. Because population is constant, market clearing requires, in per-capita terms,

$$L_t^s = L_t^d \tag{5}$$

$$s_t = k_{t+1} \tag{6}$$

Show that the conditions for market clearing and individual optimization can be reduced to the following system of first-order difference equations in k and R:

$$k_{t+1} = R_t k_t, \tag{A}$$

$$R_{t+1}^{1-\gamma} = 4k_t^\gamma R_t^{1+\gamma} \tag{B}$$

To begin, we use (3) and (4) to derive two convenient relationships; multiplying and dividing these two equations in turn we obtain

$$(3)*(4) \quad 4w_t R_t = 1 \Rightarrow w_t = 1/4R_t \tag{7}$$

$$(3)/(4) \quad w_t/R_t = k_t/L_t \Rightarrow w_t L_t = k_t R_t \tag{8}$$

Next, we substitute the savings function (6) into the capital-market clearing condition and use (8) to get (making implicit use of the labor-market clearing condition)

$$k_{t+1} = w_t L_t = k_t R_t$$

which is (A).

Then, labor-market clearing implies, using (3) and (1),

$$L_t^s = L_t^d \Rightarrow (w_t R_{t+1})^{(1-\gamma)/\gamma} = k_t/4w_t^2$$

from where

$$R_{t+1}^{(1-\gamma)/\gamma} = \frac{k_t}{4w_t^2 w_t^{(1-\gamma)/\gamma}} \Rightarrow R_{t+1}^{(1-\gamma)/\gamma} = \frac{k_t}{4w_t^{(1+\gamma)/\gamma}}$$

Raising both sides of this expression to the power γ,

$$R_{t+1}^{1-\gamma} = \frac{k_t^\gamma}{4^\gamma w_t^{1+\gamma}}$$

and using (7), $w_t = 1/4R_t$,

$$R_{t+1}^{1-\gamma} = \frac{k_t^\gamma 4^{1+\gamma} R_t^{1+\gamma}}{4^\gamma} \Rightarrow R_{t+1}^{1-\gamma} = 4k_t^\gamma R_t^{1+\gamma}$$

(iv) We have been able to reduce the model to a system of two first-order difference equations that describe the sequence of competitive equilibria in this economy. Note that if we take logs, the system becomes linear. Defining

$$\kappa = \ln k \quad \text{and} \quad \rho = \ln R$$

we can rewrite (A) and (B) as

$$\kappa_{t+1} = \rho_t + \kappa_t \tag{A'}$$

$$(1-\gamma)\rho_{t+1} = \ln 4 + \gamma\kappa_t + (1+\gamma)\rho_t \tag{B'}$$

Construct the phase diagram of the system, compute its solution, and analyze its dynamics. What would be a reasonable initial condition for this model?

Setting $\rho_t = \rho_{t+1} = \rho$ and $\kappa_t = \kappa_{t+1} = \kappa$ in (A') and (B'), we obtain the equations of the phase lines:

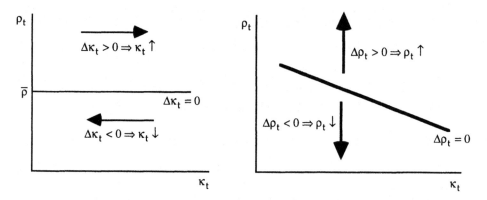

Figure A11.13. Phase lines and arrows of motion.

$$(A') \Rightarrow \kappa = \rho + \kappa$$

$$\Rightarrow \rho = 0 \tag{P.A}$$

$$(B') \Rightarrow (1-\gamma)\rho = \ln 4 + \gamma\kappa + (1+\gamma)\rho$$

$$\Rightarrow \rho = \frac{-1}{2\gamma}(\ln 4 + \gamma\kappa) \tag{P.B}$$

The intersection of the phase lines gives us the steady state. From the first equation,

$$\bar{\rho} = 0 \Rightarrow \bar{R} = e^\rho = 1$$

Using this in (P.B), we get

$$0 = \ln 4 + \gamma\kappa \Rightarrow \bar{\kappa} = -\frac{\ln 4}{\gamma} = \ln(1/4)^{1/\gamma} \Rightarrow \bar{k} = e^\kappa = (1/4)^{1/\gamma}$$

Graphically, (P.A) describes a horizontal line at $\rho = 0$. From (A') we have

$$\Delta\kappa_t = \kappa_{t+1} - \kappa_t = \rho_t \Rightarrow \frac{\partial\Delta\kappa_t}{\partial\rho_t} = 1 > 0$$

Hence, an increase in ρ_t increases $\Delta\kappa_t$, which is zero along the phase line. It follows that in the region above the phase line we have $\Delta\kappa_t > 0$, and κ_t increases over time. The arrows of motion point to the right above the phase line (Figure A11.13).

Similarly, (P.B) is downward-sloping in κ, and from (B'),

$$\frac{\partial\Delta\rho_t}{\partial\rho_t} = \frac{\partial\rho_{t+1}}{\partial\rho_t} - 1 = \frac{1+\gamma}{1-\gamma} - 1 = \frac{2\gamma}{1-\gamma} > 0$$

so $\Delta\rho_t > 0$ above the phase line, and ρ_t increases over time in that region, as indicated by the arrows of motion in Figure A11.13.

Combining the two graphs above, we obtain the phase diagram for the system (Figure A11.14). The pattern of motion indicated by the arrows suggests the existence of a saddle-point equilibrium. That this is indeed the case will be shown next.

In matrix form, the system (A')–(B') can be written

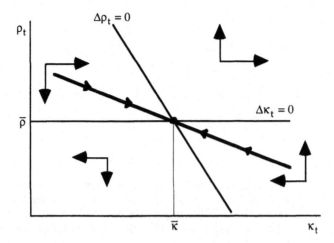

Figure A11.14. Phase diagram.

$$\begin{bmatrix} \kappa_{t+1} \\ \rho_{t+1} \end{bmatrix} = \begin{bmatrix} 1 & 1 \\ \dfrac{\gamma}{1-\gamma} & \dfrac{1+\gamma}{1-\gamma} \end{bmatrix} \begin{bmatrix} \kappa_t \\ \rho_t \end{bmatrix} + \begin{bmatrix} 0 \\ \ln 4 \end{bmatrix}$$

The eigenvalues of the coefficient matrix are therefore the solutions to the following equation:

$$\begin{vmatrix} 1-\lambda & 1 \\ \dfrac{\gamma}{1-\gamma} & \dfrac{1+\gamma}{1-\gamma} - \lambda \end{vmatrix} = (1-\lambda)\left(\dfrac{1+\gamma}{1-\gamma} - \lambda\right) - \dfrac{\gamma}{1-\gamma} = \dfrac{1}{1-\gamma}[(1-\gamma)\lambda^2 - 2\lambda + 1] = 0$$

from where

$$\lambda = \dfrac{2 \pm \sqrt{4 - 4(1-\gamma)}}{2(1-\gamma)} = \dfrac{2 \pm \sqrt{4\gamma}}{2(1-\gamma)} = \dfrac{1 \pm \sqrt{\gamma}}{1-\gamma}$$

and hence

$$\lambda_1 = \dfrac{1+\sqrt{\gamma}}{1-\gamma} \quad \text{and} \quad \lambda_2 = \dfrac{1-\sqrt{\gamma}}{1-\gamma}$$

By assumption, $\gamma \in (0, 1)$, and therefore both eigenvalues are real and positive, with $\lambda_1 > 1$. Moreover, $\sqrt{\gamma} > \gamma$, so $\lambda_2 < 1$, and the steady state is a saddle point.

To find the eigenvectors of the coefficient matrix, we solve $Ae_i = \lambda_i e_i$, that is, normalizing the second component of the eigenvector to 1 ($e_{i1} = 1$),

$$\begin{bmatrix} 1 & 1 \\ \dfrac{\gamma}{1-\gamma} & \dfrac{1+\gamma}{1-\gamma} \end{bmatrix} \begin{bmatrix} e_{i1} \\ 1 \end{bmatrix} = \begin{bmatrix} \lambda_{i1} e_{i1} \\ \lambda_{i1} \end{bmatrix}$$

from where

$$e_i + 1 = \lambda_i e_i \Rightarrow e_i = \dfrac{1}{\lambda_i - 1}$$

so, with

$$\lambda_1 = \frac{1+\sqrt{\gamma}}{1-\gamma} \Rightarrow e_{11} = \frac{1-\gamma}{\gamma+\sqrt{\gamma}}$$

$$\lambda_2 = \frac{1-\sqrt{\gamma}}{1-\gamma} \Rightarrow e_{21} = \frac{1-\gamma}{\gamma-\sqrt{\gamma}}$$

we can now write the general solution to the system as

$$\kappa_t - \bar{\kappa} = c_1 \frac{1-\gamma}{\gamma+\sqrt{\gamma}} \lambda_1^t + c_2 \frac{1-\gamma}{\gamma-\sqrt{\gamma}} \lambda_2^t \qquad \text{(GS.1)}$$

$$\rho_t - \bar{\rho} = c_1 \lambda_1^t + c_2 \lambda_2^t \qquad \text{(GS.2)}$$

where c_1 and c_2 are arbitrary constants. Any sequence $\{\kappa_t, \rho_t\}$ that satisfies these two equations is a solution to the system (A')–(B'). To definitize the solution, we have a natural initial condition, $\kappa_0 = \ln k_0$, because the initial capital stock of the economy is given. On the other hand, ρ_t is a "free variable," and its starting value is not constrained by an initial condition.[2] This observation leaves us with too many solutions. A reasonable thing to do, following the discussion in Section 2, is to assume that the economy does not embark on an explosive path, but instead moves along the unique trajectory that converges to the steady state, i.e., the saddle path of the system.

To impose this (economic) assumption on the solution, we set the constant c_1 equal to zero in (GS.1) and (GS.2) and "kill off" the explosive root of the system ($\lambda_1 > 1$). This yields

$$\kappa_t - \bar{\kappa} = c_2 \frac{1-\gamma}{\gamma-\sqrt{\gamma}} \lambda_2^t \qquad \text{(9)}$$

$$\rho_t - \bar{\rho} = c_2 \lambda_2^t \qquad \text{(10)}$$

Dividing these two equations to eliminate $c_2 \lambda_2^t$, we get the equation of the saddle path

$$\rho_t - \bar{\rho} = \frac{\gamma-\sqrt{\gamma}}{1-\gamma} (\kappa_t - \bar{\kappa}) \qquad \text{(S)}$$

To obtain an explicit expression for the saddle-path solution, we need to determine the corresponding value of the arbitrary constant c_2 in the system (9)–(10). This can be done using the natural initial condition on the capital stock. At time zero, κ_t is a given constant κ_0, and (9) yields

$$\kappa_0 - \bar{\kappa} = c_2 \frac{1-\gamma}{\gamma-\sqrt{\gamma}} \lambda_2^0$$

$$\Rightarrow c_2 = \frac{\gamma-\sqrt{\gamma}}{1-\gamma} (\kappa_0 - \bar{\kappa}) \qquad \text{(11)}$$

Substituting this result into (9) and (10), we get

$$\kappa_t - \bar{\kappa} = (\kappa_0 - \bar{\kappa}) \frac{\gamma-\sqrt{\gamma}}{1-\gamma} \frac{1-\gamma}{\gamma-\sqrt{\gamma}} \lambda_2^t = (\kappa_0 - \bar{\kappa}) \lambda_2^t = (\kappa_0 - \bar{\kappa}) \left(\frac{1-\sqrt{\gamma}}{1-\gamma} \right)^t \qquad \text{(12)}$$

$$\rho_t - \bar{\rho} = (\kappa_0 - \bar{\kappa}) \frac{\gamma-\sqrt{\gamma}}{1-\gamma} \left(\frac{1-\sqrt{\gamma}}{1-\gamma} \right)^t \qquad \text{(13)}$$

which is the solution we seek. $\qquad\qquad\qquad\qquad\qquad\qquad\qquad\qquad\qquad$ □

Problem 5.6. Social security in Diamond's model. Consider a Diamond economy like the one analyzed in Example 3.6. Population grows at a constant rate n, preferences are of the form

$$U(c, x) = \ln c + \beta \ln x \qquad \text{(U)}$$

with $\beta \in (0, 1)$, and the production function is Cobb-Douglas,

$$Y = K^{\alpha} L^{1-\alpha}$$

with $\alpha \in (0, 1)$.

We assume that wages are taxed at a proportional rate τ and that proceeds are used to finance a balanced pay-as-you-go social-security scheme. Hence, first-period after-tax income for an agent born at time t is given by

$$y_1 = (1 - \tau)w_t$$

and his second-period retirement subsidy is equal to

$$y_2 = \tau(1 + n)w_{t+1}$$

(because there are $1 + n$ young agents for each old agent).

(i) Maximize $U(c, x)$ subject to the appropriate budget constraint, and solve for the agent's savings function $s^* = s(y_1, y_2, R)$ and his indirect utility function $v(w_t, w_{t+1}, R_{t+1}, \tau)$. Taking factor prices as given, when is the agent's welfare an increasing function of the social-security tax rate?

The agent maximizes $U(c, x)$ subject to the constraints

$$c = y_1 - s \quad \text{and} \quad x = y_2 + sR$$

Solving these expressions for s and substituting the result into the utility function, the agent solves

$$\max_{s} W(s) = \ln(y_1 - s) + \beta \ln(y_2 + sR)$$

The first-order condition for the problem is

$$W'(s) = \frac{-1}{y_1 - s} + \beta \frac{R}{y_2 + sR} = 0$$

Solving this expression for s, we obtain the savings function

$$s^* = s(y_1, y_2, R) = \frac{\beta}{1+\beta} y_1 - \frac{1}{1+\beta} \frac{y_2}{R} \qquad (1)$$

Using (1), we have

$$c^* = y_1 - s^* = \frac{y_1}{1+\beta} + \frac{y_2}{R(1+\beta)} \quad \text{and} \quad x^* = y_2 + Rs^* = \frac{\beta R y_1}{1+\beta} + \frac{\beta y_2}{1+\beta}$$

Substituting these expressions into $U(c, x)$, we obtain the indirect-utility function

$$v(R, y_1, y_2) = U(c^*, x^*) = \ln\left(\frac{y_1}{1+\beta} + \frac{y_2}{R(1+\beta)}\right) + \beta \ln\left(\frac{\beta R y_1}{1+\beta} + \frac{\beta y_2}{1+\beta}\right)$$

or

$$v(R, y_1^*, y_2^*) = \ln\left(\frac{1}{1+\beta}\right) + \beta \ln\left(\frac{\beta}{1+\beta}\right) + \ln\left(y_1 + \frac{y_2}{R}\right) + \beta \ln(Ry_1 + y_2)$$

$$= \ln\left(\frac{1}{1+\beta}\right) + \beta \ln\left(\frac{\beta}{1+\beta}\right) + (1+\beta)\ln(Ry_1 + y_2) - \ln R \qquad (2)$$

Taking factor prices as given, the agent's welfare increases with the social-security tax whenever his lifetime income

$$I(\tau) = Ry_1 + y_2 = R_{t+1}(1-\tau)w_t + \tau(1+n)w_{t+1}$$

is an increasing function of τ for given values of R_{t+1}, w_t, and w_{t+1}. Because

$$I'(\tau) = -R_{t+1}w_t + (1+n)w_{t+1}$$

this will be the case when

$$(1+n)\frac{w_{t+1}}{wt} > R_{t+1} \qquad (3)$$

that is, when population growth and the rate of wage increase are sufficiently high to guarantee the agent a "return" on his social-security payments that is higher than the market interest factor.

(ii) Derive the law for motion of the capital/labor ratio, $Z = K/L$, and compute the steady-state values of Z and factor prices as functions of τ. Call these functions

$$\overline{Z} = Z_s(\tau), \quad \overline{w} = w_s(\tau), \quad \text{and} \quad \overline{R} = R_s(\tau)$$

Under what conditions is it true that $1 + n > R_s(0)$?

With a Cobb-Douglas production function, equilibrium factor prices are given by

$$w_t = (1-\alpha)Z_t^{\alpha} \quad \text{and} \quad R_{t+1} = \alpha Z_{t+1}^{\alpha-1} \qquad (4)$$

The savings function (1) can be written

$$s_t^* = s[(1-\tau)w_t, (1+n)\tau w_{t+1}, R_{t+1}] = \frac{\beta}{1+\beta}(1-\tau)w_t - \frac{1}{1+\beta}\frac{(1+n)\tau w_{t+1}}{R_{t+1}} \qquad (5)$$

and the capital-market clearing condition requires

$$K_{t+1} = L_t s_t$$

or, dividing both sides of this expression by $L_{t+1} = (1+n)L_t$,

$$Z_{t+1} = \frac{1}{1+n}s_t \qquad (6)$$

Substituting (4) and (5) into (6) and simplifying,

$$Z_{t+1} = \frac{1}{1+n}\left(\frac{\beta}{1+\beta}(1-\tau)w_t - \frac{1}{1+\beta}\frac{(1+n)\tau w_{t+1}}{R_{t+1}}\right) = \frac{1}{1+\beta}\left(\frac{\beta}{1+n}(1-\tau)w_t - \frac{\tau w_{t+1}}{R_{t+1}}\right)$$

$$\Rightarrow (1+\beta)Z_{t+1} = \frac{\beta}{1+n}(1-\tau)(1-\alpha)Z_t^{\alpha} - \frac{\tau(1-\alpha)Z_{t+1}^{\alpha}}{\alpha Z_{t+1}^{\alpha-1}}$$

$$\Rightarrow \left(1+\beta+\frac{\tau(1-\alpha)}{\alpha}\right)Z_{t+1} = \frac{\beta}{1+n}(1-\tau)(1-\alpha)Z_t^{\alpha}$$

we obtain the law of motion for Z:

$$Z_{t+1} = \frac{\beta(1-\tau)(1-\alpha)}{(1+n)\left(1+\beta+\dfrac{\tau(1-\alpha)}{\alpha}\right)}Z_t^{\alpha} \qquad (7)$$

Eliminating the time subscripts in (7), we can solve for the steady-state capital/labor ratio,

$$\overline{Z} = \left(\frac{\beta(1-\tau)(1-\alpha)}{(1+n)\left(1+\beta+\dfrac{\tau(1-\alpha)}{\alpha}\right)} \right)^{1/(1-\alpha)} \tag{8}$$

The steady-state interest factor is then given by

$$\overline{R} = R_s(\tau) = \alpha \overline{Z}^{\alpha-1} = \frac{\alpha(1+n)\left(1+\beta+\dfrac{\tau(1-\alpha)}{\alpha}\right)}{\beta(1-\tau)(1-\alpha)} \tag{9}$$

and when $\tau = 0$, it reduces to

$$R_s(0) = \frac{\alpha(1+n)(1+\beta)}{\beta(1-\alpha)}$$

Notice that $1 + n > R_s(0)$ if

$$\frac{\alpha(1+\beta)}{\beta(1-\alpha)} < 1$$

(iii) What are the effects of an increase in τ on steady-state Z and factor prices? Compute the following derivatives evaluated at $\tau = 0$:

$$\frac{Z_s'(\tau)}{Z_s(\tau)}, \quad \frac{w_s'(\tau)}{w_s(\tau)}, \quad \text{and} \quad \frac{R_s'(\tau)}{R_s(\tau)}$$

Taking logarithms of (8), we have

$$z_s(\tau) = \ln \overline{Z} = \frac{1}{1-\alpha}\left(\ln \frac{\beta(1-\alpha)}{1+n} + \ln(1-\tau) - \ln\left(1+\beta+\frac{\tau(1-\alpha)}{\alpha}\right) \right)$$

and differentiating this expression with respect to τ,

$$z_s'(\tau) = \frac{Z_s'(\tau)}{Z_s(\tau)} = \frac{1}{1-\alpha}\left(\frac{-1}{1-\tau} - \frac{\dfrac{1-\alpha}{\alpha}}{\left(1+\beta+\dfrac{\tau(1-\alpha)}{\alpha}\right)} \right) < 0 \tag{10}$$

we see that an increase in the social-security tax always reduces the steady-state capital/labor ratio. Evaluating (10) at $\tau = 0$,

$$z_s'(0) = -\frac{1}{1-\alpha}\left(1+\frac{1-\alpha}{\alpha(1+\beta)}\right) \tag{11}$$

Finally, because $w_t = (1-\alpha)Z_t^\alpha$, we have

$$\ln w_t = \ln(1-\alpha) + \alpha \ln Z_t$$

and therefore

$$\frac{w_s'(0)}{w_s(0)} = \frac{d \ln w_s(0)}{d\tau} = \alpha z_s'(0) = -\frac{\alpha}{1-\alpha}\left(1+\frac{1-\alpha}{\alpha(1+\beta)}\right) \tag{12}$$

and because $R = \alpha Z^{\alpha-1}$,

$$\frac{R_s'(0)}{R_s(0)} = \frac{d \ln R_s(0)}{d\tau} = (\alpha-1)z_s'(0) = 1+\frac{1-\alpha}{\alpha(1+\beta)} \tag{13}$$

(iv) One of the advantages of working with a model in which individual preferences are clearly specified is that this gives us a natural criterion for evaluating the desirability of possible policy alternatives. Using your previous results, and considering only its effects on steady-state welfare, when will it be a good idea to introduce a social-security scheme? To answer this question, compute the derivative of a representative individual's (maximized) welfare with respect to τ, taking into account both the direct effects of the tax and its indirect effect through the induced change in steady-state factor prices, and evaluate it at $\tau = 0$.

At a steady state we have

$$Ry_1 + y_2 = [R(1-\tau) + \tau(1+n)]w \tag{14}$$

Using (2) and (14), steady-state welfare can be written

$$V(\tau) = v[R_s(\tau), w_s(\tau), \tau]$$

$$= \ln\left(\frac{1}{1+\beta}\right) + \beta \ln\left(\frac{\beta}{1+\beta}\right) + (1+\beta)\ln w_s(\tau)$$

$$+ (1+\beta)\ln[R_s(\tau)(1-\tau) + \tau(1+n)] - \ln R_s(\tau) \tag{15}$$

Hence,

$$V'(\tau) = (1+\beta)\frac{w_s'(\tau)}{w_s(\tau)} + (1+\beta)\frac{-R_s(\tau) + (1-\tau)R_s'(\tau) + (1+n)}{R_s(\tau)(1-\tau) + \tau(1+n)} - \frac{R_s'(\tau)}{R_s(\tau)}$$

and

$$V'(0) = (1+\beta)\frac{w_s'(0)}{w_s(0)} + (1+\beta)\frac{-R_s(0) + R_s'(0) + (1+n)}{R_s(0)} - \frac{R_s'(0)}{R_s(0)}$$

$$= (1+\beta)\frac{w_s'(0)}{w_s(0)} + \beta\frac{R_s'(0)}{R_s(0)} - (1+\beta) + \frac{(1+\beta)(1+n)}{R_s(0)}$$

$$= (1+\beta)\frac{w_s'(0)}{w_s(0)} + \beta\frac{R_s'(0)}{R_s(0)} - (1+\beta) + \frac{\beta(1-\alpha)}{\alpha}$$

Using (12) and (13), this expression becomes

$$V'(0) = (1+\beta)\alpha z_s'(0) - (1-\alpha)\beta z_s'(0) - \frac{(1+\beta)\alpha - (1-\alpha)\beta}{\alpha}$$

$$= [(1+\beta)\alpha - (1-\alpha)\beta]\left(z_s'(0) - \frac{1}{\alpha}\right)$$

Now, because $z_s'(0) < 0$, the second term of this expression is negative, and $V'(0) > 0$ if and only if

$$(1+\beta)\alpha < (1-\alpha)\beta \Leftrightarrow \frac{\alpha(1+\beta)}{\beta(1-\alpha)} < 1 \Leftrightarrow R_s(0) < 1+n$$

Hence, social security may increase welfare even though it reduces savings and lowers the steady-state capital stock. This will be the case when the no-social-security steady-state interest factor is "too low," i.e., when in some sense the economy has a tendency to overaccumulate capital. (To make this more precise, consider a social planner who wants to maximize the welfare of steady-state generations subject to a resource constraint. What will be the optimal value of Z and the implied interest factor?)   □

Chapter 12

Problem 1.2. A violation of the principle of optimality

Consider an agent who lives three periods and maximizes a utility function of the form

$$V_1 = U_1 + \alpha U_2 + \beta U_3$$

where utility in period i, U_i, is a function of current and (expected) future consumption, i.e.,

$$U_1(c_1, c_2, c_3) = \ln(c_1 c_2 c_3), \quad U_2(c_2, c_3) = \ln(c_2 c_3), \quad \text{and} \quad U_3(c_3) = \ln c_3$$

and the budget constraint is of the form

$$A_{t+1} = A_t - c_t \qquad (A_1 \text{ given, and } A_4 = 0)$$

where A is wealth.

Notice that the return function is additive, but not separable over periods, as the period-1 utility, for example, depends on (expected) consumption at times 2 and 3. Hence, the assumptions of Theorem 1.1 do not hold, and as we will see, the principle of optimality fails.

(i) Compute the optimal consumption plan from the perspective of time 1, $c^1 = (c_1^1, c_2^1, c_3^1)$.

The objective function from the perspective of period 1 can be written

$$V_1 = \ln c_1 + (1+\alpha)\ln c_2 + (1+\alpha+\beta)\ln c_3 \tag{1}$$

Substituting the flow budget constraints recursively into each other, we obtain a single restriction requiring the sum of consumption expenditures to add up to initial wealth A_1:

$$c_1 + c_2 + c_3 = A_1 \tag{2}$$

Solving (2) for c_3, and substituting the result into (1), the agent solves the following problem at time 1:

$$\max V_1(c_1, c_2) = \ln c_1 + (1+\alpha)\ln c_2 + (1+\alpha+\beta)\ln(A_1 - c_1 - c_2) \tag{P.1}$$

The first-order conditions for this problem are given by

$$\frac{\partial V_1}{\partial c_1} = \frac{1}{c_1} - \frac{1+\alpha+\beta}{A_1 - c_2 - c_3} = 0$$

$$\Rightarrow \frac{1}{c_1} = \frac{1+\alpha+\beta}{A_1 - c_2 - c_3} \tag{3}$$

$$\frac{\partial V_1}{\partial c_2} = \frac{1+\alpha}{c_2} - \frac{1+\alpha+\beta}{A_1 - c_2 - c_3} = 0$$

$$\Rightarrow \frac{1+\alpha}{c_2} = \frac{1+\alpha+\beta}{A_1 - c_2 - c_3} \tag{4}$$

Using (3) and (4), we have

$$\frac{1}{c_1} = \frac{1+\alpha}{c_2}$$

$$\Rightarrow c_2 = (1+\alpha)c_1 \tag{5}$$

and substituting (5) into (3),

$$(1+\alpha+\beta)c_1 = A_1 - c_1 - c_2 = A_1 - c_1 - (1+\alpha)c_1$$

$$\Rightarrow c_1^1 = \frac{A_1}{3+2\alpha+\beta} \tag{6}$$

Using (2), (5), and (6), the remainder of the consumption plan is given by

$$c_2^1 = (1+\alpha)c_1^1 = (1+\alpha)\frac{A_1}{3+2\alpha+\beta} \tag{7}$$

$$c_3^1 = A_1 - c_1^1 - c_2^1 = A_1 - (2+\alpha)c_1^1 = (1+\alpha+\beta)\frac{A_1}{3+2\alpha+\beta} \tag{8}$$

(ii) Next, consider what happens as the agent begins to implement this plan. At time 1, he consumes c_1^1, receives utility U_1, and has leftover wealth $A_2 = A_1 - c_1^1$. He then faces the problem of maximizing utility over the remainder of his life,

$$\max V_2 = \alpha U_2 + \beta U_3$$

subject to $c_2 + c_3 = A_2$. Compute the new optimal plan, $c^2 = (c_2^2, c_3^2)$, and compare it with the last portion of c^1. Has the consumer changed his mind? How and why? Does the Bellman equation hold?

At time 2, the agent solves

$$\max V_2(c_2) = \alpha \ln c_2 + (\alpha+\beta)\ln(A_2 - c_2) \tag{P.2}$$

where

$$A_2 = A_1 - c_1^1 = A_1 - \frac{A_1}{3+2\alpha+\beta} = \frac{(2+2\alpha+\beta)A_1}{3+2\alpha+\beta} \tag{9}$$

The first-order condition,

$$V_2'(c_2) = \frac{\alpha}{c_2} - \frac{\alpha+\beta}{A_2-c_2} = 0$$

$$\Rightarrow \frac{\alpha}{c_2} = \frac{\alpha+\beta}{A_2-c_2} \tag{10}$$

can be solved for c_2^2 as a function of A_2:

$$c_2^2 = \frac{\alpha A_2}{2\alpha+\beta} \tag{11}$$

Using (9) and (7), we have

$$c_2^2 = \frac{\alpha}{2\alpha+\beta}\frac{(2+2\alpha+\beta)A_1}{3+2\alpha+\beta}\frac{1+\alpha}{1+\alpha} = \frac{\alpha(2+2\alpha+\beta)}{(2\alpha+\beta)(1+\alpha)}\frac{(1+\alpha)A_1}{3+2\alpha+\beta}$$

$$= \frac{2\alpha+2\alpha^2+\alpha\beta}{2\alpha+\beta+2\alpha^2+\alpha\beta}c_2^1 < c_2^1 \tag{12}$$

Hence, revised second-period consumption is lower than in the original plan. The agent has changed his mind because once period 1 has passed, he no longer cares about the effect of planned second- and third-period consumption on period-1 utility. □

Problem 1.7. Prove Theorem 1.6: Let (X, d) be a complete metric space, and let $T: X \to X$ be a contraction with fixed point $v \in X$. Further, let Y be a closed subset of X, and assume that T maps points in Y into some subset Z of Y (i.e., $T: Y \to Z$). Then the unique fixed point v of T in X will be in Z.

Because (Y, d) is a complete metric space, v must be in Y. To show that it is in the subset Z, note that, by assumption, T maps points in Y into points in Z; hence, Tv must be in Z, but because v is a fixed point, $Tv = v \in Z$.   □

Problem 1.11. Prove Lemma 1.10: Let $T: C(X) \to C(X)$ be the operator defined by

$$Tv(x) = \max_{u \in \Gamma(x)} \{F(x, u) + \beta v[m(x, u)]\}$$

and assume that Assumption 1.9 (monotonicity) holds. Then T maps nondecreasing functions into strictly increasing functions.

Let $v(\ )$ be a nondecreasing function, and x_0 and $x_1 \in X$ two arbitrary points in its domain, with $x_1 > x_0$. Then $v(x_1) \geq v(x_0)$, and because F is assumed to be strictly increasing in x, $F(x_1, u) > F(x_0, u)$ if u is the same, and $v[m(x_1, u)] \geq v[m(x_0, u)]$, by our monotonicity assumptions on $v(\ )$ and $m(\ )$. Moreover, the constraint set corresponding to x_1, $\Gamma(x_1)$, contains $\Gamma(x_0)$. Hence,

$$Tv(x_1) = \max_{u \in \Gamma(x_1)} \{F(x_1, u) + \beta v[m(x_1, u)]\} > \max_{u \in \Gamma(x_0)} \{F(x_0, u) + \beta v[m(x_0, u)]\} = Tv(x_0)$$

and we conclude that Tv is strictly increasing.   □

Problem 1.14. Prove Lemma 1.13: Consider the normed vector space $[C(X), \|\cdot\|_s]$, where $\|\cdot\|_s$ is the sup norm, and assume X is a convex set. The set of (weakly) concave functions in $C(X)$ is a closed subset of $C(X)$.

We will show that any convergent sequence of concave functions in $C(X)$ has a concave limit. Given a sequence of concave functions $\{f_n\}$ convergent to f, let x_0 and x_1 be arbitrary points in X, and consider the sequence of real numbers

$$\{f_n[(1-\lambda)x_0 + \lambda x_1] - (1-\lambda)f_n(x_0) - \lambda f_n(x_1)\}$$

By the concavity of f_n, this is a sequence of nonnegative real numbers, and because $\{f_n\} \to f$ (in the sup norm and hence pointwise), the sequence has a nonnegative limit

$$L = f[(1-\lambda)x + \lambda y] - (1-\lambda)f(x) - \lambda f(y) \geq 0$$

This proves the lemma.   □

Problem 1.17. Prove Lemma 1.16: Let $T : C(X) \longrightarrow C(X)$ be the operator defined by

$$Tv(x) = \max_{u \in \Gamma(x)} \{F(x, u) + \beta v[m(x, u)]\}$$

and assume that the concavity and monotonicity assumptions hold. Then T maps weakly concave functions into strictly concave functions.

Let v be weakly concave, take two arbitrary points in its domain, x_0 and x_1 in X, with $x_0 \neq x_1$, and assume that $u_0 \in \Gamma(x_0)$ and $u_1 \in \Gamma(x_1)$ solve the maximization problems for x_0 and x_1, respectively. Hence, $u_0 \in \Gamma(x_0)$ achieves $Tv(x_0)$, and $u_1 \in \Gamma(x_1)$ achieves $Tv(x_1)$. To simplify the notation, define

$$y_0 = m(x_0, u_0), \qquad y_1 = m(x_1, u_1)$$
$$x^\lambda = (1-\lambda)x_0 + \lambda x_1, \qquad u^\lambda = (1-\lambda)u_0 + \lambda u_1, \qquad y^\lambda = (1-\lambda)y_0 + \lambda y_1$$

The assumption that Γ is convex can then be written as $u^\lambda \in \Gamma(x^\lambda)$. Note that

$$Tv(x^{\lambda}) = \max_{u \in \Gamma(x^{\lambda})} \{F(x^{\lambda}, u) + \beta v[m(x^{\lambda}, u)]\} \geq F(u^{\lambda}, x^{\lambda}) + v[m(x^{\lambda}, u^{\lambda})]$$

$$\geq F(u^{\lambda}, x^{\lambda}) + v[(1 - \lambda)m(x_0, u_0) + \lambda m(x_1, u_1)] = F(u^{\lambda}, x^{\lambda}) + v(y^{\lambda})$$

$$> [(1 - \lambda)F(x_0, u_0) + \lambda F(x_1, u_1)] + [(1 - \lambda)v(y_0) + \lambda v(y_1)]$$

$$= [(1 - \lambda)Tv(x_0) + \lambda Tv(x_1)]$$

where the first inequality holds because, by the convexity of the constraint correspondence, u^{λ} is feasible for x^{λ} ($u^{\lambda} \in \Gamma(x^{\lambda})$), but is not necessarily optimal. The second holds by the concavity of $m(\ )$ and the monotonicity assumption, which ensures that $v(\ )$ is increasing. The third holds by the concavity of $F(\ )$ (strict) and $v(\ )$.   □

Chapter 13

Problem 2.7. Apply the implicit-function theorem (IFT) to compute the partial derivatives of the function $\phi(k_t, c_t)$, defined implicitly by equation (16) in the text, and determine their signs.

Rewriting (16) in the form

$$F(c_{t+1}; k_t, c_t) = \beta U'(c_{t+1})f'[f(k_t) - c_t] - U'(c_t) = 0$$

we have, by the IFT, that provided $F_{ct+1} \neq 0$,

$$\phi_k = \frac{\partial c_{t+1}}{\partial k_t} = -\frac{F_{kt}}{F_{ct+1}} \quad \text{and} \quad \phi_c = \frac{\partial c_{t+1}}{\partial c_t} = -\frac{F_{ct}}{F_{ct+1}}$$

where

$$F_{ct+1} = \beta U''(c_{t+1})f'(k_{t+1}) < 0$$

$$F_{kt} = \beta U'(c_{t+1})f''(k_{t+1})f'(k_t) < 0$$

$$F_{ct} = \beta U'(c_{t+1})f''(k_{t+1})(-1) - U''(c_t) > 0$$

and therefore

$$\phi_k = \frac{\partial c_{t+1}}{\partial k_t} = -\frac{F_{kt}}{F_{ct+1}} = -(-)/(-) < 0$$

$$\phi_c = \frac{\partial c_{t+1}}{\partial c_t} = -\frac{F_{ct}}{F_{ct+1}} = -(+)/(-) > 0 \qquad \square$$

Problem 2.8. Setting $c_t = c_{t+1} = c$ and $k_t = k_{t+1} = k$ in equations (15) and (16) in the text, draw the phase lines $\Delta k_t = 0$ and $\Delta c_t = 0$ for the system. To complete the phase diagram, determine the directions of motion along the c and k axes in each of the four regions in which the state plane (c, x) is divided by the phase lines.

The equations of the phase lines are obtained by setting in turn $\Delta k_t = k_{t+1} - k_t = 0$ and $\Delta c_t = c_{t+1} - c_t = 0$ (i.e., $c_t = c_{t+1} = c$ and $k_t = k_{t+1} = k$) in (15) and (16):

$$(15) \Rightarrow k = f(k) - c$$

$$\Rightarrow \Delta k_t = 0: c = f(k) - k \tag{P.1}$$

$$(16) \Rightarrow U'(c) = \beta U'(c)f'[f(k) - c]$$

$$\Rightarrow \Delta c_t = 0: \beta f'[f(k) - c] = 1 \tag{P.2}$$

• Working with (P.1), we have

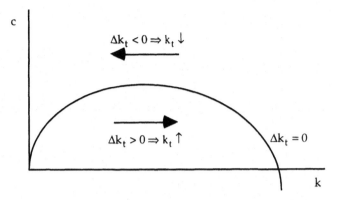

Figure A13.1. The $\Delta k_t = 0$ phase line.

$$\left.\frac{dc}{dk}\right|_{\Delta k=0} = f'(k) - 1 \quad \text{and} \quad \left.\frac{d^2c}{dk^2}\right|_{\Delta k=0} = f''(k) < 0$$

Hence the phase line $c = c(k)$ is concave. It achieves a maximum at the point k^m where $f'(k^m) = 1$. In addition, $f(0) = 0$, so the line goes through the origin; it rises at first to the maximum and then declines, intersecting the k axis again at the point where $f(k) = k$.

This information allows us to draw the phase line. To determine the direction of the arrows of motion, note that we can write, using (15),

$$\Delta k_t = k_{t+1} - k_t = f(k_t) - k_t - c_t$$

Differentiating this expression with respect to c, we find that

$$\frac{\partial \Delta k_t}{\partial c_t} = -1 < 0$$

that is, an increase in c reduces the value of Δk_t. In particular, because $\Delta k_t = 0$ along the phase line, an increase in c (which will put us above the line) makes Δk_t negative. Hence, k is decreasing over time above the phase line, and increasing below it, as shown in Figure A13.1. This is intuitively obvious, as a consumption level that is "too high" must necessarily reduce the capital stock.
- Similarly,

$$\Delta c_t = 0 \Rightarrow G(c; k) = \beta f'[f(k) - c] - 1 = 0 \qquad (\text{P.2})$$

Differentiating this equation implicitly with respect to k, we get

$$\beta\left(f''(\,)f'(k) + f''(\,)\frac{dc}{dk}(-1) \right) = 0 \Rightarrow \left.\frac{dc}{dk}\right|_{\Delta c=0} = f'(k) > 0$$

so the phase line is upward-sloping. Comparing this expression with $(dc/dk)_{\Delta k=0}$, we see that the second phase line is steeper than the first one in the region in which the latter has positive slope. Differentiating again,

$$\left.\frac{d^2c}{dk^2}\right|_{\Delta c=0} = f'' < 0$$

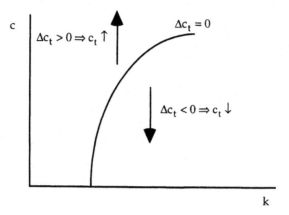

Figure A13.2. The $\Delta c_t = 0$ phase line.

so the phase line is concave. Moreover, the horizontal intercept is positive, as with $c = 0$ we have

$$f'[f(k) - 0] = 1/\beta$$

Because $f'(\ )$ is monotonically decreasing with $f'(0) = \infty$, the last expression holds only with $f(k) > 0$, which in turn requires $k > 0$.

To draw the arrows of motion corresponding to this phase line, observe that

$$U'(c_t) = \beta U'(c_{t+1}) f'[f(k_t) - c_t] \Leftrightarrow c_{t+1} = \phi(k_t, c_t) \qquad (2)$$

implies that

$$\Delta c_t = c_{t+1} - c_t = \phi(k_t, c_t) - c_t$$

so

$$\frac{\partial \Delta c_t}{\partial k_t} = \phi_k < 0$$

This result tells us that c is decreasing over time to the right of the phase line, as shown in Figure A13.2.

• Combining what we know about the two phase lines, we can draw the phase diagram for the system. It is clear that the two lines will intersect in the first quadrant, yielding a steady state $(\bar{c}, \bar{k})$. Figure A13.3 shows the intersection at a point where the two lines are upward-sloping. To see that this is indeed the case, recall that the slope of the first phase line is given by

$$\left.\frac{dc}{dk}\right|_{\Delta k=0} = f'(k) - 1$$

At the steady state we must have $f'(k) = 1/\beta > 1$, so $dc/dk|_{\Delta k=0} > 0$. $\square$

Problem 2.9. The phase diagram you have just drawn should suggest that the steady state is a saddle point. Check that this is true by showing that the eigenvalues of the Jacobian matrix for the system are positive real numbers lying on opposite sides of 1.

We have

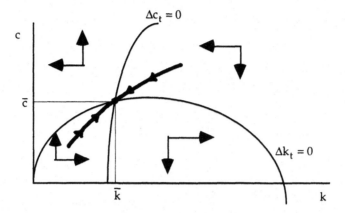

Figure A13.3. Phase diagram.

$$k_{t+1} = f(k_t) - c_t \equiv \varphi(k_t, c_t) \tag{15}$$

$$U'(c_t) = \beta U'(c_{t+1}) f'[f(k_t) - c_t] \Leftrightarrow c_{t+1} = \phi(k_t, c_t) \tag{16}$$

From Problem 2.7, we know that

$$\phi_k = \frac{\partial c_{t+1}}{\partial k_t} = -\frac{F_{kt}}{F_{ct+1}} = -\frac{\beta U'(c_{t+1}) f''(k_{t+1}) f'(k_t)}{\beta U''(c_{t+1}) f'(k_{t+1})}$$

$$\phi_c = \frac{\partial c_{t+1}}{\partial c_t} = -\frac{F_{ct}}{F_{ct+1}} = -\frac{\beta U'(c_{t+1}) f''(k_{t+1})(-1) - U''(c_t)}{\beta U''(c_{t+1}) f'(k_{t+1})}$$

At a steady state, we have $k_{t+1} = k_t = k$, $c_{t+1} = c_t = c$, and $\beta f'(k) = 1$. Hence we can simplify these expressions to

$$\overline{\phi}_k = -\frac{U'(c) f''(k) f'(k)}{U''(c) f'(k)} = -\frac{U'f''}{U''}$$

$$\overline{\phi}_c = -\frac{\beta U'(c) f''(k) + U''(c)}{\beta U''(c) f'(k)} = \frac{\beta U'f''}{U''} + 1$$

Moreover,

$$\overline{\varphi}_k = f'(k) \quad \text{and} \quad \overline{\varphi}_c = -1$$

The Jacobian matrix evaluated at the steady state is then

$$J(\overline{c}, \overline{k}) = \begin{bmatrix} \overline{\varphi}_k & \overline{\varphi}_c \\ \overline{\phi}_k & \overline{\phi}_c \end{bmatrix} = \begin{bmatrix} f' & -1 \\ \dfrac{-U'f''}{U''} & 1 + \dfrac{\beta U'f''}{U''} \end{bmatrix}$$

Hence,

$$\lambda_1 + \lambda_2 = \operatorname{tr} J = f' + \frac{\beta U'f''}{U''} + 1 > 2$$

because $f'(k) = 1/\beta > 1$ at the steady state,

$$\lambda_1\lambda_2 = \det J = f' + \frac{\beta f'U'f''}{U''} - \frac{U'f''}{U''} = f' + \frac{U'f''(\beta f' - 1)}{U''} = f' > 1$$

and

$$\Delta = \mathrm{tr}^2 - 4\det = \left(\frac{\beta U'f''}{U''} + (1+f')\right)^2 - 4f'$$

$$= \left(\frac{\beta U'f''}{U''}\right)^2 + 2\frac{\beta U'f''}{U''}(1+f') + (1+f')^2 - 4f'$$

$$= \left(\frac{\beta U'f''}{U''}\right)^2 + 2\frac{\beta U'f''}{U''}(1+f') + 1 + 2f' + (f')^2 - 4f'$$

$$= \left(\frac{\beta U'f''}{U''}\right)^2 + 2\frac{\beta U'f''}{U''}(1+f') + (1-f')^2 > 0$$

Because $\Delta > 0$, the eigenvalues of the Jacobian are distinct real numbers, and because both their product and their sum are positive, they are both positive. Finally, notice that

$$p(1) = 1 - \mathrm{tr} + \det = 1 - f' - (\beta U'f''/U'') - 1 + f' = -\frac{\beta U'f''}{U''} < 0$$

so λ_1 and λ_2 lie on different sides of 1 on the real line; see Section 2(*f*)(*ii*) of Chapter 10. Hence, the steady state is a saddle point, with one eigenvalue in (0, 1) and the other in (1, ∞).   □

Problem 2.11. Show that the function $U(k_t, k_{t+1})$ defined in the proof of Proposition 2.10 is concave.

From (1) and (2) in the proof of Proposition 2.10 we have

$$U_{11}(k_t, k_{t+1}) = U'[f(k_t) - k_{t+1}]f''(k_t) + f'(k_t)U''[f(k_t) - k_{t+1}]f'(k_t) < 0$$

$$U_{12}(k_t, k_{t+1}) = U_{21}(k_t, k_{t+1}) = -U''[f(k_t) - k_{t+1}]f'(k_t) > 0$$

$$U_{22}(k_t, k_{t+1}) = U''[f(k_t) - k_{t+1}] < 0$$

The determinant of the Jacobian matrix is given by

$$\begin{vmatrix} U_{11} & U_{12} \\ U_{21} & U_{22} \end{vmatrix} = \begin{vmatrix} U'f'' + U''(f')^2 & -f'U'' \\ -f'U'' & U'' \end{vmatrix} = [U'f'' + U''(f')^2]U'' - (f')^2(U'')^2 = U'f''U'' > 0$$

Hence, the Jacobian matrix is negative definite, and $U(k_t, k_{t+1})$ is concave (see Theorem 2.17 in Chapter 6).   □

Problem 4.1. A social planner maximizes the utility of the representative individual,

$$\int_0^\infty \frac{C_t^{1-\sigma}}{1-\sigma} e^{-\rho t} dt$$

subject to the resource constraint

$$\dot{K}_t = F(K_t, A_t) - \delta K_t - C_t, \quad \text{with } \frac{\dot{A}}{A} = g$$

Write the necessary conditions for this problem, and show that they reduce to equations (20) and (21) in the text whenever there are no taxes or subsidies.

Hence, under these conditions, the competitive equilibrium will be a social optimum.

The current-value Hamiltonian for the planner's problem is

$$H^c = \frac{C^{1-\sigma}}{1-\sigma} + \lambda\{F(K, A) - \delta K - C\}$$

This yields the following Pontryagin conditions:

$$\frac{\partial H^C}{\partial C} = C^{-\sigma} - \lambda = 0 \tag{1}$$

$$-\frac{\partial H^C}{\partial K} = -\lambda[F_k(K, A) - \delta] = \dot{\lambda} - \rho\lambda \tag{2}$$

$$\Rightarrow \frac{\dot{\lambda}}{\lambda} = \rho - f'(Z) - \delta \tag{2'}$$

Differentiating (1) with respect to time, and substituting (2') in the resulting expression, we have

$$\frac{\dot{C}}{C} = -\frac{1}{\sigma}\frac{\dot{\lambda}}{\lambda} = \frac{1}{\sigma}\{f'(Z) - \delta - \rho\} \tag{3}$$

This expression easily yields equation (20) in the text when $\tau_r = 0$. A simple manipulation of the planner's resource constraint will similarly yield equation (21) in the text when $x = 0$. $\qquad\square$

Problem 4.2. Assuming a Cobb-Douglas production function (i.e., $f(Z) = Z^\alpha$), solve for the steady-state savings rate as a function of τ_r and the other parameters of the model.

Using equations (22) and (23), the steady state savings ratio s^* is given by

$$s^* = \frac{Y - LC}{Y} = \frac{ALZ^\alpha - ALc}{ALZ^\alpha} = 1 - \frac{c}{Z^\alpha} = 1 - \frac{Z^\alpha - (\delta + g)Z}{Z^\alpha} = (\delta + g)Z^{1-\alpha}$$

from where

$$s^* = \frac{\alpha(\delta + g)}{\delta + ((g\sigma + \rho)/(1 - \tau_r))}$$

Hence, s^* is an increasing function of the elasticity of output with respect to capital (α), the rate of population growth (n), and the elasticity of intertemporal substitution ($1/\sigma$), and it is a decreasing function of the rate of discount (ρ) and the tax rate on capital income (τ_r). $\qquad\square$

Problem 4.3. One limitation of the approach we have followed is that it assumes that the economy is initially at a steady state. Otherwise the coefficients of the variational equation (the law of motion for Z_r) change over time, and this makes it difficult to evaluate $V'(\tau_r)$. It is still possible (and in fact much easier) to show that a zero tax on capital income is optimal by showing that when $\tau_r = 0$ the equilibrium path for the economy solves a closely related planning problem.

Consider, in particular, the problem faced by a social planner, similar to the one described in Problem 2.1, who maximizes the utility of the representative agent subject to the standard resource constraint and the additional restriction that he must "throw away" an amount of output equal to xA at each point in time. Write the planning problem, derive the necessary conditions for an optimum, and verify that they reduce to equations (20) and (21) when $\tau_r = 0$ in this system.

The planner maximizes

$$\int_0^\infty \frac{C_t^{1-\sigma}}{1-\sigma} e^{-\rho t} dt \tag{1}$$

subject to the resource constraint

$$\dot{K}_t = F(K_t, A_t) - \delta K_t - C_t - x A_t \tag{2}$$

where A increases over time at a constant exogenous rate g (i.e., $\dot{A}/A = g$). The necessary conditions for an optimum are almost exactly the same as in Problem 4.1, and in particular we have

$$\frac{\dot{C}}{C} = \frac{1}{\sigma}\{f'(Z) - \delta - \rho\}$$

from which it is easy to derive equation (20) with $\tau_r = 0$. In addition, the resource constraint can be written in the form

$$\frac{\dot{K}}{K} = \frac{f(Z)}{Z} - \delta - \frac{C/A}{Z} - \frac{x}{Z}$$

which is equation (18) in the text. Equation (21) then follows easily.

Hence, the planning problem yields exactly the same system of equations we have derived in the text, provided we set $\tau_r = 0$ in the latter. Hence, we can achieve the optimal path by eliminating taxes on interest. The equivalence to the planning problem brings out the reason why taxes on capital are inefficient. Because labor supply is perfectly inelastic, wage levies are, in effect, lump-sum taxes in this model, whereas taxes on capital affect the rate of return on savings and thus distort the intertemporal allocation of resources.   □

Problem 5.1

(i) Let $V_e(s)$ be the expected lifetime utility of an employed worker who shirks, $V_e(n)$ the expected lifetime utility of an employed non-shirker, and V_u the expected lifetime utility of an unemployed worker. Write the valuation equations defining $V_e(s)$ and $V_e(n)$, and explain their meaning.

Consider first a discrete-time formulation in which each period has length h and workers solve

$$\max_e \sum_{t=0}^\infty (w - E) h \beta(h)^t$$

Then the value of an employed shirker is given by

$$V_e(s) = (w - 0)h + \beta(h)\{(b + q)h V_u + [1 - (b + q)h] V_e(s)\} \tag{2}$$

In the stationary environment we have assumed, expected lifetime utility for a shirker tomorrow is the same as today. Thus if the worker chooses to shirk today, he will make the same choice tomorrow. Hence, we can define $V_e(s)$ recursively: If the worker shirks, today he gets the wage w times the length of the period. There is, however, a probability $(b + q)h$ that he will lose his job. If that is the case, next period he will get V_u; otherwise he will remain employed, continue to shirk, and get the same value $V_e(s)$ again. Because this will happen one period hence, the expression within the curly brackets (tomorrow's expected lifetime utility) must be multiplied by the time discount factor to get it in present-value terms.

To go to continuous time, let the discount factor be $\beta(h) = e^{-\rho h}$. Subtracting $\beta(h)V_e(s)$ from both sides of (2), dividing by h, and taking the limit as $h \to 0$, we have

$$\lim_{h \to 0} \frac{1 - \beta(h)}{h} V_e(s) = \lim_{h \to 0} w + \beta(h)(b+q)[V_u - V_e(s)]$$

or

$$\rho V_e(s) = w + (b+q)[V_u - V_e(s)] \tag{3}$$

$$\Rightarrow V_e(s) = \frac{w + (b+q)V_u}{\rho + b + q} \tag{3'}$$

Similarly, in the case of a non-shirker, the current "dividend" is $w - x$, and the probability of job separation is b. Hence,

$$\rho V_e(n) = (w - x) + b[V_u - V_e(n)] \tag{4}$$

$$\Rightarrow V_e(n) = \frac{w - x + bV_u}{\rho + b} \tag{4'}$$

(ii) An employed worker will choose not to shirk if $V_e(n) \geq V_e(s)$. Show that this "no-shirking" condition implies that $V_e(s) \geq V_u$, so that workers prefer to be employed, and use it to solve for the minimum wage w_m at which workers will find it optimal not to shirk. What factors determine w_m?

   An employed worker will choose not to shirk if $V_e(n) \geq V_e(s)$. Using (3) and (4), we can write the non-shirking condition (NSC) as

$$V_e(n) \geq V_e(s) \Rightarrow \frac{w + (b+q)V_u}{\rho + b + q} \geq \frac{w - x + bV_u}{\rho + b} \tag{5}$$

or, rearranging terms,

$$w \geq \rho V_u + (r + b + q)(x/q) \equiv w_m \tag{6}$$

Alternatively, using (3') and (4'), we have

$$q[V_e(s) - V_u] \geq x \tag{7}$$

Equation (6) defines w_m, the minimum wage the firm has to pay in order to prevent shirking. Note that w_m increases with the level of effort, the expected utility of unemployed workers (which lowers the cost of job loss), the exogenous quit rate (if one is leaving, one may as well cheat), and the discount rate ("punishment," which comes in the future, is discounted more heavily); it decreases with the probability of detection.

   Equation (7) tells us that in order to ensure that workers will not shirk, wages have to be high enough that workers will prefer to work. This implies that the unemployment rate will be positive – otherwise, a worker who was fired could get another job immediately, and $V_e(s) = V_u$, so (7) could not hold. □

Problem 5.2. We will now characterize a stationary equilibrium of the model.

(i) Let w_u be the unemployment benefit. Derive the expected lifetime utility of an unemployed worker, V_u, as a function of w_u and the value of an employed worker, V_e.

   By the same reasoning as in Problem 5.1, the value of an unemployed worker, V_u, must satisfy

$$\rho V_u = w_u + a(V_e - V_u) \tag{9}$$

where a is the rate at which workers find jobs and come out of the pool of unemployed.

(ii) Using the expressions for V_e $(= V_e(n))$ and V_u derived earlier, solve for V_e and V_u as functions of a and the parameters of the model. Rewrite the no-shirking condition, replacing V_u by its equilibrium value. How do unemployment benefits and the probability of finding employment affect the minimum non-shirking wage?

Using (4) and (9), we have

$$\rho V_e - \rho V_u = (w - x) + b(V_u - V_e) - w_u - a(V_e - V_u)$$

from where

$$V_e - V_u = \frac{(w - x) - w_u}{\rho + a + b} \tag{10}$$

Substituting (10) into (4) and (9), we obtain

$$\rho V_e = \frac{(\rho + a)(w - x) + bw_u}{\rho + a + b} \tag{11}$$

$$\rho V_u = \frac{a(w - x) + (\rho + b)w_u}{\rho + a + b} \tag{12}$$

Substituting (12) into (6), with $w = w_m$,

$$w_m = \rho V_u + (r + b + q)(x/q) = \frac{a(w_m - x) + (\rho + b)w_u}{\rho + a + b}$$

and rearranging, the no-shirking condition can be written

$$w \geq w_m \equiv w_u + x + (x/q)(\rho + a + b) \tag{12}$$

Hence, the critical wage increases with the size of the unemployment benefit and the rate of flow out of unemployment, both factors that tend to increase V_u.

(iii) Let N be the given labor supply. In a steady-state equilibrium, the flows into unemployment and out of it must be equal. Using this condition, solve for the probability of finding employment, a, as a function of b, L, and N, and substitute the result into the no-shirking condition. Interpret the resulting condition. The equilibrium wage and unemployment levels are determined by the intersection of the non-shirking condition and the labor demand schedule $f'(L) = w_m$. Draw both functions in the (w, L) plane, and verify that the equilibrium involves an excess supply of labor.

In a steady-state equilibrium, the flow into unemployment (bL) and out of it ($a(N - L)$) must be equal; hence,

$$a = \frac{bL}{N - L} \tag{13}$$

Substituting this expression into (12), the no-shirking condition can be rewritten

$$w \geq w_u + x + (x/q)\left(\rho + \frac{bN}{N - L}\right) \equiv w_m \tag{NSC}$$

This expression defines an upward-sloping curve in the (w, L) plane, as illustrated in Figure A13.4. As employment increases, wages must also rise, to prevent shirking. The reason is that a decrease in the unemployment rate tends to lower the expected value of the "punishment" to detected shirkers.

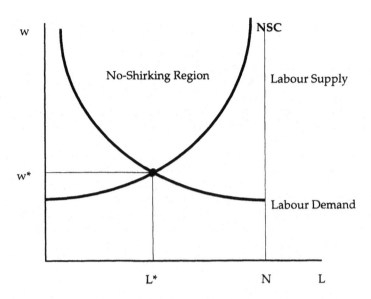

Figure A13.4. Equilibrium wage and employment levels.

To compensate for this, wages must rise, so that the loss of being fired increases.

The equilibrium wage and unemployment levels are determined by the intersection of the non-shirking condition and the labor demand schedule $f'(L) = w_m$, as illustrated in Figure A13.4. As noted earlier, the equilibrium will involve involuntary unemployment. In spite of the excess supply of labor, w^* is the equilibrium wage, because firms have no incentive to either increase (because workers are supplying effort) or decrease wages (because they are on their labor demand schedule). Unemployed workers would be happy to take a job, but cannot make a credible commitment not to shirk if the wage is lowered.   □

Problem 5.3

(i) Derive an expression that describes the evolution of the unemployment rate over time as a function of the instantaneous rate of separation (s) and the probability of finding employment, $\theta^{1-\alpha}$. Set $\dot{u} = 0$ and solve for the steady-state unemployment rate as a function of the rates of flow into and out of unemployment (assuming θ is constant).

The instantaneous change in the unemployment rate is the difference between the flows into and out of unemployment normalized by the total population. At a given point in time, a fraction $(1-u)$ of the population is employed. Multiplying this number by the instantaneous probability of separation, s, we obtain the flow into unemployment. Similarly, the flow into employment is equal to the current unemployment rate times the probability of finding a job, given by (3). Hence, we have

$$\dot{u} = (1-u)s - u\theta^{1-\alpha} \qquad (4)$$

Setting $\dot{u}$ equal to zero in (4), we can solve for the steady-state rate of unemployment as a function of θ:

$$u = \frac{s}{s + \theta^{1-\alpha}} \tag{5}$$

(ii) Let V be the value of a vacancy, J the value of a filled job, and r the discount rate. Taking into account the relevant transition probabilities and the flows of costs and benefits for an occupied job and vacant job, write the valuation equations for these two assets, J and V. Explain their meaning. Using the two asset-valuation equations (subtract one from the other), derive an expression for $J - V$ as a function of y, c, w, r, and the relevant transition probabilities.

    As in the discussion in Section 1 of the text, the general idea is the same for all the valuation equations: The expected return on each "asset," given by its current dividend plus expected capital gain expressed as a fraction of its value, must be equal to the discount (interest) rate. In the case of a vacant firm, the dividend is negative (the maintenance cost, c), and the expected capital gain is equal to the difference between the value of a filled job, J, and that of a vacant one, V, multiplied by the instantaneous probability that a vacancy will be filled, given in equation (2). Hence,

$$rV = -c + \theta^{-\alpha}(J - V) \tag{6}$$

In the case of an active firm, the dividend is the current profit (the difference between output and the wage), and the expected capital gain depends on the probability (s) that the match will be exogenously destroyed:

$$rJ = y - w + s(V - J) \tag{7}$$

Using these two expressions,

$$rJ - rV = y - w - s(J - V) + c - \theta^{-\alpha}(J - V)$$

Rearranging terms and solving for $J - V$,

$$J - V = \frac{y + c - w}{r + s + \theta^{-\alpha}} \tag{8}$$

(iii) Let E and U be the "values" of an employed worker and an unemployed worker, respectively. Write and explain the corresponding asset valuation equations, and derive an expression for $E - U$.

    By the same logic as in (ii), we have

$$rU = b + \theta^{1-\alpha}(E - U) \tag{9}$$

$$rE = w + s(U - E) \tag{10}$$

from where

$$r(E - U) = w - s(E - U) - b - \theta^{1-\alpha}(E - U) \tag{11}$$

$$\Rightarrow E - U = \frac{w - b}{r + s + \theta^{1-\alpha}} \qquad \square$$

Problem 5.4. Using the results of Problem 5.3, solve for the equilibrium wage.

    We have to solve

$$\max_{w}(E - U)^{\beta}(J - V)^{1-\beta} = \left(\frac{w - b}{r + s + \theta^{1-\alpha}}\right)^{\beta}\left(\frac{y + c - w}{r + s + \theta^{-\alpha}}\right)^{1-\beta}$$

Taking logs, this is equivalent to

$$\max \beta \ln(w - b) + (1 - \beta)\ln(y + c - w)$$

Setting the derivative of this function with respect to w equal to zero,

$$\frac{\beta}{w - b} - \frac{1 - \beta}{y + c - w} = 0 \Rightarrow \beta(y + c - w) = (1 - \beta)(w - b)$$

and solving for w,

$$w = \beta(y + c) + (1 - \beta)b \tag{12}$$

$\square$

Problem 5.5. In equilibrium, new firms enter until the value of a vacant job drops to zero, i.e., until $V = 0$.

(i) Using the valuation equations for V and J, show that

$$\frac{y - w}{r + s} = c\theta^\alpha \tag{13}$$

With $V = 0$ the valuation equations (6) and (7) yield

$$J = c\theta^\alpha \quad \text{and} \quad J = \frac{y - w}{r + s}$$

Thus

$$\frac{y - w}{r + s} = c\theta^\alpha \tag{13}$$

a condition that summarizes the "supply of jobs" in equilibrium.

(ii) Using equation (13), along with the expression for the equilibrium wage obtained in Problem 5.4 and the formula for the steady-state unemployment rate obtained in Problem 5.3, solve for the equilibrium values of u, w, and θ. Draw a diagram in the (u, θ) plane illustrating the determination of equilibrium.

Collecting previous results, we have

$$y - w = c(r + s)\theta^\alpha \tag{13'}$$
$$w = \beta(y + c) + (1 - \beta)b \tag{12}$$

$$u = \frac{s}{s + \theta^{1-\alpha}} \tag{5}$$

Using the first two equations, we can solve for θ^*,

$$\theta^\alpha = \frac{(1 - \beta)(y - b) - \beta c}{c(r + s)} \tag{14}$$

and equation (5) then gives the equilibrium rate of unemployment. Graphically, equation (14) defines a vertical line in the (θ, u) plane, and equation (5) a downward-sloping line, as shown in Figure A13.5.

Notice that in order for θ^* to be positive, it must be the case that

$$y - b \geq \frac{\beta c}{1 - \beta} \tag{15}$$

Hence, we need to impose this condition on the parameters in order to get a sensible equilibrium.

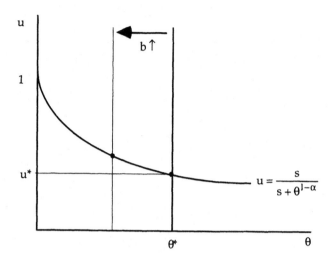

Figure A13.5. Determination of the steady-state unemployment rate.

(iii) What are the effects on the equilibrium unemployment rate of an increase in workers' bargaining power (β), an increase in the unemployment benefit (b), and an increase in the probability of structural shocks (s)?

Using equation (14), it is clear that an increase in b reduces the equilibrium value of θ, shifting the vertical line to the left. Because the other equation is not affected, an increase in the unemployment benefit increases the equilibrium rate of unemployment. The effect on θ of an increase in s is similar. Moreover, this parameter change also shifts the second line upward, which raises the unemployment rate further. Finally, it is easy to see, using equations (14) and (15), that an increase in workers' bargaining power also increases the unemployment rate.   □

Problem 5.6. Define the variables

$$X = \frac{c}{Z^\alpha} \quad \text{and} \quad R = Z^{\alpha-1} \tag{6}$$

(i) Rewrite the system (4)–(5) in terms of X and R. Solve for the steady-state values of X and Z.

Notice that

$$\frac{c}{Z} = \frac{c}{Z^\alpha Z^{1-\alpha}} = XR$$

Hence, we can rewrite (4) and (5) in the form

$$\frac{\dot{c}}{c} = \frac{1}{\sigma}\{\alpha R - (\rho + \delta)\} - g \tag{4'}$$

$$\frac{\dot{Z}}{Z} = (1 - X)R - (\delta + g + n) \tag{5'}$$

We can use these expressions to solve for the steady-state values of X and R. Setting $\dot{c}$ and $\dot{Z}$ equal to zero, we have

$$R^* = \frac{\rho + \delta + g\sigma}{\alpha} \tag{7}$$

$$S^* = 1 - X^* = \frac{\delta + g + n}{R} = \frac{\alpha(\delta + g + n)}{\rho + \delta + g\sigma} \tag{8}$$

Notice that the condition for utility to be bounded, given in equation (3), implies that $S^* = 1 - X^* < \alpha$.

Using (6), moreover, we have

$$\frac{\dot{X}}{X} = \frac{\dot{c}}{c} - \alpha \frac{\dot{Z}}{Z} = \frac{1}{\sigma}\{\alpha R - (\rho + \delta)\} - g - \alpha(1 - X)R + \alpha(\delta + g + n)$$

or

$$\frac{\dot{X}}{X} = \alpha R\left(\frac{1}{\sigma} - (1 - X)\right) - \frac{\rho + \delta + g\sigma}{\sigma} + \alpha(\delta + g + n) \tag{9}$$

and

$$\frac{\dot{R}}{R} = (\alpha - 1)\frac{\dot{Z}}{Z} = (1 - \alpha)(\delta + g + n) - (1 - \alpha)(1 - X)R \tag{10}$$

(ii) Construct the log-linearization of the system obtained in (i). Compute the eigenvalues of its coefficient matrix, and show that the steady state is a saddle point. Compute the eigenvector associated with the negative eigenvalue, and relate the slope of the saddle path to the size of the negative eigenvalue. Does anything look familiar?

Let $x = \ln X$ and $r = \ln R$. Then the system (9)–(10) can be written in the form

$$\dot{x} = \alpha e^r\left(\frac{1}{\sigma} - (1 - e^x)\right) - \frac{\rho + \delta + g\sigma}{\sigma} + \alpha(\delta + g + n) \equiv F(x, r)$$

$$\dot{r} = (1 - \alpha)(\delta + g + n) - (1 - \alpha)(1 - e^x)e^r \equiv G(x, r) \tag{10'}$$

Evaluating the partial derivatives of $F(\ )$ and $G(\ )$ at the steady state, we obtain

$$F_x = \alpha e^r e^x = \alpha R^* X^*$$

$$F_r = \alpha e^r\left(\frac{1}{\sigma} - (1 - e^x)\right) = \alpha R^*\left(\frac{1}{\sigma} - (1 - X^*)\right) = \frac{\rho + \delta + g\sigma}{\sigma} - (\delta + g + n)$$

$$G_x = (1 - \alpha)e^r e^x = (1 - \alpha)R^* X^*$$

$$G_r = -(1 - \alpha)(1 - e^x)e^r = -(1 - \alpha)(1 - X^*)R^* = -(1 - \alpha)(\delta + g + n)$$

Hence, the Jacobian of the system is of the form

$$J = \begin{bmatrix} F_x & F_r \\ G_x & G_r \end{bmatrix} = \begin{bmatrix} \alpha R^* X^* & \alpha R^*\left(\frac{1}{\sigma} - (1 - X^*)\right) \\ (1 - \alpha)R^* X^* & -(1 - \alpha)(1 - X^*)R^* \end{bmatrix}$$

and we have

$$\text{tr } J = \alpha R^* X^* - (1 - \alpha)(1 - X^*)R^* = -(1 - X^* - \alpha)R^* > 0$$

$$\det J = -(1 - \alpha)(1 - X^*)\alpha X^* R^{*2} - (1 - \alpha)\alpha X^* R^{*2}\left(\frac{1}{\sigma} - (1 - X^*)\right)$$

$$= -\frac{(1 - \alpha)\alpha X^* R^{*2}}{\sigma} < 0$$

Notice that because $\det J < 0$, the steady state is a saddle point, as claimed.

The eigenvalues of the system are given by

$$-\lambda, \omega = \frac{\text{tr} \pm \sqrt{\text{tr}^2 - 4\det}}{2} = \frac{\text{tr}}{2}\left(1 \pm \sqrt{1 - \frac{4\det}{\text{tr}^2}}\right)$$

where

$$\Delta = \text{tr}^2 - 4\det = (1 - X^* - \alpha)^2 R^{*2} + \frac{4(1-\alpha)\alpha X^* R^{*2}}{\sigma}$$

$$= R^{*2}\left((1 - X^* - \alpha)^2 + \frac{4(1-\alpha)\alpha X^*}{\sigma}\right) > 0$$

Let e_λ be the second component of the eigenvector corresponding to the negative eigenvalue, $-\lambda$, and normalize the first component to 1, so that e_λ is the inverse of the slope of the saddle path at the steady state. Then e_λ solves

$$J e_\lambda = -\lambda e_\lambda \Leftrightarrow \begin{bmatrix} F_x & F_r \\ G_x & G_r \end{bmatrix}\begin{bmatrix} 1 \\ e_\lambda \end{bmatrix} = \begin{bmatrix} -\lambda \\ -\lambda e_\lambda \end{bmatrix}$$

from where

$$G_x + G_r e_\lambda = -\lambda e_\lambda$$

$$\Rightarrow \frac{1}{e_\lambda} = \frac{-(G_r + \lambda)}{G_x} = \frac{(1-\alpha)(\delta + g + n) - \lambda}{(1-\alpha)R^* X^*} \tag{11}$$

Hence, the slope of the saddle path depends on the sign of the difference $(1 - \alpha)(\delta + g + n) - \lambda$, where the first term, as the reader will recall from Section 4(a) in Chapter 11, is the rate of convergence in the Solow model. As we will see later, this difference can be either positive or negative, so in principle the savings rate can be either an increasing or decreasing function of the interest rate, depending on parameter values. □

Problem 5.7. Next, we will consider a special case. Assume that the following restriction on the parameters holds:

$$\rho + \delta + g\sigma = \alpha\sigma(\delta + n + g) \tag{12}$$

Construct the phase diagram for the system, and compute its negative eigenvalue and the associated eigenvector.

Given condition (12), equation (9) reduces to

$$\dot{x} = \frac{\dot{X}}{X} = \alpha R\left(\frac{1}{\sigma} - (1 - X)\right) \tag{13}$$

Hence, $\dot{x} \geq 0$ if

$$\frac{1}{\sigma} \geq (1 - X)$$

$$\Leftrightarrow X \geq \frac{\sigma - 1}{\sigma} \equiv X^* \tag{14}$$

Notice that, given (3), equation (12) requires that $\sigma > 1/\alpha > 1$; hence $X^* > 0$. Figure A13.6 shows the corresponding phase line and arrows of motion.

Working with

$$\dot{r} = \frac{\dot{R}}{R} = (1 - \alpha)(\delta + g + n) - (1 - \alpha)(1 - X)R \tag{10}$$

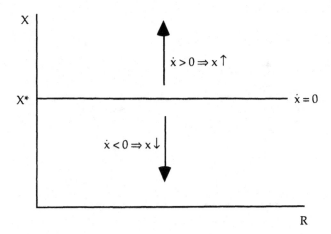

Figure A13.6. The $\dot{x} = 0$ phase line.

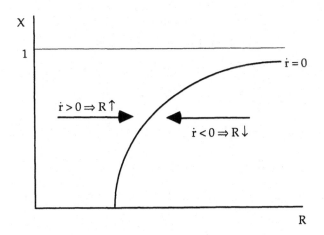

Figure A13.7. The $\dot{r} = 0$ phase line.

the equation of the $\dot{r} = 0$ phase line is

$$X = 1 - \frac{\delta + g + n}{R} \tag{15}$$

and

$$\frac{\partial \dot{r}}{\partial R} = -(1 - \alpha)(1 - X) < 0$$

Hence, the $\dot{r} = 0$ phase line is upward-sloping, with a positive R intercept and a horizontal asymptote at $x = 1$, and R decreases over time in the region to the right of the phase line, as shown in Figure A13.7.

Combining the two phase lines, we obtain the phase diagram shown in Figure A13.8. Notice that, given the pattern of the arrows of motion, the saddle path coincides with the $\dot{x} = 0$ phase line. Hence, the savings ratio remains constant over time in equilibrium, as in the Solow model.

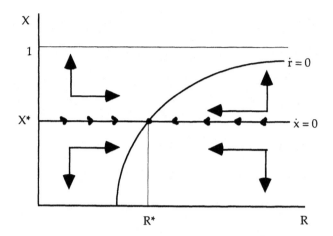

Figure A13.8. Phase diagram.

To compute the eigenvalues of the system, notice that under the assumption

$$\rho + \delta + g\sigma = \alpha\sigma(\delta + n + g) \tag{12}$$

equations (7) and (8) become

$$R^* = \frac{\rho + \delta + g\sigma}{\alpha} = \sigma(\delta + n + g) \tag{16}$$

$$1 - X^* = \frac{1}{\sigma} \Rightarrow X^* = \frac{\sigma - 1}{\sigma} \tag{17}$$

Using these expressions and previous results, we have

$$\operatorname{tr} J = -(1 - X^* - \alpha)R^* = -\left(\frac{1}{\sigma} - \alpha\right)\sigma(\delta + n + g) = -(1 - \alpha\sigma)(\delta + n + g)$$

and

$$\frac{\Delta}{R^{*2}} = (1 - X^* - \alpha)^2 + \frac{4(1-\alpha)\alpha X^*}{\sigma} = \frac{(1-\alpha\sigma)^2}{\sigma^2} - \frac{4(1-\alpha)\alpha}{\sigma}\frac{1-\sigma}{\sigma}$$

$$= \frac{1}{\sigma^2}\left[(1-\alpha\sigma)^2 - 4(1-\alpha)\alpha(1-\sigma)\right]$$

To simplify this expression, notice that

$$(1 - \alpha\sigma)^2 = [(1-\alpha) + \alpha(1-\sigma)]^2 = (1-\alpha)^2 + \alpha^2(1-\sigma)^2 + 2(1-\alpha)\alpha(1-\sigma)$$

Hence,

$$\frac{\Delta}{R^{*2}} = \frac{1}{\sigma^2}\left[(1-\alpha)^2 + \alpha^2(1-\sigma)^2 - 2(1-\alpha)\alpha(1-\sigma)\right]$$

$$= \frac{1}{\sigma^2}[(1-\alpha) - \alpha(1-\sigma)]^2 = \frac{(1-2\alpha+\alpha\sigma)^2}{\sigma^2}$$

and, using (16),

$$\Delta = (1 - 2\alpha + \alpha\sigma)^2(\delta + n + g)^2$$

Now, the negative eigenvalue is given by

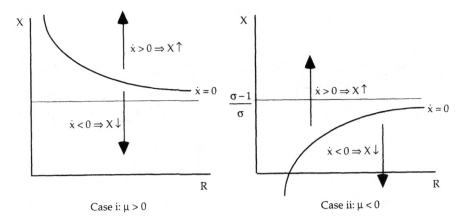

Figure A13.9. The $\dot{x} = 0$ phase line.

$$-\lambda = \frac{1}{2}(\mathrm{tr} - \sqrt{\Delta}) = \frac{-(\delta + n + g)}{2}[(1 - \alpha\sigma) + (1 - 2\alpha + \alpha\sigma)] = -(1 - \alpha)(\delta + n + g)$$

and, using (11),

$$\frac{1}{e_\lambda} = \frac{(1 - \alpha)(\delta + g + n) - \lambda}{(1 - \alpha)R^* X^*} = 0 \qquad \qquad \Box$$

Problem 5.8. Let us now return to the general case of the model. Define the parameter μ by

$$1 + \mu \equiv \frac{\rho + \delta + g\sigma}{\alpha\sigma(\delta + n + g)} \tag{18}$$

and notice that if $\mu = 0$, then we are in Problem 5.7. Write the negative eigenvalue of the system and the corresponding eigenvector as functions of μ, and relate the slope of the saddle path to the sign of μ. Draw the phase diagram of the system for $\mu > 0$ and $\mu < 0$.

Using (18), equation (9) can be written

$$\dot{x} = \frac{\dot{X}}{X} = \alpha R\left(\frac{1}{\sigma} - (1 - X)\right) - \frac{\rho + \delta + g\sigma}{\sigma} + \alpha(\delta + g + n)$$

$$= \alpha R\left(\frac{1}{\sigma} - (1 - X)\right) - (1 + \mu)\alpha(\delta + g + n) + \alpha(\delta + g + n)$$

or

$$\dot{x} = \alpha R\left(\frac{1}{\sigma} - (1 - X)\right) - \mu\alpha(\delta + g + n) \tag{19}$$

Hence, $\dot{x} \geq 0$ if

$$X \geq \frac{\mu\alpha(\delta + g + n)}{\alpha R} + \frac{\sigma - 1}{\sigma} \tag{20}$$

Hence, the $\dot{x} = 0$ phase line has a horizontal asymptote at $X = (\sigma - 1)/\sigma$. If $\mu > 0$, the phase line lies above the asymptote and is downward-sloping, and if $\mu < 0$ the line lies below the asymptote and is upward-sloping. In both cases, X increases over time in the region above the phase line, as shown in Figure A13.9.

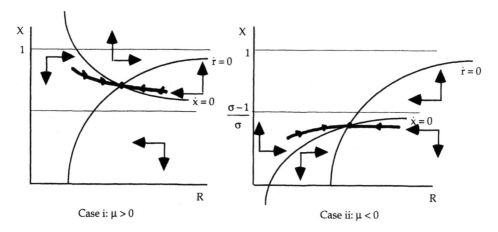

Figure A13.10. Phase diagram.

Combining this figure with the $\dot{r} = 0$ phase line, which does not depend on μ, we obtain the phase diagram shown in Figure A13.10. Notice that if $\mu > 0$, the consumption rate is a decreasing function of the interest factor. If the economy approaches its steady-state capital/labor ratio from below, the interest factor decreases over time, and the consumption rate increases. Hence, the savings rate falls with income. If $\mu < 0$, on the other hand, the savings rate increases with income as the economy approaches its steady state.

To compute the negative eigenvalue, notice that with

$$1 + \mu \equiv \frac{\rho + \delta + g\sigma}{\alpha\sigma(\delta + n + g)} \tag{18}$$

equations (7) and (8) become

$$R^* = \frac{\rho + \delta + g\sigma}{\alpha} = (1 + \mu)\sigma(\delta + n + g) \tag{21}$$

$$1 - X^* = \frac{\alpha(\delta + g + n)}{\rho + \delta + g\sigma} = \frac{1}{(1 + \mu)\sigma} \Rightarrow X^* = \frac{(1 + \mu)\sigma - 1}{(1 + \mu)\sigma} \tag{22}$$

Using these expressions and previous results, we have

$$\operatorname{tr} J = -(1 - X^* - \alpha)R^* = -\left(\frac{1}{(1 + \mu)\sigma} - \alpha\right)(1 + \mu)\sigma(\delta + n + g)$$

$$= -[1 - \alpha(1 + \mu)\sigma](\delta + n + g)$$

and

$$\frac{\Delta}{R^{*2}} = (1 - X^* - \alpha)^2 + \frac{4(1 - \alpha)\alpha X^*}{\sigma} = \frac{[1 - \alpha(1 + \mu)\sigma]^2}{(1 + \mu)^2\sigma^2} - \frac{4(1 - \alpha)\alpha}{\sigma}\frac{1 - (1 + \mu)\sigma}{(1 + \mu)\sigma}$$

$$= \frac{1}{(1 + \mu)^2\sigma^2}\left\{[1 - \alpha(1 + \mu)\sigma]^2 - 4(1 - \alpha)\alpha(1 + \mu)[1 - (1 + \mu)\sigma]\right\}$$

To simplify this expression, notice that

$$[1 - \alpha(1 + \mu)\sigma]^2 = \{(1 - \alpha) + \alpha[1 - (1 + \mu)\sigma]\}^2$$
$$= (1 - \alpha)^2 + \alpha^2[1 - (1 + \mu)\sigma]^2 + 2(1 - \alpha)\alpha[1 - (1 + \mu)\sigma]$$

Hence,

$$\frac{(1 + \mu)^2 \sigma^2}{R^{*2}} \Delta = (1 - \alpha)^2 + \alpha^2[1 - (1 + \mu)\sigma]^2 + 2(1 - \alpha)\alpha[1 - (1 + \mu)\sigma]$$
$$- 4(1 - \alpha)\alpha[1 - (1 + \mu)\sigma] - 4\mu(1 - \alpha)\alpha[1 - (1 + \mu)\sigma]$$
$$= (1 - \alpha)^2 + \alpha^2[1 - (1 + \mu)\sigma]^2 - 2(1 - \alpha)\alpha[1 - (1 + \mu)\sigma]$$
$$- 4\mu(1 - \alpha)\alpha[1 - (1 + \mu)\sigma]$$
$$= \{(1 - \alpha) - \alpha[1 - (1 + \mu)\sigma]\}^2 - 4\mu(1 - \alpha)\alpha[1 - (1 + \mu)\sigma]$$
$$= [1 - 2\alpha + \alpha(1 + \mu)\sigma]^2 - 4\mu(1 - \alpha)\alpha[1 - (1 + \mu)\sigma]$$
$$= [1 - 2\alpha + \alpha(1 + \mu)\sigma]^2[1 - B(\mu)]^2$$

with

$$1 - B(\mu) = \sqrt{1 - \frac{\mu 4(1 - \alpha)\alpha[1 - (1 + \mu)\sigma]}{[1 - 2\alpha + \alpha(1 + \mu)\sigma]^2}} \tag{23}$$

where the expression under the square-root radical is positive, because we know that $\Delta > 0$.

Using (21),

$$\Delta = \frac{R^{*2}}{(1 + \mu)^2 \sigma^2}[1 - 2\alpha + \alpha(1 + \mu)\sigma]^2[1 - B(\mu)]$$
$$= (\delta + n + g)^2[1 - 2\alpha + \alpha(1 + \mu)\sigma]^2[1 - B(\mu)]^2$$

Now, the negative eigenvalue is given by

$$-\lambda = \frac{1}{2}(\text{tr} - \sqrt{\Delta}) = \frac{-(\delta + n + g)}{2}\{[1 - \alpha(1 + \mu)\sigma] + [1 - 2\alpha + \alpha(1 + \mu)\sigma][1 - B(\mu)]\}$$
$$= \frac{-(\delta + n + g)}{2}\{2 - 2\alpha - B(\mu)[1 - 2\alpha + \alpha(1 + \mu)\sigma]\}$$

or

$$-\lambda = -[1 - \alpha - D(\mu)](\delta + n + g) \tag{24}$$

where

$$D(\mu) = \frac{B(\mu)[1 - 2\alpha + \alpha(1 + \mu)\sigma]}{2} \tag{25}$$

Using (11), (21), and (22),

$$\frac{1}{e_\lambda} = \frac{(1 - \alpha)(\delta + g + n) - \lambda}{(1 - \alpha)R^* X^*} = \frac{D(\mu)(\delta + n + g)}{(1 - \alpha)R^* X^*} = \frac{D(\mu)}{(1 - \alpha)(1 + \mu)\sigma X^*} = \frac{D(\mu)}{(1 - \alpha)[(1 + \mu)\sigma - 1]} \tag{26}$$

Notice that by (22), $X^* > 0$ requires

$$(1 + \mu)\sigma - 1 > 0 \tag{27}$$

Hence, the denominator of (26) is positive, and

$$(1-\alpha)-\alpha[1-(1+\mu)\sigma]=(1-\alpha)+\alpha[(1+\mu)\sigma-1]>0$$

so the factor multiplying $B(\mu)$ in (25) is also positive, and it follows that the sign of the slope of the saddle path is the same as the sign of $B(\mu)$. Now,

$$B(\mu)=1-\sqrt{1-\frac{\mu 4(1-\alpha)\alpha[1-(1+\mu)\sigma]}{[1-2\alpha+\alpha(1+\mu)\sigma]^2}}=1-\sqrt{1+\frac{\mu 4(1-\alpha)\alpha[(1+\mu)\sigma-1]}{[1-2\alpha+\alpha(1+\mu)\sigma]^2}}$$

By (27), the expression multiplying μ under the square-root radical is also positive. Thus, the slope of the saddle path is positive if the expression under the radical is less than 1 (i.e., if $\mu<0$). This agrees with our earlier graphical analysis. $\square$

Problem 5.9

(i) Taking as given the time path of p, write the necessary conditions for a solution to the consumer's problem. Derive an equation describing the evolution of consumption over time.

From the current-value Hamiltonian

$$H^c=\frac{c^{1-\sigma}}{1-\sigma}+\lambda\{(1-\tau)k^{1-\alpha}p^\alpha-c\}$$

we obtain

$$\frac{\partial H^c}{\partial c}=c^{-\sigma}-\lambda=0$$

$$\Rightarrow c^{-\sigma}=\lambda \tag{4}$$

$$-\frac{\partial H^c}{\partial k}=-\lambda\{(1-\tau)(1-\alpha)k^{-\alpha}p^\alpha\}=\dot\lambda-\rho\lambda$$

$$\Rightarrow \frac{\dot\lambda}{\lambda}=\rho-(1-\tau)(1-\alpha)k^{-\alpha}p^\alpha \tag{5}$$

Using (4) and (5),

$$\frac{\dot c}{c}=\frac{-1}{\sigma}\frac{\dot\lambda}{\lambda}=\frac{1}{\sigma}\{(1-\tau)(1-\alpha)k^{-\alpha}p^\alpha-\rho\} \tag{6}$$

(ii) Assume that $p=\tau y$, that is, that all tax revenue is used to finance public services. Substituting the production function in this last expression, solve for p as a function of τ and k. Substitute the result into the flow budget constraint and the transition equation for consumption. Call γ the growth rate of consumption, obtained from this step, and let β be the coefficient of k in the law of motion for k. Notice that β can be written as a simple function of γ.

We have $p=\tau y=\tau k^{1-\alpha}p^\alpha$. Solving for p,

$$p=\tau^{1/(1-\alpha)}k \tag{7}$$

and substituting (7) into (3) and (6),

$$\dot k=(1-\tau)\tau^{\alpha/(1-\alpha)}k-c\equiv\beta k-c \tag{3'}$$

$$\frac{\dot c}{c}=\frac{1}{\sigma}\{(1-\tau)(1-\alpha)\tau^{\alpha/(1-\alpha)}-\rho\}\equiv\gamma \tag{6'}$$

Notice that (6') can be written

$$\gamma = \frac{1}{\sigma}\{(1-\alpha)\beta - \rho\}$$

Hence,

$$\beta = \frac{\rho + \gamma\sigma}{1-\alpha} \qquad (8)$$

(iii) Observe that consumption grows at a constant exponential rate. Hence, once we determine its initial level, we have characterized its entire path. Integrating the flow budget constraint and imposing the transversality condition, we obtain

$$k_0 = \int_0^\infty c_t e^{-\beta t}\, dt \qquad (9)$$

Use this expression to solve for c_0.

Solving the integral in (9),

$$k_0 = \int_0^\infty c_t e^{-\beta t}\, dt = \int_0^\infty c_0 e^{\gamma t} e^{-\beta t}\, dt = \int_0^\infty c_0 e^{-(\beta-\gamma)t}\, dt = \frac{c_0}{\beta-\gamma}$$

from where

$$c_0 = (\beta - \gamma)k_0 \qquad (10)$$

where, by (8),

$$\beta - \gamma = \frac{\rho - (1-\sigma-\alpha)\gamma}{1-\alpha} \qquad (11)$$
$$\square$$

Problem 5.10

(i) Substitute the equilibrium path of consumption into the agent's objective function to obtain utility as a function of γ (or τ), $U(\gamma)$. What condition must we impose in order to guarantee that utility is bounded? Assume that this condition holds.

We shall write the utility of the representative agent as a function of γ. Using (10) and (11), we have

$$U(\gamma) = \int_0^\infty \frac{c_t^{1-\sigma}}{1-\sigma} e^{-\rho t}\, dt = \frac{1}{1-\sigma} \int_0^\infty c_0^{1-\sigma} e^{(1-\sigma)\gamma t} e^{-\rho t}\, dt$$

$$= \frac{c_0^{1-\sigma}}{(1-\sigma)[\rho-(1-\sigma)\gamma]} = \frac{k_0^{1-\sigma}(\beta-\gamma)^{1-\sigma}}{(1-\sigma)[\rho-(1-\sigma)\gamma]} = \frac{k_0^{1-\sigma}}{(1-\alpha)^{1-\sigma}} \frac{[\rho-(1-\sigma-\alpha)\gamma]^{1-\sigma}}{(1-\sigma)[\rho-(1-\sigma)\gamma]}$$
$$(12)$$

Hence, utility will be bounded whenever

$$\rho - (1-\sigma)\gamma > 0 \qquad (13)$$

We shall assume in what follows that this condition holds.

(ii) Find the optimal value of τ. Does the result "look right"? Why or why not?

Notice that we can write (12) in the form

$$U(\gamma) = B\frac{[\rho-(1-\sigma-\alpha)\gamma]^{1-\sigma}}{(1-\sigma)[\rho-(1-\sigma)\gamma]} \qquad (12')$$

where

$$B = \frac{k_0^{1-\sigma}}{(1-\alpha)^{1-\sigma}}$$

is a positive constant. Differentiating (12′),

$$U'(\gamma) = B \frac{[(1-\sigma)[\rho-(1-\sigma)\gamma](1-\sigma)[\rho-(1-\sigma-\alpha)\gamma]^{-\sigma}][-(1-\sigma-\alpha)] - [\rho-(1-\sigma-\alpha)\gamma]^{1-\sigma}(1-\sigma)[-(1-\sigma)]}{(1-\sigma)^2[\rho-(1-\sigma)\gamma]^2}$$

$$= B \frac{\left[-(1-\sigma)^2[\rho-(1-\sigma)\gamma][\rho-(1-\sigma-\alpha)\gamma]^{-\sigma}\right](1-\sigma-\alpha) + [\rho-(1-\sigma-\alpha)\gamma]^{1-\sigma}(1-\sigma)^2}{(1-\sigma)^2[\rho-(1-\sigma)\gamma]^2}$$

$$= B \frac{[\rho-(1-\sigma-\alpha)\gamma]^{-\sigma}}{[\rho-(1-\sigma)\gamma]^2} \{[\rho-(1-\sigma-\alpha)\gamma] - (1-\sigma-\alpha)[\rho-(1-\sigma)\gamma]\}$$

Hence, $U'(\gamma) > 0$ provided

$$\rho - (1-\sigma)\gamma + \alpha\gamma > (1-\sigma-\alpha)[\rho-(1-\sigma)\gamma] \Leftrightarrow \alpha\gamma > -(\sigma+\alpha)[\rho-(1-\sigma)\gamma]$$

and this last expression holds by the boundedness condition (13).

Because utility is increasing in the growth rate of consumption, γ, the government should choose τ so as to maximize

$$\gamma = \frac{1}{\sigma} \{(1-\tau)(1-\alpha)\tau^{\alpha/(1-\alpha)} - \rho\}$$

that is, so as to maximize $(1-\tau)\tau^{\alpha/(1-\alpha)}$. Taking logarithms of this expression and differentiating with respect to τ, it is easy to see that the optimal policy involves setting the tax rate equal to the coefficient of public services in the production function (i.e., $\tau^* = \alpha$).

In some sense this is precisely what we should expect. Recall that given a constant-returns-to-scale Cobb-Douglas technology, the share of output of each factor in a competitive equilibrium is equal to its coefficient in the production function. Hence, by setting $\tau^* = \alpha$, the government is essentially selling its services at their competitive price.   □

Problem 5.11. It will be convenient in what follows to work with the growth rate of per-capita consumption, denoted by g. Assuming that the share of employment in goods production, L_x, remains constant over time, solve for L_x as a function of g. Keep an eye out for scale effects, that is, reasons why a larger economy (as measured by the size of the labor force, L) may be able to grow faster.

Differentiating the reduced-form per-capita production function with respect to time, and holding the share of industrial employment constant, we can express the growth rate of output per worker as a function of the rate of technical progress. Because goods-market clearing, moreover, requires per-capita consumption to equal average output per worker, we obtain, using (2) and the labor-market clearing condition, $L_n + L_x = L$,

$$g = \frac{1-\alpha}{\alpha}\frac{\dot{n}}{n} = \frac{1-\alpha}{\alpha}aL_n = \frac{1-\alpha}{\alpha}a(L-L_x)$$

and, solving for L_x as a function of g,

$$L_x = L - \frac{\alpha}{1-\alpha}\frac{g}{a} \tag{3}$$

Notice that this expression gives us a first clue to the source of scale effects. For the same growth rate, a larger economy can have larger employment in goods production and therefore, given the same n, higher output. Because profit is, for given n, a fixed fraction of output, the incentive to do R&D will be greater in the larger economy. $\square$

Problem 5.12. Using equations (5) and (6), together with the expressions for equilibrium factor prices derived in Section 5(a) of Chapter 8, derive the following relationship between the interest rate and the growth rate of consumption:

$$r = \frac{a(1-\alpha)}{\alpha} L - \frac{\alpha}{1-\alpha} g \tag{II}$$

Interpret this condition.

Using the results of Problem 5.3 in Chapter 8, together with equations (1) and (3), we can compute the equilibrium values of w and v:

$$w = \frac{\alpha L Q}{L_x} = \frac{\alpha Y}{L_x} = a n^{(1-\alpha)/\alpha} \tag{7}$$

$$\pi = \frac{(1-\alpha)Y}{n} = (1-\alpha)n^{(1-2\alpha)/\alpha}L_x = (1-\alpha)n^{(1-2\alpha)/\alpha}\left(L - \frac{\alpha}{1-\alpha}\frac{g}{a}\right) \tag{8}$$

(Second clue on scale effects: Wages are independent of population size, but profits are increasing in it, and decreasing in g, as more research reduces output and profits.)

We will use equation (8) to compute the value of the firm, v. Notice that the only thing in this expression that is changing over time in equilibrium is n, which grows at the constant rate $\alpha g/(1 - \alpha)$. Hence,

$$n_{t+s} = n_t \exp\left(\frac{\alpha g}{1-\alpha} s\right) \tag{9}$$

and, substituting (8) and (9) into (6), the equilibrium value of the firm at time t is given by

$$v_t = (1-\alpha)n_t^{(1-2\alpha)/\alpha}\left(L - \frac{\alpha}{1-\alpha}\frac{g}{a}\right)\int_t^\infty \exp\left(\frac{1-2\alpha}{\alpha}\frac{\alpha g}{1-\alpha}s\right)e^{-rs}\,ds$$

from where

$$v_t = \frac{(1-\alpha)n_t^{(1-2\alpha)/\alpha}\left(L - \frac{\alpha}{1-\alpha}\frac{g}{a}\right)}{r - \frac{1-2\alpha}{1-\alpha}g} \tag{10}$$

Next, we return to the equal-compensation condition, (5). Using (7) and (10), equation (5) implies that

$$(w =) \quad a n^{(1-\alpha)/\alpha} = an\frac{(1-\alpha)n_t^{(1-2\alpha)/\alpha}\left(L - \frac{\alpha}{1-\alpha}\frac{g}{a}\right)}{r - \frac{1-2\alpha}{1-\alpha}g} \quad (= anv)$$

Simplifying and rearranging terms,

$$r - \frac{1-2\alpha}{1-\alpha} g = \frac{a(1-\alpha)}{\alpha}\left(L - \frac{\alpha}{1-\alpha}\frac{g}{a}\right) = \frac{a(1-\alpha)}{\alpha}L - g$$

and

$$r = \frac{a(1-\alpha)}{\alpha}L - \frac{\alpha}{1-\alpha}g \qquad (II)$$

This is the second relationship we wanted. The production side of the model implies a negative relationship between the interest rate and the rate of growth. Intuitively, the reason is the following. In equilibrium, labor must be allocated between its two uses (goods production and R&D) in such a way that its (private) marginal return is the same in both sectors. The rate of return on R&D investment is determined by the present value of the stream of monopoly profits earned by a component producer. An increase in the interest rate will reduce the discounted value of this sum and thus the market value of the firm and the incentive to do research. In equilibrium, the level of research employment must fall, implying a lower rate of growth.   □

Problem 5.13. Solve for the equilibrium values of g and the fraction of the labor force employed in research (L_n/L). Discuss the determinants of the equilibrium growth rate and the impact on both variables of an increase in the size of the labor force, L. Consider also the effects of "merging" two isolated economies into a larger, integrated one. Does anything change? To what extent is the answer to this question sensitive to the details of the specification we have used?

Using (II) and (SS) it is easy to see that the equilibrium growth rate is given by[3]

$$g^* = \frac{\dfrac{a(1-\alpha)}{\alpha}L - \rho}{\sigma + \dfrac{\alpha}{1-\alpha}} \qquad (11)$$

and that the fraction of the labor force employed in research in equilibrium is equal to

$$\frac{L_n}{L} = \frac{(1-\alpha) - \dfrac{\alpha\rho}{aL}}{(1-\alpha)\sigma + \alpha} \qquad (12)$$

Hence, the growth rate increases with population (L), the market power of firms (of which α is an inverse index), the elasticity of intertemporal substitution (σ^{-1}) and the productivity of R&D (a), and it decreases with the rate of time discount (ρ).

Consider the effect of an increase in population size in the current model. Inspection of the equilibrium conditions shows that an increase in L will shift the II schedule upward, yielding a higher equilibrium value of g. This increase in the growth rate comes from two sources. First, because in our specification the rate of innovation depends on total (rather than per-capita) R&D employment (i.e., $\dot{n}/n = aL_n$), a large economy will grow faster than a small one, even if both devote the same fraction of resources to R&D. Second, equation (12) shows that R&D employment in the large economy will also be higher in relative terms. The reason is that, given the number of firms, a larger market size implies larger profits, and therefore a greater incentive to invest in research.

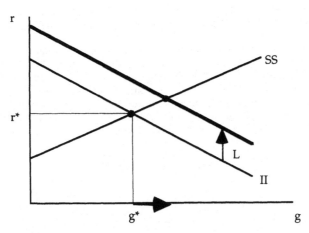

Figure A13.11. Effect of market enlargement of R&D intensity.

Suppose now that we merge two isolated economies into a larger, integrated one. In this case, both population and the number of firms will increase, and there are two separate effects to consider. The size of the market is now larger, but so is the number of competitors. The impact on profits and on the incentive to invest in R&D is uncertain ex ante. In the current model, the equilibrium value of g is independent of the number of firms, and hence the net effect will still be a higher rate of growth, but this result depends to a large extent on the details of the model's specification. In particular, we have assumed that n measures both the number of firms and the stock of technical knowledge available to potential innovators. An increase in n, then, reduces profits through lower margins, but it also reduces the cost of developing new products. In the current specification, both effects just cancel out. Hence, if integration implies the automatic pooling of (nonoverlapping) national stocks of technical knowledge, the net result will be an increase in overall R&D intensity. If this is not the case, as seems more likely, the reduction of price markups induced by greater competition will tend to lower profits, offsetting, at least partially, the positive effect of a larger market size.[4] □

Bibliography

Cohen, W., and Levin, R. 1989. Empirical Studies of Innovation and Market Structure. In: *Handbook of Industrial Organization*, ed. R. Schmalensee and R. Willig, pp. 1059–107. Amsterdam: Elsevier.

Kamien, M., and Schwartz, N. 1982. *Market Structure and Innovation*. Cambridge University Press.

Scherer, F. 1984. *Innovation and Growth: Schumpeterian Perspectives*. Massachusetts Institute of Technology Press.

Notes

1 Recall from Chapter 1 that a complex number c can be written as

$$c = a + ib = r(\cos\theta + i\sin\theta) = re^{i\theta}$$

where the last step follows from Euler's formula. Its conjugate is defined as

$$\bar{c} = a + ib = r(\cos\theta - i\sin\theta) = [\cos(-\theta) + i\sin(-\theta)] = re^{-i\theta}$$

2 It is true that in equilibrium the interest factor must be equal to the marginal product of capital and that initial capital is given. But R also depends on labor input, which is a free variable.

3 To guarantee that the II and SS schedules cross in the positive quadrant, some restrictions on parameter values must be satisfied. When this condition does not hold, we have a corner equilibrium in which R&D employment is zero.

4 The impact of market structure on the rate of innovation is a complex matter. Firms with some degree of market power may be better able to appropriate the benefits of their research, but may also be under less pressure to innovate. The literature on the topic is extensive and not very conclusive. See, for example, Kamien and Schwartz (1982), Scherer (1984), and Cohen and Levin (1989).

Author index

Subject index